THE OXFORD HANDBOOK OF

MODERN IRISH THEATRE

THE OXFORD HANDBOOK OF

MODERN IRISH THEATRE

Edited by

NICHOLAS GRENE

and

CHRIS MORASH

OXFORD
UNIVERSITY PRESS

OXFORD
UNIVERSITY PRESS

Great Clarendon Street, Oxford, OX2 6DP,
United Kingdom

Oxford University Press is a department of the University of Oxford.
It furthers the University's objective of excellence in research, scholarship,
and education by publishing worldwide. Oxford is a registered trade mark of
Oxford University Press in the UK and in certain other countries

Published in the United States of America by Oxford University Press
198 Madison Avenue, New York, NY 10016, United States of America

British Library Cataloguing in Publication Data

Data available

ISBN 978-0-91-870613-7

Jacket illustration: Marie Mullen in J.M. Synge's *The Tinker's
Wedding*, DruidSynge (2005). Photo: Keith Pattison. Courtesy
of Druid Theatre Company

ACKNOWLEDGEMENTS

WE gratefully acknowledge support from within Trinity College Dublin: the Provost's Academic Development Fund for the costs of illustrations; the Trinity Foundation and Trust and the School of English for the cost of indexing. We were fortunate also in our professional indexer, Julitta Clancy, who compiled a necessarily intricate index for this large volume. Jacqueline Baker and Rachel Platt at Oxford University Press supported the project from its beginning and were tolerant of delays in the delivery date. We very much appreciated the anonymous peer reviews they commissioned, and the book benefited as a result.

We are grateful to Chanté Kinyon for her diligent picture research. James Little and Zosia Kuczyńska worked with exemplary diligence and painstaking care as our editorial interns on the project, and without them the book would have had many errors and taken a great deal more time. A great many people responded generously to our requests to use the illustrations that add so much to this book, and they are acknowledged at the appropriate places throughout the volume; however, a special mention must be given to Mairéad Delaney, the Abbey Theatre archivist, and Barry Houlihan of the James Hardiman Library in NUI Galway. Above all, we have to say thank you to our contributors who delivered such fine and original chapters, and put up with our editorial harrying with good grace. Any remaining mistakes or omissions are exclusively our responsibility.

CONTENTS

List of Illustrations   xiii
Notes on Contributors   xix
Modern Irish Theatre: A Chronology   xxv

Introduction   1
NICHOLAS GRENE AND CHRIS MORASH

PART I NINETEENTH-CENTURY LEGACIES

1. The Inheritance of Melodrama   9
   STEPHEN WATT

2. Oscar Wilde: International Politics and the Drama of Sacrifice   24
   MICHAEL MCATEER

PART II THEATRE AND NATION

3. The Abbey and the Idea of a Theatre   41
   BEN LEVITAS

4. Theatre and Activism 1900–1916   58
   P. J. MATHEWS

5. W. B. Yeats and Rituals of Performance   72
   TERENCE BROWN

6. The Riot of Spring: Synge's 'Failed Realism' and the Peasant Drama 87
   MARY BURKE

PART III MODELS AND INFLUENCES

7. 'We Were Very Young and We Shrank From Nothing':
   Realism and Early Twentieth-Century Irish Drama   105
   SHAUN RICHARDS

8. Modernism and Irish Theatre 1900–1940   121
   RICHARD CAVE

9. Missing Links: Bernard Shaw and the Discussion Play   138
   BRAD KENT

PART IV REVOLUTION AND BEYOND

10. Imagining the Rising   155
    NICHOLAS ALLEN

11. The Abbey Theatre and the Irish State   169
    LAUREN ARRINGTON

12. O'Casey and the City   183
    CHRISTOPHER MURRAY

PART V PERFORMANCE 1

13. Design and Direction to 1960   201
    PAIGE REYNOLDS

14. The Importance of Staging Oscar: Wilde at the Gate   217
    EIBHEAR WALSHE

15. Irish Acting in the Early Twentieth Century   231
    ADRIAN FRAZIER

PART VI CONTESTING VOICES

16. Twisting in the Wind: Irish-Language Stage Theatre 1884–2014   251
    BRIAN Ó CONCHUBHAIR

17. Women and Irish Theatre before 1960   269
    CATHY LEENEY

18. The Little Theatres of the 1950s   286
    LIONEL PILKINGTON

PART VII THE NEW REVIVAL

19. Urban and Rural Theatre Cultures: M. J. Molloy, John B. Keane, and
    Hugh Leonard   307
    LISA COEN

20. Brian Friel and Tom Murphy: Forms of Exile   322
    ANTHONY ROCHE

21. Thomas Kilroy and the Idea of a Theatre   337
    JOSÉ LANTERS

PART VIII DIVERSIFICATION

22. Brian Friel and Field Day   357
    MARILYNN RICHTARIK

23. From Troubles to Post-Conflict Theatre in Northern Ireland   372
    MARK PHELAN

24. 'As We Must': Growth and Diversification in Ireland's Theatre Culture
    1977–2000   389
    VICTOR MERRIMAN

25. From Druid/Murphy to *DruidMurphy*   404
    SHELLEY TROUPE

PART IX PERFORMANCE 2

26. Places of Performance   425
    CHRIS MORASH

27. Directors and Designers since 1960   443
    IAN R. WALSH

28. Defining Performers and Performances   459
    NICHOLAS GRENE

29. Beckett at the Gate   478
    JULIE BATES

PART X CONTEMPORARY IRISH THEATRE

30. Negotiating Differences in the Plays of Frank McGuinness   497
    HELEN HEUSNER LOJEK

31. Drama since the 1990s: Memory, Story, Exile   515
    EMILIE PINE

32. Irish Drama since the 1990s: Disruptions   529
    CLARE WALLACE

33. Shadow and Substance: Women, Feminism, and Irish Theatre
    after 1980   545
    MELISSA SIHRA

34. Irish Theatre Devised   559
    BRIAN SINGLETON

PART XI IRELAND AND THE WORLD

35. Global Beckett   577
    RÓNÁN MCDONALD

36. Irish Theatre and the United States   593
    JOHN P. HARRINGTON

37. Irish Theatre in Britain   607
    JAMES MORAN

38. Irish Theatre in Europe   623
    ONDŘEJ PILNÝ

39. 'Feast and Celebration': The Theatre Festival and Modern
    Irish Theatre   637
    PATRICK LONERGAN

40. Reinscribing the Classics, Ancient and Modern: The Sharp Diagonal of
    Adaptation   654
    CHRISTINA HUNT MAHONY

PART XII CRITICAL RESPONSES

41. Irish Theatre and Historiography   673
    EAMONN JORDAN

Bibliography   695
Index   719

LIST OF ILLUSTRATIONS

The editors and publishers acknowledge the following sources of copyright material and are grateful for the permissions granted. While every effort has been made, it has not always been possible to identify the sources of all material used, nor to trace all copyright holders. If any omissions are brought to our notice, we will be happy to include the appropriate acknowledgements on reprinting.

6.1 Igor Stravinsky meets Éamon de Valera, 1 June 1963. Stravinsky was in Dublin to conduct a concert of his work. Courtesy of Irish Photographic Archive.   90

6.2 Arthur Shields armed with a loy in the 1932 production of J. M. Synge's *The Playboy of the Western World* at the Abbey Theatre. Courtesy of the Abbey Theatre and James Hardiman Library, NUI Galway.   95

7.1 *Time's Pocket* by Frank O'Connor (Abbey Theatre, 26 December 1938). Even when designed by the innovative Tanya Moiseiwitsch, the realist country kitchen set for plays such as this could have served equally well for numerous other Abbey plays of the period. Courtesy of Abbey Theatre Archive, James Hardiman Library, NUI Galway.   119

7.2 *Killycreggs in Twilight* by Lennox Robinson (Abbey Theatre, 19 April 1937). Set designer Tanya Moiseiwitsch tried to give the set a stylized touch, but there was little escaping the essentially realist aesthetic of the play. Courtesy of the Abbey Theatre and James Hardiman Library, NUI Galway.   119

8.1 Edmund Dulac's design for the Guardian of the Well in W. B. Yeats's *At the Hawk's Well*. Published in *Four Plays for Dancers* by W. B. Yeats (London: Macmillan, 1921).   126

8.2 Denis Johnston's *The Old Lady Says 'No!'* showing the Speaker (Micheál Mac Liammóir), the Flower-Seller (Meriel Moore), and the Statue of Grattan (Hilton Edwards). Photo from 1934 revival. Photograph by J. J. Mooney from Bulmer Hobson (ed.), *The Gate Theatre Dublin* (Dublin: Gate Theatre, 1934).   132

8.3 Presentational acting and direction in Hilton Edwards's staging of an ensemble sequence from *The Old Lady Says 'No!'* in the 1934 revival by the Gate Theatre, Dublin. Photograph by J. J. Mooney from Bulmer Hobson (ed.), *The Gate Theatre Dublin* (Dublin: Gate Theatre, 1934).   135

8.4 The presentational setting: four designs by Micheál Mac Liammóir for the Gate Theatre's staging of Ibsen's Peer Gynt at the Peacock Theatre (14 October 1928). From Bulmer Hobson (ed.), *The Gate Theatre Dublin* (Dublin: Gate Theatre, 1934).   136

12.1   The continuing resonance of the background to O'Casey's Dublin Trilogy
can be measured in the events commemorating the Great Lockout of 1913 a
hundred years later. This detail is from the *Great Dublin Lockout Tapestry*,
designed by Robert Ballagh and Cathy Henderson for the 1913 Committee.
Courtesy of SIPTU.   186

12.2   Poster for the first production of Seán O'Casey's *Red Roses for Me*, in the
Olympia Theatre, Dublin, 15 March 1943. Courtesy of Irish Theatre Archive,
Dublin City Libraries.   195

13.1   Tanya Moiseiwitsch's set designs for G. B. Shaw's *A Village Wooing* (30
September 1935). Courtesy of the Abbey Theatre and James Hardiman
Library, NUI Galway.   212

14.1   Micheál Mac Liammóir (left) and Hilton Edwards (right) strike a pose
outside the doors of the Gate Theatre, on Dublin's Parnell Square. Courtesy
of the Gate Theatre and Library Special Collections, Northwestern University.   218

14.2   Steven Berkoff's landmark 1988 production of *Salomé* (designed by Robert
Ballagh) indicated a new direction in the Gate's production of Wilde's work.
Photo: Tom Lawlor. Courtesy of the Gate Theatre.   228

15.1   Barry Fitzgerald as Captain Jack Boyle in Seán O'Casey's *Juno and the
Paycock* (3 March 1924). Courtesy of the Abbey Theatre and James Hardiman
Library, NUI Galway.   242

15.2   F. J. McCormick as Joxer Daly in *Juno and the Paycock* (1924). Courtesy of the
Abbey Theatre and James Hardiman Library, NUI Galway.   243

15.3   Eileen Crowe as Pegeen (right) in *The Playboy of the Western World* in
New York 1932: with Barry Fitzgerald as Michael James (centre) and Arthur
Shields (left) as Christy Mahon. Courtesy of James Hardiman Library, NUI
Galway.   244

16.1   Poster for Paul Mercier, *Sétanta*, produced by Fibín (Abbey Theatre, 28
November 2011). Courtesy of Fibín.   265

16.2   Fíbin's *Stair na gCeilteach/History of the Celts*, co-produced with
Improbable Films (13 and 14 September 2013), used video-mapping to project
images in a quarry in Camus, Connemara. Photo: Seán T. Ó Meallaigh.
Courtesy of Fibín.   266

16.3   Poster for Gearóid Ó Cairealláin's *The Wheelchair Monologues*, produced by
Aisling Ghéar theatre company (7 March 2013). Courtesy of Aisling Ghéar.   267

18.1   Anna Manahan and Pat Nolan in *The Rose Tattoo*, Pike Theatre (12 May 1957).
Photo: Derrick Michelson. Courtesy of Trinity College Dublin.   295

18.2   When Alan Simpson was arrested over the Pike Theatre's production of *The
Rose Tattoo* in 1957, the case provoked widespread public interest in Dublin,
making headlines in newspapers across the city. Courtesy of Trinity College
Dublin.   298

21.1   Donal McCann and Aideen O'Kelly as Brien and Elmina in *Tea and Sex
and Shakespeare* (Abbey Theatre, 6 October 1976). Photo: Fergus Bourke.
Courtesy of the Abbey Theatre and James Hardiman Library, NUI Galway.   346

21.2   Scene from *Talbot's Box*, with Stephen Brennan, John Molloy, Clive Geraghty, Ingrid Craigie, and Eileen Colgan (Abbey Theatre, 13 October 1977). Courtesy of the Abbey Theatre and James Hardiman Library, NUI Galway.   349

23.1   Still from *The Far Side of Revenge* (2012), film-maker Margo Harkin's documentary tracing Teya Sepinuck's 'Theatre of Witness' project (2012–14). Courtesy of Margo Harkin and Besom Productions.   383

25.1   Detail from Druid's programme for the Galway première of Tom Murphy's *Bailegangaire* (5 December 1985). Courtesy of Druid Theatre Company and James Hardiman Library, NUI Galway.   412

25.2   Flyer announcing Druid's production of Tom Murphy's *Bailegangaire* at London's Donmar Warehouse (17 February 1986). Courtesy of Druid Theatre Company and James Hardiman Library, NUI Galway.   413

25.3   Flyer announcing Druid's production of Tom Murphy's *Bailegangaire* at Dublin's Gaiety Theatre (12 May 1986). Photo: Amelia Stein. Courtesy of Druid Theatre Company and James Hardiman Library, NUI Galway.   414

25.4   Main promotional graphic for *DruidMurphy*, Irish tour 2013. Courtesy of Druid Theatre Company.   420

25.5   Brian Doherty as John Connor and the cast of *Famine*, performed as the concluding play in *DruidMurphy* (25 May 2012). Photo: Catherine Ashmore. Courtesy of Druid Theatre Company.   421

26.1   Interior of the 1904 Abbey Theatre, converted by Joseph Holloway from an early theatre, the Mechanics' Institute. Digital reconstruction courtesy of Hugh Denard: http://blog.oldabbeytheatre.net/   431

26.2   Noel Moffett's original plans for the open-air theatre on Achill Island, 1941. Note specifications for materials found on the site: 'grass sods on turf', 'sand on stone', and gorse hedging to create an al fresco green room. Courtesy of Irish Architectural Archive.   433

26.3   Photograph of Noel Moffett's open-air Achill Theatre, 1941. The house of Dermot Freyer, who sponsored the project, is visible in the background. Courtesy of Irish Architectural Archive.   434

26.4   The spectacularly curving auditorium of Robin Walker's Cork Opera House (1965). Courtesy of Simon Walker.   437

26.5   J. Neil Downes's never-realized plans for a new Lyric Theatre, on the Ridgeway Street site in Belfast (May 1967). Note the division of the auditorium, with a runway-like acting area between the two parts of the house. Courtesy of James Hardiman Library, NUI Galway.   438

26.6   Plans (never realized) for a new Abbey Theatre from 1994, drawn up by McCulloch–Mulvin Architects. The design placed an auditorium that echoed the 1904 Abbey in a contemporary shell. Courtesy McCulloch–Mulvin Architects and the Irish Architectural Archive.   440

27.1   Bronwen Casson, set and costume design for *The Sanctuary Lamp* by Tom Murphy (7 October 1975). Photo: Fergus Bourke. Courtesy of the Abbey Theatre and James Hardiman Library, NUI Galway.   450

27.2   Frank Conway, design for *Shibari* by Garry Duggan (Peacock, 4 October
       2012). Courtesy of Frank Conway.   451

27.3   Robert Ballagh, model for design of *The Importance of Being Earnest* (Gate
       Theatre, 23 July 1987). Photo: Tom Lawlor. Courtesy of the Gate Theatre.   455

28.1   Cyril Cusack in Dion Boucicault's *The Shaughraun* (Abbey Theatre, 31
       January 1967). Courtesy of the Abbey Theatre and National Library of Ireland.   461

28.2   Siobhán McKenna as the Maid in G. B. Shaw's *Saint Joan* (Gate Theatre, 18
       November 1954). Photo: Cecil Beaton. Courtesy of the Cecil Beaton Studio
       Archive at Sotheby's.   467

28.3   Donal McCann as Frank Hardy in the Abbey production of Brian Friel's
       Faith Healer (Abbey Theatre, 28 August 1980; the play premièred in New York
       in 1979). Photo: Fergus Bourke. Courtesy of the Abbey Theatre.   471

28.4   Donal McCann as Captain Boyle in Seán O'Casey's *Juno and the Paycock*
       (Gate Theatre, 15 July 1986). Photo: Tom Lawlor. Courtesy of the Gate Theatre.   472

28.5   Marie Mullen as Mary and Siobhán McKenna as Mommo in Tom Murphy's
       Bailegangaire (Druid, 15 December 1985). Photo: Amelia Stein.   474

28.6   Marie Mullen as Mary in J. M. Synge's *The Tinker's Wedding, DruidSynge* (29
       June 2005). Photo: Keith Pattison. Courtesy of Druid Theatre Company.   476

29.1   Michael Colgan standing in front of the billboard for the Beckett Festival,
       1991. Photo: Tom Lawlor. Courtesy of the Gate Theatre.   487

29.2   Telecom Éireann advertisement, the Beckett Festival, the Gate Theatre, 1–20
       October 1990; festival programme, edited by Mary Dowey (Dublin: Gate
       Theatre, 1990). Courtesy of Eircom.   488

29.3   Maureen Potter in *Rockaby* by Samuel Beckett at the Beckett Festival, the
       Gate Theatre, 1–20 October 1990. Photo: Tom Lawlor. Courtesy of the Gate
       Theatre.   490

29.4   Publicity photograph of Barry McGovern as Vladimir in *Waiting for Godot*
       by Samuel Beckett; Beckett Festival, the Gate Theatre, 1–20 October 1990.
       Photo: Tom Lawlor. Courtesy of the Gate Theatre.   491

30.1   Rosaleen Linehan as Maela in Frank McGuinness, *Carthaginians* (Abbey
       Theatre, 26 September 1988). Courtesy of the Abbey Theatre and James
       Hardiman Library, NUI Galway.   502

31.1   Bríd Brennan, Catherine Byrne, Bríd Ní Neachtain, and Frances Tomelty in a
       scene from *Dancing at Lughnasa* (Abbey Theatre, 24 April 1990). Courtesy of
       the Abbey Theatre and James Hardiman Library, NUI Galway.   516

34.1   Sorcha Kenny in ANU Productions, *Laundry* (25 September 2011). Photo: Pat
       Redmond. Courtesy of ANU Productions.   572

35.1   *Waiting for Godot* by Samuel Beckett, directed by Christopher McElroen
       (Artistic Director, Paul Chan) (Gentilly, New Orleans, 9 November 2007).
       From left to right: T. Ryder Smith as Pozzo, J. Kyle Manzay as Estragon,
       Wendell Pierce as Vladimir, and Mark McLaughlin as Lucky. Photo: Frank
       Aymami. Courtesy of Frank Aymami Photography.   589

36.1   Seán McGinley and Stephen Rea in *Ages of the Moon*, by Sam Shepard.
Directed by Jimmy Fay (Atlantic Theater Company at the Linda Gross
Theater, New York, 27 October 2010). Photo: Ari Mintz. Courtesy of the
Atlantic Theater Company.   604

37.1   Jamie Vartan, model set design, *Misterman* by Enda Walsh (Lyttleton
Theatre, 18 April 2012). Courtesy of the set and costume designer Jamie Vartan.   612

39.1   Poster for 1953 An Tóstal Festival pageant. Courtesy of James Hardiman
Library, NUI Galway.   642

39.2   Poster for 1956 An Tóstal festival pageant. Courtesy of James Hardiman
Library, NUI Galway.   643

40.1   Janet McTeer as Nora in Frank McGuiness's version of Ibsen's *A Doll's House*
(Playhouse Theatre, London 1996). Courtesy of Victoria and Albert Museum.   661

40.2   Thomas Kilroy's version of Chekhov's *The Seagull*, directed by Max Stafford-
Clark (Royal Court Theatre, 8 April 1981). Courtesy of Victoria and Albert
Museum.   663

Notes on Contributors

Nicholas Allen is Director of the Willson Center and Franklin Professor of English at the University of Georgia. He is the author of *George Russell (Æ) and the New Ireland, 1905–30* (Four Courts Press, 2003) and *Modernism, Ireland and Civil War* (Cambridge University Press, 2009).

Lauren Arrington is Senior Lecturer at the Institute of Irish Studies, University of Liverpool. She is the author of *W. B. Yeats, the Abbey Theatre, Censorship, and the Irish State: Adding the Half-Pence to the Pence* (Oxford University Press, 2010) and *Revolutionary Lives: Constance and Casimir Markievicz* (Princeton University Press, 2016).

Julie Bates is Teaching Fellow at the School of English, Trinity College Dublin, where she completed her PhD. Her book, *Beckett's Art of Salvage*, will be published in 2016 by Cambridge University Press.

Terence Brown is Fellow Emeritus of Trinity College Dublin, where he was formerly Professor of Anglo-Irish Literature. Among his many books are *The Life of W. B. Yeats: A Critical Biography* (Blackwell, 1999), *Ireland: a Social and Cultural History 1922–2002* (Harper Perennial, 2004), and *The Irish Times: 150 Years of Influence* (Bloomsbury, 2015).

Mary Burke is Associate Professor of English at the University of Connecticut, Storrs. She is the author of *'Tinkers': Synge and the Cultural History of the Irish Traveller* (Oxford University Press, 2009).

Richard Cave is Professor Emeritus of Drama and Theatre Arts, Royal Holloway, University of London. He has published extensively on Yeats's dance plays (many of which he has both edited and staged professionally); on O'Casey, Johnston, and the Gate Theatre; on Wilde, Lady Gregory, Ninette de Valois, Beckett, Friel, and McGuinness; and on stage design for Irish plays. He is editor (with Ben Levitas) of *Irish Theatre in England* (Carysfort Press, 2007).

Lisa Coen obtained her PhD. at Trinity College Dublin with a dissertation on Abbey Theatre tours in the contemporary period. She is the founding co-director of the independent publisher Tramp Press.

Adrian Frazier is Emeritus Professor of English at NUI, Galway. He is the author of *Behind the Scenes: Yeats, Horniman and the Struggle for the Abbey Theatre* (University of California Press, 1990), *George Moore 1852–1933* (Yale University Press, 2000), and *Hollywood Irish* (Lilliput Press, 2011).

Nicholas Grene is Emeritus Professor of English Literature at Trinity College Dublin. His books include *The Politics of Irish Drama* (Cambridge University Press, 1999), *Yeats's Poetic*

Codes (Oxford University Press, 2008), and *Home on the Stage: Domestic Spaces in Modern Drama* (Cambridge University Press, 2014).

John P. Harrington is Professor of English and Dean of the Faculty of Arts and Sciences at Fordham University. He is the author of *The Irish Play on the New York Stage, 1874–1976* (University Press of Kentucky, 1997) and the editor of *Irish Theater in America* (Syracuse University Press, 2009).

Eamonn Jordan is Senior Lecturer in Drama Studies in the School of English, Drama and Film at University College Dublin. He is the author of *Dissident Dramaturgies: Contemporary Irish Theatre* (Irish Academic Press, 2010) and *From Leenane to LA: The Theatre and Cinema of Martin McDonagh* (Irish Academic Press, 2014).

Brad Kent is Associate Professor in the Département des littératures, Université de Laval, Québec, and programme director of the Shaw Festival's Shaw Symposium in Niagara-on-the-Lake, Canada. He is the editor of Bernard Shaw's *Mrs Warren's Profession* (Methuen Drama, 2012) and of *Bernard Shaw in Context* (Cambridge University Press, 2015).

José Lanters is Professor of English and co-director of the Center for Celtic Studies at the University of Wisconsin-Milwaukee. She is the author of *Unauthorized Versions: Irish Menippean Satire, 1919–1952* (Catholic University of America Press, 2000) and *The 'Tinkers' in Irish Literature: Unsettled Subjects and the Construction of Difference* (Irish Academic Press, 2008).

Cathy Leeney is Lecturer in Drama Studies in the School of English, Drama and Film in University College Dublin. She is the author of *Irish Women Playwrights, 1900–1939* (Peter Lang, 2010) and editor (with Anna McMullan) of *The Theatre of Marina Carr* (Carysfort Press, 2003).

Ben Levitas is Reader in the Department of Theatre and Performance at Goldsmiths, University of London. He is the author of *The Theatre of Nation: Irish Drama and Cultural Nationalism 1890–1916* (Clarendon Press, 2002) and the editor (with David Holdeman) of *W. B. Yeats in Context* (Cambridge University Press, 2010).

Helen Heusner Lojek is Professor Emeritus of English and formerly Associate Dean of the College of Arts and Sciences at Boise State University, Idaho. She is the author of *Contexts for Frank McGuinness's Drama* (Catholic University of America Press, 2004) and *The Spaces of Irish Drama* (Palgrave Macmillan, 2011), and the editor of *The Theatre of Frank McGuinness: Stages of Mutability* (Carysfort Press, 2002).

Patrick Lonergan is Professor of Drama and Theatre Studies at the National University of Ireland, Galway. He is the author of *Theatre and Globalisation: Irish Drama in the Celtic Tiger Era* (Palgrave Macmillan, 2009), *The Theatre and Films of Martin McDonagh* (Methuen Drama, 2012), and *Theatre and Social Media* (Palgrave Macmillan, 2015).

Christina Hunt Mahony is a Research Fellow in the School of English, Trinity College Dublin, and a former director of the Graduate Center for Irish Studies at Catholic University of America, Washington, DC. She is the author of *Contemporary Irish Literature: Transforming Tradition* (St Martin's Press, 1998) and the editor of *Out of History: Essays on the Writings of Sebastian Barry* (Carysfort Press, 2006)

P. J. Mathews is a Senior Lecturer in the School of English, Drama and Film at University College Dublin. He is the author of *Revival* (Cork University Press, 2003), editor of the *Cambridge Companion to J. M. Synge* (Cambridge University Press, 2009), and co-editor (with Declan Kiberd) of *Handbook of the Irish Revival* (Abbey Theatre Press, 2015).

Michael McAteer is Associate Professor of English at Pázmány Péter Catholic University, Budapest. He is the author of *Standish O'Grady, Æ, Yeats* (Irish Academic Press, 2002) and *Yeats and European Drama* (Cambridge University Press, 2010).

Rónán McDonald is Professor of Modern Literature at the University of New South Wales. His books include the *Cambridge Introduction to Beckett* (Cambridge University Press, 2006) and *The Death of the Critic* (Bloomsbury, 2007), and he is the editor of *The Values of Literary Studies: Critical Institutions, Scholarly Agendas* (Cambridge University Press, 2015).

Victor Merriman is Professor of Critical Performance Studies at Edge Hill University, Lancashire. He is the author of *Because We Are Poor: Irish Theatre in the 1990s* (Carysfort Press, 2011).

James Moran is Professor of Modern English Literature and Drama at the University of Nottingham. His books include *The Theatre of D. H. Lawrence* (2015), *Staging the Easter Rising* (2005), and (as co-editor with Neal Alexander) *Regional Modernisms* (2013).

Chris Morash is Seamus Heaney Professor of Irish Writing at Trinity College Dublin. He is the author of *A History of Irish Theatre, 1601–2000* (Cambridge University Press, 2002), *A History of the Media in Ireland* (Cambridge University Press, 2009), and (with Shaun Richards) *Mapping Irish Theatre: Theories of Space and Place* (Cambridge University Press, 2014).

Christopher Murray is Associate Professor Emeritus of Drama and Theatre History in the School of English, Drama and Film at University College Dublin. He is the author of *Twentieth Century Irish Drama: Mirror up to Nation* (Manchester University Press, 1997), *Seán O'Casey: Writer at Work* (Gill and Macmillan, 2004), and *The Theatre of Brian Friel: Tradition and Modernity* (Bloomsbury, 2014).

Brian Ó Conchubhair is Associate Professor of Irish Language and Literature at the University of Notre Dame and currently President of the American Conference for Irish Studies (2015–17). He is the author of *Fin de Siècle na Gaeilge: Darwin, An Athbheochan agus Smaointeoireacht na hEorpa* (CIC, 2009).

Mark Phelan is Lecturer in Drama at Queen's University Belfast. He is the editor of Tim Loane, *The Comedy of Terrors: Caught Red-Handed and To Be Sure* (Lagan Press, 2008).

Lionel Pilkington is Personal Professor of English, National University of Ireland, Galway. He is the author of *Theatre and the State in 20th Century Ireland: Cultivating the People* (Routledge, 2001) and of *Theatre and Ireland* (Palgrave, 2010).

Ondřej Pilný is Associate Professor of English and Director of the Centre for Irish Studies at Charles University, Prague. He is the author of *Irony and Identity in Modern Irish Drama* (Litteraria Pragensia, 2006) and of *The Grotesque in Contemporary Drama: Off Limits* (Palgrave Macmillan, forthcoming 2016), and the editor (with Gerald Power) of *Ireland and the Czech Lands: Contacts and Comparisons in History and Culture* (Peter Lang, 2014).

Emilie Pine is Lecturer in the School of English, Drama and Film in University College Dublin, Director of the Irish Memory Studies Network, and Assistant Editor of the *Irish University Review*. She is the author of *The Politics of Irish Memory: Performing Remembrance in Contemporary Irish Culture* (Palgrave Macmillan, 2010).

Paige Reynolds is a Professor in the Department of English at the College of the Holy Cross in Worcester, Massachusetts. She is the author of *Modernism, Drama, and the Audience for Irish Spectacle* (Cambridge University Press, 2007), and the editor of an *Eire-Ireland* special issue on material culture (2011) and of *Modernist Afterlives in Irish Literature and Culture* (Anthem Press, forthcoming).

Shaun Richards is Professorial Research Fellow at the Centre for Irish Studies, St Mary's University Twickenham, London. He is the author (with David Cairns) of *Writing Ireland: Colonialism, Nationalism and Culture* (Manchester University Press, 1988) and (with Chris Morash) of *Mapping Irish Theatre: Theories of Space and Place* (Cambridge University Press, 2014), and the editor of the *Cambridge Companion to Twentieth-Century Irish Drama* (Cambridge University Press, 2004).

Marilynn Richtarik is Professor of English at Georgia State University. She is the author of *Acting Between the Lines: The Field Day Theatre Company and Irish Cultural Politics 1980-1984* (Oxford University Press, 1994) and *Stewart Parker: A Life* (Oxford University Press, 2012).

Anthony Roche is Professor in the School of English, Drama and Film in University College Dublin. He is the author of *Brian Friel: Theatre and Politics* (Palgrave Macmillan, 2011), *Synge and the Making of Modern Irish Drama* (Carysfort Press, 2013), and *The Irish Dramatic Revival 1899–1939* (Bloomsbury, 2015).

Melissa Sihra is Assistant Professor of Drama at Trinity College Dublin. She is the editor of *Women in Irish Drama: A Century of Authorship and Representation* (Palgrave Macmillan, 2007) and (with Paul Murphy) of *The Dreaming Body: Contemporary Irish Theatre* (Gerrards Cross: Colin Smythe, 2009).

Brian Singleton is the Samuel Beckett Professor of Drama and Theatre at Trinity College Dublin and a past president of the International Federation for Theatre Research. His most recent book is *Masculinities and the Contemporary Irish Theatre* (Palgrave Macmillan, 2011, revised with a new preface, 2015).

Shelley Troupe, formerly a theatre administrator, teaches at Maynooth University and the National University of Ireland, Galway, where she completed her PhD on Druid's relationship with Tom Murphy in the 1980s. She is currently writing a monograph called *Druid and Murphy: Archaeology of a Relationship*.

Clare Wallace is Associate Professor of English at Charles University, Prague. She is the author of *Suspect Cultures: Narrative, Identity and Citation in 1990s New Drama* (Litteraria Pragensia, 2006) and of *The Theatre of David Greig* (Bloomsbury, 2013), and the editor of Stewart Parker, *Television Plays* (Litteraria Pragensia, 2008).

Ian R. Walsh is Lecturer in Drama, Theatre and Performance at NUI, Galway. He is the author of *Experimental Irish Theatre: After W. B. Yeats* (Palgrave Macmillan, 2012) and the co-editor (with Mary Caulfield) of *The Theatre of Enda Walsh* (Carysfort Press, 2015).

Eibhear Walshe is Senior Lecturer in English at University College Cork. He is the author of *Oscar's Shadow: Wilde, Homosexuality and Modern Ireland* (Cork University Press, 2011), *A Different Story: The Fictions of Colm Tóibín* (Irish Academic Press, 2013), and the novel *The Diary of Mary Travers* (Somerville Press, 2014).

Stephen Watt is Provost Professor at Indiana University, Bloomington. His books include *Joyce, O'Casey, and the Irish Popular Theatre* (Syracuse University Press, 1991), *Beckett and Contemporary Irish Writing* (Cambridge University Press, 2009), and *'Something Dreadful and Grand': American Literature and the Irish–Jewish Unconscious* (Oxford University Press, 2015).

MODERN IRISH THEATRE: A CHRONOLOGY

1860	29 Mar.	Dion Boucicault, *The Colleen Bawn* (Laura Keene's, New York)
1871	27 Nov.	Gaiety Theatre opens, Dublin
	14 Nov.	Dion Boucicault, *The Shaughraun* (Wallack's Theatre, New York)
1879	22 Dec.	Star of Erin Music Hall (later Olympia Theatre) opens, Dublin
1882	Nov.–June 1883	Eoin S. Ó Cearbhaill, *Brian Boroimhe*, published in Irish, in *Irisleabhar na Gaedhilge/The Gaelic Journal* (Dublin)
1884	1 Nov.	Gaelic Athletic Association founded
	27 Nov.	Paul McSwiney, *An Bard 'gus an Fó: A Gaelic Idyll* (Steinway Hall, New York)
1886	26 Apr.	Hubert O'Grady, *The Famine* (Queen's, Dublin)
	8 June	First Home Rule Bill defeated
1891	Sept.	G. B. Shaw, *The Quintessence of Ibsenism*
1893	19 Apr.	Oscar Wilde, *A Woman of No Importance*
	31 July	Gaelic League founded
1894	21 Apr.	G. B. Shaw, *Arms and the Man*; W. B. Yeats, *The Land of Heart's Desire* [opened 29 March] (Avenue Theatre, London)
1895	23 Dec.	Grand Opera House, Belfast, opens
	14 Feb.	Oscar Wilde, *The Importance of Being Earnest* (St James Theatre, London)
1897	Summer	W. B. Yeats, Lady Gregory, and Edward Martyn compose manifesto of Irish Literary Theatre
1899	8 May	W. B. Yeats, *The Countess Cathleen*; Irish Literary Theatre first performance; first issue of *Beltaine* published same week
1900	19 Feb.	Alice Milligan, *The Last Feast of the Fianna* (Irish Literary Theatre)
1901	21 Oct.	Douglas Hyde, *Casadh an tSúgáin* (Irish Literary Theatre)
1902	2 Apr.	W. B. Yeats [and Lady Gregory, uncredited], *Kathleen ni Houlihan* (Irish National Dramatic Company)
1903	12 Jan.	J. W. Whitbread, *The Ulster Hero* (Queen's, Dublin)
	Mar.	First Irish National Theatre Society tour (London)
	8 Oct.	J. M. Synge, *In the Shadow of the Glen* (National Theatre Society) Wyndham Land (Purchase) Act
1904	25 Jan.	J. M. Synge, *Riders to the Sea* (National Theatre Society)
	Nov.	Ulster Literary Theatre founded
	27 Dec.	Abbey Theatre opens; W. B. Yeats, *On Baile's Strand*; Lady Gregory, *Spreading the News*
1905	4 May	Lewis Purcell, *The Enthusiast* (Ulster Literary Theatre)
	9 June	Padraic Colum, *The Land* (Abbey)
1906	10 Oct.	Lady Gregory, *The Gaol Gate* (Abbey)
	6 Dec.	Theatre of Ireland: James Cousins, *The Racing Lug*; Douglas Hyde, *Casadh an tSúgáin*; and a scene from Ibsen's *Brand*
1907	26 Jan.	J. M. Synge, *The Playboy of the Western World* (Abbey); riots throughout the week

(continued)

	9 Mar.	Lady Gregory, *The Rising of the Moon* (Abbey)
1908	Nov.	Cork Dramatic Society founded
1909	25 Aug.	G. B. Shaw, *The Shewing Up of Blanco Posnet* (Abbey)
1910	27 Oct.	T. C. Murray, *Birthright* (Abbey)
1911	Sept.	First Abbey tour of USA
	30 Mar.	St John Ervine, *Mixed Marriage* (Abbey)
	26 Aug.	Irish Transport and General Workers Union strike begins
1914	28 July	First World War begins
	18 Sept.	Third Home Rule Bill enacted, but suspended for duration of WWI.
1915	20 May	Patrick Pearse, *The Master* (Hardwicke St Theatre, Dublin)
1916	16 Mar.	James Connolly, *Under Which Flag?* (Irish Workers Dramatic Company, Dublin)
	2 Apr.	W. B. Yeats, *At the Hawk's Well* (Cavendish Square, London)
	24 Apr.	Easter Rising begins; rebels surrender, 29 April; leaders executed, May
	25 Sept.	Abbey première of G. B. Shaw's *John Bull's Other Island* [1904] (Abbey)
	13 Dec.	Lennox Robinson, *The Whiteheaded Boy* (Abbey)
1919	21 Jan.	Soloheadbeg Ambush begins Anglo-Irish War
	9 Feb.	Dublin Drama League first production, Srgjan Tucic, *The Liberators*; regular productions until 1929
	1 Apr.	First meeting of Dáil Éireann; declared illegal, 12 Sept.
	26 Apr.	W. B. Yeats, 'A People's Theatre' (*Irish Statesman*)
1921	9 July	Truce opens negotiations for Anglo-Irish Treaty (signed 6 Dec.); enacted 31 March 1922.
1922	14 Apr.	Anti-Treaty forces seize Four Courts, Dublin; attack by provisional government forces on June 28 begins civil war
1923	12 Apr.	Seán O'Casey, *The Shadow of a Gunman* (Abbey)
	27 Apr.	Suspension of campaign by Anti-Treaty forces
	14 Nov.	W. B. Yeats, Nobel Prize in literature
1924		An Comhar Drámaíochta founded, Dublin
	3 Mar.	Seán O'Casey, *Juno and the Paycock* (Abbey)
1925	14 Sept.	George Sheils, *Professor Tim* (Abbey)
	8 Aug.	Abbey Theatre state subsidy announced
1926	11 Feb.	Seán O'Casey, *The Plough and the Stars* (Abbey); riots throughout the week
	1 Mar.	Liam O'Flaherty, *Dorchadas* (An Comhar, Dublin)
	11 Nov.	G. B. Shaw, Nobel Prize in literature
1927	13 Nov.	Peacock Theatre opens with Georg Kaiser, *From Morn to Midnight*
1928	28 Aug.	An Taibhdheardhc opens with Micheál Mac Liammóir, *Diarmuid agus Gráinne*
	14 Oct.	First Gate Theatre production, *Peer Gynt* (in Peacock Theatre)
	12 Dec.	Oscar Wilde, *Salomé* (Gate; in Peacock)
1929	19 June	Denis Johnston, *The Old Lady Says 'No!'* (Gate; in Peacock)
	16 July	Censorship of Publications Act
	11 Oct.	Seán O'Casey, *The Silver Tassie* (Apollo Theatre, London)
1930	17 Feb.	Gate Theatre opens with Goethe's *Faust*
1931	10 Aug.	Oscar Wilde, *Lady Windermere's Fan* (Gate Theatre)
		Dorothy Macardle, *Witch's Brew* (rejected by Abbey, 1929; published)
1933	6 Feb.	Lennox Robinson, *Drama at Inish* (Abbey)
1935	29 Apr.	Teresa Deevy, *The King of Spain's Daughter* (Abbey)
1936	16 May	Teresa Deevy, *Katie Roche* (Abbey)
1937	1 July	Bunreacht na hÉireann (Constitution of Ireland) enacted
1938	10 Aug.	W. B. Yeats, *Purgatory* (Abbey)
1939	1 Sept.	Second World War begins

1940	Sept.	Ulster Group Theatre founded
1941	May	Noel Moffett and members of White Stag Group build open air-theatre, Achill Island
1948	21 Dec.	Republic of Ireland Act (effective 1949)
1950	13 Dec.	G. B. Shaw (trans. Siobhán McKenna), *San Siobhán* (translation of *Saint Joan*), (An Taibhdhearc, Galway)
1951	Mar.	37 Theatre Club established, Dublin
	Mar.	Lyric Theatre founded, Belfast
	8 May	Arts Council established, Republic of Ireland
	18 July	Abbey Theatre burns
	21 Oct.	Wexford Opera Festival founded
1952	3 July	Bord Fáilte (Irish Tourist Board) founded
1953		Pike Theatre founded, Dublin
	26 Jan.	J. B. Molloy, *The Wood of the Whispering* (Abbey)
	4 Apr.	Maurice Meldon, *Aisling* (37 Theatre Club, Dublin)
	12–22 Apr.	First All-Ireland Drama Festival, Athone
	1 June	Louis D'Alton, *This Other Eden* (Abbey)
1954	18 Nov.	G. B. Shaw, *Saint Joan* (first production, 1924; Siobhán McKenna as the Maid) (Gate)
	19 Nov.	Brendan Behan, *The Quare Fellow* (Pike)
1955	28 Oct.	Samuel Beckett, *Waiting for Godot* (Pike; Irish première)
	21 Nov.	Walter Macken, *Twilight of the Warrior* (Abbey)
1957	Feb.	Lyric Studio Theatre opens, Belfast; *Threshold* magazine first published
	3 Apr.	Samuel Beckett, *Endgame* (Royal Court, London)
	13–26 May	First Dublin Theatre Festival
	12 May	Pike Theatre prosecuted for obscenity after production of Tennessee Williams' *The Rose Tattoo*
1958	28 Apr.	Dublin Theatre Festival cancelled due to episcopal opposition
	16 June	Brendan Behan, *An Giall* (An Damer); as *The Hostage* (Theatre Royal, Stratford East; 14 Oct.)
	2 July	Industrial Development Act, to encourage foreign investment
	28 Oct.	Samuel Beckett, *Krapp's Last Tape* (Royal Court, London)
1959	2 Feb.	John B. Keane, *Sive* (Listowel Drama Group)
	28 Apr.	Eugene O'Neill, *Long Day's Journey Into Night* (Abbey)
		Thomas Kilroy, 'Groundwork for an Irish Theatre'
1960	26 Jan.	Sam Thompson, *Over the Bridge* (Ulster Bridge Productions)
	19 Sept.	Oscar Wilde and Micheál Mac Liammóir, *The Importance of Being Oscar* (Gate Theatre; in Gaiety)
1961	11 Sept.	Tom Murphy, *A Whistle in the Dark* (Theatre Royal, Stratford East, London)
	31 Dec.	RTÉ television begins broadcasting
1964	22 Sept.	Máiréad Ní Ghráda, *An Triail* (An Damer)
	28 Sept.	Brian Friel, *Philadelphia, Here I Come!* (Gate Theatre; in Gaiety)
1965	20 Sept.	Bertolt Brecht, *The Life of Galileo*, directed by Tomás Mac Anna (Abbey)
	Oct.	Cork Opera House (designed Robin Walker) opens
	1 Nov.	John B. Keane, *The Field* (Gemini Productions, Dublin)
1966	18 July	Abbey Theatre (designed Michael Scott) opens
1967	31 Jan.	Dion Boucicault, *The Shaughraun* (first produced 1874) (Abbey)
		Project Arts Centre opens, Dublin
1968	18 Mar.	Tom Murphy, *Famine* (Peacock)

(continued)

	7 Oct.	Thomas Kilroy, *The Death and Resurrection of Mr Roche* (Dublin Theatre Festival)
	Oct.	Lyric Theatre opens, Belfast
1969	14–15 Aug.	Riots in Derry and Belfast, British troops enter Northern Ireland
	23 Oct.	Samuel Beckett, Nobel Prize in literature
	11 Nov.	Tom Murphy, *A Crucial Week in the Life of a Grocer's Assistant* (Abbey)
1970	11 Jan.	Formation of Provisional IRA
1971	Mar.	Tom Murphy, *The Morning After Optimism* (Abbey); John Boyd, *The Flats* (Lyric)
1972	22 Jan.	Republic signs treaty of accession to EEC
1973		Arts Act (1973), Republic of Ireland
	8 Oct.	Hugh Leonard, *Da* (Olympia)
	20 Feb.	Brian Friel, *The Freedom of the City* (Abbey)
1975	6 Oct.	Tom Murphy, *The Sanctuary Lamp* (Abbey)
	5 July	Druid Theatre Company stage first season of plays, Galway
		TEAM theatre company founded (Dublin)
1977	13 Oct.	Thomas Kilroy, *Talbot's Box* (Abbey)
1979	5 Apr.	Brian Friel, *Faith Healer* (Longacre Theatre, New York)
	4 Oct.	Hugh Leonard, *A Life* (Abbey)
1980	23 Sept.	Brian Friel, *Translations* (Guildhall, Derry; first Field Day production)
		Arts Councils begin funding regional theatres
1983	9 May	Tom Mac Intyre, *The Great Hunger* (Peacock)
	15 May	Martin Lynch (in collaboration with company), *Lay Up Your Ends* (Charabanc)
	29 Sept.	Tom Murphy, *The Gigli Concert* (Abbey)
	9 Nov.	Christina Reid, *Tea in a China Cup* (Lyric)
1984	29 Feb.	Aidan Mathews and Operating Theatre, *The Diamond Body* (Operating Theatre)
	19 Sept.	Tom Paulin, *The Riot Act* (version of Sophocles, *Antigone*) (Field Day)
	7 Nov.	Stewart Parker, *Northern Star* (Lyric)
		Rough Magic Theatre Company founded (Dublin)
1985	16 Apr.	Tom Murphy, *Conversations on a Homecoming* (Druid)
	18 Feb.	Frank McGuinness, *Observe the Sons of Ulster* (Peacock)
	15 Nov.	Anglo-Irish Agreement
	5 Dec.	Tom Murphy, *Bailegangaire* (Druid)
1986		Macnas Theatre Company founded (Galway)
	3 Feb.	Thomas Kilroy, *Double Cross* (Field Day)
1987	16 Sept.	Roddy Doyle, *Brownbread* (Passion Machine)
	23 Sept.	Stewart Parker, *Pentecost* (Field Day)
1988		Island Theatre Company founded (Limerick)
		Red Kettle Theatre Company founded (Waterford)
	26 Sept.	Frank McGuinness, *Carthaginians* (Peacock)
1990	15 Feb.	Alan Titley, *Tagann Godot* (Abbey)
	24 Apr.	Brian Friel, *Dancing at Lughnasa* (Abbey)
	1 Oct.	Seamus Heaney, *The Cure at Troy* (Field Day)
	9 Oct.	Dermot Bolger, *In High Germany* (Gate)
	3 Dec.	Mary Robinson inaugurated as first female President of Ireland
1991	1–20 Oct.	Beckett Festival (Gate)
	18 Nov.	Billy Roche, *Belfry* (Bush Theatre, London)
		Blue Raincoat Theatre Company founded (Sligo)
		Corcadorca Theatre Company founded (Cork)
1992	11 Feb.	Patricia Burke Brogan, *Eclipsed* (Punchbag)

	23 Apr.	Seán Mac Mathúna, *The Winter Thief/Gadaí Géar na Geamh Oíche* (Peacock)
1993	13 Apr.	Calypso Theatre Company founded
		Frank McGuinness, *Someone Who'll Watch Over Me* (Abbey)
1994	19 Apr.	Bickerstaffe Theatre Company, *True Lines*
	8 Aug.	Marie Jones, *A Night in November* (DubbelJoint)
	31 Aug.	IRA cease-fire; Loyalist paramilitaries follow, 10 Oct.
	5 Oct.	Marina Carr, *The Mai* (Peacock)
		Morgan Stanley report first uses phrase 'Celtic Tiger'
1995	9 Feb.	*Riverdance* (Point Theatre, Dublin)
	9 Nov.	Antoine Ó Flatharta, *An Solas Dearg* (Amharclann de hÍde, in Abbey)
	24 Nov.	Referendum legalizes divorce in Republic of Ireland
	30 Mar.	Sebastian Barry, *The Steward of Christendom* (Royal Court, London)
1996	1 Feb.	Martin McDonagh, *The Beauty Queen of Leenane* (Druid/Royal Court)
	27 Mar.	Marina Carr, *Portia Coughlan* (Abbey)
	7 Aug.	Marie Jones, *Stones in His Pockets* (DubbelJoint)
	26 Sept.	Enda Walsh, *Disco Pigs* (Corcadorca)
	12 Dec.	Martin McDonagh, *The Cripple of Innishmaan* (RNT, London)
1997	21 May	Conall Morrison, *Tarry Flynn* (based on the novel by Patrick Kavanagh) (Abbey)
	4 July	Conor McPherson, *The Weir* (Royal Court, London)
1998	14 Jan.	Jim Nolan, *The Salvage Shop* (Red Kettle)
	10 Apr.	Good Friday Agreement
	7 Oct.	Marina Carr, *By the Bog of Cats* (Abbey)
	10 Dec.	John Hume and David Trimble share Nobel Peace Prize
1999	Nov.	*The Wedding Community Play* (Belfast Festival)
	24 Mar.	Operating Theatre, *Angel/Babel*
2000	12 Apr.	Tom Murphy, *The House* (Abbey)
	30 Oct.	Daragh Carville et al., *Convictions* (Tinderbox)
2002	1 Apr.	Conor Grimes, Martin Lynch, Alan McKee, *The History of the Troubles (Accordin' to my Da)* (Belfast)
	30 Apr.	Frank McGuinness, *Gates of Gold* (Gate)
2003		Irish Playography database launched
	10 Apr.	Owen McCafferty, *Scenes from the Big Picture* (National Theatre, London)
2005	29 June	DruidSynge (production of six plays by Synge; Druid; Town Hall Theatre, Galway)
2006	20 Mar.	Enda Walsh, *The Walworth Farce* (Druid)
	10 Oct.	Conor McPherson, *The Seafarer* (National Theatre, London)
2007	13 June	Mark O'Rowe, *Terminus* (Abbey)
	29 Sept.	Roddy Doyle and Bisi Adigun, *The Playboy of the Western World* (adaptation of play by J. M. Synge) (Abbey)
2009	3 June	Tom Murphy, *The Last Days of a Reluctant Tyrant* (Abbey)
2010	17 Sept.	ANU Productions, *World's End Lane* (first play in Monto cycle)
	21 Oct.	Theatre of Witness, *I Once Knew a Girl* (Derry)
2011	May	Lyric Theatre opens (designed by O'Donnell and Tuomey)
	28 Nov.	Paul Mercier, *Sétanta* (Fibín, in Peacock)
2012	May	Smock Alley Theatre reopens as theatre (closed since 1787)
	23 June	Druid Murphy (three plays by Tom Murphy, Druid; opens at Hampstead Theatre, London)
	14 Nov.	Owen McCafferty, *Quietly* (Abbey)
2013	23 May	David Ireland, *Can't Forget About You* (Lyric)
2014	3 Oct.	Mark O'Rowe, *Our Few and Evil Days* (Abbey)

INTRODUCTION

THE most important word in the title of this book is 'theatre'. The familiar narrative in the field has most often been that of the Irish dramatic movement from the foundational work of W. B. Yeats, Augusta Gregory, and J. M. Synge to contemporary figures such as Martin McDonagh, Marina Carr, and Enda Walsh, sometimes including (although more often excluding) the major dramatists who made their careers abroad: Oscar Wilde, Bernard Shaw, and Samuel Beckett. These playwrights are, of course, given detailed analysis in the *Handbook*. However, our aim has been to extend the conspectus to take in the full phenomenon of modern Irish theatre. So, for example, we have two sections of the book devoted to performance, in which there is an examination of the often neglected work of directors and designers in what has been a text-centred tradition, an exploration of the acting styles and playing spaces that contribute to defining any period of theatre. While the Abbey, as Ireland's national theatre, has been of central importance, chapters in this book bring out the contesting voices of women in a male-dominated arena, the position of Irish language theatre, and 'little theatres' that challenged the hegemony of the Abbey. The middle of the twentieth century saw what amounted to a new revival of Irish drama with the emergence of a generation of playwrights responding in innovative ways to a modernizing Ireland. This, however, was again diversified by the changes in the structure and funding of Irish theatre from the 1970s on, resulting in the establishment of regional companies and alternative dramaturgical directions. The contemporary period in Irish theatre has been a particularly rich one, featuring both continuities and disruptions of inherited dramatic tradition, a movement beyond scripted plays to more experimental work. In its international success, also, this more recent work affords the opportunity to look beyond Ireland itself to the impact and interactions of Irish theatre with a wider world in the UK, Europe, and the United States.

Modern Irish theatre is generally dated from 1897, the manifesto of the Irish Literary Theatre of that year mapping the way towards the 1904 establishment of the Abbey with its claim to a new national status. However, although the leaders of that national theatre movement were in reaction against the earlier forms of nineteenth-century Irish melodrama, such forms persisted as an often unacknowledged substrate of modern Irish drama. And Wilde, who was to become something like a house dramatist of the Gate Theatre from the 1930s on, can also be seen to express nineteenth-century European styles and themes. An Irish national theatre was thus created out of the multiple and often conflicting forces that sought to conceive an independent national culture in early twentieth-century Ireland, expressed both in power struggles within the Abbey itself and in other competing theatre companies. A representational realism, almost inevitably based around the rural cottage kitchen or pub, in which the small town stands in (more or less explicitly) for the country as a whole, was to win out as the dominant style of Irish theatre from 1910 on. But it was not inevitably or unequivocally so. Yeats persisted in experimenting with a variety of non-naturalistic modernist styles, and through the 1920s and 1930s theatrical influences from outside Ireland shaped the practice of the Gate Theatre, which was to become the principal dramaturgical alternative to the Abbey. Indeed, even going back to Synge's work at the Abbey in the first decade of the century, there is an argument that his work, like that of Yeats, can be just as plausibly read in the context of international modernism. At the same time, Shaw, so often written out of the narrative of Irish theatre, provided in the discussion play of ideas another model of key importance to Irish dramatists. As the country moved through revolution towards an independent national state, the urgencies of political conflict had to find expression in the theatre. For the revolutionaries themselves, drama was a crucial medium both for propaganda and for the imagining of their objectives. In the aftermath, this produced a reaction particularly in the work of Seán O'Casey, whose sceptical urban vision challenged the unifying ideals of transformative revolution. After 1922 the national theatre in the postcolonial state found itself in a new and sometimes uneasy relationship with that state and its self-image.

All three of the first Directors of the Abbey Theatre—Yeats, Gregory, and Synge—were writers, none of them with a practical background in the theatre. For the productions of the Irish Literary Theatre (1899–1901), acting companies had to be recruited from England. It was the coming together of the leaders of the aspirational national theatre with the small troupe of largely amateur or semi-professional actors trained by William and Frank Fay that gave concrete reality and an acting style to the Abbey. That style was to blossom into a practice that allowed individual invention to exist within the ensemble playing that was a necessary feature of repertory, with results that can be seen in the inspired work of actors such as Sara Allgood, F. J. McCormick, and Barry Fitzgerald. In the Abbey initially, there would have been no separately credited 'director' for a production; this was still a time when the concept of the director as the shaping figure who controlled all aspects of a theatre production was only beginning to evolve. But Yeats, with his interests in the theories of Adolphe Appia and Gordon Craig, raised awareness of stage design, and extratheatrical pageants and spectacles in the 1920s added a new dimension to the idea of performance. The collaborative work of Hilton Edwards as director and Mícheál MacLiammóir as designer at the Gate yielded productions in which lighting, costuming, and movement were integrated into a coherent whole.

Despite the crucial role of Gregory in the establishment of the Abbey as moving spirit, director, and for years their most popular playwright, modern Irish theatre history has often occluded the contribution of women. Dramatists such as Eva Gore-Booth, Mary Manning, and Teresa Deevy, actors and actor-directors Sara Allgood, Shelah Richards, and Ria Mooney, designers Dorothy Travers Smith and Tanya Moiseiwitsch have been virtually written out of the record. Almost equally neglected has been Irish-language theatre, which, in spite of the longstanding efforts of the Galway-based An Taibhdhearc and other shorter-lived companies, has struggled to maintain its presence within an overwhelmingly Anglophone population. The 1950s in Ireland is often portrayed as a period in the cultural doldrums, but it was also a time when a proliferation of small theatres and theatre companies in Belfast and Dublin enlivened audience experience by the difference of their dramaturgy and politics.

In the 1960s, Ireland's long state policy of isolationism came to an end. Playwrights at this time reacted variously to the accelerating process of urbanization and modernization, whether in the conservative quietism of M. J. Molloy, the liberationist protests against repression of John B. Keane, or the satiric exposures of a new suburban life by Hugh Leonard. Two of the major figures starting to write at this period, Brian Friel and Tom Murphy, sought innovative theatrical styles to express the social, psychological, and spiritual condition of Irish men and women caught between the attachment to home and the need to escape. Thomas Kilroy, both in his theoretical writing and in his own dramaturgical practice, helped to reconceive Irish theatre of the 1960s and 1970s.

Dublin was long the dominant centre for theatre in Ireland, with venues outside the capital largely acting as receiving houses for touring productions. This began to change significantly with the establishment of Druid Theatre Company in Galway in 1975, using their western base and local acting company to develop a distinctive playing style that allowed them to produce fresh revivals of Synge and highly successful productions of work by Tom Murphy. Druid, like other regional theatres and alternative Dublin companies, such as Rough Magic and Passion Machine, were supported by the evolving cultural policies of the Arts Council, and by the opportunity of festivals at home and abroad to showcase their work. The political violence in the North demanded attention and produced an independent initiative in Field Day, established in 1980 by Friel and the actor Stephen Rea, which was to grow into an important theatre company touring out of its centre in Derry, in which Friel's own works were central to the attempt to rethink politically divisive images of the nation. However, the violent political and sectarian conflicts threatened over time to create their own familiar, stereotyped formula of the Northern 'Troubles' play. Many individual playwrights and theatre groups within Northern Ireland have found means to resist such dramatic clichés, particularly in the period since the Good Friday Agreement of 1998 when communities have tried to come to terms with the legacy of thirty years of violence.

Plays and playing are necessarily conditioned by the spaces of performance, spaces which carry within them the traditions associated with their past. The experiences of audiences within the Abbey, itself a reconstructed music-hall venue, over the years became overlaid with memories of former productions. At times in Irish theatre there have been efforts to work against such spatial inheritance in radical modern designs (not always realized) that attempted to create a sort of ground zero of performance. More recently, in site-specific work it has been the memories of historical actuality associated with the building that are invoked. While the spaces and circumstances of production have changed over time, so have attitudes towards direction and design, particularly in the more recent period. Directors such as Tomás Mac Anna, Patrick Mason, and Garry Hynes, often working very closely with designers such as Bronwen Casson, Joe Vaněk, and Frank Conway, have expanded the parameters of Irish scenic design

Professionalization has come relatively belatedly to Irish theatre, with full training in theatre arts emerging only in the late twentieth and early twenty-first century. Some of the most significant actors of the modern period learned on the job rather than in drama schools. Cyril Cusack, Siobhán McKenna, and Donal McCann served their apprenticeship in the Abbey company, playing a huge variety of leading and supporting roles, enabling them to develop the skills that make them international stars. Marie Mullen came up from student drama to become the leading actor of Druid Theatre Company, which she helped to found. These actors, though working also in film and television, continued to play primarily in the theatre, dependent on the live rapport with audiences established as the basis of their working practice. At the same time, Irish theatre became more international, as the sector as a whole became more professionalized. For instance, the entrepreneurial skills of Michael Colgan, the long-serving managing director of the Gate, were instrumental in putting together the hugely successful Beckett Festival in 1991, in which all nineteen of Beckett's stage plays were produced together. Colgan saw this event not simply as a creative challenge, but equally as a market opportunity for reclaiming the playwright for Ireland, while also creating a show that drew on international directors and performers and had an extended afterlife in repeated revivals and eventually a cinematic re-creation as the *Beckett on Film* series.

The last twenty-five years in Irish theatre has been a period of unprecedented diversity of achievement and international success. To some extent this has come about through a continuation of forms of play production that have been become associated with the 'brand' of Irish theatre: a poetic fluency of language, a mixed skein of comic and tragic emotions, a retrospective concern with past history, and a near-archaic imagined community. An outstanding figure in this period has been Frank McGuinness, who has challenged traditional conceptions of ethnic and sexual identity, while fulfilling audience expectations of a richly layered form of Irish drama. Friel, Murphy, and Kilroy have continued to be productive, negotiating the changes in contemporary Irish society often through memory-based negotiations with the past. An Irish reputation for story-telling has been one reason for the success of a playwright such as Conor McPherson, whereas expectations of lyrical expressiveness or folklore-based drama have played into the reception of Sebastian Barry and Marina Carr. In contrast to such playwrights, who, however challenging their vision, seem to conform to traditional dramaturgical forms, there have been the sharply abrasive works of Martin McDonagh, Mark O'Rowe, and Enda Walsh. These dramatists parody conventional images of Irish theatre, and in their violent action appear to be close to a radical British 'in-yer-face' style. Many companies in this period, such as Pan Pan, Corn Exchange, Blue Raincoat, and ANU Productions have moved away from text-based work into theatre of movement and image, improvisational, and site-specific drama that no longer gives primacy to language. However, even in this period when so much has been changing, women's role in theatre has continued to be undervalued. In spite of the international success of the work of Carr, and the excitement generated by the female collective Charabanc in the 1980s and 1990s (out of which Marie Jones emerged as a playwright), it has not been until well into the twenty-first century that the achievement of women as actors, directors, and playwrights have been normalized as part of the theatrical mainstream rather than ghettoized as a separate category.

It is understandable that the Irish national theatre movement emerging from centuries of colonial domination should be preoccupied with self-image and thus to some degree in-turned. But from at least as far back as the time of Dion Boucicault in the nineteenth century, Irish drama has been a presence in a wider theatrical marketplace. Beckett has, of course, been the playwright whose European and global reception has made his Irish origins all but invisible, in spite of the fact that his work has been successfully performed in Ireland since the 1950s. His supposed universalism has been a key part of his international standing, although there have long been critical challenges to this understanding of his work. By contrast, there has been a continuous interaction between Irish theatre identified as such and other Anglophone cultures, notably in the US, with influence and impact working both ways. The London transfer has been the aspiration for many Irish plays and productions in the modern period, and London approval the mark of success. Several contemporary Irish playwrights, indeed, choose to open their plays in Britain rather than Ireland for the greater market exposure it affords. Outside London, also, British playwrights of Irish origins have dramatized the problematic nature of national and regional identity.

Festivals have provided Irish drama with an international showcase both at home and abroad. The Dublin Theatre Festival, founded in 1957, is itself a collective performance of Irish drama, while it brings cross-fertilizing influence from visiting companies from abroad. Within continental Europe the penetration of Irish theatre has been much more uneven than in Anglophone countries. While Wilde, Shaw, and Beckett are widely produced, they are not really registered as Irish. Locally, there have been traditions of playing Synge, for instance, in the Czech lands, and O'Casey in Germany, and some contemporary playwrights such as McDonagh and Walsh have been widely translated and produced, but others such as Friel, highly successful elsewhere, are less well known in Europe. If Irish drama has not always succeeded in reaching the Continent, there has been a flourishing tradition in recent times of bringing European drama home to Ireland in 'versions'—by Irish dramatists who do not themselves know the original languages of the plays they are rewriting—or in adaptations more fully assimilated to an Irish setting. The strong reputation of individual playwrights and the Irish theatre collectively has created a market for these more or less Hibernicized productions of classic drama from Greek tragedy to Chekhov and Ibsen.

Irish theatre has by now generated a substantial body of criticism, with theatre historians, political commentators, and cultural interpreters approaching the subject from different perspectives. Taken as a whole, the *Oxford Handbook of Modern Irish Theatre* displays not only the diversity of Irish theatre scholarship but also the ways in which it is evolving. The long dominance of the playwright in Irish theatre has resulted in a rich tradition of critical writing focused on the dramatic text. Within the past decade and a half, there has been a discernible performative turn in writing about Irish theatre, coinciding both with new critical approaches and with an ever more varied performance culture. More recently, it has been possible to sense a new concentration on archives in the field, as major collections such as the Abbey archive have been digitized, and the papers of writers such as Brian Friel, Thomas Kilroy, and Tom Murphy have become available for the first time. All of these movements within the field can be found within this volume.

In putting together this book, we as editors were very lucky in being able to recruit some of the most distinguished Irish theatre scholars. While we mapped out the territory and planned the structural divisions into sections and chapters to fulfil our objective of representing as full an analysis as possible of Irish theatre, we also encouraged our contributors to adopt whatever approach they felt most telling for their subject. According to the principles of the Oxford Handbook series, the chapters are more or less discrete units, each tackling a separate facet of Irish theatrical practice. Inevitably, that means there are some areas of overlap and a few gaps. We have, however, restricted cross-referencing to a minimum, mostly in cases where another author within the volume has offered a different point of view of the same subject. Full references for all cited materials appear in footnotes, but so as not to make the Bibliography too unwieldy we have restricted it to book publications. We hope that the result is a volume that can be used for information and understanding by anyone interested in a single aspect of the subject, but also will result in a more complex, nuanced, and fully comprehensive view of what is a quite extraordinary cultural product of Ireland and an important contribution to world theatre.

Nicholas Grene
Chris Morash
Trinity College Dublin, April 2015

PART I

NINETEENTH-CENTURY LEGACIES

CHAPTER 1

THE INHERITANCE OF MELODRAMA

STEPHEN WATT

DRAMAS OF EXTERIORITY

ONE of the most enduring truisms in theatrical criticism is that, much like the antago-nistic position announced by a young James Joyce after seeing a production of Hermann Sudermann's *Magda* (1893; English translation, 1896), modern drama revolted violently against the past: against Victorian-era repressions and social orthodoxy; against a theatre of cheap sentiment and stale declamation; and against such enormously popular dramatic forms as melodrama. That is to say, as a modern drama epitomized by the plays of Henrik Ibsen was becoming a 'thing of supreme importance' to him, the teenage Joyce warned his parents that they would witness first hand, as they had at the Theatre Royal in Mrs Patrick Campbell's portrayal of Sudermann's protagonist, 'genius breaking out in the home and against the home'.[1] As intimated by the title of Robert Brustein's widely influential study some half a century ago, *The Theatre of Revolt: An Approach to Modern Drama* (1964)—a book chronicling the aesthetic projects of such playwrights as Ibsen, August Strindberg, and Eugene O'Neill—Joyce's insurrection rivalled that of writers like Bernard Shaw, who, as a reviewer in the 1890s for London's *Saturday Review*, lambasted the late Victorian stage while championing the causes of a 'new' social drama and the more subtle 'highly intellec-tual' acting of such brilliant stars as Eleonora Duse.[2]

---

[1] Stanislaus Joyce, *My Brother's Keeper: James Joyce's Early Years*, ed. Richard Ellmann (New York: Viking Press, 1958), 87. Mrs Patrick (Stella) Campbell appeared as Magda at Dublin's Theatre Royal several times during Joyce's teenage years: in Mar. 1899, Aug. 1900, and July 1901.

[2] Shaw praises Ibsen as founding a 'new school of dramatic art' in *The Quintessence of Ibsenism: Now Completed to the Death of Ibsen* (London: Constable, 1913), 175. *The Quintessence of Ibsenism* originally appeared in 1891. In early June 1895, Shaw applauded Duse's 'highly intellectual' performance in *La Femme de Claude* by Alexandre Dumas *fils* (1873), hailing it as the 'the best modern acting I have ever seen'; and in a review of 15 June 1895, he compared Duse's impersonation of Sudermann's Magda favourably with that of Sarah Bernhardt, who had disappointed in a 'less

In this critical genealogy, melodrama is typically disparaged as an 'old' dramatic form reaching back as far as the 1820s and 1830s, or even slightly earlier, when so-called nautical docudrama based on sea battles during the Napoleonic era made their ways from newspapers to the stages of London theatres. Docudrama then evolved into nautical melodrama, in which ship-to-ship confrontations proved especially popular, providing audiences with high-voltage excitement, sensational action, spectacular visual effects, and a patriotic hero or more generic 'Jack Tar', sacrificing nobly for his country and battling heartless adversaries while his innocent wife languished at home.[3] In many respects a supple and versatile form, melodrama transported its audiences throughout the nineteenth century to a myriad of contemporary and historical settings: to working-class tenements in rapidly expanding cities like London and New York; to anti-colonial upheavals in distant colonies like India; to fifteenth-century Rouen and the trial of Joan of Arc; and to more Irish peasant cottages than it is feasible to count. It continues to evince its powers of attraction today, particularly in the cinema. Yet, whatever its historical and geographical representation, melodrama relies upon a predictable ensemble of characters and a repetitive trajectory of dramatic action, as it 'not only employs virtue persecuted as a source of its dramaturgy, but also tends to become the dramaturgy of virtue misprized and eventually recognized'.[4] As Peter Brooks emphasizes, melodrama is a drama of 'exteriority', as its characters do not possess complex psychologies or suffer the anguish of interior conflict. Instead, they occupy extremes in a world 'built on an irreducible Manichaeanism' where the 'conflict of good and evil as opposites' is seldom subject to compromise.[5] Villains are evil simply because they are, one might say; heroines are virtuous because they are as inherently innocent as they are desirable; and, in many instances of the genre, though not all, heroes can bravely intervene to make certain that the complications that imperilled the heroine's good name or life can be overcome.

At the same moment as Joyce revelled in Ibsen's drama, Seán O'Casey was equally diverted by melodrama's attractions.[6] As his 1938 letter to Harvard scholar Horace Reynolds indicates,[7] O'Casey (1880–1964) enjoyed Dion Boucicault's *The Octoroon* (1859) and *The Colleen Bawn* (1860), the titles of which focus attention on the plays' innocent

---

satisfactory assumption' of the same role. See George Bernard Shaw, *Our Theatres in the Nineties*, vol. 1 (London: Constable, 1932), 140–54.

   [3] For a discussion of the heritage of nautical melodrama, see George D. Glenn, 'Nautical "Docudramas" in the Age of the Kembles', in Judith L. Fisher and Stephen Watt (eds.), *When They Weren't Doing Shakespeare: Essays on Nineteenth-Century British and American Theatre*, 2nd edn. (Athens, GA: University of Georgia Press, 2011), 137–51. See also J. S. Bratton, 'British Heroism and the Structure of Melodrama', in J. S. Bratton et al., *Acts of Supremacy: The British Empire and the Stage, 1790–1930* (Manchester: Manchester University Press, 1991), 18–61.

   [4] Peter Brooks, *The Melodramatic Imagination: Balzac, Henry James, Melodrama, and the Mode of Excess* (New York: Columbia University Press, 1985), 27.

   [5] Ibid., 35–6.

   [6] See Christopher Murray, *Seán O'Casey, Writer at Work: A Biography* (Dublin: Gill & Macmillan, 2004), 43–7. Murray describes how O'Casey's older brother Isaac, 'head over heels in love with theatre' (44), staged amateur theatricals in which O'Casey took part. Isaac had nearly 100 scripts from *Dicks's Standard Plays* bound in one volume, which his younger brother took great delight in reading.

   [7] See *The Letters of Sean O'Casey 1910–1941*, vol. 1, ed. David Krause (New York: Macmillan, 1975), 700–1.

heroines and express an important relationship to America, where by the 1860s Boucicault (1820–90) had become a star. *The Octoroon; or, Life in Louisiana* is set on an antebellum plantation on the verge of ruin, and centres around the fate of a dual-heritage heroine named Zoe, an exotic object of too many men's desires. *The Colleen Bawn*, the title of which alludes to the fair Irish girl at the centre of the dramatic action, premièred at New York's Laura Keene Theatre on 29 March 1860, quickly becoming a success across America, in London, and in Dublin. In explaining his international success, Deirdre McFeely not only recalls Boucicault's lionization by Dublin reviewers, but also observes that his turn to Irish materials—at least in his own estimation—marked the inauguration of the Irish play in New York, so that now, in his words, 'other greater men, of finer genius and abilities than I possess, may hereafter give you plenty of Irish plays'.[8]

The Irish Play

Two such plays, Boucicault's *Arrah-na-Pogue* (1864) and *The Shaughraun* (1874), are set during tense moments between Ireland and England—respectively, during the 1798 rebellion of the United Irishmen and the Fenian uprising of the 1860s—and helped create an audience for even more historically specific Irish melodrama. Hubert O'Grady (1841–99) and the English-born proprietor of the Queen's Theatre Dublin, J. W. Whitbread (1848–1916), to name two of the most prolific dramatists, consistently attracted large and enthusiastic audiences with plays based (often loosely) on Irish experience and the vicissitudes of recent history: O'Grady's *Eviction* (1879), *Emigration* (1880), *The Famine* (1886), and *The Fenian* (1888), for example, and Whitbread's *Lord Edward or '98* (1894), *Wolfe Tone* (1898), and *The Insurgent Chief* (1902). At one time regarded as presenting a 'mythical land of blarney and blather'[9] populated exclusively by patriotic orators, oppressed colleens, and traitorous informers—and, as such, once consigned by scholars to an 'arid wasteland of indifference and contempt'[10]—melodrama and the 'old' Queen's Theatre to which O'Casey alluded in his reminiscence to Reynolds have received renewed attention. Séamus de Búrca's *The Queen's Royal Theatre Dublin 1829–1969* (1983) outlines the history of later nineteenth-century melodrama and other popular entertainments such as pantomime at the Queen's, complete with playbills and posters advertising Boucicault's and other plays; and in *'Buffoonery and Easy Sentiment'*, Christopher Fitz-Simon delineates the wider appeal of Irish melodrama

---

[8] Dion Boucicault, *New York Tribune*, 20 Mar. 1860, quoted in Deirdre McFeely, *Dion Boucicault: Irish Identity on Stage* (Cambridge: Cambridge University Press, 2012), 13. McFeely makes a persuasive case for the representation of nationalism, race, and class in *The Colleen Bawn*, in part by adducing parallels between Eily O'Connor—the *cailín bán* ('fair-haired girl') of the title—and Zoe, the title character of *The Octoroon* (16–21). Boucicault's implicit claim of inaugurating a genre of melodrama rooted in Irish experience is somewhat hubristic, as a decade or more before, in the wake of the Great Famine, several playwrights created plays based on the experiences of Irish immigrants in America.

[9] Hugh Hunt, *The Abbey: Ireland's National Theatre, 1904–1979* (Dublin: Gill & Macmillan, 1979), 4.

[10] Michael R. Booth, *Prefaces to English Nineteenth-Century Theatre* (Manchester: Manchester University Press, 1980), 1.

throughout the country and abroad. Because of the 'continuous touring to metropolitan centres outside Ireland' and cities within it,[11] revivals of melodramas by Whitbread, O'Grady, and others were staged regularly at the turn of the century not only in Dublin but also in Cork, Belfast, London, and—particularly in Boucicault's case—in New York, Boston, and cities across America.

It is not difficult to understand why melodrama dominated the stage for much of the nineteenth century and the earlier decades of the twentieth. At theatres like the Queen's, as Mary Trotter explains, nationalist dramas were '*popular*—affordable and accessible to all classes', including those from the working class, and '*participatory*', allowing spectators to register their views immediately and, often, loudly.[12] Such was the case, for example, at a revival of O'Grady's *The Famine* in 1899, as The *Freeman's Journal* reported on October 10 of that year:

> The attendance last night was about the largest that has been seen in the Queen's for a considerable time. The pit and gallery were simply packed [. . .] The pit and gallery were noisy, but that was evidently due to the excitement caused by the incidents of the play, and the characters [. . .] were constantly applauded or hissed according to [their] merits or demerits.[13]

Nationalist melodramas were also spectacular, occasionally featuring landmarks that induced national pride in spectators as well as offering, like most other varieties of melodrama, sensational scenes with burning buildings or boats, prison walls or towers that needed to be climbed to effect an escape. Not surprisingly, given the visual and emotive appeals of such plays, playbills for popular melodramas both identified the actors appearing in the production and provided a catalogue of highly emotive scenes and settings forecasting the excitement that awaited spectators. Brightly coloured posters advertised climactic scenes much as 'trailers' for action films do today: a poignant deathbed scene for an adaptation of Mrs Henry Wood's novel *East Lynne* (1861); a volatile slave auction in *The Octoroon* at which buyers fight over Zoe; a firing squad in Whitbread's *Wolfe Tone* that executes a traitorous lawyer in the employ of Dublin Castle, and so on.[14]

A significant number of plays in the popular repertory at the *fin de siècle* represent one or another of two types of melodrama: domestic melodrama, in which the trials of innocent heroines constitute the focus of the dramatic action; and historical melodrama, in which Irish nationalism is typically placed on conspicuous and heroic display. Both kinds of play exercised enormous appeal when the Irish Literary Theatre was founded formally in January 1899; and because both were produced with great regularity in

---

[11]   Christopher Fitz-Simon, *'Buffoonery and Easy Sentiment': Popular Irish Plays in the Decade Prior to the Opening of the Abbey Theatre* (Dublin: Carysfort Press, 2011), 1. See 4–18 for a calendar of productions of melodrama in Dublin, Belfast, and Cork between 1895 and 1904. In *Louis D'Alton and the Abbey Theatre* (Dublin: Four Courts Press, 2004) , Ciara O'Farrell connects melodrama to the offerings of 'fit-up' or travelling theatre companies—'at least' 250 of them (32)—that toured Ireland in the nineteenth and first half of the twentieth century. One of these featuring Frank Dalton, Louis D'Alton's father, conveyed O'Grady's *Eviction* to the United States soon after its première in 1880.

[12]   Mary Trotter, *Ireland's National Theatres: Political Performance and the Origins of the Irish Dramatic Movement* (Syracuse, NY: Syracuse University Press, 2001), 41.

[13]   *Freeman's Journal*, 10 Oct. 1899.

[14]   For a selection of Queen's Theatre playbills and posters, see Séamus de Búrca, *The Queen's Royal Theatre Dublin 1829–1969* (Dublin: Séamus de Búrca, 1983), 47–77.

Dublin, they constituted formidable competition for the Abbey Theatre when it opened its doors for the first time in 1904.[15] At the same time, melodrama was much more than competition. As Frank Fay, who along with his brother Willie played an essential role in the launching of the National Theatre Society, demurred in the *United Irishman* of 4 May 1901, it was the despised 'other' that a new Irish drama must both supplant and transcend: '[T]he Irishman who goes on the stage must sink his individuality and his accent as much as it is possible for him to do, otherwise he will not rise above the class of stuff that Mr Whitbread is in the habit of presenting to his patrons.'[16] Fay's assertion anticipates several modernist agendas, theatrical and otherwise: to rise above the popular, the expected, or the conventional, for example, and to facilitate the creation of more authentic characters that might reveal shallow stereotypes for what they are. Yet, is it truly possible for a writer of O'Casey's background—or for theatre professionals like Frank and Willie Fay—to forget completely the popular drama they knew so well? And what of the Irish audience? From its inception, the National Theatre Society, led by William Butler Yeats, Lady Gregory, Edward Martyn, and J. M. Synge, contemplated a kind of theatre that would 'educate and interest the public of this country in the higher aspects of dramatic art'.[17] But what if the audience's experience of theatre rendered them unwilling or unable to appreciate these 'higher aspects' of drama? What if melodrama spoke to theatregoers in ways that mapped usefully onto their experience of an ever more complicated modernity?

These last two questions pertain directly to connotations of 'inheritance' in the title of this chapter, for melodrama might profitably be construed as more than the set of dramatic conventions which the next section of this chapter will outline. Melodrama, that is, also serves as a response to the changes wrought by modernity, and as such may be regarded as a mode of thought cultivated in a Petri dish of increasingly complex economic and sociopolitical realities, some of which emerge at a velocity destined to upset the rhythms of lived experience. Elaine Hadley, for example, argues that melodrama in Victorian England ceased to be a 'localized literary convention';[18] rather, it informed fiction, journalism, politics, and more. Melodrama, she adds, is always a 'public and theatrical response to the classification of English society'; 'profoundly reactionary, if not precisely politically' reactionary, this mode both hearkened back 'to a deferential society and its patriarchal grounds for identity' and invariably idealized a life quickly being superseded by the more ruthless mechanisms of capitalism and the

---

[15]   As an example, in January 1899, when the Theatre Royal and Gaiety Theatres mounted pantomimes, the Queen's Theatre featured *Wolfe Tone* and *East Lynne*. Whitbread's *Lord Edward, or '98* was produced in April, as was Douglas Jerrold's nautical melodrama *Black Ey'd Susan* (1829). During one week in July, Boucicault's *The Shaughraun* played at the Queen's while *Arrah-na-Pogue* and *The Colleen Bawn* alternated in repertory at the Theatre Royal. *Wolfe Tone*, Whitbread's *The Irishman* (1892), John Baldwin Buckstone's *The Green Bushes* (1847), several Boucicault plays, and Hubert O'Grady's *The Famine* appeared in the late summer and autumn; and Boucicault's best-known Irish plays were reprised for three weeks in December. See Stephen Watt, *Joyce, O'Casey, and the Irish Popular Theater* (Syracuse, NY: Syracuse University Press, 1991), 201–39.

[16]   Quoted in Hunt, *Abbey Theatre*, 32.   [17]   Ibid., 39.

[18]   Elaine Hadley, *Melodramatic Tactics: Theatricalized Dissent in the English Marketplace, 1800–1885* (Stanford, CA: Stanford University Press, 1995), 8.

marketplace.[19] In making these assertions, Hadley implicitly underscores both the historically contingent quality of melodrama and the broad range of cultural work it can achieve; for by the middle nineteenth century, as North America welcomed what would grow to over two million Irish immigrants, such playwrights as James Pilgrim (1825–79) and John Brougham (1810–80) created melodramas that, instead of looking backward to an idealized past, promoted the readiness of Irish newcomers to contribute to an ever-modernizing urban America.[20] Melodrama, in short, may not always advance a 'reactionary' or conservative politics, although Victorian melodrama and much Irish melodrama may very well do so; some forms of the genre—and immigrant melodrama is one of them—induce their audiences to look forward in what are arguably politically progressive ways.[21]

Following Hadley's lead, Matthew Kaiser argues that no matter how 'profound' its 'superficiality of plot and character'—no matter how musty its contrivances—melodrama inevitably 'breaks loose from its theatrical frame' and 'infiltrates modern consciousness'.[22] Melodramatic 'logic' reshaped nineteenth-century British subjectivity, he contends, so much so that people began to 'live melodramatic lives, think melodramatic thoughts', and see the world with 'melodramatic eyes'.[23] By this logic, the inheritance of nineteenth-century melodrama not only includes familiar action, characters, language, and scenic motifs, but also implies an epistemology—a rich bequest of thought, perspective, and ways of knowing—that manifests itself at times in disguised ways in much later Irish drama. Melodrama, put by way of another theoretical lexicon, serves as a latent content or Freudian unconscious that in both overt and more subtle ways underlies the manifest content—the scripts—of writers like O'Casey, Louis D'Alton (1900–51), Walter Macken (1915–67), and others long after its heyday in the nineteenth century. It is the case, then, that no matter how residual a form it might have been in the 1940s and 1950s, or how 'old' in comparison to the 'new' theatre of revolt that eclipsed it in the 1880s and 1890s, melodrama played a crucial role in the development of the modern Irish drama. And, at times, well after Boucicault initiated his long string of successes, melodramatic conventions reappeared in altered or ironic ways recalling popular plots and characters, and generating the excitement that the most accomplished melodrama so spectacularly created on the nineteenth-century stage.

---

[19] Ibid., 11.

[20] See Kerby A. Miller, *Ireland and Irish America: Culture, Class, and Transatlantic Migration* (Dublin: Field Day, 2008). Miller estimates that during 1845–55 some 2.1 million Irish emigrated to North America, and characterizes the majority as 'unhappy exiles' suffering often from 'acute home sickness' (10).

[21] This position resembles that of Stuart Hall who, in 'Notes on Deconstructing the "Popular"', in Raphael Samuel (ed.), *People's History and Socialist Theory* (London: Routledge and Kegan Paul, 1981), 227–40, argues that the 'traditionalism' often associated with popular cultural forms has been 'misinterpreted as a product of a merely conservative impulse, backward looking and anachronistic' (227). Hadley is correct in diagnosing this impulse in Victorian and, by extension, some Irish melodrama, but immigrant melodrama is better described by Hall's notion of the 'double movement of containment and resistance' inherent to popular cultural texts (Hadley, *Melodramatic Tactics*, 11).

[22] Matthew Kaiser, *The World in Play: Portrait of a Victorian Concept* (Stanford, CA: Stanford University Press, 2012), 60.

[23] Ibid., 53.

MELODRAMA AND THE ENCROACHMENT OF MODERNITY

Kaiser makes a salient observation—and advances a thoughtful extension of Peter Brooks's emphasis of melodrama's Manichaean opposition of good and evil—when he deems modernity as 'not evil'; rather, from the vantage point of the melodramatic mode, modern life has become less fair: '[t]he capitalist market has changed the rules of the game', with the result that society has become 'more ruthlessly competitive, less cooperative' than it once was and a community's 'organic connectivity' is threatened.[24] Melodrama may thus be regarded as staging more than the opposition of good and evil, however persuasive such a thesis might be. With its foregrounding of unfairness and injustice, the victimization of the weak or powerless by seemingly invincible adversaries, melodrama moves to situations of excitement and heightened dramatic tension in which the opposition of fairness and unfairness—or fair play and foul play—obtains. This tension heightens suspense, leading audiences to wonder how an impasse will be resolved and how the entrapped will escape a life- or home-threatening predicament that always seems sanctioned by the law and enforced by its minions of soulless operatives. In the nationalist context, the unfairness is perpetrated, not surprisingly, by representatives of the English military—although 'gentlemanly' soldiers often appear as well, broadening considerably the appeal of plays like *Arrah-na-Pogue* and *The Shaughraun*—but is more often represented by the misdeeds of their Irish confederates: informants and avaricious lawyers, process servers, and the like. As featured prominently in four-colour advertisements, the action of nineteenth-century melodrama often led to a 'scene-closing tableau, in which actors froze in an arrangement that starkly revealed the dramatic conflict among opposing parties'.[25] Tireless in their invention of such situations, melodramatists also engineered action to lead to a stage-picture that replicated well-known artworks or vistas. And these tableaux were undergirded—often caused—by the vicissitudes of a relentless modernity and the essential unfairness it produced. Melodrama, in other words, anticipated social, economic, and national changes; and this is as true of Irish domestic drama as of that based on well-known historical moments or the lives of nationalist heroes.

The Colleen Bawn displays many of these characteristics, beginning, as *The Octoroon* does, with the imminent loss of a family's home. The opening set of '*the Residence of Mrs Cregan on the Banks of Killarney*',[26] like that of *The Shaughraun* at '*Suil-a-beg—the Cottage of Arte O'Neal*',[27] locates the dramatic action squarely in the Irish countryside. By the time the inaugural scene of *The Colleen Bawn* concludes, the complications driving the plot have almost all been revealed. Corrigan, denigrated in the *dramatis personae* as a 'pettifogging attorney',[28] holds a mortgage on the Cregan home, which he will gladly pay if the widowed

[24] Ibid., 55–6.
[25] Ben Singer, *Melodrama and Modernity: Early Sensational Cinema and Its Contexts* (New York: Columbia University Press, 2001), 41–2.
[26] Dion Boucicault, *Selected Plays*, ed. Andrew Parkin (Gerrards Cross: Colin Smythe; Washington, DC: Catholic University Press of America, 1987), 193.
[27] Ibid., 259.   [28] Ibid., 192.

Mrs Cregan succumbs to his odious advances; otherwise, the family will be evicted. Or, if her son Hardress marries the wealthy and exemplary Anne Chute, the Cregan home might be saved, but he cannot do so as he is secretly married to the angelic peasant girl Eily O'Connor, the Colleen Bawn. Admonishing his mother for denigrating Eily as 'a vulgar barefooted beggar', Hardress proclaims that love has made her his social 'equal' and that 'when you set your foot upon her you tread upon my heart'.[29] Desperate to manufacture a remedy, Hardress's loyal, albeit misguided, servant Danny Mann believes that seizing Eily's marriage certificate and throwing her into a lake are the only ways to preserve the family home. If she is out of the way, then Hardress might marry Anne, whose money could save the Cregan home just as the heiress Dora Sunnyside's wealth could redeem the Terrebone plantation from Northern interlopers in *The Octoroon*. In the kind of sensation scene audiences expected to see, the comic Irishman Myles-na-Coppaleen, first played by Boucicault himself, is tending his whiskey still in a nearby cave when Eily is in the most extreme danger. Myles, far from being the 'lazy, ragged' poacher Corrigan castigates in an earlier scene,[30] is the hero who, at the very moment he is needed, hears Eily's screams, shoots Danny, and rescues her from drowning.

In a manner resembling the celebrations that conclude romantic comedy, *The Colleen Bawn* and Irish domestic melodramas move towards a closing tableau that signals the restoration of a community that has been threatened—a community now revolving around the virtuous heroine and her friends. This typically requires not merely the rescue of the innocent from the clutches of the powerful, but a kind of wish-fulfilling reverie that closes historical fissures in nineteenth-century Irish society.[31] Priests, for instance, appear in Boucicault's most famous Irish plays, and in *The Shaughraun* Father Dolan remains the loving tutor of Robert Ffolliott, even though Ffolliott is 'under sentence' as a Fenian: that is, a member of an organization that would exert physical force in its pursuit of Irish nationalism and, as a result, was frequently denounced from the pulpits of Catholic churches. In addition, in Act I, Scene 3 of *The Colleen Bawn*, Father Tom endorses both the drinking and blarney often associated with the Stage Irishman in an effort to bolster Eily's flagging spirits:

> Put your lips to that jug; there's only the sthrippens left. Drink! and while that thrue Irish liquor warms your heart, take this wid it. May the brogue of ould Ireland niver forsake your tongue—may her music niver lave your voice—and may a true Irishwoman's virtue niver die in your heart![32]

The community that melodrama restores similarly annuls social class division, even if as in *The Colleen Bawn* class distinctions and their signals—the way one talks or dresses—initially form an obstacle to the projects of the play's central characters. Ever mindful of the plights of the less fortunate, characters like Anne Chute, Lady Alice Raymond in

---

   [29] Ibid., 198.   [30] Ibid., 203.
   [31] Brooks regards melodrama as inextricably connected to dreams. Echoing both Eric Bentley and Michael Booth, he notes that 'the affective structure of melodrama brings us close to the experience of dreams'. Further, he asserts that 'Bentley is surely right that the force of melodrama derives from the very origins of theatricality, of self-dramatization, in the infantile dream world' (Brooks, *Melodramatic Imagination*, 35).
   [32] Boucicault, *Selected Plays*, 208.

O'Grady's *The Famine*, and Lady Rose O'Malley in Whitbread's *The Nationalist* (1891) come to the defence of the peasants who surround them and are happily included in a revised social order.

The most consistent and popular elision of social class complications in Irish melodrama, however, involves the stage Irishman's loyal protection of the nationalist hero. From Shaun the Post in *Arrah-na-Pogue* to his counterparts in Whitbread's dramas—Shane McMahon in *Wolfe Tone*, Thady M'Grath in *Lord Edward, or '98*, and Gallopin' Hogan in *Sarsfield* (1905)—such characters consistently demonstrate that they are 'boy[s] of the right sort, true to the core', as M'Grath is heralded in the cast list of *Lord Edward*.[33] Whitbread's comic Irishmen stand ready to defend the nationalist heroes they serve from the traitors and informers who plague them, typically motivated either by lust for the hero's wife or by simple avarice. Indeed, the stage Irishman's thwarting of the villains' traps at the ends of suspenseful scenes while trouncing them physically forms a motif in many of these plays until, of course, an end to their mischief must be reached. Near the conclusion of *The Shaughraun*, Conn presents one final option to the notorious informer Harvey Duff, who pleads for mercy as an angry crowd pursues him to the edge of a precipice: 'There's death coming down upon you from above!—there's death waiting for you below! Now, *informer*, take your choice.'[34] Duff chooses the latter.

In some historically based melodrama, the informer is portrayed as re-enacting Judas's betrayal of Christ. Lord Edward's betrayer in Whitbread's play, the Barrister-at-Law Francis Magan, is described as having given Edward the 'kiss of Judas',[35] and like Christ's life, Edward's cannot be spared. In the final scene, he selflessly asks his family and friends not to weep for him and bids them a gallant 'Farewell' while his principal adversary, Francis Higgins, nicknamed the 'Shamado', sadistically predicts that as the 'icy grasp' of death afflicts the hero, the nationalist 'Rebellion' will die with him (169). The more ornately decorated final tableau of Boucicault's *Robert Emmet* (1884), the authorship of which is substantially attributable to the lesser-known playwright Frank Marshall,[36] provides a spectacular correlative to this association of the nationalist patriot with the Messiah as the concluding tableau references Michelangelo's *Pietà*. After Emmet has expired, a black flag is raised and the stage darkens. Then:

> The wall behind EMMET slowly opens. A vista of pale blue clouds appears. The figure of Ireland clothed in palest green and with a coronet of shamrocks in her hair descends slowly; and bending forward when she reaches the spot behind EMMET, she kneels. Two CHILDREN at her feet, R and L, draw slowly back the body of EMMET until his head lies looking up into her face.[37]

In some historical melodrama, therefore, a wish-fulfilling reverie cannot be sustained; the devices of traitorous informants cannot be overcome, and the essentially comic resolutions

[33] J. W. Whitbread, *Lord Edward, or '98*, in Cheryl Herr (ed.), *For the Land They Loved: Irish Political Melodramas, 1890–1925* (Syracuse, NY: Syracuse University Press, 1991), 83.

[34] Boucicault, *Selected Plays*, 324.   [35] Whitbread, *Lord Edward*, 131.

[36] For a discussion of the complications of this play's history and a correction of previous scholarship about the play, see McFeely, *Dion Boucicault*, 139–40, 169–72.

[37] Boucicault, *Selected Plays*, 397.

of domestic melodrama, with the promises of marriage or multiple marriages, cannot be celebrated. A Christ-like sacrifice can be the only conclusion.

As Irish melodrama evolved from the mid-century of *The Colleen Bawn* to the *fin de siècle*, the sense of an increasingly powerful capitalism insinuated itself into plots, attaching itself to plays' villains. So, for example, Whitbread's *The Nationalist* begins not with a single mortgage being dangled precariously over one family's future, but with attorney Patrick Flynn in the process of delivering twenty-five 'writs of ejectment'. One, designated for Peggy Donohoe, has been frustrated by a rent payment from Lady Rose O'Malley, dedicated to assisting her poor tenants. Flynn quickly becomes the target of the comic Irishman Denny O'Hea, who rebuffs Flynn's false accusation that he has witnessed an 'ocular demonstration' of Peggy's supposed love affair as the source of her rent money with a 'knockular diminstration [*sic*]'[38] of his own, and he repeats his clever witticisms and physical victories throughout the play. More to the point, Whitbread's play introduces not only nationalism but socialism as a foil to the machinations of greedy operatives like Flynn and his partner, Matthew Sheehan. Impoverished landowner Phil Hennessey, restrained legally by his father's will from accessing badly needed funds until he attains the age of 25, insists that the lowest tenant on his land 'receive the same justice as the highest' (11), and he is supported in this position by Joe McManus, a reporter for the *Daily Exposer* accused by Sheehan of promulgating 'socialist teachings' (13). This accusation, Phil and Joe's need to conceal 'League' papers from the police, and allusions to organized 'plans of campaign' pose collective action as the only response to the rapacity of a socioeconomic system that would prompt evictions on such a large scale.

Yet another intimation of an ever-expanding capitalism in later melodrama is the issue of an individual selling his or her labour—or being denied the opportunity to do so. As Ben Singer asserts when outlining the several forces associated with capitalism—including modernization, rationality, mobility, and individualism—the commodification of goods and services and 'individuals' ownership of their own labour power' effectively 'altered the social nature of the individual'.[39] When poor peasants desperate for work congregate in the Prologue of Hubert O'Grady's *The Famine*, the heartless administrator, Sackvill, and his timekeeper-accomplice, Sadler, are admonished by Sir Richard Raymond to 'act justly' and 'show no malice' to any applicant, even if in the past he did not pay his rent when he could have.[40] After Sir Richard exits, however, a conversation between Sackville and Sadler confirms that justice will not govern such decisions, intimating in the process the darker side of selling one's labour:

SACKVILL.   Have all the men presented themselves at work?
SADLER.   All except five.
SACKVILL.   Who are they?
SADLER.   Kelly, Byrne, Donovan, Haggerty, and Clancey.
SACKVILL.   Did they not make their appearance?
SADLER.   Yes, but they were five minutes late.

---

[38] J. W. Whitbread, *The Nationalist* (Dublin: W. J. Alley, 1892), 6.
[39] Singer, *Melodrama and Modernity*, 31.
[40] Hubert O'Grady, *The Famine*, repr. in *The Journal of Irish Literature* 14 (Jan. 1985), 26.

SACKVILL.   You dismissed them of course.

SADLER.   Certainly.[41]

Obsessed with punishing the O'Connor family for promoting the Land League's 'No Rent Manifesto', Sackvill makes certain that Vincent O'Connor never finds employment, which results in his wife's starvation and the devastation of his family. There are consequences for spearheading a collective response to inequity, as those punished for involvement in such labour actions as strikes know all too well, and the O'Connor family anticipates these.

The communitarian sense of labour Synge discovered in his visits to the Aran Islands between 1898 and 1902 might be juxtaposed to the quantified, micromanaged sense of work gestured to in *The Famine* and the unfairness manifested early in the play when O'Connor, refusing to abandon his family and move to the workhouse, is arrested for stealing bread to save his starving children. As Nelson Ó Ceallaigh Ritschel observes, on Inishmaan Synge found workers 'not destroyed, or alienated, by their work'—not, in other words, 'ground into a dehumanized existence by a modern capitalist system, nor did they bear the stifling morals of a conservative capitalist middle class'.[42] No 'bosses' like Sackvill plagued Inishmaan, no middle managers like Sadler. However tepidly, Irish melodrama inched toward critique of capitalism's dehumanization, the kind later decried by more political forms such as the alienated drama of the Brechtian epic theatre or agitprop drama of the 1930s. Unlike these more politically inflected genres, melodrama attributes systemic unfairness to the misdeeds of craven villains in the employment of the English government. One example is Whitbread's *The Ulster Hero* (1903), set (as so many of his plays are) during the rising of 1798.[43] The action opens in the offices of Henry Joy McCracken's Belfast factory, where the villainous Danny Niblock is rifling through a desk in search of evidence of management's involvement with the United Irishmen. Suddenly, the factory bell is sounded and laughing workers appear; Niblock is incredulous: 'Who ever heard ov boys and girls laughin' when goin' to work? It's cursin' ye should be the man who's growin' fat an' rich an' affluent on the labour ov your bones.'[44] In fact, McCracken is in love with a factory girl, Norah Bodel, and he regards his workers with such genuine affection that their workplace is anything but dehumanizing. The ruthlessness of industrial capitalism—the kind that helps destroy the Mundy family in Brian Friel's *Dancing at Lughnasa* (1990) when a newly built factory makes it impossible for Agnes and Rose to knit gloves at the small profit they once realized—is mitigated by McCracken's treatment of his workers and his love for Ireland, the latter of which leads him to the gallows.

[41] Ibid., 27.

[42] Nelson Ó Ceallaigh Ritschel, *Shaw, Synge, Connolly, and the Socialist Provocation* (Gainesville, FL: University Press of Florida, 2011), 18.

[43] J. W. Whitbread, *The Ulster Hero*, in British Library MS 1905/19 (320). The play was licensed for performance at the Metropole Theatre, Glasgow, in July 1905, and a notation cites its original production as occurring on 12 Jan. 1903 at Dublin's Queen's Royal Theatre. Reviews appeared in Dublin newspapers the next day, one in the *Dublin Evening Mail* asserting that, performed before a 'large and enthusiastic crowd', *The Ulster Hero* constitutes a 'valuable addition' to the repertory (13 Jan. 1903).

[44] Whitbread, *The Ulster Hero*.

The issues that drive both domestic and nationalist melodrama, however, scarcely disappeared as the nineteenth century came to a close. Nor did melodrama itself. On the contrary, modern writers found other uses for the characters, plots, and concerns of the genre that had attracted audiences to the Irish theatre for so long. For this reason, the opposition between a newer Ibsenite realism and a seemingly residual form like melodrama may not be so polarizing as it first appears. A melodramatic inheritance remains to be identified—and enjoyed—in plays produced long after Boucicault was the dominant force on the popular stage.

AN IRONIC BEQUEST

Near the conclusion of Seán O'Casey's *The Plough and the Stars* (1926), an exasperated Fluther Good responds sharply to a Cockney sergeant's claim that snipers shooting from rooftops during the Easter 1916 rising are not 'playing the goime'. 'Why down't they come into the owpen and foight fair!' he asks. Unable to contain himself, Fluther paints a decidedly different picture of the 'game' and its putative rules:

> Fight fair! A few hundhred scrawls o' chaps with a couple o' guns an' Rosary beads, again' a hundhred thousand thrained men with horse, fut, an' artillery . . . an' he wants us to fight fair! (*To Sergeant*) D'ye want us to come out in our skins an' throw stones![45]

Like historical melodramas based on the events of 1798 or the collective actions of the Land League, the dramatic action of O'Casey's *The Shadow of a Gunman* (1923), *Juno and the Paycock* (1924), and *The Plough and the Stars* occurs during recent conflicts in Irish history—the civil war and 1916 Easter Rising in particular. Given O'Casey's education in the popular theatre, it is hardly surprising that these plays would reveal strong traces of the melodrama he knew so well. Many of these pertain to the very issue addressed by Fluther—and melodrama: fairness and its opposite. Yet, at the same time, O'Casey substantially redacts the conventions of melodrama, rendering them ironic yet nonetheless so legible that in many ways his audiences were induced to misread the plays' plots, expecting familiar resolutions and comforts, yet typically finding neither.

Juno and the Paycock, for example, presents O'Casey's audience with highly familiar plot elements and characters: a poor family's efforts to save their home, a young nationalist's struggles to survive while fighting for Ireland, and knockabout comedians cast in the mould of the stage Irishman. At the beginning of the play, the Boyles are haunted by the possibility that Johnny, already scarred from previous fights and cowering in fear of a violent end that eventually claims him, will soon become another victim of the fighting; if that were not enough, abject poverty threatens the family's very existence. The family matriarch, Juno, worries that she can no longer buy necessary goods on credit, while at the same time her daughter Mary, for the sake of principle, is out on strike for better working conditions. Juno expresses her disapprobation of the strike, as Mary's income is crucial to the family's fragile economy:

---

[45] Sean O'Casey, *Plays 2* (London: Faber & Faber, 1998), 155.

Yis; an' when I go into oul' Murphy's tomorrow, an' he gets to know that, instead o' payin' all, I'm going to borry more, what'll he say when I tell him a principle's a principle? What'll we do if he refuses to give us any more on tick?[46]

Juno's husband, 'Captain' Jack Boyle, can hardly ameliorate their condition, as he and his pal Joxer Daly are more interested in drinking than in securing gainful employment. In true melodramatic fashion, a document—in this case, the will of a distant relative—might save them from ruin; and the handsome young schoolteacher Charles Bentham retained to write the will, resplendent with gloves and walking stick, enters the Boyle household and immediately wins Mary's affection. The opening act closes with the promise of the Boyles inheriting some £1,500–£2,000 and with the irresponsible 'Captain' singing of a renewed devotion to his wife and family. Perhaps things will work out.

Sadly, this springtime of possibility is never realized: near the end of the play, Johnny is led off to be executed, with no Mother Ireland and coronets of shamrocks to honour his sacrifice; Bentham abandons Mary, who has become pregnant and suffered the censure of her father, brother, and former co-worker; and the family home is lost, as no inheritance is forthcoming. All that remains by the final curtain are the inebriate ramblings of the 'Captain' and Joxer—and 'chassis' or chaos. The promises of domestic melodrama, in other words, seem tantalizingly within reach and are then inverted, as the community conventionally formed in the closing tableaux is sundered and all too conspicuously absent from the play's final moments. Such borrowings from melodrama, rendered often in ironic fashion, resurface in O'Casey's later plays. *Purple Dust* (1940), for instance, which O'Casey regarded as a farcical treatment of the Anglo-Irish relationship, suffered from the criticism that it invoked the tradition of the stage Irishman—the heritage of Boucicault and his imitators—although it eventually found appreciative audiences. Its December 1956 production in New York was met with praise of its 'old zest, vitality, rich humor and comic sense of character', and the consensus was that the play's 'cloud of blarney' led to 'grand, irreverent fun' for O'Casey's audience.[47] Long after Irish comic characters trounced their English adversaries in popular melodrama, Irish workmen in *Purple Dust* comically defeat the wealthy and foppish Brits Basil Stokes and Cyril Poges, who are renovating an Irish 'Tudor-Elizabethan mansion' and courting Irish women who eventually jilt them.[48] Laughably involved in high financial matters, Poges at one point attempts to purchase stocks over the telephone at the precise moment a war is to commence. Unable to do so as none are available, he indicates, as occurred so often in melodrama, capitalism's threadbare sense of ethics: 'One wouldn't imagine there'd be so many trying to cash in on splintered bodies.'[49]

Similar traces of the inheritance of melodrama mark some of the most successful plays produced by the Abbey at mid-century, including Walter Macken's *Home Is the Hero* (1952), which enjoyed a seventeen-week run, and Louis D'Alton's *This Other Eden* (1953), which ran for twenty-four.[50] Both plays recall conventions of nationalist melodrama, albeit in

---

[46] Sean O'Casey, *Plays 1* (London: Faber & Faber, 1998), 8.
[47] See Murray, *O'Casey*, 266, 382 for a summary of these reviews, all of which imply a genealogy of *Purple Dust* that leads to the melodramatic stage.
[48] O'Casey, *Plays 2*, 275.   [49] Ibid., 353.
[50] See Hunt, *Abbey Theatre*, 182. Discussing the Abbey repertory at mid-century, Hunt observes that since the 1920s O'Casey's plays had been a 'mainstay of the repertoire', but other than the 'hardy old melodrama' *The Righteous Are Bold,* no other plays from 'the repertoire of the old theatre' could be

ironic and, finally, demystifying ways. D'Alton, whose father, Frank, starred on the melodramatic stage and, in several different ventures, operated his own touring companies, was as thoroughly steeped in melodrama as his friend O'Casey.[51] D'Alton's comedy *They Got What They Wanted* (1947) featured the last appearance of the actor F. J. McCormick (1889–1947), who as a young actor played in Boucicault's melodramas and earned widespread acclaim as Joxer in *Juno and the Paycock*. The first act of *They Got What They Wanted* develops the familiar predicament of domestic melodrama, as the Murnaghan family is so deeply in debt that local merchant Owney Tubridy threatens an imminent loss of credit, although the slight possibility exists that they might inherit wealth. Bessie Murnaghan patiently endures the conversation while her husband, the unemployed Bartley (played by McCormick), remains in bed. Emerging later to announce his disdain for work—it had always 'eluded' him, in part because he couldn't stand the 'insecurity of having a job' and 'never knowing the minute you were going to lose it'[52]—he then, surprisingly, demonstrates an acumen for business dealings that leads to a newfound wealth and a happy ending to the family's dilemma. By the final curtain, Bartley has regained his old 'jauntiness', founded Murnaghan & Sons, bested Tubridy, and is preparing to attend the marriage of his daughter. The remnants of domestic melodrama, in short, find lively revision in D'Alton's play.

The template of nationalist melodrama similarly receives strong rewriting in D'Alton's *This Other Eden* and Macken's *Home Is the Hero*, with exceptionally ironic stress put on such terms as 'Eden' and 'hero'. That is to say, if melodrama in Brooks's analysis foregrounds virtue and frequently stages actions in gardens enclosed to convey a prelapsarian innocence—and if the melodramatic plot involves intruders invading this unspoiled space—then terms like 'Eden' implicitly resonate with a melodramatic tenor.[53] In *This Other Eden*, in fact, two intruders come to Ballymorgan for the dedication of a new memorial to Commandant Jack Carberry, the local IRA leader: Roger Crispin, an Englishman in town to bid on a local estate, and Conor Heaphy, a former resident returned for the celebration. In Act II, a speaker at the dedication of Carberry's statue lauds him as a 'thunderbolt in the hand of God' and 'above all' the possessor of a 'shining virtue' that led to his hatred of 'shams and lies'.[54] In one scene in a film version of the play released six years later, this homily to Carberry's virtue was extended to trumpet his 'unsullied' character and the fiction that 'drink never passed [his] lips'.[55] But, as it happens, these encomia are not entirely accurate, as Conor is discovered—to his shame—to be Carberry's illegitimate son. Moreover, and unlike the soothing texture of melodrama in which the representatives of religion support the nationalist project, Canon Moyle denounces nationalism as 'the most terrible heresy that ever afflicted the human race'.[56] The play ends with Crispin, the Englishman deemed to be more Irish than the Irish themselves, purchasing the local estate and taking Maire McRoarty with him to tour his new acquisition. The mythology of

'relied upon to pay their way'. Enjoying significant runs, D'Alton's and Macken's plays were welcome exceptions.

[51] For a brief history of D'Alton's father and melodrama, see O'Farrell, *Louis D'Alton*, 17–31.
[52] Louis D'Alton, *They Got What They Wanted* (Dundalk: Dundalgan Press, 1962), 16.
[53] See Brooks, *Melodramatic Imagination*, 29–31.
[54] Louis D'Alton, *This Other Eden* (Dublin: P. J. Bourke, 1954), 45.
[55] See Fidelma Farley, *This Other Eden* (Cork: Cork University Press, 2011), 36–51.
[56] D'Alton, *This Other Eden*, 27.

a nationalist hero as a Messiah, as the unsullied martyr in the tradition of Robert Emmet and Lord Edward Fitzgerald, is thus imploded in D'Alton's play; Ballymorgan never was Eden, and the nationalist hero never possessed unblemished virtue.

D'Alton's earlier novel *Death Is So Fair* (1937), which begins on Easter Monday, 1916, anticipates this ironic purchase of national heroism in part through the cynicism of one of its protagonists, Andrew Kilfoyle. For Kilfoyle, nationalist sacrifice is inherently performative, and rooted in both psychical failing and a sophomoric history of melodramatic sentiment: 'The Irish are the world's greatest playboys,' he exclaims. 'They will die cheerfully for the mere privilege of being able to make a highfalutin speech from the dock. They've done it for centuries with the same old props.' Yet what he terms this 'mania for acting and dramatizing life', particularly in a melodramatic way, never manifests itself in the novel.[57] Instead, cruelty and an inglorious end await Manus Considine, Kilfoyle's colleague and the closest thing to a selfless hero in D'Alton's novel.[58] The same deconstruction of heroism drives Macken's *Home Is the Hero*, as in this instance the 'hero', Paddo O'Reilly, has just returned from five years' imprisonment for killing his neighbour in an incident in a local pub. Almost killing another neighbour in a skirmish near the end of the play, Paddo, a pathetic brute of a man, leaves home for fear of repeating the accident that sent him to prison in the first place. In the play's closing scene, children dance around a bonfire and sing about tackling England and following leaders ''neath the orange, green and white';[59] but such conventions ring hollowly in the deromanticized context Macken creates by implicitly juxtaposing the narrative of a disturbed hulk of a man to the well-known narrative of nationalist heroism.

In these ways and many more, modern Irish drama reveals its ancestry in the nineteenth-century theatre. 'New' drama, however innovative and apparently radical in form, often owes a debt, acknowledged or not, to a tradition of 'old' theatre that preceded it. And so it is with modern Irish drama's indebtedness to domestic and nationalist melodrama.

---

[57] Louis Lynch D'Alton, *Death Is So Fair* (New York: Doubleday, Doran, 1938), 43. The play was first published a year earlier; D'Alton includes the middle name 'Lynch' for this edition, even though his birth name was Louis Francis Joseph Dalton. He changed his last name to D'Alton later.

[58] In *Louis D'Alton and the Abbey Theatre*, O'Farrell discusses how D'Alton 'deliberately inverts his audience's expectations' in the novel by revising the melodramatic 'template' (86). So, for example, rather than playing an innocent and much-oppressed colleen, Norah Cogan actually loves and pursues Manus Considine. After realizing that her affection for him is wasted, she yields 'to the importunities and promises' of Considine's brother, who after having 'gained her without marriage' has no plans to take her to the altar (*Death Is So Fair*, 190). See O'Farrell, *Louis D'Alton*, 85–90.

[59] Walter Macken, *Home Is the Hero* (New York: Macmillan, 1953), 114.

CHAPTER 2

....

OSCAR WILDE

International Politics and the Drama of Sacrifice

....

MICHAEL McATEER

'AU CONTRAIRE': NIHILISTS AND NATIONALISTS

....

THE extensive geographical references in Oscar Wilde's drama are worthy of attention, as they pertain to a recurrent theme of sacrifice. Their significance questions a widespread characterization of Wilde's plays as expressions of the artist's freedom to invent and subvert identity, raising instead an alternative emphasis: tensions in international political relations leading into the period of Wilde's success in London theatre. These tensions impacted significantly upon the theme of sacrifice in his drama, a theme that carried loaded meanings for a playwright coming from Ireland, with its political and religious sensitivities around the subject.[1] Although Wilde's plays are indeed full of playful subversion, he was decidedly touchy when his own consciously invented personality was sent up for ridicule. His breakthrough success, *Lady Windermere's Fan* (1892), formed the basis of a musical farce, *The Poet and the Puppets*, by Charles Brookfield and James Glover, in May that year. In a letter to his friend William Rothenstein, Wilde suggested that this piece ought to have been censored. Kerry Powell points out that Wilde had entered into negotiations with E. F. S. Pigott in the Lord Chamberlain's office over *The Poet and the Puppets*, insisting that the authors delete his own name from the text; this despite the fact that Wilde described Pigott to Rothenstein as 'a commonplace official' without artistic taste.[2] Readers can hardly call this attitude one of a dissident libertarian.

---

[1] For discussion of the question as it relates to Wilde, see Bernard O'Donoghue, 'The Journey to Reading Gaol: Sacrifice and Scapegoats in Irish Literature', in Jerusha McCormack (ed.), *Wilde the Irishman* (New Haven, CT: Yale University Press, 1998), 103–12.

[2] Kerry Powell, *Oscar Wilde and the Theatre of the 1890s* (Cambridge: Cambridge University Press, 1990), 34–5. For Wilde's letter to Rothenstein, see *Oscar Wilde: A Life in Letters*, ed. Merlin Holland (New York: Carroll & Graf, 2007), 154.

Sacrifice is one of the most significant and enigmatic aspects of Wilde's drama. Mrs Erlynne sacrifices herself as a mother for her daughter in *Lady Windermere's Fan* precisely by sustaining the impression that she is a socialite with no maternal instincts. Erlynne surrenders the hope both of revealing her true identity to Lady Windermere and of finding some reconciliation with the young woman whom she abandoned when, as Erlynne's daughter, Lady Windermere was still a child. Windermere speaks of sacrifice as the 'purification of life' to Lord Darlington, a purveyor of paradoxes in pursuit of new pleasures.[3] Dismissing this as puritanical—as Darlington himself does—overlooks the weight of feeling from *Vera, Or the Nihilists* (1880; first produced in New York, 1883) that is carried over into *Lady Windermere's Fan*. *Vera, Or the Nihilists* presents a young woman, Vera Sabouroff, who joins a secret society of nihilists in Moscow after her brother, Dmitri, is deported to Siberia for being a member of the same group. Observing the wretchedness of Russian society and falling in love with Vera, Alexis— the Czar's son—secretly goes over to the cause of the nihilists. In solemn devotion to the oath of allegiance to the nihilist order, however, Vera must kill Alexis under orders from its President, despite her feelings for him, and despite the fact that, as the new Czar, Alexis becomes a radical reformer upon his accession to the throne. The sign of regicide is to be the bloody dagger that Vera will throw from a window in the Czar's palace. Unable to bring herself to kill him, in the end she stabs herself before flinging the dagger unto the crowd gathered outside. Wilde's first play is one in which the sacrifice of everything to an ideal judged to be sacred reaches such a level of frenzy that it is easy to mistake the nihilists for automatons—one reason why the press dismissed the play so quickly upon its first performance.[4] Another was that it was political dynamite on stage. Opening in New York in August 1883, it went into performance just two years after the assassination of the Russian Czar Alexander II by a nihilist group in St Petersburg in March 1881, and in the shadow of the assassination of US President Garfield in Washington, also in 1881. The imagery through which Vera expresses the ideal of political freedom at the end of Act III is hyperbolic in its biblical aspect, anticipating most directly the tone and subject of *Salomé* (first published in French, 1893; first produced in Paris, 1896), a play that went into rehearsal in the summer of 1892 before it was refused a license, while the impressively long run of *Lady Windermere's Fan* continued. It ends with the heroine, Vera, stabbing herself in the room of the new Czar who has fallen in love with her, sacrificing herself for 'Mother Russia'.[5] The play thus ends on a question decorated with the Byronic style of its dialogue and characterization: has Vera killed herself out of love for Czar Alexis, out of love for her country, or as a failure to endure the conflict between the two?

This question would come to dominate the mythological and folk dramas of the Irish theatre movement at the start of the twentieth century. In Lady Gregory and W. B. Yeats's

---

[3] Oscar Wilde, *The Complete Plays* (London: Methuen, 1988), 36.

[4] The *New York Times* reviewer described the play as 'unreal, longwinded and wearisome', while the *New York Herald* was even more damning: 'It is long-drawn, dramatic rot, a series of disconnected essays and sickening rant, with a course and common kind of cleverness' (*New York Herald*, 21 Aug. 1883). See Karl Beckson (ed.), *Oscar Wilde: The Critical Heritage* (London: Routledge, 1974), 47–50. The play ran for just one week.

[5] Wilde, *Complete Plays*, 578.

Cathleen ni Houlihan (1902), is Michael Gillane to marry Delia or to die for 'Mother Ireland', the *Sean Bhean Bhocht*? In Lady Gregory's folk-history play *Dervorgilla* (1907), the Queen of Breffini in medieval Ireland lets her husband die by beheading in England, she having eloped with her lover, Diarmuid: a woman true to her heart's passion or a traitor to her country? Yeats's Cuchulain in *The Only Jealousy of Emer* (1919) is too enchanted by Fand, the supernatural ancient Irish goddess, to live an ordinary married life with Emer: a warrior completely submissive to the spiritual destiny of his tribe, or a man hardened to human affection?[6] Most significant of all is Patrick Pearse's *The Singer* (1916), first performed in December 1917 after Pearse's death by execution in April of the previous year. The Christian biblical imagery of *Vera* is most striking in Pearse's play through the figure of an Irish insurrectionary named MacDara. Like the Russian nihilists of Wilde's play, MacDara endeavours to harden his heart for an ideal of liberty, suppressing whatever desire that he feels for the young woman, Sighle. Instead, he is determined to 'stand up before the Gall as Christ hung naked before men on the tree'.[7] The strong homoerotic undercurrent in the messianic form of Pearse's Irish republicanism is evident here. MacDara forgoes any prospect of marital contentment with this woman for a religious ideal of sacrifice, exchanging the possibility of heterosexual love for his determination to hang 'naked' before men. Albeit for completely different reasons, Pearse may have shared Henry James's damning judgement of Wilde's drama as directed solely towards an 'unspeakable animal': the literal-minded English theatre-goer.[8] Still, MacDara's image in *The Singer* testifies to the extent to which the legacy of Wilde's religious homoeroticism was sustained in Pearse's own outlook. Far from removing the individual from sanctity, tabooed homoerotic desires accentuated Pearse's sense of the religious sphere as both beautiful and traumatic (in its intimation of a connection of sacrificial death to homosexual feeling).[9]

The significance of sacrifice to Wilde is evident in the fact that he planned to follow *Lady Windermere's Fan* with *Salomé* rather than another comedy of manners. The failure of the Lord Chamberlain's Office to grant it a license increased the opportunity for a young W. B. Yeats to get an Irish fairy play onto the London stage. Yeats's *The Land of Heart's Desire* eventually went into production at the Avenue Theatre in April 1894 as a preliminary piece to Bernard Shaw's *Arms and the Man*. In publicly expressing his

---

[6] W. B. Yeats, *Collected Works*, vol. 2: *The Plays*, ed. David R. Clark and Rosalind E. Clark (New York: Scribner, 2001), 317–28; Augusta Gregory, *Selected Plays*, ed. Mary Fitzgerald (Gerrards Cross: Colin Smythe, 1983), 153–69.

[7] Patrick Pearse, *Collected Plays*, ed. Róisín Ní Ghairbhí and Eugene McNulty (Dublin: Irish Academic Press, 2013), 228. Joost Augusteijn sees *The Singer*, written in 1915, as the closest identification made in Pearse's drama between an Irish uprising and the story of Calvary: *Patrick Pearse: The Making of a Revolutionary* (Basingstoke: Palgrave Macmillan, 2010), 295.

[8] See, Henry James to Mrs. Hugh Bell, Feb. 23, 1892 in *Henry James Letters*, vol. 3: *1883–1895*, ed. Leon Edel (Cambridge, MA: The Belknap Press of Harvard University Press, 1980), 373.

[9] Declan Kiberd observes the consonance of Wilde's fairy tales with Pearse's Christian fables for boys, but the sensuality of Wilde's writing as a prompt for Pearse's idealized homoerotic imagery in his writing on male adolescents is not taken into consideration: Declan Kiberd, *Irish Classics* (Cambridge, MA: Harvard University Press, 2001), 326–7. Elaine Sisson addresses the issue in detail in *Pearse's Patriots: St Enda's and the Cult of Boyhood* (Cork: Cork University Press, 2004), 131–52.

outrage at the refusal to grant *Salomé* a license, Wilde brought his Irish origins to the fore when declaring his intention to leave England and settle in Paris: 'I am not at present an Englishman. I am an Irishman, which is by no means the same thing.'[10] The Irish poet Derek Mahon identifies in this a precedent for the story of Samuel Beckett's response decades later to a question from a French journalist as to whether he was English—'au contraire'.[11] The prospect of Wilde setting up in France as a declaration of Irish difference provoked the mockery of the English press. With its well-known penchant for caricaturing the Irish (one of its first editors, Joseph Stirling Coyne, being an Irish native of Birr in Co. Offaly), *Punch* magazine depicted Wilde as a French conscript marching with *Salomé* in his knapsack, the caption reading: 'A Wilde Idea. Or more injustice to Ireland.'

This sudden association of dandyism with the Irish question in a leading English press outlet so soon after the death of Parnell could not have gone unnoticed by a writer like Yeats, whose love of all things Pre-Raphaelite during his 20s became entwined with his growing identification with Irish radical nationalism into the 1890s. Had Wilde's *Salomé* proved a success in England, *The Land of Heart's Desire* would have seemed puny by contrast, instead of becoming the blueprint for *Cathleen ni Houlihan*, the most politically charged piece that Yeats—with Lady Gregory—wrote for the stage. The Fenian sympathies that Wilde inherited from his mother came out strongly in 'The Irish Poets of 1848', the talk that he delivered in San Francisco in April 1882, during the course of his American tour.[12] However, Wilde never regarded the provocative nature of *Salomé* as a Fenian matter. When Mathews and Lane published the first English-language edition of the play in February 1894, they enclosed Aubrey Beardsley's quasi-caricature drawings to accompany the text within a green book-cover carrying an explicitly Irish Celtic design. Wilde was furious, describing the cover as 'quite dreadful' and telling Lane to '[u]se up this horrid Irish stuff for stories, etc'.[13]

WILDEAN GEO-POLITICS

The two plays that followed the censoring of *Salomé* in England—*A Woman of No Importance* (1893) and *An Ideal Husband* (1895)—develop the motif of sacrifice in the context of unsettling developments in international relations during the 1890s. *A Woman of No Importance* was first performed at the Haymarket Theatre in April 1893, a time during which British–American diplomacies were under considerable strain. After an extended period of dispute with Venezuela over territories that were claimed to be part of British Guiana, Britain entered into a major disagreement with the United States on the question,

---

[10] See Frances Winwar, *Oscar Wilde and the Yellow 'Nineties*, foreword by Lord Alfred Douglas (New York: Blue Ribbon Books, 1941), 211–12.

[11] Derek Mahon, 'Ellmann's Wilde', in McCormack, *Wilde the Irishman*, 148.

[12] Richard Ellmann, *Oscar Wilde* (London: Hamish Hamilton, 1987), 185–6.

[13] Oscar Wilde, *Selected Letters*, ed. Rupert Hart-Davis, 2nd edn. (Oxford: Oxford University Press, 1979), 115.

one that threatened momentarily to turn into a war in 1895.[14] In November of that year, Congressman Charles H. Grosvenor put the issue in stark terms:

> England should not be permitted to succeed in this scheme [ownership of the trans-Isthmus Canal] [. . .] The attitude of the United States towards the Venezuelan question should be that of determined opposition to any movement of England, the result of which would impair or weaken our ancient declaration of support for the Monroe Doctrine.[15]

This context lends added significance to the character of Hester Worsley in *A Woman of No Importance*. As a young American woman, Hester denounces the frivolity of the upper-class society of Hunstanton Chase. Combining in her a suffragist determination with an Episcopalian conservatism, Wilde places the theme of sacrifice within a framework of conflicting interests between the United States and Great Britain as a dangerous stand-off was developing between the two powers over their zones of influence.

Rachel Arbuthnot stands out as the sacrificial figure in *A Woman of No Importance* as the woman who was left unmarried by Lord Illingworth twenty years previously when she gave birth to their son, Gerald, leaving the young boy 'without a name'.[16] It is superficial to take the fight between them for Gerald as a struggle of the principled virtue of Arbuthnot against Lord Illingworth's world of luxury, power, and indulgence. Such a characterization is already compromised by the fact that Rachel lives a life of disguise, while Illingworth desires the ostensibly virtuous objective of developing a relationship with his son, now a young man. Beyond this, however, is the significance within the context of this family of Hester Worsley, the American whom Neil Sammells dismisses as a character who 'bores her onstage and offstage audiences with her smug faith in the great outdoors'.[17] Far from doing so at the April 1893 opening run of *A Woman of No Importance*: at Herbert Beerbohm Tree's Haymarket Theatre, her one extended speech in Act II riled the audience, provoking boos when Wilde himself was called for at the end. Specifically, this was prompted by Worsley's American Republican denunciation of English upper-class society as 'a leper

---

[14]   R. A. Humphreys described it as 'one of the most momentous episodes in the history of Anglo-American relations' and 'one of those major shocks which compel the theory of international relations to adjust itself to new facts'. Commenting on William Lindsay Scruggs's campaign in Washington in support of Venezuela's opposition to British territorial claims in South America, Humphreys makes a passing yet telling reference to Ireland: 'Twisting the lion's tail was an old game, not confined to the American Irish.' See R. A. Humphreys, 'Anglo-American Rivalries and the Venezuela Crisis of 1895', *Transactions of the Royal Historical Society* 17 (1967), 133, 145. This may serve to indicate why Wilde, an Irishman who began his career in America, would take such interest in British affairs in South America in *An Ideal Husband*.

[15]   Charles H. Grosvenor, 'Our Duty in the Venezuelan Crisis', *North American Review* 161, no. 468 (1895), 633.

[16]   Wilde, *Complete Plays*, 338.

[17]   Neil Sammells, 'Oscar Wilde and the Politics of Style', in Shaun Richards (ed.), *The Cambridge Companion to Twentieth-Century Irish Drama* (Cambridge: Cambridge University Press, 2004), 115. For the rich mixture of admiration, distaste, and fascination that Wilde felt for America following his 1882 tour, see his *Impressions of America*, ed. Stuart Mason (Sunderland: Keystone Press, 1906), 2–5. Mary Warner Blanchard gives an illuminating account of the cultural and aesthetic values shaping America in the decades leading into the period of his tour, and how his ideas were received. *Oscar Wilde's America: Counterculture in the Gilded Age* (New Haven, CT: Yale University Press, 1998), 1–44.

dressed in purple'.[18] At a time of diplomatic stand-off between Washington and London, this image would have stung many in the audience quite sharply. It is derived from the banned *Salomé*, a play in which Herod admires the healing of lepers and in which Iokanaan prophesies that Herod seated on his throne 'clothed in scarlet and purple … shall be eaten of worms'.[19]

Beerbohm Tree claimed that Wilde travelled to Belfast in 1893 to solicit his interest in producing *A Woman of No Importance*. In an interview for the *New York Times*, to accompany a 1916 New York revival of the play, he declared unabashedly that the part of Lord Illingworth had been written for him.[20] 1893 was the same year in which Beerbohm Tree produced Ibsen's *An Enemy of the People* at the Haymarket. While there is some truth in Kirsten Shepherd-Barr's judgement that this was 'a deceptively well-calculated risk', it was one amplified by taking *A Woman of No Importance* into performance as well, when the refusal of a licence for *Salomé* increased the unpredictability of the audience's reception.[21] In that 1893 run of *A Woman of No Importance*, Illingworth's attempt to kiss Hester Worsley carries a meaning beyond what Illingworth credits simply as a harmless gesture that this 'puritan' could not abide. It is loaded with connotations of the sacrilegious kiss in *Salomé*—Herod's daughter kissing the severed head of John the Baptist in a gesture at once a mystical portent and a sexual transgression. With London theatregoers denied the spectacle of this gesture to follow Salomé's striptease show before Herod—the dance of the seven veils—Rachel Arbuthnot's allusion to the power of a kiss in *A Woman of No Importance* speaks poignantly to the theme of fate that shapes Wilde's censored play. She bitterly observes how fate is released in a single gesture: 'A kiss may ruin a human life, George Harford. *I* know that. *I* know that too well.'[22] Not only is Salomé's kiss present in the background here but, equally, the Judas kiss of treachery that Wilde had adapted to the political intrigue of *Vera*.

Insisting that Gerald remain loyal to his mother if he is to leave for America rather than follow Lord Illingworth to the Continent as his secretary, Hester Worsley sees a martyrdom of womanhood in the figure of Rachel Arbuthnot.[23] Victoria White suggests that Wilde remained infantile all his life, evident in what she identifies as his failure to represent sexually active, reproductive women on their own terms. White speculates that this may lie in the possibility that he never moved beyond his mother's controlling influence.[24] The argument is plausible, particularly considering the feminist implications of the position accorded to Constance Wilde during the period of success of her husband as a dramatist.

---

[18] Wilde, *Complete Plays*, 329. Ellmann notes that the line was removed in later performances. See Ellmann, *Oscar Wilde*, 360.

[19] Wilde, *Complete Plays*, 400–2.

[20] Sir Herbert Beerbohm Tree, 'The Beginnings of *A Woman of No Importance*', *New York Times*, 30 Apr. 1916; repr. in E. H. Mikhail (ed.), *Oscar Wilde: Interviews and Recollections* (2 vols., London: Macmillan, 1979), vol. 1, 215.

[21] Kirsten Shepherd-Barr, *Ibsen and Early Modernist Theatre, 1890–1900* (London: Greenwood Press, 1997), 14.

[22] Wilde, *Complete Plays*, 372.

[23] In Act IV, Hester implores Gerald to remain loyal to his mother, describing Rachel Arbuthnot in the following terms: 'In her all womanhood is martyred' (ibid., 370).

[24] Victoria White, 'Misogyny in the Work of Oscar Wilde', in McCormack, *Wilde the Irishman*, 160.

However, *A Woman of No Importance* offers a contrary reading. Rachel's offspring, Gerald, occupies the plot centre of the play. He chooses to follow Hester and her feminist ideals not by leaving his mother behind, but by accepting Hester's sympathy for Rachel.

This matter of gender politics is framed by that of geopolitics. Whereas Hester draws Rachel and her son towards America, Lord Illingworth appears to be heading eastward. Lady Hunstanton has heard that he had been offered the position of British Ambassador in Vienna—hence his determination at the end of Act II to make Gerald agree to accept a position as his secretary, despite the opposition of Gerald's mother.[25] Thus the struggle for Gerald carries religious, cultural, and political connotations. It is the conflict between, in Hester's words, 'the largest country in the world', where people are working towards a society founded on 'a better, truer, purer basis', and a future, in Illingworth's phrasing, that 'belongs to the dandy', in which it 'is the exquisites who are going to rule'.[26] At a time when Germany's power in Europe was keenly felt through the expansionism of Bismarck and when the new Austro-Hungarian empire drew the Hapsburg dynasty eastward, the type of dinner-table prowess that Illingworth exudes would be of utmost importance in British diplomatic manoeuvres on the Continent. The lesson that the Irish Party had taught Westminster in the 1870s—through Joseph Biggar, Charles Stewart Parnell, and their fellow obstructionists—had long been absorbed: 'talk' was a weapon capable of influencing political affairs more effectively than military force in many instances.[27]

IMPERIAL SCHEMING AND NOBLE SACRIFICE

Wilde's exploration of sacrifice in geopolitical contexts was most explicit in the January 1895 production of *An Ideal Husband* by Lewis Waller at the Haymarket Theatre in London. Whereas Vienna is mentioned in passing in *A Woman of No Importance*, now its significance becomes more explicit. In contrast to Hester in the earlier play, here Mrs Cheveley arrives from the palatial old city of Mozart and the Hapsburgs. Hester Worsley may be a variant on New England puritanism in the earlier play; Mrs Cheveley, by contrast, carries a veneer of continental European intrigue and decadence in *An Ideal Husband*. She moves with ease among the rich and titled of London, and attempts to blackmail Sir Robert Chiltern—a sitting MP at Westminster—in a presumptuous, offhand manner. Cheveley's accomplishment in adopting poses necessary to her interests indicates her old association

---

[25] Wilde, *Complete Plays*, 306.

[26] Ibid., 303, 329, 345.

[27] For analysis of the Irish Party's obstructionist tactics at Westminster, including Joseph Biggar's exhausting speeches, see David Thornley, 'The Irish Home Rule Party and Parliamentary Obstruction', *Irish Historical Studies* 12, no. 45 (1960), 38–57. W. J. Mc Cormack offers an intriguing consideration of Parnell's significance to Wilde as evidenced by the theme of crime in *The Picture of Dorian Gray* carrying an undercurrent reference to Parnell's imprisonment in 1880 and the murder of Chief Secretary Cavendish in Dublin's Phoenix Park days after Parnell's release. The point is equally relevant to Wilde's plays. W. J. Mc Cormack, 'Wilde and Parnell', in McCormack, *Wilde the Irishman*, 95–102.

with Lord Goring (a 'flawless dandy'), now revived with her arrival in London.[28] In her case, the aesthete's adoption of masks is entangled with political power games that raise her mastery of style above that of a dandy's pursuit of rarefied sensations. Upon their first introduction, Sir Robert Chiltern hopes that Mrs Cheveley is not 'going to plunge us into a European war'.[29] Threatening to expose the fact that Robert sold a stock exchange speculator a Cabinet secret in order to advance his career, Mrs Cheveley at once brings down the first impression of honour that Robert exudes, and she attempts to exert influence upon the direction of British Government policy in international affairs. In exchange for an offer to keep his original act of wrongful disclosure a secret, she demands that he speak in parliament in favour of an Argentinian investment scheme (a thinly disguised allusion to the Venezuelan crisis of the time).

Cheveley may be a spy coming from Vienna, acting on behalf either of the German nation-state united in 1871 or of the Austro-Hungarian empire that extended its influence over the Balkan region from the *Ausgleich* between Vienna and Pest-Buda in 1867. She combines aesthetic subtlety with political intrigue. Following her attempt to blackmail him, Sir Robert Chiltern makes enquiries regarding Mrs Cheveley's standing in Vienna, while Lord Goring wonders whether she may be a spy.[30] Moments later, she enters the room where the two men are talking, disclosing that she had been listening to their conversation in the adjacent room, having a love of 'listening through keyholes'.[31] Were it not for the geopolitical points of interest in the play, this might all seem as frivolous as Algernon's discussion with Lane over cucumber sandwiches in *The Importance of Being Earnest*. In this instance, however, the stakes are high. In Act I, Mrs Cheveley requests Robert to refrain from submitting a commissioned report to the House of Commons concerning an Argentinian Canal financial scheme—one that Robert judges to be 'a stock exchange swindle' and 'a second Panama'.[32] She reminds him that he has experience in international canal schemes, having being Lord Radley's secretary when the Government bought shares in the Suez Canal project.[33]

Selecting an Argentinian Canal scheme as a topic for the plot of *An Ideal Husband* in 1895, Wilde was addressing a loaded subject in English politics at this time of diplomatic tensions with the United States over Britain's presence in South America. Associating the scheme with the Suez Canal project, Mrs Cheveley amplifies its significance further, given the Suez project's importance to Britain's political and economic control over India. Wilde was not alone in addressing imperial economic questions of this nature in the stylized literature of the *fin-de-siècle* period. One of the most intriguing stories to be published in the London magazine the *Yellow Book* was Netta Syrett's 'Thy Heart's Desire', which appeared in its second issue, in July 1894. Wilde was scathing about the *Yellow Book* because he was left out, when his disciples—Richard Le Gallienne, Arthur Symons, Max Beerbohm—were included. As Frances Winwar observes, Beardsley (art editor of the magazine) disliked Wilde; and in any case, it was already sufficiently risqué without adding the notoriety of the Irishman's reputation in England.[34] Syrett's story is set in an unnamed location in the Middle East where Kathleen Drayton is stationed with her husband, an employee of an oil

---

[28] Wilde, *Complete Plays*, 117–18.   [29] Ibid., 118.   [30] Ibid., 179.   [31] Ibid., 183.
[32] Ibid., 124.   [33] Ibid.   [34] Winwar, *Oscar Wilde*, 240–1.

company. Portraying Kathleen as blaming herself for his death during this time, the story deals with marital infidelity and desires awakened in an 'Oriental' location as its resources are undergoing Western commercial exploitation.[35] Published just two months after the run of Yeats's *The Land of Heart's Desire* at the Avenue Theatre in April 1894, 'Thy Heart's Desire' may have drawn its theme in part from that play, also linking a married woman's desire for mystery and exoticism in a remote setting in the west of Ireland.[36] The name that Syrett uses in her story, Kathleen Drayton, also suggests that she had read Yeats's book *The Countess Kathleen and Various Legends and Lyrics* (published in London two years before the appearance of her story in print).

The urban sophistication of dialogue and characterization in *An Ideal Husband* is far removed from the rustic metre of *The Land of Heart's Desire* and the ethereal wistfulness of 'Thy Heart's Desire'. However, Wilde's play makes emphatic a tension that underlies the contrast between these literary pieces: the other-worldly atmosphere of the former and the background of Western oil exploration in the Middle East within the latter. The counterpoint to Mrs Cheveley's sophistication and scheming in *An Ideal Husband* is the virtuous idealism through which Gertrude, Lady Chiltern, beholds her husband Robert. Mrs Cheveley challenges Robert Chiltern to balance the interests of commerce with the principle of honourable conduct in public affairs. Gertrude regards her husband's decision to recommend that the Government support the Argentinian Canal project as a betrayal of the ideals for which she holds him in her highest estimation. Mrs Cheveley's threat to expose the illegal act, through which Robert launched his career, confronts him with the prospect of destroying both his political career and his marriage.

The continental European background to *An Ideal Husband* complicates its contrast between idealism and duplicitous manipulation. The influence that Baron Arnheim had exercised upon Robert in his youth, as well as upon Mrs Cheveley, troubles the distinction between virtue and corruption in the play. Arnheim's 'gospel of gold', as Robert describes it, is one of wealth as an instrument of power over others rather than a means of gluttonous consumption; luxury is merely 'a background' to a power that he judges 'the one supreme pleasure worth knowing'.[37] The occult nature of this philosophy of power suggests itself through the obscure, cultured, and intellectual character of Baron Arnheim as Robert describes him; the Baron is a 'hidden hand' through the entire plot of *An Ideal Husband* and the movements in imperial power politics that it engages. Under pressure from the modern philosophy of power elaborated most provocatively by Friedrich Nietzsche that was disseminated in the late 1880s and 1890s by Georg Brandes and Havelock Ellis, Aristotelian virtues—particularly that of justice—are unsettled in Wilde's play.[38] Yet courage (a primary virtue in Aristotle's *Ethics*) remains a supreme ideal in *An Ideal Husband*,

[35] Netta Syrett, 'Thy Heart's Desire', *The Yellow Book: An Illustrated Quarterly* 2 (July 1894), 221–5.

[36] Yeats, *Collected Works*, vol. 2, 65–82.

[37] Wilde, *Complete Plays*, 143.

[38] For the rise of Nietzsche's influence in Wilde's lifetime, see the following essays: Georg Brandes, 'Friedrich Nietzsche: En Afhandling om aristokratisk Radikalisme' [An Essay on Aristocratic Radicalism], *Samlede Skrifter* 7 (1889), 596–664, in *Friedrich Nietzsche*, trans. A. G. Chater (London: William Heinemann, 1914); Havelock Ellis, 'Friedrich Nietzsche, I'; 'Friedrich Nietzsche, II'; 'Friedrich Nietzsche, III', *The Savoy* 2 (Apr. 1896), 79–94; 3 (July 1896), 68–81; 4 (Aug. 1896), 57–63.

even in Arnheim's shady influence over affairs. Robert presents it as the courage demanded to cast the dice, 'to stake all one's life on a single moment, to risk everything on one throw'.[39]

The Germanic name and secret influence of Baron Arnheim indicate that while investment in a South American scheme may be the issue of contest between Sir Robert Chiltern and Mrs Cheveley in *An Ideal Husband*, the play draws its audience eastward towards Central Europe. A young attaché to the French embassy in London, the Vicomte de Nanjac moves among guests at Sir Robert's *soirée* wearing one of his distinctive neckties and displaying his 'anglo-mania'; he is surprised to encounter Mrs Cheveley, having last met her five years previously in Berlin.[40] Leaving the ball, Lord Goring plans to drop in to Hartlocks, expecting to find a 'mauve Hungarian band that plays mauve Hungarian music'.[41] Mrs Cheveley is in a position to blackmail Robert because she has in her possession the letter that he wrote to Baron Arnheim when he was Lord Radley's secretary, advising the Baron to buy shares in the Suez Canal project three days before the Government announced its own purchase, enabling the Baron to make a fortune.[42] Given the rumour that Robert has heard from Vienna that the Baron's vast fortune passed to Mrs Cheveley after he died, it is evident that the Baron belonged to Viennese aristocratic circles.

Insofar as his influence extends beyond the grave through the legacy that he has bequeathed to Mrs Cheveley—a legacy that she plans to invest in a scheme of international significance economically and politically—Arnheim anticipates another figure from Austro-Hungarian territories to appear in literature just two years after *An Ideal Husband*. This is Bram Stoker's Dracula, the Transylvanian Count who plans a vampire takeover of London. Apart from his close association with Henry Irving, Stoker could not escape the influence of Wilde's theatre in the 1890s. In December 1878 he married Florence Balcombe, a woman with whom Wilde had been in love in his youth and to whom Wilde wrote soon before his departure for England that same year 'probably for good', as he confided to her.[43] Declan Kiberd sees in this 'yet another nightmare from the Irish past to be suppressed by a famous career in England'.[44] In its affinity to Count Dracula, the occult aspect of Arnheim's invisible presence in *An Ideal Husband* suggests that Wilde's Irish experience continued to haunt his drama, through a propensity that he shared with his Dublin literary compatriot to conceive Central and Eastern Europe in terms of mystery and ancient, hidden power. It is more than coincidence that less than two years after the letter to Balcombe, Wilde turned eastwards to Russia as the setting for his first play in 1880, a private copy of which he sent to Ellen Terry, then Henry Irving's leading lady at the Lyceum theatre in London (where Stoker, as it happens, was business manager).[45] Shaw would do likewise in the Bulgarian setting that he chose for his own breakthrough play of 1894, *Arms and the Man*, while Stoker established his fame for posterity in the Transylvanian setting of *Dracula*.

Within the complex frame of reference to geographies of empire in *An Ideal Husband*— moving between London, Vienna, Argentina, and Suez—Wilde explores the idea of sacrifice from a variety of perspectives. Sir Robert's sister Mabel sees his wife Gertrude as having 'a noble, self-sacrificing character'.[46] Meeting Lord Goring again after many

---

[39] Wilde, *Complete Plays*, 144.   [40] Ibid., 110.
[41] Ibid., 135.   [42] Ibid., 127.   [43] Wilde, *Selected Letters*, 21–2.
[44] Declan Kiberd, *Inventing Ireland: the Literature of the Modern Nation* (London: Jonathan Cape, 1995), 34.
[45] Wilde, *Selected Letters*, 27.   [46] Wilde, *Complete Plays*, 156.

years, Mrs Cheveley wonders that he has not 'risen to some great height of self-sacrifice', to which Goring replies that self-sacrifice should be 'put down by law', so 'demoralising' it is to the people for whom the sacrifice is being made.[47] Yet for all Arthur Goring's playful dandyism, he is the one most cognizant of the gravity of the sacrifice that Sir Robert is contemplating for the purpose of redeeming the love of his wife Gertrude; the complete sacrifice of his political career and the calumny of public disgrace. Goring warns Gertrude against accepting such 'a terrible sacrifice', certain that she would live to regret it dearly.[48] Robert's decision to denounce not only the Argentinian scheme but 'the whole system of modern political finance' *is* this sacrificial act, since he fully expects that Cheveley will destroy him in consequence. Having no prior knowledge of Arthur Goring's machinations by which he traps Cheveley into silence, Robert has completed the sacrificial act, but with political redemption rather than political ruin as its consequence, his speech greeted with wholehearted applause in Parliament. Prepared to go the further step and resign from politics at the point at which his career has reached its zenith, he takes on the character of the martyr. It is impossible to ignore Wilde's hidden and ironical inversion here of Parnell's political martyrdom four years earlier: destroyed precisely because he refused, on principle, to resign from politics when pressurized to do so. Ultimately, Gertrude refuses the sacrificial offering of his political career that Robert presents to her: 'And I will not spoil your life for you, nor see you spoil it as a sacrifice to me, a useless sacrifice!'[49]

In disturbing a British sense of contrast between the dutiful virtue of its imperial realm and the duplicitous imperial advances of continental European powers, Wilde tests the elasticity of sacrifice as an idea in *An Ideal Husband*. Doing so, the play tackles an issue that Ross Forman identifies in Matthew Phipps Shiel's *The Yellow Danger* three years later, in 1898: Victorian Britain's imperial expansion 'as concomitant with her potentially disastrous retraction from Europe'.[50] At the very heart of *An Ideal Husband*, however, is a disposition central to the concept of sacrifice that would influence the course of European politics into the twentieth century: a willingness to risk everything in a single moment. Robert admits to having done so at the beginning of his career, not simply for material gain, but for a power over others that Baron Arnheim had presented to him as a supreme value. If the play may be regarded as an *exposé* of the corrupt nature of Imperial finance, it is only as a context for a more fundamental question: the question of sacrifice.

WAGNER IN EARNEST

Early in Act III of *The Importance of Being Earnest*, the concept of sacrifice 'suffers' a most ignominious ridicule. Cecily Cardew and Gwendolen Bracknell having discovered that both Jack Worthing and Algernon Montcrieff have lied to them about their names, the two men disclose their intention to be baptized, for the second time in Algernon's case. Cecily

---

47 Ibid., 186.   48 Ibid., 208.   49 Ibid.
50 Ross G. Forman, 'Empire', in Gail Marshall (ed.), *Cambridge Companion to the Fin de Siècle* (Cambridge: Cambridge University Press, 2007), 91.

and Gwendolen are beside themselves with admiration that Jack and Algernon would do this for them, Gwendolen declaring that 'men are infinitely beyond us', when it comes to matters of self-sacrifice, Cecily concurring wholeheartedly.[51] The humour of the exchange is served not simply by the manner of the young women's reaction to this intention to take baptismal vows; it is enhanced by the recognition that the baptisms planned are attempts at self-reform. Jack and Algernon intend to get baptized in order to leave the vices of bachelorhood behind them and enter married life. In this way, the farce of *The Importance of Being Earnest* takes us back to *Vera*, a play in which Baron Raff declares that reforms in Russia 'are very tragic, but they always end in farce'.[52] Here, Wilde was paraphrasing the opening sentences of Karl Marx's 1851 pamphlet (also first published in New York), *The Eighteenth Brumaire of Louis Bonaparte*: 'Hegel remarks somewhere that all facts and personages of great importance in world history occur, as it were, twice. He forgot to add: the first time as tragedy, the second as farce.'[53] This lends an odd historico-political gloss to Lady Bracknell's immortal response to Jack's lack of parents: 'To lose one parent, Mr Worthing, may be regarded as a misfortune; to lose both looks like carelessness.'[54]

The connection between Wilde's first theatrical flop and his last and greatest theatrical success does not end there. *Vera* is knotted in deceit, almost everyone pretending to be someone else. Indeed, deception is so taken for granted that honesty itself is considered a sign of sedition. When a General of the Czar breaks in upon a conspiratorial meeting of nihilists in a secret Moscow location, Vera pretends, ironically as it turns out, that it is a rehearsal for a tragedy. General Kotemkin is unconvinced, however, precisely because Vera's answers are 'too *honest* to be true'.[55] By the end of *The Importance of Being Earnest*, Jack discovers that the name he had been assuming in London was, indeed, his real name. As General Kotemkin mistrusts honesty in *Vera*, so Jack apologizes to Gwendolen and asks her forgiveness for not having actually lied to her when he believed himself to be doing so, it being 'a terrible thing for a man to find out suddenly that all his life he has being speaking nothing but the truth'.[56]

Viewed in relation to *Vera*, the disguises of *The Importance of Being Earnest* appear as traces of a practice through which political power contests are carried on at the intersection of international and personal levels: espionage. The plot entanglements of Wilde's last play have justly earned its fame: Jack pretending to be Ernest whilst really being so without knowing it; Algernon pretending to be Jack's brother without knowing that he is, indeed, his brother; Gwendolen falling in love with a man solely because of his name without realizing that the man in question invents that name in the mistaken belief that it is not his name. This culminates in the rather incestuous conclusion that first cousins Gwendolen and Ernest are to get married, and Ernest's brother Algernon is to marry Cecily, so that the man whom Cecily always thought of as 'uncle Jack' is about to become her brother-in-law Ernest. All of this accentuates the comic brilliance of Jack/Ernest's impeccably polite yet portentously existential question: 'Lady Bracknell, I hate to seem inquisitive, but would you kindly inform me who I am?'[57] In its political circumstances, Wilde's first drama grants this apparent frivolity immediate political import. Czar Ivan is convinced that he

---

[51] Wilde, *Complete Plays*, 275.   [52] Ibid., 570
[53] Karl Marx, *Selected Writings*, ed. David McLellan (Oxford: Oxford University Press, 1977), 300.
[54] Wilde, *Complete Plays*, 234.   [55] Ibid., 52.   [56] Ibid., 288.   [57] Ibid., 286.

is surrounded by spies at the monarchical palace—worst of all, his own son Alexis.[58] All those present at the meeting of nihilists in Act I are wearing masks. When it is broken up by General Kotemkin, those present are saved from execution by Alexis removing his mask and revealing himself as the Czar's son, the General being ignorant of the fact that he has secretly gone over to the cause of the nihilists.[59]

Against the backdrop of double identities, spying, and political assassination in *Vera*, the concept of sacrificial death emerges at the play's conclusion in the suicide of Vera. It is at once political and artistic, completing the play and inaugurating the moment of revolution. The tragic suicide motif is taken up again by Wilde in that of Sibyl Vane in *The Picture of Dorian Gray*. Hers is essentially a sacrifice to art, becoming in death the Juliet of Shakespeare's *Romeo and Juliet*, whose character she failed to perform in life, thereby losing the adoration of Dorian, with whom she had fallen in love.[60] The melodrama of the whole episode is underlined in the fact that Dorian was repelled by her performance because she 'overemphasized everything that she had to say'.[61] Lurking beneath this is Wagner; upon discovering that Sibyl Vane is dead, Lord Henry Wotton and Dorian go immediately to the opera. This reaction is evidence of the misogyny that Dennis Denisoff identifies among male dandies of the *fin-de-siècle* aestheticist movement, including Wilde.[62] Earlier in the narrative, Dorian recalls meeting Lord Henry's wife at a performance of Wagner's *Lohengrin*; to Lady Victoria's clever remark that she likes Wagner's operas because it is possible to talk during the performance without being heard, Dorian responds that he never talks during the performance of 'good music'.[63]

The suicides of these Wildean women, Vera Sabouroff and Sibyl Vane, betray the influence of the sacrificial deaths of women in Wagner's operas. These include that of Elsa of Brabant at the end of *Lohengrin*, but most emphatically, the immolation of Brünnhilde at the conclusion of *Götterdämmerung*—the final Act of the Ring cycle—charging on a horse into the flames of Siegfried's funeral pyre.[64] Derek Hughes points out that Wagner almost considered women to be a different species to men, so fundamentally did he identify woman's nature as inherently sacrificial: 'Brünnhilde's very identity as a woman is itself a sacrifice.'[65] The misogynistic aspects evident in the writings of several male aesthetes of the *fin-de-siècle* (including Wilde) is partly attributable to the all-pervasive influence of Wagner in the late nineteenth century. At one time a great champion of Wagner, Friedrich Nietzsche came to view Wagner's music as representing the sickness of modern Europe. Arch-misogynist that he himself was, Nietzsche attributed the corrupting influence and the widespread popularity of Wagner's operas to his 'success with nerves, and therefore with women' in 'The Case of Wagner'. Somewhat ironically, this open letter was written

[58] Ibid., 548.   [59] Ibid., 525–38.

[60] Oscar Wilde, *The Picture of Dorian Gray*, 1891 edn., ed. Robert Mighall (London: Penguin, 2000), 80–103.

[61] Ibid., 81.

[62] Dennis Denisoff, 'Decadence and Aestheticism', in Marshall, *Cambridge Companion to the Fin de Siècle*, 48.

[63] Wilde, *The Picture of Dorian Gray*, 46.

[64] Stewart Spencer and Barry Millington (eds.), *Wagner's Ring of the Nibelung: A Companion* (London: Thames & Hudson, 1993), 350–1.

[65] Derek Hughes, *Culture and Sacrifice: Rituals in Literature and Opera* (Cambridge: Cambridge University Press, 2007), 183.

and published in 1888 just months before Nietzsche's complete breakdown early in 1889.[66] *The Importance of Being Earnest* smirks at the Wagner craze when Algernon remarks of the emphatic nature with which Aunt Augusta rings the doorbell: 'Only relatives, or creditors, ever ring in that Wagnerian manner.'[67] Nonetheless, the Germanic element within the play is significant. Lady Bracknell's seriousness, her domineering personality, and her admiration of the German language speak obviously to the figure of Queen Victoria, widow of the German Prince Albert. These same characteristics (summed up in her roar—'Prism!'— in the final scene) also bring to mind the muscularity of Wagner's warrior-goddess Brünnhilde, who reaches notes that no sane person should attempt.[68] In his acutely perceptive discussion of the influence of Wagner on *The Importance of Being Earnest*, Dieter Fuchs identifies a probable allusion to Wagnerian *Sprechgesang* in Bracknell's assertion that German is the best language for singing, her 'Valkyrie-like entrance and exit' in Act I, and the significance of Algernon playing 'The Wedding March' from *Lohengrin* as she interrogates Jack in the next room concerning his fitness to marry her daughter.[69]

Wilde's play does not give its audience Wagnerian heroic-mystical sacrifices. There is, however, more than a hint of the implacable Cathleen ni Houlihan of the Gregory–Yeats 1902 piece in the bossy Bracknell of Wilde's earlier play. As Aunt Augusta storms into Algernon's residence and demands that Jack Worthing find himself some parents fast, so the Old Woman of Beare pushes her way into the Gillanes' little cottage to demand their son for a bit of sacrificing. In any case, *The Importance of Being Earnest* presents in a chameleon way two sacrifices for love. Algernon must sacrifice his beloved Bunbury if he is to marry Cecily. Jack must kill off his brother Ernest Worthing if he is to marry Gwendolen. Doing so, Jack resurrects him, finding himself in the process to be truly Ernest. This death-and-resurrection motif, Jack/ Ernest finding himself by losing himself (found in a London station-locker in a hand-bag, as Moses was found in the Nile in a basket among reeds), brings the comic conceit of the play close to the narrative of Christ's teaching and sacrifice that runs through Wagner operas, particularly the Grail legend of *Parsifal*. The movement, from the laughter of *The Importance of Being Earnest* to the sorrow of *De Profundis* two years later, retrospectively lends a Christian sacrificial significance to the Jack/Ernest double identity: 'Most people are other people. Their thoughts are someone else's opinions, their lives a mimicry, their passions a quotation. Christ was not merely the supreme individualist, but he was the first individualist in history.'[70] In this way, *De Profundis* raises the question of the extent to which, in all its wit, duplicity, and double-play, the idea of sacrifice persists in *The Importance of Being Earnest* as one of the foremost preoccupations of Wilde's drama. Jan-Melissa Schramm reads into Wilde's discussion of Christ in *De Profundis* his abandonment of Hellenism for 'the old stories of sacrifice and martyrdom', following his imprisonment at Pentonville and then at Reading Gaol.[71]

[66] Friedrich Nietzsche, *The Case of Wagner; Nietzsche Contra Wagner; Selected Aphorisms*, 3rd edn., ed. and trans. Anthony M. Ludovici (London: T. N. Foulis, 1911), 14.

[67] Wilde, *Complete Plays*, 226.   [68] Ibid., 284.

[69] Dieter Fuchs, 'Wilde, Wagner, and the Aestheticist Debate of Representation: "What's in a Name?" *The Importance of Being Earnest*, or *Lohengrin*', *Anglistik: International Journal of English Studies* 20, no. 2 (2009), 132–3.

[70] Oscar Wilde, *De Profundis and Other Writings*, 1949 edn., ed. Vyvyan Holland (London: Penguin, 1973), 169.

[71] Jan-Melissa Schramm, 'Wilde and Christ', in Kerry Powell and Peter Raby (eds.), *Oscar Wilde in Context* (Cambridge: Cambridge University Press, 2013), 259.

De Profundis is not such a fundamental turn in direction as this implies. However far behind it has left the joviality of *The Importance of Being Earnest*, the letter to Lord Alfred Douglas can still be viewed as a last thorn-enmeshed blossoming of the sacrificial motif running through Wilde's drama as a whole.

The great impact of Wagner's opera throughout Europe in the last three decades of the nineteenth century was attributable not just to innovations that he brought to the operatic medium but also to the rise of Central/Eastern European powers in those decades: the Austro-Hungarian *Ausgleich* of 1867 and the unification of Germany under Bismarck. The secrecies, the spying and the coded gestures of Wilde's drama, its Central European points of reference, and its recurrent preoccupation with sacrifice together have a significant affinity with Wagner's *oeuvre*. We need only think of *Lohengrin*, in which Elsa's failure to keep Lohengrin's name a secret causes her sacrificial death.[72] Wagner's legacy would carry through in the Irish cultural revival that began in the 1880s. The epic scale and mystical atmosphere of Yeats's 'The Wanderings of Oisin' not only looks back to the legends of ancient Ireland and the epics of Homer. A poem praised by Wilde, it also shares in the mysticism and grandeur of Wagner's work. Wagner's *Tristan and Isolde*, after all, portrays the character of Isolde, an Irish Princess from a medieval Celtic legend. The novelist George Moore and the playwright Edward Martyn collaborated and contested with Yeats during the late 1890s and 1900s in the development of the Irish Literary Theatre. In his masterly autobiography, *Hail and Farewell!*, Moore provided a detailed and evocative account of his pilgrimages with Martyn to Bayreuth for Wagner's Ring festival in the 1890s.[73] In debates over the sources upon which the new Irish theatre movement should draw, Yeats wrote: 'Richard Wagner's dramas of "The Ring" are, together with his mainly Celtic "Parsival" and "Lohengrin," and "Tristan and Iseult," the most passionate influence in the arts of Europe.'[74]

Concluding in borderline incestuous marital arrangements and the sacrificial deaths of two fictional characters, *The Importance of Being Earnest* projects the death of fiction itself; the death of art, and (following *The Picture of Dorian Gray*) art as death. In a scene of biblical apocalypse at the end of *Götterdämmerung* that accompanies Brünnhilde's sacrificial act, the stage is engulfed in flames as the Rhine bursts its banks. Drawing on the Judeo-Christian tradition of the end-times, it is a forerunner of Europe's political catastrophes in the twentieth century. The magnificent, unsettling witticisms of Wilde's dramas, their constant play with the dangers of social and political subterfuge, and their fascination with the sacrificial act, all contribute to the sense of his theatrical achievement as a portent of the calamities that would follow the age of Wagner. Wilde did not write for Ireland, but the influence of Ireland's historical conflict with England prompted and enabled him to develop his distinctive theatrical perspectives on art, politics, and sacrifice as prophecies of this future.

---

[72] Fuchs identifies in this an influence on the character of Sibyl Vane in *The Picture of Dorian Gray*: 'Wilde, Wagner, and the Aestheticist Debate', 132–3. He further considers how the subversion of the name as foundational marker of identity in *The Importance of Being Earnest* is a send-up of Elsa's craving for knowledge of the hero's name in *Lohengrin*: 135–7.

[73] George Moore, *Hail and Farewell!* (1911), 2nd edn., ed. Richard Allen Cave (Gerrards Cross: Colin Smythe, 1985), 144–83. For accounts of Moore's trip to Bayreuth with Martyn, see Adrian Frazier, *George Moore, 1852–1933* (New Haven, CT: Yale University Press, 2000), 244–5, 275–8.

[74] W. B. Yeats, 'A Note on National Drama', in John Eglinton, W. B. Yeats, Æ, and W. Larminie, *Literary Ideals in Ireland* (London: T. Fisher Unwin, 1899), 18.

PART II

THEATRE
AND NATION

CHAPTER 3

THE ABBEY AND THE IDEA OF A THEATRE

BEN LEVITAS

REDEFINITIONS

'STOP any man in the street nowadays and ask him to describe an Irish drama,' declared William Barratt in March 1895:

> He will tell you that there is a background of soldiers or policemen, four principal 'good' people, consisting of a high-minded young Irish gentleman in tight trousers, a faithful retainer, whose name should be Larry or Thade; the charming fiancée of the young gentleman, and the merry sweetheart of the faithful retainer; and two principal 'bad' people— generally a wicked landlord and his hireling spy.[1]

The sure-fire formulas of Irish melodrama, its conventionality, and its routine sentimentality could by this stage be mockingly sketched as tired—even quaint—simplifications. The theatrical form that had held sway for half a century was increasingly out of date and place.

That ideal of unsullied honesty writ large into the staged Irishman—of 'the sparkling wit and humour, deep pathos, poetic sentiment and tender feeling'[2]—no longer seemed to fit. The 1890s in Ireland had begun in disillusion: Charles Stewart Parnell, the 'uncrowned king' of the nation-in-waiting, had been living a double life with Katharine O'Shea, the wife of a political colleague. He was no leading man. Parnell's subsequent death, following a series of rearguard contests for control of the Irish Parliamentary Party, had left Ireland in rancour, debating social and sexual ethics. For those who deemed him a scoundrel, melodrama might still seem apt,[3] but for his supporters another mood had been manifested. Suddenly Irish public life seemed an echo of the radical theatre emerging from the

---

[1] William Barratt, 'Irish Drama', *New Ireland Review* 3, no. 1 (1895), 39.
[2] J. W. Scanlan, 'Irish Drama: A Symposium', *New Ireland Review* 3, no. 2 (1895), 113.
[3] See Cheryl Herr, *For the Land They Loved: Irish Political Melodramas 1890–1925* (Syracuse, NY: Syracuse University Press, 1991), 3–19.

continent—of Ibsen's study in hypocrisy and populism, *An Enemy of the People* (1882), or even the then recently notorious *Ghosts* (1882). And no sooner had Oscar Wilde completed his comic inversions of moral duality and evasion, culminating in *The Importance of Being Earnest* (1895), than his trial and imprisonment compounded the sense that Ireland might veer into a *fin-de-siècle* vogue.

At the same time, an alternative idealism had begun to flourish. The coalescence of Irish cultural institutions in the final decade of the nineteenth century—the National Literary Society (1892), the Celtic Literary Society (1892), and the Gaelic League (1893)— became populated by young nationalists looking for redefinition. It was a natural progression to seek out a theatre to complement this process. John McGrath, literary editor of the Parnellite flagship *United Ireland*, noted in 1894 the potential for Irish theatre when W. B. Yeats's *The Land of Heart's Desire* (1894) was twinned with G. B. Shaw's *Arms and the Man* (1894) at the Avenue Theatre, London,[4] but his paper posed the question that was immediately suggested by its location: 'Certainly there is the promise of an Irish National drama, but what of the Irish National stage?'[5]

The development of the Irish National Theatre, housed at the Abbey Theatre, had its roots in this particular combination of local and transnational modernity. It began by leaving London behind and drawing Dublin closer to the Continent. Wilde's wiser friends had urged him to flee for Paris; Yeats and Shaw were invited to head for Dublin. In both can be detected a departure—an Irish cultural shift looking to resist British imperial presumptions by combining the Celt and the bohemian, merging indigenous myth and language with hostility to bourgeois populism. The Irish Literary Theatre (ILT) and its successor, the National Theatre Society (NTS), evolved as hybrid organizations: part constitutive national institution, closely allied to the cultural restructuring of Ireland in the period prior to independence, and part modern theatrical venture, allied to a wider artistic project that typically challenged accepted social norms. The anomalous tension at the heart of this possibility, between idealism and modernism, was also a founding feature of its emergence particular to Ireland's status as a European polity emerging from the British empire. The idea of a national theatre as a constitutive prerequisite to statehood had been articulated by Friedrich Schiller a century earlier, in an attempt to combine the Enlightenment ideals of Rousseau and Diderot with the Romantic ideas of an ethnic people (*Volk*) elaborated by Johann Gottfried Herder.[6] But as rapid industrialization translated into urbanization, and revolutionary ethnic nationalism developed into imperial expansionism, the concept of 'the people' had become strained by divisions of social class and gender, while popular forms of culture had become absorbed into a commercialized mass culture that resisted change.

Across Europe, twin processes of social and aesthetic resistance to conventionality generated modern theatres that took root in the cracks that appeared as processes of democratization loosened agencies of control. In Paris, André Antoine's Théâtre Libre (1887), in Berlin, Otto Brahm's Freie Bühne (1889), and in London, J. T. Grein's Independent Theatre

---

[4] John McGrath, 'North and South', *United Ireland*, 21 Apr. 1894.

[5] R., 'Two Irish Dramatists', *United Ireland*, 21 Apr. 1894.

[6] See Loren Kruger, 'The National Stage and the Naturalized House: (Trans)National Legitimation in Modern Europe', in S. E. Wilmer (ed.), *National Theatres in a Changing Europe* (Basingstoke: Palgrave Macmillan, 2008), 36–7.

(1891) were founded along the fault lines of the semi-censorship afforded by private theatre clubs. This initial efflorescence quickly proliferated into stylistic variety, in a process
that tugged at the implicit dialectical tensions between artistic and social function: so, for
instance, Paul Fort's Théâtre d'Art (1890) developed a symbolist stage in Paris, hosting an
esoteric alternative to sceptical realism.

Between Civic Theatre and Art Theatre

For the founders of the National Theatre in Ireland, such innovations were both profound
and inadequate. As a proto-state institution, the new theatre could have neither the luxury
nor the protection of the private theatre club. A theatre organized on national principles
had to take up a socially defining public position, even while it sought to adopt a stance of
artistic innovation. The tension between these divergent impulses—toward a consensus-
seeking civic theatre and toward an art-house challenge to conventionality—is evident
from the first, in the manifesto of the ILT craftily outlined by Yeats, Lady Gregory, and
Edward Martyn in 1897:

> We hope to find in Ireland an uncorrupted and imaginative audience trained to listen
> by its passion for oratory, and believe that our desire to bring upon the stage the deeper
> thoughts and emotions of Ireland will ensure for us a tolerant welcome, and that free-
> dom to experiment which is not found in theatres of England, and without which no
> new movement in art or literature can succeed. We will show that Ireland is not the
> home of buffoonery and of easy sentiment, as it has been represented, but the home of
> an ancient idealism. We are confident of the support of all Irish people, who are weary
> of misrepresentation, in carrying out a work that is outside all the political questions
> that divide us.[7]

Underlying the assured tone are telling indicators of a fraught project in which strained
expectation betrays a more tentative hope of a 'tolerant welcome' to a 'new movement'
intent on exercising 'freedom to experiment'. The prospectus confidently claims common
ground in its memorable dismissal of melodrama and stage Irish clichés, but ends with a
less easy allusion to the notionally apolitical objectives of cultural representation. In its
initial stages, the ILT necessarily courted indulgence from constructive unionist as from
elite nationalist party interests, each equally interested in co-opting cultural development
as part of their political projects. Such flexibility was politic, as opportunities to establish
the material presence of a theatre movement required funding, location, changes to law,
and social sponsorship. The manifesto's inventive projection of unity disguised a spectrum
of opinion within alliances of convenience, and uneasy coalition proved an enduring principle. The idea of the theatre would always be a contingent, historical process, tied in to
the internal and external power struggles that defined the relation between its social and
aesthetic functions.

---

[7] Augusta Gregory, *Our Irish Theatre: A Chapter of Autobiography*, 3rd edn. (Gerrards Cross: Colin
Smythe, 1972), 20.

A rich debate began around which existing models of theatre practice best suited Ireland. In the opening editorial to *Beltaine*, the journal accompanying the first productions of the ILT, Yeats declared:

> One finds the literary drama [. . .] in little and expansive theatres, which associations of men hire from time to time that they may see up on the stage the plays of Henrik Ibsen, Maurice Maeterlinck, Gerard Hauptmann, Jose Echegaray. [. . .] The Irish Literary Theatre will attempt to do in Dublin something that has been done in London and in Paris. [. . .] The plays will differ because the intellect of Ireland is romantic and spiritual rather than scientific and analytical.[8]

Yeats's proposition is notable for the way in which it took in the wider ambit of modern theatre before narrowing into symbolist preferences. Already emerging as the theatre project's chief theoretician, [9] Yeats quietly asserted the expertise he had gathered touring the Parisian avant-garde in the early 1890s. But the mode of European modernism that would best suit Irish circumstance divided opinion. George Russell (Æ) described the core problem as 'Nationality and Cosmopolitanism in Literature', and in so doing revealed a subtle set of differences. Russell's literary emphasis was in fact rather anti-theatrical: Celtic poets, he suggested, were notable for 'the faculty of abstracting from the land their eyes beheld another Ireland through which they wandered in dream'.[10] Such a proposal subtly undermined dramatic arts as a less reliable guide to nationality than more abstract forms of evocation, which had the advantage of being more resistant to outside influence. In contrast, Yeats's closer attention to the specific developments in theatrical form on the Continent picked out specific role models. The immediate comparators were Ibsen and Wagner, who had, with *Peer Gynt* and the Ring cycle, produced modern works from folk legend and ancient myth. When pressed by W. K. Magee ('John Eglinton'), who pointed out that 'the crowd of elect persons seated in the curiously-devised seats in Bayreuth does not seem very like the whole Athenian democracy thronging to their places for a couple of obols',[11] Yeats had clarified: 'I thought less of the crowds at Vienna or at Munich than of the best intellects of our time, of men like Count Villiers de L'Isle Adam.'[12] He and Maeterlinck had, Yeats suggested, 'set before us faint souls, naked and pathetic shadows already half vapour and sighing to one another upon the border of the vast abyss'.[13]

This was quite different, however, from either wandering poets or dramatizations of foundational myth. Yeats's appreciation of Maeterlinck's transition from poetry into theatre was a complex acknowledgement of differences within modes of symbolism. Like Strindberg, whose experiment in 'dream' plays was under way at the same time (*To Damascus I* was also written in 1898), Yeats found in the Belgian dramatist's dissertation on interiority—*The Treasure of the Humble*—'a great revolution of thought'.[14]

---

[8] W. B. Yeats, 'Plans and Methods', *Beltaine* 1 (May 1899), 6.

[9] See James W. Flannery, *W. B. Yeats and the Idea of a Theatre: The Early Abbey Theatre in Theory and Practice* (New Haven, CT: Yale University Press, 1976).

[10] Æ [George Russell], 'Nationality and Cosmopolitanism in Literature', *Dublin Daily Express*, 10 Dec. 1898.

[11] John Eglinton, 'What Should Be the Subject of a National Drama?', *Daily Express*, 8 Oct. 1898.

[12] W. B. Yeats, 'John Eglinton and Spiritual Art', *Daily Express*, 29 Oct. 1898.

[13] W. B. Yeats, 'The Autumn of the Flesh', *Daily Express*, 3 Dec. 1898.

[14] W. B. Yeats, ' The Treasure of the Humble', *The Bookman* 12, no. 70 (1897), 94.

Post-Maeterlinck, the poetic '[r]evelation of a hidden life'[15] could be paradoxically enhanced by the theatrical representation of surface for its effect. But it also stepped back from mythic nationalism and towards a revelation both more intimate and more cosmic.

Yeats's *parti pris* advocacy glossed over such distinctions, preferring to contrast symbolist forms with Ibsen's problem plays, schematically designated as 'criticism of life'. But Magee had proposed a subtler reading of the varieties open to modern drama. In a daring stride toward a unifying theory, he replaced Yeats's subjective/objective polarity with a model of intersubjectivity, stepping beyond the crude opposition of the 'romantic' and 'realistic'. He suggested:

> What was [their] weakness but, in the first, the innate tendency to trust fantasy too far; while the second shared the fallacy of an exclusively scientific age, which regarded truth as altogether objective, not acknowledging that man himself is a truth, not to be demonstrated scientifically but by himself to himself.[16]

This recalibration of realism was closer to the perception of modern theatre in France, where at the same Théâtre de l'Oeuvre (founded in 1893) at which Yeats had attended his productions of Villiers de Lisle-Adam and Maeterlinck, Aurélien Lugné-Poe staged Ibsen as a staple.[17] Indeed, it is a view closer to the reality of the Irish Literary Theatre, which reproduced the balance of the manifesto and the spectrum of opinion in the debates with its first productions in May 1899: Yeats's symbolist-influenced *The Countess Cathleen* (written in 1892) and Edward Martyn's attempt to transplant Scandinavian naturalism, *The Heather Field.*

Becoming the Irish National Theatre Society

Although Magee's emphasis had been on the shared modernity of urban anomie, the debut productions revealed that the moving target of modern 'man' that became the central subject of European theatre was, in the Irish context, an individual also determined in and by cultural and political resistance to British power. That *The Countess Cathleen*, in a supposedly detached artistic métier of 'hidden revelation', provoked immediate controversy was instructive. The first version of the play had been published years before its first production, but in this fresh national context the tale of abstracted aristocratic selflessness, in which the heroine barters her soul to redeem the already sold souls of starving peasants, appeared an offensive condescension. Autonomy was anti-national, falling into the gap between Villiers de l'Isle-Adam and Wagner. The furore revealed that in a culture where national symbolism was already in play, conceptual representation of aristocracy, of redemption, of

---

[15] Yeats, 'Autumn of the Flesh'.

[16] John Eglinton, 'Personality in Literature', *Daily Express*, 17 Sept. 1898. This is a curious anticipation not only of Synge's *oeuvre* but also of the dialectics of performativity and phenomenology (apropos Maurice Merleau-Ponty) elaborated by Erika Fischer-Lichte, *The Transformative Power of Performance: A New Aesthetics* (London: Routledge, 2008), 26–9.

[17] Bettina L. Knapp, *The Reign of the Theatrical Director: French Theatre 1887–1924* (Troy, NY: Whitston Press, 1988), 113.

organized religion, and indeed of hunger could never be abstracted from local, temporal specificity.

This turbulent beginning prefaced a swift radicalization of the project, brought on by the combination of the beginning of the Boer War and the royal visit by Queen Victoria in April 1900. As the ground shifted, Yeats was quick to recognize that, in circumstances in which the theatre was understood as seeking a national role, it would inevitably be designated as constitutive. This theatre would be required to engage in a practice that not merely reflected life in Ireland but also developed social and national discourse in the process of both representation and presentation. 'Because [Ireland's] moral nature has been aroused by political sacrifices, and her imagination by a political pre-occupation with her own destiny,' he argued, 'she is ready to be moved by profound thoughts that are a part of the unfolding of herself.'[18]

That Yeats constructed Ireland as a female subject was a customary trope. But that he did discloses an appropriate parallel to emerging feminist nationalism. As the Irish Literary Theatre alliance fragmented at the end of 1901, part of what constituted the Irish cultural identity was a reformulation of its theatre toward praxis: the coalescence of a theatre company, not led by established writers but drawn from grass-roots stagecraft, Gaelic league activists, and proto-feminist nationalists from the *Inghinidhe na hÉireann* (Daughters of Erin). In this context, Yeats's formula—the 'unfolding of herself' that linked nation formation with gendered identity and both with ongoing incompleteness—was also a knowing construction that positioned Irish nationalism as a process of modernity: driven by sacrifices that constituted political direction, but also in flux, constantly remade, and with opportunities for unexpected challenge and contestation. Shifting gender roles within the rubric of national becoming manifested precisely this dynamic: and, as Yeats implied, the best place to explore that performative relationship was through an artistic form constituted in performance itself.[19] It was a combination evident not merely in Yeats's theory but also in what might be considered the inaugural productions of what would become the national theatre in 1902. *Cathleen ni Houlihan* not only symbolically represented the literary tradition of the *aisling* personification of Ireland in an idealized female form:[20] the production of the play also constituted a complementary, structuring role of performative theatricality, of representation as social action. The partial reconfiguration of gender as a dynamic within cultural nationalism is evident in the unacknowledged yet also co-authored text by Yeats and Augusta Gregory, in particular in the physical rendering of the title role by Maud Gonne. In the play, Cathleen entices Michael Gillane away from marriage and into the 1798 rebellion, and is rejuvenated in the process. As political activist, actor, and muse, Gonne operated as practitioner as well as performative speech-actor, seeking renewal in the expression of what the diarist of the early theatre Joseph Holloway described as 'red hot patriotic sentiment'.

Yet, as Holloway also reported, *Cathleen ni Houlihan* was a hybrid form built around contrast: 'The matter-of-fact ways of the household and the weird, uncanny conduct of

---

[18] W. B. Yeats, 'The Irish Literary Theatre', *Beltaine* 2 (Feb. 1900), 23.

[19] See Judith Butler (*pace* J. L. Austin's 'speech act' theory of performativity), *Excitable Speech: A Politics of the Performative* (London: Routledge, 1997), 147.

[20] Susan Cannon Harris, *Gender and Modern Irish Drama* (Bloomington, IN: Indiana University Press, 2002), 62.

the strange visitor.'[21] If the work asserted symbolism as a revolutionary form capable of national rejuvenation, it also required a sure-footed mimesis and disciplined control. Crucially, the core of the national theatre company was built around a strong combination of formal rigour across a range of theatrical modes, able to respond equally well to realist satire and to symbolist evocation, and capable of physical comedy as much as tragic gravitas. The Fay brothers were just such a combination. William George Fay, a seasoned veteran of melodrama and mobile fit-up, had evolved a spare style equally adaptable for symbolist distance and economical realism, and possessed a gift for comic timing; his brother Frank gave close attention to vocal recitation and verse speech. Like Yeats, their inspiration came from the Continent rather than from British routine, and yet they were notably eclectic in what they took. Like Yeats, Frank Fay had studied closely the independent theatres of the early 1890s,[22] and as dramatic critic for the *United Irishman* (the weekly newspaper for advanced nationalists, under the editorship of Arthur Griffith) could also provide essays on the theatre Den Nationale Scene in Bergen or on the influence of Boucicault on Shaw.[23] The Fays' penchant for visual focus and stillness was derived from the veteran Benoît-Constant Coquelin, whose company produced Molière's *Tartuffe* at the Dublin Gaiety in July 1899,[24] while symbolist stage signatures such as the dreamlike effect of gauze curtaining were imported directly from Lugné-Poe.[25] (Observing an English adaptation of *Pelléas et Mélisande* at the Theatre Royal in September 1900, Frank Fay complained that their unveiled performance lacked the necessary 'gloom and joylessness [. . .] the inner meaning [. . .] was destroyed by too much light on the stage'.[26]) What became the Abbey reputation for understated economy of movement and deft characterization—misconstrued by the London critics on first encounter as an attractive mixture of naivety and affectation[27]—was a studied mode of performance, capable of swift transition into static tragedy or mobile farce, developed through a busy correspondence between Frank Fay and Yeats and in shared, devised process of rehearsal under the watchful eye of W. G. Fay, as new scripts and new actors emerged. The group that by the end of 1902 had designated itself the Irish National Theatre Society (INTS) was also an emerging school of dramatic arts, through which amateur players developed, under the tutelage of W. G. and Frank Fay, into performers of increasing confidence and authority.

[21] Joseph Holloway, *Joseph Holloway's Abbey Theatre: A Selection from his Unpublished Journal 'Impressions of an Irish Playgoer'*, ed. Robert Hogan and Michael J. O'Neill (Carbondale, IL: Southern Illinois University Press, 1967), 17.

[22] Gerard Fay, *The Abbey Theatre, Cradle of Genius* (London: Hollis & Carter, 1958), 33.

[23] Frank J. Fay, 'Dion Boucicault', *United Irishman*, 5 Aug. 1899.

[24] Chester Williams Keeler, 'The Abbey Theatre and the Brothers Fay' (PhD dissertation, University of California, 1973), 106, 226.

[25] For a different interpretation of the Fays' acting style, see Ch. 15.

[26] F. J. Fay, '"Pelleas et Melisande" at the Theatre Royal', *United Irishman*, 1 Sept. 1900.

[27] A. B. Walkley of *The Times* described the delicacy of the production: 'playing *pianissimo*, all hushed as in some sick-room, all grave and, as it were, careworn', but felt they had 'something of the self-importance of children surpliced for service at the altar': 'The Irish National Theatre', *Times Literary Supplement*, 8 May 1903, 146.

SYNGE: BEYOND UNIFYING REASSURANCE

With the coalescence of a dramatic company around the Fays, the INTS attracted new writing that emerged through the formulation of the Society along democratic, participatory lines. As it did so, however, the INTS quickly began to reproduce in microcosm wider divisions in Irish cultural politics. From late 1902 and throughout 1903, skirmishes were fought between factions in the budding organization. At first, this was largely due to resistance on the part of the Fays and Yeats to the influence of commercial styles on new writers. While symbolist renderings of Irish myth had become a staple in nationalist circles, and Irish realism and comic satire were likewise quickly established within the theatre repertoire, any overly populist or commercial style was swiftly detected and resisted. Young writers drawn to such material, as was the case with James Cousins's *Sold* (published 1902) or Padraic Colum's *The Saxon Shillin'* (published 1902)—farce and melodrama respectively—were invited to mend their ways, but not without umbrage and altercation en route. For those involved in the INTS purely as a political commitment, *The Saxon Shillin'* simply had potential as a piece of anti-recruiting propaganda: artistic quality was not an issue. For activists such as Maud Gonne, the theatre had always as its primary function the exposure of British imperial power; if the national theatre had a fundamental duty, it was to dramatize the need for resistance. But for those engaged in the Revival, theatre had a more complex role as part of a wider cultural commitment.

This was no straightforward opposition: *Cathleen ni Houlihan* had already demonstrated that the theatre could be both experimental and republican. And realism was in its own way radical: for most theatregoers, even-handed depiction of rural Ireland was already a revelation. Padraic Colum's response to advice over his early melodrama had been to return with two more subtle renderings of the small tenant farm, *Broken Soil* (1903) and *The Land* (1905), that were not only palatable to all parties but widely celebrated for mature sensibility. Some might cavil that Yeats's mythic verse plays lacked dramatic tension, but they remained for many what Gregory called the 'point of the diamond'.[28] Nevertheless, despite the common ground, once the disruptive presence of John Millington Synge had made its appearance, it became clear that the national theatre would make its way as a contested space.

When Synge's first play *The Shadow of the Glen* (1903) sparked controversy, it partly did so as a play adapting *A Doll's House* to an Irish peasant context. Nora's exit from a failed (if not entirely dead) marriage likewise took that step beyond the threshold of respectability. But whereas in Europe the opprobrium such transgression invited had been a confirmation of progressive credentials, in Ireland the accusation was of entrenching stereotypes that fed colonial attitudes. In condemning the play, Arthur Griffith (soon to found Sinn Féin) set a pattern of criticism that lasted until Synge's death. It is worth noticing that he picked out, not just an issue of content in his critique, but of form. He complained:

> It remained for a member of the Society who spends most of his time away from Ireland, and under the operation of foreign influences, to represent, in good faith no doubt, adultery

---

[28] Gregory, *Our Irish Theatre*, 52.

as a feature of Irish life, and to exhibit his utter ignorance of the Irish character by treating woman's frailty as a subject for laughter.[29]

Griffith's criticism thus divided Synge's sin into three parts: first, that he had reproduced a foreign trope (the literature of adultery) in an Irish context; secondly, that he had thereby failed to recognize Irish immunity to the moral decadence apparent in that trope; and finally, that he had compounded the error by inflecting it through comedy. Stripped of its moral indignation, this was not unperceptive. Synge had spent far longer on the Parisian left bank than Yeats, and had brought his study of the French moderns west to Wicklow and the Aran Islands. His innovation was to incorporate in this conjunction a longer tradition of Rabelaisian (or, as Griffith thought, Boccaccian) ribaldry. Synge's ability to pack together acute observation of rural Ireland, modern sexual politics, folk tradition, and poetic Hiberno-English dialogue with tightly framed dramatic construction redefined the national theatre. But his genre-shifting ability to move between theatrical modes particularly unnerved earnest nationalists. For all that the reception—and defence—of *The Shadow of the Glen* recalled serious *Kulturkampf*,[30] it was Synge's unsettling, reflexive comedy that disturbed audience responses. By comparison, the reception given to the tragedy *Riders to the Sea* (1904) was that of an audience grateful to be harrowed.

Like *Cathleen ni Houlihan*, *The Shadow of the Glen* had made ample use of the company's versatility, utilizing the spectrum of theatricality towards which the Fays had trained the group—particularly now that a crop of actors ready to take on Synge's strong female roles had emerged under their instruction: 'The fact is Miss Walker, Miss Garvey, Miss Allgood and Miss Esposito beat the men hollow,' confided Frank Fay to Joseph Holloway in March 1904.[31] Unlike *Cathleen ni Houlihan*, *The Shadow of the Glen* departed from the confluence of idealized nation and idealized woman. Instead, keen observation of poverty and misalliance came with a wry joy in physicality that celebrated sexual energy. With Synge's entrance, the formative role of theatre in the context of national identity took a shift away from unifying reassurance, away from what he described as 'unmodern, ideal, breezy, springdayish, Cuchulainoid National Theatre'. He proposed instead to 'deal with modern matters on the stage in Ireland', citing as antecedents Ibsen, Hauptmann, and Sudermann.[32] This was a manifesto not of autonomy but of interventionism. Yeats accommodated Synge's trespass in a broad defence of defamiliarization—'we must encourage every writer to see life afresh, even though he sees it with strange eyes'[33]—but it was a position adopted at least in part because Synge, like Jarry's *Ubu Roi* (1896), defied symbolist detachment with a new, 'Savage God'.

---

[29] Arthur Griffith, editorial comment on published letter from J. B. Yeats ['The Irish National Theatre Society'], *United Irishman*, 31 Oct. 1903.

[30] P. J. Mathews, *Revival: The Abbey Theatre, Sinn Féin, the Gaelic League and the Co-operative Movement* (Cork: Cork University Press), 2003.

[31] Holloway, *Joseph Holloway's Irish Theatre*, 36.

[32] J. M. Synge, *Collected Letters*, vol. 1, ed. Ann Saddlemyer (Oxford: Oxford University Press, 1983), 74.

[33] W. B. Yeats, 'Notes', *Samhain*, Sept. 1903, 7.

'No Propaganda But That of Good Art'?

Yeats's theatre activism, evolving as it did through the situations stimulated by Synge's interventionism, grew in a sense into a shared paratheatricality, constantly testing the hinterland between production and reception. In *Samhain*, the theatre's journal, he declared its guiding principle as 'no propaganda but that of good art'.[34] But having already recognized that autonomy within a national tradition was impossible, he made clear in his article defying 'Three Sorts of Ignorance' (propaganda, piety and opportunism) that the theatre would, instead, set the national agenda not by confirming its traditions but by challenging them.[35] This lapse into modernist function was too much for some in the company, who left in protest to form an alternative group. Thus the seceding National Players joined a long tradition of nationalist theatres that were never the National Theatre, from continuing melodrama at the Queen's to emerging regional groups like the Ulster Literary Theatre (1902) and the Cork Dramatic Society (1910).[36]

Yeats's combative persona was partly the product of his fascination with Friedrich Nietzsche, an encounter that required a profound shift away from the ideal of a sacred theatre. When in 1906 Yeats launched a new theatre journal, the *Arrow*, specifically to attack his enemies, he took for its masthead Wagner's 1867 essay 'German Art and German Policy':

> In the theatre there lies the spiritual seed and kernel of all national poetic and national moral culture. No other branch of Art can ever truly flourish or ever aid in cultivating the people until the Theatre's all-powerful assistance has been completely recognized and guaranteed. [37]

It was a statement that reasserted the centrality of the theatre to the national project while boldly lifting it above criticism.[38] But it was also disingenuous. Having studied *The Case of Wagner*,[39] Yeats understood that Nietzsche had chosen a lonelier road after his old mentor had written what he considered the hypocritically Christian *Parsifal*. Had not Maud Gonne done the same by converting to Catholicism and marrying John McBride? Well might she protest in her letters that 'Neiche [*sic*] is not Celtic'.[40] Yeats's forceful reaction to Synge's work betrayed a move away from Wagnerian pretensions to a monarchically

---

[34] Ibid., 4.

[35] W. B. Yeats, 'The Irish National Theatre and Three Sorts of Ignorance', *United Irishman*, 24 Oct. 1903.

[36] See Mary Trotter, *Ireland's National Theaters: Political Performance and the Origins of the Irish Dramatic Movement* (Syracuse, NY: Syracuse University Press, 2001); Ben Levitas, *The Theatre of Nation: Irish Drama and Cultural Nationalism 1890–1916* (Oxford: Clarendon Press, 2002).

[37] Richard Wagner, 'German Art and German Policy', in *Prose Works*, vol. 4: *Art and Politics* (London: Kegan Paul, 1895), 69–70.

[38] Wagner went on to declare: 'If we enter a theatre with any power of insight, we look straight into a daemonic abyss of possibilities, the lowest as the loftiest' (ibid., 70): a caveat which might have been of use to the National Theatre's critics, had they examined the original more closely.

[39] R. F. Foster, *W. B. Yeats: A Life*, vol. 1: *The Apprentice Mage* (Oxford: Oxford University Press, 1997), 584.

[40] A. Norman Jeffares and Anna MacBride White (eds.), *The Gonne-Yeats Letters 1893–1938* (Syracuse, NY: Syracuse University Press, 1994), 169.

led national *Geist*, toward a Nietzschean commitment to an aristocratic individual will and a posture of estranged revelation. *On Baile's Strand* (1904) and *The King's Threshold* (1903) were both allegories of rebellious superiority disavowing social duty that might have taken the Nietzsche–Wagner split as their matter. With the injection of capital provided by Annie Horniman, Yeats had, in theory at least, the opportunity to establish a Bayreuth for Zarathustras, beckoning like Cuchulain to 'Nestlings of a high nest,/Hawks that have followed me into air/And looked upon the sun'.[41] A tea heiress with a passion for the theatrical arts whom Yeats had been cultivating since the early 1890s, Horniman egged him on in his bid to join the *Übermenschen*, warning that he was being dragged down by his obligations to the lower orders, and that 'even Super People cannot be expected to enjoy a revolt of slaves'.[42] With a new platform for this will to power, Yeats welcomed the conflict that came with Synge's notoriety. Always a combative cultural activist, his advocacy of theatrical primacy lent him a new ferocity. 'During the years that followed,' remembered the actor Máire Nic Shuibhlaigh (Mary Walker), 'when he acquired the leadership of the Abbey, he carried it through some of its most critical years, fought all of its battles, denounced its enemies and critics with a vigour almost terrifying in its finality.'[43]

THE ABBEY

Yet the intensity of Yeats's struggle in the Abbey was also a testament to the fact that leadership was never control. The theatre that opened its doors on 27 December 1904 was resolutely a product of the movement rather than the man: a building that demonstrated how imbricated theatre was into the society that had given it shape. Architecturally, the Abbey was roughly superimposed on the footprint of the 'National Musical Hall' that had operated at the Mechanics Institute. Irish institutions were typically a blend of established national and civic functions and revivalist departures, and the new theatre was no exception. Whereas the fixtures and fittings (apart from the German lights) gave a polished veneer of Revival industry, the 'large medallions exhibiting the city arms [and] the Irish harp'[44] left over from its former life were evident high up on either side of the proscenium. Sarah Purser's stained glass windows depicting nut trees—Celtic symbols of wisdom—fronted the building beside the double glass doors of the main entrance on Malborough Street, but no one forgot the vestibule's previous use as a morgue.

That the Abbey was constituted in the fabric of a pre-existing Dublin is a useful reminder of the ways that physical housing ties in social and aesthetic function. It was a theatre defined as much by the people who frequented the space as by its playwrights, performances and performers, or managers. The designer, the same Joseph Holloway who recorded Dublin's theatrical everyday, made a fine use of the space available: an intimate

---

[41] W. B. Yeats, *The Variorum Edition of the Plays of W. B. Yeats*, ed. Russell K. Alspach (London: Macmillan, 1966), 491.

[42] A. E. F. Horniman to W. B. Yeats, 29 Dec. 1909. National Library of Ireland (NLI) MS 10,952, iv.

[43] Máire Nic Shuibhlaigh, *The Splendid Years: Recollections of Máire Nic Shuibhlaigh as Told to Edward Kenny* (Dublin: James Duffy, 1955), 15.

[44] 'New Dublin Theatre' (a preview of the interior), *Freeman's Journal*, 15 Dec. 1904.

theatre with a modest capacity of 562, and a compact stage in close proximity to the spectators, who, unusually, had no orchestra pit to separate them from the action. The best seats
in the house were the upholstered stalls, taking up the first nine rows from the stage back
to the central auditorium; immediately behind them, the wooden benches of the 'pit' situated the cheapest seats in close proximity to the dearest. No doubt to Yeats's satisfaction, a
shallow circle kept the mid-priced comparatively remote.[45] The Abbey's unusually dynamic
and involved audience meant that this cheek-by-jowl arrangement accomplished the effect
of throwing 'the little streets upon the great', heightening any conflict where reception was
divided along class lines. At first this was less pronounced, since the new theatre's competitors (and Annie Horniman's snobbery) initially required a one shilling minimum, double
the customary price. But by the time of the disturbances that greeted Synge's *The Playboy
of the Western World* a little over two years later, the doors had been thrown open to the
'sixpenny public'.[46]

The momentum of Irish national institutions and convening publics apparent in the
fabric of the Abbey were mirrored by the adjustments afforded the new venture by the
structures of law. As with Yeats's new-found access to capital, Augusta Gregory's access
to imperial lawmakers was testimony to the benefits of elite connections. And as in 1898,
when she had finessed a clause into the Local Government (Ireland) Act for the benefit
of the ILT, in 1904 Gregory deployed her formidable influence in arranging for the new
theatre to be granted a patent to put it on a par with the established Theatre Royal, Queen's,
and Gaiety. It is worth quoting the document at length, since it serves as a reminder of the
still-imperial realities of law and governance that defined Irish life, a useful counterweight
to otherwise teleological emphasis on nascent republican influence:

> KNOW YE THEREFORE that We of Our special grace, certain knowledge and mere motion
> by and with the advice and consent of Our Right Trusty and Right Well-beloved Cousin and
> Councillor William Humbel Dudley, Knight Grand Cross of Our Royal Victorian Order,
> Our Lieutenant General and General Governor of that part of Our said United Kingdom of
> Great Britain and Ireland called Ireland, DO HEREBY grant unto the said Dame Isabella
> Augusta Gregory, her executors, administrators and such assigns as are hereinafter men-
> tioned in trust for the said Annie Elizabeth Fredricka Horniman her executors or admin-
> istrators, under the restrictions, conditions and limitations hereinafter mentioned, full
> power and authority to establish and keep in the building formerly known as the Dublin
> Mechanics Institute and the Morgue of the City of Dublin and indicated in the plans depos-
> ited in Our Privy Seal Office in Our Castle of Dublin a well-regulated Theatre or Play-house
> and therein at all lawful times (except when We or Our Chief Governor or Governors of
> that part of Our said United Kingdom or Great Britain and Ireland for the time being shall
> see cause to forbid the acting or performance of any species of plays or theatrical amuse-
> ments) publicly to act represent or perform or cause to be acted represented or performed
> all Interludes, Tragedies, Comedies, Plays in the Irish or English language written by Irish
> writers or on Irish subjects and such dramatic works of foreign authors as would tend to
> educate and interest the Irish public in the higher works of dramatic art as may be selected

---

[45] See Hugh Denard and NOHO, 2011, for a carefully researched and evidenced virtual model of the
Abbey interior *c*.1904. http://blog.oldabbeytheatre.net/. Accessed 20 Nov. 2014.

[46] In D. P. Moran's phrase, 'At the Abbey Theatre', *Leader*, 7 Jan. 1905. One shilling (12 pence) was a
steep 5% of an unskilled labourer's weekly wage, at that time around £1.

by the Irish National Theatre Society under the provisions contained in part six of the Rules of the Irish National Theatre Society.[47]

The legal demarcation bears testimony to an accomplishment hedged about by tempering pressures. The remit offered a familiar bifurcation of Revival objectives ('by Irish writers or on Irish subjects') and art-house cosmopolitanism ('foreign authors as would tend to educate'), partly exposed because the wider remit had been limited after complaint from already patented competitors jealous of their custom. Executive responsibility rested with Gregory, but under the conditions stipulated by Horniman's subsidy and the process of selection determined by the INTS. Above all, the Lord Lieutenant ('Our Chief Governor') had final say, although—as became clear in the battle over Shaw's *The Shewing-up of Blanco Posnet* (1909)—he too was open to persuasion.

The result was a protracted series of power struggles. Within a year of the Abbey opening, the Realpolitik of control of the building had facilitated a transfer of power away from the INTS, converting the voluntary, democratic organization into a professionalized company with Yeats, Gregory, and Synge at the helm. There were obvious advantages to paid employment for those who had now the opportunity to devote themselves to their craft, and the Society did in the end vote for its conversion to a Limited Company by fourteen votes to one. However, the introduction of the cash nexus into proceedings also entailed a process of alienation, by which the commodification of labour provoked resentment; and for many, the prospect of a Protestant clique owning the theatrical estate looked suspiciously as if the Land Act of 1903 (offering Irish tenant farmers purchasing rights) had gone into reverse.[48] Founding members grieved at the loss of camaraderie, and by 1906 had split again to form The Theatre of Ireland.

A PEOPLE'S THEATRE

Padraic Colum's exit was particularly painful. Invited by Gregory to join the directorate, he declined. Given a choice framed as political integrity versus self-advancement, he felt his position impossible:

> Am I not to consider my own ideal at all? Am I to surrender the ideal of a National Drama? For if Mr Yeats looses [sic] his Dublin audience he will become side tracked, and the creation of a National Drama will lie with societies like those in Cork or Belfast [. . .] I am prepared to loose theatre and actors and the chance of a great training [. . .] I am faced with a tragic issue.[49]

---

[47] 'Warrant for Letters Patent for a new Theatre in the City of Dublin' (22 Dec. 1904), reproduced in appendix A of Peter Kavanagh, *The Story of the Abbey Theatre: From Its Origins in 1899 to the Present* (New York: Devin-Adair, 1950), 216–17. The edition we have in the Bibliography and have used in other references is the later edition of 1976.

[48] See Adrian Frazier's seminal study *Behind the Scenes: Yeats, Horniman and the Struggle for the Abbey Theatre* (Berkeley, CA: University of California Press, 1990).

[49] Padraic Colum to Augusta Gregory, 8 Jan. 1906, Berg Collection, NYPL.

At root Colum recognized that the Abbey would continue to exert profound influence through its commitment to artistic goals; but he was mistaken if he considered that Yeats's contempt for the Dublin audience would disable the Abbey. The fact that it did not is partly explained by the tone of this letter. Gregory's correspondence was full of the confiding remonstrance that her characteristic diplomacy naturally invited. Hers was not simply what Edward Martyn cattily described as 'tact that can only be described as genius'[50] but, at root, the winning charm of a populist. If she sympathized with Colum it was because of a shared vision of consensual theatre. While her fundamental allegiance may have been to Yeats, her plays provided a reassuring counterweight to his instinct for conflict and Synge's capacity to outrage. And she worked hard to make it count: fourteen original works in the period 1904–10, plus three translations (two Molière and one Goldoni) and two co-written works (Hyde and Yeats). Over the same period, Yeats and Synge would only produce three plays apiece. Although Fay complained of her 'milk and water' dialogue,[51] Gregory's work was considered by many to exemplify what a national theatre should perform. Celtic dramas such as *Kincora* (1905) and *Dervorgilla* (1907), tragic or comic histories like *The White Cockade* (1905) and *The Canavans* (1906), intriguing comedies of misunderstanding including *Hyacinth Halvey* (1906) and *The Jackdaw* (1909), as well as sharp nationalist reflections like *The Gaol Gate* (1906) and rabble-rousers such as *The Rising of the Moon* (1907) all went down well, confounding simplistic views of what the Abbey did. 'I really think Kincora a beautiful play,' Pádraig Pearse confided to its author, 'and (though Mr. Yeats dislikes the word) an excellent piece of *propagandism*.'[52]

Gregory formed a united front with Synge to fend off Yeats's restless chafing at the limitations of the national remit, joining forces to prevent his attempt to include more foreign masterpieces to leaven what he took to be a populist diet. They were less successful in shoring up the Fays against similar attacks. Tinkering endlessly with the verse form of *The Shadowy Waters* and *Deirdre* (1906), Yeats had grown impatient with the acting company, and sought to bring in overseas talent from England. Once again, seeking a wider modernist spectrum, he sought to qualify what the Abbey meant, moderating its national status. Despite some success in recasting *Deirdre* with the tragedienne Mrs Patrick Campbell, the form Yeats sought was to elude him until Ezra Pound introduced him to Noh theatre, conjuring *At the Hawk's Well* and subsequent dance plays from 1916 onward. More immediately damaging was the insistence on a new—if short-lived—manager for the theatre, Ben Iden Payne, whose appearance fatally undermined W. G. Fay's authority.

The *cause célèbre* of *The Playboy of the Western World*, and the rapid sequel of Synge's death, masked the effects of the Fays' departure. In part, their schooling of a generation of actors had worked too well: as once grateful protégés outgrew them, W. G.'s attempts to retain authority began—particularly for the all-conquering Allgood sisters—to feel patronizing. There is no doubt, too, that the expertise they had injected into the National Theatre took on its own momentum and established a tradition independent of its originators. But

[50]   Edward Martyn, 'A Plea for the Revival of the Irish Literary Theatre', *Irish Review* 4, no. 38 (1914), 79.

[51]   NLI, MS 10,952.

[52]   Pádraig Pearse, letter to Augusta Gregory, 29 May 1905, in *The Letters of P. H. Pearse*, ed. Seamus O Buachalla (Gerrards Cross: Colin Smythe, 1980), 94.

it is worth reflecting on the concurrence of Synge's death and the loss of the brothers' agile versatility. Lacking both, the output of the theatre reoriented toward a less elastic set of genres, dominated by a sceptical peasant realism. Revivals of Synge's plays were less well served by subsequent directors and actors who struggled to keep that balance between the ecstatic, comic, and disturbing aspects of his plays.

Despite Yeats's pressure, Synge fought hard to keep W. G. Fay in charge at least until *The Playboy* had been produced under his direction.[53] It was Fay who, in close collaboration with the author, staged the work that more than any other would define the Abbey and its relation to the nascent nation state. The formal invention of *The Playboy* had evolved within and through the capacities of the company for which he had written, and indeed of the audience he sought to provoke.[54] The result was a row of redeeming intensity. For a moment the theatre was released both from the romantic ideal of unifying ethnic cohesion and the heroic pretensions of artistic autonomy and superior detachment. After *The Playboy*, the Abbey was not only identified as a radical theatre but also became a reminder of the complexity of democratic polity, altering perspective on majoritarian populism and exposing a subsumed politics of gender and class.

The Playboy can be considered to both allegorize and manifest this process, in a production that synthesized an 'event' out of the dialectic of text and context. Christy Mahon, the would-be parricide who washes up in the Mayo shebeen at the start of the play, gathers reputation as his notoriety breeds confidence, but is caught in a crisis of reception that reverberated beyond narrative. Once Christy's projected myth of rebellious violence is thrown into question, members of his adoptive community become violent critics, and with Synge's genre-shifting synthesis of social and sexual dynamism, the fault lines between national convention and troubling modernism are likewise exposed. In a crescendo of off- and on-stage reaction at the end of the first night, the concerted outrage of affronted nationalists greeted the closing scene in which the attempted lynching of Christy by the local crowd is led by the romantic object of his affections, Pegeen Mike. Her allusion to the 'great gap between a gallous story and a dirty deed'[55] is confronted by a wider act of participation, where artistic autonomy and social agency operate in dialectical counterpoint, through an uproar in which the 'gap' between presentation and representation is bridged in an avant-gardist collapse of the art/life dichotomy.

DISSONANT IDENTITIES

Modernist detachment and nationalist convention are apparently riven in divergent courses, as the history of the National Theatre at the Abbey would seem to emphasize. But to generate angry intervention, thereby arresting the narrative of tragic estrangement, is to

[53] See Robert Welch, *The Abbey Theatre 1899–1999: Form and Pressure* (Oxford: Oxford University Press, 1999), 40.

[54] See Ben Levitas, 'Censorship and Self-Censure in the Plays of J. M. Synge', in Patrick Lonergan (ed.), *Synge and His Influences* (Dublin: Carysfort, 2011), 33–54.

[55] J. M. Synge, *Collected Works*, vol. 4: *Plays Book II*, ed. Ann Saddlemyer (London: Oxford University Press, 1968), 169.

reach precisely for the longed-for comedic marriage that will heal difference.[56] The union of Christy and Pegeen, as of avant-garde and audience, is only possible, however, when the origins of outrage—particularly the objection of bourgeois patriarchy to sexually frank women and far-from-ideal proletarians—can be obviated in utopian settlement. In other words, Synge constructed a double-negative public event that refused the refusal of modernist and nationalist theatre traditions to find common cause, where that common cause is the resolution of the national struggle in a plural, social emancipation.

Yeats was drawn into the paradox. His drift into authoritarian resentment of nationalist imperatives was evident at the *Playboy* debates hosted at the end of the fractious week. Yet while he boasted hieratically of 'the houses that bred us', he did so before a quickly assembled *dáil* of critics, amplifying dispute to preclude censorship. The poet's rightward tack secured a hearing for the most sophisticated left critique of national theatricality of the early twentieth century. Instead of seeking the founding moment of the National Theatre tradition in the manifesto of the ILT or the debut performances of the INTS, or finding the point of origin in the opening of the Abbey doors, an alternative frame for national theatre in the Irish tradition is constituted around a semi-autonomy of art event and conflict, with dissidence at the heart of Irish identity.

A legacy of this confluent episode of modernist nationality at the early Abbey was that in Ireland the theatre retained immunity from the censorship legislatively imposed after Independence, even though neither the Free State nor the Abbey Theatre could always live up to (or live down) this innovative, unstable celebration of the anti-ideal. The tradition of peasant realists who followed Synge, from T. C. Murray to John B. Keane, grew into a dominant convention as restrictive as the 'tight trousers' of the melodramatic heroes they had replaced. The dark sense of reality such plays generated was apposite enough: although the theatre was gratefully released from Annie Horniman's strangulating embrace in 1910, commercial survival—and, from 1926, the close attention of a conditional state subsidy—meant that the 'freedom' from finance or disapproving officialdom never materialized.[57] Yet despite that, there remained room for manoeuvre that allowed experimentation to continue. Lennox Robinson founded the Dublin Drama League in 1919 to ease the embargo on the production of European modernism, and in 1927 the Peacock opened and—as if hatching the cosmopolitan cuckoo in the national nest—immediately hosted the nascent Gate theatre in 1928. The tradition of not-Abbey theatre, which began with regional offshoots and local splitters and continued healthily down to the Pike (1953) and Field Day (1980), was first found in the Abbey's inaugural antagonisms.

If the Abbey did not always succeed in radicalizing nationality, its failures were instructive. At the core of the *Playboy* paradigm is exactly that paradox which recognizes that utopian projection has its main use in acknowledging imperfection, and thus serves a double function: to signpost struggle, and to allow for flesh and blood. Much modern theatre is predicated on the observation that, as a social art, it is uniquely placed to treat the interstices between idealized or imaginative invention and the inescapable situation of physical

---

[56] It thus invites the application of agency to 'complete' modernity. See Fredric Jameson [*pace* Habermas], *A Singular Modernity: Essay on the Ontology of the Present* (New York: Verso, 2002), 11.

[57] Lauren Arrington, *W. B. Yeats, the Abbey Theatre, Censorship, and the Irish State: Adding the Half-Pence to the Pence* (Oxford: Oxford University Press, 2010).

being in history. As a national theatre, the Abbey was structured, both out of the fabric of its time and under the pressure of expectation, and it was not remarkable that its own 'idea' should be a compound of contradictory visions and typically comprised makeshift alliances. But it was less predictable that it should reflexively scrutinize this relationship in such as way as to accommodate modernism in the nation's sense of itself. What Yeats called the 'fascination of what's difficult'[58]—the relentless materiality of theatre—was exactly what made it key to an unfolding national politics still finding its script. Yeats's *Four Plays for Dancers* (1922) wrought a new innovation out of that problematic, in which space literally unfolds into mythic narrative, but verse is halted by a dancing figure. Seán O'Casey brought his totally different tenor of the vaudevillian tragic to the same question, and in 1926 *The Plough and the Stars* sparked a further theatrical conflagration. Yeats upbraided the house as having 'disgraced themselves again', but he was closer in describing the ruckus as a 'recurring celebration of Irish genius'.[59] It was a reaffirmation of theatre as a testing place for the nation.

[58] W. B. Yeats, *The Variorum Edition of the Poems of W. B. Yeats*, ed. Peter Allt and Russell K. Alspach (New York: Macmillan, 1956), 260.

[59] W. B. Yeats, quoted in Christopher Morash, *A History of Irish Theatre 1601–2000* (Cambridge: Cambridge University Press), 163–71.

CHAPTER 4

··

THEATRE AND ACTIVISM
1900–1916

··

P. J. MATHEWS

BETWEEN the defeat of Gladstone's Second Home Rule Bill in 1893 and the introduction of the ill-fated Third Home Rule Bill to the British Parliament in April 1912, the dynamics of Irish nationalist politics changed irrevocably as the solidarity of support behind Parnell's Irish Parliamentary Party began to fragment and transmute into other forms of political activism and allegiance. Much of this activism was animated by a wider intellectual awakening in Irish literary circles which questioned Ireland's status as a western province of Britain, and promoted a broad spectrum of debate on cultural sovereignty and alternative models of political autonomy. This is a period when the wider availability of print technology and the rise of niche newspapers and journals greatly facilitated political organization and anti-establishment activism. During this time it was possible for Irish men and women to join a whole range of clubs, leagues, and societies dedicated to agricultural cooperation, nationalism, Fenianism, loyalism, socialism, republicanism, women's suffrage, anti-conscriptionism, Irish-language revivalism, trade unionism, pacifism, and paramilitarism, among others. Such a diversity of activism also had repercussions in the cultural arena, where literature, music, theatre and the visual arts were pressed into the service of various causes and agendas. It is no longer tenable, therefore, to think of the Irish Revival solely as a monolithic cultural movement that cohered around the influential figures of W. B. Yeats, Augusta Gregory, and J. M. Synge, and that found institutional expression when the Abbey Theatre opened its doors in 1904. Indeed, much of the recent scholarship of the period has shifted the focus away from the concentration on a highbrow literary movement to focus instead on the relationships between various interdependent cultural, social, and political forces. New critical attention to the diverse range of groups, movements, and societies dedicated to multiple forms of political action has revealed a more complex picture of Irish activism during this period.[1] Of particular importance is the role

---

[1] See e.g. Giulia Bruna and Catherine Wilsdon (eds.), 'Special Issue: Organised Spaces: Revival Activism and Print Culture', *Irish Studies Review* 22, no. 1 (2014); Catherine Morris, *Alice Milligan and the Irish Cultural Revival* (Dublin: Four Courts Press, 2012); Marnie Hay, *Bulmer Hobson and the Nationalist Movement in Twentieth-Century Ireland* (Manchester: Manchester University Press, 2009); Karen Steele, *Women, Press and Politics during the Irish Revival* (Syracuse, NY: Syracuse University Press, 2007).

that theatre-making played in binding together a multiplicity of fringe political groups, and in promoting their various aims and agendas. Significant among the vibrant theatre companies that emerged during an intense period of Irish social activism between 1900 and 1916 are the Ulster Literary Theatre, the Theatre of Ireland, and Na hAisteoirí.

ALTERNATIVE ULSTER: THE ULSTER LITERARY THEATRE

One of the striking features of the Irish Revival is the high proportion of Ulster writers, intellectuals, and activists who became involved in the wider movement. Any catalogue of significant Revival figures would have to include prominent Northerners such as Alice Milligan, Anna Johnston, George Russell, Bulmer Hobson, Roger Casement, James Cousins, Francis Joseph Bigger, Eoin MacNeill, John and Joseph Campbell, and Ernest Blythe.Yet in the popular imagination the cultural movement is more readily identifiable, geographically, with the west of Ireland. In truth, locations such as Yeats's Sligo, Gregory's Kiltartan, Pearse's Rosmuc, and Synge's Aran have significant purchase over representations of the Irish Revival. In contrast, Glenarm, Co. Antrim—a distinguished site of Revivalist cultural activity—does not impact on the wider nationalist imagination to the same degree.[2] In many important ways, however, Belfast (and its Ulster hinterland) has a legitimate claim to be considered an alternative node of Revivalist activity and achievement. Yet the contested condition of Ulster as a territory and its status as a zone of intense cultural conflict, particularly in the run-up to the Home Rule crisis of 1912, meant that Ulster Revivalism did not easily cohere around notions of place amenable to a wider Irish nationalist consciousness.

From an early stage in the emergence of the Irish theatre movement, Ulster playwrights were prominently involved. In 1900, *The Last Feast of the Fianna* by Alice Milligan (born in Co. Tyrone) was staged by the Irish Literary Theatre, while *Deirdre* by George Russell (born in Co. Antrim) was produced by W. G. Fay's Irish National Dramatic Company in April 1902 (on the same bill as *Cathleen ni Houlihan* by Yeats and Gregory). Both Milligan and Russell, writers who looked to ancient Irish myth for inspiration, were prominent theatre activists and key figures in the early Dublin theatre experiments. Another Ulster playwright, James Cousins, was among the first produced by the Irish National Theatre Society when his play *The Racing Lug* was performed in the Antient Concert Rooms in Dublin in October 1902.

It was Alice Milligan who first introduced Bulmer Hobson and David Parkhill, both Protestant National Association members interested in the ideals of the United Irishmen, to the innovations of nationalist theatre in Dublin at the beginning of the twentieth century.[3] Inspired by their Dublin visits, Hobson and Parkhill set about founding an Ulster branch of the Irish Literary Theatre in Belfast. In Dublin in 1902, both men found advice

[2] For an appraisal of Revivalist activity in the Glens of Antrim, see Eamon Phoenix, Pádraic Ó Cléireacháin, Eileen McAuley, and Nuala McSparran (eds.), *Feis na nGleann: A Century of Gaelic Culture in the Antrim Glens* (Belfast: Stair Uladh, 2005).
[3] Parkhill later wrote under the pseudonym of Lewis Purcell.

and support for their initiative from the rising generation of theatre activists, with the exception of Yeats, who refused them permission to perform *Cathleen ni Houlihan*. As Hobson recalled:

> Parkhill and I wanted to get into touch with the National Theatre Society which had been started by Maud Gonne's Daughters of Eireann. The Fays were the producers and Yeats, A.E., and all the writing crowd were actively helping. [. . .] We wanted permission to put on some of their plays and help from some of their actors. Everybody was most cordial and helpful except Yeats—haughty and aloof [. . .] we wanted to put on in Belfast Yeats' *Cathleen Ni Houlihan* [sic] and Cousins's *The Racing Lug*. Dudley Digges and Maire Quin promised to come and act in our first production. But Yeats refused permission. [. . .] Annoyed by Yeats we decided to write our own plays—and we did.[4]

Undeterred by the Yeatsian rebuff, Hobson and Parkhill pressed ahead in staging the inaugural and, as it turned out, final production of the Ulster Branch of the Irish Literary Theatre in November 1902, with performances of *Cathleen ni Houlihan* and James Cousins's *The Racing Lug* in St Mary's Minor Hall, Belfast.[5]

In the context of the subsequent development of Ulster drama, Cousins's play was arguably the most significant production that evening.[6] *The Racing Lug* is often credited as an important influence on Synge's *Riders to the Sea*.[7] This is traceable in his use of rural dialect—in this instance the dialect of the Northern coastal town of Carrickfergus—and its treatment of the drowning of a fisherman and the death of his broken-hearted wife on hearing the news. Cousins reportedly wrote the play in a matter of hours. He recalls this creative burst in his memoir:

> I awoke in my lodging [. . .] to find my mind possessed by a vivid re-creation in dramatic form of an event which had made a deep impression on my child-mind years before. A fishing-boat with an uncle and several distant relatives of my own had put out to the fishing-grounds from Carrickfergues [sic] under a large sail called a racing-lug. The lug had been taken under protest as the outcome of a charge of cowardice by one of the younger members of the crew against the cautiousness of the oldest member in the face of probable 'dirty weather.' A squall struck the boat, the big sail jammed and could not be lowered. The boat capsized, and three out of the seven were drowned, including the young man who had insisted on the lug. Something in my head shaped the event with miraculous rapidity and certainty. I seemed merely to be the spectator of a mental process which happened to be in my own brain; and when I arose, dressed hastily, and began to write it out, I felt that I was but a transcriber.[8]

---

[4] Letter from Bulmer Hobson to Sam Hanna Bell cited in Sam Hanna Bell, *The Theatre in Ulster: A Survey of the Dramatic Movement in Ulster from 1902 until the Present Day* (Dublin: Gill & Macmillan, 1972), 2.

[5] Hobson credits Maud Gonne with an important intervention: 'Maud said "Don't mind Willie. He wrote that play for me and gave it to me. It is mine and you can put it on whenever you want to"': ibid., 2.

[6] One of the recurring features of the Ulster Literary Theatre during its three-decade existence was a deep suspicion of stylized poetic drama exemplified by the Yeats–Gregory play, *Cathleen ni Houlihan*.

[7] James Cousins, *The Racing Lug*, *United Irishman*, 5 July 1902; repr. in Robert Hogan and James Kilroy (eds.), *Lost Plays of the Irish Renaissance* (Newark, DE: Proscenium Press, 1970), 39–49.

[8] James H. Cousins and Margaret E. Cousins, *We Two Together* (Madras: Ganesh, 1950), 71–2.

Notwithstanding Cousins's account of its mystical genesis, the play did inaugurate a shift away from the highly stylized poetic dramas of Yeats—and indeed of other Northern playwrights such as Russell and Milligan—towards the local and the everyday, and paved the way for a new kind of Ulster play which would flourish under the auspices of the newly named Ulster Literary Theatre (ULT) from 1904 to 1934.

The initial impulse to align a new Ulster drama initiative with the work of the various Dublin theatre groups was quickly replaced by a clear desire to retain independence from the centralizing propensities of Yeats and his circle. An attempt to articulate a new Ulster aesthetic was outlined in the inaugural issue of the ULT's magazine, *Ulad*:

> Ulad means Ulster. It is often necessary to state as much; we intend to insist. This Ulster has its own way of things, which may be taken as the great contrast to the Munster way of things, still keeping on Irish land.
>
>   Cities like Londonderry and Belfast have drawn all its best energies towards them. And though of late years the city has been more a stumbling-block to the right intellectual and artistic progress of the country, yet, in spite of influences and disabilities operating against it, a certain characteristic temperamental and mental trend has been lent to the town by the country, and a certain local intellectual activity has persisted there. We wish to locate this, and to afford it an outlet in literary expression.[9]

The tentative tone of this early manifesto recalls the uncertainty of approach evident in the famous opening statement of the Irish Literary Theatre.[10] However, one can detect in the reference to 'keeping on Irish land' a deliberate attempt to connect with a national consciousness, and yet a determined effort to articulate a regional distinctiveness. Significantly, the perceived influence of a vibrant rural culture on the character of Ulster's urban centres was singled out for special mention—a sign of things to come.

In the three decades of its existence the ULT produced forty-seven original plays, 'of which only six were mythological plays; the majority were either political satires or rural comedies with a satiric edge.'[11] In many respects, therefore, the ULT's literary impulse owed much to the Swiftian condition of occupying a precarious position between the pressures of two opposing forces—the all-pervasive contempt of Ulster unionism for cultural nationalism and the condescension and apparent decadence of a southern-focused Yeatsian cultural agenda. From this distinctive vantage point, the ULT confronted the reality of local sectarian tensions head on, in contrast to the Dublin theatre companies, who tended to construe cultural division solely along an Irish–English axis. One of the plays which best exemplifies this tendency is Lewis Purcell's *The Enthusiast*, produced in Clarence Place Hall, Belfast, in May 1905. This topical play engages with the phenomenon of agricultural cooperation that was sweeping Ireland at this time under the leadership of Horace Plunkett. The aim of this movement was to encourage small farmers to band together to improve their mutual economic prospects and break the economic stranglehold of the middleman. In Purcell's play the attempt by James McKinstry, a young Protestant enthusiast, to bring

  [9] Hanna Bell, *Theatre in Ulster*, 6.
  [10] See Augusta Gregory, *Our Irish Theatre: A Chapter in Autobiography*, 3rd edn. (Gerrards Cross: Colin Smythe, 1972), 20.
  [11] Christopher Morash, *A History of Irish Theatre 1601–2000* (Cambridge: Cambridge University Press, 2002), 148.

ideas of cooperation to his own locality is scuppered when underlying sectarian tensions overwhelm initial support for his plans. As the farmhand, Rab, relates, when asked to describe the outcome of a meeting organized by James:

> RAB: Oh, aye, Weel, as I say, I wuzn't botherin' my head much, at the start, but as far as I mind, about a dozen got up in turns an' said as it might be a good thing an' it might not, they had no knowins. Then Andy Moore got up—no' young Andy, the oul' man—an' he said they were goin' till upset the Crown and Constitution. An' at the wind up he axed Jamie if he cud gie scripture for it, an' Jamie as much as said he cudn't. Then somebody shouted 'Socialisms', and Ned Grahme—he wuz drunk—he shouted it wuz a Fenian thing, an' he kep' shoutin' that the whole time. An' sez I to myself, this is goin' to be the warm meetin'.[12]

Like his fellow ULT playwright Rutherford Mayne, Purcell consciously used local dialect and accent to emphasize Ulster distinctiveness but was eager to explore the possibilities of a broader communal consensus that might transcend entrenched sectarian divisions. Significantly, it is the older generation ('no' young Andy, the oul' man') that most trenchantly resists the cooperative rapprochement envisaged by James. The importance of *The Enthusiast* to the development of ULT was later recognized by Rutherford Mayne, who praised it as 'a genuine work of art—slight—imperfect—but vital'.[13]

If this Ulster realism became the dominant note in the ULT, it was often accompanied by an impish tendency to parody the high poetic seriousness of the Abbey Theatre. Although the works of Synge, in particular, were much parodied by subsequent playwrights such as Seán O'Casey and Denis Johnston, among the first to lampoon his distinctive peasant-speak was ULT playwright Gerald MacNamara with his play *The Mist That Does Be on the Bog* (1909), which playfully satirized the fetishization of place and landscape that was so pervasive a feature of Dublin Revivalism.[14] In his next play, *Thompson in Tir-na-nOg* (1912), MacNamara further honed his skill for parody and, like Purcell, set out to disturb the foundational myths of both unionism and nationalism. In this mythical extravaganza Andy Thompson, an Orangeman, finds himself stranded in Tír-na-nÓg, where he meets a host of Irish mythic figures from Cúchulainn to Queen Maev. Performed in 1912 at the height of sectarian tensions in Ulster over the introduction of the Third Home Rule Bill to the British Parliament, *Thompson in Tir-na-nOg* effectively undercut 'Ulster unionism's sense of divine mission' as well as 'some of the more extravagant claims of an Irish nationalism is search of historical authentication'.[15] In so doing the play clearly registered the ULT as an important interventionist force in Ulster culture and politics, and a vital counterweight to the dominance of the Abbey Theatre on a national scale.[16]

---

[12] *The Enthusiast*, originally published in *Ulad* 3 (May 1905), is reprinted in Hugh Odling-Smee (ed.), *Its Own Way of Things:* The Enthusiast *by Lewis Purcell and* Thompson in Tir-na-nOg *by Gerald MacNamara* (Belfast: Lagan Press, 2004), 29.

[13] Rutherford Mayne, 'The Ulster Literary Theatre', *Dublin Magazine* (2nd ser.), 30, no. 2 (1955), 17.

[14] Gerald McNamara was the pseudonym of Harry C. Morrow.

[15] Eugene McNulty, *The Ulster Literary Theatre and the Northern Revival* (Cork: Cork University Press, 2008), 207.

[16] *The Mist that Does be on the Bog* and *Thompson in Tir-na-nOg* are published in the *Journal of Irish Literature*, ed. Kathleen Danaher, 17, nos. 2 and 3 (1988), 58–88.

ALL ART IS A COLLABORATION: THE THEATRE OF IRELAND

The history of the Abbey Theatre during the first decade of its existence is a story of an organization lurching from one crisis to the next. Not only did the theatre produce several plays that many of its own patrons found objectionable but it also suffered a serious internal constitutional crisis that threatened to undermine the momentum behind the new initiative. This occurred when Annie Horniman, an independently wealthy theatre enthusiast from London, cultivated a friendship withYeats and offered to fund a new permanent theatre for the Irish National Theatre Society in Dublin. Yeats, not surprisingly, was a keen supporter of this proposal, seeing it as a means of securing autonomy for the theatre's directorate to pursue its own artistic priorities. Essentially, this move would professionalize the fledgling theatre group and allow it to develop on a more secure financial basis. To facilitate these developments Yeats pushed for a reorganization of the company that would introduce a new hierarchical structure of shareholders, directors, and employees. Such a reconstitution of the theatre represented a profound shift away from the egalitarian principles upon which the original theatre society was founded and, effectively, installed Yeats and his fellow directors, Gregory and Synge, as the leaders of the company.[17] It is important to bear in mind that after the end of the Irish Literary Theatre experiment, Yeats by his own account joined an existing dramatic society run by Frank and Willie Fay in early 1902.[18] It was under the auspices of this group, W. G. Fay's Irish National Dramatic Company, that *Cathleen ni Houlihan* was performed on 2 April 1902 at St Teresa's Hall in Clarendon Street.[19] Unlike the earlier Irish Literary Theatre group with which Yeats had been involved, the Irish National Theatre Society (INTS) was avowedly popular in orientation and dedicated to the training of Irish actors. Without the Horniman donation the INTS would not have been able to fund a permanent theatre in Abbey Street. However, the acceptance of this patronage led to a fundamental change in the governance of the society that would divide the members, cause a split, and lead to the establishment of a new company, the Theatre of Ireland, to rival the Abbey Theatre.

At a decisive INTS meeting on 22 September 1905, Yeats responded to the implications of the new financial situation with a proposal that the society be transformed into a joint stock company in which the theatre directors would, essentially, wield control, and the actors would be given salaries and assume the status of employees. This would effectively end the era of cooperative democracy that had characterized the company from the start, and placed Yeats in a controlling position arising from his close relationship with Annie Horniman. To a sizeable proportion of the members—including actors, backstage workers, and writers—it appeared as though Yeats had disingenuously commandeered a movement

---

[17] For a more detailed account of this history, see Ch. 3.

[18] W. B. Yeats, *Autobiographies* (London: Macmillan, 1955), 303.

[19] W. G. Fay's Irish Dramatic Company was later constituted formally as the Irish National Theatre Society in October 1902. For the best account of the complex evolution of the various theatre groups and movements during this period, see Brenna Katz Clarke, *The Emergence of the Irish Peasant Play at the Abbey Theatre* (Ann Arbor, MI: UMI Research Press, 1982).

into which he was initially welcomed as an equal partner. On 10 March 1906 a disgruntled member wrote a letter to *The United Irishman*:

> The National Theatre Society, Ltd., is a body run in the interest of one person, Mr. W. B. Yeats, who has proved himself capable of absorbing for his own personal ends the disinterested work of a large number of people given on the understanding that they were aiding in a work which was devoted primarily to the development of the highest interests of nationality in the country.[20]

The Theatre of Ireland (Cluithcheoiri-na-hÉireann) was founded in 1906 when disgruntled members Máire Nic Shiubhlaigh, Honor Lavelle, Emma Vernon, Frank Walker, Seumus O'Sullivan, George Roberts, James Cousins, and Padraic Colum left to form a new company in protest against the recent turn of events at the Abbey.[21] Other supporters of the venture included Stephen Gwynn, Thomas Keohler, Eoin MacNeill, Patrick Pearse, and Edward Martyn. Temporary rehearsal rooms were acquired in a house in High Street, and a board was elected with Edward Martyn as President and including Padraic Colum, Thomas Keohler, George Nesbitt, Dermot Trench, James Cousins, Helen Laird (Honor Lavelle), Patrick Pearse, and Thomas Kettle on the committee. Despite the formal break with their erstwhile colleagues, the new company managed to secure permission from the Abbey to rent the theatre when availability allowed.

It is significant that many of the prime movers behind the new Theatre of Ireland had had difficult relations with Yeats and suffered at the hands of his authoritarian managerial style. However, the major difference between the two groups rested on divergent ideas on the function of a national theatre. In many ways the Theatre of Ireland looked to the nineteenth-century example of Thomas Davis and the Young Irelanders, who believed that literary work should, in the first instance, serve the needs of popular nationalism. As Máire Nic Shiubhlaigh, a prominent Abbey dissident, put it:

> In those days I never thought of the National Theatre Society as a purely theatrical enterprise. It was merely a part of the larger national movement in which most of us were then participating. Even at the risk of its ultimate stagnation and death, I would, just then, have preferred the theatre to struggle on alone, administered solely from within itself, as a subsidiary part of that movement.[22]

This thinking was anathema to Yeats, who had long fought against such an instrumental approach to literary creation. The exiled members, for their part, hankered after a more collaborative and less autocratic style of theatre production embodied in the methods of George Russell. Russell, who had been an important presence during the early days of the INTS, was well known for supporting the work of younger, less experienced writers and actors. Unlike Yeats, 'he worked quietly, without any attempt to gain individual distinction'.[23] The Theatre of Ireland, then, prided itself on fostering the cooperative ethos that it

---

[20] Quoted in Adrian Frazier, *Behind the Scenes: Yeats, Horniman, and the Struggle for the Abbey Theatre* (Berkeley, CA: University of California Press, 1990), 132.

[21] Clarke, *Emergence of the Irish Peasant Play*, 40, 100.

[22] Máire Nic Shuibhlaigh, *The Splendid Years: Recollections of Máire Nic Shuibhlaigh as told to Edward Kenny* (Dublin: James Duffy, 1955), 73.

[23] Ibid., 29.

considered the Abbey to have abandoned—not just in terms of the formal organization of the theatre but also in relation to the creative process.

The new theatre initiative was set up as a non-profit-making organization to advance drama in Ireland 'through the production of plays by Irish writers in Irish and in English and such works of foreign dramatists as might be considered advisable'.[24] In reality, however, the new venture might more properly be regarded as a pioneering community theatre rather than a rival national theatre to the Abbey. The primary aim seems to have been to foster a collaborative and supportive creative milieu in which like-minded enthusiasts were encouraged to participate in theatre-making to the highest standard that local conditions would allow. Crucially, they resisted moves to professionalize their theatre practices along the lines of the Abbey. Many of the members were involved in or attended the iconic first performances of *Cathleen ni Houlihan* in April 1902, and seemed to be motivated by a desire to recreate the remarkable potency of that production in which a part-time director, six amateur actors, and two aspiring playwrights fashioned a historic theatre event out of modest resources in St Teresa's Hall, Clarendon Street.

During its six-year heyday from 1906 to 1912, the new company solicited original plays, nurtured home-grown acting talent, and fostered a cooperative approach to theatre without any member gaining financial reward. At its best it mounted productions that were equal to, and at times surpassed, the quality of those to be seen on the Abbey stage. However, the Theatre of Ireland was frequently plagued by inconsistency and poor production values. Many of the difficulties stemmed from the fact that the company never managed to secure a permanent home, and worked with meagre resources in comparison with the facilities available in Abbey Street, and also from the reality that most of those involved divided their time between their theatre commitments and paid employment elsewhere.

The aims of the new company were fairly reflected in the inaugural programme of December 1906, which consisted of a triple bill: James Cousins's folk play *The Racing Lug*; a scene from Ibsen's *Brand*; and an Irish-language play, *Casadh an tSúgáin* by Douglas Hyde. While *The Racing Lug* had been previously staged by the INTS and the ULT, and had initially received the blessing of Yeats, who pronounced it 'perfect with no need of further work',[25] Cousins was abruptly dismissed by him when his next play, *Sold*,[26] was rejected. 'Cousins is evidently hopeless,' Yeats wrote to Lady Gregory, 'and the sooner that I have him as an enemy the better.'[27] Indeed, it had been suggested that Yeats may have had Cousins in mind when he satirized George Russell's indulgence of lesser literary talents in his poem, 'To a Poet, who Would Have me Praise Certain Bad Poets, Imitators of His and Mine'.[28] The inclusion of *The Racing Lug* on the inaugural programme of the Theatre of Ireland, therefore, adds weight to the theory that many of the leading members of the new initiative had suffered at the hands of Yeats and were united in their antipathy towards him.

The decision to stage a scene from Ibsen's play *Brand* (6 December 1906) is noteworthy for a number of reasons. Ibsen's importance to the fledgling Irish theatre movement had

---

[24] Ibid., 77.   [25] William Dumbleton, *James Cousins* (Boston, MA: Twayne, 1980), 22.

[26] Published in the *United Irishman*, 27 Dec. 1902.

[27] W. B. Yeats to Lady Gregory, 26 Dec. 1902, in W. B. Yeats, *Collected Letters*, vol. 3, ed. Ronald Schuchard and John Kelly (Oxford: Clarendon Press, 1994), 285.

[28] Paul Stephenson and Margie Waters, '"We Two" and the Lost Angel: The Cousins of Sandymount and James Joyce', *James Joyce Quarterly* 37, nos. 1 and 2 (2000), 170.

been celebrated by Padraic Colum in an essay published in the *Sinn Féin* newspaper weeks after his death in May 1906.[29] The inclusion of one of his plays, therefore, was a clear attempt to align the Theatre of Ireland with Ibsen's work. This no doubt met with the approval of Edward Martyn, who was a committed Ibsenite. *Brand* is an uncompromising dramatization of the necessity of being true to one's private convictions and, surely, was carefully chosen to reflect the recent actions of the Abbey exiles in setting up their own theatre.[30] The scene the company performed from Act IV involves a poignant exchange between the protagonist, Brand, and his wife, Agnes, on Christmas Eve when a passing ragged woman begs clothes for her freezing child. Brand demands that Agnes hand over the clothes of their dead child—her last remaining tokens of connection with her son—to the stranger. Such a sacrifice embodies the 'all or nothing' philosophy espoused by Brand which is not unambiguously endorsed by the play. Taken in isolation, however, it is easy to see how a scene like this would resonate with Celticist ideas of material sacrifice for spiritual ends so prevalent in Irish drama during this period.[31]

The final play on the bill clearly demonstrated the commitment of the new theatre to the Irish language. Originally produced to resounding acclaim by the Irish Literary Theatre in October 1901, Hyde's *Casadh an tSúgáin* (The Twisting of the Rope) is the play which inaugurated a tradition of theatre *as Gaeilge*. In this highly influential folk drama, values of communal solidarity are endorsed against the threat of an interloper, as the villagers conspire to expel what they regard as the interfering presence of Hanrahan, the wandering poet. Once again the chosen play seemed to proclaim loudly the priorities and ethos of the new company. It also functioned as a fitting parable for a group that construed itself as having been taken over by an overbearing poet.

Despite the rancour in the air since the split from the Abbey, Joseph Holloway reported that the new venture 'made a good start at the Molesworth Hall'. Many of Dublin's most prominent literary figures were present to wish the Theatre of Ireland well, including George Moore, Douglas Hyde, Lady Gregory, James Cousins, and Padraic Colum.[32] A less salutary note was struck a couple of days later, however, when socialist activist and playwright Fredrick Ryan attacked both the Abbey's fondness for mythical heroes and the Theatre of Ireland's 'attempts at the production of more or less immature plays in backyard halls'.[33] From Ryan's perspective, neither the Abbey aesthetes nor the dilettante nationalists of the Theatre of Ireland were addressing the issues closest to his socialist heart. His gibe about 'immature plays' certainly had some validity given the fact that—apart from the staging of the scene from *Brand*[34]—the new

[29] Padraic Colum, 'Ibsen and National Drama', *Sinn Féin*, 2 June 1906.

[30] Given the recent turn of events at the Abbey, the protagonist Brand can be interpreted as a Yeatsian figure who cannot accept poor standards and human weakness. In Act V, Brand builds a new church for his followers because the existing one is too small.

[31] See Irina Ruppa Malone, 'Ibsen, the Irish Revival and the Debate about Cosmopolitanism', in Patrick O'Donovan and Laura Rascaroli (eds.), *The Cause of Cosmopolitanism: Dispositions, Models, Transformations* (Bern: Peter Lang, 2010), 193–200.

[32] Joseph Holloway, *Joseph Holloway's Abbey Theatre: A Selection from his Unpublished Journal 'Impressions of an Irish Playgoer'*, ed. Robert Hogan and Michael J. O'Neill (Carbondale, IL: Southern Illinois University Press, 1967), 77.

[33] Ibid., 78.

[34] Máire Nic Shiubhlaigh claimed that this production of a scene from *Brand* 'was probably one of the first occasions upon which the play had been given in these islands': *Splendid Years*, 78.

company had invested heavily in reviving plays from the early glory days of the INTS, perhaps in an attempt to reclaim that legacy, rather than offering something recognizably new to Dublin theatregoers.

In subsequent years the Theatre of Ireland continued the practice of reviving plays from the earlier phases of the Irish theatre movement such as Alice Milligan's *The Last Feast of the Fianna* and George Russell's *Deirdre*, both in 1907, and Edward Martyn's *Maeve* in 1908. Irish language versions of *Deirdre* and *Cathleen ni Houlihan* (*Caitlin Ni Uallachain*) also featured. To its credit, the company did attempt to nurture a new realist turn in Irish drama: Padraic Colum's *The Fiddler's House* (a rewrite of the earlier *Broken Soil*) offered a portrait of the peasant as artist in more obviously conventional terms than those provided by Synge. Yet the probing of the deep distrust harboured within the settled orthodoxies of rural Ireland of the bohemian spirit struck a Syngean note. Colum's next offering, *The Miracle of the Corn*, however, was less successful and is remembered only as a failed experiment in verse drama. In the words of one critic: 'It is a heavily allegorical, overtly literary, morality piece, and it added nothing to Colum's reputation.'[35] Of the May 1908 production the theatre reviewer Joseph Holloway wrote bleakly in his diary:

> When I, who am looked upon as theatre mad, say I would not willingly sit it out again, the quality of the performance may be judged as below par. No footlights were used, casting all the characters into gloomy silhouettes. Padraic Colum's play *The Miracle of the Corn* was tried for the first time on the stage, but as it was taken in such a minor key by those taking part the dialogue failed to reach us in the pit, and consequently, was not understood. The first essential of acting is to be heard. Fail in this and you fail in all. [. . .]
>
> The Theatre of Ireland has as yet to give a successful performance [. . .] and they don't seem to improve as they go along, which is the most depressing feature. Artistically they cannot hold a candle to the National Theatre Company [Abbey Theatre] whom they are in hopes of driving out of the field.[36]

Raw enthusiasm did not always make up for slapdash production standards, it would seem.

The major playwriting success of the Theatre of Ireland was Seumas O'Kelly, who was nurtured in-house. His plays *The Matchmakers* and *The Flame on the Hearth* (later retitled *The Stranger*) were staged to modest success in 1907 and 1910 respectively. Yet it was in 1909 that he was to enjoy his greatest success with *The Shuiler's Child* 'which was inspired by and dedicated to Máire Nic Shuibhlaigh'.[37] This play steered the Theatre of Ireland more directly towards the problem play tradition of the later Ibsen by taking on serious themes of child welfare, adoption, and the relationship between the travelling community and state institutions. Not only did O'Kelly's play occasion one of Máire Nic Shuibhlaigh's more memorable performances in the role of the travelling woman, Moll Woods, but the cast

---

[35] *Selected Plays of Padraic Colum*, ed. Sanford Sternlicht (Syracuse, NY: Syracuse University Press, 1986), xiii.

[36] Holloway, *Joseph Holloway's Abbey Theatre*, 112.

[37] Joan FitzPatrick Dean, 'Staging the Aesthetic: The Vagrant Artists of Padraic Colum and Seumas O'Kelly', in Patrick Lonergan and Riana O'Dwyer (eds.), *Echoes Down the Corridor: Irish Theatre— Past, Present and Future* (Dublin: Carysfort Press, 2007), 45.

also included the nationalist activist, Constance Markievicz, as the government official. As Máire Nic Shiubhlaigh recalled:

> Madame [Markievicz] was a memorable soul. To everything she did she brought much of that vigour that had made her one of the most colourful figures of the whole national scene; the idol of every young girl with a spark of nationalism. [. . .] Madame was an early member of the Theatre of Ireland [. . .] but she was rather unpredictable as an actress. On a stage her enthusiasm for the work occasionally carried her away; she could never quite sink her own vivid personality in a rôle.[38]

The admission that the frisson generated by the involvement of this celebrity national-ist was not matched by her prowess as an actress betrays much about the priorities of the Theatre of Ireland. The involvement of James Stephens, republican activist and future author of *The Crock of Gold*, in the same cast further demonstrates the concentration of committed nationalists among the membership. Furthermore, the Theatre of Ireland also functioned as an open zone for female participation and engagement. Apart from the involvement of high-profile activists such as Alice Milligan and Constance Markievicz, and highly talented actors like Máire Nic Shiubhlaigh and Honor Lavelle, the company premièred a new play, *Expiation* by Kathleen Fitzpatrick in 1910, and Jane Barlow's *A Bunch of Lavender* in 1911.

It is significant that the Theatre of Ireland began to decline in 1912, the year when debates over the introduction of the Third Home Rule Bill engendered a flurry of mili-tary activity with the foundation of the Ulster Volunteers in the North, followed by the formation of the Irish Volunteers in Dublin the following year. With many Theatre of Ireland personnel and audience members dedicating more energy to military rather than dramatic manoeuvres, impetus and support for the theatre initiative inevitably declined. Indeed, a significant number of prominent members were to take leading roles in emer-gent militant groups such as the Irish Volunteers, Cumman na mBan, and the IRB, includ-ing Constance Markievcz, Padraic Colum, Máire Nic Shiubhlaigh, James Stephens, and Thomas MacDonagh. One of the last Theatre of Ireland productions in April 1912 featured a new work, *Metempsychosis*, by future 1916 leader MacDonagh. This play was a thinly disguised satire on Yeats, many of whose foibles were recognizable in the leading charac-ter, Earl Winton-Winton De Winton. As the stage directions have it, the Earl is 'voluble, excitable, earnest, visionary' and 'a victim of ease and enthusiasm'.[39] In many respects, therefore, the Theatre of Ireland ended as it had begun: with a critique of aristocratic pre-tensions, artistic aloofness, and abstract theorizing which many associated with Yeats and his devotion to the *vita contemplativa*. Whether or not Yeats himself was aware of the jibe, it did not prevent him from paying generous tribute to the rebel's literary talent in the poem 'Easter 1916', where he asserted that MacDonagh 'was coming into his force' and 'might have won fame in the end'.[40]

---

[38] Nic Shiubhlaigh, *Splendid Years*, 100–1.

[39] Thomas MacDonagh, 'Metempsychosis: Or a Mad World: A Play in One Act', *Irish Review* 1, no. 12 (Feb. 1912), 585.

[40] W. B. Yeats, 'Easter 1916', in *Collected Poems* (London: Macmillan, 1933), 203.

'Ploughing Ahead Nicely': Na hAisteoirí

One of the distinctive hallmarks of almost every incarnation of the early Irish theatre movement was a vocal support for theatre in the Irish language. This, however, was not always backed up by a genuine commitment to staging Irish-language plays. Within the Irish Literary Theatre Lady Gregory, an Irish-language scholar of some note, and George Moore, a vocal supporter of the language, were keen to feature plays in Irish as part of the theatre's programme. As a result this group mounted the first ever professional production of a drama in the Irish language during its 1901 season. *Casadh an tSugáin* (*The Twisting of the Rope*), written by Douglas Hyde and directed by Willie Fay, was performed by Irish-speaking actors, with Hyde himself taking the lead role. Although the play was enthusiastically received by audiences and reviewers, Irish-language drama would remain marginal for most of the Revival period. In truth, the Gaelic League was hugely successful in revising attitudes and generating goodwill towards the Irish language; but it did not generate a critical mass of sufficiently competent Irish speakers necessary to sustain a vigorous theatre in the native language. Add to this the fact that no tradition of Gaelic drama previously existed, and one gets a sense of the difficulties faced by Irish-language theatre enthusiasts. As Philip O'Leary puts it, 'quite simply, there were no Gaelic plays, no Gaelic actors, and no Gaelic audiences.'[41] It was not uncommon, however, for supporters of the language to get swept up in their enthusiasm for the language and create unrealistic expectations for a Gaelic theatre.[42] In reality, however, Irish-language theatre made little impact beyond the meeting rooms and halls of the Gaelic League. Patrick Pearse offered a reality check to overblown expectations in an editorial published in *An Claidheamh Soluis* in 1906.

> Bluntly, we have hitherto got very little acting in Irish that has risen above the painfully mediocre [. . .] Two things are wrong. The first thing is that most of those who have essayed the actor's art in Irish do not know how to speak. They can only talk. The second is that they—or perhaps those responsible for their training—are enslaved by English conventions and mannerisms.[43]

Although Pearse referred specifically to acting, by implication his comments focused attention on the form that a Gaelic theatre should take. In this respect the most likely options involved a return to native traditions of the folk tale, as Hyde had done, or to translations of existing drama in English. The latter possibility was tested by the Theatre of Ireland when it performed Irish-language versions of George Russell's *Deirdre* in 1909 and *Cathleen ni Houlihan* by Yeats and Gregory in 1912, both translated by the Revd Thomas O'Kelly. Pearse himself contributed in no small way to the development of Gaelic drama, as a playwright

---

[41] Philip O'Leary, 'Poor Relations: Gaelic Drama and the Abbey Theatre', *Journal of Irish Literature* 18, no. 1 (1989), 4.

[42] Writing in the *United Irishman* on 4 May 1901, Frank Fay expressed the view that he would 'prefer to see a Theatre inaugurated here that would abolish English completely, and conduct its operations outside of the uncongenial atmosphere of an English commercial Theatre': Frank J. Fay, *Towards a National Theatre: The Dramatic Criticism of Frank J. Fay*, ed. Robert Hogan (Dublin: Dolmen Press, 1970), 54.

[43] 'Irish Acting', editorial, *An Claidheamh Soluis*, 7 July 1906.

whose works were performed by the students of St Enda's at the school, at the Hardwicke Street Irish Theatre, and at the Abbey Theatre between 1910 and 1913.[44]

By 1912 a growing realization began to take hold that while Irish theatre in English had gained considerable momentum, theatre in Irish was still languishing, with limited scripts, poor acting, and meagre resources. The mood of demoralization among the *gaelgeoirí* was eloquently expressed by a reviewer in *An Claidheamh Soluis*, who felt that 'everything is so perfect in the Abbey that the Gaelic League feels ashamed of its occasional little dramatic attempts'.[45] In an effort to raise morale and to facilitate cooperation between disparate Gaelic drama groups, a new company, Na hAisteoirí (The Actors), drawn from all the Gaelic League branches in Dublin, was formed in October 1912. The ubiquitous Edward Martyn was elected President, while Piaras Béaslaí was installed as the director of the enterprise. Founding members included Fionán Ó Loingsigh, Conchubhar Ó Coileáin, Gearóid Ó Súilleabháin, Máire Ní Dhiscín, and Brighid Ní Dhiscín.[46] Béaslaí, a committed republican, was deeply involved in the language revival and was an engaged contributor to Árd-Chúirt na hÉigse—'a group of poet-scholars dedicated to the preservation of a distinctive Gaelic poetic'. Notwithstanding this, he was far from a hardline nativist, believing instead in 'a cosmopolitan, Irish-speaking future'.[47]

The inaugural performances of Na hAisteoirí were held in the Gaelic League premises in Rutland (now Parnell) Square in April 1913. An ambitious programme included *Beart Nótaí* (A Bundle of Banknotes) by Máire Ní Shíthe and Eilís Ní Mhurchadha, the only Irish-language text of the period to 'deal explicitly and exclusively with the life of urban middle-class characters other than language activists'.[48] In contrast, the second offering of the evening, *Beirt na Bodhaire Bréige* (Two Deaf Tricksters), was an adaptation by Piaras Béaslaí of a one-act comedy, *Les deux sourds* by Jules Moinaux. A clearly delighted reviewer in *An Claidheamh Soluis* described the two performances as 'excellent', and highlighted the 'good Irish, clear enunciation and the happy choice of two plays with simple plots'.[49]

There is no doubt that Na hAisteoirí gave Irish language drama a much-needed shot in the arm at the peak of its influence between 1913 and 1917. Production and acting standards improved considerably as the company gained momentum and sustained continuity.[50] Also vital to the success of Na hAisteoirí was Piaras Béaslaí's ability to write plays that were both technically assured and amenable to a Gaelic League audience. He contributed four of the seven plays produced by the company between 1913 and 1917, and deserves recognition for adding considerably to the repertoire of Irish-language theatre at a time when this new form was in its infancy.[51] Significantly too, Na hAisteoirí toured its productions around

---

[44]   See Patrick Pearse, *Collected Plays: Drámaí an Phiarsaigh*, ed. Róisín Ní Ghairbhí and Eugene McNulty (Dublin: Irish Academic Press, 2013).

[45]   'E.O.N.', *An Claidheamh Soluis*, 19 Apr. 1913.

[46]   Pádraig Ó Siadhail, *Stair Dhrámaíocht na Gaeilge 1900–1970* (Indreabhán: Cló Iar-Chonnachta, 1993), 45.

[47]   Philip O'Leary, *The Prose Literature of the Gaelic Revival, 1881–1921: Ideology and Innovation* (University Park, PA: Pennsylvania State University Press, 1994), 77n.

[48]   Ibid., 416.   [49]   'E.O.N.', 'Na hAisteoirí', *An Claidheamh Soluis*, 19 Apr. 1913.

[50]   Ó Siadhail, *Stair Dhrámaíocht na Gaeilge*, 54.

[51]   *Beirt na Bodhaire Bréige* (The Two Deaf Tricksters), *Cluiche Cártaí* (The Card Game), *An Sgaothaire* (The Braggart), *Fear na Milliún Punt* (The Millionaire). http://www.irishplayography.com/play.aspx?playid=2551

Ireland and brought Gaelic drama to many of the smaller towns for the first time. However, much like the case of the Theatre of Ireland, a great deal of the momentum behind the enterprise was lost when events took a revolutionary turn in 1916. As Béaslaí recalled:

> Bhíomar ag treabhadh chun cinn go maith nuair a tháinig Seachtain na Cásca, agus d'imthigh scaipeadh ar Na hAisteoirí, mar ní raibh éan [sic] bhuachaill ortha ná go raibh baint aige le hobair na Seachtaine sin.

> [We were ploughing ahead nicely when Easter Week happened, and Na hAisteoirí folded because there wasn't one of those boys that didn't have something to do with the work of that Week.][52]

Béaslaí took part in the fighting in 1916 and, after the Rising, was sent to Portland Prison and later to Lewes Prison until his release in June 1917.[53] In 1923 members of Na hAisteoirí regrouped to form 'the nucleus of Gearóid Ó Lochlainn's An Comhar Drámaíochta, the Gaelic group which brought serious drama in Irish into the Abbey on a regular basis'.[54]

FOOTLIGHTS TO FOOT SOLDIERS

As the twentieth century dawned, Irish society witnessed an explosion of radical political activism across the ideological spectrum. Significantly, a huge crossover in terms of personnel working in the political and the cultural spheres is clearly discernible. One of the central figures of the period, Máire Ni Shiubhlaigh, records the extent to which clubs and societies had associations with theatrical groups: 'Many young nationalists appeared as players with amateur companies, and a lot of the political clubs led by Arthur Griffiths' Cumman-na-nGaedheal, had dramatic societies attached, either as a means of gathering funds or of disseminating propaganda.' [55] Most of these groups had clear cultural agendas—among them, encouraging regional theatre, promoting community drama, and fostering the Irish language. The most important of these companies, the ULT, the Theatre of Ireland, and Na hAisteoirí, functioned as satellites of the Abbey Theatre and challenged its role as the de facto National theatre, significantly influencing the flow of events in Abbey Street. All of them, in different ways, opposed the centralizing tendencies of an exclusive, Dublin-centred Revivalism, and were relentlessly critical of W. B. Yeats's hegemony over cultural sanction within nationalist Ireland. Of significance, too, is the porous and protean nature of these organizations, with members flowing freely across and between particular groups of activity. What is most striking, however, is the speed with which cultural energies and activities across these networks of activism transformed rapidly into military organization in response to the Home Rule crisis of 1912, and in rehearsal for armed action in the GPO in 1916.

---

[52] *Fáinne an Lae*, 5 Oct. 1918.   [53] Ó Siadhail, *Stair Dhrámaíocht na Gaeilge*, 55.
[54] Philip O'Leary, 'Poor Relations: Gaelic Drama and the Abbey Theatre', *Journal of Irish Literature* 18, no. 1 (1989), 18n.
[55] Nic Shiubhlaigh, *Splendid Years*, 141.

CHAPTER 5

W. B. YEATS AND RITUALS OF PERFORMANCE

TERENCE BROWN

In the early 1880s the Yeats family was living in Howth, a small fishing village to the north of Dublin. There in the spring of 1882 Willie Yeats, the poet-to-be, first saw his slightly older distant cousin Laura Armstrong, with whom he quickly felt himself to be in love. Seven years later, writing to Katharine Tynan, he recalled this early infatuation and its effect on him. He remembered the 'wild dash of insane genius' of the red-headed Laura, whom he had first glimpsed as she rode in a dog-cart, with her hair flying in the wind, and confessed: 'Laura is to me always a pleasant memory she woke me from the metallic sleep of science and set me writing my first play.'[1] Indeed, Yeats wrote a play for her in which she could take a main part entitled *Vivien and Time*, which was performed in the home of another Howth resident.

A DRAMATIC AESTHETIC

There is something peculiarly apt in the fact that Yeats associated this early engagement with dramatic art with an awakening from 'the metallic sleep of science', since his own dramatic practice, with its ritualistic eschewal of the conventions of theatrical realism, would seem over a lifetime to challenge in fundamental ways the materialist world-view of modern science.

Another of Yeats's early encounters with theatrical art had a considerable negative impact upon the neophyte poet and dramatist. We know that before his family had moved from London to Howth, Yeats had had the opportunity to see a production of *Hamlet* with Sir Henry Irving as the Prince of Denmark; as Yeats recalled in an autobiographical work, he had been unimpressed: 'Irving never moved me but in the expression of intellectual pride.'[2] Irving, of course, as a knighted actor-manager, stood at the apex of the commercial

---

[1] W. B. Yeats to Katharine Tynan, 21 Mar. 1889, in *Collected Letters*, vol. 1: *1865–1895*, ed. John Kelly and Eric Domville (Oxford: Clarendon Press, 1986), 155.

[2] W. B. Yeats, *Autobiographies* (London: Macmillan, 1955), 125.

Victorian theatre which Yeats was to dedicate himself to challenging as an experimental theatrical practitioner. In *The Trembling of the Veil* he wrote of Hamlet as 'the wavering, lean image of hungry speculation, that cannot but because of certain famous Hamlets of our stage fill the mind's eye'.[3] From the start of his career in the theatre, Yeats sought to sponsor a dramatic art that would fill both the minds and ears of audiences in ways that the commercial theatre, with its fascination with character acting and with elaborate sets and scene painting, in his view could not.

In May 1899 Yeats proclaimed, in what amounted to a manifesto for a theatrical revolution: 'The theatre began in ritual, and it cannot come to its greatness again without recalling words to their ancient sovereignty.'[4]

Since seeing *Vivien and Time* performed by amateurs in Howth, Yeats had had various opportunities to reflect on the contemporary theatre and on the role he might play in it. Most importantly, he had seen two of his own works performed, and had attended various productions that helped him to refine the kind of dramatic aesthetic encapsulated in the proclamation quoted above.

One of these occasions had had a particular impact upon him. In 1890 he had seen a production of the Irish poet John Todhunter's pastoral play *A Sicilian Idyll*, performed in the Clubhouse at Bedford Park, the London suburb where the Yeats family had chosen to live in 1888. The speaking of her lines by one of the actors in the play, Florence Farr, impressed Yeats deeply. He later wrote of her and a male player in the production: 'While they were on the stage no one else could hold an eye or an ear. Their speech was music, the poetry acquired a nobility, a passionate austerity that made it akin for certain moments to the great poetry of the world.'[5]

The 1890s, in which Yeats began his career as a dramatist, was a decade which culminated for the poet with the production of his play *The Countess Cathleen* in 1899. It was also a decade in which theatrical experiment was ubiquitous. In *The Trembling of the Veil* Yeats remembered how Arthur Symons brought back from Paris stories of Verhaeren and Maeterlinck. Indeed, it was in Paris that in 1894 Yeats saw de l'Isle-Adam's Rosicrucian play *Axel*. A year before, in St Petersburg, Chekhov's *The Seagull* had premièred, with its implicit assault on the conventions of bourgeois theatre and its plea for reform of the theatre in Russia. The announcement that Yeats and his colleagues prepared in 1897 for what would become the Irish Literary Theatre indicates that at work in Ireland there was a similar spirit of experimental reform to that which prepared the way for the establishment of the Moscow Arts Theatre in 1898. In a document entitled 'The Celtic Theatre' an attempt was promised to 'build up a Celtic & Irish dramatic school'. The document continued:

> Dramatic journalism has had full possession of the stage in England for a century [. . .] We hope to find in Ireland an uncorrupted & imaginative audience trained to listen by its passion for oratory.[6]

---

[3] Ibid., 142

[4] W. B. Yeats, 'The Theatre', in *Essays and Introductions* (London: Macmillan, 1961), 170.

[5] Yeats, *Autobiographies*, 120–1.

[6] R. F. Foster, *W. B. Yeats: A Life*, vol. 1: *The Apprentice Mage* (Oxford: Oxford University Press, 1997), 184.

LIMINAL SPACES

Yeats inaugurated his career as a theatrical experimentalist with the production in 1894 in London of his play *The Land of Heart's Desire*. This short drama, based on the Irish folkloric motif of the changeling, afforded its cast (which included Florence Farr's 10-year-old niece Dorothy Paget as a 'A Faery Child') the opportunity to make the speaking of verse an integral part of the play's overall effect. For at key moments in the action Yeats supplied lyric poems to be spoken by individual players. Words were being called back to 'their ancient sovereignty' in a work that displayed some of the characteristics of a ritual enactment. James Flannery, writing of Yeats's early dramaturgy, identifies the basis of its effect on audiences:

> By placing relatively uncomplicated though compelling dramatic situations within a ritualistic context and by employing the traditional techniques of ritual—poetry, song, dance, and drama with their multiple range of images reverberating amongst each other— Yeats was enabled to appeal to his audience on both a conscious and unconscious level simultaneously.[7]

Considering the 'Concept of Ritual Drama', Richard Taylor comments: 'The form of the drama itself and its projection of the relationship between the temporal and spiritual worlds is nearly always the centre of interest in Yeats's plays.'[8] The dramatic situation that unfolds in *The Land of Heart's Desire* certainly involves such a relationship. For, in an apposition the dramatist was to develop in later plays, Yeats in this work sets the lure of a transcendent, spiritualized dimension against the banal tedium of the quotidian with its dispiriting compromises.

In the play a young bride is tempted on a May Eve to end her dissatisfaction with the dreariness of a peasant marriage by submitting to the magical power of a fairy child who offers her release and fulfilment in the supernatural order. Various features of the work suggest that a ritual is being performed. And, as in a ritual, there is no real dramatic tension. We sense throughout that Mary Bruin will accede to the power of the fairies. Details of the action augment the impression that the rubric of a liturgy is being followed. The Faery Child, who rejects bread and wine, is presented with gifts of fire, milk, and honey. At one point she strews primroses from a large bowl. The cottage in which the play is set is seemingly protected from supernatural influences by a bough of mountain ash at the doorway and by a crucifix, which is removed for hiding at a crucial point by a priest at the behest of the Faery Child. At the end of the play, as distant dancing figures appear in the woods around the cottage, the Faery Child intones what amounts to a kind of spell: 'Come, newly-married bride [. . .] White bird, white bird, come with me, little bird [. . .] Come, little bird with crest of gold.'[9]

---

[7] James Flannery, *W. B. Yeats and the Idea of a Theatre: The Early Abbey Theatre in Theory and Practice* (New Haven, CT: Yale University Press, 1976), 83.

[8] Richard Taylor, *A Reader's Guide to the Plays of W. B. Yeats* (New York: St Martin's Press, 1984), 5.

[9] *The Variorum Edition of the Plays of W. B. Yeats*, ed. Russell K. Alspach (London: Macmillan, 1966), 208–9.

Yeats the neophyte playwright had been introduced to the powers of ritual in ways that undoubtedly must have influenced his early dramaturgy by his membership of the Order of the Golden Dawn. He had joined this London-based society of Rosicrucianism and ritual magic in March 1890—Florence Farr was also a devout member. In her book on Farr, Josephine Johnson makes telling reference to 'the drama, the pageantry, the complicated learning procedures attached to the system of grades' which membership in the order involved.[10] It was the hope of the Order's adepts that by the practice of ritual magic (which involved a good deal of dressing-up and ritual incantation) human consciousness could be transcended in an elevated spirituality.

In a book entitled *The Music of Speech*, published in 1909, Florence Farr wrote in terms that suggest how deeply she had been influenced by her experience in the Golden Dawn to place an intense faith in ritual. She describes how 'bodies sway to the rhythm and melody of the words, their souls melt under the breath of the infinite spirit, the sound of the words enters their innermost beings. As in a dream, so they pass away from the life of actuality into the more real ideal.'[11] One can imagine the impressionable young poet being similarly conditioned in the 1890s as he rose though the Golden Dawn's various grades to value the sounds of words and the effects of ritual as a theatrical resource. John Kelly and Eric Domville make a key point when they write of this subject:

> Shorn of its more exotic and ludicrous aspects, WBY's membership of the Golden Dawn was a sustained attempt to explore questions about the relationship of the noumenal to the phenomenal world that were central to his philosophical quest and to his identity as a late Romantic poet [...] the rites also offered him a symbolic language that he supposed was sanctioned by ancient usage.[12]

It is possible to see a play such as *The Land of Heart's Desire* as a kind of living symbol that offers audiences the opportunity to meditate upon how closely the noumenal and the phenomenal worlds are intertwined. In the opening stage direction, much is made of an open cottage door as if it is a portal to the transcendent: 'a late sunset glimmers through the trees and carries the eye far off into a vague, mysterious world.'[13] The limited action of the play unfolds therefore not so much on a conventional stage as in a liminal space.

The second of his plays that Yeats saw in production in the 1890s was *The Countess Cathleen*, which premièred on 8 May 1899 on the opening night of the Irish Literary Theatre's first season of plays. It too was marked by a ritualistic element. The stage direction to Scene 1 emphasizes that the effect of the play should almost be that of a kind of spiritual emblem or icon: 'The scene should have the effect of missal painting.'[14]

Like *The Land of Heart's Desire*, *The Countess Cathleen* offered actors the opportunity to declaim elevated verse and to chant their lines in a sacerdotal manner. The play is set at a time of famine, and the devil has sent emissaries to the starving peasants offering to purchase souls for gold so that they might buy food. The title character is a noble lady who is willing to lose her own soul as the cost of saving the people. The final scene is an impressive

---

[10] Josephine Johnson, *Florence Farr: Bernard Shaw's 'New Woman'* (Totowa, NJ: Rowman & Littlefield, 1975), 73.
[11] Ibid., 122.   [12] Yeats, *Collected Letters*, vol. 1, 488.
[13] *Variorum Plays of W. B. Yeats*, 34.   [14] Ibid., 5.

tableau in which the saintly Countess is received into Heaven, since God looks on the motive, not simply on the deed, and she has sacrificed herself from the highest possible motives, seeking to save others. The play ends with an almost Wagnerian extravaganza of stage effects. Twilight fades to the distant muttering of thunder and a rising storm. There is lightning and a visionary light. Peasants are seen to be kneeling on 'the rocky slope of a mountain [. . .] half in the light, half in the shadow, stand armed angels.'[15] The symbolic implication is that a battle for a soul has ended in victory: 'A sound of far-off horns seems to come from the heart of the light.'[16]

Where in *The Land of Heart's Desire* the appeal of fairy land was seen to be in conflict with the demands of everyday life in a peasant world, in *The Countess Cathleen* the spirituality of the poetic (as represented by the poet Aleel who devotes himself to the Countess) and the Countess's Christian virtue are in manifest contrast with the crass materialism of the devil's merchants, and with the readiness with which the peasantry strike a damning deal with them. Indeed, a contrast between Aleel's lyricism and the peasants' dialogues with the merchants expresses in linguistic terms the conflict between good and evil that lies at the heart of the play, making it seem a work of coherent, well-managed symbolism.

DRAMAS OF SUPERNATURAL TRANSFORMATION

Yeats's ability to deploy a rural demotic in this play was a theatrical resource to be developed through collaboration with his fellow playwright Augusta Gregory, which gave an earthy immediacy to the texture of a work with its gaze fixed on the transcendent. This was an ability Yeats would exploit to great effect in *Cathleen ni Houlihan*, first produced in Dublin in 1902 with Maud Gonne in the title part.

The play is set in a cottage in Co. Mayo just before the French troops arrive to support the United Irish rebellion in 1798. As a peasant family prepares for the wedding of their son to a local girl, an old woman makes an unexpected visit, interrupting the family's talk of the handsome dowry the wedding in prospect has involved. Their materialistic concerns are expressed in vividly demotic Hiberno-English dialogue which is in marked contrast with the elevated rhetoric of their mysterious visitor. It soon becomes clear to the audience, as she alludes to four green fields that have been stolen from her and to 'strangers in the house', that she is none other than Cathleen ni Houlihan, a traditional personification of Ireland. She chants and indeed sings of the sufferings of the nation. So powerful are her mesmeric utterances, as if they were the words of some magic ritual, that the prospective bridegroom is challenged to give up marriage in favour of service to the strange visitor in which he must risk his life. His reward will be that his name will be entered in the pantheon of those who have died for Ireland.

That some supernatural transformation has been set in motion by the liturgical force of the visitor's eloquence is suggested by the play's memorable curtain-line. The young boy of

---

[15] Ibid., 167. Quotations from this play are taken from the much-revised final text rather than the very different first version published in 1892.

[16] Ibid., 169.

the house is asked if he saw an old woman 'going down the path' on her departure from the cottage. He replies, 'I did not, but I saw a young girl, and she had the walk of a queen.'[17]

The penetration of everyday life by the supernatural became a preoccupation of Yeats the dramatist in the early years of his theatrical career. The folk plays he composed, exploiting the kind of Hiberno-English which had given a homely tone to *Cathleen ni Houlihan*, were open to such manifestations. *The Hour-Glass* (1903), for example, a play based on the medieval *Everyman*, climaxes with an angelic appearance. These plays, less obviously ritualistic than Yeats's later dramatic experiments would be, were nonetheless demonstrably the work of an author who valued symbolic action. One notes that the angel in *The Hour-Glass*, who comes to claim the soul of an inveterate religious sceptic, carries a golden casket, into which in a moment of pure magic the man's soul is placed with the promise that the lid will be opened in Paradise. Nor do such plays—which quickly became curtain-raising staples of the Abbey Theatre's repertoire, for all their homely dialect— indicate any diminution of faith in the power of effective speech. Tellingly, in the drolly comic peasant play *The Pot of Broth* (1902), a wandering tramp triumphs in a domestic set-ting simply by the colourful ingenuity of his talk.

It is important to recognize that Yeats's early plays were not dramatic in the conven-tional sense of presenting audiences with dramas of characters in conflict. Rather, true to his creed that highlighted the origins of theatre in ritual, the personages of his early plays seem figures in near-liturgical enactments in which they embody the way the spiritual and the material world interact. They represent, as it were, states of consciousness and spiritual awareness. The Countess, for example, is not a conflicted character, but she appears to us as the very epitome of self-sacrificial virtue. She is, to use a formulation Yeats used in his late poem 'The Circus Animals' Desertion', a 'character isolated by a deed'.[18]

A DRAMA OF CHARACTER

It is a measure of Yeats's creative energy as an experimental artist that he was not to be bound by any aesthetic doctrine, even one he had propagated himself. Accordingly, having seen plays by himself produced as ritual performances, in 1904 he had a drama of character take its place on the Abbey stage: *On Baile's Strand*.

Yeats based the action of this play on an ancient Irish saga which told a tragic tale of the heroic Cuchulain, the central figure of the Ulster or Red Branch cycle of Irish mythology. In the play Cuchulain is at the court of his uncle, Conchubar, King of Ulster and leader of the Red Branch Knights. In 1902 Yeats had attended a cycle of Shakespeare's history plays at Stratford-upon-Avon, and had been impressed by Shakespeare's creation of drama from the history of England in a way that probably encouraged him to base drama on Irish saga material (which he knew from Lady Gregory's prose work *Cuchulain of Muirthemne*). He had noted how the six plays that were 'but one play' involved a contrast between two main

---

[17] Ibid., 231.
[18] *The Variorum Edition of the Poems of W. B. Yeats*, ed. Peter Allt and Russell K. Alspach (New York: Macmillan, 1956), 630.

characters, Richard II and Henry V.[19] Yeats indeed may have been emboldened by this to make his own history play, composed with a Shakespearian amplitude of perspective, hinge in part on a dramatic opposition between two powerfully realized characters: Cuchulain and Conchubar.

In a letter to a friend in 1938, Yeats wrote of Cuchulain, who appears in five of his plays, 'Cuchulain seemed to me a heroic figure because he was creative joy separated from fear.'[20] In Conchubar's kingdom there are those who think the kingdom cannot afford the risk to stability represented by such an anarchic free spirit. The king's sons are to the fore in pressing the case that Cuchulain should be tamed, and that he should be required to take an oath of subservience. In the first part of the play, a dramatically compelling scene has the now circumspect and pragmatic king endure Cuchulain's accusation that he has betrayed the spirit of their youthful comradeship in arms to become a craven slave to domesticity, 'the threshold and the hearthstone'.[21] The force of Conchubar's argument is that because Cuchulain has no son he cannot appreciate how the king hopes to leave a secure kingdom to his heirs.

To satisfy the urgent demands of the High King's children, Cuchulain takes the oath of allegiance, with fatal consequences for himself. For a young champion arrives at the hero's assembly house, where the action of the play takes place, to challenge Cuchulain in armed conflict. At Conchubar's insistence that such a challenge, once issued, must be met, the oath-bound Cuchulain fights and kills his challenger. Upon discovering that he has in fact killed his own son, offspring of a former lover, Cuchulain in manic horror tries to do battle with the sea (Cuchulain's assembly hall gives onto Baile's strand), striking each wave as if it were Conchubar's crowned head. We are to assume that he drowns in this deranged attempt.[22]

In the first part of the play we have been given insight into the prudent, calculating character of Conchubar and have admired the heroic individualism of Cuchulain, a man who can declare with conviction:

> I'll not be bound.
> I'll dance or hunt, or quarrel or make love
> Wherever and whenever I've a mind to.[23]

In the encounter with his son, when the young man arrives to issue his challenge Cuchulain sees in him something of his lover Aoife, with whom he had a passionate affair. He sees him as a fitting son of a warrior queen (a 'fierce woman of the camp'[24]) with whom he feels burgeoning friendship:

> But I can see there's no more need for words
> And that you'll be my friend from this day out.[25]

[19] Yeats, *Essays and Introductions*, 109.
[20] W. B. Yeats to Dorothy Wellesley, 15 Aug. 1939, in *Letters*, ed. Allan Wade (London: Rupert Hart-Davis, 1954), 913.
[21] *Variorum Plays of W. B. Yeats*, 499.
[22] This is of course only one version of the end of Cuchulain; he is resurrected in *The Only Jealousy of Emer* and his final defeat dramatized in *The Death of Cuchulain*
[23] *Variorum Plays of W. B. Yeats*, 477–9.   [24] Ibid., 487.   [25] Ibid., 506.

The lyricism in their emotional exchange highlights how much of the experience of father-hood Cuchulain must lose in this tragic play, giving it an affecting poignancy, unusual in Yeats's *oeuvre*.

Unlike the ritual enactments we have considered above, *On Baile's Strand* does not in itself constitute a performance that embodies the way the eternal enters the temporal. It is not however without ritualistic elements. Cuchulain's act of oath-taking, in a 1906 version of the play, features an elaborate ritual involving three women carrying a bowl of fire. In taking his oath, Cuchulain is obliged to thrust his sword into the flames as the women chant a spell to ward off evil and witchery. Indeed, the presence of the women calls to mind the three weird sisters in Shakespeare's *Macbeth*. They give to Yeats's play, with its moments of divination and brooding awareness of fate, an eldritch atmosphere appropriate to the pre-historical era in which it is ostensibly set. The work's unity of effect makes for a powerful theatrical experience.

DRAMA AND THE MASK

Yeats experimented with what for him was a remarkable innovation in *On Baile's Strand*. He chose to frame the main action with a kind of subplot—a near-burlesque of the main plot, concerning a Fool and a Blind Man. Rather than undermining the high seriousness of the main plot or the work's unity of effect, this stratagem served to highlight by tonal generic contrast how momentous was the fateful drama being played out on stage. For 'life drifts between a fool and a blind man/To the end, and nobody can know his end.' [26]

On Baile's Strand represents an important stage in the development of Yeats's dramaturgy. His willingness to work within a Shakespearean dramatic mode is indicative of the generic flexibility which would mark his subsequent theatrical career. The play, moreover, was the first of his works for the stage for which masks were designed to be worn by actors playing specific parts.

For some years before the first production of *On Baile's Strand* Yeats had been taking a keen interest in the theories of the experimental stage designer Edward Gordon Craig, whose *On the Art of the Theatre* was published in 1905. Craig's idea for the use of screens to create theatrical sets that would not require the kind of elaborate scene painting which Yeats abhorred in the commercial theatre would prove a boon to the Abbey Theatre, with its limited stage space and resources. Craig's suggestion that masks (designs for which he himself supplied sketches) could appropriately be worn by the Blind Man and the Fool in *On Baile's Strand* confirmed Yeats's interest in a concept that would prove very fruitful for him over the decades. Though, as Richard Allen Cave points out, 'There is no record that either mask was made, or that masks of any kind were used in Abbey productions of the play during Yeats's lifetime.'[27]

---

[26] Ibid., 514.
[27] Richard Allen Cave, 'Commentaries and notes', in W. B. Yeats, *Selected Plays*, ed. Richard Allen Cave (Harmondsworth: Penguin Books, 1997), 293.

Despite this, it is clear the concept of the mask was to become very important to Yeats both as poet and as experimental dramatist. In the private journal he began to keep in 1908, we can see how he increasingly thought of the poet's role as a matter of the donning of a mask and of the acting out in lyric poems of the emotions appropriate to dramatic situations. And we can see too in the journal how, for Yeats, the kind of ritual drama to which he was dedicated was central to his creativity. In the journal he wrote that 'there is a relation between discipline and the theatrical sense', that when '[you] eliminate character from comedy [...] you get farce', and of how the 'masks of tragedy contain neither character nor personal energy'.[28]

Yeats's first play to take Cuchulain as its hero was followed by *The Green Helmet* (1910). Since Yeats remained wedded to the ideal of theatre as ritual performance (in which character is not significant), this work can usefully be seen as proof of the poet's claim about comedy and farce. The title of this play, in a version derived from a prose ur-text, includes the information that it is 'An Heroic Farce'.[29]

The farcical elements of this play consist in the way ancient heroes are not immune from bombast, vainglory, and quarrelsome wrangling as to who is most worthy of honour. That even their wives become involved in a fatuous, violent dispute about priority adds to the impression of farce at work. In the midst of noisy disorder only Cuchulain (who is scarcely a realized dramatic character in the play) is seen to rise above the general, demeaning chaos to resolve a ludicrous situation by an act of magnanimity. At the last, he is honoured for a volunteered self-sacrifice in terms which define true heroism:

> And I choose the laughing lip
> That shall not turn from laughing, whatever rise or fall;
> The heart that grows no bitterer although betrayed by all;
> The hand that loves to scatter; the life like a gambler's throw.[30]

Theatre as ritual performance as well as chant-like speech can draw on the liturgical use of colour as a visual element to be exploited theatrically. *The Green Helmet* was a near-kaleidoscope of colour effects and tonal gradations. This colourful profusion serves to highlight for the audience how crowded the stage becomes as the play proceeds and how chaotically the spectacle unfolds. When supernatural agency intervenes in the play, three black hands put out the torches, leaving the house in 'pitch black'[31] as though some liturgical ceremony is being enacted.

An Invented Form of Drama

Besides its colour effects, *The Green Helmet* was notable for its large cast, including Stable Boys and Scullions. It had its rowdy moments of an uproariously crowded stage (reminiscent of Jonsonian comedy), quite remote from the slow solemnity of a ritual performance. In the autumn of 1913 Yeats began a serious engagement with a dramatic genre that over the rest of the decade would intensify his engagement as an artist with theatre as ritual

[28] W. B. Yeats, *Memoirs*, ed. Denis Donoghue (London: Macmillan, 1972), 151–2.
[29] *Variorum Plays of W. B. Yeats*, 420.   [30] Ibid., 453.   [31] Ibid., 450.

performance. That winter, Yeats was sharing accommodation with the poet Ezra Pound. Pound had been entrusted, as literary executor, with the papers of Ernest Fenollosa, an American scholar who had spent many years in Japan, where he had studied Noh in detail. Pound made Fenollosa's findings available to his fellow poet, who quickly appreciated that this esoteric form of theatre, with its stylized masks, had much to teach him as he sought to make ritual the basis of his own drama. Over the next eight years, Yeats, influenced by the Noh, would compose a number of remarkable plays which in 1921 he would publish together as *Four Plays for Dancers*. It is not difficult to understand why Yeats was so impressed by Noh when one notes Richard Taylor's summary of Fenollosa's scholarly findings. In Noh:

> Sensuous rhythms and patterns of natural images are so arranged and ordered as to charge objective images with pure and intense emotion to disclose by direct correspondence the pattern of ideal order which existed beyond them. Fenollosa understood Nō as ritual rather than drama; not an imitation of life, but rather a transfiguration of its forms though human imagination in which universal antitheses are synthesised and reconciled.[32]

Augustine Martin writes well of the probable impact of Noh on Yeats as he composed his dance plays:

> From it he took all the elements he needed for his new genre—the sense of religion and ritual, the sacredness of place, the omnipresence of the supernatural, custom and ceremony, the eloquence of gesture, mime, dance, the dramatic power of stillness and silence; above all perhaps, an impersonality which would replace the modern naturalistic preoccupation with character and personal idiosyncrasy.[33]

An article which Yeats published in April 1916 indicates that he had grasped a key fact about Noh, its anti-illusionist nature. In 'Certain Noble Plays of Japan' he told his readership how, through the good offices of Pound and with the help of a Japanese dancer (one Michio Itō, who had trained in Tokyo and Paris), he had 'invented a form of drama, distinguished, indirect, and symbolic, and having no need of mob or press to pay its way—an aristocratic form'.[34] He advised:

> All imaginative art remains at a distance and this distance once chosen, must be firmly held against a pushing world. Verse, ritual, music, and dance in association with action require that gesture, costume, facial expression, stage arrangement must help in keeping the door. Our unimaginative arts are content to see a piece of the world as we know it in a place by itself, to put their photographs as it were in a plush or plain frame, but the art that interests me, while seeming to separate from the world and us a group of figure, images, symbols, enable us to pass for a few moments into a deep of the mind that had hitherto been too subtle for our habitation.[35]

A select invited audience (among them T. S. Eliot) were able to experience Yeats's new 'form of drama', when the first of his dance plays, *At the Hawk's Well*, was performed in

---

[32] Richard Taylor, *The Drama of W. B. Yeats: Irish Myth and Japanese Nō* (New Haven, CT: Yale University Press, 1976), 62.

[33] Augustine Martin, 'Introduction', in Masaru Sekine and Christopher Murray (eds.), *Yeats and the Noh: A Comparative Study* (Gerrards Cross: Colin Smythe, 1990), xiv.

[34] Yeats, *Essays and Introductions*, 221.   [35] Ibid., 224–5.

the drawing-room of Lady Cunard's London residence in April 1916. Her implied patron-age in making this space available lent an aristocratic patina to an occasion that emulated the nobility of a Japanese tradition. The participation of Itō gave an air of authenticity to the production, of whose performance Yeats wrote admiringly that his 'minute intensity of movement in the dance of the hawk so well suited our small room and private art'.[36]

The audience which assembled in Lady Cunard's drawing room that April in 1916 to see Yeats's work must quickly have realized that it was not a conventional drama that would be played. For *At the Hawk's Well* opens with a mysterious, ceremony-like series of actions which involve Musicians, songs, masked actors, and a strange black-clad figure. A hieratic atmosphere is created as the First Musician 'stands motionless', a 'folded cloth hanging from between his hands'.[37] Then the two other Musicians enter and, after standing a moment at either side of the stage, go towards him and slowly unfold the cloth. The impression is given that by means of this ritual a sacred space is being called into being in which the play itself can unfold. This piece of experimental theatricality was a Yeatsian invention; it is not a fea-ture of Noh. When an Old Man comes on stage he does so through the audience, subverting any sense that the play is offering the audience an action set apart from them in an illusion-ist reality, in an imitation of the real world. Most tellingly perhaps, as the Musicians unfold the cloth they sing: 'I call to the eye of the mind/A well long choked up and dry/The boughs long stripped by the wind.'[38] By this the audience is alerted to the fact that this will be a play which will take place in their imaginations. Here is no set with scenery as they might have expected. Indeed, the well of the title is symbolized by 'a square blue cloth'.[39]

The imagination of the audience has much to feed on in this play, for the poet/drama-tist supplies them in imagistic fashion with a compelling sense of a sacred place with its supernatural well (he who drinks of its occasionally full waters puts on immortality). It is a place of cloud, wind, salt sea, dry sticks, and withered hazel tree leaves, broken rocks, and ragged thorn. The sterility of the place thus evoked seems an 'objective correlative' (to use T. S. Eliot's term) of the condition of the Old Man of the play, who has waited fifty years for the miraculous waters to rise. At the moments when they have, he has been bewitched and asleep and so has missed his chance of immortality. We must see in him an image of man-hood sunk in enfeebled old age. By contrast, the Young Man who enters and declares 'I am named Cuchulain, Sualtim's son' is in the full of his heroic strength.[40]

It soon becomes clear to the audience that what they are watching is Cuchulain undergoing a kind of initiation rite. We learn that he has come from afar over the sea, and has to brave the fearsome presence of the Guardian of the Well, like a quest hero undergoing a test of his courage. The Old Man, fearful as he is of the supernatural powers which inhabit the sacred place, which he believes have cheated him of immortality, warns the Young Man of the danger he faces. Suddenly the Guardian in the guise of a hawk begins an alluring dance, yet the young man does not flinch in her presence even though the Musicians together proclaim the name of Aoife as they strike a gong, divining the terrible fate that awaits Cuchulain. The Old Man explains:

> She has roused up the fierce women of the hills,
> Aoife, and all her troop, to take your life.
> And never till you are lying in the earth
> Can you know rest.[41]

---

[36] *Variorum Plays of W. B. Yeats*, 417.   [37] Ibid., 399.   [38] Ibid., 399.
[39] Ibid., 400.   [40] Ibid., 403.   [41] Ibid., 411–12.

The play ends in praise of Cuchulain, who has embraced his heroic and tragic destiny, who accepts a full life with all its 'human faces' rather than the depleted thing which is the lot of the Old Man: 'who but an idiot would praise a withered tree?'[42]

At the Hawk's Well is a remarkable piece of theatre and marks a high point in Yeats's career as an experimental dramatist. It has a riveting austerity of atmosphere which convinces an audience that they have attended a richly meaningful ritual performance that has somehow summoned the supernatural among them. The sudden transformation when the Guardian of the Well becomes a hawk figure is a notable piece of theatrical magic which inspires appropriate feelings of awe. In Noh plays, a divine manifestation often takes place as a climax. In *At The Hawk's Well* it is as if the Guardian of the Well becomes suddenly possessed by a god who directs her movements.

Later in the month in which *At the Hawk's Well* was first performed, the Easter Rising broke out in Dublin. Yeats expressed some of his troubled feelings about this development in a further play for dancers, *The Dreaming of the Bones* (1931). This play also displays features that indicate that Yeats, who wrote it in 1917, was still influenced by Noh (one scholar has noted that it followed closely the form of the Noh dream play).[43] In this play there are three Musicians wearing masks. A central character is a Young Man, who we learn is a rebel who has fled from Dublin to the west of Ireland, where he hopes to escape arrest and punishment. He arrives at a ruined Abbey, where he encounters two masked figures of a man and a girl. These are the ghosts of Diarmuid and Dervorgilla, who invited the Normans into Ireland, setting in train the colonial oppression against which the Young Man has fought in Dublin. We learn that they are doomed to endure unfulfilled love for each other until one of their own race forgives them for their historic crime. The Young Man refuses to do so and the lovers dance, gazing passionately on each other in a state of unending longing from which they cannot awaken. The Musicians, acting like a kind of chorus, provide a poetic commentary on the scene. The imagery of their songs contrasts a vision of dry bones and of jade and agate cups with an invocation of the renewing energies of revolution.

> I have heard from far below
> The strong March birds a-crow.
> Stretch neck and clap the wing,
> Red cock, and crow![44]

The effect in this poignant play is to suggest that a beautiful archaic, aristocratic order must give way to revolution, whatever the cost.

The Easter Rising had a direct impact on Yeats, for the execution of Maud Gonne's husband, John MacBride, allowed him to propose marriage to his former lover once again. Upon rejection he proposed to Maud's daughter Iseult, who also refused his suit. Shortly thereafter in 1917 Yeats married Georgie Hyde Lees, who in the early months of their marriage had to contend with the poet's residual feelings for both Maud and Iseult. It is perhaps

---

[42] Ibid., 412, 414.
[43] Karen Dorn, *Players and Painted Stage: The Theatre of W. B. Yeats* (Brighton: Harvester, 1984), 43.
[44] *Variorum Plays of W. B. Yeats*, 776.

not surprising that Yeats's next dance play was a work that addressed the theme of sexual entanglement and jealousy.

In *The Only Jealousy of Emer* (1926, published 1919) we meet Cuchulain once again, now at the point in *On Baile's Strand* where he dies confronting the waves. He has been joined by his wife, Emer, and he himself has been possessed by a malign spirit of mischief and disorder. His ghost, wearing a mask, crouches on stage as if ready to depart for the next world. Imagery of shore, sea, and sea birds, evoked by the Musicians in the piece, call to the eye of the mind the liminal state in which the play unfolds with ritual formality.

Emer has sent for the hero's mistress, Eithne Inguba, in the hopes that her love can revive the man whom she believes is not in fact dead, merely 'bewitched'. At Emer's suggestion Eithne kisses the figure of Cuchulain, provoking Cuchulain, who is desired by the fairy Fand, into speech. Emer is offered the chance to save her husband's life if she will renounce any future matrimonial life with her husband. At the play's climax she is obliged to witness an alluring dance by Fand. And as Cuchulain almost gives way to the temptation posed by Fand, Emer makes her sacrificial, life-saving renunciation and Cuchulain is restored to heroic life.

Yeats's dance plays are an important contribution to the Irish dramatic tradition. As Katherine Worth has argued, a link of affinity can be seen stretching from Yeats's dream-like dance plays to Beckett's late ghost plays for television, such as *Ghost Trio* and . . . *but the clouds* . . . and even to moments in *Waiting for Godot*.[45] We know that Beckett was an admirer of *At the Hawk's Well*. The intensity of feeling and impression of high spiritual significance Yeats was able to generate in these ritual enactments was a powerful incentive to subsequent Irish dramatists to achieve similar triumphs of theatrical compression. One thinks of the final moments of plays such as Friel's *Faith Healer* and the dance scene in his *Dancing at Lughnasa*, or of Pyper's ghost-haunted imagination in McGuiness's *Observe the Sons of Ulster Marching Towards the Somme*, with its balletic ensemble playing.

THE SAVAGE MIND

The Japanese scholar Hiro Ishibashi quotes a critic and creator of Noh on the kind of beauty which Noh attains, who claims that it is 'calm, graceful, grave, detached, mysterious, elegant'.[46] Commenting on this, with reference to Yeats's later plays, John Rees Moore states that 'they retain more of a nightmare element than the Noh would tolerate'.[47] Certainly the fourth of the plays Yeats included in his *Four Plays for Dancers*, while still displaying the influence of Noh form, scarcely deserves the epithets Ishibashi employs. *Calvary* (published 1921, but never performed in Yeats's lifetime) focuses on Christ's crucifixion and makes of this event, which lies at the heart of the Catholic Mass, a frankly unsettling image

---

[45] Katharine Worth, 'Enigmatic Influences: Yeats, Beckett and the Noh', in Sekine and Murray, *Yeats and the Noh*, 145–58.

[46] Cited in Anthony Kerrigan (ed.), *Yeats and the Noh: Types of Japanese Beauty and their Reflection in Yeats's Plays* (Dublin: Dolmen Press, 1966), 132.

[47] John Rees Moore, *Masks of Love and Death: Yeats as Dramatist* (Ithaca, NY: Cornell University Press, 1971), 198.

of humankind's brutal indifference to spiritual realities. The climactic dance in this near-blasphemous work is that of the Roman soldiers for whom an execution is all in a day's work, who cast lots, in crass delight at a wager, for their victim's cloak.

Ritual motifs in Yeats's later plays, composed during the last two decades of his life, tend in comparison with his earlier work to involve not grave, almost liturgical action but shocking engagements with the savage mind. One remembers in respect of a play such as *A Full Moon in March* (published 1935) that T. S. Eliot's *The Waste Land* had appeared in 1922, with its literary exploitation of matter drawn from Frazer's *The Golden Bough*. In Yeats's play, in conscious echo of Wilde's *Salomé*, an erotic dance is followed by a beheading (a motif Yeats had introduced to his oeuvre in *The Green Helmet*) and a queen dancing in sexual ecstasy, the severed head in her hands. In a note Yeats explained the anthropological origins of the severed-head motif in European literature: 'It is part of the old ritual of the year: the mother goddess and the slain god.'[48] This grisly motif is further exploited in *The King of the Great Clock Tower* (1934), in which the severed head of a strolling poet sings to a queen he is deemed to have insulted, as she dances.

One senses in Yeats's later work for the theatre an impulse to push theatrical experiment as far as possible. Writing of his play *The Resurrection* (1934), he confessed that 'its subject matter might make it unsuited for the public stage in England or in Ireland'.[49] This experimental extremism sometimes resulted in the inclusion of what Rees Moore terms a 'nightmare element'. In *The Resurrection*, a Shavian play of ideas, a dialogue about the meaning of Christ's life and death between a Hebrew, a Syrian, and a Greek is interrupted by the appearance of the risen god (outside the room in which the discussion is set, a Dionysian festival is taking place). The ghost-like apparition of the Christ figure draws from the Greek a terrified declaration straight from nightmare: 'the heart of a phantom is beating.'[50] A similar frisson of supernatural terror is provoked as a notable theatrical coup in *The Words Upon the Window-Pane* (1934, published 1927), when at a commonplace Dublin séance the medium becomes possessed by the anguished spirit of Jonathan Swift, tormented by his love for two women.

In 1938 Yeats completed a play, *The Herne's Egg*, which in its defiant unconventionality—wildly remote in its brief, swift scenes from any control a ritual performance might require—seemed wilfully composed to challenge the peasant realism which had become, to Yeats's chagrin, a staple of the Abbey's repertoire (the play was not performed there in Yeats's lifetime). The play employs a huge heron as a central symbol, and even envisages putting a mechanical donkey on stage. Provocatively, the play's plot turns on the rape of a priestess of the heron's cult by seven drunken soldiers. *The Herne's Egg*, Richard Cave has argued, enters the zone of the bizarre and the grotesque, anticipating the theatre of the absurd to which Samuel Beckett would make so signal a contribution.[51] The play has the unnerving weirdness of a nightmare.

The last of his plays Yeats saw produced was *Purgatory* (1938), which premièred at the Abbey Theatre shortly before Yeats died at the end of January 1939. This short play of 223 lines of verse truly enters a nightmarish world. An old pedlar and his son arrive at a burned-out mansion, where the father tells the son the terrible family history of the place.

---

[48] *Variorum Plays of W. B. Yeats*, 1010.   [49] Ibid., 901.   [50] Ibid., 929.
[51] Cave, 'Commentaries and Notes', in Yeats, *Selected Plays*, 367.

Their ancestor had once been mistress of the house, but she had foolishly married beneath her to a groom, who fathered the Old Man. The Old Man recounts a terrible family saga, which involves his mother's death while delivering him, financial profligacy, his murder of his father, and the burning of the house in an act of vengeance. The play is a ghost play in which the Old Man's mother and father appear at a window of the house to the sound of hoof-beats, and re-enact moments of the past, as souls in purgatory must dream back their lives in an effort to expiate the consequences of their sins. In a grisly attempt to cleanse a polluted and ruined family line (the ruination of which is symbolized on stage by a tree stripped bare), the Old Man kills his son with the same knife with which he murdered his father. The terrible sense is generated by this compelling play that we are watching a nightmare from which there will be no awakening, that it will repeat itself unendingly. There is little obvious sense amid all the horror of this play of a ritual performance (the poetry in its urgent, almost fearful pace lacks the necessary formality). However, Richard Cave has argued convincingly of *Purgatory*: 'The whole experience that we have witnessed in the play has been a ritual devised by the Old Man, a rite of purgation.'[52] Be that as it may, *Purgatory* is one of Yeats's most remarkable works for theatre, arresting in its capacity to arouse great intensity of tragic emotion in a brief span of theatrical time, as Synge had done in *Riders to the Sea*.

A measure of the poet's near-lifelong commitment to drama as an art is the fact that he spent some of his last days alive working on a final play, *The Death of Cuchulain* (published 1939). In this, the hero of *On Baile's Strand* is dispatched by the Blind Man of that work. To the rhythm of pipe and drum, the killer approaches the bound and trussed Cuchulain, making his death seem like a ritual killing.

If, as Yeats asserted early in his career, drama began in ritual and the modern theatre must restore the ancient sovereignty of words, it is surely telling that his work on this play seems to have opened up a seam of words and images for the dying poet that became the basis of his remarkable death-bed poem, 'Cuchulain Comforted'. There, images of human souls as singing bird-like in their acceptance of humankind's common lot are stitched into a poem of visionary, transcendental language.

---

[52] Ibid., 376.

CHAPTER 6

....

THE RIOT OF SPRING
Synge's 'Failed Realism' and the Peasant Drama

....

MARY BURKE

It is better any day to have the row we had last night, than to have your play fizzling out in half-hearted applause. Now we'll be talked about. We're an event in the history of the Irish stage.[1]

The drama, like the symphony, does not teach or prove anything.[2]

IT is the early years of the twentieth century in an exciting new performance venue in a capital city undergoing an artistic blossoming. The culturally engaged audience has gathered for a new work by a recently emerged artist who is promising to develop into a major talent. There are two main factions in attendance: a well-heeled set, and a more combative body of audience members who see themselves as being politically opposed to the establishment contingent. Among the crowd is an iconoclastic Dublin writer who is loath to align himself with either (or indeed any) faction, whose response that evening will be noted by many. Some in the venue have been schooled by preceding performances in similar contexts to expect a work that celebrates the artist's native culture. The stage décor and costumes revealed when the curtain lifts are the result of deep research into peasant folklore, and attendees who had claimed to hope for a conventionally admiring depiction of country life appear to be about to have that expectation fulfilled. However, murmurs of disquiet are heard throughout the venue as a dissonant and brutal timbre begins to be detectable early in the performance. The action reveals a wild and pagan people engaging in primitive games and tribal violence, while the shocking plot appears to be hurtling towards a sacrificial death that will appease the frenzied community. Audience members begin to cat-call and to offer audible suggestions as to how the

---

[1] J. M. Synge to Molly Allgood, 27 Jan. 1907, in *Letters to Molly: John Millington Synge to Maire O'Neill, 1906–1909*, ed. Ann Saddlemyer (Cambridge, MA: Harvard University Press, 1971), 88.

[2] 'Preface', *The Tinker's Wedding*, in J. M. Synge, *Collected Works*, vol. 4, ed. Ann Saddlemyer (London: Oxford University Press, 1968), 3.

performance should proceed, and it becomes apparent that some may have come expecting, even wanting, to be offended. Hisses turn into loud jeers and protests. The two factions begin to attack each other with fists, and once spent, divert their violent attentions towards the performers on the stage. The fashionable audience has transformed into a mob. A piercing voice from the gallery can be heard above the mêlée, shouting for a doctor, and a well-known figure is heard stridently condemning the immorality of the young women on the stage. The demonstrations grow into a terrific uproar and it becomes impossible to hear the performance, which, nevertheless, continues. A member of the theatre management turns up the lights, the police are summoned, and the most violent offenders are ejected. At the disordered conclusion, one faction of the audience claps forcefully, while the rival contingent protests more vociferously than before. Reviews in the next morning's papers and discussions in various publications in the weeks that follow condemn the performance, or the attendees, or both. The riot makes headline news in the capital city itself and throughout the rest of Europe and North America, and the audience's astonishing behaviour goes down in the annals of performance criticism and history, forever colouring considerations of the work's merit and significance. It is later observed that one of the few audience members to remain calm and even amused by the spectacle of the riot was the previously noted Dublin writer, who would himself go on to create equally divisive works of art.

This is not, as might be supposed in a chapter with a reference to Synge in the title, an account of the disturbances that erupted in the Abbey Theatre in Dublin during the opening run of that dramatist's *The Playboy of the Western World* in late January 1907, but a description of the astounding response to the première on 29 May 1913, in the Théâtre des Champs-Élysées, Paris, of Russian composer Igor Stravinsky's avant-garde ballet and orchestral work, *The Rite of Spring* (*Le sacre du printemps*).[3] The Dublin writer in attendance was of course James Joyce, who went on to direct Synge's *Riders to the Sea* (1904) in Zurich five years later. As the outline above suggests, there are startling similarities between the audiences' actions at the Abbey and the Théâtre des Champs-Élysées, and only six years separate the two events. What is even more extraordinary, when one considers that the two disturbances have not been read side by side, is that a list of the factors that contributed to the Paris riot are remarkably similar to the sociopolitical context often provided by contemporary scholars in relation to the Dublin fracas:

> [T]he controversy surrounding the new Théâtre des Champs-Élysées and its management, the purposeful stimulation in the press of public excitement over *Le sacre*, hostility in some circles to foreign art and music at this time, and the jarring contrast of this work to other ballets in the program at the première.[4]

---

[3] The description of the disturbance on the opening night of *The Rite of Spring* is a synopsis of the many first-person accounts provided in Truman Campbell Bullard's 'The First Performance of Igor Stravinsky's *Sacre du printemps*' (PhD dissertation, Eastman School of Music, University of Rochester, 1971), 143–54. Widely-circulated (though possibly apocryphal) modernist lore suggests that James Joyce was in attendance that night. My thanks to Brigid Cohen for this information. For details of the research into folklore utilized and a synopsis of the sequence of choreographed episodes that constitute the scenario, see Pieter van den Toorn, *Stravinsky and the Rite of Spring: The Beginnings of a Musical Language* (Berkeley, CA: University of California Press, 1987), 14–15, 26–7.

[4] Bullard, 'First Performance', xiv–xv.

Why, when the parallels in the responses to the single most important works of Synge and Stravinsky seem so apparent, are these two artists never considered together?[5] Indeed, if any Irish writer is commonly mentioned in the same discussion as Stravinsky, it tends to be Joyce, whose novels are cited in numerous comprehensive considerations of modernism as decon-structions of conventional literature in the manner of Stravinsky's preceding challenges to the orthodoxies of formal music and Lisztian appropriations of folk culture. The etymology of the word 'donnybrook',[6] meaning 'a brawl', suggests a widespread stereotype of a spe-cifically Dublin predilection for riotousness. This, along with the fact that disturbances also occurred at the Abbey Theatre when Seán O'Casey's *The Plough and the Stars* was staged in 1926, contributed to the manner in which the *Playboy* riots have sometimes been understood to reveal some intrinsic partiality for violent protest within the Dublin personality or, more specifically, within Dublin cultural nationalism of the period. While the *Playboy* riots 'facil-itated the construction of a tradition of Irish theatrical disorder',[7] by contrast, the Théâtre des Champs-Élysées fracas has generally been interpreted as an isolated event that tells us something of the confusion and hostility invoked in that audience by a work that defied artistic categorization and challenged peer productions, rather than as evidence of some partiality for rioting among Parisian ballet enthusiasts. It may be an interesting exercise, therefore, to consider the antagonism that greeted Synge's *Playboy* and his earlier dramas as being similarly grounded in what the dramatist himself (in a foreshadowing of a canonical work on modernism[8]) named as 'the shock of [the] new',[9] rather than merely in the narrower context of the nation and its cultural politics. It is worth repeating that 'the jarring contrast' of *The Rite of Spring* to peer works was one of the main roots of the trouble at the Théâtre des Champs-Élysées in 1913, since the role of 'the shock of the new' has often been downplayed in accounts of why Synge's drama offended its audience. Read through such a lens, negative responses to the primitivism of Synge's works may be contextualized as much in a broader early twentieth-century European revolt against the avant-garde as in urban Revivalists' insistence on idealizing the remote Irish west and its inhabitants. For instance, although the *Rite of Spring* ruckus is not explicitly invoked, Paige Reynolds's discussion of the *Playboy* disturbances places them within this milieu of modernist provocation: 'Modernism seeks through any means possible to guarantee the life of great art; hence, the desire to shock the middle classes, or *épater le bourgeois*, is one of the signal characteristics of this movement. Shock provides an uncannily successful promotional tool.'[10] Impresario Sergei Diaghilev,

[5] Terence Brown makes a tantalizing and brief reference to Stravinsky in a discussion of Synge's account of a dream he has on Aran in which he is made frenzied by mysterious music against his will, but otherwise perceives no link between the artists: *The Literature of Ireland: Culture and Criticism* (Cambridge: Cambridge University Press, 2010), 42.

[6] Donnybrook, a district on Dublin's Southside, was for centuries the periodic location of a fair notorious for its drunkenness and violence, thus giving rise to the term.

[7] Joan Fitzpatrick Dean, *Riot and Great Anger: Stage Censorship in Twentieth-Century Ireland* (Madison, WI: University of Wisconsin Press, 2004), 10.

[8] *The Shock of the New* is the title both of Robert Hughes's influential 1980 PBS/BBC documentary television series and of his book tie-in on art's long twentieth-century avant-garde.

[9] 'Style', Synge told W. B. Yeats, was 'born out of the shock of new material': W. B. Yeats, *Autobiographies*, ed. Douglas Archibald and William O'Donnell (*Collected Works*, vol. 3) (New York: Scribner, 1999), 231.

[10] Paige Reynolds, *Modernism, Drama, and the Audience for Irish Spectacle* (Cambridge: Cambridge University Press, 2007), 75. For earlier and foundational considerations of Synge in the modernist

FIG. 6.1 Igor Stravinsky meets Éamon de Valera, 1 June 1963. Stravinsky was in Dublin to conduct a concert of his work.

Courtesy of Irish Photographic Archive.

under whose remit *The Rite of Spring* was staged, commented to Stravinsky afterwards that the riot was 'exactly what I wanted',[11] just as Synge boasted about being 'talked about' on the day following *Playboy*'s raucous opening night. First, however, it is useful to outline the sociocultural context in which Synge's works emerged in order to demonstrate how they challenged the standard play of the period on the peasant or rural theme in a manner that created enormous hostility among critics and audience members alike.

context, see Thomas Kilroy, 'Synge and Modernism', in Maurice Harmon (ed.), *J. M. Synge Centenary Papers, 1971* (Dublin: Dolmen Press, 1972), 167–79, and James Knapp, 'Primitivism and Empire: John Synge and Paul Gauguin', *Comparative Literature* 41, no. 1 (1989), 53–68.

[11] Robert Craft, *Conversations with Igor Stravinsky* (New York: Doubleday, 1959), 48.

THE RISE OF THE PEASANT PLAY

During a long struggle over the management and ownership of Irish land—gathering momentum with the Encumbered Estates Act of 1849 and the first Land Act of 1870, and culminating with the Wyndham Act of 1903—a nascent state organized itself around the ambition of landownership, and small farmers were invested with an exemplary Irishness. According to Philip Bull, 'the status given to land as the symbol of liberation from oppression was such that those who had little or no land were unable to see either their individual identity or their national and social identity in terms other than as landholders and farmers.'[12] Significantly, the movement to promote the replacement of landlords with small proprietors gained extensive backing from urban and rural dwellers alike, which goes some way towards explaining how members of a predominantly middle-class and urban Abbey audience could perceive the Irish peasant 'as a symbol of their lost identity'.[13] By the time the Abbey Theatre was founded in 1904, one year after the Wyndham Act, the greater part of Irish soil was in the possession of former tenants, and Ireland had long become a society dominated by the interests and values of smallholders. The strength and pervasiveness of this consensus explains the remarkable unanimity concerning landownership and its ties to what was perceived to be 'authentic Irishness' in the drama of the early Abbey and certain contemporaneous Dublin theatres. Plays on the theme of land and its possession or transfer that utilized various Hiberno-English dialects, Irish actors, smallholder characters, cottage settings, and action rooted in what purported to be social realism came to be known as 'peasant plays'. Many peasant play plotlines tended to centre uncritically on land and its ownership, and on rural marriage practices tied to patrilineal inheritance; even when potentially subversive peripatetic figures were depicted, the challenge to agrarian *mores* was often ultimately undermined (as will be demonstrated below in an analysis of a Padraic Colum peasant play) or functioned merely to reflect the author's own bohemianism, rather than engage meaningfully with peripatetic subcultures.[14] Just as the naturalization of proprietorship of various kinds in Victorian Irish society and culture implicitly excluded the urban working classes and the rural landless from 'Irishness' itself, the dominance of the peasant play dethroned alternative and more 'elite' modes such as poetic drama and the plays based on Irish epic or supernatural themes favoured by W. B. Yeats and by the Abbey's earliest patron, Annie Horniman.[15] Significantly, William Fay stated that his role in the early Abbey years of 'peasant [plays] director' was the National Theatre's 'most important' work.[16] According to

[12] Philip Bull, *Land, Politics and Nationalism* (Dublin: Gill & Macmillan, 1996), 179.

[13] Brenna Katz Clarke, *The Emergence of the Irish Peasant Play at the Abbey Theatre* (Ann Arbor, MI: UMI Research Press, 1982), 94.

[14] The Revival fashion for depicting tinkers and tramps as the antithesis of the expanding Irish bourgeoisie in plays such as Yeats's *Where There Is Nothing* (1902) was often merely a narcissistic elevation of the bohemian values with which the literati identified, rather than a sincere representation of life on the roads. By contrast, Synge's depictions of such groupings were exceptional for their empathetic and even-handed nature. See Mary Burke, *'Tinkers': Synge and the Cultural History of the Irish Traveller* (Oxford: Oxford University Press, 2009), 10, 58–78, 106.

[15] George Moore debated with Yeats as to whether 'the Galway dialect was possible in the mouths of heroes': George Moore, *Hail and Farewell*, vol. 2 (New York: Appleton, 1912), 360.

[16] Catherine Carswell and W. G. Fay, *The Fays of the Abbey Theatre* (New York: Harcourt & Brace, 1935), 225.

Brenna Katz Clarke's foundational study of the topic, *The Emergence of the Irish Peasant Play at the Abbey Theatre*, during the period 1902–8—'when it assumed its distinctive character', and when J. M. Synge's reputation was made—the Abbey Theatre produced 'twice as many peasant plays as poetic plays'.[17] Cumulative testimony from contemporary diaries, newspapers, and journals 'reveal how extremely popular' the peasant play was with Dublin audiences. This popularity only increased with time, since the early plays revived by the Abbey in the 1920s were predominantly of this sort, as were some of the most successful new plays of its mid-century years.[18]

PLAYS PEASANT AND PLAYERS AND PLAYWRIGHTS UNPEASANT

Although the aim of the peasant play was to present its subject realistically, the Abbey acting style was far from naturalistic. The Abbey technique of standing still was used first for both peasant and poetic plays, and likely suited the latter better; but as the theatre evolved, it became the preserve of the peasant play alone, and was intended to convey that figure's innate nobility. The stilted Abbey peasant was an 'artless' rejoinder to the over-animated stage Irishman buffoon instituted on the eighteenth-century London stage,[19] and this divergence from preceding depiction gave the impression of the mode's accuracy. Synge, for one, was unconvinced, complaining that it had 'become a fashion in Dublin, quite recently', to 'exalt the Irish peasant into a type of almost absolute virtue, frugal, self-sacrificing, [and] valiant [. . . and] though the Irish peasant has many beautiful virtues, it is idle to assert that he is totally unacquainted with the deadly sins, and many minor rogueries'.[20] Without much personal knowledge of rural Ireland in some instances, the urban Abbey audience could only surmise that what they saw was a representation of reality. For Joseph Holloway, William Fay's Peter Gillane in *Cathleen ni Houlihan* (1902) 'might have walked in off the road or come in from the fields after a day's toil'.[21] That a gossipy urban professional who was well known for attending every theatrical production in the capital city was an authority on such matters seems implausible. Audience and critics alike assumed that the Abbey peasant character had to be a realistic representation of the 'real' Irish peasant; and perhaps the more exposed a viewer had been to the earlier negative stereotype, the quicker they wished to seize the more positive stereotype as truth. The English writer and critic Max Beerbohm looked at the Dublin actors whose accents Frank

---

[17] Clarke, *Emergence of the Irish Peasant Play*, 1.

[18] George Shiels's tragedy *The Rugged Path* (1940), which concerns the struggle of a law-abiding farmer to uphold agrarian *mores* against a disordered neighbour, was seen by 25,000 people over the course of eight weeks.

[19] For a discussion of the figure's development, see Joep Leerssen, *Mere Irish and Fíor-Ghael: Studies in the Idea of Irish Nationality, Its Development, and Literary Expression Prior to the Nineteenth Century* (Amsterdam: Benjamins, 1986).

[20] J. M. Synge, *Collected Works*, vol. 2, ed. Alan Price (London: Oxford University Press, 1966), 224.

[21] Joseph Holloway, Diaries, 9 Oct. 1903, quoted in Clarke, *Emergence of the Irish Peasant Play*, 52.

Fay had had to work long and hard to obliterate[22] and really wanted to believe that he saw *actual* Irish peasants.[23]

Paradoxically, the peasant play was intrinsically entwined with the kind of popular tradition that relied on the 'buffoonery and [...] easy sentiment' condemned by the founding document of the Abbey Theatre—the 1897 Irish Literary Theatre manifesto written by Yeats, Gregory, and Martyn. Indeed, it was in this very tradition that the experienced actors of the national theatre had of necessity received their training: it is noteworthy that before gaining fame with the Abbey, the Fay brothers obtained their initial theatre experience in Ireland with companies that produced standard English farce 'such as *Paddy Miles, The Limerick Boy*, and *The Irish Tutor*—Irish only in name and with stage Irish parts'.[24] Clarke uncritically posits that the peasant play strove to use identifiably 'peasant types as characters';[25] but to Dublin audiences used to such English productions and whose ancestors had left the land one, two, or three generations previously, often the only way to 'recognize' a 'peasant type' was by the degree to which it diverged from previous popular literary and dramatic representations. The Abbey went to great trouble and expense to obtain what were considered 'authentic' islander and peasant costumes, even though Aran's famed red flannel petticoats and the hooded Kinsale cloak were both fossilized survivals of earlier general western European fashions, just as the stage Irishman's breeches had been an eighteenth-century British fashion that, once no longer modish, were represented as Irish dress in order to indicate backwardness.[26]

The 'peasant' of the Abbey stage was, to a large extent, a Dublin fantasy: it is significant that the only weekly national newspaper with a focus on country life that has survived from the early decades of the Irish State is titled the *Irish Farmers Journal* (a number of preceding Irish publications with a similar focus also used the word 'farmer' in their titles). By contrast, the one Irish publication during the period in which the Abbey emerged that utilized the word 'peasant' in its title[27] was aimed at an urban Catholic readership and concerned itself more with Abbey gossip than with—to use a phrase from *The Aran Islands*—'the price of kelp in Connemara'.[28] By Synge's lifetime, Dublin had never, in its long history, functioned as a centre of Gaelic power or culture. It began life as a Norse micro-kingdom in the ninth century and then became a royal borough of the English crown, and by the Revival the city remained the most Anglicized major settlement on the island.[29] This fact, alongside the era's rhetoric concerning the authenticity of peasant Ireland, created a defensive unease

[22] Clarke, *Emergence of the Irish Peasant Play*, 41.
[23] 'None of them, in any strict sense of the word, acts. They are exactly the same on the stage as they are (I conceive) off it': Max Beerbohm, 'Irish Players after a Performance at the Court Theatre', *Saturday Review*, 12 June 1909, quoted in Clarke, *Emergence of the Irish Peasant Play*, 53.
[24] Ibid., 14.   [25] Ibid., 2.
[26] Elizabeth McCrum, *Fabric and Form: Irish Fashion Since 1950* (Stroud: Alan Sutton, 1996), 4; Henry McClintock, *Old Irish and Highland Dress and that of the Isle of Man* (Dundalk: Dundalgan, 1950), 105.
[27] *Irish Peasant* was published in both Navan, Co. Meath, and Dublin between Feb. 1903 and Dec. 1906. It continued as *Peasant* from Dec. 1906, and was titled *Peasant and Irish Ireland* between Feb. 1907 and Dec. 1908. In its final iteration between Jan. 1909 and Dec. 1910, it was known as *Irish Nation and the Irish Peasant*.
[28] Synge, *The Aran Islands*, in *Collected Works*, vol. 2, 74.
[29] David Dickson, *Dublin: The Making of a Capital City* (London: Profile Books, 2014), xiv.

in country people living in the capital that by so doing they were being less than fully Irish. Moreover, Dublin middle-class Catholics were often of farming background, which may partially explain why they idealized rural dwellers.

Many of the actors and directors of the Abbey's early years such as William and Frank Fay were Catholic and nationalist, and all of its actors of that period were from the Dublin lower middle or working classes. This was, of course, a huge contrast to the Ascendancy roots of the theatre's then directors, Synge, Yeats, and Gregory—a heritage that drew criticism from nationalist commentators who believed that a humble tie to the land or a modest urban background was a necessary qualification for National Theatre involvement. William Fay's descent from Irish-speaking stock[30] is implied by Clarke to have provided him with an aptitude for his sometime role of peasant play director at the Abbey. Likewise, his brother Frank believed that the Abbey actors had 'most of them peasant blood, if they are not the children of peasants, and instinctively talk, move and act as peasants would'. By contrast, the 'better classes imitate [. . .] the English accent and manner'. It is among the 'working classes and the peasantry', Fay suggested, 'that you find the real live Irish'.[31] Rival dramatists were similarly dismissive of Synge's ability to represent rural Ireland accurately because of his class background. In Ulster Literary Theatre playwright Gerald MacNamara's parody of Synge's persona and dialogue, *The Mist that Does Be on the Bog* (1909), a 'tramp' is revealed to be a method-writing, establishment-class Dublin dramatist.[32] MacNamara was born Harry Morrow into a Northern Presbyterian family, and took the pseudonym 'Gerald MacNamara' in honour of his Irish-speaking Galway grandfather—a lineage that he may have felt bestowed upon him a degree of 'authenticity' lacking in his Dublin counterpart. It was a truism of the period that a writer depicting the 'Irish peasant' had to be 'peasant-born and peasant-bred' in order to reveal 'the character of the Irish people',[33] and controversies surrounding Synge's loquacious and untamed characters always centred on the degree to which the Dublin audience judged them to be a complimentary or faithful representation. The urban Catholic Abbey audience most offended by Synge often seemed to suppose that his class background precluded him from understanding the nuances of rural Irish life. Like William Fay, their assumption seemed to be that they themselves possessed an instinctive insight into rural Ireland because of an ancestry (assumed or real) that they were beginning to idealize in the heat of the Revival moment.

FAILED REALISM: SYNGE'S CRITICAL RECEPTION IN HIS LIFETIME

The increasingly defensive Synge contributed to the controversy surrounding his dramas by alternately claiming that he strove for realism and denying that his work could be

[30] See Carswell and Fay, *Fays of the Abbey*, 4.

[31] Frank Fay, 'Some Account of the Early Days of the INTS', in E. H. Mikhail (ed.), *The Abbey Theatre: Interviews and Recollections* (Totowa, NJ: Barnes & Noble, 1988), 76.

[32] MacNamara's title obviously plays on Nora's description of the isolated setting of *The Shadow of the Glen*. See Synge, *The Shadow of the Glen*, in *Collected Works*, vol. 3, ed. Ann Saddlemyer (Oxford: Oxford University Press, 1968), 49.

[33] Rowland Prothero, 'Irish Novelists on Irish Peasants', *National Review*, 12, no. 71 (1889), 598.

FIG. 6.2 Arthur Shields armed with a loy in the 1932 production of J. M. Synge's *The Playboy of the Western World* at the Abbey Theatre.

Courtesy of the Abbey Theatre and James Hardiman Library, NUI Galway.

interpreted through such a prosaic lens. His Preface to *The Tinker's Wedding* (1907) appears to attack the reductive realism of the peasant play: 'We should not go to the theatre as we go to a chemist's, or a dram-shop [. . .] in these days the playhouse is too often stocked with the drugs of many seedy problems.'[34] He recorded his admiration for Douglas Hyde's *Love Songs of Connacht*[35]—translations that almost certainly shaped the dialogue of his plays—but after the question of the realism of his dialogue erupted, he later claimed in the *Playboy* 'Preface' that his plays 'used one or two words only that I have not heard among the country people of Ireland', and that the dialogue of *The Shadow of the Glen* (1903) was aided by what

[34] Synge, 'Preface', *The Tinker's Wedding*, in *Collected Works*, vol. 4, 3.
[35] Synge, 'An Epic of Ulster', in *Collected Works*, vol. 2, 367.

he heard servant girls say through 'a chink in the floor of the old Wicklow house where I was staying'.[36] His letter to the *Irish Times* in the days after the *Playboy* unrest mixes the message entirely:

> *The Playboy of the Western World* is not a play with 'a purpose' in the modern sense of the word, but although parts of it are, or are meant to be, extravagant comedy, still a great deal that is in it, and a great deal more that is behind it, is perfectly serious, when looked at in a certain light.[37]

Both Synge and critics who have subsequently discussed the realism of his plays tend to invoke the Prefaces to *Playboy* and *The Tinker's Wedding*, which he wrote with his back to the wall immediately after the *Playboy* riots (and in anticipation of the controversy the latter play would stir if staged in Dublin).[38]

If Synge had wanted to defend his understanding of rural Ireland, it might have been more politic to draw attention to his prose works on Wicklow, West Kerry, and the west, and to his *Manchester Guardian* articles, most of which he wrote *before* the controversy. Taken as a whole, his prose works and Congested Districts articles easily function as an extended Preface that vindicates all of his 'peasant' drama as being rooted in his knowledge of rural Ireland.[39] Most importantly, however, if we are to spotlight the way in which Synge's dramas pushed the boundaries of the theatre of his day, the prose works confirm that he was artist enough to do more than simply attempt to mechanically replicate rural life on stage, since they reveal that his dramas transmute into art the base material that he personally collected and experienced.

'No drama', Synge wrote to a friend, 'can grow out of anything but the fundamental realities of life.'[40] However, his *oeuvre* is not simply an attempt to mirror the rural life documented with anthropological precision in his prose, but profoundly argumentative works of the imagination that both incorporate and transcend mundane questions of social documentary. Yeats suggests as much in his 'Preface' for the *The Well of the Saints*

---

[36] Synge, 'Preface', *The Playboy of the Western World*, in *Collected Works*, vol. 4, 53.

[37] Synge to the editor, *Irish Times*, 30 Jan. 1907, in *Collected Letters*, vol. 1: *1871–1907*, ed. Ann Saddlemyer (Oxford: Clarendon Press, 1983), 286.

[38] *The Tinker's Wedding* (published in 1907) premièred in London on 11 Nov. 1909 at the Afternoon Theatre Company at His Majesty's Theatre only after Synge's death, because he was leery of the reception it might receive in Dublin. See Synge in a draft reply to publisher Elkin Mathews [*c.*29 Jan. 1905], in *Collected Letters*, vol. 1, 105.

[39] E.g. traces of *Playboy*'s plotline are discernible in incidents outlined in 'In West Kerry'. Synge describes a racing competition on the Blasket Islands of the sort that features in the play, and puzzles over the fact that the island girls found 'romance in [the] condition' of a youth whose face was 'raw and bleeding' as a result of a fall. If the man concerned seems an amalgam of the strangely alluring Christy Mahon and his bloodied father, then Synge himself seems the prototype for the preening Christy's attachment to his mirror when he notes how a crowd gathered around 'watching [...] intently' as he shaved with the aid of a broken looking glass in the central room of a Blasket cottage. Moreover, the diversion caused by the stranger that constitutes the heart of *Playboy* is foreshadowed in Synge's account of the stir caused in Mayo by a visiting 'Chinaman', who was followed 'by a wondering crowd'. Synge, 'In West Kerry', in *Collected Works*, vol. 2, 248, 253, 255; Synge, 'Erris', in *Collected Works*, vol. 2, 326–8.

[40] Synge to Stephen McKenna, 28 Jan. 1904, in *Collected Letters*, vol. 1, 74.

(1905), which was prepared for publication while the play was in rehearsal: '[Synge] tells us of realities, but he knows that art has never taken more than its symbols from anything that the eye can see or the hand measure.'[41] Similarly, an American critic noted insightfully in 1913 that Synge's controversial play *The Shadow of the Glen* (1903) conjoins Boucicault and Ibsen.[42] William Fay's proposal, in a book published almost three decades after the *Playboy* riots, that the root of that trouble lay in the drama's dearth 'of the traditional sentiment or illusions that were then so dear to the Irish playgoer' has become a truism of Synge criticism.[43] However, Edward Hirsch's argument that the hostile reaction to *Playboy* was in response to the fact that it simultaneously asserted and denied realism as the action unfolds is a more nuanced reading of the events. This confusion is reflected in the *Irish Times* reviewer's complaint that the play's self-reflexive linguistic extravagance *was* an accurate rendition of peasant speech, but that the offensive nature of that speech meant that such a degree of realism was inadmissible on stage.[44] In reading the character of Christy as 'another example of the colonial stereotype', the audience misapprehended the degree to which he is 'a parody of the conventional [peasant play] figure'. Moreover, Synge's plays draw attention to the manner in which representing Irish peasant culture onstage would always be, in Jean Baudrillard's phrase, a copy with no original: the folkloric mock wake/viewing one's own funeral scene utilized in *The Shadow of the Glen* was familiar to the Irish reader or theatregoer of Synge's day from Maria Edgeworth's *Castle Rackrent* and Dion Boucicault's *The Shaughraun*. Synge's 'peasant plays' were in fact critiques of that category, and playfully alluded to preceding works of Irish literature. In addition, theatregoers were baffled by a naturalistic frame that was repeatedly disrupted by the extravagant language and exaggerated action. The Abbey audience had expected typical peasant plays in the social realist mode, and merely made a 'time-bound aesthetic judgment in terms of its previous literary experience'.[45] Because the method was too new, the calculated excesses of Synge's peasant plays were misread as failed realism, while the referential repetition of old tropes was seen as the restoration of the stage Irishman figure. For the extreme nationalist William Bulfin, Synge's knowingly referential style made him a kind of literary Dr Frankenstein, 'hunting for slimy, clammy, hideous things [. . .] gleaning odds and ends of humanity from graveyards and dead-houses and making a monster!'[46] In Fay's estimation, the hostility that greeted *The Shadow of the Glen* was also rooted in the fact that 'the Gaels never had a theatre of their own and therefore [had] little understanding of the functions and values of the stage'.[47] Schooled by the dominant peasant play genre (and arguably even by Synge's own prose works) to consider all writing on the Irish rural theme as mirrors held up to nature, audiences found Synge's drama wanting. In the wake of *The Well of the*

---

[41] Yeats, 'Preface', *The Well of the Saints*, in Synge, *Collected Works*, vol. 3, 67.

[42] Cornelius Weygand, *Irish Plays and Playwrights* (London: Constable, 1913), 168.

[43] Carswell and Fay, *Fays of the Abbey*, 216.

[44] Quoted in Edward Hirsch, 'The Gallous Story and the Dirty Deed: The Two *Playboys*', *Modern Drama* 26(1) (spring 1983), 91–2.

[45] Ibid., 86, 87, 93, 91.

[46] William Bulfin, quoted in Maurice Bourgeois, *John Millington Synge and the Irish Theatre* (London: Constable, 1913), 61.

[47] Carswell and Fay, *Fays of the Abbey*, 140.

Saints controversy, the *Freeman's Journal* pronounced that Synge knew 'nothing of Irish peasant religion', while *The Tinker's Wedding*, noted the *Observer* dismissively in 1910, was 'merely a study of sordid peasant life'.[48]

Of course, even when *The Well of the Saints* was admitted to have realistic elements, it was not necessarily the right kind of realism. 'The New Irish Peasant', carried in both the London *Gentleman's Magazine* in January 1906 and the April–June edition of the American publication *The Living Age* of that same year, lamented the passing of the stage Irishman—'witty, laughter-loving, lazy, unscrupulous, pious Pat'—but found Colum's 'slight, but [. . .] sympath[etic]' 'new peasant' play, *The Land* (produced at the Abbey on 9 June 1905) much more palatable than Synge's play, which 'rejoices' in 'the lack of all nobility in his puppets'.[49] In Synge's dramas, the ownership and passing on of land and the economically driven matchmaking between farming and property-owning families is a prime source of sexual and emotional repression, and he found the hysteria surrounding Nora's choice of a tramp over her financially secure but cold farmer husband in *The Shadow of the Glen* to be an evasion of 'the fundamental realities' of life: 'I restored the sex-element to its natural place, and the people were so surprised they saw the sex only.'[50] 'The shopman', Synge complained in 1908, 'says that a work of art is not artistic if it is unwholesome.'[51] Synge's drama rebukes the sanitized Revival fantasy of the Irish peasant, ultimately harking back to what he saw as the unruliness that was always acknowledged in ancient Irish literature. Indeed, his review of Lady Gregory's *Cuchulain of Muirthemne* (1902) subtly critiques her expurgation of the 'barbarous features'—that is, the sex and violence—of the source material.[52] Rather than celebrate the cottage as a symbol of security, as occurs in typical peasant plays such as Gregory's *Twenty-Five* (1903) or *The Land*, Synge foregrounds landless subcultures that reject such values in *The Shadow of the Glen*, and, of course, in *The Tinker's Wedding*. In his prose piece 'The Inner Lands of Mayo', Synge records a resident's complaint that returned female emigrants were skewing the local marriage market, as their savings (rather than any physical attribute) made them an attractive prospect.[53] *Playboy*, *The Shadow of the Glen*, and *The Well of the Saints*—in which young Molly acts in her own best economic interests by ultimately settling for the aged but solvent Timmy, despite flirtations with the tramp Martin Doul—similarly depict the unhappiness or necessary pragmatism of the settled woman forced into a loveless match for its financial security. Nevertheless, the strain of Ibsenite realism in Synge's stress on rural women's rationality in the face of their dearth of options was, yet again, not the *right kind* of realism. *Playboy* was, the *Freeman's Journal* famously thundered, 'an unmitigated, protracted libel upon Irish peasant [. . .] girlhood'.[54]

---

[48] *Freeman's Journal*, 6 Feb. 1905; *Observer*, 14 Nov. 1910, quoted in Nesta Jones, *File on Synge* (London: Methuen Drama, 1994), 47, 38.

[49] 'The New Irish Peasant', *Living Age* 249 (Apr.–June 1906), 301–3.

[50] Synge to Stephen McKenna, 28 Jan. 1904, in *Collected Letters*, vol. 1, 74.

[51] Synge, 'Various Notes', in *Collected Works*, vol. 2, 348.

[52] Synge, 'An Epic of Ulster', in *Collected Works*, vol. 2, 370.

[53] Synge, 'The Inner Lands of Mayo', in *Collected Works*, vol. 2, 330.

[54] Quoted in Máire Nic Shiubhlaigh, *The Splendid Years: Recollections of Máire Nic Shiubhlaigh as Told to Edward Kenny* (Dublin: Duffy, 1955), 81.

Padraic Colum and the Exemplary
Peasant Play

What then did the Dublin audience of the period judge to be the right kind of realism in a play with a contemporary rural Irish setting? Dramas by Padraic Colum almost always appear in accounts of the most noteworthy examples of the peasant play. Colum fitted the image of the 'peasant playwright' because he often declared that he was 'Catholic, of peasant stock, and had been born in the workhouse in Longford', without mentioning the fact that his father had been the workhouse master.[55] An analysis of Colum's *The Fiddler's House* (1907), produced in the same year as *Playboy*, will provide an example of the kind of drama against which Synge's work was measured. *The Fiddler's House*, a revised version of *Broken Soil* (1903), was staged on 21 March 1907 by the Theatre of Ireland in the Rotunda after Colum broke with the Abbey (although the play went on to become a staple of the Abbey roster). Given the staging of both plays in the same year in the same small city, it is certain that they had many audience members in common, not least Colum's father, who played a prominent role in inciting one of the *Playboy* riots.[56] *The Fiddler's House* concerns musician Conn Hourican's desire to return to the road after a five-year stint in a house. Conn had previously been accompanied by his daughters Maire and Anne on his rambles, but settled with his children when Maire inherited her grandmother's house and small farm. The erstwhile rover's desire to wander is portrayed as innate and irrepressible. Anne hopes to marry James, the son of a neighbouring farmer, but her suitor's father disapproves of a woman who has neither property nor dowry,[57] and the couple will have to wait until James's sprightly father dies before gaining self-determination. As in *The Shadow of the Glen*, *The Well of the Saints*, and *Playboy*, Colum situates his story within an agrarian Ireland in which monetary concerns determine choice of marriage partner and even possibility of union; Conn is disgusted by the values of a society in which people 'would leave the best fiddler at the fair and go and look at a bullock'.[58] Conn's daughters enjoy the comfort conferred by their new life, but, disinclined to see Anne denied happiness, Maire signs the farm over to her younger sister. Subsequently, Maire feels compelled to return to tramping with her father in order to make room for the young couple, despite the fact that it is clear that she prizes the respectability bestowed by landownership. Where *The Fiddler's House* departs from Synge's work is in its suggestion that vagabondage is a necessary sacrifice to be embraced by the few so that the majority may enjoy living on the land. Throughout the play, Colum privileges the supposed romance of Conn's favoured lifestyle over the pragmatism and avarice of small-farming Ireland, but the play's conclusion pragmatically intimates that the settled lifestyle has primacy. The pre-eminence of the artist is perceived to be

---

[55] Sanford Sternlicht, 'Introduction', in Padraic Colum, *Selected Plays*, ed. Sanford Sternlicht (Syracuse, NY: Syracuse University Press, 2006), vii.

[56] Dean, *Riot and Great Anger*, 217–18.

[57] Maire notes: 'We were brought up different to farmers, and maybe we never gave thought to the like': Padraic Colum, *The Fiddler's House* (Dublin: Maunsel, 1907), 32.

[58] Ibid., 7.

a privilege of ancient Ireland that the forward-thrusting proto-state cannot afford.[59] James himself dabbles in poetry, but his farming responsibilities will necessarily take precedence over his redundant artistic skills. In *The Land*, the day on which former tenants will purchase their holdings from their old landlord is referred to as 'the day of the redemption'.[60]

Colum similarly mythologizes the new landed class in *The Road Round Ireland* (1926), an account of his travels in post-partition Ireland that was marketed to the lucrative Irish-American market: 'Landlordism', Colum declares, 'can never again pile rent upon the householder here or eject him from his holding; his acres are part of the sixteen million acres that the farmers of Ireland now own.'[61] Such details suggest a commitment to social realism, but Colum's writing often achieved its vaunted realism by excising what Synge considered to be the most unsavoury aspects of rural life. For instance, Colum's best-known poem, the much-anthologized 'An Old Woman of the Roads' (1905), simultaneously celebrates the life of the woman of the road and the small farmer's wife, by portraying the rambler's unvarying wish for 'a little house';[62] but it is notable that the threat of sexual violence to the female vagrant intimated by another old woman of the roads—this one in Synge's *The Tinker's Wedding*[63]—is entirely absent in Colum's sentimental poem.

SYNGE AND PARIS

Synge and Stravinksy may be aligned as artists whose attempts to push the boundaries of art and representation were profoundly misunderstood in their lifetimes. Synge's dramas and Stravinsky's symphonies (or, to be more precise, his orchestral work) do not, indeed, 'teach or prove anything', other than that Paris audiences in 1913 were as susceptible to the shock of the new as their Dublin counterparts in 1907. Of course, the city that incubated the Russian composer's controversial work and the whole early twentieth-century avant-garde movement in art, music, and literature was also a place with which Synge was deeply familiar. The Irishman sporadically resided in Paris between 1895 and 1902, where he lived almost exclusively on the Rive Gauche, the centre of all things countercultural. Although the *Irish Independent* sniffily suggested in 1903 that 'Synge knows more about the boulevards of Paris than the fishing folk of Aran',[64] his years in the French capital do not receive the degree of attention given to his periodic trips to the islands by contemporary scholars. Synge's stint in France is often treated as though 'he had taken a wrong turn and his creative life only began when he returned to Ireland'.[65] Rejecting the weight given to Yeats's

---

[59] 'In the day's of Ireland's glory [...] the men of art had their rights and dues': ibid., 47.

[60] Colum, *The Land*, in *Selected Plays*, 6.

[61] Padraic Colum, *The Road Round Ireland* (New York: Macmillan, 1930), 23.

[62] Padraic Colum, 'The Old Woman of the Road', in *Selected Poems*, ed. Sanford Sternlicht (Syracuse, NY: Syracuse University Press, 1989), 26.

[63] In Act II of *The Tinker's Wedding,* Mary mutters that 'a woman would never know the things might happen her and she walking single in a lonesome place': Synge, *The Tinker's Wedding*, in *Collected Works*, vol. 4, 39.

[64] Quoted in Ulick O'Connor, *Celtic Dawn: A Portrait of the Irish Literary Renaissance* (London: Hamish Hamilton, 1984), 235.

[65] Katharine Worth, *The Irish Drama of Europe from Yeats to Beckett* (London: Athlone Press, 1978), 121.

dismissal of Synge's Paris years,[66] Mark Mortimer suggests that the budding playwright's time in the French capital is crucial to understanding his artistic development:

> In Paris, he read widely and retained what was appropriate to his own intellectual and aesthetic growth. In Paris, he learned much from the lectures he went to at the University [. . .] attending the lectures of d'Arbois de Jubainville on Celtic civilization and languages, he returned to a study of the Irish language and acquired a knowledge of, and a love for, Irish mythology. In Paris, away from the shrill voices of narrow nationalists and blinkered unionists, he became aware of his Irish identity [. . .] he saw many great plays and laid the foundations for his work as a dramatist [. . .] and learned the trade of writing.[67]

In various journal and newspaper articles, Synge outlined French art, theatre, and literature to the Irish reading public, and interpreted the Irish Literary Revival for the French. Moreover, the protagonist of Synge's patently autobiographical first play, *When the Moon Has Set* (*c*.1900–1903), is an artistic upper-middle-class Irishman recently returned from Paris, and the young man from Ireland who has immersed himself in the artistic scene of Paris is forever marked by the experience, as Synge suggests in a 1908 review of the exhibition at the Municipal Gallery of Modern Art in Dublin:

> Perhaps no one but Dublin men who have lived abroad can quite realise the strange thrill it gave me to turn in from Harcourt-street—where I passed by to school long ago—and to find myself among Monets, and Manets and Renoirs, things I connect so directly with the life of Paris.[68]

Culturally, Synge was as French as he was Irish—a fact that allies downplayed in order 'to defend him against the charge of being "Frenchified" [. . .] levelled by extreme nationalists and smug pietists in Dublin'.[69] However, Synge admitted to the influence of the fashionable French literature he had been exposed to in a 1907 draft preface for the Cuala Press edition of his poems: 'They were written from five to eight years ago and, as is obvious enough, in Paris among all the influences of the so-called decadent and symbolist schools.'[70] All in all, the *Irish Independent* review of *The Shadow of the Glen* that suggested that Synge's drama emerged from 'the gaiety of Paris' and Arthur Griffith's accusation that it stank of 'the Latin *Quartier*' are perceptive, if not exactly admiring.[71] There is more admiration for this cultural hybridity in the observation of Synge's earliest biographer, the French scholar Maurice Bourgeois, that Synge was 'one of the few Irish writers who Europeanized Ireland without degaelicizing it'.[72] Unfortunately for Synge, however, the Dublin audiences of

---

[66] Yeats claimed to have told Synge: 'Give up Paris. You will never create anything by reading Racine, and Arthur Symons will always be a better critic of French literature. Go to the Aran Islands': W. B. Yeats, *Collected Works,* vol. 4: *Early Essays,* ed. Richard J. Finneran and George Bornstein (New York: Scribner, 2007), 216–17.

[67] Mark Mortimer, 'Synge and France', in Joseph McMinn (ed.), *The Internationalism of Irish Literature and Drama* (Gerrards Cross: Colin Smythe, 1992), 92–3.

[68] Synge, 'Good Pictures in Dublin', in *Collected Works,* vol. 2, 391.

[69] Mortimer, 'Synge and France', 87.

[70] Robin Skelton, 'Introduction', in Synge, *Collected Works,* vol. 1, xiii.

[71] Quoted in David H. Greene and Edward M. Stephens, *J. M. Synge 1871–1909* (New York: New York University Press, 1989), 159.

[72] Bourgeois, *John Millington Synge,* 63.

his day did not appreciate the fact that he had, as he had claimed, married realism and experiment, reality and joy.[73] Synge was a Janus of Irish literature, looking backwards to Boucicault and near-contemporary peasant plays and forwards to the achievements of Irish modernism. Gregory Dobbins notes that although Synge's work is 'formally more conservative' than the most celebrated texts of Irish modernism, it shares the 'critique of the construction of tradition found in later texts'.[74] Synge's drama is a bridge between the kind of social realist peasant play exemplified by Colum and the iconoclastic chapter in Irish literature ushered in by the future director of *Riders to the Sea* who sat calmly in the Théâtre des Champs-Élysées in 1913 as those around him rioted. Bourgeois translated *Playboy* into French for its 12 December 1913 production at the Théâtre de l'Oeuvre, Paris, some seven months after the opening of *The Rite of Spring*. Audiences and critics alike were exasperated by the play's 'unchecked flood of language' and wild action.[75] 'It took many years for Ireland to learn', noted William Fay, 'that in J. M. Synge she had produced a great dramatist.'[76] It also took Paris many years to welcome its adopted son's most famous play, but the city did so decisively in 1954,[77] when Cyril Cusack took on the role of Christy Mahon at the Sarah Bernhardt Theatre during the first International Theatre Festival. 'It was accounted one of the two major contributions to the Festival,' Cusack records, 'the other being Brecht's production of *Mutter Courage*.' Paris had been the incubator of some of the most important experimental works of the early twentieth century, from *The Rite of Spring* to *Finnegans Wake*, and in Paris, in Cusack's estimation, the *Playboy* finally 'found its true home and audience'.[78]

---

[73] 'On the stage one must have reality, and one must have joy [...]': Synge, 'Preface', *The Playboy of the Western World*, in *Collected Works*, vol. 4, 53–4.

[74] Gregory Dobbins, 'Synge and Irish Modernism', in P. J. Mathews (ed.), *The Cambridge Companion to J. M. Synge* (Cambridge: Cambridge University Press, 2009), 137.

[75] See Gérard Leblanc, 'Synge in France', in S. B. Bushrui (ed.), *A Centenary Tribute to John Millington Synge, 1871–1909: Sunshine and the Moon's Delight* (New York: Barnes & Noble, 1972), 266–7.

[76] Carswell and Fay, *Fays of the Abbey*, 141.

[77] A 1941 Marcel Herrand production was only a moderate success, since it 'missed the deeper issues': Leblanc, 'Synge in France', 267.

[78] Cyril Cusack, 'A Player's Reflections on *Playboy*', *Modern Drama* 4, no. 3 (1961), 304.

PART III

MODELS AND INFLUENCES

CHAPTER 7

···

'WE WERE VERY YOUNG AND WE SHRANK FROM NOTHING'
Realism and Early Twentieth-Century Irish Drama

···

SHAUN RICHARDS

W. B. Yeats's article 'A People's Theatre', published as an open letter to Lady Gregory in the *Freeman's Journal* on 26 April 1919, stated that the success of the Abbey Theatre was for him 'a discouragement and a defeat' in that it lacked the 'mysterious art' that he desired. Feeling excluded from the direction of the theatre, Yeats contrasted his isolation with 'some young Corkman, all eyes and ears, whose first rambling play we have just pulled together or half together'.[1] Years later, in notes written in 1934 for *The Only Jealousy of Emer* (1919), Yeats expanded on his position and moved to identify the 'young Corkman':

> About 1909 the first of the satirists appeared, 'The Cork Realists', we called them, men that had come to maturity amidst spite and bitterness. Instead of turning their backs upon the actual Ireland of their day, they attacked everything that made it possible.[2]

In identifying 'about 1909' as the moment of change, Yeats is referring implicitly to the Cork playwright Lennox Robinson, whose first play, *The Clancy Name*, was staged at the Abbey in October 1908, with Robinson being appointed manager of the theatre in the March of the following year—a move which led George Russell to comment that this was 'a strange end to the poetic playhouse Yeats wanted'.[3] However, as Yeats perceptively reflected, 'only a change in European thought' could have produced a situation in which 'romantic dreaming' rather than raw reality was the subject of drama, and he bowed to the inevitable public triumph of 'mechanical philosophy'.[4]

---

[1] W. B. Yeats, *Collected Works*, vol. 8: *The Irish Dramatic Movement*, ed. Mary Fitzgerald and Richard J. Finneran (New York: Scribner, 2003), 128, 131.
[2] *The Variorum Edition of the Plays of W. B. Yeats*, ed. Russell K. Alspach (London: Macmillan, 1966), 568.
[3] Quoted in R. F. Foster, *W. B. Yeats: A Life*, vol. 1: *The Apprentice Mage 1865–1914* (Oxford: Oxford University Press. 1997), 415.
[4] Yeats, *Variorum Plays*, 568.

While Yeats's symbolist-influenced drama was firmly part of the European avant-garde and stylistically more innovative than the plays of the Cork Realists—Robinson, T. C. Murray, and R. J. Ray (the pen name of Robert J. Brophy)—they, in Robinson's words, 'were very young and we shrank from nothing'. And in lines that convey the modern movement to which they aligned themselves, Robinson continued: 'We knew our Ibsen and the plays of the Lancashire school, we showed our people as robbers and murderers, guilty of arson, steeped in trickery and jobbery.' Indeed, he noted, Lady Gregory told him that he had 'waded through blood' before coming to write *The Whiteheaded Boy*, his successful family comedy from 1916.[5] But it was that commitment to criticism that characterized the realist revolution in Irish theatre and allied it, although often in complex ways, to the movement whose origins are to be found in continental Europe, particularly France, in the last decades of the nineteenth century.

'Truthful, Objective, and Impartial'

In his seminal article 'On Realism in Art', Roman Jakobson identified the aspiration to artistic realism as the characteristic of 'any artistic movement which aims at conveying reality as closely as possible and strives for maximum verisimilitude', but observed that in the nineteenth century 'one specific artistic movement was identified as the ultimate manifestation of realism in art and was made the standard by which to measure the degree of realism in preceding and succeeding artistic movements'.[6] In a clear definition of realism, Linda Nochlin writes of its aim as being 'to give a truthful, objective and impartial representation of the real world, based on meticulous observation of contemporary life'. It is in that concern with the contemporary, 'one of the central issues, if not the very crux, of nineteenth-century realism', that it engages with the political shift in which class becomes a crucial aspect of art.[7] Indeed, suggests Philip Beitchman, while realism is marked by empiricism, materialism, and the belief 'that the world can be understood', the fact that realism begins around 1870, at the time of the brief socialist revolution of the Paris Commune, means that it 'also conveys images, prospects and representations of a class struggle then surfacing as an increasingly unavoidable issue confronting humanity'.[8]

The underpinning of realism's social agenda is best captured in Émile Zola's essay 'The Experimental Novel' (1880). Although Zola is known as the theorist of naturalism, it is only distinguishable from realism in its codification of what is a shared theatrical practice. Both, in Patrice Pavis's words, 'advocated a total reproduction of unstylized, unembellished reality, stressing the material aspects of human existence'.[9] The sets were made up of real objects, the language aimed to reproduce that specific to a character's social class

---

[5] Lennox Robinson, *Curtain Up: An Autobiography* (London: Michael Joseph, 1942), 22.

[6] Roman Jakobson, 'On Realism in Art', in Ladislav Matejka and Krystyn Pomoska (eds.), *Readings in Russian Poetics: Formalist and Structuralist Views* (Cambridge, MA: MIT Press, 1971), 38, 39.

[7] Linda Nochlin, *Realism* (Harmondsworth: Penguin, 1990), 13, 103.

[8] Philip Beitchman, *The Theatre of Naturalism: Disappearing Act* (New York: Peter Lang 2011), 5.

[9] Patrice Pavis, *Dictionary of Theatre: Terms, Concepts, and Analysis* (Toronto: University of Toronto Press, 1998), 236.

and psychology, and the acting style continued the aim of mimetic realism; the whole was performed behind the 'invisible fourth wall' in a world into which the audience looked at the meticulously rendered 'slice of life'. While playwrights more conventionally described as realists, such as Ibsen, did not follow meticulously the naturalist ideal of the scientific method derived from Claude Bernard's *An Introduction to the Study of Scientific Medicine* (1865), they did observe Zola's directive 'to analyse facts and to master them'.[10]

The view that drama should be an art of analysis was anathema to Yeats. In the debate 'What Should Be the Subject of a National Drama?', published in the Dublin *Daily Express* in 1898 and in book form the following year, he argued that the task was to 'liberate the arts from "their age" and from life', convinced 'that all men will more and more reject the opinion that poetry is "a criticism of life" and be more and more convinced that it is a revelation of a hidden life'.[11] This was resisted by John Eglinton, who stressed that the epic subjects of the present, and therefore of a national theatre which looked forward, were 'the steam-engine and the dynamo [. . .] the kinematograph, phonograph, etc.'.[12] 'In short,' he said, 'we need to realize in Ireland that a national drama or literature must spring from a native interest in life and its problems.'[13] Only three years earlier, Bernard Shaw's 'The Problem Play: A Symposium' (1895) famously concluded that '*A Doll's House* will be as flat as ditch-water when *A Midsummer Night's Dream* will still be as fresh as paint; but it will have done more work in the world; and that is enough for the highest genius, which is always intensely utilitarian.'[14] However, the social problems towards which Shaw felt drama should be directed were no more the concern of Eglinton than they were of Yeats. Far from embracing European trends, Eglinton stated: 'In London and Paris they seem to believe in theories and "movements" [. . .] and we are in some danger of being absorbed into their error.'[15] According to Pascale Casanova, the advent of realism coincided with 'the semantic and political shift that led from the idea of the people as a nation to that of the people as a class';[16] but Eglinton's concern with the contemporary did not engage with the pressing issue of social division. To introduce this contentious element would have shattered the necessary fiction of an undivided people directed to the goal of national liberation. Early twentieth-century Irish theatre did develop production and performance styles similar to the realist theatre practice of the continent, but, as argued by Frank Fay, the only reality to which theatre should be directed was that of Ireland's colonial condition: 'This land is ours, but we have ceased to realise the fact. We want a drama that will make us realise it.'[17]

[10] Émile Zola, 'The Experimental Novel', in *The Experimental Novel and Other Essays*, trans. Belle M. Sherman (New York: Haskell House, 1964), 13.

[11] W. B. Yeats, 'John Eglinton and Spiritual Art', in John Eglinton, W. B. Yeats, Æ, and W. Larminie, *Literary Ideals in Ireland* (Dublin: T. Fisher Unwin, 1899), 36.

[12] John Eglinton, 'Mr Yeats and Popular Poetry', in *Literary Ideals in Ireland*, 43.

[13] John Eglinton, 'What Should Be the Subjects of a National Drama?', in *Literary Ideals in Ireland*, 13.

[14] G. B. Shaw, 'The Problem Play: A Symposium', in E. J. West (ed.), *Shaw on Theatre* (London: MacGibbon & Kee, 1958), 63.

[15] Eglinton, 'What Should be the Subjects of a National Drama?', 13.

[16] Pascale Casanova, *The World Republic of Letters* (Cambridge, MA: Harvard University Press, 2004), 225.

[17] Frank J. Fay, *Towards a National Theatre: The Dramatic Criticism of Frank J. Fay*, ed. Robert Hogan (Dublin: Dolmen Press, 1970), 53.

THE EXAMPLE OF REALISM

The debate over 'What Should Be the subject of a National Drama?' took place at what was, as P. J. Mathews argues, 'a hugely significant moment, not only in Irish cultural history, but also in terms of the development of Irish politics [...] between 1899 and 1905, Ireland was mutating both politically and culturally in all kinds of interesting ways.'[18] Theatre had a key role in this ferment of cultural–political activity, and its centrality as a consciousness-raising and consciousness-shaping enterprise was clearly articulated—above all that it should counter the commercial theatre's diet of plays, largely of English origin, which were, in the words of the nationalist polemicist D. P. Moran, 'vulgar, pointless, uninteresting drivel'.[19] The quest was then for a model of theatre whose objective was not commercial and whose subject matter was unremittingly Irish.

In the late summer of 1897, Yeats, Augusta Gregory, and Edward Martyn issued a statement of their intention to establish an Irish Literary Theatre; their first productions—Yeats's *The Countess Cathleen* and Martyn's *The Heather Field*—took place in May 1899. In January, Yeats had written to the Dublin *Daily Express* announcing that this new theatre initiative hoped to do for Irish theatre 'what the Theatre Libre and the Theatre l'Oeuvre have done for French dramatic literature'.[20] The Théâtre Libre was founded by André Antoine in 1887, the Théâtre de l'Oeuvre by Aurélien Lugné-Poe in 1893; Yeats was familiar with both through his sojourns in Paris, having absorbed the message of Antoine and famously attending the première of Alfred Jarry's *Ubu Roi* at Théâtre de l'Oeuvre in 1896. The two theatres, however, had different aesthetic objectives, and Yeats admired their independence from commercial imperatives rather than (especially in the case of Antoine) their theatrical style. Antoine was the primary innovator in realist staging, taking furniture from his own house for the set of Léon Hennique's adaptation of Zola's novel *Jacques Damour* in 1887. This was disparaged by Yeats; as he wrote to Frank Fay in August 1904, Antoine was 'a realist, he cared nothing for poetry [. . .] He despised it and did something to drive it from the stage.'[21]

However, it was not only Antoine's example of a theatre independent of commercial considerations which was spreading across Europe; so too was the dedication to staging what was increasingly referred to as 'the new drama' of realism. In 1889 Otto Brahm founded the Freie Bühne in Berlin, and in 1890, George Moore, himself soon to become directly involved in the Irish Literary Theatre in Dublin, published 'On the Necessity of an English Theatre Libre'. J. T. Grein, who established the Independent Theatre in London in 1891, also responded by asking rhetorically, 'What has been done in France, cannot it be done, too, in England?'[22] News of the Théâtre Libre's independence, and the plays championed by

---

[18] P. J. Mathews, *Revival: The Abbey Theatre, Sinn Féin, the Gaelic League and the Co-operative Movement* (Cork: Cork University Press in association with Field Day, 2003), 1, 4.

[19] D. P. Moran, 'The English Mind in Ireland: Drivel at the Gaiety', *The Leader*, 22 Sept. 1900, 56.

[20] W. B. Yeats, *Collected Letters*, vol. 2: *1896–1900*, ed. Warwick Gould, John Kelly, and Deirdre Toomey (Oxford: Clarendon Press, 1997), 338.

[21] W. B. Yeats, *Collected Letters*, vol. 3: *1901–1904*, ed. John Kelly and Ronald Schuchard (Oxford: Clarendon Press, 1994), 642.

[22] J. T. Grein and C. W. Jarvis, 'A British "Theatre Libre"', *Weekly Comedy*, 30 Nov. 1889, repr. in James Woodward, *English Theatre in Transition 1881–1914* (London: Croom Helm, 1984), 175–7.

Antoine, circulated among radical thinkers and theatre people across Europe, aided, in the Anglophone world, by William Archer, who translated Ibsen and proselytized in the cause of theatrical realism. Frank Fay and his brother William, who were active in the amateur theatre world of Dublin, learned of Antoine through a 1901 article by Archer; as William Fay later recorded, 'Antoine's example proved of great service and inspiration to us, for he was not a man of the theatre when he began, but a man engaged in business and had to try his experiment without capital.'[23] It was through Archer that they also heard of Ole Bull and the establishment of the Norwegian National Theatre. These two examples of non-commercial ventures, the latter dedicated to the cause of national independence, determined them to direct their amateur theatrical company to creating a similar theatre for Ireland; and, having worked successfully with the Irish Literary Theatre in 1902, they united with Yeats's initiative as the Irish National Theatre Society.

For all participants in the new venture, the ideal of a non-commercial theatre was modelled on Antoine's example, and the Fays were alert to his staging of a new style of play but, as William Fay recorded, 'with only newspaper reports and articles to help us we could not really find out how these new plays differed from the old'.[24] Above all, they were unfamiliar with the specifics of the staging and acting styles developed by Antoine in order to represent fully the revolutionary force of realist plays. However—and crucially, with regard to the form of realism they developed—while the independent theatres in continental Europe and England staged (and, in the case of the Freie Bühne and the Independent Theatre, opened with) Ibsen's *Ghosts*, the play did not feature in the planning of the major figures in the new company. For J. M. Synge, writing in his preface to *The Tinker's Wedding*, 'the drama, like the symphony, does not teach or prove anything',[25] and he rejected both Ibsen and Zola for 'dealing with the reality of life in joyless and pallid words', judging that 'the intellectual modern drama has failed'.[26] The Fay brothers were sympathetic to this view, Frank claiming that the dialogue in plays they produced had a lifelike fidelity to that of the peasants, and so was 'wonderfully interesting' and 'often even unconsciously poetic'.[27] Such an aesthetic had no place for the dialogue of the Ibsenite drawing room, or the Zolaesque demi-monde. However, the main reason for Ibsen's absence from the stage of both the Irish Literary Theatre and the Irish National Theatre Society was because his realist plays 'expose the core values of Irish nationalists such as female purity, household respectability, individual sacrifice for the good of the community, as hypocritical constructions threatening individual freedom'.[28] It is then not surprising that there were only three productions of Ibsen in Dublin between 1889 and 1904, when Irish theatre was in its formative years: a production of *An Enemy of the People* by the English actor-manager Beerbohm Tree in September

[23] Catherine Carswell and W. G. Fay, *The Fays of the Abbey Theatre* (London: Rich & Cowan, 1935), 108.

[24] Ibid.

[25] J. M. Synge, *Collected Works*, vol. 4, ed. Ann Saddlemyer (London: Oxford University Press, 1968), 3.

[26] J. M. Synge, 'Preface', *The Playboy of the Western World*, in *Collected Works*, vol. 4, 53–4.

[27] Frank Fay, 'Some Account of the Early Days of the INTS', in E. H. Mikhail (ed.), *The Abbey Theatre: Interviews and Recollections* (London: Macmillan, 1988), 74.

[28] Irina Ruppo Malone, 'Ibsen, the Irish Revival and the Debate about Cosmopolitanism and Nationality in Irish Literature', in Patrick O'Donovan and Laura Rascaroli (eds.), *The Cause of Cosmopolitanism: Dispositions, Models, Transformations* (Bern: Peter Lang, 2011), 192.

1894; an amateur production of *A Doll's House* by the Dublin Players Club in December 1897; and a further production of this latter work in June 1903 which was stage managed by George Moore and funded by Edward Martyn, two of the most vocal and active advocates of Ibsenite realism.

Beerbohm Tree's performance style 'eliminated almost all of the qualities of Ibsen's work that had inspired the independent theatres in the first place';[29] but for the Fays, who attended the production, it served to demonstrate that realist drama 'demanded from the actor an entirely new technique'.[30] This involved stripping away the rhetorical delivery and melodramatic gestures employed by Beerbohm Tree, and focusing instead on a simplicity which Frank Fay recognized was a necessity for the fledgling company and its potential playwrights: 'There are a few hints I would give Irishmen who wish to write Irish plays to be played by Irish actors. One of these is to remember that they will have to be acted by amateurs and that at present, and for a long time to come, simplicity and not subtlety should be aimed at.' That simplicity, however, was linked to an authenticity that was claimed to be absolute in every respect. As Frank Fay summarized their practice, 'Most of the plays in the company's repertoire are peasant plays, that is plays dealing with peasant life. They are dressed exactly as in real life, the dresses being specifically made by the tailors employed by the peasantry, and the properties are absolutely correct.'[31] And along with the recreation of visual reality went that of movement for, as a programme for the Abbey's 1906 UK tour declared, 'The players of the company are all familiar with the ways of the Irish peasantry, and in their acting care is taken to keep close to the actual movements and gestures of the people.'[32]

GEORGE MOORE AND IRISH REALISM

However, 'Paul Ruttledge'—a thinly disguised George Moore—criticized the reality of their performances in an article published in September 1904, mere months before the first productions at the Abbey in the December of that year. The article, 'Stage Management in the Irish National Theatre', referenced 'Antoine' seven times as a positive example, as opposed to what Moore termed 'Mr Fay's method, or want of method in presenting the play on the stage'. In particular, he said, 'the actors and actresses in a National Theatre play scramble about practically anyhow, and they remind one very often of three little boys and a little girl reciting a story on a barn door.'[33] Moore was certainly more familiar with the style of realist theatre than anyone else in Dublin, having regularly attended performances

---

[29] Michael Boguki, 'The Art of Making-Up: Ibsen, Ireland and Metropolitan Performance', *Modernist Cultures* 5, no. 2 (2010), 292.

[30] Carswell and Fay, *Fays of the Abbey Theatre*, 109.

[31] Fay, *Towards a National Theatre*, 76.

[32] Programme distributed in Cardiff, Glasgow, Aberdeen, Newcastle, Edinburgh, Hull, 26 May–9 July 1906: Ann Saddlemyer (ed.), *Theatre Business: The Correspondence of the First Abbey Directors: William Butler Yeats, Lady Gregory and J. M. Synge* (Gerrards Cross: Colin Smythe, 1982), 321.

[33] Paul Ruttledge (George Moore), 'Stage Management in the Irish National Theatre', *Dana* 5 (Sept. 1904), 150–2.

at the Théâtre Libre, and even interviewed Antoine, but his concept of realism had more in common with its European roots than its Irish adaptations. For while he argued that 'the labour dispute' in his 1893 play *The Strike at Arlingford* was 'an externality' to which he attached 'little importance', its references to 'socialist leaders and the capitalists' and to 'non-unionist labour'[34] clearly raise issues of class conflict. It was not an Irish play, being set in Co. Durham in England and premièred by J. T. Grein's Independent Theatre; it does, however, make clear Moore's dramatic principles, which came into full play in the world of Dublin when *The Bending of the Bough*—his revision of Martyn's unproduced *The Tale of a Town* (1900)—was staged in the second season of the Irish Literary Theatre in 1900.

By comparison to the other two plays in the season, Martyn's *Maeve* (1900) and Alice Milligan's *The Last Feast of the Fianna* (1900), Moore's play was indeed radical. Though set in 'the present time', Martyn's eponymous heroine dreams of Queen Maeve and 'ancient Irish harpers, chieftains, warriors', all of whom appear on stage,[35] while Milligan's play is set in 'A banqueting hall in the house of Fionn Mac Cumhal'.[36] Moore's stage sets of a corporation meeting hall, a domestic drawing room, and a hotel sitting room are a world away from the heroic age, and its content was even more so. Martyn's original play 'takes place during the present time at a coast town of West Ireland',[37] and while Moore's work is set in Northhaven, whose corporation is in a financial dispute with Southaven, these are thinly disguised version of Ireland and England, their populations being, respectively, a 'mainly Celtic people' and a 'mainly Saxon people'.[38] Northhaven, however, is riven by petty quarrels, self-interest, and the failure of its natural leader, and its cause is lost. The play, as with *The Strike at Arlingford*, oscillates between the male protagonist's engagement with the cause and his personal life, with the result that politics fades intermittently into the dramatic background. However, as argued by Adrian Frazier, 'by staging contemporary problems in realistic settings, even presenting the very images of public people of different classes and religions, *The Bending of the Bough* made dangerously explicit the divisions within Ireland.'[39]

FREDERICK RYAN, PADRAIC COLUM, AND IRISH REALISM

Apart from Moore, Fred Ryan and Padraic Colum were among the few dramatists in the early years of the National Theatre Society who looked to address pressing contemporary issues. Ryan's *The Laying of the Foundations* premièred in the October of 1902 and was reprised that December in the first season of the Irish National Theatre Society. Described by Yeats as a play of 'a slightly socialist tinge',[40] it focuses on council corruption, and

---

[34] George Moore and Edward Martyn, *Selected Plays*, ed. David B. Eakin and Michael Case (Gerrards Cross: Colin Smythe, 1995), 2, 5, 9.

[35] Ibid., 270.

[36] Alice Milligan, *The Last Feast of the Fianna* (London: David Nutt, 1900), 7.

[37] Moore and Martyn, *Selected Plays*, 300.   [38] Ibid., 64.

[39] Adrian Frazier, *George Moore, 1852–1933* (New Haven, CT: Yale University Press, 2000), 287.

[40] In John Kelly, 'A Lost Abbey Play: Fredrick Ryan's *The Laying of the Foundations*', *Ariel* 1, no. 3 (1970), 35.

while only the second act is extant, lines such as 'Patriotism, to the capitalist, is for use only at election times'[41] gives a clear sense of a realist agenda far removed from the play with which it shared the opening bill—James Cousins's *The Sleep of the King* (1902), featuring Con, High King of Erinn, and his son, Connla 'Of the Flowing Golden Hair'. Colum's *The Land* (1905) concerns plans for marriage and land merger between the Cosgars and the Dourases, two farming families in the Irish Midlands, but is as directly concerned with the state of contemporary Ireland as Ryan's 'socialistic' urban drama. For while the play finally endorses an explicitly nationalist agenda, its dynamic comes from Ellen Douras's choice of emigration to America rather than an arranged marriage with Matt Cosgar, declaring 'I can't go into a farmer's house [. . .] it's my freedom I want'.[42] Although, as Colum noted, the play 'was written to celebrate the redemption of the soil of Ireland—an event made possible by the Land Act of 1903', he was equally concerned to show 'that it was not altogether an economic necessity that was driving young men and women out of the Irish rural districts; the lack of life and the lack of freedom there had much to do with emigration.'[43]

LENNOX ROBINSON AND IRISH REALISM

Both Ryan's exposure of municipal corruption and Colum's drama of tensions within the rural heartland were aspects of contemporary Ireland largely shunned by their immediate contemporaries. But what influenced the future direction of the drama was not so much the content of the broad spectrum of plays but the style of production that had been developed by the Fays. Lennox Robinson recorded his reaction to seeing the Abbey company in Cork in 1907: 'It came on me in a flash, as a revelation, that play-material could be found outside one's own door, at one's own fireside.' For while, he noted, 'the time of realistic Irish drama was yet to come [. . .]' these players behaved on the stage like human beings.' Accordingly, when he wrote *The Clancy Name* (1908) just a few months later, his objective was realism; the play, he said, was 'as harsh as the stones of West Cork, as realistic as the midden in front of an Irish farm-house'.[44]

The one-act play focuses on the day of Mrs Clancy's triumph in paying off a loan that enabled her to save the farm in the aftermath of her husband's death. Now her hopes are all for arranging a successful marriage for her son, John, and the ratification of the family's respectability. Her hopes are dashed, however, by John's admission that he is responsible for the death of a neighbour, a subject that has threaded its way through the conversations in the play. John's intention is to give himself up to the police, but Mrs Clancy attempts to dissuade him, and for reasons that are all to do with 'The Clancy Name': 'I'm not going to let you disgrace the family name, John. Think of your father's three brothers, all priests; think of your aunt married to a gentleman in Dublin; think of me, a poor widow woman, who's always been respected and looked up to by the neighbours.'[45] However, in a rapid sequence

---

[41] Frederick Ryan, *The Laying of the Foundations* in *Lost Plays of the Irish Renaissance*, ed. Robert Hogan and James Kilroy (Newark, DE: Proscenium Press, 1970), 32.

[42] Padraic Colum, *Three Plays: The Fiddler's House, The Land, Thomas Muskerry* (Boston, MA: Little, Brown, 1916), 130, 132.

[43] Ibid., vii.   [44] Robinson, *Curtain Up*, 18–19.

[45] Lennox Robinson, *Two Plays: Harvest; The Clancy Name* (Dublin: Maunsel, 1911), 76.

of off-stage events, John saves a child from being crushed by a runaway cart but allows himself to be struck fatally. He is carried back into the family home, where his dying words appear to be implicating him in the murder but, to Mrs Clancy's relief, he dies—a fact she greets 'with a terrible quiet satisfaction'.[46]

In Robinson's view, the significance of the play—and that of its successor, *The Cross Roads* (1909)—was that they 'brought for the first time on an Irish stage harsh reality. It was part and parcel of what the younger generation was beginning to think about Ireland.' While Robinson recognized that the cause of national liberation had demanded that they 'had to represent [themselves] to the world as the purest and noblest of people', now was also the moment when 'we must criticize ourselves ruthlessly'.[47] Reviews, however, were almost wholly negative, judging the play melodramatic and, in the case of the *Freeman's Journal*, 'a shocking and libellous picture' of Irish country people.[48] Despite these reactions, *The Clancy Name* ushered in what Robinson termed, 'a series of bitter, critical plays'.[49] For while national independence was the dominant item on the cultural and political agenda, the young realists were concerned with a society that sought political freedom while remaining oblivious to its own hypocrisy, corruption, and abuse of power. Consequently, as Ben Levitas argues, their plays foregrounded 'the material issues that had already begun to corrupt the clean lines of Irish cultural forecasting'.[50]

The Rise of the Realists

As evidenced by the list of productions collected in *The Rise of the Realists 1910–1915*, dramas such as those initiated by *The Clancy Name* were a significant, but not dominant, part of the plays staged not only at the Abbey but also by the Cork Dramatic Society, the Ulster Literary Theatre, and the Theatre of Ireland, the Dublin-based group that split from the National Theatre Society when Yeats abandoned its democratic origins and led the move to become a limited company.[51] But while Lady Gregory's comedies, plays such as Douglas Hyde's *The Tinker and the Fairy* (1912) or melodramas such as P. J. Bourke's *When Wexford Rose* (1913), continued to be produced, they lacked the power and immediacy of the realists, who eschewed romance, mysticism, and evocations of anti-colonial rebellions.

Irish realism was distinguished by a sense of moral outrage rather than any overt political agenda. It exposed the failings of the indigenous Irish—both the peasantry and the professional classes—rather than the excesses of the colonial elite. But irrespective of the social background of the main characters, the drama was frequently occasioned by

[46] Ibid., 83.   [47] Robinson, *Curtain Up*, 21–2.

[48] Robert Hogan and James Kilroy (eds.), *The Abbey Theatre: The Years of Synge, 1904–1909* (Dublin: Dolmen Press, 1978), 225.

[49] Robinson, *Curtain Up*, 21–2.

[50] Ben Levitas, *The Theatre of Nation: Irish Drama and Cultural Nationalism 1890–1916* (Oxford: Clarendon Press, 2002), 182.

[51] Robert Hogan, Richard Burnham, and Daniel P. Poteet, *The Modern Irish Drama*, vol. 4: *The Rise of the Realists 1910–1915* (Dublin: Dolmen Press, 1979), 442–73.

inter-generational conflict. This applied equally to plays staged by the Abbey, the Ulster Literary Theatre, and the Cork Dramatic Society. Rutherford Mayne's *The Turn of the Road*, which was produced in Belfast in 1906, lacks some of the harshness of the Cork Realists, but in his dramatization of the Granahans—the Co. Down farming family whose concern is for money and land consolidation through marriage, as opposed to their son, Robbie John, whose love is music—Mayne does stage a fundamental aspect of the realist view: that the old are mercenary while the young are idealistic. In Daniel Corkery's *Embers*, which was staged in Cork in 1909, this is given a specific political turn as the idealism of Lawrence Kiely is contrasted to the materialism of his father, William, whose only concern is that Lawrence's nationalist politics will affect his business. William accuses Lawrence of 'robbing and destroying us' and, when Lawrence expresses his bafflement at what this means, responds 'I'm talking about contracts, do you hear, half-year contracts. Do you know what I'm talking about? Is there a board or an institution in the whole country will ever look at me again?'[52] It is clear that William's contracts are acquired through bribery—a corruption in which his wife is complicit—and one of the driving moral imperatives of the realists was to force home the message that unless Irish society cleansed itself then its future, politically independent or otherwise, would be one of decline and degeneration. This is nowhere more directly addressed than in Seamus O'Kelly's *The Bribe* (1913), described by Robinson as 'a cold, taut work' on 'the bribery and corruption which too often plays its part in the making of public appointments in Ireland'.[53]

The Bribe dramatizes the election for the post of doctor to the Garrymore Union, a position for which Dr Power O'Connor is prepared to bribe the board's chairman, John Kirwan, to ensure that his son, Jack, succeeds him. The best man for the job, Dr Luke Diamond, has been brought up by his widowed mother who 'lived on slops and scraps'[54] to educate him, but she is despised by the middle-class Mrs Kirwan for her 'smell of herrings and onions'. Despite Luke's qualifications, he is unable to overcome the corruption and vested interests of the Irish middle class, who are engaged in abuses equivalent to English colonialism: 'When men talk of patriotism and then sell their votes they are the gets of that bribery and corruption which put this country upon the cross, crucified for over a hundred years.' Luke himself speaks of canvassing for the post and being made to feel like 'the slave of the past generation approaching the landlord'.[55] Dr O'Connor's reference to 'half-baked socialists like Diamond', and his condemnation of 'this immoral and deadly subdued rage that is continually seeking the overthrow of the established and even divine authority', makes clear that there were class-based political divisions in Irish society— a fact that became brutally clear in the Dublin Lockout which still preoccupied the city when the play premièred at the Abbey in December 1913. The consequences of appointing Jack Power are devastating, as his incompetence leads to the death in childbirth of Kirwan's wife and baby. This is the destruction of the future on both an individual and a national level, for, as Luke Diamond observes: 'The man who sells his vote today will sell

---

[52] Richard Burnham and Robert Hogan (eds.), *The Cork Dramatic Society: Lost Plays of the Irish Renaissance*, vol. 3 (Newark, DE: Proscenium Press, 1984), 28.

[53] Robinson, *Curtain Up*, 74.   [54] Seamus O'Kelly, *The Bribe* (Dublin: Maunsel, 1914), 41.

[55] Ibid., 3, 25, 8–9.

his soul to-morrow. The channels to public life must be kept open to the best intellects or there will be no progress.'[56]

The sense of a future blighted was a dominant concern of the realists, and the death of the younger generation is a frequent conclusion to a number of the plays—fatalities usually caused by the corruption, incompetence, or ingrained prejudices of the old. This is forcefully dramatized in St John Ervine's Belfast-set play *Mixed Marriage,* which was produced at the Abbey in March 1911. Praised by the *Irish Times* as a play 'that cuts right into a throbbing question which is of the gravest importance to every person in this country,'[57] it dramatizes the effect of religious sectarianism on the Protestant Rainey family at a time of industrial unrest. As later in Seán O'Casey's plays, the mother is full of practical humanity, judging that 'Cathlicks is jus like wurselves, as good as we are an' as bad as we are, an' no worse,'[58] while John Rainey, the father, although initially prepared to ignore his own prejudices and act as a voice of moderation in order to retain the unity of the striking workers, will not countenance the marriage of his son to a Catholic: 'A'm agin a man marryin' out o' his religion, an A'll stick til that no matter what happens.' As a consequence of his withdrawal from the action, the workers split along sectarian lines and a riot ensues in which Nora, the fiancée of Rainey's son, is killed. The play ends as Rainey, 'as if dreaming', mutters 'A was right. A know A wus riht.'[59]

While the play was seen as flawed—the Freeman's Journal arguing that St John Ervine 'has given us a satisfactory piece of propagandist work, but he has not given us a play'[60]— it does demonstrate many of the strengths of the realist movement; the dialogue has an uncompromising authenticity, and in its engagement with issues of politics and industrial action it comes closer than did many contemporary works to the semantic and political shift which Pascale Casanova argued led to the idea of the people as a class.[61] In the play, class-consciousness is destroyed by religious prejudice, but as the ending demonstrates, the audience is to learn from Rainey's befuddled assertion that he was right, and to think and act in opposition to those values.

The urban setting of *Mixed Marriage* was, however, an exception, as was its engagement with issues of industrial action. The majority of the realist plays focused on rural or small town settings where the dominant issues were those of mean-spirited materialism, hypocrisy, corruption, and callous indifference to the feelings of others. As starkly realized in Padraic Colum's *Thomas Muskerry* (1910), in which the eponymous protagonist is the ageing master of the workhouse in Garrisowen, a town where 'everybody's in debt to everyone else', this even involves members of one's own family, for Muskerry is at the point of retirement and his daughter is intent on acquiring his pension: 'We can't think of fifty pounds a year to go out of our house.'[62] The reviewer of the *Leader* saw her as possessing 'all the harshness of a Goneril or a Regan', and as in Shakespeare's play, the old man is destroyed by what *Sinn Féin*'s Ella Young described as his 'grasping daughter' and her 'incapable, inexorable family'.[63] Weakened by a stroke brought on from these pressures, Muskerry dies on a pauper's bed having suffered 'loss of my trust, the loss of my dignity, my self respect'.[64] The bleakness of these money-bound lives in which debt determines

[56] Ibid., 11, 13, 9.   [57] Hogan et al., *The Rise of the Realists,* 122.
[58] St John Ervine, *Mixed Marriage* (Dublin: Maunsel, 1911), 5.   [59] Ibid., 37, 55.
[60] Hogan et al., *The Rise of the Realists,* 122.   [61] See n. 16.
[62] Colum, *Three Plays,* 151, 162.
[63] Hogan et al., *The Rise of the Realists,* 28, 29.   [64] Colum, *Three Plays,* 197.

the nature of family relations is powerfully realized, and a society in which emotions are stunted is exposed, for the characters, as Young noted, are those 'one could find in any little decaying Irish town'.[65]

THE REALISM OF R. J. RAY

This laying bare of the denied side of Irish society is the dominant concern of the realists—nowhere more so than in the plays, all unpublished, of R. J. Ray, especially *The Casting Out of Martin Whelan*, staged at the Abbey in September 1910, and *The Gombeen Man*, performed by the Abbey company at the Royal Court Theatre, London, in November 1913. Martin Whelan is a wealthy Australian, the child of Irish emigrants, who comes to Ballintrosnan where he is looking to be elected as an MP. He is accepted until it is discovered that he is the grandson of Tim Magrath, who 'gave Crown evidence that put the rope around the neck of the man that shot Lord Morton's agent'. Now seen as 'the breed of the informer',[66] he is rejected by all except Ellen Barton, who is prepared to leave her family and marry him. Both Whelan and Ellen are seen as free of the narrow thinking of the town, and are scathing in their condemnations. Ellen refers to the 'little tin pot minds' and Whelan concludes, ''tis most likely we'll become a Nation some day, and if the Ballintrosnan mind is the Irish mind, 'twill be the sorry day for Ireland.' Ray's presentation of the nationalist council confirms the judgements of the young couple as he shows a world which is riddled with cronyism: a complaint about the building of a pump cannot be supported 'because the contract will go to Con Collins as true and sound a man as stands in Ballintrosnan', nor, for similar reasons, will they stop 'more clay than mortar going between the stones' in a new bridge.[67] The subsequent loss to Ireland of the young and intelligent echoes the conclusion of *The Bribe* from the same year, and in *The Gombeen Man* Ray goes even further in dramatizing a society whose future is tainted by the corruption of the powerful in its present.

Stephen Kiniry, the Gombeen Man, dominates Crutanmore by making loans and then acquiring farms and shops when his debtors are unable to pay. As he says of himself, 'I'm the man that's looked down upon and cursed and some would like to see me going to the gallows, and others would like to see me dead and damned.'[68] He seeks to disinherit his son, a man driven to drink through his father's abuses, by having a child with his second wife, whom he acquired through the mortgage he holds on her father's farm; but as she has not borne a child after four years of marriage he tries to drive her to suicide. However, his brutality has made her half-mad, and at the end of the play, with 'the pleasant light of madness in her eyes', she announces that she is pregnant but, as she

[65] Hogan et al., *The Rise of the Realists*, 29.
[66] R. J. Ray, *The Casting-Out of Martin Whelan* (prompt script), in National University of Ireland Galway, Abbey Theatre Digital Archive, 4300_PS_0001, 32.
[67] Ibid., 25, 55, 38, 39.
[68] R. J. Ray, *The Gombeen Man* (prompt script), National University of Ireland Galway, Abbey Theatre Digital Archiv 1599_PS_0001, 18.

has been told by an old beggar women, her madness will reappear in the baby. Kiniry has already been bested in business by the priest's brother, who has loaned money to one of Kiniry's debtors, and for reasons of cronyism rather than kindness ('for he knows what the priest and the bishop think of you, and being a builder, when the priest hears of this, I needn't tell you who'll get the contract for the new church on Mullane's Island'), and his future is now shadowed by the damaged birth-to-be. As his son says at the close of the play, 'there'll be bitterness and sorrow every day of your life till you're laid in Crutanmore.'[69] The play dramatizes the callousness of one individual, but the original title, *Gombeenism*, suggests a level of mercenary maliciousness which permeates the national psyche, leading not just to death but to degeneration, as the future is blighted by endemic levels of corruption.

There is no redemption offered in these plays; audiences are simply presented with the fallen state of their world. For the *Irish Times, The Casting Out of Martin Whelan* 'is an excellent political sermon, whose text is taken from life as we find it in Ireland',[70] and the play, like other contemporary realist works, does have an almost religious zeal to its denunciations: an exhortation to abandon sin or suffer. The condition of corruption tends to be a given, with the plays focusing on its consequences rather than mapping a causal chain from origins to outcomes; the faults are personal rather than structural, and in this sense the judgements are moral rather than political. As this will indicate, the realists were more concerned to chastise than analyse, and their impulse, in Ben Levitas's phrase, was 'to sour an already turning perception of Irish life'.[71] The most extreme example, which inverts all ideas of peasant purity, is T. C. Murray's bleak *Birthright* (1910), whose implication of all four members of the Morrisey family in the violent outcome to the drama suggests the House of Atreus, while the fratricidal conflict of Hugh and Shane evokes that of Cain and Abel: all set in '*The interior of a farmhouse kitchen in the County Cork*'.[72] Played out in two acts which move from evening to midnight, the play dramatizes the growing disgust of Bat Morrisey, the 'hard faced' father, with his elder son, Hugh, whom he judges to have a 'quare nature' 'with his sporting, an' his fiddling, an' his *ráméis* about the Irish' which takes precedence over work on the farm. Finally Bat determines to disinherit Hugh in favour of his younger son, Shane, whom Hugh accuses of being 'a grabber', while Shane gives vent to his pent-up anger at their childhood in which their mother always favoured Hugh, 'taking him to the town to see the fair an' the circus, an' leaving me at home thinking bitter things in my heart'. The brothers begin to struggle and, in a powerful on-stage climax, Shane strikes Hugh with a hurley: '*The latter tries to ward off the terrible blow, but without success. He is felled to the ground*' and Shane, '*dazed and horrified ... staggers out into the night*'.[73] As 'An Philibin' wrote in the *National Student*, 'in practically direct sequence we have been given *The Cross Roads, Thomas Muskerry, Harvest, The Casting Out of Martin Whelan*, plays the power of which no one may deny; but also eminently depressing. It remains to state that *Birthright* is temperamentally in close agreement with its predecessors.'[74]

[69] Ibid., 74, 54, 79.   [70] Hogan et al., *The Rise of the Realists*, 43.
[71] Levitas, *Theatre and Nation*, 183.
[72] T. C. Murray, *Selected Plays*, ed. Richard Allen Cave (Gerrards Cross: Colin Smythe, 1998), 29.
[73] Ibid., 34, 55, 57.   [74] Hogan et al., *The Rise of the Realists*, 49.

'AREN'T THE PICTURES LOVELY?'
THE DECLINE OF IRISH REALISM

Robinson was a key figure in many of these productions, directing *Mixed Marriage, The Gombeen Man, The Bribe, Thomas Muskerry*, and his own *Harvest* (1910). However, his commitment to criticism had demonstrably subsided by the time of *The Whiteheaded Boy* (1916), whose amiable attitude to the Geoghegans—the play's family—is established in its set directions:

> Aren't the pictures lovely? They're all enlarged photographs of William's family. That's William himself over the chimney-piece, and that's his brother that died in Boston hanging between the window and the door. The priest in the plush frame is Father Maguire, no relation, but a lovely man.[75]

As Robinson acknowledges, there was a brief return of social criticism in Seán O'Casey's Dublin Trilogy (1923–6) when 'The bubble of false sentimentality which we Cork realists had pricked years before was beginning to be blown up again', but the impetus was largely over'.[76] In his 1942 autobiography, Robinson named his realist colleagues Murray, Ray, and O'Kelly, and then added, 'one could continue the list to the point of boredom.'[77] This dismissive attitude towards the drama of social criticism of which he was a key member is confirmed in *Drama at Inish* (1933), which is set in the Seaview Hotel, run by John Twohig, who is also the owner of the Pavilion, the town's theatre. In an attempt to improve the fortunes of the town in the summer season he invites the De La Mare Repertory Company rather than the 'too vulgar altogether' comic troupes about which there had been complaints.[78] Dedicated to 'the great plays of Russia, an Ibsen or two, a Strindberg', the company has a devastating effect, leading audiences to socially destabilizing responses to the plays. Hector De La Mare is delighted: 'We have lifted the stone, we have exposed Inish … it's wonderful. We have a mission here, a duty.' But his enthusiasm is countered by Mrs Twohig's assertion that 'we were all more or less happy and comfortable, good tempered and jolly—until these plays began to put ideas into our heads', and the company's contract is terminated, their place taken by a circus. The play closes as the music of the circus band is heard and 'the room is flooded with sunshine'. As John Twohig declares to his wife: 'We've put back the old stone, Lizzie, thank God.'[79]

In *The Wretched of the Earth*, Frantz Fanon noted that 'the behaviour of the national landed proprietors is practically identical with that of the middle classes of the towns', and that both, rather than putting their resources at the disposal of the people, act in 'the shocking ways' of the traditional bourgeoisie, using 'class aggressiveness' to benefit only themselves.[80] The realists staged this 'national bourgeoisie', but, while they suggested the

---

[75] Lennox Robinson, *Selected Plays*, ed. Christopher Murray (Gerrards Cross: Colin Smythe, 1982), 66.

[76] Robinson, *Curtain Up*, 140.   [77] Ibid., 22.   [78] Robinson, *Selected Plays*, 205.

[79] Ibid., 207, 252, 251, 255.

[80] Frantz Fanon, *The Wretched of the Earth* (Harmondsworth: Penguin, 1967), 121–5.

FIG. 7.1 *Time's Pocket* by Frank O'Connor (Abbey Theatre, 26 December 1938). Even when designed by the innovative Tanya Moiseiwitsch, the realist country kitchen set for plays such as this could have served equally well for numerous other Abbey plays of the period.

Courtesy of the Abbey Theatre and James Hardiman Library, NUI Galway.

FIG. 7.2 *Killycreggs in Twilight* by Lennox Robinson (Abbey Theatre, 19 April 1937). Set designer Tanya Moiseiwitsch tried to give the set a stylized touch, but there was little escaping the essentially realist aesthetic of the play.

Courtesy of the Abbey Theatre and James Hardiman Library, NUI Galway.

negative national consequences of such behaviour, their condemnation did not develop into analysis, Robinson simply commenting that the characters in their plays 'were for the most part avaricious, mean, drunken, brutal'.[81] It was not until decades later that Tom Murphy staged characters who were the products of history, dramatizing Kevin Whelan's

---

[81] Robinson, *Curtain Up*, 21.

view that '[a] certain amount of iron entered the Irish soul in the Famine holocaust',[82] with a brutal focus on self-survival being the result. In the interim, while realism as a style of production continued to dominate Irish theatre, the generation that 'shrank from nothing' progressively came to accept that a country concerned with independent statehood was not committed to self-criticism and self-correction, especially as the class largely subjected to the wrath of the realists was also the dynamo of independence. As Ireland progressed towards independence, 'a society dominated by farmers and their offspring in the professions and in trade, believed that they had come at last into their rightful inheritance',[83] and realism degenerated into a verisimilitude of the surface, far removed from its original impulse: when playwrights felt that 'we must criticize ourselves ruthlessly.'[84]

[82] Kevin Whelan, 'Pre and Post-Famine Landscape Change', in Cathal Póirtéir (ed.), *The Great Irish Famine* (Dublin: Mercier Press, 1995), 32.

[83] Terence Brown, *Ireland: A Social and Cultural History 1922–1985* (London: Fontana, 1981), 99.

[84] Robinson, *Curtain Up*, 21.

CHAPTER 8

MODERNISM AND IRISH THEATRE 1900-1940

RICHARD CAVE

Towards a Definition of Modernism

THE terms 'modernism' and 'modernist' (as distinct from 'modernity' and 'modern') seem to aim at precise definition as descriptors of early twentieth-century cultural change. However, a survey of the ways in which the terms over time have been applied shows that, far from achieving exactitude of discrimination, they tend to be elastic to the point of being opaque and nebulous. In the sphere of drama, both as text and in performance, what overtly stylistic features would Strindberg, Maeterlinck, Wedekind, Claudel, Pirandello, Artaud, Brecht, and Lorca (to take a random sample) appear to have in common, though each has regularly been termed a modernist playwright? As a perusal of the online catalogue of any library's holdings under the heading of 'modernism' will show, the term is consistently deployed in relation to the widest range of manifestations of cultural and social endeavour, from architecture, poetry, and the novel, through dance, painting, philosophy, music, forms of political resistance, journalism, fashion, feminism, furniture styles, ethics, literary editing, translation, to history, the body in space, and politics; and this list does not include volumes devoted to specific authors, artists, or designers, or to specific national cultures. (My sample relates simply to the acquisitions made by the London Library between 2010 and 2014.)

No form of cultural change happens conveniently overnight, so there is inevitably considerable disagreement in volumes devoted to aspects of modernism over how precisely to date the origins of such a process of change. In the context of Irish theatre, should one, for example, include discussion of Wilde or Shaw, seeing that, though of Irish descent, they pursued their respective careers as dramatists in England? Should one consider Yeats a modernist playwright from the time in 1913 when he worked in Stone Cottage with Ezra Pound (deemed by many the high priest of literary modernism) and discovered Japanese Noh?[1] If so, how would one designate earlier plays, such as *The Land of Heart's Desire* or

---

[1] See James Longenbach, *Stone Cottage: Pound, Yeats, and Modernism* (Oxford: Oxford University Press, 1988).

The Shadowy Waters (both subsequently revised heavily but dating from 1894), which clearly demonstrate the influence of Maeterlinck and Villiers de l'Isle Adam, exponents of Symbolism, a style that cultural and literary critics have generally termed modernist?

To ease a mounting sense of confusion, perhaps it would help to list some of the recurring features that critics and historians have detected in works they give this label:

- a crisis of confidence in all forms of authority, literary, artistic, political, and social (even in the authority of the actual creator and the tyranny within theatre of established conventions and audiences' expectation of the intellectual comfort to be derived from such conventions being adhered to as traditional);
- as a consequence of the former point, a stylistic preoccupation with techniques of dislocation, fragmentation, ironic juxtapositions and montage, abstraction, stylization, minimalism, avoidance of closure within forms, and a consequent embracing of silence, uncertainty, the void;
- an engagement with myth as informing the complexities of the present;
- a focus on interiority and forms of consciousness, since exterior modes of shaping and organizing experience were deemed wanting;
- the extension of this focus into darker, more threatening modes for exploring identity (symbolism, expressionism, existentialism, surrealism, absurdism);
- an imperative within all forms of art and applied art to examine, dissect, or interrogate the fundamental nature of the medium (the resulting self-reflexivity in theatre provoked an enthusiasm for parody and pastiche, a deliberate confusing of what previously were deemed 'high' and 'low' genres, games with diversity of style, and a confident evolution of new devices of meta-theatre);
- the cultivation of international perspectives, influences, and contacts which extended beyond Europe to America, Africa, Polynesia, and the Far East.

Needless to say, all such traits were pursued in a spirit of fierce iconoclasm and resistance to the work of an immediately preceding generation. To judge by this list alone, it is not surprising to find a recent Oxford Handbook on the subject choosing to refer not to modernism but to modernisms.[2]

THE IRISH THEATRICAL CONTEXT

Resistance had long been a feature of Irish drama well before the onset of modernism: under English colonial rule, English cultural values had held sway, dictating acceptable literary and theatrical styles, forms, and plot structures. From the date of the Roman Catholic

[2] See Peter Brooker, Andrzej Gasiorek, Deborah Longworth, and Andrew Thacker (eds.), *The Oxford Handbook of Modernisms* (Oxford: Oxford University Press, 2010). Of the wealth of critical literature studied in preparing this chapter, the most informative and influential have been the following: Malcolm Bradbury and James McFarlane (eds.), *Modernism: A Guide to European Literature 1890–1930* (Harmondsworth: Penguin, 1976); Gabriel Josipovici, *The Lessons of Modernism* (Basingstoke: Macmillan, 1977); Christopher Butler, *Modernism: A Very Short Introduction*

Relief Act, passed by the English Parliament in 1829, actor-dramatists of the likes of Tyrone Power (1787–1841) and Dion Boucicault (1820–90) began subtly to undermine the structures and conventions of melodrama and comedy to encourage audiences to sympathize morally with a range of Irish sensibilities; the strategy in both instances carried political intent.[3] Wilde worked within this tradition, manipulating the devices of traditional comedy of manners repeatedly to expose the depths of hypocrisy latent in upper-class English society, implicitly questioning their fitness for rule. In the process he deliberately redeemed from ignominy and abjection several stereotypes vilified by contemporary playwriting: the woman with a past in Mrs Erlynne in *Lady Windermere's Fan* (1892), the fallen woman in Mrs Arbuthnot in *A Woman of No Importance* (1893), the dandified man-about-town in Lord Goring in *The Ideal Husband* (1895). Wilde's comedies eschew earnest moral judgement in favour of breadth of understanding, and so offer a critique of English cultural values.[4] Where Wilde ran stylish rings round English assumptions of moral authority, Shaw used comedy to run circles round English pretensions to intellectual superiority, exposing how their confidently emphatic assertions of what they viewed as right thinking were just so much bombast and hot air. From *Widowers' Houses* (1892) through *Man and Superman* (published 1903, staged 1905), *John Bull's Other Island* (1904), and *Major Barbara* (1905), to *Heartbreak House* (written 1916–17, published 1919, staged 1920) and beyond, Shaw found rich humour in the capacity of English men (but rarely English women, who are generally characterized as far more pragmatic) to convince themselves that what in fact best serves their own self-interest is the highest form of philanthropy. Broadbent in *John Bull's Other Island* may stand as representative: he is a prize ass, his bombast is shocking for its want of sensitivity, but he relentlessly gets his way in Ireland financially, socially, and emotionally, while those with whom he is doing business are laughing uproariously at his total lack of self-awareness. And it is not an act on his part. Broadbent is no manipulating stage Machiavellian; rather, as Shaw presents him, he is a complete innocent and his innocence is lethal.

There is no denying the political commitment underpinning the dramaturgical strategies in Wilde and Shaw, but it is arguable whether such strategies might be labelled 'modernist'. An exception may be made perhaps for Shaw's fantasy plays, such as *Back to Methuselah* (1922) and *Too True To Be Good* (1932), on account of their games with style, illogical progressions in plotting, and in the latter case an ending which, by showing the ever-loquacious Aubrey prosing on and on till silenced only by the descent of an impenetrable fog, seems to anticipate Beckett's characters and their absurd posturings before the void, especially Lucky's solipsistic monologue in *Waiting for Godot*. Chiefly, Wilde and Shaw have too great a need of the forms they are subverting and of the particular audience expectations that such forms invite to consider breaking with those formal moulds in a serious, iconoclastic fashion. Rather, their preferred way is to tease audiences into new levels of awareness, to take them by surprise when they have rendered them vulnerable

(Oxford: Oxford University Press, 2010); and Michael Levenson (ed.), *The Cambridge Companion to Modernism*, 2nd edn. (Cambridge: Cambridge University Press, 2011).

  3 See Richard Allen Cave, 'Staging the Irishman', in J. S. Bratton (ed.), *Acts of Supremacy* (Manchester: Manchester University Press, 1991), 62–128.

  4 See Richard Allen Cave, 'Wilde's Comedies', in Mary Luckhurst (ed.), *A Companion to Modern British and Irish Drama: 1880–2005* (Oxford: Blackwell, 2006), 213–24.

through laughter; their way is not to astound, scandalize, disconcert, or offend. They are more accurately seen as precursors of modernism—which is not an observation one would choose to make of their younger contemporary, Yeats.

W. B. Yeats as Modernist Playwright

In founding the Irish Literary Theatre with Lady Gregory and Edward Martyn in 1899, Yeats was determined to establish a company and repertoire that owed nothing to English influence or personnel, though it was not until the opening of the Abbey Theatre in 1904 that this objective was fully realized.[5] But it was not his enterprising involvement with theatre business that propelled Yeats into modernism, but rather his independent and personal quest to create a stage for poetry, though from his early experiments with the otherworldly nuances of Symbolism it was clear that Yeats would always work to accommodate such influences as Maeterlinck's plays within decidedly Irish contexts and themes.[6] His was a relentless quest for an original dramatic form that would allow for a concentrated focus on the interior being of his characters, one where the surface realism favoured by most contemporary dramaturgy could be pared away, allowing audiences 'to pass for a moment into a deep of the mind that had hitherto been too subtle for [their] habitation'.[7] Believing staunchly in the value of tradition, Yeats turned first to the medieval morality drama as filtered through Marlowe's *Doctor Faustus* for *The Hour-Glass* (1903) to examine the consciousness of an atheist at the point of death; then to Shakespearean tragic structuring with *On Baile's Strand* (staged 1904), with its independent but complementary levels of plotting to define the complexities of Cuchulain's self-awareness at the moment he realizes he has slain his own son; and in *Deirdre* (staged 1906), to the greater concentration allowed by Racine's neoclassical focus on the climactic moments of a tragic action to depict Deirdre's choice of one of several possibilities for ending her story 'right' in a manner that will satisfyingly ensure her status in myth.[8] Such forms, however, were familiar, not strange enough to disturb spectators, troubling them with the sense of suddenly inhabiting otherness. That dimension came with Yeats's discovery in 1913 of Japanese Noh theatre with its minimalist staging techniques, sung dialogue, choric utterance, masks, and dance, all in the service of communicating a poetic text poetically and symbolically. (Noh possessed a dramaturgy and stagecraft that had the sharp precision and immediacy of the dream state, quite distinct from the emotional vagaries and threatening indeterminacies of Maeterlinck's Symbolism.)

That Yeats well understood the form and significance of Noh as text and performance is evident from his essay 'Certain Noble Plays of Japan';[9] but his own practice, which

---

[5] There were but few exceptions to this stricture over the years, notably Florence Darragh, Mrs Patrick Campbell, Ben Iden Payne, Hugh Hunt, and Tanya Moiseiwitsch.

[6] For an alternative discussion of Yeats's relationship with modernism in the theatre, see Ch. 5; for a wider discussion of the impact of European modernism in Irish theatre of the early twentieth century, see Chs. 3 and 6.

[7] W. B. Yeats, *Essays and Introductions* (London: Macmillan, 1961), 225.

[8] W. B. Yeats, *Variorum Edition of the Plays*, ed. Russell K. Alspach (London: Macmillan, 1966), 377.

[9] Published originally as the introduction to a selection of Noh plays 'from the manuscripts of Ernest Fenollosa, chosen and finished by Ezra Pound', *Certain Noble Plays of Japan* (Dundrum:

culminated in *Four Plays for Dancers*, moulded the constituent features of his Japanese model wholly to suit his creative needs while always retaining the hieratic quality of Noh in performance. Immediately he began to experiment with changing an actor's mask in view of the audience (*The Only Jealousy of Emer*, published 1919, not performed in Yeats's lifetime) or surrounding a human face with masked actors (*The Dreaming of the Bones*, published 1919, performed 1931). However, it was the potential of the danced component that he extended beyond its function in the Japanese prototype, where it tends to depict the central character's realization in joy, sorrow, or horror of his or her future destiny. In Yeats's plays dance tends to be more dynamic, an enacting of a process of psychological change too profound for verbal definition; and the dance involves more than one participant. In *At The Hawk's Well* Cuchulain is lured by the Hawk-Woman's patterns of movement to follow her, as if mesmerized, to choose a heroic future over longevity but mindful of what he is sacrificing in consequence. In *The Only Jealousy of Emer*, Fand, the sea goddess, tries by encircling Cuchulain to win him to obey her will and follow a life of sensual oblivion; but the danced sequence is presented as a play within the play that is watched by his wife, Emer, who is moved by what she witnesses to sacrifice her own future emotional security to free him from Fand's wiles. The dance provokes Emer to triumph over her deep-rooted jealousy, which is as restrictive of Cuchulain's integrity as Fand's erotic scheming. Similarly, the dance which expresses all the misery and frustration of Diarmuid and Dervorgilla at being condemned throughout eternity to be judged rather than understood is not itself the climax of *The Dreaming of the Bones*; rather, it is how the repetitive cycles of the dance excite the young gunman watching the ghostly lovers to assert his nationalist beliefs and suppress his instinct for compassion. The Roman soldiers, relatively minor characters in *Calvary*, exuberantly rollick around Christ's cross in a display of wild, mindless energy that challenges the Messiah's altruistic sense of purposeful mission in which his whole identity has been invested till now. What interests Yeats, and what his dramaturgy captures, is less a state of psychological completion than a process of transition, a moment of inner change.

This detailed examination of the principal features of Yeatsian dance-drama has been a necessary prelude to appraising how they map onto the templates, given above, that determine modernism. There is here no direct imitation of a European theatrical model (though Noh shares some clear elements with classical Greek tragedy); and no attempt to flatter an audience's expectations or values (the audience is required to work to shape meaning throughout the performance, and so is required to share in the creative process; instead of offering authoritatively precise guidance as to meaning, Yeats invites spectators to make of a performance what they will). Theatrical realism is resolutely avoided, given Yeats's deployment of sung dialogue for the choruses of Musicians who frame and comment on the action, intimating but never directing ways of interpreting what is being played out; his use of masks (all the productions Yeats oversaw favoured full-head masks) or, for the Musicians, mask-like make-up; his dependence on minimalist staging and stylized props

Cuala Press, 1916); it was subsequently included in W. B. Yeats, *The Cutting of an Agate* (London: Macmillan, 1919) and in *Essays and Introductions* (London: Macmillan, 1961), 221–37. It can also be found in *Collected Works*, vol. iv, *Early Essays*, ed. Richard J. Finneran and George Bornstein (New York: Scribner, 2007), 163–73. See also W. B. Yeats, *Four Plays for Dancers* (London: Macmillan, 1921).

(the well presided over by the Hawk-Woman is to be represented by a small square of blue cloth, while the stage curtain is replaced by a token cloth which the Musicians unfold and refold to mark the beginning and the end of the action); the use of a variety of poetic forms for stage dialogue that owe nothing to Shakespearean blank verse; the bold intrusion of direct address to spectators by the Musicians; and Yeats's increasing reliance on extended sequences of dance rather than spoken text as his chosen medium of expression at times of the greatest psychological and emotional intensity, which are approached through calculated modes of stylization. Most of these strategies and formal devices are deliberately meta-theatrical, as Yeats delights in confronting spectators with startling experiences of otherness.

Three of the plays contain highly meta-theatrical experiences of a play-within-the-play, at once an emblem of moving yet further into an interior world and a self-reflexive challenge

FIG. 8.1 Edmund Dulac's design for the Guardian of the Well in W. B. Yeats's *At the Hawk's Well*. Published in *Four Plays for Dancers* by W. B. Yeats (London: Macmillan, 1921).

to spectators about how they shape their own responses to what they view, since they enter and watch that world along with a responsive onstage audience. The focus throughout is on movements of consciousness; but the medium used for such an exploration is action not within the contemporary world of naturalism or realism but in the seemingly distanced world of myth, which is suddenly made more immediate by the extreme theatricality of the presentation than would be the case if Yeats had resorted to a more traditional, narrative-based dramaturgy. Clearly, most of the criteria that define a work as modernist are met by the *Four Plays for Dancers*.

EXPERIMENTAL THEATRE IN DUBLIN 1920–1930

Yeats was to work variations on the pattern of these dance plays for most of his future career as playwright, expanding (*The Words upon the Window-Pane*, 1930) or refining (*The King of the Great Clock Tower*, 1934) on the components, as if eager to experiment, continually pushing the form to new limits, the better to define more intricate depths of consciousness (social, sexual, and political). Yeats's own international venture drew unprecedentedly on a rarefied Asian dramaturgy, but he was ever-conscious of the need for a national theatre such as the Abbey had become to embrace drama from a wide international spectrum, both to keep audiences fully conversant with styles of theatre practice and to offer creative stimulus to Irish dramatists. To this end he gave his support to Lennox Robinson in founding the Dublin Drama League as a kind of experimental club theatre that flourished between 1919 and 1941, in which subscriber–members decided policy and elected a play-selection committee, and a further committee to oversee performances by visiting companies.[10] Over seventy productions were mounted, generally for two performances only on Sunday and Monday nights when the Abbey was otherwise closed; staging the plays gave younger Abbey actors, male and female, a chance at direction, while performing in them helped expand the actors' technical and vocal skills.The range of dramatists is impressive: Andreyev, Chekhov, Benavente, Strindberg, Schnitzler, Sudermann, O'Neill, Lenormand, Claudel, Pirandello, Shaw, Molnár, Glaspell, Flecker, Toller, Cocteau, T. S. Eliot, Wilde, and Buchner (as well as stagings of Yeats's dance plays, Euripides' tragedies, and try-outs for St John Hankin, Blanaid Salkeld, and Lord Dunsany).[11]

European and American modernism had certainly come to Dublin; but productions of expressionist plays—the one major, modernist theatrical style to impact on theatres throughout both continents after the Great War—were noticeably limited before 1930 in the League's repertory to plays by Toller and O'Neill. The situation was remedied after

[10] There had been sporadic attempts by Robinson to broaden the Abbey's own repertoire—e.g. in 1913 plays by Hauptmann, Strindberg, and Tagore were included in bills alongside Irish plays—but these were random and exceptional cases.

[11] For an account of the Dublin Drama League and full listing of productions, see Brenna Katz Clarke and Harold Ferrar, *The Dublin Drama League: 1919–1941* (Dublin: Dolmen Press, 1979); also Robert Hogan and Richard Burnham, *The Years of O'Casey 1921–1926* (Gerrards Cross: Colin Smythe, 1992). From 1929 performances grew less frequent (there had been 4–6 meetings annually till then) and were now sometimes at the Torch Theatre or the Gate Theatre rather than the Abbey.

the establishing of the Gate Theatre in October 1928 by Hilton Edwards and Micheál Mac Liammóir; there had been less publicized, often amateur groups like Dramick and the New Players, whom Denis Johnston affectionately recalled staging 'Ireland's first expressionist productions in the drawing rooms of private houses with the aid of a complicated set of curtains, wires, cardboard boxes, and sheets of beaver board, worthy of Heath Robinson'.[12] Edwards and Mac Liammóir by comparison were fiercely professional. Expressionism, however, had begun influencing Seán O'Casey and Johnston's playwriting before this. Both men were resident in London in 1926, regularly attending performances at Peter Godfrey's Gate Theatre Studio in Covent Garden (the formative model too for Edwards and Mac Liammóir's policy and values), which as another club venue, opening in October 1925, staged German and American expressionist dramas otherwise banned by the British censor alongside highly iconoclastic revivals of established classics.[13]

Seán O'Casey as Modernist Playwright

It would be wrong to suggest that O'Casey's engagement with the tenets of expressionism dates from his encounter with Godfrey's theatre in London: *The Plough and the Stars*, which deploys overtly expressionist techniques from its second act onwards, was after all staged in February 1926 and completed some time before then. Writing that year of his friend's style, Johnston is categorical, stating: 'it is becoming more and more clear that as a realist he is an impostor', and arguing that his drama is 'far too pregnant with meaning to be bound by the four dismal walls of orthodox realism'.[14] This is perceptive. In *The Shadow of a Gunman* (1923) eerie bursts of supernatural knocking undermine Davoren and Shields' pretensions to heroism and build up an ominous tension, disrupting the surface realism of the action as it moves to its climax. The setting for *Juno and the Paycock* (1924) takes on a symbolic relation to the characters' fortunes: from a realist presentation of a drab tenement, it transforms into a parody of a bourgeois parlour that epitomizes Juno's pathetic aspirations to gentility, before being stripped to become a stark impersonal void, the tragic emblem of the dysfunctional family she has struggled to hold meaningfully together. Throughout *The Plough and the Stars*, expressionist strategies intrude into the realistic presentation of the characters' private lives to show how external militaristic, nationalist, and political agencies lay waste people's efforts at creating a modicum of private security (Nora's carefully nurtured love nest; the pub as a congenial haven for their menfolk; Bessie's attic refuge from the street fighting below). Those external forces, in exceeding the limits of realism, define its shortcomings. Another mode of presentation is required, and hence the vastly distorted image of the Speaker urging Dubliners to

[12] Denis Johnston, 'The Making of the Theatre', in Bulmer Hobson (ed.), *The Gate Theatre Dublin* (Dublin: Gate Theatre, 1934), 12–14. The Gate seasons started in the Peacock Theatre at the Abbey, but moved to their premises in Cavendish Row for their third season in February 1930.

[13] See 'Peter Godfrey and the Gate', in Norman Marshall, *The Other Theatre* (London: John Lehmann, 1947), 42–52.

[14] Denis Johnston, 'Sean O'Casey: An Appreciation (1926)', in Ronald Ayling (ed.), *Sean O'Casey: Modern Judgements* (London: Macmillan, 1969), 85.

rebellion that repeatedly dominates the setting in the pub or the amplified voices and gunshots of the English Tommies that surround and eventually take callous and casual possession of Bessie's room in the final scene. Throughout all three plays there are for spectators deeply unsettling inconsistencies of tone, shifts between a painful seriousness and at times a music-hall gaiety. Nothing in these characters' lives (or in the ways that O'Casey chooses to present them) can be viewed with certainty: mutability prevails; the characters' attempts to determine their existence prove futile and their near-wilful jollity is exposed as absurd. This is a calculated, hybrid style in which the disjunctions are deliberate and the underlying objective is determinedly political.

Johnston in his 'Appreciation' drew an informative comparison: 'Like Toller, he [O'Casey] is a poet of the revolution, and his chiefest and only concern is the sordid misery of the common people.'[15] Toller's most-performed play throughout Europe in the 1920s bore the significant title *Masses and Man*, and concerned the fate of the individual trapped within the limiting confines of his or her class.[16] This was similarly the theme of the other German expressionist work to impact on O'Casey, Georg Kaiser's *From Morn to Midnight* (written in 1912, staged 1917), with which Godfrey had had a conspicuous success at the Gate in London in 1926; it is the theme too of O'Casey's first overtly expressionist play, *The Silver Tassie*, a significant change in style that led to the rejection of the play by Yeats and the Abbey in 1928. Shaw greeted its production by Charles Cochrane at the Apollo Theatre, London, in November 1929 as 'a famous achievement', writing ecstatically that the play epitomized 'a new drama rising from unplumbed depths to sweep the nice little bourgeois efforts of myself and my contemporaries into the dustbin'.[17] Comparisons with German models can be extended only so far, however: the language and vision of the second act, especially, which evokes life in the trenches in the Great War, are wholly unique. The soldiers' dialogue embraces parodied quotations from a wealth of working-class cultural influences: snatches of popular song and nursery-style rhymes and rhythms, bursts of music hall repartee, fragments of the Bible, and a black parody of the Mass are interspersed with the dreary meandering speech of the totally exhausted, crass exhortations of establishment figures, cries of the dying, and embarrassed orders from the men's leaders. The spiritual abjection of the soldiers is paramount, as they inhabit a broken landscape that resembles an image from Dante's *Inferno*.[18] The power of O'Casey's conception for this scene gives a greater purposefulness to the shifting tones of his customary dialogue in the two ensuing acts, where audiences observe men wounded physically and mentally struggling to find a place again in 'ordinary' life, while their relations and friends are desperate to find the right tone with which to converse with them. The dark qualities of the dialogue now have a direct reference point back to the horror of the trenches, while the moments of gaiety seem forced, anxious, embarrassed, thoughtless, or plain uncaring. The dramaturgy may move through discordant styles, but the conception of the play overall has a precise organic structure.

[15] Ibid., 84.
[16] Toller's play was first staged brilliantly by Jürgen Fehling at the Berlin Volksbühne in 1921 and by the Dublin Drama League in 1925.
[17] The letter was published in *The Times* (London), 26 Nov. 1929.
[18] The setting of the Apollo production was created by Augustus John in response to O'Casey's directions.

There is no denying the modernist credentials of *The Silver Tassie*: O'Casey has evolved a dramatic speech that owes nothing to realism for Act II, which percolates into the remaining acts of the play, so that the aim is wholly subversive politically in treating the impoverished with insight and seriousness of intent. The presentation of the conditions undergone by the lower classes is an indictment, informed by O'Casey's Marxism, of all forms of authority that foster the continuance of such ways of life; the style is fragmented, experimenting with diverse performance modes that are sharply juxtaposed to effect a political, social, and emotional commentary on the action; the subject, the sufferings of the working classes throughout the Great War, is of international reference; and international too is O'Casey's engagement with German expressionism, though the influences undergo a sea change into a uniquely Irish manifestation. Though this is not seemingly a play about the interior lives of the characters, O'Casey does contrive a dramatic means to imply through the structuring of his action an interiority for his central character, Harry Heegan (even if Harry lacks the intellectual and verbal means to articulate his miseries), which finally shapes his great cry of outrage: 'The Lord has given and man hath taken away!'[19] His life has been a vast betrayal of his virility and humanity.

O'Casey's next two plays, written in self-imposed exile in England after the Abbey's rejection of *The Silver Tassie*, develop his interest in expressionism into a markedly more schematic and oppositional dramaturgy. *Within the Gates* (1934), for example, has four acts in which each is set at four different times of day from dawn to dusk and in a different season from spring to winter; the same groupings of characters (all visitors to a large public park) drift by or settle on the benches and we learn of their mostly petty preoccupations, while a plot of sorts is intimated about the paternal relationship of a bishop to a young woman who, threatened with heart trouble, is pressingly anxious to find a partner and conceive a child. It would seem a satirical exercise veering between social comedy and the sentimentally tragic were it not for the sense of threat occasioned by an audience's growing awareness that the play is set during the Great Depression. A band of down-and-outs invade the stage and try to envelop the body of the dying woman, but they are fended off by the monumental figure of the grieving bishop and a young poet, who has cared for her and uses all his strength of purpose to prevent her being assimilated in her dying into anonymity. It is a strangely period piece, modernist in method but weakened by a lack of focus (Jannice, the young woman, never attains a status in the action comparable to Harry Heegan's in *The Silver Tassie*); the darker allegorical purpose of the action is not established soon enough to prevent the central group of characters from appearing to be caught up in sentimental melodrama.

Equally schematic, and deliberately so, is *The Star Turns Red* (1940), an anti-fascist morality play, which shows the struggle between the Red Guards, the militant wing of the trade union movement representing the political interests of the proletariat, and the Saffron Shirts, a fascist army representing the establishment supported by the Catholic Church.[20] The setting is dominated by two vast windows, through one of which spectators see a representation of looming factory chimneys belching smoke and occasionally fire,

[19] Sean O'Casey, *Collected Plays*, vol. 2 (London: Macmillan, 1949), 102.
[20] The play was not staged at the Abbey Theatre until directed by Tomás Mac Anna in 1978.

while through the other appears a church spire, overhung by a vast star (it is Christmas and the star is the Star of Bethlehem). Civil war in the community is patterned by a breakdown in family relations ending in murder. By the end the star has moved to hang over the chimneys and steadily turns red throughout the final scene, as a priest breaks rank with his superior to come to the comfort of the grieving poor. The constituent elements hang more cogently together here: the colour coding helps clarify the political allegiances of a large cast of characters; the two sides voice the opposed styles of rhetoric that propel them into action, but do so around tableaux depicting various states of desperation experienced by the central family which demand humanitarian rather than cerebral responses. Verse supplants prose when individuals take on representative, choric status; music and song are used to enhance an audience's perception of the nature of the two warring parties; music-hall style patter and comic 'business' are deployed to belittle the self-aggrandizing pretensions of the establishment figures, who rely on the Saffron Shirts to protect their interests. Through all the conflict passes the self-possessed figure of Red Jim, Union Leader, keen-eyed observer, calming and consoling sympathizer, who asserts the rights of man (even when seemingly facing defeat) over the demands of the Church or any institution that demoralizes and demonizes working men and their families. The play, which is highly theatrical in its chosen modes of presentation, is a moving reflection on the emotional and political turmoil that defined the Thirties. Its success, compared with *Within the Gates*, derives from the fact that, in performance, it is a densely layered experience for spectators: a political play that is also a family drama; a moral allegory that relies on a powerful symbolism; an appeal for left-wing solidarity that uses a panoply of expressionist effects to communicate its urgency. That layering determines the play's modernism.

DENIS JOHNSTON AS MODERNIST PLAYWRIGHT

Layering strategies are the key to the dramaturgy of Denis Johnston, arguably the most experimental of Irish playwrights before 1940. A glance through the range of his plays shows that he could command a great variety of styles from realism (*The Moon in the Yellow River*, 1931; *Storm Song*, 1934; *The Scythe and the Sunset*, 1958) to whimsical comedy (*The Golden Cuckoo*, staged 1939, revised 1956); from translations of German expressionism (*Blind Man's Buff*, 1936, an adaptation of Toller's *The Blind Goddess*, which Johnston later transformed into an Irish murder mystery in the realist mode, *Strange Occurrence on Ireland's Eye*, staged 1956) to a morality play that is also an exercise in historical realism, interrogating the life of Swift (*The Dreaming Dust*, staged 1940); and he was a master of satire, parody, and pastiche. However, the two plays directed by Hilton Edwards at the Dublin Gate Theatre Studio are his major contribution to Irish modernism: *The Old Lady Says 'No!'* (staged 1929, but many times revised thereafter) and *A Bride for the Unicorn* (1933).

The first is an interior drama in a special sense: an amateur actor playing the role of Robert Emmet in the revival of a romantic melodrama is accidentally hit over the head and in a concussed state wanders out into post-Independence Dublin, which allows Johnston to contrast the imagined future for an Ireland free of English domination which fuelled Emmet's rebellious rhetoric with the realities of Dublin's political and cultural life in the late 1920s. The dream state of his hero enables Johnston to pursue liberties with time, place,

FIG. 8.2 Denis Johnston's *The Old Lady Says 'No!'* showing the Speaker (Micheál Mac Liammóir), the Flower-Seller (Meriel Moore), and the Statue of Grattan (Hilton Edwards). Photo from 1934 revival. Photograph by J. J. Mooney from Bulmer Hobson (ed.), *The Gate Theatre Dublin* (Dublin: Gate Theatre, 1934).

style, as situation after situation melds into another by processes of free psychological association and mind-play that are reminiscent of the ways Joyce presents the wanderings of his Ulysses (Bloom) in Nighttown. However, Johnston's presiding goddess is not the Circe-like Bella of *Ulysses* but a constantly shape-changing woman, who is a richly comic amalgam of Emmet's beloved Sarah Curran, Maud Gonne in her role as Yeats's Cathleen ni Houlihan, a blowsy Dublin flower-seller (somewhat reminiscent of Shaw's Eliza Doolittle at her most earthily forthright), and one of O'Casey's mourning mothers. The very conception of this character shows the degree to which the layering is permeated and controlled by a sharp, educated wit, as Emmet's (and the spectator's) dream shades first into nightmare and then delirium.

Johnston exploits his ear for idiomatic speech rhythms brilliantly, as he guys a Trinity student and his flapper girlfriend who, posing as Bright Young Things, are at first too naive to respond to their sexual instincts and later too sophisticatedly bored to remedy their lost opportunity. Equally pointed in its satirical impetus is Johnston's attack on the would-be intelligentsia who populate an 'at home', given by the Minister for Arts and Crafts and his lady, with its toadying dramatist, novelist, and artist, grouped inseparably on a sofa like the three wise monkeys, an ingratiating Lady Trimmer, and a much-put-upon daughter, whose role is that of general entertainer at her mother's command whenever the conversation stalls. The self-centred occupants of the room quickly start speaking all at once, and the resulting nonsensical babble of voices virtually drives Emmet mad. Johnston's is a dark vision for all the wild humour of the play, as repeatedly the grand ambitions for Ireland conceived by her one-time lauded patriots are shown to have been betrayed, politically, socially, and culturally, while the rhetoric of the past has become jaded and sentimentalized through constant, mindless reiteration. The layering technique carries the force of Johnston's indictment, allowing for continual juxtaposition of past with present, the innocent voice of hope with the jaundiced dismay of experience, the vigour of the dramatist's invention with the banality of the material he is forced to deal with, the structure of a vaudeville-style revue with the passion of a moralist. *The Old Lady Says 'No!'* is a dramaturgical tour de force.

A Bride for the Unicorn, though as complex as *The Old Lady*, has a different structure, influenced by Johnston's familiarity with the plays of Ernst Toller, especially *Hoppla!*, which he directed for the Dublin Drama League in 1929.[21] Influenced in part by Reinhardt's 1911 staging of the medieval morality play *Everyman* (*Jedermann*) at Salzburg, expressionist playwrights began imitating its series of disconnected episodes, which they termed 'stations' after the manner of the Stations of the Cross.[22] Johnston draws on this concept in shaping the career of his Everyman figure, Jay, who is also modelled on Jason of the Argonauts, since his life's journey is a voyage of discovery into the unknown and unforeseen. (Joyce's *Ulysses* is again a latent presence.) Jay pursues an ideal, represented by a dancing masked woman through a life that repeatedly fails to live up to his expectations. The 'stations' show his marriage, work as a stockbroker, reunions with his college friends, an affair, before moving into more surreal representations of his fears (menacing shadow figures), his deepening conscience (a courtroom in which he is on trial and a bizarre wartime episode), his apparent reconciliation with his ideal, his death, and his funeral. For Jay, unlike Everyman, there is seemingly no redemption, since every 'station' has been significantly lacking in any spiritual dimension or positive moral action (even the masked woman is little more than a casual sexual conquest, however much she permeates Jay's future consciousness, crippling his power fully to engage with others). Each scene follows a distinctive dramatic style. The dysfunctionality of the marriage is defined by flatly uttered dialogue which contains the characters' stage directions as well as conventional speech. The affair is presented as a disturbing confrontation with Jay's former mistress and a shrewdly calculating, juvenile daughter who dismisses her father's pretence at sentimentality with brutal frankness: 'You only love a Daughter. I'm not just somebody's daughter. I'm Me.'[23] Johnston's stage directions ask for clear cultural references: to Marlowe's *Dr Faustus*; Dante's *Inferno* (though Jay's guide is not Virgil, but a drunken Orpheus); images and colour effects in the staging reminiscent of Dali's paintings. There are echoes in the shadow sequence of O'Neill's *The Emperor Jones* (staged in 1927 by the Drama League) and Ibsen's *Peer Gynt* (staged 1928 by the Dublin Gate Theatre Studio),[24] while the theories and practice of Freud and Jung underlie the whole conception. As spectators of *A Bride for the Unicorn*, we live not in the nightmare that is the individual's perception of history (the theme of *The Old Lady Says 'No!'*), but in the trauma of a modern psyche.

[21] This was under Johnston's theatrical pseudonym, E. W. Tocher.
[22] *Everyman* survives in English and Dutch versions, but was modernized by von Hofmannsthal for Reinhardt.
[23] Denis Johnston, *Dramatic Works*, vol. 2 (Gerrards Cross: Colin Smythe, 1979), 68.
[24] Edwards and Mac Liammóir's company was so named during their first two seasons (1928–9), when it was performing in the Peacock Theatre, the Abbey's studio space. The company took its more familiar name, the Dublin Gate Theatre, after it acquired its own premises in Cavendish Row.

MODERNIST PERFORMANCE

Given Johnston's free use of dance, song, mime, mask-work, ensemble movement, choric speaking and singing, and varied styles of acting, it is clear that highly versatile performers are essential for staging either of these plays. The same observation may be made concerning the plays of O'Casey and Yeats: in eschewing realism and naturalism, the modernist drama demanded new technical skills of actors, designers, and directors. Working with the experienced actor Henry Ainley, Yeats found it impossible in rehearsal to achieve the effects he wanted, once he had the actor don a mask: Ainley continued to move and speak in the manner of his particular training.[25] Yeats despaired too of finding a sensitive choreographer and performer to realize the climactic danced sequences of his plays until he met Ninette de Valois in Cambridge in 1926, where she was acting as what we would now term 'movement director' for the expressionist productions of her cousin Terence Gray.[26] Gray's Cambridge Festival Theatre, like Peter Godfrey's Gate Theatre Studio, employed a self-styled modernist ensemble, using the newest techniques of what he termed 'presentational methods' (as distinct from the representational method of realism). The new method was both iconoclastic in its rebuttal and mockery of traditional stagecraft and experimental in its openness to ways of stirring audience receptivity and response. Expressionist theatre was the formative influence, and its impact can be traced throughout Europe and America: it initiated a time of theatrical exchange. The American trainee director, theorist, and critic Kenneth Macgowan, who was studying with Reinhardt in Germany, invited his friend, the future designer Robert Edmond Jones, to join him in touring theatres there and recording productions. Macgowan described, while Jones sketched what they encountered; the volume which resulted, *Continental Stagecraft*,[27] was rapidly issued in England and influenced a generation of practitioners, including in Ireland Hilton Edwards and Micheál Mac Liammóir, who founded the Dublin Gate Theatre on presentational principles.

Presentational theatre meant meta-theatre—the theatre theatrical—a mode of staging that was quite open about its techniques of making illusion. The aim involved simplicity and economy of means to stimulate spectators' imaginations. Yeats had advocated just such principles in 1904, when the Abbey Theatre opened: an avoidance of fussy movement; the deployment of but two colours in costumes offset by a third in the setting; a scenic art and corresponding styles of direction and acting that honoured the power of suggestion.[28] The result was to throw increased emphasis on the actor and on drama as performance. Mask-work requires a special mode of delivery for speech and in mime and movement a careful timing and emphasis, which excite the spectator's attention by the difference from conventional theatre, as the actor's whole body (rather than simply the voice) becomes the prime medium of expression.

---

[25] See W. B. Yeats to John Quinn, 2 Apr. 1916, in *Letters*, ed. Allan Wade (London: Hart-Davis, 1954), 610–11.

[26] See Richard Allen Cave, *Collaborations: Ninette de Valois and William Butler Yeats* (Alton: Dance Books, 2011). Terence Stannus Gray and Idris Stannus (Ninette de Valois) were cousins and of Irish descent.

[27] Kenneth Macgowan and Robert Edmund Jones, *Continental Stagecraft* (New York: Harcourt, Brace, 1922).

[28] See W. B. Yeats, 'The Play, The Player, and the Scene', *Samhain* (Dec. 1904), 24–33.

FIG. 8.3 Presentational acting and direction in Hilton Edwards's staging of an ensemble sequence from *The Old Lady Says 'No!'* in the 1934 revival by the Gate Theatre, Dublin. Photograph by J. J. Mooney from Bulmer Hobson (ed.), *The Gate Theatre Dublin* (Dublin: Gate Theatre, 1934).

The relatively new invention of electricity began to be used creatively for more than illumination: spotlights could be sharply angled to highlight particular features of a scene, shadow effects and silhouettes were introduced to enhance mood and intimate a sense of place, while the arrival of coloured lighting allowed deft evocations of atmosphere. Settings, avoiding painted backcloths and wing-pieces, became more architectural through organizations of rostra, curtains, and screens onto which images (on occasion, whole settings) might be projected. It was possible to use a basic arrangement of rostra throughout a play and create different scenes by the introduction of curtains or subtle changes in the lighting states. The dynamic of productions changed immediately. Audiences no longer waited in the dark while used settings were taken down and new ones built up, as happened in the old scenic theatre; now action could flow, tensions be sustained and augmented, juxtapositions and rhythmic contrasts be exploited. Moreover, by using three-dimensional architectural settings to offset groupings of actors at different heights or across vacant spaces to define shifting power relations between characters, the art of stage proxemics entered a new phase. Johnston's two plays *The Old Lady Says 'No!'* and *A Bride for the Unicorn* took full advantage of all these developments: his dramaturgy assumed this particular style of staging as a necessity.

THE GATE THEATRE, DUBLIN

Continental Stagecraft not only explained how major expressionist plays were mounted in Germany, but also demonstrated how the techniques devised for this endeavour might

FIG. 8.4 The presentational setting: four designs by Micheál Mac Liammóir for the Gate Theatre's staging of Ibsen's Peer Gynt at the Peacock Theatre (14 October 1928). From Bulmer Hobson (ed.), *The Gate Theatre Dublin* (Dublin: Gate Theatre, 1934).

be used to stage more traditional plays by means other than the scenic method, upheld throughout the nineteenth century. Leopold Jessner at the Schauspielhaus in Berlin, celebrated for his use of rostra organized in stepped formations (*Jessner Treppen*), staged such pared-down productions of Shakespeare's *Richard III* (1920), *Othello* (1921), and a modern-dress *Hamlet* (1926).[29] The sheer scenic economy of these productions, allowing for a rapid turnover of plays for a repertory theatre, excited immediate imitation.[30] Presentational techniques were seen as a godsend internationally to ambitious but financially pressured amateur or semi-professional troupes, which now linked their efforts through correspondence and journals and created the Little Theatre movement.[31] This is the context in which to appraise Edwards and Mac Liammóir's establishment of the Gate Theatre, as supporting a consciously international repertory, while 'experimenting in methods of presentation free from the conventional limitations of the commercial theatre'.[32]

[29] The first two are admirably described and illustrated by Macgowan and Jones, and their account may have influenced Johnston's production of *King Lear* for the Abbey in 1928, with expressionist settings by Dorothy Travers Smith.

[30] E.g. Gray directed Shakespeare, Greek tragedy, Sheridan, Congreve, Wilde, Yeats, Maeterlinck, Synge, Shaw, Glaspell, Elmer Rice, Rostand, and O'Neill in this manner at Cambridge, 1926–33. See Richard Allen Cave, *Terence Gray and the Cambridge Festival Theatre* (Cambridge: Chadwyck-Healey, 1980).

[31] The best, most informative of the journals was *Theatre Arts Monthly* (1924–39), which though American-based was international in outlook.

[32] Hilton Edwards, 'Production', in Hobson, *Gate Theatre*, 21.

Working first in the minute Peacock Theatre at the Abbey and subsequently in their own not much larger premises, the production team were faced with the need like most Little Theatres to create infinite riches within very little room. Nothing daunted, they opened with Ibsen's epic *Peer Gynt* in the former (1928) and with Goethe's equally epic *Faust* in the latter (1930). Though both plays contain an infinite number of scenic locations, the pair deployed what was an innovative device in Dublin: a permanent unit setting, a structure that could be turned, adapted, hung with curtains, and subtly lit or cross-lit to suggest myriad changing places. *Peer Gynt* used two blocks of rising rostra which, placed back to back, evoked mountain-tops; drawn apart, the two blocks presented a cottage interior when 'between them was fitted a wall with a door and a little gable-shaped roof'.[33]

Faust was played inside a setting involving three angled, proscenium-arched spaces, each of which could be prepared independently to create a location from which the action spilled onto the main acting area, while the rest of the stage was left dark. Productions celebrated the inventive ingenuity of designer and director, and required audiences actively to engage imaginatively with their work to shape meaning. The unit setting undergoing diverse variations was constant in Gate Theatre stagings for decades to come; it was perhaps the most enduring legacy modernist theatre in Europe and America gave to twentieth-century production methods.

The plays of Yeats, O'Casey, and Johnston and the enduring style and methodology of Gate Theatre productions are notable not so much for challenging the tenets and practice of realism as for recovering and exuberantly rejoicing in the potential of all the arts that make up theatre, pushing at the limits and limitations of dramatic expression and demanding new approaches to acting, stage movement, design, and direction. Modernist expression in other art forms (painting, sculpture, architecture, poetry, and the novel) turned in this period to exploring the inherent fundamentals of the chosen medium, as did the modernist theatre. The Gate Theatre aimed 'to put at the disposal of our audiences all the riches of the theatre, past, present, and future, culled from the theatres of all the world and irrespective of their nationality. A theatre limited only by the limits of the imagination.' Modernism worked with all the available elements that constitute the fabric of drama in performance, the text and its staging, and in the process rediscovered, as Hilton Edwards hoped, the 'Theatre Theatrical'.[34]

[33] Ibid., 24.   [34] Ibid., 21-2.

CHAPTER 9

....

MISSING LINKS
Bernard Shaw and the Discussion Play

....

BRAD KENT

THE origins of modern Irish theatre have been most commonly dated as May 1899, when the Irish Literary Theatre was launched, or December 1904, when the ILT's successor, the Abbey Theatre, staged its first plays. From this moment on, Irish drama had an institutional bulwark—tenuous though it might prove over the years—to nurture its development and contribute towards the national consciousness that was being forged through the broader Irish Revival. This dating is challenged by Oscar Wilde and Bernard Shaw, who considered themselves the double-barrelled 'great Celtic school', their outsider status as Irishmen in England giving them a subversive perspective that challenged the dominant morality in the early 1890s.[1] Yet if one were pressed to provide a precise place and date for when the seeds of modern Irish theatre were sown, the best candidate would be when W. B. Yeats's *The Land of Heart's Desire* and Shaw's *Arms and the Man* were staged at London's Avenue Theatre on 21 April 1894. In addition to launching the careers of Ireland's first Nobel laureates of literature, three of the main tensions that have dogged Irish theatre since were in evidence that night: works that alternately fed into and sought to explode romantic conventions; the Irishness of a play set in a non-Irish locale and performed outside Ireland, though written by an Irish writer; and the methods of underwriting a non-commercial but nonetheless 'important' drama. As to the latter, the production was funded by Annie Horniman, the British heiress who later subsidized the Abbey. Looking back on that night and the audience's cheering of Shaw's play, Yeats reminisced: 'from that moment on, Bernard Shaw became the most formidable man in modern letters, and even the most drunken of medical students knew it.'[2] At best, Shaw had limited success for another ten years, appealing mainly to the avant-garde and a new generation of theatre practitioners who sought to overturn tired traditions. Rather, the hyberbole in Yeats's retelling reveals his acceptance several decades later that Shaw had won out over him in the fight for the soul of drama, especially in Britain, but in Ireland, too.[3]

---

[1] Oscar Wilde, *Complete Letters*, ed. Merlin Holland and Rupert Hart-Davis (New York: Henry Holt, 2000), 563. They also referred to themselves as 'the Hibernian School'.

[2] W. B. Yeats, *Autobiographies* (London: Macmillan, 1955), 282.

[3] For the most compelling account of Shaw's influence on the British stage, see Christopher Innes, *Modern British Drama: The Twentieth Century* (Cambridge: Cambridge University Press, 2002).

Shaw's shadow is cast across all efforts to establish a national theatre in Ireland. Even though he was not approached or involved, he haunted those first performances by the ILT through Edward Martyn's *The Heather Field*—a play that bore the influences of Henrik Ibsen and Richard Wagner, the two artists that Shaw had written of in what should be regarded as two of the earliest modernist manifestos, *The Quintessence of Ibsenism* (1891) and *The Perfect Wagnerite* (1898). And Yeats had asked Shaw to contribute something for the Abbey to perform on the opening night. In most historical academic accounts, though, Shaw's place in the field of Irish theatre is marginal, if not wholly obscured. One reason often given for this is that Shaw left Ireland for the lures of England. He explained his decision for his move from Dublin in 1876 as being necessitated by environment:

> London was the literary centre for the English language, and for such artistic culture as the realm of the English language (in which I proposed to be king) could afford. There was no Gaelic League in those days, nor any sense that Ireland had in herself the seed of culture. Every Irishman who felt his business in life was on the higher planes of the cultural professions felt that he must have a metropolitan domicile and an international culture: that is, he felt that his first business was to get out of Ireland.[4]

Yeats, too, moved to London, but he often shifted between the two capitals and devoted a great deal of energy to founding and running the Abbey Theatre, whereas Shaw was long involved in trying to establish a national theatre in England. Audience was also a principal difference, Yeats writing mainly for the Irish, Shaw writing mainly for the English. As a result, Shaw is often considered as the last in a great line of Irish playwrights who made England their physical and imaginative home, inheriting the mantle of Farquhar, Goldsmith, Sheridan, Congreve, Boucicault, and Wilde.[5]

Much of this narrative parrots the Irish culture wars of the early twentieth century. In surveying the opinions of some polemical writers of the Gaelic Movement in this period, Philip O'Leary concludes that 'Shaw seems to have inspired little interest in the Gaelic circles of his native Dublin, and that little negative', mainly because he was 'considered the most irrelevantly "Anglo" of all contemporary Anglo-Irish writers'. He stresses, however, 'that this was not a question of ability, but rather of identification and commitment', before sweepingly concluding: 'Shaw was never welcomed back to the fold by his countrymen.'[6] This opinion receives a surprising amount of acceptance in canonical academic circles, despite the fact that the Gaelic Movement as it is thus defined hardly represented all Irishmen.[7] The move to exclude Shaw infiltrated the academy in the early 1930s in the eminent figure of Daniel Corkery, the Professor of English at University College Cork. In his influential *Synge and Anglo-Irish Literature*

[4] Shaw, 'Preface', *Immaturity* (London: Constable, 1931), xxxiv.
[5] See e.g. Christopher Innes, 'Defining Irishness: Bernard Shaw and the Irish Connection on the English Stage', in Julia Wright (ed.), *A Companion to Irish Literature*, vol. 2 (Oxford: Wiley-Blackwell, 2010), 35–49.
[6] Philip O'Leary, 'Lost Tribesman or Prodigal Son? George Bernard Shaw and the Gaelic Movement', *Éire-Ireland* 29, no. 2 (1994), 52–3, 56, 57, 64.
[7] See e.g. Gearóid O'Flaherty, 'George Bernard Shaw and Ireland', in Shaun Richards (ed.), *The Cambridge Companion to Twentieth-Century Irish Drama* (Cambridge: Cambridge University Press, 2006), 122–35.

(1931), Corkery argued that those who wrote in and for other countries could not lay any claim to the title of an Irish author, regardless of their outlook or subject matter; those who did so were 'expatriates', which he clarified was 'not the right word to apply to such writers as, for instance, Swift, Goldsmith, Shaw—writers for whom Ireland was never a *patria* in any sense'.[8] Shaw rebuffed such efforts many years later: 'Certain English historians, and even some Gaelic Leaguers, have tried to steal Swift and Berkeley, Sheridan and Yeats (to say nothing of myself) as Anglo-Irish. There never was any such species as Anglo-Irish; and there never will be.'[9] Thus began what would be an uphill battle to repatriate him.

Shaw's Plays in their Irish Contexts

In many ways, Shaw's politics were born of his Irish experience. Land and rent—contentious issues in a colonized Ireland—were two major concerns of the socialist Fabian Society, which Shaw joined in 1884. Shaw made his socialist turn upon hearing a lecture by the American political economist Henry George, who advocated the nationalization of land. This policy attracted Shaw, whose uncle Frederick, the chief of staff of Dublin's Land Valuation Office, got him a job as a clerk in an estate agent's office, a position that he held for the four years before he left Ireland. His sensitivity to the necessity of social welfare policy was already heightened by his Dublin childhood experiences: 'my esthetic hatred of poverty and squalor, and of the species of human animal they produce, was acquired [. . .] in the slums into which my nursemaid took me on her visits to her friends.'[10] Produced by the Stage Society in 1892, Shaw's first play, *Widowers' Houses*, introduced his method of provocation in portraying a social ill such as urban poverty not as the product of unscrupulous villains like the landlords and agents of melodrama, but rather the result of an inherently unjust system. In doing so, he displaced the responsibility onto the audience as complacent participants.

Shaw had developed his technique from studying the plays of Ibsen. He first lectured on the Norwegian playwright on 18 July 1890 as a part of a series that the Fabians held on 'Socialism in Contemporary Literature'. Michael Holroyd suggests that Shaw was motivated to rework the lecture into a book the next year, when the Parnell scandal exploded.[11] This makes some sense when one considers the lengths to which Shaw admired Ibsen's attacks on conventions, most famously on marriage as a bourgeois, patriarchal institution in such plays as *A Doll's House* (1879) and *Hedda Gabler* (1890). At the same time, Shaw's journalistic writings charged that the real issue in the Parnell affair was not the immorality of the Parnell–O'Shea relation, but rather the naturalness of that relation as against the unnaturalness of

[8] Daniel Corkery, *Synge and Anglo-Irish Literature* (Cork: Cork University Press, 1947), 3.

[9] Bernard Shaw, *The Matter with Ireland*, ed. David H. Greene and Dan H. Laurence (London: Rupert Hart-Davis, 1962), 295–6.

[10] Bernard Shaw, *Sixteen Self-Sketches* (London: Constable, 1949), 24.

[11] Michael Holroyd, 'Introduction', in Bernard Shaw, *Major Critical Essays* (London: Penguin, 1989), 11.

marriage laws.[12] Ibsen's challenge to social conventions was, however, importantly accompanied by a concomitant challenge to aesthetic form and structure. Shaw noted that the tripartite movement of exposition, situation, and unravelling conclusion in the popular 'well-made' plays of Eugène Scribe and Victorien Sardou was transformed in Ibsen's *oeuvre* into exposition, situation, and discussion. This discussion, Shaw argued, was now 'the test of the playwright'.[13] In his own plays, discussion often fails to lead to any resolution, instead leaving the audience with an open end that begs for debate outside the theatre. The discussion play, which Shaw developed out of the play of ideas, found its apotheosis in several of his works, perhaps most notably in the Don Juan in Hell scene from *Man and Superman* (1905), in *Getting Married* (1908), and in *Misalliance* (1910).[14] Yet Seán O'Casey reminds us that it courses throughout Shaw's *oeuvre* and that it is a source of his genius:

> No one can write about ideas without creating persons to express them; but it is one thing to have an idea in a head and quite another to place it in a play. It takes a master-mind to do that so that it will appeal to the imagination of an audience. Shaw and Ibsen are masters of this fancy. Shaw's plays are packed with punches for all kinds of reforms, yet there's hardly one of them that isn't glittering with the fanciful guile of a dramatist.[15]

The primacy of ideas in Shaw's work might be another source of his marginalization from the Irish narrative. Fintan O'Toole claims:

> Ideas have always sat uneasily in the Irish theatre. Plays which take it on themselves to interpret the world for us, to add to our understanding of politics and history, have generally been either ignored or travestied. The theatre of ideas needs styles of production which we are unused to.[16]

Typically, Shaw's reaction when Yeats asked him to contribute something to the Abbey Theatre was to write a discussion play, *John Bull's Other Island* (1904), that would run, when performed without excisions, for more than four hours—rather contrary to a movement that was to make its reputation with brisk one-act plays. When Yeats refused it, Shaw shrugged off the rejection, claiming that it 'was uncongenial to the whole spirit of the neo-Gaelic movement, which is bent on creating a new Ireland after its own ideal, whereas my play is a very uncompromising presentment of the real old Ireland'.[17] Yet he had forewarned Yeats, writing in June 1903 that his new play would be 'frightfully modern—no banshees nor leprechauns'.[18]

---

[12] Shaw, *The Matter with Ireland*, 25.   [13] Shaw, *Major Critical Essays*, 160.

[14] See Christopher Innes, '"Nothing But Talk, Talk, Talk—Shaw Talk": Discussion Plays and the Making of Modern Drama', in Christopher Innes (ed.), *The Cambridge Companion to George Bernard Shaw* (Cambridge: Cambridge University Press, 1998), 162–79.

[15] Sean O'Casey, *Blasts and Benedictions: Articles and Stories*, ed. Ronald Ayling (London: Macmillan, 1967), 25.

[16] Fintan O'Toole, *Critical Moments: Fintan O'Toole on Modern Irish Theatre*, ed. Julia Furay and Redmond O'Hanlon (Dublin: Carysfort Press, 2003), 50.

[17] Bernard Shaw, *John Bull's Other Island; How He Lied to Her Husband; Major Barbara* (London: Constable, 1930), 13.

[18] Bernard Shaw to W. B. Yeats, June 1903, in Dan H. Laurence and Nicholas Grene (eds.), *Shaw, Lady Gregory and the Abbey: A Correspondence and a Record* (Gerrards Cross: Colin Smythe, 1993), xi.

As he was later to note, 'in a modern Irish play the hero doesnt sing that "Ould Ireland" is his country and his name is Molloy; he pours forth all his bitterness on it like the prophets of old.'[19] This is a fitting description of Larry Doyle, the protagonist of *John Bull's Other Island*, who, like Shaw, has gone to London to carve out a life for himself and has wound up staying. His return eighteen years later is not as a weepy-eyed sentimental émigré, but rather as a calculating partner in a multinational syndicate who has come back both to tie up loose personal ends and to close a deal to develop his native Rosscullen. Larry is obsessed with facts, finding romanticized 'dreaming, dreaming, dreaming' to be unproductive. In this way, the play dissects a number of stereotypes, and in particular those that had been propagated through the stage Irishman. Tim Haffigan, the first character introduced, has all of the traces of this figure: loquaciousness, drinking alcohol to excess, witty turns of phrase, and a hardy stock of clichéd Irish sayings. While these work on Larry's English partner, Tom Broadbent, to great comic effect, they raise Larry's ire. When Haffigan is confronted by Larry, he betrays his Glasgow accent, sheds his groomed Irish persona, and hurries out of the door having touched Broadbent for several pounds. Larry chastises Broadbent for believing in the stereotype: 'Man alive, dont you know that all this top-o-the-morning and broth-of-a-boy and more-power-to-your-elbow business is got up in England to fool you, like the Albert Hall concerts of Irish music? No Irishman ever talks like that in Ireland, or ever did, or ever will.'[20] The unmasking of the stage Irishman *on stage* allowed Shaw to emphatically explode 'those two hollowest of fictions, the Irish and English "races"'.[21] Here he was actually in line with the directors of the ILT and the Abbey, whose main objective was to 'show that Ireland is not the home of buffoonery and of easy sentiment, as it has been represented'. Where Shaw parted with them was in their believing that Ireland is 'the home of an ancient idealism' as a desirable alternative and not simply the other side of the same coin.[22]

Instead of appealing to facile patriotism, Shaw reveals the ways in which nationalism serves as a smokescreen to obscure pressing socioeconomic concerns. When the play shifts to Ireland in the second act, the audience encounters the newly established landed bourgeoisie, the beneficiaries of the 1903 Wyndham Act that subsidized the transfer of land from landowners to tenants. These men do not seek to help raise up their fellow countrymen, but rather watch them anxiously, keep them in their places, and exploit them mercilessly, as is evidenced in their heartless treatment of Patsy Farrell. Meanwhile, they allow themselves to be bamboozled by the soft-nationalist rhetoric of Broadbent. Failing to realize that Broadbent's liberalism allows for multinational corporations and transnational capital to move freely across borders, they are in the process of having their recently won freedom taken away: their land is mortgaged to the hilt and about to be foreclosed and their businesses are tied to conglomerates, all of which are controlled and orchestrated by the syndicate. Larry strikes at this early on, lamenting that an Irishman 'cant be intelligently political: he dreams of what the Shan Van Vocht said in ninety-eight. If you want to interest him in Ireland youve got to call the unfortunate island Kathleen ni Hoolihan and pretend she's a little old woman.'[23]

[19] Shaw, *The Matter with Ireland*, 25.   [20] Shaw, *John Bull's Other Island*, 83.
[21] Ibid., 18.
[22] Augusta Gregory, *Our Irish Theatre: A Chapter in Autobiography*, 3rd edn. (Gerrards Cross: Colin Smythe, 1972), 20.
[23] Shaw, *John Bull's Other Island*, 87. For a discussion of the play in relation to gendered politics and the Irish context, see Brad Kent, 'The Politics of Shaw's Women in *John Bull's Other Island*', in D. A.

In a discussion play, dramatic action arises through the jab and thrust of conflicting ideas, each given a fair airing in its own turn. This is most evident in *John Bull's Other Island* through the competing utopian visions of Ireland—utopias that are marked with constant references to dreaming and imagination. For the bourgeoisie of Rosscullen, utopia is the ownership of their small corner of the earth and their belief that this somehow makes men of them; for Hodson, Broadbent's valet and English advocate of Home Rule, it is a Parliament in Westminster that is free of nationalist politics so that attention might be paid to relieving the plight of the urban poor. The main struggle, though, is between the vision of Larry and Broadbent and that of Father Keegan, the unorthodox defrocked priest. While the arch-capitalists align themselves with the forces of progress in viewing land development, economic growth, and efficiency as key to the future, Keegan unmasks their greed and inhumanity in the pursuit of Mammon, viewing the earth—as it is and as these men propose to continue to transform it—as hell. Shaw's sympathies shift gradually over the course of the play from Larry to Keegan, who at the end offers his own utopia:

> In my dreams [Heaven] is a country where the State is the Church and the Church the people: three in one and one in three. It is a commonwealth in which work is play and play is life: three in one and one in three. It is a temple in which the priest is the worshipper and the worshipper the worshipped: three in one and one in three. It is a godhead in which all life is human and all humanity divine: three in one and one in three. It is, in short, the dream of a madman.[24]

In Shavian fashion, this vision is undercut as Keegan walks away, Broadbent simply dismissing him as a potential 'attraction' for the tourists, and leaving Larry to close the play by looking for a site on which to build their hotel.

Despite the obvious resonances in a contemporary Ireland defined by its globalized economy and inequitable distribution of resources, the relevance of *John Bull's Other Island* is denied by critics who are likely antipathetic to Shaw's socialism, having labelled it with the kiss-of-death and patently false charge of being 'dated'. Rejected by the Abbey, it went on to enjoy a successful run at London's Court Theatre, a non-commercial venture managed by Harley Granville-Barker and J. E. Vedrenne from 1904 to 1907 that was a proto-Shaw repertory theatre, with his plays accounting for 701 of its 988 performances.[25] At a Royal Command Performance, King Edward VII reportedly laughed so hard that he broke his chair and thereby cemented Shaw's celebrity as the day's leading dramatist. The play's dissection of the politics and economics at work behind the Irish question was perceptive enough to draw the sitting Prime Minister, Arthur Balfour, and several other Members of Parliament to view it on more than one occasion. Belfast-born manager James B. Fagan later directed the play in London in the autumn of 1921, which coincided with negotiations on the Anglo-Irish Treaty.[26] Watching a revival of it at the Abbey in 1923, with Ireland just

---

Hadfield and Jean Reynolds (eds.), *Shaw and Feminisms: On Stage and Off* (Gainesville, FL: University Press of Florida, 2013), 73–92.

[24] Shaw, *John Bull's Other Island*, 181.

[25] Dennis Kennedy, *Granville Barker and the Dream of Theatre* (Cambridge: Cambridge University Press, 1985).

[26] Christopher Innes, 'Bernard Shaw and James B. Fagan, Playwright and Producer', *SHAW* 30 (2010), 100

emerging from its civil war, Lady Gregory wrote to Shaw that she had at first feared that 'the complete change in political circumstance' would affect its reception, 'but that made no difference in the delight in the play'.[27] It is perhaps most telling that before the Abbey finally staged it in 1916, it was Granville-Barker and Vedrenne who first brought the play to Ireland in touring productions in 1907 and 1909

Shaw's perceived importance to Irish theatre was signalled by Lady Gregory when she offered to make him an Abbey director in June 1909 following the death of J. M. Synge. He politely declined. The two did collaborate, however, over the course of the following months, when Shaw's *The Shewing-up of Blanco Posnet* (1909) was banned from being staged in Britain. In this one-act play Blanco Posnet, a rogue of the first order in the wild American West, is threatened with lynching for the crime of stealing a horse. He is only caught by the authorities when he sees a woman nursing a child who is dying of croup and offers her the steed to help. In the end, in the best melodramatic fashion, he is saved from the gallows when the woman arrives to testify on his behalf, but not before the child has died and Blanco has repeatedly cursed God and charged officials for having carnal relations with a prostitute. The blasphemy and sexual explicitness sank the play in the eyes of the censor. But Dublin being beyond the jurisdiction of British censorship legislation, Lady Gregory rightly saw the play as being a way of defying authority and garnering some much-needed nationalist credit for the Abbey in the wake of the divisions caused by the controversy surrounding the 1907 production of *The Playboy of the Western World*. The population sided with the theatre in its public struggle with British officials, who sought to dissuade the directors from staging the play; the Abbey won the day when it became a resounding success. At the end of the affair, Shaw wrote to Lady Gregory: 'Of the fifteen countries outside Britain in which my plays are performed, my own is by no means the least lucrative; and even if it were, I should not accept its money value as a measure of its importance.'[28] To ensure the Abbey's continued success, he returned the royalties they sent him when they later toured the play in America.[29]

At least in institutional terms, this newfound Irish respect for Shaw was not by any means unconditional. Facing massive unpopularity in Britain following the publication of *Common Sense About the War* (1914), a pamphlet aimed at deflating British jingoism and attempts to demonize the Germans, Shaw wrote *O'Flaherty V.C.* (1915), another one-act play that he offered to the Abbey. Set in an Irish estate based on Lady Gregory's Coole Park, where he had spent a significant amount of time vacationing earlier that year, Shaw warned Gregory before delivering the manuscript that the depiction of the Irish 'will make the Playboy seem a patriotic rhapsody by comparison'.[30] Dennis O'Flaherty, who returns to Ireland having been awarded the Victoria Cross for exceptional bravery, joined the British army not out of any sense of duty or love of the Empire, but rather to get away from his overbearing, hyper-nationalist mother. Of the authorities, he says that 'if there was twenty ways of telling the truth and only one way of telling a lie, the Government

---

[27] Laurence and Grene, *Shaw, Lady Gregory and the Abbey*, 170.

[28] Gregory, *Our Irish Theatre*, 221.

[29] Shaw to Lady Gregory, 18 June 1912, in Laurence and Grene, *Shaw, Lady Gregory and the Abbey*, 76.

[30] Shaw to Lady Gregory, ibid., 95.

would find it out'.[31] And for good measure his potential love interest, Tessie, is not 'an ideal Irish colleen', but rather a calculating lass whose wooing O'Flaherty recognizes as a brazen attempt to get her hands on his pension should he be maimed or killed.[32] Having lived in France, where he has 'been as good as married' to more than one woman and tasted the delights of French cuisine, he has become dissatisfied with Irish life and the dim future that it holds out for him.[33] In the end he returns to the field of battle, preferring the relative calm of war to the headaches of home. The double-edged criticism of the play—the even-handedness of its negative portrayal of Ireland and unmasking of the brutalities of war and government propaganda—caused the Abbey to reject the play, much to the relief of the military authorities, who had been quietly lobbying them to do so behind the scenes. It appears that the Abbey directors feared alienating all people: nationalists, the government, and those who would be sensitive to the possibility that the play might be a satire of a real local war hero, Lance Corporal Michael O'Leary, who had recently been decorated with the Victoria Cross and whose image adorned recruiting posters all over Dublin.

With the exception of almost annual revivals of *Blanco Posnet*, Shaw's plays were not staged at the Abbey until 1916, by which time the theatre was mired in financial difficulties. J. Augustus Keogh, who took over as Abbey director that summer, was a Shaw enthusiast. His first production was *Widowers' Houses*, Lady Gregory informing Shaw that it was well received, with 'great applause on the slum question'. Looking for a way to make the Abbey solvent again, she hit upon the idea of 'a season of G.B.S.—our Irish Shakespeare'.[34] That autumn and winter Keogh produced Shaw's *Candida* (1894), *John Bull's Other Island*, *Arms and the Man*, *Man and Superman*, *The Inca of Perusalem* (1915), *The Shewing-up of Blanco Posnet*, and *The Doctor's Dilemma* (1906). Although the season did not bring in the hoped-for returns, leading to Keogh's replacement by Fred O'Donovan in April 1917, Shaw's plays remained fixtures at the Abbey, with several of them performed almost every year over the next two decades, and more at other theatres in Dublin and across the island.[35]

This attention to Shaw, coupled with the country's slide into rebellion and war, generated a more intense reciprocal interest on his part. Throughout this turbulent period, Shaw worked on his magnum opus, the five-part *Back to Methuselah* (1920), which runs from the Book of Genesis to 31920 AD, or 'As Far as Thought Can Reach'. Shaw set the fourth part of this science fiction epic on Burrin Pier in 3000 AD. By this time, the capital of the British empire has long moved to Baghdad. With the shift east, the Irish were left to themselves; but ever the contrarians, they emigrated to other countries where the national question was still alive to make nuisances of themselves until all claims of nationality were conceded the world over. 'Think', the Elderly Gentleman says, 'of the position of the Irish, who had lost all their political faculties by disuse except that of nationalist agitation, and who owed their position as the most interesting race on earth solely to their sufferings!'[36]

[31] Bernard Shaw, *Heartbreak House; Great Catherine; Playlets of the War* (London: Constable, 1930), 219.

[32] Ibid., 203.   [33] Ibid., 222.

[34] Lady Gregory to Shaw, 12 Aug. 1916, in Laurence and Grene, *Shaw, Lady Gregory and the Abbey*, 118–19.

[35] See Nicholas Grene and Deirdre McFeely, 'Shaw Productions in Ireland, 1900–2009', *SHAW* 30 (2010), 236–59.

[36] Bernard Shaw, *Back to Methuselah* (London: Constable, 1930), 155.

Eventually the younger generations abandoned their notions of Irish exceptionalism upon returning home to the south coast of Galway Bay, finding the promised land of milk and honey barren. As the Anglo-Irish War raged, Shaw's moral to the leaders of both sides was to let the Irish determine their own future and get down to more advanced issues of governance, or suffer interminable conflict and the stifling of political maturation. In a play that illustrates Shaw's doctrine of creative evolution, the national question is depicted as both a tiresome impediment to progress and a means to that end.

Although Shaw did not set any of his dozens of other plays in Ireland, this does not mean that it fails to register in them. For example, his two major works to bracket *Methuselah*, *Heartbreak House* (1919) and *Saint Joan* (1924), are brimming with Irish resonances. *Heartbreak House* has commonly been read as an adaptation of Anton Chekhov's *The Cherry Orchard* and a statement on the decline of European aristocracy, but it is also in line with the tradition of Big House literature, with its dislocated and disconnected inhabitants infiltrated by Ellie Dunn, one of many Irish characters to people Shaw's plays set outside the country. Shaw wrote the part of Ellie for Ellen O'Malley, believing that only an Irish actor could replicate the musical quality of Ellie's speeches and emphasize her outsider status.[37] *Saint Joan* features a strong national heroine who, unlike Cathleen ni Houlihan, seeks men to fight alongside, not for her. It was completed in August 1923, just following the end of the Irish Civil War, while Shaw and Charlotte enjoyed their last Irish vacation deep in Republican Kerry. It is rather difficult to hear Joan assure her comrades that they 'will live to see the day when there will not be an English soldier on the soil of France' and later implore them to press on and not sign a treaty after some victories in battle, without recognizing the powerful analogy with the contemporary Irish context—an analogy made stronger by Shaw's comparison in the preface of Joan and the executed Irish rebel Roger Casement.[38] In this light, *The Devil's Disciple* (1897), a melodrama set in the United States during the Revolutionary War that features not one but two rebellious heroes, could also be considered analogous to the Irish context, particularly given that it was written as the country prepared the centenary celebrations for the 1798 Rebellion. Shaw even prohibited it from performance at the Abbey during the First World War to prevent inflaming national sentiments.[39]

Shaw's Impact on Irish Letters

While Shaw's role in the foundation of modern Irish theatre and his engagement with Ireland and Irish issues are essential aspects of his writings, his importance to the country is also traced through his influence on the generations of Irish writers who have followed in his wake. One of the effects of this inspiration was the establishment of a theatrical

[37]   Shaw to St John Ervine, 23 Oct. 1921, in *Collected Letters, 1911–1925*, ed. Dan H. Laurence (London: Max Reinhardt, 1985), 741–4.

[38]   Bernard Shaw, *Saint Joan; The Apple Cart* (London: Constable, 1930), 69.

[39]   Shaw to Lady Gregory, 22 Aug. 1922, in Laurence and Grene, *Shaw, Lady Gregory and the Abbey*, 122.

subgenre: the reformist municipal politics play. The earliest of these, *The Laying of the Foundations*, was by Fred Ryan, a devoted Shavian, a journalist, and the first secretary of the Irish National Theatre Society. Premièred by the Irish National Drama Company at the Antient Concert Rooms on 20 October 1902, the play was greeted by Yeats as 'excellent. It is a really astonishing piece of satire.'[40] In 1914, the Abbey offered another glimpse into municipal politics with *The Lord Mayor*, a play by Shaw's childhood friend Edward McNulty. McNulty was instrumental in Shaw's formation, the two spending much of their adolescence together and corresponding when McNulty moved from Dublin to Newry to work at a branch of the Bank of Ireland, their letters 'illustrated with crude drawings and enlivened by burlesque dramas'.[41] This collaborative apprenticeship was continued in later years, McNulty writing to Shaw as he worked on *The Lord Mayor* to ask him for advice on stage technique.[42] In both *The Laying of the Foundations* and *The Lord Mayor*, men are placed in positions of power at City Hall by established councilmen. These elder politicians use patriotism as an outward sign of their benevolence and solidarity with the people, but it merely serves to gloss over their quietly profiting from graft and insider deals. The newcomers eventually become aware of the systemic corruption, reject offers to look the other way, and promise to engage in a war of ethics by ridding the land of those who refuse to care about the people and do anything about the tenements that are 'unfit for beasts' and should be 'pulled down as unsafe'.[43] As in Shaw's *oeuvre*, the issues of poverty and an unfair system underpinned by corruption are discussed not in the slums and among their dwellers, but in the halls and homes of the powerful who have the capacity to instigate and enforce reform through the Fabian method of permeating legislative authorities.

This tradition is developed with Oliver St John Gogarty's *Blight*, first staged at the Abbey on 11 December 1917.[44] Gogarty's play opens in a dilapidated tenement room, with its protagonist, Tully, leading the people in what appears to be the groundswell towards a popular reform movement. By the end of the play, Tully uses his newfound wealth and seat on the Corporation simply to enrich himself, calling into question the ability of those who infiltrate the system to resist being co-opted by it. However, Tumulty, the righteous character in the play, fails to undergo a conversion that parallels that of Tully, and Tully's conversion happens offstage, somewhere between the second and third acts. Such ideological conversion and the awakening of conscience are central dramatic moments in the discussion play, the characters functioning as conduits for the audience. The provocation of the play is further undermined by Tumulty's shrill didacticism, making the play more akin to the work of another Shaw favourite, Eugène Brieux.

---

[40] Robert Hogan and James Kilroy, 'Introduction', in *Lost Plays of the Irish Renaissance*, ed. Robert Hogan and James Kilroy (Dixon, CA: Proscenium Press, 1970), 11.

[41] Shaw, *Sixteen Self-Sketches*, 33.

[42] Shaw to Edward McNulty, 9 June 1914, in Laurence and Grene, *Shaw, Lady Gregory and the Abbey*, 88–9.

[43] Frederick Ryan, *The Laying of the Foundations*, in Hogan and Kilroy, *Lost Plays of the Irish Renaissance*, 25.

[44] James F. Carens offers good evidence to argue that the play should be solely attributed to Gogarty, countering claims that co-authorship should be given to the Dublin lawyer Joseph O'Connor, who informed Gogarty's knowledge of Dublin slum life. See James F. Carens, 'Introduction', in *The Plays of Oliver St. John Gogarty*, ed. James F. Carens (Newark, DE: Proscenium Press, 1971), 9–10.

Certainly the most famous Irish playwright to have been directly influenced by Shaw is
Seán O'Casey, who wrote that around 1912, when he was an active Gaelic Leaguer: 'I abandoned the romantic cult of Nationalism [...] and saw the real Ireland when I read the cheap
edition of Shaw's *John Bull's Other Island*; hating only poverty, hunger, and disease.'[45] This
conversion later led a still relatively unknown O'Casey to ask Shaw to provide a foreword
for his completed collection of essays on Irish labour and nationalism, *Three Shouts on a
Hill*. Shaw rejected the offer, saying that O'Casey would have to publish his book on its own
merits, adding: 'You ought to work out your position positively & definitely. This objecting
to everyone else is Irish, but useless.'[46] O'Casey took the comments to heart and kept the
letter in his wallet. When he came to make his own mark, with his first play, *The Shadow
of a Gunman* (1923), O'Casey signalled his indebtedness to Shaw from the outset. In a stage
direction as novelistic in its attention to detail and as psychologically penetrating of character as any that Shaw wrote, O'Casey borrows a line from Louis Dubedat, the troubled artist of *The Doctor's Dilemma*, to describe his own artist, Donal Davoren, as being devoted to
'the might of design, the mystery of colour, and the belief in the redemption of all things by
beauty everlasting'.[47] While O'Casey also excels at presenting a range of competing view-
points in his plays, it is perhaps in perspective rather than form that the two writers have
the most in common, both being leftists and inveterate contrarians, their plays steeped in
humanity and threaded with humour. Looking back on Shaw's career, O'Casey admired
him as

> a leader who carried a flag of rebellion against every wrong, every pious fraud, every stupid-
> ity that institutional and conventional interest used to keep themselves up and the mass of
> people down. A leader who went forward, not with a threat, not even with a frown, but with a
> laugh flying like a pennon from his pointed spear of thought.[48]

Shaw remained supportive throughout O'Casey's life, and was one of the prime forces
that buoyed him when the Abbey rejected *The Silver Tassie* (1928), calling it 'a hell of a play'
and haranguing Yeats and Gregory for having botched the situation.[49] Such gestures, which
were typical expressions of the man and his writings, led O'Casey to say that Shaw 'is one of
my great friends, anam-chara—soul-friend—as we say in Ireland, & has been for so many
years, long before I met him in the flesh'.[50]

Shaw's generosity was experienced by many younger Irish writers and theatre practitioners. When Yeats and Gregory hired a young Lennox Robinson as the Abbey's director
in 1909, they wrote to Shaw asking if the fledgling playwright could apprentice under him.
Shaw immediately secured Robinson a place at the Duke of York's, where Charles Frohman

---

[45] Sean O'Casey, *Under a Colored Cap: Articles Merry and Mournful with Comments and a Song*
(London: Macmillan, 1963), 263.

[46] Shaw to Seán O'Casey, 3 Dec. 1919, in *The Letters of Sean O'Casey, 1910–41*, ed. David Krause, vol. 1
(London: Cassell, 1975), 88.

[47] Sean O'Casey, *Three Dublin Plays*, ed. Christopher Murray (London: Faber & Faber, 1998),
4; Bernard Shaw, *The Doctor's Dilemma; Getting Married; The Shewing-up of Blanco Posnet*
(London: Constable, 1930), 165.

[48] Sean O'Casey, *The Green Crow* (London: W. H. Allen, 1987), 177.

[49] Eileen O'Casey, *Cheerio, Titan: The Friendship between George Bernard Shaw and Eileen and
Seán O'Casey* (London: Papermac, 1991), 50.

[50] Seán O'Casey to Charlotte F. Shaw, Nov. 1931, in *The Letters of Sean O'Casey*, 440.

had begun a repertory theatre with Shaw, Barker, and Dion Boucicault Jr as directors. Robinson studied under the three men for the better part of six weeks, and took back much of what he had learned to shape the Abbey for the next five years. When he returned to head the Abbey again in 1919, he directed no fewer than thirty productions of Shaw's plays over the following decade and a half, and many of his own plays of this later period betray his intimacy with Shaw's techniques. Robinson tipped his hat most obviously to him in rewriting *Crabbed Youth and Age* (1928) for publication in 1956, one character recalling her honeymoon in London where she saw Sybil Thorndike star in *Saint Joan* and bumped into a friendly Shaw in the street.[51]

The Ulster writer St John Ervine had his career similarly touched by Shaw. Ervine, though, was more in the O'Casey mould of Shavian acolytes, and experienced a comparable shock to his nature when he first came into contact with Shaw—through Forbes-Robertson's touring production of *The Devil's Disciple* at Belfast's Grand Opera House in October 1900.[52] He was further transformed when he attended a Shaw lecture on religion shortly after he had emigrated to London, recollecting that it 'was extraordinarily startling to a young man, fresh from Belfast and still influenced by his fathers' faith'.[53] Ervine later became a committed socialist who received strong support from Shaw to take over as part of a generational shift in the Fabian Society. When his first full-length work, *Mixed Marriage* (1911), was being performed in London by the Irish Players, Ervine recalls Shaw publicly complimenting the play as 'almost as good as one of his [...] to do me a good turn'.[54] This might have been in part because of Ervine's depiction of the entrenched sectarian divide preventing social and industrial reform in Northern Ireland, a point of view that Shaw would have endorsed but that most Fabian colleagues denied. Francis Sheehy-Skeffington even lamented that *Mixed Marriage* was nothing more than 'one of Mr Bernard Shaw's plays with part of the preface expressing his political views thrown in'.[55] Ervine appears to have been content with such a comparison, later sending Shaw the manuscripts to *Jane Clegg* (1913) and *John Ferguson* (1915), to which Shaw responded with 'long, valuable letters of advice about them'.[56] While Ervine remained indebted to Shaw as a model and valued his contribution of establishing the play of ideas, he was still critical of aspects of Shaw's work, notably what Ervine considered to be Shaw's excessive verbosity.[57] Yet he also did Shaw good turns, getting the ban lifted so that an unexpurgated production of *Blanco Posnet* could be played at the Liverpool Repertory Theatre in 1916; and his acclaimed biography of Shaw was awarded the 1956 James Tait Black Memorial Prize.

The generation of Irish writers that followed O'Casey, Robinson, and Ervine was likewise strongly affected by Shaw, in many cases replaying their conversion narrative. Renowned short story writer, essayist, and biographer Seán O'Faolain noted that watching

[51] Lennox Robinson, *Selected Plays*, ed. Christopher Murray (Gerrards Cross: Colin Smythe, 1982), 130.
[52] St John Ervine, *The Theatre in My Time* (London: Rich & Cowan, 1933), 87–94.
[53] St John Ervine, *Some Impressions of My Elders* (London: George Allen & Unwin, 1923), 221.
[54] St John Ervine, *Bernard Shaw: His Life, Work and Friends* (London: Constable, 1956), 412.
[55] Lauren Arrington, 'St John Ervine and the Fabian Society: Capital, Empire and Irish Home Rule', *History Workshop Journal* 72 (autumn 2011), 62.
[56] Ervine, *Some Impressions*, 223.
[57] St John Ervine, *How to Write a Play* (London: George Allen & Unwin, 1928).

performances of Robinson's *Patriots* (1912) and *John Bull's Other Island* profoundly affected him, having previously only been treated to the Victorian melodrama and musicals that toured through his native Cork.[58] When he turned his hand to write his one play, *She Had to Do Something* (1938), O'Faolain included a stab at a long Shavian preface of his own. Kate O'Brien, perhaps the most outstanding novelist of the post-independence period, wrote of seeing her first Abbey play, *Man and Superman*, as 'a nervous, green convent-school creature, just up from Limerick', but on emerging:

> I felt as if I had been filled within by some very brittle, burning kind of light. I was aston-ished; and I was to remain enclosed in that condition for nights and days. Shaw's proposi-tions, rapid, mad, uncatchable, rang about my brain—like icicles clashing. I thought that I would never sleep again, never be able to sit still, or hear what people said, or eat my supper [. . .]. I have never forgotten the shock of it, or the tingling refreshment.[59]

Teresa Deevy confessed that reading *Heartbreak House* had inspired her to write 'a fan-tasy in the Russian manner on *Irish* themes'; she never did so, but from that moment she devoted herself to serious playwrighting.[60] Louis D'Alton expressed his admiration for Shaw in penning *This Other Eden* (1953), an update of *John Bull's Other Island* that shows how a half-century on, the gombeen men have indeed taken over Ireland, developing the country and exploiting the lower classes as Keegan had feared.[61]

Denis Johnston, another member of this cohort, had a more conflicted relationship with Shaw. In assembling a collection of his plays for publication, Johnston recalled attending Barry Jackson's Malvern Festival in the early 1930s where Shaw advised him that 'all good playwrights ought—like himself—to explain themselves in prefaces'. However, while he had always listened to Shaw 'with becoming respect, I have usually tried to do the opposite [...]. Nevertheless I now find myself writing six prefaces for various reasons that do not include any wish to obey the instructions of Good Old Wencelas of Ayot St Lawrence—a monarch who was always a pleasure to read, a headache to listen to, and utter confusion to agree with.'[62] Johnston's comparative anxiety perhaps stems from the fact that he felt the need to distance himself from Shaw's influence, as is evident in the underlined pas-sages and scribbled critical marginalia throughout his personal copy of Shaw's *Sixteen Self Sketches*.[63] *The Scythe and the Sunset* (1958), set during the Easter Rising, owes its title to O'Casey's *The Plough and the Stars* (1926), but the diverse opinions of the characters, the dramatic action forged from debate, and the tempered to and fro of argument and counter-argument are distinctly Shavian. Johnston recognized the links between form and content, labelling his play an 'antimelodrama'—a Shavian genre if ever there were one—because while most representations of national struggles romanticized the rebels and villainized the oppressive forces, he found it difficult 'to accept these shopsoiled axioms as a matter

---

[58] Seán O'Faolain, 'Shaw's Prefaces', *Bell* 12, no. 5 (1946), 425–32.

[59] Kate O'Brien, *My Ireland* (London: B. T. Batsford, 1962), 117.

[60] 'Teresa Deevy', in Matthew Hoehn (ed.), *Catholic Authors: Contemporary Biographical Sketches* (Newark, NJ: St Mary's Abbey, 1952), 121.

[61] For a comparison of the two plays, see Fidelma Farley, *This Other Eden* (Cork: Cork University Press, 2001).

[62] Denis Johnston, *The Old Lady Says 'No!' & Other Plays* (Boston, MA: Little, Brown, 1960), 8–9.

[63] Denis Johnston Collection, Trinity College Dublin Library, OLS JOH 22.

of course'.[64] However, his most Shavian play is *The Moon in the Yellow River* (1931), which follows Tausch, a German engineer come to develop post-independence Ireland by build-ing a hydroelectric works. The threatened destruction of the works by a group of diehards initiates extended discussions on the merits of progress. Blake—the Republican leader whose name is perhaps a nod to William Blake, an important influence on Shaw and author of the dialectical *The Marriage of Heaven and Hell*, a copy of which is looted for one of the characters in *The Scythe and the Sunset*—views progress as dangerous and killing the people, whereas Tausch sees it as relieving and helping humanity. These men are, in effect, Shaw's idealist and efficient realist, the debate between them and the other characters peppered with such philosophical and artistic heavyweights as Aquinas, Nietzsche, and Dante. Dobelle, the local, well-travelled, sophisticated engineer who has brought Tausch to Ireland, in the end rejects the works before they are blown up, arguing as though he has been lifted from one of Shaw's plays: 'It is right that men should murder each other for the safety of progress. I admit it. That is why I am against right and believe in wrong [...]. It is always evil that seems to have made life worth while, and always righteousness that has blasted it.'[65]

In *Some Impressions of My Elders*, Ervine claims that 'Mr Shaw was incontestably the supreme figure among these men of mind who stimulated and influenced the young men and women of the Early Twentieth Century. I doubt whether any one has ever captured or held the fancy of young men as Mr Shaw captured and held our fancy.'[66] When Shaw lay on his deathbed, he tried to pass the torch, whispering to Eileen O'Casey, Seán's wife, that it was up to Seán now. But O'Casey demurred, writing to Peadar O'Donnell: 'it is up to each of us to see that we use the courage, the wit, and the wisdom of G. B. S. for the achieve-ment of peace in the world, commonsense in international relationships everywhere, and a strong heart with a ready hand to fight on till fear, want, and ignorance be banished from among the nations of the earth'.[67] This was, in part, the challenge that many of those who came in his wake recognized as having jolted them from the conventional mentality of their parochial and provincial communities. The admission of Shaw's artistic merit, formal innovation, and political relevance by successive generations of writers who were among the leading voices of their times attests to the need to account for Shaw's role in the develop-ment of modern Irish letters.

---

[64] Johnston, *The Old Lady Says 'No!'*, 5.   [65] Ibid., 74.
[66] Ervine, *Some Impressions*, 25.
[67] *The Letters of Sean O'Casey, 1942–54*, ed. David Krause (New York: Macmillan, 1980), 753.

PART IV

REVOLUTION
AND BEYOND

CHAPTER 10

....

IMAGINING THE RISING

....

NICHOLAS ALLEN

1916

....

THE Easter Rising was the violent consequence of decades of political and cultural
unrest in Ireland. This unrest had its deepest roots in the colonization of the island
from the sixteenth century, and took its immediate energy from the controversies that
attended the progress of Home Rule through the imperial Parliament. If the coming
of the First World War forestalled a possible civil war, it also brought Ireland's troubled status as a small nation into problematic focus. Many Irish people decided that
the best way to secure Ireland's future as a self-governing member of whatever federation survived the war was to support Britain. Indeed, in 1914 there would be a split in
the nationalist Irish Volunteer movement when a section of its members committed to
service in the British army in the belief that self-government would be the reward of
victory over Germany and its allies. The minority who refused this arrangement dedicated themselves to continued disaffection, and saw the First World War as an opportunity to weaken further the already fraught connection with empire. However, few in
either camp imagined they would break it utterly, not least since the litany of rebellion
in Ireland against British rule was long and disappointing. In short, the rebellion was
by no means inevitable, even up to the final moments before Patrick Pearse read the
Proclamation of the Irish Republic at the General Post Office in Dublin. At the same
time, its legacy has proved inescapable: 'before it,' Fearghal McGarry writes, 'the great
majority of Irish Catholics backed the moderate constitutional nationalism of the Irish
Parliamentary Party: after it, popular support shifted decisively towards Sinn Féin and
its more radical goal of a republic.'[1]

---

[1] Fearghal McGarry, *The Rising. Ireland: Easter 1916* (Oxford: Oxford University Press, 2010), 8.

PEARSE AND THE DRAMA OF SELF-SACRIFICE

The Easter Rising was a small-scale and audacious insurrection that began on Monday 24 April 1916 and lasted barely a week.[2] Its symbolic transformation into a key event of Irish history was secured in part by the execution of its leaders. Of these, the central figure was Patrick Pearse, a lawyer by training and schoolteacher by profession. The nationalist movement brought together militants, dissidents, educationalists, and cultural activists in a series of societies and associations that rose and fell as their members considered Ireland's relationship with Britain in the context of larger events in the imperial world. The progress of the Home Rule Bills was a constant barometer for radical politics, and the possibility of a constitutional settlement of Ireland's status within the Union undercut the separatists' message. Consequently, doubt is a common theme in the plays of Pearse and his cohorts, a condition that is resolved by their characters' exemplary acts of self-sacrifice.

The theatre was important to a generation of Irish radicals because it represented a space for the self-government of what Declan Kiberd calls a 'renovated consciousness'[3] free from the slavery of colonial imitation. The playhouse provided a stage whereby their motives could be expressed in front of a clearly defined audience, which was more often the cast of supporting characters than it was the stalls.[4] This lends many of the plays of Pearse, James Connolly, and (to a lesser extent) Thomas MacDonagh a didactic quality that locates the works in their immediate time and place. The dramatic culture of twentieth-century Dublin was infinitely more complex than a sample of the rebels' plays would suggest, as the public had a wide choice of theatres, cinemas, and music halls to attend. Everywhere, however, there was evidence of war. The British Red Cross Society staged a children's play, *The Enchanted Garden*, at the Abbey Theatre in December 1916 that had children dressed as sunshine, rain, elves, pages, Mephistopheles, Galway peasants, and the various countries in Europe.[5] Elsewhere, theatre revues advertised turns including acrobats, cycling comedians, Japanese entertainers, and Chief Kawbawgam, the American Indian tenor.

The plays of Pearse and company were in contrast a kind of morbid anti-theatre in which the central figure is a sensitive young man supported by an older male mentor and a chorus of chaste women who may, after the fact, include his mother. In this sense, the theatre of rebellion was a cautious gathering of a doubtful audience that was as unsure as its playwrights of the new social contract they were engaged jointly in imagining.[6] In 1916,

---

[2] For more historical background, see Charles Townshend, *Easter 1916: The Irish Rebellion* (London: Allen Lane, 2005).

[3] Declan Kiberd, *Inventing Ireland* (London: Jonathan Cape, 1995), 203.

[4] For more on the relationship between history, politics, and performance, see Ben Levitas, *The Theatre of Nation: Irish Drama and Cultural Nationalism, 1890–1916* (Oxford: Clarendon Press, 2002).

[5] 'Dublin and District', *Irish Times*, 20 Dec. 1916.

[6] Declan Kiberd understands this moment differently in his reading of the rebellion and theatre. Kiberd points to W. B. Yeats's enthusiasm for Victor Hugo's maxim that 'in the theatre a mob becomes a people' as evidence that the 'rebels' play was staged to gather an Irish audience and challenge an English one'. This is an attractive idea but to a degree avoids the extreme caution Pearse exhibits on the issue of charisma and leadership in his theatre, so little of which is actually dramatic: Kiberd, *Inventing Ireland*, 204.

theatre was a rehearsal for a rising in which dramatists and actors were activists, much to the astonishment of Joseph Holloway: 'when he read the proclamation he was startled to find that an assortment of playwrights and producers had endorsed the document.'[7] For the rebels, drama helped embody ideas that were otherwise abstract—as indeed did military training—and Ben Levitas has identified the Hardwicke Street Theatre as 'a forum for strategic debate about the military tactics of the Irish Volunteers'.[8] This overlap was typical of the shifting boundaries between culture and politics in early twentieth-century Ireland, and is symptomatic of its condition as a colonial society in which the unavailable practice of representative politics was sublimated into other cultural forms. It is also true that the 'IRB could hardly conduct an explicit public debate about their rebellion, and so the playhouse provided an alternative meeting place for ideological and tactical discussions'.[9]

This is the basis on which some critics have identified the Easter Rising as a theatrical act in itself. This idea has caused controversy, because it liberates the rebellion from the responsibility to possess a democratic mandate for its revolutionary violence. It also enters ground prepared by the rebels themselves, given their idea of morality in the theatre—an idea that is problematic, given the killing of civilians in the Rising. One of the fundamental criticisms of the Easter Rising was the rebels' disregard for the general population in their situation of revolutionary violence in the packed urban hub of Dublin. To some critics, this suggested a deficit at the heart of the Irish republican project in general, which was a preference for radical rhetoric over and above a commitment to citizenship and social justice—which is very much the point of Seán O'Casey's later assault on the legacy of Patrick Pearse in his Dublin trilogy, as we shall see.[10]

At issue generally was not an idea of Ireland so much as an idea of audience. Pearse understood the opportunity the theatre offered to imagine a political community that had deep and organic roots in social history. In part this reflects another longstanding tendency of Irish nationalism: the symbolic configuration of specific social classes into a representative idea of Ireland itself. If this was a necessity in the long battle for self-determination it required, according to expediency, the exclusion of certain other classes—and their problems—from public and, eventually, aesthetic discourse. So it was that Pearse and company turned to rural Ireland as a dramatic resource; and so it was that Seán O'Casey shocked as he broke the taboo of putting the urban working class—the audience of mass entertainment in Dublin—on stage a decade later.

It is a particular quirk of this period that the shock of the new was veiled so deceptively in the fabric of the past. Dublin audiences experienced theatre as a history lesson staged in the country cabins of an Ireland very far from the complex, urban society in which they lived. The fabric of their daily lives was stripped away by a drama whose simplicity was a rebuke to imperial pretention; the smallholding was a metaphor for the self-sufficiency that made Sinn Féin so dangerous politically to the British idea of a world interconnected by trade and held by force. The little dramas of Pearse and company were freighted with a host of cultural implications, many of which had material effects. If these plays were minor in

---

[7] James Moran, *Staging the Easter Rising: 1916 as Theatre* (Cork: Cork University Press, 2005), 16.

[8] Ibid., 19.   [9] Ibid., 19.

[10] Still the best rejoinder to critical false equivalence that can underpin such judgements is Seamus Deane's essay 'Wherever Green is Red', in Máirín Ní Dhonnchadha and Theo Dorgan (eds.), *Revising the Rising* (Derry: Field Day, 1991), 91–105.

their artistic dimension, they were major indicators of the fault lines underlying the Easter Rising. The theatre was a gathering of ideas and forms in a contested public space, and as such the drama was a proxy for much larger stresses that had not yet found their form in political life.

Patrick Pearse 'drew from his radical English artisan father unusual qualities of character and intellect',[11] and was an early and enthusiastic advocate for the Irish language through the Gaelic League. He took his degree at the Royal University, after which he was called to the Bar, where he pleaded only one case. Pearse's abiding interest was in the education of children, which he believed should allow the individual to develop their abilities according to his or her own interests. To Pearse, the role of the teacher was that of mentor and role model. He looked for analogues for this relationship in Irish history, and created a culture—some have said a cult—of the heroic that the pupils shared with their teachers in the production of masques, plays, and spectacles at St Enda's, the boys' school that Pearse founded in Cullenswood House, Rathmines, in Dublin in 1908.[12] Ruth Dudley Edwards suggests that Pearse's interest in the theatre is 'a key to his prevailing convictions',[13] and many of the boys who first attended the school were active members in the rebellion eight years later. Many of them also acted in or provided the audience for the ten plays and pageants that Pearse wrote. These dramas ranged over a wide ground, and exhibit crucial elements of his thinking: *The King* (1912), *The Singer* (1917), and *The Master* (1915), for example, explore Pearse's thinking about sacrifice, faith, and leadership, all of which he considered to be the necessary foundations of rebellion.[14]

PEARSE'S *THE KING*

The King was written in Irish and produced in the grounds of St Enda's in June 1912. It was revived in May 1913 for a showing in the Abbey Theatre, where it was staged with Tagore's *The Post Office* (1912) as a fundraiser for St Enda's. This connection continued later, as Tagore staged Pearse's play in his own school in Bengal in 1915.[15] In 1912, Pearse was not yet an apostle of armed insurgency, and *The King*'s dramatization of war is set in an ancient monastery with a small cast of boys, an Abbot, monks, a King, and his warriors. This male

[11] J. J. Lee, *Ireland 1912–1985* (Cambridge: Cambridge University Press, 1989), 37.

[12] For a brilliant study of Pearse's engagement with ideas of boyhood and education, see Elaine Sisson, *Pearse's Patriots: St Enda's and the Cult of Boyhood* (Cork: Cork University Press, 2004).

[13] Ruth Dudley Edwards, *Patrick Pearse: The Triumph of Failure* (London: Victor Gollancz, 1977), 142.

[14] In saying this I am conscious of the rebuke that '[c]ritics familiar with the Irish language have long interested themselves in Pearse's pioneering role as a literary theorist and innovator. But by and large [...] commentators working solely in English have tended to deal with his literary writings in a cursory fashion [...] In particular, Pearse's writings on and work in the theatre are too often seen as mere adjuncts to an ideological journey from educational and language enthusiast to political revolutionary': Róisín Ní Ghairbhí and Eugene McNulty, 'Introduction', in Patrick Pearse, *Collected Plays*, ed. Róisín Ní Ghairbhí and Eugene McNulty (Dublin: Irish Academic Press, 2013), 3.

[15] Ibid., 35.

society is a miniature of Pearse's ideal state: martial, religious, and homosocial.[16] The plot is simple: the King is defeated in battle, and returns in disarray to the monastery, where he is admonished for his failings. He is willing to relinquish his crown if a successor with a clean conscience can be found, and the Abbot decides that it must be one of the boys in his foster-age. Giolla na Naomh, the servant of the saints, is chosen.

The King's essential themes all foreshadow the issues with which Pearse wrestled in his own journey towards rebellion. The play is concerned with the idea of righteousness, a condition tempered by doubt and secured by self-sacrifice in service of the community. The Abbot is the gatekeeper of all judgements, handily absolving the Church from any political critique. 'The nation is guilty of the sins of its princes,' he says, and so the heroes' sacrifice in war goes unrewarded, as a God that demands obedience will not give victory to an unright-eous King:

> THE ABBOT.   Do you think that an offering will be accepted from polluted hands? This King has shed the blood of the innocent. He has made spoils and forays. He has oppressed the poor. He has forsaken the friendship of God and made friends with evil-doers.[17]

Complicity is a subsidiary evil in Pearse's play, and is the antithesis of fraternity, which is the basis of life in the monastery. Given that advanced nationalism outside the theatre was built on the principles of self-sufficiency and masculine vigour through the practice of sport and paramilitarism, the audience could see clearly through the thin veil of the past that Pearse drew on stage. Giolla na Naomh is not a character in any recognizable sense but a cipher. He accepts kingship not out of desire for the privilege of rank but rather because he understands that death will follow, and with it the resurrection of his people. One of the most problematic of Pearse's legacies is his equation of national life with individual death. The idea of blood sacrifice was not uncommon in Europe, and it might be argued that Pearse seems anomalous only because he did not act on behalf of an established state. Still, Pearse's formula for Irish liberation is by any standard a curious blend of the martial and the erotic, as the preparation for Giolla na Naomh's kingship shows:

> THE ABBOT.   Let this child be stripped that the raiment of a King may be put about him. *(The child is stripped of his clothing.)* Let a royal vest be put next the skin of the child. *(A royal vest is put upon him.)* Let a royal tunic be put about him. *(A royal tunic is put about him above the vest, and sandals upon his feet.)* Let the royal mantle be put about him. *(The King takes off the royal mantle and it is put upon the child.)* Let a royal diadem be put upon his head. *(The King takes off the royal diadem and it is put upon the child's head.)* Let him be given the shield of the King. *(The shield-bearer holds up the shield.)* A blessing upon this shield! May it be firm against foes![18]

---

[16] Dudley Edwards suggests that *The King* exhibits three key aspects of Pearse's thinking at this time: 'his growing preoccupation with the sacrifice of Calvary [...] his belief in the essential purity of childhood [...] the necessity of sacrificing the young and the sinless to save a decadent nation': *Patrick Pearse*, 142.

[17] Pearse, *Collected Plays*, 153.   [18] Ibid., 159.

The veneration of the child's body encodes Pearse's attention to the immature state of Ireland. The intimate affection for Giolla na Naomh on the part of the Abbot and the King secures the survival of this state in the bond it builds between the survivors who observe the boy before he rides off to die. The shared male gaze is confirmation for a covert community that its ambitions might soon transform the symbolic terrain of the public sphere. This moment is barely visible in the theatre as Giolla na Naomh dies in the press of battle. The play ends with the corpse's return and the admonition not to mourn:

> THE ABBOT.   Do not keen this child, for he hath purchased freedom for his people.
> Let shouts of exultation be raised and let a canticle be sung in praise of God.[19]

The absolute conflation of heroism with the Church promised a bond that had not always been strong between militant republicanism and the majority religion. Different orders of the Catholic Church had varying or no sympathy with the nationalists: Declan Kiberd has argued that the rebel's religiosity was 'that of a generalized mystical Christianity rather than something specifically Catholic in overtone'.[20] The last point to make about *The King* is the transactional nature of Giolla na Naomh's sacrifice. The Abbott's idea that the child 'purchased' freedom for Ireland is a small but significant trace of the material reality of the imperial society in which Pearse lived, and which much of his rhetoric was designed to deny. By the late nineteenth century, Dublin was enmeshed in a network of world trade that Britain had built through force and ingenuity in the previous decades.[21] Pearse's recurrent idea in his drama of a substitution of one life for a nation seems symbolic of his part in a wider culture in which the global flow of things through daily life was a common experience. The substitution of mourning for celebration by the investment of youth in the national project was soon to be an idea orchestrated on a massive scale with the beginning of the First World War. Even here, in the little dramas of a Dublin schoolteacher, lies the pattern of a wider culture in Britain and its empire that led to catastrophe on a grander scale than anything the Easter rebels ever let loose.

PEARSE'S *THE SINGER*

The Singer was not performed until after Pearse's death in May 1916, when it played in the Foresters' Hall in Dublin in December 1917 and in Liverpool the following year.[22] It is a more developed staging of Pearse's ideas, as it contains all the signature elements of *The King* but adds to it a more varied chorus of voices. Women lead the early part of the play through a conversation between a mother and her foster daughter about the two sons of the family who prepare for insurgency. Each of these boys—Colm and his brother, MacDara, the eponymous singer—represents a different thread of the republican tradition; the play

---

[19] Ibid., 164.   [20] Kiberd, *Inventing Ireland*, 207.
[21] For an account of this sometimes ramshackle rise, see John Darwin, *The Empire Project: The Rise and Fall of the British World-System, 1830–1970*, rev. edn. (Cambridge: Cambridge University Press, 2011).
[22] Pearse, *Collected Plays*, 201.

flirts with the dangerous idea that the old methods of physical force have not worked because they had no symbolic aspect. The surprise is that MacDara has admitted he no longer believes in God—a nod no doubt to the ascendancy of Ibsen in the modern theatre. MacDara's experience of community outside the village is of rejection and poverty, his songs considered blasphemous and his passions dangerous. He has survived partly by teaching, first in a school from which he was asked to leave, and second as a tutor of a young boy. MacDara's theory of education blends seamlessly into Pearse's erotic vision of male community—a vision at the heart of the idea of self-sacrifice that he built into republican separatism:[23]

> MACDARA.   The true teacher must suffer and do. He must break bread to the people: he must go into Gethsemane and toil up the steep of Golgotha [. . .]. Sometimes I think that to be a woman and to serve and suffer as women do is to be the highest thing. Perhaps that is why I felt it proud and wondrous to be a teacher, for a teacher does that. I gave to the little lad I taught the very flesh and blood and breath that were my life. I fed him on the milk of my kindness; I breathed into him my spirit.[24]

MacDara assumes upon himself a God-like animation that extends to the final scene, when he walks off stage to an unknown fate, unarmed and naked. The Gethsemane surrender of the weak to the powerful is monstrous egotism when considered objectively; on stage it is a political tempest of image and words that disorients any simple response to the play.

Pearse used similar tactics in *The Master*, which was first performed by the Irish Theatre at Hardwicke Street in May 1915. This play is set at a transitional moment in Irish society between heroic and Christian cultures. The central conflict is between a King and a teacher, Daire and Ciaran. Both have known each other since boyhood, and the play amplifies Pearse's earlier adoration of the young male body. Again, the plot is simple: Daire demands proof from Ciaran that his new religion has power in a culture that relies on the strength of heroes to survive; Ciaran doubts his faith in face of the King, a doubt answered by the commitment of his young disciple to the new God. The King threatens one of Ciaran's pupils, Iollann Beag, with death before a paralysed Ciaran:

> IOLLANN BEAG.   Fear not, little Master, I remember the word you taught me . . . Young Michael, stand near me!
> *The figure of a mighty Warrior, winged, and clothed in light, seems to stand beside the boy. Ciaran bends on one knee.*
> DAIRE.   Who art thou, O Soldier?
> MICHAEL.   I am he that waiteth at the portal. I am he that hasteneth. I am he that rideth before the squadron. I am he that holdeth a shield over the retreat of man's host when Satan cometh in war. I am he that turneth and smiteth. I am he that is Captain of the Host of God.
> *Daire bends slowly on one knee.*

---

[23] For a discussion of this idea in wider context, see Joseph Valente, *The Myth of Manliness in Irish Nationalist Culture, 1880–1922* (Champaign–Urbana: University of Illinois Press, 2011).
[24] Pearse, *Collected Plays*, 220.

CIARAN.   The Seraphim and the Cherubim stand horsed. I hear the thunder of their
    coming ... O Splendour!
He falls forward, dead.
CURTAIN.[25]

Pearse's insistent admixture of the mystical and the martial summons a series of tangled cultural strands from the Revival period. The angelic appearance of the Archangel Michael has all the lustre of a George Russell painting, the *faux* folk resignation of Iollan Beag all the sentimental self-abnegation of a suffering people who might finally, through the process of theatre, be provoked into action by the sight of their passivity. This is the complexity of Pearse's drama. It makes the visionary historical because it binds the aesthetic to sedition in a dialectic that by alchemy transforms art into action. If Pearse had dramatic insight, it was that theatre was one of those few places, like the platform and perhaps the street, where the future could unfold in all the violence necessary to rob the old symbols of their power. This is the idea dramatized in *The Master* and amplified in the Easter Rising. Both, perhaps, were bad art, but neither can be judged on anything but its own revolutionary terms.

Pearse sowed these ideas in the broken ground of a Dublin rocked by the Lockout and the constant parade of armed men, and his plays are part of a mosaic that includes his militant speeches, his poetry, his essays, and his plotting. The boundary between the meeting hall and theatre was thin, and Pearse crossed it with bravura. The miniature adjustments of radical praxis embodied in the plays are difficult to understand a century after the event. These plays do, however, live in the minute gestures they make towards the larger questions of empire and nation that were soon to tear the wider world apart. For that reason alone, Pearse's dramas command a continuing interest far in excess of their actual achievement, or otherwise, as theatre.

CONNOLLY AND MACDONAGH: DRAMAS OF DOUBT

Of course, Pearse did not act alone. The Irish Volunteers were joined in the Easter Rising by a contingent of the Irish Citizen Army under the control of James Connolly. Connolly was born into poverty in Edinburgh and served briefly in the British army as a young man before committing himself to the cause of labour, a commitment that took him to America and Ireland. As a thinker, 'Connolly was in a class of his own by the standards not only of Irish socialist but of Irish capitalist thought of his generation'.[26] By March 1916 he was prepared for armed rebellion. From his base at Liberty Hall, he organized printing, protests, and publicity stunts in a building that also housed the Irish Workers' Dramatic Company. Under armed guard by the citizen volunteers, the company produced Connolly's play *Under Which Flag?* on 16 March 1916, in counterpoint to Lady Gregory's romance of the 1798 rebellion, *The Rising of the Moon* (1907), which played in the Abbey Theatre the same week. Connolly's play was a dramatic disaster, which Seán O'Casey watched horrified from the stalls, appalled by the sentimentality and glittering tinsel. Indeed, the experience

---

[25] Ibid., 196–7.   [26] Lee, *Ireland*, 37.

stayed with O'Casey to the degree that he made fun of Connolly's play a decade later in *The Plough and the Stars*.[27] Francis Sheehy-Skeffington's verdict was 'all propag.; no construction'.[28] Connolly's intentions as a playwright were simple. His play was an incitement to rebellion and an indictment of recruiting because it made stark the complex reasons that prompted many to join the British army. The play's moral centre is a blinded Fenian called Dan McMahon, who was played by Seán Connolly. Weeks later, the actor killed Constable James O'Brien at the public entrance to Dublin Castle;[29] O'Brien was the first victim of the Easter Rising. Seán Connolly was killed shortly afterwards when he was shot as he tried to raise a rebel flag over the City Hall—the same flag that had been used in the production of Thomas McDonagh's *When the Dawn is Come* (1908).

James Connolly's play is set in a country cabin, complete with singers and musicians. It proceeds with a peppering of Irish English, with the words '*scran*' and '*greeshog*' two low points in a fast-declining dialogue that presents two options for its characters: one is to emigrate to America; the other is to join the British army. America is a false freedom, where wage slavery replaces the tyranny of landlords. The Queen's shilling is also tainted as a base metal that carries the guilt of exploitation home from the colonies: 'and every bit of food that's bought with a soldier's money has blood on it, the blood of the people murdered to keep the bloody Empire going!'[30] The masculine attraction of soldiery is not lost on the play's women. Mary O'Neill, a neighbour of the main male characters, imagines what it will be like to wait for her beau if he enlists. As she thinks of him she sings:

> O the horses were capering and prancing,
> Their accoutrements shone like a star,
> She saw her young lover advancing,
> Young Edward the gallant hussar.[31]

In contrast, the parade of shopkeepers and clerks engaged in Fenian drill has no such romance. Like Pearse, Connolly suggested that blood alone would pay for the transformation from mockery to myth. This was not a motif of demented nationalism alone, since the idea of blood sacrifice also bound Ireland to the empire—a fact recognized both by moderates and radicals. *War Illustrated* reported John Redmond's speech 'The Miracle of Ireland', in which he celebrated the bravery of the Irish divisions in Gallipoli and Salonika. 'War is a terrible ordeal for all of us,' admitted Redmond, 'but we Irishmen have one consolation, namely, that the blood our country is willingly shedding in this great cause will seal forever the reconciliation of the two nations.'[32] So Connolly's play entered a competition for men and ideas that constitutionalists were as keen to win as the militants.

One of the more charismatic figures in this struggle was Thomas MacDonagh, a minor poet and innovative critic whose posthumous *Literature in Ireland* remains a classic. He

[27] Sean O'Casey, *Autobiographies* (2 vols., London: Macmillan, 1963), 646.
[28] Francis Sheehy-Skeffington, diary entry dated 26 Mar. 1916, National Library of Ireland (NLI), MS 40,479/4.
[29] McGarry, *The Rising*, 1.
[30] James Connolly, *Under Which Flag?*, in *Four Irish Rebel Plays*, ed. James Moran (Dublin: Irish Academic Press, 2007), 114.
[31] Ibid., 116.
[32] John Redmond papers, NLI MS 15277/8: news clipping from speech called 'The Miracle of Ireland', published in *War Illustrated*.

had the broadest training in drama, which shows in the literary construction of *When the Dawn is Come* (1908), the play of his that describes events that are most like the actual events of the rebellion itself. The play is closer to Pearse than Connolly in its celebration of Thurlough MacKieran, the stoic male character who leads the action. MacKieran is, more developed than Pearse's leads, as a schemer and a warrior, an intellectual and a strategist. *When the Dawn is Come* owes a debt to Elizabethan drama in its tragic construction, and the play is trapped in the old world of representative action, whereby the fate of one character stands as a symbol of the wider community's progress. This leads to the odd situation whereby a play set fifty years in the future combines speech patterns from a past century with images of battle that were long superseded by the modern military. MacDonagh, like Pearse, set his insurgent plays in a kind of abstract time and place that shunned the modern world. There are no foreign characters in any of the plays, no rifles, artillery, or hint of aircraft. There are no British characters either, as all MacDonagh's intermediaries are native spies, which rather forestalls the possibility of creative dialogue.

When the Dawn is Come stages splits and intrigue, death and the risk of all for the reward of a free Ireland. Its central merit is the way in which it dramatizes questions that even the most far-sighted volunteer commander could barely imagine. Early in the play, MacKieran is offered the compromise of limited self-government at the price of an annual subvention to the alien exchequer, an offer that foreshadows the terms of the Anglo-Irish Treaty in 1922. MacKieran rejects it, and wins the day in a fierce battle that happens offstage. But the internal squabbling that he and his fellow commanders indulge in is born of MacDonagh's real experience as an agitator in the radical movement. The Anglo-Irish Treaty was secured eventually by a Civil War with its own share of executions carried out between former comrades-in-arms. MacDonagh was no innocent in this culture of intrigue: he was with Pearse on the Supreme Council of the Irish Republican Brotherhood when the militants outmanoeuvred the more cautious elements of the older generation.

All of these rebel plays are to some degree dramas of self-doubt resolved by action. The formula is surprising in the context of a militant cohort that subsequent history has taken to be convinced of its right to rebel. This confidence is less remarkable dramatically. *Hamlet* was the established theatrical archetype for the troubled man, and Shakespeare was much in the early twentieth-century public mind, since April 1916 marked the tercentenary of his death. From the beginning of the war, a fierce rivalry flared between England and Germany over the ownership of *unser Shakespeare*, the national poet kept alive during the dull stretches of the nineteenth century by Continental scholarship.[33] In retaliation, Shakespeare was staged anew in Dublin, London, and all points beyond; Sir James Barrie, the creator of *Peter Pan*, took the opportunity to claim Shakespeare as Scottish in a short skit, *Shakespeare's Legacy* (1916); and in *Ulysses*, Stephen jokes that Shakespeares were as common as Murphys.[34]

---

[33] In this construction, Shakespeare was the antecedent of Goethe, and proof that Saxon genius had transferred from England to Germany in the intervening centuries. 'We Germans', writes the prospectus to a German edition of *Hamlet* reported in the Irish press, 'find ourselves in Goethe's "Faust" and in Shakespeare's "Hamlet" in our proper metaphysical environment, in that longing for heaven which rises over all terrestrial anxiety. Shakespeare is one of Ours. In the midst of war we are now paying homage to his genius by an edition of "Hamlet" the like of which has never been presented by an English publisher to Shakespeare's own countrymen': 'German Homage to Shakespeare', *Irish Independent*, 21 Apr. 1916.

[34] James Joyce, *Ulysses* (London: Alma Press, 2012), 438.

A few short weeks before the rebellion, a production of *Hamlet* was staged at the Abbey Theatre by the local branch of the British Empire Shakespeare Society. This was not *Hamlet* as we now know it, but three performances closing with 'the Fortinbras Scene', with profits going to the British Red Cross. The library of Trinity College Dublin exhibited the first four folios of Shakespeare's work, while Belfast planned a public meeting in the City Hall for May, with recitals to follow.

The original date for the memorial of Shakespeare's death had been planned for Sunday 23 April, which was also the original date also for the outbreak of the rebellion. Shakespeare played his part in the rebellion as a source of comparison for the volunteers with historical precedent in the plays. Seosamh de Brun was a member of the garrison at the Jacob's factory, where he found a ramshackle *internationale* of acquired weaponry and uniforms. There the volunteers prepared for an assault that never came, putting barbed wire in the yard and knocking through walls for secure communication. In the boredom of cigarettes and rest, the men apparently made free with the Jacob's staff library, provided by the factory's Quaker owners, as De Brun was later to recall. 'The book-case in the library was broken open and pillaged. I can distinctly remember the interest evoked by quotations from "Julius Caesar", the battle of Pharsalia, etc.'[35] It is intriguing to imagine the discussions provoked by Shakespeare's *Julius Caesar*, or possibly Caesar's *Commentaries on Civil War* with its treatment of the battle of Pharsalia, the defining conflict of the Roman Civil War and the defeat of a larger army by a smaller, in a culture threatened with its own violent upheavals.

When the Dawn is Come ends, as these plays before rebellion do, with the death of the central character. Suffering tied the rebels' agenda to the larger cultural narrative of religious devotion, and prepared the playwrights themselves for the possibility of execution for their proposed treason. Many members of Irish society thought these plays were foolish dramas, but the rebellion proved them something more. Pearse, Connolly, and MacDonagh must have watched the fall of the final curtain in their plays with a certain trepidation, and if nothing else the playwrights' rehearsal of death on the Dublin stage undoes the idea sometimes put forward that the rebels were unprepared for the consequences of their uprising. The last words of *When the Dawn is Come* go to Father John as he bends over the fallen body of Thurlough MacKieran: 'Hush! Hush!', he says, 'Our voices are vain in the ear of the world. Pray for his soul. Peace at last for his soul!'[36]

O'CASEY'S DUBLIN TRILOGY AND BEYOND

In reality, there was little chance that a violent uprising would secure peace in Ireland. The Easter Rising was followed by a guerrilla War of Independence, partition, and a Civil War that left deep and still visible fissures in Irish society. The administration of the Free State after 1922 owed little to the ideals of community expressed in the Proclamation of the Irish Republic, which was never a representative document. But its aspirations of liberty and equality created a benchmark of comparison against which the state was always lacking. This fact would have remained a footnote to Irish cultural history but for the intervention

---

[35] Bureau of Military History, Witness Statement 312 (de Brun), 9.
[36] Thomas MacDonagh, *When the Dawn is Come* (Dublin: Maunsel, 1908), 53.

of Seán O'Casey, whose Dublin trilogy of *The Shadow of a Gunman* (1923), *Juno and the Paycock* (1924), and *The Plough and the Stars* (1926) form the iconic image on stage of the rebellion period. O'Casey revolutionized Irish theatre by his introduction of a new cast of characters and speech to the Dublin stage. The people of the inner-city slums are at the core of his plays, and their struggles to survive are in obvious contrast to the dreamy motivations of the romantics for whom they are asked to suffer in the name of Ireland.

Of the three plays, *The Plough and the Stars* was concerned most directly with the Easter Rising. It caused consternation among the cast and audience when first produced in the Abbey Theatre in February 1926. A decade on, the Easter Rising had very personal meanings for many of the people involved in the play's production. Its sharpest critics were republican women, who saw the play as a further step in the undoing of the rebels' high ideals—ideals already undermined to disastrous extent by the surrender, as they saw it, of the Anglo-Irish Treaty. In this context, O'Casey's play was less emblematic of the rebellion than it was of another phase in a cultural war in which Pearse, Connolly, and MacDonagh had fought previously.[37] The theatre, again, was a crucial part of this long process of Irish cultural dislocation from the British Empire—a process that continued long after independence with the Abbey Theatre riot that attended a production of *The Plough and the Stars*.[38] The occasion of one section of the audience's disaffection was the display in the play of rebel flags in a pub whose barman chats with a prostitute who regrets the political enthusiasms of her potential clients:

> You'd think they were th' glorious company of th' saints, an' th' noble army of martyrs thrampin' through th' streets of paradise. They're all thinkin' of higher things than a girl's garthers .[39]

This is a brilliant subversion of the dramatic conventions established by Pearse and company. The Easter rebels were concerned to give their rebellion a just rhetorical shape because they were concerned that violence should not obscure the justice of their claim to national sovereignty. A decade later none of this mattered to O'Casey, who knew too well that the poor were still trapped in the tenements. He pushed the point home with his bloodthirsty quotations from Patrick Pearse in 'The Voice of the Man'.[40] Pearse's fascination with

---

[37] This wave of post-revolutionary change posed new challenges for the actors on stage, as Christopher Morash observes of F. J. McCormick, who played Jack Clitheroe. 'When Clitheroe, resplendently foolish in full green dress uniform, calls out "Death for th' Independence of Ireland" at the end of act II of *The Plough and the Stars*, it required a form of acting very different from the quiet understatement of the first generation of Abbey actors': Christopher Morash, *A History of Irish Theatre 1601–2000* (Cambridge: Cambridge University Press, 2002), 175.

[38] Nicholas Grene reminds us that the riot occurred on the fourth night, not the first, and that the majority of the audience did not in fact object to O'Casey's play: *The Politics of Irish Drama: Plays in Context from Boucicault to Friel* (Cambridge: Cambridge University Press, 1999), 140.

[39] Sean O'Casey, *The Plough and the Stars*, in *Plays 2* (London: Faber & Faber, 1998), 49.

[40] 'Among the four speeches made by the Speaker outside the window in *The Plough and the Stars* (1926) is one celebrating the outbreak of World War I [...]. The actor who first played the Speaker mimicked Pearse's voice and mannerisms; there has never, in the Abbey tradition, been an attempt to present the Speaker ironically. O'Casey allowed Pearse's words to have their full effect (although he did, in fact, omit two sentences which make a difference to the meaning), which is to celebrate bloodshed in a nationalist cause as heroic. The play itself, of course,

bloodshed is grotesque in a context where death is the inescapable consequence of poverty, the implication being that a cult of self-sacrifice is the product only of bourgeois fantasy. O'Casey's plays dramatized the unintended—because unconsidered—consequences of rebellion for the people who suffered most and gained least from Irish Independence. In doing so, they liberated the Irish stage from its thrall to forms of dialogue and setting that had calcified into rural kitchen dramas at a far distance from the complexity of everyday life.[41]

O'Casey was one of many dramatists who took the Easter Rising as their subject, and *The Plough and the Stars* had a direct influence on Brendan Behan's later play, *An Giall* (1958), which shared his criticism of Pearse. Denis Johnston's *The Scythe and the Sunset* (1958) also exhibits O'Casey's influence in its ironic dialogue and dilapidated setting. The *Scythe and the Sunset* uses the rebellion to coop together civilians, militants, and an Irish soldier of the British army in a café overlooking the General Post Office. James Moran has observed that Johnston overturns the gender politics of O'Casey's play because no man fires a shot.[42] This is part recognition of the reality of women's involvement in the rebellion and part reflection of the gendered, and prejudicial, habit of figuring republicanism post-Civil War as hysterical and irrational. *The Scythe and the Sunset* finishes with a dialogue between the rebel Tetley and his prisoner, Palliser. They are both Irish, and Tetley offers Palliser the opportunity to escape the burning building that they are in:

TETLEY.   Listen, Palliser, I know that you people have a pride in your past. But isn't it our turn now?

PALLISER.   (*softening*) Of course it is. I know what's coming, and there's no hard feeling so long as I don't have to be part of the audience. When we built an Empire, Tetley, we didn't have much in the way of big battalions. But we had life and an interest in ourselves. Now we're tired of being what we are, and we play the other fellow's game because we're sick of winning. I see it all as if it had happened already. Ireland's only the start. We're going to go on winning every war, but piece by piece we're going to give it all away—not because we're licked, but because we're bloody well bored. So don't be too proud of yourselves. It won't be the first time that people like you have loosened the foundations of a civilization—and at Easter too, by gad.[43]

Johnston's inversion of a national narrative that claimed victory over a world empire is part of a broader tradition of post-revolutionary disaffection that began with O'Casey. The dialogue dramatizes the idea of Ireland's imaginative insularity post-rebellion, and as such

overturns that notion': Christopher Murray, *Twentieth-Century Irish Drama: Mirror up to Nation* (Manchester: Manchester University Press, 1997), 91.

[41] The polemicist D. P. Moran hated the Abbey after Synge for its 'Pegeen Mikes', and he poured scorn on the young men in cloaks with long hair and pale faces who 'hear lake water lapping even when stirring their punch'. Yeats's 'Celtic Note', said Moran, was one of the most glaring frauds that the credulous Irish people ever swallowed': Donal McCartney, 'Hyde, D. P. Moran, and Irish Ireland', in F. X. Martin (ed.), *Leaders and Men of the Easter Rising: Dublin 1916* (London: Methuen, 1967), 50.

[42] Moran, *Staging the Easter Rising*, 114.

[43] Denis Johnston, *The Old Lady Says No! and Other Plays* (Boston, MA: Little, Brown, 1960), 97.

articulates a certain nostalgia for the global association secured by union with Britain. The idea grew over the later twentieth century that the Easter Rising destroyed more than it created—an idea that focused on the character defects of its major figures. Hugh Leonard's *The Patrick Pearse Motel* (1971) focused again on this central, and increasingly controversial, figure of the rebellion. Pearse's erotic vision of a bodily commitment to Irish republicanism rang false to generations of artists who were well aware of the cultural conservatism of the independent state. Sex became a subject through which became visible other forms of politics that intruded negatively in the personal life of Irish citizens. The figure of Pearse evolved into a cipher for everything that went wrong after independence, despite his death in the rebellion, and will remain a problematic figure for so long as the ideals of the Irish republic for which he fought are considered to be relevant to the lives of its citizens.

The human consequences of social suffering were the central subject of literature in Ireland during the twentieth century. This was evidence less of the political commitment of generations of writers born in the shadow of the rebellion than of the consequence of a cultural inheritance shaped by the incoherent institutions of a state built from civil war. Plays about the Easter Rising exhibit more than a historical narcissism with Ireland as its subject. They can be, as O'Casey showed, dramatizations of the ideas that rebellion expressed—ideas that the state was not equipped, or enthusiastic, to apply. The plays of Pearse, Connolly, and MacDonagh were political and didactic. They were not representative of the vibrant cultures of public entertainment with which Dublin audiences were familiar through touring companies, revues, and the cinema; and it took O'Casey to realign the political event of the Easter Rising with the urban reality of the city in which the rebellion took place.

For all that, theatre was the public platform on which ideas of Ireland were tested in correspondence with turmoil in the state. This tradition has continued into the present with Sebastian Barry's *The Steward of Christendom* (1995), in which memories of the revolutionary period and its violence lap over the confused consciousness of an elderly Thomas Dunne, a one-time member of the Dublin Metropolitan Police. The Easter Rising was one of a series of violent events that mark the history of twentieth-century Ireland, and not their origin. The rebellion shared a public space with theatre and other forms of creative expression, in which we might include political agitation. The heat of this connection was felt most at the point before ignition, and this was the incendiary power of Pearse and company's plays. The impact of these dramas, and their aftermath in the century to follow, is hard to see precisely because their message burnt so intensely. The image is best caught by Yeats in his elegy for Robert Gregory, like the rebels another victim of a world at war:

> Some burn damp faggots, others may consume
> The entire combustible world in one small room
> As though dried straw, and if we turn about
> The bare chimney is gone black out
> Because the work had finished in that flare.[44]

---

[44] W. B. Yeats, 'In Memory of Major Robert Gregory', in *Collected Works*, vol. 1: *The Poems*, 2nd edn., ed. Richard Finneran (New York: Scribner, 1997), 144.

CHAPTER 11

....

THE ABBEY THEATRE AND THE IRISH STATE

....

LAUREN ARRINGTON

From the foundation of the modern Irish State, the Abbey Theatre enjoyed a position of privilege. As the self-proclaimed Irish National Theatre, the Abbey was an important cultural signifier of continuity between the ambitions of the Revival and the establishment of the Irish Free State. The value of the theatre—as perceived by the successive Provisional Government, Cumann na nGaedheal, and Fianna Fáil governments—permitted an extraordinary degree of freedom in its programme. Despite a growing conservatism that saw the institution of the Censorship of Films (1923) and the Censorship of Publications (1929), there was never legislative censorship of the theatre. That is not to say that the state did not attempt to control the theatre's programme, or that censorship did not occur. The Abbey was tethered to the state by a subsidy on which its survival depended; yet the theatre's directors used the ostensible freedom of the theatre in Ireland as a point of difference in order to defy attempts at government interference. Privately, the directors compromised the theatre's programme, censoring plays that they believed were of sound artistic merit in order to ensure good relations with the state. Throughout the 1920s and 1930s, the theatre's politics, represented in its programme and in the actions and statements of the directors, were in constant flux.[1]

By 1923 a series of wars, forced closures due to curfews, and a dearth of suitable new plays for production had left the theatre near financial collapse. The directors, W. B. Yeats, Augusta Gregory, and Lennox Robinson, believed that a subsidy from the new Free State government could rescue the Abbey from ruin. A formal relationship with the Abbey was mutually attractive to the Provisional Government and to its successor, Cumann na nGaedheal.[2] The new political elite believed that support for the National Theatre might reinforce the government's claim to authority in a state that had emerged from violent dissent

---

[1] For a more detailed discussion of the issues raised in this chapter, see Lauren Arrington, *W. B. Yeats, the Abbey Theatre, Censorship, and the Irish State: Adding the Half-Pence to the Pence* (Oxford: Oxford University Press, 2010).

[2] The Provisional Government was a transitional administration in effect from Jan. to Dec. 1922. The Irish Free State was established in Dec. 1922, after the signing of the Anglo-Irish Treaty. Cumann na nGaedheal was the first party elected to government, in 1923.

over questions of democracy, the nature of independence, and the very idea of Ireland. While the Abbey's directors sought the state's endorsement of the theatre as national, the government believed that the theatre could endorse a given political party as representative of the nation. The theatre and the state were caught in a double bind: mutually reliant but often working from conflicting ideas about what representation meant. This relationship became even more fraught after the change of government in 1932, as the values of the Catholic Church in Ireland were insinuated into the policies of Fianna Fáil, and lay organizations such as the Catholic Truth Society established a firm grasp on daily life.

EDUCATION, REPRESENTATION, AND THE CAMPAIGN FOR A STATE SUBSIDY

Cumann na nGaedheal had a strong educational ethos. The party pledged 'To carry on the National Tradition; and To utilize the powers of Government in the hands of the Irish people as well as other forms of public activity for the fullest development of the Nation's heritage'.[3] Of course, the heritage to which the party's manifesto referred was very recent: the Irish Revival had been at its height just twenty-five years earlier. The party's cultural programme attempted to create a sense of continuity and to elide the fracture and dissent that marred the myth of national progress from the Revival to the Free State. The Abbey Theatre, the Gaelic League, and the Gaelic Athletic Association were the most prominent cultural artefacts of the Revival, exemplars of the 'National Language, Literature, games and Arts' that Cumann na nGaedheal pledged itself 'to preserve and foster'.[4] The Abbey directors, desperate for financial aid, took advantage of their own history and, in a letter to President Cosgrave, positioned themselves in accordance with Cumann na nGaedheal's cultural programme:

> By tradition and accomplishment our Theatre has become the National Theatre of Ireland, it should no longer be in the possession of private individuals, it should belong to the State. Having created it and fostered it through twenty years we believe we can now confidently trust it to the Irish Nation.[5]

This wholesale offering was a bluff. Yeats knew that neither the Provisional Government nor the Cumann na nGaedheal government that followed had the resources or the expertise to manage a theatre. He had written to Gregory as early as October 1922 to say that he was 'convinced that the government will not give a penny *unless we remain in control* [. . .] Cosgrove [*sic*] does not want to be bothered with control of a theatre.'[6] Yeats used his

---

[3] John Regan, *The Irish Counter-Revolution 1921–1936: Treatyite Politics and Settlement in Independent Ireland* (Dublin: Gill & Macmillan, 1999), 36–7.

[4] Ibid.

[5] Yeats and Gregory to Cosgrave, 27 June 1924 [*recte* 1923], in W. B Yeats, *Collected Letters*, Accession letter no. 4577, Oxford University Press (InteLex Electronic Edition, http://www.nix.com/collections/130), 2002.

[6] Yeats to Gregory, 22 Oct. 1922, ibid., no. 4197.

personal connections with Desmond FitzGerald, who served as Minister for Publicity in the Provisional Government and then as Minister for External Affairs in the Free State, to approach Eoin MacNeill, the new Free State's Minister for Education. Both Fitzgerald and Ernest Blythe, Minister for Finance, urged the Abbey's directors that 'a good report from Education would be of great value and might get the matter through Finance where the real opposition would be'.[7]

In fact, when the Abbey made an official appeal, Cosgrave forwarded the report to MacNeill in the Department of Education with a note attached saying that he was 'against giving assistance'.[8] Cosgrave had served as Minister for Finance in the Provisional Government and was keenly aware of the heavy war debt that burdened the new state. By summer 1923, the Free State's expenditure was far exceeding its revenue, with an estimated deficit for the financial year in 'excess of a million pounds'.[9] It was probably this financial conservatism rather than any outright philistinism that lay behind Cosgrave's advice. However, the Abbey had an important ally in Ernest Blythe. Blythe anticipated the intangible benefits to the government's cultural programme that support for the theatre would bring.[10] It was, as Yeats had foreseen, 'the psychological moment': the Abbey could take advantage of 'the practical men without interference from the literary amateurs who are for the most part hiding their republican heads'.[11] This proved to be true: Cumann na nGaedheal had an unambiguously laissez-faire approach to the Abbey's programme, and it was not until Fianna Fáil (who styled themselves 'the Republican Party') came to power in 1932 that the state attempted to directly interfere with the theatre's productions.

Regardless of which government was in office, the state encouraged a commitment to the Irish language in the Abbey. In early negotiations on the subsidy, Robinson encouraged Yeats and Gregory to include plays in Irish in the repertoire, or else to show an intention to develop a separate theatre devoted to plays in the Irish language. The directorate responded by letting the Abbey premises to the Gaelic Players, an independent amateur company; in addition to providing a source of revenue for when the theatre was dark, the relationship had the effect of aligning the Abbey with Irish-language drama while relieving the directors of the burden of producing it. It was a prescient move. In advance of the grant's first renewal in 1926, the *Catholic Bulletin* criticized the Abbey for being a burden on the taxpayer and not in any meaningful sense an 'Irish Theatre', but the Abbey was in a strong position to refute this.[12] Irish language plays would equally be essential to the Abbey's campaign for a large-scale building project in the 1930s. The directors would include in that proposal a plan to stage six productions in Irish annually; yet it was common knowledge

[7] Robinson to Gregory, 13 July 1923, Berg Collection, NYPL. See also Robert Hogan and Richard Burnham, *The Modern Irish Drama*, vol. 6: *The Years of O'Casey, 1921–1926: A Documentary History* (Gerrards Cross: Colin Smythe, 1992), 158; and Yeats to Gregory, 6 July [1923], Yeats, *Collected Letters* no. 4344.

[8] Robinson to Gregory, 13 July 1923, Berg Collection.

[9] Regan, *Irish Counter-Revolution*, 147.

[10] Robinson to Gregory, 13 July 1923, Berg Collection. See also Hogan and Burnham, *Years of O'Casey*, 158, and Yeats to Gregory, 6 July [1923], Yeats, *Collected Letters* no. 4344.

[11] Yeats to Gregory, 22 Oct 1922, Yeats, *Collected Letters* no. 4197.

[12] Editorial, *Catholic Bulletin* 16, no. 1 (1926), 4.

that these plays were not popular with audiences, so in return for supporting the 'National language', the directors were able to leverage a request for an additional grant of £1,000.[13]

Remarkably, the Abbey directors were also able to use the Free State's educational policy as a way of securing support for some of their most experimental work. In 1919, Robinson and Yeats had founded the Dublin Drama League, an independent experimental company that staged modern European plays in translation and the work of contemporary avant-garde playwrights such as Eugene O'Neill. This experimental work could not be staged at the Abbey Theatre because of a confluence of financial pressures and popular expectations of what constituted the artistic remit of the Irish National Theatre. The League's productions inspired Yeats and Robinson to create a smaller performance space that could accommodate more experimental plays by Irish playwrights. The Abbey building desperately needed renovation, so the directors incorporated the construction of a new performance space into their plans. Although the theatre had 'between three and four thousand pounds' to its credit when the subsidy came up for renewal in 1927, Robinson described the theatre as being financially vulnerable. He wrote to Blythe: 'the Theatre could not be said to be in a safe financial position unless it had laid by a large sum of money—£10,000 say.'[14] Robinson was bold in positing such a preposterous amount, but Blythe seems to have been unflinching, and he endorsed Robinson's claim that the new experimental space could 'be looked upon as *educational* work'. Aesthetically, the experiments at what would become the Peacock Theatre were educational in the best sense, but these plays did not comply with the idea of a 'national' education that was essential to both Cumann na nGaedheal and Fianna Fáil's cultural politics. In fact, this mattered very little. The Peacock was a small space and accommodated small audiences. It was also used principally for productions by the Dublin Drama League and the new company established by Hilton Edwards and Micheál Mac Liammóir, the Gate Theatre. Since these productions did not occur under the auspices of the Abbey, they attracted little attention and no government interference.

THE LEGACY OF PUBLIC INVESTMENT AND POPULAR OWNERSHIP

The directors' claim that the Abbey constituted the National Theatre of Ireland was important to creating a sense of public ownership that would sustain the theatre over the long term. However, the ideological investment of the state and the people in the concept of a national theatre was also at the heart of the theatre's most famous controversies. The reception of Seán O'Casey's *The Plough and the Stars* (1926) exemplified the legacy of public ownership of the Abbey, as the play became an important test of the theatre's relationship with the Irish State and the state's response to popular demand for intervention. As a result of the theatre's first subsidy in 1925, the economist George O'Brien had been appointed to the Abbey directorate. His official role was to oversee the theatre's finances, but he was also

---

[13]   27 Mar. 1936, Abbey Theatre Minute Book, NLI Acc 3961/NFC 98 (6) and 1 Sept. 1937, Abbey Theatre Minute Book, NLI Acc 3961/NFC 98 (7).

[14]   Robinson to Blythe, 6 July 1927, Earnán de Blaghd Papers, Dublin, NLI MS 20,706.

governed privately by a strong sense of Catholic morality. This was not immediately evident to the Abbey's directors. When he first read the manuscript of *The Plough*, O'Brien
regarded it as 'excellent' and believed it would be 'very successful at the Abbey'. However,
when the theatre's manager, Michael Dolan, expressed reservations about O'Casey's
language—particularly the song 'sung by the "girl-of-the-streets"'—O'Brien lost his
nerve.[15] He wrote privately to Yeats, objecting to O'Casey's use of religious language, pro-
fanity, explicit sexual phrases, and the character Rosie Redmond: 'The lady's professional
side is unduly emphasised in her actions and conversation [. . .] The song at the end is an
example of what I mean.'[16] He then went so far as to propose that 'the numerous references
to "lowsers" and "lice"' should be changed. Yeats refused to compromise: 'To eliminate any
part of it on grounds that have nothing to do with dramatic literature would be to deny all
our traditions.'[17] O'Brien attempted to gain purchase by suggesting that an offence to 'public
opinion' might 'make it difficult or impossible for the Government to continue or increase
their subsidy'.[18] Although he later disavowed any intention to blackmail the directors, this
was certainly the way that his argument was received. Gregory was emphatic: 'If we have
to choose between the subsidy and our freedom, it is our freedom we choose.'[19] Privately,
Yeats, Gregory, and Robinson agreed that aspects of the play, including Rosie Redmond's
bawdy song, would have to be altered for production, but they kept this secret from O'Brien
in order to make it clear to him that the government representative on the board of directors did not have the power to censor plays.

In addition to the government-appointed director overstepping his bounds, some of
the actors were afraid to be associated with roles that challenged religious orthodoxy. In
rehearsals for *The Plough*, F. J. McCormick and Eileen Crowe refused to deliver some of their
lines. Crowe objected to saying 'I never had a child that was not born within the border of the
ten Commandments', and McCormick went so far as to refuse to speak the word 'snotty'.[20]
For O'Casey, this was the last straw. He stood by his use of 'snotty' as well as 'Bum, Bastard',
and 'Lowsey', and argued that other plays, such as Shaw's *The Devil's Disciple* and George
Shiels' *Paul Twyning*, had included those words and had not met any objection. O'Casey
wrote to Robinson, briskly withdrawing *The Plough* from production: 'The play itself is
(in my opinion) a deadly compromise with the actual; it has been further modified by the
Directors but I draw the line at a Vigilance Committee of the Actors.'[21] Catholic vigilance
associations were lobbying for legal reforms in the Free State that would institutionalize
religious morality. The 'Associated Æsthetes'—as the *Catholic Bulletin* referred to George
Russell, Yeats, Gregory, Robinson, and other prominent Protestant writers and artists—
were a prime target. As Dolan, McCormick, and Crowe's objections illustrate, actors were
not free from the pervasive climate of moral policing, but again the directorate refused to

[15] Dolan to Gregory, 1 Sept. 1925, Dublin, NLI MS 22,557.
[16] For the song as it originally appeared, see Robert Lowery (ed.), *A Whirlwind in Dublin: The
Plough and the Stars Riots* (Westport, CT: Greenwood Press, 1984), 10.
[17] Yeats to O'Brien, 10 Sept. 1925, Yeats, *Collected Letters* no. 4772.
[18] O'Brien to Yeats, 13 Sept. 1925, entry on 20 Sept. 1925, in Augusta Gregory, *Journals*, ed. Daniel
J. Murphy, vol. 2 (Gerrards Cross: Colin Smythe, 1987), 42.
[19] 20 Sept. 1925, *Journals*, 39.   [20] 10 Jan. 1926, ibid., 57.
[21] O'Casey to Robinson, 10 Jan. 1926, in *The Letters of Sean O'Casey*, vol. 1: *1910–1941*, ed. David
Krause (London: Cassell 1975), 165–6.

bow to conservative pressures. Yeats orchestrated a compromise to save the production, permitting Crowe and May Craig (who played 'A Woman') to change parts. However, the short-term solution did not prevent these morally minded actors from periodically interfering with plays that they believed were injurious to popular religious practices. A decade later, for example, Michael Dolan objected to Cormac O'Daly's play *The Silver Jubilee* because one of the characters in it, presented as a hypocrite, was a member of the Catholic Young Men's Society (a thinly veiled reference to the popular Catholic Young Men's Association). In the case of that play, the theatre was in a less secure position, and the directors believed that it was necessary to compromise the text in order to secure negotiations with the state. Yet in 1926 the directors silenced the moral objections to *The Plough*, and the play was staged with few adjustments to the script.[22]

The riots over *The Plough* were a response to perceived political rather than moral offences, and were not driven by the state but rather by individuals who stood in opposition to the state. Government ministers did have reservations about O'Casey's play, but these concerns were expressed privately. The consummate playgoer and diarist Joseph Holloway overheard James Montgomery, the first Free State Film Censor, remark caustically on *The Plough*'s opening night, 'This is a lovely Irish export.' Holloway noted that after the play he heard Montgomery say that he believed the Free State should not have appointed a director to the theatre's board at all, since it might lead to the belief that the state endorsed the Abbey's productions: 'They should have given a grant unburdened by any restrictions or not at all'!.[23] This perspective would prove prescient in the wake of the riots that erupted on the fourth night of *The Plough*'s run. Members of Cumann na mBan, led by Hanna Sheehy-Skeffington, protested that O'Casey's play degraded the memory of the Easter Rising, and that it desecrated the tricolour by having the flag carried into a public house. O'Casey's defence was that the flag was not 'symbolical or representative' of Republicanism but rather symbolized 'the whole of Ireland'.[24] As Montgomery feared, these arguments created the opportunity for public critiques of the relationship between the theatre and the state. The *Evening Herald*, which had initially published a long, favourable review of *The Plough*, went on to attack the play as 'repulsive' and argued that 'such a play would not be permitted by the Government of any other country—certainly not in America, France, Germany, or under Mussolini at the present time'.[25] Another reviewer argued that censorship was the solution to stopping 'a recurrence of those unfortunate protests'.[26] The Censorship of Films Act (1923) had been designed primarily to protect young audiences and lower-class people, who were believed to be less discriminating and therefore more susceptible to immoral influences.[27] There was growing support for a similar censorship of publications (eventually enacted in 1929), to which Yeats and Robinson were publicly opposed. (Gregory was more cautious and refrained from aligning herself with any cause that might prove injurious to the Abbey.) Importantly, Hanna Sheehy-Skeffington attacked the government subsidy, but she did not support the calls for official censorship that

[22] For these and other changes to O'Casey's script, see Nicholas Grene, 'The Class of the Clitheroes: O'Casey's Revisions to The Plough and the Stars Promptbook', *Bullán* 4, no. 2 (1999/2000), 57–66.
[23] 15 Feb. 1926, Holloway, 'Impressions of a Dublin Playgoer', Dublin, NLI MS 1,899, 321.
[24] '"The Plough and the Stars", Author Replies to Republican's Charges, A Piquant Debate', *Irish Independent*, 2 Mar. 1926, in O'Casey, *Letters*, vol. 1, 177–80.
[25] *Evening Herald*, 12 Feb. 1926.   [26] 'The Abbey Melee', ibid.
[27] Peter Martin, *Censorship in the Two Irelands, 1922–1939* (Dublin: Irish Academic Press, 2006).

came from some quarters. Rather, she thought that the state should not sponsor a theatre that failed to uphold the nation's values. Ireland was the only country, she argued, where 'a State-subsidised theatre [could] presume on popular patience to the extent of making a mockery and a byword of a revolutionary movement on which the present structure claims to stand'.[28] In her view, the answer was not institutional control but 'the free censorship of popular opinion' that she and her fellow members of Cumann na mBan had attempted to exercise through the riots.[29] Sheehy-Skeffington also argued that the Abbey directors had prohibited free expression when they summoned the police to suppress the protest. Yeats had behaved as though the theatre was a 'kept house', and—she cautioned—'any theatre lost more than the subsidy it received by giving up its freedom.'[30]

Cumann na mBan's protest laid the foundations for the *Catholic Bulletin*'s campaign against the Abbey's 'subsidised attack on Irish Nationality'.[31] The *Bulletin* challenged the subsidy from several angles. One article accused 'this subsidised system of pouring scorn on the ideals of Easter Week', while another argued that the government had given the Abbey an £850 annual subsidy but at the same time had refused to support the work of the Dublin Industrial Development Association, thereby implying that the funds supporting O'Casey's offensive play might have been used instead to alleviate the poverty that was his subject.[32] These challenges to the subsidy arose just a few weeks before the government grant to the Abbey came up for annual review. At first, the protests seemed to have hit their mark. The Cumann na nGaedheal TD (member of the Dáil) for Wexford, Osmond Esmonde, interrupted Blythe's introduction to the vote on the subsidy, which had been increased—without explanation to the Committee on Finance—to £1,000. Esmonde argued that in approving the grant, the government was 'asked to subsidise the new stage Irishman who is being invented by a modern playwright'; he called for reform of 'the board for selecting plays to be acted in the theatre [which] should be representative of the whole nation, and not any small clique or minority'.[33] Other ministers spoke up in support of Esmonde; Thomas Nolan (Cumann na nGaedheal TD for Limerick), for example, argued that the subsidy should be withdrawn 'and that the education should be given in some other way'. Several TDs complained about the lack of disclosure regarding the theatre's management and showed a total lack of knowledge that the government had a representative in place on the board. Again, Blythe proved to be essential to defending the theatre's grant. He summarized the history of the subsidy, discussed O'Brien's appointment, and concluded by arguing that 'financial stringency' should not be exercised by starving cultural institutions that 'develop the talents of the people in regard to literature and the drama'. The grant was not only renewed but increased, and the debates in the Dáil over the nature of the Abbey's productions served as a platform for campaigns against theatrical censorship. The day after the finance committee's vote, the *Irish Times* published an editorial arguing:

> everybody knows that the Abbey would refuse to sell its birthright—its ideals in art, its intellectual standards, its liberty of prophesying—for the *Dail*'s annual mess of pottage [. . .]

[28] Hanna Sheehy-Skeffington to *Irish Independent*, 15 Feb. 1926, in O'Casey, *Letters*, vol. 1, 167–8.
[29] Ibid., 168.   [30] ' "The Plough and the Stars", Author Replies to Republican's Charges'.
[31] Editorial, *Catholic Bulletin* 16, no. 3 (1926), 242–3.
[32] Ibid., 244; and 'Kevin', 'Far and Near', *Catholic Bulletin* 16, no. 3 (1926), 281.
[33] Vote 21, Miscellaneous Expenses, Dáil Eireann, vol. 16 (22 June 1926). http://www.oireachtas-debates.gov.ie/D/0016/D.0016.192606220021.html. Accessed 9 Mar. 2007.

the *Dail*, being as now constituted, utterly unfit to discuss questions of art or letters, would make itself and Ireland ridiculous in the eyes of the world.[34]

The Abbey Theatre's role as a public face of the nation, abroad and within Ireland, was a central concern of the Cumann na nGaedheal and Fianna Fáil governments. In fact, during the Irish Civil War, the capital's theatres had been a space for contesting the identity of the nation. In March 1923, the Minister for Home Affairs in the Republican government (the alternative government established by the anti-Treaty opposition), Padraig O'Ruitleis, demanded that all theatres close as an act of mourning for Republicans who had been executed by Free State forces. The Free State Army was dispatched to the Abbey to ensure that the theatre stayed open. This symbolic act endorsed the Abbey as the theatre of the new state, but it was also an act of protection, since Yeats's role as a senator had the effect, in Gregory's words, of making the Abbey 'a good target'.[35] After the Civil War, the first Cumann na nGaedheal government saw the potential for the theatre to work as a tool for unification, or at least for the presentation of a unified idea of the nation. In the first discussion of a subsidy for the Abbey in the Committee on Finance, Blythe argued, 'I think we must have this sort of institution, and the sort of activities it stands for, in this country if we are to keep the affection of the citizens of the country for the country in the way we would like it to be kept.' [36] By the time of the *Plough* riots, Cumann na nGaedheal's position as the majority seemed secure, and it would have been against the government's political interest to kowtow to the demands of the Republican women of Cumann na mBan.

In addition to the potential for the Abbey to act as a platform to endorse the power of the state, both the government and Irish citizens were keenly aware of the international prestige of the theatre and its capacity to bring tourists to Dublin. Increasing tourism, it was hoped, would boost the blighted postwar economy. This point had also been raised by Blythe in the first vote on the theatre's subsidy. He had argued that the Abbey above any other agency had made 'the name of this country [so] favourably known abroad'.[37] Similarly, at the Abbey's twenty-first birthday celebration, held in advance of the first occasion of the subsidy's renewal in 1926, Blythe praised the Abbey as 'a most important national asset' and commended its role in creating 'an interest in, and respect for, Ireland in places where, but for the Abbey, there would have been neither'.[38] Since the Abbey's role in advertising the nation had been a significant argument to justify the government's subsidy, it is unsurprising that there were objections within and outside government to *The Plough*. After the riots, Blythe successfully emphasized the theatre's educational role in order to manoeuvre the renewal and increase of the grant, but *The Plough* did not cease to

[34] 'Dail and Stage', *Irish Times*, 23 June 1926, in Holloway, 'Impressions', NLI MS 1,902.

[35] Augusta Gregory, 25 Mar. 1923, in *Journals*, ed. Daniel J. Murphy, vol. 1 (Gerrards Cross: Colin Smythe, 1978), 444.

[36] Dáil Éireann, vol. 11 (13 May 1925), 'Committee on Finance. Miscellaneous Expenses (Vote 21)'. http://historical-debates.oireachtas.ie/D/0011/D.0011.192505130012.html. Accessed 24 Oct. 2005. Morash writes that 'the matter [i.e. the subsidy] was not voted on in the Dáil' and that Yeats 'announced that the government would be giving the Abbey an annual subsidy of £850' at the dinner on 8 Aug. See Christopher Morash, *A History of Irish Theatre, 1601–2000* (Cambridge: Cambridge University Press, 2002), 163.

[37] Dáil Éireann, vol. 11 (13 May 1925), 'Committee on Finance. Miscellaneous Expenses (Vote 21)'.

[38] 'Abbey Theatre: Coming of Age Celebration', *Irish Times*, 28 Dec. 1925.

be controversial. In 1930 the play was cause for further objection when it became known that the Abbey planned to perform it alongside two other controversial plays, *John Bull's Other Island* and *The Playboy of the Western World*, at the height of 'the Tourist season'.[39] The *Nation* argued against the productions:

> That State-subsidised playhouse seems to take a perfect delight in caricaturing our people for the amusement of foreigners [. . .] is it necessary that we be continually portrayed to foreign visitors as peasants feted for killing their 'das' or as cravens such as people [in] the 'Plough and the Stars'? [. . .] Big audiences for Motor Race week and Horse Show week were already certain. The Directors could have given them the finest plays on the theatre's magnificent list. Instead it chooses to give them Seán O'Casey's 'Plough and the Stars' lest any of them go away with respect for our War of Independence, and Synge's 'Playboy' to be taken as typical peasant life.[40]

The article went on to suggest that the Abbey directors colluded 'in cracking a joke against the crude Irish with any Tom Dick or Harry who crosses the Channel to see the motor speeders in Phoenix Park or the military jumpers in Ballsbridge'.

The annual horse show at the Royal Dublin Society was the most important occasion in the Abbey Theatre's year for reviving profits. In the interim between the critique of the theatre's programme by the *Nation* and the opening of Horse Show Week a fortnight later, the Abbey directors silently adjusted the theatre's programme. *The Plough* and *John Bull's Other Island* were withdrawn, and Gregory's *The Rising of the Moon* and Brinsley MacNamara's comedy *Look at The Heffernans* were scheduled to play on alternating nights.[41] This drastically changed a programme of plays that were famous for their controversies into a tepid programme of a new play—a proven crowd-pleaser—and two classics. (*The Playboy* was now accepted as an enjoyable part of the Abbey's repertoire by all but the most conservative audiences.) Although a direct motive is impossible to ascribe, it seems as if the change was calculated to keep the Abbey financially afloat—not only in terms of satisfying audiences during Horse Show Week but also in order to secure the continuance of the state subsidy, which had seemed precarious in the most recent financial debate.

In addition to attracting tourists to Dublin, the government subsidy put the theatre under pressure to tour within the country. In the 1927 subsidy debate, Thomas Johnson, Minister for Labour, suggested that state funding could be used to 'extend the activities of the society to the country', which would provide a broader benefit beyond a Dublin audience. However, Johnson's suggestion was problematic given the Abbey's history of touring within the country. In June 1924, the Abbey players had organized as a private enterprise a tour of *Juno and the Paycock* to Cork. The local manager had opposed the religious and sexual references in the play and demanded the rewriting of a large portion of the script. Gregory recorded the controversy in her journal: 'Dolan had to arrange (between two performances) that the young man [Bentham] should marry her [Mary] but should desert her later because she had not brought the expected fortune.'[42] Again, in 1927 when the Abbey toured T. C. Murray's *Autumn Fire* and Lennox Robinson's *The Big House* to Cork, local Catholic vigilance societies organized a boycott. The protesters were criticized by Dublin's

---

[39] 'Why Those?', *Nation*, 19 July 1930.   [40] Ibid.
[41] Abbey Account Book 1925–32, Abbey Theatre Archives.
[42] Gregory, 3 June 1924, in *Journals*, vol. 1, 541.

Evening Herald for being uneducated and prudish 'patriots'.[43] Yet the conservatism of provincial audiences, which combined religious orthodoxy with political opinion, was a portent of the challenges that the Abbey would face when Fianna Fáil came to power in 1932.

THE ABBEY UNDER FIANNA FÁIL

Yeats expected Fianna Fáil to withdraw the annual subsidy to the Abbey.[44] The theatre had lost a valuable ally when Blythe left his post as Minister for Finance, but he still served as Cumann na nGaedheal TD for Monaghan, which Robinson believed offered some hope. However, it was clear that Fianna Fáil was going to demand compliance with the party's ideology if the subsidy were to continue. Yeats anticipated this, and in the spring of 1932 he published the introduction to his play *Fighting the Waves* in which he combined his frustration with the change in government with his concern for the freedom of the theatre.[45] He contrasted the Abbey's early plays—his own plays in verse and Gregory's folk drama, plays 'full of vague suggestion'—with the recent vogue for a vulgar 'school of satire that has for its subject the actual life of the village and the slum'. He lamented a lack of imagination in the statesmen who shaped the identity of modern Ireland:

> [I]f the Irish Government at the establishment of the Free State had done something no revolution of strong farmers, clerks and lawyers would permit, have founded a school that could have substituted, as only a literature without satirical or realist prepossessions could, positive desire for the negative passion of a national movement beaten down into party politics, compelled for a century to attack everything, to suspect everybody.[46]

Almost three decades earlier, Yeats had written 'An Irish National Theatre and Three Sorts of Ignorance' in response to Arthur Griffith's attack on *The Shadow of the Glen*.[47] This introduction to *Fighting the Waves* was a similar defence of artistic freedom against a blinkered religious nationalism, which demanded a 'representative' drama that embodied party ideology rather than artistic vision.

When Augusta Gregory died on 22 May 1932, the government moved quickly to attempt to institute control over the theatre. Just two days after her death, Fianna Fáil's executive council met to select her successor to the Abbey board.[48] Their first choice, Arthur Clery, had been a vocal opponent of both *The Playboy* and *The Shadow of the Glen* and had encouraged people to protest 'if they find their *National* theatre tending towards immoral,

---

[43] D. O'C., 'The "Kill-Joys"', *Evening Herald*, 9 Feb. 1927, in Holloway, 'Impressions'. NLI MS 1,907.

[44] Yeats to Olivia Shakespear, 9 May 1932, Yeats, *Collected Letters* no. 5668.

[45] Yeats, 'Introduction to *Fighting the Waves*', *Dublin Magazine* 7, no. 2 (1932), 7–11.

[46] Ibid., 8.

[47] Yeats, 'The Irish National Theatre and Three Sorts of Ignorance', *United Irishman*, 24 Oct. 1903, in W. B. Yeats, *Uncollected Prose*, ed. John P. Frayne, vol. 2 (London: Macmillan, 1975), 306–8. Also see David Krause, 'Sean O'Casey and the Higher Nationalism: The Desecration of Ireland's Household Gods', in Robert O'Driscoll (ed.), *Theatre and Nationalism in Twentieth-Century Ireland* (London: Oxford University Press, 1971), 120.

[48] Memorandum. Extract from Cabinet Minutes, 'Abbey Theatre: Appointment of a Director', 24 and 27 May 1932, NAI TAOIS/S 6284 A.

anti-Christian or anti-human propaganda'.[49] To the government's disappointment, Clery was unwilling to take up the post of director, and before the executive council could proceed very far in recommending another candidate, the state's lack of authority came to light. Walter Starkie, George O'Brien's successor, still held the post of government director, and the state was not entitled to appoint regular members to the theatre's board of directors. The issue of a new director would not be raised again for another year, when Starkie took Gregory's place, and the post of government-appointed director became vacant.

In the meantime, Yeats and the Abbey Players embarked for North America. These were separate but complementary enterprises. Yeats was travelling on a lecture tour to fundraise for the Irish Academy of Letters, which had been organized in opposition to the censorship of publications, but the freedom of the theatre was a constant subject of his speeches. In Cleveland, Ohio, he argued:

> You've got to treat the theater as if it were part of an educational system [. . .] A subsidy enables a theater to perform unpopular plays, to keep ahead of public opinion and to shape it. We have had a subsidy for years, a small one, and we have produced plays unpopular at the time which became part of the life of the country. Without a subsidy a theater must produce best sellers only. A play isn't like a book. When I was a young man I was published by publishers who knew my book would not be popular but who were willing to face a risk for the sake of the future. Theaters cannot do that, and great vitality is sacrificed.[50]

As his lecture tour progressed, Yeats's references to the Abbey's relationship with the Irish state increasingly gave voice to the rising antagonism between the theatre and the Fianna Fáil government. In Toronto, he went so far as to declare that the new government would be continuing the grant that began under Cumann na nGaedheal. This was a pre-emptive move that was calculated to make it difficult for Fianna Fáil to withdraw its support.[51]

Just a few months later, the threat of government interference with the Abbey's productions was finally realized. The spark was the Abbey's recent tour of the United States, during which they performed Synge's *Playboy* and *Shadow of the Glen* as well as O'Casey's *Juno*. The American political party Fianna Fáil, Incorporated objected to the Abbey's representation of 'the Irish character' and argued that there were

> thousands of good clean wholesome plays which might be presented and which would have a tendency to help us in our efforts to elevate our race and our people and to keep them before the other peoples of the world as decent, worthy and God-fearing people and at least the equals of the people of any other nation.[52]

Fianna Fáil, Inc. proceeded to lobby Fianna Fáil in Ireland to withhold the theatre's subsidy, which the Americans argued wasted the hard-earned money of Irish taxpayers on these 'plays, with their filthy language, their drunkness [*sic*], murder and prostitution'. At first, the government attempted to handle the party's complaints with diplomacy. The Secretary for the Department of External Affairs, J. P. Walsh, wrote a letter clarifying that

[49] Arthur Clery, *The Idea of a Nation*, ed. Patrick Maume (Dublin: University College Dublin Press, 2002), 49–50.

[50] W. B. Yeats in interview with *Cleveland Plain Dealer*, quoted in Karin Margaret Strand, 'W. B. Yeats's American Lecture Tours' (doctoral thesis, Northwestern University, 1978), 216–17.

[51] Ibid., 218.   [52] Memorandum, Fianna Fáil, Inc., 21 Dec. 1932, NAI TAOIS/S 6284 A.

the subsidy was to support 'the National Theatre Society, Ltd.', not the Abbey Players who had undertaken the American tour. In fact, the Irish consulate had refused to allow the players to include the official seal of the Free State on the publicity circulars for that tour.[53] Fianna Fáil, Inc. would not be so easily appeased, and Walsh forwarded the matter to the Department of the President.[54]

Yeats launched a counter-campaign in an interview with the pro-de Valera *Irish Press*. When he was asked about the American protests, he argued that the Abbey Players had gone 'to America as ambassadors of Irish taste', and he echoed the government's concerns by arguing, 'We have got to keep the Irish in America linked up with our nation, we must not lose them.' However, Yeats insisted that this link must be a cultural, not a political one. As a further demonstration of the cultural link between the two countries, Yeats produced his *Sophocles' King Oedipus* in January 1933 as a benefit for the Irish Academy of Letters. He explained that *Oedipus* had recently been produced by the University of Notre Dame, an institution with a strong Catholic and Irish identity. This was proof of the liberality of Irish audiences in the United States and an implicit argument against theatrical censorship: 'Ireland had no censorship, and a successful performance [of his *Oedipus*] might make her proud of her freedom.'[55]

Yeats's manipulation of the press was a frequent tactic in shaping the theatre's relationship with the state. Despite Fianna Fáil, Inc.'s influence, in the face of controversy the Fianna Fáil executive council voted to include the grant in the next budget. Even so, J. J. McElligott, the secretary to the Minister for Finance, wrote a threatening letter to Lennox Robinson:

> It will be understood that in considering the advisability of continuing the Grant hitherto made the Minister could hardly disregard representations of this kind. It might even happen that if the representations were of sufficient weight and substance he would be compelled to make the continuance of the grant conditional on an undertaking that, in the event of another American Tour being contemplated in the future, the repertoire of plays should be such as not to arouse criticism of the nature indicated.[56]

Without waiting for a reply, the government immediately exercised a further measure of control by reducing the grant to £750. This reduction was not entirely punitive, since it was in keeping with Fianna Fáil's cuts to the public sector, including reductions to the salaries of civil servants. Yet the 1933 budget does show how different the policies of Fianna Fáil were to those of Cumann na nGaedheal, which had increased the theatre's grant in the same budget that it reduced old-age pensions.

Fianna Fáil was far from finished with dealing with the Abbey directorate's rebellion. In the same letter in which McElligott relayed the state's threat to the theatre's funding, he informed Robinson that the executive council had appointed Professor William Magennis as the new government director, replacing Starkie, who had now taken Gregory's post. This

---

[53] M. Murphy (for Consul General) to Secretary, Department of External Affairs (28 Dec. 1932), NAI TAOIS/S 6284 A.

[54] At this time, the Department of the President referred to the President of the Executive Council, Éamon de Valera. The office of the Taoiseach (Irish for 'chief') was established by the 1937 constitution.

[55] Quoted in Strand, 'W. B. Yeats's American Lecture Tours', 277.

[56] J. J. McElligott to Robinson, 27 Feb. 1933, NLI MS 21,957.

was an incredible affront. Magennis was a regular contributor to the *Catholic Bulletin*, a vocal opponent of modern literature, and a public opponent of W. B. Yeats.[57] Yeats replied immediately, bypassing McElligott and writing straight to de Valera. He argued that the government was bowing to the whims of reactionaries. He argued that there had been no protest from 'the Great Catholic University of Notre Dame' when he had spoken there on tour, and in New York some Irish-Americans had defended the Abbey against Fianna Fáil, Inc.'s attacks. One of these allies was Patrick Farrell, who had an influential position as the director of the Irish Theatre and the Museum of Irish Art, and had issued a public statement proclaiming the aesthetic value of the Abbey's touring productions.[58] Although Farrell's influence was artistic and lacked the weight of the lobby of Fianna Fáil's funders in New York, Yeats threatened to publish Farrell's correspondence and his own indictment of the government's policy. As a final flourish, he declared that the Abbey directorate refused Magennis's appointment and 'any further financial assistance' from the government.[59] This was a similar manoeuvre to the directorate's offer of the entire theatre and its management to Cosgrave during the early campaign for a subsidy. Yeats now drafted a letter to the press in which he shamed Fianna Fáil and recounted support for the Abbey from important, educated audiences in the United States. These were people who appreciated 'the Irish intellectual movement' and all it had done to raise 'the prestige of the Irish Race in America'.[60] Before the letter was printed, Yeats had a last-minute audience with de Valera, during which the two managed to reach a degree of agreement. Magennis was withdrawn as the government's appointment to the directorate; Yeats would withhold his letter to the press, which would allow de Valera to save face, and the Abbey would keep its subsidy.

The Abbey's touring programme continued to be the subject of debate. For the next tour to the United States, in the summer of 1934, the directors included Synge and O'Casey in their programme: *Riders to the Sea*, *The Shadow of the Glen*, *The Well of the Saints*, *The Playboy of the Western World*, *The Shadow of a Gunman*, *Juno and the Paycock*, and *The Plough and the Stars*. For the first time in the theatre's history, the directors submitted their touring programme to the government in advance of departure. While this might seem like a display of compliance in the wake of Fianna Fáil, Inc.'s protest, in reality it was more of a taunt. Ten days before the government wrote to the Abbey regarding their plans for the tour, the Abbey directors leaked to the press reports of the government's opposition to their production of *Playboy* and *The Plough*. Yeats declared that 'the Abbey Theatre was not to be regarded as a minor branch of the civil service', and he threatened to give up the subsidy rather than sacrifice the 'liberty of the Theatre'.[61] De Valera could only reply mildly: 'the selection of plays for production by the Abbey Company is, of course, a matter for the Directors of the National Theatre Society'; in other words, it was beyond the government's remit. The government asked merely that the directors make it 'clear that the Government is in no sense responsible for the selection of plays'.[62] As a consequence

[57] R. F. Foster, *W. B. Yeats: A Life*, vol. 2: *The Arch-Poet* (Oxford: Oxford University Press, 2003), 464.
[58] Peter Kavanagh, *The Story of the Abbey Theatre* (Orono: National Poetry Foundation, 1984), 159.
[59] Enclosure, TS (copy) Yeats to McElligott, 1 Mar. 1933, NLI MS 21,957.
[60] Yeats to the Irish Newspapers [1 Mar. 1933], Yeats, *Collected Letters*, no. 5827.
[61] 'Abbey Theatre Tour Surprise', *Irish Independent*, 7 Apr. 1934.
[62] Department of the President to Robinson, 17 Apr. 1934, NLI MS 21,957. See also Foster, *Yeats*, vol. 2, 465, 742.

of his meek response to Yeats's coup, de Valera was challenged by members of his party in the Dáil, who reminded him of the previous year's protests. Several Fianna Fáil TDs asked that government's approval of the theatre's productions be made a condition of the grant. However, de Valera stood firm and Yeats published a corrective in the *Sunday Times* that allowed the President to save face.[63]

There were occasions when it was in the Abbey's interest to comply with the state's conservatism. The most extreme example of this is the decisions that were made during the Abbey directors' campaign for a new theatre building. Yeats and his fellow directors foresaw the opportunity to amalgamate the Abbey Theatre with other Dublin theatres, including the Gate, under the auspices of a single National Theatre. This would reduce competition, provide the Abbey with a new building (which was desperately needed), and ensure the future of the Irish National Theatre Society. During the secret negotiations, the directors lost the leverage they had enjoyed through the public controversies that had allowed them to use the power of the press to effectively bully the government into submission. When the government-appointed director Richard Hayes (formerly the Censor of Films, appointed to the Abbey's board in 1934) objected to a new play by Cormac O'Daly, *The Silver Jubilee*, because he believed its plot was morally offensive, the directors returned the script to O'Daly, recommending censorial changes. In rehearsal, the script was subjected to further censorship, as the same members of the company who had objected to aspects of *The Plough* now opposed O'Daly's representation of the Catholic clergy. As the plans for reconstruction gained momentum, another play, Paul Vincent Carroll's *The White Steed*, was declined for production because, as Holloway recorded, 'the Abbey Directors voted it too anti-clerical'.[64] Yeats also withheld his play *The Herne's Egg* in order to avoid endangering the theatre's relationship to the state. Frank O'Connor, who was then serving on the board of directors, recalls in his autobiography *My Father's Son* a conversation with Yeats during which O'Connor asked, 'Hasn't it occurred to you that we have created vested interests?' Yeats replied, 'bitterly, "Did you think I wasn't aware of it?"'[65]

The aesthetic principles of education and representation that Yeats and Gregory set out at the founding of the Abbey Theatre enabled the directorate to cultivate a relationship with the state that ensured the theatre's place as the Irish National Theatre. Yet this was a relationship that demanded compromises on both sides. Even so, at least during Yeats's lifetime, the Abbey directors were able to resist the complete ideological co-option of the theatre, and any compromises to artistic freedom were made willingly in order to ensure the continued alliance of the theatre and the state.

[63] 'A Misunderstanding Corrected', *Sunday Times*, 7 Oct. 1934, in Yeats, *Uncollected Prose*, vol. 1, 500.

[64] Joseph Holloway, *Joseph Holloway's Irish Theatre*, ed. Robert Hogan and Michael J. O'Neill (3 vols., Dixon, CA: Proscenium Press, 1968–70), vol. 3, 15.

[65] Frank O'Connor, *My Father's Son* (London: Macmillan, 1968), 191.

CHAPTER 12

....

O'CASEY AND THE CITY

....

CHRISTOPHER MURRAY

INTRODUCTION
....

IN his classic study *The City in History*, Lewis Mumford reminds us that it was through the city in ancient Greece that drama was fostered and, with its dialogue, the growth of 'urban self-consciousness'. Indeed, the ancient city was itself a theatre, 'in which common life takes on the features of a drama heightened by every device of costume and scenery'. The 'human dialogue', in all its freedom, humour, and variety of expression, emerged from ritual and dramatic action.[1] It is a startling thesis Mumford advances, albeit one that those immersed in theatre and the arts are instinctively happy to see advanced in a sociological and anthropological history. It is good, too, to have Mumford's definition of the city as 'a place designed to offer the widest facilities for significant conversation'.[2] This is a claim particularly suited to Dublin city, founded by the Danes in the ninth century, and the history of its secular theatre, developed by the colonizing English from its origins—as elsewhere in Europe—in the dramatization of biblical narrative within church, cathedral, and eventually urban settings.[3] Mumford's concept of the city seems well suited to Dublin, where self-consciousness and conversation have proved leading, not to say dominating, features of its culture and specifically its theatre.

Seán O'Casey was born in Dublin only two years before James Joyce. Unbeknownst to each other they shared the intimate city (population around 250,000) at the same time, Joyce seeing it as a centre of paralysis, O'Casey as a site of injustice to the poor. Although there was a class difference between them and O'Casey had little formal education, both writers shared a love–hate relationship with their native city, O'Casey's aesthetic being

....

[1] Lewis Mumford, *The City in History: Its Origins, its Transformations, and its Prospects* (Harmondsworth: Penguin, 1966), 138.

[2] Ibid., 139.

[3] A. M. Nagler, *A Source Book in Theatrical History* (New York: Dover, 1959), 39–53. See also Alan J. Fletcher, *Drama, Polity and Performance in Pre-Cromwellian Ireland* (Cork: Cork University Press, 2000), and Desmond Slowey, *The Radicalization of Irish Drama 1600–1900: The Rise and Fall of Ascendancy Theatre* (Dublin: Irish Academic Press, 2008).

the more tragic and political. What Stanislaus Joyce said of his brother holds good for O'Casey: it was 'the comprehending love of an artist for his subject'[4] that characterized their scathing criticism of the place. Where Joyce adopted scrupulous meanness as his version of realism, verging towards Zola, O'Casey was from the belated outset of his career as writer closer to the styles of the Bible, Boucicault, and Shakespeare, where generosity of spirit went hand-in-hand with rhetoric and lyricism. The god governing O'Casey's imagined version of Dublin city could never be remote, 'refined out of existence, indifferent, paring his fingernails'[5] as Joyce imagined. O'Casey would seem, in his aesthetic, to favour his own creation Juno Boyle's sentiment: 'Ah, what can God do agen the stupidity o' men!'[6] Joyce was fundamentally a humanist intent on providing exemplars of the individual's struggle for freedom and moral decency;[7] O'Casey, on the other hand, as a socialist, was intent on a search for a wider form of fulfilment, for which the workers' trade union established in Dublin in 1909 by his idol James Larkin provided the clearest image and programme.

Nevertheless, while community comes first in O'Casey's ethical understanding of the relationship between the individual and society, it is a mistake to overlook his interest in the individual's plight.[8] *Within the Gates* (1934) is partly about the imperative to resist conventional mores; in *Red Roses for Me* (1943), for all its emphasis on social regeneration, the hero responds angrily to his lover's attempt to draw him away from strike action: 'Go to hell, girl, I have a soul to save as well as you.'[9] In this chapter I focus on how, beginning with *The Harvest Festival* (written 1919), O'Casey had in mind the necessity to see social change as dependent on individual commitment, and how in the three great Dublin plays—*The Shadow of a Gunman* (1923), *Juno and the Paycock* (1924), and *The Plough and the Stars* (1926)—he foregrounded the tragedy inherent in a liberation struggle in which individual participation was delusive. In that context *Red Roses for Me* not only rewrites *The Harvest Festival* but also rewrites history, and in particular rewrites Patrick Pearse's idea of a revolution as Christian sacrifice, which O'Casey originally spurned. The trajectory, then, arrives at an idealized portrait of a city on the brink of redemption.

The Harvest Festival, from its first publication in 1979, has not had a good press. Ronald Ayling, O'Casey's literary executor and bibliographer, terms it 'apprentice work' and affirms that 'the writing is oratorical rather than dramatic'.[10] Yet Ayling thought well enough of this work—which was rejected for production by the Abbey and remains unstaged—to include it in the 1984 edition of O'Casey's *Complete Plays* (volume 5), thus rendering it in some degree canonical. Heinz Kosok is less indulgent: 'it might be argued that a distinct

⁴ Stanislaus Joyce, *My Brother's Keeper* (1958) (London: Faber & Faber, 1982), 234.

⁵ James Joyce, *A Portrait of the Artist as a Young Man* (Harmondsworth: Penguin, 1960), 215.

⁶ Sean O'Casey, *Complete Plays* (5 vols., London: Macmillan, 1984), vol. 1, 86.

⁷ Declan Kiberd, *Ulysses and Us: The Art of Everyday Living* (London: Faber & Faber, 2009), 10–15, 347–57.

⁸ Accordingly, Herbert Goldstone's study may be regarded as inspecting only one side of the equation, admirable though his analysis is. See Herbert Goldstone, *In Search of Community: The Achievement of Seán O'Casey* (Cork: Mercier Press, 1972).

⁹ O'Casey, *Complete Plays*, vol. 3, 172.

¹⁰ Ronald Ayling, 'Seeds for Future Harvest: Propaganda and Art in O'Casey's Earliest Plays', *Irish University Review* 10, (1980) special issue on Seán O'Casey, ed. Christopher Murray, 25, 32.

disservice has been done to [O'Casey's] reputation by its publication.'[11] James Moran limits his comments to situating *The Harvest Festival* as an early draft of *Red Roses for Me*.[12] The significant point, however, about O'Casey's first surviving full-length play, apart from its obvious autobiographical elements, is its mytho-poetic structure—its being governed by a dominating dramatic image. For the first time, O'Casey interrogated and ironized what an eponymous symbol can release within a community when superimposed on a social situation where class warfare cuts across other levels of 'actuality'. As a common labourer who gloried in the new creed of Larkin's syndicalism, O'Casey had a vision of a new Jerusalem; as a practising Protestant into his early 30s, he was quite familiar with the annual harvest festival of thanksgiving hosted by his spiritual father, the Revd E. M. Griffin, in his parish church of St Barnabas in Dublin's East Wall. What this festival embodied is well described by the English writer Laurie Lee, born in the Cotswolds in 1914: 'The year revolved around the village, the festivals round the year, the Church round the festivals, the Squire round the Church, and the village round the Squire.' [13] The young people liked the harvest festival best, and virtually everyone participated: it was all about 'the continuity of growth'.[14] The East Wall area, where O'Casey lived, was a kind of urban village containing a working-class area.[15] He matured within its sustaining but unsustainable values. As the pace of Irish history accelerated in the second decade of the twentieth century, traditional Anglo-Irish cultural values and allegiances came under attack from militant nationalists, socialists, and Irish-language enthusiasts. In his play, O'Casey would bring these two worlds, the old and new, into harsh opposition, so that a new kind of secularized, urban harvest festival could be adumbrated.

For all its faults, *The Harvest Festival* is prologue to the three great Dublin plays to which *Red Roses for Me* is the epilogue. Such is the summary of my argument. In *The Harvest Festival*, set mainly in a churchwarden's parlour where his wife is discovered piling up cabbages to be taken to the parish church, a workman, Tom Nimmo (perhaps from *nemo*, 'nobody'), is engaged in tiling her fireplace. Tom admires the cabbages: 'One of them 'ud make a dinner for a navvy's [docker's] family.' Later we are introduced to such a docker, who is on strike. O'Casey satirizes the churchwarden's wife, Mrs Williamson, who laughs at the idea that she has grown the cabbages herself: 'Oh! dear no; thank God we are able to buy everything we want.'[16] She explains the festival to Tom, a Roman Catholic, who only knows of a version 'held in a barn with plenty of singin' an' dancin' an' lashin's of drink'. The horrified Mrs Willamson, to underline the sectarian rift which also marks a socio-economic one, responds, 'we know better than that'.[17] When O'Casey's hero, Jack Rocliffe, enters, his unskilled status further extends the class-divided society O'Casey is trying to depict. A strike is pending, and Jack is all for it (as Tom is not):

> If this strike develops much more there will be a Harvest Festival in Dublin, in which the Labour Leaders will be the clergy, the strikers the congregation; in which curses will be prayers,

[11] Heinz Kosok, *O'Casey the Dramatist* (Gerrards Cross: Colin Smythe; Totowa, NJ: Barnes & Noble, 1985), 7.

[12] James Moran, *Seán O'Casey* (London: Bloomsbury, 2013), 104, 236.

[13] Laurie Lee, *Cider with Rosie* (London: Hogarth Press, 1959), 223.   [14] Ibid., 268.

[15] Alan Simpson, 'O'Casey and the East Wall Area in Dublin', *Irish University Review* 10 (1980), 41–51.

[16] O'Casey, *Complete Plays*, vol. 5, 414.   [17] Ibid., 415.

FIG. 12.1 The continuing resonance of the background to O'Casey's *Dublin Trilogy* can be measured in the events commemorating the Great Lockout of 1913 a hundred years later. This detail is from the *Great Dublin Lockout Tapestry*, designed by Robert Ballagh and Cathy Henderson for the 1913 Committee.

Courtesy of Pádraig Yeates and SIPTU.

hymns will be lamentations, the choir will be police and soldiers, the seed will be the blood of the proletariat, and the crop will be the conception of the New Idea of Labour in Ireland.[18]

As Jack is a Protestant and beloved of the rector of St Brendan's, biographically he is O'Casey's first dramatic self-portrait. Although its complexity of class and religious affiliations renders the play difficult to read in relation to the 1913 Lockout, such is its main historical source. O'Casey was emotionally and physically involved in that long and divisive dispute (which ended in humiliation for Jim Larkin), and its bitterness served to shape his militant socialism thereafter. It happened that the 1913 Lockout is also the key to the Irish Citizen Army's involvement in the 1916 rebellion, although the disaffected O'Casey, a founder member and drafter of its constitution, stood aside.[19]

[18]   Ibid., 418.

[19]   Pádraig Yeates, *Lockout: Dublin 1913* (Dublin: Gill & Macmillan, 2000) and *A City in Wartime: Dublin 1914–18* (Dublin: Gill & Macmillan, 2011). See also Sean O'Casey, *The Story of the Irish Citizen Army* (1919) (London: Journeyman Chapbook, 1980).

The plot of *The Harvest Festival* makes its indirect way to Jack's being shot while sup-porting the strike. Then follows an awkward death scene at the Rockliffes' 'poorly fur-nished' but fully described tenement room in Act II,[20] leaving a whole act during which the actual harvest festival takes place while Jack's body is refused entry to the church. This is the central *agon* of the play, meant as synecdoche for the struggle in Dublin between imperialism and socialism. Unfortunately, as the play's critics point out, O'Casey's struc-ture is such that the protagonist who should advance the workers' argument is killed too soon, and the representative of the employers, Sir Jocelyn Vane, has an easy target in the rector who wishes to accept Jack's body in church. Vane informs him: 'If you are deter-mined to identify yourself, and through yourself, to identify the Church, with those who have committed themselves to the overthrow of established Society [. . .] then, sir, you will not have Sir Jocelyn Vane with you.'[21] The rector capitulates; new battle lines are drawn as Jack's comrades sing the socialist anthem, 'The Red Flag'. This finale suggests that the play was not revised until after 1917, when, as O'Casey says, 'A Terrible Beauty [was] Borneo' in the USSR and 'not in Ireland'.[22] By allowing the stirring anthem to end *The Harvest Festival*, O'Casey indicates his willingness to permit anachronism to strengthen effect, as he does later in lending the Covey in *The Plough and the Stars* a full-blown commu-nist consciousness in 1915–16. In 1919, when he submitted the play to the Abbey, O'Casey found that the directors, and in particular W. B. Yeats, had no time for subversive harvest festivals. Forced to adapt to the Abbey's aesthetic, O'Casey would make the Covey a fool as well as a Marxian theorist. At any rate, the Covey remains alive in the play (as reso-lute non-combatant) in order to carry on the argument that only a proletarian revolution made sense in Dublin at that time.

Language and Politics

For the purposes of this chapter I look here at the three Dublin plays under two headings. The first is language as it reflects upon Dublin city, and the other is politics as they derive from Pearse's nationalism and Larkin/Connolly's socialism. In relation to language—or urban dialogue, to revert to Lewis Mumford—the salient fact about O'Casey's plays is the interaction of life and art. With him, this was not a constant. In the trilogy, he aimed for and achieved mimesis of Dublin speech in its liveliness and rhetorical flourishes, but in his later plays the poetical qualities latent in his work from the outset were given free rein. This shift in style, blatant in *Red Roses for Me*, led to derision from those Irish critics of the 1940s who could not see beyond the naturalistic speech of the earlier work. But the shift was rather a further development away from naturalism, to which he became increasingly hos-tile after 1926. In describing the wit of Northside Dubliners, oral historian Kevin C. Kearns attributes to his witnesses the belief that 'Seán O'Casey didn't invent a single thing. All he

---

[20] O'Casey, *Complete Plays*, vol. 5, 434.   [21] Ibid., 466.

[22] Sean O'Casey, *Autobiographies* (London: Macmillan, 1963), vol. 2, 138. It is my view that the single act published along with the first edition of *The Harvest Festival* is an early and not a revised act.

did was keep his ears open.' Therefore his language was '*totally* authentic'.[23] Gabriel Fallon, a native Dubliner, cast as Mr Gallogher in the première of *The Shadow of a Gunman*, testifies to that:

> As I reached stage level my ear caught some of the richest Dublin dialogue I had ever heard, at least on the stage of the Abbey. It was spoken by F. J. McCormick with that proud consciousness of origin that marks the true-born Dubliner, every nuance charged with an intensity of meaning.[24]

Reviews of *The Shadow of a Gunman* and the succeeding plays make it plain that the first audiences packed out the Abbey because they recognized the language as theirs and the characters as sympathetic.[25] That much is incontestable. But what Kearns really shows is that demotic Dublin speech came to be heard as 'like O'Casey'. O'Casey became established as the *inventor* of Dublin speech while imitating and elaborating its rhetorical mannerisms. He was, in fact, impatient with the contemporary notion of dramatic realism as reproducing rather than representing actuality, claiming that '[t]his rage for real, real life on the stage has taken all the life out of the drama'.[26] The question of O'Casey's language, then, is a lot more complex than commentators such as Raymond Williams and Seamus Deane have suggested, each of them tending to see the plays' politics sacrificed to the elaboration of 'idle talk'.[27] Rather, O'Casey's Dublinese is theatrically heightened in pursuit of alienation effects.

The advance from *The Harvest Festival* to *The Shadow of a Gunman,* in showing greater mastery of dialogue, characterization, and plot structure, also involved a development of performativity for comic purposes. It is a device which accords with the distinction Colbert Kearney makes between oral and literary culture: 'Oral culture is characterized by a sense of language as performance rather than description.'[28] From the greeting of his opening words, Mr Gallogher's absurd letter to the Irish Republican Army meets the approval of his on-stage audience:

MRS. HENDERSON.   There's a beginnin' for you, Mr. Davoren.
MINNIE.   That's some swank.

[23] Kevin C. Kearns, *Dublin Tenement Life: An Oral History* (New York: Penguin, 2000), 143. Italics in original.
[24] Gabriel Fallon, *Sean O'Casey: The Man I Knew* (London: Routledge & Kegan Paul; Boston, MA: Little, Brown, 1965), 5.
[25] See Robert Hogan and Richard Burnham (eds.), *The Modern Irish Drama*, vol. 6: *The Years of O'Casey, 1921–1926: A Documentary History* (Gerrards Cross: Colin Smythe; Newark, DE: University of Delaware Press, 1992).
[26] Sean O'Casey, 'The Green Goddess of Realism', in *The Flying Wasp* (London: Macmillan, 1937), 123.
[27] See Raymond Williams, *Drama from Ibsen to Brecht* (London: Pelican Books, 1973), 163. See also Seamus Deane, 'Irish Politics and O'Casey's Theatre', in Thomas Kilroy (ed.), *Sean O'Casey: A Collection of Critical Essays* (Englewood Cliffs, NJ: Prentice-Hall, 1975), 149–58.
[28] Colbert Kearney, *The Glamour of Grammar: Orality and Politics and the Emergence of Sean O'Casey* (Westport, CT: Greenwood Press, 2000), 7. See also Bernice Schrank, ' "You Needn't Say No More": Language and the Problems of Communication in Seán O'Casey's *The Shadow of a Gunman*', *Irish University Review* 8 (1978), 91–112.

TOMMY.   There's a lot in that sayin', mind you; it's a hard wallop at the British Empire.[29]

The comic participation of those on-stage draws in the audience to participate likewise. There is mockery involved, but no condescension. Actors of the calibre of F. J. McCormick (the first Seumas Shields, the first Joxer Daly), Barry Fitzgerald (the first Captain Boyle, the first Sylvester Heegan), and Sarah Allgood (the first Juno)—all Dubliners—knew exactly how to calibrate the shifts in tone and meaning called for in O'Casey's dialogue. Like the ancient Greeks in the theatre, they were 'hypocrites' but they were not thereby liars: they well understood the meaning of stage truth. So did O'Casey, whose characters are often in this sense hypocritical, contradicting themselves in order to save face, whereby they become both knowable and lovable.

Theatricality, then, is central to O'Casey's language, even where flamboyance is concerned. His early interest in theatre lay in nineteenth-century melodrama and the sensational style of play and acting to be found at the old Queen's Theatre. Shakespeare's history plays provided another enduring influence, and as a young man O'Casey acted in Dublin with his brother in a small fit-up. Dion Boucicault was perhaps the nearest to a model, with Shaw to follow, in prioritizing entertainment as theatrical value. He came to write sketches for Delia Larkin's Irish Workers' Dramatic Club at Liberty Hall, and although it has been said that O'Casey did not know music hall because he was 'priggishly idealistic' as writer this is manifestly untrue.[30] In fact, he was very interested in music hall, and in November 1917 organized a variety evening at the Olympia for charitable purposes. The little plays with which he was associated at Liberty Hall and St Laurence O'Toole's Club around this time, and occasionally acted in, were farces, and the acting style would have been in line with variety theatre—that is, exaggerated, the opposite of naturalistic. Even in *The Harvest Festival*, where he was trying to do something quite different, the characterization of the middle-class figures, especially the husband and wife routine, is mainly over the top. For example:

WILLIAMSON.   Who the hell put these things [cabbages] on the table? Do you hear me asking a question Mrs. Williamson? (*Raising his voice*) Are you damn well deaf Mrs. Williamson?
MRS WILLIAMSON.   'I hear you calling me.'
WILLIAMSON.   Look here, I've had enough of your sarcastic answers. Who put these on the table?
MRS WILLIAMSON.   Maybe, my dear love, they grew there.
WILLIAMSON.   (*fiercely flinging them on the floor*) Let them grow somewhere else, then. Where did you put the books I left there? Do you hear me talking to you?
MRS WILLIAMSON.   Don't you think if you opened your eyes a little you might find them?

[29] O'Casey, *Complete Plays*, vol. 1, 117.
[30] Adrian Frazier, *Hollywood Irish: John Ford, Abbey Actors and the Irish Revival in Hollywood* (Dublin: Lilliput Press, 2011), 66. See Christopher Murray, *Seán O'Casey, Writer at Work: A Biography* (Dublin: Gill & Macmillan, 2004), 110–11.

WILLIAMSON.   (*walking over to her, and catching her by the arms*) You will make me lose my temper, will you? Do you want me to knock you down?

MRS WILLIAMSON.   Whether I wish it or not, I'm sure you would like to do it. Ever since I married you I am hourly expecting that demonstration of affection, dear.

WILLIAMSON.   (*loudly*) And if you don't change your tune, you'll get what you're expecting.[31]

There is always this exaggeration in O'Casey's dramatic style. His scenes are often vaudeville sketches, like the above, that outrageously mimic domestic friction; no audience would mistake them for naturalism. Mrs Williamson obviously pauses too long to tax her husband's patience; his violence towards her is never intended to come to blows. Though lacking a real punch line, the excerpt indicates what in the three Dublin plays is trademark O'Casey: a paradoxical mimicking of self-consciousness.

O'Casey was very much at home in the Abbey once *The Shadow of a Gunman* was accepted for staging in 1923. Even for *The Silver Tassie* (1929), written in London, he shaped his characterization to suit the acting style of the Abbey company. Thus the straight man/funny man routine, a central element of all three Dublin plays, is carried into the *Tassie*. Shields and Davoren, Boyle and Joxer, Fluther and the Covey, Simon and Sylvester, all bear a family resemblance. Indeed, Mr and Mrs Grigson in the *Gunman* may be seen as close relatives of Mr and Mrs Williamson in *The Harvest Festival* (although better developed). These are all in their way music-hall performers. To be incapable of impromptu performance, as Joxer fails to master a song in Act II of *Juno*, is to be disgraced. In O'Casey's dramaturgy, the central characters are always simply passing the time while in the background something a lot more 'real' is being sidelined. What should be peripheral is made central. Two worlds coexist in parallel. Diversion rules, in accordance with O'Casey's principle of juxtaposing scenes for ironic contrast—a strategy he borrowed from Shakespeare's *Henry IV* plays, in which the playful and subversive Boar's Head tavern scenes contrast dialectically with the serious conflict over kingship taking shape offstage. This dramatic schism became central to O'Casey's tragicomic technique.

As to the politics, this juxtaposition principle provides one key. In *The Shadow of a Gunman*, the protagonist or central character, Donal Davoren, declares he has 'no connection with the politics of the day' and does not want 'any connection'.[32] This lack of connection defines his character. As Act I ends, and he has decided to play out the 'shadow' reputation of an IRA man which Minnie Powell and the other tenement residents have awarded him, Davoren muses on the two names he has typed, 'Minnie, Donal; Donal, Minnie'.[33] There is no conjunction. At the end of the play, when Minnie is killed offstage, Davoren is terrified his name will be found on her person. He breathes again when it is clarified that his name was literally obliterated by her blood. The portrait of this artist offered on-stage is of an aesthete to whom the community means nothing. The anti-hero is born to the Irish stage. Davoren thinks he can live in a bubble while Dublin is torn apart around him. O'Casey subjects him to severe reprimand, although some see the final state of Davoren as insufficiently changed. The point is nevertheless underlined that going 'on the

---

[31] O'Casey, *Complete Plays*, vol. 5, 428–9.   [32] O'Casey, *Complete Plays*, vol. 1, 112.
[33] Ibid., 124.

run' (O'Casey's original title) is not an option in civic life. What Reena in the later Dublin play *Behind the Green Curtains* (1962) says in rebuke to the self-involved Senator Chatastray voices O'Casey's own view: 'No one and nothing can be left alone in this world. As long as you're alive, you'll have to bear being touched by th' world you live in.'[34] Apart from Davoren, several of the characters in the *Gunman* are shown up once the Black and Tan raid threatens their comfort zone. For the audience also, the same point holds. The problem is the one Herbert Blau raises in defining an audience: 'it is not an entity to begin with but a consciousness constructed.'[35] O'Casey would expose his audience to creative confusion.

O'Casey's novelty lay in presenting on stage the 'conditions which all Dubliners knew more or less at first hand'.[36] There had been tenement plays before this but none involved with contemporary urban warfare. O'Casey was in the audience when *Blight*, by Joyce's erstwhile friend Oliver St John Gogarty, was staged at the Abbey in December 1917. One of the first tenement plays seen in Dublin, after A. P. Wilson's *Victims* (1912) and *Slough* (1914), *Blight* ticks several boxes for O'Casey: a drunken layabout who resembles Captain Boyle in *Juno*, the successful use of Dublin working-class speech, and the setting itself, its poverty thrust in the face of the audience. But the subtitle of *Blight* is ominous: *The Tragedy of Dublin: An Exposition in Three Acts*. Gogarty clearly intended to be didactic: 'This city will continue to be the breeding ground of disease, vice, hypocrisy and discontent.'[37] Elizabeth Mannion has suggested that the play was too 'hot' for the Abbey management, for although successful, it was revived only briefly in 1918 and then disappeared.[38] O'Casey barely mentions the play, coupling it with a few other Abbey plays seen before his first was accepted and remarking that he had seen 'nothing that he could try to imitate'.[39]

The politics of the Irish Civil War form the background of *Juno and the Paycock*, when the split over acceptance of the Treaty had Free Staters fighting Irregulars (a.k.a. Die-hards, or the IRA). Once again, 'background' is not quite the word; politics inevitably burst onto the stage. The focus is on Johnny Boyle, physically and psychologically damaged after his experiences in the wars in Dublin. This portrait of a man really 'on the run' is juxtaposed with a domestic plot in which Captain Boyle has a life-changing stroke of luck, which actually destroys the family. The unusually 'well-made' plot reflects the influence of Abbey playwright Lennox Robinson, who regarded *Juno* as exemplary.[40] It is unique among the Dublin plays for its unity of theme and action, whereby Johnny's story of betrayal and evasion of responsibility is juxtaposed with the theme of betrayal in the Mary/Bentham, Jerry Devine/Mary love stories and with Captain Boyle's irresponsibility. The tit-for-tat killings

---

[34] O'Casey, *Complete Plays*, vol. 5, 304.

[35] Herbert Blau, *The Audience* (Baltimore, MD: Johns Hopkins University Press, 1990), 25, cited in Chris Morash and Shaun Richards, *Mapping Irish Theatre: Theories of Space and Place* (Cambridge: Cambridge University Press, 2013), 8.

[36] Nicholas Grene, *The Politics of Irish Drama: Plays in Context from Boucicault to Friel* (Cambridge: Cambridge University Press, 1999), 133.

[37] Oliver St John Gogarty, *Poems and Plays*, ed. A. Norman Jeffares (Gerrards Cross: Colin Smythe, 2001), 507. It is noteworthy that Jeffares does not attribute dual authorship to *Blight*.

[38] Elizabeth Mannion, 'The Dublin Tenement Plays of the Early Abbey Theatre', *New Hibernia Review/Iris Ēireannach Nua* 14, no. 2 (2010), 78.

[39] O'Casey, *Autobiographies*, vol. 2, 96.

[40] Lennox Robinson, *Towards an Appreciation of the Theatre* (Dublin: Metropolitan Publishing, 1945), 16–19.

that make up the play's background percolate via newspapers and the dramatic entrance of
Mrs Tancred. Here the juxtaposition of the Boyles' carnival with the widow's grief transforms the mood of the play. Afterwards, Juno is overwhelmed with guilt at blotting out this
neighbour's sorrow. And while Captain Boyle, another of O'Casey's figures cocooned from
reality, insists that Mrs Tancred's litany of assassinations is none of their business, Juno's
reply is aimed at the wider community: 'I'd like to know how a body's not to mind these
things; [. . .] Hasn't the whole house, nearly, been massacreed?' She names three families
recently bereaved before the present instance, 'an' now, poor Mrs Tancred's only child gone
west with his body made a collandher of. Sure, if it's not our business, I don't know whose
business it is.' The image of the colander shocks through its familiarity. Although Boyle
insists that such matters do not affect them, 'an' we needn't give a damn',[41] Juno's thinking
stamps the politics of responsibility on the play from here until the end, when she has to
deal with the murder of her own son as part of the tragic pattern.

The Plough and the Stars is more complex in its use of politics. Here O'Casey severely
tested his Dublin audience and found it wanting. The violent protesters on the fourth night
(11 February 1926) of the first production were in essence declaring that O'Casey didn't 'give
a damn' about the men who died in 1916. They were also complaining that since Dublin's
Abbey Theatre was now enjoying a government subsidy (since 1925) as Ireland's national
theatre, it was unacceptable that a negative representation of the 1916 Rising should appear
in it. The protesters mainly comprised the women's auxiliary of the IRA, Cumann na
mBan.[42] Theirs was a different response than had greeted Synge's Playboy of the Western
World in Dublin in 1907, as Yeats relished when he sent for the police: 'and this time it will
be their police!'[43] In the new Free State, Yeats enjoyed his minority status in the face of a mob
whose Gardaí Síochána were representative of the country's Catholic majority. O'Casey,
however, was overwhelmed by the audience hostility, and the memory remained vivid
when he recalled the night years later:

> They said he was a renegade, a friend to England, and that he would soon have a government
> pension. They said he had held up Ireland's sacred name to ridicule for the sake of the money
> he'd get for doing it; and that it was he who, sooner or later, would feel the shame, and not
> Ireland.[44]

But what exactly were the politics that underlay The Plough and the Stars? In a word, they
were revisionist before the term was coined. Hence the dislike of the Plough by Irish critics
with a republican bias such as Seamus Deane,[45] Declan Kiberd,[46] and George Watson.[47] The
best response to this negative view of O'Casey came from David Krause.[48] In 1916, O'Casey's

[41] O'Casey, Complete Plays, vol. 1, 56.

[42] Murray, Seán O'Casey, 172–6. See also Robert Lowery (ed.), A Whirlwind in Dublin: The Plough
and the Stars Riots (Westport, CT: Greenwood Press, 1984).

[43] Fallon, Sean O'Casey, 92.   [44] O'Casey, Autobiographies, vol. 2, 150.

[45] Seamus Deane, 'Irish Politics and O'Casey's Theatre', Threshold 24 (spring 1973), 5–6.

[46] Declan Kiberd, Inventing Ireland: The Literature of the Modern Nation (London: Jonathan Cape,
1995), 218–38.

[47] G. J. Watson, Irish Identity and the Irish Literary Revival: Synge, Yeats, Joyce and O'Casey, 2nd
edn. (Washington, DC: Catholic University of America Press, 1994).

[48] David Krause, 'The Plough and the Stars: Socialism (1913) and Nationalism (1916)', New Hibernia
Review 1, no. 4 (1997), 28–40.

own politics would still have been governed by the events of the 1913 Dublin Lockout. Therefore, he had no time whatsoever for the alliance Connolly forged between the Irish Citizen Army and Pearse's Volunteers. That much is plain from his *Story of the Irish Citizen Army* (1919). In that regard the Covey in the *Plough* speaks for O'Casey: the flag of the ICA had no place in a nationalist struggle, '[b]ecause it's a Labour flag, an' was never meant for politics. [. . .] It's a flag that should only be used when we're buildin' th' barricades to fight for A Workers' Republic!'[49] If it had no place on a nationalist stage either, factually the flag *was* part of the 1916 Rising alongside the tricolour; here representation attempts to reveal historic contradiction, a point lost on the protesters. O'Casey's view of Labour had soured between 1916 and 1926. In the absence of Larkin, otherwise occupied in Sing Sing, the new trade union leaders were pygmies in O'Casey's eyes who lacked any vision for the future of Labour in Ireland. In *The Cooing of Doves,* a satirical one-act rejected by the Abbey in September 1923 and listed among O'Casey's lost play-scripts until it came up for auction in 2005, O'Casey gives harsh treatment to all political parties attending an election meeting being held outside a public house, in which the play is set, but he is hardest of all on the Labour men. There are two of them, one more belligerent than the other; neither has O'Casey's sympathy. Thus The Republican Labourer, a rabid IRA man, the civil war having been lost, knows only anger:

> The spirit of Ireland lives, in seculo seculorum! Some of them ud like to fix the Ne Plus Ulthra of the Nation, but theres men left that wont let them do it! (*Loudly*) The Irish Republic lives! (*He lifts his glass above his head*) The Republic, One and Invisible![50]

He means, of course, in reference to the partition of Ireland in 1922, 'indivisible', but the joke is directed at the metaphysics of the republican debate. The Socialist Labourer, who anticipates the Covey, regards himself as an intellectual when he mocks The Forester (a version of Uncle Peter):

> Your Shan Van Vok, an your Irish Freedom! No more our ancient Sirelandll shelter the despot an the slave! But theyll shelter the despot, ay, an give him a good job too! But the day of the common peoplell come when the workers'll stand on the principles enunciated by Fintan Lalor, that the ownership of Ireland, moral an material, is vested of right in the people of Ireland![51]

During the play, those within the pub hear a commotion outside and shouts of '*Throw the Bolshies into the river; They ought to be plugged. We want none o the red flag here*' (p. 349). Dublin was not yet ready for a true Harvest Festival. O'Casey slotted the rejected *Cooing of Doves* into his *Plough* 'with but a few minor changes'.[52] He thus imported into a play set in 1916 political ideas and attitudes that belonged to Dublin in the election year of 1923. The Republicans in his 1926 audience were unprepared to listen, although in time *The Plough*

---

[49] O'Casey, *Complete Plays*, vol. 1, 181.

[50] 'Sean O'Casey's *The Cooing of Doves*: A One-Act Play Rediscovered', ed. and introduced by Christopher Murray, *Princeton University Library Chronicle* 68, nos. 1 and 2 (2006–7), 342. O'Casey's spelling and punctuation are retained.

[51] Ibid., 353.

[52] Sean O'Casey, '*The Plough and the Stars* in Retrospect (1960)', in *Blasts and Benedictions*, ed. Ronald Ayling (London: Macmillan, 1967), 98.

was to be the most frequently performed of all his plays at the Abbey. Perhaps the audience had not taken full note of the last scene in *Juno*, where the fakery of Captain Boyle towards 1916 represents an attitude O'Casey wished, through mockery, to extend in the *Plough* to the whole enterprise of 1916. It is not that O'Casey was mocking the Rising, which he regarded as a tragic mistake. With great courage, he was holding up to scrutiny a pious attitude towards heroism which by 1926 represented denial of credit to those who had fought in the 1914–18 war. His next play, *The Silver Tassie*, would address this denial with passion and bitterness.

O'Casey's revisionism appears in tandem with the objective details of his 1926 play. Today, when so much has been published to record the 1916 Rising, it is still surprising how much O'Casey got right. The republished memoir by W. J. Brennan-Whitmore, for example, has the same details O'Casey singles out: the looting, the barricades in the streets off O'Connell Street, the snipers, the distraught figures lost in the maelstrom (like the Woman from Rathmines), the shock to Dubliners of the artillery firing from the British vessel *Helga* on Liberty Hall, and above all, perhaps, the incendiary bombs which spread fire along the two sides of O'Connell Street, reducing the city centre to an inferno.[53] The Imperial Hotel, where O'Casey locates Jack Clitheroe's last stand, in reality a building under Brennan-Whitmore's command, flew the Plough and the Stars ensign by Connolly's orders, according to his biographer.[54] By Thursday of Easter Week Brennan-Whitmore was wondering, 'Should we stick it out and be burned to death?' like Clitheroe.[55] The historian Charles Townshend verifies the Covey's response to one of Pearse's speeches given to the Figure in the Window in Act II: Connolly himself said that Pearse's lines represented the thinking of 'a blithering idiot'.[56] The speech in question, one of four O'Casey lifted from Pearse's published writings, is the Voice's third speech, a second extract from Pearse's 'Peace and the Gael'.[57] The fact is that O'Casey was himself a historian; his 'maverick' status merely represented his dramatic genius. But what Charles Townshend calls O'Casey's 'dyspeptic perspective—he [O'Casey] would have called it honesty—was not endorsed by any significant public figure for almost half a century',[58] that is, until the 1966 jubilee was well out of the way.

RED ROSES FOR DUBLIN

'It was time for Sean to go.' Thus begins the final chapter of O'Casey's *Inishfallen, Fare Thee Well* (1949). This playwright was not for burning. Dublin city had let him down: 'He would stay no longer to view life through a stained-glass window.'[59] London would be his city

[53] Commandant W. J. Brennan-Whitmore, *Dublin Burning: The Easter Rising from Behind the Barricades* (1996) (Dublin: Gill & Macmillan, 2013).
[54] Donal Nevin, *James Connolly: 'A Full Life'* (Dublin: Gill & Macmillan, 2005), 650.
[55] Brennan-Whitmore, *Dublin Burning*, 111.
[56] Charles Townshend, *Easter 1916: The Irish Rebellion* (London: Penguin, 2006), 114. Connolly wrote in *The Workers' Republic*, 25 Dec. 1915: 'We do not think that the old heart of the earth needs to be warmed with the red wine of millions of lives. We think anyone who does is a blithering idiot.' See Nevin, *James Connolly*, 702.
[57] Patrick Pearse, *The Coming Revolution: The Political Writings of Patrick Pearse* (Cork: Mercier Press, 2012), 169–71.
[58] Townshend, *Easter 1916*, 348.   [59] O'Casey, *Autobiographies*, vol. 2, 231.

Olympia Theatre

Commencing Monday, 15th March, 1943 Nightly at 7.30 p.m.—Thursday at 7 p.m.

FIRST PRODUCTION

OF

RED ROSES FOR ME

A Play in Four Acts   By SEAN O'CASEY

CHARACTERS:

MRS. BREYDON	Ann Clery
AYAMONN (her son)	Dan O Herlihy
EEADA	Sheila Carty
DYMPNA } Mrs. Breydon's neighbours in	Gertrude Quinn
FINNOOLA in the house	Cepta Cullen
SHEILA MOORNEEN	Sheila May
BRENNAN O' THE MOOR	John Stephenson
(owner of a few oul' houses)	
A SINGER	John Richards
ROORY O'BALACAUN (a zealous Irish Irelander)	W. O'Gorman
MULCCANNY (a mocker of sacred things)	Seamus Healy
REV. E. CLINTON (Rector of St. Burnupus)	Michael Walsh
SAMUEL (Sexton to the church)	Luke McLoughlin
INSPECTOR FINGLAS (of the Mounted Police and	
Rector's churchwarden)	Austin Meldon
1st MAN } neighbours in the next house to	Joseph O'Dea
2nd MAN } Breydon's	Patrick Nolan
DOWZARD } members of St. Burnupus' select	John McDarby
FOSTER } vestry	Wilfrid Brambell
A LAMPLIGHTER	John Allen
1st RAILWAY MAN	Pat Nolan
2nd RAILWAY MAN	Gerrard McCarthy

CITIZENS, STRIKERS, ETC.: Miss Mignon Rumbold, Messrs. Burke, S. Burke, Byrne, N. Byrne, Bloomfield, Carroll, Healy, Larkin, Merrigan, Morris, O'Neill, Penston, Quinn, Scanlon, D. Smyth, M. Smyth and Tobin.

SYNOPSIS OF SCENES:

ACT I.
TWO-ROOMED HOME OF THE BREYDONS.

ACT II.
THE SAME.

ACT III.
A DUBLIN STREET, BESIDE A BRIDGE OVER THE LIFFEY.

ACT IV.
PART OF THE GROUNDS ROUND THE PROTESTANT CHURCH OF ST. BURNUPUS.

NOTE: In this Act the Curtain is lowered for a few seconds to denote the passing of a few hours.

TIME: A LITTLE WHILE AGO.

There will be Intervals of Ten Minutes between the Acts.

THE PLAY PRODUCED BY SHELAH RICHARDS.

Settings designed by RALPH CUSACK. Painted by RALPH CUSACK assisted by ANNE YEATS. Constructed by CHARLES BOLGER.

STAGE DIRECTOR }	For Richards-	CECIL FORD
STAGE MANAGER }	Walsh Productions	SHEILA CARTY
ASSISTANT STAGE MANAGER		ANNE YEATS
STAGE MANAGER }		LORCAN BOURKE
ELECTRICIAN }	For Olympia	FRED BEASLEY
MUSICAL DIRECTOR }	Theatre	ROBERT BOLTON

FIG. 12.2 Programme for the first production of Séan O'Casey's *Red Roses for Me*, in the Olympia Theatre, Dublin, 15 March 1943.

Courtesy of Irish Theatre Archive, Dublin City Libraries.

now, where *Juno* was being fêted. He took a three-year lease on a flat, and quipped in interview: 'It may mean three years' penal servitude for me, but, begorra, it cannot be worse than Dublin.'[60] In London, he would settle down, marry, and write *The Silver Tassie* and *Within the Gates* (1934). The former has little to do with Dublin (although three acts of it are set there), as its focus is on the broad question of the First World War and its horrors: O'Casey was expanding the anti-war feeling which fuelled the *Plough* in order to condemn the inhumanity of a far greater conflict. From a distance he watched in a blend of anger and amusement as the Free State turned into de Valera's ideal, theocratic nation. O'Casey would write one-act plays—*Hall of Healing* (1952) and *Bedtime Story* (1952)—satirizing the new Dublin that emerged from this counter-revolution. He saw the parallel between this mid-century

[60] *Irish Independent*, 7 July 1926, cited in *Joseph Holloway's Abbey Theatre: A Selection from His Unpublished Journal 'Impressions of a Dublin Theatregoer'*, ed. Robert Hogan and Michael J. O'Neill (Carbondale, IL: Southern Illinois University Press, 1967), 270.

city and 'a neurotic patient in facing a long-buried infantile trauma that has stood in the way of his normal growth and integration'.[61] He would have agreed that the problem was 'to transmute physical mass into psychic energy' (607). It is within this area that he composed *Red Roses for Me*. It stands apart from the later satirical plays, but it vindicates Maxwell's comment that 'it is on the relationships between the early and the later plays that any assessment of O'Casey must turn'.[62]

Red Roses is a rewriting of history—personal, social, and urban—as fantasy. In revisiting *The Harvest Festival*, O'Casey revisits in a new spirit the class conflict arising from Jim Larkin's great crusade to provide Dublin workers with a greater sense of their destiny. Larkin's statue in that messianic pose commands modern Dublin today, with prose by O'Casey lending it symbolic power.[63] The elements of fantasy which sustain the autobiographies (which he was writing at this time) had already appeared in *The Star Turns Red* (1940), a transitional play which seeks to combine 'Red' Jim Larkin in 1913 with the clash between fascism and communism in the 1930s. This play was cathartic for O'Casey, purging poisonous feelings about postcolonial Dublin with a surge of optimism deriving from the memory of lost possibilities. Indeed, Susan Cannon Harris argues that the shift towards fantasy in *The Star* marks a major reorientation by O'Casey from the 'Abbey realism' he equated with bourgeois values. In Act II of that play, in keeping with O'Casey's 'revulsion' against the new men leading Larkin's old union, 'the union hall [setting] becomes the last bastion of realism and its discontents'.[64] There is an epiphanic passage in *Pictures in the Hallway* (1942) where the 60-year-old writer recalls a vision of the city experienced one spring evening before he was 20, which bears direct relation to the crucial Act III of *Red Roses for Me*:

> Numerous empty lorries, floats, vans, and drays were flowing quickly past him, each of them, under the magic sky, looking like flaming chariots making for a battle front. He saw golden arrows of the sun shooting up side streets, leading from the quay to God knows where. Here the hard, set, and leering faces of roughs leaning against a corner had changed into sturdy faces of bronze where the sun's shadow lingered [. . .]. The bridges looked like golden pathways, growing grey dauntlessly, turning from pride to get gentleness and peace. He left the crippled handcart by the side of the street, and went over to lean upon the river wall to gaze at Dublin in the grip of God. [. . .] The great dome of the Four Courts shone like a golden rose in a great bronze cup.[65]

It is a vision of Dublin before the fall into history, a city identified with God. The young O'Casey experiences such ecstasy prompted by the city's beauty that he composes a song on the spot, a hymn to work and God, seen as intertwined. As he moves on he encounters a young woman who does a dance in which he joins while others clap their hands. Encouraged by the changing colours of the evening light young Johnny cries out: 'Th' sword of light is shining!' When the experience passes, Johnny makes his way up the darkening

[61] Mumford, *City in History*, 599.
[62] D. E. S. Maxwell, *A Critical History of Modern Irish Drama 1890–1980* (Cambridge: Cambridge University Press, 1984), 97.
[63] Paula Murphy, 'Let Us Rise: The Background to Oisín Kelly's Immortalization of Big Jim Larkin Commissioned by the Workers of Ireland', *Irish Arts Review* 30, no. 4 (2013–14), 114–17.
[64] Susan Cannon Harris, 'Red Star versus Green Goddess: Sean O'Casey's "The Star Turns Red" and the Politics of Form', *Princeton University Library Chronicle* 68, nos. 1 and 2 (2006–7), 384.
[65] O'Casey, *Autobiographies*, vol. 1, 379–80.

quays in a religious fervour, thinking, 'A holy city's our city of Dublin [. . .] more ancient than Athens; more sacred than Rome; as holy as Zion.'[66]

O'Casey incorporates this scene into Act III of *Red Roses*. He does away with the anti-hero, and, consciousness and cause being aligned, a modern hero becomes possible in Ayamonn Breydon, who is less a fresh take on Red Jim[67] than a compound. Gone, too, is the 'political nihilism' visible in *The Plough and the Stars*.[68] The expressionist, panoramic Act III settles Ayamonn in his sense of mission as he too, like his prose counterpart Johnny, is fired by his vision of the city 'in th' grip o' God!'[69] In the play, however, something quite strange is going on. It is as if Larkinite Ayamonn is donning the religious mantle of Patrick Pearse. Can it be that, having reconciled himself with Yeats in 1935 (leading to the staging of *The Silver Tassie* at the Abbey), O'Casey was now also reconciling himself with the dead Pearse? In the transformation scene, where Ayamonn rouses the supine people, there is a shift from the self-regarding religiosity Johnny evinces in *Pictures in the Hallway* to the charisma his counterpart Ayamonn reveals when he inspires the down-and-outs to sing lustily in chorus to Dublin: 'We vow to release thee from anger an' envy,/To dhrive th' fierce wolf an' sly fox from thy gate.'[70] Ayamonn's role is Christ-like, as Larkin is fused with Pearse as model: 'Life springs from death,' wrote Pearse.[71] In Act IV, in contrast to the last act of *The Harvest Festival*, Ayamonn is involved with a *spring* church festival, with images of resurrection, like the cross made of daffodils. When challenged by the churchwarden over the stakes Ayamonn is prepared to die for, namely a wage increase of one shilling for all unskilled workers, his reply is theological rather than Marxist: 'A shilling's little to you, and less to many; to us it is our Shechinah, showing us God's light is near; showing us the way in which our feet must go.'[72] *Shekinah* is defined in the *Concise OED* as 'the glory of the divine presence, represented as light or interpreted (in Kabbalism) as a divine feminine aspect'. A small sign, says Mumford, 'may be the harbinger of a larger transformation'.[73] And so Ayamonn altruistically dies for his vision of the future.

Accordingly, O'Casey comes round to a vision of the city totally at odds with that under-pinning the early Dublin plays. Through a romantic representation of what might have been, *Red Roses for Me* is a dream play which signifies what may yet be. History is laid aside for myth. It is at this point Joyce comes into the picture again. If by 'a commodius vicus of recirculation'[74] O'Casey returns with *Red Roses* to the environs of *The Harvest Festival* it is not without the stirrings caused by the publication of *Finnegans Wake* in 1939, which he read and admired. Bizarrely, when the *Irish Times* received the novel for review they attributed it in their 'publications received' to Seán O'Casey. Believing it was not an error but a form of Dublin malice, he nevertheless sent '[a] deep bow to James Joyce'.[75] Before its transformation, O'Casey refers to Dublin in *Red Roses* as 'a bleak, black, an' bitther city',

---

[66] Ibid., 382–3.

[67] Emmet O'Connor, *James Larkin* (Cork: Cork University Press, 2002), 113.

[68] Maxwell, *Critical History*, 102.   [69] O'Casey, *Complete Plays*, vol. 3, 200.

[70] Ibid.   [71] Pearse, *The Coming Revolution*, 112.

[72] O'Casey, *Complete Plays*, 211.   [73] Mumford, *City in History*, 601.

[74] James Joyce, *Finnegans Wake*, 3rd edn. (London: Faber & Faber, 1964), 3.

[75] Sean O'Casey to James Joyce, 30 May 1939, in reply to Joyce's (postmarked 26 May) alerting O'Casey to what he termed a 'misprint—if it is a misprint', in *The Letters of Sean O'Casey*, vol. 1: *1910–1941*, ed. David Krause (New York: Cassell, 1975), 800. Joyce's letter is included on 799.

as if undergoing the paralysis Joyce diagnosed in *Dubliners* (1914). Then, caught up in the ecstasy of the visionary moment, Ayamonn salutes Dublin as 'Fair city', potentially beautiful and proud, that potential to be realized through the people's revolution. It will be not quite Joyce's 'soft morning, city', redeemed from history, but close enough.[76] It will depend on an impulse outside Joyce's interest but one Yeats formulated in reimagining a dialogue between Pearse and Connolly in 1916: 'There's nothing but our own red blood/Can make a right Rose Tree.'[77] O'Casey's teleology is apocalyptic. The rather peculiar use of the personal pronoun in the title of O'Casey's play actually asserts the notion of altruism. The loved one, the Shekinah, bestows the roses on 'me' in recognition of personal sacrifice. The self is identified with the city, '[f]or the city should be an organ of love'.[78] O'Casey internalizes his symbols, be they roses or daffodils. Whereas the expressionist second act of the *Tassie* 'attempts to show the war through the spectacles usually worn by James Joyce', as one reviewer commented in 1929,[79] O'Casey's language has now become flagrantly poetic, defying naturalism more strongly than ever before. The actual harvest festival which lay at the centre of his first version of *Red Roses* now becomes an Easter ritual involving the fruit-sellers of Dublin's streets—a rewriting of Easter 1916. Ayamonn becomes a Celtic hero, wielder of the Sword of Light (referring to the god Nuada, whose weapon gave the title to the journal Pearse edited, *An Claidheamh Soluis*). The city itself, Eblana, merges with the statue which goes missing[80] and is transformed by the choric figure Brennan on the Moor (with a lick of paint); Brennan, associated with folklore, is closely linked to Ayamonn as artist and virtual rebel. Thus *Red Roses* is a great mishmash of realism, fantasy, history, and myth, difficult to stage and yet successful on stage (though less in Dublin than in London and New York). Its highly stylized form marks it out as O'Casey's greatest tribute to a city he earlier saw falling into ruin through exploitation and misdirected warfare. Just this once, he was able to see that city less as the modern megalopolis which Mumford feared was in danger of becoming a centre of death than, strangely, as St Augustine did in his *City of God*, containing the possibility of a new Jerusalem.

[76] Joyce, *Finnegans Wake*, 619.

[77] W. B. Yeats, *Collected Works*, vol. 1: *The Poems*, ed. Richard J. Finneran (New York: Scribner, 1991), 183.

[78] Mumford, *City in History*, 655

[79] T. H., 'Apollo [Theatre]: "The Silver Tassie", 11 October 1929', *Theatre World*, Nov. 1929, 14.

[80] The crown of Our Lady of Eblana incorporates the emblem of Dublin castle. See Heinz Kosok, 'The Image of Dublin in Anglo-Irish Drama', in Maurice Harmon (ed.), *The Irish Writer and the City* (Gerrards Cross: Colin Smythe; Totowa, NJ: Barnes & Noble, 1984), 30–1.

PART V

PERFORMANCE 1

CHAPTER 13

···

DESIGN AND DIRECTION TO 1960

···

PAIGE REYNOLDS

EARLY TWENTIETH-CENTURY DESIGN AND DIRECTION

···

THE collaboration between text and image necessary to produce a rich experience for audiences may seem of obvious importance in our understanding of Irish theatre. However, studies of modern Irish drama have generally spotlighted the surfeit of talented individual writers and their dramatic texts, thanks in part to views successfully advanced by Yeats and the early Abbey Theatre that cast the visual world of stagecraft as something to be repressed in favour of poetry and movement on stage. The disregard of, and even disdain for, the visual and material world of theatre stems in part from its association with the English commercial theatre that toured Ireland to entrance (or corrupt) Irish audiences. For many theatregoers of the nineteenth century, design and direction meant the elaborate stagecraft and artificial performance styles of the popular theatre. For instance, W. G. Fay, who toured Ireland with a variety of popular melodramas before becoming the leader of the early Abbey company, worked on a production of J. W. Whitbread's *The Irishman* (1892) which staged a climactic scene around a fully functioning two-storey mill requiring 2,000 gallons of water for each performance.[1] The description of this dazzling set conveys the allure of visual spectacle on the popular stage, though direction in this context was frequently less impressive. The Irish actor Máire Nic Shiubhlaigh lambasted the 'military foot-drill' of English touring companies, condemning direction that choreographed the supporting cast around the 'idiosyncrasies' of the star, and produced a 'robot effect; a lack of spontaneity' on stage.[2]

---

[1] Catherine Carswell and W. G. Fay, *The Fays of the Abbey Theatre: An Autobiographical Record* (New York: Harcourt, Brace, 1935), 60–2.

[2] Máire Nic Shiubhlaigh, *The Splendid Years: Recollections of Maire Nic Shiubhlaigh as Told to Edward Kenny* (Dublin: James Duffy, 1955), 9.

Like other independent theatres established during the late nineteenth century, the Irish Literary Theatre (ILT) intended to produce original drama and to renovate these tired stage practices of the commercial theatre. The founders of the ILT—Lady Gregory, Edward Martyn, and Yeats—largely regarded the visual aspects of theatre as something to repress in order to heighten the power of poetry. As George Moore contended, 'scenery should be strictly limited, if not abolished altogether; dresses and furniture as much as scenery beset the imagination and prevent the spectator from union with the conception of the poet.'[3] This primacy of the word remained a central ideological tenet of iterations of the Irish national theatre springing from the ILT. Yet the theatre poached talent from abroad to heighten the power of those words through design and direction. For instance, the English actor Florence Farr, who had directed both Shaw's *Arms and the Man* (1894) and Yeats's *The Land of Heart's Desire* (1894) in 1894 in London, was invited by Yeats to help stage *The Countess Cathleen* in 1899 for the ILT in Dublin. Farr not only played the part of Aleel in this production but also directed it, composed the music, and designed the set and props.

The success of the April 1902 production of Gregory and Yeats's *Cathleen ni Houlihan* and George Russell's *Deirdre* by Frank and W. G. Fay's National Dramatic Company high-lighted the value of experienced directors and scenographers. Frank Fay was a theatre critic with a vested interest in foreign innovations in stagecraft, and had worked with amateur companies in Ireland and abroad as a voice and acting coach; his brother, W. G. (Willie) Fay, came with years of experience as an actor and member of various stage crews. This 1902 production signalled a merger of direction styles: the Irish actors 'chanted' their lines, which reflected the commitment of both Yeats and Frank Fay to in verse speaking, though the chants were often in 'very marked accents' that produced, at least for the diarist Joseph Holloway, an effect 'not impressive, to put it mildly'.[4] Until the Fays departed the Abbey in 1908, they developed and directed the muted and realistic performances, characterized by restrained movement and Irish accents, that became a trademark of the theatre.

In 'The Reform of the Theatre' (1903), Yeats called for sweeping reforms in dramatic texts, as well as in performance and scenography. He announced the necessity 'to simplify both the form and colour of scenery and costume', asking for single-colour backgrounds that resembled the background of a painted portrait to 'harmonise' with the performers, and demanded 'nothing unnecessary, nothing that will distract the attention from speech and movement'.[5] These ideas were partially realized by the production offered in tandem with this lecture—Yeats's *The Hour-Glass*, which Lady Gregory described as 'our first attempt at the decorative staging long demanded by Mr Yeats'.[6] W. G. Fay directed the production; the set was designed by T. Sturge Moore and Robert Gregory; the costumes were designed by

[3] George Moore, 'Is the Theatre a Place of Amusement?', *Beltaine* 2 (Feb. 1900), 8–9.

[4] Joseph Holloway, *Joseph Holloway's Abbey Theatre: A Selection from the Unpublished Journal 'Impressions of a Dublin Playgoer*, ed. Robert Hogan and Michael J. O'Neill (Carbondale, IL: Southern Illinois University Press, 1967), 16.

[5] W. B. Yeats, 'The Reform of the Theatre' (1903), in W. B. Yeats, [untitled], *Samhain*, Sept. 1903; repr. in *Collected Works of W. B. Yeats*, vol. 8: *The Irish Dramatic Movement*, ed. Mary Fitzgerald and Richard J. Finneran (New York: Scribner, 2003), 28. For more on Abbey stage design, see Helen O'Donoghue, *Scene Change: One Hundred Years of Theatre Design at the Abbey* (Dublin: Irish Museum of Modern Art, 2004).

[6] Augusta Gregory, *Our Irish Theatre: A Chapter in Autobiography* (New York: Capricorn Books, 1965), 107. See also Liam Miller, *The Noble Drama of W. B. Yeats* (Dublin: Dolmen Press, 1976),

Robert Gregory and made by Honor Lavelle, a member of the company. Nic Shiubhlaigh, who played the Angel that night, described the stage:

> The scenery, such as it was, was calculated to centre the onlookers' attention principally on the dialogue and action. A background of dark-green tapestries; a rough desk, bearing a heavy book, open to show an illuminated text; a tasselled bell-pull and a wrought-iron bracket holding the hour-glass; these were the only properties employed. Costumes merged into the background, only those of two of the ten characters having tints of warmth in them.[7]

The company's English patron Annie Horniman also contributed to these early experiments in scenography by designing and making elaborate costumes for Yeats's *The King's Threshold* (1903), *The Shadowy Waters* (1904), and *On Baile's Strand* (1904).[8]

Accounts of the design and manufacture of sets at the Abbey reveal the collaborative, and frequently haphazard, nature of their early productions. Lady Gregory, who predictably effaced her influence in design and direction, described the 1905 staging of her play *Kincora*:

> A great deal of unpaid labour went into it. Mr. Fay discovered a method of making papier mâché, a chief part of which seemed to be the boiling down of large quantities of our old programs, for the mouldings and the shields. I have often seen the designer himself on his knees by a great iron pot—one we use in cottage scenes—dying pieces of sacking, or up high on a ladder painting his forests or leaves.[9]

The theatre's long-time carpenter and scene painter Seaghan Barlow recalled being abandoned to build the set Robert Gregory had designed for his mother's play *The Image* (1909), while Robert went to the Tramore races. As Barlow worked, Lady Gregory demanded the brush and began painting trees herself to demonstrate the proper technique.[10]

At the Abbey, there was also a dynamic relationship between the text and design. For example, Synge's *The Playboy of the Western World* (1907) was originally written with several settings, but ultimately unfolded in a one-room shebeen, with characters peering out of windows to observe the action unfolding elsewhere. Gregory recalled this revision, noting: 'We all tried at that time to write our plays so as to require as little scene-shifting as possible for the sake of economy of scenery and of stage hands.'[11] And the ease with which traditional box sets could be crafted for the small Abbey stage, according to Richard Cave, may have supplemented the claustrophobia of plays like T. C. Murray's *Birthright* (1910).[12]

Elizabeth Bergmann Loizeaux, *Yeats and the Visual Arts* (Syracuse, NY: Syracuse University Press, 2003), 87–116, on Yeats's Abbey aesthetics.

[7] Nic Shiubhlaigh, *Splendid Years*, 33–4.

[8] For valuable accounts of women designers, see Ann Saddlemyer, 'Designing Ladies: Women Artists and the Early Abbey Stage', *Princeton University Library Chronicle* 67, nos. 1 and 2 (2006–7), 163–99.

[9] Gregory, *Our Irish Theatre*, 107–8.

[10] Lennox Robinson, *Ireland's Abbey Theatre: A History 1899–1951* (London: Sidgwick & Jackson, 1951), 71. This history provides first-hand accounts from early Abbey crew members.

[11] Gregory, *Our Irish Theatre*, 132.

[12] Richard Allen Cave, 'On the Siting of Doors and Windows: Aesthetics, Ideology and Irish Stage Design', in Shaun Richards (ed.), *The Cambridge Companion to Twentieth-Century Irish Drama* (Cambridge: Cambridge University Press, 2004), 97.

The cottage and later tenement aesthetics of the early Abbey represented important advances from the spectacle of popular theatre and the middle-class drawing rooms of European realism.[13] The directors of the Abbey attempted to manifest in design and direction the authenticity they intended to convey in their plays, even using actual peasant cottages as a source for props, a principle realized by Synge's request for objects from Inishmaan for the 1904 production of *Riders to the Sea*. As Lennox Robinson recalled, Yeats was deeply attentive to design matters at the Abbey: 'After watching a realistic play, he would make a dozen criticisms [. . .] I had hung the pictures too high, the farmer's daughters were too clean—('Smear cow-dung on their faces!' I remember him exclaiming,) some actor's wig was atrocious, the scene was too dark.'[14]

From its early days, the Abbey looked beyond Ireland's shores for inspiration in design and direction. Yeats, for instance, 'found it useful to have confirmation from Frank Fay's studies of theatrical history for theories of speech, gesture, costumes, scenery and music'.[15] Yeats often cited the influence of Adolphe Appia, the Swiss scenographer best known for his designs for Richard Wagner, but admitted, 'I cannot understand what [he] is doing.'[16] Appia's innovations included the rejection of the flat painted background scenery of nineteenth-century theatre for a more three-dimensional setting and an insistence on rhythmic and unified movement from performers, and he developed the creative use of lighting to establish mood—all innovations from which Irish theatre practitioners would draw. Yeats also collaborated with Charles Ricketts, the British stage designer, who designed costumes and settings for a 1908 revival of *The Well of the Saints* (1905) and a London production of *The King's Threshold* (1903) in 1914. In his work with the Noh, Yeats turned to the French designer Edmund Dulac, who designed the costumes, set, and makeup, as well as composing the music for the April 1916 production of *At the Hawk's Well*, staged in Lady Cunard's London drawing room and later reproduced at Yeats's house in Merrion Square. Seán O'Casey, who attended the Dublin production, described the scene:

> Zither and flute and drum, with Dulac's masks, too full of detail for such an eyeless play, couldn't pour the imagination into the minds of those who listened and saw. The unfolding and folding of the fanciful cloth couldn't carry the stage into the drawing-room. [. . .] a Japanese spirit had failed to climb into the soul of a Kelt.[17]

The most lauded outside influence on the Irish stage of this period was the English scene designer and theorist Gordon Craig.[18] The son of the actor Ellen Terry, Craig began

---

[13] For a study of the peasant play, see Brenna Katz Clarke, *The Emergence of the Irish Peasant Play at the Abbey Theatre* (Ann Arbor, MI: UMI Research Press, 1982). For urban aesthetics on stage, see Nelson Ó Ceallaigh Ritschel, 'The Alternative Aesthetic: The Theatre of Ireland's Urban Plays', in Stephen Watt, Eileen Morgan, and Shakir Mustafa (eds.), *A Century of Irish Drama: Widening the Stage* (Bloomington, IN: Indiana University Press, 2001), 17–33, and Elizabeth Mannion, 'The Dublin Tenement Plays of the Early Abbey', *New Hibernia Review* 14, no. 2 (2010), 69–83.

[14] Lennox Robinson, '[Yeats] As a Man of Theatre', *The Arrow*, summer 1939, 21.

[15] Gabriel Fallon, *The Abbey and the Actor* (Dublin: National Theatre Society, 1969), 16. See Frank J. Fay, *Towards a National Theatre: The Dramatic Criticism of Frank J. Fay*, ed. Robert Hogan (Dublin: Dolmen Press, 1970).

[16] W. B. Yeats, *Explorations* (London: Macmillan, 1962), 179.

[17] Sean O'Casey, *Inishfallen, Fare Thee Well* (London: Macmillan, 1954), 373.

[18] See James W. Flannery, 'W. B. Yeats, Gordon Craig, and the Visual Arts of the Theatre', in Robert O'Driscoll and Lorna Reynolds (eds.), *Yeats and the Theatre* (Toronto: Macmillan, 1975), 82–108, and Alan Tomlinson, 'W. B. Yeats and Gordon Craig', *Ariel* 3, no. 3 (1972), 48–57.

his career performing in Irving's company. Like Appia, Craig sought unity among the elements of theatrical production. His tome *On the Art of the Theatre* (1911) celebrated simple scenery and lighting, argued that meaning should be conveyed by movement, and advocated that designers draw inspiration first from the play's text. Craig famously called for the use of masks on stage, a tactic deployed in plays such as *At the Hawk's Well* and *The Death of Cuchulain* (1949). The 1903 production of Yeats's *The Hour-Glass* employed Craig's theories, and in January 1911 the Abbey revived *The Hour-Glass* in order to use a new set of tall portable screens Yeats had made to Craig's specifications, as well as costumes and masks Craig designed for the production. Yeats explained the value of the screens: 'it enables one to use light in a more natural and beautiful way than ever before. […] One enters into a world of decorative effects which give the actor a renewed importance.'[19]

These innovations, celebrated as an alternative to the Abbey's cottage settings, were not 'one size fits all'. Craig's screens and costumes augmented the language of Yeats's morality play, and the coherence in this vision was crucial to the success of the 1911 production, which critics regarded as an improvement over the 1903 staging. However, Lady Gregory's *The Deliverer* (1911), which unfolds in ancient Egypt, was produced that same night with the same screens and was less successful. Thanks to awkward use of the screens, and the production's uneasy brew of Kiltartan dialect and Egyptian costumes, *The Deliverer* 'was perhaps a severe trial to which to subject a stage-setting which aims at creating a mood'.[20] As this reviewer described: 'The setting of Lady Gregory's play was extremely simple. The screens were placed slantwise across the stage and were folded so as to suggest pillars. The lighting was from the top and the sides. One did not get, however, the sense of space which was intended by the artist.'[21]

The uniquely detailed press accounts of the stage design for these two plays reveal that Craig's screens drew attention not only to the productions on view, as Yeats had hoped, but also to new ways of visualizing the imaginative worlds conjured by the Abbey playwrights. Even the *Irish Times* noted that 'the new methods of staging will subject not only the acting, but the plays themselves to more exacting scrutiny'.[22] This became explicit in a review of a subsequent Abbey production, Lord Dunsany's fantastical *King Argimines and the Unknown Warrior* (1911), which W. J. Lawrence dismissed in part because '[o]ne expects much better staging than this now that the Abbey directorate has openly flouted the scenic methods of the traditional stage, and has called in the services of Mr Gordon Craig to amend them'.[23] The first productions with Craig's screens (which were used at the Abbey until destroyed in the 1951 fire) also demonstrated the synchrony necessary among the elements of drama: the screens worked best with symbolic plays, not the realist plays that composed the bulk of the repertory. The evening thus confirmed the Abbey's repeated assertion that experiment came at the cost of occasional failure.

---

[19] *Evening Telegraph*, 9 Jan. 1911, quoted in Robert Hogan, Richard Burnham, and Daniel P. Poteet (eds.), *The Modern Irish Drama*, vol. 4: *The Rise of the Realists 1910–1915* (Dublin: Dolmen Press, 1979), 101.

[20] *Freeman's Journal*, 13 Jan. 1911, in Hogan et al., *The Rise of the Realists*, 106.   [21] Ibid., 105.

[22] *Irish Times*, 14 Jan. 1911, in Hogan et al., *The Rise of the Realists*, 109.

[23] W. J. Lawrence, *The Stage*, Feb. 1911, in Hogan et al., *The Rise of the Realists*, 112.

Direction at the Abbey continued to be a collaborative and sometimes clumsy process. Barlow was one of many who recalled Yeats's insensitive 'habit of interrupting actors in the middle of a speech',[24] and Nic Shiubhlaigh bemoaned the deliberate lack of direction when rehearsing her role as Nora Burke for Synge's *The Shadow of the Glen* (1904).[25] The role of the director at the Abbey was more officially articulated with the arrival of Lennox Robinson. After a brief stint with Charles Frohman's company in London, where he observed the directing styles of Shaw and Granville Barker among others, Robinson joined the Abbey in 1909 as director and manager. He instituted the practice of naming a play's director in the programmes, and he directed the Abbey School of Acting for many years. Robinson honed his skills not only as the director of the increasing number of realistic productions on view at the Abbey—including his own work—but also by leading the Dublin Drama League.

The Dublin Drama League (1919–29) was founded by Robinson, Ernest Boyd, James Stephens, and Yeats to stage innovative foreign drama on nights when the Abbey was dark. Though the resources for this company were limited, it nonetheless provided an opportunity for set designers like the Abbey's Seaghan Barlow and Dorothy Travers-Smith, as well as artists like Beatrice Campbell, Louis Le Brocquy, and Norah McGuinness, to design productions for plays by Strindberg, Pirandello, and Buchner. A review of the company's Irish première of Eugene O'Neill's *The Emperor Jones* in 1927, directed by Robinson and designed by Travers-Smith, noted 'a clever use of curtains and the exceptionally fine lighting equipment of the Abbey' which 'secured a theatrical spectacle that for convincing realism was a magnificent setting [. . .]The ghosts and 'ha'nts' of [Jones's] fear-distorted imagination were reproduced to give a creepy feeling even to the audience'.[26] The DDL also staged plays by Yeats, including a 1926 production of *The Only Jealousy of Emer* (1922), choreographed by Ninette de Valois with scenery and masks designed by Norah McGuinness, who also performed the role of The Woman of the Sidhe.

Robinson's work with the DDL no doubt influenced the first production of *The Plough and the Stars* (1926), Seán O'Casey's four-act drama set in Dublin tenements during the week of the Easter Rising. Famous for the riots that attended its 1926 première, *Plough* also provides a snapshot of Abbey direction during this period. As director, Robinson frequently sat in rehearsals, according to the actor Shelah Richards, with his eyes covered, listening to the dialogue:

> He was utterly uninterested visually [. . .] Sets just did not matter much to him, nor did the costumes, and I am sure that he never looked at the players' make-up [. . .] Sad and a pity because vocally he was absolutely splendid.[27]

As an audience member at *Plough*, Holloway failed to see this 'splendid' vocal direction manifest on stage, complaining: 'The actors rattle through those interminable word-twisters in a gabby, inflectionless manner.'[28] Nonetheless, accounts of the preparations for

[24] Robinson, *Ireland's Abbey Theatre*, 75.   [25] Nic Shiubhlaigh, *Splendid Years*, 42–3.
[26] '"Emperor Jones": Production by the Dublin Drama League', *Irish Times*, 17 Jan. 1927.
[27] See Robert Hogan and Richard Burnham (eds.), *The Modern Irish Drama*, vol. 6: *The Years of O'Casey 1921–1926: A Documentary History* (Gerrards Cross: Colin Smythe 1992), 293.
[28] Ibid., 295.

Plough confirm the rich collaborative nature of production at the Abbey by recounting the back-and-forth between director and playwright in matters of casting and direction, noting O'Casey's dramaturgical research on costumes or the placement of a tricolour in a pub.[29]

THE GATE THEATRE

The Abbey's staging of *Plough* also subtly demonstrated the pervasive influence of a new aesthetic in the Dublin theatre—that of German expressionism.[30] The off-stage figure of The Man in the Window, who speaks the words of the unnamed Republican hero Patrick Pearse, was suggestively inconsistent with the stark naturalism of this tenement play. Throughout the 1920s, small companies like Edward Martyn's Irish Theatre and the New Players (which produced expressionist plays in private drawing rooms using crude sets built from curtains, wires, and cardboard boxes) also staged experimental drama and offered Irish audiences early, if unpolished, examples of avant-garde design and direction.[31] But there remained, and with good reason, a widespread perception that realist and naturalist aesthetics prevailed on the Irish stage.

Enter Hilton Edwards and Micheál Mac Liammóir, whose inventive direction and design at Dublin's Gate Theatre provided a new aesthetic for theatre audiences of this period. The meeting of Edwards and Mac Liammóir in June 1927 is a seminal moment in the mythology of modern Irish theatre. Both men, in their 20s at the time, were travelling with the touring company of Anew McMaster, and each had a long acting career already behind him. Both were born in England and had toured in various professional productions: Mac Liammóir as a child actor for Sir Herbert Beerbohm Tree, Edwards with Charles Doran's Shakespearean Company. Both were steeped in the acting and design traditions of nineteenth-century popular theatre, and understood the power of a strong performance and a visually compelling stage. They first worked together in 1928, when they staged *Diarmuid agus Gráinne* (Diarmuid and Grainne) for Taibhdhearc na Gaillimhe, the Irish-language theatre they helped to found in Galway. This play, performed entirely in Irish and inspired by the mythic love story from the Fenian Cycle, was written and designed by Mac Liammóir (self-taught in Irish, like Gregory and Synge before him), and directed by Edwards. This collaboration revealed their shared passion for innovative direction and design, and introduced a principle that distinguished their work in the Irish theatre: 'we', Mac Liammóir explained, 'revealed the importance of the visible, as well as the audible.'[32]

[29] See Robert G. Lowery (ed.), *A Whirlwind in Dublin: The Plough and the Stars Riots* (Westport, CT: Greenwood Press, 1984).

[30] See Michael McAteer, 'Expressionism, Ireland and the First World War: Yeats, O'Casey, McGuinness', in Edwina Keown and Carol Taaffe (eds.), *Irish Modernism: Origins, Contexts, Publics* (Bern: Peter Lang, 2009), 65–80.

[31] See Jerry Nolan, 'Edward Martyn's Struggle for an Irish National Theatre, 1899–1920', *New Hibernia Review* 7, no. 2 (2003), 88–105, for a history of Martyn's engagement with foreign drama and experiment.

[32] Richard Pine (with Richard Cave), *The Dublin Gate Theatre 1928–1978* (Cambridge: Chadwyck-Healey, 1984), 21. This invaluable history is accompanied by a series of slide images and informative appendices.

Established in 1928, the Gate Theatre imagined itself as part of the larger international Little Theatre Movement, which had inspired America's Provincetown Players among others—companies that could take intellectual and aesthetic risks thanks to low-cost venues and small audiences. Its founding prospectus announced the opening of 'the Dublin Gate Theatre Studio [. . .] for the production of modern and progressive plays, unfettered by theatrical convention'. Modelled after the London Gate Theatre Studio, it promised to produce a new play with a short run every two weeks, as well as offering lectures, discussions, and painting exhibitions to small audiences. Expressly not a national theatre, it promised a 'Continental repertoire' and 'all plays of a suitable nature'[33]. Like other Irish theatres, the Gate was highly collaborative, and supported Denis Johnston, Daisy Bannard Cogley, Gearóid Ó Lochlainn, Gordon Campbell (second Baron Glenavy), Norman Reddin, Edward Pakenham (sixth Earl of Longford), and his wife, Christine—along with a roster of talented designers, craftspeople, and performers, including Orson Welles, who at age 16 made his stage debut in the company's 1931 production of *Jew Suss* (1929).[34]

To some degree, the Gate was formed as a reaction against the theatrical naturalism of the Abbey. Mac Liammóir credited Edwards with successfully challenging this limited and limiting aesthetic, and with introducing a more coherent style of direction:

> It was his arrival on the Irish scene that was the first signal for the searchlights of interest and understanding to be turned, not away from the author, who at the Abbey had been pre-eminent from the beginning even over the actor, but equally upon the director and his art. It was he who introduced to Dublin methods of production, décor, and lighting, handling of mass effects, experiments in choral speaking, in scenic continuity, in symphonic arrangements of incidental music, of mime and gesture, hitherto barely understood.[35]

Mac Liammóir was an equal partner in imagining and realizing this theatrical revolution, designing virtually all of the costumes and sets during the theatre's early years.

While other Irish companies had attended haphazardly to European innovations in scenography, the Gate consistently presented a fully realized experimental aesthetic on stage. In particular, it developed stage techniques drawn from expressionism, whose dominance on the experimental stage of this period was partially credited to Appia and Craig.[36] In its quest to represent interior mental states on the stage, expressionist scenography emphasized abstraction and distortion through evocative colours in makeup, costume, and setting, as well as exaggerated imagery on stage, the dramatic use of light and shadow, and highly choreographed movement. It also demanded new forms of stage design: it generally incorporated variant stage levels and demanded quick scene changes. Thus, theatrical expressionism required that audiences adjust to new modes of representing space and time on stage. Other influences at the Gate resemble a roll-call of internationally influential

[33] Ibid., 25.

[34] See John Cowell, *No Profit but the Name: The Longfords and the Gate Theatre* (Dublin: O'Brien Press, 1988).

[35] Peter Luke (ed.), *Enter Certain Players: Edwards, Mac Liammóir, and the Gate 1928–1978* (Dublin: Dolmen Press, 1978), 15.

[36] See Elaine Sisson, 'Experimentalism and the Irish Stage: Theatre and German Expressionism in the 1920s', in Linda King and Elaine Sisson (eds.), *Ireland, Design, and Visual Culture: Negotiating Modernity, 1922–1992* (Cork: Cork University Press, 2011), 39–58.

scenographers and directors: Léon Bakst, who designed exotic costumes and sets for the Ballets Russes; Norman Bel Geddes, whose futurist set and costume designs appeared on Broadway and in film; Constantin Stanislavksi, whose techniques for drawing out more realistic performances were developed at the Moscow Art Theatre; Peter Godfrey, who directed expressionist drama at London's Gate Theatre Studio.

As the Abbey had discovered before them, the Gate was challenged and inspired by the limitations of physical spaces and resources. The first production of the Dublin Gate Studio Theatre was staged in the rented space of the Peacock Theatre in October 1928, with a production of Ibsen's verse drama *Peer Gynt*. Edwards identified the goal of this production as 'the conquest of space', and set about creating the vast setting required by this play on the Peacock's 16-foot stage.[37] He created a sense of 'unlimited space' by painting the back wall 'a neutral blue-grey, and flooding it with light from eight 500-watt lanterns, thus achieving an illusion of shadowless and infinite sky' to create the effect of a cyclorama.[38] For the mountain scenes, two sets of steps were placed back-to-back on stage, their projected shadow suggesting the Norwegian peaks. Actors, silhouetted or under spotlights graduated in colour, thus appeared to ascend or descend these mountain peaks. Valley scenes were played between the separated sets of steps; hut scenes played with a wall and roof placed between the stairs; desert scenes meant the removal of stairs from the stage and a single ground row of amber lights at the front stage to suggest an endless horizon. A few deliberately artificial decorative mountains and trees were placed on the stage, as a concession to the audience. But in fact, playgoers in the sold-out theatre appeared to accept the demands on their visual imagination with little complaint, awarding the production 'spontaneous and frantic' applause.[39]

The unified vision of this 1928 *Peer Gynt* led the influential critic C. P. Curran to cite Edwards's 'great skill' as a director.[40] The play required a large cast, so members of the company performed several roles, with Edwards starring as Peer (Mac Liammóir was in Galway for much of the run). In his direction, Edwards stressed the 'rhythmical speaking of the verse', and used the play's original incidental music by Edvard Grieg. Here, Edward's understanding of large-scale spectacle was evident, even on the small stage: 'This rhythm was carried into the movements of the crowds, the group movements of the peasants, trolls, and the Saeter girls, and, in fact, all movements whether of mass or individual were, according to a definite rhythmic pattern, related to the design of the settings.'[41]

In 1930, the company moved from the Peacock to the renovated New Rooms in the Rotunda, a site in Dublin known for popular theatre and cinema screenings. The Gate now had a larger stage with a passage behind the stage for actors, as well as a proscenium, a pit for lights, and a second small proscenium that would host the string orchestra (with Bay Jellett, Cathleen Rogers, and Gretta Smith) that became part of its regular staff. The 1932

---

[37] Hilton Edwards, 'Production', in Bulmer Hobson (ed.), *The Gate Theatre Dublin* (Dublin: Gate Theatre, 1934), 24. See also Irina Ruppo Malone, 'Ibsen and the Irish Free State: The Gate Theatre Company Productions of *Peer Gynt*', *Irish University Review* 39, no. 1 (2009), 42–64.

[38] Edwards, 'Production', 24.

[39] Micheál Mac Liammóir, *All for Hecuba* (1946) (Boston, MA: Brayden Press, 1967), 64.

[40] Christopher Fitz-Simon, *The Boys: A Biography of Micheál Mac Liammóir and Hilton Edwards* (Dublin: Gill & Macmillan, 1994), 53.

[41] Edwards, 'Production', 25.

revival of *Peer Gynt* demonstrated the improvements allowed for by the new site: now, the full score by Greig was played by a hidden orchestra, the steps on stage were surrounded by coloured curtains, and the lanterns were hidden in the light pit.

This move to a larger theatre also meant the Gate could 'leave the three-act or five-act form of conventionality and to demand many and short scenes'[42]—an effect that was realized in what might be its most renowned original production, Denis Johnston's *The Old Lady Says 'No!'* (1929). Johnston's satire of the Free State was rejected by the Abbey, and its original title, *Shadowdance*, was replaced, according to legend, with this new title capturing Gregory's decree. *The Old Lady Says 'No!'* opens with a stage actor, 'The Speaker', performing the role of the Irish nationalist hero Robert Emmet. The Speaker suffers a head injury and becomes convinced he actually is Emmet—a plotline likely adapted from Pirandello's *Henry IV* (1921), which had been staged in 1924 by the Dublin Drama League. The play follows The Speaker on a hallucinatory and humorous journey through the streets of Dublin, where he observes the various failures of the post-Independence state. The play and its staging drew from surrealism and expressionism: the music, lights, and rapid scene changes called for by Johnston and designed by Edwards and Mac Liammóir were intended to convey the protagonist's nightmarish experience.

The opening scene of the play began with the curtain down, the theatre filled with the noise of tramping feet and voices chanting the 'Shan Van Vocht'. As the sound faded, the curtain opened to reveal the play's setting. Reviews praised Edwards's blocking of the crowd scenes, with Johnston singling out the 'mass movements of crowds that have to be carried out in a manner not dissimilar to a ballet' on a 16×12-foot stage, and commended the boldly imagined series of curtains designed by Mac Liammóir that were quickly swept across the stage and into the wings to accommodate the rapidly changing scenes.[43] Working as lighting designer and director, Edwards 'discovered a seemingly unconscious rhythm in the lines spoken by the shadows and had introduced them with a pulsation of light and the notes of a drum beaten with varying *tempi*'.[44]

The range and variety of Gate productions in these early years are impressive. Their innovative direction and design was applied to work as diverse as a 1928 production of Eugene O'Neill's *The Hairy Ape* (1922), which Lady Gregory praised for Edwards's lighting of the stoke-hole scene which 'made the stage look like a picture of Rembrandt',[45] and a popular 1934 production of Shakespeare's *Julius Caesar*, which offered a massive pediment that 'held in turn a garlanded bust of Caesar, an immense globe, and Caesar's throne [. . . and] a pulpit for Brutus and Anthony, with the mob thronged on or about the steps'.[46] Ironically, the remarkable design and direction of the Gate so powerfully dominate its historical narrative that, with the exception of Denis Johnston, few of its plays and playwrights have received sustained attention.

The eclectic nature of the visual world of the early Gate was evident not only on stage but also in *Motley*, the theatre's little magazine edited by the playwright and performer Mary Manning, which displayed the wide-ranging influences on the theatre's aesthetic,

---

[42] Ibid., 32.

[43] Denis Johnston, 'A Note on What Happened', in *Selected Plays*, ed. Joseph Ronsley (Gerrards Cross: Colin Smythe, 1983), 85.

[44] Mac Liammóir, *All for Hecuba*, 80.   [45] Ibid., 66.

[46] Review from the *Manchester Guardian*, cited in Pine, *Dublin Gate Theatre*, 74.

including public spectacle, cabaret, pantomime, and Russian art. *Motley*'s close attention to early cinema also exposes the Gate's complicated relationship with film. In 1935, Johnston and Manning premièred their film adaptation of Frank O'Connor's *Guests of the Nation* at the Gate.[47] Yet the early Gate maintained a strange ambivalence, and even defensiveness, about media technologies, with Edwards asserting, '[t]he theatre at its best has always depended upon brain rather than machinery'.[48] Nonetheless, the 1933 production of Johnston's *A Bride for the Unicorn* merged traditional theatrical styles drawn from mime and musical comedy, with a radio gramophone and loudspeakers in the theatre.

The influence of design and direction at the Gate casts a long shadow. Of Edwards and Mac Liammóir, Orson Welles claimed 'my debt to them can never be measured', and critics have identified not only the impact of their direction, lighting, and set design on *Citizen Kane* (1941), but also the similarities in plot between the film and David Sears' play *The Dead Ride Fast*, which premièred at the Gate in 1931, with Welles in the cast.[49] The film collaborations between Edwards, Mac Liammóir, and Welles continued through Welles's 1952 film adaptation of *Othello* (chronicled in Mac Liammóir's *Put Money in Thy Purse*), Edwards's film *Return to Glenascaul* (1953), and the failed *Chimes at Midnight* (1966). The influence of the Gate would also appear in Manning's astonishing stage adaptations of James Joyce's *Finnegans Wake*. First staged in America in 1955 by the Poets' Theatre, this production—along with her 1966 adaptation of 'Ivy Day in the Committee Room'—was heavily influenced by the Gate's commitment to expressionism. Later, Brian Friel cited the importance of his early theatrical 'education' at the Gate, claiming, 'I came out from under the Edwards–Mac Liammóir overcoat.'[50]

Experiment in Mid-Twentieth-Century Irish Theatre

Ireland's national theatre took notice of the innovations in direction and design at the Gate and gingerly began to tinker with the 'Abbey style'. Denis Johnston was invited to direct the very first Shakespeare on the Abbey stage, a 1928 production of *King Lear* with a 'futurist' set by Dorothy Travers-Smith.[51] And in 1935, the theatre once more looked abroad for guidance in direction and design, bringing in as director Hugh Hunt, who in turn hired the designer Tanya Moiseiwitsch.[52] An Englishman with a long track record in theatre, Hunt took on a variety of roles at the Abbey, as a playwright and actor, lighting designer, and manager.

---

[47] See 'Guests of the Nation', *Irish Film and TV Research On-Line*, Trinity College Dublin, http://www.tcd.ie/irishfilm/showfilm.php?fid=56631. Accessed 10 Oct. 2014.

[48] Edwards, 'Production', 33.

[49] 'Orson Welles and the Gate Theatre', in *Scéalta Átha Cliath*, dir. Darren Chan, TG4 (transmitted 17 Nov. 2011).

[50] Mac Liammóir, *Enter Certain Players*, 21.

[51] Hugh Hunt, *The Abbey: Ireland's National Theatre 1904–1979* (New York: Columbia University Press, 1979), 143.

[52] Ibid., 152.

FIG. 13.1 Tanya Moiseiwitsch's set designs for G. B. Shaw's *A Village Wooing* (30 September 1935).

Courtesy of the Abbey Theatre and James Hardiman Library, NUI Galway.

A student at the Old Vic Theatre in London, who had worked there with Tyrone Guthrie, Moiseiwitsch was well versed in a variety of aesthetic traditions, ranging from Arts and Crafts to Bauhaus. Her first production was F. R. Higgins's *A Deuce o' Jacks* (1935), whose set Joseph Holloway considered 'too fantastical for words'.[53] Between 1935 and 1939, she created, at a breakneck pace, the costumes and settings for over fifty productions, ranging from Synge's *Playboy* in 1935 to Shakespeare's *Coriolanus* in 1936; and her collaboration with Hunt on the first production of Paul Vincent Carroll's *Shadow and Substance* in 1937 drew international acclaim. The position of resident designer was subsequently held by a roster of talents including Anne Yeats (1939–40), Alicia Sweetman (1943–6), and Tomás Mac Anna (1947–66), whose design for a 1965 production of Brecht's *The Life of Galileo* (1943) was heralded as 'a break-through in lighting, production, and acting'.[54] From the early 1940s, the artist Seán Keating provided designs for the setting and costumes for occasional productions of *Playboy* and *Well of the Saints*.

Regular innovations in design and direction at the Abbey stalled during the mid-twentieth century. However, Ria Mooney did attempt to import new tactics during her tenure as Abbey director. An actor, Mooney had played Rosie Redmond in the notorious 1926 Abbey première of O'Casey's *The Plough and the Stars* and performed with Eva

[53] Cited in Denis Behl, 'A Career in the Theatre', in T. J. Edelstein et al., *The Stage is All the World: The Theatrical Designs of Tanya Moiseiwitsch* (Chicago, IL: Smart Museum of Art, 1994), 36.

[54] Hunt, *Abbey Theatre*, 184. A mistake in Hunt's text makes it appear as though the date of this production was 1956; it in fact opened on 20 Sept. 1965, as Hunt himself makes clear in his list of Abbey productions, p. 268.

Le Gallienne's Civic Repertory Theatre in New York City. After returning to Ireland, she founded the student-run Experimental Theatre at the Peacock in 1937 to encourage young playwrights and performers, as well as to develop production and design practices. Anne Yeats, for instance, began her work on costumes and sets with Mooney's company. Mooney was appointed by Ernest Blythe in 1948 to serve as the Abbey's artistic director, a position she held until 1963. Serving under Blythe's conservatism, Mooney nonetheless successfully staged dozens of original scripts, as well as revivals ranging from Yeats's *The Dreaming of the Bones* (1949) to Behan's *The Quare Fellow* (1956).

Both the Abbey and the Gate rejected *The Quare Fellow*, due in part to the demands presented by its large cast and its technical requirements. Thus, the 1954 world première of Behan's play was staged at Dublin's Pike Theatre, where the 'atmosphere of claustrophobia and isolation' necessary to the play was, according to Carolyn Swift, conveyed through Alan Simpson's expressionist lighting and prison sets composed of 'five white door frames constructed in perspective (by Seán O'Shea) and holding plain numbered doors'.[55] Mooney's subsequent restaging of *The Quare Fellow* at the Abbey was unfairly dismissed as 'unimaginative' despite praise for the 'highly effective settings of Tomás MacAnna'.[56] The Pike was also the first to stage Beckett's *Waiting for Godot* in 1955. Simpson's direction heightened the slapstick and cross-talk of the popular theatre, the costumes drew in part from the films of Charlie Chaplin, and the largely barren stage—dressed in 'backcloths daubed in black, green and brown to vaguely suggest an Irish bogland and gloomy sky'[57]—was inspired by the minimal stagecraft of the early Abbey and existentialist aesthetics.

SPECTACLE AND PAGEANTRY

Like productions on traditional theatre stages, public spectacle—which includes a vast range of consciously executed live events, from funerals to historical re-enactments to automobile races—cannily engaged direction and design to convey its messages.[58] Nationalist organizations, for instance, regularly harnessed the power of spectacle

[55] Cited in Ian Walsh, *Experimental Irish Theatre: After W. B. Yeats* (New York: Palgrave Macmillan, 2012), 174.

[56] See James P. McGlone, *Ria Mooney: The Life and Times of the Artistic Director of the Abbey Theatre, 1948–1963* (London: McFarland, 2002), 168.

[57] Dougald McMillan and Martha Fehsenfeld, *Beckett in the Theatre* (London: John Calder, 1988), 82. For a detailed account of this production, see Christopher Morash, *A History of the Irish Theatre 1601–2000* (Cambridge: Cambridge University Press, 2002), 199–208.

[58] Studies specifically addressing the range of spectacle and pageantry during this period include Sara Brady and Fintan Walsh (eds.), *Crossroads: Performance Studies and Irish Culture* (Basingstoke: Palgrave Macmillan, 2009); Joan FitzPatrick Dean, 'Pageants, Parades, and Performance Culture', in John P. Harrington (ed.), *Modern and Contemporary Irish Drama*, 2nd edn. (New York: Norton, 2009), 613–22; Joan FitzPatrick Dean, *All Dressed Up: Modern Irish Historical Pageantry* (Syracuse, NY: Syracuse University Press, 2014); Paige Reynolds, *Modernism, Drama, and the Audience for Irish Spectacle* (Cambridge: Cambridge University Press, 2007); Paige Reynolds, 'Spectacle and Performance in (and out of) Modern Irish Theatre', in Anthony Roche (ed.), *The Irish Dramatic Revival 1899–1939* (London: Methuen, 2015).

to advance anti-imperialist ideals to large audiences. In April 1900, Queen Victoria sponsored a 'Children's Treat' in Phoenix Park to generate support for the Boer War; in response, a group of Irish nationalist women organized the Irish Patriotic Children's Treat, hosting activities for roughly 20,000 children to promote Irish nationalism.[59] Later, Cumann na mBan (League of Women), a Republican organization, hosted open-air festivals of music, verse recitation, comedy skits, and singing that 'carefully avoided' the music-hall pattern and championed nationalist ideals.[60] Spectacles such as these were not important simply because they stimulated nationalist sentiment; they also played a role in the establishment of more traditional forms of Irish theatre. The informally organized group of women who produced the Irish Patriotic Children's Treat, for example, resulted in the formation of Inghinidhe na hEireann (Daughters of Ireland), which was crucial to the foundation of the Abbey. Large audiences also attended this organization's popular *tableaux vivants*, 'living pictures' that staged moments from Irish history or myth.[61] The ongoing commitment to and enthusiasm for forms of historical pageantry were evident as well in the productions staged by Patrick Pearse.[62] This easy interaction between fictional narratives on the dramatic stage and actual events in public spaces may explain why citizens sometimes understood political happenings in Ireland, such as the 1916 Easter Rising, in explicitly theatrical terms.[63]

Following Independence, the Irish Free State regularly employed public spectacle to represent itself as mature both politically and culturally to audiences at home and abroad. These large-scale public events were intended to incubate national pride, to soothe political turmoil in recently partitioned Ireland, and to lure tourists to the island. In 1924, for instance, the Cumann na Gaedheal government successfully revived Aonach Tailteann, an ancient Irish festival incorporating native sport and cultural pursuits.[64] The Tailteann Games promised spectators sixteen days of pageantry and competitive sport celebrating all things Celtic. Before live audiences, participants competed in a wide variety of Irish and international sports such as hurling and athletics, pastimes including chess, sailing, and billiards, and contests in dancing, theatrical performance, literature, and crafts. The dialogue between spectacle and traditional theatre was again evident: the winning plays of the 1924 and 1926 Tailteann competitions were produced by the Gate.

[59] For accounts of this event and the subsequent formation of Inghinidhe na hEireann, see Janette Condon, 'The Patriotic Children's Treat: Irish Nationalism and Children's Culture at the Twilight of Empire', *Irish Studies Review* 8, no. 2 (2000), 167–78; D. A. J. McPherson, *Women and the Irish Nation: Gender, Culture, and Irish Identity, 1890–1940* (Basingstoke: Palgrave Macmillan, 2012), 125–30; and Mary Trotter, *Ireland's National Theatres: Political Performance and the Origins of the Irish Dramatic Movement* (Syracuse, NY: Syracuse University Press, 2001), 73–99.

[60] Nic Shiubhlaigh, *Splendid Years*, 160.

[61] Maria Tymoczko, 'Amateur Political Theatricals, *Tableaux Vivants*, and Cathleen ni Houlihan', in Warwick Gould (ed.), *Yeats Annual* 10 (New York: Macmillan, 1993), 33–64.

[62] See Elaine Sisson, *Pearse's Patriots: St Enda's and the Cult of Boyhood* (Cork: Cork University Press, 2005); and Trotter, *Ireland's National Theatres*, 137–66.

[63] See James Moran, *Staging the Easter Rising: 1916 as Theatre* (Cork: Cork University Press, 2005).

[64] See Mary McKernan, 'A Historical Account of the Three Phases of Aonach Tailteann' (master's thesis, Springfield College, 1981); Mike Cronin, 'Projecting the Nation through Sport and Culture: Ireland, Aonach Tailteann and the Irish Free State, 1924–32', *Journal of Contemporary History* 38, no. 3 (2003), 395–411; Reynolds, *Modernism*, 156–98; Louise Ryan, *Gender, Identity, and the Irish Press 1922–1937* (Lewiston, NY: Edwin Mellen Press, 2002), 16–35.

The two Dublin Civic Weeks staged in 1927 and 1929 offer another compelling example of the Free State's use of political spectacle, and its effect on traditional theatre. Like Aonach Tailteann, Dublin Civic Week offered audiences an astonishing assortment of activities, including lectures, sporting competitions, concerts, and dances. During the 1927 Civic Week, an opening parade through Dublin showcased hundreds of mythic, legendary, and historical figures drawn from the Irish past; the 'Grand Pageant of Dublin History' and 'Historical Pageant and Tableaux' offered audiences short historical episodes; and in the popular military tattoo, Free State soldiers participated in mass gymnastics, military processions, and dramatic re-enactments before an audience in the tens of thousands.[65] For the 1929 Civic Week, Mac Liammóir staged *The Ford of the Hurdles*, a historical pageant composed of seven episodes depicting mythic and historical events including 'The Rape of Dervorgilla' and the 1916 Easter Rising. So popular were these productions that in 1933, at the invitation of Orson Welles, Edwards and Mac Liammóir travelled to America, and while there presented the 'Pageant of the Celt' in Chicago's enormous Soldier Field.[66] The adept staging of crowd scenes on the Gate stage suggests that spectacles such as these inspired new forms of theatrical design and direction. As Edwards noted, 'I was always for crowd work, the big scene, the sort of Cecil B. De Mille effect on a tiny stage.'[67]

Though these events generally unfolded outside the traditional confines of the theatre, many of them were elaborately designed and directed. The 1932 International Eucharistic Congress held in Dublin, for example, was a religious spectacle characterized by astonishingly elaborate, and expensive, scenography calculated to showcase, before a national and international audience, an Ireland united in its Catholic identity.[68] The Dublin Congress, with its busy week of Masses and meetings for Catholic religious and lay people from across the globe, temporarily transformed the city: two ornamental pylons were temporarily erected to mark entrance to the city; buildings throughout the city were bedecked with flowers and shrubs; informally erected shrines were put in place by local residents. These decorations turned Dublin into an elaborate stage set designed to conceal the poverty and decay infecting the country after years of political strife and a worldwide economic depression. Like the other spectacles staged during this period, the Eucharistic Congress drew an astonishingly large audience. An estimated one million people attended the final open-air Mass in Phoenix Park, and the events of the Eucharistic Congress, including John McCormack's performance of 'Panis Angelicus', were broadcast throughout Ireland by the new Irish radio station.

The Republic took up the cause of self-celebrating spectacle to buoy national esteem and draw tourists to the island. In 1953, it organized and hosted An Tóstal (The Festival), which offered the public parades, sporting competitions, and art festivals designed to showcase

---

[65] Joan FitzPatrick Dean, 'Rewriting the Past: Historical Pageantry in the Dublin Civic Weeks of 1927 and 1929', *New Hibernia Review* 13, no. 1 (2009), 20–41.

[66] Fitz-Simon, *The Boys*, 82–3.   [67] Pine, *Dublin Gate Theatre*, 75.

[68] Rory O'Dwyer, *The Eucharistic Congress, Dublin 1932: An Illustrated History* (Dublin: Nonsuch, 2009), 116. See also G. K. Chesterton, *Christendom in Dublin* (London: Sheed & Ward, 1932); John Paul McCarthy and Tomás O'Riordan, 'The 31st International Eucharistic Congress, Dublin, 1932', in *The Pursuit of Sovereignty and the Impact of Partition, 1912–1949*, UCC Multi-Text Project in Irish History, http://multitext.ucc.ie/d/The_31st_International_Eucharistic_Congress_Dublin_1932. Accessed 16 Mar. 2014.

Irish culture. As with previous public spectacles like Aonach Tailteann and the Eucharistic Congress, Dublin was bedecked with banners, shields, and other decorations intended to convey national pride. Of these, the most celebrated was the 'Bowl of Light', a large copper bowl with illuminated plastic flames that was intended as a permanent monument. On the night it was unveiled, the 'Bowl of Light' drew a crowd in the thousands to O'Connell Street. Within weeks, however, a drunken student from Trinity College had tossed the bowl into the Liffey. The legacy of An Tóstal lives on in Ireland, evident through the Tidy Towns competition and 'The Gathering', a 2013 celebration similarly designed to draw tourists to an economically struggling Ireland.[69]

---

[69] For film footage, see 'On This Day 1953 *An Tóstal*', RTÉ Archives, http://www.rte.ie/archives/2013/0404/379686-an-tostal-1953/. Accessed 22 May 2014.

CHAPTER 14

....

THE IMPORTANCE OF
STAGING OSCAR
Wilde at the Gate

....

EIBHEAR WALSHE

IN this chapter, I consider the enabling status of Oscar Wilde as house dramatist at the Gate Theatre in Dublin, starting with the iconic 1928 staging of *Salomé*, the first professional production of the play in Ireland and the UK. This production led on to a series of Wilde plays staged there throughout the 1930s, thus starting a lifelong association with his work. From there, I discuss the one-man show *The Importance of Being Oscar*, staged in 1960 by the Gate Theatre founders, Micheál Mac Liammóir and Hilton Edwards. My argument in this chapter is that Mac Liammóir and Edwards were key in shaping popular cultural perceptions of Wilde's drama and his persona in Ireland in the twentieth century. In turn, productions of Wilde's own work set the tone and style for the programme of drama produced by the Gate Theatre. In my book *Oscar's Shadow*,[1] I argue that Wilde's homosexuality was a contested discourse within twentieth-century Ireland—a discourse that became enmeshed with debates around Irish cultural nationalism. Ireland was undergoing a period of radical self-fashioning in the years after Wilde's disgrace, particularly in the years before political independence in 1922, and therefore perceptions of his sexuality and his plays became part of this cultural volatility. Furthermore, Wilde's writings create a kind of imaginative mutability, both hinting at and, at the same time, containing his sexuality for key figures in the Irish Renaissance like Yeats, Shaw, and Gregory. From 1922 onwards, Wilde begins to disappear from the imaginative landscape of the new Irish State, and so the Gate Theatre provided a crucial locus for the staging of acceptable and palatable versions of Wilde. This is true, I would argue, right up to the present, with highly stylized, lushly staged, and commercially successful revivals of Wilde at the Gate under the directorship of Michael Colgan from 1983 onwards to the 2015 production of *The Importance of Being Earnest*. However, I would contend that any potential for these current Wilde productions as radical, or as reflecting his iconic status in contemporary queer discourse, is only sometimes realized, and that, for the contemporary stagings in the Gate, Wilde the charming dandy is often more acceptable than Wilde the queer artist.

---

[1] Eibhear Walshe, *Oscar's Shadow* (Cork: Cork University Press, 2011), 149.

DISPLACED PERSONS

In the early part of the twentieth century, Wilde was an uneasy figure within Irish cultural discourse, a difficult writer to place and categorize. The most important figure for Wilde's visibility in Ireland was actor and dramatist Micheál Mac Liammóir. Born Alfred Willmore in London in 1899, he Gaelicized his name and reinvented himself as an Irishman when he moved to Dublin as a young man, later setting up the Gate Theatre with his life partner, the director Hilton Edwards. The Gate Theatre was founded in 1928 by Edwards and Mac Liammóir to provide a less insular, more cosmopolitan alternative to the state-subsidized Abbey Theatre, and maintained a counterbalance to the peasant dramas and rustic comedies of establishment theatre with a programme including Wilde, Coward, Ibsen, Pirandello, Eugene O'Neill, and Anouillh. Just as significantly, Mac Liammóir and Edwards were openly gay public figures. In a state where homosexuality was criminalized until 1993, and the homoerotic was censored and expunged from all official literary and cultural discourse, Mac Liammóir and Edwards survived, and even flourished, as Ireland's only visible gay couple. When Mac Liammóir died in 1978, the president of Ireland attended

FIG. 14.1 Micheál Mac Liammóir (left) and Hilton Edwards (right) strike a pose outside the doors of the Gate Theatre, on Dublin's Parnell Square.

Courtesy of the Gate Theatre and Library Special Collections, Northwestern University.

his funeral, as did the Taoiseach and several government ministers, while Edwards was openly deferred to and sympathized with as chief mourner. Wilde was a vital part of their acceptable and popular public personas, but their various engagements with Wilde changed with each phase of the development of the Gate Theatre, and could be ambivalent, depending on the cultural mode of the day.

'Micheál Mac Liammóir', supposedly Cork-born Irish actor and writer, never actually existed. It was a name and a personal history conjured up by London-born actor Alfred Willmore, when he left England for Ireland in 1917. Willmore, born in Kensal Green in London in 1899, had no Irish connections whatsoever. He had been a success as a child actor, working with Sir Herbert Beerbohm Tree amongst others, and then had attended the Slade School of Fine Art. Just before graduating from the Slade, however, Willmore abandoned his studies and went travelling. In the short term, he was fleeing Britain because of conscription, and possibly because of the attentions of an older, wealthy lover. To escape association with this newly forged 'deviant' sexual role, Willmore reversed Wilde's own journey of self-consummation. He left London for Dublin, embracing Celticism and remaking himself as an Irishman, finding in the role of the Irish mystic artist a defence against the taint of Wildean aestheticism and decadence.

By his own account, Mac Liammóir's meeting with Edwards in June 1927, where both were acting with the travelling company of Anew McMaster in Enniscorthy, Co. Wexford, was a pivotal moment in the construction of his fictive persona. Private and public roles, and national and sexual identities, were resolved and anchored for Mac Liammóir in his partnership with Edwards. (Alfred Willmore's decision to remake himself as the Cork man Micheál Mac Liammóir may have had something to do with the fact that he and Edwards, out of work and penniless, moved on directly from Wexford to Cork, formulating plans for a new Irish theatre in the southern capital.) In a professional sense, the actor/designer found the ideal director, with Edwards's exacting production values checking and harnessing Mac Liammóir's lyricism and self-dramatization. The two were to live together for fifty years. However, Edwards provided the perfect Saxon foil against which Mac Liammóir could define his own invented Celticism, and his literary reincarnation as poet of the Celtic Twilight. Throughout his life, in his various autobiographical writings, Mac Liammóir was to tell and retell the narrative of this youthful decision to leave London and to adopt Dublin as his theatrical base, each retelling involving a creative reordering of the narrative to accommodate and to justify his assumed mask or persona: 'Here is London, a huge impersonal web of shadow and movement and like a vast motherly hen, the night broods and waits. [. . .] Home again to Ireland, to a new Ireland, maybe.'[2]

In essence, Alfred Willmore reconstructed himself as the neo-Celtic thespian Mac Liammóir, a disciple of Yeats and of the Celtic Twilight, because the Yeatsian mask would enable Willmore to dissent and separate himself from British masculinist heterosexuality. In other words, with the shadow of Wilde and the Wilde trials making the homoerotic suspect and questionable in Britain, the Yeatsian mode of artistic being offered a more acceptable role for the sexually ambiguous actor and dramatist, and so Willmore reinvented himself, taking on the mantle of the Celtic Revival. Yet Wilde remained key in his success at maintaining this fictive persona, and his autobiographies turn on a series of

---

[2] Micheál Mac Liammóir, *All for Hecuba* (London: Methuen, 1946), 25.

evasions and screenings, obscuring his English origins and veiling his sexual identity, delicately treading a balance between artistic license and downright 'fiction', i.e. invention. His dramatic and autobiographical writings—in particular, *An Oscar of no Importance* (1968) and his play, *The Importance of Being Oscar* (1963)—are key in assessing Wilde's evolving importance for the Gate Theatre and for the evolution of Mac Liammóir's own dramatic imagination.

WILDE AT THE GATE: THE 1920S AND 1930S

It is worth setting the context for the kind of Ireland in which the Gate was founded. Ireland had achieved political autonomy in 1922, and what was being gradually constructed in the late 1920s and into the 1930s was an official or state version of the idea of 'Irishness'. This national identity actively supported and promoted the ideal of linguistic, economic, and cultural self-sufficiency as a necessary adjunct to political independence, and had a certain idealism inherited from earlier revolutionary times. It has been argued that, as a result, intellectually and culturally, Ireland became stagnant in the late 1930s and 1940s, with what Terence Brown describes as 'the devastating lack of cultural and social innovation in the first decade of Irish independence'.[3] He goes on to state: 'an explanation for this social and cultural conservatism of the new state is, I believe, to be found in the social composition of Irish society.' With the building of an overwhelmingly Catholic state of twenty-six counties, the sense was that all the radicalism of the previous decades was now gone. Roy Foster argues:

> The rigorous conservatism of the Irish Free State has become a cliché: what matters most about the atmosphere and mentality of the twenty-six county Ireland in the 1920s is that the dominant preoccupation of the regime was self-definition against Britain—cultural and political.[4]

The consolidation of the idea of an independent Irish identity led, amongst other measures, to the introduction of censorship in 1929, and this has been seen as an intensification of Catholic influence on the idea of an Irish state. Censorship in Ireland had one target: the expression and depiction of sexuality. Tom Inglis writes: 'The inculcation of Victorian prudery throughout Irish society was not a universal or homogeneous process. It was a strategy of a new class of tenant farmer that emerged in the social space between the peasantry and the Protestant ascendancy class.'[5] One result was a profound antipathy towards all public notions or acknowledgement of the body and a denial of the existence of homosexuality; hence, any discussion of homosexuality and of Wilde would be fraught with difficulty. Despite this, however, productions of Wilde's plays continued to be staged all over Ireland

---

[3] Terence Brown, *Ireland: A Social and Cultural History 1922–2002* (London: Harper Perennial, 2004), 7.

[4] R. F. Foster, *Modern Ireland 1600–1972* (London: Penguin, 1988), 517.

[5] Tom Inglis, 'Origins and Legacies of Irish Prudery; Sexuality and Social Control in Modern Ireland', *Eire Ireland* 40, nos. 3 and 4 (2005), 21.

throughout the 1930s and 1940s, and were central to the artistic programme of the Gate Theatre.

In that first year at the Gate, Wilde was an initial obvious choice for the Gate in terms of its directors' own artistic influences. As Richard Pine puts it, 'fired by the spectacle of the Russian ballet which he had seen in London in 1912–13 and subsequently in Monte Carlo (1925–1927), Mac Liammóir's choice of theatre was in some ways bound to be exotic.'[6] The Dublin Gate Theatre opened with an ambitious staging of *Peer Gynt* in October 1928. *Salomé* was their first Wilde production, in December 1928, followed by a 1931 staging of *Lady Windermere's Fan* and *An Ideal Husband* in 1933, with a 1937 touring version of *The Importance of Being Earnest* going first to Cairo and then onwards to Sofia and Bucharest in 1939. Then in 1945 the Gate adapted *The Picture of Dorian Gray* for the stage.

The engagement of Edwards and Mac Liammóir with Wilde at this early stage of their careers came with a lively sense of being rebellious, young, and controversial; they were determined to make their mark on the presentation and staging of Wilde in the city of his birth, despite any unease with his sexuality and his downfall. In an interview, Hilton Edwards states:

> A number of people disliked my treatment of *The Importance of Being Earnest*. One critic going as far as to call it pantomime [. . .] To which I reply that the actual wit may have been very subtle in the day, but the fact that the epigrams have been so plagiarised since and the style has become so well-known makes it very much broader as compared to present day dialogue. To my surprise I found that the method necessary for the delivery of lines was anything but subtle.[7]

Wilde was their means of making a bold theatrical statement. Joan Fitzpatrick Dean describes the reason for which *Salomé* was chosen:

> [It was written] by an Irishman whose Irishness was rarely celebrated. In its first twenty-five years of operation, the Abbey had produced only one play by Wilde, *The Importance of Being Earnest* in 1926. The very antithesis of Abbey Theatre's sense of what an Irish play was, *Salomé* was a styled parable of decadence.[8]

As well as that, *Salomé* had again been refused a license for performance in London by the Lord Chamberlain only the previous year. Mac Liammóir's attraction to Wilde's theatre came from his attraction to the slightly suspect visual legacy of *fin-de-siècle* decadence, and he relished the whiff of homoeroticism:

> What is generally understood as the 'Nineties' in literature and in the theatre, indeed in the whole attitude towards art and life, collapsed with the debacle of Oscar Wilde, and the reactions in his own country and in England, where his influence has been far more marked, were both violent and manifold.[9]

---

[6] Richard Pine (with Richard Cave), *The Dublin Gate Theatre* (Cambridge: Chadwyck-Healey, 1984), 21.

[7] Mary Manning, 'Processional', *Motley* 11, no. 7 (1933), 7.

[8] Joan Fitzpatrick Dean, *Riot and Great Anger: Stage Censorship in Twentieth-Century Ireland* (Madison, WI: University of Wisconsin Press, 2004), 129.

[9] Micheál Mac Liammóir, *Theatre in Ireland* (Dublin: Three Castles, 1964), 43.

Salomé opened on 12 December 1928; Mac Liammóir recalled later:

> The play we had most fun with that season was probably *Salomé* [. . .] we had a lovely set in black and silver and viperish green with the entire cast stripped almost naked [. . .] So, naked and with a few elaborately painted head-dresses and loin cloths, it was played on a series of black curving steps and green cube-like thrones, and ours was the first public performance in these islands, a fact in which we took a modest pride that was only a little damped by the fact that two of the minor parts, chosen for their physique, spoke in rich and incurable Dublinese. It won for us a few more adherents and a handful of busybodies who had heard of Wilde's personal tragedy and of our sartorial economies and who decided that a visit to the Peacock would be cheaper than a weekend in Douglas or Ostend and who went away disappointed, never to return.[10]

It seemed to have been a lively if uneven production, and reviewers found fault with some of the elements of the staging—for example with voice training and accents: 'Constantine Curran referred in the review of *Salomé* to a murmuration of untrained local accents.'[11] In his memoir, *An Oscar of No Importance*, Mac Liammóir writes:

> Although our presentation was tumultuously applauded by our miniscule capacity audience—the Peacock theatre where we offered our first seven or eight productions, seated just one hundred and two people—some of the critics were wary in their opinion about our choice of the play [. . .] But we were at once amused and dismayed to find that some enthusiastic moralists (were they leaders or followers of *Maria Duce* were they Plymouth Brothers?) had scrawled *Degenerates!* and sometimes *Decadents!* across our posters and we went about Dublin feeling important and dangerous, a stimulating emotion for hard-working people who are still in their twenties.[12]

This exciting sense of danger and challenge to conservative Dublin theatre was to modify somewhat with the years, but the playwright Denis Johnston, who saw this production, later wrote: 'Personally I am glad that I saw *Salomé* in the Peacock in 1929 and with all deference to Mac Liammóir, I think he is wrong now in thinking he was wrong then.'[13]

The context for this slightly provocative staging of their first Wilde play was the fact that, in terms of engagement with Wilde, Mac Liammóir's theatrical career had three distinct phases: the Yeatsian phase in the 1930s and 1940s; an interlude of stagnation during the 1950s; and finally the Wildean phase of the 1960s and 1970s. W. B. Yeats did afford him a secure artistic mode within which to become an aesthete without the taint of Wildean sexuality: 'Celticism has swept through, paling the colours and purging the fatty richness of a masterpiece and turning Wilde's monstrous orchid into a wet bulrush.'[14] Mac Liammóir claims Yeats as an emblematic muse figure: 'I had read Yeats' "Ireland and the Arts" for the first time at fourteen.'[15] At one point, Edwards rails jealously against the overweening influence Yeats has had on Mac Liammóir: 'Yeats was your god. He had shaped everything in your programme before you met him.'[16] How precisely did Mac Liammóir engage with

[10] Mac Liammóir, *All For Hecuba*, 71.   [11] Pine, *Dublin Gate*, 36.
[12] Micheál Mac Liammóir, *An Oscar of No Importance* (London: Heinemann, 1968), 35.
[13] Denis Johnston, 'Dublin Theatre', *Bell* 3, no. 2 (1941), 151.
[14] Mac Liammóir, *All for Hecuba*, 45.   [15] Ibid., 32.
[16] Ibid., 215.

Yeats as a mentor figure within his own theatrical activity? There is undoubtedly some manifestation of Yeatsian influence in his *Diarmuid and Grainne* (1928)—an influence later acknowledged in his one-man show *I Must Be Talking to my Friends* (1963) and in his study *W. B. Yeats and his World* (1977), written with the poet Eavan Boland. However, in *All for Hecuba*, there is no accounting for Mac Liammóir's lack of contact with Yeats's own Abbey Theatre, or for the profoundly divergent programmes in these two Dublin theatres, or even for the fact that Mac Liammóir, during Yeats's time at the Abbey, appeared in only two productions. His one recorded meeting with Yeats reflects something of the unease of their relationship: 'I felt that he only half approved of me as an exponent of the Celtic Twilight, which in those days of self-conscious virility was at its lowest ebb, and I, in my heart, agreed with him. These were no times for echoing the vanished rhapsodies of the Nineties.'[17]

Towards the close of *All for Hecuba,* he writes of the death of Yeats and, referring to Ireland's artistic soul, asks the question: 'What new stamp would be pressed into the changing wax, softened again into shapelessness with the death of the poet?'[18] Mac Liammóir may have been talking about Ireland, but there is also a sense that Yeats proved an unsatisfactory and inadequate personal muse for Mac Liammóir himself. Wilde was more relevant as a figure of emblematic dissent. There was a clear sense that by the beginning of the 1950s the Gate had failed to sustain itself as an integrated and consistent force within Irish theatre. As Terence Brown comments: 'Neither [Gate nor Abbey theatres] managed quite to create that sense of new awakening that had characterised the early years of the Irish literary theatre.'[19] In *All for Hecuba*, Mac Liammóir has Edwards attacking him for his obsession with his supposed Irishness, blaming their enforced residence in Dublin for a certain staleness in their work. In his pamphlet *Theatre in Ireland* (1950), he allows that 'a period of uncertainty, even perhaps of stagnation, in the Irish theatre and its literature may be at hand'.[20] By 1957, Edwards was urging Mac Liammóir to leave Ireland. Yeats dwindled as a source of inspiration for Mac Liammóir because, ultimately, as a writer, he found Wilde to be a more direct source of personal revelation. One of the code terms for the homosexual in Mac Liammóir's time was 'unspeakables of the Oscar Wilde sort',[21] as used by E. M. Forster in his novel *Maurice*. As his career progressed into the 1960s, he returned to the unspeakable Wilde to speak again at a time where attitudes towards homosexuality were changing. This new Wilde was to be modified and made safer.

WILDE'S 'RE-INGREENCARNATION'

In 1954, the centenary of Wilde's birth, Mac Liammóir wrote to some of the Irish newspapers suggesting that members of the public might subscribe to the placing of a suitable tablet on the facade of the house in which Wilde had been born, at 21 Westland Row, Dublin. The renewed interest in Wilde culminated in the widely performed *The Importance of Being Oscar*, presenting an acceptable version of Wilde, his life, and his writings for a wide

---

[17] Ibid., 70.   [18] Ibid., 229.   [19] Brown, *Ireland*, 167.
[20] Mac Liammóir, *All for Hecuba*, 222.
[21] E. M. Forster, *Maurice* (Harmondsworth: Penguin, 1975), 136.

audience in Ireland and elsewhere. The many performances of this popular show were crucial for the process of cultural acceptance and rehabilitation of Wilde's name in Ireland. The text was created by Mac Liammóir and Edwards and then directed by Edwards, and first performed on 15 September 1960 at the Curragh Barracks in Co. Kildare, for Irish army officers and their families. When it opened in Dublin in the Gaiety Theatre, Christopher Fitz-Simon records: '*The Importance of Being Oscar* opened [...] to a very warm response. All the reviews next day were more than favourable.'[22]

In an article headed, 'Three hours of triumph for Mac Liammóir', the *Irish Press* reviewer commented: 'Mac Liammóir painted Wilde's life with a gentle brush.'[23] In a thoughtful review in the *Irish Times*, the writer commented that 'this triumph belonged to two people, Oscar Wilde and Micheál Mac Liammóir', although making the shrewd point that 'all of Wilde was not shown to us, that his sins were smoothed over by his regret'.[24] The *Irish Independent* applauded the humour and wit of the performance, and made the point about the representation of Wilde that 'we began to see him in the round, have a fuller understanding of him and though there is much to deplore, the feeling in the end was one of compassion for the man and of a greater understanding of his many-sided genius'.[25] This success led to a series of American and European tours and, eventually, a television dramatization, bringing a measure of financial success for the pair. The biographer Micheál Ó'hAohda calls this time in their career the 'Re-ingreencarnation'.[26]

Given that the name of Wilde had been employed throughout the twentieth century as a shorthand code for homosexual identity, Mac Liammóir's reading of Wilde in *The Importance of Being Oscar* was very partial, shaped by a need to present an acceptable version of Wilde and of his fate. Wilde was central to the success of the Gate Theatre, but when it came to their most successful Wildean show, the openly gay Mac Liammóir and Edwards achieved this success by heterosexualizing Wilde. Taking their cue from *De Profundis*, they reconstructed Wilde as helpless victim, sidestepping any details of his sexual 'downfall' and finding tragedy and pathos in his fate. Mac Liammóir performed his 'safe' version of Wilde's life in theatres, schools, and on television all over Ireland from 1960 to 1970, and thus facilitated a sea change in Irish attitudes towards Wilde. In his 1968 memoir of the show, published under the title *An Oscar of No Importance*, Mac Liammóir permitted himself some frank speculation on Wilde's sexuality:

> How fortunate he was. Not merely because without the catastrophe he would be remembered as the author of a handful of underrated and little read books and plays, but, by the very nature of the scandal that ripped the last rags of decency from him, posthumous writers can discuss him and his work with complete frankness, as no other homosexual artist, leading a discreet and reasonable private life, can even in our time be discussed.[27]

[22] Christopher Fitz-Simon, *The Boys: A Biography of Micheál Mac Liammóir and Hilton Edwards* (Dublin: Gill & Macmillan, 1994), 230.
[23] 'Three hours of triumph for Mac Liammóir', *Irish Press*, 20 Sept. 1960.
[24] 'Mac Liammóir at the Gaiety', *Irish Times*, 20 Sept. 1960.
[25] 'Humour and Wit in Wilde Recital', *Irish Independent*, 20 Sept. 1960.
[26] Micheál Ó hAodha, *The Importance of Being Micheál: A Portrait of Mac Liammóir* (Kerry: Brandon Press, 1990), 159.
[27] Mac Liammóir, *Oscar of No Importance*, 37.

In this version of his downfall, Mac Liammóir fixates on Wilde the tragic hero, and not on Wilde the rebel—Irish or otherwise. Edwards introduced the published text of the performance in the following terms: 'It shows him to have been aware, from the first, of the inevitability of his tragedy.'[28]

In his narrating within *The Importance of Being Oscar*, Mac Liammóir chose to distance himself from Wilde, recounting his life and his writings rather than impersonating Wilde directly. This allowed him to construct a Wilde of his own making. Edwards and Mac Liammóir took Wilde's fall from grace as their theme, and saw that fall as a consequence of his fatal glorification of the erotic: 'I did but touch the honey of romance / and must I lose a soul's inheritance?'[29] However, the honey of Wilde's romance in this version is predominantly heterosexual. Wilde's key act of transgression—his infatuation with Lord Alfred 'Bosie' Douglas—is referred to in one telling phrase: 'that tiger life'.[30] Setting a tone of world-weary despair and ennui, Mac Liammóir keeps all his sexual referents strictly heterosexual. In the first half of the presentation, Wilde's passion for Lily Langtry and his love for Constance, his wife, are recounted. Indeed, the readings from *Salomé* and *The Picture of Dorian Gray* concentrate on Herod's lust for Salomé rather than on her eroticization of Iokanaan's body, and on Dorian's murderous instincts rather than on Lord Henry's and Basil's love for Dorian's beauty. After these straight moments from Wilde's writings, Mac Liammóir inserts a short interval. During the interval, Wilde's affair with Bosie, his 'tiger life' with London rent boys, and the three trials are presumed to have taken place, but they remain unseen and undramatized. In the second act, the play deals solely with Wilde's prison writings and the consequences of Wilde's sexual 'deviancy' are concentrated on, rendered with pathos and melodrama. Wilde's dignity in prison and in exile, his composed yet passionate reproach to Bosie in *De Profundis*, and the stark, anguished compassion of *The Ballad of Reading Gaol* all serve to increase sympathy with the erring outcast. His final fable, *The Doer of Good*, although dealing with lust and the despair of the erotic, is firmly heterosexual.

However, playing Wilde, or at least interpreting Wilde as predominantly straight, led to questions that Mac Liammóir was not quite ready to answer. Joan Fitzpatrick Dean has researched the two North American tours of *The Importance of Being Oscar*, and her account of these various reviews reveals that there was a greater cultural difficulty with Wilde and with the hidden theme of his homosexuality in the United States than in Ireland. The first American performance of the show began in the Lyceum Theatre on Broadway on 14 March 1961, and led to a four-week season. American reviews, positive in many ways, were, at the same time, as blunt as they could be about the gay implications of the subject and of the production, often alluding to the show's appeal to a 'specialized' audience. Joan Fitzpatrick Dean has written about the bristling over any sympathetic treatment of homosexuality.[31] Despite some hostility, *The Importance of Being Oscar* returned to the United States in October 1961 for an extended tour, where the First Lady, Jackie Kennedy, attended a performance of the play in Washington.

[28] Hilton Edwards, 'Introduction', in Mac Liammóir, *Importance of Being Oscar*, 5.
[29] Mac Liammóir, *Importance of Being Oscar*, 15.   [30] Ibid., 37.
[31] See Joan Fitzpatrick Dean, '*The Importance of Being Oscar* in America', in John P. Harrington (ed.), *Irish Theater in America: Essays on Irish Theatrical Diaspora* (Syracuse, NY: Syracuse University Press, 2009), 109.

In *An Oscar of No Importance*, Mac Liammóir recounts an incident during his later South African tour of the show, when a journalist challenged him directly on the subject of Wilde's sexuality and, by implication, his own:

> 'You', began a small, plump, very firm-looking lady, gazing at me through her spectacles as though she would burrow into the depths of my soul, 'are going to act as Oscar Wilde?' 'Not act as him: I try to interpret him'. 'Well then, I would be interested to know, as you have chosen him rather than another writer, what is your own attitude to the question of male homosexuality?' I gazed back at her in a prolonged moment of silence, as of deep cool waters whose apparent tranquillity might be haunted by many sharks. [. . .] Did she mean among cattle or human beings? But I never received an answer.[32]

It is worth pointing out that neither Edwards nor Mac Liammóir felt confident enough to come out at this stage in their careers and, in fact, no mainstream Irish writer was to define themselves as openly lesbian or gay until 1993. They did feel sufficiently confident as to the climate of public opinion on Wilde, however, to present the show all over the world; indeed, the 1960s were an important decade for the republishing of Wilde's texts and his rehabilitation as an artist. Although emboldened by the success of the one-man show, there is evidence that they were still hesitant about highlighting the homoerotic in their theatrical work. Indeed, it was not until Mac Liammóir was in the final decade of his life that he wrote his most directly 'gay' play, *Prelude in Kazbek Street* (1973). Changes in British law and in censorship in the theatre and the experience of working on Wilde all had a cumulative effect on Mac Liammóir's writings on the homoerotic.

> It is no accident, then, that the English legislation governing both theatre and homosexuality was reformed when the Labour Party was elected with a big majority on a modernizing platform in 1966. [. . .] The Wolfenden proposals were enacted in 1967 and theatre censorship was abolished in 1968. [. . .] It enabled many gay men and lesbians to refuse the discreet spirit of the law and, with varying degrees of flamboyance, to come out.[33]

Mac Liammóir's memoir *An Oscar of no Importance* is a revealing account of the way in which the one-man show on Wilde brought him face to face with the nature of Wilde's sexuality and with the implications for his own creativity. *An Oscar of No Importance* is, as the title suggests, a mirror text for *The Importance of Being Oscar*. All the evasions of the stage play are dealt with directly in the memoir. In considering the relationship of the play to the memoir, it seems as if Mac Liammóir found the public arena of theatre, as yet, an unsafe place in which to speculate on Wilde's sexual nature. Where the play concentrates on the heteronormative aspects of Wilde's life and writings, the memoir displays no such reticence. It opens with surprising directness, relating a childhood incident where he quizzed his embarrassed father as to the exact nature of Wilde's unspeakable crime, eventually provoking this outburst: ' "What was wrong with Oscar Wilde? He turned young men into women." '[34] In the course of the memoir, Mac Liammóir explores his professional and personal bonds with Wilde, 'that magician whose name was my secret for evermore'.[35] He even

---

[32] Mac Liammóir, *Importance of Being Oscar*, 138.
[33] Alan Sinfield, *Out On Stage* (New Haven, CT: Yale University Press, 1999), 265.
[34] Mac Liammóir, *Oscar of No Importance*, 1.   [35] Ibid., 4.

allows himself to theorize on Wilde's sexual identity. He claims a more direct kinship with Wilde than in his previous writings. As a result of Mac Liammóir's Wilde show, new versions of Wilde's sexuality could be accommodated and presented in mainstream social discourse in Ireland, permitting a contemporary reclaiming of Wilde the gay Irishman: Mac Liammóir had effected a revolution.

WILDE AT THE GATE: REINVENTION AND RENEWAL

The current engagement by the Gate with Wilde continues the fruitful and commercially successful relationship established by Mac Liammóir and Edwards. There were some versions of Wilde after this one-man show, with a production of *The Importance of Being Earnest* in 1971 and *An Ideal Husband* in 1972; but by the time Michael Colgan took over the running of the Gate Theatre in 1983, in the words of the *Irish Times*, 'he had inherited a theatre that had fallen on hard times. Mac Liammóir and Edwards, its founders, had grown old without making any real provision for successors.'[36] The Dublin Gate needed renewal and reinvention and, significantly, *Salomé* was to prove an iconic text for Colgan as it had been for Mac Liammóir and Edwards. In a sense, as Ireland changed its laws and its attitudes, the Gate's new versions of Wilde became more subversive.

Key to this was Steven Berkoff's landmark production of *Salomé* with Olwen Fouéré as Salomé and Alan Stanford as Herod, with original music composed by Roger Doyle. This was first produced in 1988 to great acclaim before being toured and then revived in Dublin in 1989 and 1990. It was received as a truly subversive version, based on a highly ritualized use of stylized movement, decadent costuming, and gender recoding. In the *Irish Times*, Berkoff was interviewed about the fact that 'mime and stylized movement is central to Berkoff's work, as anyone who caught his mould-breaking production of Oscar Wilde's *Salomé* at the Gate will know':

> The responsibility for me creating it was really Michael Colgan at the Gate, and he took it to the Edinburgh Festival. I'd wanted to do *Salomé* all my life. And while every lazy director and producer keeps regurgitating Oscar Wilde's plays of wit, nobody, but nobody, touches *Salomé* where he wanted to leave wit behind and go into his passion, into his heart and soul, into his beliefs, into his imagination.[37]

The eroticism of the production was commented on in the *Irish Times*, where Olwen Fouéré was described in these terms: 'It is a miraculous performance: at times she is so erotic that the audience is almost baying.'[38] This exciting radicalism was not to be a feature of subsequent Gate productions of Wilde, successful as they have been.

To conclude, I would argue that, to some extent, the challenging eroticism of this landmark production of a Wilde text in the Gate was absent in subsequent productions. In the twenty-first century, more commercially appealing, plush versions of his plays reflected the

---

[36]   Fergus Lenihan, 'Michael Colgan: Producer Par Excellence', *Irish Times*, 5 Dec. 1987.
[37]   Penelope Dening, 'Good at the Bad Stuff', *Irish Times*, 10 Oct. 1998.
[38]   Kevin Myers, 'An Irishman's Diary', *Irish Times*, 10 May 1988.

FIG. 14.2 Steven Berkoff's landmark 1988 production of *Salomé* (designed by Robert Ballagh), indicated a new direction in the Gate's production of Wilde's work.

Photo: Tom Lawlor. Courtesy of Gate Theatre.

notion of Wilde the dandy, rather than Oscar the sexual rebel and outcast. As public perceptions of Wilde moved him from shadow and silence, performances of his plays reflected the class, gender, and politics of each of his interpreters in Ireland. Wilde, more than any other writer, lends himself to this constant reinvention, because of the playful, subversive, performative nature of his writings and his dramas. Thus, throughout the first decade of the twenty-first century, both gay and straight Irish culture sought to appropriate Wilde as a potent symbol of affirmation and a signal for a reinvented Irish cultural openness and modernity. This led to two versions of Wilde, reflected in versions of his plays staged at the Gate.

In the centenary year of Wilde's death, in December 2000, President Mary McAleese visited a centenary exhibition about Wilde in the British Library:

> Reflecting on a 'hesitancy' of ownership of Wilde in Ireland and Britain, Mrs McAleese said that on the anniversary of his death, Ireland was 'justly, joyfully' celebrating his work and life but in the past, 'Irish people have sometime been unsure how to regard him'.[39]

Ireland was still a little unsure of Wilde: his cultural presence continued to be reformulated in the Celtic Tiger years and thus become more self-consciously modernized and a token of

---

[39] Rachel Dowling, 'President Celebrates Wilde's Centenary in London', *Irish Times*, 1 Dec. 2000.

modernity and acceptance. On the one hand, the logo of the Dublin Gay Theatre Festival, a fringe festival that began in 2004, claimed Wilde as a central figure for contemporary Irish gay identities. At the same time, in 2007, in line with their policy of naming their ferries for Irish literary figures, Irish Ferries christened their most recently acquired luxury cruise ship, which sails between Ireland and France, the *Oscar Wilde*. Enniskillen was also busy revising its former unease with one of Portora's most famous students when the Oscar Wilde Festival was launched in 2002, keeping him firmly mainstream and acceptable.

The Gate now reflects a more mainstream identification with Wilde, with high production values, expensive sets and costuming, and a West End polish for each new production. From 1984, with the first production of *A Woman of No Importance*, Wilde plays have followed at regular intervals: *The Importance of Being Earnest* in 1987, and once again in 2004 and in 2015; *Salomé*, originally in 1988, but revived in 1989, 1990, 1993, 2000, and 2007; *An Ideal Husband* in 1989, 1999, and again in 2014; an adaptation of *The Picture of Dorian Gray* in 1995; *Lady Windermere's Fan* in 1997, 1998, and 2005; and *A Woman of No Importance* once again in 2012.

However, it could be argued that the potential for a radical, queer version of a Wilde play on the Irish stage went elsewhere. An all-male production of *The Importance of Being Earnest* was staged at the Abbey Theatre in 2005—a production which staged the play itself in the last year of Wilde's own life in Paris. In the play, Wilde takes various roles, and the French rent boys take the parts of the main characters in the play. The gay subtext is thus brought to the fore, and the conjunction of Wilde's Irishness and the mainstream nature of his subversive sexuality are made plain in an essay in the *Irish Times* on 27 July 2005 called 'A Peek through Oscar's Glasses', which incorporates an interview with the director:

> Conall Morrison's all-male *The Importance of Being Earnest* at the Abbey Theatre bravely places Oscar Wilde as a character in the play; Conall Morrison knows that directing *The Importance of Being Earnest* for the Abbey Theatre this month will be a challenge. [. . .] Morrison sees it as a way to bring out the serious and courageous questions that Wilde's play, cloaked in glittering comedy, dared to ask.[40]

In this production, the same actor, Alan Stanford, played Wilde in the preface to the play and then took the part of Lady Bracknell and of the servant Lane (breaking down barriers of gender and class), while men also played Cecily, Gwedolen, and Miss Prism. The play was well received, however, perhaps because Morrison's production stayed safely within gender divisions, with little or no physical contact between the men. Rather, there was an emphasis on containing any potential sexual subtexts within the play; it created little or no disturbance for its Dublin audience, happy to see Wilde updated but not queer, and this is also true for Gate Theatre productions of Wilde.

On the Irish stage, I would argue that the performance of radical queerness was happening elsewhere, outside commercial and mainstream theatre. In his edited collection of plays, *Queer Notions*, in 2010, Fintan Walsh collected a number of plays and short performances from contemporary Irish drama in recent times, principally written and staged in the years following the decriminalization of homosexuality in 1993. This collection includes plays, experimental performances, and one-man shows, all remapping the

---

[40] Belinda McKeon, 'A Peek Through Oscar's Glasses', *Irish Times*, 27 July 2005.

permitted terrain of contemporary Irish dramatic writing. In his introduction, Walsh describes the time frame in which these queer plays were created in Ireland:

> Written and performed between 2000 and 2010, the pieces both challenge, but also strive to imagine alternative ways of being with others, and being in the world. The works are queer in so far as they explore tensions surrounding sexual difference in the broadest sense, in a manner that illuminates and interrogates issues that affect a wide range of people, including those who neither identify as Irish nor queer.[41]

These plays mark the division between mainstream theatre and a more subversive queer theatre in Dublin, between the Dandy Wilde and Queer Wilde; both, however, are legacies of Wilde as 'the invisible but by no means inaudible bond who made the road I was facing less chilly,' as Mac Liammóir once wrote; 'that magician whose name was my secret for evermore.'[42]

[41] Fintan Walsh, *Queer Notions: New Plays and Performances from Ireland* (Cork: Cork University Press, 2010), 4.

[42] Mac Liammóir, *Oscar of No Importance*, 25.

CHAPTER 15

···

IRISH ACTING IN THE EARLY TWENTIETH CENTURY

···

ADRIAN FRAZIER

IRISH, ENGLISH, AND FRENCH ACTING AT THE CLOSE OF THE NINETEENTH CENTURY

··

In the 8 July 1899 issue of the *United Irishman*, Frank Fay reflected on the sad condition of Irish acting: 'In the last century, we gave Quin, Macklin, Barry, and Peg Woffington, Mossop and Sheridan (father and son) to the English stage. What has become of our historical ability?'[1] For an Irish star in the galaxies of London's West End, he could point only to Ada Rehan. She had been born in 1859 in Limerick, then emigrated at age 6 with her parents to New York, where she learned to act with American stock companies and with Boucicault's company too. Established as a leading lady, she crossed back over the Atlantic to anchor many Shakespeare productions in England. Had he been including Irish stars of the current American stage, Fay could have mentioned Kilkenny-born James O'Neill, another actor apprenticed to Boucicault. O'Neill graduated to play character parts opposite his idol Edwin Booth, before achieving fame and wealth as the Count of Monte Cristo (first played by O'Neill on 11 February 1883), with ashes-in-the-mouth grandeur from the point of view of his playwright son in *Long Day's Journey into Night* (1956). Given Frank Fay's emerging antipathy to the 'Irish play' of the period,[2] he refused to name Hubert O'Grady as a credit to his country, though O'Grady—yet another student of Boucicault—was an actor-manager who formed his own 'Irish National Company' in 1877. The posters for the company described Hubert O'Grady as 'the greatest Irish actor in the world'. At the time, this was not much of a boast.

---

[1] Frank J. Fay, *Towards a National Theatre: Dramatic Criticism*, ed. Robert Hogan (Dublin: Dolmen Press, 1970), 20.

[2] A nationalistic attitude no doubt encouraged by Arthur Griffith, the editor of the *United Irishman*, and its principal benefactor, Maud Gonne.

The great English actors at the turn of the century were the actor-managers and their leading ladies, figures such as Squire and Mrs Bancroft, Henry Irving and Ellen Terry, Wilson Barrett and Caroline Heath, Johnston Forbes-Robertson and Beatrice Campbell, as well as Frank and Mrs Benson. Generally, the actor-manager was a tall man, with presence and long hair, and some powerful pipes. He had risen through the ranks of an established acting company, from non-speaking parts, to young gentleman parts, to the hero's best friend or antagonist, and finally to leading man. Shakespeare had been essential to his curriculum. Once successful, he took the lease of a West End theatre, acquired the regular services of a crowd-pleasing leading lady, and if possible married her (wedlock was a secure contract, a burnt offering to Victorian values, and a big saving to him). 'To the great actor-managers,' J. B. Booth observed, 'their theatres were, to a very large extent, their homes; in their private suites they received and entertained their friends at supper after the play.'[3] Writers were employed, sometimes in teams, by the actor-manager to refashion classics, dramatize popular novels, or manufacture new vehicles for the actor-manager's particular talents. Henry Irving, for instance, developed a signature spasmodic parade across the stage, like a man 'trying to run across a ploughed field', which worked best when accompanied by chiaroscuro lighting and alarmed witnesses.[4] This was the sort of thing a writer was required to take into consideration when developing scenes. The actor-manager typically invested heavily in elaborate costumes, magnificent properties, chromolithographic backgrounds, and special effects never before seen on stage. The growing celebrity status of the actor-manager tended to disgust literary men, not just the poets and novelists but aspiring playwrights too. 'Mummer worship,' George Moore called it.[5] He conceded that Henry Irving was admirable 'as a shopman'. 'But as an artist I despise him [. . .] [I] look back with yearning to those times when theatrical audiences did not require real fountains and real trees.'[6]

Before Herbert Beerbohm Tree founded the Royal Academy of Dramatic Art in 1904, the training open to aspiring English actors principally came through apprenticeships within the companies of actor-managers. The Bensons formalized and commercialized these apprenticeships. A year of touring with the company was offered to paying students, with practice in bit parts, and training in 'Elocution, Dancing, Fencing, Callisthenics, Rehearsal, and general technique'.[7] There had been nothing in the nineteenth century like the Paris Conservatoire or Comédie-Française in any English-speaking country, to provide a settled standard of professionalism among actors.

In the same series of *United Irishman* articles in which Fay lamented the break in the long tradition of great Irish actors, he found fault with the present state of the profession in Britain. Beerbohm Tree brought the Haymarket Company's Sheridan season to the Gaiety Theatre, Dublin, in 1900, and Fay was there taking notes. 'It is a mistake', he wrote in the September 29 issue of the *United Irishman*, 'to make people pass to and fro in the street scene, first act, during the dialogue between Fag and Thomas [. . .] [I]t is out of place in an

[3] J. B. Booth, *Sporting Times: The 'Pink 'Un' World* (London: T. Werner Laurie, 1938), 28.

[4] William Archer, quoted in Michael Holroyd, *A Strange Eventful History: The Dramatic Lives of Ellen Terry, Henry Irving, and Their Remarkable Families* (London: Chatto & Windus, 2008), 175.

[5] George Moore, 'Mummer Worship', *Universal Review* 2 (Sept.–Dec. 1888), 105–18.

[6] George Moore, 'Our Dramatists and Their Literature', *Fortnightly Review* 46, no. 275 (1889), 630.

[7] Quoted by Michael Sanderson, *From Irving to Olivier: A Social History of the Acting Profession in England 1880–1983* (London: Athlone Press, 1985), 35.

artificial play like *The Rivals*.[8] Apart from the spectacular effects and the 'big acting,' this pointless walking about on the forestage, Fay thought, was the curse of English acting—just people looking for the limelight. It distracted the actors from proper articulation. British actors seemed to believe, as Arthur Symons put it (Fay had been reading Symons), that whatever was wrong with a play, you could fix by 'Crossing Stage to Right'.[9]

To discover 'a new standard of performance which would be characteristically Irish',[10] Fay directed the attention of young Irish actors (he had taken on students such as Dudley Digges, Sara Allgood, and Máire Nic Shiubhlaigh) to the French masters of the craft.[11] Reviewing Benoît-Constant Coquelin's Cyrano at the Gaiety in July 1899,[12] Fay falls into the unfortunate habit of those who praise acting they like: they call it 'natural' or 'lifelike'. A film exists of Coquelin in a sword-fighting scene from *Cyrano de Bergerac* in 1900, and his acting, although very fine, is nothing like life.[13] The French actor famously had the ability, by a prolonged effort of muscles, to remake his face for every part, so that whereas playing Mascarille in *Les Précieuses ridicules* he was 'delicate and extravagant, a scented whirl-wind', as Tartuffe, he had a 'great fish's face, heavy, suppressed, with lowered eyelids and a secret mouth, out of which steals at times some stealthy avowal'.[14] His face is otherwise transfigured for Cyrano: all the features above the upper lip are lifted, and a blasé expression is imparted to the whole. He is self-assurance manifest. The effect is not all accomplished by a prop nose, as was commonly the case with later actors in the role. As Coquelin administers a lesson in fencing to an unfortunate opponent, with many an accustomed flourish of the plumed hat, the lace-cuffed hand, and the foil, he utters without drawing an obvious breath a musical monologue, occasional notes being almost sung, others breaking out in nasal pronouncements that must have produced some effluvia. It is an astonishingly accomplished performance, a single whole from the beginning of the fencing lesson to the end, when the opponent is gracefully and quickly borne from the stage by attendants. The clockwork accuracy of the teamwork and speed of the scene are dreamlike.

Certainly, Fay meant to direct the future of Irish acting away from British customs of the time to the politically less threatening, and aesthetically more impressive, example of the celebrity graduates of the French Conservatoire. But commending the example of Réjane, Coquelin, and Sarah Bernhardt to his young pupils was setting the bar very high. Young Irish actors might imitate the ensemble playing of the French, or the lightness, briskness, and variety of tempo in their voicing, as opposed to the way 'every scene gets the same emphasis [. . .] distracted by [. . .] fiddle-faddle business' on the English stage.[15] But the

---

[8] Fay, 'The Haymarket Company at the Gaiety Theatre', in *Towards a National Theatre*, 50.

[9] Arthur Symons, 'On Crossing Stage to Right', quoted by Fay, 'Irish Acting', in *Towards a National Theatre*, 99.

[10] Máire Nic Shiubhlaigh, quoted in Gabriel Fallon, *The Abbey and the Actor* (Dublin: National Theatre Society, 1969), 12.

[11] Máire Nic Shiubhlaigh, *The Splendid Years: Recollections of Máire Nic Shiubhlaigh as Told to Edward Kenny* (Dublin: James Duffy, 1955), 9.

[12] Fay, 'M. Coquelin in Dublin', in *Towards a National Theatre*, 16.

[13] 'Cyrano de Bergerac', https://www.youtube.com/watch?v=xpxlZrEnPz4. It is the first film ever made with both colour and sound.

[14] Arthur Symons, 'Coquelin and Molière: Some Aspects', in *Plays, Acting, and Music: A Book of Theory* (London: Duckworth, 1903), 12.

[15] Frank J. Fay, 'Sarah Bernhardt', in *Towards a National Theatre*, 94.

sense of peril, like a lion entering a cage, that Bernhardt created on her entrance, or the throbbing, monotonous music of her recitation, *pianissimo, largamente, tempo rubato*— these are not things that are easy to copy, nor would they lead the way to the future of the stage. She was the last of the sacred monsters.

More attainable as a model was the example of André Antoine, also frequently described by Fay in his *United Irishman* articles. Fay had not actually seen Antoine's company, but he had read all about it. What he admired was Antoine's outsider status ('other managers treated him as if he were an "enemy of his country"'), his success in spite of having been only a gasworks employee prior to the foundation of his company, his reliance on gifted amateurs united by idealism, his appreciation for new writing, and the unschooled naturalism of his playing.[16] Even if young Irish actors could not mirror, because they could not see, the players of Antoine's Théâtre Libre, the precedent of his success was fortifying. Much could be accomplished by teamwork, desophisticated freshness, and service to new writing.

THE FIRST PERFORMANCE OF *CATHLEEN NI HOULIHAN* AND 'ABBEY TRADITIONS'

These highly self-conscious reflections on the art of acting by Frank Fay antedate the first production of Yeats and Gregory's *Cathleen ni Houlihan* and Æ's *Deirdre* on 2 April 1902. Prior to that performance, Fay had been coaching his student actors by means of breathing exercises and the voice lessons used by singing-masters for Italian opera. Sara Allgood recalled her classes with Fay:

> I used to go up to the hall in Camden street every Saturday—after I had finished my work in the [antique] shop, clutching my few shillings (wages) in my little hand—and with him I would work on my breathing; my Ah's and Oh's; my poetry reading; deportment; principles of voice production; the secret of articulation; how to pitch the voice. Then he would make me walk across and up stage, with books balanced on my head for poise; how to make an entrance; how to sit, and so on. He would get so intent on his teaching that time would be completely forgotten. I would work there all during the afternoon for about five hours without a stop.[17]

Udolphus Wright, another student from 1902, recalled,

> He would make us sound a's and l's for hours, raising and lowering the key. He insisted on distinct final d's and t's. The ends of our sentences had to be well out. Shrp! [*sic*][18]

---

[16]   Frank Fay to Maire Garvey, 1 Sept. 1904, Dublin, NLI MS 8320, fo. 8.

[17]   Sara Allgood, 'Memories', typed copy, Belfast, Public Record Office of Northern Ireland. The information about techniques of the Italian singing masters is from W. G. Fay and Catherine Carswell, *The Fays of the Abbey Theatre: An Autobiographical Record* (New York: Harcourt Brace, 1935), 32.

[18]   'Abbey Veteran Tells Story of Early Associates', *Sunday Times* (Chicago), 12 Mar. 1933. Dublin, Abbey Theatre scrapbooks.

Working with patriotic volunteers from Inghinidhe na hÉireann ('Daughters of Erin') and Cumann na nGaedheal ('Society of the Gaels'), Frank Fay and his brother W. G. Fay instructed the young actors (mostly just teenagers) to stand still, face the audience, and recite their words clearly in their native accents. Early photographs show a line of roughly costumed speaking statues, an even distance from the apron of the stage. The *mise en scène* is ridiculously simplistic by West End standards.

Into this emerging ensemble of student actors, W. B. Yeats helicoptered a celebrity, Maud Gonne, his Muse and the Honorary President of Inghinidhe na hÉireann. The rehearsal period for this play was to take on a fateful significance. It became the point of reference for the freshly invented 'traditions' of Abbey acting. Uncertainty about who was in charge prevailed from the start. W. G. Fay was the manager of the amateur company. His brother Frank was in charge of speech. Maud Gonne had the title role. Yeats had a strong interest in the outcome as (supposed) author. Then George Moore, as the only one with experience of the professional stage (though very, very little), arrived as uninvited expert consultant.

On 17 March 1902, Maud Gonne made a change to the end of the play, so that the hero decisively rushes out to die in battle, rather than vacillating at the door. Yeats was told afterwards. Moore, watching the second rehearsal, declared the acting 'the silliest he ever saw'.[19] One of the amateurs, Maire Quinn, was, he declared, utterly incompetent, but as Quinn was Gonne's protégée, and the girlfriend of the company's best actor, Dudley Digges, she had to stay. As for Maud Gonne, Moore argued that as Cathleen she should not just come in and sit by the stage hearth. She must, he explained, 'wander round the cottage all the time, and make most of her remarks from the front of the stage'.[20] This, of course, was the contemporary mode of the English stage—'Cross stage to right'. Gonne was determined that Cathleen should 'sit down and rock herself over the fire' until she heard her friends (the French troops); then she would rise.

The play was performed on the tiny stage of St Teresa's Total Abstinence Hall, with a full but entirely sober house. Gonne made her way through the crowd to the stage, wearing a stagey mop of long white horsehair, and hunched under a black cloak, but everyone knew who this 6 ft 2 in. female must be. As the play unfolded, Yeats was disconcerted by the peasant comedy side of the play (why were people laughing?), but then found himself swept away by the 'weird power' of Maud Gonne; 'creepy' was Joseph Holloway's word for her acting.[21] Gonne rose at the ending as if mounting a speaker's platform, focused her eyes in a thousand-yard stare, and gave an oration in a quavering, spine-tingling voice, as if over the grave of a patriot in Bodenstown cemetery: 'They shall be reee mem berrrrdd forEVER!'[22] The combination of a simplistic rendering of peasant life and an other-worldly revelation aimed at the audience was startlingly effective.

[19] W. B. Yeats to Augusta Gregory, 22 Mar. 1902, in W. B. Yeats, *Collected Letters*, vol. 3: *1901–1904*, ed. John Kelly and Ronald Schuchard (Oxford: Clarendon Press, 1994), 162.

[20] A. Norman Jeffares and Anna MacBride White (eds.), *The Gonne–Yeats Letters 1893–1938* (London: Hutchinson, 1992), 151.

[21] W. B. Yeats to Augusta Gregory, 3 Apr. 1902, in Yeats, *Collected Letters*, vol. 3, 166–8; 'Holloway Diaries: A Dublin Playgoer's Impressions', NLI MSS 1798–1808, 3 Apr. 1902, 169.

[22] 'The well-known Nationalist orator did not address the other actors as is usual in drama, but spoke directly to the audience, as if she was addressing them in Beresford Place [...]. She can scarcely be said to act the part, she lived it': review in *All Ireland Review*, quoted in Samuel Levenson, *Maud Gonne* (London: Cassell, 1976), 195.

Overall, was this acting good or bad? Yeats at first thought that perhaps Moore was right about its contemptible amateurism. Within a few days, however, he changed his mind. The young people of Fay's company were 'trying to act with wonderful simplicity & naivety'.[23] This was the right method for an Irish movement: begin like children, but theorize it like adults.

Some weeks later, in London on 20 June 1902, Yeats saw Sarah Bernhardt with Édouard de Max in *Phèdre*. Here is where, Yeats wrote, 'Mr Fay had gone for his model'.[24] It was naturally gifted, classically trained acting that Fay admired all right—'the art there is in being quite still'—but surely Max and Bernhardt on stage were far from what the Irish National Theatre Society (INTS) had so far achieved.[25] When it had accomplishments to its name, they would be far other than those of the Comédie-Française.[26]

The best description of early Abbey acting is by the English critic C. E. Montague:

> In a world of things overdone, like the stage, mere quietude has the value of epigram, like a thing soberly said in a newspaper. Throughout one-half of Lady Gregory's *The Rising of the Moon* there is scarcely a movement: merely that no one should strut or fret tickles you. Miss Maire O'Neill, as Nora, in *The Shadow of the Glen*, stands almost stock still through a scene where most English actresses would pace the stage like lionesses in a zoo. The result is that when she does move you can see the passion propel her like a screw. In Mr Yeats's *Kathleen ni Houlihan* the average stage manager would have thought everything under-acted; he would have made the whole cast sweat and squirm up to the climax in a geometrical progression of muscular agonies [. . .]. They seem all alike to have seized on the truth that the way to do big things in an art [. . .] is to become as a little child, so long as you do it without thinking all the time what an engaging child you are.[27]

It was, Montague reflected, like looking through an uncurtained window into a lighted room; the movements and stillnesses of the people within acquired a value both from one's own presence at the spy-hole and from the unawareness of the Irish natives (that the actors themselves were all Dubliners, and not all were Catholics, did not break in upon the spectator's illusion). Their actions seem 'slower, graver, more controlled'. Because no one 'rants, trumpets, or booms', 'no one frisks about', the spectator needs to watch carefully for hints of what is in progress.

Of course, on the tiny Dublin stages on which the INTS acted, no one was going to frisk about, or limpingly lope like Henry Irving 'trying to run across a ploughed field'. Even when the company got its own theatre through the charitable offices of Annie Horniman, the Abbey stage was just 21 feet wide and 15 feet deep, on which often sizeable casts had to find a spot to stand. Standing still right where actors had been told to stand was a necessary professional fact of life. A big gesture could push a fellow actor into the wings. A large cast was confined to something like a recitation by a chorus in costume. As for hogging the limelight, no spots had been picked out by a lighting plan; the stage was evenly lit throughout. Some of the effects of Abbey acting in its first years were thus the results of simple

[23] Yeats to Henry Newbolt, 5 Apr. 1901, in Yeats, *Collected Letters*, vol. 3, 169.
[24] W. B. Yeats, *Collected Works*, vol. 8: *The Irish Dramatic Movement*, ed. Mary FitzGerald and Richard J. Finneran (New York: Scribner, 2003), 236, n. 8.
[25] Symons, 'On Crossing Stage to Right', 100.   [26] Fay, 'Irish Acting', 97–101.
[27] C. E. Montague, *Dramatic Values* (New York: Macmillan, 1911), 51–2.

naivety, limited means of production, and the strict supervision of the Fay brothers, who kept a lid on the individual histrionic ambitions of members of the ensemble. A further factor in the development of a house style was the repertory nature of the company and the relative coherence in terms of style of the plays in repertory (dialogue inflected by Hiberno-English, either a mythical heroic or peasant west-of-Ireland *mise en scène*).[28] In short order, these effects of the conditions of the Irish theatre's origins were codified as ideals that the INTS had consciously pursued: fine speech, teamwork, and restraint.[29]

Such restraint in acting did not suit Yeats's plays, but it worked particularly well with the kind of plays written for the INTS by Lady Gregory and almost everyone else. These plays frequently had 'stranger in a cottage' plots, in which an 'artist-disturber' figure arrives, coming through the door of the box set, while the audience—not through a keyhole, but through the invisible fourth wall—watches the anthropologically 'real' life of those in the cottage or tenement react to the arrival of an agent of change.[30] This is the set-up for everything from *The Playboy of the Western World* (1907) to *Juno and the Paycock* (1924). The very habits of life of cottiers had an interest for those in Dublin like that of an exhibit of exotics at a World's Fair—perhaps even more so than to those outside Ireland. More interesting still was to see how those simple cottiers or slum-dwellers would behave if disturbed. Let us imagine we send in a man to say to an island woman: Your last son has just been drowned. Or to those in remote rural pub, a lad who says: I just killed my da, will you hide me? Or to a young wife in a mountain cabin, a tramp who says: Come away on the roads with me. Or to a slum-dwelling family in debt: The surprise inheritance you briefly thought you were getting, you're not. What will they say then and how will they say it?

After six years, several tours of the United Kingdom, and the public-relations triumph of an Abbey production of Yeats's *Deirdre* guest starring Mrs Patrick Campbell (1907), the INTS was sufficiently sure of itself for Yeats to encapsulate their truly Irish 'traditions' for the British Association in 1908:

> Quite apart from the traditions of the ordinary theatre, we have built up an art of acting which is perhaps peculiar to ourselves. Our players, instead of specialising, as most other actors do, to represent the life of the drawing room, which is the same all over the world, have concentrated themselves upon the representation of what is most characteristic in one nation. I think I can say with perfect sincerity that until our people learnt their business what is most characteristic in Irish life had never been set upon the stage at all. I doubt if the Irish accent had ever been accurately spoken there. In rehearsing our plays we have tried to give the words great importance, to make speech, whether it be the beautiful and rhythmical delivery of verse or the accurate speaking of a rhythmical dialect, our supreme end. Almost all our playwrights in the same way give to the vividness and picturesqueness of their style a principal consideration. We believe that words are more important than gesture, that voice

---

[28] In 1908 Yeats explained the Abbey playwrights' preference for the west of Ireland: 'Connaught is Ireland; Dublin is half England—shabby England perhaps we should call it': scrapbook containing press cuttings for the period of 1907, Dublin, Abbey Theatre, NLI REF 25, 491, 1907–8, Abbey Theatre Digital Archive at National University of Ireland, Galway, ADM_00003644, p. 64.

[29] Christopher Morash, *A History of Irish Theatre* (Cambridge: Cambridge University Press, 2002), 140.

[30] 'Artist-disturber' is James Pethica's phrase in 'Lady Gregory's Abbey Theatre Drama: Ireland Real and Ideal', in Shaun Richards (ed.), *The Cambridge Companion to Twentieth-Century Irish Drama* (Cambridge: Cambridge University Press, 2004), 62–78.

is the principal power an actor possesses, and that nothing may distract from the actor and what he says we have greatly simplified scenery. When we wish to give a remote poetical effect we throw away realism altogether and are content with suggestion. This is the idea of the Japanese in their dramatic art [. . .].[31]

Character and Ensemble Acting after the Fay Brothers

Yet by 1908 this 'Abbey style' had in fact already begun to change. The Abbey had outgrown the Fay brothers. The dispute that caused W. G. Fay's January 1908 letter of resignation to be quickly snapped up by the Abbey directors (Yeats, Gregory, and Synge) had complex causes, including the fact that Abbey owner, Annie Horniman, detested W. G. Fay.[32] But another chief source of conflict within the ensemble was that the actors rejected the hot-tempered forms of 'restraint' W. G. Fay tried to impose on them, not just in rehearsal and casting but in performance style too. Sara Allgood, J. M. Kerrigan, and Arthur Sinclair were maturing into actors of range, personality, and charisma. A set-up in which the Fay brothers ruled the roost, took the big roles, and resented emerging talent was unacceptable to them. Once W. G. Fay had left the Abbey and joined Charles Frohman's tour of Irish work in America, he gave a revealingly resentful interview to the Chicago *Mail*:

> The real trouble with the drama nowadays is that people do not go to the theatre to see plays, but to see stars, to study the personality of those who wear holes in the carpet standing where the limelight falls in chunks. In my company, I will have no stars.[33]

So the Abbey would not have him.

How big a loss, in terms of acting quality, were the Fays? W. G. Fay had a subsequent career in minor roles on the English stage and in movies. He can be seen as the Irish gardener for an aristocratic British family in *Spellbound* (1941). Remarkably short compared with others in the scene, he pours out stage-Irish clichés without pause. He has a fretful set to his brow, and leans aggressively in to his interlocutors, nodding his head and producing quick mechanical gestures. The rapid unvarying pace of his speech makes what he has to say nearly senseless, setting up his impatient dismissal by the lady of the house, 'Thank you, Johnnie.' Admittedly, the part does not give Fay much of a chance to show what he can do, but Barry Fitzgerald in a similar role as gardener in *Bringing Up Baby* (1938) is both lovable and unforgettable.

---

[31] Clipping from the *Weekly Stage*, 20 Sept. 1907, Abbey Theatre: scrapbook containing press cuttings for the period of 1907. NLI REF 25, 491. Abbey Theatre Digital Archive, National University of Ireland Galway, ADM_00003644, fo. 61.

[32] Adrian Frazier, *Behind the Scenes: Yeats, Horniman, and the Struggle for the Abbey Theatre* (Berkeley, CA: University of California Press, 1990), 176–9.

[33] 'Willie Fay on the Drama', *Mail* (Chicago), 20 May 1908: Abbey scrapbook, Hardiman Library, NUI Galway, T13/A/392. Where newspaper articles are unpaginated, this is because the material is derived from folders of clippings in the Hardiman Library.

Frank Fay did not find the success, however limited, of his brother on the English stage or in the movies, perhaps because, in spite of a red face, big ears, and a big nose, he had no gift at all for comic parts. Arthur Shields, who later became the Abbey's leading man, recalled getting lessons from Frank Fay around 1913.

> I was a sort of favourite in the class at that time, however; [Frank Fay] was a strange fellow. Frank was a great speaker of verse; unfortunately, he was a very tiny little man, with a big nose, and it sometimes seemed ridiculous—very ridiculous. Last time I can remember him being on the Abbey stage was one period when he came back again and he tried to win his audience by shouting his part. In a small theatre, it was so ridiculous, really ridiculous. Poor man, it's a shame that people have to leave that group [the Abbey Theatre], but I suppose it was necessary. [34]

Fay settled in Dublin and, though bitter about the Abbey, continued to work privately as a voice coach, and taught a number of those who later wound up in the Abbey Company, such as F. J. McCormick and Gabriel Fallon.[35]

Sara Allgood, her sister Maire O'Neill, J. M. Kerrigan, and Arthur Sinclair remained in the Abbey as the main draws. Sinclair had had little training before joining the company, nor did he appear to require any. Watching him, Allgood concluded that acting 'is purely an instinctive art, and sometimes education is a handicap'.[36] Off-stage, Sinclair was a dandy, with lovely golden hair, oiled and parted in the centre, à la Oscar Wilde. On-stage, with Allgood in Lady Gregory's adaptation of *The Rogueries of Scapin*,

> Mr Sinclair was the imperturbable, scheming, sly Scapin [. . .] he delivered almost every word [. . .] with an air of comic earnestness combined with a roguish twinkle in the eye. His description of the terrors of litigation was really masterly, his many-voiced mimicry in the sack scene was well managed, and his final victory and pardon were achieved with great drollery.[37]

To those with long experience of playgoing, Sinclair's depiction of an Irish drunk was the best example of a turn always popular with actors and audiences. 'Hand upon my heart,' declared George Moore in an interview with the *Boston Evening Transcript* in 1911, 'it is impossible for me to say I ever saw a better actor than Arthur Sinclair of the Abbey Theatre in his best parts, such as the father in *The Playboy*.'[38] In 1916, Sinclair started his own company with other ex-Abbey players, such as Maire O'Neill, Fred O'Donovan, Sydney Morgan, and sometimes Sara Allgood, which played in the UK, Australia, and the USA.

Sara Allgood, even if she learned what Frank Fay had to teach, was born with an imperishable gift, a really beautiful contralto voice. She excelled at singing and verse recitation even before she began to act with the INTS (a small part in *The King's Threshold*, 2 October 1903). She soon took over the role of Maurya in *Riders to the Sea* from Helen Laird, and made it her own. Lady Gregory came to believe that Allgood was essential to the success

---

[34] Arthur Shields, interview with Herbert Gans, n.d., Hardiman Library, NUI Galway, T13/A/392.
[35] Fallon, *The Abbey and the Actor*, 24.   [36] Allgood, 'Memories', 59–60.
[37] 'The Abbey Theatre', *Evening Telegraph*, 28 Aug. 1908, Hardiman Library, NUI Galway, T13/A/392.
[38] 'George Moore on the Irish Theatre', *Boston Evening Transcript*, 23 Sept. 1911, Hardiman Library, NUI Galway, T13/A/392.

of her own plays, such as *Spreading the News*. The playwright became a kind of prisoner of the actress's vanity thereafter, always urging on the other directors Allgood's case for high wages. Yet Allgood had range beyond the Abbey's one-acts, and the desire for a bigger stage on which to display her talents. Mrs Patrick Campbell, after playing with Allgood in *Deirdre*, borrowed her for the London production of that play. Then Annie Horniman employed Allgood to play Isabella in a 1908 Manchester Gaiety production of *Measure for Measure*. The critics for the *Manchester Courier* and the *Daily Dispatch* were swept away by the Irish visitor: 'Wedded to great comeliness is a mellow contralto voice, with a sweet and plaintive note in it which thrills the hearer.' 'Were the other characters impersonated by mediocrities, we should still be interested if Isabella were gifted with the power to make us envisage her agony of spirit, her mental horror, her womanly insult, and Miss Sara Allgood has that power.'[39]

The power is there to witness in a number of films. Alfred Hitchcock made a poor job of his effort to turn *Juno and the Paycock* into a successful 1929 movie, but in the film's last minutes Allgood's acting must have been lifted directly from her recent performances on stage as Juno, her greatest role. After hearing of the death of her son Johnny, she pleads in a motherly way with her daughter Mary, just jilted and pregnant, not to lose hope and faith; she pats her often on the back, and gives her little kisses on the cheek ('I forgot [. . .] your poor old selfish mother was thinking of no one but herself'), then sends Mary off. Left alone on stage, Allgood wanders back across the set, muttering, wringing her hands slowly, then fingering the buttons on her dress. She walks over to Johnny's empty bed, talking as if to the infant she brought into the world. Then without a visible transition, she folds her hands in prayer and looks up to the plaster crucifix hung on the wall, 'Mother of God, have pity on us!' Her prayer for her darling son ends in tears with the phrase, 'who was riddled with bullets'. Stretching her arms upward to God on high, she prays, 'Take away these hearts of stone.' The arms slowly drop and the voice dies with 'Give us your own eternal love'. It is a fluid, physically graceful, and truly just performance, much, much more than 'crossing stage to right'.

Allgood could also anchor comedy, though she never played for laughs. In the film of the West End and Broadway hit, *A Storm in a Teacup* (1937), she holds together, by means of an artificial but apparently real grief about the putting down of her little unlicensed dog, a slightly farcical romantic comedy with Rex Harrison, Vivien Leigh, and Cecil Hardwicke. Without the faux-tragic performance by Allgood, this photoplay might have been just too silly to be popular. In general, Hollywood directors concluded that films were often better with Allgood in the cast, even if in a small part, one for an ageing and quite round Irishwoman. She was cast in fifty-four films, and was nominated for an Oscar for her Juno-like part as the mother in John Ford's *How Green Was My Valley* (1941) (a film that, with Shields, Barry Fitzgerald, and Maureen O'Hara in the cast, is an all-around Abbey homage).[40]

[39] Abbey Theatre: scrapbook containing press cuttings for the period of 1907. NLI REF 25, 491. Abbey Theatre Digital Archive at National University of Ireland, Galway, ADM_00003644, fo. 40.

[40] Adrian Frazier, *Hollywood Irish: John Ford, Abbey Actors, and the Irish Revival in Hollywood* (Dublin: Lilliput Press, 2011), 147–74.

Allgood's sister Molly, who appeared under the stage name Maire O'Neill, did not have Sara's contralto voice or 'commanding cadence',[41] but she had her own gifts and ultimately became a very finished actress, first as Synge's betrothed (he pestered her with schoolmasterly advice in his letters) and later as Arthur Sinclair's wife. In her early days, Molly was thinner, prettier, younger, and more lyrically emotional than Sara, and thus went more easily into the romantic female leads like Pegeen Mike in *The Playboy of the Western World* (a part written for her by Synge). Molly left the Abbey in June 1911, when she married the *Guardian* journalist George Mair, and never returned, though she joined other ex-Abbey players in Sinclair's company when the mismatch with Mair petered out. She did not have the movie career of Sara Allgood, but Molly shows the qualities that made her a favourite of British audiences in Hitchcock's *Juno*. She is sly, insincerely platitudinous, liquored, and Dublin 'cute' in her cagey ensemble playing as Maisie Madigan with Joxer and the Captain.

The exodus of actors driven out of the Abbey by the Ulster Protestant manager St John Irvine post-Easter 1916 made room for a great new generation of Irish actors. Several of these, including F. J. McCormick, Barry Fitzgerald, and May Craig, had actually acted previously at Queen's Theatre, Dublin, home of the broadly humorous, often melodramatic Irish acting that Fay and Yeats had regarded as anathema at the birth of the Irish dramatic revival. It may be that a less supercilious attitude to the artistry of Queen's, even the admission that artistry was at work there, helps to explain new developments in characterization on the Abbey stage of the 1920s. Actors introduced subtextual or extratextual business of their own invention to the characters as written. The resultant characterizations in themselves became a source of pleasure for the 1920s and 1930s Dublin audiences. What, the playgoer thought in anticipation, will F. J. McCormick come up with tonight? The roles were not always played the same way from one production to another in the repertory, and everything was left to the momentary inspiration of the players. Barry Fitzgerald said he liked working for the Abbey better than for other theatres because '[t]here every actor, once he's shown himself to be one of the company, is allowed to develop his role with more liberty than anywhere else'.[42] This had never been the case under W. G. Fay.

Experience at Queen's may not be the only cause of a looser and deeper approach to character. Even before the departure of J. M. Kerrigan in 1914, the Abbey actor was studying more than the text in the preparation for a role. 'Often we'd sit for hours in the Green Room,' Kerrigan recalled, 'discussing the "other life" of the characters in our current play—that is, what those characters would do in situations besides those in which they were involved on the stage'. And Arthur Shields agreed that their actual approach was parallel to that of Stanislavski:

> I don't know whether you'd call it the Method or not, but we based our acting on observation of real characters we saw around us. I remember about 1912, J. M. Kerrigan taking me out to Donnybrook to a public house. 'Watch that barman now,' he said. Then when we got back to the Abbey he made me give an impression of the barman, and criticized me where he thought I should improve it.[43]

---

[41] 'Old Wine in New Bottles', *Mail* (Chicago), 20 Nov. 1908.

[42] Interview with Barry Fitzgerald, *Chicago Daily News*, 15 Mar. 1933, Hardiman Library, NUI Galway, T13/A/392.

[43] 'Two Actors Relive the Great Days at the Abbey Theatre', *The Times*, 28 Jan. 1963, 5.

FIG. 15.1 Barry Fitzgerald as Captain Jack Boyle in Seán O'Casey's *Juno and the Paycock* (3 March 1924).

Courtesy of the Abbey Theatre and James Hardiman Library, NUI Galway.

Barry Fitzgerald recalled that when working on the role of the Captain in *Juno*, 'for nights and days I sat listening to the playwright, Seán O'Casey, read the play or tell stories of the old Captain who was the original of Captain Boyle. I took my cues from O'Casey's descriptions and impersonations of the old man.'[44]

While the actors were still told about the Abbey traditions—restraint, teamwork, clarity of voice—they did not abide by the old instruction never to move until it was time for a single and pre-ordained dramatic gesture. There is a 1925 clip made by British Pathé with cameos by the principals of the Abbey ensemble.[45] The film is silent, but one can

[44] Interview with Barry Fitzgerald, *Chicago Daily News*, 15 Mar. 1933.
[45] 'Brilliant Irish Artists 1925', http://www.britishpathe.com/video/brilliant-irish-artists/query/abbey+theatre. Accessed 10 July 2014.

FIG. 15.2 F. J. McCormick as Joxer Daly in *Juno and the Paycock* (1924).

Courtesy of the Abbey Theatre and James Hardiman Library, NUI Galway.

still see the 'physical work' of the actors—twenty seconds each of Fitzgerald as Captain Boyle, McCormick as Joxer, Arthur Shields as Johnny, May Craig as Maurya, and others. F. J. McCormick is particularly interesting, given the scarcity of his work captured on film. The number of 'tics' or personal mannerisms he packs into his stationary portrayal of Joxer is notable. The byplay with the cigarette, the turning away from the view, and looking back over the shoulder, the repeated faux refusals of this and that, the hand gestures signalling 'Oh, not at all, not at all' when he is actually determined to snap up what is on offer, are a seamless stream of epiphenomena from an obliquely impenetrable and possibly empty psyche. O Joxer, he was a gas man!

Unlike that of F. J. McCormick, the inventiveness of Barry Fitzgerald is widely evident in movies. He was the first Abbey actor to win an Academy award, for his work in 1944 as the old priest opposite Bing Crosby in *Going My Way* (his Protestantism went without mention in the Free State's rejoicing). Hitchcock's bad *Juno* again contains proof of an Irish actor's good acting. Fitzgerald, with top billing, has just a brief bit at the very beginning of the film as The Orator, a new part apparently adapted from the Patrick Pearse off-stage role in *The Plough and the Stars*. He is giving what should be a blood-curdling, rabble rousing speech, of the sort first delivered by Maud Gonne in *Cathleen ni Houlihan*. With his thumbs under his vest at his lapels, he begins, 'We have thought together and fought together', then repeats himself, before, as he takes out his pipe, he concludes, so 'we have always won' (for Irish rebels, a comical inaccuracy). He then repeats himself in fugal variations as he absentmindedly waves about the lit match in one hand and the pipe nestled in the other. Will he ever get the flame to the pipe's bowl? Suddenly, a machine-gun opens fire from a high window in a tenement, and the speaker and his audience scatter. The parody of Irish male blustering heroism could not be less bitter or more charming. Fitzgerald had the trick of making something out of nothing, and something lovable too.

F. J. McCormick, however, remained Dublin's favourite actor. Barry Fitzgerald, after a sojourn in London to work with O'Casey and others in the late 1920s, felt on his return that

FIG. 15.3 Eileen Crowe as Pegeen (right) in *The Playboy of the Western World* in New York 1932: with Barry Fitzgerald as Michael James (centre), and Arthur Shields (left) as Christy Mahon.

Courtesy of the Abbey Theatre and James Hardiman Library, NUI Galway.

he would never conquer resentment against his wider ambitions and his Protestantism. He was disinclined to return to the Abbey from Hollywood after the filming of John Ford's *The Plough and the Stars* in 1936.

F. J. McCormick and his wife, Eileen Crowe, returned to take their places as the now unchallenged leading lights, to reign almost like Squire and Mrs Bancroft at the Abbey. On McCormick's death, after a brief stint filming *Odd Man Out* in 1947, Ernest Blythe, the Abbey's artistic director, memorialized him in the *Capuchin Annual*:

> We tend unconsciously to associate the idea of patriotism with some sort of political or military activity. But there could be no more practical or admirable patriotism than that of a man like F. J. McCormick, who, of choice, devoted his matchless talents almost exclusively to the enrichment of the cultural life of his own people and who in all his work kept before him the ideal of enhancing Ireland's renown, sacrificing great monetary rewards rather than give the hallmark of his name and reputation to a part which might reflect unfairly on his country or his people.[46]

The unnamed traitors in Hollywood, who took parts that 'might reflect unfairly on their country', were Dudley Digges, J. M. Kerrigan, Una O'Connor, Barry Fitzgerald, his brother Arthur Shields, Sara Allgood, Maureen O'Sullivan, and Maureen O'Hara, all internationally respected for the quality of their work and well paid in Hollywood.

ANEW McMASTER AND THE GATE

Outside of the Abbey, its tradition, and its school, there was one other influential academy of Irish acting, the travelling company of Ulsterman Anew McMaster. Six foot one, graceful, and with 'eyes the colour of harebells', McMaster was one of the last actor-managers of the old school, and an epitome of the type.[47]

From 1912, when he fell in love with Marjorie, the sister of Alfred Willmore (later known as Micheál Mac Liammóir), McMaster was associated with the boy who would become the star of the Gate Theatre, Dublin. By 1912, McMaster had already been touring Ireland with the O'Brien fit-up company. In 1925 he married Marjorie and formed his own band of Shakespeareans. In March 1927 he hired Mac Liammóir for a part in *Romeo and Juliet*, and in June in Enniscorthy added Hilton Edwards. These two, soon a couple, went on the following year to establish an Irish-speaking theatre, the Taibhdhearc, in Galway. This was only the first of McMaster's gifts to the theatre, Irish and worldwide. Those who began their careers with McMaster in Ireland, at three or four pounds a week, include Coralie Carmichael, T. P. McKenna, Milo O'Shea, and Harold Pinter.[48]

---

[46] *Capuchin Annual*, ed. Father Senan (Dublin, 1948), 151–2.
[47] Mac Liammóir's phrase, quoted in Carl Paul Falb, 'A World Elsewhere: The Stage Career of Anew McMaster' (PhD dissertation, Ohio State University, 1974), 6.
[48] Morash, *A History of Irish Theatre*, 177; pay scales from Falb, 'A World Elsewhere'.

Boucicault concluded that 'Shakespeare spells bankruptcy', but McMaster made him pay in one country town after another for forty years.[49] McMaster was the noble tragic soloist, with grandiloquence in spades. Pinter described his heroic powers of vocalization:

> His voice was unique: in my experience of an unequalled range. A bass of extraordinary echo, resonance, and gut, and remarkable sweep up into tenor, when the note would hit the back of the gallery and come straight back, a brilliant, stunning sound. I remember his delivery of this line: 'Methinks (bass) it should be now a huge (bass) eclipse (tenor) of sun and moon (baritone) and that th'affrighted globe (bass) Should yawn (very deep, the abyss) at alteration.' We all watched from the wings. [50]

Although uneven, McMaster at his best was reportedly as good as Laurence Olivier.

In the beginning, Mac Liammóir and Edwards at the Gate Theatre, Dublin, aspired to do something quite modernist, as with their first production in the Peacock, *Peer Gynt* (1928), modelling themselves on Diaghilev and Nijinsky of the Ballets Russes.[51] However, what endured as the Gate tradition was romantic grandiloquence of the McMaster strain in plays by Wilde, Shakespeare, and Shaw, all the lavish Anglo-Irish or British theatrical starriness that could never appear in a kitchen comedy at the Abbey. This second tradition in Ireland has often been a saving grace. That it flowered from the very romantic root of the actor-manager tradition, which the Irish revival was born to eradicate, is a pleasant paradox.

In 2007, one could see these two traditions of performance still thrillingly in conflict (it is the subject matter as well as the style of the play) in the Druid Theatre production of Eugene O'Neill's *Long Day's Journey into Night*, with American star James Cromwell in the lead—what a surname, for Connaught!—and utterly controlled Irish players like Marie Mullen in support. This creative polarity between grandiloquence and restraint may reasonably be expected to continue.

Is there such a thing as Irish acting? Irish actors, like Irish dancers, it is often remarked, are limited in their physical skills: the footwork may be fancy, and the mouth-music magical, but everything in between is often static. The Abbey under the Fays (1902–8) and under W. B. Yeats (until 1939) attempted many improvements in actor training—some of them radical, like inviting Ninette de Valois, a graduate of Ballets Russes, to start an Abbey Theatre School of Ballet (1927–33). From 1937 Ria Mooney brought her years in the New York company of Eva Le Gallienne to bear as teacher in the Abbey and Gaiety acting schools (1937–66). Training in performance in Ireland, however, did not keep pace with training in France, England, or the USA.

Education aside, there are certainly Irish speech-ways and customs peculiar unto themselves that can be accurately or artistically used as the material for performance. There is also a natural desire on the part of people to see themselves represented by their own kind.

[49] The sentiment was common in the late nineteenth and early twentieth century. See Joseph Hatton, *Henry Irving's Impressions of America*, vol. 1 (London: Sampson, Low, Marston, Searle, & Livingston, 1884), 86.

[50] Harold Pinter, *Mac* (London: Pendragon, 1968), 11–12.

[51] My thanks to Des Lally for permission to borrow this insight into the importance of Diaghilev and Nijinsky to Mac Liammóir and Edwards, explained by him at greater length at the English and Drama Graduate Research Day, Galway, 12 May 2014.

Perhaps in a very small island nation like Ireland, there is an even greater desire to watch one another pretend, and to mimic the idiosyncrasies of local people and local ways of being that are rarely seen on global media. Both the Abbey and the McMaster tours gave birth to a thriving amateur tradition, thriving in the sense that audiences in numbers gather to watch their relations and their neighbours on stage. That is the heart of any living tradition of acting—the pleasure people take in pretending to be someone else on stage, for the enjoyment of their friends—and it is the cradle for the apparently random arrival of infant genius.

PART VI

CONTESTING VOICES

CHAPTER 16

TWISTING IN THE WIND
Irish-Language Stage Theatre 1884–2014

BRIAN Ó CONCHUBHAIR[*]

THE IRISH LITERARY REVIVAL

DESPITE a strong tradition of storytelling, dance, and music, formal stage drama came late to the Irish language. Theatre in Irish, such as it is, began not in Ireland but in the first Steinway Hall on 14th Street, Manhattan, where the New York Society for the Preservation of the Irish Language staged Paul McSwiney's libretto *An Bard 'gus an Fó: A Gaelic Idyll* on Thanksgiving 1884.[1] Two years earlier in Ireland, *Irisleabhar na Gaedhilge/ The Gaelic Journal* published Eoin S. Ó Cearbhaill's historical play *Brian Boroimhe* from November 1882 to June 1883. Less formally, but no less importantly, Douglas Hyde and Norma Borthwick entertained workhouse children at a party hosted by Lady Gregory at Coole Park in December 1898 with a Punch and Judy show in Irish, inspired by *Imtheacht Chonaill/The Passing of Conall*, attributed to Eoin Ó Gramhnaigh, at Letterkenny's Aonach Thír Chonaill on 18 November 1898.[2] In Dublin, Conradh na Gaeilge/the Gaelic League performed John Cannon and Michael Rogers' *The Dentist/An Fiaclóir* in Blackrock on 24 April 1900, while Belfast hosted a production of *Eilís agus an Bhean Déirce* by 'Cú Uladh'

[*] The author gratefully acknowledges comments by James W. Hamrick, Brendan Kane, Caitlín Nic Iomhair, Philip O'Leary, James S. Rogers, and Mary Trotter.

[1] Published by the New York Society for the Preservation of the Irish Language in 1884 and subsequently published in *An Gaodhal*, Dec. 1884–Mar. 1885. Pádraig Denn's 'Aighneas an Pheacaigh leis an mBás', a dramatic dialogue between a repentant sinner and the devil, appeared in print in 1814. It is claimed that Seán Ó Neachtain's translation of Boucicault's *Colleen Bawn* in the *Galway Pilot* in 1895 is the first translated play in Irish. For mid-nineteenth-century. verse plays see Seán Ó Morónaigh (ed.), *Drámaíocht ó Dhúchas* (An Comhlachas Náisiúnta Drámaíochta, 2005). For plays dating back to the seventeenth century., see Philip O'Leary, *Prose Literature of the Gaelic Revival, 1881–1921: Ideology and Innovation* (University Park, PA: Pennsylvania State University Press, 1994), 296, n. 56.

[2] Published in the *Freeman's Journal* in Irish, 19 Nov. 1898, and in English, 21 Nov. 1898. See Mary Trotter, *Ireland's National Theaters: Political Performance and the Origins of the Irish Dramatic Movement* (Syracuse, NY: Syracuse University Press, 2001), xx–xxi.

(Peadar Toner Mac Fhionnlaoich) on 1 November 1900, subsequently performed on 27 August 1901 in Dublin's Antient Concert Rooms by the Fay brothers and the Ormonde Dramatic Society.[3]

The Revival's most famous play, however, is the Irish Literary Theatre's production of Douglas Hyde's one-act play *Casadh an tSúgáin* ('Twisting of the Rope/Weaving the Rush').[4] Performed by the Gaelic League's Keating Branch at the Gaiety Theatre, Dublin, on 21 October 1901, it was not only the first Irish-language play to receive a professional production, but the first to feature an all-Irish cast.[5] Significant for these attributes alone, it is more remarkable for plotting 'the future direction of the Irish theatre'[6] and marking 'the first time that audiences would watch a play set entirely in a cottage interior. By 1911, the company would have used more or less the same set sixteen times, and by the middle of the twentieth century it would be embarrassingly ubiquitous.'[7]

The play's origins lie in discussions between Yeats and Hyde at Coole Park in late August 1900 about alternate versions of a local folk tale and its theatrical potential. On 27 August Yeats provided a scenario that Hyde, by 29 August, crafted into a one-act dramatization combining both men's differing conceptions of the folk tale.[8] Though often dismissed as 'light, unassuming, and as unpretentious as its author . . . as a start toward folk-drama that exploited the Gaelic-Catholic-peasant theatre tradition, *The Twisting of the Rope* could not fail'.[9] The text, like many Gaelic League plays, showcased traditional music, song, dance, and vernacular crafts in the performance scenes, and allowed audiences to participate in a manner not dissimilar to popular Victorian performances. But not all plays romanticized rural life, and Pádraic Ó Conaire's 1908 *Bairbre Ruadh* (Red Barbara) offers a social critique akin to Shaw and Ibsen. Produced by Na Cluicheoirí in the Abbey in 1913, it dramatizes Bairbre's social dilemma: marry Cuimín, the servant boy she loves, or save her fatherless family from financial hardship through an arranged marriage.

These initial plays set the tone and established a pattern for the revival period where amateur Gaelic League groups staged plays for recreational and propagandist purposes. While *Feiseanna* (cultural fairs) and excursions to Irish-speaking regions and historic sites dominated the summer seasons, language classes and plays marked the League's winter programmes. Such plays as were written and performed in this period fall, largely, into two broad groups: historical pageants designed to teach history and inspire national pride,[10] and farces intended to entertain and improve linguistic practices

---

[3] Published in *Ulster Herald*, Jan. 1902. The emergence of Irish-language theatre in Belfast and Dublin can be attributed to the routes of English touring companies. The Belfast–Dublin–Cork axis emerged in the 1730s and survived into the 1890s. See Christopher Morash, *A History of Irish Theatre 1601–2000* (Cambridge: Cambridge University Press, 2004), 104–6.

[4] See Anthony Roche, *The Irish Dramatic Revival 1899–1939* (London: Bloomsbury, 2015), 7–9, 27.

[5] See Madeleine Humphries, *The Life and Times of Edward Martyn: An Aristocratic Bohemian* (Dublin: Irish Academic Press, 2007), 152–3.

[6] Morash, *History of Irish Theatre*, 121.   [7] Ibid.

[8] See Janet Egleson Dunleavy and Gareth W. Dunleavy, *Douglas Hyde: A Maker of Modern Ireland* (Berkeley, CA: University of California Press, 1991), 219.

[9] Douglas Hyde, *Selected Plays*, ed. Gareth W. Dunleavy and Janet Egleson Dunleavy (Washington, DC; Catholic University of America Press, 1991), 15–16. For its subsequent influence, see Anthony Roche, *Contemporary Irish Drama: From Beckett to McGuinness* (Dublin: Gill & Macmillan, 1994), 50.

[10] Joan Fitzpatrick Dean, *All Dressed Up: Modern Irish Historical Pageantry* (Syracuse, NY: Syracuse University Press, 2014).

for actors and audiences alike. Numerous Gaelic League branches embraced drama as a social and educational tool. Prominent in Dublin were the radical and Munster-oriented Craobh an Chéitinnigh (the Keating Branch),[11] An ArdChraobh (the Senior Branch), and Craobh na gCúig gCúigí (Branch of the Five Provinces); prolific outside of Dublin were the Galway city branch, Aisteoirí Thamhna on Tawain Island off Galway, Craobh an Pharóiste Thuaidh (Cork), and Craobh Bhealach an Doirín (Ballaghaderreen, Roscommon). Like many cultural groups formed during the revival, few concerned themselves primarily with producing plays.[12] A 1913 effort to improve the quality of productions led to the formation of two dedicated theatre groups in Dublin: Na Cluicheoirí (The Players), closely associated with Edward Martyn, and Na hAisteoirí (The Actors), founded by Piaras Béaslaí.[13] Irish-language theatre stagnated in the aftermath of the Easter Rising, frozen by the unpredictability of the hostilities during 1916–22, and restricted by actors' involvement in military and political affairs.

Dramatically, the Revival period bequeathed little to posterity: Irish-language theatre remained a nomadic, amateur, occasional endeavour. The typical revival play—a propagandistic piece and/or a humorous farce, often, but not always folkloric[14]—was written and performed by, and for, a Gaelic League membership for the express purpose of buttressing cultural and linguistic nationalism in a naturalistic style.[15] Actors were part-time enthusiasts, writers were almost universally cultural nationalists writing out of a patriotic duty rather than literary vocation or artistic inspiration, and performances formed enjoyable opportunities for social congress in Irish. Mary Trotter writes that 'the intimate bond between audience and actors in these grassroots performances evoked the popular spirit of the movement',[16] yet their plays generally suffered from common structural weakness.

Edward Martyn, a senior Gaelic League member, had co-founded the Irish Literary Theatre with Yeats and Gregory, but subsequently broke with them in early 1902.[17] Such political rifts and cultural arguments among the Abbey leadership subverted Irish-language theatre's opportunities for professional development. In separating from the Abbey, along with Máire Nic Shiubhlaigh, and founding the Theatre of Ireland in 1905, Martyn arguably diluted the Irish-language element in the fledgling Abbey.[18] One could contend that the Irish language absented itself from the Abbey before the Abbey shunned

[11] Notable members included Mairéad Ní Chinnéide, Seán O'Casey, Ernest Blythe, Pádraig Ua Duinnín, and Cathal Brugha.

[12] See Morash, *History of Irish Theatre*, 193.

[13] See Pádraig Ó Siadhail, *An Béaslaíoch* (Dublin: Coiscéim, 2007), 209–17. See also O'Leary, *Prose Literature*, 306–8.

[14] For the gender implications of folkloric adaptations, see Trotter, *Ireland's National Theaters*, 91–2. For construction of plays, see O'Leary, *Prose Literature*, 313–15.

[15] See Lionel Pilkington, *Theatre and Ireland* (London: Palgrave, 2010), 54–60. See also Trotter, *Ireland's National Theaters*, 7.

[16] Ibid., 6–7.

[17] Humphries, *Edward Martyn*, 155; Jerry Nolan, *Six Essays on Edward Martyn (1859–1923), Irish Cultural Revivalist* (Lampeter: Edwin Mellen Press, 2004), 134–7.

[18] The Theatre of Ireland committed to producing a play in Irish alongside every English play; members included Gearóid Ó Lochlainn and P. H. Pearse. See Gearóid Ó Lochlainn, *Ealaíon na hAmharclainne* (Dublin: Clódhanta Teo, 1984), 44. See also O'Leary, *Prose Literature*, 315.

Irish.[19] A combination of factors may account for the Abbey's ostracism of Irish from 1912 to 1938: the Martyn and Nic Shiubhlaigh split in 1905–6 to form the Theatre of Ireland in 1906; the Fays' 1908 emigration;[20] P. H. Pearse's attacks in *An Claidheamh Soluis*;[21] the 1907 Synge riots where Yeats testified in court against Gaelic League members such as Béaslaí;[22] and the 1926 O'Casey protests in which Gaelic Leaguers were again to the fore.

IRISH-LANGUAGE THEATRE IN DUBLIN

The Free State's contribution to Irish-language theatre as part of a deliberate nation-building project consisted of An Comhar Drámaíochta (The Drama Union) in Dublin and Taibhdhearc na Gaillimhe in Galway. Founded in 1924, An Comhar Drámaíochta staged plays, both Irish-language originals and translations, on the first Monday of each month and a Sunday matinée when possible from October to April on the main Abbey Theatre stage.[23] Due to a 1924 government subsidy of £600 from minister Ernest Blythe—who subsequently granted the Abbey £850—An Comhar Drámaíochta had a financial base.[24] Comprised of surviving remnants of Na Cluicheoirí and Na hAisteoirí, it emerged from a five-play mini-festival in the Gaiety in July 1923 and was initially charged with organizing Irish-language theatrical productions, but it quickly became a production company. Gearóid Ó Lochlainn's return from Copenhagen, where he had worked with Danio Biofilm, added theatrical expertise and a European elan to an established, albeit informal and loose, amateur acting structure.[25] In 1925–26 An Comhar performed thirty-seven plays, sixteen of which were new. But perceived as anti-Republican and largely ignored by the Gaelic League, it only offered limited runs of two nights and suffered from a dearth of professional actors and directors, lack of equipment, want of original scripts, and small audiences. Its most controversial production was Liam O'Flaherty's expressionist three-act play *Dorchadas* (Darkness), performed in March 1926 at the risk of protest less than a month after O'Casey's *The Plough and the Stars*.[26] In an effort to benefit from longer runs and more frequent productions, An Comhar relocated in August 1929 to the new 102-seat Peacock, where productions ran for a month. Micheál Mac Liammóir replaced Béaslaí as director, and not only transported An Comhar to the Gate but transformed it in the period 1930–34 into the Gate's Irish-language surrogate producing European classics in translation.[27] By the mid-1930s An Comhar had stagnated. Widely criticized, it faced the annual subsidy's

[19] Jerry Nolan attributes the League's failure in comparison to the Abbey's success to the absence of a Yeats-like figure 'to pull together the proliferation of amateur drama projects into coherent artistic realization': *Six Essays on Edward Martyn*, 137–8.

[20] See O'Leary, *Prose Literature*, 295.   [21] Ibid., 281–4, 316–19.

[22] See Nicholas Grene, *Synge: A Critical Study of the Plays* (Basingstoke: Macmillan, 1975), 8–10.

[23] Philip O'Leary, *Gaelic Prose in the Irish Free State 1922–1939* (Dublin: UCD Press, 2004), 465.

[24] For the annual amount, see Peter Kavanagh, *The Story of the Abbey Theatre* (Orono: National Poetry Foundation, 1984), 211–12.

[25] See http://www.ainm.ie/Bio.aspx?ID=345.

[26] See Liam O'Flaherty, *Darkness* (Dublin: Arlen House, 2014).

[27] Ó Lochlainn, *Ealaíon na hAmharclainne*, 37.

withdrawal. The need for a specific, small-sized theatre appeared more pressing than ever. Hopes of securing a dedicated space in a new Abbey theatre in the late 1930s floundered when the Second World War, the Abbey, and Blythe intervened.

The Abbey staged its first Irish-language play, Hyde's *An Tincéar agus An tSídheog* (The Tinker and the Fairy),[28] in February 1912. On 9 May 1938, the Abbey returned to Hyde—whose presidential inauguration was announced in April—and staged his *Casadh an tSúgáin*. A production of Séamus de Bhilmot, *Baintighearna an Ghorta* (The Famine Peeress)—directed by Frank Dermody, recently recruited from *An Taibhdhearc*—followed quickly in December. 1939 brought a new Irish-language literary competition and the staging of the winning entry, Séamus Ó hAodha's *Donnchadha Ruadh* (Red Donnchadha), which had shared first place with Séamus de Bhilmot's *Baintighearna*. 1941 brought the Bulgarian army to Athens and Blythe to the Abbey, and after a twenty-six-year hiatus, the Abbey produced six plays in Irish in four years. Irish-language theatre, absent since 1912, was suddenly centre stage. Blythe's skilful manipulations saw the Abbey cannibalize An Comhar Drámaíochta and its annual grant. The move dissatisfied all concerned: former An Comhar actors and directors felt shunned; Abbey actors faced language examinations. Nor did Irish-language theatre prosper. Whatever Blythe's motives—creating a bilingual Abbey, improving the quality of Irish-language theatre, forging the future of Irish theatre according to his own design—the results were deleterious. It remains unclear if the quality of theatre produced in Irish was a contributing factor to, or a symptom of, the Abbey's marked decline in the period. But An Damer's subsequent success suggests that while ability in Irish became a shibboleth at the Abbey, it achieved little of substance for theatre in Irish.

Ironically, it was disaffected An Comhar actors who inadvertently provided Blythe with an enduring formula for successful theatre in Irish, or at least with a veneer of success. Disenfranchised from the Abbey, former members established Compántas Amharclainne na Gaeilge (the Irish-Language Theatre Company) in 1941, and their 1944 Christmas pantomime at the Gaiety proved a financial and popular success. Their short-lived venture offered a formula that would repeatedly prove viable for Irish-language theatre: simple, accessible, and comprehensible language; recognizable plot lines; physical movement; and humour that enticed non-fluent speakers. Public demand extended the initial run from 25 to 30 December to two weeks. Their 1945 pantomime competed with the Abbey's *Muireann agus an Prionsa* (Muireann and the Prince). Initially scheduled for five nights, it ran for forty-four.[29] Suddenly, Irish-language productions were popular and profitable, and Blythe replicated the formula on a larger, better-resourced scale.[30]

The success of the Abbey's annual pantomimes increased its annual grant from £600 to £1,000, and created an impression of successful Irish-language theatre. The Abbey produced pantomimes almost annually for the next twenty-five years. Yet while pantomimes

---

[28] First produced in George Moore's garden at Ely Place, Dublin, on 19 May 1902. See Hyde, *Selected Plays*, 17–18.

[29] Pádraig Ó Siadhail, *Stair Dhrámaíocht na Gaeilge 1900–1970* (Indreabhán: Cló Iar-Chonnacht, 1993), 87.

[30] See Philip O'Leary, *Writing Beyond the Revival: Facing the Future in Gaelic Prose 1940–1951* (Dublin: UCD Press, 2011), 281–386.

attracted large audiences and created an illusion of dramatic activity, they masked a declining number of plays produced in Irish, and their meagre audiences.[31] Fiscal responsibility led to a reduction in the number of poorly attended, but expensive, full-length Irish-language plays from the late 1940s onwards, and a move to more economical one-act plays. Such one-acts—quicker to rehearse and cheaper to produce (£30 rather than £100–£200)—were sprung, often unannounced, on unsuspecting audiences after the advertised full-length play in English. Like insurgents in a guerrilla army, these plays appeared, often without warning, and disappeared without trace, serving a twofold purpose: confirming that the Abbey was indeed producing Irish-language plays and that those audiences, on paper, were as large as those attending the preceding English-language play.[32]

The 1950s continued a steady retreat from full-length plays: three between 1951 and 1967; no original full-length play between 1945 and 1953.[33] The 1951 fire further reduced the number of plays and threatened the budget, as compliance with Dublin Corporation's regulations required substantial capital expenditure.[34] Despite the pantomimes, the Abbey consciously withdrew from Irish-language theatre in the late 1940s, less than ten years after devouring An Comhar Drámaíochta, to focus on developing a core bilingual Abbey. No full-length play in Irish has been staged on the main Abbey stage since 1969.[35] The exclusion spawned new theatre companies, and the most pertinent in this regard was the 37 Theatre Club on Baggot Street, which produced Maurice Meldon's bilingual play *Aisling* in 1951, directed by Barry Cassin, and described as the most interesting and stimulating new Irish play since *The Old Lady Says 'No'*.[36] Revived at the Gate in 1959, it remained one of the 'most original and entertaining plays of its generation'.[37] The paucity of Irish-language drama, more pronounced during the enforced absence from Abbey Street, led to protests. Such criticism was tempered by promises, attributed to Blythe, that a new theatre—the New Peacock—would be dedicated to Irish-language drama. The assurance offered a tonic: a permanent, reasonably sized, dedicated theatrical space in the city centre for Irish-language theatre. This new space's potential impact was as boundless as the promises made: plays in Irish forty weeks per year, summer plays for tourists.[38] The closing lines in Ó Lochlainn's slim 1966 volume address that hope in expectant terms.[39] However, the Peacock's opening years provided further evidence of retreat. From 33% of the productions being in Irish in 1967, the number declined to 25% in 1968 and 1969, and precipitously to 7% in 1970.[40] A gala performance

[31] See Robert Welch, *The Abbey Theatre, 1899–1999: Form and Pressure* (Oxford: Oxford University Press, 1999), 145.

[32] See O'Leary, *Gaelic Prose*, 458–503 and *Writing Beyond the Revival*, 281–407; see also Ó Siadhail, *Stair Dhrámaíocht na Gaeilge*, 89. One such play, possibly among the last, was Blythe's translation of Gregory's *The Gaol Gate* as *Geata An Phríosúin*, performed by Aisteoirí Loch Con Aortha after John Power's *The Irishwoman of the Year* in May 1966 at the Queen's Theatre.

[33] Ó Siadhail, *Stair Dhrámaíocht na Gaeilge*, 89.

[34] Ibid., 90. See also Liam Miller, 'Eden and After: The Irish Theatre 1945–1966', *Studies: An Irish Quarterly Review* 55, no. 219 (1965), 231–5.

[35] Ó Siadhail, *Stair Dhrámaíocht na Gaeilge*, 93.

[36] 'New Play By Maurice Meldon', *Irish Times*, 7 Apr. 1953.

[37] '*Aisling* Revived at the Gate', *Irish Independent*, 28 Oct. 1959.

[38] Ó Siadhail, *Stair Dhrámaíocht na Gaeilge*, 91–3. See also Welch, *The Abbey Theatre*, 184.

[39] Ó Lochlainn, *Ealaíon na hAmharclainne*, 58.

[40] Ó Siadhail, *Stair Dhrámaíocht na Gaeilge*, 89.

of Hyde's *An Pósadh* (The Marriage) on 16 May 1968, honouring the Belgian king's state visit, apparently, marked the last Irish-language Abbey production, excluding panto-mimes, on the main stage.[41]

Two major trends in Irish-language playwriting emerged at the Peacock after 1970: pantomime/revue-type performances (such as *Scéal Scéalaí*) and adaptations of classic texts. But significant original work also emerged: the Abbey has produced nineteen original Irish-language plays since 1971, including canonical works such as Alan Titley's *Tagann Godot* (Godot Arrives)[42] (1990) and Seán Mac Mathúna's *The Winter Thief/Gadaí Géar na Geamh-Oíche* (1992). A subsequent radio version of Titley's play won 'best foreign language play' in Australia and a public reading followed, leading to a full production in the Peacock, where Mac Anna hyped the farcical elements to the level of spectacle. In *Tagann Godot*, the titular character's arrival creates a philosophical and intellectual dileama—once the major life questions are answered, what is left to ponder?

Seán Mac Mathúna's *The Winter Thief/Gadaí Géar na Geamh-Oíche*, written in 1985, is a teasing historical play set at the start of the War of Independence in an Irish-speaking part of Kerry–Cork borderlands where an IRB organizer—based on Blythe—is tasked with transforming locals into effective soldiers, and bloods them by executing a 'traitor' from amongst them. The play explores the harsh difference between theoretical cultural nationalism and the brutality of war in a bilingual region dealing with encroaching modernity. Ironically, sacrificing the 'traitor'—the local storyteller and keeper of ancestral memory—requires forfeiting tradition and cultural history. The *Irish Press* declared it 'one of the more important plays to be staged in Dublin for some time' and 'as dramatic in significance as anything on stage'.[43] The *Sunday Independent* similarly lauded it as offering 'rivetingly innovational (or revisionist, depending on your politics) views of Irish heritage [...] epic in philosophical terms ... simple to the point of domesticity in presentation'.[44] Staged at the Peacock, in English and Irish on alternate nights, it offered audiences an uncompromising depiction of what the struggle for independence entailed. Patsy McGarry cautioned against labelling it revisionist.

> To describe its stance as revisionist is far too simple. It goes much deeper. This play looks at the anatomy of revolution—any revolution—and recoils. *A Winter Thief* is a protest on behalf of ordinary life against the brutish demands of the heroic. It argues for the story that entertains in preference to the one that inspires.[45]

Nevertheless, an irate audience member interrupted the preview to verbally condemn the author, who also received threatening telephone calls.[46]

---

[41] Siobhán McKenna, with UCC's Drama Soc, read *Caoineadh Airt Uí Laoghaire*, adapted by Seán Ó Tuama and directed by Alan Young, on 6 Apr. 1969 on the main Abbey stage. The last play to receive a full production and extended run on the main stage appears to be Liam Ó Briain's translation of Dion Boucicault's *An Cailín Bán* (The Colleen Bawn) in Dec. 1967 in lieu of a Christmas pantomime. An adaptation of *An Baile Seo 'Gainne* appeared on the main stage in Dec. 1968.

[42] See Welch, *The Abbey Theatre*, 242–4.

[43] Patsy McGarry, 'Winter Thief a Protest on Behalf of Humanity', *Irish Press*, 23 Apr. 1992.

[44] Emer O'Kelly, 'Garry's Year', *Sunday Independent*, 7 June 1992.

[45] McGarry, 'Winter Thief'.

[46] Paddy Woodworth, 'Abbey Travels Well', *Irish Times*, 2 May 1992.

Antoine Ó Flatharta, the only Irish-language playwright to establish a productive relationship with the Abbey in the 1980s–1990s, had five original plays produced there.[47] Fintan O'Toole opines that plays such as *Gaeilgeoirí* (Irish Enthusiasts) and *Imeachtaí na Saoirse* (The Events of Freedom) present Irish as a problematic medium, and that Ó Flatharta's 'best work in Irish, indeed rises far above naturalism by making the two languages work almost like dramatic characters, arguing and interacting with each other'.[48] *An Solas Dearg* (The Red Light), directed by Deirdre Friel in 1995, explores the consequences of the communications industry's impact on Connemara's linguistic and cultural ecosystem. The play focuses on the fractured mother–son relationship of a middle-aged suburban midlands hipster and fervent language activist, long transplanted to Connemara, committed to preserving indigenous culture by instructing local youth in movie production. His local protégée's success at an international film festival in tandem with his mother's sale of the ancestral home—refuge to Cumann na mBan and IRA men during the War of Independence—creates an ideological and spiritual crisis that animates the play. In identifying the linguistic politics that animate *An Solas Dearg*, O'Toole also credits it with tackling 'inescapable complexities' and taking 'the pulse of a broader Irish culture'. Moreover, O'Toole contends it 'shows that Irish does add something to the theatre, and therefore to the wider culture […] It is an untranslatable play, and when something can't be translated, you know that what it contains is irreplaceable.'[49]

Touring the Irish-speaking *gaeltachtaí* became a distinctive feature in the 1990s, when adaptations such as Macdara Ó Fátharta's 1996 *Cré na Cille* (Graveyard Clay), Tom Mac Intyre's 1998 *Caoineadh Airt Uí Laoghaire* (Lament for Art O'Leary), and Mac Intyre's 1999 *Cúirt an Mheán Oíche* (The Midnight Court) all toured.[50] Yet Titley's assessment that 'the Abbey's retreat from Irish-language theatre was not, so to speak, dramatic, it was certain and slow and sure-footed'[51] is accurate. The Abbey 'has mounted just one full-length Irish-language production in the past 15 years (Aodh Ó Dómhnaill's *Idir an Dá Shúil* in December) and you'd have to go back to the 1960s to discover the last in-house Irish-language production that graced its main stage.'[52] In 1999 Robert Welch argued: 'when one compares the resurgence in literature in Irish, especially poetry, with writing for the theatre, the contrast is dispiriting and, perhaps, not a little baffling.' He went on to suggest that the Abbey's next phase in rediscovering its tradition 'will be an exciting drama in Irish; not the parousia, the waiting for the Gaelic redeemer, of Blythe, but the insouciant fire and confidence of a Titley or a Ní Dhomhnaill'.[53]

The intervening fifteen years have offered no such evidence of rediscovery. Since 2006 the Abbey has commissioned some seventy-six plays: 'Twenty-five have been produced, seven are due for production and a further twelve are still in development.'[54] None was in

[47] *Gaeilgeoirí* (1981); *Imeachtaí na Saoirse* (1983); *Ag Ealaín in Éirinn* (1986); *Aois na hÓige* (1986); *An Fear Bréige* (1991); *An Solas Dearg* (produced by Amharclann de híde at the Abbey in 1995).
[48] Fintan O'Toole, 'Through the Medium', *Irish Times*, 28 Nov. 1995.   [49] Ibid.
[50] In 1967 the Abbey toured Synge's *Chun na Fairrge Síos* [sic] (Riders to the Sea) translated by Tomás Ó Muircheartaigh, and Boucicault's *An Cailín Bán*, and in 1969 Ní Ghráda's *Breithiúnas* (Verdict) and Robinson's *Is Glas Iad na Cnuic* (The Far Off Hills).
[51] Alan Titley, *Nailing Theses* (Belfast: Lagan Press, 2011), 272.
[52] Caomhan Keane, 'Irish Language Theatre', *Irish Times*, 13 June 2011.
[53] Welch, *The Abbey Theatre*, 250.
[54] 'Wanted: New Plays for Our National Theatre, Without the Risk', *Irish Independent*, 27 Nov. 2014.

Irish. The Abbey's responsibility, if any, to Irish has remained a vexed question ever since its foundation, and even more so since the annexation of An Comhar Drámaíochta. In 1960–70 the Abbey produced more than thirteen original plays in Irish, three adaptations, and numerous pantomimes. In 1970–80 the Abbey produced four original plays in Irish, one translation, and some nine adaptations, revues, and pantomimes—albeit often for very limited runs, often only three nights or less. Between 1980 and 1990 ten plays: six new plays, two bilingual plays[55], and two adaptations. 1990–2000 brought two original plays (*Tagann Godot*, 1990, and *Gadaí Géar na Geamh-Oíche*, 1992) and three adaptations of classic Irish texts (*Cré na Cille*, 1996; *Caoineadh Airt Uí Laoghaire*, 1998; and *Cúirt an Mheán Oíche*, 1999). The period 2000–2009 witnessed Synge's one-act: *Chun na Farraige Síos* (Riders to the Sea), translated by Tomás Ó Flaithearta, staged for one night in 2004 to mark its centenary, and *Gach Áit Eile* (All Other Places, 2009), a reading of three commissioned twenty-minute pieces followed with *Bí ag Scríobh* (Be Writing). *Sétanta* (2011), produced by Fíbín in association with the Abbey in 2011, is the only full Irish-language production in the period 2000–2013. Fíbín returned in 2014 to perform *Réiltín*, a coming-of-age story of a 20-year-old intent on becoming a singer during the economic crisis. It was also the Dublin Theatre Festival's first Irish production in seventeen years. In the 1980s and early 1990s the Abbey produced the decade's most significant Irish plays: *Tagann Godot, Gadaí Géar na Geamh-Oíche, Solas Dearg*, and *Gaeilgeoirí*: the same cannot be said from the mid-1990s and beyond. The Abbey is now irrelevant to contemporary Irish-language theatre, and the 1990s may be considered an end date for the national theatre's engagement with theatre in the first official language.

The Abbey's mid-century inertia around the language question and the need to provide a professional stage for a new generation of Irish-language dramatists created an opportunity. The first of these, An Damer, emerged from Gael Linn's cultural agenda in 1955.[56] Typically, An Damer produced five to seven productions annually, three of which were original plays.[57] Gael Linn rented the Damer Hall, beneath the Dublin Unitarian Church in St Stephen's Green, in 1955 for £400, and secured 400 subscribers to attend yearly performances.[58] The initial season led to calls for higher production standards which saw Frank Dermody appointed director, after returning from London.[59] Gael Linn's Roibeárd Mac Góráin secured the promise of a full-length play from Brendan Behan for An Damer and *An Giall*, deemed 'a landmark in the history of drama in Irish',[60] appeared in the underground theatre on Bloomsday 1958. Described by the *Irish Times* as a production of 'high quality',[61] a radio version, adapted by Pádraic Ó Néill and produced by Micheál Ó Garbhaigh, aired on RTÉ to coincide with Joan Littlewood's English-language version *The*

[55] Bilingual plays such as *Gach Neach Beo* (1984) and *Dialann Ocrais* (1987, first produced in Hull in 1982) are considered Irish-language plays here.

[56] See Mairéad Ní Chinnéide, *Scéal Ghael-Linn* (Indreabhán: Cló Iar-Chonnacht, 2013).

[57] See Roibeárd Mac Góráin, 'Scannáin, Amhráin agus Drámaí', in Stiofán Ó hAnnracháin (ed.), *An Comhchaidreamh: Crann a Chraobhaigh* (Dublin: An Clóchomhar Tta, 1985), 75.

[58] Mairéad Ní Chinnéide, *An Damer: Stair Amharclainne* (Dublin: Gael Linn, 2008), 13–14.

[59] Ibid., 18.

[60] Declan Kiberd, 'Introduction', in Brendan Behan, *Poems and a Play in Irish* (Dublin: Gallery Books, 1981), 9.

[61] *Irish Times*, 17 June 1958.

Hostage at the Theatre Royal, Stratford East, in 1958.[62] Set in a Dublin brothel, owned by a fanatical, Oxford-educated Irish-Irelander and managed by an old IRA man, the drama centres on a young English soldier who discovers that he is not only a hostage but a pawn in a wider political game and faces retaliatory execution if an IRA man in Belfast gaol hangs. The play's success led to a second week of performances, the first such occasion for An Damer.[63] Declan Kiberd considers it to offer 'a sharp critique of idealism, a critique which often comes perilously close to downright nihilism [. . .] Its unabashed experimentalism and expressionist sequences proved that a Gaelic Modernism had belatedly arrived.'[64] The significant differences between *An Giall* and the 'drastically modified' *The Hostage* include additional characters who 'contribute nothing to the plot of *The Hostage*, but they contribute a great deal to its tone, which is very different from that of the original'.[65] *The Hostage* rather 'panders to popular conceptions of the Irish', with Littlewood 'making it bawdy and peppering it with allusions to most of the popular issues of the day'.[66] Controversy regarding a later Behan play, *Lá Breá sa Roilig* (A Fine Day in the Cemetery), led to Dermody's departure in 1961 and signalled not only Mac Anna's advent as An Damer's leader but a significant change in style: spectacle over characterization.[67] Mac Anna's tenure saw the 1962 production of *Cúirt an Mheán Oíche* for the Dublin Theatre Festival, and a creative relationship with Eoghan Ó Tuairisc resulted in *De Réir Rúibricí* (According to Rubrics, 1961) and *Lá Fhéile Mhichíl* (St Michael's Feast Day, 1963, 1964).

It was Mac Anna, recently returned from Germany, who reportedly reshaped Máiréad Ní Ghráda's script of *An Triail* in Brechtian fashion.[68] Ní Ghráda, formerly Blythe's secretary and a founding member of An Comhar Drámaíochta, had had short plays staged by An Comhar and the Abbey. She came to prominence, however, in her two final plays, *An Triail* (The Trial) and *Breithiúnas* (Verdict), which was when she abandoned naturalism for expressionism. As part of the 1964 Dublin Theatre Festival, the Gaiety produced Brian Friel's *Philadelphia, Here I Come!* and Eugene McCabe's *The King of the Castle*, while An Damer produced *An Triail*, which explored the plight of single mother Máire Cassidy, pregnant with the child of a married man who disowns her. Surviving a Magdalene Laundry but abandoned by all, she kills herself and her daughter rather than rear her in such a society. The subsequent inquest structures the play with the audience as jury. Coinciding with Michael Viney's investigative journalism on 'illegitimacy' in the *Irish Times*, the play offered 'illegitimacy, crystalized into a searing drama that challenges every aspect of the nation's treatment of this social problem',[69] and became a cause célèbre 'as much for the topicality of her subject and the courage of her treatment as for

[62] Ibid. See *Irish Press*, 8 Sept. 1958.   [63] *Sunday Press*, 22 June 1958.

[64] Behan, *Poems and a Play in Irish*, 9–10.

[65] Richard Wall, 'An Giall and The Hostage Compared', *Modern Drama* 18, no. 2 (1975), 165–6. BBC Radio 3 broadcast Lorcán Ó Treasaigh's translation on 19 May 1989 and 12 Aug. 1988. See also Roche, *Contemporary Irish Drama*, 64.

[66] Wall, 'An Giall', 171.

[67] See Ní Chinnéide, *An Damer: Stair Amharclainne*, 37–8. *Lá Breá sa Roilig* was subsequently produced as *Richard's Cork Leg* in 1972.

[68] See, however, Tomás Mac Anna, *Fallaing Aonghusa: Saol Amharclainne* (Indreabhán: Cló Iar-Chonnacht, 2000), 163.

[69] L. Mac G., 'An Triail is Viney Stressed on Stage', *Irish Times*, 23 Sept. 1964.

the dramatic efforts'.[70] The London *Times* critic Harold Hobson reviewed it glowingly, as
did Peter Lennon, despite his evaporated Irish, in the *Guardian*, expressing the feeling
that Ireland was 'straining intellectually at those seams stitched so scrupulously by the
old ladies of the revolution a couple of generations ago'. Yet despite its obvious relevance
for contemporary Ireland, he questioned the play's universal value.[71] It became a phenomenon extending beyond the confines of Irish: an English translation at the Eblana
and a television version on Teilifís Éireann in February 1965 quickly followed, leading to
unfounded hopes that more plays in Irish might be televised.[72]

An Damer followed up in 1965 with *Spéir Thoirní* (Thundery Sky), Liam Ó Murchú's play
on race relations involving a West Indian woman attending UCD while financing her studies through domestic service. Other significant An Damer productions include Críostóir
Ó Floinn's controversial 1968 *Cóta Bán Chríost* (Christ's White Coat) and Siobhán Ní
Shúilleabháin's 1975 *Cití* (Kitty). *Cóta Bán Chríost*, written during Ó Floinn's Liverpool
exile in the early 1960s, unsurprisingly proved controversial.[73] A three-act play, structured
on the rosary's Annunciation, Agony, and Resurrection, it features Father Iúd, a 40-year-
old priest in rural Ireland, and Máire, a 25-year-old woman, who appears, pregnant and
single, at his door on Christmas night. Claiming an immaculate conception, she is less
a virgin than a virago bent on revenge. Rejected by the Abbey as 'obscene agus blasphemous'[74] and condemned by Mac Anna as 'a dirty play about a priest and a woman running
off together',[75] it was directed by Noel Ó Briain at An Damer, where it played for six weeks
to full houses.[76] Translated as *The Order of Melchizedek* but 'mutilated in production'[77] at
the Gate in 1967, it led to its author's dismissal as a teacher. In addition to original plays, An
Damer specifically produced translations previously unperformed in Dublin, such as Jean
Giraudoux's 1929 *Amphytron 38* (performed by Compántas Chorcaí in 1957), Diego Fabbri's
1955 *Processo a Gesù* as *An Chúis in Aghaidh Íosa* in 1960, and Armand Salacrou's 1945 *Les
nuits de la colère* as *Oícheanta na Feirge* in 1960. In doing so they extended the range of
plays available in Dublin and attracted a wider audience.[78] An Damer turned professional
in 1978 with the assistance of a state subsidy (£80,000), the termination of which in 1981
signalled its demise. During its tenure, An Damer proved that Irish-language theatre in
Dublin could not only attract audiences but produce work of significance.

In 1982, under Ray Yeates's directorship, Deilt (Delta) emerged to fill the vacuum created by An Damer, and Seán Ó Broin's *Daoine ar an Dart* (People on the DART), staged
on DART trains, appeared as part of the 1987 Dublin Theatre Festival. Stage productions included Antoine Ó Fathartha's *An Fear Bréige* (Scarecrow, 1991) and Nuala Ní
Dhomhnaill's adaptation of An Seabhac's *Jimín* (Little Jimmy, 1985). Deilt collaborated
with Na Fánaithe (The Wanderers) to produce Seán McCarthy's adaptation of *Bullaí*

[70] Sean J. White, 'Theatre Festival '64', *Irish Press*, 24 Sept. 1964. See Éamon Ó Ciosáin, 'Máiréad
Ní Ghráda agus a saothar liteartha', in Máiréad Ní Ghráda, *Breithiúnas: Dráma Dhá Ghníomh*
(Dublin: An Gúm, 1996), 96–7.
[71] Peter Lennon, 'Dublin Theatre Festival', *Guardian*, 26 Sept. 1964.
[72] See Ní Chinnéide, *An Damer: Stair Amharclainne*, 48–9.
[73] Críostoir O'Flynn, *A Writer's Life* (Dublin: Obelisk Books, 2001), 4–68.
[74] Diarmuid Ó Grainne, 'Agallamh na Míosa', *Comhar* 51, no. 8 (1992), 6.
[75] Críostóir Ó Floinn, 'The Order of Melchizedek', *Furrow* 19, no. 9 (1968), 532.
[76] O'Flynn, *A Writer's Life*, 54.   [77] Ó Floinn, 'Order of Melchizedek', 531.
[78] See Fiachra Ó Marcaigh, 'An Damer: Bás nó Beatha?', *Comhar* 40, no. 12 (1981), 6.

Mhártain at the Druid Lane Theatre in 1989 prior to a national tour. Deilt folded, to be replaced by Amharclann de hÍde (Hyde's Theatre), a professional Irish-language theatre company in 1992. It suffered the enduring limitations that afflict every Irish-language theatre in Dublin—the lack of a permanent venue.[79] Nevertheless, Amharclann de hÍde produced predominantly original plays including Liam Ó Muirthile's *Feur an Tae* (The Tea Man, 1995), Éilís Ní Dhuibhne's *Milseog an tSamhraidh* (The Summer Dessert, 1997), Alan Titley's *An Ghráin agus an Ghruaim* (Hate and Gloom, 1999) and, in collaboration with Aisling Ghéar, Celia de Fréine's powerful exploration of direction provision and treatment of refugees, *Nára Turas é in Aistear* (May It Not Be a Journey in Vain, 2000). Among the company's legacies is the space they created for women dramatists and directors. With the closure of Amharclann de hÍde, there is no professional or semi-professional theatre company in Dublin other than Mouth on Fire, established in 2010 by Melissa Nolan and Cathal Quinn, who have produced several of Beckett's plays in Irish. As in the revival period, theatre in Irish is now an amateur endeavour, led primarily by Aisteoirí Bulfin.[80]

Irish-Language Theatre in Galway

Proximity to Ireland's largest *gaeltacht*, the presence of a university officially committed to the language, and An Chéad Chath (the Army's Irish-speaking first battalion) rendered Galway a natural location for Irish-language theatre. In December 1927 a committee formed Taibhdhearc na Gaillimhe, and in 1928 Blythe authorized government funding (£600),[81] Micheál Mac Liammóir and Hilton Edwards signed contracts, and, critically, a 211-seat hall was identified as a venue. The staging of Mac Liammóir's *Diarmuid agus Gráinne* (Diarmuid and Gráinne) on 27 August–2 September 1928 marked the official opening. Its success was in every sense a triumph for Mac Liammóir.[82] Attracting full houses and critical acclaim, the play dramatized the well-known medieval love tale of the Irish hero Fionn and his wife to be, Gráinne, who willingly elopes with the dashing Diarmuid. The *Manchester Guardian* noted the production's 'lavish scale, the mounting and lighting effect being especially beautiful'.[83]

Mac Liammóir's *Prunella* followed quickly in October 1928. But the drama was both on and off stage. An Taibhdhearc's committee members differed considerably in political allegiances, artistic ideologies, and creative visions. This variance held particularly true in the case of

---

[79] Titley, *Nailing Theses*, 275–6.

[80] Guthanna Binne Síoraí (Eternal Sweet Voices), formed in 2012 by Gabriel Rosenstock and Cathal Quinn, use musicians, actors, singers, and dancers to stage the works of significant Irish poets in English and Irish. Mouth on Fire, established in 2010 by Melissa Nolan and Cathal Quinn, is a theatre company dedicated to performing Samuel Beckett's works, in particular the shorter, less commonly performed pieces, often using unconventional and site-specific locations. In addition to *Téip Dheireanach Krapp* (*Krapp's Last Tape*) (2014), they have staged *Teacht is Imeacht* (*Come and Go*) (2013) and *Ag Taibhreamh ar an … nGrá / Dreaming of … Love* (2012).

[81] See Seán Stafford, 'Taibhdhearc na Gaillimhe: Galway's Gaelic Theatre', *Journal of the Galway Archaeological and Historical Society* 54 (2002), 183–214.

[82] See Morash, *History of Irish Theatre*, 120–1.

[83] 'Gaelic Theatre in Galway', *Manchester Guardian*, 29 Aug. 1928.

Liam Ó Briain and Séamus Ó Beirn, who advocated differing visions for An Taibhdhearc: Ó Briain, a Dublin-born professor of French, favoured international theatre translated into Irish as a source for inspiring future authors and cultivating audiences; Ó Beirn, a Galwegian medical doctor closely associated with the Galway island of Tawain, more nativist and more practical, favoured a financially viable popular theatre that would attract patrons. In 1929 An Taibhdhearc staged original dramas by Hyde, Micheál Breathnach, Tomás Ó Ceallaigh, and translations of Irish and European classics by Lady Gregory, Chekhov, Molière, and Martínez Sierra. By the end of 1929 Mac Liammóir's bilocation between Dublin and Galway became an issue. Blythe ensured a transfer for Frank Dermody, a Chicago-born corporal in An Chéad Chath who had appeared in *Diarmuid agus Gráinne*, to Dublin's Cathal Brugha Barracks specifically to study with Mac Liammóir and Edwards at the Gate.

Dermody, having served his apprenticeship, became manager and secretary of An Taibhdhearc in 1931. He appeased both factions by producing translations—both continental European and English-language plays, including Ó Briain's translation of Synge's *Deirdre of the Sorrows* as his initial production—as well as original drama in Irish. The year 1936 saw thirteen productions and 1937 saw eighteen, assisted presumably by an increase in the government grant from £600 to £1,000. Dermody accepted the directorship of the Abbey School of Acting in October 1938, and in January 1939 Walter Macken returned from London as manager/play director. Under Macken's direction An Taibhdhearc staged ninety-seven productions, including seventy-six plays in 1939–47, and underwent renovation in 1944 resulting in improved dressing rooms, storage, and heating. Credited with consistently high-quality productions, Macken resigned on 17 December 1947, frustrated by the ongoing tensions between competing demands for original plays and translations.[84] After a Londoner, a Chicagoan, and a Galwegian, An Taibhdhearc finally turned the artistic keys over to Ian Priestly Mitchell, a Dubliner with little, if any, Irish. The 1950 staging of *San Siobhán* (a version of G. B. Shaw's *Saint Joan*) recaptured the hype and success of Mac Liammóir's inaugural *Diarmuid agus Gráinne*. It was translated by and starred Siobhán McKenna, who also co-directed it with Ian Priestly Mitchell. Mac Liammóir returned in 1953 to direct *Diarmuid agus Gráinne* to celebrate the theatre's twenty-fifth anniversary. A production of *An Triail* marked the fortieth anniversary, and Alan Simpson produced Behan's *An Giall* (The Hostage) in 1970 and the following year directed *Ag Fanacht le Godot* (Waiting for Godot).[85] The last production in the 'old' theatre was Mozart's *Così fan tutte*.[86] An Taibhsín, purchased in 1973 as a rehearsal space, was sold in 1977 to fund the building's permanent acquisition from the Augustinians, the theatre's former landlords. On St Patrick's Day 1978, President Patrick Hillery opened Críostóir Ó Floinn's *Cluichí Cleamhnais* (Engagement Games) in a refurbished theatre, minus the old balcony, with tiered seating for 200, new dressing rooms, and an enlarged foyer. October 1978 marked An Taibhdhearc's golden jubilee and the staging of a musical version of *Diarmuid agus Gráinne*.

Ó Floinn's *An Spailpín Fánach* (The Migrant Labourer), a bilingual account of Pádraic Ó Conaire's life, marked the sixtieth anniversary in 1988 and ushered in a reinvigoration

[84] Stafford, 'Taibhdhearc na Gaillimhe', 206.
[85] See Dick Byrne, 'Beckett as Gaeilge', *Irish Times*, 16 Apr. 2012.
[86] Other performances include Mozart's *Così Fan Tutti* (1977), Donizetti's *Lucia Di Lammermoor* (1980), Verdi's *La Traviata* (1984), and Verdi's *Macbeth* (1998).

of An Taibhdhearc's original aims: promotion of Irish-language drama and performance, diversity in programming, and a recommitment to Irish-language opera. The year 1990 commenced with *Seoda ón Opera* (Jewels from the Opera), a miscellany of operatic and musical items from previous shows including *Aida, La Traviata, The Merry Widow, The Mikado*, and *Madame Butterfly*. An Taibhdhearc returned to its roots in 1991 by appointing Huddersfield-born Trevor Ó Clochartaigh, who had co-founded Na Fánaithe in 1987. In 1994 'the show went on' despite an early morning blaze in the theatre during a week-long production of Synge's *Uaigneas an Ghleanna* (The Shadow of the Glen) and *Chun an Farraige Síos* (Riders to the Sea), translated by Tom Sailí Ó Flaithearta. Given the permanent tension between cultivating original work in Irish and staging European translations, it was apt that Seán Ó Tarpaigh selected Friel's *Aistriúcháin* (Translations) for his maiden production as artistic director in November 1995.[87]

In 1999, in addition to premièring Mac Mathúna's Civil War three-act *Hulla Hul* (Tally-ho), published as *Duilleoga Tae* in 2015, which explores events when a Free State soldier takes refuge in a Republican household, the board endorsed a new artistic policy that committed An Taibhdhearc to staging fewer productions but fully resourcing each production to a professional level. Darach Mac Con Iomaire's appointment on 11 September 2000 as artistic director led to several high-quality experimental productions. In 2002 An Taibhdhearc produced Macdara Ó Fátharta's adaptation of Máirtín Ó Cadhain's *Cré na Cille* (Graveyard Clay) and another version in 2006 directed by Mac Con Iomaire. A bitter breakdown in relations between the director and the board played out publicly in 2005. In November 2007 a fire caused serious structural damage, but during its extended closure An Taibhdhearc continued to stage plays, concerts, and events at various locations throughout the city—including the Black Box and Druid Lane. President Michael D. Higgins opened a refurbished 148-seat An Taibhdhearc on 28 September 2012. Successful collaboration with Joe Steve Ó Neachtain and Micheál Ó Conghaile resulted in extremely popular productions of *Níor Mhaith Linn do Thrioblóid* (Sorry for Your Trouble, 2000), *In Ainm an Athar* (In the Name of the Father, 2006), and *Faoi Dheireadh Thiar* (Eventually, 2008); all delved into social and cultural change in Ireland and proved that audiences in droves will attend certain types of play on certain conditions. Ó Conghaile's plays *Cúigear Chonamara* (2003), *Jude* (2007), and *Go dTaga do Ríocht* (2008) explore social issues in contemporary Connemara in stark and unrelenting fashion. As part of the 2014 Galway International Arts Festival, An Taibhdhearc collaborated with Moonfish on *Star of the Sea*, based on Joseph O'Connor's 2004 novel. Described as 'accessible to non-Irish speakers' and employing surtitles, it sold out for the entire run and earned positive reviews. Nor is Moonfish the only innovative company exploring new modalities in Irish theatre.

The stated artistic mission of Fíbín (Frenetic), based in Galway and established in 2003, is to promote the Irish language through an eclectic blend of music, puppetry, and masks. In an effort to transcend linguistic barriers and overcome attitudinal prejudices, it harnesses boundless energy and embraces puppets, masks, visuals, and music to bring stories to life. Such an approach to theatre in many ways recognizes the popularity of Irish-language pantomimes

[87] Friel rejected a bilingual production of *Translations*. See Christopher Murray, 'Palimpsest: Two Languages as One in Translations', in Donald E. Morse, Csilla Bertha, and Mária Kurdi (eds.), *Brian Friel's Dramatic Artistry:'The Work Has Value'* (Dublin: Carysfort Press, 2006), 103.

FIG. 16.1 Poster for Paul Mercier, *Sétanta*, produced by Fíbín (Abbey Theatre, 28 November 2011).

Courtesy of Fíbín.

from the 1940s to the 1960s and the successful use of masks by Na Fánaithe, an important and highly innovative Galway-based troupe prominent in the late 1980s and early 1990s. Fíbín came to national prominence in December 2011 with their acclaimed production of Paul Mercier's *Sétanta* at the Peacock. Typical of Fíbín's productions, *Sétanta* was innovative, exceedingly visual, and chock-full of masks and puppets, with five actors playing fifty characters.

In 2013 it marked its tenth birthday with *Stair na gCeilteach/History of the Celts*, a video-mapping performance and co-production with Improbable Films (Madrid). Their distinctive style is so 'unapologetically physical, that the question of language seems redundant; the language of the play is beautiful, but the fact that it is Irish rather than English is hardly

FIG. 16.2 Fíbín's *Stair na gCeilteach/History of the Celts*, co-produced with Improbable Films (13 and 14 September 2013), used video-mapping to project images in a quarry in Camus, Connemara.

Photo: Seán T. Ó Meallaigh. Courtesy of Fíbín.

worth commenting on.'[88] Emphasizing spectacle and theatrics, it arguably exemplifies Mac Liammóir's vision for An Taibhdhearc in 1928.

IRISH-LANGUAGE THEATRE IN BELFAST

Aisling Ghéar (A Bitter Vision), founded in 1997 in West Belfast, represents the most sustained, innovative, and progressive theatrical experiment in Irish in recent decades.[89] Pioneering in overcoming language barriers and expanding its audience through technology, Aisling Ghéar provides individual headsets and a simultaneous translation service from Irish into English for each performance. By design or not, there is a delicious irony in the fact that Aisling Ghéar's first performance on 2 February 1997, Pádraig Ó Snodaigh's full-length play *Leaba Dhiarmada* (Diarmuid's Bed) was a nod, if not a response, to Mac Liammoir's 1928 *Diarmuid agus Gráinne*, in which the disturbed ghosts of Diarmuid and Gráinne seek revenge on builders who desecrate their graves. Other full-length original works include Biddy Jenkinson's dark morality play *Ó Rajerum* (From Rajerum, 1999); Gearóid Ó Cairealláin's *In Ainm an Rí* (In the King's Name, 2000), in which a bored housewife escapes her daily drudgery by fantasizing about Elvis, and *Mise, Subhó agus Maccó* (Myself, Subhó and Sonny, 2000), Biddy Jenkinson's exploration of the Celtic Tiger's dark social underbelly.[90] In 2014 Aisling Ghéar produced Nuala Ní Neill's bilingual *The Fadgies*, a thirty-minute site-specific play, and *The Wheelchair Monologues*, a one-man show,

[88] Ruth Kennedy, 'Sétanta', *Irish Theatre Magazine*, 6 Dec. 2011.

[89] For earlier groups, see Lionárd Ó Coigligh, 'Drámaíocht Ghaeilge i mBéal Feirste', in *Fearsaid* (Béal Feirste: Cumann Gaelach na hIolscoile, 1956), 61–5.

[90] An Lab (The Lab), founded in Dingle, Kerry, in 2008, revived *Mise, Subhó agus Maccó* directed by Áine Moynihan, in 2014 and toured nationally. The death of John Corrie (1 Dec. 2014), a homeless

FIG. 16.3 Poster for Gearóid Ó Cairealláin's *The Wheelchair Monologues*, produced by Aisling Ghéar theatre company (7 March 2013).

Courtesy of Aisling Ghéar.

written/performed by Gearóid Ó Cairealláin (2014) detailing his life experiences before suffering a haemorrhagic stroke. Dave Duggan's multilingual sci-fi drama *Makaronik*, set in 2084, features two officials—Diarmuid and Gráinne—supervising Makaronik's ('Macaronic') linguistic archive, toured in November 2014.

CONCLUSION

Irish-language theatre entered the twenty-first century facing many of the same challenges and impediments as 100 years ago. Theatre remains a litmus test of Irish as a communal language and public art form. It highlights the aspirations of a bilingual society and pinpoints the contradiction between the dream and reality. That there is no sustained tradition of regular, seasonal Irish-language theatre in Dublin remains a function of cost, availability, and production. The fundamental problem is a mismatch between supply—a limited number of theatre companies—and demand—a fractured audience, scattered throughout the country, unaccustomed to attending semi/professional productions. Radio stations and

man, in the shadow of Leinster House underscored the play's social impact. See Áine Ní Éalaí, 'Mise Subhó agus Maccó', *Tuairisc*, 8 Dec. 2014.

TG4, the Irish language television channel, have successfully employed technology to unite a fragmented linguistic community, attract those of limited ability, and create a linguistic, if physically dispersed and diverse, audience. Recent trends—use of technology, individual headsets, instantaneous translation and surtitles—suggest theatre is learning and adapting for the twenty-first century rather than relying on pantomimes and translations of classic plays to expand audiences. Mouth on Fire's impressive project of staging Beckett's works in Irish aside, it falls on Aisteoirí Bulfin to carry the torch in Dublin, but there are considerable limits to what an amateur group can achieve.

An Taibhdhearc also faces many of the problems it confronted in the 1930s and 1940s: the need to procure new scripts and strike a balance between translations and original work; and secure funding to verify itself as the 'national theatre for the Irish language'—serving the entire Irish-speaking community throughout the island by undertaking nationwide tours like the Abbey in the 1990s and currently Aisling Ghéar, or targeted tours to include cultural festivals such as Oireachtas na Gaeilge like Aisteoirí Bulfin or Salamander. Closely associated with Darach Ó Scolaí, Salamander have toured his plays—*An tSeanbhróg* (The Old Shoe), a tragicomedy alternative narrative of Irish history; *An Braon Aníos* (The Drop Down), that depicts the farcical scene when the international search for Osama bin Laden comes to a globally warming Connemara, and *Coinneáil Orainn* (Keep on Going), where government inspectors hunt down the last Irish speaker—at festivals and events attended by Irish speakers.

Many issues plaguing theatre in Irish are perpetual: the lack of a dedicated space in Dublin, a diverse and dispersed audience, political and ideological disputes, the vexed role of translation, and the dearth of professional actors and professional trained directors. While the hindrances are many and the challenges great, the manner in which different individuals and groups respond to these perennial challenges sheds light on the evolving and ever-changing nature of Irish cultural life. The emergence of Aisling Ghéar in Belfast as well as the advent of creative and energetic troupes such as Na Fánaithe, Amharclann de híde, Salamander, and Fíbín speak to a subversive and creative energy that is neither simple nor symbolic but real and engaged. Its own history and its ongoing shared interaction with the English-language tradition shed new light on both traditions because, while written in Irish, a minority language, the compass of Irish-language drama is international. The purview of a minority within a minority, it nonetheless addresses issues of national and global significance. The Irish language may well serve as a symbolic marker and significant absence in plays such as Friel's *Translations*, Murphy's *Famine*, and Bolger's *In High Germany*, but Irish-language theatre is neither absent nor insignificant. Rather, it boasts a rich and distinguished history that interacts and intersects with the English-language tradition in unusual and surprising ways.

CHAPTER 17

....

WOMEN AND IRISH THEATRE BEFORE 1960

....

CATHY LEENEY

INTRODUCTION

WOMEN's contribution to Irish theatre continues often to be considered as a separate topic. Gender conservatism corrals women's creative energies away from the mainstream: as the title of this chapter indicates, women are in relationship ('and') to Irish theatre which is thus naturalized as men's, but recognizing women's work also needs to happen, whatever the context. The aim here is to explore necessarily selected aspects of what some women have achieved as writers, performance activists, and theatre-makers, and to suggest the value of that achievement in changing how the story of Irish theatre has been told: its periodization, its omissions, its values, issues of training and professionalism, and its national significance. Women's work points towards how gender limits are men's problem as well as women's, towards the deeper structures of cultural authority, the artistic requirements of the class whose interests control theatrical production, and the expectations of audiences.

There are two stages in the consideration of a separatist approach to women in theatre in Ireland. First, the potential gain and excitement at the recovery of what has been lost or undervalued; then (what has proved to be a more problematic stage) an integration of this recovery into canonical judgment, a disruption of the canon, and acknowledging how reassessment in gender terms has the potential to unbalance existing models of how Irish theatre has operated, has energized or stultified the fluid thing that is the nation— fluid in identity, gender, class, aspiration, and in willingness to confront the operations of power.[1]

---

[1] See Cathy Leeney, 'Introduction', in *Irish Women Playwrights 1900–1939: Gender and Violence on Stage* (New York: Peter Lang, 2010), 1–18; Melissa Sihra, 'Introduction: Figures at the Window', in *Women in Irish Drama: A Century of Authorship and Representation* (Basingstoke: Palgrave Macmillan, 2007), 1–22.

WOMEN, THEATRE, AND NATION

Women's early twentieth-century engagement with cultural and political nationalism, their creative output, and their access to the machinery of representation connects with their fight for rights as full citizens. This was swiftly followed by their subsequent exclusion from and betrayal by the foundling Free State. Their journey has been mapped by feminist historians as clashes arose between prioritizing suffrage over national freedom; Owens comments that 'most advocated [gender] equality, but believed it would follow automatically on political independence'.[2] Some saw clearly how Irish women were doubly disadvantaged under colonial rule; 'the first step on the road to freedom is to realize ourselves as Irishwomen—not only as Irish or merely as women, but as Irishwomen doubly enslaved, and with a double battle to fight,' wrote Constance Markievicz, somewhat eliding the difficulties of tackling both causes together.[3] Pressure was regularly put on women to prioritize the nation over their own pressing concerns as putative citizens, a tension that continues to be played out in present-day women's negotiation between engagement with feminist as opposed to other issues.

Women's sense of excitement and energy at the chance to act, to realize the ideal of national autonomy, is palpable in accounts of the early 1900s by Mary Colum, Margaret and James Cousins, Augusta Gregory, and Alice Milligan.[4] The atmosphere of vigour, aspiration, and shared purpose is very effectively captured in Mary Trotter's account of the theatre and cultural nationalism in the 1900s and 1910s.[5] The 'vivid' faces that Yeats met in the evening rush hour on Dublin streets, on their way from work to meetings, rehearsals, concerts, or tableaux and performances, belonged to women too; they saw an opportunity to participate in furthering ideals that had the potential to transform the public spheres of culture and politics, and that could empower them as citizens and as women. Whether women rejected the politics of violence in the form of recruitment into the British army or in relation to nationalist struggle through membership of armed rebel groups, either way they were subject to extreme condemnation; at the same time, martial women who were keen to fight alongside men to gain Irish independence were judged to be betraying their sex and were invited instead to be an image of the nation rather than an agent for national liberation. Stereotypes of the female fell into these two categories: the icon inspiring national sacrifice for nationhood, or the materialist wife/mother detesting violence and war, more concerned with the survival of the family. Historical examples include Constance Markievicz née Gore-Booth, whose armed participation in the rising of 1916, captured in striking photographs, still has the power to reveal the masculinist unease with Irish woman as warrior.[6]

---

[2] Rosemary Cullen Owens, *A Social History of Women in Ireland 1870–1970* (Dublin: Gill & Macmillan, 2005), 111. See also Margaret Ward, *In Their Own Voice: Women and Irish Nationalism* (Dublin: Attic Press, 2005).

[3] Quoted in Owens, *Social History*, 112.

[4] Augusta Gregory, *Our Irish Theatre*, 3rd edn. (Gerrards Cross: Colin Smythe, 1972); Catherine Morris, *Alice Milligan and the Irish Cultural Revival* (Dublin: Four Courts Press, 2012).

[5] Mary Trotter, *Modern Irish Theatre* (Cambridge: Polity Press, 2008), 5–60.

[6] Mary Caulfield, 'Fashion Advice: Constance Markievicz's "Unmarked", "Mismarked" and "Remarkable" Women', in Rhona Trench (ed.), *Staging Thought: Essays on Irish Theatre, Scholarship and Practice* (Bern: Peter Lang, 2009), 191–203.

New Historiography

As the discipline of theatre and performance studies develops in Ireland away from drama and towards theatre as collaborative practice, as a spatio-temporal event, and as a cultural activity in the public sphere, the key roles played by women and their important interventions into theatrical culture require acknowledgement. Research by feminist scholars has opened the field of Irish theatre and performance to gendered analysis, and in the process redefined the spaces and cultural purposes of performance, extending outside theatre buildings and into public spaces. Mary Trotter's reconception of Ireland's national theatre as a plural entity—national theatres—destabilizes canonical definitions of how, where, and to what effect performances take place.[7] Paige Reynolds has developed analysis of public events within a performance frame, revealing how women's performance creativity often found expression outside theatres, in public or community settings, involving deeply collaborative practices that undermine the individual-centred structure of patriarchal theatre histories.[8] These critical interventions have yet to fully realize their potential to reframe Irish theatre studies, to relocate originary moments.

Already Reynolds's and Trotter's analysis proposes 1900 as a key year, in place of 1904, when the Abbey Theatre was founded. Inghinidhe na hEireann (Daughters of Ireland) was founded in 1900, arising out of the organization by a group of women of a Children's Treat, which was a response to Queen Victoria's Treat which had taken place as part of her visit to the capital earlier that year. The alternative Treat was attended by 20,000, who were introduced in the process to a sense of pride in Ireland and to the idea of republicanism. The scale of the occasion far outstripped the number (5,000) that the English queen had attracted, and from this shared enterprise grew Inghinidhe na hEireann.[9] 1900 was also the year of the first performance of Alice Milligan's *The Last Feast of the Fianna*. That performance inspired W. B. Yeats to recognize that Irish theatre needed Irish performers in whose voices the true quality of Irish identity could be heard. Milligan's skill in arranging tableaux based on Irish history, music, and dance inspired Inghinidhe to adopt performances in mobile popular formats to entertain wider audiences through an engagement with Irish history, culture, and myth.[10] Inghinidhe na hEireann effectively invented performance as a site of political and ideological empowerment through tableaux vivants; their concerts and entertainments constitute one point of origin of the Irish theatre movement and its formative role in cultural nationalism.

---

[7] Mary Trotter, *Ireland's National Theaters* (Syracuse, NY: Syracuse University Press, 2001).

[8] Paige Reynolds, *Modernism, Drama and the Audience for Irish Spectacle* (Cambridge: Cambridge University Press, 2007).

[9] Trotter, *Ireland's National Theaters*, 83; Margaret Ward, *Unmanageable Revolutionaries* (Dingle: Brandon; London: Pluto, 1983), 48–9.

[10] Trotter, *Ireland's National Theaters*, 73–100; Joan Fitzpatrick Dean, *All Dressed Up: Modern Irish Historical Pageantry* (Syracuse, NY: Syracuse University Press, 2014).

PACIFISM AND NATIONALISM: ICON OR SUBJECT?

Markievicz's sister Eva Gore-Booth writes a pacifist and proto-feminist reimagining of Irish mythic tropes, dissolving them into an image of woman as defining ethical value; Gore-Booth's is an essentialist vision of the female as a source of and a resource for resistance to violence, with profound philosophical and moral implications. Augusta Gregory's *The Gaol Gate* (1906) and Gore-Booth's *The Buried Life of Deirdre* (1916/17) serve to contrast how performance in the theatre can be a site for the exploration of differing views of women's roles and potentials in times of violence.

In *The Gaol Gate* (1906) Gregory explores the binary trope of womanhood: icon or subject.[11] But Gregory's contribution began earlier with her co-authorship of *Cathleen Ni Houlihan* with W. B. Yeats (performed 1902). She was not fully recognized as co-author of the famous play for many decades. With Maud Gonne in the part of the Old Woman in its first staging, Yeats's belief that the play had inspired patriots to sacrifice their lives for Ireland distracts from its dual representation of women: Cathleen herself, the Old Woman, icon or symbolic figure, a classic sovereignty trope on the one hand; and the 'real' women Bridget Gillane (who loses her son) and Delia Cahel (who is abandoned by her husband-to-be) on the other. Both Bridget and Delia are silent and heart-broken at the play's end: '*Bridget takes Delia, who is crying silently, into her arms.*'[12]

The action of the play is the invasion of family domestic space where a dowried love match has been finally concluded; into the cottage kitchen comes an archetypal figure, an Old Woman as she is named in the text, who speaks the rhetorical language of heroic sacrifice for Ireland, for her 'four green fields' to be recovered for her from the hands of the 'strangers in the house'.[13] The house of Ireland then is positioned as at once metonymic of and in opposition to the house as family home. Finally, the son of the family goes with the Old Woman, his foreseen blood sacrifice renewing her, transforming her abject age into beautiful, youthful, queenly dignity. As the creator of much of the dialogue of the play (Yeats supplied the idea and action from a dream he had), Gregory chose the detail of how the real women and men are represented, extrapolating Bridget's point of view in particular through the dialogue with her husband, where she defends her contribution to the maintenance of the house and the continuity of the family and its future: 'If I brought no fortune I worked it out in my bones, laying down the baby Michael that is standing there now, on a stook of straw, while I dug the potatoes, and never asking big dresses or anything but to be working.'[14] The visceral immediacy of her description stresses her surrender of her physical self that parallels the surrender required by the Old Woman in the men she recruits. Bridget's husband, Peter, values her role: 'You are the best woman in Ireland [. . .]', yet in adding 'but money is good too'[15] he reasserts the market value of the bride-to-be. The patriarch is the one who handles the money and plans its positive impact on the household's future; it is through the roles of producer of children, unpaid worker, and bringer of

---

[11] *The Gaol Gate*, in Lady Gregory, *Selected Writings*, ed. Lucy McDiarmid and Maureen Waters (Harmondsworth: Penguin, 1995), 356–62.

[12] *Kathleen Ní Houlihan*, in Gregory, *Selected Writings*, 311.   [13] Ibid., 306.

[14] Ibid., 303.   [15] Ibid., 303.

dowry that Bridget and Delia dramatize the deeper emotional, physical, and social costs of nationalist ideology.

Viewed in relation to this analysis, Gregory's later play *The Gaol Gate* can be seen as both a prequel and a sequel to *Cathleen*, focusing intensely on the process whereby the Old Woman comes into being, for in the later work we meet Mary Cahel, mother of Denis Cahel, a rebel who has been arrested and detained in Galway Gaol. At her side is her daughter-in-law Mary Cushin (a matured development on Delia in the earlier play), wife of Denis and mother of their child.

The 'prequel' reading of the play suggests it is a dramatization of how women's experience of political rebellion left them with a choice between loss of their men (with all the profound disadvantages that involved in a patriarchal societal structure) and glorifying that loss as their sole means of active participation in the fight for independence. The figure of the Old Woman is somewhat awe-inspiring in *Cathleen Ni Houlihan*; her power is unchallenged and mysteriously beyond resistance; Michael's reaction to her is described in supernatural terms: 'he has the look of a man that has got the touch.'[16] In *The Gaol Gate* Gregory returns the audience to the process whereby the mythic Old Woman comes into being out of a specific situation of political resistance, how Irish women faced an irresolvable choice: between their care for their sons or husbands in proselytizing for their blood sacrifice, and their care for their sons or husbands in protecting the welfare of the family and of their dependents. Gregory's 1906 play puts the process on stage; no other Irish drama of the period achieves this analysis.

Based on a set of real events, the play 'fused Christian iconography with republican ideals', as McDiarmid and Waters have described it.[17] The critics are inaccurate, however, when they say that in the play 'the two Marys of Galway inscribe the death of the male victim with meaning: they will make great praise' for Denis Cahel.[18] On the contrary, Gregory's dramaturgical structure creates a variety of potential meanings in performance as the tragedy of Mary Cushin turns into the triumph of Mary Cahel. In recognizing both women's great speeches in the play, the first by Mary Cushin, and the second and final speech of the piece by Mary Cahel, Gregory marks the complex of attitudes and artistry in the tradition of *caoineadh* or keening, which was a public cultural discourse developed and practised by women. *Caoineadh* offered a space for women to grieve for their losses, but also a rare opportunity to speak their truths, to make complaint: 'Irish women poets could manipulate the themes and verbal formulas of the lament to construct and transmit a rhetoric of resistance to male domination in general.'[19] *Caoineadh* held this disruptive potential while it could also express the more official function of grief, forgiveness of past wrongs, and hagiographic recuperation. *Caoineadh* could set the record, the story of a single private life appropriated into history and myth. This is the action of Mary Cahel's lament. By placing it at the end of her play, Gregory recognizes the political power of such discourse and the difficulty of resistance to it which, arguably, is dramatized in Mary Cushin's silence. Mary Cushin's earlier *caoineadh*, in contrast, is one of complaint. At

---

[16] Ibid., 310.   [17] Ibid., xxxi.   [18] Ibid.

[19] Angela Bourke, 'More in Anger than in Sorrow: Irish Women's Lament Poetry', in Joan Newlon Radner (ed.), *Feminist Messages: Coding in Women's Folk Culture* (Urbana: University of Illinois Press, 1993), 163.

that point in the effectively controlled exposition, the women know that Denis is dead, but they fear that he died with the stain of traitorous informer on his name. Thus, Mary Cushin foresees her fate as a widow, heartbroken and disgraced, cast out from her community, without comfort or resources. Although she admits she would not begrudge his death were he to have died a hero, she quickly defends her bond with her husband regardless of what she then believes is his lost honour. Antigone-like, she wishes to carry out the respectful ritualized laying out of the body and the arrangement of his funeral. Her grief is for the loss of her life companion and for the material hardship and loneliness that will result for her diminished family. When the wife discovers that Denis was hanged, and thus was after all a hero and not an informer, she does not rejoice. Rather she curses those who took his life so violently, and those whom he saved by taking the blame while they were the real perpetrators.

Most crucially, Gregory poises the drama between the wife's pain, abject loss, and future precarity and the mother's salvaging of his death to transform it into ideological victory. At the end, the breaking dawn is a sign of rebirth and celebration for Mary Cahel, and a sign of painful loss for Mary Cushin, ironically illuminated: the machinery of theatrical representation splits between speech and image. The silence of Mary Cushin speaks through the stage picture. She says nothing and exits separately from Mary Cahel.

Their two paths map the binary of women's position in discourses of patriotism, national struggle, and achievement of independent statehood; nation was to be male-identified and women's rights were to bow to its priority. The cultural contests that arose throughout the 1920s and 1930s played out the subordination of women's personal lives to the life of the nation. The Constitution of 1937 demands their confinement in the (unpaid) domestic realm, and defines their role as covalent with maternity, although control over their fertility was withheld by legal means, through social discourses of sexual guilt, and by the illegal detention of women and girls on this basis. *The Gaol Gate* is a theatrically accomplished and highly nuanced staging of women's vexed relationship with postcolonial nationalism, when women were doubly othered, or, in postcolonial terms, were 'other of the ex-other', as Ailbhe Smyth succinctly describes it.[20]

NEW SUBJECTS IN THE OLD CULTURE

Radically different in her view of women's potential roles and aspirations, Eva Gore-Booth chose the unpopular path of pacifism. From the time she left Ireland in 1896 to live and work in Manchester, she abandoned her privileged 'big house' upbringing at Lissadell in Co. Sligo, but not its landscape or mythological vocabulary. Gore-Booth wrote poetry and poetic plays alongside her campaigning for labour and suffrage causes. When the mainstream English suffrage movement entered into a trade-off between promised votes for women in return for support for military recruitment in the First World War, and 1916 saw the involvement of her sister in the Easter Rising, Gore-Booth's thoroughgoing pacifism

[20] Ailbhe Smyth, 'The Floozie in the Jacuzzi', *Irish Review* 6 (1989), 10.

led her to complete *The Buried Life of Deirdre*, a work she had developed over a number of years, but which took over her imagination during the winter of 1916/17.[21]

Gore-Booth takes on the beautiful and doomed Deirdre, who had attracted W. B. Yeats (in 1907) and J. M. Synge (in 1908). The story is a triangular one of love, jealousy, and revenge arising from the King Conor's desire for Deirdre, who elopes with Naisi. In Gore-Booth's hands, however, Deirdre takes on an extraordinary, gender-fluid identity, occupying synchronic or suprahistorical time, named by Julia Kristeva 'monumental time' which is linked with matrix space, anterior and fluid.[22] As a result, Deirdre dominates the play. The impact is radical. Through reincarnation, Deirdre is no longer a fateful object of desire; rather, her desire shapes the play. In a previous life she has been an ancient king whose actions are at the root of the cycle of violent retribution in which Conor and Naisi are caught. Thus Deirdre expiates her own guilt and creates the possibility of breaking the cycle. As a Christ figure, the mythic queen chooses self-sacrifice and redeems the world. What results, in theatrical terms, is a unique structure, refusing entirely the teleology of tragic narrative and proposing in its place a ritual form that does not end in death but overcomes it through a spatial image of a passageway, 'very deep and very long',[23] that is death leading to reincarnated or renewed life.

Over the three acts of *The Buried Life of Deirdre* images of the natural world, of grass, trees, water, fire, sea, mist, and shifting spaciousness seem to suggest values of landscape staging and, most certainly, symbolist spaces in the style of Maurice Maeterlinck. Nature, Gore-Booth believed, belonged to women; she identified the man-made environment as just that, in a literal sense a sphere made by and for men, in metonymic relation to the lived values of power through hierarchy and violence: 'Men have got their pomp and pride—/All the green world is on our side.'[24]

The play presents such an unfamiliar model of the Deirdre myth, is so resistant to the punitive placing of the heroine, that it is at once deeply strange and also invigorating. The touches of humour, when Deirdre teases Naisi for his self-importance, fracture a dream quality arising from the refusal of conventional tragic narrative, which is displaced by a theatre of ritual suggestion, incantation, and trance. The aim patently connects with W. B. Yeats's ambitions as a dramatist, but in her essentialist focus on women as a source of agency and ethical impulse, Gore-Booth is forced to delve deeper dramaturgically, to undermine and reshape the dramatic structure involved in the originary tale of erotic love and chivalric loyalty that demands the tragic guilt and doom of the heroine.[25] *The Buried Life of Deirdre* sees the pathos of Naisi's offstage death, a sacrificial crisis that lies at the cusp of a momentous possibility: the triumph of Mannanan, the deity of 'freedom and the universality of loving'.[26]

[21] Eva Gore-Booth, *The Buried Life of Deirdre*, in *Plays*, ed. Frederick Lapisardi (San Francisco, CaA: EMText, 1991), 151–217.

[22] Julia Kristeva, 'Women's Time', in *The Kristeva Reader*, ed. Toril Moi (Oxford: Blackwell, 1986), 188–213.

[23] Gore-Booth, *Plays*, 197.

[24] Eva Gore-Booth, 'Women's Rights', in *Poems*, ed. Esther Roper (London: Longman Green, 1929), 409.

[25] Proinsias NacCana, 'Women in Irish Mythology', *Crane Bag* 4 (1980), 523.

[26] Eva Gore-Booth, 'Introduction' to *The Buried Life of Deirdre*, in *Plays*, 152.

The essentialist valuing of women's experience in Gore-Booth's writing— women's attitudes and values seen as different from and superior to men's—arguably overtakes separatism, since it involves a Neoplatonic transcendence of gender difference itself. Its core feminism, though, reflects what Rosi Braidotti defines as 'the critical and living experience of discovering new woman-based modalities of existence, creation and communication of knowledge'.[27]

The new historiography of Irish theatre from the woman's point of view is marked by an anti-progressive model where initial energy was gradually ground down by lack of opportunity, discouragement, and misogynist ideology. Those early decades of the twentieth century had their missed opportunities too, however—sites of denial that reveal the caution, the embedded egos, and the self-censorship of theatre practitioners and institutions. Pre-dating well-known examples such as the Abbey's rejection of Seán O'Casey's *The Silver Tassie* (1926) is the failure of that theatre to stage Augusta Gregory's *Grania*, a play begun by Gregory in 1910 and published in 1912.[28] Owing much to the naturalist/symbolic emotional drama of Strindberg and late Ibsen in its crypto-new woman figure, a Celtic queen in a gold dress, the play negotiates with the vulnerability of desire for a man in a patriarchal world, involving *jouissance*,[29] betrayal and loss, and finally the cost of deciding to re-enter a patriarchal social structure. It is as if Gregory follows Ibsen's Nora of *A Doll's House* as she slams the door and goes out into the world to become a human being, and tracks the ugly pragmatics of the heroine's exposure, survival, and punishing acknowledgement of a deep need for integration. Gregory's version follows the tale of Grania's promised marriage with Finn, which she abandons when she sees Diarmuid again, a young man she met years before. The couple spend seven years wandering in the wilderness but finally consummate their love. Finn tracks them down, disguised as a beggar. He taunts Diarmuid, making him jealous of the King of Foreign who has kissed Grania, and in tackling his rival Diarmuid is killed. After this point Gregory purposefully creates her own twist in the story.

Grania reveals the agon of woman as agent of her own destiny in a context where destiny is defined by men. Twenty-first-century critiques of feminism grapple with how women may achieve change from within the structure. Grania's fight to survive with her dignity intact, to come in from the wilderness, inside the walls of the patriarchy—a transition that demands all of her intelligence and steely rationality—is a journey that resonates with present-day women's experience. A triangular love relationship is at the centre of the play, and the twist that Gregory makes begins with Diarmuid's betrayal of Grania in death, as he erases her from his memory and sees only Finn. Finn cries out to Diarmuid: 'you are my son and my darling, and it is beyond the power of any woman to put us asunder.'[30] But here Gregory departs from the traditional versions of the tale, in which she is taken as a virtual slave by Finn. She refuses to be a victim and instead takes the action into her own hands and argues her way back into the narrative and into a space for herself. This is a remarkable moment in which she refuses to be crushed by the homosocial relationship between the two men, asking: 'why should I be always a widow that went so long a maid?'[31] Because of

---

[27] Rosi Braidotti, *Patterns of Dissonance* (London: Polity Press, 1991), 12.
[28] Gregory, *Selected Writings*, 383–421. Richard Allen Cave, 'Dangers and Difficulties of Dramatizing the Lives of Deirdre and Grania', in Jacqueline Genet and Richard Allen Cave (eds.), *Perspectives of Irish Drama and Theatre* (Gerrards Cross: Colin Smythe, 1991), 1–16.
[29] *Jouissance* is defined by Julia Kristeva as women's extreme joy or bliss, 'breaking the symbolic chain, the taboo, the mastery': *Kristeva Reader*, 154.
[30] Gregory, *Selected Writings*, 416.   [31] Ibid., 420.

the power of the relationship between the two men she is freed of her role as a sexual object and fills the space left by lost *jouissance* with a more pragmatic form of desire, for personal and public power, as a subject within the fold. Her exit is a reversal of Nora's; she re-enters society, courageously, but at a cost.

TRAINING AND PROFESSIONALISM

The Irish theatre movement developed largely out of amateur participation. With no producing repertory theatres where ambitious professionals could learn in a systematic way, directors, designers, and technical collaborators grew their skills through practice. Passionate enthusiasm and hard work for little monetary reward substituted for training through the commercial theatre or repertory system, in a context that specifically aimed to challenge the dominance of popular theatre seen as representing colonial values. There was, however, a hunger for expertise and training; three women exemplify how professionalism could positively impact on standards of production, and aesthetic awareness and achievement.

In the sphere of design, Tanya Moiseiwitsch arrived at the Abbey Theatre as a very young, relatively inexperienced designer. She had trained at London's Central School of Arts and Crafts, apprenticed for half a year at the Old Vic Theatre, and assisted Ruth Keating (designer) at the Westminster Theatre, where the director Hugh Hunt met her and invited her to travel with him to Dublin and undertake the Abbey Theatre adventure. She was hugely talented, flexible, and quickly found how to collaborate effectively with directors. The English repertory system had prepared her for a fast turnover of work, but not for the rigidly tradition-bound attitudes of the Abbey players towards settings and costumes, which they regarded as aspects of production that could be endlessly recycled. Her training in researching historical contexts and design styles raised the visual awareness of audiences and inevitably of other practitioners.[32] Several gifted women artists worked in theatre design, including Norah McGuinness, Dorothy Travers Smyth, and Anne Yeats, who succeeded Moiseiwitsch when she left the Abbey in 1938 to work with Tyrone Guthrie;[33] but Moiseiwitsch was perhaps the first professional stage designer to work in Irish theatre, and she opened the way for a succession of extraordinarily talented designers, women and men, who followed.

As an actress and a director, Ria Mooney took the opportunity, while in the US with an Abbey Theatre tour, to stay on in New York and work with Eva Le Gallienne at the Civic Repertory Theatre. Le Gallienne was a remarkable figure, originally English, an accomplished and highly successful actress, director, and producer who, in her disillusion with commercial theatre in the 1920s, founded the CRT in 1926, contributing significantly to the development of repertory theatre in the US. The company produced thirty-four plays

---

[32] Denis Behl, 'A Career in the Theatre', in T. J. Edelstein et al., *The Stage is All the World: The Theatrical Designs of Tanya Moiseiwitsch* (Chicago, IL: Smart Museum of Art, 1994), 38.

[33] Elaine Sisson, 'Experimentalism on the Irish Stage: Theatre and German Expressionism in the 1920s', in Linda King and Elaine Sisson (eds.), *Ireland, Design and Visual Culture, 1922–1992* (Cork: Cork University Press, 2011), 39–58.

until the depression of 1933 hit. Mooney would have seen and been involved with productions of a wide range of European and American works, as Le Gallienne's programming included classics of the European and world canon as well as American plays. As a director and actress back in Dublin (she had created the part of Rosie Redmond in the 1926 Abbey production of O'Casey's *The Plough and the Stars*), Mooney was assured enough to direct at the Abbey from 1936, and she ran the Abbey School of Acting—where she was a demanding teacher—while she sustained a professional career and a remarkable level of productivity as actress and director through the 1930s and up to 1963. In the midst of all this she also established the Gaiety School of Acting in 1944. From 1948 she was director in residence at the Abbey—effectively artistic director, although Ernest Blythe had to be reckoned with.[34] She dealt with the company's move to the Queen's Theatre as a result of the Abbey fire in 1951. Mooney's work was associated with the playwright Teresa Deevy at a number of levels. In 1935, when Deevy was fast establishing herself as an Abbey playwright, Ria Mooney played Annie Kinsella in *The King of Spain's Daughter*. Later, under her artistic directorship of the Peacock Theatre, and in spite of Ernest Blythe's constraining presence, Mooney made possible the staging of Deevy's *Light Falling* in 1948, and she directed revivals of *Katie Roche* in 1949 and 1954. This was in the face of Blythe's rejection of Deevy's *Wife to James Whelan* in 1942, when he made it clear to the author that further work from her would not be welcomed at the Abbey. Mooney balanced her work between theatres and companies, the Abbey, the Gate, and other Dublin companies. She appeared in her own adaptation of *Wuthering Heights*, for example, at the Gate Theatre in 1934 and in 1935.

The difficulties that faced Ria Mooney in the Ireland of the time and the Irish theatre of the time were very considerable. She was single, earned her living through the theatre, and had to choose her battles in a world where women, and especially single women, were excluded from men's power networks. Through years of unrelenting pressure of work for the Abbey at the Queen's Theatre, she still found spaces in which to resist the masculinist prejudices of many of her colleagues.

The apotheosis of discipline and training in performance is most associated with dance. In the development of dance in Ireland, Ninette de Valois had a profound influence; it was through her association with the Plays for Dancers of W. B. Yeats that she began her work at the Abbey Theatre. De Valois was born Edris Stannis and came from Co. Wicklow. Her family moved to England while she was still a child; she attended classes with Edouard Espinosa and studied with Enrico Cecchetti, joining the Léonide Massine–Lydia Lopokova Company to tour for over ten years in a wide range of productions. In 1923 she was accepted into the Ballets Russes and became a soloist in 1925. Returning to England to found her own Academy of Choreographic Arts in London, she worked with Terence Gray at the Cambridge Festival Theatre. Gray experimented with abstract performance spaces and searched for a performance style that would work within those spaces, and de Valois developed abstract expressionist choreography connecting diverse classical and innovative elements. At Cambridge she met Yeats; it was an epiphany for the poet-dramatist, who asked her to establish a School of Ballet at the Abbey. From 1927 to 1934 de Valois choreographed, and often performed in, fourteen dance programmes at the Abbey (and sometimes elsewhere) as well as creating choreographies for four of Yeats's plays. *Fighting the Waves* in

34 www.abbeytheatre.ie/archives. Accessed 3 Sept. 2014.

1929 featured de Valois as Fand, a temptress come from the Country Under Wave to seduce Cuchulain from his mortal life. De Valois's performance was striking, and drew delighted reviews from critics.[35] She went on to appear in *At the Hawk's Well, The Dreaming of the Bones,* and lastly, in *The King of the Great Clock Tower* in 1934, her final appearance at the Abbey. Through de Valois, Yeats saw his Plays for Dancers staged somewhat as he had imagined them. With *Fighting the Waves,* despite mixed responses, he declared it 'my greatest success' and de Valois's contribution to be 'extraordinarily exciting'.[36] The poet's gift for choosing collaborators was once again confirmed in de Valois, but this went far beyond her role in bringing plays for dancers to performance life for audiences. De Valois, temporarily, changed the terms upon which the potential of theatre performance was assessed outside of realism, producing visible physical virtuosity and expressivity of a standard equal to the great stages of Europe.

De Valois's Abbey School of Ballet, as Victoria O'Brien writes, 'trained and produced an influential generation of Irish dancers, choreographers, teachers and artistic directors'.[37] De Valois's work as a choreographer and as a dancer set a level of both professional accomplishment and potential that had not been seen in the theatrical renaissance until then. Her commitments in London after 1933, at the Old Vic Theatre, Sadler's Wells, and in her development of the Royal Ballet Company, as she 'went on to transform dance in the twentieth century',[38] meant a huge loss for Irish theatre and for Yeats; but she inspired those she trained, many of whom maintained a ballet and dance culture over generations in Ireland, where the great touring companies of Diaghilev, Nijinsky, Massine, or Balanchine were never seen.

ACTS OF RESISTANCE: FACING THE 1930S AND 1940S

At the end of the 1920s and into the 1930s, Irish women were increasingly subject to retrogressive legislation that restricted their access to civil rights as equal citizens.[39] Recognition of abuses was suppressed in favour of the maintenance of a false image of the Saorstát or Free State.[40] In the theatre, women's resistance to growing conservatism was visible in playwrights' work, and in how theatrical institutions tried to censor or control representations made by women, either through the production process or by the simpler method of not staging the plays in the first place.

Margaret O'Leary's *The Woman* was produced in 1929 at the Abbey Theatre; Lisa Fitzpatrick has traced how the play was produced and performed, with Yeats insisting that 'the heroine must die' at the end of the play. O'Leary did change the final scene, as

---

[35] Richard Allen Cave, *Collaborations: Ninette de Valois and William Butler Yeats* (Alton: Dance Books, 2011), 47–70; W. B. Yeats to Olivia Shakespear, 24 Aug. [1929], in W. B. Yeats, *Letters,* ed. Alan Wade (London: Rupert Hart-Davis, 1954), 767–8.

[36] Yeats's letter to Shakespear, quoted in Cave, *Collaborations,* 68–70.

[37] Victoria O'Brien, *A History of Irish Ballet from 1927 to 1963* (Bern: Peter Lang, 2011), 7.

[38] Ibid., 37–8.   [39] Owens, *Social History,* 251–79.   [40] Ibid., 260–1.

Fitzpatrick points out, to imply strongly that Ellen plans to kill herself, but drew the line at staging her death, and effectively refused the finality of Yeats's opinion.[41]

Dorothy Macardle submitted *Witch's Brew* to the Abbey in 1929. She already had a track record of production at the theatre, but *Witch's Brew* was rejected. The text was published in 1931 and reveals the spiritual–supernatural element that is characteristic of much of Macardle's fiction and several of her plays. Given her active political allegiance with republicanism and the way, in *Ann Kavanagh* (1922) and *The Old Man* (1925), she used the stage to problematize political–historical violence, *Witch's Brew* stands out, as it distances itself from realist contexts and adopts a symbolic style that distances the audience. Since the play very clearly concerns the patriarchal power of church and state (the latter here allegorized in the family structure) to alienate women to the point of their withdrawal from life itself, Macardle coded her critique, but perhaps not ambiguously or subtly enough.

The action opens in an archaic setting: the claustrophobic space of a primitive cabin, decked with animal skins and earthen vessels. A terrifying storm rages outside, while Una lies at the edge of death, victim of an unspecified illness. Her mother-in-law, Aine, and sister-in-law Nessa attend her, and await the return of Una's husband who has gone in search of the monk Kieran. Despairing of the husband, Aine switches her reliance to 'the old Gods' in the shape of Blanid, who enters *'out of the darkness, her black hair streaming, rags wet and dishevelled [. . .] as though blown by the wind'*[42]. Visually and theatrically Blanid and the potion of blood and milk that she prepares onstage, which turns the space red and which writhes like serpents, is potentially visually exciting for an audience, and creates an expectation of transformation for Una, who has been characterized by the 'drive of forgetfulness and death' that Julia Kristeva calls the 'semiotic'.[43] Una's revival on taking the potion is alarmingly violent and disruptive, angry, and full of blood lust.[44] It is not until Kieran's entrance and his parallel blood sacrifice (which is however limited to cutting a finger) that symbolic order is reasserted, and blood retrieved from its female and pagan associations and reappropriated as a Christian symbol of redemption. The monk and the husband, church and state, close in on Una once again, and Una reverts to her longing for death. Macardle presents a killing entrapment for her; her obliteration as a subject is ensured as she sinks back into deathly unconsciousness while the circle of authority embraces her once more.

Mary Manning was Dorothy Macardle's pupil at Alexandra College in Dublin in the 1920s, and the younger woman, in her plays of the 1930s for the Gate Theatre, took up an exploration of gendered struggle for self-determination and expression in the face of a deeply conservative and restrictive era. Manning's characters were the young adults of the middle class inner suburbs of the city; they were mostly non-Catholic, somewhat privileged, and their horizons stretched to London and mainland Europe, and to neocolonial opportunity in the then British Empire. Manning's wit and precocious talent in conceiving theatrical structures and sparkling dialogue led quickly to her first success, *Youth's the Season?* in 1931, at the Gate Theatre. It was received with enthusiastic praise by the Gate

[41] Lisa Fitzpatrick, 'Taking Their Own Road', in Sihra, *Women in Irish Drama*, 69–86.
[42] Dorothy Macardle, *Witch's Brew: A Drama in One Act* (London: H. F. W. Deane, 1931), 6, 9.
[43] Julia Kristeva, 'Modern Theater Does Not Take (a) Place', *Sub-Stance* 18/19 (1977), 132.
[44] Macardle, *Witch's Brew*, 17.

audience, and several plays followed at the venue. Manning's theatrical style brought together the social comedy forms of Wilde and Noel Coward with expressionist elements in staging, including non-naturalistic lighting changes and uses of space, patterning of action, language and silence, and the invasion of the scenic space by an off-stage sonic world. These strategies work to draw attention to a reflexive presentation of character as performative, and gender is at the heart of the performance: masculinities and femininities dance around each other in a choreography of forced conformity with he-man/she-woman binaries, and thinly coded nonconformity. As the category gender multiplies into queerness, so categories of national and class identity are satirized, fracture, and fall apart. Manning does not avoid the requirement of the theatre of the period: that this resistance to compulsory heterosexual (and national) norms must be punished. The darkly violent ending of *Youth's the Season?* does not, however, reinstate conventional values, but demolishes the play itself in an image of panic and chaos.

The construction of a cultural life in the new state was promoted across the decades of the twentieth century in theatre by figures from Augusta Gregory to de Valois, Ria Mooney, and Phyllis Ryan (whose Gemini Productions was a key factor in the development of the independent theatre sector in playing contemporary international works), while Carolyn Swift, co-founder of the Pike Theatre, created one of the vital 'little theatre' sites for new and experimental work in 1950s Dublin, working in the tradition of Daisy Bannard Cogley before her.[45] In Belfast, Mary O'Malley took on the challenge of developing a theatre of non-realist poetic performance with W. B. Yeats's drama at the core. Her initiative in 1951 grew into the Lyric Theatre.[46]

Three playwrights wrote to explore how Irish society dealt with those unfortunate enough not to fit into the narrow spaces shaped by fearful and disabling conservatism: Teresa Deevy, Maura Laverty, and Máiréad Ní Ghráda (whose work is discussed elsewhere in this volume).[47] From the 1930s to the late 1950s their plays raised difficult questions around family failure, violent control of sexual energies, state interference in personal lives, sexual hypocrisy, and the double standard. All three writers deliberately set out to confront audiences with those struggling for social, personal, or economic power, whether through the circumstances of their birth or their failure to submit to social control. Expressionism plays a significant part in the work of all three. Deevy's ability to conceive characters who are bursting with creative and emotional energies, who are crazily ambitious, naive, and unwilling to accept defeat, marks out her work as an important exploration of the contortions that result from lack of opportunity, prejudice, violence, and fear of women, while it is also a theatrical chronicle of wasted potential. Deevy's female anti-heroines (Ellie Irwin, Annie Kinsella, Katie Roche) are not mere victims; they are determined to grab hold of life, proud, infuriating, wilful, and twisted into incoherence

[45] Madame Bannard Cogley, also known as Toto, was Helen Carter, a soprano, a cabaret and theatre producer at the Little Theatre and later at her Studio Theatre Club, and a member of the Gate Theatre Board. See Nicholas Allen, *Modernism, Ireland and Civil War* (Cambridge: Cambridge University Press, 2009), 57.

[46] Mary O'Malley, *Never Shake Hands with the Devil* (Dublin: Elo, 1990).

[47] For analysis of 1940s work by Elizabeth Connor at the Abbey Theatre, see Ian R. Walsh, *Experimental Irish Theatre: After W. B. Yeats* (Basingstoke: Palgrave Macmillan, 2012), 74–94. For a discussion of Ní Ghráda's *An Triall*, see Ch. 16.

by the weight of disregard for their personhood, and by their extreme isolation in a society where they search in vain for an image of heroism or greatness within their reach. These are young women doubly alienated, caught in contradiction 'between the conscious self, which is conscious in so far as it is able to feature in discourse, and the self which is only partially represented there—which constitutes the source of possible change', as Catherine Belsey points out.[48] And it is the crisis of change that stalls the forward movement of both Ellie in *A Disciple*, also titled *In Search of Valour* (1931),[49] and Katie in *Katie Roche* (1936).[50]

Deevy's work through the late 1920s, 1930s, and 1940s spans media (theatre, radio, and television) and a range of theatrical styles. Two central figures, whose inner states ramify through two plays and through the wider social and ideological contexts of the action, serve as an introduction to the wider work. Both are motherless, convent-reared, 'illegitimate', both are domestic servants, poor, without prospects, alone. Ellie Irwin and Katie Roche exemplify the brutal social control of girls and young women in the young Irish state. Their containment speaks of the politics of the personal, of ambition, desire and its thwarting.

Ellie Irwin is named in homage to Shaw's Ellie in *Heartbreak House*, which formatively impressed Deevy when she saw it staged in London around 1920. The Shavian Ellie is ambivalently pragmatic, romantic, ruthless, and amoral, so that, lacking the full-length form that allows Shaw's anti-heroine to develop this whirligig of aspects, Deevy's reincarnation may be said to flash through this complex of states with giddying drive. The clearly expressionist style in *A Disciple* makes possible a more complex reading of the instability of *Katie Roche*, challenging the view of the play as a 'grand little piece of typical Abbey domestic naturalism'.[51] Rather, Katie herself is a dissonant element in a theatrical form that struggles to contain her and her drama.

Stage directions in *A Disciple* specify Ellie Irwin's space as '*tumbledown . . . slanting and uneven*',[52] and it works both as externalizing her internal state of mind and as analogous to the state of the nation in Ellie's terms. The dialogue weighs in to support the strong sense of psycho-emotional crisis and extremity in the representation of the stage space; a heavy zinc door repeatedly slams shut from off-stage, defining the room as a prison, while images of worms and of the subterranean add to the declamatory and staccato dialogue to make the space at once tortured and grave-like.

Deevy's writerly awareness of Synge is distilled in the latter part of Ellie's search for a hero. Since she has already internalized the idea that she can never be heroic herself, she looks to Jack the Scalp, a comically deromanticized Christy Mahon figure, to be her vicarious hero. However, Deevy pointedly departs from *The Playboy* narrative—Pegeen's betrayal of her lover through social cowardice; in *A Disciple* it is Ellie who challenges Jack to defy convention, terrifying him with her determination to be his partner in more than lawlessness; he protests, 'I'm willing to shoot whoever you'd like but ... I'm a respectable man.'[53]

---

[48] Catherine Belsey, *Critical Practice* (London: Routledge, 1980), 85.

[49] Teresa Deevy, *A Disciple*, or *In Search of Valour*, *Dublin Magazine* 12 (1937), 29–47.

[50] Teresa Deevy, *Katie Roche*, in *Teresa Deevy Reclaimed*, vol. 1, ed. Jonathan Bank, John P. Harrington, and Christopher Morash (New York: Mint Theater Company, 2011), 57–102.

[51] Fintan O'Toole, 'Second Opinion: What Katie Doesn't Do', *Irish Times*, 26 Apr. 1994.

[52] Deevy, *A Disciple*, 29.   [53] Ibid., 47.

Ellie's alienation from social norms, through her origins and her dissatisfaction with the demeaning roles society lays before her, is far more directly communicated than Katie Roche's parallel milieu. What is gained in *Katie Roche* is the sense of Katie's entitlement to aspiration that is beyond laughter or the grotesque. Katie Roche is a thwarted subject, as trapped as Ellie, but sufficiently knowing to try to play the patriarchy at its own game. Ellie Irwin twists Synge's *Playboy* ending, shaping it into fury, contrary to Pegeen's heart-rending acknowledgement of deep loss. Ellie cannot stand outside the system of power that circulates around her; rather she is part of what Foucault calls the 'carceral continuum', in which inside and outside collapse into one another.[54] Deevy's expressionist style mirrors exactly the psychological thematic of the play: the impossibility of maintaining self independently of social forces.

Katie Roche is the only play of Deevy's that has been repeatedly revived at the Abbey Theatre.[55] As the third in a series of plays (including *The King of Spain's Daughter* in 1935) featuring young powerhouse women, its intensity combined with its patterns of interference, miscommunication, misalliance, and failed connection show how, from the late 1920s to the late 1930s, Deevy dramatizes a progressive silencing of personal discourses of resistance as those unshielded by privilege are overwhelmed by and unable to escape from punishing systems of control. Like Foucault's convict in his history of prison systems, Katie pays for her 'crime' of illegitimacy and desire: 'by the labour [s]he provides [Katie is an unpaid domestic servant] and by the signs she produces.'[56] Image defines what dialogue stops short of; Katie is the on-stage sign of one captured by oblique and normalized patriarchal and class control.

Marriage—a defining ritualized transformation—is, ironically, the nexus of stasis in the play. Katie marries Stan, an architect who is old enough to be her father and who was in love with Katie's mother, but the transformation is botched and re-botched through the rest of the play until Stan demands Katie's removal from all that she has ever known. They will travel away together to make a new life, and her attempt to meet this as an opportunity ('I was looking for something great to do—sure now I have it') looks like a desperate performance of optimism in the light of her wisdom minutes earlier when she reflects, 'I don't think we can start afresh. [. . .] Won't we bring ourselves with us?'[57]

The play denies the romantic notion of individual triumph over circumstance. Instead it enacts the inner vacillations of Stan, Katie, and her young admirer Michael, their convictions and passions reduced to momentary outbursts interrupted by withdrawal, doubt, and quiet desolation. The patterned flow of exits, entrances, silences, impotent protests, and disarming uncertainty externalizes the emotional landscape of both the characters and the society they endure. The setting in the living room of a small cottage in a village reads in realist terms in the script, but operates as an image of the domesticated carceral space seen in *A Disciple*. The front door of the cottage opens directly into this room, a choice that

---

[54] Michel Foucault, *Discipline and Punish: The Birth of the Prison*, trans. Alan Sheridan (London: Penguin, 1991), 299.

[55] *Katie Roche* premièred in 1936, touring to London, Cambridge, and New York in 1938; it was revived by the Abbey Theatre under the direction of Ria Mooney in 1949 and 1954 at the Queen's Theatre, returning to the Abbey stage (Joe Dowling directing) in 1975 and to the Peacock Theatre in 1994 (directed by Judy Friel).

[56] Foucault, *Discipline and Punish*, 109.   [57] Deevy, *Teresa Deevy Reclaimed*, vol. 1, 102, 101.

allows Deevy to explore the liminal zone of the doorway and its effectiveness in leading to change. The space outside, at times, operates as a sphere of freedom and movement, but this is never how it is for Katie.[58] She stands on the threshold and can glimpse possibility, but through her own or others' responses, the sense of potential turns to dust.

An image of surprising directness in Act II realizes in action the oppression of Katie by violence that is otherwise occluded. Already in Act I Katie has invited 'Holy Reuben', a local vagrant and spiritual adviser, into the cottage and heard from him about the circumstances of her origins; he tells her that her father was already married with a family, her mother a beauty: 'the strength of passion: it swept them both.'[59] But on his return in Act II, Reuben assaults Katie violently, beating her across her shoulders with his stick. He then announces to her that he is her father. It is impossible to read Reuben as a father merely in the sense of a realist dramatic exposé; his status as an archetypal figure in the action is further strengthened in Act III when he inveighs against Katie, threatening that humiliation is what she needs.[60] In a telling triangular scene Katie is between Stan and Reuben, patriarchal allies, but refuses to be a victim. Rather she puts (as she says) her strength against both men. *Katie Roche* strains realist conventions to reach beyond the individual concerns of characters and dramatize the structures that have trapped them and their internalization of those forces.

Katie Roche is a feminist play in nascent form. Katie is no facile female ideal; she is vigorous, aspirational, and proud.[61] She counters oppression with a will to power of her own. But we see Stan and Michael suffer too as a result of the stifling social mores of class and sexual hypocrisy. Stan is almost as trapped as Katie, unwise certainly, prone to withdrawal as a solution, but also struggling to break his own silence, to change. Through Katie's crises and desires, the play extrapolates those of Stan and Michael and those of society. The stylistic instability of the piece, between realism and expressionism, opened up here by reference back to *A Disciple*, signals a different kind of subject at the play's centre: a Stanislavskian nightmare of confused motivations and objectives, taut with the crises of fractured consciousness that expressionism exposes.

Expressionism emerges as an important source of stylistic vocabulary through which to express the crisis of power and identity in early twentieth-century Irish theatre. Its significance in the work of Manning and Deevy, remodelling the precedents of German expressionists and of Denis Johnston, allowed them to express the uneasy traffic between inner consciousness and outer social pressure. Later, in the 1940s, 1950s, and early 1960s, the work of Maura Laverty at the Gate was effectively staged by Hilton Edwards in fluid expressionist stagings. Laverty's novels had been consistently subjected to censorship in Ireland, and Micheál Mac Liammóir and Edwards invited Laverty to dramatize *Lift Up Your Gates* (1946), which was the third of her novels to be banned. It became *Liffey Lane*, and its success, along with later work by Laverty, sustained the continuation of the Gate Theatre.[62] The fight of Chrissie Doyle to stop her 4-year-old brother from being placed in an orphanage is

[58] Anthony Roche, 'Woman on the Threshold: J. M. Synge's *The Shadow of the Glen*, Teresa Deevy's *Katie Roche*, and Marina Carr's *The Mai*', *Irish University Review* 25 (1995), 150–7.

[59] Deevy, *Teresa Deevy Reclaimed*, vol. 1, 63.   [60] Ibid., 98.

[61] See Sue-Ellen Case's exploration of definitions of feminist theatre in *Feminism and Theatre* (Basingstoke: Palgrave Macmillan, 2008), 112–32.

[62] Christopher Fitz-Simon, *The Boys: A Biography of Micheál Mac Liammóir and Hilton Edwards* (Dublin: Gill & Macmillan, 1994), 169–76.

at the centre of the action. The play's inherent critique of policies that victimized the poor for their poverty was effectively staged in (for Dublin) innovative theatrical fashion. For the time being, theatre was dodging the tight censorship to which literature was victim; but Laverty's plays have yet to be recognized as important.

CONCLUSION

The cultural and social value of Irish theatre is enhanced through the inclusion of women playwrights' work, clarifying our understanding of the gendering of national ideologies, the operations of power in society, how the theatre has reflected, exposed, and critiqued the intersections of public life and private lives over the twentieth century, and questioned the assumed values of social order and privilege. Women's enthusiasm for the ideal of national independence meant that they were actively determined to make theatrical interventions as part of a utopian belief that political change would be accompanied by changes in their civic and legal status. Many of the key figures in this chapter are associated with the period between 1900 and 1940, and from the late 1930s onwards women's work faced greater censoring challenges as their ambitions were stymied by gendered postcolonial mimicry of exclusion and oppression that arose from patriarchal national insecurity and lack of daring. The energy of 1950s economic changes that revived aspects of national political life did not affect attitudes to women in Ireland. Women's cultural participation was marginalized until they took matters into their own hands in the 1960s and 1970s; but it took even longer for the theatre to begin to reflect the changes in women's social status. How women survived as citizens of lower status is important in our understanding of this later period, in the mid-twentieth century. The so-called second renaissance in Irish theatre is significantly limited to men's work. When women began to make inroads into the fenced-off civil and social rights that held them in check, the drama of their struggle—probably the profoundest change in Irish society that has taken place in that period—has not been recognized; it must be sought out, acknowledged, and understood.

CHAPTER 18

THE LITTLE THEATRES OF THE 1950S

LIONEL PILKINGTON

HISTORIOGRAPHY

'SHORT-LIVED ventures in make-shift theatres' is Michael Sheehy's fleeting reference to Ireland's little theatres in the 1950s. Published in 1968, Sheehy's *Is Ireland Dying?* argues that the dearth of theatrical activity in Dublin in the previous decade provides yet another instance of the debilitating effect of the Irish government's failure to support or develop a properly representative national culture. In addition to what he takes as the self-evident failure of the Abbey under Ernest Blythe ('a costly piece of hypocrisy, no longer tolerable to a Government with any liberal or realist pretensions')[1] and 'the collapse' of the Gate Theatre, Sheehy remarks: 'the Irish theatre fell on hard times, and had to depend on short-lived ventures in make-shift theatres as in the Gas Company in Dun Laoghaire, or the Eblana in the basement of the central bus depot.'[2] Variations on this view are widely held, and contribute to a more general characterization of the period as culturally arid and bleakly authoritarian. In the words of novelist John Banville, this was a time in which Ireland appeared as 'monolithic, impregnable, eternal' and as a 'demilitarised totalitarian state' marked by an 'intellectual isolationism'.[3] In general, cultural commentators have become used to the idea of 1950s Ireland as 'a lost decade' and as existing in negative contrast to what is seen as the long-awaited and belated programme of economic modernization heralded by Seán Lemass and T. K. Whitaker in the late 1950s. That theatre history hails the 1960s for its resurgence of Irish dramatic writing—most notably, the production of plays by Brian Friel,

---

[1] Michael Sheehy, *Is Ireland Dying? Culture and the Church in Modern Ireland* (London: Hollis & Carter, 1968), 148.

[2] Ibid., 147.

[3] John Banville, 'Memory and Forgetting: the Ireland of de Valera and Ó Faoláin', in Dermot Keogh, Finbarr O'Shea, and Carmel Quinlan (eds.), *Ireland in the 1950s: the Lost Decade* (Cork: Mercier Press, 2004), 26.

J. B. Keane, Thomas Kilroy, and Tom Murphy—renders all the more compelling this view of the 1950s as culturally deprived.[4]

And yet the experience of many who participated in various forms of theatrical activity in the 1950s offers an entirely different impression. Actor and director Dan Donovan (formerly of Compántas Chorcaí and Cork's Everyman Theatre) remarks in interview, 'the only possibilities we entertained [in the 1950s] were that things would get better',[5] and activist and writer Margaretta D'Arcy describes working with the 37 Theatre Club in the early 1950s as taking part in a whole new movement that was like 'a regular Phoenix Ascending'.[6] 'I know the fifties officially were dull and terrible,' comments the critic John Devitt: '[E]migration was high and all that. But things were happening then—the town was alive with talk.'[7] Repeatedly, then, and in a manner that confirms Michael G. Cronin's recent assessment of the period as one of 'epistemic change',[8] the reminiscences of many who lived through this period recall a scenario of optimistic political possibilities and of a rambunctiously exciting social and cultural life that centred on a dynamic and multifarious theatrical activity.

Information about Ireland's little theatres, however, is sporadically available. While in some cases, such as the Pike Theatre Club, the Lyric Players' Theatre, and the Lantern Theatre Club, there exist considerable well-catalogued archival collections, for many other similar initiatives such as the 37 Theatre Club, Globe Theatre Company, 66 Theatre Club, Gemini Productions, and the Pocket Theatre, there is a striking paucity of publicly accessible archival resources. Accordingly, research for this chapter is indebted to the generous assistance of a variety of individuals: Mary Clark, Margaretta D'Arcy, Christopher Fitz-Simon, Maureen Frawley, Oona Frawley, Kieran Hoare, Barry Houlihan, Aidan Kane, Marie Kennedy, Felix Meehan, Michael O'Brien, and Bob Quinn.

VENUES AND INFLUENCES

Whereas in Paris, what was referred to as *théâtres de poche* (pocket theatres) could sometimes accommodate audiences of up to 300,[9] Ireland's little theatres tended to have a much smaller seating capacity, ranging on average from forty to sixty. The most common type of location was the city-centre basement, close to a public house (or several) and inexpensive to rent. 'At one stage,' remarks John Devitt, 'I don't think that you could have delivered coal in the [Dublin] city centre without burying an amateur company.'[10] Walking along Baggot

---

[4] For an alternative view, however, see Brian Fallon, *An Age of Innocence: Irish Culture 1930–1960* (Dublin: Gill & Macmillan, 1998), 262–7.

[5] Quoted in Vera Ryan, *Dan Donovan: An Everyman's Life* (Cork: Collins Press, 2008), 88.

[6] Margaretta D'Arcy, *Loose Theatre: Memoirs of a Guerrilla Theatre Activist* (Victoria, BC: Trafford, 2005), 168.

[7] John Devitt, with Nicholas Grene and Chris Morash (eds.), *Shifting Scenes: Irish Theatre-Going, 1955–1985* (Dublin: Carysfort Press, 2008), 33.

[8] Michael G. Cronin, *Impure Thoughts: Sexuality, Catholicism and Literature in Twentieth-Century Ireland* (Manchester: Manchester University Press, 2012), 116.

[9] See Jean-Yves Guérin, *Le Théâtre en France de 1914 à 1950* (Paris: Honoré Champion, 2007), 337.

[10] Devitt, *Shifting Scenes*, 50.

Street in the early 1950s, Margaretta D'Arcy describes her sense of excitement when she first came across the basement premises of 37 Theatre Club:

> One basement was different; it pulled the passer-by up sharply. A black-curtained window, an enigmatic black door, a discreet sign on the open gate: 37 Theatre Club. How many others were as intrigued, excited, delighted, as I was, when they first went down the stone steps and through that black door.[11]

Apart from city-centre basements (also home to the Studio Theatre Club in Upper Mount Street, the Eblana at Busáras, and the 66 Theatre Club), other venues for little theatres included a restored coach-house at Herbert Street (Pike Theatre Club), the two Dublin-area showcase theatre venues for the Alliance and Dublin Consumers' Gas Company at D'Olier Street and at Dun Laoghaire (Globe Theatre Company), and Mary and Pearse O'Malley's suburban drawing room at Ulsterville House in Belfast (Lyric Players' Group). The Gas Company Theatre in Dun Laoghaire was an especially well-known destination: notoriously uncomfortable, this was the home to Godfrey Quigley's Globe Theatre Company and then (from 1959) to the 66 Theatre Club.

Ireland's little theatre movement in the 1950s draws on a diverse range of national and international influences: from older Dublin-based theatre and dance initiatives to the 1950s scene of London's club theatres and the *théâtres de poche* of the Parisian left bank. In Ireland, as in London and in Paris, little theatres were associated with modernist experimentation and with an anti-authoritarian avant-garde. What in London was known as the 'club device' was a way of evading the stringent censorship rulings of the English Lord Chamberlain. Plays were performed as club performances because they would otherwise have been subject to censorship, often on the grounds of implied or explicit homosexual references or because of other offences to bourgeois decorum.[12] In addition, the very flagrancy and accumulative effect of club performances contributed, over almost two decades, to the 1968 abolition of censorship in the United Kingdom. In Paris, where little theatres were sometimes described disparagingly as 'the street urinals of the left bank' ('*les pissotières de la rive gauche*'),[13] such theatres had a reputation as laboratories of modernist experiment, demanding from their audiences heightened forms of participation and response.[14] If such theatres were small and uncomfortable, this was viewed as an essential part of their modernist and anti-bourgeois character.

But Ireland's little theatre phenomenon in the 1950s drew just as heavily on the country's prodigious amateur theatre movement, the extraordinary porous boundaries that existed between amateur and professional theatre, and Dublin-based theatre groups associated with socialist or left-leaning political activism. Immediate predecessors included enterprises such as Roibeárd Ó Faracháin and Austin Clarke's Dublin Verse Speaking Society (1938–44), Austin Clarke's Lyric Theatre (1944–52), the socialist New Theatre Group (1937–43), and Erina Brady's Dublin Dance Theatre Club (1948–51). Each of these

---

[11]   D'Arcy, *Loose Theatre*, 169.

[12]   See Dominic Shellard, *British Theatre Since the War* (New Haven, CT: Yale University Press, 2000), 38–9; Dennis Kennedy (ed.), *The Oxford Companion to Theatre and Performance* (Oxford: Oxford University Press, 2010), 105–6.

[13]   See Guérin, *Le Théâtre en France*, 336.   [14]   Ibid., 338–9.

combined theatre and dance with a range of other educational and cultural self-improvement activities such as poetry reading, lectures on drama and literature, and, invariably, some degree of political and social debate.[15] Mary O'Malley, who went on to found the Lyric Players Theatre in Belfast, began her involvement in theatre with the socialist New Theatre Group in the 1940s and then became a member of Clarke's Lyric Theatre. 'We [New Theatre Group] played in little sheds and derelict buildings,' O'Malley recalls, adding that debates ranged 'from birth control to poetry in the theatre'.[16] In a manner that looks forward to the diverse activities of the Lyric Players Theatre in the mid-1950s, the New Theatre Group established a Playgoers' Circle that encouraged discussion of contemporary theatre and produced plays by Clifford Odets (*Waiting for Lefty*, 1935), *Awake and Sing*, 1935), Bernard Shaw (*Heartbreak House*, 1919), W. H. Auden and Christopher Isherwood (*On the Frontier*, 1938), and Denis Johnston (*The Golden Cuckoo*, 1939).[17] The New Theatre Group was anti-capitalist and a 'worker's theatre',[18] but was also dominated by a broadly Fabian philosophy of workers' education and cultural self-improvement. With trade unionists admitted at half price and the unemployed admitted for free, this initiative of the late 1930s and 1940s offered a powerful model of theatre that was politically active, socially inclusive, and interested in the production of international plays.

Other less overtly political influences were groups such as the Dublin Verse Speaking Society, the Lyric Theatre, and the Dublin Dance Theatre Club. As with the New Theatre Group, each of these groups combined an eclectic mix of cultural activities and social engagement, and championed variations of a defiant and exuberant bohemianism. Bringing together theatrical performances, musical recitals, discussion, and lectures, these groups were crisscrossed by a network of complex inter-involvement, with a plethora of overlaps between those who were involved in these earlier ventures and those involved in later groups like the 37 Theatre Club, the Pike Theatre Club, and the Lantern Theatre Club. Moreover, the Lyric Players Theatre was named in tribute to Clarke's Dublin-based Lyric Theatre,[19] and Donagh MacDonagh's play *Happy as Larry*, premièred by Clarke's Lyric Theatre in May 1947, went on over a decade later to serve as the opening production of the Lantern Theatre in November 1957. In addition, key members of the Pike Theatre Club in the 1950s—choreographer June Fryer and actor Patrick Nolan—had been prominently involved with the Dublin Dance Theatre Club.

The Dublin Dance Theatre Club was a particularly important influence on the little theatre phenomenon. Its performances took place in Erina Brady's tiny Harcourt Street Studio (audience capacity twenty-five) and, as Aoife McGrath points out, these performances were characterized by an experience that, at least for the *Irish Times* theatre critic Seamus Kelly, was regarded as disconcertingly proximate.[20] The reminiscences of Jacqueline Robinson—a

---

[15] See Ian R. Walsh, *Experimental Irish Theatre: After W. B. Yeats* (Basingstoke: Palgrave Macmillan, 2012), 102; Tina Hunt Mahony, 'The Dublin Verse Speaking Society and the Lyric Theatre Company', *Irish University Review* 4, no. 1 (1974), 65–73.

[16] Mary O'Malley, *Never Shake Hands with the Devil* (Dublin: Elo, 1990), 34.

[17] See H. Gustav Klaus, *Strong Words Brave Deeds: The Poetry, Life and Times of Thomas O'Brien Volunteer in the Spanish Civil War* (Dublin: O'Brien Press, 1994), 151–2.

[18] Thomas O'Brien, quoted in ibid., 149.   [19] See O'Malley, *Never Shake Hands*, 57–8.

[20] See Aoife McGrath, *Dance Theatre in Ireland: Revolutionary Moves* (Basingstoke: Palgrave Macmillan, 2013), 61.

dancer who worked with Brady—offer an invaluable account of the transformative atmosphere generated by Brady's dancing and by her dance classes:

> On stage she could appear as an angel or a witch, and as it were, an epitome of womanhood! In the intimacy of her studio, we knew her as exacting and considerate, aloof and tender, cold and passionate, ever filled with the desire to go further, deeper, with no compromise, into the veracity of the art of dance to which she was devoted and to bring us along that same path. We looked at her dancing, and were taken into another world.[21]

Brady's barefoot dancing style ('ballet without ballet shoes') was influenced by the Mary Wigman School in Dresden and by Brady's work as a choreographer for the Théâtre Mogador and by the Académie de Danse in Paris. In 1939 Brady founded the Irish School of Dance Art at 39 Harcourt Street, and by 1942, Jacqueline Robinson and June Fryer were protégées who went on to cooperate (in 1944) with Austin Clarke's Lyric Theatre Company for a production of a piece combining poetry and dance and based on Samuel Ferguson's poem *The Fairy Thorn* (repeated at the Peacock Theatre in April 1946).[22]

What each of these dance and theatre initiatives has in common is an emphasis on the experience of performance and, in particular, on the spectator's physically intimate relationship to the actor's voice and moving body. To the extent that these theatre initiatives were often self-consciously artistic and experimental, Ireland's little theatre movement in the 1950s may also be related to the much earlier US-based Little Theatre movement.[23] Thus Austin Clarke's Lyric Theatre Company, the Dublin Verse Speaking Society, the Dublin Arts Theatre, the 37 Theatre Club, as well as Cork's longstanding Little Theatre Society and Compantás Chorcaí,[24] were all attracted to the notion of smaller and more exclusive theatre venues set apart from the commercial theatre and thus freer to perform contemporary European or US modernist drama. Symptomatic of this view are David O'Leary's comments on behalf of the Dublin Arts Theatre describing a November 1951 production of Jean Anouilh's *Antigone* as 'the first step in our endeavour to found a theatre club in Dublin' in order 'to present a wide range of plays including those seldom, if ever, seen in the normal commercial theatre'.[25]

Another influence on Dublin's little theatre movement of the 1950s was the Bernadette Players (or 'Bernos' as they were nicknamed by their participants), an amateur theatre company that was well known in 1950s Dublin. The group was started by Father Mick Murphy and was originally based at his church in Rathmines and its nearby parish hall. From the recollection of Maureen Frawley (neé Foley), who acted with the Bernadette Players from 1951 to 1961, Father Mick was 'theatre mad' and co-wrote all of the shows—many of which involved complex dance routines—with Pat O'Rourke. Only O'Rourke's name was ever associated with the theatre group due to the embargo on priests being associated with theatre. Actors who were directly involved in the Bernadette Players included Donal Donnelly

---

[21] Jacqueline Robinson, quoted in Deirdre Mulrooney, *An Illustrated History of Dance and Physical Theatre in Ireland* (Dublin: Liffey Press, 2006), 89.

[22] Ibid., 99.

[23] See Dorothy Chansky, *Composing Ourselves: The Little Theatre Movement and the American Audience* (Carbondale, IL: Southern Illinois Press, 2004).

[24] See Ryan, *Dan Donovan*, 61–7, 76–83.

[25] Dublin City Archives, Irish Theatre Archive (ITA), R1/04/53.

(his last show with the Bernos was in 1951[26]), Michael Dunne, Denis Boothman, Bernard Frawley, Bob Quinn, Chris McDonald, and Noreen and Kevin Cunnane. The actor Milo O'Shea attended performances regularly, as did Lord Longford, who sought to recruit actors for the Gate. As well as the close links between the Bernadette Players and professional institutional theatres like the Abbey, the Gate, and the Gaiety, there was a close overlap between the Bernos' pantomime-like topical revues (such as *Snow White and the 7 Corkmen* and *Aladeen and the E.S.B.*, December 1955) and the late-night satirical revues that were such an important part of the repertoire of the Pike Theatre Club and the Lantern Theatre. Often the Bernos' pantomimes would be played first in December, with three months of performances in Dublin, followed by a tour of parish and community halls around Ireland and, in at least one instance, a trip to England. From sketchy newspaper reports and the vivid accounts of some of its participants, the Bernos' productions were exuberant and ever-alert to opportunities for social commentary and satire.

THE 37 THEATRE CLUB

One of the earliest and most prodigious of Dublin's little theatres in the 1950s was the 37 Theatre Club. Established by Barry Cassin and Nora Lever in March 1951 and located initially in a large basement room of 37 Lower Baggot Street, the 37 Theatre Club had a stated policy of introducing 'new plays and new artistes as well as plays of unusual interest' with a monthly schedule of productions. With a seating capacity of forty this was, according to its own 1953 souvenir programme, 'the smallest professional theatre in Ireland'. [27] Margaretta D'Arcy's collection of memoirs *Loose Theatre* recounts the early involvement of Trinity College students, John Gibbon and Michael Frier, and of the young American actor Jack Aronson, who played the part of Mr Zero in Elmer Rice's *The Adding Machine* (1923).[28] The choice of Rice's expressionist play with its satire of repressed needs and desires is illustrative of what was a recurrent emphasis in many of the smaller Dublin-based theatres in this period: the association of a healthy social life with uninhibited heterosexuality. D'Arcy recounts that 'their [that of Frier and Gibbon] talk was all of existentialism and Sartre and Simone de Beauvoir, who would not accept the exclusivity of the sexual relationships between men and women' (165). For D'Arcy, the 37 Theatre Club represented a vitally important element in 1950s Irish theatre and laid 'the foundations for the new post war theatre and a new generation of Irish actors: Anna Manahan; Pauline Delaney; Norman Rodway' (168–9), while Ian Walsh cites the 37 Theatre Club as existing at the centre of Dublin's bohemian life in the 1950s.[29] D'Arcy provides a vivid description of what it was like to step into the intimate space of the 37 Theatre Club:

> As soon as you came in, as a member of the audience, you found yourself immediately in the theatre, with the slightly-raised stage to your left, at your very elbow. To your right, against the wall, was the table where you bought your ticket. I suppose the little room held about forty for a full house. It was always warm, heated by a paraffin stove [. . .]. In the interval

---

[26] See 'Bernadette Players' Colourful Show', *Irish Times*, 28 Dec. 1951.   [27] ITA, R1/04/57.
[28] See D'Arcy, *Loose Theatre*, 162.   [29] Walsh, *Experimental Irish Theatre*, 103.

the black curtain that separated the auditorium and stage from the dressing-room area was drawn back and coffee, tea and biscuits were served; because it was a club, their price was included in the ticket. I seem to recall that the audience took its refreshments in company with the cast who were preparing for the next act, coming and going out collecting their props, their clothes hanging up along the wall, the make-up mirror with the sticks laid out, and the intermingling smells of greasepaint, coffee and paraffin.[30]

In January 1953, the 37 Theatre Club moved to a 170-seater space on the second floor of an old Georgian building at 51 Lower O'Connell Street. The move to the larger theatre allowed the paying of wages and the installation of a box office.[31] Here a variety of new plays were staged, including Maurice Meldon's *Aisling* (1953)—a satire on nationalist politics and the treatment of women—which ran from March until May; less enthusiastically received were new plays such as Cecil ffrench Salkeld's *Berlin Dusk* (1953) and Seamus de Faoite's *Harrigan's Girl* (1953). By January of the following year, the O'Connell Street premises were condemned as unsafe, and the 37 Theatre Club moved again, this time to a series of venues including the basement premises of 36 Lower Baggot Street. From this point on, the 37 Theatre Club's production of plays became more sporadic, and many of its actors—including Anna Manahan, Norman Rodway, and Maurice Meldon—went on to join other theatre initiatives.[32]

PIKE THEATRE CLUB

By far the best known of Dublin's little theatres in the 1950s was the Pike Theatre Club. Founded by Carolyn Swift and her husband, Alan Simpson, in 1953, the Pike was situated in the south city centre at 18A Herbert Lane. This was a location that was set apart from the traditional theatre districts of Dublin, but conveniently proximate to some of the public houses that featured prominently in the social and cultural life of 1950s Dublin: Doheny and Nesbitts, McDaids, the Catacombs, and 'Lampshades' Ryans.[33] Like the 37 Theatre Club, the Pike Theatre Club was, unmistakeably, a little theatre, with a mere 3.6 square metre acting space and approximately sixty seats for spectators. Described by Simpson as 'a revolutionary force of small means [. . .] to stir up the theatrical lethargy of post-war Ireland',[34] the Pike's programme of plays reflected an outlook that was conspicuously and self-consciously cosmopolitan. As issues of the *Pike Newsletter* repeatedly stress, the plays that were chosen for performance tended to be those that had recently acquired an avant-garde reputation in Paris or London. Performances were done in a style that was beatnik, technically skilful, and flamboyantly energetic. The Pike's slick self-presentation was enhanced by the fact that Liam and Josephine Miller's recently established Dolmen Press printed many of its programmes and posters, as well as its quarterly newsletter.

---

[30] D'Arcy, *Loose Theatre*, 169–70.   [31] Ibid., 171
[32] See Walsh, *Experimental Irish Theatre*, 144–5.
[33] See Christopher Morash, *A History of Irish Theatre 1601–2000* (Cambridge: Cambridge University Press, 2002), 200; Carolyn Swift, *Stage by Stage* (Dublin: Poolbeg, 1995), 122.
[34] Alan Simpson, *Beckett and Behan and a Theatre in Dublin* (London: Routledge & Kegan Paul, 1962), 1.

The prevailing atmosphere in the Pike Theatre Club was that of physical proximity: 'no seat in the theatre', Morash observes, 'was more than four rows from the stage.'[35] Typically, the subject matter concerned the tensions between social convention and a volcanic, heterosexual libidinousness. Thus Jacquetta Hawkes and J. B. Priestley's play *Dragon's Mouth* (1951) was selected for production in 1953 partly because of its 'terrific success' in London's Winter Garden and partly because it showed 'two men and two women in a situation calculated to break down the ordinary barriers of reticence and politeness which usually restrain civilized human beings'.[36] Similarly, in 1954, Tennessee Williams's play *Summer and Smoke* (1948) was chosen for production on 3 May because of the play's 'remarkable insight into mental and sexual frustration'.[37] In other words, long before the controversy associated with Simpson's production of *The Rose Tattoo* (1951) in May 1957, the Pike showed a persistent interest in the dramatic performance of bodies inscribed by desire and fighting the constraints of social convention. Indeed, when Marie Bryant visited Dublin in July 1953 and was unable to find a theatre willing to host a performance that included her risqué calypso lyrics ('Please, Mister, Don't You Touch My Tomato', 'He Has the Biggest Water Melon in Africa'), Simpson made a point of inviting Bryant to perform at one of the Pike's late evening follies, on 10 July 1953.[38] With her rambunctious international reputation, Bryant's performance at the Pike was a coup.

Undoubtedly, what propelled the exponential growth of the Pike Theatre Club in the early days of its existence were its late-night revues or 'follies.' These, rather than the Pike's more traditional theatre productions, soon made the little theatre at Herbert Street a favourite destination for late-night cultural entertainment. After the sparsely attended *Dragon's Mouth* in 1953, the *Pike Newsletter* announced its next production as 'The Follies of Herbert Lane: An Intimate Late-Night Revue' with the curtain rising at 22:45 and a finish time of 00:15.[39] However, as Swift writes in her autobiography, the actual finish time of the performances was often much later; the curtain was seldom brought down before 00:45, and there were also occasions (specifically, in 1957) when the follies finished as late as 01:45. The follies consisted of a sequence of short satiric skits that included dance and song, and entailed a range of contemporary references. The objects of satire ranged from church-sanctioned prudery to social institutions like the Gaelic Athletic Association to the cross-examination of Patrick Kavanagh during the latter's libel case against the *Leader* in 1954.[40]

The Pike's satire also included the productions taking place in other more mainstream Dublin theatres. Swift relates, for example, how one actress—Deirdre McSharry—performed an impersonation of Siobhán McKenna who was then playing the title role in a Gate Theatre production of Bernard Shaw's *Saint Joan*. Despite the satire of acting styles and, in particular, of the Abbey Theatre's often portentous naturalism, the relationship between the Pike and Dublin's larger institutional theatres was close and highly involved. Indeed, one of the reasons why the Pike's follies were scheduled at such a late hour was in order to facilitate many of the Pike's actors who conducted a 'cross-town-sprint' from the larger theatres to the little theatre on Herbert Street. Swift recounts how, on one occasion, Milo O'Shea

---

[35] Morash, *History*, 202.
[36] Dublin, Trinity College Dublin (TCD), Pike Theatre Collection, MS 10813/383/1.
[37] *Pike Newsletter*, no. 1 (1953), in TCD, Pike, MS 10813/383/3.   [38] Swift, *Stage by Stage*, 131.
[39] *Pike Newsletter* 2 (1954), in TCD, Pike, MS 10813/383/2.
[40] See Antoinette Quinn, *Patrick Kavanagh: A Biography* (Dublin: Gill & Macmillan, 2001), 325–9.

played thirteen roles in an Irish version of Cinderella—*Bláithín agus an Mac Rí* (1953)—with the Abbey at the Queens Theatre before then rushing across the city to play no fewer than eleven roles at a revue in the Pike.[41] In other instances, the same actor responsible for the voice-over on a radio advertisement would then appear at the Pike in an overt parody of that advertisement.[42]

What made the Pike's follies so successful was their combination of exuberant irreverence, contemporary satire, and superb technical skill, evident as much in the speed of set changes as in their song and dance routines.[43] *The Follies of Herbert Lane* opened in December 1953 and continued until March 1954 and, largely as a consequence, membership at the Pike increased from 270 to 1,200. With subscription prices set at two guineas (about €64 in today's money), this meant that the Pike was also doing well financially: by the end of 1954 the *Pike Newsletter* outlines ambitious new plans to purchase an additional premises and also to develop an educational dimension to its activities:

> Other activities, such as lectures on theatrical subjects, social gatherings to meet local and visiting celebrities, etc., are planned. It is also hoped to start a theatrical library and to take out subscriptions to all theatrical periodicals.[44]

Although these plans did not materialize, their ambitious tone indicates a new confidence, and it was in this context that Simpson and Swift announced a first production of Brendan Behan's *The Quare Fellow* in the autumn of 1954. Directed by Simpson, and with the recorded singing voice of Behan as the prisoner in the punishment cells, the play's opening night (19 November 1954) was reviewed positively by the *Irish Times*, who described the play as distinctively 'modern': '[I]t rounds off neither character nor situation, but "passes the buck", as it were, to the customer [. . .] There is no progression nor development of any of the characters.'[45] The large cast and small size of the Pike as a venue contributed powerfully to the way in which Behan's play insists that audiences take responsibility for the Irish state's reliance on violently coercive mechanisms for social control. This was the Pike's first straightforward theatrical production that was both well received and well attended, and provided an incentive for Simpson and Swift to seek permission from Samuel Beckett to perform a translated version of *En Attendant Godot*. After various legal delays (helpfully documented in detail in Morash's *History of Irish Theatre*), *Waiting for Godot* was finally performed on 28 October 1955. This was a production that softened the play's disconcertingly anonymous setting by presenting Vladimir and Estragon as members of the Dublin working class,[46] by rendering the production's backcloth as 'suggestive of Irish bogland and gloomy sky',[47] and by having Pozzo portrayed in a manner reminiscent of an Anglo-Irish landlord with Lucky as his much-abused footman.[48] The production ran from October 1955 until February 1956 before moving for a week at the Gate in March 1956 and then on to a tour of various Irish towns and cities.

[41] Swift, *Stage by Stage*, 117.   [42] Ibid., 134.   [43] Ibid., 114–15.
[44] *Pike Newsletter* 6 (1954), in TCD, Pike, MS 10813/383/6.
[45] Anon., 'The Quare Fellow at the Pike', *Irish Times*, 20 Nov. 1954.
[46] Morash, *History*, 202.   [47] Simpson, *Beckett and Behan*, 131–2.
[48] Morash, *History*, 202–3.

THE ROSE TATTOO

In addition to the first performances of Behan's *The Quare Fellow* and Beckett's *Waiting for Godot*, the Pike Theatre Club features prominently in Irish cultural history because of Simpson's controversial production of Tennessee Williams's *The Rose Tattoo* in May 1957. The decision to stage the European première of *The Rose Tattoo* at the Pike was consistent with the Pike's long-term emphasis on producing performances that stressed the irrepressibility of heterosexual desire and the folly of institutions and conventions—particularly Irish ones—that sought to repress and frustrate such desire. Even by these standards, however, Simpson's production of *The Rose Tattoo* was deliberately and extraordinarily provocative.

FIG. 18.1 Anna Manahan and Pat Nolan in *The Rose Tattoo*, Pike Theatre (12 May 1957).

Photo: Derrick Michelson. Courtesy of Trinity College Dublin.

This is, after all, a play that begins with a scene in which the play's protagonist Serafina della Rosa eulogizes her husband's prowess at love-making and ends with a scene in which Serafina encourages her by now 15-year-old daughter, Rosa, to have sexual intercourse with her boyfriend. Close to the end of the play, in Act III, Scene 2, the onstage dialogue between Rosa and her boyfriend Jack is punctuated by the orgasmic sounds of Serafina making love, and in the play's final scene (Act III, Scene 3), Serafina's lover, Alvaro, is described as crouching 'in a leap-frog position' over the partly undressed sleeping teenager.[49]

With a sequence of narrative action that might best be described as histrionically neo-Freudian, then, *The Rose Tattoo* stresses that a female heterosexuality unrepressed by the strictures of Roman Catholicism is an indispensable ingredient for the set of broad sociopolitical adaptations required of Sicilian immigrants in the southern United States by a modern, US-dominated global economy. For Swift and Simpson, the analogy with Ireland was transparent: *The Rose Tattoo* had been chosen for production because 'the play has a theme of religion versus primitive superstition and should appeal particularly to an Irish audience'.[50] To this extent, Swift and Simpson's production of *The Rose Tattoo* was consistent with the Pike's earlier repertoire of plays as well as with Clarke's Lyric Theatre and its production of Donagh McDonagh's *Happy as Larry* (1946). An implicit priority here is not just a reinvigorated idea of theatre as a crucial site for modernity, but also the idea of the actor's body as revealing this modernity by means of an uninhibited heterosexuality.

Simpson's production of *The Rose Tattoo* was fully consistent with a key aspect of the Pike Theatre Club's agenda: its determination to expose Ireland's traditional social restrictions on sexual expression as prudish, antiquated, and damaging to the country's modernization. To this extent, Simpson's production merely accentuated what is a core preoccupation in Williams's play: the notion that releasing female heterosexuality from the inhibiting mediation of Roman Catholicism is indispensable to the integration of Italian immigrants into a modern and United States-dominated capitalist economy. Indeed, the play's climactic moment of revelation comes when Serafina describes the statue of the Virgin Mary as 'just a poor little doll with the paint peeling off'[51] and then blows out its vigil light.

In Irish cultural history, the reputation of Simpson's production is dominated by Simpson's arrest and detention by Garda 'Special Branch' detectives for producing 'for gain an indecent and profane performance'.[52] Most recently, Gerard Whelan argues very convincingly that this act of draconian force against Simpson was prompted by the government's concern that if action was not taken against the production of Williams's play, there would be a strong possibility that the Roman Catholic Archbishop of Dublin (John Charles McQuaid) would make a public statement criticizing the government for its ineffectuality in not censoring indecent material.[53] Given the then Fianna Fáil government's determination to weaken the powers of the censorship board, such a statement could have exposed the Minister for Justice to political attack. But concentrating on the damaging

---

[49] Tennessee Williams, *The Rose Tattoo and Other Plays* (London: Penguin, 2001), 107.
[50] See *Pike Newsletter* 15 (1957), in TCD, Pike, MS 10813/383/14.
[51] Williams, *Rose Tattoo*, 101.
[52] 'Charge of Presenting Indecent Play', *Irish Press*, 25 May 1957.
[53] See Gerard Whelan with Carolyn Swift, *Spiked: Church–State Intrigue and The Rose Tattoo* (Dublin: New Island Books, 2002).

effect of the state's actions against Simpson—or the distracting irrelevance of whether or not an actual condom may have been dropped on stage in the course of the performance—massively underestimates the subversive effect of the play in performance. Specifically, this was a production that made overt that which the satirical action of the follies had merely suggested: that a somatic Irish modernity—now so necessary to Ireland's new climate of state modernization—could and should spill over into the realm of the erotic. What made the performance of *The Rose Tattoo* so provocative in performance, therefore, was precisely the same use of actor–character analogy that was such an important element in the follies. In the same way as the pleasure of hearing Godfrey Quigley's parody of a radio advertisement relied on one's familiarity with Quigley's actual radio advertisement, or the fun of watching Milo O'Shea's comic mimes in the follies was increased by one's delight in recognizing O'Shea from his roles at the Gaiety, so Simpson's casting of *The Rose Tattoo* suggested an association—or transference—between actor and role. Indeed, Williams's play is explicitly concerned with the idea of libidinal transference. The play's central hypothesis is that a rose tattoo appears on Serafina's breast when her love-making leads to conception, and it is this conceit that underlines the play's claim that heterosexual desire is a drive that simply cannot—and should not—be resisted. Anna Manahan—then 33 years old and herself recently and tragically bereaved (Manahan married the actor Colm Ó Ceallaigh in 1955 and Ó Ceallaigh died of polio in 1956[54])—played the part of the distraught Serafina who laments the unexpected loss of her husband and, especially, their orgasmic sexual relationship. As is recounted in Joan FitzPatrick Dean's book *Riot and Great Anger: Stage Censorship in Twentieth-Century Ireland*, Manahan's performance was extraordinarily powerful—'a remarkable performance that was beautifully shaded' according to the *Irish Press*, and 'her greatest triumph' according to the *Dublin Evening Mail*.[55] The 19-year-old Kate Binchy was cast as Serafina's highly sexualized 15-year-old daughter Rosa delle Rosa who, in the first three scenes of the play, is portrayed as 12 years old, and who is described throughout the play as craving to lose her virginity. As Swift points out, a vital ingredient to the performance was the contrast between the visible 'delicacy and innocence' of this actress and the role's suggestion of 'the sexual maturity of a hot-blooded Italian'.[56] In Manahan and in Binchy's case, what was also suggested—none too subtly—was that such libidinal instincts could be shared (and, in performance, were shared) by the actresses themselves.[57]

Simpson's arrest in May 1957 did not lead to a prosecution, and the state dropped its charges in June of the following year. However, the effect of the case on the Pike Theatre Club was devastating. Because no actual case was taken against Simpson and the Pike, Simpson possessed no mechanism in order to recover the massive legal costs that had been

[54] See Micheál Mac Liammóir, *Each Actor on His Ass* (London: Routledge & Kegan Paul, 1961), 197–9.

[55] See Joan FitzPatrick Dean, *Riot and Great Anger: Stage Censorship in Twentieth-Century Ireland* (Madison, WI: Wisconsin University Press, 2004), 157.

[56] Swift, *Stage by Stage*, 265.

[57] I elaborate on this episode in Irish cultural history in Lionel Pilkington, 'Theatre, Sexuality and the State: Tennessee Williams's *The Rose Tattoo* at the Dublin Theatre Festival', in Nicholas Grene and Patrick Lonergan (eds.), *Interactions: Dublin Theatre Festival 1957–2007* (Dublin: Carysfort Press, 2008), 23–33.

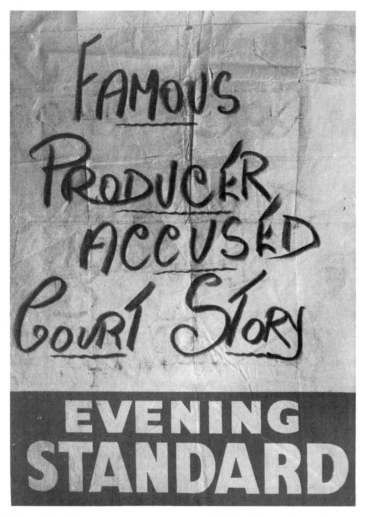

FIG. 18.2 When Alan Simpson was arrested over the Pike Theatre's production of *The Rose Tattoo* in 1957, the case provoked widespread public interest in Dublin, making headlines in newspapers across the city.

Courtesy of Trinity College Dublin.

involved in hiring a senior council in order to formulate a defence. While the Pike Theatre Defence Fund had raised £200, the costs incurred by the Pike Theatre Club were £2,500, leaving Swift and Simpson heavily in debt. Damaging also to the Pike's depleted finances and to its reputation was Lord Longford's decision to cancel the production's move to the Gate Theatre. This, combined with the view that Simpson's production had gone too far in provoking the state,[58] led to a major withdrawal of support from the Pike's list of subscribers; by 1961, the Pike Theatre Club had collapsed as an independent theatrical entity.

[58] See Swift, *Stage by Stage*, 261.

Lantern Theatre Club

The Lantern Theatre Club (1957–75) was founded by Josephine and Patrick Funge, and was situated (until 1962) in a basement premises at 127 Lower Baggot Street. Its interest in proclaiming a subversive, libidinal energy through performance may be detected in its choice of Donagh McDonagh's verse play *Happy as Larry* as its opening production. A former production of Austin Clarke's Lyric Theatre Group, McDonagh's play is explicitly concerned with the irrepressibility of heterosexual desire: Larry is 'happy' to the degree that he discovers this to be a reassuring truth that no convention can suppress. Jim Phelan's comment on the production suggests the extent to which this emphasis made the Lantern Theatre Club conform to the expectation of 'the true intimate theatre so beloved by many Dubliners'.[59] Like the Pike, the Lantern was a theatre project that combined the traditional theatre production of plays with devised pieces (Padraic Colum's *Road Round Ireland* in 1964 was its most famous success) and a series of satirical revues, mostly written by Fergus Linehan and known as *Lanternscope*. From what one can judge from the evidence, however, it seems as if the Lantern stopped short of Swift and Simpson's penchant for trenchant provocation. While the Pike's 'follies' and many of its productions stressed the contagious sexuality of the performing body, *Lanternscope* performances tended towards a somewhat milder form of social satire, with targets of caricature that ranged from working-class Dublin accents to the ways in which expanding state organizations (such as the Electricity Supply Board and the Irish Tourist Board, Bord Fáilte) and an American-oriented consumer culture attempted to infiltrate almost every aspect of people's personal lives. Parodies of toothpaste, tobacco, and body deodorant advertisements were combined with satires of state-sponsored tourism ventures, mocking references to a homosexual amateur dramatics adjudicator, and a short vignette, 'Light and Shadow' by Darrach Connolly, dealing with the topic of heterosexual loneliness.[60] Like the Pike's 'follies', but in the somewhat milder context of T. K. Whitaker's reforms, the Lantern's revues were often excoriating exposures of national claims.

Lyric Players Theatre

A final example that illustrates the sense of political possibility often associated with little theatres is the Lyric Players Theatre in Belfast, established by Mary O'Malley in March 1951. Named in honour of Austin Clarke's Dublin-based Lyric Theatre, the Lyric Players Theatre (or Lyric Players Group as it was sometimes called) remained an entirely amateur and private operation until 1960. Admission to the theatre was free and by invitation, and performances took place in the Belfast residences of Pearse and Mary O'Malley, first at their home at Ulsterville House and then, from 1952, at their house at Derryvolgie Avenue. As Mary O'Malley recounts in *Never Shake Hands with the Devil*, the idea of establishing a

---

[59] Jim Phelan, 'Actors Construct Intimate Theatre', *Irish Pictorial*, 16 Nov. 1957.
[60] Dublin, National Library of Ireland, Lantern Theatre Club Collection, MS 40,184.

private amateur theatre arose when, in 1949, she devised a Christmas entertainment for the (Catholic) Newman Society at Queen's University Belfast. Operating in a period in which 'unionist control [in Northern Ireland] was total',[61] the Lyric Players asserted the possibility of an all-Ireland cultural organization that refused Northern Ireland's prevailing anti-Catholic discrimination. Nevertheless, this was an initiative that was, from its beginning, closely associated with an assertion of nationalist identity in Northern Ireland. Plays from the Abbey Theatre (by Yeats and Lady Gregory) featured prominently on the repertoire, there were regular visits by Dublin-based dramatists and intellectuals, and the logo for the Lyric Players consisted of the head of the young Cuchulain superimposed on a harp. As a signatory to the letter delivered to the delegates to the Belfast PEN conference in 1953, Mary O'Malley was on record as opposed to what was described in the letter as a 'spurious [Ulster] regionalism' designed to 'ignore or play down the larger background of Ireland', and to the ways in which 'regionalist' writers rendered 'the political and economic domination of the Unionist Party [. . .] taboo as a subject as is the victimization of political opponents'.[62]

But the programme of plays presented by the Lyric Players was decidedly non-political, featuring especially the verse plays of Austin Clarke and W. B. Yeats as well as several productions of plays by William Shakespeare. Only Lauro de Bosis's anti-fascist play *Icaro* (1927) could be said to harken back to O'Malley's time with the socialist New Theatre Group, or indeed to chime with O'Malley's own work as a Belfast Labour councillor. Only very rarely—as when the Lyric Players performed Yeats and Gregory's *Cathleen Ni Houlihan* at the same time as the 1953 coronation celebrations—can one detect the smallest nationalist *parti pris* element to the selection of plays. What the Lyric sought to achieve, rather, was a broad-based cultural movement based on a fundamentally bourgeois conception of all-Ireland cultural traditions. In the words of Mary O'Malley, performances provided 'an opportunity for free discussion and the furthering of friendships'.[63] Writing in June 1956, Mary and Pearse O'Malley allude to this broad agenda as a 'movement' that attempts 'to integrate as closely as possible the poet and the painter with the player, producer and theatre craftsman'. 'While it is our policy to present any play considered suitable in world theatre', they concluded that 'a special place is reserved for the Irish dramatist and artist and we hope that the work of the Lyric Players will encourage creative activity.'[64] This sense of the theatre as a cultural movement was reinforced by the establishment of a drama school in 1956,[65] by the opening of the Lyric's Studio Theatre in 1957, and by the setting up of the literary magazine *Threshold* in the same year. Performances of literary drama were followed by coffee and sometimes by suppers designed to facilitate post-show discussion, and there were annual Christmas and St Patrick's Day parties and entertainments.[66] On the face of it, this does not appear as a radical or divisive initiative. However, as a little theatre prominently associated with a broad-based Irish nationalism and sponsored by a newly confident Catholic middle class, the Lyric Players Theatre encountered increasing unionist and state hostility when, in the 1960s, it became a professional company.[67]

[61] O'Malley, *Never Shake Hands with the Devil*, 60.   [62] Ibid., 66–7.   [63] Ibid., 71.
[64] Mary and Pearse O'Malley, 'The Lyric Players, Belfast: 1951–1956' (unpublished brochure, *c.*20 June 1956), in Galway, NUI Galway, James Hardiman Library, T4/476.
[65] O'Malley, *Never Shake Hands with the Devil*, 87.
[66] Conor O'Malley, *A Poet's Theatre* (Dublin: Elo Press, 1988), 24.
[67] See Lionel Pilkington, *Theatre and the State in Twentieth-Century Ireland: Cultivating the People* (London: Routledge, 2001), 186–90.

Conclusion

This chapter's account of the little theatre movement in 1950s Ireland has been selective; quite evidently, there is much more work that needs to be done in terms of document-ing, and also critically reflecting on, this extraordinary cultural phenomenon. Apart from the reminiscences and memoirs of some of its participants and Ian Walsh's useful *Experimental Irish Theatre After W. B. Yeats*, the little theatre phenomenon in Ireland has received little scholarly attention. This is partly a result of a dominant tendency in Irish cultural history that views Ireland's political modernity as following on from T. K. Whitaker's 1958 insistence on the primacy of inward capital investment and an export-driven economy, and the corollary view that Ireland's postwar period (1945–58) is to be viewed as backward and culturally benighted. Another important reason for our scholarly inattention is the author-centred tendency of Irish theatre history and the ways in which a national theatre history tends to favour naturalistic or neo-naturalistic forms of drama that can be identified clearly as 'representative'. Something of the unset-tling effect of the little theatre phenomenon on the orthodoxies of Irish theatre history may be glimpsed in Thomas Kilroy's 1959 essay 'Groundwork for an Irish Theatre'. Here Kilroy argues that none of the 'small theatre clubs' of the 1950s are 'ever likely to pro-duce a new movement in Irish playwriting', and argues that the 'one great deficiency' of the Irish theatrical scene in the late 1950s is that 'it excludes the writer and keeps him at a distance':[68]

> It is a theatre which *provides for* the community, but it is very seldom, in any significant way, *of* it. [. . .] The policies of our theatres, almost without exception, are determined by talented directors or actors with a keen eye for material which will exploit their talents to the fullest. [. . .] This has imposed a pattern on the Irish theatre for the past ten or fifteen years. It has not been a very inspiring period in our theatre and the Irish writer, except in one or two instances, has been as remote from it as a member of any ordinary trade or profession.[69]

Kilroy's argument is that constructing a theatre movement around talented actors or direc-tors leads to a social fissiparousness, and that this anarchic state of affairs is to be contrasted to the kind of unity and representational authority that is generated by the production of plays by native dramatists: '[A] theatre [. . .] which creates something permanent absorbs some of the conflicting, topical social issues around it *and gives a public interpretation of current values.*'[70] We need a playwright's theatre rather than one of devised performances, Kilroy suggests, in order to create a more fully functioning national culture.

A related point blocking an appreciation of the little theatres, then, is that while many of the 'lost' Irish dramatists of this period—Donagh MacDonagh, Maurice Meldon, and Austin Clarke, for example—fit very awkwardly into a naturalistic or nationalist paradigm, many little theatres were not organized around particular *Irish* playwrights (Clarke's Lyric Theatre is an obvious exception). Instead, they were much more concerned either with

---

[68] Thomas Kilroy, 'Groundwork for an Irish Theatre', *Studies: An Irish Quarterly* 48, no. 190 (1959), 192.
[69] Ibid., 194.   [70] Ibid., 192, my emphasis.

staging productions of United States or European dramatists or with devised performances that stressed the improvisatory responsiveness of theatre to a particular political context. In all of this, there was an emphasis on the sheer physical versatility of actors in performance. In this regard, the experience of acting on stage and of theatregoing in general demonstrated a collective investment in the practice and possibility of political change— and indeed this can be connected to a range of other cultural and political phenomena in Ireland in this period.[71] In the case of the social and political commentary evident in the pantomimes of the Bernadette Players, the Pike Theatre Club's 'follies', or the Lantern Theatre Club's satiric revue *Lanternscope*, what is in evidence is a broad-based political optimism: not only a sense that the political and social status quo could be critiqued as antiquated and as badly in need of reform, but also an impression that such reforms could and would be achieved in the context of a Western international consensus concerning the salutary effects of the modern. Putting actors and spectators in very close quarters to one another, then, little theatres generated a participative atmosphere similar to that of a movement. It was an atmosphere that suggested a communal investment in change and social renewal. Often, this resulted in disquieting political implications for particular ruling groups—as in the instance of the Catholic Church as an institution and the Pike Theatre Club's suggestion that heterosexual activity outside marriage could be celebrated without fear, or in the case of Ulster unionism and the Lyric Players Theatre's suggestion that an inclusive, non-sectarian, and all-Ireland culture could be affirmed and celebrated in 1950s Belfast.

Finally, Ireland's little theatre movement signals a set of new possibilities regarding women's participation in Irish cultural life. Phyllis Ryan (Gemini Productions), Nora Lever (37 Theatre Club), D. Bannard Cogley (Studio Theatre, Mount Street), Mary O'Malley (Lyric Players Theatre), Josephine Funge (Lantern Theatre Club), Anna Manahan (37 Theatre Club and Pike Theatre Club), Carolyn Swift, June Fryer, and Pauline Bewick (Pike Theatre Club) are just some of the many women who were centrally involved in terms of little theatre organization, direction, production, acting, and design. Recognizing the extent of this participation is not without difficulty since, as Siobhán O'Gorman has argued in relation to the Pike, this participation was often concealed by a patriarchal tradition that insisted on men's innate priority as artistic directors.[72] A closely connected point is that the sexuality that was being celebrated was consistently heterosexual. As Dan Rebellato has pointed out in relation to British theatre in 1956, revitalizing theatre in the 1950s was seen as connected to a project to rid theatre of its effeminate or 'queer' associations and proclaim a new, reinvigorated heterosexuality.[73]

All these considerations, however, have one point in common: the 'politics' of the little theatre groups is to be found far less in manifestos, policy statements, or even the subject

---

[71] See e.g. Tomás Finn, *Tuairim: Intellectual Debate and Policy Formation: Rethinking Ireland, 1954–1975* (Manchester: Manchester University Press, 2012).

[72] See Siobhán O'Gorman, '"Hers and His": Carolyn Swift, Alan Simpson and Collective Creation at Dublin's Pike Theatre', in Kathryn Syssoyeva and Scott Proudfit (eds.), *Women, Collective Creation, and Devised Theatre* (New York: Palgrave Macmillan, forthcoming) 121–38.

[73] See Dan Rebellato, *1956 and All That* (London: Routledge, 1998).

matter of the plays chosen for performance, but in the various ways in which theatrical performance could be deployed as a way of asserting new forms of social and political possibility. In this respect, the physical nature of theatrical experience and the proximity, intimacy, and interconnections between audience and performer constitute the little theatres' most important element.

PART VII

THE NEW REVIVAL

CHAPTER 19

....

URBAN AND RURAL THEATRE CULTURES
M. J. Molloy, John B. Keane, and Hugh Leonard

....

LISA COEN

By the 1950s distinct strands of rural and urban Irish theatre were prompted by the clash of traditional mores with major social and political changes in Ireland. A new generation of Irish playwrights would emerge in this period, for whom growing modernization, inward investment, and a newly acceptable emphasis on personal success clashed awkwardly with the ideological impoverishment carried along by a monolithic Church. Three playwrights, M. J. Molloy, John B. Keane, and Hugh Leonard, came to represent the rural and urban sensibility of theatre at that time. All three were interested in how traditional Irish values and practices fitted in with the Ireland emerging around them. The ways in which they reacted to an urbanizing, modernizing culture illustrates how the theatre of their generation was conditioned by a national perspective that was failing to assimilate profound societal change. Molloy, essentially conservative, promoted ideas of self-sacrifice, while Keane implicitly endorsed a liberal humanist protest against repression. Hugh Leonard's satires on suburbia wrote out rural Ireland as a thing of the past, although he retained some vestiges of the country kitchen play in his work.

All three were produced by amateur dramatic societies in their early careers and throughout the later twentieth century. Though they all three found their way on to the national stage in the Abbey Theatre, Molloy's work was to disappear from professional theatre and he became something of a laureate of the Irish amateur dramatic scene. Keane's great popularity with amateur drama competitions could arguably be cited as a reason for the late acceptance of the playwright by the national theatre. Popular as they were for amateur theatre groups, both John B. Keane and Hugh Leonard did go on to achieve international success as a result of their Abbey Theatre productions. The Ireland these playwrights described was one straddling its recent past and rapidly changing present, trying to assimilate modernization, emigration, the changing importance of the Catholic Church in Irish society, and changing attitudes to sexuality. Nationalist rhetoric became increasingly irrelevant as it failed to address the practical concerns of many young Irish men, as Bull McCabe's grotesque co-opting of it to justify murder shows in Keane's *The Field*.

The popular success of these playwrights indicates an ability to strike a chord with audiences, and as such offers something of an insight into the duality of Ireland: rural isolation and a declining way of life in an emptying countryside due to unwanted emigration, and Ireland the emerging economic success story. M. J. Molloy's work, inspired by his interest in preserving folklore gathered in his native Galway, looked back, fixated on a pre-Famine moment in Ireland that was the crucible of a recognizable, lingering trauma. John B. Keane looked to the past too, and how an increasingly modern Ireland was a thin veneer for the tradition, ritual, and power dynamics that prevailed. In Hugh Leonard's mostly suburban world, the past is a resented authority, but personal past a more important scar tissue than national past for many of his characters. All three wrote out of the aftermath of trauma that had redefined Ireland (famine, war, civil war). Molloy was concerned with preserving, and paying deference to, folkloric pre-Famine Ireland, while Keane and Leonard looked to the more global/modern Ireland of the 1950s onwards. Each placed their characters against different Irelands—wild, untamed, unknowable, and ancient, versus modern, controlled, cerebral, and yet, because of the very instability of the social contexts, often neurotic about the authenticity of the individual self.

M. J. MOLLOY

M. J. Molloy, called 'the greatest master of Irish folk theatre since Synge' by Robert O'Driscoll,[1] was born in Milltown, Co. Galway. Molloy, like Synge, took a great interest in the declining ways of life in the west of Ireland, and undertook detailed preservations of the folklore he was exposed to at gatherings held in the 'visiting house' of a neighbour. While Molloy shared Synge's urge to reach an authentic rural Ireland, he was an insider with arguably better access and, perhaps because of this, was inspired to record and preserve, rather than borrow from and experiment. Molloy's characters arrive ready-made, borrowed from his experiences and the stories he heard, and speak a more accessible, albeit still fanciful, form of Hiberno-English than Synge's.

Molloy trained for the priesthood, but his studies were interrupted by tuberculosis. A first visit to the Abbey Theatre in 1937 led him to begin writing plays in tandem with his recording of local folk histories. Molloy became preoccupied with making 'a protest against the cruel, unromantic, mechanistic mentality of modern times'.[2] After a number of years being produced in amateur dramatic events, he won a playwriting competition at the Abbey Theatre in 1941. *Old Road*, a play about emigration and poverty in 1930s Galway, was produced in the Abbey in 1943 and again in 1944; thereafter Molloy had a number of his plays staged in the Abbey in the 1940s, 1950s, and sporadically throughout the latter half of the twentieth century. His most regularly staged plays returned to the decline of rural life, as in the case of *The Visiting House* (1946), or religion and tradition with *The King of Friday's*

[1] M. J. Molloy, *Selected Plays*, ed. Robert O'Driscoll (Gerrards Cross: Colin Smythe, 1998), vii.
[2] Ibid., xv.

Men (1948) (where the tradition is that of stick-fighting). *The Paddy Pedlar* (1953) is set in 1840, in which famine and the desperation of starving men are set alongside the gruesome discovery of a corpse in a pedlar's bag. *The Wood of the Whispering* (1953) is set in rural Ireland in 1950 and concerns the descendant of the local big house, Sanbatch Daly, living in wretched poverty. The play's preface excoriates emigration forced on a diminishing population by bad government policies.

Though from the 1960s on Molloy was less often performed at the Abbey, his work became a staple of amateur drama groups throughout the country. He himself cited the years the Abbey spent based in the Queen's Theatre as disastrous for him, and for other writers.[3] Molloy believed music-hall-style work found a more sympathetic hearing at the new venue, and believed the decreasing interest in his folk-based rural plays was caused by the change in theatre and mood. Molloy withdrew into his farming as a more stable source of income, which consequently lowered his writing output. His later plays struggled to find professional productions, and his style of playwriting fell out of fashion.

Molloy identified rural people adrift in a present burdened by a legacy of slavery and fear. We see something of that legacy in *The King of Friday's Men*, set in 1787, where the people of Kilmacreena live with and accept a landlord who enforces the feudal custom of *droit de seigneur*, and at the start of the action the choice has fallen on Una, the young girl who has just got engaged to Owen. In the background is the violence of the shillelagh fighters gathered for their annual event, and it is Bartley, the strongest and most famous of the shillelagh fighters, who will eventually rescue Una from the landlord's pressgang and allow her to marry honourably. Despite this nominally happy outcome, however, the play's message is unremittingly bleak, advocating stoicism in the face of unrelenting political privation.

The King of Friday's Men concerns itself with people destined for 'odd jobs'. Bartley, the shillelagh fighter who never settled down and now takes an interest in beautiful, 17-year-old Una, resigns himself to the fact that she does not love him and will marry Owen because he is younger and more attractive. Bartley at 33, with a shillelagh-battered face, is too elderly and ineligible to hope to marry in this sparse countryside. Rory, a tragi-comic character, is the son of the celebrated bard Cormac, who does not inherit his gift for composing and similarly wastes his youth before he finally realizes this. Both retreat to 'Joyce country' (the Cornamona–Clonbur area of Connemara) to live out their lives as bit players. For Rory and Bartley, the betrayal lies in their preparation for greatness: Bartley a well-known and respected shillelagh fighter, Rory, son of the bard, who hopes to inherit his gift. Both anticipate an illustrious future, and both have it taken away. In a sense they are deprived of the heroic destiny to be expected of Irish characters on a stage. Unlike Cuchulain in Yeats's *At the Hawk's Well*, Bartley will fade into obscurity despite his having chosen the heroic life, and Rory is an aspiring shaughraun denied the eloquence and wit typical of a stage Irish poet.

In spite of the brutal political oppression suffered by the characters in *The King of Friday's Men*, in the stage directions of the third act Molloy compares their situation favourably with that of his own generation. The eighteenth-century characters enjoy the 'three essentials of food, shelter and marriage' and are happier in their subjection than

---

[3] Ibid. In fact, Molloy's plays went on being produced by the Abbey fairly regularly until 1964, after which there was a long gap before *Petticoat Loose* (1979), his last play to be performed there.

their descendants, 'who are denied the last of the three' (48). Nevertheless, for Molloy, it was the legacy of past slavery that caused the relentless emigration that he saw as draining the countryside of its people and culture. *The King of Friday's Men* looks toward the psychological damage of the Irish rural people, which in Molloy's view continued to affect the rural people ever since. This long-term historical retrospect is reflected in his preface to his later play *The Wood of the Whispering*:

> For forty years Ireland has been free, and for forty years it has wandered in the desert under the leadership of men who freed their nation, but who could never free their own souls and minds from the ill-effects of having been born in slavery. [. . .] But country people know all about it, and they know the background of this play, the comedy of the eccentric old bachelors, and the tragedy too. So it was no coincidence that its first amateur performance were by two tiny rural villages: Inchovea in County Clare and Killeedy in County Limerick, which between them won half a dozen drama festivals with it—before their dramatic societies were shattered by emigration. Every activity is hit by a falling population; and every activity is helped by an expanding population.[4]

The one-act play *The Paddy Pedlar* is set in 1840, the decade in which the Irish potato famine would decimate the landscape. The play is ostensibly concerned with the comic behaviour of Ooshla (a name related to the Irish 'duine uasal' meaning 'gentleman'), who has squandered some money with which he was entrusted for the marriage of the young woman Honor. He attempts to retrieve it by stealing from a passing pedlar, who guards a sack so carefully it is presumed to be full of stolen valuables. The pedlar in fact is carrying his mother's corpse to Leitrim, where he intends to bury her. Ooshla's philosophy of life is expressed in his dialogue with Thady, Honor's fiancé:

> OOSHLA.   [. . .] My course of life was that I passed a year one time spending her money, and lost the habit of work, so I had to have the other tenant farmers do the work for me the same as they do for the gentlemen, their landlords. But I couldn't take their crops openly the same as the landlords do. All I could do was take enough to keep me living of spuds and oatmeal in the midnight, when the world is in bed. [. . .]
>
> THADY.   But, Ooshla, 'tis God's law that all should work, but the gentlemen.
>
> OOSHLA.   (*quickly and solemnly*) That's it, work for all but the gentlemen, so no work for Ooshla, because God appointed Ooshla to be a gentleman too.[5]

Here the logic behind Ooshla's thievery (and nickname) is explained: if absentee landlords can legally take crops from the tenant farmers, then Ooshla's behaviour is just as legitimate. Neither are properly entitled, by Molloy's way of thinking, and the difference in Ooshla's theft is that it neither exceeds his needs nor is it intended as a sustainable way to live. The irony is that Ooshla plans to rise above his 'roguery', and the landlords implicitly do not. This suggests that the logic at play causes the inevitable distortion of people's behaviour because of the imposition of an unnatural authority. In Molloy's plays the individual usually only rebels and overcomes the master temporarily, and happy endings are a compromise rather than a complete accomplishment.

---

[4] Ibid., 111–12.   [5] Ibid., 91.

The play, though comic, is inherently dark, as it is concerned with poverty, desperation, deceit, and death. The conclusion again ends with the marriage of the heroine, but requires the displacement of Ooshla from his home. Despite the positive outcome of marriage for Honor to Thady, the play's setting of 1840 indicates that the couple have yet to experience greater destitution, and Ooshla will almost certainly die as an elderly, homeless pedlar during the Famine.

The Wood of the Whispering is set in the west of Ireland close to the time of the play's composition in 1953. Here, the country has been depopulated by emigration, and marriage is no longer an act of love but of economics. Characters like Sanbatch Daly, Jimmy, Paddy, and Hotha are comic bachelors whose oppressive poverty and social exile have undermined their humanity and sanity. John Devitt observed that the play 'mirrors the despair and frustration of the fifties when unemployment and emigration took their terrible spiritual toll'.[6] The set of *The Wood of the Whispering* is almost post-apocalyptic in the destitution around Sanbatch's meagre possessions. He lives a hand-to-mouth existence among the trees, and even they will be soon cut down. Sanbatch is the dominant character in the play; having lost his farm and seen the decline of the area, his remaining energy is devoted to encouraging as many marriages between young people as he can, while trying to make money with an 'invention'.

Sanbatch seeks to coax the reclusive Sadie into marrying her one-time fiancé Hotha (from the Irish *háta*, 'hat', because of the character's eccentric headwear). Hotha refused to marry Sadie when they were young, and now Sadie, a symbol of the declining population, has apparently lost the ability to speak:

> SANBATCH.   The time she was in her bloom th' oul' Depression was on, and no farmer around could afford to marry a girl that had no fortune. So she had to stop with her father and mother till they died, and then she was left alone and the lonesomeness and the darkness and the trees defeated her at last. 'Tis two years now since she spoke to anywan or went out amongst the neighbours. She spends the day and night within there thinking and ever thinking about how she lost herself.[7]

Sanbatch tries to reintegrate Sadie into society, and to make her 'marriageable'. He and Sadie live somewhat like Beckett's Hamm and Clov, in that they are a codependent pair passing the time in an endgame scenario. In Molloy's play, however, the outcome is entirely positive, and Sadie is won back to society by Sanbatch's self-sacrifice and Hotha's music.

The Wood of the Whispering records a diminishing class. Those who remain in the country, like Sadie, retreat into insanity because of a loneliness Sanbatch sees as compounded by a sort of *poena damni*, because to his mind even God has left, or will not tolerate their poverty in the church:

> SANBATCH.   [...] The young priest was talking to me about it and about the unsane [*sic*]. 'A lot are in the asylum for leading a bad life,' he said. 'Father,' I ses, 'there's more in the asylum from want of married life. 'Tis easy for the priests and nuns

[6] John Devitt, 'Murphy and Molloy', *Irish Catechist* 7, no. 3 (1983), 55–8.
[7] Molloy, *Selected Plays*, 119.

to live straightforward; they have God every morning. But we can't go to Mass on a Sunday itself, we're gone so old, some of us, and more of us are so starved and raggedy. If only we had good learning! The finest thing in the world is to be a little crazy, and to have great learning.'[8]

For Molloy, Sanbatch's being perceived by God defines his humanity. On a basic level, Sanbatch is excluded from a normalizing social ritual; it is a demoralizing and destructive experience. This is continued in the play; in the second act, for instance, Kitty enters and says 'God save all here, except the dog!'[9] Kitty is being a typical light-hearted Molloy heroine, and the remark is not an unusual one in Catholic, rural Ireland. The dog, like all animals, is not considered to have a soul or to be capable of religious salvation in Catholicism, so had Kitty not added that disclaimer to her blessing, she would have blasphemed. As Sanbatch finds himself outside of the dominion of religious consolation because of his clothes, his life is valued as little as the dog's. He too, thinks himself unworthy of divine help, telling his dog:

> SANBATCH.   I wouldn't miss you, Leggy, or be lonesome at all, if I was a good Christian, and could pass the time thinking ever more about the Sacred Mysteries up there. But I'm as greedy for the world as ever I was.[10]

Sanbatch, in complete despair and at a loss of all hope, embarks on an alchemical endeavour, declaring he has the solution to all the problems of the village and his friends, holding up a copper tube.

Sanbatch's invention succeeds but only briefly, and its seizure by the police precipitates his great gesture of hopelessness, in which he is tied Christ-like to a tree and offers himself to be taken to the asylum in Ballinasloe so that the remaining characters may sell his land and make use of his meagre resources. Instead, a practical solution is found in the young couples' agreeing to marry. Financial plans are therefore agreed, so Sanbatch is saved. The catalyst for the agreement in *The Wood* was Sanbatch's sacrifice, and this trope of salvation arising from despair, because only the truly damned can be saved, recurs in Molloy's writing. The authorities—church, state, police—cannot be depended on to effect a change for the better; rather, solutions come from within, from a necessary attainment of individual resources. As O'Toole argues, 'only the outsider can have the possibility of achieving wholeness.'[11] Molloy's characters compel action and change around them. When a transcendence occurs, it is rarely by means of traditional support structures like church and governing authority or under the demands of strict morality and convention, but in magical moments like Sadie's being coaxed back to sanity through music in *The Wood of the Whispering*.

The importance of Molloy's legacy is in his representation of rural Irish characters on their own terms, not merely as aesthetic symbols. That is not to say Molloy's characters do not speak in an extravagant, exaggerated speech, but their representation is more of an

[8] Ibid., 135–6.   [9] Ibid., 138.   [10] Ibid., 143.
[11] Fintan O'Toole, '*Homo Absconditus*: the Apocalyptic Imagination in *The Gigli Concert*', *Irish University Review* 17, no. 1 (1987), 99.

archaeological discovery and unfolding of a way of life to which Molloy strives to give a hearing. The cultural revival in the early twentieth century was, at its most ambitious, an attempt to break down, recast, and reassert Irish identity in literature, poetry, and theatre by encouraging indigenous art forms to show a distinct culture worthy of, and entitled to, independence. Less experimental, Molloy was no less effective for reaching a broad Irish audience through the frequent amateur dramatic productions of his work. Through such productions, Molloy continued as a nationwide presence, even after he lost favour with the Abbey.

Molloy shares with Synge an interest in valorizing the traditional rural Ireland diminishing before his eyes. The environments in which he sets his plays act as a stark criticism of the decimation of a culture, but his answer is not to offer a call to arms so much as present the quietly resigned result. In the self-sacrificing characters in his work, Molloy offers a social therapy that draws on the Catholic Church's teaching. The outcast Bartley and Rory are the 'king of Friday's men' of their play's title, those whose lives are given for others like their God who died on Good Friday. At the same time, where Synge, in the aborted weddings of his plays, ultimately frustrates the expectations of comedy, Molloy does provide conventional, if not entirely happy, endings, a feel-good feature of his work that may have contributed to his popularity with amateur drama competitions.

D. E. S. Maxwell argued, 'M. J. Molloy is the Irish dramatist whose work exemplified both the poetry which prose may attain and its dramatically enfeebling self-indulgences.'[12] Molloy's prose was criticized for standing 'midway between Shiels's thinning of the language and Synge's thickening of it [. . .] a tone lacking in Irish drama since the death of Synge and the early plays of Fitzmaurice'.[13] Nonetheless, Molloy's influence on fellow playwrights such as Tom Murphy should not be overlooked. Molloy's work was performed by the amateur drama society in which Tom Murphy acted as a young man in Tuam, and Molloy himself was on hand to be consulted. Plays such as *The King of Friday's Men*, *The Paddy Pedlar*, and *The Wood of the Whispering* share the dialectic of exile, violence, and paralysis of Irish life which is found in Murphy's plays. In Molloy, Fintan O'Toole argues, Murphy found 'at least the possibility of a non-naturalistic theatre which could yet reflect the reality of the world around him'.[14]

John B. Keane

Similarly popular with amateur dramatic societies, John B. Keane (1928–2002) was a playwright and novelist from Listowel in Co. Kerry. Keane emigrated to the UK like many of his generation and worked as a labourer for a time, but returned and opened a pub in Listowel in 1955. His first major play, *Sive*, was rejected by the Abbey, but went on to win the All-Ireland Amateur Drama Finals in 1959, thus ending up on the Abbey stage. Over the course

---

[12] D. E. S. Maxwell, *A Critical History of Modern Irish Drama 1891–1980* (Cambridge: Cambridge University Press, 1984), 145.

[13] Robert Hogan, *After the Irish Renaissance: A Critical History of the Irish Drama Since 'The Plough and the Stars'* (Minneapolis, MN: University of Minnesota Press, 1967), 87, 96.

[14] Fintan O'Toole, *Tom Murphy: The Politics of Magic*, 2nd edn. (Dublin: New Island, 1994), 34.

of his career he was to write over twenty plays, as well as a number of novels and many books of essays and letters. As with Molloy, the rural characters of Keane's writing reflect the Ireland of the playwright's time. His characters straddle two ways of life: traditional Ireland and its power dynamics deformed by illegitimate authorities (empire, commerce) and the changing Ireland that, along with economic growth saw a gradually liberalizing view of sexuality.

Keane's work, like Molloy's, is derived from personal experience; he often confessed to eavesdropping as a way to build a corpus of authentic vocabulary. But where Molloy recorded the trapped figures of a declining Ireland, the entrapment of Keane's characters comes from adherence to traditions that are not compatible with modern Ireland. *Hut 42* (1962) deals with the difficult reality of emigration, inspired by Keane's own experience as a migrant worker in England as a young man. *The Field* (1965), set in the bar of a public house in Carraigthomond, a small village in the south-west of Ireland, treats the clash of a tribal, traditional way of life with economic development that undermines the power dynamic of a village. *Sharon's Grave* (1960) also deals with the theme of land obsession, this time in 1930s Ireland. *Sive* (1959) confronts the way poverty and tradition has made buying and selling in marriage an accepted means of economic survival, while *Big Maggie* (1969) is a powerful and prescient argument for Irish women's right to control their bodies and their sexuality. On that theme, *The Chastitute* (1980) is a dark comedy about rural depopulation, like *The Wood of the Whispering*, which makes marriage less likely, especially in the context of retrograde church ideology in Ireland. If Molloy's treatment of these subjects was defiant but quiet, Keane's plays dramatize comparable situations with increasing frankness and anger, frequently ending with the death of his characters. Unlike Molloy, Keane was critical of church as well as state, as is most evident with the address of the land-hungry Bull McCabe to the priest in *The Field*:

> You're wrong there, Father. You have your collar and the Sergeant, his uniform. I have my fields and [my son] Tadhg [. . .] There's two laws. There's a law for them that's priests and doctors and lawmen. But there's no law for us. The man with the law behind him is the law . . . and it don't change and it never will.[15]

Keane is anti-clerical, and broadly critical of the church, but does not stray so far from verisimilitude as to make Bull McCabe an atheist. For the Bull, his prayers are a straight line to his god, and Father Murphy is merely another bureaucrat in a corrupt system to whom he pays dues he can ill afford.

The Field, perhaps Keane's best-known work, largely because of the internationally successful 1990 film version, is set in 1965, the year of its production. The crux of the play is the tension between the village's domineering quasi-leader, Bull McCabe, and William Dee, an emigrant returned from England who wishes to buy the field Bull has long coveted. Dee is an outsider to the residents of Carraigthomond; originally from Galway, he has lived in England for twelve years. Dee only returns reluctantly, for the sake of his wife. Moreover, his interest in the field is even less romantic than Bull's: he announces his intention to use it as a site for developing building materials. Bull speaks for the shocked

---

[15] John B. Keane, *Three Plays: Sive, The Field, Big Maggie* (Cork: Mercier Press, 1990), 166. It is from this edition of 'new revised texts' that all quotations from Keane are taken.

reaction of the villagers to such a use of the land: "'Tis a sin to cover grass and clover with concrete.'[16] As such, Dee can easily be seen as a signifier of the imposition of industry on rural Ireland. The relentlessness of modernization and the power of money to undermine the most stubbornly held local influence generate a potent sense of panic in the play, and Dee's murder by Bull is as understandable as it is savage. Keane's success in the play is to create a wholly unlikeable protagonist whose behaviour is somehow justified within the terms of the play. Bull is no Christy Mahon, but his character also offers persuasive eloquence and makes comprehensible to audiences how his commitment to the land gives way to violence.

In a simple free-market economic sense, Dee has the means and therefore the right to buy the field. In terms of the unspoken laws of the community, McCabe's hard work and dedication to making the land healthy and profitable in the years he has rented it outweigh Dee's claim to industrialize the field. The play deftly mediates between the natural moral outrage of McCabe's act of murder and the audience's understanding of the reasons for its cover-up

The Field explores many salient fears, particularly the loss of tradition through inexorable modernity and the potential for commercialism to literally pave over Ireland's rural heritage: Dee proposes locating a cement works in the field in question. The unseen 'tinker' characters to which the others refer are fluid and mobile. The most disturbing thing about them from the rural community's point of view, it would seem, is not just the social status they represent but also the fact that they are not tied to the land and bear no loyalty to it. And while Dee's character represents capitalist expansion, the Bull represents the power of money to corrupt the morality of ordinary people: it is Bull who places the land above human life, and his actions, though designated as immoral by the play, are crucially rendered understandable, almost forgivable, particularly in his last speech defying the priest and the Sergeant quoted above.

In *Sive* the old woman, Nanna Glavin, is a cipher of traditional Ireland in that she represents community and modest ambition (that is, she just wants a smoke). Her daughter-in-law Mena is the villain of the piece, but motivated by fear of poverty as well as a pressure to succeed. The play concerns arranged marriage in rural Ireland as an accepted practice of Mena's generation, justified by economic circumstance, and made possible by the church's stigmatizing of illegitimate children that facilitates what amounts to a trafficking of women by ostensibly respectable members of the community. Sive, an illegitimate child now 17, lives with Mena and Mike (who is her uncle). In spite of her love for the young workman Liam Scuab, she is compelled by her aunt to marry the elderly Séan Dóta, for which the family will receive a large sum of money as dowry. Keane presents Mena as a hard-nosed character (specifying even in the stage directions that her hair should be 'tied sharply in a bun' to make her less sympathetic),[17] but her plans are presented as socially acceptable: Sive is a burden and should make herself useful and repay a debt to her family in the only currency she has; she is fortunate to get a husband at all. The outcome is Sive's suicide and the genuine remorse of everyone involved. Mena's selling off of her husband's niece is desperate but ruthless, and the resultant suicide is an unsubtle moral. Keane would return in later plays to Irish society's commodification of women's bodies.

[16] Ibid., 130.   [17] Ibid., 11.

Big Maggie, first produced in 1969 at the Opera House, Cork, by Gemini Productions, opens in a graveyard, where a 'near middle-aged woman dressed in black' attends the funeral of her alcoholic and philandering husband. The widowed Big Maggie takes control of the shop and the farm. Her newfound freedom and expression of her agency see Maggie alienate her children until she is alone, and the play ends with her powerful monologue in which she curses 'the stifling, smothering breath of the religion that withered my loving and my living and my womanhood'.[18] Maggie's speech is a furious broadside against the dysfunction of the Irish family in a misogynist culture.

The strength of Keane's dramaturgy lies in the dramatic conflict of old values with practical realities. Couching it as he often did in farcical humour was a means to deliver a denunciation of contemporary Ireland and the cracks in the facade of Catholic respectability. Keane's theatre of Irish naturalism is less about celebrating or recording a declining way of life than about highlighting the social pathologies of rural Ireland. So, in *The Chastitute*, Keane addressed another kind of sexual deformation. John Bosco McLaine is a 'chastitute', a bachelor farmer who is celibate by circumstance, not choice. The play treats with comedy his attempts to find a mate, but closes with his frank confrontation with loneliness and suicidal thoughts. John Bosco's circumstances are brought about by depopulation as well as church repression, and the legacy continues in Hugh Leonard's plays, such as *The Patrick Pearse Motel*. Both treat the topic with a degree of humour, as a way to criticize the infantilism of adult sexuality that passed for respectability and piety.

The compromise between humour and anger in Keane helped to make difficult subjects more palatable. His plays look like throwback cottage-kitchen naturalism, but in fact they bravely challenged an Irish society that was repressive but depended on transactional sex under the guise of piety. Tending toward melodrama, Keane's work can suffer from a production style standardized by repetition and dependence on the light relief of laughter. But thoughtful stagings can emphasize Keane's incisive eviscerations of social and clerical hypocrisy, and the damage they can inflict on people hemmed in by poverty and obedience. And though Keane's themes now seem well-worn, his was a lone voice at the time.

It is generally accepted that Keane's recognition by the Abbey Theatre was slow to happen. Robert Welch argues that Keane's work was rejected as too folksy by a theatre that was trying to move away from a reputation for being stuck in a rut of producing peasant plays.[19] Keane's work, for all its prescient feminism and strong criticism of church hypocrisy, was still mostly set in kitchens. His being ignored was arguably an over-correction. After *Sive*, he submitted a number of plays to Ernest Blythe, only to be rejected. It was the popularity of Keane's work in amateur drama productions that maintained his career, but arguably this popularity undermined his reputation with the national theatre, while its turning away from Keane was damaging to the theatre's own status as 'national'. Ignoring Keane's work, which was produced all over the country, reinforced the sense that the theatre had nothing to say to people outside Dublin. However, in 1985 a production by Ben Barnes of *Sive* in the Gaiety Theatre, Dublin, was the beginning of a revival that eventually saw Keane embraced by the Abbey. Barnes's production involved the reduction of the play from three acts to two, and that significant alteration was enough to reinvigorate the play. Professional

[18]   Ibid., 234.
[19]   See Robert Welch, *The Abbey Theatre 1899–1999: Form and Pressure* (Oxford: Oxford University Press, 1999), 217.

productions increased in the 1980s with Ben Barnes's Abbey staging of *The Field* in 1987, which went on to tour Russia. In 1999 the Abbey belatedly recognized his importance, presenting him with a Gradam Medal (the Abbey Theatre's highest award) 'in recognition of his exceptional contribution to Irish cultural life'.[20]

Hugh Leonard

Christopher Morash argues that Tom Murphy's *The Sanctuary Lamp* (1976) and Kilroy's *Talbot's Box* (1977) 'could easily be read as the theatrical products of a modernizing urban society pulling away from a more traditional rural hinterland'.[21] At the same time, Hugh Leonard was writing plays set in contemporary, suburban Dublin that turned perceptibly away from the lonesome west.

Hugh Leonard was the pseudonym of John Keyes Byrne, born in Dublin in 1926 and raised by adoptive parents in the affluent suburb of Dalkey. In his autobiographical works, such as *Home Before Night* (1979) and *Out After Dark* (1989), as well as later newspaper columns in the *Sunday Independent*, Leonard painted a picture of a happy child who recoiled against the snobbery he perceived in his schoolmates and who was frustrated in his own disappointing academic work and attempts to write. Leonard entered the Irish civil service in 1945. The Land Commission branch of the service had an amateur dramatic society ('Lancos') which he joined, beginning soon after to write plays. Initial works were for amateur production. *The Italian Road* was submitted to an Abbey Theatre competition in 1954 but was unsuccessful in a year of no winners. It was for this play he would adopt the pen name 'Hugh Leonard'.

Leonard submitted *The Big Birthday* to the Abbey Theatre (it was a retitling of *Nightingale in the Branches*), and this was accepted and staged. Leonard's career throughout the 1950s was characterized by radio plays and enough commercial success to merit resigning his day job, before working for Granada Television in Manchester as a script editor. Leonard wrote for television, film, and theatre in the 1960s in the UK, before returning to Dublin in the 1970s. In 1976 he became literary editor for the Abbey Theatre, and in 1978 was the programme director for the Dublin Theatre Festival.

Leonard cited an early visit to the Abbey, where he saw *The Plough and the Stars* with Cyril Cusack as the Young Covey, as the impetus behind his decision to write for the theatre. Despite his later association with the Abbey, he was outspoken on the theatre's rejection of his plays, which tended to be more popular than critically acclaimed. As such, Leonard felt that he did not have the Abbey's legitimizing stamp, and was inclined to set himself apart:

> The Abbey was the one you shot for, really. All you did was try to please Ernest Blythe and if you pleased Ernest, you were in. He liked political plays and he liked plays dealing with the Troubles and things like that.[22]

[20] Carol Taaffe, 'An Introduction to "Sive" and John B. Keane', http://www.abbeytheatre.ie/resources/abbeysive/feature_727.html. Accessed 25 Oct. 2014.

[21] Christopher Morash, *A History of Irish Theatre* (Cambridge: Cambridge University Press, 2002), 251.

[22] 'Hugh Leonard in conversation with Pat Donlon', in Lilian Chambers, Ger FitzGibbon and Eamonn Jordan (eds.), *Theatre Talk: Voices of Irish Practitioners* (Dublin: Carysfort Press, 2001), 252.

Nevertheless, Christopher Morash argues that *A Life* (1980), along with *Da* (1973) and *Time Was* (1976),

> emerge not only as hugely entertaining pieces of theatre [. . .] but also as important social commentaries on a society that, in spite of a slowing of the economic growth of the 1960s, was continuing to become more dominated by the values of an urban middle-class.[23]

Christopher Fitz-Simon describes Hugh Leonard as 'the most prolific and the most technically assured of modern playwrights'.[24]

Leonard's award-winning, semi-autobiographical play *Da* ran for two years on Broadway, and led to a major film adaptation starring Martin Sheen and Barnard Hughes. *Da* is set in Dalkey 1968, with some flashbacks. The main character, Charlie, is taken to be a version of Leonard as a young man. Charlie returns to his Dalkey home from London on the death of his adoptive father, and the play is concerned with Charlie's attempt to deal with the death, his own difficulties in fitting in and moving on. Charlie speaks to a number of ghosts, primarily his father, throughout. As in Friel's *Philadelphia, Here I Come!*, the problems of an Irish man and his decent but infuriating father are played out through conversations between real and incorporeal characters, but when Charlie is set to leave Ireland at the end of the play, unlike Gar, his father follows him.

A Life (1980) is set in the contemporary Dublin of the 1970s. The critical and popular reception of the play was extremely positive. Leonard was by then known for his preference for self-conscious representations of suburban life in lieu of what he criticized as the trappings of cliché and insularity in Irish drama:

> My belief is that our attitude towards Irish writing is as parochial as the communal tap-water and the horse-trough at the end of the village street. Poets, novelists, and playwrights— unless the name happens to be Yeats or Joyce or Beckett—write about Irishmen first, as a separate species that is, and mankind a very distant and unimportant second.[25]

A Life is contemporary, irreverent, engages with Irish theatrical history as well as contemporary dramaturgy in trying to forge a new image for the national theatre. *A Life* shares with *Da,* and many of Leonard's texts, a preoccupation with mortality. The text is a cross-section of a small community and characterized by ironic metaphor. It is divided into three playing areas: a modern living room in the present; a kitchen in the past; and an old bandstand situated in 'all that remains of what was called the commons of Dalkey', 'before the country became one vast builder's yard'.[26] This set, and the physical comedy it occasions, shares more with Alan Ayckbourn's *How the Other Half Loves*, originally staged in Britain in 1971 but performed at the Peacock the year before the production of *A Life*, than any Synge or O'Casey.

The main characters in *A Life* are presented as their current and younger selves: Drumm was Desmond, Dolly/Dorothy, Mary/Mibs, and Kearns/Lar. Drumm, a minor character from *Da*, now a dying bureaucrat, recalls the circumstances that led to his current situation

---

[23] Morash, *History of Irish Theatre*, 249.

[24] Christopher Fitz-Simon, *The Irish Theatre* (London: Thames & Hudson, 1983), 191.

[25] Hugh Leonard, 'Irishness in a Changing Society', in *Selected Plays* (Gerrards Cross: Colin Smythe, 1988), 19–20.

[26] Ibid., 358.

and prepares for death by attempting to resolve old grudges. Confronting mistakes in the past and antagonizing his wife Dolly, his former love interest Mary and her husband Kearns, he positions himself as 'accountant' at the end of his life:

> DRUMM: [. . .] I need to know what I amount to. Debit or credit, that much I am owed. If the account is to be closed, so be it: I demand an audit. [. . .] I seem to have access to everyone's file but my own.[27]

Nostalgia, such as it exists in the play, is reserved for a bitter character who appears to have failed by the play's end in coming to a point of self-realization. In his opening speech, which is also to be his conclusion, Drumm evokes

> Bernard Shaw's observation that whereas Ireland's men are temporal, her hills are eternal. Any child familiar with the rudiments of geology could have told him otherwise, but then even Shaw was not immune to his countrymen's passion for inexactitude.[28]

What Leonard does in this opening text by proxy is to put Shaw in the unlikely position of wistful and loquacious Irishman, the stereotype Shaw satirized in *John Bull's Other Island*. In distancing himself from overzealous, parochial Irish cliché, Drumm goes so far as to show up Shaw to effect his point.

The setting, while still in the familiar territory of an Irish domestic sphere, is also a palimpsest. In Mary's modernized Edwardian house, Drumm's attention is drawn to the redecoration:

> MARY: It was too dark. The old people, that's them dead and gone, they went in for that: no sunlight, everything morose and dusty. I thought we'd get into the fashion.[29]

Tellingly, Mary has changed the furniture and no longer reserves a reception room for the patrician figure of the priest, but has failed to get 'the smell of beeswax and the lavender' out, an acknowledgement of the difficulty in shedding stereotypes.[30] However, in spite of the almost anonymous suburban banality of Leonard's text, it is conspicuously a play about people talking in a kitchen.

A Life is also a play about disappointment and disillusion, especially the past, which imposes itself upon the characters' attempts to move on. Drumm is irretrievably bitter and socially abrasive because of his schoolteacher father's abusive insistence on education. Yet Drumm's rejection of the past is ambivalent: 'I wanted my father alive and myself an orphan.'[31] Mibs is put in the position of being obliged to marry Lar when her father opens a letter intended for her, and consults with the priest, who, like Friel's Canon Mick O'Byrne is an arid community leader, failing as spiritual interpreter. The younger Drumm, making reference in his speech to de Valera, the irreverence of which he is informed, will draw more boos than appreciative laughs, as Ireland is apparently still passively deferential to the old conservative government. Desmond tries to impress the young Mibs with what he makes out to be the success of a public speech he made: 'It was too crowded', 'I clowned, so they laughed a lot'; 'the history professor from Trinity, he got a rough time of it'.[32] The

---

[27] Ibid., 335.   [28] Ibid., 305.   [29] Ibid., 314.   [30] Ibid.
[31] Ibid., 319.   [32] Ibid., 358.

audience learns from the older Drumm that he was in fact heckled and very little of his speech was heard.

According to Fintan O'Toole, Irish theatre after the 1950s was characterized by the convergence of traditional and modern Ireland, represented in the splitting of character:

> Playwrights such as Friel and Murphy started to place their characters in two different Irelands at the same time, creating two opposed moral and psychological worlds—a traditional one and a modern one—in which their characters have to live. Doomed to live by old values in a new world, they can literally do nothing right, for what they perceive to be right is no longer, by the lights of the new world, so. The split personality takes over. Gar O'Donnell in *Philadelphia, Here I Come!* divides between a public and a private self. Hugh Leonard's Charlie in *Da*, and the entire cast of characters in *A Life* split into past and present selves. In a slightly different configuration, Tom Murphy in almost all of his plays, divides the self between two characters, often brothers, sometimes friends or mortal enemies, who appear to be separate but who emerge as two halves of the one whole.[33]

The co-presence of traditional Ireland with the hastily evolving globalized society is one contributing factor to this split-personality disorder in Irish theatre.

Love in the Title (1999) highlighted Leonard's interest in recovering family history and a repair of the damage to the Irish family caused by empty rectitude. In this play, contemporary Ireland, in the guise of the granddaughter, engages with two past generations of Irish women, in her mother and grandmother. Meeting in a liminal, rural space with a large rock, the women, aged chronologically in reverse (that is, the grandmother is the youngest, the granddaughter the eldest), talk about their lives, usually colliding at a comical impasse when one's social propriety is contrasted with another's. Their experiences and values are based on the very different Irelands that they embody: from the naive and devout grandmother, Cat, the bourgeois and uptight mother, Triona, to the apparently liberal but isolated granddaughter, Katie. It was a very effective device of Leonard's to show the rapid social changes that Ireland had undergone, especially as far as women were concerned; and the naming of the characters, often referred to by Leonard in his journalism as 'the three Kates', is suggestive of another famous Cathleen on the Irish stage. Setting the play in what might have been a field with a large rock in the middle afforded the audience a pastoral scene, while the playful naivety of the young grandmother offered a reverberation of Friel's Mundy sisters in *Dancing at Lughnasa*. The more modern granddaughter was a proxy for contemporary Irish women, or indeed any woman that identified herself as the modern, enlightened product of a repressed socially conservative mother, such as Triona, the middle 'Kate'.

Writing for television and film may have been instrumental in Leonard's technical accomplishment in his work; it may also be why his work was often pushed into the realm of 'middle-brow' and 'saying something with a small "s"'.[34] Leonard was credited for his witty dialogue and engaging stories, but not generally held up as a playwright of artistic importance. The perspective that his upbringing afforded him, as well as his often-cited contempt for parochial theatre, offered a new perspective in Irish theatre: his was a suburban context for Kathleen Ni Houlihan. But although Leonard was ostensibly cosmopolitan,

---

[33] Fintan O'Toole, 'Play for Ireland', *Irish Times*, 12 Feb. 2000.
[34] Leonard, *Selected Plays*, 4.

he was as defiantly local as writers like Molloy and Keane, in his marking of place names and local idiom.

What all three playwrights share is that ostensible saying 'something with a small "s"' which amounted to an amassing of a complex interweaving portrait of Irish society. All three gathered the sound and images of a recognizable, local Ireland, which found eager audiences seeking theatre that spoke to the anxieties of a nation in domestic settings. This too is played out in the demonstrable importance of Molloy, Keane, and Leonard to the amateur drama scene in Ireland, which in turn shows the importance of amateur drama's ability to elevate playwrights to a national status, transcending ideological agendas of directors and notional audiences.

CHAPTER 20

··

BRIAN FRIEL AND TOM MURPHY

Forms of Exile

··

ANTHONY ROCHE

EXILE AND THE IRISH WRITER

IN 'Reflections on Exile', Edward Said writes: 'James Joyce *chose* to be in exile: to give force to his artistic vocation. In an uncannily effective way […] Joyce picked a quarrel with Ireland and kept it alive so as to sustain the strictest opposition to what was familiar.'[1] As aspiring Irish playwrights emerging at the end of the 1950s, neither Brian Friel nor Tom Murphy opted for permanent exile, though it must have offered its temptations. In 1963, Friel left his home in Derry to spend several months observing rehearsals at the new Guthrie Theatre in Minneapolis, invited there by the famed director Sir Tyrone Guthrie. The time in America and his first exposure to the process of live theatre enabled the writing of Friel's break-through play, *Philadelphia, Here I Come!*. Despite describing this period as 'my first parole from inbred claustrophobic Ireland',[2] there is no sense in the phrase that Friel desired a permanent exile. He returned with his family to Ireland, where he lived for the next fifty years, defiantly building a worldwide career in theatre from the Northern fastnesses of Derry and Donegal. Encouraged by the success of his first full-length play, *Whistle in the Dark*, in London in 1961, after its rejection by the Abbey Theatre, Tom Murphy spent the rest of the decade in England. But though London may have introduced Murphy to new theatrical techniques, the plays he wrote found no productions there; and it was the successful staging of *Famine* and *A Crucial Week in the Life of a Grocer's Assistant* under the auspices of the new Abbey and Peacock in the late 1960s that brought him home to Ireland, where he has lived and written his plays for the past forty-six years.

---

[1] Edward W. Said, *Reflections on Exile and Other Literary and Cultural Essays* (London: Granta Books, 2001), 182.

[2] Brian Friel, 'Self-Portrait (1972)', in *Essays, Diaries, Interviews: 1964–1999*, ed. Christopher Murray (London: Faber & Faber, 1999), 42.

The situation for Irish playwrights who began practising their trade after the Second World War is arguably different from those predecessors who chose exile, as so many earlier dramatists had done. The country was liberalizing in the 1960s, and Irish writers could now contribute to that critique from within. There remains the issue of existential homelessness, the estrangement of the writer from any society, and the urge to rethink aesthetic norms that Theodor Adorno memorably encapsulated in the phrase: 'no poetry after Auschwitz'. Edward Said, in 'Reflections on Exile', writes of Adorno:

> [his] reflections are informed by the belief that the only home truly available now, though fragile and vulnerable, is in writing. [. . .] Adorno says with a grave irony, 'it is part of morality not to be at home in one's home'.

Returning to the theme of exile, Said adds, 'To follow Adorno is to stand away from "home" in order to look at it with the exile's detachment.'[3]

No word or concept in the plays of Friel and Murphy comes under more pressure than that of 'home'. It is an unstable, tenuous, problematic concept, very different from the old-fashioned secure version of hearth and homeland. The term in the titles of Murphy's *Conversations on a Homecoming* (1985) and Friel's *The Home Place* (2005) is layered with irony. If Friel and Murphy returned to live and work in Ireland, they did so as inner émigrés, writers for whom the notion of home was elusive and the stance towards the society critical.

EMIGRATION IN THE 1950S AND 1960S

The most literal form of exile historically experienced by the Irish was and is emigration, and this in turn forms the subject matter of Friel and Murphy's early drama. One of the most negative factors in the 1950s and early 1960s was the sheer number of people leaving the country. Diarmaid Ferriter gives the figures in *The Transformation of Ireland*: 'Between 1951 and 1961, 412,000 people emigrated from Ireland.'[4] There had been a slight rise in population for the first time in a century (i.e. since the Great Famine) but that slight surplus was 'consumed by emigration on a scale startling by international standards'.[5] It comes as no surprise that playwrights of this period like M. J. Molloy (1917–94) should make emigration one of their central subjects. The topic would surface throughout Friel's drama, whether it is the hedge-school student Maire's wish to learn English in order to emigrate from nineteenth-century Ireland in *Translations* (1980) or the fate that awaits two of the Mundy sisters, Agnes and Rose, when they emigrate to England in the 1930s in Friel's most autobiographical play, *Dancing at Lughnasa* (1990). For Tom Murphy, his childhood in Tuam, Co. Galway, was deeply influenced by the emigration experienced in his own family. As Fintan O'Toole describes it: 'During the Second World War, as the Irish building trade slumped into depression, Jack Murphy, his father, went to work in Birmingham and stayed there

---

[3] Said, *Reflections on Exile*, 184–5.
[4] Diarmaid Ferriter, *The Transformation of Ireland 1900–2000* (London: Profile Books, 2005), 465.
[5] Ibid., 463.

for the rest of his working life.[6] As the youngest of ten children, Murphy had to witness his older nine siblings going into exile one by one. *A Whistle in the Dark* is set in England rather than 'at home' in Ireland, focusing on an all-male emigrant family, the Carneys. *A Crucial Week in the Life of a Grocer's Assistant* (1969, though written earlier) is crucial for the title character, John Joe Moran, because by the end of it he has to decide whether to emigrate or not. Murphy, like Friel, has returned to the topic of exile and emigration throughout his career, making it central to such plays as *Conversations on a Homecoming* and *The House* (2000). Neither of these two great playwrights has been entirely absorbed in their plays by the topic of emigration. They could see through and beyond it into other serious issues that ensured a lifetime of writing plays. But they could also see deeply into it.

PHILADELPHIA, HERE I COME! 'THE EXILE'S DETACHMENT'

What becomes clear in the course of *Philadelphia, Here I Come!* is that Gar O'Donnell is not emigrating from Co. Donegal to Philadelphia the following morning because of economic necessity. He is in regular full-time employment, working for his father in the family grocery shop. In Episode II we meet his three best male friends, collectively known as 'the boys', even though like Gar they are all in their mid-20s. The suggestion is that all three of 'the boys' are still living with their parents, something the collective description is meant to soften by making them sound younger than they are. Almost all the young women of the neighbourhood appear to have emigrated; we hear of one, Annie McFadden, home for the holidays. But Gar is in employment, as we know from the detailed exchanges with his father, S. B. O'Donnell, about the day's economic transactions relating to the shop, most of them staggering in their banality.

Gar is not the first of his family to emigrate. Indeed, his passage to Philadelphia has been enabled by his mother's sister, Aunt Lizzie. She is now self-styled 'Elise', an act of personal refashioning made possible by her relocation. As the important flashback scene covering their return to Ireland the previous summer reveals, Gar's childless aunt and uncle have invited him to come and live with them as a surrogate son in their Philadelphia home, where they have found him employment working in a hotel. Gar tries to encourage Lizzie to recall his parents' wedding day, but instead she keeps being drawn to remembering the economic details of her and husband Con Sweeney's decision to emigrate, even if she and her husband argue over the precise details. The date was 1937 (Con says 1938), the same year her older sister Maire got married to S. B. O'Donnell. The expectations of her mother were made clear with regard to her remaining four unmarried daughters: '[S]he thought that just because Maire got this guy with a big store we should all of got guys with big stores.'[7] Lizzie married Con in default of his having a 'big store' or any expectations and the couple emigrated to the US with '[n]othing in our pockets [and] [n]o job to go to',[8] where he got his first job with a construction company. These dates, of Maire's marriage to S. B.

[6] Fintan O'Toole, *Tom Murphy: The Politics of Magic* (Dublin: Raven Arts Press, 1994), 26.
[7] Brian Friel, *Plays 1* (London: Faber & Faber, 1996), 62.   [8] Ibid., 61.

O'Donnell and Lizzie and Con Sweeney's emigration, hover around 1937, the year of the new Irish Constitution with its declaration that it protected and arguably valorized the role of women in the home as wife and mother.

Much of what is presented in *Philadelphia, Here I Come!* was the stock-in-trade of the emigration play, as realistically rendered. This is particularly the case in relation to the play's cast of characters: the surly, uncommunicative father; the lovable housekeeper; the three rowdy male friends; the returned Yanks, and so forth. In Said's words, 'to stand away from "home" and regard it with the exile's detachment', Friel invented the brilliant device of the two Gars, the public man that all of the other characters see and interact with, and the private man who voices his inner thoughts that only he can hear. I have already argued elsewhere that the unrestrained language and behaviour of Private Gar was most likely suggested to Friel by the experience of watching Tyrone Guthrie in rehearsal in Minnesota: 'Private Gar has freedom of movement to roam around the stage while Public Gar and the other "realistic" characters are bound to and by the prescribed rituals of their everyday dialogue and routines.'[9] Nowhere is this more apparent than in the scene where Gar Public retreats to the bedroom but Gar Private stays in the kitchen to confront his father, who is engaged in his nightly game of draughts with Canon Mick O'Byrne, the parish priest. What most marked the atrophy of the 1950s in Ireland was the fact that the aged revolutionaries were still in charge—de Valera and his Fianna Fáil government—with the severe and authoritarian John Charles McQuaid as the face of the Catholic Church. Both forces of state and church are present in *Philadelphia*'s angriest scene. S. B. O'Donnell is not only Gar's father but his employer, aged 67 but with no intention of retiring or handing over the business to his sole son and heir, even to keep him from emigrating. But S.B. is also, as Scott Boltwood has pointed out, a county councillor and hence someone with a political role in maintaining the stifling status quo represented in the play: 'his position as "county councillor" further denotes both local influence and institutionalization into the bourgeois ruling class, such as it is in rural Donegal.'[10] The critique directed at S. B. O'Donnell and the Canon is only possible with the overtly theatrical device of Gar Private. His presence throughout the play involves a good deal of irreverence and parody, a freeing up of the stage to a greater range of expression, both physical and verbal, than strict realism would allow. His presence keys two crucial flashbacks that have induced Gar to emigrate: the visit the previous summer of his aunt and uncle, already examined, and the break-up with his beloved, Kate Doogan, in face of the social intimidation represented by her wealthy father. More absolutely, the device of the two Gars utilizes theatrical techniques to subject the culture to examination and critique, to expose a poverty of spirit and a cultural incoherence where a totality has traditionally been asserted:

> [T]here's an affinity between Screwballs and me that no one, literally no one could understand—except you, Canon (*Deadly serious*) [. . .] because you could translate all this loneliness, this groping, this dreadful bloody buffoonery into Christian terms that will make life bearable for us all. [. . .] Isn't this your job?—to translate? Why don't you speak, then? Prudence, arid Canon? Prudence be damned! Christianity isn't prudent—it's insane!'[11]

---

[9] Anthony Roche, *Brian Friel: Theatre and Politics* (Basingstoke: Palgrave Macmillan, 2011), 40.

[10] Scott Boltwood, *Brian Friel, Ireland, and the North* (Cambridge: Cambridge University Press, 2007), 56.

[11] Friel, *Plays 1*, 88.

This speech serves as a reminder that Brian Friel entered St Patrick's College, Maynooth as a seminarian, but emerged with his BA as a lay graduate. Gar Private's is not an attack upon religion *per se* but upon an institution that has calcified. Gar Private departs the kitchen with one of the play's most memorable and resounding lines: 'To hell with all strong silent men!'[12] It is as much a curse and a judgement on the political and religious leaders of the time as it is on the two old men bent over their game, studiously ignoring the central fact of Gar's imminent emigration.

THE LOVES OF CASS MCGUIRE
HOMES AND INSTITUTIONS

The play Friel wrote after *Philadelphia, The Loves of Cass McGuire* in 1966, is in many ways a sequel. Where the 25-year-old Gar O'Donnell emigrates from Ballybeg to the USA, the 70-year-old Cass McGuire returns home to Ireland after fifty years in New York. (Unusually for Friel, no specific locale or county is indicated, only that her family meet Cass off the boat at Cork.) Cass returns to the 'new Ireland' of the 1960s, which is enjoying the first flush of material prosperity. This precursor of Celtic Tiger Ireland is represented through the figure and family of her brother, Harry McGuire, a successful businessman, whose four children have all trained for the professions. The family relative they welcome home shocks their bourgeois notions. Cass is verbally coarse, physically raucous, smokes incessantly, and is frequently drunk. She speaks a brash, vital New Yorkese acquired in the fifty years she spent working in a busy hash-house, which her family repeatedly refer to as a restaurant. She has some bawdy set-pieces she likes to perform and, far from being euphemistic about natural functions, takes care to stress all the syllables in the word 'ur-eye-nal' when she drops it into the conversation.[13] It also turns out that the 'maiden aunt', as she is repeatedly described, may be anything but. Her stories of her exile in New York frequently refer to Jeff Olson, a man with whom she lived for many decades but to whom it becomes equally clear she was not married. It is her partner's death that has precipitated Cass's return to Ireland. But that Ireland, certainly as represented by her upwardly mobile brother and his bourgeois family, has great difficulty in accommodating the unruly presence of Cass McGuire. We learn in the opening scene of her drunken night on the town, which Harry has covered up by paying for the breakages and 'squaring' things with the police. Plans soon emerge for the old woman to be installed in a home, ironically entitled Eden House, which Cass repeatedly refers to as 'the workhouse'[14] because the home has been built on the site of one. The play seems even more prescient now in its demonstration of how Irish women who did not conform to the expected model of maidenly or marital submissiveness were incarcerated over many of the twentieth century's decades in what the play describes as 'an asylum'[15].

As the date of Gar's parents' marriage in 1937 is politically suggestive, so are those of Cass McGuire's exile. She had left Ireland, we are told, some fifty-one or fifty-two years earlier, at

---

[12] Ibid., 89.   [13] Brian Friel, *The Loves of Cass McGuire* (Dublin: Gallery Books, 1984), 15.
[14] Ibid., 15, 16, 25.   [15] Ibid., 67.

the age of 18, and in the drafts of the play Friel keeps making minor alterations to the date, suggesting 1914 or 1915 as the date of her departure. The date that looms behind Friel's revisions is 1916, which would make the date of her return to Ireland 1966, the year in which *The Loves of Cass McGuire* was first produced and the fiftieth anniversary of the Easter Rising. Far from either endorsing or condemning the Rising, the characters in the play to whom Cass returns—the affluent extended family of the McGuires—make no reference to nationalist or republican politics whatsoever. The drama's political references proceed from and are located within the context of Eden House. At the end of Act I, when Cass fiercely declares her desire to maintain her independence and sense of self in the place to which she has been confined, the man who runs odd jobs there supports her with the cry: 'Up the Republic!'[16] The one other area in the play where there are references to the Irish political struggle, so lacking in the Ireland of the 1960s, is in the past: Cass's teenage years before she emigrated, and in particular her fifty years in New York's Hell's Kitchen. At the beginning of Act II, Cass breaks the fourth wall by directly addressing a monologue to the audience— the only ones with whom she can share her political dreams. She recalls the Christmas of 1942 when Jeff Olson gave her a brooch, shaped like a shamrock with 'green and white and orange diamonds'.[17] Cass returns from one form of exile to another, to inner exile in an Ireland that in no way lives up to what she had imagined. The fantasy constructions of her time in New York lead Fintan O'Toole to speculate 'that even Cass's American history is all in her head'.[18] Her mythical reminiscences of life in the US join up with the surreal scenarios enacted not just by Cass but by the various other characters in Eden Home to provide the political subtexts to the 'reality' of the affluent, modernizing Ireland that Harry McGuire's family embodies. I find the play less uncertain than O'Toole does when he argues that it 'betrays an underlying uncertainty about whether or not its overwhelming sense of homelessness is caused by emigration'.[19] To re-invoke Adorno: 'it is part of morality not to be at home in one's home.' This point is beautifully made when Harry visits his sister in Eden House on Christmas Day, and reveals that none of their children is returning home for the holiday and that none of them is as successful as their parents have been pretending. The fluidity of the play's careful intermingling of reality and fantasy climaxes when Harry ends his confession to Cass by saying he wishes he could stay with his sister rather than returning to the physical comforts and supposed consolations of the dream home he has constructed for his wife and family.

MURPHY THE OUTSIDER

Tom Murphy's very first play, *On the Outside*, was written in 1959 (with his friend Noel O'Donoghue) but not staged professionally until 1974. Although not overtly concerned with emigration as its theme (as the following two full-length plays were), it displays a

[16] Ibid., 33.   [17] Ibid., 34.
[18] Fintan O'Toole, *Critical Moments: Fintan O'Toole on Modern Irish Theatre*, ed. Julie Furay and Redmond O'Hanlon (Dublin: Carysfort Press, 2003), 234.
[19] Ibid., 233.

form of exile in its graphic depiction of its two young male protagonists, Joe and Frank, as outsiders in the society to which they ostensibly belong. The play is set 'outside a dance-hall',[20] and that is where the action remains, despite the young men's dogged efforts to gain access. At first, the emphasis is on economics, with the placard outside the dancehall inscribed with the six shillings required to gain entrance. It rapidly becomes clear that neither Joe nor Frank can afford to pay for themselves, let alone anyone else. (The women experience no such difficulty.) One of them has four shillings, the other four and sixpence, though Joe had to 'borrow that just before I came out here'.[21] The rest of the money has likewise to be got from someone else. A drunk who joins their company is won over by their plight and, in a reversal of the social norm, gives them the handout he might instead be soliciting. In an elaborate and funny piece of mime, he shakes out coins on three successive occasions, all of which amounts to a grand total of 'sixpence halfpenny'.[22] One of the other males, Mickey Ford, declares his financial superiority not only by immediately entering the hall but by arriving in a car. They are reluctant to 'touch'[23] him financially, since it is a source of shame and will become known inside the hall. Driven to it by the extremity of their need, they approach Mickey but are rebuffed by being told he needs the money to buy petrol for his car. Neither Joe nor Frank is willing to trust the other sufficiently to back one of them to go in on both their behalves. But there are more than economic considerations at play. Murphy is one of the great dissectors of class in Irish drama, and these considerations arise when the young men gain (temporary) access to the hall on two occasions during the play. Frank goes in first to argue with the woman in the box office, but she in turn complains to the bouncer and Frank is ejected. On the second occasion, they manage to gain a pair of passes but are once more ejected by the bouncer, who recognizes Frank from the earlier altercation. The exchange with the bouncer makes clear that the two young men are being excluded for reasons that are finally more social than financial: 'You watch your filthy tongue and keep away from here if you know what's good for you.'[24]

The topic of emigration emerges in the play when it becomes clear that the dance is being held during the two weeks the local emigrants return annually from England. As in Friel's *Philadelphia*, the returned women emigrants are considered as being more sexually experienced than the stay-at-home virgins. As usual with the young Irish male of the time, the women's sexual prowess is based on hearsay and wish-fulfilment rather than direct experience:

MICKEY.   There's a Jane in there that's nursing in England home on holidays. What a woman! Full of your arms, you know. (*He winks*)
JOE.   There's nothing like the ones that spend a while in England. Them are the ones to get.[25]

Joe elsewhere queries Mickey's American accent and is told, not that Mickey has ever been to the US, but that he 'has an uncle in America and they get letters at home from him'.[26] Mickey Ford has four brothers on the inside at the dance, returned émigrés all, but from

---

[20] Tom Murphy, *Plays: 4* (London: Methuen Drama, 1997), 167.   [21] Ibid., 172.
[22] Ibid., 184.   [23] Ibid., 175.   [24] Ibid., 185.   [25] Ibid., 176–7.   [26] Ibid., 179.

England rather than the US. They are used to physically threaten Joe and Frank. Where the emigrant woman's body is sexualized, the male's is represented as inherently violent, something which *A Whistle in the Dark* will explore. At one point, Frank memorably compares the town to a tank, a 'huge tank with walls running up, straight up. And we're at the bottom, splashing around all week in their Friday night vomit',[27] while the bosses are on top spitting down on them. When he finally resolves to take action against the sense of exclusion he experiences, his proposed solution is to emigrate: 'I'm not sticking around here much longer. England.'[28] Murphy's next two plays would dramatically put that ready proposition to the test and find it wanting.

A WHISTLE IN THE DARK: THE IRISH IN ENGLAND

Frank's attempt to resolve the conflicts of class and identity by emigrating to England points the way that Murphy's drama is to go in his first full-length play, *A Whistle in the Dark* (1961). Usually in an Irish play about emigration, the setting is Ireland, with the foreign country of exile only conjured verbally, as a place of otherness which is not fully real. But Murphy's play is set throughout in England rather than Ireland, in Coventry, something which is rarely seen again in Irish theatre until Jimmy Murphy's *Kings of the Kilburn High Road* (2000) and Enda Walsh's *The Walworth Farce* (2005). Walsh's play derives from Murphy's the same sense of double setting, with a real England outside the door, and a surreal sense of displaced Irishness represented within. In the case of Murphy, the play opens on a conventional lower-middle-class bourgeois interior, the home of Michael Carney and his English wife, Betty; but it is one that his three brothers seem intent on destroying as they hurl objects at each other in the opening scene, breaking a china cup against the wall.[29] This is mirrored in the fragmentation of Murphy's language, which breaks up the imprisoning formality of syntactically complete English to admit an Irish hybrid. Where Michael seeks to conform to the norms of the society to which he has emigrated, for the rest of the Carneys to fit into an English scheme of things is at some level to suppress the distinguishing marks of Irishness:

HARRY.   You're not a Paddy?
MICHAEL.   We're all Paddies and the British boys know it.
HARRY.   So we can't disappoint them if that's what they think. Person'lly, I wouldn't disappoint them.
MICHAEL.   You won't fit into a place that way.
HARRY.   Who wants to?
MICHAEL.   I do.[30]

---

[27] Ibid., 180.   [28] Ibid., 190.
[29] In Murphy's revision for the 2012 Druid production, the play opened with an expository scene between Michael and Betty, not the chaotic scene of previous productions.
[30] Murphy, *Plays: 4*, 14.

The Carneys are aware that they are part of a broader stream of immigration into England in the early 1960s, and feel a degree of kinship with these other outsiders who own a dual allegiance: 'Blacks, Muslims. They stick together, their families and all.'[31] There are parallels with Greek drama (and Murphy's play is a tragedy), not least in the way the House of Carney pits itself against the Muslims ('that's fair; we're Catholics') and the House of Mulryan, and the warriors talk of their pride in ways that recall pagan virtue rather than Christian sin. The west of Ireland characters think and feel in tribal terms; their loyalties are organized around the family, with Dada as the hitherto undisputed chief from whom they take both direction and orders. This is virtually an all-male society, the men making up the warriors of the tribe, while the women are relegated to the background (as with Michael's English wife, Betty, and the absent Carney mother, back home in Ireland). But the faction-fighting of the Carneys has been displaced from an Irish rural hinterland to a modern English urban setting. In this locale, their activities are no longer appropriate and are as much directed against their surroundings and ultimately at each other. The violence in the play is also viewed in Joycean demythologizing terms as an undignified set-to in the toilet of a public bar. The deliberately squalid details and setting make a mockery of and seriously qualify the brothers' claims to heroic status.

England appears to offer the prospect of change, of anonymity and a new beginning. At least it did to Michael Carney, the character in the play most obviously torn between the life into which he was born and the life he is trying to make. He has sought to evade a crippling psychological inheritance by a geographic act of exile, by moving to a new and open space in which he can remake himself. But Michael's past catches up with him in *A Whistle in the Dark* as much as it does with Christy Mahon in Synge's *The Playboy of the Western World*. He tries throughout to play a double role: husband to Betty, brother and son to the Carney men. The ties of legal marriage do not operate on Michael with the same compelling atavistic force as the blood ties of family kinship. At the end of the play, even as he has fought to show up their father's bogus authority, Michael no longer recognizes Betty; as he once more enters into and takes on his familial identity, she becomes a stranger to him.

A Crucial Week in the Life of a Grocer's Assistant: Should I Stay or Should I Go?

Where *A Whistle in the Dark* is a tragedy about emigration, Murphy's *A Crucial Week in the Life of a Grocer's Assistant* (originally titled *The Fooleen*) is a comedy on the same subject. Although explicitly referenced as being set in 1958—'Jesus job! I can earn seven ten a week anywhere in 1958!'[32]—the play was not staged until its première in Dublin at the newly reopened Peacock Theatre in 1969. It provides a fascinating complement to Friel's *Philadelphia, Here I Come!* and a contrast to *A Whistle*. The week is crucial in the life of John Joe Moran because it is the one wherein he has to decide whether to emigrate

---

[31] Ibid., 10.   [32] Ibid., 125

or not. John Joe is even older than Gar O'Donnell, conscious at 29 that 30 is coming up, but still referred to by the inquisitive neighbour, Mrs Smith, as 'the boy, John Joe! Off to work, darlin', now, the boy!'[33] Mrs Smith always appears clutching her rosary beads in her fist and trailing her daughter, Agnes, who, despite chewing sweets unbeknownst to her mother and wearing ringlets, is only a year younger than John Joe. He is off to work as the assistant in a grocery shop, but not one run by a relative. In the second scene, which is set there, the shop is entered by one Pakey Garvey, who like John Joe used to work there, has emigrated to England, and has returned for his father's funeral. Pakey is smartly dressed and has come to pay Mr Brown for the coffin. Because Pakey is a paying customer, Mr Brown is determinedly polite to him, even in the face of all the insults Pakey sends his way. When they are alone, John Joe tries to probe Pakey on the quality of life in England, asking what there is 'apart from the money over there'; but his friend can only retort: 'Apart from *what*?'[34] John Joe puts in a good to middling word in defence of his employer, clearly states that he 'never had any wish to leave', and declares after Pakey exits: 'Well, if it's that good, what're you so bitter about?'[35] In this key scene, Murphy dramatizes what Emilie Pine has termed 'the uneasiness of the home community about the return of the emigrant'.[36]

The play makes the bedroom a site of fantasy, not by the device of splitting the central character but by making it the location of the play's dream sequences. Indeed, this is how *Crucial Week* opens: with John Joe's 19-year-old girlfriend Mona climbing into his bedroom, dressed in a slip. There is more sexual foreplay than any realistic staging in the 1950s or 1960s would have allowed. But the boundary between waking and sleeping becomes hard to draw when John Joe's mother enters to banish Mona and we realize from her fantastical description of the girl—'that hussy of a clotty of a plótha of a streeleen of an ownshook of a lebidjeh of a girleen'[37]—that John Joe is still asleep. There is a gradation between fantasy and reality in Murphy rather than any clear-cut distinction, as there would be in his 1971 play, *The Morning After Optimism*, with an aging ponce and whore confronted with their idealized younger selves in a fairy-tale forest. But the fantastical language of many of the characters and the difficulty in telling whether they are talking to themselves or engaging in keen-eared dialogue gives an air of fantasy to even the most realistic of scenes. Mona, when she is actually in the haybarn with John Joe, spends less time rolling in it than in the dream sequences; but what she is luring him towards is not sex but emigration, couched in the Yeatsian cadence of a fairy-like call to 'come away'.[38] The emigration is held out by her as a means to overcome and lessen if not abolish the class divide between them, which he feels acutely.

Where S. B. O'Donnell was to the fore in *Philadelphia*, and the mother an absent if still potent presence, John Joe's mother dominates the Moran household. Her relationship with her son is a suffocating one, and comes freighted with reminders of how much she has sacrificed for him, to the point where John Joe expresses the wish that he might be rich so he could 'pay her off'.[39] Mother rarely if ever leaves the house, preferring to

---

[33] Ibid., 97.   [34] Ibid., 101.   [35] Ibid., 104.

[36] Emilie Pine, 'The Homeward Journey: The Returning Emigrant in Recent Irish Theatre', *Irish University Review* 38, no. 2 (2008), 312.

[37] Murphy, *Plays: 4*, 94.   [38] Ibid., 114.   [39] Ibid., 114.

peer out the window and see what the neighbours are up to; John Joe's father is alive, but only barely so, a vestigial figure in the household (his job, appropriately, is digging graves) who sits on a box in the corner and stares vacantly into space. The efforts of the son to make contact with his father are occasional but moving. He is entirely overlooked and dismissed by his wife, who is consumed by the relationship with her son. John Joe appears for most of the play to be an only son. But there are brief, passing references to an older brother, Frank, who has emigrated. In the play's climactic and cathartic scene, when John Joe exits his home and takes to the street in the middle of the night to shout out all the secrets of the parish, he does not spare the Moran household and their guilty secret: 'My brother Frank done jail in America. Fourteen months, drunk and fighting a policeman. Say a prayer for him.'[40] Even though Frank is out of the country, the neighbours can still intuit something is amiss by the failure of the postman to deliver any of the usual dollar-stuffed letters to the Morans from the USA. When his mother responds to her son's criticisms by suggesting he follow his brother into exile, John Joe responds: 'we're half-men here, or half-men away, and how can we hope ever to do anything.' His mother points out that his parents are not 'forcing [him] to stay', but he is equally clear that he is 'not being forced to go either'.[41] John Joe's resolve to stay does not come easily; and the demons he has to cope with are succinctly embodied in the question: 'Do you feel guilty for every cigarette you smoke? And how can I do anything until I find out what's wrong with that?'[42]

THE EARLY 1970S: PROBLEMATIC EXILE

Both Brian Friel and Tom Murphy took up emigration again (briefly) at the beginning of the 1970s. Friel's *The Gentle Island* (1971) begins with an extraordinary scene of mass emigration, as the island's entire remaining population other than one family leaves for the UK. The scene unbalances the rest of the play, which concentrates on the Sweeney family and their complicated, ultimately tragic response to the arrival on the 'gentle' island of a gay couple from Dublin. Friel's dissatisfaction with the play may be gauged by the fact that he essentially rewrote it nine years later as *Translations* (1980), which contains a similar structure but with the two male outsiders now associated with the British army in the 1830s. Tom Murphy's *The White House* was originally a two-act play when staged at the Abbey Theatre in 1972. One act told of the impact on 1960s Ireland of the visit of American president, John F. Kennedy. The other act was set in the 1970s, when the returned emigrant Michael comes home with his ideals intact to confront the disillusionment of those who have remained behind. The relationship of the two acts remained problematic. Murphy solved the dilemma when he reworked the play as *Conversations on a Homecoming* with Druid Theatre Company in Galway in the following decade. Murphy's solution was to eliminate one of the two acts (that set in the 1960s) and develop the other, where the idealistic earlier decade is not represented but recalled.

[40] Ibid., 160.   [41] Ibid., 162.   [42] Ibid., 152.

THE SANCTUARY LAMP AND FAITH HEALER: METAPHYSICAL EXILE

Throughout the 1970s Friel and Murphy grew increasingly dissatisfied with the social realism they had undermined in their plays about emigration—by splitting Gar O'Donnell into two characters, by directly staging John Joe Moran's dreams—and instead developed a more overtly symbolic dramaturgy. As already indicated, Murphy's *The Morning After Optimism* was set in a fairy-tale forest which appeared to offer a refuge from their everyday sordid lives for Jimmy and Rosie. In *The Sanctuary Lamp* (1975), the Murphy play I will concentrate on from this decade, the set is an empty church at night, its abstractness further developed by the fact of the play's being set in a city which is not named and which seems likelier to be in England than in Ireland. Brian Friel wrote a succession of plays in the 1970s which were staged at the Abbey Theatre. *The Freedom of the City* (1973) and *Volunteers* (1975) were his most political, a response to the developing Troubles in Northern Ireland, where he had been raised a Catholic Nationalist and where he still lived with his family. Friel followed these two political plays with a move into a more Chekhovian mode, with *Living Quarters* (1977) and *Aristocrats* (1979). The family structure was enriched and complicated by the presence of three sisters in each, creating a fluid theatrical ensemble.

In both plays, several grown-ups in the families returned briefly from exile: Helen, the divorced eldest daughter in *Living Quarters*, from London; Casimir, the only son in *Aristocrats*, from Hamburg where his alleged happy marriage is described by another character as a 'fiction'[43] and where one suspects his suppressed homosexuality may more readily be expressed. In 1979 Friel produced another play, his most theatrically experimental and arguably his best, in *Faith Healer*. I will briefly consider Murphy's *The Sanctuary Lamp* and Friel's *Faith Healer* in tandem, since they are both plays that set the stakes much higher than anything they had so far written by representing not a literal exile but a spiritual one.

The Catholic Church was coming under increasing strain in the 1970s; as Diarmaid Ferriter puts it: 'some of the indicators of a demise in the power of the Church were already in place.'[44] The number of clergy declined, and the most alarming sign of all was the precipitate decline in vocations. Mass attendance did not decline significantly but Irish Catholics were much more selective in those areas of belief and dogma they chose to follow (particularly in relation to human sexuality). When he returned to Ireland in the 1970s, Tom Murphy accepted an invitation to work as a member of the International Commission of English in the Liturgy and spent several years absorbed in refashioning a new religious language in the vernacular. But, as Fintan O'Toole records, Murphy told the Commission that he was not a Catholic, and the experience of working on a liturgy in English did not alter that fact.[45] It helps to explain the extent to which religious imagery and language inform *The Sanctuary Lamp*, a play dedicated not to the ends of Mother Church but to addressing the still pressing spiritual needs of characters cut adrift in an increasingly post-Catholic world (and one which caused walkouts at the Abbey in scenes reminiscent of Synge and

---

[43] Friel, *Plays 1*, 291.   [44] Ferriter, *Transformation of Ireland*, 732.
[45] O'Toole, *Tom Murphy*, 184–5.

O'Casey). When one man in *The Sanctuary Lamp* directs a threat of violence at the other, it is couched in the following terms: 'Unless you resolve to suffer and die things will not get better says the Lord! Speak up, speak up, Lord, your servant is listening!'[46] As Shaun Richards remarks, 'Murphy's theatre is a secular theatre in its location, but I'd suggest it is profane in the original sense of *profanum*, outside the temple, but not disconnected from sacred concerns.'[47] Friel's *Faith Healer* opens, appropriately enough, '*in darkness*'. As the lights come up they disclose the title character alone on stage, '*his face tilted upwards, his eyes shut tight*' as he intones words we do not understand, the names of Welsh and Scottish villages rather than the words of the Latin ritual, which he does 'just for the mesmerism, the sedation, of the incantation'.[48] Frank goes on to describe his faith healing as 'a vocation without a ministry',[49] but in certain ways he resembles the priest Friel had once thought of becoming. Throughout the play, Frank Hardy is plagued with doubts as to whether his faith healing will work; most of the time, it does not. But these doubts that assail him—as to whether he is a charlatan or a genuine mystic—may be termed questions of belief.

In this play, Friel has reduced the setting and props to a minimum. The banner proclaiming 'The Fantastic Francis Hardy/Faith Healer/One Night Only' and the fifteen chairs indicate that we are directly present at one of Frank's 'performances'[50] (the word he always uses to describe the faith-healing ritual). He directly addresses the audience in the first and last of the play's four monologues, just as his wife, Grace, and Cockney manager, Teddy, do in the other two. The audience in the theatre, therefore, stands in for the physically damaged people who have sought out Frank in the fringes of Wales and Scotland; and we realize that the play is a rehearsal of the very process it describes. With the bare boards exposed, and with the characters so explicitly addressing and acknowledging the audience, *Faith Healer* is explicitly a meta-dramatically self-conscious work about the theatre, and about a certain kind of theatre, a theatre of ritual rather than realism.[51] We come looking for the 'miracle' of theatre even though experience tells us, and Frank confirms, that 'nine times out of ten, nothing at all happened'.[52] His opening monologue raises the audience's hopes and at the same time shows why they are foolish to be so wooed; it is an act of calculated theatrical defiance. Frank's pitch leaves the audience free to regulate the degree of its credulity at will but also sets its cap at transcendence—a risky business, indeed. The set of *The Sanctuary Lamp* is the interior of a church; and its various symbolic props are turned to their own particular uses by the three characters, but with remaining traces of their original symbolic function. When a down-and-out beggar is hired as a clerk by the Monsignor, who spends his days reading Hermann Hesse since no one comes to the church any longer, one of Harry's few tasks is to keep the sanctuary lamp of the title lit. In this way, some light is provided but also some hope of a saving spiritual connection, however attenuated. The confession box is soon put on its side, and its hollowed-out interiors provide a convenient

---

[46]   Tom Murphy, *Plays: 3* (London: Methuen Drama, 1997), 142.

[47]   Shaun Richards, 'Response', in Nicholas Grene (ed.), *Talking About Tom Murphy* (Dublin: Carysfort Press, 2002), 63.

[48]   Friel, *Plays 1*, 331.   [49]   Ibid., 333.   [50]   Ibid., 343.

[51]   On this aspect of the play, see Nicholas Grene, 'Five Ways of Looking at *Faith Healer*', in Anthony Roche (ed.), *The Cambridge Companion to Brian Friel* (Cambridge: Cambridge University Press, 2006), 60–2.

[52]   Friel, *Plays 1*, 334.

place for the characters to sleep. But the need to confess, to open up about one's private hopes and fears to another human being, does not go away so readily. When Harry talks to his friend Francisco about 'the first time' he had sex, the latter responds: 'What's with the confession?'[53] The church's pulpit is a central presence. Formerly, Harry was a strong man in a circus; and he makes more than one attempt to lift it off the ground. Finally, he is successful, ironically when Francisco is occupying the pulpit to deliver a sermon. Harry is a lapsed Jew; Francisco an Irish Catholic raised by the Jesuits. The latter stands in the pulpit to denounce an institutional Christianity, the members of which 'cannot agree among themselves on the first three words of the Our Father' and instead proclaim a Jesus who is 'total man' and will call to his side on the Day of Judgment not the sheep-like clergy but the goats, 'all those rakish, dissolute, suicidal, fornicating goats, taken in adultery and what-have-you'.[54]

The two plays push beyond realism in the theatrical ways already indicated, but most of all in their approach to and treatment of life and death. We take Frank Hardy's first monologue at face value. The second, by his wife, Grace, rapidly raises doubts about the veracity of Frank's version of their relationship. Grace's monologue refers to the death of a baby she bore Frank in Kinlochbervie that has formed no part of his account of their stay in that Scottish village. But further than that, her account also indicates that Frank has died on the night of his homecoming to Ballybeg in Ireland, when he fails to cure the crippled McGarvey. Grace's monologue is set in London a year after Frank's death and sees her making a perilous, pill-laden return to normality without the man to whom she has dedicated her life. The manager, Teddy, picks up the narrative in the third monologue, confirming certain details of the previous two, contradicting others, but adding the key detail that he was called to identify Grace's corpse during that period in London. The play concludes with Frank giving a heightened account of how he faced his end. The entire drama, therefore, appears to be set in some kind of theatrical afterlife (à la Beckett's *Play*) in which the characters are endlessly fated to retell the interwoven stories of their lives together. No religious terms are used to describe this region, just as the name of God is never used other than as an expletive in Friel's play. It could be called Limbo, which is finally the place that Murphy's Francisco wishes to go after his death—or rather wishes he had gone after his birth and prior to baptism: 'I thought—same as any other sensible baby would—that Limbo was the place to get to.' You would not get to see the face of God but, as Franscisco continues, 'what baby, I ask you, gives a burp about the face of God. No, the only thing that babies feared was the hand of God, that could hold your little baby body in his fist, before dipping you into the red hot coals of hell. Then take you out again [before dipping you] into the damp black heat of purgatory.'[55] *The Sanctuary Lamp* is haunted by the ghosts of dead babies, Harry's daughter Teresa and the teenage Maudie's infant Stephen; Francisco also confirms that Harry's wife, Olga, with whom he has had an affair, is dead of an overdose, in ways that strikingly parallel the fate of Friel's Grace Hardy. The three characters central to both plays draw together in the face of death, the fourth character whose presence can be sensed all the way through.

The Sanctuary Lamp and *Faith Healer* are a very different order of theatre from the naturalistic norm, and from much of what Tom Murphy and Brian Friel had written earlier in

---

[53] Murphy, *Plays: 3*, 137.   [54] Ibid., 154–5.   [55] Ibid., 159–60.

their careers. The exile now is spiritual; but both plays also feature a strand of literal emigration. Although he is from Ireland, Frank Hardy has plied his faith healing trade in the Celtic fringes of Wales and Scotland. When he seeks to renew his gift by going back to Ireland, the homecoming proves fatal. Francisco in *The Sanctuary Lamp* is an Irishman in exile in England, as with so many of the characters in early Murphy. But if these later plays reveal connections with the earlier, the reverse is also true. When *Philadelphia, Here I Come!* and the other works discussed in this chapter are viewed in the light of *The Sanctuary Lamp* and *Faith Healer*, the emphasis on literal emigration recedes and the metaphysical plight of the central characters is instead foregrounded. The flight from self-awareness that all of the protagonists in these plays seek to enact by going into exile is placed in serious question, never more succinctly than in Gar Public's final answer to Gar Private's asking why he has to leave: 'I—I—I don't know.'[56]

---

[56] Friel, *Plays 1*, 99.

CHAPTER 21

··

THOMAS KILROY AND THE IDEA OF A THEATRE

··

JOSÉ LANTERS

In the 1960s and 70s, when Ireland was undergoing major social, cultural, and economic changes, Thomas Kilroy's academic writings helped shape the debate about how Irish theatre might best reflect and respond to this unsettling process of modernization, while his plays of the era, in their subject matter as well as their technique, exemplified how the limited range of conventions and approaches that dominated the mid-twentieth-century Irish stage might be broadened and transcended. Looking back on the 1950s, Kilroy has remarked on the 'peculiarity' of that decade: 'its odd mixture of stagnation and incipient struggles to break free, its collision of an older Ireland and an Ireland about to be reborn.' Although the Dublin theatre scene was then, as Kilroy himself concedes, 'very alive', this was not true of new Irish writing for the stage.[1] The productions Kilroy saw in the Irish capital in the second half of the 1950s that excited him—at the Gate Theatre, sometimes at the Abbey, but also in small venues like Alan Simpson's Pike Theatre—were of mainly European and American plays. Particularly stimulating among those was Hilton Edwards's 1957 staging of Shakespeare's *Julius Caesar* in fascist costume and his production of Brecht's *Mother Courage* in 1959; but the arrest of Simpson that same year on the grounds of obscenity in his production of Tennessee Williams's *The Rose Tattoo* at the Pike (where Kilroy worked in the box office) showed that there were still some risks Irish theatre-makers could ill afford to take. The Irish plays that caught Kilroy's attention in 1957 were Denis Johnston's *The Old Lady Says 'No!'* (1929) at the Gate, which proved 'a revelation of energetic theatricality', and Jim Fitzgerald's staging of seven plays by W. B. Yeats at the Globe Theatre in Dun Laoghaire, which taught the aspiring playwright 'how Yeats's idea of theatre could still speak to the later twentieth century'.[2] But in 1957 these Irish works were already decades old; new Irish writing was unimaginative by comparison.

---

[1] Thomas Kilroy, 'A Memoir of the 1950s', in Gerald Dawe, Darryl Jones, and Nora Pelizzari (eds.), *Beautiful Strangers: Ireland and the World in the 1950s* (Oxford: Peter Lang, 2013), 9.

[2] Thomas Kilroy, 'A Playwright's Festival', in Nicholas Grene and Patrick Lonergan (eds.), *Interactions: Dublin Theatre Festival 1957–2007* (Dublin: Carysfort Press, 2008), 11.

As a student in the 1950s, Kilroy's involvement in drama at University College Dublin provided him with valuable insight into the practice of acting and stagecraft; but it was in England, where he worked during the summer months, that he was introduced to a different kind of theatre from that with which he was familiar at home. What was 'freeing and exciting and interesting' about young playwrights like John Osborne, Arnold Wesker, and John Arden was that 'they were reading English culture in such a close way', whereas the Irish plays of his day, by and large, 'read Irish culture without any angle'.[3] The generation of playwrights that emerged in Ireland in the early 1960s—Kilroy, Brian Friel, Tom Murphy, John B. Keane, and Hugh Leonard prominently among them—had to contend with a powerful theatrical tradition shaped by the likes of J. M. Synge and Seán O'Casey but which had, by the 1940s and 1950s, become pedestrian under the influence of a narrow-minded nationalism and Catholicism. The new generation could only approach that tradition with a degree of iconoclasm, which in Kilroy's case initially entailed writing what amounted to a manifesto of sorts: drawing on the innovative practices and approaches he had encountered outside Ireland, he set out his ideas for what the modern Irish theatre should be in an article published in the summer 1959 issue of the journal *Studies*.

'GROUNDWORK FOR AN IRISH THEATRE'

In 'Groundwork for an Irish Theatre', Kilroy makes two fundamental points: that the theatre at its best should be a community, and that its constituent members—writer, actor, director, designer—should be 'very responsive to the demands of the society about it', in that an ideal theatre 'absorbs some of the conflicting, topical, social issues around it and gives a public interpretation of current values'.[4] Arguing that 'the Irish theatre is badly in need of new worthwhile Irish plays',[5] and that younger writers would be encouraged by an environment where they could work alongside actors and directors, Kilroy advocated the creation of a theatre workshop along the lines of Joan Littlewood's Theatre Workshop at the Theatre Royal, Stratford East, which had successfully produced Brendan Behan's *The Quare Fellow* (1956) and *The Hostage* (1958), and the experimental playwright's workshop established at London's Royal Court by George Devine as an effort to create a theatre that would be part of the intellectual life of the country. As for Kilroy's second point—that Irish dramatists 'are inclined to shirk the painful, sometimes tragic problems of a modern Ireland which is undergoing considerable social and ideological stress'—his suggestion was that a communal approach to theatre that would 'keep playwrights alive to the experiments and advances of modern stage-craft' would also encourage serious dramatists to 'fulfil the role of commentator on current values, practising espionage for everyman'.[6]

In the decade following Kilroy's passionate call for an engaged and vibrant Irish theatre supportive of young talent, new playwrights struggled to make their mark, often from a base outside the country. In 1960, Tom Murphy's *The Iron Men* (winner of a national

---

[3] Sara Keating, 'Hearing Voices', interview with Thomas Kilroy, *Irish Times*, 2 Feb. 2008.
[4] Thomas Kilroy, 'Groundwork for an Irish Theatre', *Studies* 48, no. 190 (1959), 192.
[5] Ibid., 193.   [6] Ibid., 195–6.

script-writing competition) was turned down for the Abbey Theatre by Ernest Blythe (who not long before had also rejected Behan's *The Hostage* and Keane's *Sive*); Murphy would spend the rest of the 1960s in England where the play, revised as *A Whistle in the Dark*, was produced in 1961 by the Theatre Workshop at Stratford East, from where it moved to the West End. Murphy suggested in the early 1970s that the move to England had also entailed a breaking away from 'the naturalism to which the Irish theatre is clinging', although Irish themes like emigration and violence remained part of his work. Blythe, who still considered *A Whistle in the Dark* 'rubbish' after it opened at the Olympia Theatre in Dublin in 1962,[7] was also to reject Murphy's *The Fooleen*, which was finally staged at the Abbey in 1969, revised and retitled *A Crucial Week in the Life of a Grocer's Assistant*. Brian Friel had three plays produced in Ireland between 1960 and 1963, including *The Enemy Within* at the Abbey (1962), but did not hit his theatrical stride until he had spent a number of months observing Tyrone Guthrie's directorial work at his theatre in Minneapolis. The revelatory nature of that experience he later likened to 'some kind of explosion in the head' that made him realize the limitations of the works he had written for the stage up to that point.[8]

In Kilroy's view, the play Friel completed after his return from the USA, *Philadelphia, Here I Come!* (1964), marked the beginning of contemporary Irish theatre, along with *Stephen D* (1962), Hugh Leonard's adaptation of James Joyce's *Stephen Hero* and *A Portrait of the Artist as a Young Man*. Leonard wrote the play while working for Granada television in Manchester and could not understand why it was so successful, since he regarded the work as 'more of an arranging job than anything else'.[9] Indeed, what was striking in these plays was less their material than, in Kilroy's words, 'the sensibility of both writers' which was 'modern, alive to the dislocating perspectives of the mid-century and the fluidity of expression possible on stage with modern lighting, design and direction'. The technical inventiveness of *Stephen D* and its 'cinematic lay-out of differing planes of action and time-scales' impressed him. Friel's play divided its main character into a 'private' and a 'public' Gar O'Donnell to be played by two actors, and also split the stage, leaving a 'generous apron' as a 'fluid' space 'to be occupied by the imagination of the audience'. Both plays imposed 'a new kind of theatrical imagination upon traditional material', a mixture Kilroy came to see as typifying his own work and that of his contemporaries over the next twenty-five years.[10]

THE O'NEILL

In 1964, Kilroy sent the script of his first play, *The O'Neill* (1969), to Hilton Edwards, whose work at the Gate Theatre he admired. The play includes some Brechtian influences—notably the technique of embedding 'realism inside highly stylized staging' which Kilroy knew appealed to Edwards[11]—and has a non-linear plot, but for the developing playwright,

    7 Fintan O'Toole, *Tom Murphy: The Politics of Magic* (Dublin: New Island, 1994), 7.
    8 Brian Friel, 'An Observer in Minneapolis', in Paul Delaney (ed.), *Brian Friel in Conversation* (Ann Arbor, MI: University of Michigan Press, 2000), 39.
    9 'Leonard: Difficult to Say "No"', in Des Hickey and Gus Smith (eds.), *A Paler Shade of Green* (London: Leslie Frewin, 1972), 194.
    10 Thomas Kilroy, 'A Generation of Playwrights', *Irish University Review* 22, no. 1 (1992), 136–7.
    11 Kilroy, 'A Playwright's Festival', 15.

formal experimentation was less important than 'the representation of reality through the individual imagination'. While Kilroy 'reacted against Irish realism or naturalism' in his early plays, he nevertheless greatly valued accuracy in the theatre 'to the social scene, or towards emotion, or the intense focus of the actor'.[12] Edwards liked the fresh approach of *The O'Neill* to its historical material as well as its freedom of form, but economic restraints prevented him from accepting a play with a cast of twenty-five. By 1966, Kilroy had submitted both the revised *O'Neill* and *The Death and Resurrection of Mr Roche* to the Abbey Theatre. The former play was, eventually, accepted for production at the Peacock—the Abbey's space for new and contemporary work—although the opening had to wait until 30 May 1969. Tomás Mac Anna, the Abbey's artistic adviser, found *Mr Roche* interesting reading and its theme—male sexual frustration and homophobia—'very much up to date',[13] but subsequently informed Kilroy that the managing director (Ernest Blythe, who was about to retire from the position) had turned it down on the grounds that the work was 'not in our line of territory'.[14] It was staged at the Olympia in 1968 as part of the Dublin Theatre Festival, where it was well received. Kilroy suspects that, without that success, *The O'Neill* might not have made it to the Peacock stage at all.

Kilroy took his inspiration for his play about Hugh O'Neill from Seán O'Faolain's biography of that last great Gaelic chieftain, *The Great O'Neill* (1942), which provides a fascinating account of a man raised, and torn, between two cultures: the traditional way of life of the Irish clans and the modern customs of English courtiers and politicians. Writing the play sparked in the playwright an interest in the cultural and psychological split within Irishness, a topic he went on to explore in a series of lectures and essays which considered the difference between the Anglo-Irish and the Irish dramatists. The Anglo-Irish playwrights, Kilroy argued in his 1969 Thomas Davis lecture, have in common that there is about their work 'that quality of cool, dispassionate observation [...] one associates with an external viewpoint',[15] which produces a theatre of artifice and ideas. Irish writing, he suggested in a later article, is more expressive of emotion but displays 'a curious intellectual resistance [...] to the life of intelligence', which 'reflects a rooted prejudice within the country as a whole' perpetuated by an educational system 'marked by fear, restrictiveness and a lack of confidence in the human mind'.[16] In Kilroy's view, theatre should always have mind as well as body: hostility to ideas in the theatre is 'simply a failure to recognize the depth of passion which can be conveyed through thinking'.[17]

One reason why Kilroy has always felt an affinity with the intellectual passion and creative distancing of the Anglo-Irish playwrights is that he, too, by nature and temperament has found himself 'in some profound way alienated' from his own culture and from the prevailing mode of social realism in Irish drama.[18] What attracts him in the Anglo-Irish

---

[12] Keating, 'Hearing Voices', 7.

[13] Tomás Mac Anna, letter to Thomas Kilroy, 30 Dec. 1966, Thomas Kilroy papers, James Hardiman Archives, NUI Galway (NUIG), MS P103/47(5–6).

[14] Tomás Mac Anna, letter to Thomas Kilroy, 22 Feb. 1967, NUIG, MS P103/57(1).

[15] 'Tradition of Irish Drama Discussed: Thomas Davis Lecture', *Irish Times*, 27 Oct. 1969.

[16] Thomas Kilroy, 'The Writers' Group in Galway', *Irish Times*, 8 Apr. 1976.

[17] Thomas Kilroy, 'The Intellectual on Stage', *Irish Pages* 7, no. 2 (2011), 100.

[18] Gerald Dawe, 'An Interview with Thomas Kilroy', in Gerald Dawe and Jonathan Williams (eds.), *Krino 1986–1996: An Anthology of Modern Irish Writing* (Dublin: Gill & Macmillan, 1996), 230.

tradition is that 'what is being dramatised [. . .] is the intelligence of the playwright himself [. . .] which mediates between us and the stage action'.[19] About *The O'Neill*, Kilroy said in 2004: '[it] had a lot of the stylistic interests that I still have today, such as making the stage a very prominent thing in the play itself. I love [. . .] the fact that plays have this kind of artifice'.[20] The action of *The O'Neill* is episodic and non-linear: each of its two acts begins after O'Neill's victory over the English at the Battle of the Yellow Ford in 1598, but the first uses a flashback technique to show the events leading up to that moment, whereas the second takes us forward to the defeat of the Irish at Kinsale three years later. Kilroy breaks the illusion of reality only in the opening scene, when the English Sir Robert Cecil impatiently interrupts the reading of the Irish victory demands, signalling the character's anger and frustration, but also subtly shifting his role to that of a stage director in order to accommodate Lord Mountjoy's request to 'begin at the beginning again', so that he (and we) may understand 'O'Neill and his Irish wars':

> O'NEILL.   Must I go back over all that, again?
> CECIL.   I'm afraid so. We must go back once more before we can go on.[21]

The play soon abandons such overt frame-breaking techniques, but its use throughout of quick successions of brief scenic episodes reflects the 'cinematic' techniques and 'differing planes of action and time-scales' Kilroy had admired in Leonard's *Stephen D* and Friel's *Philadelphia, Here I Come!*

THE DEATH AND RESURRECTION OF MR ROCHE

Around 1959, Kilroy began the play that became *The Death and Resurrection of Mr Roche* by trying to write about an assault on a prostitute, in an attempt to address the sexual violence of the Dublin he knew in the 1950s. The play resisted him until he substituted a gay man for the female character, which 'concentrated the play on maleness, on the dynamic within which the dysfunctional world of the play had its roots and grounding'.[22] For Kilroy, the choice of a homosexual character also constituted a personal liberation from the forces of fear, guilt, and hypocrisy that dominated Irish culture at the time. *The Death and Resurrection of Mr Roche*, directed by Jim Fitzgerald, premièred in November 1968 as part of the Dublin Theatre Festival. It was, according to a review in the *Evening Herald*, 'the first play by an Irish writer in which the title role is that of a homosexual',[23] although Kilroy stressed that the work is about 'the ambiguous sexuality of men who drink together and make this their way of life' rather than about homosexuality.[24] 'What is wrong with these men', Kilroy wrote in his notes for the 1971 New York production, 'is that they live in a social

---

[19] Thomas Kilroy, 'The Anglo-Irish Theatrical Imagination', *Bullán* 3, no. 2 (1997–8), 6.

[20] Thierry Dubost, 'An Interview with Thomas Kilroy, 2001', in *The Plays of Thomas Kilroy: A Critical Study* (Jefferson, NC: McFarland, 2007), 138.

[21] Thomas Kilroy, *The O'Neill* (Oldcastle: Gallery Press, 1995), 12.

[22] Kilroy, 'Playwright's Festival', 13.

[23] J. J. F[inegan], 'Saturday Night in Dublin', *Evening Herald*, 8 Oct. 1968.

[24] Seamus Kelly, 'No "Idle Tiers" for Plays', *Irish Times*, 5 Oct. 1968.

setting which inhibits sexual encounters with girls.'[25] Elsewhere he described *Mr Roche* as being 'satirical of Irish society, particularly the male "jarring" [drinking] element', and characterized it as disturbing, truthful, and 'very funny'.[26]

After a night in the pub, the 'jarring' fraternity of the play—national school teacher Seamus, car salesman Myles, and an unnamed failed medical student turned morgue attendant ('Doc')—gather at the apartment of Kelly, a civil servant of their party, for more drinking. The dingy, two-room flat where Kelly has lived for the last fifteen years is located in the basement of a Dublin Georgian house that has seen better days. Kelly's background is rural and poor, but a secondary education made possible by a scholarship enabled him to take the civil service examination and find a position in the capital. Whereas Seamus, who became a national school teacher via a similar route, has married and relocated to the suburbs, Kelly has not changed, something Seamus finds worrying: 'what was healthy then is sick now.'[27] Kelly's separation from his origins allows him now to idealize the cottage of his birth as 'a natural place to live in', and to romanticize farming activities like the digging of turnips, 'with the roots black and wet' (58–9)—the implication being that he experiences his current state as unnatural in its aridity and rootlessness. In Kelly's circumstances, Kilroy reflects a series of symbolic displacements that show, in Anthony Roche's words, how the character 'is trying to live up to a variety of conflicting images and is uncertain in all of them'.[28] Kelly's nostalgic fantasy coupled with his hysterical homophobia amount to what Joseph Valente calls 'a species of nationalist false consciousness, a failure to reckon with how significantly Irish cultural heritage has been implicated in and constituted through the very sorts of queer dislocations that are so often repudiated in its name'.[29]

Mr Roche is initially a peripheral character: he turns up late with his young friend Kevin and it seems that he, not Mr Roche, was the one originally invited to the party. Before he arrives Myles has already branded him as 'the queer', but of the four men, only Kelly vehemently objects to the presence of 'the likes of him'; when Doc points out that Mr Roche has been to the flat before, Kelly awkwardly counters: 'That says nothing. That means I've seen enough of him.'[30] In his notes to the director of the play's New York production Kilroy stressed that Mr Roche is not camp but 'a very typical Dublin homosexual, of good, sober background, a self-employed business-man perhaps'. Indeed, Seamus remarks to Kelly that he would never have known that Mr Roche was a homosexual.[31] When *The Death and Resurrection of Mr Roche* opened in 1968, reviewers were inclined to refer to Mr Roche as 'a queer' and to depict his condition as unhappy, but while they were at times bemused, they were not hostile. If there was shock, it was at the 'coarse, realistic speech' of the characters which was 'too close to life for the general comfort':[32] in the opening scene, for example, Kelly addresses Seamus as 'y'auld tool of a schoolmaster' and 'you auld bugger', while he

[25] Thomas Kilroy, notes on *The Death and Resurrection of Mr Roche* for Mike Kellin, director of the play's New York production (New Theatre Workshop, 1971), NUIG, MS P103/68(1).
[26] Kelly, 'No "Idle Tiers"', 15.
[27] Thomas Kilroy, *The Death and Resurrection of Mr Roche* (Oldcastle: Gallery Press, 2002), 55.
[28] Anthony Roche, *Contemporary Irish Drama: From Beckett to McGuinness* (Dublin: Gill & Macmillan, 1994), 194.
[29] Joseph Valente, 'Self-Queering Ireland?', *Canadian Journal of Irish Studies* 36, no. 1 (2010), 27.
[30] Kilroy, *Death and Resurrection*, 15.   [31] Ibid., 60.
[32] Allen Wright, 'More Real Drama Off-Stage Than On', *Scotsman*, 12 Oct. 1968, 2.

later complains that '[s]ome whore came around here last week and lifted every fuckin' glass in the place',[33] language that graphically captures the play's themes and the characters' ways of thinking. J. W. Lambert noted in the *Sunday Times* that 'any attempt at a harsh truth about modern life still doesn't go down too well in Dublin', and that he 'had a distinct impression of pursed lips' on the play's opening night.[34] Brian Friel admired the play, and Kilroy's frank treatment of an uncomfortable subject paved the way for—and perhaps inspired—the gay couple (although never overtly identified as such) in Friel's *The Gentle Island* (1971); they, like Mr Roche, are scapegoats, in a brutal familial conflict that mirrors and presages the violent divisions on the island of Ireland in the early 1970s.

When Kelly and his friends start taking out their frustrations on the outsider in the course of *The Death and Resurrection of Mr Roche*, their underlying misogyny emerges in the way they, and in particular the macho car salesman Myles, feminize Mr Roche as they abuse him. Myles's treatment of Mr Roche says much of his attitude to the women he claims to be sexually conquering by the score: 'Oh, you dirty devil. *(Whips behind and catches Mr Roche about the chest)* Are you wearing your bra tonight, Agatha?'[35] Young Kevin is in the bathroom being sick when the others shove his friend in on top of him and hold the door closed while Mr Roche beats on it from the inside. Clearly the water closet here serves as the homosexual closet, and the 'joke' shakes Mr Roche to the core as he fears that 'the door may never be opened'.[36] Later, provoked by Mr Roche's outspoken disapproval of their nights of heavy drinking which have become 'the way we chain ourselves together, no freedom, no joy',[37] the men push him into what Kelly refers to as his 'holy-hole'—a small cellar within his basement. When they pull him out, he has stopped breathing, and panic ensues, particularly on the part of Kelly.

Fearful of being implicated in a scandal, Myles and Doc, accompanied by Kevin, take Mr Roche's body away in the car to be 'discovered somewhere else', but Kelly remains distracted by worries about the 'terrible reputation' the men will acquire if their association with Mr Roche were to become public knowledge.[38] Left alone together in the small hours of the morning, Seamus and Kelly awkwardly end up sharing intimacies. Seamus reveals that the repetitive sameness of his middle-class, married life is slowly driving him mad; Kelly confesses that once, when drunk and lonely, he had a sexual fumble with Mr Roche. Seamus feels unfairly implicated in Kelly's guilt by the knowledge of what he wishes the other had kept to himself. The uncomfortable revelation is the trigger for him to depart and assert his orthodox heterosexuality: 'We'll have to have you out to the house sometime too. [. . .] Oh, it's not too bad now.'[39]

When Myles, Kevin, and Doc return to Kelly's flat, they are surprisingly accompanied by Mr Roche, miraculously revived by a sudden heavy downpour that occurred just as they were attempting to deposit his body in the canal. In Anthony Roche's words, 'as Kelly emerges from the closet, Mr Roche, representing that aspect of Kelly which the latter has always sought to deny, simultaneously emerges from a death-like state with his *alter-ego*'s confession'.[40] The 'holy-hole', then, in its function as a cellar within a basement, a double

[33] Kilroy, *Death and Resurrection*, 13, 16.
[34] J. W. Lambert, 'Kilroy Is Here', *Sunday Times*, 13 Oct. 1968.
[35] Kilroy, *Death and Resurrection*, 41.   [36] Ibid., 35.   [37] Ibid., 41.
[38] Ibid., 46, 60.   [39] Ibid., 64.   [40] Roche, *Contemporary Irish Drama*, 195.

'hole' in which secrets can be buried, serves as the closet of repression, but as a 'holy' retreat it is also the sacred, liminal space of a rite of passage towards 'wholeness'—the transitional space between one context of meaning and another. We learn that Roche himself experienced his 'resurrection' in such sacred terms; indeed, to celebrate 'the beginning of life again' (74), he insisted to the others that they all wait in the park to see the sun rise before returning to Kelly's basement. Once there, he relates what happened:

> (*As he speaks, the tone should shift radically from all that has gone before.*) Breaking up over the roof-tops into particles of silver and gold. And the streets opened up before it. And each tree yawned and shook, the leaves splintering. I was witness to it. (*Pause. Quietly*) Then the clock began again. Tick-tock. Tick-tock. Tick-tock. I had come back, you see. Seconds, minutes, hours, days again, as before. I was so—so overcome to be back. The old heartbeat again. And the journey still stretching out ahead. (*He resumes his seat, gingerly, smiling to himself.*)[41]

Commenting on the script some months before the play's opening, Hilton Edwards expressed 'some puzzlement' about the reason for Roche's resurrection, and confessed to being 'somewhat worried by the change of the nature of the technique'. To his mind, the shock of the resurrection was already sufficiently dramatic 'without taking the audience into another and un-prepared-for dimension'; he also conceded that his concerns were 'probably all poppycock'.[42] By contrast, Fintan O'Toole contends that 'you can't play *Mr Roche* as a naturalistic drama of psychology and motivation' because Mr Roche is a 'richly empty figure. He is what he is perceived to be by others.'[43] Given the play's preoccupation with the male drinking culture of the 1950s, however, the naturalistic aspect cannot be altogether ignored: it is precisely the successful negotiation of the drama's several layers and techniques that poses a challenge to directors and actors. In his notes for the New York production, Kilroy stressed that Roche is the only character 'who steps outside the play's "realism"' and, in the last act, is removed onto 'a plane of mystery, enigma'. The actor playing Roche should convey the transition by speaking in a 'gradually heightened monotone, the voice of [a] man gradually infatuated by his own, quasi-mystical rôle'. As Fintan O'Toole puts it, in the hands of theatre practitioners who understand what the play's unusual technique requires, the parallels with sacrificial rituals created within Kilroy's 'visionary, apocalyptic style [...] are a testament to humanity's power to transform itself'.[44]

Christopher Murray suggests that *Mr Roche* explores comic motifs that go back as far as 'phallic rituals in honour of Dionysus', but that Kilroy turns everything inside out: 'there is no real celebration, no fertility', and the 'comic glory' of the play 'arises from Mr Roche himself': he is 'the unacknowledged, unrecognised god of comedy himself, a Dublin Dionysus'.[45] For Fintan O'Toole, on the other hand, what makes the play shocking is the way in which it uses the rituals and symbols of Catholicism 'in giving us Jesus as a genteel, middle-aged Dun Laoghaire homosexual'. But O'Toole argues that Kelly, in some ways

[41] Kilroy, *Death and Resurrection*, 74–5.
[42] Hilton Edwards, letter to Thomas Kilroy, 17 May 1968, NUIG, MS P103/57(4).
[43] Fintan O'Toole, 'Mr Roche Earns His Place in the Repertoire', *Irish Times*, 3 June 1989.
[44] Ibid.
[45] Christopher Murray, 'Mr Kilroy's Modern Mummers', programme note for Thomas Kilroy, *The Death and Resurrection of Mr Roche*, directed by Ben Barnes (Dublin: Abbey Theatre, 1989).

Roche's alter ego, also undergoes a rite of passage of sorts, and that, at the end of the play, he should be seen to go through 'a moment of utter nakedness, of emotional truth'. The irony on which the final part of the play turns 'is the fact that Kelly (not Roche) is alive at all. To feel that wonder we have to feel that at some stage he had died.'[46] 'Resurrection equals new life, shedding of old personality,' Kilroy wrote in his New York notes: 'What does Mr Roche offer Kelly? [. . .] New chance to grasp life? To understand self? I think something like that.'

The sacrifice of a scapegoat—an outsider upon whom a community projects its own shortcomings and towards whom it deflects the violence that would otherwise be vented on its own members—deprives that community of 'knowledge of the violence inherent in themselves with which they have never come to terms' and which, therefore, has not been removed at all.[47] In Kilroy's comedy, Mr Roche has turned up in Kelly's life twice and returns again after Kelly thought he had been killed. Roche teases Kelly: 'Ah, but I'm not here at all! I'm only a ghost, old chap. [. . .] I'm dead, remember?'[48] By now it is the Sunday morning after a long night, and the men resume the routine of their respectable lives by preparing to go to Mass. 'Go off and pray,' Mr Roche tells Kelly: 'For all the dead and the living dead.' When Kelly frantically denies being 'dead', Mr Roche replies: 'Precisely. You understand me perfectly.'[49] The church Kelly suggests to his friends is St Mary's, Gayfield, 'down there beside the Royal Hospital for Incurables. [. . .] They're enclosed—'.[50] The subtle linguistic play—one of Kilroy's characteristic ways of 'meeting [his] audience at the level of challenge'[51]—suggests that it is Kelly and his friends who are closeting themselves again, away from the truth of their lives: they have not fundamentally changed. Yet the language also suggests that the orthodox perspective has been queered, and the closet door cannot be completely shut again. Mr Roche, therefore, is not going anywhere: cheerful and enigmatic, he will be waiting in the flat until Kelly returns, while young Kevin sleeps off his sickness in Kelly's bed.

TEA AND SEX AND SHAKESPEARE

In 1969, in spite of the two successful productions now under his belt, Kilroy was still smarting from the battles he had had to fight to get to this point, and bitter about the continued lack of opportunities for young writers in Ireland and the absence of real social engagement in Irish drama.

His own next play, however, focused on the personal: *Tea and Sex and Shakespeare* (1976), although a farcical comedy, involves its protagonist in 'a painful revolution where all the violent confrontations take place between the individual and himself'.[52] The idea for the play was already brewing in 1972, when Kilroy told Elgy Gillespie that 'it takes place inside the mind of one man; it's a fantasy play and a marriage play, I think, and about the alienation of the intellectual, too.'[53] In more recent years, Kilroy has spoken about the crisis in

[46] O'Toole, 'Mr Roche'.

[47] René Girard, *Violence and the Sacred*, trans. Patrick Gregory (Baltimore, MD: Johns Hopkins University Press, 1977), 82.

[48] Kilroy, *Death and Resurrection*, 78.   [49] Ibid., 80.   [50] Ibid., 81.

[51] Dubost, 'An Interview with Thomas Kilroy, 2004', 145.

[52] Caroline Walsh, interview with Thomas Kilroy, *Irish Times*, 25 Nov. 1975.

[53] Elgy Gillespie, interview with Thomas Kilroy, *Irish Times*, 26 Apr. 1972.

FIG. 21.1 Donal McCann and Aideen O'Kelly as Brien and Elmina in *Tea and Sex and Shakespeare* (Abbey Theatre, 6 October 1976).

Photo: Fergus Bourke. Courtesy of the Abbey Theatre and James Hardiman Library, NUI Galway.

his personal life in the early 1970s—when giving up teaching to become a full-time writer coincided with his divorce, which left him with three children to raise—that formed the starting point for *Tea and Sex and Shakespeare*: the play gave him 'enormous difficulty' and 'came out of a personal [...] breakdown' which brought with it the fear that he might 'never write again'.[54] Out of these private circumstances emerged Kilroy's growing preoccupation in his plays with loneliness, gender roles, and what a character in a later play calls the 'sexual zoo',[55] which was already evident in *Mr Roche* and would become increasingly central in many of his later works.

Tea and Sex and Shakespeare is a comedy of despair with farcical elements, the kind of comedy that, Kilroy argues, 'draws on hysteria and the hysterical'.[56] In writing the play,

[54] 'Thomas Kilroy in Conversation with Gerry Dukes', in Lilian Chambers, Ger Fitzgibbon, and Eamonn Jordan (eds.), *Theatre Talk: Voices of Irish Theatre Practitioners* (Dublin: Carysfort Press, 2001), 243.

[55] Lord Alfred Douglas in Thomas Kilroy, *My Scandalous Life* (Oldcastle: Gallery Press, 2004), 22.

[56] Mária Kurdi, '"The Whole Idea of Writing Historical Fictions Is Paradoxical": Talk with Irish Playwright Thomas Kilroy', *HJEAS: Hungarian Journal of English and American Studies* 8, no. 1 (2002), 266.

Kilroy was translating his own sense of failure into the experiences of his protagonist, a struggling writer named Brien, whose inner turmoil is expressed on stage within what the opening stage directions describe as a 'surrealistic' setting meant to reflect Brien's unconscious. The tension between the writer's need for solitude and the emotional isolation created by that need is expressed at the beginning of the action when, in the morning, Brien steps onto the landing of Mrs O's boarding house and announces to the empty space: 'Going to do a bit of the writing now. Get that first act going.'[57] He locks himself in his room and sits at the typewriter, but no original words come. Tormented by writer's block, Brien finds himself assaulted by figments of his imagination, which assume the forms of people close to him but which are used as expressionistic devices to perform his emotions, including depression, guilt, anger, jealousy, sexual frustration, and anxiety about his marriage, talent, class, and economic status. His wife, Elmina, who is at work, keeps popping out of the wardrobe to berate him about his inability to pay the bills and his sexual inadequacy, which, as he exasperatedly explains, is a direct result of his creative endeavour. His wife's disapproving parents keep barging in through the walls of his room to have tea and to remind him that he is not 'one of them'; their condescension creates feelings of inferiority and sparks rebellious behaviour. The landlady is forever in and out with cups of tea and sweeping brushes, while her attractive teenage daughter Deirdre keeps asking for Brien's advice about her studies of Shakespeare. Brien suspects his elusive neighbour Sylvester, whose wardrobe ranges from a long black coat and hat to a series of increasingly flamboyant outfits, to be conducting a torrid affair with Elmina, notwithstanding his ambiguous sexuality; Sylvester keeps insisting on parking his suitcases in Brien's apartment—the 'baggage' of his marriage which Brien is, in the end, no longer able to ignore. All these personified anxieties preventing Brien from writing his play have to be recognized and, to some degree, exorcized, in the course of the action.

For Kilroy, writing *Tea and Sex and Shakespeare* was 'like cutting through immense, tangled undergrowth and it meant numerous wrong directions'.[58] Mary Manning read the script and found the dialogue 'brilliant', but worried that the 'total lack of exposition' would cause 'total confusion' in an audience; she cautioned that the play would need 'a director who understands it', and did not think such a person could be found in Dublin.[59] The Abbey Theatre approached English freelance director Max Stafford-Clark to work with Kilroy on rewriting parts of a script that was 'much less structured' and 'much less neat' than *Mr Roche*:[60] indeed, the version of *Tea and Sex and Shakespeare* produced at the Abbey in 1976 as part of the Dublin Theatre Festival lacked, as Kilroy himself acknowledges, a workable shape to contain the surrealistic projections of Brien's imagination. It was the collaborative effort of writer, director, and actors—Donal McCann played the part of Brien with a flawless 'intelligence of apprehension and timing'[61]—that rescued the play. For its revival by Rough Magic in 1988, Kilroy made extensive revisions in collaboration with director Declan Hughes, imposing a shape whereby the surreal action emerges from 'some sort of pedestrian normality' and returns to it at the end.[62]

[57] Thomas Kilroy, *Tea and Sex and Shakespeare* (Oldcastle: Gallery Press, 1998), 14.
[58] 'Kilroy in Conversation with Dukes', 243.
[59] Mary Manning, letter to Thomas Kilroy, n.d., NUIG, MS P103/450(1).
[60] Elgy Gillespie, interview with Max Stafford-Clark, *Irish Times*, 5 Oct. 1976.
[61] Seamus Kelly, 'Kilroy's *Tea and Sex and Shakespeare*', *Irish Times*, 7 Oct. 1976.
[62] 'Kilroy in Conversation with Dukes', 243.

The reception in Ireland of *Tea and Sex and Shakespeare* in 1976 exposed the fault line between theatre traditionalists and modernists: the play 'had a very ambiguous success, attracting a cult following and total rejection in equal proportions'.[63] While many reviewers were of the same opinion as Seamus Kelly, who detected the spirit of Denis Johnston, James Joyce, and Flann O'Brien in the radically innovative play and concluded that Kilroy deserved 'a golden cap and bells' for his desperately comical depiction of the human condition,[64] a sour note was introduced by Desmond Rushe, who frowned upon the play's 'four letter words, double-meanings and a couple of attempted sex scenes' and urged the Abbey Theatre to return to the manifesto of its founders 'in the hope of dredging something that might set its values straight'.[65] Commenting on the 1988 production of the revised text, Fintan O'Toole suggested that *Tea and Sex and Shakespeare* 'uses the theatrical conventions, particularly those of farce, with a knowing subversiveness that ultimately remains a brilliantly clever but arid exercise in talking shop'.[66] By then, however, Kilroy had already shown, in *Talbot's Box* (1977), that such technical and metatheatrical mastery could also be paired with deep feeling.

TALBOT'S BOX

The idea for a play about Matt Talbot, Dublin's working-class 'saint', was already in Kilroy's mind in the late 1960s, but gathered momentum in the early 1970s when Talbot's potential canonization was much in the Irish news. For most of his adult life, Talbot worked as an unskilled labourer in Martin's timber yard and lived a life of fasting and prayer; after his death in 1925 it was discovered that underneath his clothes, he had bound his body with chains and cords as a form of penance. Although regarded by many as a saintly man, he was reviled by others for not taking strike pay during the great lock-out of 1913. Kilroy initially intended to use the figure of Talbot to satirize the nature of religious asceticism and martyrdom, which he considered sadomasochistic; that notion shifted as Kilroy, in the course of working on *Talbot's Box*, became increasingly fascinated by the unknowable nature of the mystic's private experience, and by 'the way individuals of exceptional personality invite manipulation and the projection of the needs of others'. As he felt himself compelled to find 'some kind of respect' for Talbot, his focus came to rest on the tensions between the extreme individualism of an inaccessible man and the claims of family, community, and society on him. The issue then became to capture a seriocomic note that would convey both these aspects.[67] In *Talbot's Box*, various characters representing Talbot's antagonists are played by four actors, referred to as 'first man', 'second man', 'woman', and 'priest figure', the latter also to be played by a woman. Talbot is the only figure to remain 'himself' throughout the play. The Abbey Theatre issued a contract for *Talbot's Box* in August 1975, although the play, directed by Patrick Mason, did not make it onto the (Peacock) stage until

[63] Lesley Adamson, 'Matt Talbot Is Dublin's Twenties Saint', *Guardian*, 22 Nov. 1977.
[64] Kelly, 'Kilroy's *Tea and Sex and Shakespeare*', 9.
[65] Desmond Rushe, 'Abbey: Tricks, Gags and Pretensions', *Irish Independent*, 6 Oct. 1976.
[66] Fintan O'Toole, 'Second Half Smash', *Sunday Tribune*, 17 July 1988.
[67] Thomas Kilroy, 'Author's Note', in *Talbot's Box* (Oldcastle: Gallery Press, 1997), n.p.

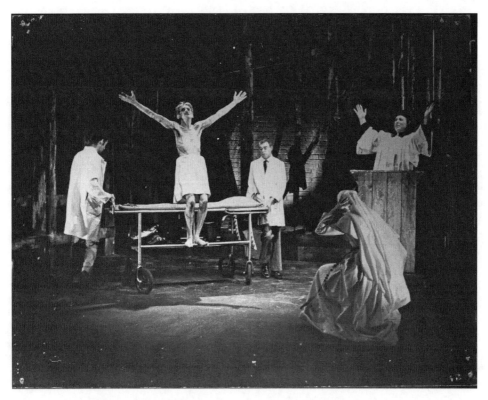

FIG. 21.2 Scene from *Talbot's Box*, with Stephen Brennan, John Molloy, Clive Geraghty, Ingrid Craigie, and Eileen Colgan (Abbey Theatre, 13 October 1977).

Courtesy of the Abbey Theatre and James Hardiman Library, NUI Galway.

the Dublin Theatre Festival of 1977. The production subsequently went to the Royal Court in London.

Kilroy's archived notes outlining the broad parameters of what would become *Talbot's Box* reveal that he started with the idea of 'an enactment within an enclosed space'.[68] The opening stage directions of the completed text suggest that when the lights go up, they should reveal '*a huge box occupying virtually the whole stage, its front closed to the audience. The effect should be that of a primitive, enclosed space, part prison, part sanctuary, part acting space.*' The front of the box is opened out from within to reveal: '*Three walls, perhaps with daubed signs and objects of a religious shrine. All the actors, costumes and props required in the play are already within the box.*'[69] The box was meant to represent both the world made by man and the body, the prison of the flesh. It should be made of timber: throughout the play, carpentry associates Talbot with Jesus, and in that way timber connects his worldly life to his inner mysticism. Anthony Roche sees in the box a 'flexible metaphor' that suggests 'a coffin, a confession box, a witness stand, a wooden bulwark

---

[68] Thomas Kilroy, notes for 'The Talbot Play', NUIG, MS P103/9(1).

[69] Kilroy, *Talbot's Box*, 9.

constructed by Talbot the carpenter against the encroaching chaos and Tom Kilroy's own box of theatrical tricks'.[70] For Nicholas Grene, the theatrical image of the box 'is there to represent inner and outer simultaneously'. The effect for him is 'not just of a Brechtian anti-illusionism', there being 'an element of ritual in the opening of the box at the beginning, the closing of it at the end, an effect comparable to the folding and unfolding of the cloth that frames Yeats's plays for dancers'.[71]

Dublin audiences found *Talbot's Box* in many ways a theatrical revelation. John Devitt, who confessed to being of a generation for whom 'Matt Talbot was a very special figure', remembered in an interview late in his life the 'very vivid production' and Kilroy's unusual angle of approach; his sense was of 'a playwright handling radioactive material' and he felt there was 'a certain kind of coldness and rigour about the play, and about the production' which startled him.[72] Kane Archer, reviewing the play in the *Irish Times*, called it 'a miracle of theatre', although 'what it communicates may be beyond description': the audience is 'caught in a kaleidoscope, whirled through patterns of history, a hundred attitudes, riding on great waves of laughter to be cast upon a beach of quietude, of mystery, of something that even in the text itself goes far too deep for speech'. The collaborative nature of Kilroy's kind of theatre was evident to this reviewer: to bring the text to life, 'Tony Wakefield has created the brilliance and the darkness; Patrick Mason has given unity to an almost unimaginable diversity of means', while among the faultless acting performances, John Molloy's depiction of Talbot stood out for its 'great integrity and understanding' and was perhaps 'the finest piece of work that this fine actor has ever done'. The end result was a 'single, complex experience' of 'theatrical mastery that denies its own brilliance'.[73] Declan Hughes, who was a very young director when he revived *Talbot's Box* in 1984 as Rough Magic's first evening show, considered the play's 'sheer theatricality [...] unusual, perhaps unprecedented, on an Irish stage'. For him, its effect was 'overwhelming' and it 'changed irrevocably' the way he felt about theatre.[74]

Kilroy's adoption of a 'free-flowing, theatrical style' at a time when he had become 'more attracted to pure theatrical playfulness'[75] owed much to the work of Peter Brook, particularly his production of Peter Weiss's *Marat/Sade* which Kilroy had seen at the Royal Court in 1964, and to Maurice Béjart's adaptation of Flaubert's *La Tentation de Saint Antoine* which he saw in Paris in 1967, with Jean-Louis Barrault in the title role. Both Brook and Barrault were strongly influenced by Antonin Artaud and the ideas he put forward in *The Theatre and Its Double*. Béjart's 'hallucinatory staging' of the saint's temptation had a huge effect on Kilroy's 'sense of what stage choreography could be'.[76] It was, as Kilroy

⁷⁰ Roche, *Contemporary Irish Drama*, 201.
⁷¹ Nicholas Grene, 'Staging the Self: Person and Persona in Kilroy's Plays', *Irish University Review* 32, no. 1 (2002), 71.
⁷² John Devitt with Nicholas Grene and Christopher Morash, *Shifting Scenes: Irish Theatre-Going, 1955–1985* (Dublin: Carysfort Press, 2008), 85.
⁷³ Kane Archer, '"Talbot's Box" at the Peacock', *Irish Times*, 14 Oct. 1977.
⁷⁴ Declan Hughes, 'Visceral Force and Haunting Lyric Beauty', *Irish Times*, 27 Apr. 2011.
⁷⁵ Kurdi, '"The Whole Idea"', 261.
⁷⁶ Christopher Innes, 'Immortal Eyes and Fearful Symmetry: Towards a Drama of Vision', *Irish University Review* 32, no. 1 (2002), 173.

remembers it, 'an extraordinary production, a kind of total theatre in its day. [. . .] Coming from Dublin theatre and seeing this kind of work in the sixties was just mind-blowing.'[77] Patrick Mason helped Kilroy find analogous techniques for *Talbot's Box*: 'It was Patrick who "discovered" the strong, almost frontal physicality and imagery in the play. I like to think all of that was there in the text but Patrick was wonderful in bringing it out and showing the possibilities.'[78]

In the opening scene of *Talbot's Box* the protagonist is lying dead on a trolley when the other actors knowingly set the play in motion:

FIRST MAN.   Right! What've we got here on this fine Sunday morning back in 1925 in the morgue of Jervis Street Hospital in the city of Dublin?

He strips the sheet off the trolley. The body is that of a frail old man, bald, with a white moustache. A white towel is about the waist but otherwise it is naked with the torso, arms, shoulders and legs painted garishly with stripes of red and blue.[79]

The faintly ridiculous towel and the obviously fake welts and bruises caricature the iconic image of Christ's sacrificial body, something blasphemously reinforced by the morgue attendant's exclamations of 'Christ Almighty!', 'God Almighty!', 'Begod', 'For Christ's sake', and 'Jaysus' throughout the subsequent dialogue.[80] The irony, however, is less a means of questioning Talbot's sincerity than it is a way of suggesting the manipulation of his public image after his death by political and religious entities to serve their own ends. This theme is verbalized as the morgue attendants discuss what is to be done with the body: 'If we can't put a label on him we can't shove him in wan of the drawers.'[81] Society is intolerant of the extremist and the outsider when he is alive, and eager to incorporate and integrate him into the existing structures once he is safely dead.

The holy man is theatrically resurrected and presented to the world as a spectacle that will at different times take the form of 'a sorta trial', 'an entertainment', a 'kind of temptation of the saint', or a 'sorta quiz show'.[82] On his cue—'Ladies and Gentlemen! We give you—Matt Talbot! Servant of God!'—Talbot rises on his trolley and binds himself with the cords and chains. Then, suddenly, he

flings both arms out in the shape of crucifixion. As he does so, blinding beams of light shoot through the walls of the box, pooling about him and leaving the rest of the stage in darkness. The other four figures cringe back, the women screaming. A high-pitched wailing cry rises, scarcely human but representing human beings in great agony. As it reaches its crescendo it is of physical discomfort to the audience. The four figures race about, hands aloft, to block the lights.[83]

John Devitt recalled vividly the remarkable performance of Molloy as Talbot in the 1977 production, and commented on 'how strange and uncanny he was in the resurrection scene'.[84] For this brief but unsustainable moment the audience share something of the

---

[77] Dubost, 'An Interview with Thomas Kilroy, 2001', 128.
[78] 'Kilroy in Conversation with Dukes', 244.   [79] Kilroy, *Talbot's Box*, 11.
[80] Ibid., 11, 12, 13, 14, 16.   [81] Ibid., 12.   [82] Ibid., 11.   [83] Ibid., 17.
[84] Devitt, *Shifting Scenes*, 68.

agony and ecstasy experienced by Talbot when he enters into what Kilroy in his notes for the play refers to as his 'immediate relation' with 'the Absolute', while the four figures cannot bear the light and attempt to separate Talbot from his inner illumination.[85] The moment over, Talbot dresses in trousers, boots, an old shirt, frock-coat, and derby hat, and is ready to be put through scenes from his life.

Talbot's two compulsions of prayer and work express the paradox of his conviction: that the happiness of God can only be known through physical suffering. Kilroy iconically depicts Talbot's physical labour in the timber yard by having him shoulder a heavy plank under whose weight he eventually collapses, as Christ did under the Cross on the road to Calvary. Within the play, the symbolic timber box that literally frames the action is echoed in descriptions of the boxy room in which Matt Talbot lives. There, visions of the world made whole come to him: 'Nothing twisted 'n broken as it is in this world. Everything straight as a piece of good timber, without warp.'[86] Outside the room, such wholeness is forever elusive. Analogous to Christ who, before his crucifixion, experienced a night of anguish in Gethsemane, Talbot in his final moments expresses doubts about the visions that came to him in his room, and admits to fearing death. In his closing reverie, however, he becomes childlike in his acceptance as he identifies with the boy Jesus, the carpenter's apprentice, who also left home to set out alone towards his inevitable destination:

> The old man worked at the bench, shavin' the yella timbers in the sunlight. An' the boy used help him. […] No need for words. Nuthin' was heard but the sound of timber. Then wan day […] the boy left. […] The old man came to the door with him. They kissed wan another. Then the mother came like a shadda from the house 'n she kissed the boy too. Then the boy walked down the road in the dust 'n the hot sun. An' way in the far distance of the city he could hear them, the sound of the hammers 'n they batin' the timbers inta the shape o' the cross.[87]

Through this visionary narrative, the elements of Talbot's own broken background—the violent, alcoholic father who forced drink upon his sons, the poverty of the Dublin slums, the back-breaking labour—are made 'straight as a piece of good timber, without warp'.[88] But Jesus walks away from his harmonious family life towards a certain, cruel death inflicted with the tools of his own trade. In the Christian narrative that Talbot follows in his own life, the opposites of wholeness and suffering inescapably lead into each other with the logic of a Moebius strip.

Anthony Roche observes that *Talbot's Box* 'examines its own processes and so must defend the integrity of the singular vision repeatedly put at risk by the necessary efforts to render it public as drama'.[89] In the play's final moment, the doors of the box are closed by the two men and the woman, leaving Talbot inside and the figures outside '*looking in through cracks in the walls from which bright light comes which illuminates their faces*'.[90] Talbot inside the box cannot convey the experience of leaving behind worldly desire, whether it means becoming one with God or dissolving into the void; those outside the box can only know what it means still to want the fulfilment that is promised inside. The tangible means of approximating that knowledge—a posthumous examination of Talbot's

[85] Thomas Kilroy, notes for *Talbot's Box*, NUIG, MS P103/90(4).
[86] Kilroy, *Talbot's Box*, 23.   [87] Ibid., 63.   [88] Ibid., 23.
[89] Roche, *Contemporary Irish Drama*, 205.   [90] Kilroy, *Talbot's Box*, 63.

life—has just been shown to be inadequate, except insofar as the play's ending has shifted the focus of characters and audience alike from trying to define Talbot to an awareness of what lies beyond representation.

From the very beginning of his career as a playwright Kilroy has been drawn to a theatre of artifice and illusion: the kind of theatre that 'never for one moment pretends to be anything else but theatre', where anything is possible, and where ideas can have free play.[91] Realistic elements are by no means absent from Kilroy's *oeuvre*, and he often builds his plays around historical figures and situations; but his aim is always to find gaps in the historical record that can be filled by the imagination, so that the focus is on uncertainty and possibility rather than on known facts. Overt theatricality is also a way of accommodating an important theme in his work: that of spiritual or artistic quest—'the efforts of the individual to find a personal vision beyond material reality'.[92] Not unlike Peter Brook, whose theatrical aim Kilroy understood to be 'a vision of life and theatre as a search, a quest',[93] Kilroy considers his plays to be 'provisional [...] an attempt at something'[94]: what happens on stage is 'a way of alerting the audience to an issue',[95] of stimulating thought and provoking questions. It is certainly the case that, as Phil Dunne suggests, Kilroy has 'grappled with the realities of contemporary Ireland', exposing some of the nation's dark sides and anticipating major attitudinal shifts in Irish society regarding, for example, the Catholic Church, nationalism, sex, and the status of women and homosexuals; but he has never done so by adopting a sociological approach. Instead, by stressing the artifice and imaginative possibilities of the stage, Kilroy makes audiences aware of the layers and complexities of such realities, while also suggesting different ways of knowing, experiencing, configuring, or transcending those given circumstances. In this way, not only has he been a 'commentator on current values, practising espionage for everyman', as he put it in his 1959 *Studies* article, but his theatre has often come close to occupying a 'sacred' space: 'the space where prefiguration occurs'.[96]

---

[91] 'Kilroy in Conversation with Dukes', 242.   [92] Kurdi, '"The Whole Idea"', 259.

[93] Thomas Kilroy, 'The Power of the Process', review of *Peter Brook: A Biography* by Michael Kustow, *Irish Times*, 19 Mar. 2005.

[94] Dubost, 'An Interview with Thomas Kilroy, 2004', 154.   [95] Ibid., 147.

[96] Phil Dunne, 'An Uncluttered Window on Irish Life: The Work of Thomas Kilroy', *Studies* 89 (2000), 145.

PART VIII

DIVERSIFICATION

CHAPTER 22

....

BRIAN FRIEL AND FIELD DAY

....

MARILYNN RICHTARIK

THE story of Brian Friel and Field Day is, in large part, the story of his professional and personal relationships with Stephen Rea and Seamus Deane. Younger than himself, both helped him recover the energy and enthusiasm of youth. But Field Day also sprang from mid-life crisis, as all three encountered limitations and disappointments in their careers; running their own theatre company and publishing outlet allowed them to claim greater control over their work. Friel loved and respected Rea and Deane for their personal qualities, but also for their ability, in their different ways, to demonstrate to him what he had achieved in his drama. In long talks and letters, many preceding the establishment of Field Day, they helped each other formulate a political position they did not find articulated elsewhere, one equally alienated from London and Dublin and convinced of the potential efficacy of a spiritual and intellectual hunger deriving from the North of Ireland. Friel and Rea shared theatre: a belief in its transformative power, a desire to bring it to people who might otherwise never see a professional production, an interest in its practical challenges, and a commitment to the highest professional standards. Friel and Deane shared Derry, the gerrymandered Northern Irish city in which both had come of age, along with a writing vocation and rigorous striving for excellence. Art, criticism, and politics were intimately connected in all their thinking. All three had ambitious goals for Field Day and, for a decade or more, devoted most of their professional endeavours to the company. While the other directors—Seamus Heaney, Tom Paulin, David Hammond, and, for a time, Thomas Kilroy—also made significant contributions to Field Day, Rea has commented, with fairness, 'Field Day's energy was really the chemistry between me and Brian, plus Seamus Deane.'[1]

Much archival material pertaining to both Friel and Field Day has become available since the start of the twenty-first century. In 2000, Friel donated his papers to the National Library of Ireland in Dublin. The following year, Emory University in Atlanta, Georgia, acquired Paulin's papers, including an incomplete set of minutes of Field Day board meetings. The Field Day Archive, consisting of over 17,000 items compiled from records formerly kept at the company's offices and from the private collections of Deane and Rea,

---

[1] Cormac Ó Duibhne, '"Talk About the Play!" An Interview with Stephen Rea', *Princeton University Library Chronicle* 68, nos. 1–2 (2006–7), 581.

was donated to the National Library of Ireland in 2008; Field Day published a book by the archivist listing the contents in 2007.[2] Deane's personal papers joined Paulin's in Emory's Manuscript, Archives, and Rare Book Library in 2011. Although his Field Day archive went to Dublin, the Emory papers include correspondence with individual board members which sheds light on the personalities behind the company. The most revelatory future scholarship on Friel and Field Day will doubtless draw on these archives. Deane's son Ciarán first made public some of the documents and letters contained in Deane's papers and the Field Day Archive in a lively essay on Field Day's origins published in 2009,[3] for example, and Aidan O'Malley's intimate knowledge of the Friel papers and the Field Day Archive helps to make his monograph on Field Day the most comprehensive examination of the company to date.[4]

Archival research should prompt the reconsideration of a common view of the company stated forcefully in 1999 by Christopher Murray:

> [T]here were two Field Days and not just one. There was the Field Day established by Friel and Rea to write, perform, and tour plays throughout Ireland north and south. And there was the Field Day which was largely Seamus Deane's invention, a cultural experiment dedicated to intervening in the Northern situation and changing it. [. . .] Brian Friel [. . .] set up the Field Day Theatre Company only to see it overtaken by intellectuals who wanted to use it to promote a debate in which Friel as artist had no part to play.[5]

'Art and criticism' were indeed 'competing on the Field Day board'.[6] The resulting tension, however, is better seen as one *within* individual directors than as one *between* them. Letters from Friel to Deane dating back to the late 1960s indicate that the conception of Field Day as a theatre company taken over by academics for polemical purposes does justice to none of the principals.[7] In particular, Friel's willingness to allow Deane to act as Field Day's spokesman has obscured the central role that he himself played in determining its activities in both the theatrical and publishing spheres.

FRIEL, REA, AND THE FOUNDING OF FIELD DAY

Friel met Stephen Rea in 1973, when Rea played Skinner in a Royal Court production of his play *The Freedom of the City* (1973). Rea later recalled: 'There was an instant rapport between

[2] Cormac Ó Duibhne, *The Field Day Archive* (Dublin: Field Day, 2007).
[3] Ciarán Deane, 'Brian Friel's *Translations*: The Origins of a Cultural Experiment', *Field Day Review* 5 (2009), 6–47.
[4] Aidan O'Malley, *Field Day and the Translation of Irish Identities: Performing Contradictions* (Basingstoke: Palgrave Macmillan, 2011).
[5] Christopher Murray, 'Palimpsest: Two Languages as One in Brian Friel's *Translations*', *Hungarian Journal of English and American Studies* 5, no. 1 (1999), 85–6.
[6] Marilynn J. Richtarik, *Acting Between the Lines: The Field Day Theatre Company and Irish Cultural Politics 1980–1984* (Oxford: Oxford University Press, 1994), 254.
[7] I wish to thank Richard Rankin Russell for drawing my attention to these letters, and Brian Friel for allowing me to quote from them. I am also grateful to Emily Bloom and Jonathan Williams for editorial suggestions and to Mary Grace Elliott for research assistance.

us, we seemed to be thinking about the same kind of things.'[8] Though Rea had grown up in Belfast in a Protestant family, Friel found him 'remarkable' as 'one of the few Northern people who has no instinctively sectarian reaction to the situation in the North'.[9] Rea also impressed Friel, as he impressed other playwrights with whom he developed close relationships (including Trevor Griffiths, Sam Shepard, and Stewart Parker), with his intellectual approach to acting.[10] 'I believe that acting is about getting out of the way of the material, not imposing yourself between the material and the people receiving it', Rea has remarked,[11] and he habitually evinced a fidelity to dramatic texts that further endeared him to Friel.[12]

In 1975 Rea starred at the National Theatre in London, as Christy Mahon in J. M. Synge's *The Playboy of the Western World*, and the next year he honed his acting skills playing Clov in a production of *Endgame* directed by Samuel Beckett himself at the Royal Court.[13] Barely 30, Rea had reached the pinnacle of the English stage, yet he remembered in 2001:

> When I was away in England, I always felt that I was preparing myself to come back. [. . . England has] probably the most achieved theater in the world. But I always felt that I was working for someone else. [. . .] Peter Hall offered me a choice at that time. He said: 'Change your accent and you can do anything you want in this theater.' [. . .] I did not change my accent.[14]

Rea encountered Friel again early in 1979, when he played Eamon in the first production of *Aristocrats*, at the Abbey Theatre.[15] Even in Ireland, Rea found, 'our own situation wasn't being expressed', but he felt he had more in common with Friel than ever: 'It was purely instinctive. We both wanted the same things and we decided to work together to achieve them.'[16]

Around this time, Rea heard that the Arts Council of Northern Ireland had money to fund theatre initiatives in the North.[17] He took the idea of starting a theatre company to Friel, asking him for a new play: 'Everybody has to make a pilgrimage once in their lives, and I made mine, and he gave me the play [*Translations*]. ... He hadn't written it at the time and he did say that the fact that he was writing it for this new company may have influenced the outcome in some way.'[18] Friel, who believed that '[t]he dramatist ought to be able to exercise complete control over the realisation of his characters',[19] must have been attracted by

[8] Fintan O'Toole, 'Stephen Rea: The Great Leap from the Abbey', *Sunday Tribune*, 23 Sept. 1984.

[9] Charles Hunter, 'Stephen Rea: Actor-Manager With a Mission', *Irish Times*, 19 Sept. 1987.

[10] O'Toole, 'Stephen Rea'; Marilynn Richtarik, *Stewart Parker: A Life* (Oxford: Oxford University Press, 2012).

[11] Luke Gibbons and Kevin Whelan, 'In Conversation with Stephen Rea: 2 February 2001, Yale University', *Yale Journal of Criticism* 15, no. 1 (2002), 13.

[12] Hunter, 'Stephen Rea'.

[13] Alex Renton, 'Ireland's Leading Rebel', *Illustrated London News*, Jan. 1989, 60–1; O'Toole, 'Stephen Rea'; Richtarik, *Stewart Parker*, 166; Christie Hickman, 'Stephen Rea, Fringe Actor Par Excellence', *Drama* 149 (1983), 23–5.

[14] Gibbons and Whelan, 'In Conversation', 7.

[15] Brian Friel, *Plays 1* (London: Faber & Faber, 1996), 250.   [16] O'Toole, 'Stephen Rea'.

[17] Martine Pelletier, '"Creating Ideas to Live By": An Interview with Stephen Rea', *Sources* 9 (2000), 52.

[18] Stephen Rea, quoted in Ciarán Deane, 'Brian Friel's *Translations*', 18.

[19] Brian Friel, quoted in Ciaran Carty, 'Finding Voice in a Language Not Our Own' (1980), in Paul Delaney (ed.), *Brian Friel in Conversation* (Ann Arbor, MI: University of Michigan Press, 2000), 142.

the chance to do just that, and the benefits of having a performer of Rea's calibre committed in advance to his next play probably did not escape him, either.

During the most intense phases of their collaboration on Field Day, Friel and Rea were in daily contact, by telephone, in person, and/or by post.[20] Friel's letters to Rea and others held in the Field Day Archive document his attention to detail and the interest he took in every aspect of theatre management, including (but not limited to) the writing and commissioning of scripts, casting of plays, securing of funding from both governmental and private entities, location of venues, choice of incidental music, issues of direction, questions of set and lighting design, overseeing of the company's office, costing of productions, and publicizing of the company's activities. With *Translations* still touring, Friel informed Seamus Deane:

> The modest little enterprise we [Friel and Rea] ventured on has suddenly engulfed us and we're daily bombarded with problems about contracts & fire-insurance & trucking sets & costume bills etc. etc. But the freedom to compose the *whole* thing has been an exhilaration and we'd [. . .] go again. And almost certainly will.[21]

Despite their mutual reluctance to discuss them at the inception of the Field Day project, Friel and Rea had political as well as artistic reasons for founding a theatre company. As Rea commented in 2005, 'You couldn't not be affected by the collapse of society in the North. Everybody was affected and in some sense maimed by it. [. . .] [A]nd if you were in the business of theatre or writing or acting you had to attempt a principled response'.[22] Set in 1833, *Translations* presents Friel's archetypal northwestern Irish small town at a moment of transition between its traditional identity as Baile Beag and its later incarnation as Ballybeg; the incursions of imperialism and modernity are represented dramatically by the British army surveyors and orthographers preparing the first Ordnance Survey map of the area and the (British) national school that will soon replace the hedge school which provides a focus for the action. The play makes palpable the loss entailed by a language shift, and the risks run by those who attempt to cross a cultural divide, but also the need to adapt to the changing 'landscape of . . . fact', to make of the English language a 'new home'.[23]

In addition to the themes of the play, Field Day's theatrical practice had a political dimension partly derived from Rea's understanding of the motives animating the founders of the

---

[20]   Ciarán Deane, 'Brian Friel's *Translations*', 18.

[21]   Brian Friel, letter to Seamus Deane, 3 Oct. 1980, Atlanta, Georgia, Emory University Manuscript, Archives, and Rare Book Library (MARBL), MSS 1210, box 1, folder 11. Quotations from these letters appear by kind permission of Brian Friel and of Emory University Library.

[22]   Stephen Rea, quoted in Ciarán Deane, 'Friel's *Translations*', 18.

[23]   Friel, *Plays 1*, 419, 444. Both Richtarik and O'Malley offer readings of Field Day's plays in monographs devoted to the company, as does Carmen Szabo in *'Clearing the Ground': The Field Day Theatre Company and the Construction of Irish Identities* (Newcastle upon Tyne: Cambridge Scholars, 2007). Readers desiring a brief overview of Field Day's theatrical life may consult Marilynn Richtarik, 'The Field Day Theatre Company', in Shaun Richards (ed.), *The Cambridge Companion to Twentieth-Century Irish Drama* (Cambridge: Cambridge University Press, 2004), 191–203. See also Richard Pine, *The Diviner: The Art of Brian Friel* (Dublin: University College Dublin Press, 1999); Anthony Roche, *Contemporary Irish Drama: From Beckett to McGuinness* (Dublin: Gill & Macmillan, 1995) and *Brian Friel: Theatre and Politics* (Basingstoke: Palgrave Macmillan, 2011); and Elmer Kennedy-Andrews, *The Art of Brian Friel: Neither Reality Nor Dreams* (Basingstoke: Macmillan, 1995).

Irish Literary Theatre: 'They were a radical bunch who realized that the time they were living in was a time of crisis and they decided to found a theater which would make a stance
against. It was an oppositional gesture.'[24] One such gesture made by Field Day's founders
was their decision to perform the play in Derry's Guildhall.[25] This building, Rea recollected,
'was hopeless in terms of the theatrical and technical achievement of the show' but had 'a
huge symbolic value because it was the Unionist headquarters and we were doing this play
about identity, language and domination'. Another practical choice signalling a political
disposition was to seek funding from the Arts Council of the Republic of Ireland as well as
that of Northern Ireland, allowing Field Day to tour throughout the island. Rea has called
this an 'essentially [...] political statement: we were northern but we belonged to the whole
country, whatever we were talking about we wanted to address the whole country'[26].

The whole country appeared to be listening. Rea found it 'immensely stimulating to go
to different towns and feel a different response'.[27] In his view, 'the great value of drama, and
I don't think I've ever seen it as poignantly and as clearly as at the opening of *Translations*,
is that it offers ideas in an unthreatening way [...]. It doesn't harangue the audience, it suggests things and they complete them.'[28]

Their perception of an audience hungry for what drama had to offer enhanced the excitement of the project for Friel and Rea. In December 1980, Friel tentatively outlined the 'principles' animating Field Day, including:

> [A] belief that theatre in Ireland can originate outside the metropolis; the sounding of an
> Irish dramatic voice that is not pitched to be heard outside of this island [...], the forging of
> a theatre company that recognises the entire island as its terrain; a sense that in these rapidly
> changing times in this country the theatre is a unique platform for the exploration of these
> changes.[29]

These principles, which Friel had been formulating through much of the 1970s in conversation and correspondence with other Irish artists and intellectuals, would continue to
inform Field Day's practice.

FRIEL AND DEANE

The poet and critic Seamus Deane featured prominently among Friel's contacts in the
period preceding Field Day's founding. They had known each other for nearly two decades.
In 1961, after completing an honours degree in English at Queen's University Belfast, Deane
returned to Derry, where he had grown up in the Catholic ghetto known as the Bogside,
to teach in a secondary school. He also worked at a distance on a master's degree, and his
graduation picture appeared in a local newspaper. Shortly after this, one fateful day in 1963,

[24] Ó Duibhne, '"Talk About the Play!"', 580.   [25] Richtarik, *Acting Between the Lines*, 23–7.
[26] Pelletier, 'Creating Ideas to Live By', 53–4, 52.
[27] Gibbons and Whelan, 'In Conversation', 9.
[28] Ó Duibhne, '"Talk About the Play!"', 579.
[29] Letter from Brian Friel to Paddy Kilroy, 2 Dec. 1980, quoted in Ciarán Deane, 'Friel's
Translations', 9.

he and his wife were hitchhiking in Donegal, and Friel, recognizing him from his photograph, picked them up.[30] Friel and Deane thus met near the beginning of their respective careers as playwright and critic. Friel's second stage play, *The Enemy Within*, had premièred the previous year at the Abbey, and earlier in 1963 he had spent several months learning stagecraft by observing the Irish director Tyrone Guthrie at work in his new theatre in Minneapolis[31] (a period Friel later referred to as 'my first parole from inbred claustrophobic Ireland').[32] Deane, too, enlarged his sphere of experience that year, embarking on doctoral study at Cambridge University.[33]

Friel's time abroad influenced *Philadelphia, Here I Come!* (1964), the play that brought him to international prominence. Meanwhile, Deane enjoyed his own first stint in the US after finishing his doctorate, teaching at Reed College in Oregon and the University of California at Berkeley from 1966 to 1968.[34] His last class at Berkeley ended abruptly with the incursion of police; upon his return to Ireland, he found a similarly fraught political situation as the civil rights movement intensified in the North.[35] Determined to contribute as an intellectual through the provision of 'informed commentary', he worked with other young writers and academics and the publisher Michael Gill to start a review called *Atlantis* dedicated, in part, to examining Ireland 'in an international perspective'; before the journal's launch he renewed his acquaintance with Friel, who became a 'founder sponsor' of the enterprise.[36]

Over the next several years, as Northern Ireland descended further into violence, Deane's critical and political concerns increasingly intertwined. In the summer of 1974 he published an essay entitled 'The Writer and the Troubles', in which he presented Friel as more 'bluntly and openly involved in the whole crisis than either Heaney or [Derek] Mahon' and expressed the worry that, at times, 'The author yields his privacy to the pressure of the public event, and in so doing, simplifies both.' Deane generalized from *The Freedom of the City*:

> Brian Friel's problem has always seemed to me to be the classic one whereby a man must find in a particular crisis its universal implication and is sorely tried by the problem of timing the moment at which he should, in any given play, move from one to the other. [. . .] If the movement is mistimed the language becomes obtrusive, full of claims, demanding that we allegorise its normal meanings into a meaningful pattern. [. . .] His people have one language which he mimics beautifully; he has another language in which he then passes judgement on those whom he has mimicked.

Nonetheless, Deane believed that 'it is when [Friel] comes closest to the actuality of the Northern crisis, and when he risks sententiousness and judgement, that he comes

[30] Seamus Deane, interview with Marilynn Richtarik, Derry, Northern Ireland, 21 Feb. 1995.

[31] Scott Boltwood, *Brian Friel, Ireland, and The North* (Cambridge: Cambridge University Press, 2007), 15–16, 217.

[32] Brian Friel, 'Self-Portrait' (1972), in *Essays, Diaries, Interviews: 1964–1999*, ed. Christopher Murray (London: Faber & Faber, 1999), 42.

[33] Seamus Deane, interview with Richtarik, 21 Feb. 1995.

[34] *The Field Day Anthology of Irish Writing*, vol. 3, ed. Seamus Deane (Derry: Field Day, 1991), 1434.

[35] Seamus Deane, interview with Richtarik, 21 Feb. 1995.

[36] Richtarik, *Acting Between the Lines*, 90; letters from Friel to Seamus Deane dated '27 July' and '10 November' [probably 1969], MARBL, MSS 1210, box 1, folder 10.

close to his best work. [. . .] He is a dramatist whose most important play has still to come.'[37]

Friel, whose difficulty in getting his plays produced had been growing in proportion to his ambitions for them, found Deane's analysis gratifying. They met in person again around this time, and that meeting initiated a correspondence which established real intimacy between them. 'I think', Friel ventured, 'that as writers we share [. . .] the common reflexive emotive response that every Derry Catholic inherits.' He believed this 'inheritance' created difficulties for him as a writer:

> [A] Derry Catholic [. . .] is incapable of working within either the classic tragic or comic form. [. . .] So you try to fashion your own feebler forms [. . .]. But no matter how apt your forms may appear, the seams begin to crack [. . .] when the pressure is greatest—and I suspect these are the moments when you tell me my sense of timing in language is uncertai[n.] What I'm saying is that it is not the timing but the form that's at fault.[38]

Soon after writing this, Friel solicited Deane's comments on a draft of his play *Volunteers*, which would be produced at the Abbey the following year. He described Deane's response as 'lucid and articulate and honest and generous and *very* welcome and ultimately disturbing which makes it all the more valuable'. Friel agreed with Deane's critique of the script's naturalistic style, but Deane's other question, about the philosophy informing the play, posed a more fundamental challenge to him:

> I don't know. I don't even know if I should know with any finality. *Freedom* and *Volunteers* are certainly genuine soundings and I'll certainly assume whatever tiny self-revelations they offer me. But I don't either push off from some concrete base nor do I expect to arrive at some final conclusion.[39]

Despite their different perspectives on dramatic art, Friel experienced Deane's attempts to abstract meaning from his plays as bracing and continued to send him work in progress, including drafts of *Faith Healer, Aristocrats*, and *Translations*; Deane, in return, showed Friel his second poetry collection, *Rumours* (1977), before its publication. In a warmly encouraging letter from the late 1970s, Friel explained why he valued Deane's opinions:

> [W]hat I think you don't know or refuse to believe about me [. . .] is that I live with a perpetual and persistent sense of failure. [. . .] [A] true and quiet recognition that for 20 years I have failed in varying degrees to integrate whatever my emotional experience into a communicable vehicle. And what you have done for me in the past has been to identify with some precision those areas of failure; so that even now, even weighted by a back-log of very flawed work, I may be able to function more truly, with a glimmer of confidence.[40]

In striving to push his artistic achievement closer to his vision, Friel sought out Deane's reactions precisely because he expected them to push him beyond his self-defined limits.

[37] Seamus Deane, 'The Writer and the Troubles', *Threshold* 25 (1974), 14–16.

[38] Brian Friel, letter to Seamus Deane, 'Sunday' [probably summer 1974], MARBL, MSS 1210, box 1, folder 10.

[39] Brian Friel, letter to Seamus Deane, 11 Nov. 1974, MARBL, MSS 1210, box 1, folder 10.

[40] Brian Friel, letter to Seamus Deane, '5 May', MARBL, MSS 1210, box 1, folder 10.

Along with constructive criticism of Friel's work, Deane offered its author a comprehensive description of it from the perspective of a sensitive and sympathetic outsider. Replying to Deane's 'mini-monograph' on *Aristocrats* several months before its première, Friel declared:

> A lot of what you said surprises me. I suppose it shouldn't. At my time of day I ought to have made many of these abstractions myself and been aware of the overlapping themes in the plays. But I never have. And to be presented with persistent themes and obsessions, with a 'Frieldom', a territory I never ever thought of, is a bit startling and, I suppose if it weren't such a sickly landscape, heartening.

Armed with Deane's observations about the plays, Friel reverted to an earlier insight of his own:

> I kept thinking how accurately you were defining (through me) an Irish Catholic, more specifically a Northern Catholic, most specifically a Derry Catholic: the (my) obsession with death; the refusal to subscribe to institutional authority; the inability to establish an alternative personal authority (lapsed Pape); the 'grotesques' who respect the very authority that abuses them (Provos + Church); and the Wessex characters who have always been outside the walls and are on the point of entry (they have, like most Derry [people], a residue of Donegal in their metabolism).

Friel proceeded to elucidate an explicitly political context for his constant feeling of failure, issuing a challenge to Deane in the process:

> [W]hat you have demonstrated to me is that like a true Derry Pape I have structured failure (social, political, cultural) into a half-sustaining philosophy. [. . .] And when I wonder why it may be true the only answer I can suggest is that we can never find realization in the Northern state where we are permitted only to be *their* concept of us. And even if the Northern state were to disappear, we would be misfits in the now super-county-council Republic because our concept of ourselves finds no reflection in that shabbiness. So we remain loyal citizens to a state of mind. So in fact we're doomed to spiritual exile [. . .].
>
> The alternative to all this [. . .] is to pitch the voice towards England. This [. . .] usually evokes a welcoming response. It also provides a home, a warmth, a complete culture, standards of comparison, a common language of criticism—all the consolations of good digs.

Concluding this early exposition of what Scott Boltwood, in his monograph on *Brian Friel, Ireland, and The North*, has characterized as the subaltern perspective that would become central to Field Day, Friel implicitly rejected the English alternative, at the risk of seeming to validate 'this here': 'Anyhow. Let's stay as we are. Let's articulate what we have.'[41]

Deane took Friel's hint in the introduction he wrote for a selection of Friel's plays first published in 1984, which opens with the statement: 'Brian Friel was born into, and grew up in, the depressed and depressing atmosphere of the minority Catholic community in Northern Ireland', proceeding to a comparison of Derry—whose 'political tension', 'strange apathy', 'bad social conditions', and 'general feeling of desolation' had 'profoundly impressed themselves on Friel's writing in which the same blend of disappointment and

---

[41] Brian Friel, letter to Seamus Deane, 3 Oct. [1978], MARBL, MSS 1210, box 1, folder 10; Boltwood, *Brian Friel.*

unyielding pressure is found time and again to characterize the experience of his protagonists'—with Donegal, 'a powerful image of possibility' for the playwright; Deane saw the
auras of the two as fused in Ballybeg. Against this background, Friel's ongoing, if futile,
search for a 'consolatory or counterbalancing agency which will offer an alternative' to politics made him an 'exemplary figure' for Deane, who ended his essay by contending: 'No
Irish writer since the early days of this century has so sternly and courageously asserted the
role of art in the public world without either yielding to that world's pressures or retreating
into art's narcissistic alternatives.'[42]

By then, Deane had become a semi-official spokesman for Friel, having also introduced a
selection of his short stories published by the Gallery Press five years earlier. That piece had
pleased Friel, who wrote to Deane that 'because I respect you and because I don't know [. . .]
"The Work" in any objective way, I'm genuinely grateful for these guide-lines and thank
you warmly and formally because the intuitive part of me recognises the truth of them.'[43]
Clearly, by the time he and Rea founded Field Day, Friel had come to rely on Deane—not
to tell him what to do, but to show him what he had already accomplished. He, in turn, had
influenced Deane, encouraging him to seek literature's meaning beyond the confines of
texts themselves.

FRIEL, DEANE, AND FIELD DAY

This dynamic between them made it natural for Friel to ask Deane to 'put words on the aspirations of Field Day' in January 1981 during the pre-production stages of Friel's Hiberno-
English version of Anton Chekhov's *Three Sisters* (1981), the company's second production.
Deane responded with 'What is Field Day?', a programme note which thrilled both Friel
and Rea with its combative tone.[44]

> Field Day is inventing an audience. [. . .] It finds itself in terms of its new audience. [. . .]
> Field Day is also a political gesture, smacking of Northernness [. . .]. It involves a double
> secession—from the North and from the Republic. It is like the Abbey in its origin in that it
> has within it the idea of a culture which has not yet come to be in political terms. It is unlike
> the Abbey in that it can no longer subscribe to a simple nationalism as the basis for its exist-
> ence. [. . .] It is also given to the idea of renovation, of adventure, of going out from the estab-
> lished to a new consciousness.[45]

Heaney probably had this piece in mind when he recollected that Deane 'in a sense wrote
our mission statement',[46] notwithstanding that Deane was not yet officially involved with

---

[42] Seamus Deane, 'Introduction', in *Plays 1*, 11–12, 22.
[43] Brian Friel, letter to Seamus Deane, 4 Sept. [1979], MARBL, MSS 1210, box 1, folder 10.
[44] Brian Friel, letters to Seamus Deane, 29 Jan. 1981 and 12 Mar. [1981], MARBL, MSS 1210, box 1,
folder 11.
[45] Seamus Deane, 'What is Field Day?', programme for Brian Friel, *Three Sisters*, directed by
Stephen Rea (Derry: Field Day, 1981).
[46] Seamus Heaney, quoted in Maurice Fitzpatrick, *The Boys of St. Columb's* (Dublin: Liffey,
2010), 198.

Field Day when he wrote it. Friel asked him to contribute to the programme again the following year, and Deane's 1982 note represented one of the first public airings of the postcolonial interpretation of Irish culture that Field Day would popularize.[47]

Deane, Heaney, Hammond, and Paulin were invited to join Field Day in the summer of 1981. Rea remarked in 2000, 'With these four men [. . .] it wasn't just going to be left to those outside who would see those wonderful creative artists doing things.' Instead, 'we would actually define what it was we were doing ourselves.'[48] He regarded Deane's contribution as especially significant, recalling: 'He started to write program notes that some people were offended by. [. . .] [W]e weren't just doing plays. We were doing plays for a reason. [. . .] We sought to be provocative in lots of ways.'[49]

Friel had begun thinking about 'extending' the membership and activities of the company even before the *Translations* tour ended. Among other things, he hoped (in vain) that the involvement of other artists would allow him to 'take respite from the daily pressures of Field Day'.[50] Deane remembered that, at one of the board's early meetings, Friel asked the new members to 'develop a publishing venture', adding, 'He also said we should do something to engage with the political mess and crisis in the North, and that we should make a point of addressing a general audience in what we were doing.' It seemed to Deane 'that Field Day provided an opportunity to write in a milieu more politically charged than was available to me as a university teacher.'[51]

Few who know Friel's work can doubt his political interests, but, given his carefully cultivated reputation as a recluse, some may be surprised to learn that he also had impressive political skills. In managing Field Day's operations, he deployed techniques of organization and persuasion likely acquired through childhood observation of his father, a schoolteacher and nationalist politician.[52] The archives offer ample evidence of his active guidance of Field Day in the pursuit of an ambitious cultural agenda encompassing both publishing and theatrical endeavours. As early as 1974, Friel had expressed his belief that 'it's high time the articles of constitution of Lit. in this country were redefined' and stated his desire to form 'a working party' for that purpose;[53] despite his public talk of impermanence and 'fluxiness' in Field Day's early years,[54] privately Friel was always thinking beyond the next production and urging other board members to do the same. Judging from the minutes of the Field Day board meetings, mostly written by Deane, Friel would report on theatrical productions and problems but otherwise typically said little, preferring to listen to the others deliberate various potential courses. This did not mean he lacked strong opinions and preferences, however. Friel worked to shape Field Day's agenda *between* meetings: speaking

---

[47] Brian Friel, letters to Seamus Deane, 16 Mar. [1982] and 17 July 1982, MARBL, MSS 1210, box 1, folder 11; Seamus Deane, 'In Search of a Story', programme for Brian Friel, *The Communication Cord*, directed by Joe Dowling (Derry: Field Day, 1982).
[48] Pelletier, 'Creating Ideas to Live By', 56.
[49] Gibbons and Whelan, 'In Conversation', 10–11.
[50] Ciarán Deane, 'Friel's *Translations*', 30–4.
[51] Yu-chen Lin, 'Field Day Revisited (I): An Interview with Seamus Deane', *Concentric* 33, no. 1 (Jan. 2007), 205.
[52] Fintan O'Toole, 'Friel's Day', *Irish Times*, 7 Jan. 1989.
[53] Brian Friel, letter to Seamus Deane, 13 Oct. 1974, MARBL, MSS 1210, box 1, folder 10.
[54] For Friel's public statements on Field Day's aims in the early 1980s, see Richtarik, *Acting Between the Lines*, 112–39.

and corresponding with individual directors, seeking their suggestions and insights, and offering arguments for the projects he favoured in terms geared to the person he sought to convince.

Publishing Projects

At a meeting on 24 October 1982, the board discussed the future of Field Day. Various publishing projects were mooted at this time: an annual Field Day magazine or an Irish Review of Books (neither of which then went any further since no one wanted to edit either), books of essays, a reader for schools and colleges, a version of the nineteenth-century *Cabinet of Irish Literature*,[55] and a pamphlet series. Heaney was deputed to investigate the market for essay collections, Hammond and Heaney volunteered to develop the textbook idea, and Deane promised to prepare an outline of his proposed 'Cabinet' for the next meeting.[56] The range of proposals suggests the degree to which board members felt themselves torn between the notion of occasional, topical productions and the wish to make a more lasting and significant ideological contribution to Irish literary culture. Friel appeared to come down in the middle of that debate in a letter sent to all directors a few days later, though it seems probable that he had already set his heart on a new Cabinet but thought it prudent to build up to it with a concession to members who preferred to think of Field Day as travelling light. Before leaving the site of the meeting, he reported:

> David Hammond and I had a chat about the discussions of the previous day. We both felt (a) that they were valuable, (b) that the notion of exploring the Reader idea was less than ambitious but good enough—if only as a first step and (c) that the potential of the Pamphlet idea hadn't been fully explored.

In the rest of the letter, Friel expounded on the advantages of pamphlets, which 'could be done cheaply' and 'produced as frequently or infrequently as we wished'. Heaney's planned open letter to the editors of an anthology containing some of his poems who had added the word 'British' to the book's title without his prior knowledge had already been mentioned as a good opening salvo, and Friel agreed that 'the pitch would be clearly marked by that first utterance'. Further pamphlets could be written by other board members and commissioned from others, including artists, intellectuals, and politicians, some of whom, Friel believed, should be 'people from outside the island'. Ideally, he suggested, the first pamphlet could be published immediately, with more to follow as soon as possible—even

---

[55] *The Cabinet of Irish Literature: Selections from the Works of the Chief Poets, Orators, and Prose Writers of Ireland. With Biographical Sketches and Literary Notices* was an influential four-volume. anthology of Irish literature first published in 1879–80, reprinted repeatedly during the late nineteenth century, and issued in a revised edition in the early twentieth century. For its publication history, editors, aims, and versions, see Margaret Kelleher, '*The Cabinet of Irish Literature*: A Historical Perspective on Irish Anthologies', *Éire-Ireland* 38, no. 3/4 (2003), 68–89.

[56] Minutes of the Field Day board meeting of 24 Oct. 1982, MARBL, MSS 880 [Tom Paulin papers], box 52, folder 1.

before the next meeting, scheduled for less than three months hence, when larger initiatives would be considered once again.[57]

The pamphlet project turned out to be more involved than Friel imagined initially. The board decided to issue pamphlets in groups of three for greater impact, which led to a delay while Deane and Paulin wrote pieces to accompany Heaney's in the first set, published in September 1983; a second set (with pamphlets by Deane, Richard Kearney, and Declan Kiberd) followed in May 1984. These first two sets were generally read as nationalist manifestos and praised or excoriated as such.[58] Writing to Deane in June 1984, Friel admitted to being 'concerned that the Northern/Protestant/Unionist readers (all one of them) seem to have classified us as hostile/Green Nat./wholly Free State based and oriented' and asked how they might change that perception,[59] preparing the way for Paulin's proposal (in a memo from August 1984 which Friel had urged him to write) that Field Day widen the franchise.[60] At the September 1984 board meeting, members agreed to focus on the Protestant idea of liberty in the third set of pamphlets, launched in May 1985.[61]

Field Day published two more sets of pamphlets, in 1986 and 1988, but Friel and the other directors were more preoccupied in this period with the company's largest undertaking of all, *The Field Day Anthology of Irish Writing*. From its introduction in October 1982, the concept of a contemporary 'Cabinet of Irish Literature' engendered much discussion at Field Day board meetings. In January 1983, Deane described the project in more detail, emphasizing the need for a sustained joint effort in the production of an anthology he estimated at the time would take two years to complete; that June, he submitted for the board's consideration an abbreviated version of one section, and Heaney agreed to contact W. W. Norton in New York to see if the press would like to publish the anthology on that side of the Atlantic—they responded with interest falling short of a commitment. The minutes of subsequent meetings reveal continuing lack of consensus among board members as to the venture's feasibility.[62] On two separate occasions, in September and December 1984, Deane recorded the board's resolve to proceed with the Cabinet, at least in Ireland, with or without the involvement of Norton, but his private correspondence with Friel shows that they both understood that the issue remained far from settled. That November, Friel confided his suspicion that Heaney thought the project 'too ambitious'.[63] The following February, after the matter had supposedly been decided for the second time, he wrote that he anticipated '*enormous* difficulties over the Cabinet', adding, 'And I believe we must overcome them.' In the same letter, he told Deane about a long talk he had had with Hammond on the subject. Hammond worried that Deane would be overworked, the cost of the anthology would be 'horrendous', and the market 'proportionately tiny', and Friel thought him

---

[57] Brian Friel, letter to Seamus Deane, 28 Oct. 1982, MARBL, MSS 1210, box 1, folder 11.

[58] Richtarik, *Acting Between the Lines*, 140–90.

[59] Brian Friel, letter to Seamus Deane, 21 June 1984, MARBL, MSS 1210, box 1, folder 11.

[60] Tom Paulin, memo to the Field Day board of directors, 17 Aug. 1984, MARBL, MSS 880, box 52, folder 1.

[61] Minutes of the Field Day board meeting of 8–9 Sept. 1984, MARBL, MSS 880, box 52, folder 1; 'The Protestant Idea of Liberty', *Derry Journal*, 21 May 1985.

[62] Minutes of the Field Day board meetings of 9 Jan. 1983, 5 June 1983, 8–9 Sept. 1984, 1–2 Dec. 1984, MARBL, MSS 880, box 52, folder 1.

[63] Letter from Brian Friel to Seamus Deane, 8 Nov. [1984], MARBL, MSS 1210, box 1, folder 9.

'almost right on all scores'. Nonetheless, he expressed his own determination to proceed, while acknowledging his anxiety about where the money to do so would come from.[64]

The anthology and the question of how to pay for it informed Field Day's decisions in 1984 to draw up a five-year plan and to devote more attention to fundraising, despite board members' resistance to the idea of the company's becoming an institution. By March 1985, discussion had proceeded from whether or not to commit to the project to specific plans for the outline of the volumes (then projected at two) and technical and financial issues related to their production. While Deane devoted himself to supervising the editing of the anthology, Friel endeavoured to ensure he would have the funds needed to bring it to fruition. After efforts to entice Irish businessmen to subsidize it proved largely fruitless, the company concentrated on Irish-American sources such as the American Ireland Fund. Believing that only he and Heaney had the name recognition in the US to hope to raise significant amounts of money there, Friel overcame his aversion to public occasions sufficiently in 1986 to suggest a fundraising tour of American cities with large Irish populations.[65] In March 1987, Friel, Deane, Heaney, and Paulin travelled to Boston, New York, and Washington, DC, to participate in events to benefit the anthology, with Friel expressing the hope that 'it will be the kind of book that will end up in everyone's home'.[66] Friel's advocacy remained unflagging even as the anthology hit the inevitable snags caused by contributors' tardiness in presenting copy and inability to contain their sections within the parameters laid down for them. At a point when publication had already been delayed from its projected date, the board had to decide whether to allow the anthology to be bound in three volumes instead of the planned two, which would further delay publication while money was found for a third volume; Friel and Heaney spoke strongly in favour of the proposal and carried the day.[67]

Friel's support for the anthology, and for Deane, was personal as well as official. In March 1989, when Deane considered stepping back from the company, Friel exhorted him to remember how central his role had been in terms revealing of the way Friel himself saw the relationship between art and criticism within Field Day:

> [Y]ou *alone* gave both cohesion and then voice to the vague & confused political aspirations of F. D. [. . .] and it is something that gives me *great* pleasure. [. . .] [W]hen F. D. goes, all that will remain, the only tangible remains, will be the Anthology and the pamphlets. And those are your monuments. [. . .] F. D. owes its significant stature and the potency of its voice to you; and almost only you. Of course SR & I do the plays. But in fact they could be done *outside* F. D. And of course I hassle & write letters & nudge & prod & beg & cajole & spit & kiss. But those are the tasks of the convenor, of the energetic nanny, of the leg-man.

Before Deane made any final decision about his future involvement with Field Day, Friel concluded, he should remind himself 'how important you are to F. D. and—if it doesn't sound too inflated—to this country'.[68] Deane remained on the board.

[64] Letter from Brian Friel to Seamus Deane, 10 Feb. 1985, MARBL, MSS 1210, box 1, folder 11.

[65] Minutes of the Field Day board meetings of 8–9 Sept. 1984, 1–2 Dec. 1984, 30–31 Mar. 1985, 7 July 1985, 9–10 Nov. 1985, 12 Jan. 1986, 14 June 1986, 21 Sept. 1986, 21 Feb. 1987, 30 Aug. 1987, MARBL, MSS 880, box 52, folder 1.

[66] Brian Friel, quoted in 'US Field Day for Begging Bowl Big Four', *Irish News*, 30 Mar. 1987.

[67] Jonathan Williams, email to the author, 18 May 2014.

[68] Brian Friel, letter to Seamus Deane, 'St. Patrick's Day' [1989], MARBL, MSS 1210, box 1, folder 9.

Even without management responsibility, Deane would have been all but overwhelmed by Field Day business in the late 1980s, as he oversaw the finishing touches to the anthology. This was published in the autumn of 1991 and immediately met with attacks both expected and unexpected.[69] Despite the disappointing initial reception of the work, Friel's faith in it remained unshaken, as evidenced by a letter to Deane at the end of 1991 in which he reiterated that

> [W]hat you have achieved in the Anthology is magnificent. [. . .] Nobody else in the country could have done it. Nobody else possesses the breadth of vision, the scholarship, the magnanimity of spirit, the dedication, the creative energy. But because you are still emotionally hooked into it, it will be some time before you become aware how enormous, how valuable, how essential this text is for the country now and how necessary it will be for generations to come.[70]

Nearly a year later, with Deane still sunk in depression, Friel implored, '[p]lease don't talk about "contamination by association" with the Anthol. I AM PROUD TO BE ASSOCIATED WITH IT.'[71]

The End of Friel's Involvement with Field Day

Since Friel was always his own toughest critic, his feelings about the theatrical side of Field Day (touching directly on his own area of expertise) were more ambivalent—despite the company's premièring of several of the most important Irish plays of the 1980s, any list of which should certainly include Kilroy's *Double Cross* (1986) and Parker's *Pentecost* (1987) as well as *Translations*. O'Malley perceptively analyses various factors contributing to the dissolution of the original board of directors. Space here permits only a cursory survey of Friel's probable reasons for ending his association with Field Day. These included artistic differences with Rea that became more pronounced over time; the deleterious effect that his work as a theatre company manager was having on his writing; and his uncomfortable recognition that the company's production values no longer met his own high standards and were unlikely to improve without his minute attention to them, which, in the interest of self-preservation, he no longer felt able to give.

In retrospect, the impracticality for a theatre company of a management structure requiring the consensus of six or seven strong-willed individuals for any important decision is readily apparent; that this structure lasted as long as it did testifies to the strength of the friendships that bound Field Day's members, though these came under unavoidable strain along the way. Friel's decision to let the Abbey produce *Dancing at Lughnasa* (1990) led to an open rift between him and Rea, who likely interpreted it as a vote of no confidence in Field Day. His rationale for seeking a change probably had more to do with his sense that

[69] For a detailed discussion of the anthology and its original reception, see Richtarik, *Acting Between the Lines*, 'Postscript'.
[70] Brian Friel, letter to Seamus Deane, 27 Dec. 1991, MARBL, MSS 1210, box 1, folder 12.
[71] Brian Friel, letter to Seamus Deane, 11 Oct. [1992], MARBL, MSS 1210, box 1, folder 9.

the production of this avowedly autobiographical play would be stressful enough without his having personal responsibility for every aspect of it. Whatever Friel's motivation, however, Field Day was not equipped to handle a breakdown in communication between its founders. Friel believed that the company's productions of Heaney's *The Cure at Troy* (1990) and Kilroy's *The Madame MacAdam Travelling Theatre* (1991) suffered as a result,[72] and he and most of the other directors were ready to call it quits by early 1992. Rea argued passionately for the continuance of Field Day's theatrical mission, although O'Malley observed: 'it is notable that many of his submissions on its behalf in the early 1990s are letters, faxes and transcriptions of telephone conversations forwarded to meetings he could not attend because he was engaged in different projects abroad.'[73] Deane supported Rea in his desire to revive the theatre side of Field Day, but, as Friel tried to explain to him in October 1992, 'to put on a large production requires a full-time producer [. . .] and we now don't have a producer. I really don't have the energy or the time. And S. R. can't be expected to pack in his career and come here.'[74]

Matters came to a head in late 1993, when Friel, Hammond, Heaney, and Paulin learned that Rea had applied on behalf of Field Day for a grant to produce Frank McGuinness's version of Chekhov's *Uncle Vanya* (1995). They threatened to dissolve the board in protest, but Rea and Deane eventually persuaded a majority to support the production, which they voted to do on 21 January 1994. Three days later, Friel informed his colleagues that he would be resigning.[75] In his absence, the other directors were left like siblings after the death of a parent, and the rest of the original board remained intact little more than a year after his departure. According to Kilroy, who served on the board from 1988 to 1992, Friel had played 'an enormous role' in holding the disparate elements of Field Day together with his ability 'to entertain many different strains of opinion around him, steering them and driving them to their boundaries': 'He was [. . .] the chairman of the whole enterprise.'[76]

[72] Brian Friel, letter to Seamus Deane, 14 Feb. 1991, MARBL, MSS 1210, box 1, folder 12.
[73] O'Malley, *Field Day*, 174–5.
[74] Brian Friel, letter to Seamus Deane, 11 Oct. [1992], MARBL, MSS 1210, box 1, folder 9.
[75] O'Malley, *Field Day*, 182–3.
[76] Kilroy, 'Friendship', *Irish University Review* 29, no. 1 (1999), 87.

CHAPTER 23

....

FROM TROUBLES TO POST-CONFLICT THEATRE IN NORTHERN IRELAND

....

MARK PHELAN

The central danger of all writing about the Troubles is the danger of cliché.[1]

THERE has long been an expectation that playwrights from the North of Ireland must engage with the Troubles. The best of this work has interrogated the causes and consequences of political violence on culture, society, and imagination in the North; however, the sense of obligation to engage with the conflict has inspired and enervated in equal measure. As early as 1972, Frank Ormsby published his 'Write-an-Ulster-Play Kit' in *The Honest Ulsterman*, signalling just how swiftly drama dealing with the conflict had ossified into stock characters and scenarios.[2] It was certainly the case that stock characters, dialogue, and drama in the form of fatalistic tragedies, black comedies, thrillers, and sensationalized spectacle abounded in theatre as much as they did in fiction and film. Narratives of tribal revenge and thwarted romance also proliferated, as the dramaturgy of love-across-the-barricades and melodrama conveniently removed complex causes of political violence to present a murderous Manichaean struggle between good and evil; right and wrong; taigs and prods; 'two men fighting over a field'—all of which, it could be argued, absolved the state from its responsibility whilst expropriating audiences of their political agency by presenting the ongoing conflict as inevitable and intractable.

While it is possible to identify the tropes that marble three decades of drama from Northern Ireland, and this in turn provides a convenient shorthand to sift through what is a large body of work, as a taxonomic system it can be reductive. Such reductionism is compounded further by the fact that theatre in the North is so frequently siloed into single chapters

[1] Rónán McDonald, 'Between Hope and History: The Drama of the Troubles', in Dermot Bolger (ed.), *Druids, Dudes and Beauty Queens: The Changing Face of Irish Theatre* (Dublin: New Island, 2001), 233.
[2] Frank Ormsby, 'The Write-an-Ulster-Play Kit', *Honest Ulsterman* 36 (1972), 2–3.

appearing as codas in edited collections and books that are much more concerned with Irish theatre on the rest of the island, constructing a canonical and compositional position that reinforces the impression of the North as 'a place apart'. This critical relegation—and the deeper partitionist structural purview it reflects and reproduces—also lends itself to a narrow engagement with Northern dramatists.

Consider, for instance, Owen McCafferty: one of Irish theatre's most prolific and significant playwrights, who is grievously neglected by scholars of Irish theatre.[3] The only explanation for this is that the Troubles *still* remains the dominant meta-narrative mis-shaping discourse about theatre and politics in the North, so that artists like McCafferty, who opt to deal obliquely with the conflict, end up being overlooked and ignored. Tellingly, scholars who have written about Northern theatre tend to concentrate almost exclusively on plays and playwrights that explicitly engage with the Troubles, hence the canonical prominence of writers and companies such as Graham Reid, Martin Lynch, Gary Mitchell, Anne Devlin, Field Day, and Charabanc.

Today, however, the forms and themes that critics like Anthony Roche once claimed distinguish Troubles drama as 'a new genre'[4] in Irish theatre now appear exhausted, utterly inadequate in capturing the complexities, contradictions, and ambivalences of life in post-conflict Northern Ireland. Indeed, as the North slowly emerges into a putatively post-conflict period, scholars of Irish theatre need to recognize this transformation and to redress its critical neglect by engaging with the rich plenitude and complex flux of new forces, forms, and themes shaping contemporary theatre practice in Northern Ireland. For the purpose of this chapter, it may be best to broadly map some of the forms, tropes, and themes of what is often collectively classified as 'Troubles drama' so that these can be compared to the veritable explosion of work produced in the era following the 1998 Good Friday Agreement, which I am loosely constellating under the prefix 'post-conflict drama'.

1969–1998: Sure Every Week Is Historic in This Place

In some respects, the dramaturgical blueprint for the 'Troubles play' appeared the year before Ormsby's 'Write-an-Ulster-Play Kit', in John Boyd's *Flats* (1971). Along with similar plays like Wilson John Haire's *Within Two Shadows* (1972) and Patrick Galvin's *Nightfall to Belfast* (1973), these Troubles plays of the early 1970s are critiqued by Lionel Pilkington as emblematic of a problematic dramaturgy which presents 'the persistence

---

[3] David Grant's entry in John Bull (ed.), *British and Irish Dramatists since World War II* (Detroit: Thomson Gale, 2005), 151–7, and my own entry in Martin Middeke and Peter Paul Schnierer (eds.), *The Methuen Guide to Contemporary Irish Playwrights* (London: Methuen Drama, 2010), 194–212, remain the only academic overviews of his work. McCafferty is only name-checked twice in Tom Maguire's landmark study of Northern Irish theatre, *Making Theatre in Northern Ireland: Through and Beyond the Troubles* (Exeter: Exeter University Press, 2006).

[4] Anthony Roche, *Contemporary Irish Drama,* 2nd edn. (Basingstoke: Palgrave, 2009), 159.

and unassimilability of sectarian division'. By doing so, Pilkington argues, they absolve 'the theatre spectator of all responsibility [as] this portrayal of the conflict in terms of an irresolvable social pathology tends to foreclose the possibility of its political solution'.[5] In many plays written by Northern authors, political violence dwells darkly in the wings, malevolently encircling the stage world, sometimes entering and interrupting, but mostly affecting action from offstage. Stewart Parker's *Pentecost* (1987), set in the haunted sanctuary of a Belfast house during the civil unrest of the Ulster Workers' Council strike of 1974, exemplifies this tradition. Indeed, the play might even stand as an appropriate metaphor for Belfast's theatres, and notably the Lyric, which remained open during the darkest days of the Troubles in spite of the ongoing state of chaos that surrounded it. Given the brutal nature of the Troubles, it is unsurprising that theatre audiences sought some sort of release or relief from the conflict outside; however, it was precisely such middle-class escapism that is attacked in Bill Morrison's *Flying Blind* (1977), which satirized those who wilfully sought to ignore the conflict. Set in a single suburban living room, its central character listens to Charlie Parker records on stereo headphones, avoiding what the play calls 'the old, mindless, useless, sectarian conflict'[6] that is unseen off-stage.

Christopher Murray also identifies another common motif in Troubles drama: the 'Romeo & Juliet *typos*'.[7] This recurrent narrative of the national romance is a wearily familiar form that functions, as Joe Cleary observes, as an emotional, albeit enfeebled, allegorical appeal for political reconciliation.[8] There are legions of examples of this sentimental tradition, from Wilson John Haire's *Bloom of the Diamond Stone* (1973), Christina Reid's *Did You Hear the One about the Irishman?* (1987), and Graham Reid's *Remembrance* (1984). Thomas Kilroy even goes so far as to suggest that one of the classic plays of the Irish dramatic canon, Brian Friel's *Translations* (1980), follows this narrative arc, pointing out that the characters Yolland and Maire resemble a Romeo-and-Juliet couple.[9] Although this form has since faded into a clichéd convention, it is one that some playwrights in more recent work have sought to rehabilitate by reconfiguring the transgressive nature of a cross-community relationship so that it instead violates geographical, generational, and sexual boundaries as well as sectarian ones.

Indeed, there was an ambitious attempt to redeem this trope through a logistically complex, site-specific staging of a literal cross-community wedding. *The Wedding Community Play* (1999) was performed across one of Belfast's oxymoronically named 'peace walls', with audiences transported to terraced homes in both the nationalist enclave of Short Strand and its surrounding Protestant heartland of East Belfast; small audiences were then triaged into even smaller groups to experience an immersive performance in which they eavesdropped on the domestic tensions and sectarian suspicions that suffused the wedding preparations, before being bussed once more to a local church and nightclub for the wedding service and reception. Although community theatre in the North has been criticized

---

[5] Pilkington, *Theatre and State*, 209.

[6] Bill Morrison, *Flying Blind* (London: Faber & Faber, 1978), 34.

[7] Christopher Murray, *Twentieth Century Irish Drama: Mirror up to Nation* (Manchester: Manchester University Press, 1997), 192.

[8] See Joe Cleary, 'Domestic Troubles: Tragedy and the Northern Ireland Conflict', *South Atlantic Quarterly* 98, no. 3 (1999), 526–7.

[9] Thomas Kilroy in *The Story of Field Day*, BBC NI documentary, 2006, dir. Johnny Muir.

for further reinforcing single-identity communities, *The Wedding Community Play* represented 'the first truly cross-community drama venture'.[10] At the same time, however, the caustic fallout afterwards from those in the Protestant community who felt their contributions had been misrepresented provides a cautionary warning against assuming that this extraordinarily ambitious and effective piece of theatre, which thrilled metropolitan festival audiences, had a transformative impact at a grass-roots level on its host communities.

Perhaps the most pervasive—and pernicious—of the modalities of representing the North portrays the Troubles as modern-day tragedy, a problem compounded by the fact that this appellation is as ubiquitous in drama as it is in the discourse of historians, political commentators, and the media. Irish playwrights have rich form in translating Greek tragedies into local vernacular, and several of these engage with the Troubles, including Tom Paulin's *The Riot Act* (1984) and Seamus Heaney's *The Cure at Troy* (1990). The attraction of such appropriation is obvious, given that tragedy is predicated on irreconcilable conflict. However, what is unsettling, especially in light of trenchant twentieth-century critiques of tragedy as a reactionary form by practitioners like Brecht and Boal, is the ease with which many theatre scholars uncritically engage with (and endorse) this approach.[11] As Pilkington and Shaun Richards astutely observe, tragedy, though based on an 'insoluble conflict' which Murray and others have argued is emblematic of the North, can be profoundly problematic given that it forecloses possibilities and depoliticizes conflict by naturalizing the conditions which precipitate it. Moreover, tragedy removes the political agency of audiences by reproducing an enveloping, enervating fatalism which precludes meaningful political engagement or action, both on- and off-stage, as we are encouraged to 'accept what we are witnessing in the North is "the working out of tragic destiny" '.[12]

We can register the change that has taken place in Ulster dramaturgy since 1998 in Owen McCafferty's version of *Antigone* (2008), which self-consciously shifts the emphasis away from its eponymous heroine to focus on the flawed figure of Creon, to the extent that McCafferty even contemplated retitling the play *Creon*. Set in the aftermath of a civil war, the political connotations of Sophocles' tragedy for post-conflict Northern Ireland were obvious, but McCafferty studiously avoided labouring any such allegorical connection. Not only is Creon cast as a much more complicated (and sympathetic) figure, a man whose martial mindset is poorly suited to the requirements of peacetime governance, but the play's chorus is reduced to a single 'Old Man' who appears from the outset, exhausted, stacking twenty-six body bags that belong to both sides of the fratricidal war. Throughout the play his wry, weary observations undercut the rhetorical hubris of the play's high-born protagonists. He later reveals that as he spends every day sewing and stacking body bags, he is simultaneously searching for his own son, who was slaughtered in the same battle as

[10]   David Grant, 'Orality and the Ethics of Ownership in Community-Based Drama', in S.C. Haedicke et al. (eds.), *Political Performances: Theory and Practice* (Amsterdam: Rodopi, 2009), 55–70.

[11]   Indeed, for Christopher Murray the situation in the North 'appeared to be insoluble conflict, which is the essence of tragedy': *Twentieth-Century Irish Drama*, 187.

[12]   Shaun Richards, 'In the Border Country: Greek Tragedy and Contemporary Irish Drama', in C.C. Barfoot and Rias van den Doel (eds), *Ritual Remembering: History, Myth and Politics in Anglo-Irish Drama* (Amsterdam: Rodopi, 1995), 192; Lionel Pilkington, 'Language and Politics in Brian Friel's *Translations*', *Irish University Review* 20, no. 2 (1999), 291–4.

Antigone's brothers. The Old Man's rough vernacular speech signifies his social position as altogether lower than the aristocratic class and caste of Creon and Antigone, and this freights the play with a class politics that contests the paternalistic precepts of Aristotle's *Poetics*, whereby only the high-born qualify as tragic. This crucial element leads to an extraordinary confrontation towards the end of the play when the ordinarily servile Old Man suddenly challenges Antigone, as she wallows in her grief, with the no less keenly felt loss of his beloved son, bellowing in her face: 'Yours is not the only grief!'[13]

This is not to say, however, that playwrights prior to 1998 did not challenge the politics of cliché or the traps of convention in their work. Stewart Parker's *Northern Star* (1984), set in a crumbling cottage on the slopes of Cave Hill in the aftermath of the 1798 Rising, is an Irish history play like no other in that it both contains and critiques the Irish theatrical canon. Stylistically, it ventriloquizes the speech, setting, and style of several Irish playwrights from Sheridan to Beckett, whilst structurally the play is shaped according to the 'Seven Ages of Man', from Shakespeare's *As You Like It*. The play opens with the first age: that of Innocence (Sheridan), then proceeds to the second age, Idealism (Boucicault), followed by Cleverness (Wilde), Dialectics (Shaw), heroism (Synge), compromise (O'Casey), and knowledge (Behan and Beckett), each written in the distinctive style of the respective playwrights. This metatheatrical structure is integral to the meaning of the play. For example, the opening stage of Innocence aptly labels the naivety of Belfast's urbane intellectual classes who believed that the lofty French ideals of *liberté, égalité, fraternité* could be transplanted to Ireland where they could transcend territorial and tribal divisions. 'We were city boys. What did we know about two men fighting over a field?' says the play's protagonist, Henry Joy McCracken, at one point.[14] By the Age of Knowledge, however, those sublime principles have been drowned in sectarian slaughter and military massacre. Thus, context and content are thematically connected. The Age of Knowledge plays out in prison and is written in the style of Behan, with explicit references to *The Quare Fellow*'s setting and dialogue. Political history, theatrical tradition, personal biography, and the canon of Irish drama are thus compressed in *Northern Star*'s cat's cradle of politics, historiography, and art.

However, Parker was less interested in the metanarrative of Irish history than in its marginalia. So, in *Northern Star*, the 1798 Rising is the frame, not the focus, of the play. Likewise, in his 1975 play *Spokesong*, the Home Rule crises, the First World War, and the Troubles are but backgrounds to what the play claims as the most important date in Irish history—1887— when Belfast-born John Dunlop invented the pneumatic tyre. Likewise, the Ulster Workers' Council strike of 1974 is the offstage context for *Pentecost* (1987), and the sinking of the *Titanic* is reduced to a subterranean SFX in his radio play *The Iceberg* (1975), which focuses instead on the purgatorial plight of two shipyard workers, Danny and Hugh, a Catholic and a Protestant, killed in the construction of Belfast's 'proudest offering to the Empire—and to the world!', whose ghosts wander Titanic's decks on her maiden voyage.[15]

In what is surely the most evocative stage direction in all of Irish drama, *Northern Star* is set in '*Ireland, the continuous past*':[16] *Northern Star* and *Pentecost* are history plays about the future. By the same token, *Spokesong*'s environmental politics, and the character of Frank

---

[13] Owen McCafferty, *Antigone* (London: Nick Hern Books, 2008), 32.

[14] Stewart Parker, *Plays: 2* (London: Methuen Drama, 2000), 59.

[15] Stewart Parker, *The Iceberg*, *Honest Ulsterman* 50 (1975), 33.   [16] Parker, *Plays: 2*, 3.

Stock's appeal for fleets of free bicycles to be supplied for the city, offers a prescient civic vision that has since materialized in many metropolitan capitals throughout Europe. Moreover, *Northern Star*'s appeal for a shared and civic politics, *Iceberg*'s history from below, and *Pentecost*'s expressionistic imagining of the possibility of political compromise and accommodation all collectively reveal Parker to be a visionary artist, capable of opening out new theatrical forms and ideas in a situation that impelled so many of his peers in the opposite direction.

WOMEN'S TROUBLES

Monica McWilliams, the founder of the Northern Ireland Women's Coalition, draws attention to the vital contribution of women to the public sphere in Northern Ireland:

> From the civil rights campaigns of the sixties, to the community projects and women's centers in the mid 1970s and 1980s, women in Northern Ireland have played a central role in the development of alternative political structures. Women have created safe, yet, subversive spaces where they can organize together around issues of concern which cross the sectarian divide all the while 'agreeing to disagree' on the more divisive ones . .[17]

Charabanc Theatre Company was very much a theatrical manifestation of this movement: a collective company founded by a number of actors (Marie Jones, Maureen McAuley, Eleanor Methven, Carol Scanlon [now Moore], and Brenda Winter) frustrated with the lack of work for women in a male-dominated dramatic scene. The subject of its inaugural production, *Lay Up Your Ends* (1983), was the hitherto largely forgotten 1911 strike by mill girls protesting against their horrific working conditions. Developed through an innovative process of collaborative research, the play was an extraordinary success, praised for 'convincingly portray[ing] the contradictions, difficulties and resilience of working class women dogged by grinding poverty.'[18] One reviewer praised the play's adroit handling of a myriad of political issues such as 'trade unionism, class issues, poverty and sectarian animosity,'[19] and yet neglected to mention its overt feminist politics. This was to miss the way in which the bawdy badinage of the millworkers in the play explicitly connects the sexual and industrial economies as the women mock the way in which sexual reproduction and child-rearing are conducted on the same principles of mass production that operate in the mills:

> FLORRIE.   Accordin' to Mary Galway, the mill trade's been fallin' off. They say there's too much pilin' up in the warehouse and they have to cut back on production.
> BELLE.   (*Entering, having heard what the others were saying*) That's what you should tell your Alfie, Ethna, next time he's lukin' his way w'ye—'hey Alfie, the house's full, I'm cuttin' production!'[20]

[17] Monica McWilliams, 'Struggling for Peace and Justice: Reflections on Women's Activism in Northern Ireland', *Journal of Women's History* 6, no. 4/7, no. 1 (1995), 32.
[18] Lyn Gardner, '*Lay Up Your Ends*', *City Limits*, cited in Ophelia Byrne, *State of Play: The Theatre and Cultural Identity in Twentieth Century Ulster* (Belfast: Linen Hall Library, 2002), 71.
[19] Jane Bell, 'Dramatic View of Life in a Mill', *Belfast Telegraph*, 16 May 1983.
[20] Martin Lynch and Charabanc Theatre Company, *Lay Up Your Ends* (1983), typescript in Linen Hall Library, Belfast, 15.

Charabanc's work is not only significant for its feminist politics, connecting the personal with the political, and for its collective creation, but also for its decision to perform in community halls and centres across the sectarian divide, in rural and urban venues, North and South, and in working-class areas where live theatre had never been brought before. In pioneering this form of portable theatre, Charabanc set the scene for the later proliferation of community theatre groups.

The work of Charabanc is also significant for its trenchant engagement with class, and in the years since *Lay Up Your Ends* Northern Ireland's thriving community theatre sector has consistently engaged with class issues. The same has been true of some established playwrights like Graham Reid, Martin Lynch, and Robin Glendenning, who have all explored how both class and educational systems reproduce sectarian identities, while Marie Jones, Christina Reid, and Anne Devlin have interrogated the complex nexus of class and sectarian politics as it shapes gender roles and relations. Devlin's *Ourselves Alone* (1985) invokes the republican movement to accuse it of relegating and restricting women's agency in real social terms, while simultaneously elevating women as iconic symbols of struggle as Kathleen Ni Houlihan, Mother Ireland, or the grotesquely mutilated character of Aunt Cora, who has been blinded and maimed by a cause for which she's ceremonially, if cynically, wheeled out every Easter. Devlin dramatizes how these gender roles and relations are regulated by domestic violence—a taboo subject also broached by Graham Reid's poignant *Remembrance* (1984) and which has belatedly become a critical issue in the politics and theatre of post-conflict Northern Ireland. Indeed, it is possible now to look back to Northern theatre before 1998, and see in some work the prescient traces of concerns that will emerge more forcefully after the Good Friday Agreement, whether racism in Christina Reid's *The Belle of Belfast City* (1989), or sexual orientation in plays such as Frank McGuinness's *Carthaginians* (1988). This work has collectively helped contribute to a new form of civic politics and performance that has been built on in the later work of Colin Bell, Tim Loane, and TheatreofplucK, the North's only queer theatre company.

PERFORMING THE PEACE

One of the most distinctive, if debilitating, features of the otherwise successful peace process in the North is the fact that there is no state mechanism or apparatus in place to undertake any form of truth recovery, with the resulting vacuum unsatisfactorily filled by a welter of charitable, statutory, and community organizations. This political failure to deal with the past means that artists—particularly theatre artists—have had an enormously important role to play in the ongoing processes of conflict transformation. Even the most cursory inventory reveals a vast repertoire of work produced over the past decade or more. Some have been produced by local theatre companies in Belfast and Derry; some are authored by ex-combatants (Laurence McKeown, Robert Niblock, Brian Campbell, Sam Miller, Danny Morrison, Brenda Murphy), others by professional playwrights (Owen McCafferty, Martin Lynch, Gary Mitchell, Abbie Spallen, Damian Gorman, Tim Loane, Stacey Gregg, Rosemary Jenkinson, Dave Duggan, David Ireland, Marie Jones, Jimmy McAleavey). Yet more work has been commissioned by organizations actively involved in ongoing processes of conflict transformation and transitional justice (e.g. Healing Through Remembering, WAVE, Consultative

Group on the Past, Victims' Commission). All of it draws on theatre and performance to assimilate traumatic history into public memory, and to engage with legacies of the past and the politics of reconciliation.

The utopian possibilities of reconciliation and redemption, the 'miracles/And cures'[21] of Heaney's *The Cure at Troy*, however, are once more suppurating wounds in the work of younger Northern playwrights like Tim Loane and Gary Mitchell, who deal with the political fallout from what often seems to be a faltering peace process. Mitchell's loyalist thriller-tragedies, set against the backdrop of a political process perceived by many of his protagonists as a 'sell-out', have attracted international critical acclaim. His work is a vital counterweight to official narratives of the peace process, dramatizing the dystopian urban underside to Heaney's promissory desire for hope and history to rhyme on the far side of revenge. Mitchell's importance is that he also places centre stage a constituency and community of working-class loyalists wholly unused to seeing themselves before the footlights, and certainly not in a sympathetic, if utterly unsentimental, light. Tellingly, in a significant body of drama, there are no Catholic characters in any of Mitchell's plays (bar one Catholic murdered at the start of *Tearing the Loom*, 1998). Mitchell instead focuses on a supposedly single-identity community to reveal, not one that is united and uniform, but a violently fissiparous fraternity that, after being united in a war against republicans, has now lost this sustaining opposition and is disintegrating dangerously, just at the moment that many republicans are progressively migrating into constitutional politics. Mitchell's work provides a vital insight into how so many within working-class loyalist communities have increasingly felt alienated, disillusioned, and disenfranchised by the 'new dispensation' of the Good Friday Agreement to offer a 'profoundly pessimistic reading of post-Agreement Northern Irish society'.[22]

His plays are also startling for their fierce critique of the hypermasculine codes of paramilitary culture, and for female characters who frequently contest the 'armed patriarchy'[23] around them with a political agency that rejects the passive roles of mothers, wives, and daughters. Mitchell's work led to his own family being attacked in his native Rathcoole, from which he had to flee under paramilitary threat in an incident that led to an enforced hiatus in his career. That almost all of his stage plays have been set within the militarist milieux of the loyalist Ulster Defence Association (UDA) seemed to signify a worrying lack of development in his work, but his recent *Re-Energise* (2013) and *Demented* (2014), both still set in the loyalist Rathcoole, are positive signs of his evolution as a writer as well as the possible emergence of post-conflict drama, for neither feature any paramilitary involvement.

Tim Loane's political comedies of the peace process, *Caught Red Handed* (2002) and *To Be Sure* (2007), are acerbic 'parodies of esteem', as both attack Sinn Féin and the Democratic Unionist Party, recalling the earlier political double act of Joseph Crilly's *Second Hand Thunder* (1998) and *McQuillan's Hill* (2000). Loane's comedies offer a damning critique of the cynicism and chicanery that underpinned the North's peace process, as well as the new

---

[21] Seamus Heaney, *The Cure at Troy* (London: Faber & Faber, 1991), 77.

[22] Wesley Hutchinson, 'Engendering Change in the UDA: Gary Mitchell's *Loyal Women*', *Estudios Irlandeses* (2005), 67.

[23] Linda Eagerton, cited in Margaret Gonzalez-Perez (ed.), *Women and Terrorism: Female Activity in Domestic and International Terror Groups* (London: Routledge, 2008), 120.

orthodoxies it has generated; along with Mitchell, Loane was one of the first playwrights to do so. Their intervention was all the more important given what many see as the mainstream media's unwillingness, in the interests of maintaining the equilibrium of the peace process, to investigate the causes and consequences of the past four decades of political violence. Indeed, Gary Mitchell claims: 'BBC Northern Ireland told me I wouldn't be working with them any more unless I wrote about the peace process and it would have to be positive.'[24] It is in this context that Mitchell and Loane's plays are so important. Not only do they set out to 'rock the boat' by asking awkward questions, but they also offer difficult, dissident answers—something which imbues their work with an ethical aesthetic integrity. After all, as Stewart Parker, observes, 'the easy answer constitutes an artistic abdication'.[25]

RE-INHABITING THE PAST

'Plays and ghosts have a lot in common,' Stewart Parker once wrote.[26] As if in confirmation, several site-specific productions have directly engaged with Belfast's troubled past, if only to imagine its future, so that the narrative of the play is shared by the place of performance. One stunning example of this was Tinderbox and Field Day's co-production of Parker's *Northern Star* in Rosemary Street Presbyterian Church on the 1998 bicentenary of the United Irishmen's Rising. The Church itself was where Henry Joy McCracken worshipped, as did the Presbyterian founder of the United Irishmen, William Drennan, so the story of *Northern Star* was ghosted with its history and meaning. When the performance reached the final line of McCracken's unfinished speech beginning 'Citizens of Belfast ...', time and space collapsed as an audience was collectively hailed to remember the past and to continue its story.

Likewise, Tinderbox's *Convictions* (2000) ghosted the site-specific setting of the dilapidated Crumlin Road Courthouse, the impact of which derived largely from the auratic experience of the place. Featuring seven short playlets, each named for an area in the building, written by different authors and performed in different spaces, *Convictions* transported small audiences to view these scenes in different sequences. For instance, Owen McCafferty's *Courtroom No. 1* hauntingly used the court as a purgatorial setting for a dialogue between a nameless victim of the Troubles and the disembodied voice of his unseen interrogator. The victim seeks answers in the vain hope of finding some form of closure or resolution to his plight; however, his hope for release or redemption is continually denied. Similarly, Daragh Carville's contribution was set in the *Male Toilets* of its title, where a jaded photographer and PR man meet whilst above them the former courthouse is being launched as a tourist information centre and heritage site. Lamenting the days when Northern Ireland 'had an identity ... a brand', the photographer goes on to wonder:

PHOTOGRAPHER.   What if there were a way we could keep Northern Ireland in the public mind. Internationally, I mean? [...] Just the odd wee bomb ... Think of the

[24] Cited by Henry McDonald, 'Playwright Hits Back Against Intimidation', *Observer*, 29 Jan. 2006.
[25] Stewart Parker, *Dramatis Personae* (Belfast: John Malone Memorial Committee, 1986), 18.
[26] Parker, *Plays: 2*, xiii.

publicity ... Just like the old days ... Put us back on the map. Make Belfast—a boom town again.[27]

Carville's jaunty joke is itself an embryonic example of a kind of Ulster ostalgie, to borrow a term that emerged in the former East Germany: a sentimental belief in the 'good old bad old days' that has informed and inflected later work, such as Beano Niblock's *Reason to Believe* (2009) and, arguably, Martin Lynch's hugely successful *History of the Troubles (Accordin' to my Da)* (2002) and *Chronicles of Long Kesh* (2009), which repackage the Troubles as a long series of comic set pieces. Lynch's West Belfast war zone is inhabited entirely by lovable rogues, chancers, characters, where affable paramilitaries and unflappable communities endure and even enjoy everything the Troubles can throw at them. Some commentators regard such comic, carnivalesque treatments as testifying to Belfast's infamous gallows humour, whilst others spuriously suggest this is a therapeutic response to collective trauma. However, at no stage in either play are the politics, ethics, and aftermath of political violence considered.

Former Loyalist UVF (Ulster Volunteer Force) prisoner Beano Niblock has expressly acknowledged the influence of Martin Lynch, whose work he seeks to emulate; unsurprisingly, his debut play, *A Reason to Believe*, was a harmless comedy about two loyalist paramilitaries who resolve to spice up their empty lives by attempting one last bank job, which farcically plays out to comic effect. Like Lynch's plays, there is a complete avoidance of any political discussion or reflection on why they were sent to prison in the first place, which in many ways mirrored Niblock's own position, as he persistently refused in a newspaper interview to confirm that he had been imprisoned for a particularly grisly murder.

By contrast, another former prisoner of Maze/Long Kesh, the hunger striker Laurence McKeown, adopts a different approach in *The Official Version* (2006), which is set in the prison and was staged by Dubbeljoint Theatre Company. Now derelict and empty, in McKeown's play the prison site is being toured by the mother and sister of a former prisoner, as well as by a history student who is being personally guided round the facilities by a former prison governor. The play opens up complex issues as to how to handle this politically charged space, which itself becomes a metaphor for how the North's politicians have failed to deal with the past, whereby they do nothing since they cannot agree. Should the prison be preserved and protected or demolished and forgotten? The family of the republican inmate hold it to be 'a sacred place';[28] its former governor maintains it 'should be demolished in its entirety [...] It should be bull-dozed into history.'[29] When the play opened in West Belfast at the republican Roddy McCorley Social Club, surrounded by prison memorabilia, with a minute's silence reverentially observed in memory of dead republican hunger strikers from the 1980s, it was possible to wonder which version was now 'the' official version, as the conditions of the play's production made it clear that the counter-narrative had a new form of official endorsement. To make matters even more complex, the actor playing the part of the prison governor, Gerry Doherty, was a former IRA prisoner of Maze/Long Kesh, who had been imprisoned for attempting to blow up Derry's Guildhall—Dubbeljoint's next venue for the play.

---

[27] Daragh Carville, *Male Toilets*, in *Convictions* (Belfast: Tinderbox, 2000), 36–7.
[28] Laurence McKeown, *The Official Version*, unpublished script in possession of the author, 7.
[29] Ibid., 40.

Whilst all the above plays represent very different responses to the legacy of the Troubles, most of them do not have the potential to play far beyond the North given the specificity of their humour, topicality, and subject matter. This is certainly not the case for the work of Owen McCafferty. McCafferty's importance as a post-conflict playwright lies in the fact that he writes about those who played no part in the conflict, the ordinary people living in extraordinary circumstances. This approach is what distinguishes *Scenes from the Big Picture* (2003) as one of the finest plays written by an Irish playwright in the past twenty years. Joycean in its ambition and vision, *Scenes* presents a prismatic perspective of an entire city in a single day as a collage of short scenes flit, flux, and fade to produce the eponymous 'big picture' of contemporary life in a modern city. Although setting the play in Belfast, McCafferty deliberately decontextualizes the city, decoupling it from those overdetermined images of conflict that have served only to caricature the place. Certain incidents do elliptically invoke the recent past: an inherited allotment yields a secret cache of buried weapons and a drug dealer is kneecapped, but this is the historical backwash of the Troubles; it does not shape the narrative, for McCafferty seeks to stage a much more complex picture of a city emerging out of conflict.

Set in a rural border backwater and comprising monologues by three characters, Abbie Spallen's *Pumpgirl* (2006) seems to have little in common with *Scenes*, but its portrait offers a fascinating counterpart to the other's big picture. The play is set in the hinterland of rumour and ragwort of south Armagh, on the Northern side of the border and in the midst of republican fiefdom of fuel smugglers that have left Pumpgirl's petrol station 'on its last legs'—'on the wrong side of a fluctuating exchange rate'. [30] This is a landscape changed utterly by demilitarization as road blocks, border bases, and military watchtowers have all been removed in what were the most striking materializations of the peace process. And yet, even though the topography of South Armagh is so deeply inscribed by the politics of conflict, *Pumpgirl* never directly references the Troubles, because the Troubles are over. The era no longer governs everyone's lives, even though its legacy inscribes the very language and landscape of the play. The character of Hammy describes racing his motor cars 'up by the new hotel that got bombed in '94', whilst the secluded scenic spot where Pumpgirl meets him for their trysts is where 'two Prods were took and killed about fifteen years ago'. [31] This elliptical presence of the past has an unsettling effect, instilling a haunting sense of how history, landscape, language, and memory have been mis-shaped by acts of political violence that have reinscribed the border areas with an altogether new form of *dinnseanchas*.

BEARING WITNESS

It has been observed that 'the end of conflict is not the end of violence for women'. [32] Pumpgirl's story is beguilingly told in the voice of a young tomboy, whose decency and innocence makes her brutal gang rape all the more horrific. It also opens up a traumatic

---

[30] Abbie Spallen, *Pumpgirl* (London: Faber & Faber, 2006), 7.

[31] Ibid., 16, 20.

[32] Fionnuala Ní Aoláin, Dina Francesca Haynes, and Naomi Cahn, *On the Frontlines: Gender, War and the Post-Conflict Process* (New York: Oxford University Press, 2011), 71.

FIG. 23.1 Still from *The Far Side of Revenge* (2012), film-maker Margo Harkin's documentary tracing Teya Sepinuck's *Theatre of Witness* project (2012–14).

Courtesy of Margo Harkin and Besom Productions.

issue that Northern Irish theatre has begun to bring into the light, notably the way in which the sexual and physical abuse of women was completely silenced throughout the Troubles. In this, the North is not unique. Many countries emerging out of conflict are confronted with the reality of epidemic levels of violence against women, masked by more public forms of violence. As Mary K. Meyer notes, 'during the 1996–7 IRA ceasefire, reported incidents of domestic violence increased owing to the fact that victims were more likely to report such crimes to police than during periods of armed conflict.'[33]

The renewed ability to see sexual violence in a post-conflict society is developed powerfully in the Theatre of Witness project, *I Once Knew a Girl* (2010). Based in Derry, Theatre of Witness is run by Teya Sepinuck, who, through a series of workshops with non-actors, composes scripts based on their life experiences that are derived from a series of interviews, workshops, and rehearsals that the 'cast' revise, edit, approve and perform. These performances resemble a form of verbatim or documentary theatre, but one in which the performed stories are not derived from reportage, legal tribunals, or documentary evidence, but from the lived experience as expressed by the same individuals who perform the collaboratively produced script themselves.

The all-female case of *I Once Knew a Girl* included, amongst others, a serving PSNI officer, a former IRA quartermaster, and Kathleen Gillespie, the widow of Patsy Gillespie, who had been vaporized in the first IRA proxy bomb along with five soldiers. This extraordinary production showed theatre's capacity to participate in the wider political process

---

[33] Mary K. Meyer, 'Gender Politics in the Northern Ireland Peace Process', in Mary Ann Tétreault and Robin L. Teske (eds.), *Partial Truths and the Politics of Community* (Columbia, SC: University of South Carolina Press, 2003), 203.

through its ability to manifest through performance what was hidden, in this case a shared experience of sexual and physical violence that crossed political and sectarian divides. Both the policewoman, Maria, and the IRA volunteer, Anne, had been exploited and abused by male figures of authority; moreover, each equally assumed that their suffering did not matter in the context of the 'real' violent struggle convulsing their respective communities. 'I've been raped more than once,' says Maria. 'I never told anyone 'cause compared to all the violence during the Troubles, I thought it was insignificant. But it wasn't. It's happened to too many of us.'[34] And from the opposite side of the conflict, Anne tells a similar story. Collectively, these testimonies also reveal how patriarchal organizations like the police and the IRA, operating in militarized masculinist culture of secrecy, institutionally reproduced sexual violence and colluded in the oppression of women, who now must struggle 'to make public the private violence they experience'.[35]

Like an earlier Theatre of Witness play, *We Carried Your Secrets* (2009), developed by victims and perpetrators of political violence, *I Once Knew a Girl* was followed by facilitated discussions between performers and audiences, which in itself 'generat[ed] an extensive archive of reflective responses from many of those who saw it'.[36] A comparison might be drawn here with the South African Truth and Reconciliation Commission, of which Catherine Cole claimed that its efficacy as a spectacle came from the fact that 'its public enactment was also about people speaking and being heard'.[37] This is where the importance of the Theatre of Witness lies: its post-show discussions, generated by the performance, provided a public forum for civic debate. The 'actors' in these performances—individuals whose politics, memories, and identities were often violently opposed—also participated in the post-show discussions, just as they had shared stage space with one another. As a cast, their camaraderie and deep affection for one another was palpable, even though they remained deeply divided by their political convictions. For many, this in itself seemed indicative of the potential of theatre as a site for peace and reconciliation.

PEACE AND RECONCILIATION

If Troubles drama has been largely defined by the expectation that artists deal with the conflict, perhaps post-conflict theatre in the North can be similarly defined by an expectation that it should play some sort of role in the processes of truth and reconciliation. David Ireland's *Everything Between Us* (2010), like David Park's novel *The Truth Commissioner*, envisages how a notional Truth and Reconciliation Commission would pan out, with its

---

[34] Teya Sepinuck, 'I Once Knew a Girl', directed by Teya Sepinuck (Derry: The Playhouse, 2010), unpublished script, 15. [The editors wish to thank Teya Sepinuck for providing us with the unpublished script to this play.]

[35] Alice Mc Intyre, *Women in Belfast: How Violence Shapes Identity* (Westport, CT: Praeger, 2004), 57.

[36] David Grant and Matthew Jennings, 'Processing the Peace: An Interview with Teya Sepinuck', *Contemporary Theatre Review* 23, no. 3 (2013), 315. http://www.10.1080/10486801.2013.806323. Accessed 23 Nov. 2014.

[37] Catherine Cole, *Performing South Africa's Truth Commission: Stages of Translation* (Bloomington, IN: Indiana University Press, 2010), 6.

black South African female Chair assaulted on the first day of hearings in a racist attack by an MLA's sister. Derry playwright, Dave Duggan, opts for an alternative approach in *AH6905* (2005), whose treatment (literally) of the supposed need for a Truth Commission is handled in an allegorical fashion, as the North's body politic is cast in the form of a patient awaiting a medical procedure to have the truth cut out of him. Laurence McKeown and Brian Campbell's *A Cold House* (2003), whose title is a reference to Unionist leader David Trimble's Nobel speech in which he conceded unionism had since partition created a 'cold house for Catholics',[38] stages the almost insuperable difficulties of any such process, whereby truth leads only to recrimination as the cold house of a former RUC officer is repaired by a former republican prisoner, who arrives to fix the boiler.

Mick Duke's *Revenge* (2004) explores, in lieu of justice, how the possibility of reconciliation can be supplanted by the primal compulsion for vengeance. Set on the eve of the wedding of a character who had lost his first fiancée and most of his face when his first wedding was blown up by an anonymous bomber, Duke's play critically examines the urge to seek vengeance. *Revenge* plays with ideas of the cyclical nature of grief, guilt, and history, revealing how those collaterally caught up in the aftermath of atrocity often end up endlessly reliving and replaying their trauma. Mobilizing a large community chorus as a vast host of the dead who appear on-stage as ghostly shades summoned for the pending nuptials, *Revenge* is staged in a strange kind of dreamscape in which the revenants entice the grieving parents with the possibility of revenge as the guilt-ridden bomber appears as an unexpected guest.

Produced in the immediate aftermath of the North's prisoner releases, whereby all paramilitaries had been freed from Maze/Long Kesh under the terms of the Good Friday Agreement, *Revenge* possessed a poignant political valence. However, where *Revenge* staged the encounter between the victim and the perpetrator of violence in a dreamscape, the next play to stage such a confrontation, McCafferty's *Quietly* (2012), did so in a form of heightened realism. *Quietly*, like so many Irish plays, is set in a pub, and Alyson Cummin's meticulously realistic set was modelled on the original design and decor of the Rose & Crown Bar on the Lower Ormeau Road, which once served as the local for McCafferty's father. It was a public house and, like all too many in the city, was reduced to a charnel house when in 1972 the UVF bombed it in a sectarian attack. It is this atrocity, and its imagined aftermath, that is so deftly handled in *Quietly* as the fictional bomber, Ian Gibson, enters the bar he blew up, where he has arranged to meet Jimmy, the son of one those killed in the attack.

In *Quietly*, McCafferty reminds us of the redemptive possibilities of truth, and that the reconciliation it can release need not be state-sanctioned or sponsored, nor can it be imposed or instrumentalized. Jimmy initially embodies the understandable tendency to seek for truth in recrimination rather than reconciliation; 'this is me playin my part in the truth and reconciliation process,'[39] he says to Ian at one point. However, as the play progresses, McCafferty reminds us all that meaningful reconciliation means much more than simply telling our stories (as with the Theatre of Witness); it is equally about listening to others, and this an exchange and experience that theatre transacts all the time, and in a public and participatory forum.

---

[38] http://www.davidtrimble.org/speeches_nobelprize.htm. Accessed 16 Nov. 2014.
[39] Owen McCafferty, *Quietly* (London: Faber & Faber, 2012), 30.

At the start of the play, Jimmy cannot bring himself to listen to Ian's account of his actions on that fateful day, constantly interrupting and correcting him, seeking to coerce his narrative into one that shores up his own:

JIMMY.   just say what happened—simple enough isn't it—the facts are the truth—
    isn't that why you're here to tell the truth and be reconciled
IAN.   no—and there's more to the truth than facts.[40]

Ian's retort that the facts alone are not sufficient are not the weasel words of someone trying to excuse his actions, nor are they an attempt to evade his responsibility; it is simply the view that truth is perspectival and positional. In the closing scene, Ian offers Jimmy his hand in a gesture which Jimmy eventually accepts, though with the admonition: 'don't ever come back here again.'[41] It is a gesture freighted with symbolism, as formal handshakes between public figures on opposite sides of the conflict have become markers of historical change. In *Quietly*, McCafferty has suggested that 'there is no huge gesture about it, it is a male way [. . .] of ending something. It's finished.'[42] It is an uneasy, unsettling act. Both men have reached an understanding, and there is a reconciliation of sorts, but no expectation that they will meet one another again.

After *Quietly* opened in Dublin's Peacock Theatre in 2013, McCafferty recalled being emotionally upset afterwards by its impact, belatedly realizing that, in many ways, he had written *Quietly* about his generation, about 'the Belfast we grew up in and how it affected us'.[43] As such, it seems the last in a cycle of plays (*Mojo-Mickybo*, 1998, *Closing Time*, 2002, *Scenes from the Big Picture*) that deal with Troubles and their aftermath; and though there may never be any clean break, this seems a sensibility that is shared in the work of a younger generation of writers like David Ireland, Rosemary Jenkinson, Lisa Magee, and Lucy Caldwell, Stacey Gregg, and Abbie Spallen.

CONTINUITY AND CHANGE

One striking new motif that can be traced through a wealth of new plays over the past decade has been the theme of change, specifically the transformation of Belfast. A slew of plays feature the returned émigré, usually someone who fled Belfast during the Troubles but who has now returned home to find a city they barely recognize. In the Kabosh Theatre Company's site-specific *Two Roads West* (2009), an audience of four share a black taxi tour with a returned local who is re-familiarizing herself with a city in which she feels a stranger. Likewise, in McCafferty's *The Absence of Women* (2010), two down-and-out navvies in a dead-end dosshouse discuss coming home to the city they have heard has been transformed. In Graham Reid's *Love Billy* (2013), the eponymous hero (first made famous by Kenneth Branagh in the *Billy* television plays in 1982–4), is utterly discombobulated as he wanders around his old stomping ground, unable to find anything familiar from the old days.

[40] Ibid., 35.
[41] Ibid., 51.   [42] Owen McCafferty in conversation with the author, 8 May 2014.
[43] Ibid.

While no one would dispute that many of the features of Northern Ireland's confessional politics remain as entrenched as ever, it is equally true that the North is changing, and theatre reflects this perhaps more than any other art form. At the time of writing in June 2014, two shows running simultaneously at the recently rebuilt Lyric and MAC theatres perfectly exemplify this: David Ireland's *Can't Forget About You* (2013) and TheatreofplucK's *Tuesdays at Tesco's* (2014). Ireland's play offers a novel take on the love-across-the-barricades motif, as the character of Stevie has been jilted by his Catholic girlfriend, to the exultation of his bigoted big sister, but on the rebound ends up in an even more socially transgressive relationship with an otherwise 'perfect' Martha (she is a Glasgow Protestant) who is, crucially, considerably older. During pillow talk after some wild lovemaking, both learn a little more about each other, with Martha discovering Stevie's policeman father had been killed in a mortar attack on an RUC station when his mother was pregnant with him; and though Stevie is palpably reticent to discuss the issue, Martha starts talking about the Troubles with a gauche combination of ignorance, horror, and curiosity:

MARTHA.   I don't understand it. I don't understand how it could have happened.
STEVIE.   What?
MARTHA.   The Troubles. How we let that happen. Like why it went on. And why it suddenly stopped. [...] And I listen to you and—I mean I know we've only just met but you seem so *normal*—and you and your family, and all the other people I meet here, I think how did any of you manage to grow up normal? How did you manage to live with all that violence in your city for so long and why do you, why do you all seem so lovely and friendly when you lived through *that*? And how could you have done that to each other when you're all so *nice*?
    I don't . . . I don't get it. I don't understand it. I don't understand how . . .
    (*She shakes her head in bewilderment and looks to him for an answer.*)
STEVIE.   Yeah. Can we stop talking about it now?
MARTHA.   Why? [. . .]
STEVIE.   It's just so fucking boring!
MARTHA.   What is?
STEVIE.   The Troubles! [. . .] I'm so sick of talking about it and hearing about it[44]

After this exchange, the Troubles are not mentioned again. In its understated way, this seems to mark a significant moment in Northern drama.

At the same time as Ireland's play was being performed at the Lyric, the new MAC venue hosted the latest production by the North's only queer theatre company, TheatreofplucK: *Tuesdays at Tesco's*, a version of Emmanuel Darley's French original *Mardi à Monoprix* (2009). An architecturally impressive new theatre and gallery in an area of Belfast city centre being promoted as the 'Cathedral Quarter', the MAC, which opened in 2012, is a vibrant symbol of the post-conflict regeneration of the city. In some respects, this makes the decision to stage *Tuesdays at Tesco's* in the venue all the more resonant. The play takes the form of a monologue about a middle-aged transgendered woman, Pauline, looking after an elderly father who refuses to accept or to acknowledge his child's

⁴⁴ David Ireland, *Can't Forget About You* (London: Bloomsbury, 2013), 41–3.

transformation, pointedly using her birthname, 'Paul', whilst scorning her appearance and identity. *Tuesdays* was performed in the MAC's ground-floor exhibition space, the rear wall of which is wholly made of glass facing onto the busy passageway that leads into the new piazza-style courtyard at the front of the building, surrounded on all sides by fashionable restaurants and bars. Peter Quigley played Pauline from the street outside, whilst the small audience watched from within the theatre into which sound was broadcast, so that the solid glass wall constituted a transparent, if impermeable, fourth wall. It was a stunningly simple yet complex staging, leaving Quigley to negotiate his drag performance among the 'civilians' passing through, many of whom reacted with amusement, curiosity, or fright. All of this inflected Pauline's narrative of having to endure daily a heteronormative society which reacts to and rejects her appearance and identity, and where her own father maligns her even as she carries out her kindly ministrations. Pauline bears all with good grace, but an encounter while carrying out the most mundane task of shopping at Tesco's with her father upsets her, and in an emotional outburst, performed right up against the glass wall, Pauline poignantly pleads for tolerance, 'I am a woman and I go with my father on Tuesdays to Tesco's [...]. [M]y name is Pauline. [...] It's all quite normal.'[45]

In post-conflict Northern Ireland, far too much emphasis remains on the politics of orange and green, rather than the grey areas in betweenor the positions of the LGBT community, women, and immigrants, all of whom get short shrift. Since the signing of the Good Friday Agreement, the North's peace process has placed enormous political capital on ensuring the 'normalization' of politics, culture, and society, as signalling a successful post-conflict evolution from war to peace. A byword for demilitarization, decommissioning, and the stability of democratic structures, alongside the massive inward investment and regeneration of the North's economy, 'normalization', as TheatreofplucK reminds us, is a heteronormative process that is an inadequate metric of political progress. If *Can't Forget About You* suggests we should learn to stop talking about the past, TheatreofplucK suggests some of the things that we should learn to begin discussing.

---

[45] Emmanuel Darley, *Tuesdays at Tesco's* (*Mardi à Monoprix*), trans. Matthew Hurt and Sarah Vermande (London: Nick Hern Books, 2011), 17.

CHAPTER 24

....

'AS WE MUST'

Growth and Diversification in Ireland's Theatre Culture 1977–2000

....

VICTOR MERRIMAN

THEATRE in Ireland is often imagined as a national conversation, to the extent that Brian Friel could declare, in accounting for its global reach, 'We are talking to ourselves, as we must, and if we are overheard in America, or England, so much the better.'[1] Over thirty years later, this might seem a tongue-in-cheek comment, but its context was a thoughtful reflection on language, identity, and drama as his *Translations* (1980) premièred at Derry's Guildhall. Friel characterizes theatre as a public necessity in a country struggling historically with colonial modernities,[2] emigration, and—by the late twentieth century—the vicissitudes of independence and political partition.[3] It also broaches the question of who constitutes the 'we' involved in, or excluded from, the public forum provided by Irish theatre. In the midst of bloody mayhem in Friel's home place, Derry, he and others turned to culture to intervene in history, mobilizing 'images of the past embodied in language'[4] to expose and interrogate problems long thematized as Ireland's historical burden by theatre-makers from Dion Boucicault to Bernard Shaw, from Seán O'Casey to Samuel Beckett. Independent Ireland is itself a function of crises and aspirations converted into dramas, as James Moran[5] and Kathleen Gough[6] have shown: in Ireland, theatre matters.

Late nineteenth-century activists used cultural means to imagine a nation, including indigenous language, 'native' games, religion, and theatre. The National Theatre Society

---

[1] Brian Friel, quoted in Christopher Murray, 'Friel's "Emblems of Adversity and the Yeatsian Example"', in Alan Peacock (ed.), *The Achievement of Brian Friel* (Gerrards Cross: Colin Smythe, 1993), 81.

[2] David Lloyd, *Irish Times: Temporalities of Modernity* (Dublin: Field Day, 2008).

[3] Morash, Christopher, '"Something's Missing": Theatre and the Republic of Ireland Act', in Ray Ryan (ed.), *Writing in the Irish Republic: Literature, Culture, Politics 1949–1999* (Basingstoke: Macmillan, 1999), 64–81.

[4] Brian Friel, *Plays 1* (London: Faber & Faber, 1998), 445.

[5] James Moran, *Staging the Easter Rising: 1916 as Theatre* (Cork: Cork University Press, 2006).

[6] Kathleen M. Gough, *Kinship and Performance in the Black and Green Atlantic: Haptic Allegories* (London: Routledge, 2014).

was established in 1904, and played a very significant part in anticipating not only the desired nation but also its predictable silences, contradictions, and cruelties. When 'the English', in the words of Stewart Parker's doomed patriot, Henry Joy McCracken, 'finally bequeath[ed] us to one another',[7] and erstwhile paramilitaries and recent foes took on the work of 'founding and forging' a state,[8] one of their first tasks was to respond to a request from the directors of the National Theatre Society for annual subsidy. In grant-aiding the Abbey and Peacock theatres, the independent state acknowledged both the importance of cultural work to civil and civic life and public responsibility for enabling it to happen. The annual grant-in-aid was not a blessing unalloyed, nor was it ever sufficient to the ambition—or, all too often, the basic needs—of the National Theatre Society. It may even have had the unintended outcome of instantiating an idea of theatre as a function of Dublin living in the Irish Free State—an attitude which arguably ensured a dearth of professional activity in cities and towns outside the capital in subsequent decades. The scale and distribution of theatre provision and the sluggishness of its development was, of course, a function of more than a narrowness of outlook on the part of Dublin's political classes. Like all aspects of life in independent Ireland, theatre experienced the various and cumulative impacts of severe social, economic, and cultural challenges facing a small autonomous state on the fringe of northwestern Europe. This chapter offers a reflection on the remarkable development in range, distribution, and quality of theatre activity during the final quarter of the twentieth century, when—as it were—something happened.

When Druid Theatre Company presented its first season at the Fo'castle Theatre, Dominick Street, Galway, in 1975, a retrospective glance might regard that moment as the lighting of a creative fuse, with implications for how Irish theatre would be understood in terms of where, how, when, by whom, and for whom it would be made from that moment on. What followed now appears as the moment of the independent company; by most standards, not least the size of the country, the range of companies which began producing professional work in Ireland between 1977 and 2000 is remarkable. *Views of Theatre in Ireland*[9] records the repertoire of fifty-two professional companies active in the period 1990–94. While some groups flared only to quickly fizzle out, many left an impression on theatre-making which endures in the early twenty-first century. A review of their establishment and distribution reveals two common features, ever-present, regardless of whether or not they achieved longevity and the respect of audiences and peers: first, companies were formed when a group of individuals decided to establish and seek to sustain a collective structure for producing plays; secondly, their success and longevity related directly to the degree of material support which was made available to them, including access to public funds and suitable performance venues. It is possible to speak of the emergence of such companies as a series of 'diversifications', specifically because professional theatre infrastructure in Ireland testifies, like most public institutions, to the residual influence of modes of colonial administration which had dominated most aspects of Ireland's civil and civic life for over two centuries: it was overwhelmingly located in Dublin. Thus, from the 1970s, 'diversification' meant that production indigenous to 'the regions' gradually

---

[7] Stewart Parker, *Stewart Parker: Plays* 2 (London: Methuen Drama, 1984), 81

[8] David Lloyd, *Anomalous States: Irish Writing and the Post-Colonial Movement* (Dublin: Lilliput Press, 1993), 60.

[9] *Views of Theatre in Ireland* (Dublin: An Chomhairle Ealaíon, 1995), 184 93.

replaced tours by the Irish Theatre Company (1974–82), itself established in response to the demise of the fit-up touring companies of earlier times.

THE ESTABLISHMENT OF THE ARTS COUNCIL

In pursuit of sustainability, Druid followed the example of the National Theatre Society in 1926, seeking grant-in-aid, not from government directly, but from a state body established at 'arm's length' from government, 'to stimulate public interest in the arts; to promote the knowledge, appreciation and practice of the arts; and to assist in improving the standards of the arts'.[10] An Chomhairle Ealaíon/the Arts Council was established by statute in 1951, and remains by far the most significant source of arts funding in the Republic of Ireland. It had a lengthy gestation, with champions on both sides of the post-Civil War political divide: James Bodkin—cultural policy adviser to President W. T. Cosgrave, who led independent Ireland's first government—and Patrick Little TD—a Fianna Fáil minister for many years, and persistent advocate of state provision for the arts.[11] Bodkin first proposed to Cosgrave that the state establish a body similar to what is now recognized as an arts council, and John A. Costello, Taoiseach (1948–51), one of Cosgrave's successors in the Fine Gael party, prepared the necessary legislation some twenty years later, only to see his political nemesis, Éamon de Valera, returned to office in time to preside at the inaugural meeting of An Chomhairle Ealaíon. According to the Arts Act (1951), 'the expression "the arts" means painting, sculpture, architecture, music, drama, literature, design in industry, and the fine arts and applied arts generally.'[12] The council quickly set out its priorities, distancing itself, in principle if not in practice, from concerns that it might merely serve an idea of the arts as a complementary aspect of polite Dublin society.

An Chomhairle Ealaíon's first annual report (1953)[13] identifies an acute concern with structural issues which have exercised policymakers, publics, and artists ever since. At that time, the National Theatre Society was funded directly by the Department of the Taoiseach, and the preponderance of the Council's initial awards of grants-in-aid for drama went to support amateur activity. However, the report records that financial assistance was 'also given to two professional dramatic companies towards meeting losses incurred, and to a third company to be specifically applied to the provision of theatre accommodation'.[14] The significance of these funding decisions emerges more fully when they are read in conjunction with the single policy recommendation offered in the report. Indicating a concern for the range and quality of theatre available to people living in rural areas and small towns, the Council argued:

[A]n amateur drama company should be judged not only by the excellence of the production of a play in a competition, but by its service to the community, and that amateur societies

---

[10] 'The Arts Act (1951)', quoted in Brian Kennedy, *Dreams and Responsibilities* (Dublin: An Chomhairle Ealaíon, 1988), 251–6.

[11] Ibid., 79–80.   [12] Ibid., 251.

[13] An Chomhairle Ealaíon/The Arts Council, *Annual Report 1951–53* (Dublin: An Chomhairle Ealaíon, 1953). All annual reports will be cited hereafter as *ACE* followed by the year.

[14] Ibid., 3.

should be encouraged to have a small repertoire rather than to continually perform one play at various competitions.[15]

Thus, from the very outset, resources, venues, and access to theatre outside Dublin were established as policy priorities.

The political act of establishing an arts council created a climate in which expectations of increased arts funding—and, eventually, coherent arts strategy—were inevitably raised. Given the Council's modest funding base, and even more modest ambition during its first twenty years, lack of progress on such expectations produced simmering frustrations, not only among artists but also among those they dismissed as bureaucratic gatekeepers. Successive annual reports from 1951 to 1973 provide a record of struggle: constant lobbying of government, real institutional grasp of the demanding realities of artists' lives, and commitment to achieving adequate resources for arts policy in the teeth of perennial underfunding. Even in the early 1990s, when the situation had manifestly improved, writer Dermot Bolger described his personal experience as a Council member as that of 'constantly having to say "No" to decent people doing good work'.[16] It is also worth bearing in mind that, from 1952 to 1973, the Council's own organizational resources were negligible; it had practically no staff.[17] Despite its constant assertion of itself as a voice for what would come to be known as the cultural sector, the relatively small reservoir from which members were appointed, the disproportionate influence of certain members of the council,[18] and its location adjacent to Government Buildings nourished a popular view that members and officials of the Arts Council themselves constituted an exclusive—and elitist—'arts establishment'.[19]

PROJECT 67

As the 1960s progressed, the government began implementing a Programme for Economic Expansion (1959),[20] reconceptualizing independent Ireland as a small, open economy; Irish television began broadcasting in 1961, bringing audiences coverage of critical debates exciting Europe and the USA. In 1966, artists from across a range of disciplines mobilized in Dublin to contest their exclusion from public life, and from dialogues both with each other and with potential audiences. Manifesting both discontent and future intentions, Project 67 emerged as a bold and deliberate intervention in what was an all-but-moribund, Dublin-centred cultural life. Initiated by Colm O Briain, Jim Fitzgerald, and others, Project 67 'began in Autumn 1966 with a season of plays, poetry readings, concerts and films at the Gate Theatre, and an exhibition of the works of four artists, John Behan, Charles Cullen, Michael Kane and John Kelly'.[21] The objective was to direct public attention

---

[15] Ibid.   [16] Private correspondence, May 1994.
[17] Kennedy notes: 'Throughout the 1950s, the Council staff was comprised of a Secretary and a short-hand typist': Kennedy, *Dreams and Responsibilities*, 100.
[18] Ibid., 138.   [19] O Briain, interview with author, 16 June 2014.
[20] T. K. Whitaker, *First Programme for Economic Expansion (1958–63)* (Dublin: Government Publications, 1958).
[21] Kennedy, *Dreams and Responsibilities*, 151.

toward new work, individual artists, and the glaring absence of venues in which to experiment with performance forms. The theatre programme was almost a manifesto in its own right, consisting of three plays of the contemporary avant-garde: Harold Pinter's *The Lover* (1962), Murray Schisgal's *The Tiger* (1962), and *Double Double* (1962) by James Saunders;[22] Imprimatur Productions staged the festival of plays at the Gate Theatre, negotiating a lease from Longford Productions for the post-Dublin Theatre Festival period. With a tenancy secured in a central venue, Project 67 organized a range of events—including a reading of Friedrich Dürrenmatt's *The Visit* and a seminar on censorship for which Edna O'Brien travelled from London—and provided a context in which 'a group of individuals decided to form a National Association of Drama for Young People (NADRYP)'.[23]

Colm O Briain qualifies Kennedy's emphasis on Project 67's affront to an arts establishment unchanged in composition or priorities since 1951, emphasizing that its principal purpose was practical rather than political or symbolic: 'The establishment wouldn't give us any work at the time. We wanted to make work for actors, to create energy and opportunities for a younger generation of artists—there were only two art galleries in Dublin at the time, for instance.'[24] Nor was its critique confined to Dublin: O Briain 'advised the Arts Council that Ireland should have local and regional arts centres where various art workshops and studios would be gathered together in free association'.[25] Such objectives informed the group's Project Gallery (1967), 'to provide a blanket cover for the arts, to allow ideas to interact freely between artists and their public who have become separated from art'.[26] The Project Gallery itself engendered the Project Arts Centre (1969), which hosted an eclectic programme of work across and between art forms, and has operated since 2000 from bespoke premises built on the site of its home since 1974, in East Essex Street, Dublin.

The environment confronted by Project 67 underwent significant change with the passing of the Arts Act (1973), which revised the founding articles of An Chomhairle Ealaíon, especially in the area of staffing; there would henceforth be a dedicated director with specialist staff, and less than a decade after articulating Project 67's critique, Colm O Briain was appointed inaugural director of An Chomhairle Ealaíon. Thus, a radical perspective took hold at the centre of one of the most beleaguered yet doggedly transformative state agencies of independent Ireland. The purview of the Council's work from 1973 was more or less the same, with one addition: the insertion of 'the cinema' after 'drama' in the Act's definition of 'the arts'. It was a decision taken subsequent to the Act's amendment, however, that occasioned a watershed in policy toward drama and theatre in Ireland:

> The Minister for Finance announced in December that he was transferring responsibility for the Abbey Theatre, the Gate Theatre, the Irish Theatre Company, the Irish Ballet Company and the Dublin Theatre Festival to the Council from his Department. Although the transfer takes effect from the beginning of 1976, discretion with regard to the grants for these organisations will not operate until 1977. This change marks an important development in the role of the Arts Council as a national body [. . .] and makes it responsible for administering funds four times greater than before.[27]

[22] All three plays were performed by the company: Colm O Briain, Gillian Hanna, Bob Carlisle, and Dinah Stabb (dir. Jim Fitzgerald).
[23] O Briain, interview with author.   [24] Kennedy, *Dreams and Responsibilities*, 151.
[25] Ibid.   [26] O Briain, quoted in ibid.
[27] ACE 1975, 9

This major policy intervention had been flagged by the Taoiseach, Liam Cosgrave, during the Dáil debates on the Arts Act (1973), when he argued that the transfer of such significant bodies to the council 'would represent a more efficient and organised way of distributing state funds to the arts'.[28] Thus, in the year of Druid Theatre Company's foundation, the state greatly increased the amount disbursed directly by the Council in support of professional theatre-making.

Twenty years after its first report, the Council's Annual Report (1973) was the last produced under the terms of the 1951 Act, and offers evidence of both change and continuity over the period: funding amateur drama, rather than professional work, remained a priority. Grants-in-aid to professional companies in 1973 privileged those mainly or exclusively touring work outside of Dublin, and the council made some modest funding available to support educational initiatives.[29] By 1975, the impact of the amended Act was already clear, and the Annual Report shows a huge shift in priorities in Council funding: of a total allocation to Drama of £13,514.00, 78% was spent on supporting five professional theatre organizations. The size of the grants to two of these—the Everyman Playhouse, Cork (30%) and Siamsa Tíre, the National Folk Theatre, Tralee (11%)[30]—indicates a real commitment to developing professional theatre outside Dublin, a policy direction emphasized as follows:

> One innovation introduced in 1975 was the creation of a Fellowship for an Apprentice Producer which in its first year is with Siamsa Tíre, the National Folk Theatre based in Kerry. The Fellowship was awarded to Bríd Dukes, who has a background in professional theatre, having worked with the Abbey and with independent companies. Siamsa Tíre is planning to build a theatre in Tralee, half the cost of which is being carried by Roinn na Gaeltachta and Bord Fáilte. The Council gave a grant to Siamsa Tíre to undertake a study of small theatres in Europe and America and the findings will be made available to any other organisation intending to build a small local theatre.[31]

The Arts Council's doggedness in transforming Ireland's cultural landscape is well illustrated in what is claimed here as an 'innovation'. As a new scheme, it most certainly justifies that description, but from its first Annual Report (1951), cited earlier, the council had its eye clearly fixed on theatre's role as a 'service to the community', grounding its support for the development of professional productions outside Dublin, in respect both of company initiatives and of venues adequate to their realization. The example of Druid Theatre Company, which rapidly outgrew its converted coach-house in Dominick Street, demonstrates how this policy objective was implemented from 1975. The Council's Annual Report (1978) recorded:

> [T]he company has been operating in thoroughly unsuitable facilities and has found it difficult to find new premises, since commercial property in Galway is expensive to rent. However by the end of the year the company had located a premises in Courthouse Lane and once the venue has been converted Druid Theatre will re-open in 1979.[32]

Druid Lane Theatre opened in May 1979, only for the Council's next Annual Report (1980) to warn: 'The theatre succeeds in achieving a very high seat occupancy and may have

[28] Kennedy, *Dreams and Responsibilities*, 173.
[29] *ACE 1973–74*, 16–17.   [30] *ACE 1975*, 13.   [31] Ibid., 12.   [32] *ACE 1978*, 11.

reached the limit of its capacity to earn.'[33] The company's reputation for high-quality work, and the growth of theatre audiences in Galway, in and out of the festival season, combined to create a need for a yet bigger venue almost immediately—a need finally met in 1996, when Druid's production of Martin McDonagh's *Leenane Trilogy* opened at the newly converted Town Hall Theatre. Indefatigably, the 1981 report reiterates that 'growth in the number and professionalism of theatres outside Dublin is potentially the most important development which the Council can assist in the area of theatre'.[34] Accordingly, the Council funded venues including Belltable Arts Centre, Limerick, Cork Opera House, Druid Lane, Siamsa Tíre, Everyman Playhouse, and the Hawk's Well Theatre, Sligo (due to open the following year).[35]

NEW COMPANIES

What might be called the Druid model of company foundation and repertory development is repeated in the histories of Rough Magic (Dublin, 1984), Pigsback (Dublin, 1988–96), Gallowglass (Clonmel, 1990), Island (Limerick, 1988–2008), Meridian (Cork, 1991–2009), Corcadorca (Cork, 1991), and Blue Raincoat (Sligo, 1991), among others. Unlike Druid, however, and with the exception of Blue Raincoat, none of these companies developed as a venue-based theatre ensemble, relying instead on seasons presented at established or emerging local venues and on access to touring—a central plank of Arts Council policy toward 'regional development' almost since its inception, and which was funded between 1982 and 1990 by direct grant aid to companies.[36] The report for 1985 noted that, following the Council's highly contentious—and high-risk—decision to cease support for the Irish Theatre Company (one of the organizations transferred to its care in 1975), 'the Council is very encouraged by the number of companies which have *come into being in order to operate within the Council's Touring Scheme*. Amongst these are Smock Alley, Playwrights and Actors Company, Rough Magic, and Deilt Productions' (my italics).[37] Rough Magic celebrated twenty-five years of award-winning work in 2009, overcoming a venue-less existence in the capital city by developing a partnership with Project Arts Centre.

If there is merit in discussing a 'Druid model', it must be acknowledged that it is not the only route to company formation. The development of arts centres and festivals played a very significant role in the emergence of Macnas (Galway, 1986), and Bickerstaffe Theatre Company (Kilkenny, 1994–2001). Interestingly, neither the existence of a world-renowned opera festival (1951) nor one of the first regional arts centres enabled the establishment of a significant theatre company in Wexford. There were efforts, including Wexford Theatre Workshop, later Riff Raff Theatre—a short-lived Arts Centre Theatre Company (1986)—and writer Billy Roche's Pocket Youth Theatre Company (1987), but the leap made in Sligo, Galway, or Cork was never made in Wexford. In neighbouring Waterford, a robust community arts movement, Waterford Arts for All, engendered Red Kettle (1988), Little Red Kettle, and Waterford Spraoi, nurturing a wide range of playwrights and providing a platform for Jim Nolan's impressive body of dramatic works.

---

[33] *ACE 1980*, 26.   [34] *ACE 1981*, 23.   [35] *ACE 1981*, 26.
[36] *Views of Theatre in Ireland*, 194–6.   [37] *ACE 1985*, 16.

SUBSIDIZED THEATRE

This discussion has, thus far, foregrounded publicly funded companies, but the Irish theatre scene has always sustained a successful core of commercial production companies, led by theatre producers/directors who assembled seasonal casts and production crews to produce and tour popular plays. Phyllis Ryan's[38] Gemini Productions was probably the most notable commercial production company, offering regular work to theatre artists over many decades. Godfrey Quigley Productions, Noel Pearson Productions, Chris O'Neill (Take 4), and Arthur Lappin and Ben Barnes's Groundwork Productions toured viable shows nationwide, with Pearson also transferring work to London's West End, the British regional circuit, and—in the case of Martin McDonagh—to Broadway. Pearson's tour of Druid's *The Leenane Trilogy* attracted large appreciative audiences, and earned Tony Awards for Garry Hynes and Anna Manahan (1998).

While theatre awards ceremonies rightly celebrate artistic endeavour, and lavish thanks are extended to bodies sponsoring the ceremonies themselves, the role of the Irish state in enabling the theatre is rarely acknowledged. Over the years, it has not been unusual for compères and even award recipients generally to ignore or dismiss the reality that almost all Irish theatre is subsidized, directly or indirectly—however inadequately or unevenly—by public funds. In clarifying the extent and impact of indirect subsidy of commercial theatre, the Arts Council's Annual Report (1979) exposes the range and interpenetration of relationships between commercial interests and directly funded organizations:

> An awareness of the needs of independent managements is essential to a comprehensive theatre policy. In recent years subsidy has been granted to some independent managements, particularly through access for their productions to the Gate Theatre for six months of the year. Such productions benefit to the extent of £3,000 per week from the annual Arts Council grant to the Gate. If one adds to this the guarantees offered through the Dublin Theatre Festival some independent companies have benefited considerably, if indirectly, from Arts Council support. These indirect subsidies are rarely seen as significant, or acknowledged as such. In addition to these indirect subsidies the Council introduced in 1979 a *Memorandum on Aid to Independent Managements*, which envisages support for the commissioning of new Irish plays and guarantees against loss on their productions. The Memorandum also offers subvention for touring productions, and interest-free loans to assist with pre-production and equipment costs.[39]

1990S DEBATES

It is important to bear these facts in mind when evaluating the gradual realization of public policy objectives, responding to a vision tentatively formulated in the Council's first

---

[38] For an assessment of her life and work, see 'Phyllis Ryan', Irish Theatre Institute, http://www.irishtheatreinstitute.com/page.aspx?t=phyllis_ryan&contentid=2007. Accessed 20 Sept. 2014.

[39] *ACE 1979*, 28.

report, and boldly expanded and articulated as a 'Statement of Intent' in *The Arts Plan 1993–1995*:

> As the statutory body entrusted with stimulating public interest in the arts and promoting their knowledge, appreciation and practice, the Arts Council believes that everyone in Ireland has an entitlement to meaningful access to and participation in the arts. The Council understands that it has a primary responsibility to encourage and maintain high standards especially in the living contemporary arts. It also understands that it has a clear responsibility to foster those structures which assist and develop dialogue between artists, the arts and the communities from which they emerge.[40]

The Plan, presented to government in 1994 by the state's first minister for Arts, Culture and Gaeltacht, Michael D. Higgins, drew on research commissioned on cultural work in Ireland to enable a political case to be made for honouring commitments inherent in the idea and operation of an Arts Council. In expanding the first Council's assertion of the need for 'service to its community', its use of plural 'communities' reflected the zeitgeist of its moment: an inclusive multiculturalism crystallized in the election and seven-year presidency of Mary Robinson.

The welcome accorded to the Plan was somewhat mixed, with heated objections focused on the designation of cities outside Dublin as 'centres of energy and excellence'[41]—Waterford was designated Centre of Excellence for Drama. The Council responded to widespread expressions of dissatisfaction by commissioning a *Review of Theatre in Ireland* (1995–6), a wide-ranging—and unprecedented—exercise in policymaking by public consultation. In evaluating the merits of criticism of the Plan's Drama proposals, the Council was struck less by what was said and more by who was saying it: what the review would refer to as the Theatre of the Nation had found a voice, and, alongside manifestos written by Patrick Mason articulating the National Theatre's purpose (1993–5), policymakers had to engage with reconfigured terms of debate around theatre provision in the Republic of Ireland. Accordingly, the *Review* was structured in three phases. Phase I was a sociological review of the state of play, published in *Views of Theatre in Ireland* (1995), with reflective essays by theatre artists and policymakers external to Ireland, but from countries of commensurable scale: Helena Kaut-Howson, Director, Theatr Clwyd, Wales; Neil Wallace, Scotland; Eduard Delgado, Catalonia. The volume was completed by a detailed overview of theatre practices across community, youth, and educational contexts, written by Declan Gorman, the *Review*'s administrator.

Phase II tested ideas and perceptions among theatre practitioners and interested members of the public at eight meetings spread geographically throughout the country, including Waterford, Cork, Galway, Monaghan, Longford, and Dublin, openly addressing questions which until that moment had been posed and answered only implicitly in funding decisions responding to policy advances and retreats and crisis management. The *Review*'s work culminated in a policy document, *Going On* (1996),[42] which drew on the critical insights of the review process to produce practical proposals supported by a critical

[40] An Chomhairle Ealaíon, *The Arts Plan 1993–1995* (Dublin: An Chomhairle Ealaíon, 1993), 6.
[41] Ibid., 4.
[42] An Chomhairle Ealaíon, *Going On* (Dublin: An Chomhairle Ealaíon, 1996).

mass of theatre-makers. The *Review* gave impetus to Theatre Shop, an initiative which blossomed into the Irish Theatre Institute,[43] and provided a context for the development of Theatre Forum.[44] These organizations underpin a dynamic, self-reflexive, and engaged community of theatre professionals, generating opportunities for artists and publics and participating in and initiating critical public discussion on state and local policies on theatre and related art forms. This period also saw the Council introduce ring-fenced funding for a National Theatre Archive at the Abbey Theatre—a key policy objective of its then artistic director, Patrick Mason.

The *Theatre Review* exposed a performance landscape developed over the previous two decades, diverse in purpose, practice, and constituencies. These included subsidized companies and artists involved in making Irish Language Theatre, Youth Theatre, Theatre-in-Education, and Dance Theatre, as well as festival organizations, including Dublin Theatre Festival and its associated Dublin Theatre Festival Fringe. Theatre in the Irish language has had an iconic home at An Taidhbhearc in Galway since 1928, and has been staged in Dublin, at the Abbey and Peacock, the Gate, An Damer (1955–1981), Project, and, latterly, at the axis centre, Ballymun. The most celebrated playwright of the century was Mairéad Ní Ghráda, whose *An Triail* is arguably the best-known drama in Irish, embarking on its eleventh consecutive tour in a production by Belfast-based Aisling Ghéar (2014).[45] *Playography na Gaeilge 1901–2010*[46] records 355 original dramas among 796 stage performances in Irish, testifying to the endurance of theatre in Irish since the first performance of Douglas Hyde's *Casadh an tSúgáin* in 1901. The national broadcaster, RTÉ, made an important contribution to the public profile of dramatic writing in Irish, providing work for writers, translators, and actors in radio and television. Almost all plays in Irish were produced either in Galway (39.5%) or in Dublin (58.2%)[47] over the period considered; the public presence of the language outside Gaeltacht areas received a very significant boost with the establishment of Teilifís na Gaeilge, now TG4, in 1996. Since then, opportunities for writers, translators, actors, and audiences increased exponentially, not least because of the popularity of the station's long-running twice-weekly soap opera, *Ros na Rún*.

Mary Robinson's election as President of Ireland in 1990 crystallized the radical changes in Irish society in the aftermath of the cultural civil wars of the 1980s. When her electoral success was followed by the election to government of a Labour party which had nominated her for office and explicitly identified with her politics, the dividend for artists was the appointment of Michael D. Higgins as the state's first ever cabinet member with a brief for arts and culture.[48] During the 1990s, companies—including Wet Paint Theatre Company, Glasshouse Productions, and Calypso Productions—began explicitly to address cultural politics and social justice. Wet Paint Theatre Company (1984–91) was part of Wet Paint Arts, an activist organization directed by a dynamic collective, including actor, director, and dramaturge David Byrne and Niall O Baoill. Wet Paint Arts developed a young people's theatre network among Dublin communities ravaged by the recessions of the 1980s,

[43] See http://www.irishtheatreonline.com/. See also http://www.irishplayography.com.

[44] See http://www.theatreforum.ie/.

[45] See 'Aisling Ghéar', Irish Theatre Online, http://www.irishtheatreonline.com/. http://www.irishtheatreonline.com/ita/company.aspx?Company_ID=27. Accessed 20 Sept. 2014.

[46] *Playography na Gaeilge 1901–2010* (Dublin: Irish Theatre Institute, 2011).   [47] Ibid., 16, 17.

[48] Michael D. Higgins served from 1993 to 1997, and was elected President of Ireland in Nov. 2011.

abandoned to low educational attainment, unemployment, and the encroachment of drug pushers and paramilitaries. Glasshouse Productions, founded by Katy Hayes, Clare Dowling, Siân Quill, and Caroline Williams, 'produced ten shows [...] including new plays by Clare Dowling, Trudy Hayes and Emma Donoghue, and in addition hosted discussions and debates on the role of women in contemporary Irish theatre'[49] between 1990 and 1996. The company's achievement was considerable, and its position clear, according to Katy Hayes, who offers, in passing, a commentary on the shape of Irish theatre at that time:

> Glasshouse was a project founded in 1990 to present and promote the work of women in the theatre. Inspirational predecessors would include Charabanc in Northern Ireland and Trouble and Strife in the UK. Ireland has never had an easy relationship with the feminist movement, and Irish theatre even less. The notion of a politically focused group was alien. [...] We had never had the upsurge in political drama that had emerged in the UK in the Seventies and Eighties, the neo-Brechtian yawp that produced voices like Howard Barker, Caryl Churchill and Sarah Daniels, and companies like Trouble and Strife and Joint Stock. This is an aesthetic environment which provides a natural home for feminism. Irish theatre was firmly rooted in realism, and Irish theatre produced 'intimate plays of Irish life' and did it rather well. So we spotted a gap in the canvas, as it were.[50]

Wet Paint also organized conferences and symposia, publishing reports and position papers to provoke and inform public debate on cultural politics. Calypso Productions went further, in tandem with a programme of radical theatrical interventions between 1993 and 1999:

> Calypso's mission is simple, practical and humble. We want to change the world ... We are all world citizens. Some of us are lucky enough to have inherited life saving rights, life enhancing social opportunities and life affirming creative possibilities. With those rights and privileges comes a responsibility to defend them for ourselves and for others.[51]

Those others included both people on the margins of Irish society—Travellers, in Charlie O'Neill, *Rosie and Starwars* (1997), refugees and asylum seekers in Declan Gorman's street festival, *Féile Fáilte* (1997), or Donal O'Kelly's *Farawayan* (1998), and women in the prison system in Paula Meehan's *Cell* (1999)—and populations at risk from the transnational military/industrial complex, in Donal O'Kelly's *Hughie on the Wires* (1993) and Donal O'Kelly and Kenneth Glenaan's *The Business of Blood* (1995), or neoliberal economic policies in Donal O'Kelly's *Trickledown Town* (1994).

A renewed sense of theatre's sociocultural purpose was very much in the air in late 1980s and early 1990s Ireland. According to Siân Quill:

> In the same year that Ireland welcomed its first female President, [Glasshouse], as a company, aimed to give Irish women a voice in the theatre. Historically, it was male voices that were heard at all levels of the theatre system—from writers to management. To change that,

[49] Katy Hayes, Clare Dowling, Siân Quill, and Caroline Williams, 'People in Glasshouse: An Anecdotal History of an Independent Irish Theatre Company', in Dermot Bolger (ed.), *Druids, Dudes and Beauty Queens* (Dublin: New Island Press, 2000), 132.

[50] Ibid., 134–5.

[51] Calypso Productions, 'Information and Action on Arms' (educational resource materials accompanying *The Business of Blood*) (Dublin: Calypso Productions, 1995), n.p.

one had to fight the system. That fight was informed by feminism. Glasshouse would make no apology for that.[52]

EXPANSION AND DIVERSITY

A theatre of ideas had been established in Ireland by the founders of the Abbey Theatre. By the early 1990s Field Day Productions, Druid Theatre Company, and—especially under Patrick Mason's artistic directorship—the National Theatre itself were explicitly engaged with burning debates, pressing crises, and thwarted or emerging aspirations of the day. If the Abbey's work was that of provoking 'national conversation', Field Day's project provided an unprecedented critical platform for understanding the various forms in which nationalist politics was practised, represented, and interpreted. Before it was 10 years old, Druid Theatre Company had evolved a coherent artistic programme pointedly characterized by Fintan O'Toole as a 'long demythologization of the West'[53] of Ireland. Garry Hynes confirmed that whatever the circumstances of the dramatic world, her reference point was an actually existing location, its people, and their living conditions. In reviving M. J. Molloy's *The Wood of the Whispering* (1953), she made use of 'a sociological study of parts of western Ireland in the 1950s [... that] had nothing to do with the characters but gave a wonderful sense of a community and how that community was breaking up. That absolutely inspired the production of the play that eventually evolved.'[54]

The pursuit of a theatre of ideas by Glasshouse, Wet Paint, and Calypso was both different from and in dialogue with this commitment in already established companies and institutions. They challenged their own generation with theatre exploring themes articulated in progressive cultural politics, both nationally and internationally. Their success in doing so was sometimes spectacular, as in the case of Wet Paint's award-winning production of Dermot Bolger's *The Lament for Arthur Cleary* (1989),[55] but proved difficult to sustain. Wet Paint Theatre Company ceased operations in 1991 and Glasshouse in 1996. Following personnel changes in 1999, Calypso Productions lost its political edge, closing down in 2006. Many of the artists and administrators involved, however, continue to make important contributions to theatre and public life more generally. Dermot Bolger's career as a playwright began with a Wet Paint commission, and led to a major trilogy of plays in Ballymun's axis theatre, demonstrating how a theatre of the local might engage not only with its own audiences and their stories but also with professional writers and makers of theatre, the broader public, and the state itself.

---

[52] Hayes et al., 'People in Glasshouse', 135.

[53] Fintan O'Toole, *Critical Moments: Fintan O'Toole on Modern Irish Theatre*, ed. Julia Furay and Redmond O'Hanlon (Dublin: Carysfort Press, 2003), 181.

[54] Quoted in Helen Manfull, *Taking Stage: Women Directors on Directing* (London: Methuen, 1999), 49.

[55] *The Lament for Arthur Cleary* was premièred by Wet Paint Arts on 18 Sept. 1989 at Project Arts Centre, Dublin, toured extensively, and won an Edinburgh Fringe First award in 1990.

A similar extension of the social mission of Irish theatre can be seen in the emergence of theatre-in-education (TiE) in this period. In particular, TEAM Educational Theatre Company (Dublin, 1975) and Graffiti Theatre in Education Company (Cork, 1984) created and toured bespoke TiE programmes to schools across Ireland. TEAM's artistic direction was renegotiated regularly over a thirty-five-year history, and the company commissioned works by distinguished playwrights, including Mary-Elizabeth Burke-Kennedy, Bernard Farrell, Frank McGuinness, Jim Nolan, Jim Sheridan, and Michael West. Graffiti benefited from consistency of artistic direction by founder/director Emelie Fitzgibbon, who also wrote regularly for the company. In contrast to TEAM—productions of works by well-known writers Enda Walsh and Raymond Scannell notwithstanding—Graffiti has tended to develop and nurture relationships with specialist TiE writers, notably Roger Gregg. Both companies looked internationally for models of good practice, and Fitzgibbon also played a leading role, with Eilis Mullan and Paddy O'Dwyer of Dublin Youth Theatre (1977), in establishing and developing NAYD (National Association of Youth Drama), a significant network of artists and educators, with strong transnational associations.

Outside Dublin, theatres were renovated, refurbished, or built from the ground up, and companies were involved either in generating performance spaces or in occupying them, once built. Some companies—Meridian and Corcadorca in Cork, for instance—were explicitly involved in projects exploring aspects of how life was lived among the people who came to see their plays (Johnny Hanrahan and John Browne's *Craving*, 1998; Enda Walsh's *The Ginger Ale Boy*, 1995, and *Disco Pigs*, 1996), while others were concerned more broadly with theatre aesthetics. Blue Raincoat Theatre Company was co-founded in Sligo by Étienne Decroux alumnus Niall Henry[56] and Malcolm Hamilton, and set out to explore the former's commitment to ensemble playing and the latter's writing, building an impressive company of actors and developing their own venue in the process. Red Kettle Theatre Company drew on the prodigious capacities of writer Jim Nolan, designer Ben Hennessy, stage manager Jim Daly, and producers T. V. Honan and Liam Rellis, placing Waterford life on-stage alongside ambitious programmes of classical drama and new writing. These indicative examples suggest the quality and diversity of the Theatre of the Nation, and its fundamental achievement: a redrawing of the map of Irish theatre production companies, lighting up venues across the country which had been restricted, historically, to a diet of amateur shows and occasional touring by professional fit-ups and their successors.

The extraordinary development of artistic capacity was accompanied by a parallel growth in funded performing arts venues—from nineteen (eleven theatres and eight arts centres) in 1983 to fifty-five (twenty-eight theatres and twenty-seven arts centres) by 2001.[57] More recently, Chris Morash and Shaun Richards record the opening of more than eighty theatres across the Republic of Ireland and Northern Ireland, giving a total

---

[56] Henry's 2001 Peacock interpretation of *The Playboy of the Western World* is generally regarded as a thrilling postmodern reimagination of Synge's classic play. See Anthony Roche, *Synge and the Making of Modern Irish Drama* (Dublin: Carysfort Press, 2013). It is important to acknowledge the contribution of the dramaturge Jocelyn Clarke to 'a dazzling metatheatrical' (224) production. The general neglect of the role of dramaturge in Irish theatre is worthy of a chapter in itself.

[57] *Auditoria: A Review of Planning, Programming and Provision for Performing Arts Venues in Ireland* (Dublin: An Chomhairle Ealaíon, 2004), app. 1, 32–3.

of ninety-five professional venues by 2014.[58] The *Auditoria* report identifies the primary policy enabler of that expansion as the Cultural Development Incentive Scheme (CDIS), established in 1996 by Michael D. Higgins, which provided €25,517,444 in capital grants to improve the physical infrastructure available to cultural organizations. *Auditoria's* research informants are drawn from a wide range and geographical distribution of early career arts professionals, central and local government officials, and hardy veterans of decades of struggle. *Auditoria* was established by the arts councils in Dublin and Belfast in 1999, and by the time it reported in 2004, a new Arts Act (2003) had been passed by Dáil Éireann,[59] Ireland was in the throes of an economic boom, and the Council directorship changed,[60] for only the fourth time since the position was established in 1973. Change may have come very slowly for artists and publics, but when it began to take effect, it had an unstoppable momentum, due to the commitment of particular people, legislators, artists, and significant enablers. Mapping personal and professional relationships among those involved in the diversification of Irish theatre will have to await another opportunity; what is clear is that individuals really mattered in shaping what it became possible to aspire to. The point is self-evident in the careers of Garry Hynes, Patrick Mason, Lynne Parker, or Phyllis Ryan, for instance, and the contributions of the Glasshouse collective and Irish Theatre Institute directors Siobhán Bourke[61] and Jane Daly,[62] Niall O Baoill, and David Byrne of Wet Paint Arts is a matter of record. The significance of individual vision and commitment is no less important in the case of those who supported Irish theatre, even when their public role was that of bearing unpalatable news of contraction and recession.

A scene played out on Merrion Square in 1982 speaks of the intimacy in Ireland of theatre-makers, policy-makers, and the general public: An Chomhairle Ealaíon decided that year to cease funding the Irish Theatre Company (ITC), ending eight years of high-quality work, and shifting policy on touring in a way that would—with later modifications—ultimately enhance the sustainability of theatre companies in regional towns and cities. The policy move was addressed in the Drama section of that year's Annual Report, which concluded:

> The decision to withdraw support from the Irish Theatre Company was made reluctantly. It was an unpleasant necessity and the Council regrets all the anguish that it caused the theatre fraternity, fully understanding the concern that this change of direction caused. However, by the end of the year the action taken proved to be the correct one. In addition to the touring scheme the Council provided guarantees to a new agency, the National Touring Agency, which is the main vehicle for providing management services both to production companies and to the venues using the touring scheme.[63]

Among the many immediate casualties of that decision was ITC administrator Phelim Donlon, who led a protest by members of Irish Actors Equity from the company's city centre

---

[58] Chris Morash and Shaun Richards, *Mapping Irish Theatre: Theories of Space and Place* (Cambridge: Cambridge University Press, 2013), 15.

[59] See http://www.irishstatutebook.ie/pdf/2003/en.act.2003.0024.pdf.

[60] Directors (1977–2000) include Colm O Briain (1973–83), Adrian Munnelly (1983–97), and Patricia Quinn (1997–2002).

[61] Former producer with Rough Magic Theatre Company, and Rough Magic Films.

[62] Former company manager, Druid Theatre Company, and freelance producer and consultant.

[63] *ACE 1982*, 16

offices to the Arts Council. As a crowd of people 'from all over the country'[64] watched, and the Irish Transport and General Workers' Union Band played, Donlon delivered a letter of protest to Council Chairman James White, Director Colm O Briain, and Drama Officer Arthur Lappin, who came out of the building to acknowledge the protest. Two years later, Donlon was appointed to succeed Lappin as the Council's Drama Officer, going on to play a central role in policy direction and implementation, especially during the Review of Theatre in Ireland, and becoming Director of the *Auditoria* project in 1999. Colm O Briain later became a key policy adviser to Michael D. Higgins at the Department of Arts, Culture and Gaeltacht (1993–7), and played a central role in developing CDIS, whose impact laid the ground for *Auditoria*. As that letter changes hands, a discerning glance can identify the combination of people and qualities of genius, passion, principle, and endurance, which came to underpin a diverse and challenging theatre nation.

[64] Phelim Donlon, interview with author, 22 May 2014.

CHAPTER 25

....

FROM DRUID/MURPHY TO *DRUIDMURPHY*

....

SHELLEY TROUPE

In November 2011, the Galway-based theatre Druid announced a large-scale theatrical event consisting of three plays by Tom Murphy: *Conversations on a Homecoming*
(1985), *A Whistle in the Dark* (1961), and *Famine* (1968).[1] Druid's press release championed
DruidMurphy as '[a] major celebration of the work of Tom Murphy and the largest touring project in Irish theatre in 2012'.[2] Later, Druid's co-founder and artistic director, Garry
Hynes, described *DruidMurphy* as an 'archaeological dig' into Ireland's past, and hence a
way of understanding contemporary Ireland.[3] However, the announcement also marked
a revival of Druid's relationship with Murphy, a partnership that began in 1983 when the
company contracted him as its writer-in-association but that formally ended three years
later. This affiliation proved significant for both parties. For Druid, the alignment with
Murphy in the 1980s assisted its development both as a national and as an international
touring company; for Murphy, it provided 'a degree of rejuvenation' for his work (to use
his own words).[4] To do so, Druid both gave new life to some of Murphy's older plays and
premièred two highly acclaimed works in 1985: *Conversations on a Homecoming* and
Bailegangaire.[5]

[1] The company opened in July 1975 as Druid: The Repertory Theatre of Galway. In current literature,
the company refers to itself as Druid or Druid (Ireland) rather than Druid Theatre Company or Druid
Theatre. Therefore, I use Druid. The assistance of the following institutions and funding agencies
in the completion of this study is warmly acknowledged: the Irish Research Council; the Moore
Institute and the Discipline of English at the National University of Ireland, Galway; and the English
Department at the Maynooth University.

[2] 'Press Release: Druid Announces DruidMurphy', Druid, 25 Nov. 2011, http://www.druid.ie/news/
press-release-druid-announces-druidmurphy. Accessed 20 Sept. 2014.

[3] Eric Gorde, 'A Dark Irish Voice Revisits His Rage', *New York Times*, 27 June 2012, http://mobile.
nytimes.com/2012/07/01/theater/druidmurphy-three-tom-murphy-plays-at-lincoln-center.html?_
r=0. Accessed 26 June 2014.

[4] Ronit Lentin, 'Playwright Returns from his Exile', *Irish Press*, 26 Sept. 1983.

[5] Although *Conversations* is often considered a new play, it is a one-act reworking of Murphy's two-
act play *The White House*, which premièred at the Abbey as part of the 1972 Dublin Theatre Festival.
Murphy wrote *Bailegangaire* for Druid, but the play has origins in two prequels, television dramas
that were written c.1981: *Brigit* and *The Contest* (alternatively titled as *The Challenge* and *Fatalism*).

This chapter provides an archaeological exploration of its own by analysing the relationship between Druid and Tom Murphy to reveal how Druid's relationship with Murphy in the mid-1980s was crucial to its construction as the extremely successful international touring company that we know today. It carries out this excavation by assessing the relative positions both of Druid and of Murphy in the Irish theatre world of 1983, drawing not only on play texts and reviews but also on less often considered visual materials such as programmes and posters. By unearthing these materials, we glimpse the groundwork for *DruidMurphy* almost thirty years later.

DRUID FROM 1975 TO 1983

From the outset, Druid was a company that was firmly rooted in Galway, but which had wider ambitions. In 1975, recent University College Galway graduates Garry Hynes and Marie Mullen teamed with semi-professional actor Mick Lally to form what was called at that time Druid: The Repertory Theatre of Galway. The company gave its first performances in the Jesuit Hall, a rented activity room at a local secondary school that seated an audience of about 200. Beginning on 3 July 1975, Druid presented John Millington Synge's *The Playboy of the Western World* (1907) in repertory with Kevin Laffan's *It's a Two-Foot-Six-Inches-Above-the-Ground World* (1970) and Brian Friel's *The Loves of Cass McGuire* (1966). From the outset, however, Druid indicated that it had bigger plans: while the company worked to create a local identity, it also expressed interest in touring. In her inaugural programme note, Garry Hynes stated that Druid sought to provide 'a means of expression of the community in which it is rooted, serving education, recreational and creative needs'; and early on, the company announced (but did not realize at the time) a tour to Clifden, in Co. Galway.[6]

In those early years, Druid both consolidated its Galway base and began moving further afield. In August 1975, the company introduced lunchtime theatre to Galway, presenting those performances in the tiny Fo'castle Theatre (a converted event room in a local hotel), which seated forty-two audience members during evening performances and thirty-six at lunchtime. Two years later, in 1977, Druid made its Dublin debut, presenting Leonard Melfi's *Birdbath* (1965) at the Project Arts Centre; in 1978 the company played Writers' Week in Listowel, Co. Kerry, with three works by Synge: *In the Glens of Rathvanna* (a compilation of Synge's prose writings), *The Shadow of the Glen* (1902), and *The Tinker's Wedding* (1909).[7] By May 1979, Druid had built its own theatre in a converted warehouse in Galway City Centre. Colloquially known as Druid Lane Theatre, it gave the company a base from which to tour more widely while maintaining a presence in Galway.

In September 1980, Druid's first international tour took the company to the Edinburgh Festival Fringe, where they presented four works: Garry Hynes's original revue based on

---

Brigit was broadcast on RTÉ television in January 1988. *The Contest*, retitled *A Thief of a Christmas*, premièred at the Abbey in 1985.

[6] Jerome Hynes (ed.), *Druid: The First Ten Years* (Galway: Druid Performing Arts and Galway Arts Festival, 1985), 79; 'Druid Players a Big Hit', *Connacht Sentinel*, 15 July 1975.

[7] *The Tinker's Wedding* was first published in 1907 but premièred in 1909.

Oscar Wilde's life, *The Pursuit of Pleasure* (1977); an original play written by Hynes that explored Ireland's relationship with England during the reign of Elizabeth I called *Island Protected by a Bridge of Glass* (1980); and two one-act plays by Galway-born playwright Geraldine Aron, *Bar and Ger* (1975) and *A Galway Girl* (1979). *Pursuit* and *Island* both won Scotsman Fringe First Awards, while *Island*'s original music (written and performed by local traditional Irish music band, De Dannan) won a Radio Forth award. The company's success in Edinburgh had a marked impact on their profile back in Ireland. Upon Druid's return to Galway, the company's success was honoured by a mayoral reception, and the national media began to take notice. For instance, one Belfast paper noted: 'Druid is a small but dynamic company. Somebody should invite them up. After Edinburgh there'll be no stopping them.'[8] There was also an attempt to schedule *Island* as part of the 1980 Dublin Theatre Festival, but Druid pulled it from the programme when the Festival refused to meet the company's required guarantee.[9] The *Irish Times* noted the irony of this situation: 'And so, Dublin festival-goers were denied a chance of seeing this remarkable group of professionals from the west who scored such a splendid success at Edinburgh.'[10] For Druid, the experience confirmed that it was possible to create an Irish national reputation through international success from a base outside of Dublin.

Druid's 1982 reinterpretation of *The Playboy of the Western World* developed further this new dynamic of the local, national, and international.[11] After opening the play in Galway, Druid toured *Playboy* to the 1982 Edinburgh Festival Fringe (along with lunchtime performances of *The Shadow of the Glen*), before bringing it to that year's Dublin Theatre Festival. The *Irish Times* hailed it as 'definitive'—an honour conferred on all of Druid's future performances of the play.[12] After stops in Sligo and Cork, Druid staged *Playboy* on two of the three Aran Islands in October 1982. These island performances further increased Druid's national visibility when they were filmed for an Irish television documentary, *Back to the Cradle*, that was broadcast nationally.[13] In November 1982, the production initiated Druid's touring to Northern Ireland with stops at Derry's Guildhall and the Belfast Civic Arts Theatre, the latter as a part of the Belfast Arts Festival.[14]

During 1982 and 1983, Druid consolidated its touring reputation and circuit, presenting productions on both sides of the Irish border and in Dublin by offering tours of such plays as Richard Brinsley Sheridan's *The Rivals* (1775) and M. J. Molloy's *The Wood of the Whispering*

[8] *Irish Post*, *c.*11 Sept. 1980, in Galway, James Hardiman Library (JHL), MS Druid Theatre, T2/343.

[9] Declan Burke-Kennedy, 'Druid "Scandal" Threat', *Sunday Journal*, 5 Oct. 1980. Dublin audiences waited until June 1981 when *Island Protected by a Bridge of Glass* appeared at the Abbey's Peacock Theatre for six performances along with three lunchtime performances of Geraldine Aron's *Bar and Ger*.

[10] Michael Finlan, 'An Irishman's Diary', *Irish Times*, 23 Oct. 1980.

[11] *Playboy* also served as Druid's first production in London when it appeared at the Donmar Warehouse in Feb. 1985; however, the company turned down an extended run in London to première *Conversations* in Galway in Apr. 1985.

[12] David Nowlan, 'Theatre Festival First Nights: *The Playboy of the Western World* at the Olympia', *Irish Times*, 28 Sept. 1982.

[13] 'Back to the Cradle', RTÉ1, 11 Jan. 1984.

[14] Druid toured a revival of this production of *Playboy* in Feb./Mar. 1985 with visits to Clifden, Castlebar, Kiltimagh, Ballaghadereen, Ballinamore, Shercock, Carlow, Callan, Clonmel, London's Donmar Warehouse, and, upon its return, Limerick's Belltable Arts Centre.

(1953). During these years, Druid created a regional touring network that became known as the Unusual Rural Tour, or URT, visiting small towns such as Lisdoonvarna in Co. Clare, Rossaveal and Milltown in Co. Galway, Westport in Co. Mayo, and Ballyshannon and Ballybofey in Co. Donegal. Indeed, Druid took *Wood* on a URT prior to playing at the 1983 Dublin Theatre Festival, so that, for instance, audiences in Ballybofey saw the play before Dublin audiences did. Given Dublin's longstanding centrality in the Irish theatre world, this may have seemed counterintuitive; in fact, however, it only served to consolidate Druid's reputation as a national company, particularly in contrast to the much more Dublin-centred Abbey. '[I]t is not praising the Druid company too highly', commented one Dublin newspaper at the time, 'to say they are the Abbey Theatre of the West.'[15]

Tom Murphy to 1983

In many respects, Tom Murphy's 1983 appointment as Druid's writer-in-association made perfect sense in terms of the ways in which the company was defining itself in a new configuration of the local, the national, and the international. From an early age, Tom Murphy's background attuned him to the problems of place and belonging for which Druid were finding new solutions. Born in Tuam, Co. Galway, in 1935, Murphy's parents were 'buff shams', country people originally from about five miles outside of the town; and his work has always shown a sympathy with people on the outside of a tightly knit community.[16] He would later speak of becoming 'acutely aware of the class divide' when he was attending Tuam's Vocational School, conscious of the schism between blue- and white-collar workers.[17] This sense of being on the outside was further intensified by the departure of his father (and many of his siblings) for England to earn a living; they would always be outsiders there, but equally would feel a sense of distance when they returned to Ireland.

Murphy's earliest work addressed these experiences of displacement directly, and the production history of his first full-length play mirrors those experiences further. His first play, written with his friend Noel O'Donoghue, was entitled *On the Outside* (1959), and its setting—outside of a dancehall where two young men without the price of admission wait in deepening frustration—acts as a physical metaphor for social exclusion. Murphy's next play, originally entitled *The Iron Men*, deals with a family of Irish emigrant labourers in England who belong neither in Ireland nor in England and who ultimately spiral into self-destructive violence. Not only is this play about migration, but its early production history has a migratory arc that both looks back to the experiences of Murphy's own family, and, to some extent, prefigures the trajectory of Druid thirty years later. After winning a playwriting award in the amateur All-Ireland Drama Festival, *The Iron Men* was rejected by the Abbey Theatre's Managing Director, Ernest Blythe, who felt such people did not exist in Ireland. The play was subsequently picked up for a London première. Retitled *A Whistle*

---

[15]   William Rocke, 'The Abbey of the West Packs 'Em In', *Sunday Press, c.*4 Dec. 1983, in JHL, MS Druid Theatre T2/367.
[16]   John Waters, 'The Frontiersman', *In Dublin*, 15 May 1986, 26.
[17]   Joe Jackson, 'Making the Words Sing', *Hot Press*, 4 Apr. 1991, 18.

in the Dark because there was a film running in London at the time called *The Iron Men*, it opened on 11 September 1961 at the Theatre Royal, Stratford East.[18] *Whistle* attracted considerable critical attention and notoriety, much of which focused on the play's raw on-stage violence; it subsequently transferred to the West End. In the wake of all this interest, a Dublin production opened the following year. As Druid would later find, the best way to achieve recognition in Ireland was first to succeed outside Ireland.

The success of *Whistle* prompted Murphy to move to London in 1962, which both gave him a psychological distance from which to examine Ireland impartially and put him in an environment of experiment with dramatic form. There he wrote *A Crucial Week in the Life of a Grocer's Assistant* (1969), which mixes the main character's dreaming and conscious states, while *Famine* (1968) adopts the alienation techniques of Brecht's Epic Theatre. By 1971, Murphy had returned to Ireland. The initial reception accorded to plays of the mid-1970s such as *The Sanctuary Lamp* (1975) and *The J. Arthur Maginnis Story* (1976) was unenthusiastic, however, and precipitated the playwright's two-year hiatus in writing. Murphy's *The Blue Macushla* (1980) and his 1981 adaptation of Liam O'Flaherty's *The Informer* (1925) met with poor critical and audience responses; however, Murphy's career rebounded in 1983 with revivals of *The Morning After Optimism* (1971) at Dublin's Project Arts Centre in April, and Red Rex's production of a rewritten version of *The Blue Macushla*. The latter toured, before playing the 1983 Dublin Theatre Festival alongside the Abbey's première of *The Gigli Concert* (and, incidentally, alongside two productions by Druid: Molloy's *The Wood of the Whispering* and Aron's *A Galway Girl*). *The Gigli Concert* went on to win the Harvey's Irish Theatre Award for Best Play, and Godfrey Quigley received a Harvey's Best Actor award for his role. In a sense, the careers of Murphy and Druid converged at the 1983 Dublin Theatre Festival. When it was announced on the eve of the Festival that Tom Murphy was to become Druid's writer-in-association, there was little doubt that both were in the ascendant.

THE DRUID/MURPHY PARTNERSHIP

'In the 1980s', Garry Hynes later recalled, 'we became very conscious in Druid that we needed to engage with new writing, engage with it in the level of working with an established writer, not just through presenting new work by young writers.'[19] Up until 1983, Druid had been engaged with new writing primarily through its relationship with playwright Geraldine Aron, a Galway-born writer (although resident in South Africa) who was commissioned to write *Same Old Moon* in celebration of Galway's quincentennial in 1984. However, it was clear that Murphy and Druid were kindred spirits in more ways than one. First, although both parties had vigorously undermined pastoral representations of the west of Ireland, they were also both very strongly rooted in Galway: from the centre of Tuam to Druid's theatre in Galway is just over thirty kilometres. Second, as working artists,

---

[18] Dublin, Trinity College Dublin (TCD), Tom Murphy papers, MS11115/6/2/3.
[19] 'Playwrights in Profile: Tom Murphy', *Drama on One*, RTÉ Radio 1, transmitted 18 Mar. 2007. http://www.rte.ie/drama/radio/player.html?clipId=3494807. Accessed 26 June 2014.

both have generated considerable creative energy from reworking—sometimes radically—the same material. Druid's penchant for revitalizing work is clearest in the company's multiple versions of Synge's *Playboy of the Western World*, which it staged first in 1975 and then revisited in fresh productions in 1977, 1982, 2004, and 2005. By the same token, Murphy's work is marked by the fact that there are multiple published versions of his plays. For example, *Conversations on a Homecoming* first appeared in a Gallery Press edition in 1986. Of the three subsequent versions from Methuen at least two were revised prior to publication.

The partnership rooted Druid even more firmly in the west of Ireland, and paired the company with a playwright who took a collaborative approach to production. At the same time, though, the relationship gave the company material with which to extend both its national reputation and its international touring reach. Initially in 1984 the company revived two of Murphy's earlier works, *Famine* and *On the Outside*; but it was the two new works premièred in 1985 (in April and December, respectively) that would really bring the partnership to world attention. For instance, Druid gave its first American performances in 1986 (at the Pepsico SummerFare Festival in Purchase, New York), pairing Murphy's *Conversations on a Homecoming* with Synge's *The Playboy of the Western World*. And, in January 1987, Druid toured to Australia for the first time, where *Conversations* was once again the featured production.[20] From that point onwards, Druid (and, indeed, Druid/Murphy) was without question as much an international as a regional or a national theatre company.

Accommodating Language

As these plays toured, however, Druid adapted the ways it presented itself and its work to meet the expectations of different audiences; this process makes it clear that the affinity between Druid and Murphy goes beyond their connection to Galway. Instead, the complexities that arise with creating work for audiences who are local, national, and global come into focus. To complicate matters further, although both Murphy and Druid are deeply rooted in the west of Ireland, both work actively against prior constructed meanings of that place, unearthing what Una Chaudhuri calls the 'geopathology' of the area. Chaudhuri defines the term as representing '[t]he problem of place—and place as *problem*', a phenomenon that she says 'appear[s] as a series of ruptures and displacements'.[21] This sense that place is a 'problem' has been very much a feature of Murphy's work from the beginning. For the character of Frank in *On the Outside*, the town in which he lives is a tank from which he cannot escape. For the peasants in *Famine*, when the potato blight kills their main food source and their landlords evict them from their homes, a rupture occurs, and the place in which they live is suddenly different from what it has been. At that point, a sense of profound displacement occurs, and Murphy captures it by using Brechtian devices

---

[20] Druid intended *Bailegangaire* to serve as its Australian première, but Siobhán McKenna's death in Nov. 1986 precluded this from happening.

[21] Una Chaudhuri, *Staging Place: The Geography of Modern Drama* (Ann Arbor, MI: University of Michigan Press, 1997), 55.

such as labelling each scene with a (sometimes ironic) caption or breaking the narrative into abrupt scenes. In short, throughout his work, Murphy's Ireland is a site of discontent in which most of his characters cannot find satisfaction or remain at home.

This sense of dislocation continues in the plays Murphy produced with Druid in the 1980s, and (as is the case with much of Murphy's earlier work) it finds a focus in language. In *Bailegangaire*, for instance, we learn that the character of Mary chose to leave Ireland for England to pursue a career in nursing. She left behind her sister, Dolly, with her grandmother, Mommo, who had raised them after their parents' deaths. However, when the play opens, Mary is back in Ireland caring for the now senile and bedbound Mommo, who endlessly retells the same story without bringing it to a conclusion (that is, until Mary does so at the play's end). Mary's position as a returned migrant is rootless and isolating. Further, her language in the play captures a dilemma common to many of those who migrate: a feeling of instability and confusion related to feelings of placelessness. Mary deals with this situation through the process of 'language accommodation' through which, as Raymond Hickey notes, people 'adapt their speech to that of their interlocutors, perhaps, in an effort to […] be socially accepted by them'.[22] Mary's speech patterns change depending on the circumstances in which she finds herself. Her experience of migration is expressed through a complex form of language accommodation which was shaped by two factors: her education and her long-term self-exile in England. In England, she changed the way she spoke in an attempt to fit in with her new environment, taking on a more standardized pronunciation and sentence structure. And at the beginning of *Bailegangaire*, Mary's way of speaking contrasts directly with Mommo's and Dolly's speech, as the following exchange illustrates (emphasis added):

> MOMMO.   But to come to Bailegangaire so *ye*'ll have it all.
> MARY.   Aren't *you* going to say hello to her?
> DOLLY.   What's up with *yeh*?[23]

Here, as elsewhere early in the play, Mary uses a more standardized form of English grammar and pronunciation. In this example, she uses a standard pronunciation of the word 'you', while Dolly and Mommo use 'yeh' and 'ye', respectively—the latter an archaic usage, while Dolly's 'yeh' is kind of hybrid of archaism and adopted Americanism. Throughout the course of the play, however, Mary begins to adapt her language as she becomes more and more absorbed in Mommo's narrative. Ultimately, Mary's participation in finishing Mommo's story marks her acceptance of her position as a returned migrant. After Mary reveals the ending of Mommo's story, she ends the play with a short speech; the subtle shifts in her language indicate the change that has taken place:

> To conclude. It's a strange old place alright, in whatever wisdom He has to have made it this way. But in whatever wisdom there is, in the year 1984, it was decided to give that—fambly . . . of strangers another chance, and a brand new baby to gladden their home. [24]

---

[22] Raymond Hickey, *A Dictionary of Varieties of Language* (Oxford: Wiley–Blackwell, 2014), 12.

[23] Tom Murphy, *Bailegangaire* (Dublin: Gallery Press, 1986), 18. Although *Bailegangaire* was subsequently published in the Methuen edition of Murphy's work, the Gallery Press edition differs from the Methuen edition, and is closest to the text used in the original performance.

[24] Ibid., 76.

Here, Mary incorporates Mommo's language with the more standardized language she learned through her education and through working in England. She maintains her pronunciation of the word 'old' rather than incorporating Mommo's 'auld', but equally adopts Mommo's pronunciation of the word 'family' as 'fambly'. Similarly, her sentence structure maintains a fairly standardized form with the exception of the awkward 'in whatever wisdom He has to have made it that way', and the incorporation of the archaic word 'gladden'. Thus, with the story finally finished, Mary tentatively accommodates her speech to the language with which she grew up, which hints at an acceptance of her return and her altered place in her childhood home.

ACCOMMODATING IMAGES

If *Bailegangaire* stages a complex and subtle form of linguistic accommodation, Druid employs what I call production accommodation by changing the images that represent Murphy's plays from location to location, packaging the work in different ways for particular audiences. For instance, the images used to promote the 1985 première of *Conversations on a Homecoming* encouraged awareness of the American themes in the play by using a likeness of American President John F. Kennedy. However, for the December 1986 and February 1987 Galway performances, the actors, rather than the Kennedy image, were used to promote the show. When *Conversations* visited Australia in January 1987, more stereotypically Irish iconography such as the colour green and shamrocks was used to market the show. And a photograph of actors with pints appeared on the programme cover of the 1987 London production, promoting an equally stereotypical image of Ireland.

Similarly, instances of production accommodation are found in the promotional materials used for Druid's touring production of *Bailegangaire*, with the play's theme of migration stressed only in the posters used for the Galway and London performances. The image from the programme for the Galway opening in December 1985 is particularly striking: a black illustration on a green background that captures migration in an especially subtle manner (Fig. 25.1).[25]

The green here does not seem to have any signifying power in relation to stereotypical Irishness; and the programme is dominated by an apparently simple silhouette of a woman, dressed in what can be interpreted as travelling clothes, carrying some sort of satchel. However, closer examination shows that there is an element of cognitive optical illusion about the image: it is not possible to determine if she is arriving or leaving. Looking at her feet, it seems she is simultaneously walking toward and away from the reader. This ambiguity is further emphasized by the blurred shadow in the image, which once again does not allow the viewer to determine in which direction the woman is walking. Viewed as a whole, the image parallels Mary's conflicted position as a returned migrant who cannot decide whether she will stay or leave again. As Dolly says of her: 'Suitcase packed—How many times? [. . .] You're stayin', you're going' [. . .] Fuck off!'[26]

---

[25] JHL, Druid Theatre MS T2/129.   [26] Murphy, *Bailegangaire*, 60.

FIG. 25.1 Detail from Druid's programme for the Galway première of Tom Murphy's *Bailegangaire* (December 1985).

Courtesy of Druid Theatre Company and James Hardiman Library, NUI Galway.

However, this image was overshadowed on the cover of the flyer used to market the London performances. Added colours, a hand-drawn title on the left of the page, and the inclusion of text, of which the word 'Druid' was most prominent, drew attention away from the figure of the travelling woman (Fig. 25.2).[27]

The prominence of 'DRUID THEATRE COMPANY' obscured Murphy's name, which was reduced to such an extent that it became part of the play's subtitle: 'BY TOM MURPHY'. This decision implies confidence in Druid's reputation in London to sell tickets

[27] JHL, Druid Theatre T2/128.

FIG. 25.2 Flyer announcing Druid's production of Tom Murphy's *Bailegangaire* at London's Donmar Warehouse (February–March 1986).

Courtesy of Druid Theatre Company and James Hardiman Library, NUI Galway.

due to the company's success with *Playboy* the previous year. Likewise, when the show returned to Ireland for performances at Dublin's Gaiety Theatre, the flyer drew the viewer's attention to 'DRUID THEATRE COMPANY', adding a production photo of Siobhán McKenna as Mommo, which suggests that while a Druid production was the main attraction for potential ticket buyers, the actor's likeness was also important for ticket sales, since she had been a popular Abbey actress who found international success in film and on Broadway (Fig. 25.3).[28]

[28] JHL, Druid Theatre T2/128.

FIG. 25.3 Flyer announcing Druid's production of Tom Murphy's *Bailegangaire* at Dublin's Gaiety Theatre (May 1986).

Photo: Amelia Stein. Courtesy of Druid Theatre Company and James Hardiman Library, NUI Galway.

Since Tom Murphy's name is highlighted by black lettering on an orange background, it seems that there was greater anticipation that the playwright would be recognized in Dublin than in London. His name is also of a similar font size as the lettering used for McKenna's, Marie Mullen's (Mary), and Mary McEvoy's (Dolly) names.[29] In short, from Galway to London to Dublin, the play was variously promoted as being primarily about emigration, Druid itself, and as a vehicle for a famous actor.

---

[29] It is worth noting that in 1986 McEvoy was a prominent cast member of *Glenroe*, a highly rated soap opera on Irish television. As such, her name would have had a high degree of recognition among Irish audiences.

ACCOMMODATING PRODUCTIONS

This kind of production accommodation is not limited to the images that represented the play: the production also changed subtly in performance as the play toured, responding to differing sets of circumstances in the world outside the theatre. This is, in part, a function of something noted by Tom Murphy himself: *Bailegangaire* sets up a contrast between an idealized west of Ireland with the realities of life in rural Ireland at the time of performance. In a 1986 interview with *In Dublin* magazine, Murphy discussed the underlying tension between tradition and modernity that he saw in Ireland:

> I've been struck in recent times at the extraordinary anomalies that exist in the country. I've been spending a lot of time in the west, in Connemara, where for instance [. . .] you'll see a man up to his knees in mud carrying plastic bags of turf out of the bog, but he has a walkman on his head.[30]

The amalgamation of temporalities that Murphy observed in the world around him are also present in *Bailegangaire*, in which, to borrow a phrase from Edward Soja, 'inextricably intertwined temporal, social, and spatial relations are constantly being reinscribed, erased, and reinscribed again'.[31] Just as *On the Outside* found a forceful stage image for the experience of social exclusion in the closed door of a dancehall, *Bailegangaire* finds a stage image for the temporal disjunction of tradition and modernity in the kitchen-cum-bedroom of a traditional thatched cottage inscribed in a contemporary time period, where there are factories and helicopters outside the door. In his review of the Galway première, Fintan O'Toole reflects on this juxtaposition: 'The Ireland of the play is the Ireland of 1984, caught between one failed dream and another, the dream of a rural Gaelic idyll, and that of a bright new industrial paradise.'[32]

When the play was performed in Galway, the audience was aware that in the imagined space of *Bailegangaire* there is a factory down the road from the cottage and its closure is imminent. The same was true outside the theatre where, in the real space of Co. Galway in 1985, the Tuam Sugar Factory in Murphy's home town faced closure (indeed, it did close in 1987). In his set design, Frank Conway captured the tension of these colliding worlds by creating a design in which both the interior and the exterior of the cottage were visible at the same time. As one reviewer at the time notes:

> The set is constructed on a slant, and appears to be suspended and, apart from Mommo's big bed, is dominated by a crude electricity pole at the edge of the stage. This also appears to be an effort to keep reminding the audience that this play is happening in 1984 and not rural Ireland twenty years ago.[33]

---

[30] Waters, 'Frontiersman', 28.

[31] Edward Soja, *Thirdspace: Journeys to Los Angeles and Other Real-and-Imagined Places* (Malden, MA: Blackwell, 1996), 18.

[32] Fintan O'Toole, 'The Old Woman's Brood', *Sunday Tribune*, 8 Dec. 1985.

[33] Cathy Halloran, 'Latest Offering from Pen of Tom Murphy a Christmas Treat', *Connacht Sentinel*, 10 Dec. 1985.

Another critic remarks, 'Frank Conway's setting captures perfectly the prison of the house, and the starry electric world beyond is perfectly lit in Roger Firth's lighting design'—although the play itself leaves open the question of whether or not that 'starry electric world' will be just another disappointment, as Mary found upon emigrating to England.[34]

Indeed, that 'starry electric world' posed particular problems for London critics, some of whom could not reconcile what they took to be the play's hopefulness with Murphy's reputation. Writing in the *Guardian*, Nicholas de Jongh states: 'Garry Hynes's production, then, allows a glittering vista of stars and romantic music to draw the piece towards a conclusion of inexplicable optimism.'[35] John Barber of the *Daily Telegraph* also found the play's conclusion problematic: 'It seemed a soft old finisher for so tough-minded and eloquent a playwright.'[36] De Jongh and more particularly Barber would seem to be perpetuating a stereotype of Murphy's writing as hard-hitting and dangerous—a perception that originated with the London reception of his 1961 play *A Whistle in the Dark*, of which *The Times* had commented that it seemed determined to convince the audience that 'the whole world consists of stupid fighting animals'.[37] De Jongh and Barber's inability to reconcile their expectations with what was actually staged contrasts with John O'Riordan's review in *Plays and Players*, which recognizes that in *Bailegangaire*, Murphy and Druid were creating a stage space in which 'all the traditional elements, the turf fire, the Paul Henry cottage [...] blend with modernist approaches such as new humanism and faith in youth, suffused in a realist fantasy of hope and home-in-exile'.[38] Indeed, Colm Tóibín, who saw the play in all three venues, remarks on a change in the production that addresses precisely the debate over the play's ending: 'On its opening night in Galway in December there were stars in the sky at the end, this was dropped when I saw the play in the Donmar Warehouse in London.'[39] This observation suggests that the stars were cut *after* the play opened in London (but before its move to Dublin), implying that Druid was responding to those critics who found the ending too sentimental.

When the play returned to Ireland in May 1986, Druid presented it at Dublin's Gaiety Theatre and a new issue of accommodation arose. While Druid's theatre in Galway sat an intimate audience of around 100, and the Donmar Warehouse (where *Bailegangaire* played in London) held about 250, the Gaiety's capacity at the time was over 1,000. When *Bailegangaire* returned to Ireland, there was some concern in the pre-production press commentary that the larger space would overwhelm the play. Marie Mullen defended the choice of location for the Dublin production: 'despite its size, it seems to be a very intimate theatre. The seats are all fairly close and once you feel that the audience is near, it's easier to go for them.'[40] For the most part, reviewers agreed that it had been possible to re-create the sense of intimacy in the larger space, but noticed that this involved adapting the stage: 'It is still the same closely knit production as in the tiny Druid Theatre last December,' observed

[34] David Nowlan, 'Bailegangaire: Druid Theatre Galway', *Irish Times*, 6 Dec. 1985.
[35] 'Bailegangaire', *Guardian* [c.21 Feb. 1986], in JHL, MS Druid, T2/388.
[36] 'Theatre: Great McKenna', *Daily Telegraph* [c.21 Feb. 1986], in JHL, MS Druid, T2/388.
[37] 'A Terrifying Play', *Times*, 12 Sept. 1961.
[38] John O'Riordan, 'Bailegangaire', *Plays and Players* (Mar. 1986), 34.
[39] Colm Tóibín, 'The Old Woman's Brood', *Sunday Independent*, 18 May 1986.
[40] Graham Sennett, 'Better Late Than Never', *Evening Press* [c.10 May 1986], in JHL, MS Druid, T2/391.

one reviewer, 'but now the kitchen-cum-bedroom has been pushed forward beyond the front curtain line to try to capture some of the intimacy of the Galway playhouse.'[41] Moving the set forward on the stage tacitly acknowledged that a memory of Druid's more intimate space in Galway persisted on the stage, and that the production had a home elsewhere. Kay Hingerty of the *Cork Examiner* noted: 'There is a difference in our reception of the play, seen from the distance of the Gaiety auditorium, but it is just a different kind of viewing, by standing back as one would from a great painting.'[42] Hingerty's point is well made. For audiences watching *Bailegangaire* in Dublin's Gaiety Theatre, at least four spaces were in play at any one moment: the fictional space on the stage, the real world of Ireland outside the theatre to which it referred, the Gaiety Theatre in which the play was being performed, and a memory (or even an imagined memory) of the 'home' production in Galway; to these could be added a fifth space, the exilic space of the London production. In this interplay between the theatre space and the text, we see a performative realization of the wider experiences of homelessness and displacement that have figured in Murphy's work from the outset.

From Druid/Murphy to *DruidMurphy*

Although Druid toured *Conversations on a Homecoming* off and on until November 1987, the company's contract with Tom Murphy ended in early 1986. There were a number of reasons for the parting of the ways; for both Murphy and Hynes, however, the break signalled the beginning of a period of closer involvement with the Abbey Theatre. Murphy became the Abbey's first playwright-in-association in April 1986, a post he held until 1989; and the role's creation itself indicates the National Theatre's recognition that it needed to catch up with its newer rival. Hynes directed *A Whistle in the Dark* for the Abbey later that year. In 1991, Hynes became Abbey's artistic director, a job she held until 1994. During her time at the Abbey, she scheduled a number of Murphy's plays, including three of the four shows that Druid had presented during its partnership with Murphy: *Famine, On the Outside*, and *Conversations on a Homecoming*. By the time Garry Hynes left the Abbey and returned to Druid, few would have disputed that Druid was any less Ireland's national theatre than the Abbey.

At the same time, however, Druid continued to develop the international reputation it had established during its initial period of association with Murphy. While continuing to tour regionally, Druid presented *Playboy* at the Sydney Festival in January 1988, followed by Frank McGuinness's *Factory Girls* (1982) in Glasgow and London in May 1988. Although it was five years before Druid next toured a production internationally with Vincent Woods's *At the Black Pig's Dyke* (1992) at the Tricycle Theatre in London in 1993, the company expanded its touring network by presenting Woods's play at Toronto's du Maurier World Stage Festival in 1994, marking the company's first Canadian performances. At that point,

---

[41] John Finegan, 'Gaiety Triumph for Tom Murphy', *Evening Herald* [c.14 May 1986], in JHL, MS Druid, T2/391

[42] Kay Hingerty, 'Mommo at the Gaiety', *Cork Examiner* [c.19 May 1986], JHL, MS Druid, T2/391.

Druid began to develop a relationship with London Irish playwright Martin McDonagh. As had been the case with Druid's involvement with Murphy a decade earlier, the association significantly enhanced its international profile. Druid presented McDonagh's *The Beauty Queen of Leenane* (1996) in Ireland, the UK, and eventually New York, where it transferred to the Walter Kerr Theatre on Broadway, and garnered four Tony Awards in 1998. Arguably, in 1997, Druid's involvement with McDonagh led to the company's first venture into what Jonathan Kalb calls 'marathon theater', which would characterize *DruidMurphy*: Druid staged all three of McDonagh's Leenane plays as a single extended performance (as well as producing them singly).[43] *The Leenane Trilogy* played Galway, London, Cork, and Dublin in 1997 before going on to Sydney, Australia, the following year. The international success of *The Leenane Trilogy* prompted a return to Synge's work as marathon theatre; called *DruidSynge*, the event staged virtually all of Synge's theatrical canon as a single day-long performance. *DruidSynge* toured internationally to Edinburgh in 2005 followed by Minneapolis and New York in 2006.

In contrast to Druid's commitment to the pursuit of international touring, Murphy stayed close to the Abbey in the same period, which kept his work primarily inside Ireland. Since the dissolution of the original partnership in 1986, Murphy has premièred only two plays outside of the country: *She Stoops to Folly* (an adaptation of Oliver Goldsmith's *The Vicar of Wakefield*) at California's South Coast Repertory Theatre in 1995, and *The Alice Trilogy* at London's Royal Court Theatre in 2005. In 2001, the Abbey Theatre presented a six-play season of Murphy's work, 'Tom Murphy at the Abbey'. At that time, the *Guardian* critic Michael Billington noted: 'the paradox of Murphy [. . .] is that one of Irish theatre's proudest possessions is also one of its least-known exports.'[44] And, in 2003, the Abbey's artistic director, Ben Barnes, observed that 'the impetus [of the 2001 season] was to honour Tom's contribution to the Abbey and to the Irish theatre but also to try and heighten the profile of Tom's work internationally'.[45]

Druid staged only one of Murphy's works during this period: John Crowley's production of Murphy's *The Blue Macushla* in 1995 as part of that year's Galway Arts Festival. Murphy only really became seriously reinvolved with Druid in 2009, when Garry Hynes directed *The Gigli Concert* as the production to inaugurate the company's newly refurbished theatre. To mark Druid's thirty-fifth anniversary in May 2010, Garry Hynes and Mikel Murfi co-directed a weekend of performances entitled 'From Galway to Broadway and Back Again', which brought together excerpts from plays Druid had produced since its inception. Among the selections were scenes from Murphy's *Bailegangaire* and *Conversations on a Homecoming*, which brought Murphy and Druid back together on familiar ground, and opened a discussion that would lead to *DruidMurphy* in 2012.

Announcing *DruidMurphy* in November 2011, Druid noted: 'This latest collaboration is also a testament to Druid's commitment, and ability, to bringing theatre to audiences in Ireland and worldwide.'[46] As with their previous work, the places of performance were significant. Although Druid presented *DruidMurphy* in Galway in May 2012, the official

[43] Jonathan Kalb, *Great Lengths: Seven Works of Marathon Theater* (Ann Arbor, MI: University of Michigan Press, 2011).

[44] Michael Billington, 'Which Side Are You On, Boys?', *Guardian*, 13 Oct. 2001.

[45] 'Sing On Forever', *Arts Lives*, RTÉ 1, transmitted 11 Mar. 2003.

[46] 'Press Release: Druid Announces DruidMurphy'.

opening was held the following month in London when *DruidMurphy* was included as part of the London 2012 Cultural Olympiad, indicating the importance Druid places on the balance between pleasing its local base of spectators while courting global audiences. The event then toured to and from Ireland including international stops at New York's Lincoln Center Festival, the Oxford Playhouse, and Washington DC's Kennedy Center for the Performing Arts. These international visits were interspersed with Irish performances in places such as Cork, Clifden, the Aran Islands, and Murphy's hometown of Tuam.

Accommodating History

In his 2009 exposé of Celtic Tiger Ireland, Fintan O'Toole notes that the country's artistic community could not 'manage the kind of realist epic that would give a multi-layered and shifting society a sense of where it was and how it got there'.[47] Certainly, *DruidMurphy*, Druid's 'archaeological dig' into Ireland's past, responds to the state of the nation in the wake of the financial crisis that left Ireland bankrupt. Presented in reverse chronological order, the three plays unearth the ravages of return migration (*Conversations on a Homecoming*), the migrant experience (*A Whistle in the Dark*), and the experience of pre-migration (*Famine*). An analysis of some of the company's design choices for *DruidMurphy*, and in particular *Famine*, reveals Druid and Murphy's ability to absorb and react to events in the world outside of the theatre. Indeed, the 2012 production of *Famine* exemplifies Murphy's original intention for the play which, the playwright noted in 1984, is 'not really about the history of the Irish Famine at all. Living in the 1960s, I found that I was a Famine victim, that it wasn't over.'[48] The 2012 production asserted the interconnection between past and present, which began when Druid unveiled the project's primary promotional image in November 2011 (Fig. 25.4).

There is a sense of overall ambiguousness in this picture (similar to the image used to promote *Bailegangaire*). For example, the shadow of the figure behind the man implies, perhaps, the rootlessness and placelessness felt by those, such as Mary in *Bailegangaire*, who migrate. At the same time, though, the shadow represents the ghosts of those who previously migrated. This illustration begins to bridge the temporal gap between Murphy's 1968 play and Ireland in 2012 when we consider the man and the cottage. Although the man's hairstyle and trench coat evoke the 1950s, the ruined cottage on the shore serves as a reminder not only of John Connor's razed cottage in *Famine* but, for a contemporary audience, of the many unfinished ghost estates that now blight the Irish landscape. Whether the man is leaving on a boat or contemplating departing on a dock cannot be determined; but the beacon emanating from the lighthouse suggests that his future will be metaphorically brighter in the distance, at a remove from his homeland. The lifebelt and the empty bottle of alcohol also resist a firm categorization. While drink could be interpreted (for better or for worse) as a lifebelt, the idea that the process of migration itself will serve to

[47] Fintan O'Toole, *Ship of Fools: How Stupidity and Corruption Sank the Celtic Tiger* (London: Faber & Faber, 2010), 185.

[48] Flyer for Druid's 1984 production of *Famine*, JHL, MS Druid, T2/99.

DRUID presents in a co-production with
QUINNIPIAC UNIVERSITY CONNECTICUT, NUI GALWAY
LINCOLN CENTER FESTIVAL and GALWAY ARTS FESTIVAL

Druid

DruidMurphy
PLAYS BY TOM MURPHY
DIRECTED BY GARRY HYNES

FIG. 25.4 Main promotional graphic for *DruidMurphy*.
Courtesy of Druid Theatre Company and James Hardiman Library, NUI Galway.

'bail him out' seems more likely, particularly to an audience in 2012 that remembers Irish property developers who attempted to avoid litigation by emigrating. The clearest tie, however, between Murphy's play and Druid's contemporary production of it is the rain in the promotional image, which is linked to Druid's physical set, as can be seen in the production photograph reproduced in Fig. 25.5.

Here the depiction of the rain is carried from the image to the back of the stage, where it is represented by a flat made of tarnished corrugated metal (another nod to the unfinished and decaying houses scattered throughout present-day Ireland): the audience has figuratively been (rain)swept into the theatre and into the world of *DruidMurphy*. This production photograph also draws attention to the intermingling of temporalities in terms of the costuming. As John Connor (played by Brian Doherty), centre, examines his failing potato crop, notice the juxtaposition of his modern-day leather trench coat with the other men's

FIG. 25.5 Brian Doherty as John Connor and the cast of *Famine*, performed as the concluding play in *DruidMurphy* (25 May 2012).

Photo: Catherine Ashmore. Courtesy of Druid Theatre Company and James Hardiman Library, NUI Galway.

flat caps and waistcoats; and the characters' boots are also of the contemporary period. The hooded sweatshirt worn by the character of Malachy and the modern-day metal crutches on which the character of Mickeleen relies (neither shown here) are also production choices that insist, in Brechtian fashion, that the audience make a connection between the nineteenth-century period shown on stage and the world outside the theatre.

The correlations between Murphy's play and Druid's production resonated with critics such as Alexander Gilmour, who found that all the plays in the *DruidMurphy* cycle 'lack the mood of cosy detachment that often accompanies period pieces: they feel urgent and visceral.'[49] Just as *DruidMurphy* interweaves the past and present to provide, in O'Toole's words, 'a sense of where [Ireland] was and how it got there', this chapter has excavated Druid's and Tom Murphy's thirty-year relationship to demonstrate where they were and how they got here.

[49] Alexander Gilmour, 'DruidMurphy, Hampstead Theatre, London', *Financial Times*, 26 June 2012; http://www.ft.com/intl/cms/s/2/d4c8d81a-bf6d-11e1-bb88-00144feabdc0.html#axzz3BVA7jgwd. Accessed 19 Aug. 2014.

PART IX

PERFORMANCE 2

CHAPTER 26

PLACES OF PERFORMANCE

CHRIS MORASH

PICTURES IN THE ASHES

IN 1951, Lennox Robinson ended his authorized history of the Abbey Theatre with a post-script, in which he recorded the burning of the building on 17 July that year. 'Almost from the day in 1904 when the Theatre was opened it had been harshly criticised,' observed Robinson wryly. 'It only needed this little tragedy (for, really, the loss of the Abbey build-ing is a small thing in its history compared with the early death of Synge, or the death of F. J. McCormick) to realise how deeply rooted is the Abbey Theatre in the national life of Ireland.' The destruction of the physical theatre building opens up an interesting ambigu-ity for Robinson in what is meant by 'the Theatre'. 'The stage, the scene-dock, the green-room, wardrobe-rooms, paint-room and dressing-rooms disappeared,' he notes, 'but [...] willing helpers from the street rescued all our lovely pictures.' One would have thought that the parts of the theatre building where plays were physically produced, such as the stage or even the scene-dock, would have been the essential element of the building's fabric. Instead, for Robinson 'the theatre' truly resides in the building's ghostly double, of which the portraits in the foyer are the closest approximation. Indeed, he goes further, and sug-gests that it was only when the bricks and mortar of the building had disappeared, ran-domly dispatched by the most insignificant and arbitrary of agents ('a cigarette butt—a fused wire?'[1] he wonders idly), that the spectral theatre could be seen, like a spirit visibly leaving the body at the moment of death.

When we read Robinson's description of 'the Abbey' floating free of its ashes, we are reminded that theatre buildings are what Pierre Nora calls a site of memory, or *lieu de mémoire*: 'any significant entity, whether material or nonmaterial in nature, which by dint of human will or the work of time has become a symbolic element of the memorial herit-age of any community'.[2] To begin to understand the 'places of performance' in modern

---

[1] Lennox Robinson, *Ireland's Abbey Theatre: A History 1899–1951* (London: Sidgwick & Jackson, 1951), 183.

[2] Pierre Nora, 'From *Lieux de Mémoire* to Realms of Memory: Preface to the English-Language Edition', in *Realms of Memory*, ed. Lawrence D. Kritzman, trans. Arthur Goldhammer (New York: Columbia University Press, 1996), xvii.

Irish theatre, then, is to do more than simply list the buildings or stages in which Irish theatre has been performed, although this is the empirical ground of the task. 'Traditional ways of analysing drama and theatre have tended to focus on what happens on stage or in the script,' Ric Knowles reminds us in *Reading the Material Theatre*, arguing instead for a 'materialist semiotics' that would concentrate on 'the material conditions, both theatrical and cultural' through which a performance is both produced and received.[3] 'The entire theatre, its audience arrangements, its other public spaces, its physical appearance, even its location within a city', insists one of the pioneers of this work, Marvin Carlson, 'are all important elements of a process by which an audience makes meaning of its experience.'[4] At the same time, as Robinson's reflections on the Abbey fire suggest, something more (or at least other) than a purely materialist semiotics of places of performance are required if we are to grasp the more elusive task of understanding the ways in which piles of bricks and mortar (even those which may not physically exist any longer, or which may never have existed in the first place) constitute the *lieux de mémoire* around which the imaginary map of modern Irish theatre has been drawn.

Before we begin to trace the function of the places of performance in modern Irish theatre, however, it will be useful to establish a working definition of what we mean by a 'theatre'. In this respect, we can begin with Hanna Scolnicov's observation that 'the theatrical space has two main characteristics: It is cut off from the everyday, and within its boundaries it achieves freedom from the everyday.'[5] Understood in these terms, a theatre is effectively an act of framing, and (as Robinson recognized) theatres are thus built by actors and audiences as much as they are built by architects. Indeed, some of the most spatially innovative Irish theatre of the twenty-first century has taken this recognition as its starting point, whether in ANU Productions' work in Dublin[6] or in Tom Swift's site-specific work with The Performance Corporation. The latter's *Lizzie Lavelle and the Vanishing of Emlyclough* (2007), for instance, was a site-specific work written for a sand dune in Co. Mayo, while ANU's 'Monto Trilogy' has excavated memories from Dublin's north inner city to create work that reinscribes city streets and abandoned buildings with layers of traumatic historical memory. In both cases, the transformation of an otherwise anonymous space into a theatre exists only for the duration of the performance; when the performance is complete, the space either simply blows away or lapses once again into the urban flow of the city.

The ephemeral nature of the theatre space in such site-specific work allows us to see more clearly one of the defining features of a designated theatre building, such as the Abbey or the Gate Theatre. Rather than allowing blind forces (the wind, the rhythms of the city) to erase the traces of performance, in a designated theatre the site of performance remains 'cut off from the everyday', and hence traces of performance are allowed to overlay one another and sediment over time, added to by audiences who return like hungry revenants

[3] Ric Knowles, *Reading the Material Theatre* (Cambridge: Cambridge University Press, 2004), 9–10.

[4] Marvin Carlson, *Places of Performance: The Semiotics of Theatre Architecture* (Ithaca, NY: Cornell University Press, 1989), 2.

[5] Hanna Scolnicov, 'Theatre Space, Theatrical Space, and the Theatrical Space Without', in James Redmond (ed.), *Theatrical Space* (Cambridge: Cambridge University Press, 1987), 12.

[6] See Brian Singleton, 'ANU Productions and Site-Specific Performance: The Politics of Space and Place' in Fintan Walsh (ed.), *'That Was Us': Contemporary Irish Theatre and Performance* (London: Oberon Books, 2013), 21–36.

to the same spot. Portraits and framed posters in the foyer remind the audience of past (and, indeed, future) events as soon as they step through the door; a seat in the auditorium may be the same seat from which the audience member watched a particularly memorable performance, perhaps ten or twenty years ago. We can be jolted into this awareness when (as has happened with both the Gate and Abbey Theatre auditoria) the house has been remodelled, and there is an uncanny moment when the older room overlays the new room, and we find ourselves looking for seats that no longer exist. This ghosting effect is both more intense and more fleeting on the stage itself. The specific spot, where, say, JPW in *The Gigli Concert* sings, or Juno delivers her final speech, is consecrated by the act with an intensity rarely encountered outside in the everyday; but that consecration of space can only last for the duration of the performance, and the curtain call at the end is like sand being kicked over a smouldering fire, clearing the stage of memories for the next performance, lest the ghosts of past performances block up all the exits.

At the level of performance, so too at the level of architecture: in both, the determining spatial dynamic is a continuous dialectic of haunting and exorcism. 'An old theatre may be a sacred place,' writes the theatre architect and design consultant Iain Mackintosh, 'and the ghosts of past productions are a reality and, if friendly, a benign presence.'[7] Likewise Marvin Carlson reminds us in *The Haunted Stage* that 'certain dramatists, certain companies, certain actors, certain designers, often remain for years or even decades at a particular location, and so the audience memories of the previous work of those various theatre artists are reinforced by the fact that much or all of that previous work was experienced in the same physical surroundings.' Carlson refers to this constellation of memories collectively as a theatre's 'ghosts'.[8] In Irish theatre over the past century or so (and this may be true of theatre generally), these spectral places of performance, or *lieux de mémoire*, sometimes have a greater reality than their brick-and-mortar counterparts, as Lennox Robinson recognized when he refused to mourn the ashes of the 1904 Abbey after the portraits had been salvaged. At the same time, running counter to the story of modern Irish theatre as a narrative of hauntings is a tale of exorcisms, a repeated and deliberate clearing away of the spectral past so that something new might emerge.

NIGHTS IN THE HAUNTED ABBEY

The history of the places of performance occupied by the Abbey provides us with perhaps the most intense (and conscious) instance of strong haunting in Irish theatre—and likewise of its opposite, the most vigorous (and, once again, conscious) attempt at architectural exorcism. It is worth remembering, then, that what became the Abbey began its life in unhaunted spaces—or, at the very least, spaces where the ghosts were no help. The first production by the Irish Literary Theatre on 18 May 1899, of Yeats's *The Countess Cathleen*, took place in a rented venue, the Antient Concert Rooms, on what was then Brunswick (now

---

[7] Iain Mackintosh, *Architecture, Actor and Audience* (London: Routledge, 1993), 84.

[8] Marvin Carlson, *The Haunted Stage: The Theatre as Memory Machine* (Ann Arbor, MI: University of Michigan Press, 2003), 143.

Pearse) Street. We get a sense of the polite ghosts who haunted this particular venue by recalling that it was in an (admittedly fictional) 'upper room' in the Antient Concert Rooms that the music students in Joyce's short story 'The Dead' held their annual concert; and, as the narrator tells us primly, they 'belonged to the better-class families on the Kingstown and Dalkey line'.[9] As the Irish Literary Theatre changed its name and personnel, they moved through a series of venues, including the Gaiety Theatre in 1900 and 1901, the tiny St Teresa's Total Abstinence Hall on Clarendon Street in 1902, and then the Molesworth Hall in 1903 and 1904. In each of these locations, the meanings of the performances were shaped by the site of performance.

For instance, in October 1901 the Irish Literary Theatre produced Yeats's and George Moore's *Diarmuid and Grania* and Douglas Hyde's *Casadh an tSúgáin* in Dublin's 1,400-seat Gaiety Theatre. Built in 1871, the Gaiety has retained its basic configuration of stalls, galleries, and boxes in a deep horseshoe-shaped auditorium, facing a large stage with the full set of Victorian stage machinery. Its mission was (and, indeed, largely remains), in many respects, the exact opposite of the self-conscious localism and nationalism of the Irish Literary Theatre: 'to give the public of Dublin [...] the best in variety and excellence that the world can afford: in short, it was to host touring productions, largely from England.'[10] So, even before the curtain had opened in 1901, Yeats had despaired of the production on account of the audience it would draw. 'Here we are going through all sorts of trouble & annoyance', he complained to Lady Gregory, 'for [...] an audience [...] that prefers Boucicault to us.'[11] For Yeats, already beginning to formulate the views that would later lead him to seek ever smaller and more exclusive audiences, there is a recognition that a theatre carries with it memories of past productions, which in turn help to shape an audience's horizon of expectations. Having said this, his assessment of the Gaiety audience as a mob who 'prefer Boucicault' was neither entirely fair nor accurate; it was in the Gaiety, after all, that Sarah Bernhardt had performed in 1881, as did Constant-Benoît Coquelin later, in performances that profoundly influenced Frank Fay in developing a performance style for the Abbey. However, regardless of the accuracy of Yeats's assessment, he nonetheless displayed a keen sense of the power of the memories of place.

Likewise, when *Cathleen ni Houlihan* and Æ's *Deirdre* played on 2 April 1902 in the Hall of the St Teresa's Total Abstinence Association (which sat no more than 200 in an auditorium facing a shallow, unraked stage), it prompted Yeats to praise the production for 'its simplicity'.[12] That simplicity was possible not only because the tiny stage lacked any machinery for scenic effects; it was equally because the Hall was, in comparison with the Gaiety, an anonymous empty space, not strongly associated with any past performances. It was, in that sense, a site in which it was possible to begin again with essentials of performance; and, in that respect, all appearances of the dingy hall to the contrary, there is a sense in which St Teresa's Hall can be understood as perhaps the first modernist site of

---

[9] James Joyce, *The Dead*, ed. Daniel R. Schwarz (New York: Bedford/St Martins, 1994), 22.

[10] Joseph Holloway, *Souvenir of the Twenty-Fifth Anniversary of the Opening of the Gaiety Theatre, 27th November, 1871* (Dublin: Dollard, 1896), 11.

[11] W. B. Yeats to Augusta Gregory, [Oct.] 1901, in *Collected Letters*, vol. 3: *1901–1904*, ed. John Kelly and Ronald Schuchard (Oxford: Clarendon Press, 1994), 118.

[12] W. B. Yeats, 'The Acting at St Teresa's Hall', in *Collected Works*, vol. 10: *Later Articles and Reviews*, ed. Colton Johnson (New York: Scribner, 2000), 87.

performance in Irish theatre, in that it was not so much disenchanted as unenchanted, a relatively blank slate.

When the company moved yet again in 1903, to the Molesworth Hall, the venue may have been only a few minutes' walk away either from the Gaiety Theatre (on Dublin's South King Street) or from St Teresa's Hall (on Clarendon Street), but change in location nonetheless changed the meaning of the company's work. Richard Schechner reminds us of the signifying role of 'the liminal approaches and leavings of performance—how the audience gets to, and into, the performance space, and how they go from that place'.[13] The location of a given theatre 'within the mental or experiential map of a community or a city', comments Carlson, 'obviously will affect the operations of, and audience attitude towards, that theatre.'[14] Located on a street connecting the National Library of Ireland and the Royal Irish Academy, and boasting an impressive neo-Gothic facade, the Molesworth Hall was a fashionable venue, used for charity events, light musical recitals, and public meetings, usually associated with Tory Anglican interests. As such, at a point in the Irish National Theatre Society's history when there were already defections from the company on the grounds that it was not 'national' enough, playing the Molesworth Hall had a signifying power that had little to do with what took place on the stage itself.

Against this background, then, the move in 1904 to the venue that had been the Mechanics' Institute on Abbey Street was as much about finding a space that could be made anew as it was about ending the company's early nomadism. Dublin theatres in the early twentieth century were largely clustered south of the River Liffey, radiating out from College Green: the Gaiety near the south end of Grafton Street, the Theatre Royal on Hawkins Street, the Queen's Royal Theatre on Brunswick Street, and the Empire Palace (renamed the Olympia Theatre in 1927) on Dame Street. Although less than a ten-minute walk away, the Abbey, located on the north side of the river, was outside this zone, in close proximity to one of the most notorious parts of Dublin at the time, the area of the north inner city known as 'the Monto', the red-light district where Joyce sets the 'Nighttown' episode of *Ulysses*. There was certainly an audience for whom the Mechanics' Institute was a place with memories, among whom was Seán O'Casey, who recalls in his *Autobiographies* acting as a young man on its stage before 'a rough-and-randy crowd who came to while away the time'.[15] However, by keeping ticket prices high (one newspaper account of the new theatre in 1904 ran with the headline: 'The Horniman–Yeats Theatricals: No Low Persons Wanted'[16]) and the number of seats relatively small, the original Mechanics' audience were effectively left out in the cold. 'The small number of seats in our theatre', Yeats observed with satisfaction of the 562-seat house, 'would have kept away that kind of drama which spoils an audience for good work.'[17]

[13] Richard Schechner, *Essays on Performance Theory 1970–1976* (New York: Drama Book Specialists, 1977), 122.

[14] Marvin Carlson, 'The Theatre *ici*', in Erika Fischer-Lichte and Benjamin Wihstutz (eds.), *Performance and the Politics of Space: Theatre and Topology* (London: Routledge, 2013), 22.

[15] Sean O'Casey, *Autobiographies*, vol. 1 (New York: Carroll & Graf, 1984), 299.

[16] 'The Horniman–Yeats Theatricals: No Low Persons Wanted', *Universe*, 14 Jan. 1905, in 'The Abbey Theatre Scrapbooks', vol. 2; NLI MSS 19,844 and 19,845.

[17] W. B. Yeats, 'The Irish Dramatic Movement', in *Collected Works*, vol. 8: *The Irish Dramatic Movement*, ed. Mary Fitzgerald and Richard J. Finneran (New York: Scribner, 2003), 44.

For the predominantly middle-class audience of the early Abbey, Dublin's north inner city was effectively *terra incognita*, and so like gentrifiers and modernizers everywhere, they could imagine it as empty because they had little or no contact with the original inhabitants. As a theatre space, it was waiting to be made anew. Among modernist theatres, of course, this kind of spatial appropriation was not unusual. Carlson recounts a leading Parisian theatre critic of the 1890s, Jules Lemaître, making his way among disoriented Parisian theatregoers searching out an early production of Antoine's Théâtre-Libre in what was then the dangerous and unfashionable neighbourhood around Place Pigallle, 'peering at the signs on the street-corner through their glasses [. . .] We looked like three kings, in overcoats, in search of a hidden and glorious manger.'[18] Similar journeys would be made in 1909 by New York audiences who ventured south of Houston Street to Alice Lewishohn's Neighbourhood Playhouse,[19] or, later in the century, by London audiences who made their way to the Tricycle Theatre in Kilburn, well away from the West End.

The transformation of the Mechanics' Institute into the Abbey Theatre also provides the first instance of a pattern that will repeat itself over the next century in the production of Irish places of performance: it begins with a gap between vision and realization. When the building was first acquired, Yeats's patron, Annie Horniman, wrote: 'I am having a plan of the Bayreuth Theatre sent to Mr [Joseph] Holloway [the architect responsible for the conversion], so that he can see how the seats are arranged.'[20] In taking Wagner's theatre as her model, Horniman demonstrated her clear intent that the Abbey was to be a modernist theatre, taking as its template the exemplary instance of a theatre building in which, as Iain Mackintosh puts it, for 'the first time [. . .] the traditions of theatre architecture were successfully challenged by an artist who had radical ideas about the conjunction of actor and audience'.[21] In this regard, Horniman's acquisition of a set of plans of the Festspielhaus in 1904 can be placed beside Yeats's enthusiasm for Edward Gordon Craig's experiments with scenic space, 'the great innovator here in the matter of scenery', as Yeats enthused in 1903.[22] For both Yeats and Horniman in those years, the 1904 Abbey was to constitute a year zero for Irish theatrical space.

However, their architect had other ideas, and in the end Joseph Holloway did very little to the interior of the Mechanics' Institute to transform it from a horseshoe-shaped Victorian music hall to a modernist auditorium. In doing little, however, he produced a theatrical space that turned out be to architecturally ideal for creating a sense of community among the audience. Under ordinary circumstances, the deep horseshoe of the balcony meant that audience members were constantly watching one another, and, along with the proximity of the stage to the stalls, could hear the words of a writers' theatre spoken, however softly, and could feel the infectious spread of laughter. Under extraordinary circumstances, the balcony provided an ideal pulpit for making speeches, and was used as such on two occasions:

[18] André Antoine, *Memories of Théâtre-Libre*, trans. Marvin Carlson (Coral Gables, FL: University of Miami Press, 1964), 47; cited in Carlson, 'Theatre *ici*', 23–4.

[19] See John Harrington, *The Irish Play on the New York Stage* (Lexington, KY: University of Kentucky Press, 1997), 76–8.

[20] Annie Horniman to George Roberts, 12 May 1904, Harvard Theatre Collection, Houghton Library, bms Thr 24 (109).

[21] Mackintosh, *Architecture, Actor and Audience*, 44.

[22] W. B. Yeats to John Quinn, 6 Feb. 1903, Yeats, *Collected Letters*, vol. 3, 312–13.

FIG. 26.1 Interior of the 1904 Abbey Theatre, converted by Joseph Holloway from an early theatre, the Mechanics' Institute. Digital reconstruction courtesy of Hugh Denard: http:// blog.oldabbeytheatre.net/

during the riots that met *The Playboy of the Western World* in 1907, and *The Plough and the Stars* in 1926. The intimate proportions of the house were proportionate to the small stage (6.3 metres wide, 4.2 metres high, and only 4.5 metres deep), with no fly tower nor traps, and very limited wing space. As such, the Abbey stage could accommodate a single realist box set, but struggled with anything beyond a simple set change, and so the argument has been made that the predominance of peasant realism, set in domestic interiors, on the early Abbey stage prior to 1951 was, at least partly, a sensible response to the available performance space. The 1904 Abbey stage was a good place to put a kitchen or a tenement room in front of a tightly knit audience who could hear every word and laugh together at the jokes; it was, in other words, ideal for realist peasant comedies, or the tenement plays of Seán O'Casey.

FIELDS AND GATES

At the same time, a counter argument to this kind of spatial determinism can be found by taking a ten-minute walk north of the Abbey Theatre. The Gate Theatre, on Parnell Square, is built on one of the oldest performance sites in Ireland. The Gate is contained within the complex of buildings attached to the Rotunda Maternity Hospital, whose adjacent pleasure gardens and rooms for music recitals, theatrical performances, and fêtes had been designed to fund the hospital in the 1740s. At first glance, then, the building might seem to harbour rich memories of the vibrant Irish theatre world of eighteenth-century Ireland, with the ghosts of Peg Woffington and Thomas Sheridan stalking the wings. However, when the architect Michael Scott (who would later work on the 1966 Abbey) converted a set of rooms in the Rotunda into the Gate Theatre in 1930, he made no attempt to build an eighteenth-century stage, which would have involved an extended forestage. Instead, he designed a simple proscenium arch 6.6 metres wide (opening into a stage of the same depth), flanked on either side by two smaller performance platforms (which were subsequently removed). When the expressionist-influenced scenic designs of the Gate's directors, Hilton Edwards and Micheál Mac Liammóir, were produced on the Gate's stage, the spatial statement was clear: the Gate would create its own memories. There were to be no bewigged ghosts here.

Indeed, Scott's work on the Gate in 1930 would be echoed again in the twenty-first century, when the oldest purpose-built theatre building in Ireland (or indeed England, for that matter), Smock Alley, which dates from 1662, was renovated, after several centuries as a warehouse, a church, and an exhibition centre. When Smock Alley reopened as a theatre in 2013, it was not configured as an eighteenth-century stage, but as an intimate, transverse auditorium, which quickly found favour with some of Ireland's most innovative post-dramatic theatre producers. Like the Gate in 1930, Smock Alley in 2013 evoked the spirit of eighteenth-century theatre only in the intimacy of its audience–actor proxemics. However, while Smock Alley has largely been a venue for hire, the Gate was able to impose its own aesthetic on the space. In spite of the relatively small stage, and the fact that the fabric of the eighteenth-century protected building leaves no scope for traps, flies, or even adequate wings (as late as 2002, the job of loading sets was described as 'Dickensian'[23]), Edwards and Mac Liammóir created scenic spaces that, in their forthright theatricality, defied the limitations imposed by architecture. 'The theatre is not life', declared Edwards in the Gate's magazine, *Motley*. 'No realistic trimmings will make it so.'[24] So, if Gate audiences have little sense that they are on the site of an eighteenth-century place of performance, they do know what is meant by a 'Gate play', a concept most would associate with Edwards and Mac Liammóir, whose spirits—conjured, as at the Abbey, by portraits in the foyer—continue to be evoked by the current director, Michael Colgan.

In making existing historical sites of performance their own, the two major Irish producing theatres of the first half of the twentieth century, the Gate and the Abbey, embodied spatially a kind of enforced modernity that shaped Irish theatre as a whole. In the period of the Literary Revival, art forms such as poetry, music, or the visual arts could turn back to models of satisfyingly indigenous antiquity from pre-Norman Ireland; theatre, by contrast, had been introduced to Ireland initially as a court entertainment associated with Dublin Castle in the early seventeenth century, and as a result Irish theatre was never going to have a fully indigenous form—and it was this recognition that led, briefly, to a remarkable apparition on a remote hillside near Dooagh, on Achill Island in Co. Mayo.

A former British Labour Party candidate, and Irish language and dancing enthusiast, Major Dermot Freyer, had moved to the island just after the outbreak of the Second World War. There he met members of an influential group of Irish modernist artists, the White Stag Group, led by two other English expatriates, Basil Rakoczi and Kenneth Hall, who spent time in the area in the early 1940s. Although the White Stag artists never quite developed a coherent aesthetic, with influences ranging from a surrealism concerned with the

[23] Edel Morgan, 'Gate Raises Curtains on Plans for New Facilities', *Irish Times*, 21 Feb. 2002.
[24] Anon. [Hilton Edwards], 'Realism', *Motley* 1, no. 7 (1932), 3.

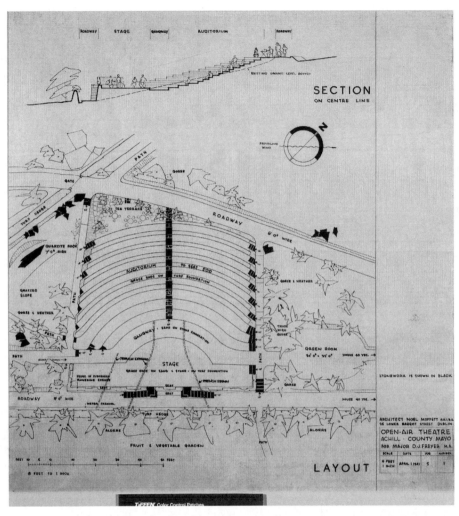

FIG. 26.2 Noel Moffett's original plans for the open-air theatre on Achill Island, 1941. Note specifications for materials found on the site: 'grass sods on turf', 'sand on stone', and gorse hedging to create an al fresco green room.

Courtesy of Irish Architectural Archive.

unconscious mind (Rakoczi was a practising psychoanalyst) to abstraction, symbolism, and primitivism, by 1941 they were nonetheless, as one commentator puts it, 'recognised as the leading "cutting edge" artists in Ireland'.[25] The White Stag exhibitions would also nurture an important generation of Irish artists, including the composer Brian Boydell, painter Patrick Scott (who in the 1950s worked in the architectural firm of Michael Scott), and a young Irish architect named Noel Moffett (who had also worked with Michael Scott). When Freyer commissioned Moffett to create a distinctively Irish theatre in Achill, Moffett

[25] S. B. Kennedy, *The White Stag Group* (Dublin: IMMA, n.d. [2005]), 25.

FIG. 26.3 Photograph of Noel Moffett's open-air Achill Theatre, 1941. The house of Dermot Freyer, who sponsored the project, is visible in the background.

Courtesy of Irish Architectural Archive.

responded with enthusiasm, cutting a 500-seat amphitheatre into the hillside above Dooagh using only available local materials: a low stage wall was made from turf, steps were cut from native quartzite, and even the green room was a planted screen of gorse, open to the elements. The vista behind the acting area looked out over Clew Bay with the Twelve Bens of Connemara, and Croagh Patrick beyond. 'Watching the superb panorama,' wrote Eamon Briscoe for the *Irish Press*, 'it was easy for me to imagine the harmony which would exist between the place and the players.'[26] If, as Seamus Deane writes, 'soil is what land becomes when it is ideologically constructed as a natal source', this was a theatre of the soil. [27] Although owing more than a little debt to a classical Greek amphitheatre in its shape, and later described as 'one of the most eccentric architectural schemes ever undertaken in Ireland', Moffett's Achill theatre can still claim to be the purest attempt to produce an indigenous Irish place of performance in the first half of the twentieth century.[28] It was, however, predictably doomed by west of Ireland weather and demographics (the nearest town, Keel, even today has a population that would barely fill the seats); there are no records of performances in the space, and Moffett's visionary performance space is now an indistinguishable hollow in the surrounding heather, completely reabsorbed by the materials from which it was built.

[26] Eamon V. Briscoe, 'Open-Air Theatre', *Irish Press*, 2 May 1941.

[27] Seamus Deane, 'Land and Soil: A Territorial Rhetoric', *History Ireland* 2, no. 1 (1994), 31.

[28] *Presenting Architecture: An Exhibition of Twentieth-Century Drawings and Models* (Dublin: Irish Architectural Archive, 2005).

DREAMS AND EXORCISMS

From a perspective that sees theatre-building as clearing a space for performance, the Abbey fire of 1951 might appear not as an interruption to a continuous tradition, but as an opportunity, a fresh start for the spatial project of an exorcized modernity to which Yeats and Horniman aspired, unsuccessfully, in 1904. Giving the initial brief to rebuild the Abbey to architect Michael Scott may have seemed initially like an act of continuity; after all, he had done design work on the Gate in 1930, had remodelled the Abbey auditorium and redesigned the entrance canopy in 1925, and had in fact acted on its stage as a young man. However, in precisely the period that Scott and his colleagues worked on the Abbey commission, their firm was asserting itself as the most important single force for architectural modernism in twentieth-century Ireland. During those years, one of Scott's partners, Robin Walker (who had been a student of Le Corbusier), returned to Ireland after an influential period studying under Mies van der Rohe in Chicago, while a new associate with equally strong Miesian leanings, Ronnie Tallon, also joined the firm. While working on the Abbey project, for instance, Tallon took the lead in designing the Donnybrook campus of the Irish broadcaster RTÉ, creating a scheme with characteristic steel and glass oblong cubes and reflecting ponds. Collectively, Scott, Tallon, and Walker would go on to produce some of Ireland's most iconic modernist buildings, using light, space, and a forthright honesty in their materials that is still the firm's signature fifty years later.[29] 'The materials are concrete, iron and glass', their spiritual father, Mies van der Rohe once wrote. 'Ferroconcrete buildings are essentially skeleton structures. Neither pastry nor tank turrets. [...] That means skin and bone structures.'[30] Also working as a consultant for the Abbey design team was the French theatre architect Pierre Sonrel, who had published with Le Corbusier in the volume *Architecture et dramaturgie* in 1950, further enhancing the consciously internationalist aesthetic of the new Abbey. [31] If, following Mies van der Rohe's dictum, materials determine structure, in Noel Moffett's Achill theatre, a sod of turf from Dooagh was unique to that place, but a concrete block is a concrete block anywhere in the world. It has no nationality. So, as the journal *Build* reported in 1966, Scott may have been instructed to 'recreate the sense of intimacy between players and audience, which was such an essential feature of the original Abbey theatre',[32] but they did so (as one member of the team put it) by trying 'to forget about every theatre built before'[33]—including the 1904 Abbey Theatre.

There would be many critics of the 1966 Abbey, including Scott himself, who later said: '[there is] no graciousness about it, it's crushed, the public areas are too small and

---

[29] Scott was first given the commission to design a new Abbey in 1951. While working on the project, he was joined by Robin Walker and Ronnie Tallon; they became Michael Scott and Associates in 1959, Michael Scott and Partners in 1966 (the firm to which the Abbey was attributed), and Scott Tallon Walker in 1972, the name by which the firm is known today.

[30] Mies van der Rohe, cited in Claire Zimmerman, *Mies van der Rohe* (Cologne: Taschen, 2006), 10.

[31] André Barsacq et al., *Architecture et dramaturgie* (Paris: Flammarion, 1950).

[32] 'The New Abbey: A Triumph in Detail and Complexity', *Build* 2, no. 6 (1966), 54.

[33] 'Abbey Theatre: The End of an Era', *Build* 2, no. 6 (1966), 53.

the stage is not deep enough'—to which he might have added that there was inadequate rehearsal, dressing room, storage, and office space. [34] However, in his defence, Scott would argue that all of the inadequacies of the design were forced upon him by the one act of remembrance that would not be denied, apparently at the behest of Ernest Blythe, the Abbey's long-serving managing director. that the new building occupy the site of the original 1904 building. 'Limitations of space', as a spokesperson for the firm put it at the time, 'presented several structural problems which required more of ingenuity than the application of advanced structural theory.'[35] And, indeed, it took ingenuity to fit the 157-seat flexible space of the Abbey's second stage, the Peacock (capable of being configured either as a proscenium, or with the audience on either two or three sides of a central playing area), into the footprint of the original building, tucked into the subterranean level under a main auditorium that sat 628 people, facing a stage 22 metres wide and 8.5 metres deep. While no one would deny that these stages have seen some memorable performances over the ensuing decades, the building as a whole is a collision between an architectural act of willed amnesia and an institutional longing for remembrance. That tension was clear from the night the theatre opened with a celebration entitled *Recall the Years*, which began with the original Abbey stage carpenter, Seaghan Barlow, striking the gong salvaged from the original building. Such acts of conjuration would be repeated in the decades that followed. Thirteen years later, at the celebrations for the theatre's seventy-fifth anniversary in 1979, the chair of the Abbey board, Michael O Aodha, told the audience that there were 'ghosts in the wings'.[36]

Those ghosts were the last things on the minds of architects such as Robin Walker and Michael Scott in the heady days of the 1960s, when dreams of even more radical buildings lay just beyond those buildings that they actually built. 'We all made schemes, endless schemes, before a design was finally accepted', Ronnie Tallon later recalled of the Abbey project.[37] Among the reported sixteen different designs (and five full models) that Michael Scott and his partners created, for instance, was one by Robin Walker, which would have extended the site to the River Liffey, and would have contained, as Scott later described it, 'a theatre with two stages back to back. For certain productions, you'd lift a screen between the two stages and have the two as one, so you would have a theatre with two audiences facing each other.'[38]

As they were imagining these radical actor–audience relationships, the firm was also making anew another of Ireland's major theatres, the Cork Opera House. Originally built in 1855 on the banks of the River Lee, the Opera House was destroyed by fire not long after the Abbey, in December 1955. The original Cork Opera House presented a curving, rotunda-like facade to the river, and was one of the city's landmarks, rich in theatrical ghosts; by contrast, the replacement building by Robin Walker, which opened in October 1965, was a defiantly modernist building, presenting the sheer cliff of an almost uninterrupted blank wall to the river. What was (and remains) most striking about Walker's Cork

[34] Dorothy Walker, *Michael Scott, Architect in (Casual) Conversation with Dorothy Walker* (Kinsale: Gandon, 1995), 199.
[35] 'The New Abbey: A Triumph in Detail and Complexity', 54.
[36] Caroline Walsh, 'Theatre's Past Recalled', *Irish Times*, 28 Dec. 1979.
[37] John O'Regan (ed.), *Michael Scott 1905–1989* (Kinsale: Gandon, 1993), 8.
[38] Walker, *Michael Scott, Architect*, 169.

FIG. 26.4 The spectacularly curving auditorium of Robin Walker's Cork Opera House (1965).

Courtesy of Simon Walker.

Opera House, however, is the auditorium, which remains largely intact. In the Cork Opera House, Walker created a 1,000-seat space which retains the intimacy of a Victorian theatre, by combining the clean lines of modern materials with a curving balcony and a reimagined version of the boxes, or loges, of a traditional opera house. It would be arguably the most architecturally important theatre interior in Ireland of its time.

What makes the Cork Opera House and the unbuilt Abbeys of 1966 something more than the idiosyncratic speculations of an energized creative team is that the same process was being mirrored, on a smaller scale, by the Lyric Theatre in Belfast. The Lyric had been founded by Mary and Pearse O'Malley in 1951 in a tiny converted room in their home in Derryvolgie Avenue in a prosperous residential area of Belfast. However, as early as 1959 the O'Malleys had been talking to J. Neil Downes, an architect living around the corner on the Lisburn Road, about building a new theatre. In 1959, Downes drew what he at one point called a 'Design for an Intimate Theatre' (with perhaps an echo of Strindberg), which would have been an innovative complex of theatre and gallery spaces, whose multiple levels and pitched roofs made the single building resemble a condensed village, clustered around a gently curving performance space.[39] When funding for a new theatre became a possibility a few years later, however, Downes drew up a completely new (and more ambitious) set of plans in 1965 for a 326-seat theatre, this time featuring a three-quarter thrust stage, shaped

[39] J. Neil Downes, 'Small Theatre for Belfast for Mrs Mary O'Malley', Job 11 (24 Oct. 1959); Lyric

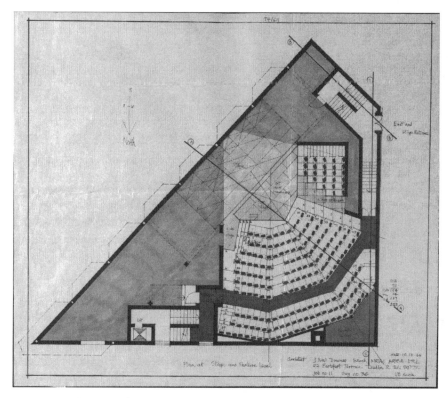

FIG. 26.5 J. Neil Downes's never-realized plans for a new Lyric Theatre, on the Ridgeway Street site in Belfast (May 1967). Note the division of the auditorium, with a runway-like acting area between the two parts of the house.

Courtesy of James Hardiman Library, NUI Galway.

not unlike the Guthrie Theatre in Minneapolis (whence Brian Friel, who had links to the Lyric, had returned after an influential residency in May and June 1963).[40]

Finally, when funding to build the new Lyric Theatre was confirmed, Downes went back to the drawing board and drew up a third set of plans in May 1967, this time for the triangular site that had been identified on Ridgeway Street. The 1967 plans imagined a foyer with glass bubble-like windows opening the public areas out to the Lagan River. This auditorium was his most innovative yet, in which steeply raked seating with a balcony was divided vertically into two asymmetrical sections, with a catwalk-like acting area running between the two seating areas, feeding into a three-quarter thrust stage.[41] Whether intended as a spatial commentary on a divided society united around a single stage, or simply as a new way of thinking about the audience–actor relationship, Downes imagined an

Theatre Archive, NUIG: T4/595.

[40] J. Neil Downes, 'Lyric Players Theatre, Belfast', Job 11 (8 June 1965); Lyric Theatre Archive, NUIG: T4/598.

[41] J. Neil Downes, 'Lyric Players Theatre, Belfast', Job 11 (drawings dated from 10 Oct. 1966 to 8 May 1967): Lyric Theatre Archive, NUIG: T4/618.

Irish theatre space that in some respects echoed Walker's unbuilt vision of two audiences facing one stage on the Abbey site. When describing Downes's work to Samuel Beckett (who was invited to lay the foundation stone in 1965), Mary O'Malley wrote that he had 'made a special study of European architecture during the past three years'.[42] However, where Scott and his colleagues in Dublin were disciples of Miesian purity, Downes took his bearings elsewhere, later arguing that the built environment should foster memories of place, and 'modern building activity should add to this store and not seek to destroy and replace it as has so often happened, particularly where the Bauhaus philosophy has held sway.'[43]

As in Dublin, so in Belfast, however: like the more utopian ideas for the Abbey, this visionary Lyric was not to be. The builders, Sir Alfred McAlpine and Sons, went ahead with their own design, which involved a much more conventional auditorium facing a proscenium arch stage with a small forestage in a building that made a functional attempt to use an awkward site.[44] Downes promptly disassociated himself from the entire enterprise. 'I have, at all times, advised you to the best of my ability on the question of the new theatre,' he wrote formally to Pearse O'Malley on 10 March 1968. 'None the less, I regret that I would be unhappy to be associated with this building.'[45]

Untethered Space

If the modernist theatres of the 1960s were acts of exorcism (from which the Gate increasingly stood out as a place still comfortably hosting the spirits of its founders—paradoxically so, considering its original modernist aesthetic), they bequeathed to the decades that followed a disenchanted Irish theatre landscape. As Tomás Mac Anna (who was appointed as the theatre's artistic adviser in 1966) complained later to theatre historian Robert Welch, 'no self-respecting ghost would find himself (or herself) dead' in the 1966 Abbey. [46] The Abbey's energetic artistic director from 1993 to 1999, Patrick Mason, showed a particularly acute sense that the Abbey needed to reactivate memories of its origins. 'I see this National Theatre as one that will be cognizant of its past, true to its best traditions,' he wrote in 1996, 'but bold enough to respond to the creative demands of a burgeoning number of theatre artists and practitioners.'[47] Rather than pretending that there were ghosts where there were none, he began in the early 1990s talking to Iain Mackintosh of Theatre Projects Consultants, who brought together a team headed by McCullough–Mulvin Architects. They drew up a number of schemes that gave architectural form to the acknowledgement that Scott's 1966 building had been too efficient in exorcizing the spirits of the early Abbey.

---

[42]   Mary O'Malley to Samuel Beckett (16 April 1968); Lyric Theatre Archive, NUIG: T4/807(1).

[43]   J. Neil Downes, 'The Nature of Conservation', *RIAI Bulletin*, Sept. 1978, 2.

[44]   Alfred McAlpine and Sons, 'Lyric Theatre' (1968), Lyric Theatre Archive, NUIG: T4/619.

[45]   J. Neil Downes to Pearse O'Malley, 10 Mar. 1968, Lyric Theatre Archive, NUIG: T4/817 (14).

[46]   Robert Welch, *The Abbey Theatre 1899–1999: Form and Pressure* (Oxford: Oxford University Press, 1999), 179.

[47]   Patrick Mason, *The National Theatre: Artistic Policy* (Dublin: Abbey Theatre, 1996), 1.

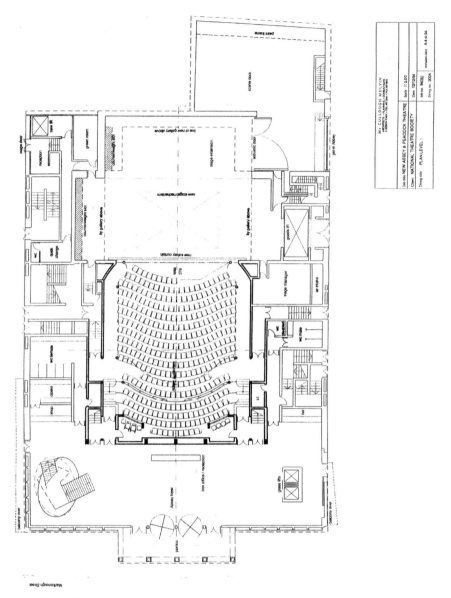

FIG. 26.6 Plans (never realized) for a new Abbey Theatre from 1994, drawn up by McCulloch–Mulvin Architects. The design placed an auditorium that echoed the 1904 Abbey in a contemporary shell.

Courtesy McCulloch–Mulvin Architects and the Irish Architectural Archive.

Consciously using the existing site and drawing on its historical resonances, the team decided that one way to overcome its shortcomings was to build upwards (although other schemes envisaged acquiring adjacent properties), and they proposed a six-storey contemporary structure, containing two performance spaces. The Peacock, on the top of the building, was once again to be a flexible black box or studio theatre, arguably the classic modernist theatrical space. However, in the main auditorium there was to be a kind of return of the repressed, with a reintroduction of the tight curving horseshoe (with an added second-level balcony) and proportions of the 1904 Abbey, facing a stage that mirrored the proscenium cube of Holloway's building.[48] In 1994 few architects were designing theatres like this, so the message was clear: the ghosts were being welcomed home. In this respect, the unbuilt McCullough–Mulvin design can stand as an emblem of the tensions in Irish theatre space over the preceding ninety years.

As the economy began to boom in the late 1990s and early 2000s, the sense that Scott's building needed replacing gathered momentum. In 2000, the then Minister for Arts, Síle de Valera, proposed a version of McCullough–Mulvin plan, to be completed in time for the Abbey's centenary in 2004. From that point onwards, possibilities multiplied; one proposal, which would have broken completely with any spatial memories, involved a building on a completely new site in George's Dock, in the redeveloped Docklands area. The site of the Carlton Cinema on O'Connell Street was then proposed, as were the former Coláiste Mhuire buildings on Parnell Square which share the same block as the Gate (thereby creating Dublin's missing theatre district), and, finally, the General Post Office, site of the 1916 Easter Rising. Of all the proposed sites, this latter provoked the most intense public debate about the ways in which spectral traces of the past could inflect performances in the present. 'What could better stir the artistic imagination than this iconic combination?' asked senator and conservation campaigner David Norris. 'The relationship between the Rising and the literary renaissance, between Pearse and Yeats, already exists.'[49] However, with the economic collapse of 2008, the prospect of a new Abbey faded, and by 2012 the *Irish Times*' architectural correspondent Frank McDonald could look back on the theatre's years of speculative wandering as 'a long-running farce with a large cast of characters'.[50] Meanwhile, in a narrative arc with some parallels, the Abbey's sister modernist theatre, the 1968 Lyric, was demolished, and a new building opened on the site in May 2011. Designed by O'Donnell and Tuomey (whose work, such as their 2008 Venice Biennale piece, *Within You Without You*, is deeply concerned with memory and place), the new Lyric coincidentally echoed some of the features of Downes's unbuilt plans, particularly in its public areas. It has a steeper auditorium than its predecessor, and a multi-level foyer with a strongly communal feeling, in which windows open out to the Lagan, just as Downes had imagined they would.

The spatial restlessness of two of the main producing theatres on the island in the period since 1990 can be understood as part of a wider, and more profound, transformation of the places of performance in Ireland. Until the late 1970s, virtually all theatre funding on the island went to the three main theatres: the Abbey, the Lyric, and the Gate. However, policy changes in arts funding in both jurisdictions in the late 1970s initiated a new regional awareness, and this led to subsidies being given to companies outside Dublin and Belfast, which in turn led to calls for new theatre buildings that were equally geographically

[48] McCullough–Mulvin Architects, *A Theatre for the 21st Century: The New National Theatre Drawings* with Theatre Projects Consultants, Ove Arup & Partners, Varming Mulcahy Reilly Associates, Mulcahy McDonagh & Partners. Job 94032 (12 Dec. 1994).

[49] David Norris, 'Iconic Marriage of Yeats and Pearse in Abbey GPO', *Irish Times*, 15 Oct. 2009.

[50] Frank McDonald, 'Long-Running Farce with a Large Cast of Characters', *Irish Times*, 27 Sept. 2012.

dispersed. As of 2014, there were ninety-five professional performance venues scattered throughout the island; only nine of these (primarily the big professional theatres and surviving Victorian theatres) were built prior to 1980. Twelve were built in the decade of the 1980s, but the majority appeared during the economic boom of the 1990s and early 2000s, while twelve were built perhaps surprisingly—after the economic collapse of 2008. Geographically, there are the expected clusters in Dublin, Belfast, Galway, and Cork, but now, for the first time, professional theatre spaces are also scattered through every county. In some cases, the building of a theatre in one town led to a demand for a theatre from a neighbouring town, creating local mini-clusters; in other cases, the opposite was true, and when a community became aware that they were not in easy proximity to a theatre, there was demand for a new performance venue; in yet other cases, decisions to locate theatres in a given town was more strategically political. Whatever their origins, however, these new theatres all cater for their local audiences. This is equally true of the necklace of theatres that ring the capital—the Pavilion Theatre in Dún Laoghaire, the Civic Theatre in Tallaght, Draíocht in Blanchardstown, and axis in Ballymun—and of Áras Éanna, the seventy-seat venue on Inisheer, the smallest of the Aran Islands. Likewise, most of these venues incorporate a small gallery or other arts space, and usually the names are intended to invoke a local sense of place. The 380-seat Solstice Arts Centre in Navan, for instance, is not far from Newgrange, a Neolithic site aligned to the winter solstice, while the 162-seat Balor Theatre in Ballybofey, Co. Donegal, is named after a mythological creature associated with nearby Tory Island. Likewise, in Galway, Druid Theatre Company did the equivalent of hanging a portrait in the foyer when they renamed their studio space in Druid Lane after one of their most distinguished actors, the late Mick Lally.

Whether the defining place of performance in Irish theatre in the first half of the last century could be said to reside among the ashes of the Abbey Theatre or to have briefly flourished amid the gorse on Achill Island, the defining space of the national theatre in the twenty-first century may well be found not in a single building, but in this dispersed map. However, relatively few of these new spaces are producing houses, and so most have struggled to create that intense, layered sense of theatrical haunting that continues to linger among the portraits in an older producing theatre. In the end, however, the tasks of these two configurations of theatrical space may not be all that different, as in the increasingly globalized, radically despatialized Ireland of the twenty-first century, the need to state the claims of place by nourishing places of performance as *lieux de mémoire* will be felt ever more strongly.

CHAPTER 27

....

DIRECTORS AND DESIGNERS
SINCE 1960

....

IAN R. WALSH

For Peter Brook, the acid test for the ephemeral art of theatre is 'what remains' once the performance has ended. It is a 'literal acid test', as what marks the 'essence' of a performance is the 'central image of the play' burnt into memory.[1] Such an image is not created by the writer alone, but is shaped by the collaboration of the director, the design team, and the actors. The theatre is a collaborative art form that requires a team of artists working together to create a production for an audience. However, Irish theatre is rarely written about in these terms. It has been characterized as a writer's theatre, and most critical writing concerns plays and playwrights. Few books consider the work of the director, let alone the designer, in the creation of the piece. And yet it is to the emergence of the director and innovation of stage design that the development of modern theatre has been traced, moving from the hierarchical system of playwrights and actor-managers in the nineteenth century to the contemporary theatre company made up of a team of creative artists, a movement away from the staging of mimetic representational drama to a 're-theatricalisation'[2] of the theatre. By examining the work of directors and designers in Ireland since 1960, this modern progression can also be clearly charted. Despite some dominant perceptions, Ireland has never been fully cut off from the experimentations of the wider theatrical world. It is in the figure of the director and the designer working in Ireland that this is most clearly illustrated, as I hope to make evident in this brief survey. With their roots in the nineteenth century, the director and modern theatre designer were figures 'shaped in the forges of nationalism and internationalism'.[3] Indeed, in the current globalized world contemporary designers and directors 'are themselves migrants across different traditions and geographical landscapes'.[4] Such cultural exchange was accelerated after 1960 with greater ease of travel, better dissemination of theories and practice through the development of

---

[1] Peter Brook, *The Empty Space* (London: MacGibbon & Kee, 1968), 136.

[2] Erika Fischer-Lichte, *The Show and the Gaze of Theatre: A European Perspective* (Iowa City, IA: University of Iowa Press, 1997), 62.

[3] 'Introduction', in Maria M. Delgado and Dan Rebellato (eds.), *Contemporary European Theatre Directors* (London: Routledge, 2010), 4.

[4] Ibid., 16.

theatre education in the universities, and the creation of international theatre festivals—the latter affording theatre artists the opportunity to develop their work by showcasing it to new audiences whilst also being exposed to new practices and the experimentation of others. The development of theatre education in Ireland did not gain momentum until the 1980s, but theatre artists began to train and travel abroad from the late 1960s, and the Dublin Theatre Festival, established in 1957, continues to connect Irish theatre makers to the leading explorers of the ever-changing landscape of contemporary international theatre practice.

Despite such cross-fertilization of practice, Irish theatre has been distinguished by its continued emphasis on and commitment to the written text. The theatre internationally has seen the arrival of many auteur-directors such as Robert Wilson, Tadeusz Kantor, or Robert Lepage, who control all the various elements of the stage and bind them to one singular artistic vision. But such a figure has yet to surface in Ireland, where direction and design remain inextricably linked with play-writing. Indeed, many Irish directors have also written plays and many playwrights have had success as directors—just as many directors have also worked as designers and some designers as directors. That most theatre in Ireland continues to show concern with the joy, freedom, and tyranny of words does not justify the singular privilege enjoyed by the playwright in the critical reception of the work. Directors and designers do not merely interpret playwrights' work but are fundamental to the 'shaping, representing, positioning and creating' of the theatrical experience.[5] This is as true of new writing as in the revival of older work, but direction and design are more often identified and commented upon in the production of canonical work. In Ireland, directors' reputations have often been made not in their staging of Shakespeare but in their revivals of Synge, O'Casey, and Yeats. But, as will be made clear when examining the work of individual directors, the creative energies released in these productions of established plays often transfers into approaches taken to new work, with these in turn rejuvenating further revivals. This is of course also true for the designers who are often made invisible in the commentary on revived work where the sole authorship of the production is assigned to the director in place of the playwright.

STRIPPING IT BACK

The influential figures that gain prominence in the 1960s and 1970s are all defined by a stripped-back aesthetic that ran counter to the naturalistic 'peasant play', with its cast of familiar small-town types and cottage-kitchen setting that had come to dominate the Irish stage. Interestingly, they are associated with very different theatrical institutions and arrive at this common aesthetic from very different directions.

The first of those I will examine is Jim Fitzgerald, who worked as both a director and designer. Fitzgerald was a largely self-educated man who got his start with the New Theatre group in Dublin during the 1940s. Spurred on by this experience he left for England,

[5] Ibid., 18.

joining the Unity Theatre[6] and later working with Joan Littlewood's Theatre Workshop[7] in Stratford East. These experiences were greatly to influence Fitzgerald's directing style when he returned to Dublin in 1954, where, after a short spell with Lord Longford's company at the Gate Theatre, he found himself as the principal director and designer for Godfrey Quigley's Globe Theatre and later for Phyllis Ryan's Gemini Productions. Fitzgerald first garnered attention for his work on canonical Irish works. He applied the techniques learnt with Unity and Littlewood to seven of Yeats's plays performed as part of the Dublin Theatre Festival to much acclaim, and he had a successful tour with a production of O'Casey's *Juno and the Paycock*. These achievements led to his selection by Brendan Smith to be the director of the ill-fated *Drums of Father Ned* for the Theatre Festival in 1958. With this controversy behind him, Fitzgerald continued with the Globe to direct productions of such international writers as Willliams, Miller, Betti, and Lorca. But he is most remembered for his role in the productions of two new Irish plays written for the Dublin Theatre Festival: Hugh Leonard's *Stephen D* (1962) and Thomas Kilroy's *Death and Resurrection of Mr Roche* (1968).

Leonard's play was an adaptation of James Joyce's *Portrait of the Artist* and was originally conceived as a one-man show, but buoyed by Fitzgerald's enthusiasm and designs the piece grew to finally have a cast of thirty. Ryan writes of Fitzgerald's final design:

> There was a rostrum right along the back of the stage, outlined against a deep blue cyclorama. In its centre there was a square piece like a large window, and at the sides flights of steps. Hanging in front of these simple pieces was a yellow scrim curtain which looked like gauze, and lifted away easily. The rest of the stage was bare. Fitz explained that the actors, plus a few spot-lights and minimal props, would create the illusion of all the other locations.[8]

Such a scenic arrangement may seem unremarkable in light of contemporary practice, but for the Irish theatre of 1962 this was a novel and bold approach. It allowed for dynamic, quick scene changes that perfectly suited Leonard's episodic script, which moved quickly from private fantasy to public confrontation. What Fitzgerald searched for in production was an 'overall cohesion that can guide a disparate collection of actors'.[9] This cohesion was shown to have been guided in practice through the tremendous creative energies of the director:

> Quick as a flash, sharp as a blade and divil for repartee, he darts hither and thither, rushes on the stage, moves an actor, fetches a prop, does the sound effects, scuffles to the back of the auditorium, curses volubly and smokes incessantly. The small, vulpine and intensely perceptive Jim Fitzgerald coaxes and blasts his cast with an energy and enthusiasm which is a joy to behold.[10]

[6] The Unity Theatre that grew from the Workers Theatre Movement was known for producing Piscator-like 'Living Newspaper' documentary theatre pieces, satirical pantomimes, and plays by Brecht, Odets, and O'Casey.

[7] Littlewood's Theatre Workshop, world-famous for its productions of *Oh, What a Lovely War* and later Brendan Behan's *The Hostage*, promoted an aesthetic that rejected representational settings in favour of suggestive and atmospheric lighting plans and sets comprising ramps, revolves, and scaffolding.

[8] Phyllis Ryan, *The Company I Kept* (Dublin: Town House, 1996), 174.

[9] 'Gabriel Fallon and Jim Fitzgerald Talking about the Abbey', *Irish Times*, 28 July 1962.

[10] David Nowlan, 'Festival Prologue', *Irish Times*, 21 Sept. 1962.

Thomas Kilroy's *Death and Resurrection of Mr Roche* is a very different play to Leonard's *Stephen D*. It is more Aristotelian than epic in its dramaturgy, with the action taking place over an evening in a fixed place. Kilroy's play was rejected by the Abbey, but in the rejection letter Tomás Mac Anna wrote: 'if Jim Fitzgerald is interested, then its success at the Gate or Olympia is assured.'[11] Kilroy did send the play to Fitzgerald, who agreed to stage it, and this most original Irish playwright has credited Fitzgerald as giving him his start in theatre. Kilroy writes of Fitzgerald:

> He was [. . .] a director of genius, particularly of actors in close, intimate, physical situations and at the same time a terrific reader of the text. He was a highly intelligent, well-read man who was deeply subversive of all conventional thought and practice.[12]

It was alcoholism that was to be the undoing of Fitzgerald, and the reason he never became more successful internationally despite the great success of *Stephen D* abroad. His star began to fade in the 1970s, although there were notable television productions and a double bill of Yeats plays—*The Herne's Egg* and *Purgatory*—staged at the Peacock in 1973, but he no longer was the charismatic force he had once been. His great legacy, other than the seminal productions mentioned, was in his collaboration in 1966 with Colm O Briain in organizing Project 67, 'the first attempt at cross-fertilisation of the arts in Ireland'.[13] This consisted of a series of events that ran for three weeks at the Gate Theatre including plays, music performances, and art exhibitions. This was the genesis for what later developed into the Project Arts Centre in Dublin.

Mary O'Malley, like Fitzgerald, began her theatrical career with the New Theatre Group in Dublin, but it was her successes at the Lyric Theatre in Belfast, which she founded, that made her name as a director. Inspired by Austin Clarke's theatre company dedicated to verse drama, she founded the Lyric Theatre at the back of her home on Derryvolgie Avenue, off the Malone Road in Belfast in 1951. The theatre later moved to larger premises on Ridgeway Street in 1968, and the current state-of-the-art theatre, which sits impressively on the banks of Belfast's River Lagan with a capacity of 390 seats, was opened officially by Brian Friel in 2011. Between 1951 and 1968 O'Malley directed 140 of the 180 productions staged by the Lyric, while also acting as artistic director. Her directing practice was informed by the limitations of the initial studio space and her dedication to the verse dramas of W. B. Yeats. Productions under O'Malley at the Lyric were thus noted for an economy of design, dynamic movement, and the actors' delivery of poetic speech. Her commitment to this Yeatsian aesthetic led her to favour more experimental works in her programming. The plays of Lorca and Brecht were given repeated stagings, as were O'Casey's later, expressionistic pieces. New works by Brian Friel and Patrick Galvin were also staged under O'Malley's artistic direction. But it is for the productions of twenty-three Yeats plays that she is remembered. Ulick O'Connor wrote: 'Stunning productions of *The Herne's Egg*, *The King of the Great Clock Tower*, *The Green Helmet* left you drained of every emotion except wonder. Once an awed member of the audience greeted her: "Hail Mary full of Yeats." '[14] The

---

[11]   Thomas Kilroy, 'A Playwright's Festival', in Nicholas Grene and Patrick Lonergan, with Lilian Chambers (eds.), *Interactions: Dublin Theatre Festival 1957–2007* (Dublin: Carysfort Press, 2008), 15.
[12]   Ibid., 18.   [13]   'Director Who Worked at the Cutting Edge', *Irish Times*, 20 Sept. 2003.
[14]   Ulick O'Connor, 'Mary O'Malley', *Irish Independent*, 7 May 2006.

dedication to Yeats's drama and the minimal abstracted aesthetic also proved inspiring to designers who worked at the Lyric,[15] where the plays were 'designed to a narrow colour scheme' with costumes similarly created with a 'simplicity of line and colour'.[16] The Lyric defiantly remained open throughout many of the worst years of the Northern Irish conflict, and O'Malley continued to deliver innovative and challenging productions, sometimes without heat or electricity. For instance, despite continuous power cuts in 1974 during the Ulster Workers Strike, she staged O'Casey's *Red Roses for Me*, a play concerning the 1913 Dublin Lockout. The boundaries between art and life seemed to dissolve in this production, as evidenced in O'Malley's account:

> The Workers' Strike was on the stage and the Workers' Strike was all around [. . .] in the city [. . .] One evening when there were about forty-five in the audience, two elderly ladies turned up with rugs and flash lamps. The funeral scene that night was lit only by Tilly lamps [. . .] the scene set against Colin Middleton's impressionistic background was never more moving.[17]

Unfortunately, after the move to Ridgeway Street, the restrictions imposed by Equity and the need to secure Arts Council funding meant that O'Malley could no longer run the theatre as a cooperative. Her dream of a permanent company that would specialize in the style of theatre she had developed over the past twenty years could not be sustained. In 1976 she resigned as a trustee of the theatre and the Lyric Company was dissolved. The theatre continued to produce new and canonical work, but the particular aesthetic developed under O'Malley's directorship did not remain. She is remembered now more often for her significant role as a cultural and political figure rather than as an innovator of Irish theatre practice. Bernard Adam in her obituary in 2006 wrote:

> From the start Mary O'Malley had been operating a kind of cultural peace process in Northern Ireland. She looked to the literary heritage of the island as a whole and strove mightily to use drama to promote debate and historical understanding in a community that found the simplicities of sectarianism so seductive.[18]

Tomás Mac Anna similarly viewed the theatre as a place of 'debate and historical understanding' but also of revolution. Indeed, he was responsible for the last riot at the national theatre in 1970 when he staged a political revue about the situation in Northern Ireland entitled *A State of Chasis*. In his first of three tenures as artistic director of the Abbey (first entitled artistic adviser), he revolutionized the output of the national theatre through his design and staging of European modernists as well as his encouragement of a new generation of playwrights. He first came to the Abbey as a designer, but with his fluency in the Irish language he was soon promoted to producer of Gaelic plays. As part of this role Mac Anna had to pen, direct, and design an annual pantomime in the Irish language. The demands of the pantomime meant that he had to learn how to stage scenes with a large cast

---

[15] Designers at the Lyric included Basil Blackshaw, Deborah Brown, Alice Berger Hammerschalg, Marie and Edna Boyd, Terence Flanagan, Rowel Friers, and Colin Middleton.

[16] Conor O'Malley, *A Poets' Theatre* (Dublin: Elo Press, 1988), 44.

[17] Mary O'Malley, *Never Shake Hands with the Devil* (Dublin: Elo Press, 1990), 256.

[18] Bernard Adam, *Irish Independent*, 29 Apr. 2006, http://www.independent.co.uk/news/obituaries/mary-omalley-476063.html. Accessed 29 Sept. 2014.

and become expert at transitions to several locations whilst also incorporating choreography and song into his productions. Also, with a lack of Irish-language plays he had to select and stage Irish-language adaptations of plays, the selection of which would favour Continental European dramatists rather than British playwrights. Thus the role of director of Irish-language plays schooled Mac Anna in a type of staging that was in direct contrast to the naturalistic style employed in the production of the Abbey's (by this time) signature realist dramas of peasant life. As he put it himself:

> I produced all the plays in Irish, mostly one-acts presented after, not before, the main attraction; and of course, the Christmas pantomimes, eighteen in all between the Abbey and the Queens. My work was completely in contrast to that of Ria Mooney, where she found herself producing play after play in the same naturalistic style, I was romping through Gheon, Jalabert, Benevente, Molière and Chekhov in styles all the way from late Guthrie to music-hall.[19]

With such a background, it is not surprising that his later productions would be characterized as Brechtian. He visited the Berliner Ensemble in 1967 and helped design and advised on their production of O'Casey's *Purple Dust*. But he denied Brecht as an influence. When his production of Máiréad Ní Ghráda's *An Triail* (1962), which employed placards and had actors double up in roles, was praised for being Brechtian, he claimed it was not intentionally so but was 'exactly the thing I was doing in the Gaelic plays for years and years'.[20] However, like Brecht he conceived of the 'theatre as something revolutionary', but claimed that it was the Russian director Meyerhold that he most emulated.[21] Nonetheless, he staged and designed an influential production of Brecht's *The Life of Galileo* for the Abbey at the Queens Theatre in 1965. John Devitt recalled going to see this performance:

> It was physically exciting performance, with a swirl of the crowds coming on. You knew it had been rehearsed, but it didn't feel like that: he got that rough, edgy quality. He had a way of breaking up the production, so that you were taken away on a wave and then you were suddenly shocked and stopped still.[22]

In 1974 Mac Anna staged Brecht's *The Resistible Rise of Arturo Ui* at the Abbey and, perhaps more significantly, at the Lyric in Belfast, where the play's theme of protectionism had a particular relevance at this time and 'its grim humour could be appreciated'.[23] His 1966 production of Lorca's *Yerma* at the Queens was distinguished in its use of movement and colour, which drew from a palette of lemon yellows and deep reds conveying both the heat of the Spanish location and the fiery temperaments of the characters. In terms of Irish playwrights, Mac Anna directed revivals of O'Casey's Dublin trilogy, but more significantly he also gave the later, expressionistic plays such as *Cock A Doodle Dandy*, *The Star Turns Red*, and *Purple*

---

[19] Tomás Mac Anna, 'Ernest Blythe and the Abbey', in E. H. Mikhail (ed.), *The Abbey Theatre: Interviews and Recollections* (Basingstoke: Macmillan, 1988), 170.

[20] 'Tomás Mac Anna in Conversation with Karen Carleton', in Lillian Chambers, Ger Fitzgibbon, and Eamonn Jordan (eds.), *Theatre Talk* (Dublin: Carysfort Press, 2001), 281.

[21] Ibid.

[22] John Devitt in conversation with Nicholas Grene and Chris Morash, *Shifting Scenes: Irish Theatre-Going, 1955–1985* (Dublin: Carysfort, 2008), 42.

[23] O'Malley, *Never Shake Hands with the Devil*, 256.

Dust their first productions at the Abbey as well as at the Lyric. His greatest success with a new play was Frank McMahon's adaptation of Brendan Behan's biographical *Borstal Boy* (1967). Mac Anna's staging again had all the hallmarks of epic theatre: the performance took place on an unadorned open stage stripped back to the back wall in a design by Christopher Baugh, the changing spaces of the different scenes were mapped out by an elaborate lighting design plotted by John Wickham of the Royal Shakespeare Company, and the dramaturgy relied on the use of a narrator figure (Brendan Behan played by Niall Tóibín to much acclaim) who introduced and linked the scenes. The production went on to Broadway, winning the Tony award for best play in 1970. Mac Anna also directed Tom Murphy's first play at the Abbey, *Famine*, in 1968, after Murphy's earlier play *A Whistle in the Dark* had famously been rejected by Ernest Blythe. Murphy's play about the nineteenth-century potato famine perfectly suited Mac Anna's style, making use of Brechtian effects that afforded audiences some critical distance from this most emotive of events in Irish history. Mac Anna continued to direct successfully into the 1980s, but the one-time rebel inevitably began to seem part of an old guard as a new generation of artists began to emerge with a fresh approach.

DEVELOPING DESIGN

Linking this old and new guard of directors are three designers that joined the Abbey Theatre in the late 1960s and early 1970s and went on to significantly shape the development of design in Ireland over the next thirty years. This trio were Bronwen Casson, Wendy Shea, and Frank Conway.[24] These designers brought a new professionalism and internationalism to design, with all three receiving formal training at the National College of Art and Design in Dublin and then going on to complete specialized courses in theatre design in London: Casson and Conway at Sadler's Wells, while Shea attended the stage design course at Regent Street Polytechnic. This education marked a shift in approach away from the design of scenery towards a designing for the space.

Casson looked to international companies for inspiration. She was affected by the Berliner Ensemble's production of *Coriolanus* in London in 1966, and greatly admired the work of Ariane Mnouchkine, working with her Théâtre du Soleil in the mid-1970s.[25] In 1978 she was awarded an External Affairs grant to visit Berlin, and learned from exciting productions that were taking place there at the time. These influences are discernible in her versatile productions, which showed a preference for combining abstraction with realism. This preference found particular expression in her design for a revival of Yeats plays at the Peacock in the 1970s and again in the 1990s but also in new plays such as Tom Murphy's *The Sanctuary Lamp* (1975). She realized to great effect Murphy's vision of characters locked inside the 'metaphorical monster that is a church'[26] with an 'abstract and atmospheric

[24] Casson joined the National Theatre in 1968, with Wendy Shea following her in 1971, and Frank Conway started to work in the theatre from the mid-1970s.

[25] Caroline Walsh, 'Caroline Walsh Talks to Stage Designer at the Abbey, about Her Work', *Irish Times*, 20 Sept. 1976.

[26] Tom Murphy quoted in Christopher Morash, *A History of Irish Theatre, 1601–2000* (Cambridge: Cambridge University Press, 2002), 250.

FIG. 27.1 Bronwen Casson, set and costume design for *The Sanctuary Lamp* by Tom Murphy (Abbey Theatre, 7 October 1975).

Photo: Fergus Bourke. Courtesy of the Abbey Theatre and James Hardiman Library, NUI Galway.

arrangement of church pillars, pulpit, pew and confessional'[27] that was 'shot through with shafts of darkness'.[28]

In the late 1970s and early 1980s Casson was to join a team of theatre-makers: playwright Tom Mac Intyre, director Patrick Mason, and actor Tom Hickey in their experiments at Peacock in a devised imagistic theatre style that led to several ingenious productions, the most successful being the adaptation of Patrick Kavanagh's *The Great Hunger* (1983). Casson's choice of props and designs brought deeper explorations of the relationships between the actors, objects, and space in these performance experiments. Her costume designs have been described as 'beautiful as works of art in themselves',[29] and were given an exhibition in 1979.[30] For Joe Vaněk they 'successfully [capture] the essential spirit of the characters in the simplest of terms'.[31]

Wendy Shea's costume designs also reflect a 'merciless eye for the foibles of the characters' she clothes.[32] This is unsurprising when we consider that she also worked as a newspaper cartoonist and painter. Her set design has been characterized as moving 'seamlessly between bold, structural dynamics'.[33] Where Casson has been associated with designing

[27] Fintan O'Toole, *Critical Moments: Fintan O'Toole on Modern Irish Theatre*, ed. Julia Furay and Redmond O'Hanlon (Dublin: Carysfort Press, 2003), 193.

[28] Morash, *History of Irish Theatre*, 150.

[29] Joe Vaněk, *Scene Change: One Hundred Years of Theatre Design at the Abbey* (Dublin: Irish Museum of Modern Art, 2005), 43.

[30] Pro-Quidnunc, 'An Irishman's Diary', *Irish Times*, 28 Feb. 1979.

[31] Vaněk, *Scene Change*, 43.   [32] Ibid.   [33] Ibid.

FIG. 27.2 Frank Conway, design for *Shibari* by Garry Duggan (Peacock, 4 October 2012).
Courtesy of Frank Conway.

for Yeats's plays, Shea has a connection to Beckett's work, designing costumes and sets for *Waiting for Godot* in 1976 and collaborating with director Ben Barnes on three of Beckett's shorter pieces, *Not I, Footfalls*, and *Play*, all presented at the Peacock in 1981. In terms of new plays at the Abbey, Shea has a particular association with Friel debuts, designing on *Volunteers* (1975), *Living Quarters* (1977), and *Aristocrats* (1979). For Kilroy's *Talbot's Box* (1978) in collaboration with director Patrick Mason she 'found a visual metaphor for this gulf between "extreme individualism" and "community" in the box of the play's title, a huge structure out of which all materials for the play emerge after the curtain rises'.[34] Her set design for Frank McGuinness's *Carthaginians* at the Peacock in 1988 saw 'a surrealistic burial mound extend from the small stage out into the auditorium so that entering was [in Sarah Pia Anderson's words] "like going down into the earth"'.[35] Such a design broke down the division between spectators and actors as in the 'same sort of suggestion made by environmental theatre.'[36]

Frank Conway has worked successfully as a director but is better known as a designer. As well as designing for the Abbey, he has also been resident designer for Druid Theatre

[34] Morash, *History of Irish Theatre*, 250.
[35] Helen Leusner Lojek, *Contexts for Frank McGuinness's Drama* (Washington, DC: Catholic University of America Press, 2004), 128.
[36] Ibid.

Company. As such he has been a long-time collaborator with director Garry Hynes, and has been behind the design for such landmark Druid productions as the première of Murphy's *Bailegangaire* (1985) and *Conversations on a Homecoming* (1985). In terms of revivals of the Irish canon, Conway has been most associated with productions of O'Casey's plays, working with directors Tomás Mac Anna, Joe Dowling, Stephen Rea, and most radically with Garry Hynes in a controversial production of *The Plough and the Stars* in 1991.

In the 2012 production at the Peacock of a new play, *Shibari*, by Garry Duggan that takes place in contemporary Dublin, Conway's set design consisted of the iconographic Irish country kitchen (hearth, kitchen table, sacred heart, and votive light) hung upside down from the ceiling and washed over with a deep red paint. Here he literally turned the old design of the Abbey on its head, and this seemed apt for a designer who did 'bring a new aesthetic' to the national theatre where he had reduced sets 'to a sumptuous monumental eloquence with only a few props and furniture to aid story-telling and location'.[37]

THEATRICALLY COMPLEX DIRECTION AND DESIGN

The directors to emerge in the late 1970s and who came to dominate the theatrical landscape throughout the 1980s and 1990s were less reactive to the naturalistic staging of the past. They brought a renewed emphasis on the psychology of character into theatrically complex productions that radically reinterpreted canonical works while also discovering appropriate approaches to new plays manifest with dramaturgical invention.

Indicative of this change is the work of Joe Dowling, whose career in theatre began as an actor at the Abbey theatre in the late 1960s. He trained at the Abbey School and then joined the company. Frustrated that the national theatre was losing younger audiences, he went to the then artistic director, Hugh Hunt, and pleaded for something to be done. Hunt sent him to Manchester to see some of the theatre-in-education companies that were running effectively there. On his return Dowling set up the Young Abbey, which was a touring company that would bring productions to younger audiences.[38] It was with this company that he first began to direct, but he soon graduated to the Abbey main stage after having served as an assistant director to Mac Anna, who remained a lifelong mentor. He was then made director of the Peacock and subsequently became, at 29, the youngest-ever artistic director of the Abbey in 1978. While at the Abbey he directed the premières of a number of important Irish plays, including Brian Friel's *Living Quarters* (1975) and *Aristocrats* (1979). He also made a success of Friel's *Faith Healer* in the Abbey in 1980 after its disastrous première on Broadway. This production is most often remembered for Donal McCann's stellar performance as the titular faith healer, Frank Hardy. By 1985 Dowling had resigned his post, disgusted at the interferences of the Abbey board in the management of the theatre. He went on a year later to exact revenge when he made a worldwide success of O'Casey's *Juno and the Paycock*, a favourite of the Abbey repertoire, at the rival Gate Theatre. The international acclaim garnered for

---

[37] Vaněk, *Scene Change*, 43.
[38] Dowling has had a lifelong commitment to theatre education. He went on to set up the Gaiety School of Acting in Dublin and to found a theatre education programme in the Guthrie Theatre.

this production eventually led Dowling to the directorship of the prestigious Guthrie Theatre in Minneapolis, from which he retired in 2015 after a highly successful career.

Although mentored by Mac Anna, Dowling's directing style did not follow that of the older man. Where Mac Anna favoured spectacle, composition, and distancing effects Dowling's style with its focus on character is more intimate in its effects. Where Mac Anna followed Meyerhold and Brecht, Dowling the actor-director looked to Stanislavski in his approach. He writes: 'The directorial function is to draw the best from all the elements—actors, designers, technical crew, in order to fully realize the intentions of the text.'[39] For Dowling, the director leads a creative team that aims to serve the text. The director and designer do not impose their ideas on the play, but use the text as a guide and mine it for inspiration. Noted collaborators in his influential Irish productions included the actors John Kavanagh and Donal McCann, as well as designers Wendy Shea, Frank Hallinan Flood, and Consolata Boyle, who designed the costumes for the Gate production of *Juno*. Boyle is better known now internationally for her film work, but she worked for many years in the theatre in Ireland, with notable credits for Field Day Theatre Company in the 1980s, including the première of Friel's *Translations* and Kilroy's *Double Cross*. In directing new plays by Friel,[40] Dowling learnt that 'it is the minutiae of the work which provide its most important exploration'.[41] For him it is the 'the unspoken things, the silences, the misunderstandings, the deliberate confusions and the tricks of memory' in Friel's plays 'which tell us the stories and maintain the narrative drive'.[42] This attention to the minutiae of the text and to the deep exploration of its given circumstances so important to his work on Friel is what led to his reinvigoration of *Juno and the Paycock* at the Gate. Christopher Morash writes of this production:

> Dowling broke with the comic sentimentalism which had traditionally characterized productions of the play, instead emphasising stylistic contrasts within the text, playing some scenes to bring out the music hall influences, and others with a graphic realism which contradicted the myth of picturesque poverty that the play is often made to support.[43]

Of course Dowling's direction was as always complemented by an appropriate design team. Frank Hallinan Flood's claustrophobic set and Consolata Boyle's ragged costumes emphasized the squalor and deprivation of O'Casey's Dublin. But this production was made particularly memorable by Dowling's take on the ending of the play, in which John Kavanagh's Joxer steals the Captain's (Donal McCann) last sixpence as he collapses to the ground unconscious with drink. In this Joxer was revealed as a malevolent parasite rather than a broad figure of fun, and the Captain's desperate fate was sealed. This small bit of invented stage business by Dowling has been the knockout punch that has left all contending revivals of *Juno*, before and since, cold.

---

[39] Joe Dowling, 'Staging Friel', in Alan J. Peacock, *The Achievement of Brian Friel* (Gerrards Cross: Colin Smythe, 1992), 188.

[40] Dowling also directed the première of *The Communication Cord* (1983) for Field Day Theatre Company and Friel's adaptation of Turgenev's *A Month in the Country* for the Gate in 1992.

[41] Peacock, *Achievement of Brian Friel*, 180.   [42] Ibid.

[43] Christopher Morash, 'Directors, Directing and Production Styles', in Peter Nagy, Phillippe Rouyer, and Don Rubin (eds.), *World Encyclopaedia of Contemporary Theatre*, vol. 1: *Europe* (London: Routledge, 1994), 481.

Where Dowling brought a renewed emphasis on character psychology, director Patrick Mason has taken this further by searching for the deeper structures within texts which has manifested itself in the creation of 'emotively powerful visual images'[44] in his productions. Mason trained at the Central School of Speech and Drama, and subsequently taught there in 1972. That same year saw him arrive in Dublin to take up a position as voice coach in the Abbey. He then left Ireland to become a lecturer in performance studies at Manchester University in 1975, but returned to the Abbey as a resident director in 1978. After a long association with the national theatre, where he directed seminal productions of plays by Friel, Leonard, Murphy, Kilroy, Mac Intyre, and in particular Frank McGuinness,[45] he became artistic director from 1991 to 1999. Mason credits his collaborations with Mac Intyre and actor Tom Hickey on a range of productions at the Peacock between 1982 and 1989 as influencing his development:

> I think it was the intensity and energy of that contact that really jolted me out of a more literal, realist kind of reading of text into a far more emblematic, symbolic reading of text and action. Since the work I did was trying to find some kind of synthesis between these two aspects of the work.[46]

Another influence on Mason's approach has been his extensive direction of opera. From opera he has learnt that '[t]heatre needs music, because music heightens energy. It is an irresistible force. With strict realism so much energy is concentrated on the introverted struggle to get an actor to project internal states. Music is extrovert.'[47] With Friel's *Dancing at Lughnasa* (1990), a play that relies heavily on music and tableaux for its effects, Mason found the perfect piece in which to display the maturation of his style. This was most clear in the scene in which all the sisters temporarily forget themselves in a wild liberating dance. Under Mason's direction the five personalities of the women began to sound and signal individually, only to then harmonize and dissolve into each other, becoming ecstatic in a transcendent *coup de théâtre*. The production became a theatrical phenomenon, with long runs in the West End and Broadway, culminating in Mason's Tony award for Best Director in 1992. A further contributing factor to the success of *Lughnasa* was the set design by Mason's long-time collaborator Joe Vaněk. The achievement of this set was the way it managed to portray both form and content of the play in its visual representation and spatial configuration: behind a small apron, which was the space of the narrator, were a table, chairs, and dresser that represented a cottage interior. These bits of furniture sat within two large white walls angled to create a triangular depth of space. A wedge of long reeds of golden corn was raked up against the high walls, signifying the harvest time in which the action takes place but also the nostalgic form and atmosphere of the play: the 'golden haze of memory'[48].

---

[44] Ibid.

[45] Mason is closely associated with the work of Frank McGuinness, and directed the premières of *The Factory Girls* (Abbey), *Observe the Sons of Ulster Marching Towards the Somme* (Abbey), *Dolly West's Kitchen* (Abbey/Old Vic, London), *Gates of Gold* (Gate Theatre, Dublin), and *The Hanging Gardens* (Abbey).

[46] Chambers et al., *Theatre Talk*, 320.

[47] Frank McGuinness, 'Mothers and Fathers', *Theatre Ireland* 4 (1983), 16.

[48] Derek West, 'Riches to Spare', *Theatre Ireland* 29 (1992), 28.

FIG. 27.3 Robert Ballagh, model for design of *The Importance of Being Earnest* (Gate, 23 July 1987).

Photo: Tom Lawlor. Courtesy of the Gate Theatre.

Vaněk's work (including over twenty productions with Mason) is distinguished in its elegance of design, visually beautiful with a keen delineation of space suitable to the playability of text. His designs of other landmark new plays such as McGuinness's *Observe the Sons of Ulster Marching towards the Somme* and Kilroy's *The Secret Fall of Constance Wilde* were integral to the success of these productions. Vaněk has also built a reputation for producing fresh design concepts with Mason for revivals, largely of the Anglo-Irish canon, including productions of Farquhar, Sheridan, Wilde, and Shaw at the Gate.

Interestingly, Vaněk was not the designer for one of Mason's most successful revivals, *The Importance of Being Earnest* at the Gate in 1987. Here, Mason, with collaborators costume designer Nigel Boyd and set designer Robert Ballagh, created a dangerous production of Wilde's comedy of manners that spoke to the contemporary, escaping the presentation of the play as harmless affectation or a museum piece. This was achieved by making parallels between the Victorian world of Wilde's drama and Thatcher's Britain. The cast were styled by Boyd to look like the British Royal Family, and Ballagh's set favoured cold abstraction over naturalistic Victorian clutter, presenting an undressed stage with a chequered black-and-white floor and a giant portrait of the Empress of India dominating the back wall. This was all framed by an opulent marble proscenium arch with gold finishing. Ballagh, a trained architect, is better known as a visual artist, but in the 1980s he created a series of influential sets distinguished by an emphasis on suggestive structures over mimetic detail, chief among them his design for Steven Berkoff's expressionistic production of Wilde's *Salomé* at the Gate in 1988.[49]

[49] See Robert Ballagh and J. Graeve, *Robert Ballagh on Stage: Theatre Set Design by Robert Ballagh* (Dublin: Project Arts Centre, 1990).

Like Mason, Garry Hynes has also won a Tony award for Best Director and has the distinction of being the first female to hold that honour. Hynes was co-founder of Druid Theatre Company in 1975 and has been its artistic director from 1975 to 1991 and from 1994 to the present. She was artistic director of the Abbey Theatre from 1991 to 1994. She has no formal training in theatre, but instead learnt her trade through directing productions for the student drama society whilst attending University College Galway. As a student in the early 1970s she spent her summers working in the United States, where she managed to see productions of the then vibrant theatrical avant-garde in New York. She went to the Performing Garage as well as seeing the work of Joe Chaikin and Meredith Monk. With the actor Marie Mullen, whom she met at the university, and actor Mick Lally she formed Druid Theatre Company in Galway; in their first season, in an attempt to attract tourists, she directed J. M Synge's *The Playboy of the Western World*. This opportunistic decision was to have a long-term effect on her practice:

> In my own development as a director, the discovery of Synge as a writer was an epiphany, one of the shock things. It completely influenced everything I've done since and continues to do so.[50]

With the combination of these two influences Hynes was to bring a fresh energy and approach characterized by 'rawness and attack' to both canonical and new Irish plays.[51] In playwright Tom Murphy she found a pugnacious and provocative kindred spirit from her native Galway. With Druid, and in collaboration with Frank Conway as designer, she would direct successful productions of Murphy's *Conversations on a Homecoming* (1985) and *Bailegangaire* (1985). In the 1980s she revived Synge's status in the Irish theatre, producing several groundbreaking productions of *The Playboy of the Western World*, transforming what had become regarded as a dated curiosity of peasant life into a theatrically vital piece that combined dirty realism with a savage energy. In 2005 she fulfilled a lifetime's ambition and staged all of Synge's plays in an international touring production entitled *DruidSynge*. Hynes most controversial revival was her 1991 production of O'Casey's *The Plough and the Stars* at the Abbey. Again she collaborated with Conway on this, her first production as artistic director of the National Theatre. She radically reimagined the play, employing an expressionistic production style with a young cast, estranging this most familiar of Irish plays, foregrounding the play's universal condemnation of poverty and violence. Conway's set consisted of a large raked platform with a 'huge, white, false proscenium [surrounding] the action. Scrawled on it with black paint the rallying cry of the 1916 Uprising, "We serve neither King nor Kaiser, but Ireland".[52] Most of the actors had shaved heads and were made pale and sickly with white makeup. The usually comedic character of Fluther was transformed into a raging alcoholic by a burly Brendan Gleeson, and the prostitute Rosie Redmond was no longer an old embittered whore with a heart of gold but a victimized young woman, played by Lorraine Pilkington. At the opening of Act III audiences had to endure a painfully slow walk across the stage by the consumptive child Mollser, played by Ruth O'Brian. And the bodies of the dead soldiers were dragged off leaving a

[50] Chambers et al., *Theatre Talk*, 201.
[51] Nagy et al., *World Encyclopaedia of Contemporary Theatre*, 478.
[52] Steven Griffith, 'The Plough and the Stars', *Theatre Journal* 44, no. 1 (1992), 97.

shocking trail of red blood over the white stage. In the late 1990s Hynes found in the plays of Martin McDonagh a similar sensibility to her own which interrogated the traditional representation of Ireland with daring, irreverence, and a contemporary perspective. It was for Druid's production of *The Beauty Queen of Leenane* that she was awarded the Tony in 1998.

Since the late 1990s a dominant directorial presence has been that of Conall Morrison, who has also proved to be an accomplished playwright. A young Morrison sent a script to Brian Friel. '"Too much dialogue" was Friel's opinion. "Don't tell me show me".' [53] This lesson has never been forgotten by Morrison, who is known for his attention to visual detail and his musical sensibility. This approach was most evident in his own adaptation of Patrick Kavanagh's novel *Tarry Flynn* at the Abbey in 1997. Here, Morrison worked with designer Francis O'Connor,[54] who created 'a playland of a set: all ladders, runways, trap doors, revolves, and a winding bicycle ramp that snaked its way into the audience'.[55] Theatre reviewer Michael C. O'Neill captured the vigour of this imaginative production when he wrote:

> Tarry Flynn freely interprets the spirit of Kavanagh's novel in audaciously theatrical ways: talk of an approaching automobile is highlighted by a miniature remote controlled car motoring across the set; shutters fly open to reveal statues of the saints taunting Tarry in his dreams; Uncle Petey descends into Tarry's world by walking vertically down the upstage wall; and, after she is mated, a cow smokes a cigarette.[56]

COMPANIES, STYLE, AND PLAYWRIGHT-DIRECTORS

In the last twenty years Irish theatre has seen an explosion of new companies led by a director with a regular design team and acting ensemble. These companies are generally made distinct not by the director's approach or the production of a particular dramatic canon but by their allegiance to particular modes of presentation. There are those that specialize in physical styles such as Corn Exchange (*commedia*), Barabbas (clowning), Loose Canon (Grotowski), Blue Raincoat (Decroux) and others such as Kabosh, Performance Corporation, and ANU, which produce important community-inspired, site-specific work. Fishamble Theatre Company, with director Jim Culleton, specializes in producing new writing, while companies such as Theatreclub, Brokentalkers, and thisispopbaby challenge traditional roles in the creating process with company-devised pieces. However, most of these companies are still involved with the production of texts, and some such as Corn Exchange and Performance Corporation have resident writers. Directors such as Mikel Murfi of Barabbas, Annie Ryan of Corn Exchange, and Jason Byrne of Loose Canon have

[53] Eileen Battersby, 'An Actor's Director with the Necessary Fire and Passion', *Irish Times*, 15 Aug. 1998.

[54] O'Connor is one of a new generation of designers that also includes Monica Frawley, Aedin Cosgrove, and Sabine Dargent, who have collaborated with directors across companies and theatres, furthering the professionalism and inventiveness of design on Irish stages.

[55] Michael C. O'Neill, '*The Cripple of Inishmaan* by Martin McDonagh; *Tarry Flynn* by Patrick Kavanagh; Conall Morrison Review', *Theatre Journal* 50, no. 2 (1998), 260.

[56] Ibid.

built very successful independent careers as directors outside their companies, blending their style or discipline with that of the requirements of certain texts, theatres, or companies with thrilling results.

One of the longest-running companies that is the exception and does not specialize in any one style of theatre is Rough Magic. This company, like Druid, grew from a group of friends who met at university (Trinity College Dublin, this time), and has been driven by artistic director Lynne Parker. Rough Magic began by producing work of contemporary international writers in the 1980s, but then later produced new Irish writing and some revivals of canonical Irish plays. The company's productions, particularly those directed by Parker, have been characterized by a sense of cleverness and playful theatricality. This style was most evident in their award-winning musical *Improbable Frequency*, written by Bell Helicopter and Arthur Riordan, that premièred in the 2004 Dublin Theatre Festival and went on to enjoy several revivals and tours in the following years.

Some of the younger directors to emerge who direct across companies, theatres, and countries, such as Selina Cartmell, Wayne Jordan, and Tom Creed, have made work that once again favours overt stylization similar to those in the 1960s but now with a postmodern edge. Jordan has made a name at the Abbey with a well-received production of O'Casey's *The Plough and the Stars*, and Cartmell has directed exciting new work by Tom Mac Intyre at the Peacock and Marina Carr at the Abbey, while Creed has made a reputation presenting the work of Lynda Radley and a well-received adaptation of Beckett's novel *Watt* by Barry McGovern at the Gate. But it is Pan Pan Theatre with director Gavin Quinn and designer Aedin Cosgrove that have been behind some of the most radical contemporary reimaginings of the Irish canon in recent years. Chief amongst these has been their production of *The Playboy of the Western World*, translated by Yue Sun into Mandarin and performed by an all-Chinese cast in 2006. This provocative production saw the Irish she-been of Synge's play 'transposed to a modern setting of a hairdressers and foot massage parlour, otherwise known as a "Whore Dressers" on the outskirts of Beijing'.[57]

The final trend to identify in terms of directing and design in Ireland is that of contemporary playwrights who direct and collaborate closely with designers in the production of their own plays. An early practitioner of this type of involvement was Frank McGuinness, and he has been followed by Conor McPherson, Enda Walsh, and Mark O'Rowe. These are different from the auteur-directors, as they are primarily playwrights who still produce a working script before rehearsals begin. It is then that they begin a collaborative process with a creative team as directors of their own script which will further develop in rehearsal until its final presentation. These playwrights, with their public status as equally competent directors, make it particularly difficult for criticism to continue to ignore the role of the director and designer in the creation and success of Irish theatre. I began with Brook's concept of the after-image that remains after a theatrical performance, but I hope this survey has persuaded the reader that directors and designers have not just made an impression on Irish theatre but are, and have always been, vital to its creation and continuance.

---

[57] 'The Playboy of the Western World', http://panpantheatre.com/shows/the-playboy-of-the-western-world/. Accessed 20 July 2014.

....

CHAPTER 28

DEFINING PERFORMERS
AND PERFORMANCES

....

NICHOLAS GRENE

In the Abbey Theatre there is a portrait of F. J. McCormick (1890–1947) by Cecil ffrench Salkeld: it is called 'The Vacant Throne', and was commissioned as a memorial to the actor after his death. McCormick stands in front of a chair with a crown on it, surrounded by images of him costumed in some of his best-known parts: King Lear; General Burgoyne in Shaw's *The Devil's Disciple*; Oedipus in Yeats's version of *Oedipus the King*.[1] McCormick's acting was legendary in his own time, but there are probably now few people alive who can remember him in his finest theatrical performances. Unlike his long-term acting partner Barry Fitzgerald, who went on to a Hollywood career and appeared in numerous films including *The Quiet Man* (1952), McCormick remained essentially a theatre actor all his life. Once the audiences who watched him on-stage are gone, the crucial eyewitness testimony to his distinction is gone too. Theatre is, by definition, a live art form; in the well-known aphorism of Edwin Booth, 'the actor is a sculptor who carves in snow'. How then to analyse the achievement of major Irish actors, even in a later period, when there begin to be full audio and video recordings of their stage performances?

The period since the 1950s has been a rich one in Irish acting talent. Many highly accomplished performers have made national and international reputations for themselves. Some, like Fiona Shaw, Kenneth Branagh, and Sinéad Cusack, have based their careers primarily outside Ireland. Others have worked both at home and abroad: Ray McAnally, T. P. McKenna, Colin Blakely, Bríd Brennan. Liam Neeson, Gabriel Byrne, and Brendan Gleeson all started as stage actors but are now best known for their cinema work, while Stephen Rea has been almost equally distinguished in both. It must always appear arbitrary to highlight a few performers at the expense of others. The four actors on whom this chapter is focused, Cyril Cusack (1910–93), Siobhán McKenna (1922–86), Donal McCann (1943–99), and Marie Mullen (1953–), have been chosen because, in spite of their work in film and television, they have been most celebrated as stage performers. And, though playing many non-Irish parts, their national origins were in each case a crucial dimension to their identity as actors: all four were fluent Irish speakers. One way to measure the achievement of a

---

[1] See Ulick O'Connor, 'The Abbey Portraits', *Irish Arts Review* 21, no. 3 (2004), 106–7.

major theatre actor is to point to certain key roles that they have defined for their generation. The aim of this chapter is to explore in relation to these four performers the contexts for such defining performances and the specific skills used to create them. In addition to theatre reviews and recordings (where they exist), I have relied heavily on the memories of fellow theatre professionals or audience members in seeking to capture the quality of the work.[2]

Cyril Cusack

One of the first productions in the new Abbey Theatre in 1967 was a highly successful staging of Dion Boucicault's *The Shaughraun* with Cyril Cusack in the lead. Seamus Kelly, drama critic of the *Irish Times*, saluted the occasion:

> [T]he greatest Playboy of this reviewer's time returned to his old home to give us what must be the greatest Conn since Boucicault created the part. [. . .] Cyril Cusack was, of course, a superb Shaughraun. Every shrug, every wink, every last dropped inflexion was dropped right into the audience's lap [. . .] It was a great comeback by a great Abbey artist, and the whole house rose to it.[3]

This was an actor at the height of his powers in a part he loved.

It was the first time the Abbey had ever staged a Boucicault play, and it was controversial, particularly when chosen to represent the theatre internationally at the World Theatre Festival season in London in 1968. For it was specifically to oppose such stage Irishry that the national theatre had been founded. 'We will show', thundered the manifesto writers of the Irish Literary Theatre in 1897, 'that Ireland is not the home of buffoonery and easy sentiment, as it has been represented.'[4] Cusack, however, had no such objection to the old-fashioned forms of melodrama, because he had grown up with them. As a child actor he had toured with his mother, Alice Violet Cusack, and her partner, the actor-manager Breffni O'Rorke, in a fit-up company, and he always looked back nostalgically to 'the peripatetic life, the makeshift shows, and the melodramatic fare'.[5] From 1944 to 1961 he was himself the actor-manager of Cyril Cusack Productions, recruiting companies to stage individual shows in which he generally had the starring role. Cusack was an Abbey-trained actor, playing there with occasional breaks from 1932 to 1945; but he can also be seen as a transitional figure, sharing many of the older features of the nineteenth-century star performer.

---

[2] I am extremely grateful to the following for their generosity in sharing their memories with me: Catherine Cusack, Sinéad Cusack, Joe Dowling, Christopher Fitz-Simon, Brian Friel, Margaret Mac Curtain, Patrick Mason, Marie Mullen, Tom Murphy, and Max Stafford-Clark. Where their views are cited in this chapter and not otherwise attributed, they are taken from my conversations with them.

[3] Seamus Kelly, ' "The Shaughraun" at the Abbey', *Irish Times*, 1 Feb. 1967.

[4] Augusta Gregory, *Our Irish Theatre: A Chapter in Autobiography*, 3rd edn. (Gerrards Cross: Colin Smythe, 1972), 20.

[5] Bridget Hourican, 'Cyril James Cusack', *Dictionary of Irish Biography* (Cambridge: Cambridge University Press, 2009).

FIG. 28.1 Cyril Cusack in Dion Boucicault's *The Shaughraun* (Abbey Theatre, 31 January 1967).

Courtesy of the Abbey Theatre and the National Library of Ireland.

Acting in Dublin in the 1930s gave plenty of opportunity for learning on the job. In his first years at the Abbey, Cusack was cast in a whole range of roles, not only in new plays by St John Ervine, Teresa Deevy, and George Shiels—all within the first four months of 1936—but also in *Macbeth* (Malcolm, 1934), and in the first Abbey production of *Candida* (Marchbanks, 1935).[6] Singled out from his initial Abbey appearance in a one-act play about the Civil War—A. P. Fanning's *Vigil* (1932)[7]—Cusack would have learned from the by

---

[6] See Lennox Robinson, *Ireland's Abbey Theatre: A History 1899–1951* (London: Sidgwick & Jackson, 1951), 160–2.

[7] Joseph Holloway commented on 24 Oct. 1932 in his unpublished journal, 'Impressions of a Dublin Playgoer': 'This young actor is the son of Breffni O'Rourke and shows great promise as an actor and has a very soft musical voice': Dublin, NLI, MS 1964.

then established style and practice of the experienced actors with whom he worked: F. J. McCormick, Barry Fitzgerald, Arthur Shields, Eileen Crowe, and Ria Mooney. It was ensemble acting in which the performers, with very limited rehearsal time, had to be able to work together to find their own places on stage.

This was the context for Cusack's playing of what was to be one of his signature roles, Christy Mahon in *The Playboy of the Western World*. According to his own account, his initial performance in the part on 26 July 1936 produced a strong protest from F. R. Higgins, one of the Abbey directors, against what was felt to be acting out of line with the theatre's tradition. Cusack's innovation, he felt in retrospect, was 'to play in a "style" compounded of the purely theatrical with a form of naturalism perilously near to being simply representational, two apparently conflicting elements which nevertheless are present and compatible in the work of Synge.'[8] It seems to have been the naturalistic dimension to Cusack's Christy that made Higgins so angry, in its challenge to the more stylized delivery of the part that had become normal in previous Abbey revivals. This was certainly what was thought most impressive in Cusack's acting at this early stage of his career. Micheál Mac Liammóir paid tribute to him in a comment ostensibly in 1938: 'He is by far the finest of the younger Irish actors [...] his sense of the detail of reality is well-nigh perfect; to the smallest things that help us to believe in a character he brings delicacy and precision.'[9]

Cusack had many opportunities to reprise his Christy Mahon, not only in an Abbey revival of 1943 but also in productions in Britain and, eventually, in his own company's staging that went to the first Paris Theatre Festival in 1954. Some critics felt that his musical lyricism in the part was achieved at the expense of other dimensions to the character. So James Agate, reviewing the 1939 Mercury Theatre production in London, commented: 'There should be Pistol as well as Romeo in this Irish lover, and the master of braggadocio as well as the wistful wooer.'[10] The record made of the 1954 production tends to support Agate's view.[11] Cusack's Playboy is wonderfully melodic, never missing a beat of the rhythmic lines, but a vulnerable, boyish character in need of the masterful love of Siobhán McKenna's Pegeen.

Shaw was one of Cusack's most admired playwrights, and his plays provided the actor with a whole range of roles. However, he was best suited to parts where he could command the theatre from an apparently marginal position: the waiter William in *You Never Can Tell* (Abbey, 1978) and, above all, Peter Keegan the unfrocked priest in *John Bull's Other Island* (Irish Theatre Company, 1980). Keegan is the wise madman of Shaw's play, adrift from the rest of the community, but commenting on it with piercing insight. Cusack had a virtuoso set-piece at the beginning of Act II, where the St Francis-like Keegan indulges a whimsical conversation with a grasshopper. At the beginning of Act IV there is a split scene in

[8] Cyril Cusack, 'A Player's Reflection on *Playboy*', in Thomas R. Whitaker (ed.), *Twentieth Century Interpretations of* The Playboy of the Western World (Englewood Cliffs, NJ: Prentice-Hall, 1969), 50.

[9] Micheál Mac Liammóir, *All for Hecuba* (1947), rev. edn. (Dublin: Progress Press, 1961), 328. This passage comes in what Mac Liammóir represents as a press conference in Belgrade during the Gate Theatre's tour of the Balkans, though the autobiography is fairly evidently fictionalized.

[10] James Agate, '"The Playboy of the Western World"', *Sunday Times*, 29 Jan. 1939.

[11] The recording was made in 1955 and included Milo O'Shea as well as Cusack and Siobhán McKenna in the cast: Naxos Audiobooks, NA287612.

which a crowd at one side of the stage laugh uproariously at Barny Doran's repeated tell-ing of the story of the pig and the motorcar, while on the other the sternly unamused ex-priest plays backgammon with Nora Reilly. Such was Cusack's presence that the audience, Christopher Fitz-Simon remembers, had eyes for nothing but the backgammon. Fintan O'Toole, reviewing a 1987 revival of the play at the Gaiety Theatre, commented on Cusack's Keegan: 'The role, full of self-deprecating wryness and understated fury, could have been written for him and he brings to bear on it all his characteristic sense of irony. His final attack on Broadbent is all the better for its quietness and his way with biting innuendo is matchless.'[12] Cusack's understated style made his surges of energy, as in this indictment of the predatory capitalist 'development' of Rosscullen, all the more effective.

The youthful Cusack cultivated a boyish, vulnerable charm; in later years, it was with a twinkly avuncular air that he wooed audiences. He was an actor who liked to be liked. Patricia Boylan, who knew him when she was a trainee actress at the Abbey in the 1930s, observed: 'Cyril's performances, in general, angled for a little sympathy for his characters, however unworthy of it they might have been.'[13] For this reason, he gave some of his best performances in roles that offered very little opportunity for this sort of ingratiation with the audience. In Brian Friel's *Crystal and Fox* (1968) he played the part of Fox, the actor-manager who wilfully alienates all the other performers in his troupe, and might have been read as a satiric portrait of Cusack himself, who had a name for selfish upstaging. Cast as Chebutykin, with his three daughters in Chekhov's *Three Sisters* (1990), in what was to be his last stage performance, he conveyed with chilling effectiveness the moral nullity of the drunken doctor. Drumm, the arid, embittered civil servant facing death in Hugh Leonard's *A Life* (1979) gave him another opportunity to play against type: 'As Cyril Cusack plays [Drumm], his voice winding round the other players like a thread soaked in acid, his face crumbling into wincing grimaces at the follies of his companions, Drumm is a figure who goes straight into the memory and stays there.'[14]

'Cusack is [. . .] the nearest thing in Europe to a *born* actor and with a unique reper-toire of histrionic skills.'[15] Whether or not there is such a thing as a born actor, from the beginning of his career Cyril Cusack showed some of the gifts for which he became cel-ebrated: his musical voice, his capacity for drawing an audience to him, the detailed obser-vation that enabled him to create living characters on stage. He was well capable of the knowing theatricality he showed off to such good effect in *The Shaughraun*. But his key quality was an understated naturalness that made the seemingly ordinary extraordinary. Fitz-Simon commented on how remarkably his skills as a cinema and television actor, where close-ups are possible, could be replicated in the theatre: Cusack was able to make tiny physical gestures and an apparently natural speaking voice produce telling effects even in a large auditorium. He was not an ensemble player, however, and had little time for direc-tors. When Patrick Mason, who worked with Cusack on *You Never Can Tell* and *John Bull's Other Island*, was asked what it was like directing him, he replied, 'You didn't.' Whatever

[12] Fintan O'Toole, 'Shaw's National Question', *Sunday Tribune*, 13 Sept. 1987.
[13] Patricia Boylan, *Gaps of Brightness* (Dublin: A. & A. Farmar, 2003), 107.
[14] I[rving].W[ardle]., 'Festivals of the Year: Theatre', *The Times*, 5 Dec. 1979.
[15] W. J. Igoe, 'Stage Irish?', *The Month*, Apr. 1980, cutting in Cyril Cusack papers, NLI MS 32,836, vol. 7.

the part he played, he was the star of his own show, which made for a competitive environment when cast opposite another star performer like Siobhán McKenna.

Siobhán McKenna

They were notably paired in a 1968 Abbey production of *The Cherry Orchard*, directed by Maria Knebel of the Moscow Art Theatre. The part of the useless uncle Gayev, with his eccentric mannerisms of sucking sweets and playing imaginary billiards, was perfect for Cusack. McKenna was also in her element as the estate owner Ranevskaya, the grandest of *grandes dames*. Both performances won the highest praise:

> As the dispossessed owner [Siobhán McKenna] gives the best performance of her career. Gorgeous in sweeping velvet and black plumes, she catches every mood of the generous, attractive and temperamental woman who has thrown her life away in frivolities. Cyril Cusack is equally magnificent in his portrayal of the charming ineffectual Gayev.[16]

However, McKenna complained that 'Cyril Cusack sucked sweets during some of her best lines'.[17] That undercutting was not accidental. Sinéad Cusack told me that, as an adoring 17-year-old, she heard her father's lines as Gayev and complimented him on the magnificence of his performance. 'Yes,' he said, 'I am coming in three notes below Siobhán and three paces behind.' The upstaging actor was cynical about McKenna's histrionics when they were cast as Fluther Good and Bessie Burgess in a 1976 Abbey production of *The Plough and the Stars*. Timing her death scene during the play's run, he commented acidly: 'Siobhán took two seconds longer tonight before she gave her last gasp.'[18]

Cusack was born into show business, playing his first stage part at the age of 6. By contrast, Siobhán McKenna, the Belfast-born daughter of a mathematics professor, growing up in Galway, had no theatrical background. She was recruited to act in the Irish-language theatre An Taibhdhearc when a student in University College Galway, simply because of her fluency in Irish, the language of the family at home. After graduation, she seems to have had no particular acting ambition when called to audition at the Abbey and given a contract there in 1944. F. J. McCormick was her mentor, who encouraged her not to accept a starring role she was offered in a film in her first year in the Abbey: 'Please stay at least three years,' she remembered him as saying. 'You could become an overnight star, but I also think you could become a real actress.'[19] In spite of her success in the film *Daughter of Darkness* (1948), she resisted a cinema career and continued to make her way as a 'real actress' in theatre both in Dublin and in London.

McKenna was first cast as Pegeen Mike by the actor director Shelah Richards. Richards was bent on getting rid of the 'old Synge-song thing' characteristic of traditional Abbey

---

[16] Maureen O'Farrell, *Evening Press*, 13 Oct. 1968, quoted in Micheál Ó hAodha, *Siobhán: A Memoir of an Actress* (Dingle: Brandon, 1994), 111–12.

[17] Ibid., 112.   [18] Ibid., 149.

[19] Siobhán McKenna, 'I Modelled Joan on My Mother', in E. H. Mikhail (ed.), *The Abbey Theatre: Interviews and Recollections* (Basingstoke: Macmillan, 1988), 209.

productions of the play, and coached McKenna in the new style she wanted instead for a production she took to the Edinburgh Theatre Festival in 1951. The American actor Carroll O'Connor, playing Michael James, spoke of the impact of McKenna's Pegeen: 'She used her magnificent voice, capable of the most wonderful contrasts—of great emotional power, and soft, deep gentleness—as I have never heard her use it.'[20] It was Seamus Kelly, however, who foresaw her potential with the right Christy: 'Miss McKenna is a fine dramatic actress [. . .] who if cast opposite Cyril Cusack might give us the greatest Pegeen Mike since Máire O'Neill.'[21]

She was given that opportunity in July 1953 when she joined Cusack's own production company in a staging of the play directed by the young actor Jack McGowran. Cusack was of course already known in the part of Christy, so the challenge was for McKenna to find the right style to partner him. The *Irish Times* reviewer thought that in the first act, 'Miss McKenna stresses Pegeen's shrewishness with too much stridency for my taste.' However, the romantic side of the character was developed, culminating in her 'sensitive and virtually flawless interpretation of the love scene in Act III', while the famous last line was daringly delivered in a whisper.[22] This was the production shown at the Theatre Festival in Paris in June 1954 to great acclaim. The red-haired McKenna as Pegeen was particularly admired for 'son ardeur de fille sauvage, [. . .] sa voix rauque, [. . .] ses taches de rousseur' (her wild girl's passion, her husky voice, her freckles).[23] The lifelike naturalness of the acting was celebrated in the French reviews, and it is clear that an element within this reaction was the association of McKenna/Pegeen with the stereotypical Irish colleen.

This was also a dimension in the reception of her most internationally successful role as the Maid in Shaw's *Saint Joan*. She first played the part in her own Irish translation, *San Siobhán*, at An Taibhdhearc in 1950, which led to the invitation of Micheál Mac Liammóir and Hilton Edwards to repeat the role in English at the Gate.[24] This hugely successful production, which opened in November 1953, with Edwards as Cauchon, Mac Liammóir as Warwick, and Jack McGowran as the Dauphin, led to a London revival directed by John Fernald. It was the London reviews of this production that really confirmed McKenna's international reputation: 'If Irish actress Siobhan McKenna can follow up on her achievement as Bernard Shaw's Saint Joan last night, she may become one of the greatest actresses alive.'[25] In the Irish-language version of the play, the French characters in the play were differentiated from the English by using different dialect forms; in English, McKenna played Joan with a Galway accent against the received standard English pronunciation of the other

[20] Ó hAodha, *Siobhán*, 45.   [21] Quoted in ibid., 34.

[22] 'The Playboy of the Western World', *Irish Times*, 21 July 1953.

[23] Christine de Rivoyre, 'Une troupe irlandaise joue "Le Baladin du Monde Occidentale" de Synge', *Le Monde*, 29 June 1954.

[24] For a detailed account, see Maureen Murphy, 'The Joan of a Generation: Siobhán McKenna's *San Siobhán*', in Michael Kenneally and Rhona Richman (eds.), *From 'English Literature' to 'Literatures in English'* (Heidelberg: Universitätsverlag Winter, 2005), 239–50. No copies of *San Siobhán* appear to have survived, in spite of the best efforts of Margaret Mac Curtain, McKenna's cousin, to locate one in archives or family papers.

[25] John Barber, 'Siobhan—She's Super', *Daily Express*, 29 Sept. 1954.

actors. This was a feature of her performance picked up by many reviewers and often linked to Joan's convincing spirituality:

> [A]mong the many Joans that I have seen I hail Siobhan McKenna, with her rich and lovely Irish brogue, as the most moving, and the most believable and the most fit for the company of the saints. Cropped-haired, stocky, feminine—blending the earthy and the spiritual—here was a Joan whose innate simplicity and common sense formed a firm and rocklike basis to perfect faith and perfect inspiration.[26]

An Irish Joan, coming from the western periphery, in her unsophisticated innocence carried complete conviction as the inspired Maid.

She played the part again in the US in 1956, where she was hailed by Elliot Norton as 'the greatest Joan of our generation, and on the basis of this performance, one of the greatest living actresses'.[27] Her New York Saint Joan gave her the career high-point accolade of appearing on the cover of *Life* magazine.[28] With successful performances in Shakespeare as well—Viola and Lady Macbeth at Stratford, Ontario under Tyrone Guthrie—McKenna by the end of the 1950s looked set to go on to a major international career. For a number of reasons, it did not quite work out like that. With her family base in Dublin, it was difficult for her to manage extended periods working abroad. And stage acting in Ireland and Britain was not all that financially rewarding. McKenna had been paid £12,000 for her part in *Daughter of Darkness*, but for her first London run in *Saint Joan* she was getting just £12 a week.[29] Even in *The Cherry Orchard* in 1968, she and Cusack would have been paid at the top rate for senior actors at the Abbey—£26 a week.[30] Like Cusack, she set up her own company, Quest Productions, in the mid-1970s, but it was not a great financial success. Though she continued to act and to direct, notably in her much admired one-woman show, *Here are Ladies* (1970), with which she toured the world for years, her histrionic performance style began to seem like old-fashioned overacting.

As a young woman, McKenna was acclaimed for her glamour and beauty, but she was never afraid to take on parts where she made herself look ugly. Thus, in Brian Friel's *The Loves of Cass McGuire* (1966, Abbey 1967), she gave a bravura performance in the title part as the 'blowzy, boozy, vulgar Irish-American emigrant. [. . .] Siobhán did not shirk looking awful for a change. Her costume and make-up were as outrageous as her splutters and spits. She wore wads of padding all over.'[31] That willingness to appear physically repulsive was one dimension to the extraordinary achievement of her last stage role as Mommo in Tom Murphy's *Bailegangaire*, the part that for many of those who saw it reinstated the sense of McKenna's extraordinary ability. The senile grandmother sitting up

[26] Elizabeth Frank, 'The Best St. Joan I Have Ever Seen', *News Chronicle*, 29 Sept. 1954.
[27] Elliot Norton, 'Irish Actress is Great in "Joan"', *Boston Globe*, 20 Aug. 1956. A recording of this production can be accessed at: https://archive.org/details/BernardShawsSaintJoan. Accessed 10 Oct. 2014.
[28] *Life Magazine*, 10 Sept. 1956.
[29] Thomas Wiseman, 'Miss McKenna Gets Ready to Pack Up—After a Success on a Shoe-String', *Evening Standard*, 2 Oct. 1954.
[30] See Ó hAodha, *Siobhán*, 107.   [31] Ibid., 107–8.

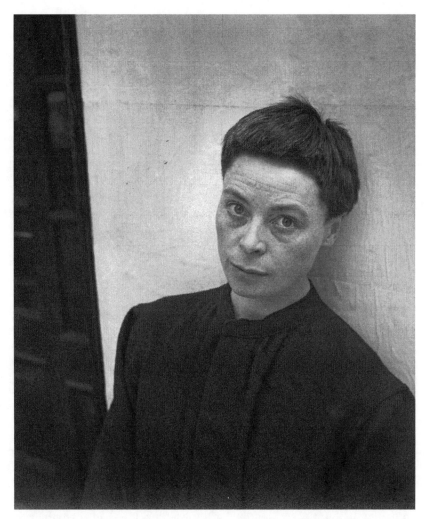

FIG. 28.2 Siobhán McKenna as The Maid in G. B. Shaw's *Saint Joan* (Gate, 18 November 1954).

Photo: Cecil Beaton. Courtesy of the Cecil Beaton Studio Archive at Sotheby's.

in bed spitting out bits of her food, her apparently toothless face framed by the mass of uncombed red-brown hair, with an expression varying from lost vacancy through dark brooding to malevolent spite, was not a pretty spectacle. The role of Mommo stuck in the bed narrating, literally endlessly, the story of the laughing contest, and 'how the place called Bochtán [. . .] came by its new appellation, Bailegangaire, the place without laughter' suited her perfectly.[32] According to Tom Murphy, she was a perfect mimic, who could imitate not only the voice but the body language of others in conversation. This allowed

---

[32] Tom Murphy, *Plays: 2* (London: Methuen, 1993), 92.

her to differentiate all the characters in the story, not to mention the laughter of the con-
testants. She also had a remarkable memory for the very long and demanding part; Marie
Mullen, cast as her carer granddaughter Mary, was astonished at how well she knew the
lines even before rehearsals started. And it cannot have made it easier when Murphy, seeing how far over-length the play was at dress rehearsal stage, cut some thirty-five minutes
out of the script.

All the reviewers of the Druid production of the play when it opened in Galway agreed
that this was an extraordinary return to form for McKenna. Fintan O'Toole's salute to the
performance was also a recognition of the significance of the play in the history of Irish
theatre going back to *Cathleen ni Houlihan* (1902).

> Siobhán McKenna emerges in *Bailegangaire*, as she has not done in Ireland in recent years,
> as a great actress. Her grand style and the amazing range of her voice work here not as mere
> display but as a superbly disciplined and well-aimed performance. The scale of her style,
> the fact that Mother Ireland hovers in the background of her stage persona, is exactly right
> here, precisely because she *is*, in one dimension of Mommo, Mother Ireland. But it is not the
> Mother Ireland of long and noble suffering, weeping and wailing. It is a Mother Ireland who
> spits and urinates.[33]

When the production transferred to the Donmar Warehouse in London, the critics were
somewhat more critical of the play but not of McKenna's performance:

> There is something witchlike about her trembling fingers, her sidelong glances as she
> speaks now to the quilt, now to the floor, speaking from some long-unspeakable past
> [. . .] The booms and cackles of her laughter, the invention and variety of tone that enable
> her to people the remembered scene, all are conjured up in her unstrained, unfaltering
> voice.[34]

The wonder of McKenna's achievement in this part could only be increased by the
knowledge that she was seriously ill at the time she played it. A heavy smoker, she had been
diagnosed with lung cancer years before; according to Margaret Mac Curtain, she had told
her family but no one involved in the production knew. She was to die in November 1986,
just months after performing as Mommo for the last time. It was an appropriately heroic
ending for a larger-than-life performer. 'The queen of Irish theatre', Tom Murphy called
her; 'she worked in big colours, big strokes.'[35] Allowing for the rhetoric of graveside ora-
tions, there was truth in Brian Friel's eulogy. Defining the term 'star' in the theatre, as 'an
actress who was unique in that she personified an idea a country has of itself at any particular time', Friel declared 'Siobhán was our pre-eminent Irish star, indeed our only star. For
people of my generation, she personified an idea of Ireland.'[36] And for non-Irish audiences
as well, that 'idea of Ireland' was crucial to the significance of her Pegeen Mike, her Joan,
and her Mommo.

[33] Fintan O'Toole, 'The Old Woman's Brood', *Sunday Tribune*, 8 Dec. 1985.
[34] Jeremy Kingston, 'Bailegangaire, Donmar Warehouse', *Times*, 21 Feb. 1986.
[35] From the documentary directed by Brian Reddin, *Siobhán*, TG4, 2001.
[36] Quoted in Ó hAodha, *Siobhán*, 180.

DONAL McCANN

In the laudatory reviews of the 1967 *Shaughraun*, it was not only Cusack who won the reviewers' praise: 'It was a great night too, for one of the most junior members of the company. Donal McCann's Captain Molineux was not only engaging. It was a comedy performance as neatly timed as Cusack's own.'[37] On its transfer to London, his Molineux, played with an 'r' lisp, was picked out as 'a superlative performance by Donal McCann who translates British moral rectitude into physical comedy—bouncing nervously up and down on his heels, and rooted to the spot until the situation calls out an approved spur to gentlemanly behaviour at which he is off like a greyhound'.[38] These were among the first of many critics' tributes to the acting skills and character creation of McCann.

In 1967 he was indeed still one of the most junior members of the Abbey company, though he had been with them for over three years. Like McKenna before him, he had served his apprenticeship playing parts in English and in Irish, appearing initially in the potboiling comedies of his father, John McCann.[39] He had already had a major success as the title character in *Tarry Flynn* (1966)—the stage adaptation of Patrick Kavanagh's novel—one of the first shows staged at the new Abbey. He was to partner Peter O'Toole in the Abbey's first production of *Waiting for Godot* (1969) and played with him also in *Arms and the Man* (Gaiety 1969). One of the advantages of being a young Abbey actor in the 1960s was to have the benefit of learning from senior members of the company, even if that brought some anxiety of influence. McCann, for instance, much admired the work of Philip O'Flynn, and when, much later, in 1986, he was cast as Captain Boyle—a part O'Flynn had played for years—he told his fellow actor Garrett Keogh: 'The only thing I want to do […] is to get Philip O'Flynn's voice out of my head.'[40]

Through the 1970s McCann was primarily based in London, extending his reputation in theatre and particularly television, becoming very well known as Phineas Finn in *The Pallisers*, the BBC adaptation of Trollope's political novels.[41] However, McCann's personal life was troubled at this time by the break-up of his marriage, depression, and drinking. McCann was widely known to be an alcoholic. He was drunk on stage in Tom Murphy's *The Blue Macushla* (1980), contributing to the play's failure, according to the playwright. He failed to show up at all for a performance of *Arms and the Man* at the Abbey (1982), resulting in a four-year absence from the stage. Yet it was in this period that he gave one of his outstanding performances in Brian Friel's *Faith Healer* (1979, Abbey 1980).

According to Joe Dowling, the director of the play, McCann arrived drunk for early rehearsals, and had to be given an ultimatum: stay dry or the production would be pulled.

---

[37] Kelly, '"The Shaughraun" at the Abbey'.

[38] Irving Wardle, 'Abbey Restored to Old Eminence', *Times*, 23 May 1968.

[39] What appears to have been his first performance with the Abbey, then still in exile in the Queen's Theatre, was in John McCann's *Put a Beggar on Horseback*, 2 Dec. 1963.

[40] Garrett Keogh, 'Goodnight Sweet Prince', in Pat Laffan and Faith O'Grady (ed.), *Donal McCann Remembered* (Dublin: New Island, 2000), 56.

[41] Lawrence William White, 'McCann, Donal Francis', in *Dictionary of Irish Biography* (Cambridge: Cambridge University Press, 2009). Most of the biographical data on McCann in this chapter are drawn from this source.

Though this condition was met and the actor did not resume drinking until after the end of the run, the figure of Frank Hardy, self-destructive alcoholic that he is, constantly tormented by the nature of his intermittent gift of faith healing, must have had a special resonance for McCann. At one level McCann was confident enough of his powers. Passing 'The Vacant Throne', that Abbey picture of F. J. McCormick, the actor Garrett Keogh remembers McCann remarking, 'Here! You can tell them, the [. . .] throne is vacant no longer!'[42] Yet Dowling says that McCann could never be satisfied with his own performance, however much and often it was praised. A quotation from a press interview with the actor suggests the combination of arrogance and dread that gave such authority to his performance as Hardy: 'Okay who am I to disagree with other people's judgement that I am the best actor to come out of the country in years and I am both aware and fearful of my talent.'[43]

In the first of his two monologues as Frank Hardy, he had to hold an audience for thirty-five minutes on a stage bare of everything but a few empty chairs and the tatty banner advertising 'Francis Hardy Faith Healer One Night Only'. It was done with an extraordinary mixture of charm, storytelling skills, and a sense of mesmerizing power that turned the theatre audience into the patients the faith healer came to cure. Acting in low relief through the narration, he could drop into a perfect mocking version of his Cockney manager Teddy's voice, authenticated when Teddy's monologue was heard. For other speakers, such as the wedding guests in the Ballybeg pub, or the clipping read out from a Welsh paper, there was just a slight colouring of the accent. It was very unshowy by comparison with McKenna's virtuoso ventriloquism in *Bailegangaire*, but just as effective. It expressed Hardy's capacity to make people up, to bring them into a life dependent on his sketching of them. Yet there were also moments when he played an impersonation of himself, sitting head in hands on the chair waiting for the people to appear for his 'performance'. McCann as Hardy was at once charlatan and shaman, live drunk and dead ghost, and a consummate actor aware of all the parts he was playing.[44]

McCann's triumphant return to the theatre after four years' absence came with his performance as the Captain in Joe Dowling's production of *Juno and the Paycock* (1986) at the Gate. Dowling and producer Michael Colgan took a risk in casting McCann, given his unreliable reputation, and even during rehearsals there was an embarrassing incident when the actor appeared in court charged with burglary, having broken into a house in a state of extreme drunkenness. In the event, it proved a risk well worth taking. Dowling had reconceived the play as a much darker work than it had become in cosy comic renderings at the Abbey, stressing the background of poverty and long-term unemployment. McCann's Boyle fitted well with this vision of the play. The production and the very talented cast were all praised, but in Colm Tóibín's view: 'The power of the production lies in the way McCann rescues the Captain from being a comic figure, too lazy to work, and a drunken bully. [. . .] His lies about his legs are rendered as self-deception: his refusal to work seems to arise from some deep spiritual enervation.'[45] Clive Barnes summed up a widespread feeling when the

---

[42] Keogh, in Laffan and O'Grady, *Donal McCann Remembered*, 55.

[43] Michael Sheridan, 'Return of the Captain', *Irish Press*, 15 July 1986.

[44] Though I saw the original production in 1980, this description is largely based on the archival recording of the 1990 Abbey revival of the play; my thanks to Mairead Delaney, the Abbey archivist, for making it available to me.

[45] Colm Tóibín, 'Dowling's "Juno" Has Sheer Magic', *Sunday Independent*, 20 July 1986.

FIG. 28.3 Donal McCann as Frank Hardy in the Abbey production of Brian Friel's *Faith Healer* (Abbey, 28 August 1980; the play premièred in New York in 1979).

Photo. Fergus Bourke. Courtesy of Abbey Theatre.

production transferred to New York: 'McCann [. . .] has redefined the role for all time, or at least any future of living memory.'[46]

As actors age, they move up the range from *jeune premier* through character parts to the great older roles. McCann always regretted being a few inches too short for romantic leads and, dying of pancreatic cancer at 56, he never lived to play Lear. But his last stage performance as Thomas Dunne in Sebastian Barry's *The Steward of Christendom* (1995) gave him a Lear-like part. Many reviews of the play indeed made the comparison with Lear— not surprisingly, given that the character is the mad father of three daughters, formerly in authority as superintendent in the Dublin Metropolitan Police, now incarcerated in

---

[46] Clive Barnes, 'Night of Irish Irony a Shining Emerald', *New York Post*, 22 June 1988.

FIG. 28.4 Donal McCann as Captain Boyle in Seán O'Casey's *Juno and the Paycock* (Gate Theatre, 15 July 1986).

Photo: Tom Lawlor. Courtesy of Gate Theatre.

a workhouse/mental asylum, stripped to a pair of grey long johns. Dunne is onstage for the whole play, rambling in mind-slip memory from early childhood through his man-hood years as policeman, husband, and father, through to his present senile self. When the play opened in the small Royal Court Upstairs, there was virtually unanimous praise for the play, the Out of Joint production directed by Max Stafford-Clark, and the perfor-mance: 'Donal McCann as Thomas Dunne is outstanding. He looks like a medieval saint with sad simian features and a mouth that opens to an O, then freezes in twisted contem-plation of the story he tells. He passes his hand over his shaven head, as if checking that he still exists.'[47] When the play moved to the Gate in Dublin, the Irish critics pitched the

---

[47] Kate Kellaway, 'Hail to Christendom', *Observer*, 9 Apr. 1995.

eulogies even higher:[48] 'this is a performance by Donal McCann such as I have never seen on any stage, and which I am unequivocally certain will rank as one of the great international milestones of the century.'[49]

How was such distinction achieved? Brian Friel spoke of McCann's intuitive theatrical intelligence, a quality that cannot be learned. Sebastian Barry called his style one of 'extravagant minimalism',[50] and he certainly had the capacity to make less do more theatrically. Stafford-Clark pointed to the physicality of his acting and his powers of perfect recall. When he had established a particular gesture, such as the hands behind the head used recurrently in *Steward*, he could reproduce it precisely every time. He was difficult to direct, both Dowling and Stafford-Clark agreed. He would listen to directors, act on their notes if they fitted with his conception of the part, and otherwise ignore them. He worked enormously hard, and for the duration of the run of a play could live like a monk with a completely disciplined routine. For all his problems with alcohol and his almost equal addiction to gambling on horses or dogs, no one ever doubted the utter seriousness of his commitment to his acting, and no one who saw him in his best roles will ever forget the experience.

MARIE MULLEN

'[A]s the old woman Siobhán McKenna gives a performance of astonishing virtuosity; but I think I shall remember for equally long the radiant goodness that Marie Mullen brings to the role of the grand-daughter Mary.'[51] This is a remarkable tribute to Mullen's acting in *Bailegangaire*, given the competition. Cast as the resident carer Mary, unable to communicate with her senile grandmother, Mommo, who refuses to recognize her, for much of the first act of the play she has nothing to do but to listen in frustration to the story she has heard so often she knows it by heart. That, though, gives her the opening to recite parts of the tale when Mommo has fallen asleep, mimicking the old woman's manner. When Mary suddenly decides that instead of trying to still Mommo, she will urge her on to the end, the character becomes the dynamic agent of the play. Acting with the veteran performer was a learning opportunity for Mullen, then in her early 30s. The play became a moment at which one generation of Irish actors could hand over to another.

The case of Marie Mullen is significantly different from that of the other three actors considered in this chapter, as she is still very much alive and working. At the time of going to press, she has just moved up into McKenna's role as Mommo in a new Druid production of *Bailegangaire*.[52] It is not possible to attempt a retrospective on her work as with Cusack, McKenna, and McCann; judgements are necessarily provisional. She is unlike the other

---

[48]   David Nowlan, 'Observing the Son of Christendom—Dying', *Irish Times*, 28 Apr. 1995.

[49]   Emer O'Kelly, 'Old Man's Nightmare', *Sunday Independent*, 30 Apr. 1995.

[50]   Quoted in the documentary directed by Bob Quinn, *Donal McCann: It Must Be Done Right*, RTÉ, 1999.

[51]   Francis King, 'The Love and Horror of War', *Sunday Telegraph*, n.d., NUIG, James Hardiman Library, McKenna papers, T20/40/9.

[52]   Produced autumn 2014, in tandem with *Brigit*, a new play by Murphy which is a prequel to *Bailegangaire*.

FIG. 28.5 Marie Mullen as Mary and Siobhán McKenna as Mommo in Tom Murphy's *Bailegangaire* (Druid, 15 December 1985).

Photo: Amelia Stein.

performers, also, in that the great bulk of her acting has been with Druid, the theatre company she helped to establish in 1975. But she resembles the earlier actors in that she developed through the apprenticeship of student, then professional, acting rather than being trained in a regular drama school. She is similar, too, in working mainly in theatre rather than film and television.

In Druid's first season in 1975, Mullen played Pegeen Mike opposite Mick Lally's Christy Mahon. By her own account, however, she was only a moderately good Pegeen. She really came into her own in the 1980s productions of the play, cast as the Widow Quin. The director Garry Hynes chose to see the character as much younger than she has often been played, with a live sexual chemistry between herself and Christy (Maeliosa Stafford). There was a dramatic moment in Act II, after the Widow had made her appeal to Christy, when Mullen moved forward towards him, arms apart with expectant tenderness in her face, only to be dashed by his 'Aid me for to win Pegeen'.[53] A moment's dismay was followed by a switch

[53] I am reliant here on the televised recording of the 1986 production in the Donmar Warehouse, London, broadcast by Channel 4, a copy of which is held in the Druid archives, James Hardiman Library, NUIG.

back to her habitual look of cunning and guarded cynicism. Watching that performance in comparison with her role as Mary in *Bailegangaire* and the later Maureen in Martin McDonagh's *The Beauty Queen of Leenane* (1996) makes one aware of the similarity of the parts—all of them ageing, sexually frustrated young women—and how differently Mullen played them.

It was the vulnerability of Mary that was most obvious, her need for love in the relationship with Mommo. Mullen enacted exactly the character as described in Murphy's opening stage direction: 'A "private" person, an intelligent, sensitive woman, a trier, but one who is possibly near breaking point. It is lovely when she laughs.'[54] Mary had none of the knowingness of Mullen's Widow Quin and none of the Widow's sexual urgency. McDonagh's lampoon style made for another sort of characterization again with Maureen, the part for which Mullen won a Tony award when the Druid production of the play transferred to Broadway in 1998. Superficially a lonely and frustrated woman, caught in the trap of looking after her tyrannically demanding old mother—a situation strikingly similar to that of Mary in *Bailegangaire*—she has a psychotic dimension to her personality, driving her to torture and finally murder, conveyed by Mullen with a frighteningly frenetic energy.

There has been no question of typecasting with the parts Mullen has played. In its early years, Druid experimented with contemporary US drama and with Jacobean tragedy. In a spell with the Royal Shakespeare Company in 1989, she played in *King Lear* and *The Man of Mode*. In the 2007 Druid production of *Long Day's Journey into Night*, she was cast as Mary Tyrone opposite the American actor James Cromwell. But the long-planned project of *DruidSynge*, the production of all six of Synge's plays together, was conceived to some extent as a showcase for Mullen's versatility within a single idiom of Irish drama.[55] This was very much the reaction of audiences and critics watching her performance:

> Marie Mullen [. . .] appears in no less than five significant roles, embodying an astonishing range of Synge's powerfully drawn female characters, defining each with indelible artistry, humor and compassion. [. . .] Ms Mullen's achievement may well come to rank among the legendary acting accomplishments of the era. She is a great actress, delivering an astonishing series of performances here.[56]

For Mullen herself, it was the part of Maurya in *Riders to the Sea*, the first play in the cycle when they were acted together, which she found most challenging. She had difficulty reaching the core of the role in rehearsals, and initially, she says, the words of the last great speech 'felt like sawdust'. It was only when she realized that the play was 'a lament from start to finish', with the whole cast as extensions of Maurya in a communal pool of emotion, that she found her way into it. There was an extraordinary shift of gear, then, for the gloriously comic part of the wild tinker woman Mary Byrne in *The Tinker's Wedding*, kitted out in modern leather coat and wellington boots.

Having to play Mary Byrne, the blind beggar in *The Well of the Saints*, immediately after this was the most testing in terms of energy: 'I used to charge down after *Tinker's Wedding*

---

[54] Murphy, *Plays: 2*, 91.

[55] Garry Hynes, interview with the author, 9 July 2013; an edited version of this interview was published in *Irish University Review* 45, no. 1 (2015), 117–25.

[56] Charles Isherwood, 'Nasty, Brutish and Gloriously Long', *New York Times*, 25 Aug. 2005.

FIG. 28.6 Marie Mullen as Mary in J. M. Synge's *The Tinker's Wedding, DruidSynge* (29 June 2005).

Photo: Keith Pattison. Courtesy of Druid Theatre Company.

and I'd get dressed for Mary Doul and I'd a pain in my stomach from shouting and screaming as the tinker woman. And I can remember thinking can I get breath to get the first speech out.' There was a welcome break before her appearance as Widow Quin in *Playboy* and finally Lavarcham in *Deirdre of the Sorrows*. Michael Billington summed up the impression of many, calling Mullen 'the greatest Irish actress since Siobhán McKenna'.[57]

This sort of accolade is suggestive of the sense of continuity and inheritance in the perception of the Irish acting tradition. Marie Mullen succeeds Siobhán McKenna in the role of Mommo, having played opposite her thirty years before. A young Donal McCann, near the start of his career, shares the stage with Cyril Cusack, coming belatedly to the great comic starring role of the Shaughraun. The iconic parts of Irish drama are there as the challenges for each generation of Irish actors like the equivalent Shakespearean roles in Britain. But because the pool of actors is much smaller, there is a more acute awareness of the actors' predecessors: McCann had to get Philip O'Flynn's voice as Boyle out of his head before he could occupy the role; Cyril Cusack said that he 'went in at number four' as Christy at the Abbey, the fourth actor to play the part.[58] The style of acting, also, can be seen as part of a distinctive tradition. The members of the original Abbey company, trained by the Fay brothers, were famous for the detailed observation of their low-key, naturalistic performances. Though this tended to become an Abbey 'manner' over time, the refreshing

---

[57] Michael Billington, 'Synge for Your Supper ... and Breakfast and Lunch', *Guardian*, 19 July 2005.
[58] Speech at the opening of the first Synge Summer School in Rathdrum, 1991.

changes in style of Cusack playing the Playboy, or of Dowling directing *Juno*, were in the direction of renewing that original realism.

None of the four actors looked at in this chapter had a full drama school training; they may be among the last Irish performers of whom that is true. Most actors now graduate from the Lir, Ireland's National Academy for the Performing Arts, founded in 2011, from the Gaiety School of Acting, or from drama schools in Britain. In place of such professional training, Cusack, McKenna, and McCann, working as members of the regular Abbey repertory company, were afforded the opportunity to play an astonishing range of roles very early in their careers, and something similar was true for Mullen in Druid. This not only allowed them to showcase their versatility. It also gave them a special rapport with Irish audiences who saw them so often in so many parts, which promoted the awareness of their star quality: McCann could feel that he was occupying the throne left vacant by F. J. McCormick. These are actors who achieved international success, not merely local celebrity. But the basis for that success, and perhaps the continuing preference of all four for theatre performance over film and television, was the special intimacy of playing to live audiences in relatively small auditoria in the benchmark parts of Irish drama.

CHAPTER 29

··

BECKETT AT THE GATE

··

JULIE BATES

THE way Michael Colgan tells it, the Beckett Festival at the Gate Theatre in 1991 arose out of a moment of dithering.[1] He visited Beckett in Paris in 1988 to follow up on a recent Gate production of *Waiting for Godot* directed by Walter Asmus. This production had originally been planned for the National Theatre in London, but they had rejected Beckett's choice of Asmus as director. When Colgan learned this, he offered Beckett the Gate. At their meeting in 1988, Colgan was planning to suggest that the Gate might stage *Krapp's Last Tape* and was hoping to discover what he described as another 'poverty', where Beckett had encountered difficulties in staging one of his plays as he wished, and that the Gate might oblige.

> And when I was talking to him, I couldn't make up my mind, I started dithering a bit and I said I'd really love to do *Krapp's Last Tape*, and of course you're talking to this great man and you love it all, and then I said like a gibbering idiot, but I'd like to do *Endgame* and of course I'd love to do *Happy Days*—so it was one of those conversations, and he said 'What do you want to do?' and I said 'Well Sam I'm going to be honest with you, I'd like to do all of them.' And he said 'You can't be serious' and it was *exactly* at that moment between my sentence and his and my next sentence that I got the idea to do all of them—it wasn't that I went to him with this or I'd had the idea in the bath or on a walk. And I often wonder to this day did he inspire that in some way by saying 'You can't be serious'.

From this moment of dithering, a feat of organizational bravura resulted. The 1991 Beckett Festival at the Gate was a masterfully ambitious, novel, and successful series of events that involved the first ever retrospective of Beckett's nineteen stage plays, as well as television and radio productions by RTÉ, and a series of lectures and exhibitions in Trinity College Dublin. Over three weeks, from 1 to 20 October 1991, the cultural landscape of Dublin was dominated by Beckett.

---

[1] In November 2013 I interviewed Michael Colgan, and in December 2013 and May 2014 I explored the archives of the Gate Theatre on Parnell Square in Dublin. I thank Colgan for his generosity in granting permission to draw on material from the interview and archives. All subsequent quotations from Colgan, unless otherwise credited, are from this interview.

Producer-Unfriendliness of Beckett's Works

Colgan was a relatively young theatre director of 38 when he made the outrageous suggestion to Beckett that the Gate stage all his plays at once; yet despite the momentary loss of poise he describes as precipitating this idea, he never once lost sight of the challenges inherent in producing Beckett's works. Many years later, describing the thought process that led to his inspired suggestion in 1988, Colgan relates how, as a 'devotee' of Beckett's drama, it was extremely difficult to identify one of the nineteen plays as his preference. However, he adds, 'I certainly didn't want to do the little ones because they weren't producer-friendly, so it was either going to be *Endgame, Happy Days* or *Krapp.*'

Despite his awareness of the difficulties posed by Beckett's late works, Colgan's proposal to stage all Beckett's plays, including the brief, allusive later pieces, may have had its origin in his recognition that the non-commercial nature of these plays largely consigned them to student productions. Colgan made this observation rather ruefully in an interview with Ciaran Carty that appeared in the *Sunday Tribune* before the Festival, in recollection, perhaps, of his own formative experiences as a student in Players Theatre in Trinity College. In this interview, Colgan related how he explained the practical fundamentals of theatre to Beckett:

> I spoke to Sam about how the plays sadly—and I have to be cautious about how I say this—had become the domain of the avant-garde or students, how we all started off our careers with a Beckett play because it's hard to be found out. Normal commercial plays are two hours twenty minutes long with nine actors and two sets and a fifteen minute interval to get people home at the right time. Sam didn't cater for anything like that. He wrote a play for seven minutes and another for twelve and another for twenty-six. It's impossible to do a twenty-week run of *Footfalls* because it would start at 8pm and end at 8.15pm. Therefore it can't attract the money nor afford actors like Anthony Hopkins or Albert Finney. I was explaining to Sam that there was a problem there and that the only way to overcome it might be to do all the plays together and make it an event.[2]

Notwithstanding Colgan's sublime confidence in lecturing Beckett on the principles of successful writing for the stage—and then drawing on the exchange as an anecdote when promoting the Festival—it was still a moment of calculated risk-taking on his part to propose a full retrospective of Beckett's work. Such an undertaking meant that Beckett's truncated late plays, more suited perhaps to art galleries than theatres, would be staged in Dublin at a time when Colgan perceived there to be little appetite for avant-garde or experimental theatre. Calculated and extremely successful risk-taking, however, has largely defined Colgan's career.

---

[2] Ciaran Carty, 'Shutting the Gate with a Promise', *Sunday Tribune*, 15 Sept 1991. Where newspaper articles are unpaginated, this is because the material is derived from clippings in 'The Beckett Festival 1991' folder, Dublin, Gate archives, PF77e.

COLGAN AT THE GATE

Beckett is not, of course, the only important playwright with whom Colgan has developed a successful working relationship at the Gate; such was the success of the Beckett Festival in 1991 that it opened the door for two festivals of Harold Pinter's work in 1994 and 1997. Pinter was involved on both occasions as a director and actor, something that gave Colgan great satisfaction, given his lasting regret that the Beckett Festival did not come about until after Beckett's death in 1989. Colgan also had an extremely positive and loyal professional relationship with Brian Friel, having premièred many of his works over the years. Just as the Gate marked the occasion of Pinter's 75th birthday in 2005 by staging two of his plays, it also celebrated Friel's 80th birthday in 2009 with a season of his works called 'Gate Friel'.

Colgan's development of lasting personal and professional relationships with three such significant playwrights has led to many of the high points in his career, but it also gives some indication of the theatrical range he has brought to the Gate. He combines a love for the avant-garde, experimental, and provocative with an unhesitating business acumen and desire to be at the centre of things, pulling strings and directing operations. His instinct for grand gestures and determination to make them a success has made him enormously influential in determining audience tastes over many decades in Ireland. That Beckett recognized Colgan's talents in this regard is certain, for Beckett repeatedly asked about the progress of what he described as 'Michael's plan' after their meeting in 1988. For all his horror of promotion, Beckett also wanted his work to find an audience, and Colgan must have appeared as exactly the sort of ringmaster, lobbyist, aesthetic champion, and organizational dynamo that Beckett needed.

In an article that appeared in the *Irish Times* in 2013, Fintan O'Toole assessed Colgan's thirty-year career at the Gate, beginning with a description of how he found himself in the job in the first place. A plan had been contrived to save the Gate from its steady decline and dwindling reputation after the loss of its charismatic founders, Micheál Mac Liammóir and Hilton Edwards. The board of the Gate, headed by the architect Michael Scott, proposed a rota of four directors—Garry Hynes, Patrick Mason, Sean McCarthy, and Pat Laffan—to take turns programming the theatre for three months each year, while Douglas Kennedy, then manager of the Peacock Theatre, would be what they described as the overall 'coordinator' of the theatre. Colgan intervened, telling first Pat Laffan and then Michael Scott that it was a terrible plan. As O'Toole described it, Scott responded by offering Colgan the role of coordinator, who made a 'breathtakingly arrogant' counter-offer:

> [Colgan] would not become a coordinator. He would become artistic director, managing director, company secretary and a member of the board. In effect, the Gate would become Michael Colgan's theatre. Scott offered him the job. Colgan then insisted that the job offer be rescinded so he could be interviewed properly by the Gate board. They obeyed: he was already in charge.
>
> And then he woke up at 4am, sitting bolt upright, his neck wet with terror, realising just how far his ego had carried him beyond all sensible norms. [. . .] He decided there and then to call Joe Dowling, former artistic director of the Abbey, and ask him to take on the same role at the Gate.
>
> 'I'd step aside and be the managing director and there was no doubt that was where my forte was, in administration. That was where I felt myself most confident.'[3]

3 Fintan O'Toole, 'The Gatekeeper', *Irish Times*, 30 Nov. 2013.

BECKETT IN THE IRISH IMAGINATION IN 1991

Confidence is something Colgan identified as an essential component of the success of the Beckett Festival, for it first of all required, in his telling of events, the breaking up of fallow ground in the Irish imagination to create an audience for Beckett's work. Colgan describes how, having come to know Beckett 'and being in some sort of awe of this man who wrote so beautifully and so carefully', he saw his role in part as seeking to 'redress unjustifiable neglect' by promoting Beckett's work and reputation in Ireland. (Ever the pragmatist, Colgan was quick to follow this comment by noting drily: 'There's a lot of justifiable neglect, you know—I'm not going to be doing a festival of Arrabal.') Moreover, Colgan explains how he had for a long time been amazed that the Abbey and Peacock theatres relatively rarely staged any work by Beckett—something that worked in his favour given the dynamic of 'permanent opposition' that existed between the Gate and the Abbey. These assertions, however, only tell part of the story of Beckett's place in the Irish imagination before the Festival at the Gate in 1991.

In 1984, J. C. C. Mays asserted that Beckett's 'incorporation into the Irish tradition' had been a 'recent' phenomenon.[4] Mays described how, until the mid- to late 1970s, Beckett was absent or marginal in the curriculum at University College Dublin and in various Irish academic publications, and observed of Beckett's place in the popular Irish imagination at this time, 'Ignorance was compounded by defensiveness, and people didn't think much about Beckett because the word was that he didn't think much of them.'[5] In Colgan's opinion, this was still the case in 1991, and he identifies himself as one of the very few with an interest in Beckett at the time. While Rónán McDonald may have concluded his 2009 assessment of Beckett's academic reception in Ireland with the observation that 'Beckett is both absent and present in Irish studies, just as Ireland is absent and present in Beckett's own work', it is however important to challenge Colgan's retrospective assessment of Beckett's neglect in Ireland in the late 1980s and early 1990s.[6] In terms of theatrical performances, Colgan himself had enjoyed recent success with Barry McGovern's I'll Go On in 1985, the commissioning of which had brought him into contact with Beckett in the first place; while at an institutional level, it was in 1992 that Trinity College Dublin named its theatre department after Beckett, in a gesture to celebrate its quatercentenary by honouring one of its most successful alumni.

In fact, Beckett's plays had enjoyed a long pedigree in Dublin theatres for decades before Colgan ever intervened on his behalf with the Festival at the Gate. The first productions of Waiting for Godot at the Pike and Abbey theatres were landmark cultural events in the life of the city. Christopher Morash has identified the Dublin response to the Pike's production of Waiting for Godot in 1955 as one that 'belies the image of Ireland in the 1950s as an intellectually timid cultural wasteland'.[7] Waiting for Godot

[4] J. C. C. Mays, 'Young Beckett's Irish Roots', Irish University Review 14, no. 1 (1984), 18.

[5] Ibid., 22.

[6] Rónán McDonald, 'Groves of Blarney: Beckett's Academic Reception in Ireland', Nordic Irish Studies 8, no. 1 (2009), 33.

[7] Christopher Morash, A History of Irish Theatre: 1601–2000 (Cambridge: Cambridge University Press, 2002), 206.

broke records for the longest continuous run in Irish theatre history from October 1955 to February 1956 at the Pike, then moved to the Gate until March, and travelled to eight further venues around the country until June 1956, a total of over 150 performances.[8] Morash, moreover, described how the production entered contemporary Irish popular culture: 'The pantomime actor, Jimmy O'Dea, introduced Godot into his variety routines, and a cartoon in one of the Irish daily papers showed a puzzled policeman explaining to his colleague that a suspicious-looking vagrant claimed to be "waiting for Godot".'[9] Morash concluded his assessment of the 1955 production at the Pike by describing it in the very terms used by Colgan to identify the 1991 Festival at the Gate as a unique and hitherto unprecedented event in Irish theatrical history: the popular and commercial success of experimental theatre: 'In a sense, the Pike Theatre production of *Waiting for Godot* heralded the arrival in Ireland of that oxymoronic beast, a mainstream *avant-garde*.'[10]

More than a decade later, the production of *Waiting for Godot* at the Abbey in December 1969, with Peter O'Toole as Vladimir and Donal McCann as Estragon, was so successful that Christopher Murray has described it as a 'watershed' in the history of Beckett productions in Ireland, due to its effect of making Beckett a figure of the theatrical establishment in Ireland: 'Before this, Beckett's plays made their way in Dublin's basement theatres or experimental halls; now, in the year when he won the Nobel Prize and was awarded a Litt.D by Trinity College Dublin, Beckett was to be honoured by [the] national theatre.'[11] Indeed, Gus Smith suggested in the *Sunday Independent* that the Abbey's production of *Waiting for Godot* was of such cultural significance that '[h]istorians may well mark down Monday December the first as the night when the "modern" Abbey Theatre became a truly National Theatre in the widest sense of the word'.[12]

Colgan's suggestion that Beckett's theatre was overlooked in Ireland before the Festival at the Gate is further challenged by Murray's observation that *Waiting for Godot* was 'the winning play in the all-Ireland amateur drama festival in 1980, a fact which contrasts sharply with the trend twenty years earlier, when conventional Irish plays were usually the festival winners.'[13] Similarly, Colgan's comments about the neglect of Beckett's work by the Abbey and Peacock are directly contradicted by the Abbey archives, which list productions of *Waiting for Godot, Endgame, Happy Days, Krapp's Last Tape, Act Without Words, Catastrophe, Come and Go, Footfalls, Nacht und Träume, Not I, Play, Rockaby, That Time,* and *What Where* between 1969 and 1990. In fact, Murray concluded his 1984 survey of theatrical productions of Beckett's work in Ireland by noting how, in this

[8] See ibid., 207–8, and Christopher Murray, 'Beckett Productions in Ireland: A Survey', *Irish University Review* 14, no. 1 (1984), 105.

[9] Morash, *A History of Irish Theatre*, 208.   [10] Ibid.

[11] Murray, 'Beckett Productions in Ireland', 114. In fact, Beckett's honorary degree had been awarded by Trinity College ten years earlier, in 1959.

[12] Gus Smith, quoted in Hugh Hunt, *The Abbey: Ireland's National Theatre, 1904–1978* (Dublin: Gill & Macmillan, 1979), 207.

[13] Murray, 'Beckett Productions in Ireland', 103.

period, the Abbey and Peacock had supplanted the Gate as the theatres most likely to produce Beckett's work:

> It would quite simply be impossible to get together anywhere else in the Irish Republic at present the acting talent, the scene designers, the lighting experts and the directorial talent which the Abbey has at its disposal. In Ireland's theatre history the national theatre was for much of its history well behind such theatres as the Gate (which had no subsidy until 1971). The new Abbey, however, developed artistically to the point where, by about 1980, it had superseded the Gate.[14]

Despite this evidence of established and ongoing interest in Beckett's theatre, Colgan adopted a narrative while promoting the Festival that Beckett was unjustly ignored in Dublin in 1991, and has maintained this narrative ever since. In his letters to sponsors seeking funding for the Beckett Festival, Colgan carefully framed it as a belated homecoming for Beckett. Writing to the project coordinator of AIB in application to the bank's 'Better Ireland' scheme in May 1991, Colgan summarized the purpose of the Festival as an imaginative reclamation:

> Because Samuel Beckett lived in France and was an internationally-renowned writer, his Irish heritage and the great contribution it made to his work have in the past sometimes been overlooked. Through our partnership with Trinity College and with RTÉ we believe we are in a unique position to redress that imbalance, and to celebrate in a fitting way the life and work of one of Ireland's greatest writers.[15]

In interviews with newspapers to promote the Festival, Colgan was more explicit about its aim to take Beckett back from the French.[16] He proceeded to shape the media narrative as one of atoning for the unjustified neglect of Beckett by his places of origin. Most media outlets followed this line, and the coverage, accordingly, gives the impression that Beckett was little known or loved in Ireland at the time.

The *Irish Times* described how plans for the Festival received 'a new impetus with Beckett's death at the end of 1989, when Colgan read a French writer describing his demise as '"a great loss to the French nation"', and determined to 'reclaim Beckett's work for Ireland, though not in any exclusive or chauvinistic sense'.[17] The *Sunday Press* carried a similar quote from Colgan:

> Samuel Beckett lived the best part of his life in Paris and the fear is that in the not too distant future he will be regarded as French and not Irish. 'A lot of our great writers have been

---

[14] Ibid., 119–20.

[15] Letter from Colgan to Aideen O'Carroll, Project Coordinator, AIB, 30 May 1991, 'The Beckett Festival 1991' folder, Dublin, Gate archives, PF77e.

[16] It is important to note that Colgan, from the start, tried to get the French government and cultural institutions involved. Jack Lang, the French Minister for Culture and Communications, gave an address at the 1991 Festival, and Colgan persevered until French material was included in the programme for the Beckett Centenary Festival held at the Gate in 2006—he believes that this is why the French government presented him with the award of Chevalier de l'Ordre des Arts et des Lettres: 'In 2006 I beat the French down, I said you really need to have some things in this Festival that are French, I think they got guilt-ridden about being so angry with me, that's why they made me one of those Chevaliers.'

[17] Paddy Woodworth, 'Playing Sam Again', *Irish Times*, 28 Sept. 1991.

hijacked' says Colgan, 'because they lived most of their lives outside Ireland. Congreve, Sheridan, Shaw, Wilde. The Beckett Festival at the Gate is all about Bringing Beckett Home.'[18]

These excerpts sound the note of many contemporaneous journal and newspaper articles and reviews of the Festival. Typical titles included 'Beckett Comes Home' in *Plays International*, 'Bringing Beckett Home' in the *Sunday Press*, and 'Beckett Brought Home in Radiant Darkness' in the *Irish Times*. Such pieces are a testament to Colgan's prowess as a publicist, but they overlook Beckett's wider status in Ireland in the decades after he won the Nobel Prize. Indeed, the degree to which Beckett was already established in the Irish imagination before the Festival is indicated by a poem published by Paul Durcan in 1987, the title of which this chapter echoes. 'The Beckett at the Gate' opens with a positively Beckettian speaker bristling with irritation about the constant promotion of McGovern's *I'll Go On* by his fellow Dubliners, and features a recurring line that emphasizes just how difficult it was to avoid Beckett in Dublin in 1987: 'Have you not been to the Beckett at the Gate?'[19]

CREATION OF THE 1991 BECKETT FESTIVAL

Colgan's ambitions for the Festival were assisted by two notable coincidences: in 1991 Dublin was designated City of Culture by the European Union, the two most obvious legacies of which are the Irish Museum of Modern Art and the Dublin Writers Museum. The year also happened to be the quatercentenary of Trinity College, Beckett's alma mater. Tom Mitchell had become Provost in 1991, and was very receptive to Colgan's suggestion that Trinity partner the Gate for the Festival and host lectures, seminars, readings, and exhibitions. Colgan then approached RTÉ and made them a partner to facilitate the production of Beckett's radio and television plays. Having arranged this, Colgan decided that for the Festival to be truly 'comprehensive' and to represent accurately the range of Beckett's creative interests, it should also feature the visual arts, so he organized an exhibition, mostly of etchings or prints, in the Douglas Hyde Gallery in Trinity. These works, by the contemporary artists Jasper Johns, Louis le Brocquy, Robert Ryman, S. W. Hayter, and Avigdor Arikha, had either been created in collaboration with Beckett, were responses to his texts, or were portraits of the man. The exhibition also featured a number of drawings by the Irish artist Brian Bourke, who was appointed artist-in-residence at the Gate and Trinity for the duration of the Festival and created a series of drawings called 'Beckett in Rehearsal'.

In his review of the Festival, Anthony Roche provides an overview of its scale, and the form of imaginative repossession of Beckett involved in the Festival's extensive programming:

> Whenever an expatriate Irish writer dies and is buried abroad, there is often talk of returning the coffin to Ireland. A much more significant act of cultural reappropriation was the courageous decision by Michael Colgan, artistic director of the Gate Theatre, to mount a

---

[18] William Roche, 'Bringing Beckett Home', *Sunday Press*, 29 Sept. 1991.
[19] Paul Durcan, 'The Beckett at the Gate', in *A Snail in My Prime: New and Selected Poems* (London: Harvill, 1993), 131.

festival which would stage all nineteen plays by the late and very much lamented Samuel Beckett in the city of Beckett's birth. But Colgan was not content to leave it there. Rather, he collaborated with Beckett's alma mater, Trinity College, to inaugurate their 400th anniversary by mounting a series of lectures, symposia, book and library exhibitions, in tandem with the festival and in honour of one of their most distinguished twentieth-century graduates.[20]

While acknowledging that even without all the complementary events, the intention to stage nineteen plays in three weeks was a 'huge undertaking' and that people thought he was crazy, Colgan, looking back, is at pains to emphasize what an 'exhilarating' experience it had been, to dream up and organize the Festival: 'I had hit the moment perfectly I think, by accident, I can't take credit for that. But now you look at DruidSynge and you look at the Murphy festival at the Abbey and nobody had done it before—it seemed to me the most obvious idea.' Colgan suggests that 'all the really great ideas are the simple ones', and compares the Beckett Festival with another of his coups at the Gate, reiterating the role of chance and timing in such achievements:

> I mean, people gave me great credit in 1990 for doing *Three Sisters* with the three Cusack girls, but you know, you can't claim that as an idea—I can claim credit for landing the fish, but not for putting the hook in the mouth—I mean, Cyril Cusack's daughters—when they were running around the garden in their childhood there would have been people talking about 'the three sisters', you know—but landing it was important.

Luck may certainly have been an element in both celebrated events, but the material in the archives of the Gate testifies eloquently to the vital roles played by Colgan's determination and chutzpah in realizing such projects.

A letter from Rupert Murray, the Festival Coordinator, to Colgan on 21 August 1991 gives an idea of the scale of Colgan and Murray's ambitions, not to mention their sheer nerve. Murray presents Colgan with a to-do list, top of which is the item: 'Contact Jonathan Miller—see does he have any interest in Beckett—if so will he give a public lecture at 5pm on Tuesday 2 October in the Edmund Burke hall (capacity 400).' The remaining items are similarly ambitious shots in the dark, with Murray asking Colgan to secure Melvyn Bragg, Mel Gussow, Terence Brown, Tom Murphy, and Michael Bogdanov as participants in a debate for which they did not yet have a motion. The penultimate item was for Colgan to find 'glitzy names to open the two major exhibitions' of visual art in Trinity.[21]

Colgan's solution to this final request by Murray was to convince the President of Iceland, Vigdís Finnbogadóttir, who was visiting Ireland at the time, to join Mary Robinson, then President of Ireland, in opening the exhibition in the Douglas Hyde Gallery. With an eye on how the overall Festival should be presented, Colgan arranged for the Taoiseach, Charles Haughey, to open it. I asked Colgan if Haughey was a fan of Beckett's work, a question that prompted much mirth. Colgan's response speaks volumes of the gulf that he perceives as then existing between Beckett and the Irish political establishment, and indeed the general

[20] Anthony Roche, 'Beckett Festival at the Gate Theatre', *Irish Literary Supplement*, 15 (Spring 1992).
[21] Letter from Rupert Murray to Colgan, dated 21 Aug. 1991, 'The Beckett Festival 1991' folder, Dublin, Gate archives, PF 77b.

population, as it does of his recognition that an ambitious festival created to celebrate the work of an artist of Beckett's stature offered great cultural capital to a political figure such as Haughey:

> No. Not at all. Sure at that time nobody liked Beckett. Nobody knew Beckett. The truth was that there were some people who might have had a sense of what *Krapp's Last Tape* might have been or *Endgame*, and they might have known something of *Godot*, but nobody had a clue, they didn't know he had written *Footfalls* or *Ohio* or any of that—so it was a ridiculous thing to do, to put on all his plays at the Gate—and to do all nineteen of them. But Haughey would have appreciated the scale of the gesture.

Before Beckett died he had made clear to Colgan certain preferences for how his work was to be presented. Colgan explains how he studiously honoured these requests in the programming for the Festival, and has done ever since:

> Sadly I didn't get the money together to do it while he was alive, but he did talk to me about it and he told me certain things that he wanted done. He certainly didn't like the idea of any of the four big plays being with any other play, and since then I've taken that on, to a ridiculous extent you know—I mean *Eh Joe* is twenty-eight minutes long and people kept saying, oh you should put it on with this or that—No!

Beckett's desire for the four full-length plays to be performed separately left fifteen shorter plays from the total of nineteen. This determined Colgan's approach: 'I got the idea that I'm leaving those four, and four from nineteen leaves fifteen and then I decided to put the other five into triple bills, and then I tried to break them up in terms of gender, the female voice and time balance.' In his review of the Festival, Anthony Roche praised Colgan's choice of structure to carry the programme, identifying this 'complex feat of engineering' as one of the reasons the Festival was such a success: 'The three "big" plays, *Waiting for Godot, Endgame*, and *Happy Days*, would occupy the main evening slot; and around this spine, he placed programmes of three plays apiece in the lunchtime and late night slots.'[22] A sense of the almost overwhelming number of performances, events, and talks is given by the breathless introduction to 'a highly selective summary' of the Festival that appeared in the *Irish Times*: 'If the programming at the Gate Theatre seems complex, it is simplicity itself compared to the plethora of events at TCD, supplemented by a variety of broadcasts on RTÉ.'[23]

Given the number of events scheduled to take place over the three weeks, it soon became clear that the Festival programme would be an important document. Colgan had a photograph in mind for the cover and contacted Richard Avedon to request permission to use it:

> I've no wish to flatter, but your photographs of Sam are without question the best that I've seen and as an image for the event we would very much like to use one of them with the words 'The Beckett Festival'. The photograph not only captures the man but sends a strong signal of his humility which I feel is entirely necessary to balance such words as 'The Beckett Festival'.[24]

---

[22] Roche, 'Beckett Festival at the Gate Theatre', 15.
[23] Author unidentified, 'Beckett Festival events', *Irish Times*, 28 Sept. 1991.
[24] Letter from Colgan to Richard Avedon, 5 June 1991, 'The Beckett Festival 1991' folder, Dublin, Gate archives, PF 77e.

FIG. 29.1 Michael Colgan standing in front of the billboard for the Beckett Festival, Gate Theatre, 1991.

Photo: Tom Lawlor. Courtesy of the Gate Theatre.

Colgan then proceeded to note the ephemerality of theatre, and to emphasize the priority attributed by the organizers to the programme and other records of the Festival: after the three weeks of the Festival, he explained, 'it all becomes a memory but it is our hope that that which is left behind—letters, brochures, programmes, etc.—will give an accurate sense of the tribute which was paid to this unique man in the city of his birth.'[25] Avedon granted permission, and his striking double photograph of Beckett, facing the camera and then casting his eyes down and away, featured on the front of the programme and on much of the publicity material for the Festival, including the billboard advertisement in Fig. 29.1 which captures Colgan's proprietorial—and entrepreneurial—approach to the Festival.

The Festival programme is a unique document and valuable record of the tribute paid by Colgan to Beckett, and the occasionally maniacal lengths to which people were pushed to realize his aims. One gets a sense of how maddening an experience it must have been to have collaborated on such an ambitious and sprawling project, with Colgan constantly changing his mind and making ever greater demands right up to the wire, in a letter of resignation sent at the end of August by Irish International Advertising which includes the line: 'Given that the relatively simple task of producing a poster has still not been resolved after three weeks, the prospects for the catalogue are horrendous.'[26]

This observation was perceptive. Colgan had charged £1,000 for each advertisement in the programme, a lot of money at the time, but was troubled by the prospect of the advertisers' messages appearing on the facing pages to Beckett's writing: 'I didn't want Beckett to be sullied by ads for Marlborough Lights and things.' So, once the process of designing the advertisements was under way, Colgan insisted that they had to be in black and white, to create a clean aesthetic. A little later, he told the sponsors that although the advertisements were all the size of a full page, he had decided that they could include no imagery other than the company logo. Finally, at the eleventh hour, he contacted them and said 'I can't bear the

---

[25] Ibid.
[26] Letter from Irish International Advertising, 9 Fitzwilliam Square, to Rupert Murray, 27 Aug. 1991, 'The Beckett Festival 1991' folder, Dublin, Gate archives, PF 77b.

idea of some advertising executive writing in the programme, so the line you use for your advertisement has to come from Beckett.' Once they had recovered from the shock, Colgan recalled, 'they were brilliant—they got all their marketing people to go through the night because I gave them very little notice.' Indeed, the advertisements are perhaps the most memorable feature of the text. Examining the programme, one can imagine the advertising men and women sitting up late at night, scanning page after page of Beckett's writing to find a line they might use. Many came up with truly inspired choices. Fig. 29.2 illustrates the advertisement for Telecom Éireann that appeared in the programme.

Other adverts included the pensions and investment company Standard Life, who adopted Pozzo's rather pointed line about the value of human intercourse: 'One Departs Wiser, Richer, More Conscious of One's Blessings'. Independent News and Media, composed of the *Evening Herald, Irish Independent*, and *Sunday Independent* newspapers, went

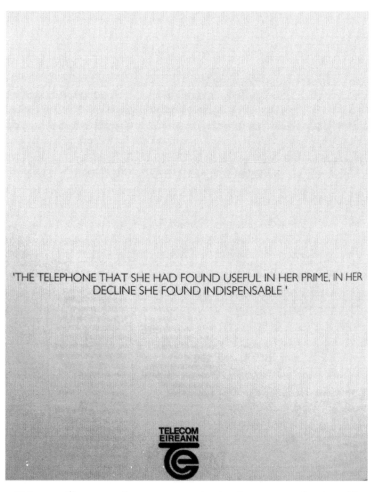

FIG. 29.2 Telecom Éireann advertisement, the Beckett Festival, Gate Theatre, 1–20 October 1991; festival programme, edited by Mary Dowey (Dublin: Gate Theatre, 1990).

Courtesy of Eircom.

for the succinct 'Trilogy'; while Bord Fáilte cleverly used the opening stage directions for *Waiting for Godot*: 'Act I "A Country Road. A Tree. Evening"'. The national airline Aer Lingus drew on Maddy Rooney's ecstatically weightless phrase from the radio play *All That Fall*: 'And Overall the Clouding Blue'; while the National Lottery used the title and refrain of one of Beckett's best-known plays to come up with a caption that surpasses any advertisement they have used since: 'Happy Days'.[27]

RECEPTION OF THE 1991 BECKETT FESTIVAL

The Festival sold out. In the Gate archives, there is a list of the fourteen countries from which visitors travelled.[28] The archives also contain many telegrams and notes sent by well-wishers who could not attend the Festival for various reasons, but wanted to express their support. Among these telegrams is a message sent from Prague Castle on 1 October by Václav Havel:

> At the time when Samuel Beckett was lying on his deathbed, several posters appeared on the walls of the Prague Metro with the significant words: 'Godot has come!' It was these posters among hundreds of others which caught one's eye, and their meaning was clear even to those who had never come across Beckett's play. The atmosphere of our new-found freedom could not have been better expressed, and no one could have paid a greater compliment to the dramatist than did that unknown author of those handwritten posters. In the course of your Festival you will, over twenty days, be presenting all of Beckett's plays. In this way Samuel Beckett has posthumously returned to the city of his youth. I wish you a fruitful meeting with the great writer.[29]

A note of regret was also sent by Edward Albee: 'Given all the foolish festivals in this world, a sensible—an essential—one is a rarity. Beckett festivals are an essential and are, therefore, alas, still a rarity. I congratulate Dublin on its essential good sense in honouring the greatest playwright of the twentieth century.' A more poignant message came from Billie Whitelaw, who sent a telegram to say: 'I'm sorry the way things ended up. It is unlikely I will perform Beckett professionally again. Good luck I'm sure you will all have a much deserved success. With love and sadness'. Messages of thanks and congratulations also arrived from participants, including Linda Ben-Zvi, who noted 'The more I think of your undertaking—nineteen Beckett plays in three weeks—the more I marvel at the quality of the work and at the "chutzpah" it took to conceive of such a project and to pull it off. You do have style.'[30]

In an astute casting decision that asserted the connections between Beckett's writing and the popular stage, two prominent Dublin comic actors were invited to participate in

[27] See *The Beckett Festival: 1–20 October 1991* (Dublin: Gate Theatre, 1991), 68, 40, 52, 12, 49.

[28] Australia, Belgium, Canada, Finland, France, Germany, Holland, Israel, Italy, Japan, Poland, Sweden, UK, and US.

[29] This and subsequent telegrams and documents are unnumbered and held in the folder: 'The Beckett Festival 1991', PF 77a. Unless otherwise indicated, these are typed, undated copies of handwritten letters or telegrams received by the Gate.

[30] Linda Ben-Zvi, typed note with letterhead from the Department of English, Fort Collins, Colorado, 21 Oct. 1991.

FIG. 29.3 Maureen Potter in *Rockaby* by Samuel Beckett at the Beckett Festival, Gate
Theatre, 1–20 October 1991.

Photo: Tom Lawlor. Courtesy of the Gate Theatre.

the Festival. Adele King (more commonly known as 'Twink') performed in *Not I*, while
Maureen Potter played Woman in *Rockaby* and Voice in *Footfalls*. These decisions aroused
some scepticism in the press in advance of the productions. Colm O'Briain, the director of
Not I, was asked by the *Irish Times* to justify his decision to cast Twink as Mouth: 'But if it's
not a laugh, why Twink?'; while a *Sunday Press* interview with Potter during rehearsals for
Rockaby played up the dissonance between Potter's familiar, down-to-earth nature and the
intimidatingly mysterious, not to say pretentious, demands of Beckett's theatre. The piece
concluded by quoting a Dublin taxi driver: 'Always the comedienne, she tells about the taximan who asked her recently what she was doing now. She told him she was rehearsing a
Beckett play. "Oh, that fella," says the taximan, "I think he's a bit heavy for you, Maureen." '[31]

Reviews of Potter's performance, however, were positive. Matt Wolf suggested that even
if Billie Whitelaw had not been filming a television series during the Festival, her attendance would still have been unlikely because 'she wanted to shake free the perception of
being a "Beckett actress" ', with the result that such 'Whitelaw-originated roles' as Woman
in *Rockaby* and the 'tortured, shuffling May in *Footfalls*' were now open to reinterpretation:

> As it turned out, Maureen Potter, who played Maisie Madigan in the Gate's now-legendary
> 1988 *Juno and the Paycock*, was an apt inheritor of the former role, rocking herself 'off'
> life and into the motherly embrace of death, substituting defiance for Whitelaw's justly
> acclaimed air of panic.[32]

Wolf was less enthusiastic about the Festival's production of *Not I*, but for technical reasons, praising 'Adele King's canny reading of the part', but expressing frustration with 'the
lighting designer's inability to blacken the stage' entirely.[33] Claudia Harris, in her review

---

[31] Author unidentified, 'Waiting for Twink', *Irish Times*, 14 Sept. 1991; William Roche,
'Comedienne is Relishing the Challenge', *Sunday Press*, 29 Sept. 1991.

[32] Matt Wolf, 'Just How Irish is Samuel Beckett?', *American Theatre*, Dec. 1991, 56.

[33] Ibid., 57.

FIG. 29.4 Publicity photograph of Barry McGovern as Vladimir in *Waiting for Godot* by Samuel Beckett; Beckett Festival, Gate Theatre, 1–20 October 1991.

Photo by Tom Lawlor. Courtesy of the Gate Theatre.

for *Theatre Journal*, similarly gestured to the considerable technical demands of the late plays in her brief assessment of their failure, relative to the success of the longer plays: '*Not I* and *Act Without Words II* did not work, for both of these the staging and conception were flawed. But those were the only unsuccessful productions.'[34]

A common feature in reviews of the Festival was a comparison of Walter Asmus's *Waiting for Godot* with Les Blair's concurrent production in London, featuring Rik Mayall and Adrian Edmondson, with a set designed by Derek Jarman. Without exception, reviewers praised the Dublin production at London's expense. Michael Billington, in his review for the *Guardian*, proclaimed the 'terrific Gate production of *Waiting for Godot*' its 'undoubted highlight':

> After the self-indulgent shtick of the current London version, this was a pure, clean production combining phenomenal speed with profound pain. Above all, Barry McGovern's anxious, attenuated Didi and Johnny Murphy's stubby, hirsute Gogo, locked together in a celibate parody of marriage, proved just how much the play gained from being played with Irish speech-rhythms. This was *Godot* in its true, magnificent colours: a lyric poem about life's meaninglessness.[35]

---

[34] Claudia Harris, 'The Beckett Festival by Samuel Beckett', *Theatre Journal* 44, no. 3 (1992), 406.

[35] Michael Billington, 'Mothers and Marvellous Meaninglessness', *Guardian*, 17 Oct. 1991.

Matt Wolf celebrated Barry McGovern as a 'near-ideal Vladimir, a logician baffled by the ceaseless illogicality of his surroundings', and noted that McGovern's Vladimir was 'memorably complemented by the comically abject Estragon of Johnny Murphy'.[36]The publicity still of McGovern as Vladimir demonstrates the costumes designed by Louis le Brocquy, while McGovern's abject pose, bent over at the waist towards his feet like a collapsed puppet, provides a strong visual echo of the Avedon photographs of Beckett which were so integral to the promotion of the Festival.

AFTERMATH OF THE 1991 BECKETT FESTIVAL

In his review for the *Irish Literary Supplement*, Anthony Roche noted that audiences increased as the Festival developed momentum, and in his analysis of the makeup of the audiences in attendance throughout the Festival, identified its most significant achievement:

> They were built up from a number of constituencies: the academic, secured by the Trinity association; the foreign, drawn by the international name of Beckett in world theatre and the rare opportunity to see all of his plays within a span of days; an older Dublin audience, who remembered the earlier productions and in some cases, the man himself; but, most surprising and rewarding of all, the Gate season drew a young audience, contributing most with their untutored hunger for what was on offer.[37]

This appetite for more was felt not only in Dublin. As soon as the Festival concluded, Colgan began receiving offers to bring it on tour. From the start, Colgan had been planning to tour some productions from the Festival, but he had not anticipated such keen demand. Some plays were brought to Chicago, Toronto, and Melbourne, while the Festival in its entirety travelled to the Lincoln Centre in New York in 1996, and then the Barbican in London in 1999. All these tours were celebrated, but Colgan expressed concern that they were becoming what he describes as a 'bit of a circus', and conceived the Beckett on Film project at least in part to 'kill' the tour: 'Dublin, London, New York was enough.'

In 1998, Colgan and the producer Alan Moloney created the production company Blue Angel Films to produce Beckett on Film, together with RTÉ, Channel 4, and the Irish Film Board. They did so with the support of the Beckett Estate, and to ensure that the films would adhere to Beckett's stage directions, which the Estate wished to uphold, Colgan and Moloney sought writer-directors who they hoped would have more fidelity to the text than was likely in an actor-led project. The actors and directors they recruited included some famous figures: David Mamet directed Harold Pinter and John Gielgud in his final acting appearance in *Catastrophe*; Atom Egoyan directed John Hurt in *Krapp's Last Tape*; Neil Jordan directed Julianne Moore in *Not I*; and Anthony Minghella directed Kristin Scott-Thomas, Juliet Stevenson, and Alan Rickman in *Play*. The films were first screened in 2001 and were warmly received. More interesting than the awards won by the project, however,

---

[36] Wolf, 'Just How Irish is Samuel Beckett?', 57.
[37] Roche, 'Beckett Festival at the Gate Theatre', 15.

are the challenges it faced in seeking to translate to the medium of film a body of work that declared itself, in this effort of translation, profoundly and stubbornly theatrical.

One of the most pronounced shortcomings of several films arose from the directors' introduction of space which broke the claustrophobia of each piece and disrupted the hypnotic effect of Beckett's stage images. *Waiting for Godot* was filmed in a quarry. With the generous grey skies stretching above and behind the characters' badinage and the broad road running into and out of their way, it was difficult to feel them trapped in any meaningful way. *Happy Days* was also filmed in a broad, open space. Patricia Rozema's preference for long shots to indicate the isolation of Winnie in this scorched and gusty location meant that much of Rosaleen Linehan's precise manipulation of the small objects she used to sustain herself in such an aggressively inhospitable environment was lost—the effect of which was a corresponding loss of interest in her scenario. *Not I* was similarly marred by Neil Jordan's cinematic instinct to pull away from the startling violence and sensuality of a mouth, teeth, and tongue swollen to fill the whole screen, to emphasize that this mouth belonged to Julianne Moore, and to include in shot the alarming-looking contraption like an electric chair in which she was strapped, a reference to the daunting stage machinery used by Billie Whitelaw in 1973 at the Royal Court. Anthony Minghella's *Play* cleverly emphasized its status as a film, using spliced images and recorded snatches of monologue which were punctuated with the sound of the camera 'eye' moving in or out; but it too suffered from the same cinematic instinct of pulling away from the three urns to reveal a landscape pockmarked with tormented figures. The scale of the loss experienced in each film illustrated the vital importance in Beckett's theatre of the physical and emotional identification of the audience with the figures on-stage. By introducing a framing narrative outside the bleakly delimited scenario described by Beckett, the films paradoxically weakened the interest and impact of these pieces.

The Beckett on Film project may have halted the Gate's tours of the Festival, as Colgan had wished, but the Gate has continued to be the main producer of Beckett in Ireland since 1991, with Colgan responsible for attracting actors of the stature of John Hurt, Michael Gambon, Liam Neeson, and Ralph Fiennes to the Gate. In his assessment of the 1991 Festival, Anthony Roche reports a conversation he had with Colgan 'at 12.25am after the final performance', where they agreed that the Festival had been such a success because the audience had responded so well.[38] Twenty-two years later, Colgan tells me that of all the high points in his career, his proudest and most exhilarating moment came at the end of the first late-night performance of *Breath* at the Festival. The play ended and was immediately met with cheers, applause, and roaring by a Dublin audience that Colgan felt in no small part responsible for creating. Recalling their response, Colgan beams and lifts his hands: 'And they got it.'

But of course they had been 'getting it' for a considerable time already. The Festival at the Gate took place almost four decades after the first such response to Beckett's theatre in Dublin. What was extraordinary and definitively new about the 1991 Beckett Festival was its scope: performances of Beckett's entire *oeuvre* were complemented by talks, workshops, exhibitions, radio, and television plays—and all of it aggressively marketed to the degree that it was impossible to be unaware of it. Colgan's continued intellectual and artistic as

[38] Ibid.

well as personal devotion to Beckett is evident, and he describes himself as a 'missionary' or 'proselytizer' rather than a producer of Beckett's work. The 1991 Festival may not have been the original and decisive imaginative reclamation of a neglected writer that he skilfully presented to the media, but the importance he attaches to a Dublin audience's ecstatic response to *Breath* identifies Colgan's legacy in Irish theatre. He may not have been responsible for 'bringing Beckett home', but for three decades now he has successfully brought Dublin audiences to Beckett at the Gate.

PART X

CONTEMPORARY IRISH THEATRE

NEGOTIATING DIFFERENCES IN THE PLAYS OF FRANK MCGUINNESS

HELEN HEUSNER LOJEK

> The Other precisely *reveals* himself in his alterity not in a shock negating the I,
> but as the primordial phenomenon of gentleness.
>
> Emmanuel Levinas[1]

IN the impressive body of work he has produced since the early 1980s, Frank McGuinness has populated the stage with characters who encounter a variety of Others. This chapter focuses on the best-known original plays from his extensive *oeuvre*: *Observe the Sons of Ulster Marching Towards the Somme* (1985), *Carthaginians* (1988), *Someone Who'll Watch Over Me* (1992), *Mutabilitie* (1997), and *Gates of Gold* (2002). Each of them incorporates slightly different perspectives on the general topics of Other, difference, and identity. Dramatic form reinforces those thematic concerns, and both characters and audiences must confront their own realities and negotiate differences.

McGuinness's biography includes factors likely to have enhanced the necessity to note and negotiate differences. A gay member of a working-class family whose nationalist/Catholic orientation matched their side of the Irish border, he was also a resident of Donegal, which the border separated from its traditional province of Ulster, making the northernmost part of the island part of the southern Irish Republic. Proximity to a border only fourteen miles away allowed for regular trips across it to Northern Ireland, which retained political ties with the United Kingdom and to a city known as Derry or Londonderry, depending on the namer's political and cultural orientation. Explosion of the island's Troubles in 1972 (during McGuinness's first year at University College Dublin) emphasized the wide gap between some members of societies on either side of a narrow and permeable border.

The trajectory of McGuinness's career coincides with important years of identity politics in Ireland. The question of nationality that has vexed multiple countries has been an

---

[1] Emmanuel Levinas, *Totality and Infinity: An Essay on Exteriority*, trans. Alphonso Lingis (Dordrecht: Kluwer Academic, 1991), 150.

ongoing concern in the Republic since before independence. Responding to complexities of emigration and (more recently) immigration, the Irish constitution and Irish law
created shifting definitions of citizenship. A 2004 constitutional amendment reversed
a 1999 amendment and removed the right of automatic citizenship from children born
in Ireland to non-Irish parents, thus restricting the meaning of Irish identity and com
plicating or simplifying the issue, depending on one's viewpoint. The Irish immigrant
population rose 143% between 2002 and 2011, and Central Statistics Office figures show
that in 2012 approximately one in nine residents of the Republic had been born somewhere else. Half a million residents spoke neither Irish nor English at home. In *Dolly
West's Kitchen* (1999), Rima laments the fact that Ireland 'did nothing' to save the Jews
during the Second World War. 'If any country should have opened the door to any people
facing what they are facing', Ireland should have.[2] Rima's comments are a relatively rare
instance of references to immigration in McGuinness's plays, which do not feature characters from immigrant or non-English/Irish-speaking backgrounds. The issues of identity and difference raised by his plays, though, may be compellingly examined against
the background of Ireland's changing demographics. In *Someone Who'll Watch Over Me*,
American Adam inquires 'What is an American?' and Irishman Edward provides the
simplest of definitions: 'Someone born in America.' Adam, though, asserts a more complex sense of identity, noting that an American is 'a valuable asset', though not one that
is 'loved'.[3] It is one of many ways the plays resonate against the discussion of national
identity.

Frequently 'identity politics' in the context of Ireland refers to the sectarian divide
between the nationalist/Catholic and Unionist/Protestant factions, but terms like Other,
identity, and difference are broad and complex, with multiple referents. Gender identity and the identity associated with sexual orientation are also commonly discussed in
an Irish context, and the increasing equality of rights for gays and women[4] can be cited
as evidence Ireland has joined an emerging consensus among Western nations, even
as it has sometimes experienced a 'perceived crisis of masculinity'.[5] Responding to the
'perplex[ing]' paradox that 'in the modern world everyone can, should, will "have"
a nationality, as he or she "has" a gender', Benedict Anderson explored the meaning of
nationality.[6] Notions of gender are now receiving the same careful thought. The appeal
of McGuinness's works for non-Irish audiences indicates that his framing of such issues
reaches beyond Ireland. Arguably all of his plays concern the negotiation of difference.
His first success (*The Factory Girls*, 1982), for example, includes lesbian characters and is

[2] Frank McGuinness, *Plays 2* (London: Faber & Faber, 2002), 228.   [3] Ibid., 118–19.
[4] A 1988 European Court of Human Rights decision led to the decriminalization of homosexuality
in the Republic. The 1993 Sexual Offences Act equalized the sexual code for homosexuals and
heterosexuals. The Equal Status Act (2000) protects nine categories of identity, including gender,
race, religion, age, and sexual orientation. The 2010 Civil Partnership Bill provides parallel rights for
partnerships and married couples. A vote on a constitutional amendment allowing same-sex marriage
was passed and enacted in law in 2015.
[5] Ed Madden, ' "Gently, Not Gay": Proximity, Sexuality, and Irish Masculinity at the End of the
Twentieth Century', *Canadian Journal of Irish Studies* 36, no. 1 (2010), 71.
[6] Benedict Anderson, *Imagined Communities* (London: Verso, 1983), 5.

literally about negotiation—in this case negotiations between workers and management and between women and men.

Observe the Sons of Ulster Marching Towards the Somme

When *Observe the Sons of Ulster* first opened on the Abbey's Peacock stage, audience and media attention was captured by the play's demonstration that sectarian identity boundaries in Ireland could be crossed with intelligence and understanding. McGuinness had defied the comforting 'truth' that individuals with his background could not treat Northerners from the Unionist/Protestant tradition with sympathy. And he had allowed characters to mock such sacred cows as the Easter Rising. The First World War setting provided a historical distance that in part defused traditional antagonisms, but it was impossible to consider the play outside the 1980s tensions during which it appeared, and it has since become an iconographic demonstration that boundaries of divergent identities may be crossed with understanding.

The play's widespread success outside Ireland, in areas where the red hand of Ulster on the cover of the 1986 Faber edition means nothing, suggests the importance of themes beyond those of Irish identity. *Observe the Sons of Ulster* toured successfully in France, Belgium, and Germany. Numerous productions in Australia, the United States, and Canada, and a Polish translation/production indicate the success with which the play captures themes about war, class, and sexual orientation that are not exclusive to Ireland. From the perspective of thirty years and an increasingly successful peace accord, the play's consideration of differences beyond the Unionist/nationalist divide emerges with greater clarity.

The Elder Pyper's opening monologue in *Observe the Sons of Ulster* lets audiences know from the start where events will end. The play's non-chronological development is not unique. Predecessors include Tennessee Williams' *The Glass Menagerie* (1944) and Brian Friel's *The Freedom of the City* (1973)—both plays likely to have influenced McGuinness. Irish audiences would have entered the theatre knowing the outcome of the Battle of the Somme that is the background of *Observe the Sons of Ulster*. The opening monologue, though, reveals that Pyper, the character least tied to Ulster Loyalism before the battle, will survive to become its adherent. Observing Pyper's interaction with fellow soldiers throughout the remainder of the play enables audiences to appreciate, without necessarily approving of, the events and negotiations of differences that lead to his final position. As Chris Morash and Shaun Richards put it, 'in the continuous "now" that is stage time, the dead rise, memories become present' and 'the hold of the past on the present' is powerfully revealed—and revealed to be powerful.[7] The play closes with the Elder and Younger Pypers reaching toward each other, a visual image of attempts to bridge differences between past and present. (The script does not specify whether the Pypers actually

[7] Chris Morash and Shaun Richards, *Mapping Irish Theatre: Theories of Space and Place* (Cambridge: Cambridge University Press, 2013), 91.

touch, and different productions have staged the moment in different ways.) Robert Welch has linked McGuinness's use of 'horrified recollection' to techniques used by both Beckett and Friel.[8] The non-chronological development is a potentially destabilizing factor that may also be seen as an example of 'queer time' which refuses to fall into standard narrative development.[9]

McGuinness has been, as David Cregan notes, at the forefront of Irish theatrical 'representations of gender and sexuality', and in the process has contributed to the dislodgment of 'identities [that] [. . .] often centre on issues of sectarianism' or the ongoing connections and frictions between Ireland and Great Britain.[10] *Observe the Sons of Ulster* is part of that contribution. Pyper is openly gay, though his narrated relationship with a French woman suggests the complexity of sexual orientation, as do the ancient androgynous figures he and Craig encounter on Boa Island. His relationship with Craig is loving and healing, but Craig is surely correct that, if they survive, life for them 'might be many things, but it won't be together'.[11] The other six men exist along a continuum of the sexual spectrum. Only one indicates that he is married, and there are few references to heterosexual relationships. The focus on somewhat neatly paired soldiers is central to exploration of a variety of identities and reactions, including reactions to Pyper, which change from discomfort to acceptance. McIlwaine deliberately echoes Pyper's early assertion that he has 'remarkably fine skin for a man'.[12] McIlwaine and Anderson, the most 'macho' of the eight soldiers, have not fully accepted Pyper, continuing to believe there is something both mad and 'rotten'[13] about him, but the bonds of war have encouraged appreciation of Pyper's heroism and loyalty to the cause—as he has developed appreciation of and solidarity with them.

McGuinness's script allows productions to find their own ways to the play's implications. It does not require that Pyper and Craig kiss; it does not suggest that Craig's invitation to 'Carve me' or Crawford's request to 'Give us a scratch' be accompanied by suggestive physical contact.[14] The script does, though, allow for such intimacies. Early productions included little suggestive physical contact between the men, even in scenes where it makes sense. More recent productions are more likely to have openly sexual contact. The play's language provides clear indications of couplings that are sexual as well as comradely, but the stage directions do not specify physical contact, and so productions have been able to develop not only in the changing Irish environment, but also in the realities of the environments where they take place.

The script deals with differences in addition to the nationalist/Unionist and heterosexual/homosexual identities on which commentary has focused. Pyper, for example, is not just a soldier with reservations about the war, but also an artist who is a member of a privileged class that Millen believes has 'contacts up above' that will 'watch over' him[15]— language that prefigures the title of McGuinness's later play, where 'watching' gains

---

[8] Robert Welch, *The Abbey Theatre 1899–1999: Form and Pressure* (Oxford: Oxford University Press, 1999), 210.

[9] See e.g. Elizabeth Freeman, *Time Binds: Queer Temporalities, Queer Histories* (Durham, NC: Duke University Press, 2010).

[10] David Cregan, '"There's Something Queer Here": Modern Ireland and the Plays of Frank McGuinness', *Australasian Drama Studies* 43 (2003), 67.

[11] Frank McGuinness, *Plays 1* (London: Faber & Faber, 1996), 192.   [12] Ibid., 109, 147.

[13] Ibid., 147.   [14] Ibid., 150, 179.   [15] Ibid., 173.

complex personal, religious, and political overtones. Social class identity matters. Pyper realizes that attempting to escape his origins and become an artist has revealed only 'the bad joke they [his Protestant fathers] had played on me in making me sufficiently different to believe I was unique, when my true uniqueness lay only in how alike them I really was'.[16] Family and class differences must both be negotiated.

Scholarship, like productions, is inevitably tangled in the realities of times and places. The play was originally received as a remarkable instance of cross-cultural understanding in a divided island. It was and is that. As tensions between sectarian factions decreased and the rights of gays were increasingly recognized, scholarship matched productions in being increasingly open to exploring the play's range of sexual identities. Following the death of his parents in 1996 and 1997, McGuinness (who had never been secretive about his own homosexuality) was more direct in discussing the appearance of homosexual characters in his plays. His openness impacted productions and aided scholarly understanding.

CARTHAGINIANS

Robert Welch's 1999 observation that *Observe the Sons of Ulster* marks 'a profound shift in Irish theatrical thought, practice, and intent'[17] is an acknowledgement of the play's complexities of subject and form. Three years later McGuinness's *Carthaginians* continued that expansion of Irish theatrical thought, practice, and intent. Set in Derry, Northern Ireland, in the aftermath of Bloody Sunday (the 1972 occasion when the British army killed thirteen peaceful civil rights marchers), the play focuses on seven characters of varying ages gathered in a cemetery that features seven headstones.[18] Images of death dominate: Greta tends a dead bird; Maela is in denial about her daughter's death from cancer; Seph has apparently condemned rebels to death by giving their names to the British army; and Carthage, of course, is the dead city whose parallels with Derry echo throughout. Death, as Dido reminds the others, is the familiar great equalizer: British, Irish, Catholics, Protestants, 'We're all dead.'[19] These Derry residents wait in the cemetery for resurrection of their dead, and the time frame echoes that of Easter weekend, from Wednesday to early Sunday morning, when Dido (the only one awake) leaves Derry—and leaves the audience to decide what happened: 'whatever you want to believe, I suppose.' His belief that 'While I walk the earth, I walk through [...] the streets of Derry' is a reminder of the interweaving of past and present, like Tom's similar interweaving in *The Glass Menagerie*. Dido's final words—a series of 'Watch yourself' blessings[20]—are another prefiguring of McGuinness's later play.

Carthaginians does not deal directly with Bloody Sunday, and neither members of the British army nor marchers appear. The play shares with *Observe the Sons of Ulster* an approach that avoids direct representation of historical events, and an absence of bitterness

---

[16] Ibid., 164.   [17] Welch, *Abbey Theatre*, 209.

[18] McGuinness slightly revised the script between its first publication in 1988 and the 1996 Faber *Plays 1* edition. It is the earlier edition that specifies 'a maximum of seven' monuments that 'should resemble [. . .] those of the grave chambers found at Knowth': Frank McGuinness, *Carthaginians and Baglady* (London: Faber & Faber, 1988), [4].

[19] McGuinness, *Plays 1*, 344.   [20] Ibid., 379.

FIG. 30.1 Rosaleen Linehan as Maela in Frank McGuinness, *Carthaginians* (Abbey Theatre, 26 September 1988).

Courtesy of the Abbey Theatre and James Hardiman Library, NUI Galway.

about individuals on the opposite side of the firing line. The Ulster soldiers insist they themselves are responsible for their presence at the Somme. (Pyper: 'We led ourselves here'; Moore: 'orders are only orders when you follow them'; Craig: 'We joined up willingly'.)[21] In *Carthaginians*, when Paul asks 'Who will guide me through this city of hell?' Greta suggests he is himself in charge: 'Do you not guide yourself?'[22]

A wide variety of sexual orientations appear flagrantly in *Carthaginians*, including that of strutting, vamping Dido, 'queen of Derry', a beloved figure in the McGuinness canon. In 1988, Paul's reference to the 'European Court of Justice'[23] (removed from the 1996 edition)

[21] Ibid., 177, 168, 188.   [22] Ibid., 309–10.   [23] McGuinness, *Carthaginians*, 30.

would have reminded audiences of the European Court's 1988 decision that Ireland's anti-gay legislation violated fundamental human rights; and the play is notable for its insistence that audiences and characters alike must learn to negotiate differences in sexual orientation. These Derry residents are generally successful in negotiating not only these differences but also differences in age, gender, and relationship to the Troubles.

A Lebanese sailor/lover has given Dido his nickname, which links him to ancient Carthage, whose original settlers came from what is now Lebanon.[24] When the play premièred in 1988, Lebanon was in the midst of a disastrous civil war that was, like the Northern Irish conflict, rooted in postcolonial conflicts of religion and culture. For all their clear differences, Lebanon and Ireland were linked by sectarian violence, both religious and political. Connections between the postcolonial conflicts are subtle but persistent. As Diya M. Abdo has pointed out, Dido seeks to rewrite a national narrative and fashion a new identity. His attempt at 'rewriting the national self' is facilitated by his 'performance of subversive identities and sexualities'.[25] Dido, 'patriot and poof',[26] is an engaging parodist whose focus is serious.

Carthaginians' clearest exploration of sectarian differences comes in the play-within-the-play, 'The Burning Balaclava', a romp written and directed by Dido that mocks the stale, predictable iconography of the Troubles and resonates against the understanding that gender and sexuality are performances. Dido's pen name (Fionnuala McGonigle) shares initials with Frank McGuinness. Dido deliberately casts his friends in cross-gender roles. All the characters have the same surname, though their varying sectarian identifications determine the spellings: Doherty, O'Dochartaigh, Dogherty, O'Doherty, Docherty. Characters are Protestant, Catholic, Irish, and British, but Dido describes them all as 'tormented'.[27] The stereotypical cross-cultural love affair features a parent who instructs his daughter to murder her lover, who comes from a different faction. A British working-class soldier wonders why he is in Derry. Dido assures us that some folks are Catholic in bed and some Protestant, but some convert. Music comes from sentimental Irish and American sources, including *West Side Story*, whose cross-cultural lovers dream of 'a place for us'. Characters are involved in the Troubles for complex reasons that include profit, religion, and allegiance to sects.

It is difficult to distinguish one character from another when reading 'The Burning Balaclava', but in performance, wardrobe pieces clarify the roles. It is a funny piece, having a go at multiple constituents and constituencies. The British soldier declares 'We never shoot on sight' (337),[28] though there was widespread conviction in the 1980s that the British army did just that. There is a 'terrorist of the year'. A 50-year-old Derry housewife profits from the Troubles by knitting balaclavas. 'Violence is terrible, but it pays well,'[29] she declares, echoing another common belief in 1980s Northern Ireland. Dido's play parodies

---

[24] See Elizabeth Butler Cullingford, 'British Romans and Irish Carthaginians: Anticolonial Metaphor in Heaney, Friel, and McGuinness', *PMLA* 111, no. 2 (1996), 222–39; James Liddy, 'Voices in the Irish Cities of the Dead: Melodrama and Dissent in Frank McGuinness's *Carthaginians*', *Irish University Review* 25, no. 2 (1995), 278–83.

[25] Diya M. Abdo, 'Redefining the Warring Self in Hanan Al-Shaykh's *The Story of Zahra* and Frank McGuinness' *Carthaginians*', *Pacific Coast Philology* 42, no. 2 (2007), 218.

[26] McGuinness, *Plays 1*, 302.   [27] Ibid., 331, 332, 334.   [28] Ibid., 337.

[29] Ibid., 344.

icons like Juno's 'Sacred Heart' speech in O'Casey's *Juno and the Paycock* and the news photograph of Father Edward Daly raising a white handkerchief in an effort to get a Bloody Sunday shooting victim to safety.[30] Maela insists, 'If you're going to laugh at other people, you should learn to laugh at yourself,'[31] a belief that clearly underlies Dido's play, in which an absence of outward solemnity mingles with a great deal of seriousness about the shifting meanings of the protracted Troubles. 'The Burning Balaclava' has a hint of camp that delights in parody but never reduces life in Derry to parody. Any perceived difference between comedy and tragedy is bridged.

If Dido's casting requires that individuals walk in the shoes of others, though, the experience does not result in lasting understanding. Dido may insist that his parody is 'just like real life', but one after another his friends dismiss it as 'Shite. [. . .] Shite incredible. [. . .] Shite incarnate.'[32] Audiences, one hopes, will have reacted differently, recognizing that 'The Burning Balaclava' is not comic relief, but a powerfully felt examination that in many ways is as solemn as the litany of the names of the Bloody Sunday dead and the reiteration of the names of Derry streets. The incantation of names (a literary device McGuinness has used in several plays) is powerful. Comedy may be equally powerful. Dido has produced a 'ridiculous' example of outsider art that is as complex as life itself.

SOMEONE WHO'LL WATCH OVER ME

Someone Who'll Watch Over Me (1992) was also inspired by real events, in this case the terrorist taking of hostages in Lebanon in the 1980s.[33] There is less time between the actual events and the play's première than was the case for either *Observe the Sons of Ulster* or *Carthaginians*, and the varied nationalities of the hostages allow for negotiating differences both among Irish, Northern Irish, and British, and among Irish, British, and American— a juxtaposition of Anglophone cultures that also occurs in McGuiness's *Dolly West's Kitchen*. Since the hostages spend the entire time chained to a wall, exploration of differences takes place in language—differences in English (the common language that divides), in cultural references, in class, and in sexuality. In the London première Adam was played by Ghanaian-born British actor Hugh Quarshie, and on the subsequent US tour African-American actor James McDaniel had the role. No racial difference for the characters is specified in the script, however, and the play is often performed without it. In the opening scene, when only the American and the Irishman are on stage, differences are immediately obvious: in culture; in attitudes toward physical exercise, religion and money; and in language (the difference between 'shithead' and 'shitehead' being only one example). When the Englishman arrives, differences in class and the traditional hostility between

---

[30] Rita Duffy's 2006 painting *Cloth*, depicting a crumpled white handkerchief on a background of browns and olive greens, is a recent reference to Father Daly's effort.

[31] McGuinness, *Plays 1*, 329.   [32] Ibid., 344–5.

[33] The play is dedicated to Irishman Brian Keenan, released in 1990 following four years in captivity. Keenan, who wrote an introduction to the script, tells his story in *An Evil Cradling* (New York: Viking, 1993). Englishman John McCarthy (held for five years, some of the time with Keenan) and Jill Morrell have written another personal account in *Some Other Rainbow* (New York: Bantam, 1993).

the Irish and the English emerge, and the American seeks to defuse tensions. It is a rough parallel to Irish peace negotiations in the 1990s, when the United States acted as mediator. After Adam has been taken away and presumably shot, the Irishman and the Englishman re-enact Englishwoman Virginia Wade's 1977 Wimbledon championship match. The male hostages play women, and the Irishman plays the queen of England who applauds Wade— the cross-gender, cross-cultural 'casting' replicating that of 'The Burning Balaclava'. After a disputed serve the Irishman appeals to the absent Adam, whom he terms 'the umpire. What should I do, Adam?'[34]—another reminder of the role of a mediator in resolving differences. Cross-gender casting that combines humour and seriousness is nothing new. The 1949 musical *South Pacific* is one example, as are two works with prison settings—Athol Fugard's 1973 South African drama *The Island* (performed in Dublin in the 1980s) and the 1985 film *Kiss of the Spider Woman*. Those works share a focus on the need to be, as one *South Pacific* song puts it, 'carefully taught'. Like those examples, McGuinness's plays suggest the performative elements of gender and demonstrate the extent to which humour is a sign of survival, if not of triumph. When Adam and Edward insist that Michael laugh[35] they defy their captors and signal their emotional resistance and survival, part and parcel with their stand against gravity.

If a production follows the script's directions about costume, the linguistic and cultural differences are accompanied by colour-coding that indicates such differences might not be definitive. The Irishman has a blue t-shirt and white shorts; the American a black t-shirt and grey shorts; the Englishman a white t-shirt and black shorts. The three develop bonds of affection because (but not only because) they must unite to resist '[t]he enemy'—Arabs who have imprisoned them.[36] The characterizations have large elements of stereotype, but the prisoners are aware that '[w]hatever else about this place, we're in it together'[37]—a fact emphasized by the Arabs' failure to distinguish between the (pre-European Union) green passport of neutral Ireland and the burgundy passport of Britain. When the American and the Irishman, who have previously discussed their heterosexual preferences and powers, gang up on the Englishman, whose effeminacy belies his status as a heterosexual widower, the Englishman reminds them, 'We are in this together', and the three agree that they are all 'bollockses' in danger of going mad.[38] Because the men are chained to the wall, there are no opportunities for physical contact, but the possibility of sexual attraction and perhaps engagement is discussed.

In this play, as in *The Factory Girls, Observe the Sons of Ulster*, and *Carthaginians*, it is tempting to decide that out-group hostility is what has led to in-group solidarity among these speakers of varying dialects of English; but McGuinness presents a more complicated picture. Edward closes the gap between genders when he writes an (imaginary) letter home telling his wife that his daughter is a better footballer than her brothers; Adam recognizes that his foster sisters and brothers are actually his sisters and brothers despite their different DNA, and he deliberately blurs the distinction between cultures: 'Arab? English Arab? Irish Arab?'[39] He reads both the Bible and the Koran and notes parallels between the sacred texts. Irishman Edward, who by the end of the play has adopted the American's exercise regime, listens closely to Englishman Michael's tale of his father's

---

[34] McGuinness, *Plays* 2, 148.   [35] Ibid., 104–5.   [36] Ibid., 105.   [37] Ibid., 95–6.
[38] Ibid., 112.   [39] Ibid., 122, 120, 124.

war experience which demonstrated that, like the Spartans, the English have learned that '[t]he bravest men sometimes behave like women'.[40] Gender is one more permeable boundary.

Before his captors remove Adam, the three hostages imagine inviting the Arabs to join them in a party: 'Take the weight off your feet.... *The same the world over*. Have a drink if you like. We won't tell. Join us.'[41] The breaking of bread together is an image of similarity and solidarity in a variety of cultures and a repeated motif in McGuinness plays. In the Christian tradition, references to breaking bread together indicate shared resources (as in the parable of the loaves and fishes) and communion. They also acknowledge that a shared meal may reveal that strangers are not strangers after all, as happened when the disciples recognized that the individual they had thought was a stranger was in fact the risen Christ (Luke 24). Coupled with reiterated declarations that individuals are responsible for their own destinies—'We're at our own [mercy]'; 'Could it be you only had your silly selves to blame [for the Irish Famine]?'[42]—images of shared food and drink require audiences to consider not only commonalities but also responsibilities that may not be relegated to those who seem different, regardless of how convenient that shift of responsibility might be.

Commonalities are not always positive, and their implications can be difficult to discern. When Adam reads the Koran's injunction 'To you, your religion, to me, my religion', what might seem an endorsement of tolerance reminds Edward of the intolerance he remembers 'at home', where '[s]cared wee shits' insist they are right and God is neither merciful nor compassionate.[43]

The captors remain off-stage, and their voices are never heard. McGuinness has stressed his unwillingness to depict Arab culture, with which he is personally unfamiliar, but commentators from the Arab world cast an interesting light on that decision. Amal Aly Mazhar, for example, sees in the play 'a consistent strategy of negation of the hostile Other', and points out that the captors are referred to not as Lebanese (which the Beirut setting would suggest they are) but only as 'the Arabs' or 'the terrorists'. The result is a generalized 'threat of the cultural Other' and a manifestation of 'unresolved and unresolvable hostility and misunderstanding'. Only the American, she notes, 'attempts to understand the culture of the hostile Other', but even he 'bursts out in a savage tirade' and is eventually killed. The hypothetical invitation for the captors to join the captives at a party which seems to be a drinking party, she points to as a disparagement of the captors' presumed Muslim faith with its prohibition of alcohol. [44]

Heba-T-Allah Aziz Ahmed Selim, whose graduate work was supervised by Mazhar, notes that because 'the Arab captors do not get the opportunity to represent [their culture] themselves' there is 'an atmosphere of menace and intimidation around them'. She sees in the play a 'negative image'[45] of the sort Edward Said described:

---

[40] Ibid., 158.   [41] Ibid., 137–8, emphasis added.   [42] Ibid., 128, 131.   [43] Ibid., 126.

[44] Amal Aly Mazhar, 'Inter/Transcultural Communication in Frank McGuinness' *Someone Who'll Watch Over Me*', in Mona El Halawany and Mohamed Abdel Aaty (eds.), *Proceedings of the Seventh International Symposium on Comparative Literature* (Cairo University, 2003), 71, 72, 74.

[45] Heba-T-Allah Aziz Ahmed Selim, 'Intertextuality as a Structural Element in Selected Plays by Frank McGuinness' (master's thesis, Cairo University, 2008), 209.

> For the general public in America and Europe today, Islam is 'news' of a particularly unpleasant sort. The media, the government, the geopolitical strategies and [. . .] the academic experts on Islam are all in concert: Islam is a threat to Western Civilization.[46]

Selim is building on Eamonn Jordan's earlier analysis that the absence of the terrorists increases the menace, but whereas Jordan sees McGuinness's strategy as a 'clever' avoidance of the difficulty of 'adequately representing' the captors,[47] Selim finds it a manifestation of colonial 'othering'.

It seems unlikely that McGuinness could have written dialogue for the captors that observers from the Arab world would have regarded as allowing the captors to represent their culture themselves. Inevitably such dialogue would exist in the context of authorship by someone personally unfamiliar with the captors' culture. The reactions of Mazhar and Selim, though, cast light on the question of negotiating differences. In *Observe the Sons of Ulster* McGuinness powerfully represented the Northern Irish Protestant community of which he was not a part, and reactions from both sides of the sectarian divide were generally positive, indicating that his portrayal of the Other had succeeded. In that play, his negotiation of differences was aided by the shared language of the two Irish communities, and by the fact that he had lived in Northern Ireland for two years and visited often. The strategy he adopted in *Someone Who'll Watch Over Me* is very different. Arab culture is represented primarily through quotes from the Koran and by Adam's paralleling of passages from the Islamic sacred text with passages from the Bible. Among other things, those parallels are reminders that the Koran regards both Christians and Jews as 'people of the Book', and that Islam's sacred text is seen as completing the sacred texts of those religions. Edward's suggestion that Michael is 'a book man'[48] resonates against the commonality of 'people of the Book'. Use of passages from the Koran is one way of letting the captors' culture speak for itself, and McGuinness has indicated that he worked with both the Everyman translation of the Koran and the Penguin text. 'I chose the "watched" verses because of the remarkable connections between [their?] imagery and the words of the song that the play takes its name from.'[49]

Mazhar recognizes and appreciates Adam's use of the Koran, which she sees as a 'significant' acceptance of 'religious and cultural diversity'.[50] She takes exception, however, to what she sees as McGuinness's 'dramatic ingenuity' which 'does not entitle him to tamper with, or attempt to distort a sacred text'.[51] For a Western reader who does not read Arabic and is not intimately familiar with the Koran, that is a difficult charge to evaluate. Quotes from both Islamic and Judeo-Christian texts seem accurate enough to me, but I recognize my status as an Other in consideration of the Koran. Mazhar's contention that the play 'seeks to consolidate a neo-orientalist ideology [...] and to consolidate the culture of intolerance

---

[46]   Edward Said, *Covering Islam* (New York: Vintage, 1997), 144. Quoted in Selim, 'Intertextuality', 189.

[47]   Eamonn Jordan, *The Feast of Famine: The Plays of Frank McGuinness* (Bern: Peter Lang, 1997), 167, 185.

[48]   McGuinness, *Plays 2*, 107

[49]   Handwritten note from McGuinness to Selim, reproduced in the appendix to her thesis.

[50]   Amal Aly Mazhar 'Self/Other in Past and Present Irish Writing: The Cases of G. B. Shaw and Frank McGuinness', *Cairo Studies in English* (2008), 16.

[51]   Ibid., 16.

and misunderstanding'[52] does seem wide of the mark. It may be that the play consolidates a culture of intolerance, though I do not find that in the text. Clearly, though, McGuinness did not seek to do that. Parallels between the Koran and the Bible (particularly the Song of Solomon, with its parallel imagery, references to Lebanon, and intriguing shifts of gender) negotiate differences by revealing powerful similarities. The refusal to put words in the mouths of the captors seems a sign of respect rather than an effort to silence the Other.

Mazhar's and Selim's responses represent careful engagement with the text and provide an interesting example of trans/intercultural critical communication. An alternative perspective is to remember that the views of a character are not necessarily those of the author, and to recognize that the captors too have difficulties recognizing nuanced cultural differences. They have provided a copy of the Bible, in the apparent belief that all English speakers come from the Judaeo-Christian tradition. They fail to distinguish between residents of the neutral Irish Republic and residents of British Northern Ireland. They also apparently fail to share Adam's perception that Americans are more valuable because they come from a wealthier, more powerful nation. For the captors, English-speaking cultures are all one. There is, however, evidence that at least one of the captors 'wept' and did not wish to kill Adam.[53] Arguably, the play makes the point not only that it is difficult to understand the Other, but also that individuals on both sides of the divide have made the effort to do so.

MUTABILITIE

Five years after *Someone Who'll Watch Over Me*, McGuinness's *Mutabilitie* (1997) premièred. A decidedly undocumentary drama, *Mutabilitie* imagines a Catholic Shakespeare arriving in Ireland and encountering Protestant Spenser. (Never mind that, though Spenser was in fact a Protestant in service to the British empire in Ireland, there is no record that Shakespeare was either Catholic or a visitor to Ireland.) This mixture of fact and fantasy allows for exploration of differences in culture and identity. Add a traditional Irish bard (*file*)—though untraditionally, McGuinness's File is female—two actors who arrive with Shakespeare, and a dispossessed Irish king and his family, and the result is a complex web of intertextuality that allows full scope for audacious use of references to sixteenth-century literature and culture. Isolating a particular strand in the text makes the entire web vibrate. Quotations from Spenser's caustic *View of the Present State of Ireland* coexist with references to Irish myth and various parts of the Shakespearean canon. Historical accuracy is not the play's goal, and revered figures in both English and Irish culture are treated with humour bordering on satire. If McGuinness is not serious about sticking to the 'facts' of history, though, he is clearly serious about exploring important historical and cultural issues.

The play's London première (preceded by a staged reading in Dublin) came after the initial ceasefire in Northern Ireland, but well before peace was firmly established. Violent clashes between Irish factions continued to make headlines, and in 1996 the Provisional IRA ended their ceasefire with a bomb blast in London. For both Irish and English audiences,

---

[52] Ibid., 11.   [53] McGuinness, *Plays 2*, 143.

Mutabilitie would have resonated against those late twentieth-century national and cultural clashes. File makes that connection specific, noting that the world is approaching the end of the sixteenth century and inquiring whether war must 'continue for another hundred years [...] And another [...] And another [...] And another'.[54] Those added hundred-year increments conclude at the end of the twentieth century, when the play premièred. Other episodes make similar points about negotiation of differences. A cross-cultural love affair like the one Dido parodied again bumps against generational differences: File insists that tribal/religious/family loyalty trumps individual affection, because 'That is a decree from God',[55] and demands that Annas (Irish king Sweney's daughter) kill her English lover. There is ongoing consideration of whether individual artists owe primary loyalty to their nations and cultures or to their individual voices. McGuinness himself pointed to that conflict when he noted that File's 'artistic journey' was facilitated by Shakespeare, who gave her 'confidence to speak for herself, rather than for her tribe or for her tradition'.[56] McGuinness is here noting what Seamus Heaney described as 'the quarrel between free creative imagination and the constraints of religious, political, and domestic obligation'.[57]

Mutabilitie is often discussed in the context of the Troubles and tensions between Irish communities. The play's depiction of postcolonial tensions between Ireland and England is also clear, and postcolonial analysis dominates the recent study by Noha Mohamad Mohamad Ibraheem. Her chapter on *Mutabilitie*, subtitled 'A Postcolonial Irish Perspective of Shakespearean Intertexts', offers the advantages of a detailed examination of Shakespearean connections and of a non-Western (Egyptian) perspective on postcolonial issues.[58] Postcolonial examination has illuminated the text of *Mutabilitie* in important ways, and the play includes familiar elements of the Irish–English dichotomy. English colonizers are seen (by both English and Irish) as motivated by economic concerns. Spenser's household regards making servants of the descendants of an Irish king as a way of 'saving' them. The English are Protestant, and the Irish are Catholic (though McGuinness includes ample indications that Irish Catholicism is informed by pre-Christian faiths). Edmund (Spenser) believes 'it is a just cause, this Protestant cause, it is a great one.'[59]

Mutabilitie is a nuanced discussion of colonialism and postcolonialism, firmly situated in the particulars of Irish history. The play is full of opposing accents, religions, and status. It is also full of indications that the differences involved are not so different. Spenser's wife Elizabeth acknowledges that the English hate the Irish, but recognizes that the Irish 'hate us'.[60] The English describe the Irish as 'savages' and 'animals', but File perceives the English as a 'savage race'.[61] The Irish queen Maeve reminds File that, although Edmund is the 'queen's spy', File serves her king as Edmund serves his queen. The English poet is 'no different' from the Irish bard.[62] Both Edmund (a Protestant) and Shakespeare

---

[54] Frank McGuinness, *Mutabilitie* (London: Faber & Faber, 1997), 58–9.   [55] Ibid., 27.

[56] Frank McGuinness, 'New Voices in Irish Theatre', interview with Joseph Long, *Études irlandaises* 24, no. 1 (1999), 11.

[57] 'Introduction' to Seamus Heaney, *Sweeney Astray: A Version from the Irish* (London: Faber & Faber, 1983), n.p.

[58] Noha Mohamad Mohamad Ibraheem, ' "Belated" Shakespearean Mosaics, Modern Shakespearean Intertexts: Al-Duwayri's *Shakespeare Malikan* (1995), McGuinness' *Mutabilitie* (1997) and Norman and Stoppard's *Shakespeare in Love* (1998)' (master's thesis, Cairo University, 2013).

[59] McGuinness, *Mutabilitie*, 10.   [60] Ibid., 10.   [61] Ibid., 8–9, 13.   [62] Ibid., 31.

(a Catholic) suffer from writer's block. The Irish may have lost their native language to English, but the colonized have made English their own and created a superior dialect—just as, by the twentieth century, they have adopted theatre (not a native Irish genre) from the English and excelled at it.

McGuinness uses the stage spaces of the theatrical tradition inherited from the English to reinforce consideration of differences and how they might be negotiated. The English abide in the world of the castle, the Irish in the forest—locations that coexist on a divided stage. The Irish, though, are an integral part of the castle environment, and the English do appear in the forest. What might initially seem a firm distinction, then, indicates instead a breachable border. The play also has sections, comparable to sections in *Observe the Sons of Ulster*, during which interwoven dialogue encourages contemplation of the intersections of worlds. The title *Mutabilitie* and File's mutabilitie song[63] are reminders of Spenser's Mutabilitie Cantos, but also parallel Shelley's 'Mutability' (1816), with its French Revolution association, its balanced opposites, and its indication that different tunes derive from different experiences. The only constant is mutability, and McGuinness's plays have multiple examples of ways in which dying skills and changing times impact individual lives as well as cultural realities. In *Observe the Sons of Ulster* Craig recognizes that the blacksmith business he shares with his father is a 'dying skill' and sees 'the motor business' as the future, despite the reality that people cling 'to whatever's there in their time'.[64] Michael in *Someone Who'll Watch Over Me* has lost his university post because '[t]hey're not teaching much Old and Middle English these days. A dying concern.'[65] File's position as a bard is seriously diminished; Queen Maeve's 'glory is past';[66] and by the end of the play England's dominance of Ireland has also diminished.

The play's conclusion suggests a way of negotiating differences in twentieth-century Ireland. The Anglo-Irish (largely Protestant) population in the Republic, and the Unionist (largely Protestant) community in Northern Ireland retain to varying degrees affinities with England, whence many of their ancestors came, but they are Irish and may hardly be sent 'home' to England. When Edmund and his family flee, they leave behind a child who in some ways represents those contemporary populations. The Irish discuss what to do:

ANNAS.   We have a child.
NIALL.   An English child.
DONAL.   A hostage.
HUGH.   We have a child. He is to be fostered as our own. Reared as our own. Nurtured like our own, and natured like his own, as decreed by our laws, our customs, our religion.[67]

Hugh's decision is coloured by the fact of his own 'lost child',[68] who has perhaps been killed by File to prevent her child's becoming subservient to the English. The different versions of the child's death are reminiscent of the varying accounts of the birth of Grace's dead child in Brian Friel's *Faith Healer* (1979). Hugh's language in describing what he says File has done parallels Lady Macbeth's (I.vii). A mother in Toni Morrison's *Beloved* (1988)

[63] Ibid., 43.   [64] McGuinness, *Plays 1*, 116.   [65] McGuinness, *Plays 2*, 106.
[66] McGuinness, *Mutabilitie*, 31.   [67] Ibid., 100–1.   [68] Ibid., 96.

makes a similar decision to kill her child rather than allow the child to become a slave. Determination to adopt the English child is followed by a communal meal (comparable to one at the end of McGuinness's *Dolly West's Kitchen*) during which the child is given the little milk available. The sixteenth-century English 'remnant', then, is absorbed into the Irish community, not as a hostage, but as one of their own. Implications for twentieth-century Ireland are clear. File has earlier advised Elizabeth to follow Edmund's example in loving Ireland: 'It has become your land. Love it.'[69] Elizabeth is unable to love Ireland, but the play's hopeful end suggests that the Irish may be able to love all the English sons and daughters left in Ireland, who are now their own.

Mutabilitie is a complex play, and it is difficult to consider its multiple layers and implications in a relatively short space. The Irish/English difference is not the only way questions of identity are raised, and some of the other differences rise to greater prominence now that the Irish/English clashes have subsided. Personal identity beyond the realm of nationality is one of those issues. Sweney has forgotten who he is.[70] Edmund, echoing Shakespeare's stage Irishman Macmorris in *Henry V*, asks 'What is my nation?'[71] The Irish are astonished to discover that the English actors may play 'kings or queens or men and women. [...] They can be in love or hate each other, kiss and kill each other, and not love nor die.'[72] Language in this passage reflects awareness that gender roles and sexual orientations involve a level of role-playing. Theatre is everywhere. Identity rests on shifting sands, and though File tells William that the 'riddle of who you are' has been solved,[73] finally the solution holds no more certainty than do current conspiracy theories and debates about who wrote the plays attributed to Shakespeare.

As if these complexities were not enough, *Mutabilitie* raises other questions. The power relationship between men and women is considered, and the play suggests that servants may have far more power than their masters realize. William has arrived not only as a Catholic Englishman but also as a gay Englishman—'He's mad. And he's molly. [. . .] he's into men.'[74] (The terse alliteration of 'mad' and 'molly' echoes Dido's description of himself as 'patriot and poof'.) There are suggestions of incest.[75] Opposing accents, religions, status, gender, sexuality, and nationality are the substance of the play, but the mutability of cultures, texts, and identities makes it difficult to settle on a single vision of almost anything.

GATES OF GOLD

Discussing Irish theatre in the 1990s, Robert Welch noted: 'The Troubles and their implications also raised afresh the issue of identity, and the relationship between culture, territories, and traditions.'[76] That cogent summary may be effectively applied to many of McGuinness's works, but recognition that he deals with additional aspects of identity is also important. As David Cregan noted, no other Irish playwright has 'dealt with issues of gender diversity and sexual "deviance" as consistently as McGuinness'.[77] Increasing critical

---

[69] Ibid., 42.   [70] Ibid., 54.   [71] Ibid., 51.   [72] Ibid., 25.   [73] Ibid., 55.
[74] Ibid., 37.   [75] Ibid., 38–9.   [76] Welch, *Abbey Theatre*, 209.
[77] David Cregan, 'Irish Theatrical Celebrity and the Critical Subjugation of Difference in the Work of Frank McGuinness', *Modern Drama* 47, no. 4 (2004), 671.

attention to such issues is evident in twenty-first century Irish studies.[78] Seán O'Faoláin's (perhaps apocryphal) observation that an Irish queer is someone who prefers women to drink no longer applies, and little outrage or even surprise accompanies revelations about the sexuality of prominent historical and cultural figures. David Norris is no longer 'the only gay man in Ireland', and his observation that the terms 'Irish' and 'homosexual' are mutually exclusive no longer holds, even in public perception. McGuinness remains, as Fintan Walsh has observed, the playwright whose '*oeuvre* [...] has consistently explored the relationship between homosexuality and the production of knowledge in an Irish context'.[79] He has done that more often and more openly than any other Irish playwright, and has been an impetus for changing perceptions.

In *Gates of Gold* (2002) McGuinness again created a play originating in historical events. Inspired by the lives of Hilton Edwards and Micheál Mac Liammóir, who founded Dublin's Gate Theatre (where the play premièred), it presented what Eibhear Walshe has termed 'the nature of unspectacular and ongoing gay life' and addressed 'central questions of the assimilation of the dilemma of gay identity within familial and emotional relationships'.[80] An ageing, long-term gay couple confront the death of one partner. They have founded a Dublin theatre, and conversations are peppered with references to and quotations from theatrical scripts. Conrad, the less flamboyant partner, must watch Gabriel decline in ways that wigs and makeup cannot disguise. They are a loving couple, whose relationship has endured infidelities, silliness, and the hostility of a society in which homosexuality has remained both generally unacceptable and illegal. They are also a couple whose involvement in theatre means they have lived generally public lives. Their familial relationship is remarkably similar to the familial relationship of any long-term heterosexual couple—marred by occasional cruelty, marked by a tendency to bring up ancient grievances, graced by deep commitment. Their agony as they confront their final separation is palpable. At the end of the play the stage directions specify that they kiss—physical contact that is not specified in *Observe the Sons of Ulster*.

One possible reaction to *Gates of Gold* is that it normalizes this gay couple and thus neutralizes the political power and meaning of the queer. Another would be to apply McGuinness's 1985 encapsulation: 'To recognize difference is the best way to begin the process of unity.'[81] Or, to modify that formulation, to recognize unity is the best way to negotiate difference. Each of these approaches can be illuminating. The body of McGuinness's work as a whole, though, makes it abundantly clear that he has never sought to neutralize gay realities, and that he is above all interested in individuals rather than in crowds or political statements. Morash and Richards declare of *Observe the Sons of Ulster*: 'the play persists not because it is political [. . .] but because it is theatrical.'[82] That evaluation applies

---

[78] See e.g. Colm Tóibín's *Love in a Dark Time* (Sydney: Pan Macmillan, 2001), Brian Lacey's 'Terrible Queer Creatures': A History of Homosexuality in Ireland (Dublin: Wordwell, 2008), David Cregan's *Deviant Acts: Essays on Queer Performance* (Dublin: Carysfort Press, 2010), Fintan Walsh's edited collection *Queer Notions: New Plays and Performances from Ireland* (Cork: Cork University Press, 2010), and the *Canadian Journal of Irish Studies* special issue, 'Queering Ireland' (2010).

[79] 'The Flaming Archive', introduction to Walsh, *Queer Notions*, 7.

[80] Eibhear Walshe, 'Opposite Camps: Gay Fiction 1', *Graph 7* (1989), 13. Walshe was not discussing McGuinness's work.

[81] 'Over the Top', interview with Fintan O'Toole, *Sunday Tribune*, 17 Feb. 1985.

[82] Morash and Richards, *Mapping Irish Theatre*, 92.

to the bulk of McGuinness's work, which is theatrical in part because it is interested in individuals. As McGuinness himself said, 'Theatre is a perfect, subversive place for resisting the herd instinct.'[83]

Gates of Gold resembles McGuinness's other works in its blend of the humorous, the fantastic, the poignant, the serious—like Gabriel's fatal illness (a combination of heart disease and bowel cancer), it juxtaposes extremes. Like *Dolly West's Kitchen*, it portrays a gay couple neither apologetic nor in the closet nor doomed to early isolation and death. It also negotiates differences other than those unique to the gay community.

Gabriel and Conrad must negotiate differences any couple would recognize, including their familial situation with Gabriel's sister and his nephew. On a larger level, the play is about the transition from life to death', and the divided set provides a visual aid for that contrast as well as for the contrast of public and private lives. The living room is 'beautifully proportioned' and dominated by the colour red. The bedroom (or dying room, since that is where Gabriel is confined) has a 'large brass bed' with blue and white linens.[84] The rooms are spare, but the stage directions call for one of McGuinness's most realistic sets. As Alma nurses Gabriel and helps him learn to die, he metaphorically nurses her and helps her learn to live. Conrad and Gabriel may lament their childless state, but Conrad's celebration of their life together is moving and healing: 'Two men met. They had a marriage. It lasted. [. . .] though they hurt and could hate each other more than man could bear, he did not want to let the love of his life pass away.'[85]

McGuinness has long embraced and celebrated dissonance, bridging the gap between his academic life and his creative life, while recognizing that those lives may not—perhaps should not—merge or synthesize. Plays that followed *Gates of Gold*—*There Came a Gypsy Riding* (2007) and *The Hanging Gardens* (2013)—examine the sort of family from which Gabriel and Conrad are excluded by their sexuality, but they share with *Gates of Gold* a concern with how individuals survive pain and sorrow and the death of loved ones and continue to live.

The sometimes ferocious intensity with which McGuinness refuses to let differences have the final say is allied with his refusal to sweep away complexity and nuance. The form and tone of his drama are clear reflections of that determination. Split stages, overlapping dialogue, colour-coding of sets and costumes—those staging choices reflect a commitment to recognizing and negotiating differences. The same commitment is evident in his refusal to choose between 'reality' and 'fantasy'; between high and low culture; between comedy and tragedy; between parody and seriousness. Repeatedly he has written plays inspired by historical events, which involves him and his characters in negotiating the relationship between past and present. Repeatedly he has laced his dialogue with intertextual references to a range of high and low culture predecessors

Joseph Valente's reminder that 'the queer contestation of hetero-normativity comes to implicate normativity at large'[86] provides a valuable way to consider McGuinness's work. In the face of common Irish and British confidence that society's norms are heterosexual,

[83] 'Foreword' to Walsh, *Queer Notions*, vii.
[84] Frank McGuinness, *Gates of Gold* (London: Faber & Faber, 2002), n.p.   [85] Ibid., 65.
[86] Joseph Valente, 'Self-Queering Ireland?', *Canadian Journal of Irish Studies* special issue, 'Queering Ireland', 36, no. 1 (2010), 26.

middle-class, and Christian (and, in the case of Ireland, republican), McGuinness echoes Beckett's 'Au contraire'. That 'Au contraire' echoes again in face of the comfortable notion that theatre is high culture and must avoid what *Mutabilitie*'s Sweney calls 'the talk of vulgar women'.[87] McGuinness's work presents no unbridgeable chasm between past and present or *this* and *that*. Differences overlay and influence each other. Comfortable in the no-man's-land of in-betweenness and ambiguity, he is willing to be disruptive and push against gravity, even while respecting borders. It is all part of negotiating differences.

[87] McGuinness, *Mutabilitie*, 14.

CHAPTER 31

DRAMA SINCE THE 1990S
Memory, Story, Exile

EMILIE PINE

IN April 1990 Brian Friel's play *Dancing at Lughnasa* premièred at the Abbey Theatre in Dublin. Against the background of Joe Vaněk's vibrant set of a cottage kitchen and wheat fields ripe for harvest, Friel granted an insight into the lives of his five 'brave' Donegal Mundy sisters, lives at once rich and narrow, expressive and repressive, loving and lonely. This play marked for Friel a move away from the political dramas of Field Day and, in its huge national and international success, became a beacon for Irish drama on a global stage. Audiences were attracted to the intimacy of the play's connection to the central female characters, the sense of community that the play fosters, and the gentle tension between nostalgia and elegy. In many ways *Lughnasa* is freighted with the prominent concerns and tropes that characterize Irish theatrical culture at the end of the twentieth and beginning of the twenty-first century: the role of memory and history; the emphasis on storytelling in the theatre; and a growing awareness of the condition of internal exile for many Irish, be they returning emigrants or unwanted 'others'. These three thematic and formal areas mark out a theatrical terrain that so much of Irish drama has crossed and recrossed, and this chapter will consider these continuities within the tradition of Irish theatre, though the plays discussed here often bring new voices and new emphases to that tradition.

MEMORY AND HISTORY

Lughnasa is framed as a memory play, narrated by the adult Michael, as he revisits his childhood and the summer of 1936. The play thus continues Friel's engagement with the past, seen in plays like *Translations* (1980) and *Making History* (1988)—an engagement shared by other playwrights in this period including Sebastian Barry, Tom Mac Intyre, Elizabeth Kuti, and Tom Murphy. These writers not only remember the pasts they stage but, through their dramatic inquiry, rethink and revise moments in Irish history which often have significance for the present moment.

In December 1990 Mary Robinson was elected the first female President of Ireland, signifying a shift in the national view of women after the conservative results of referenda during

FIG. 31.1 Bríd Brennan, Catherine Byrne, Bríd Ní Neachtain, and Frances Tomelty in a scene from *Dancing at Lughnasa* (Abbey Theatre, 24 April 1990).

Courtesy of the Abbey Theatre and James Hardiman Library, NUI Galway.

the 1980s on divorce and abortion. Though Friel could not have anticipated Robinson's election, *Lughnasa* nevertheless resonated with this political shift through its evocation of the limited lives of women in the year before de Valera's new Constitution of Ireland (1937) would define women's place as mothers in the home (a definition still unchanged). In 1990, the coexistence of a chauvinistic constitution with a female President produced a tension which is mirrored in *Lughnasa* as the Mundy sisters are simultaneously empowered stage presences and voices yet disempowered socially and economically.

Lughnasa is, like so many of Friel's plays, set in Ballybeg in Donegal, and begins with Michael, the play's narrator, summoning up the past: 'When I cast my mind back to that summer of 1936 different kinds of memories offer themselves to me.'[1] As Michael speaks, describing the family's acquisition of a wireless, 'Marconi', as well as the return of his prodigal uncle, Father Jack, he is surrounded by a motionless tableau of his mother, Chris, and four aunts, Kate, Maggie, Agnes, and Rose Mundy. Over the course of the play we get to know these five women and to feel a kinship with them as they face social and economic challenges. Their brother, Father Jack, has returned from decades as a missionary priest

---

[1] Brian Friel, *Plays 2* (London: Faber & Faber, 1996), 7.

to Uganda, but he has returned in some disgrace, having forsaken Catholic doctrine for African ritual. Kate, as schoolteacher, is the main breadwinner of the family but her job is threatened by Jack's unconventional return, as well as by the public shame of Michael's illegitimacy. The family's financial precariousness is underlined when a local factory takes away Agnes and Rose's livelihood as hand-knitters, which leads in turn to their emigration. *Lughnasa* is thus both elegiac and nostalgic, replaying and pausing the moments before the dissolution of the family unit as they enjoy the last of the summer warmth before the harvest.

Michael's narration admits to a feeling of 'unease, some awareness of a widening breach between what seemed to be and what was, of things changing too quickly before my eyes'.[2] Michael's introduction of the idea of change is significant, partly for the play's setting in 1936, during the Spanish Civil War and the lead-up to the Second World War. Change is also prominent on a more local level: the opening of a textiles factory is only one example of the modernization programme of the Free State. Though Friel's stage may look like the well-worn Abbey country cottage, the pace of change, which proves catastrophic for the family, and the explosion of repressed emotions within the family belie this traditional setting. The new wireless is a symbol which connects both pagan Ireland and its modern counterpart; in its representation of technology, manufacturing, and national broadcasting the radio is clearly an emblem of modernity, yet when it suddenly jolts into life, playing the '*very fast [...] raucous sound*' of a céilí band, it provokes the women into dancing wildly, as they cast off their domestic roles and become 'other', demonstrated when Chris dons a surplice and Maggie masks her face with flour.[3] At the end of the dance, when the music stops abruptly and brings the women to a halt, they self-consciously realize that the freedom of the dance ironically acknowledges the self-censorship that they more usually perform. Despite this self-censorship, the Mundy sisters are unable to shape or control their reality, and this is highlighted by the intervention of Michael as narrator at key points of the plot, for example when he halts the action on-stage to inform the audience of the emigration and death of Agnes and Rose. These moments display Michael's control of the plot, and suggest that though his memories reanimate the past, these fragments of personal history remain firmly under the control of the present, and his supervening master-narrative.

If *Lughnasa* is a memory play, then it also belongs to the strong tradition of Irish history plays, a tradition that Friel helped to shape with plays such as *Translations, Making History*, and *The Home Place* (2005). *Lughnasa* is distinguished by its awareness of female subjectivity, which is representative of a growing emphasis in Irish theatre on bringing women to the fore, most evident since Tom Murphy's *Bailegangaire* (1985). This emphasis can be traced across many genres, but is particularly relevant to history plays, as a focus on gender enables playwrights to angle their gaze at often overlooked dimensions of Irish society. Tom Mac Intyre's *What Happened Bridgie Cleary* (2005) dramatizes the real-life history of Bridget Cleary, who was burned to death by her husband for infidelity, and her death covered up by the accusation that she had been 'taken' by the fairies.[4]

---

[2] Ibid., 8.   [3] Ibid., 35–6.
[4] The play follows the lead of pioneering history work by Angela Bourke in *The Burning of Bridget Cleary* (London: Pimlico, 1999).

Mac Intyre situates Bridgie in an afterlife, from which she directly addresses the audience, her husband, and her lovers. Through a powerful soliloquy for the man she truly loved and lost, Mac Intyre enables Bridgie to fully voice her uncensored sexual desires. Throughout the play, however, the knowledge of how Bridgie came to this place of limbo in the afterlife, which she describes as 'gloom', is a poignant contrast to her compelling narrative power and embodiment.[5] For Bridgie, the choice to satisfy personal desire over marital duty results in her death, yet Mac Intyre ultimately refuses to let this punishment silence her. Elizabeth Kuti is another playwright who explores the tension between fulfilling approved social roles and following sexual impulses, for both men and women, in her play *The Sugar Wife* (2005), set in Dublin in the 1850s. The central character is Hannah Tewkley, a devout Quaker and wife to prosperous tea-merchant Samuel. When the couple host Alfred, an English abolitionist, and Sarah, a freed slave, Hannah is compelled to reassess her and Samuel's religious beliefs, though she ultimately re-pledges her commitment to serving the poor, and denying personal and sexual vanity. Kuti provides in Hannah a portrait of a woman who is not driven to moral compromise by economic necessity, but who nevertheless struggles to reconcile personal longings and ideals with bitter realities.

The 1930s has proved a rich period setting for drama, and Friel is not the only playwright to mine this seam; Sebastian Barry's *The Steward of Christendom* (1995) is set in 1932, and explores the afterlife of the transition from colonial to postcolonial statehood through the character of Thomas Dunne, once chief superintendent of the Dublin Metropolitan Police and now a senile inmate of an impoverished rural asylum. Over the course of the play, Dunne recalls his loyalty to Queen Victoria and the British crown and his pride at being a policeman. Dunne's soliloquy on Victoria is a high point of the play's rhetoric, yet the emotional depth of the play derives from Dunne's longing for his son Willie, who died a soldier in the Great War. In the last moments, Barry brings together past and present, son and father in a moving tableau as the ghost of Willie listens while his father narrates a story of his own childhood and father. As the story ends, Willie helps Dunne to bed and then 'lies in close to him',[6] placing his arm 'protectively across his father's chest'.[7] The play thus closes with an implicit act of forgiveness and acceptance between three generations of father and son, and this familial togetherness compensates for the social hardship, political disjuncture, and anachronism of Dunne's situation, the last Catholic Loyalist in the Free State. This is a more successful closing image than Barry creates in his 2009 play *Tales of Ballycumber*, set in the present, in which he illustrates the tragic outcome of holding a stronger allegiance to ghosts than to the living. *Tales* thus suggests, especially if set alongside history plays, that for the past to function as an enabling presence it must be framed and kept at both a temporal and a critical distance.

---

[5]   Tom Mac Intyre, *What Happened Bridgie Cleary* (Dublin: New Island, 2005), 3.
[6]   Sebastian Barry, *The Steward of Christendom* (London: Methuen, 1996), 65.
[7]   Philip Roberts and Max Stafford-Clark, *Taking Stock: The Theatre of Max Stafford-Clark* (London: Nick Hern Books, 2007), 194. Barry continued to develop these characters, and Willie and Dunne's relationship finds its fullest expression in his novel *A Long Long Way* (London: Faber & Faber, 2005).

STORYTELLINGS

If the concern with history and with family is at the heart of Irish theatre, as the reconciliation at the end of *Steward* indicates, then an equally central feature is storytelling. Indeed, to address the audience directly, and thus to gain their sympathy and understanding, is one of the main ambitions of Irish playwrights from Macklin and Boucicault to today. This is obvious in both *Lughnasa*, which is framed by the figure of an on-stage narrator, and *Steward*, which orchestrates closure through Willie's act of listening to his father's stories. This interplay between teller and listener is at the heart of many plays which, though different in form, have at their core a longing for contact and validation. Friel, in *Faith Healer* (1979) and *Molly Sweeney* (1994), has been a formative influence on this genre, which became an identifiable trend in the 1990s and 2000s, particularly in the work of Conor McPherson, Marie Jones, Eugene O'Brien, and Colm Tóibín. The storytellers of these plays are simultaneously vulnerable and resilient, confessional and assertive, as they gesture to the social conditions of loneliness in modern Ireland.

Molly Sweeney continues many of the themes of *Lughnasa* as Friel represents the condition of living on the margins in rural Ireland. The play interweaves the personal stories of Molly Sweeney, her husband, Frank, and her surgeon, Mr Rice, as they address the issue of Molly's blindness. Though the quest to restore Molly's sight through a series of surgeries is partially successful, the restoration of sight results in Molly's profound disorientation, as she is unable to relearn the world and her place in it. This is particularly poignant given that Molly's previous sensory connection to the world, through smell, taste, touch, and sound, was both intimate and unselfconscious. Through newly seeing eyes Molly encounters the world afresh, but her reaction to that world reveals sight as the least reliable, and perhaps least perceptive, of the senses. Molly's disorientation causes her to retreat from reality and to find consolation in a liminal world somewhere between the real, the imagined, and the remembered, and so Friel exposes the fallacious idea that to be healed physically is to be made whole psychically.

The hope of something better than reality drives many monologists, including Kenneth in Marie Jones's *A Night in November* (1994). Where *Molly Sweeney* is structured around three speakers and their interwoven monologues, *A Night in November* has a single speaker: Kenneth McAllister, a Protestant dole clerk from Belfast. These two plays are linked, not only by their year of production, but also in the thematic concern with the idea of transformation; yet where Molly's transformation results in disintegration and reduction of the self, Kenneth's transformation is revitalizing. Kenneth's Damascene conversion comes at a football match between Northern Ireland and the Republic of Ireland, when he belatedly realizes the violence underlying the bigoted Unionist culture he has previously unthinkingly accepted. This sea-change finds expression in Kenneth's rebellious support for the Irish Republic's football team during the 1994 World Cup. In following the team—literally—to New York, Kenneth is able to go outside the narrow cultural and urban boundaries of Belfast and connect to a more expansive sense of himself outside politics and through a more open sense of his own masculinity, both of which engender a new sense of belonging. This reading of the Irish football team as an enabling force outside the political stalemate of Northern Ireland is somewhat simplistic; one might question how much of this newfound spirit of inclusiveness can be maintained once Kenneth returns home after his brief holiday romance with Irishness. Nevertheless, the success of Jones's play testifies to a market demand for narratives which permit optimism, an optimism which linked to the Celtic-Tiger growth of the Irish economy in the 1990s and the slow but hopeful development of the Peace Process in Northern Ireland.

Kenneth is exceptionally fortunate in his discovery and attainment of community via a national narrative of sporting success. Jones's next plays, *Women on the Verge of HRT* (1995) and *Stones in His Pockets* (1996), are less upbeat, confronting the realities of disappointing marriages and young male suicide, with plots driven by exploitation and loneliness. These are two themes also explored by Eugene O'Brien in the double monologue *Eden* (2001), as Billy and Breda reach crisis point in their marriage. Billy is keen to impress the audience from the outset with his masculine prowess, though it is implicit from the beginning that his boasts are driven by the fear of not measuring up to the achievements of other men. Competitive masculinity leads to a debauched night during which Billy assaults a young woman, Imelda, in the false hope that this will raise his social status and cure his impotence. Breda is also intent on seduction—of her husband—hoping that her weight loss will rekindle Billy's interest. Both husband and wife seek not only validation but also a healing through recognition of the value and status of the self by the other. For neither is this healing forthcoming, though Breda does attain some resolution via sex with an alternative partner.

Billy's quest to seduce Imelda Egan is a symptom of his desire for another life, a fantasy he bases on a picture of a country scene, complete with haystacks, shepherds, and milkmaids. This retreat into the pastoral highlights the romanticization of the rural and of patriarchy, in a period when the Irish landscape was increasingly urbanized and suburbanized, and in which gender roles were becoming more balanced. Billy's inevitable failure to seduce Imelda is offset by Breda's unexpected and tender sexual encounter with a stranger on her journey home, suggesting her new ascendancy over her husband. The play ends without reconciliation, underlined by the staging in which the characters, though they sit on either end of a single bench, only address the audience and never each other. Formally, this approach was echoed several years later in Sebastian Barry's *The Pride of Parnell Street* (2007), another double monologue delivered by a married couple. Here again, husband and wife Joe and Janet deliver their stories about the violent breakdown of their marriage, caused in this case by Joe physically assaulting Janet. The marriage is never rehabilitated, but the two actors do come together on-stage in the play's final moments, as Janet visits the dying Joe, creating for the audience the possibility of healing the rupture, even if this is only viable because of the sacrifice of the hyper-masculine character.

O'Brien's emphasis on the failure of communication and the disintegration of the powerbase for macho performance are concerns shared by the playwright Conor McPherson, perhaps the most internationally recognized of Ireland's monologist playwrights. Yet his most successful play situates the act of storytelling in a communal setting. *The Weir* (1997) is set in a run-down rural pub where Brendan serves a small band of local men, Jack, Jim, and Finbar, and the action covers a single evening when the locals are joined by the new occupant of a nearby cottage, Valerie, who has moved to the area from Dublin. Valerie disrupts the masculine and rural pub through both her gender and her association with the city, which reverses the usual transition of young people from country to town.

One of the effects of Valerie's presence is that the men strive to entertain her with local tales of the supernatural. Jack tells a story of fairies agitating at the very house that Valerie has recently moved into. Building on this atmosphere, Finbar then tells a story of a young girl convinced that she is being haunted—an incident that had such an effect on him that it contributed towards his own move from the isolated countryside to the town. The stories become increasingly troubling, as Jim next relates how he saw a ghost in a graveyard who asked Jim to bury him in a plot allotted to a young girl. At this point the men realize that the storytelling has gone too far, and when Valerie excuses herself, they turn on Jim: 'Jaysus. That's some fucking story. To be telling a girl, like. Perverts out in the country.'[8] Yet Valerie, it seems, can hold her own; when she returns to the group she relates her own story of how she has been haunted by the ghost of her daughter who drowned when very young. This personal tragedy silences the men and makes them self-conscious about the implications of their own stories; in attempting to give Valerie an impression of traditional culture—fairies, ghosts, rural isolation—the men realize that they have actually undermined the 'peace and quiet' that she is seeking as solace for the traumatic loss of her daughter.

The Weir thus presents to an audience traditional folk-tale material with a modern edge, yet the play as a whole is more prosaic than ghostly as the sense of rural decline and loneliness lends the bar and its community a downbeat atmosphere. If the men constitute an on-stage community they do so against a background seemingly devoid of family—though Finbar is married, his wife is barely a presence in his life, Valerie is separated, and the other three men are unmarried, suggesting a general and pervasive social alienation. Though Valerie's presence might imply a form of rejuvenation, her own trauma prevents any easy happy ending to the play, while shadowy references to 'perverts' and lost children mark the stories as more disturbing than simply a comment on rural stagnation.

Valerie's ability to tell a good story, and to challenge masculine control of the act of storytelling, is mirrored by two female-centred dramas: Tom Murphy's *Alice Trilogy* (2005) and Colm Tóibín's *Testament* (2011). Murphy's Alice is seen at three stages of her life: as she struggles in her 20s to deal with the limits of motherhood and domesticity, in her 40s with lost love and, finally, in her 50s, with the death of her son. Though Alice interacts with other characters, including an alter ego Al, who anticipates Marina Carr's Scarecrow in *Woman and Scarecrow* (2006), her narrative is also a private one that only the audience is privy to, particularly in her final scene, 'At the Airport', as she waits for her son's coffin to be flown home. Alice struggles to make sense of her life through a series of disconnected thoughts and questions, veering away from the certainty of a master-narrative, and obliquely allowing the audience to see a core self which resists coherence and absolute definition. We can also read this impulse to move away from fixed assumptions in Colm Tóibín's play *Testament*. Told from the perspective of Mary, mother of Christ, from her exile in Ephesus, this monologue powerfully asserts a different perspective as Mary recounts the distance created between mother and child by his destiny, and the impact on her own life of Jesus's notoriety and persecution. Again, as with all these monologues, the audience is granted access to the prize of interior authenticity over public personality, though both versions of the self are, of course, crafted and shaped; indeed, Tóibín's writing is self-consciously and poetically constructed. This authenticity certainly resonates with the

---

[8] Conor McPherson, *Plays: Two* (London: Nick Hern Books, 2004), 52.

founding ideals of the national theatre in 1904, 'to bring upon the stage the deeper thoughts and emotions of Ireland'.[9] Beyond this, however, the consistent emphasis in monologue drama on the necessity that stories are actively listened to and witnessed represents a protest by Irish playwrights that these ideals are, in Irish society, more honoured in the breach than the observance.

OUTSIDERS: FAILED HOMECOMINGS

In *The Weir*, the bar regulars Jack and Jim are archetypal outsiders, typical of those liminal figures who find their place of belonging temporarily in the theatre (or in this case, the pub). Though their community is temporarily challenged by Valerie's arrival, she is quickly incorporated into the intimate group, as the men renegotiate the relative status of insider/outsider positions by contrasting Valerie's welcome arrival with the unwanted influx of summer tourists, the true outsiders. This suspicion of people from outside Ireland attaches itself not only to tourists but also, more pervasively, to immigrants. Yet though immigration into Ireland has been increasingly the norm since the mid-1990s, Irish theatre continues to focus on emigration, and in particular the dispossessed returning emigrant, as a dramatic trope. Indeed, the theme of dispossession is a quality vital to the work of many Irish playwrights, from Friel to Murphy to Dermot Bolger. The idea of belonging is, of course, one of both philosophical longing and physical necessity, and Friel, Murphy, and Bolger engage with the failure to belong by focusing on different forms of failed homecomings.

Friel's *The Home Place* is set in the '[s]ummer of 1878', within the grounds and walls of the Lodge of Ballybeg, the home of Christopher Gore, his son David, and their household, including housekeeper Margaret O'Donnell, who is loved by both father and son.[10] The Lodge becomes a fulcrum for colonial and anti-colonial tensions when Christopher's cousin Richard visits on an anthropometric mission to measure and racially categorize the local people. Unsurprisingly, this occupation creates conflict between the Gore household and the local anti-colonial resistance, led by Con Doherty. Refusing this confrontation, Christopher asks his cousin to leave, in an attempt to appease Doherty and avoid the fate of fellow Anglo-Irish landlords who have been attacked and killed. Though set forty-five years after *Translations* and almost three centuries after *Making History*, *The Home Place* maps a similar struggle between Anglo-Irish and Gaelic, encapsulated in the ambivalent 'home place' reference of the title to both the Lodge in Donegal and the family estate in Kent, England.

At several points in the play, music underlines this ambivalence, as Clement O'Donnell, local schoolmaster and Margaret's father, rehearses his choir to sing Thomas Moore's 'Oft in the Stilly Night'. Moore, who was thought of as Ireland's national poet yet lived in England, dependent on English patronage, seems an apt musical emblem for a play which

---

[9] Manifesto of the Irish Literary Theatre, 1897, quoted in Augusta Gregory, *Our Irish Theatre: A Chapter in Autobiography*, 3rd edn. (Gerrards Cross: Colin Smythe, 1972), 20.

[10] The Lodge may also be read as another incarnation of Ballybeg Hall of *Aristocrats* (1979).

demonstrates the porous nature of English–Irish relations. When the song is heard it has a comparable effect to that of the music in *Lughnasa*, which transports the Mundy sisters to a sense of 'otherness'; here Friel describes the music as '*ethereal* […] *wondrous*',[11] and it has the power to enrapture Margaret, who herself plays a double role as 'chatelaine' of the Big House and citizen of Ballybeg. The song, first published in Moore's *National Airs* (1807), is also featured in James Joyce's *A Portrait of the Artist as a Young Man*, and both Friel and Joyce exploit its national and its personal significance, the lyrics written by Moore to commemorate the death of his young son. The solemnity underlines both the coming split between Christopher and David over the latter's successful wooing of Margaret, as well as the sense of an ending for the Gore family in Donegal.

If departure is in the air at the end of *The Home Place*, then arrival is the issue for both Bolger and Murphy as they dramatize the struggle of former emigrants' attempts at home-coming. In *In High Germany* (1990) Dermot Bolger explored the theme of an emigrant's national allegiance, basing the monologue play on Eoin's journey around Germany to watch the Irish football team play in Euro '88.[12] At the end of the play, Eoin returns to his German girlfriend, Frieda, in Hamburg. Bolger, however, picks up the story in 2010 in *The Parting Glass*, as Eoin attempts to return to Ireland with Frieda and son Dieter, when Frieda's job gives them an opportunity to move to Kildare. Eoin sees the return as a chance to resolve 'phantom pain inside me',[13] though the booming Celtic Tiger economy means he does not return to the Dublin he knows but to a distant suburb of the urban sprawl that now extends into the next county. When Frieda is killed in a traffic accident, and the economy enters recession, Eoin must cope with both emotional and financial dislocation. Eoin reconstructs his life, with the aid of his son Dieter, and finds a new sense of belonging in a newly multicultural Ireland. *The Parting Glass* is typical of Bolger's work in demonstrating the healing power of emotional connectivity, demonstrating home is something more metaphysical than a point on a map.

Yet for many emigrants, home is inherently rooted in the local, and this is certainly the case for Tom Murphy's emigrants in plays like *The Wake* (1998) and *The House* (2000).[14] These plays draw on Murphy's longstanding interest in the liminal figure of the emigrant from *A Whistle in the Dark* (1961), *A Crucial Week in the Life of a Grocer's Assistant* (1969), *Conversations on a Homecoming* (1985), and *Bailegangaire* (1985). In *The House*, Murphy focuses on the problem of homecoming, as Christy attempts to return to Ireland after years living and working in England. For Christy, though he lives and works nearly fifty weeks of the year in England, his hometown remains the place by which he defines himself. Christy wants to come home permanently and reintegrate into the community, in particular the de Burca family, to whom he cleaved when his mother worked for them in the Big House. Christy's fantasy revolves around owning the Big House for himself, a fantasy he achieves by the end of the play but at a huge cost, with the death of Suzanne, the youngest de Burca daughter, at his hands. Christy's confession of his role in Suzanne's death causes in turn the

[11] Brian Friel, *Plays 3* (London: Faber & Faber, 2014), 495.
[12] *In High Germany* later became a RTÉ television drama, directed by Brian MacLochlainn, in the 'Two Lives' drama series in 1994.
[13] Dermot Bolger, *The Parting Glass* (Dublin: New Island, 2011), 13.
[14] *The Wake* is based on Murphy's 1994 novel *The Seduction of Morality* (New York: Little, Brown, 1994).

death of her mother, while his friend Kerrigan feels betrayed at being tricked into giving Christy an alibi. It is a much-diminished community, then, into which Christy finally reincorporates himself, and Murphy questions whether, without community, a home place can offer a meaningful sense of home.

First produced in 2000, the play is set in the 1950s, when migrant workers labouring in England was a social norm;[15] and though this practice was no longer the case in 2000, the play still spoke to the social issues of Celtic Tiger Ireland, such as the sacrifices made to achieve social status through ownership. However, by the time of the play's successful 2012 Abbey revival, the necessity of emigration was once more to the fore of Irish social consciousness and the play resonated even more noticeably. In *The House*, the influx of returning emigrants every summer generates an ambivalent mixture of resentment and pleasure in the locals and, while the local pub sponsors the first drink for the men back from abroad, as a celebration of their return, it also sponsors the last drink before their annual re-emigration. Indeed, there is ambivalence on both sides as, for both the home community and the returning emigrant, the process of return causes huge emotional and social upheaval. In fact, the drunken behaviour of one of Christy's fellow returnees, Goldfish, results in his court appearance, where the judge declares: 'I don't know where you come from.'[16] The futility of Goldfish's attempts to establish his right to call 'this town' home is an indication of the dislocation felt by emigrants, and the failure of the idea of home to be either elastic or inclusive. Inevitably, though Bolger and Murphy only address returning emigrants, their work, alongside plays by Bisi Adigun, Roddy Doyle, Donal O'Kelly, and Charlie O'Neill, gestures towards the reality for thousands of immigrants to Ireland who are excluded and marginalized to a far greater extent than Eoin and Christy.

The permanency of exile is the subject of Sebastian Barry's 1990 play *Prayers of Sherkin*, in which three families, a community of millenarians, live on the small island of Sherkin off the south coast of Cork in the 1890s.[17] The community have left their homes in Manchester in England searching for a New Jerusalem, but have not found the bounty they had hoped for, instead facing a declining community and no prospects for marriage within their sect. This poetic drama follows the emotional journey of the daughter, Fanny, as she negotiates a place for herself between her religious beliefs and her desire for a generative family. On a trip to the mainland, Fanny meets Patrick Kirwan, an eccentric lithographer, and forms a bond. Though their conversation is limited and strange, it is the dance that she performs for him that is captivating. In response to a song being sung off-stage, Fanny dances, as Michael in *Lughnasa* suggests, 'as if language had surrendered to movement'.[18] Here Barry uses the dance as a courting ritual, echoed by Patrick's two subsequent sea journeys across to the island to propose to Fanny.

The play is a gentle exploration of the quietude of a religious community who hold their beliefs sincerely and see themselves as apart from others (rather than being excluded by mainstream society, it is their own choices that lead to their sequestering), and whose

---

[15] In this, the play is reminiscent of John B. Keane's *Many Young Men of Twenty* (1961).

[16] Tom Murphy, *The House* (London: Methuen, 2000), 101–2.

[17] The play grew out of Barry's earlier long poem, *Fanny Hawke Goes to the Mainland Forever* (Dublin: Raven Arts Press, 1989). Fanny Hawke was a distant relative of Barry's, and Barry's writing of her story unlocked a personal history that he has continued to exploit in plays and novels since.

[18] Friel, *Plays 2*, 107.

strongest connection to the national community is via their candle-making for the local convent. The dramatic tension is forged by the choice that Fanny must make, between maintaining fealty to a dying way of life and marrying Patrick and having her own children, fusing the two traditions. In the end, inspired by a vision of their founder, Matt Purdy, Fanny chooses to move to the mainland and all that goes with that choice—permanent alienation from her own family, as she will be outcast and shunned. Her leavetaking is tender but final, and in this permanency, though Barry locates Fanny's story in a particular religious and cultural period, he also acknowledges the finality and exile inherent in any migratory journey and the process of othering that follows.

Outsiders: Internal Exiles

Murphy's career-long dissection of the operations of Irish small-town life is a focus shared by the work of Jim Nolan, in plays such as *The Salvage Shop* (1998), and, strikingly, in the work of Billy Roche, with plays such as *The Cavalcaders* (1993) and *Lay Me Down Softly* (2008). In the late 1980s and 1990s Roche gave a voice and shape to disenfranchised men in the 'Wexford Trilogy': *A Handful of Stars* (1988), *Poor Beast in the Rain* (1989), and *Belfry* (1991). Roche's plays are often set outside the family and family home—in pool halls, betting shops, carnivals, and barbershops—spaces which allow him to explore the dynamics of small communities. The final play of the 'Wexford Trilogy', *Belfry* (1991), is set in the town's Catholic church and considers the isolation inherent in men's lives through the characters of Father Pat, Artie, the church sacristan, and Dominic, an illegitimate boy with learning difficulties, who helps in the church. The play begins with a monologue as Artie relates his sense of his life being measured out by the 'lonely bell' of the belfry which 'tells me that I'm goin' to live a long, long time'.[19] Artie's greatest fear is that at the end of his long life he will have only a small funeral, with none to mourn him.

In an attempt to break out of his isolation, Artie has an affair with Angela, a married local woman who arranges the flowers in the church. The affair, though short-lived, finally allows Artie to express the full range of his emotions and represents his only contact with a woman in the play, other than his ailing and vindictive off-stage mother. Artie's sense of isolation is not unique in the play, and Father Pat, though a spiritual guide to others, is lost himself, repeatedly succumbing to bouts of alcoholism. Even Angela's husband, Donal, is revealed in the closing scene as not just an angry cuckold, but rather a forsaken man powerless before his wife's serial affairs. And Dominic, who is only a teenage boy, is the least cherished character in the play.

Dominic's special needs mean that he is a difficult boy to manage, but he heeds Artie's authority even if he is also mischievous, ringing the church bells to the tune of the Rolling Stones' *I Can't Get No Satisfaction*, and climbing on the roof. These repeated minor misdemeanours prove too much for his uncle and aunt, who commit Dominic to an Industrial School. At the point of his committal, Dominic's aunt reveals that she is, in fact, his biological mother, thus explaining some of her husband's antipathy towards him. Dominic does

---

[19] Billy Roche, *The Wexford Trilogy* (London: Nick Hern Books, 1992), 127.

not go easily and repeatedly runs away; on one of these escapes he is hit by a car and killed outright. The death of the youngest character is an obvious indictment of the ways that community fails its most vulnerable, and the role that institutions play in these failures. Similar failures define the work of Marina Carr, in plays such as *Portia Coughlan* (1996), *By the Bog of Cats* (1999), and *On Raftery's Hill* (2000). Carr's characters are marginal in the extreme, and though these plays are not overt social critiques, the suicides and self-sacrifices of the central female characters, who find no support in their communities, are nevertheless condemnations of family and society.

The tension between family, church, and institution is explored in turn by Thomas Kilroy in plays such as *Talbot's Box* (1977) and *The Secret Fall of Constance Wilde* (1997). In *Christ Deliver Us!* (2010), a tragedy that might also bear the title of 'history play', Kilroy transposes Frank Wedekind's German *fin-de-siècle* play *Spring Awakening* to mid-century Ireland. The play focuses on the fates of three teenagers—Winnie, Mossie, and Michael—who, like Dominic in *Belfry*, struggle to exist within the repressive atmosphere and social rules of small-town Ireland. By the end of the play, Winnie and Mossie are dead, from childbirth and suicide respectively; it is no coincidence that of the three central teenagers, the character who survives is from the most affluent family. The deaths of Winnie and Mossie are a clear accusation against the conjoined power of church and family which foster a society that is lethal to its next generation. The play's first production in 2010, a year after the publication of the Ryan Report, which documented institutional abuse into the mid-1990s, makes this accusation all too relevant for twenty-first-century Ireland.

The 1990s and 2000s witnessed a significant opening up of a culture of silence which had surrounded religious-run institutions for children and women, from orphanages and industrial schools to Magdalene laundries. The arts played a significant role in breaking that silence, from novels and memoirs to documentaries and plays. In theatre, Patricia Burke Brogan pioneered this movement with her play *Eclipsed* (1992), which had a major impact at the Edinburgh Festival that year. Without this play it is hard to imagine later dramatic explorations of similar subject matter, from Mannix Flynn's *James X* (2003) to the Abbey's documentary play *No Escape* (2010), compiled by Mary Raftery, to *Laundry* (2011) by ANU Productions and *The Blue Boy* (2011) by Brokentalkers.

In *Eclipsed*, Burke Brogan sets up a dialogue between past and present, by alternating the action between the present day and 1963; in the present, Rosa is searching for evidence of her mother, Brigit, who was incarcerated in the laundry after her birth. Rosa's search triggers a flashback to the days of the laundry when Brigit and the other inmates, Cathy, Mandy, and Nellie-Nora, cleaned the dirty laundry of the local bishop and the Athlone seminary. Though the women dream of the outside world and, in particular, of finding their children, they realize that they are not wanted by society; Mother Victoria shouts at one point: 'No one else wants them! No one else wants them!',[20] a sentiment that the women clearly internalize as Brigit describes them, herself included, as '[t]he outcasts! The women nobody wants!'[21]

In scenes which are reminiscent of Friel's *Lughnasa*, the women console themselves for their imprisonment through play-acting and dance, entering into a communal fantasy which makes it possible for them to express an interior freedom struggling against a

---

[20] Patricia Burke Brogan, *Eclipsed* (Knockeven: Salmon Publishing, 1994), 31.   [21] Ibid., 34.

repressive society. The four female inmates perform a mock wedding scene between Mandy and a mannequin, which is dressed up in the bishop's soutane to represent Elvis. Like the dance in *Lughnasa*, this scene provides a forum for the women to unleash some of their pent-up energies, yet it also helps them to dispel some of that energy, thus enabling them to return to their work in the laundry. Where in *Lughnasa* the explosion of energy disturbs the Mundy sisters as a portent of change and unacknowledged anger, the more harmonious and socially sanctioned marriage plot in *Eclipsed* paradoxically grants a release that maintains the status quo.

The women are ruled in the play by two nuns, Mother Victoria and Sister Virginia; the former is a harsh disciplinarian who fundamentally believes the laundry women must pay for their 'sins', while Sister Virginia is more compassionate to the women and critical of the patriarchal structures of the church. The role of Sister Virginia brings to the play not just the presence of a good nun but, in a move that resonates with Tóibín's *Testament*, a reimagining of Christianity as a female- and mother-centred religion, in which a Christ borne by a woman 'performed [his] first miracle at [his] mother's request'.[22] Indeed, Sister Virginia's emphasis on the vital role of women in Christ's life highlights the harsh treatment of women by the Catholic Church. These tensions are brought to a head when Cathy dies during an escape attempt, and Brigit challenges Sister Virginia to give her the keys. Brigit does escape, but Brogan does not disclose what happened to her, and this ambiguity, much like the disappearance of Agnes and Rose in *Lughnasa*, is disquieting. Equally unsettling is the present-day situation in which Nellie-Nora meets Brigit's daughter Rosa but declines Rosa's invitation to leave the convent because, after decades of institutionalization, she cannot, saying, 'I—I don't go out much.'[23]

The separation of Ireland's others from mainstream society into institutions is a deep and far-reaching trauma both directly confronted and tacitly acknowledged by Irish playwrights. Yet the end of the twentieth century and the beginning of the twenty-first have also seen plays which succeed in their attempts at reconciling otherness and thus moving away from a condition of internal exile. Frank McGuinness's work has consistently represented an imaginative impulse towards healing, generosity, and inclusiveness. In the 1990s, the fulcrum of this impulse could be seen in *Someone Who'll Watch Over Me* (1992) and *Dolly West's Kitchen* (1999). *Dolly West's Kitchen* is set in Donegal during the Second World War when the Free State was a neutral country, but there were British and American soldiers stationed across the border in Northern Ireland. The play represents a coming together of these elements, when the matriarch, Rima, invites three soldiers across to her home. This act of boundary-crossing upsets the balance of the Free State household, yet this upheaval provokes positive change and creates a new community; the dance of these characters is challenging but also creative. Rima's three children—Justin, Esther, and Dolly—are all transformed through love; Justin acknowledges his homosexuality through his love for American soldier Marco Delvarico, Esther has an affair which provokes a reunion with her husband, and Dolly reconnects with her former lover, the British officer Alec. Though these relationships are all begun while the men are stationed in Northern Ireland before seeing action, the bonds are only confirmed after they return from battle traumatized by what they have seen and in desperate need of healing. McGuinness's work demonstrates

---

[22] Ibid., 31.   [23] Ibid., 76.

the power of possibility, that through trauma and self-exile something new and more hopeful can emerge.

CONCLUSIONS

The decades since the opening night of *Lughnasa* have witnessed a broadening of the Irish stage to include new forms, such as site-specific, devised, and documentary theatre. The state has undergone huge transitions in these years too, through the Celtic Tiger, the ongoing Peace Process, and the global economic crisis, and it is as yet unclear how exactly the nation has weathered these changes. Formal shifts have enabled Irish theatrical culture to remain current, to keep pace with social and economic change, and to reflect the new faces and voices of Ireland. Nevertheless, more traditional forms and themes have also been sustained, as shown by the plays discussed in this chapter. The continuing importance of the rural and the family at the heart of Irish drama, and the continuation of storytelling as a structural device for new Irish plays, demonstrate the richness derived by keeping faith with foundational elements.

These continuities within the theatre may seem paradoxical given the massive shifts in Irish society and life outside of the theatre, yet this emphasis on an anchoring stability (at least dramaturgically) does not mean that these plays either ignore or turn their back on changing social tides. Indeed, the continued importance of the history play (particularly to the stages of the Abbey Theatre), though it may suggest a conservative impulse, uses the backward glance to relate the past to the present moment, as seen through both Burke Brogan's *Eclipsed* and Kilroy's *Christ Deliver Us!* We should therefore not essentialize these playwrights as pure traditionalists, nor assume that tradition is synonymous with stasis, especially given Irish playwrights' alertness to contemporary social signifiers. McPherson's *The Weir*, for instance, draws on fairy lore, but includes Valerie's urban world within the scope of the supernatural, while the failure of Billy's playboy performance in O'Brien's *Eden* is due to a shift away from patriarchy and its attendant power relations. Equally, though Friel's *Lughnasa* and Murphy's *House* are set in the 1930s and 1950s, they resist easy nostalgia for a simpler time. Such attunement to social context allows these plays to speak to, as well as for, a modern Ireland, a dialogue which is, at heart, cathartic in both its acknowledgement of personal and (by implication) national crises, and in its yearning for reconciliation through understanding. As these plays continue to perform a vital role on the Irish stage, it is clear that that act of reconciliation, of then and now, tradition and change, self and other, is a journey in progress, not a final destination.

CHAPTER 32

....

IRISH DRAMA SINCE THE 1990S
Disruptions

....

CLARE WALLACE

IN the midst of his seminal dystopian novel *Brave New World*, Aldous Huxley stages an encounter between past and future. John, an inhabitant of one of the last 'uncivilized' remnants of the old world, meets Bernard Marx and Lenina Crowne, citizens of World State, who are on a tour of the Savage Reservation, and who invite John to return with them. John is an autodidact outsider, schooled only in primitive customs and the works of Shakespeare. He greets the prospect of being transported to London, the heart of progress, with a rapturous exclamation borrowed from *The Tempest*: 'O brave new world that has such people in it. Let's start at once.' To which his interlocutor Bernard Marx responds quizzically: 'You have a most peculiar way of talking sometimes […] And, anyhow, hadn't you better wait till you actually see the new world?'[1] It is an episode replete with dramatic irony for the consequences of John's rapid relocation to a world where scientific progress, sexual liberation, and rampant consumerism reign are plainly far from harmonious. Like the beleaguered John Savage of *Brave New World*, Ireland in the last decade of the twentieth century seemed to be catapulted into a dubiously defined realm of progress, the consequences of which are still unfolding. The futuristic flavour to the former Taoiseach Bertie Ahern's 1998 proclamation—'The cynics may be able to point to the past. But we live in the future'—provides the starting point for Roy Foster's study of Ireland's recent past, *Luck and the Irish* (2007). For Foster, the politician 'was expressing the zeitgeist more profoundly than perhaps he knew': Ireland indeed seemed to be in 'fast-forward mode, as transformations accumulate[d] in economic practice, in social and religious experience, in cultural achievement and in political relationships, both at home and abroad.'[2] From the vantage point of the present, it is easy to be disenchanted about the outcomes of the Celtic Tiger era: so much went drastically wrong and so few who rode the gravy train were brought to account, even after the wheels had fallen off. Yet something momentous also took place that

---

[1] Aldous Huxley, *Brave New World* (London: Granada, 1977), 116.
[2] R. F. Foster, *Luck and the Irish: A Brief History of Change, 1970–2000* (London: Allen Lane, 2007), 1.

has had a deep and heterogeneous impact upon Irish social and cultural life generally, and theatre specifically.

This chapter will consider some key developments in new writing from 1990 to 2007—a remarkably creative period for Irish theatre and the discourse around it, which coincides with Ireland's rise and fall as 'an icon of the globalisation process'.[3] As Foster puts it: 'Accompanying this [process] has been [. . .] a striking efflorescence in the creative arts. The achievements and insights of writers are themselves part of the story, and so is the marketing of the culture industry.'[4] Simultaneous with the ongoing contributions of the group of largely established writers treated by Emilie Pine in the previous chapter, work by a dynamic new generation of playwrights emergent in the 1990s energized and, in some highly provocative ways, intervened in Irish theatre. A cluster of these new playwrights—Marina Carr, Martin McDonagh, Conor McPherson, Enda Walsh, and Mark O'Rowe—achieved substantial success both in Ireland and internationally, and are now widely recognized as the principal voices of the turn-of-the-century wave of new Irish writing. Since the work of Marina Carr is treated in the following chapter, the focus here is confined to McDonagh, McPherson, O'Rowe, and Walsh—a remit that regretfully perpetuates a gender-imbalanced view of playwriting in the period and points to the ongoing inequities in the representation of women in theatre-making.

In attempting to understand what these writers bring to Irish theatre, context is pivotal, but manifold. None is writing *about* the Celtic Tiger; indeed, as Eamonn Jordan cautions in *Dissident Dramaturgies*, one must remain alert to complexities of context and the pitfalls of ad hoc reasoning.[5] In retrospect it is also clear that their work says a great deal about the disorientations and impulses of the era, though always in indirect, elliptical ways.

In *Twentieth-Century Irish Drama*, Christopher Murray suggested:

> Irish drama is a long, energetic dispute with a changing audience over the same basic issues: where we come from, where we are now, and where we are headed. Alternatively, these questions comprise history, identity, home or a sense of place, and visionary imagination.[6]

While this definition is capacious enough to accommodate vastly different forms of theatrical activity, it is instructive to consider the fractures that appeared in the late 1990s and early 2000s. One of these, delineated insightfully by Patrick Lonergan, is what happens when Irish theatre becomes a commodity marketed to a purportedly global audience.[7] Another question contingent upon this is whether the issues are still basically the same at all, given the transformations in how the world is perceived spatially and temporally in the wake of globalization. In our introduction to the section on Irish theatre in *Irish Literature Since 1990: Diverse Voices*, Ondřej Pilný and I reflected on how various formal and thematic threads might continue to be traced in new Irish drama. The tragic–mythic,

---

[3] Fintan O'Toole, 'Irish Culture in a Globalised World', in Munira H. Mutran and Laura P. Z. Izarra (eds.), *Kaleidoscopic Views of Ireland* (São Paulo: Universidade de São Paulo, 2003), 76.

[4] Foster, *Luck and the Irish*, 4.

[5] Eamonn Jordan, *Dissident Dramaturgies* (Dublin: Irish Academic Press, 2009), 10.

[6] Christopher Murray, *Twentieth-Century Irish Drama: Mirror Up to Nation* (Manchester: Manchester University Press, 1997), 224.

[7] See Patrick Lonergan, *Theatre and Globalisation: Irish Drama in the Celtic Tiger Era* (Basingstoke: Palgrave, 2009).

the experimental, the lyric–narrative, the melodramatic–comic, and the history–memory play were among the most recurrent, and these tendencies 'at times intermingle, at times diverge, and at other times cut across each other with turbulent effect'.[8] That said, while many of these approaches can readily be observed in the work of the new playwrights of the 1990s, they are often reoriented, at times even derailed. Working in the slipstream of advancing, anarchic postmodernity, these writers are disruptive in often highly ambivalent ways that present keen interpretive challenges to their audiences.

MARTIN McDONAGH: AFTER AUTHENTICITY

Martin McDonagh burst onto the Irish and British theatre scenes in 1996; four of his plays— *The Beauty Queen of Leenane* (1996), *The Cripple of Inishmaan* (1996), *A Skull in Connemara* (1997), and *The Lonesome West* (1997)—were produced in swift succession, followed by *The Lieutentant of Inishmore* (2001), *The Pillowman* (2003), *A Behanding in Spokane* (2011), and *Hangman* (2015). One of the most commercially successful new playwrights of the era, McDonagh's work has sparked extensive and intense critical debate, in particular in relation to the plays up to 2001, all of which use Irish settings. Most controversy surrounding McDonagh originates from two entangled areas: the first concerns his personal position in relation to his subject matter; the second, the treatment and perceived purpose of that subject matter.

McDonagh's provenance is hybrid; born in London to Irish parents, he holds dual citizenship, but the fact that he has never lived in Ireland certainly was an aspect of the anxiety and scepticism expressed by some commentators about the plays set in the west of the country. He has countered by claiming: 'I've always felt half-Irish, half-English. The suggestion seems to be that I'm not allowed to write about where my parents are from. I hate that idea of authenticity, that you must be tied down only to what you know first-hand.'[9] The question whether he is perceived as an outsider whose comedy works at the expense of his characters and the audiences who enjoy them, or an insider who dismantles rote notions of cultural identity with postmodern aplomb, recurs in different guises as a feature of the plays' reception.

Another dimension to responses has been the image McDonagh projected in the media in the 1990s as a rebel, out to disrupt the 'cycle of boredom' of British drama[10] bent upon 'some kind of punk destruction of what's gone before',[11] while boasting of his ignorance of theatre and preference for cinema. This public posturing worked to win McDonagh attention in the UK at a time when London stages were crowded with work by new playwrights.[12]

---

[8] Clare Wallace and Ondřej Pilný, 'Home Places: Irish Drama since 1990', in Scott Brewster and Michael Parker (eds.), *Irish Literature Since 1990: Diverse Voices* (Manchester: Manchester University Press, 2009), 46.

[9] Dominic Cavendish, 'He's Back, and Only Half as Arrogant', *Telegraph*, 6 Apr. 2001.

[10] Richard Zoglin, 'When O'Casey Met Scorsese', *Time*, 13 Apr. 1998, 215.

[11] Matt Wolf, 'Martin McDonagh on a Tear', *American Theatre* 15, no. 1 (1998), 48.

[12] As described at length in Aleks Sierz's *In-Yer-Face Theatre: British Drama Today* (London: Faber & Faber, 2001).

His first play, *The Beauty Queen of Leenane*, won over the critics, but his press image served to make him a memorable personality. That image some found amusing, an extension of the subversive playfulness of his work; others have marshalled McDonagh's remarks in order to castigate him. A vivid example is Mary Luckhurst, who, on the basis of various comments the playwright had made in newspapers and an analysis of *The Lieutenant of Inishmore*, dismissed him as 'a thoroughly establishment figure who relies on monolithic, prejudicial constructs of rural Ireland to generate himself an income'.[13] Nevertheless, the difficulty lies in how much weight to give McDonagh's provocative statements about theatre, since many of his most quoted comments are throwaway, rather than a part of a considered artistic agenda.

Of all McDonagh's work to date, it is the Connemara and Aran Island plays that most directly address Irish dramatic tradition to expose questions of representational practice and politics. McDonagh is without question a gifted writer, whose raucously grim humour and tightly plotted plays blend hilarity, cruelty, and absurd exaggeration with a lively sense of provocation. His contribution to the changing landscape of Irish theatre in the 1990s and early 2000s comes in the guise of a reorientation of stage reality that refracts two associated historical forms—the Irish play and the peasant play—through the prism of a late twentieth-century ironic sensibility. Consequently, the Connemara and Aran plays parade postmodern tendencies in their heavy dependence on recycling, ironic detachment, and 'bad' taste: what they circulate are representations of representations with no guaranteed recourse to a 'truthful' original.[14]

One of the greatest challenges McDonagh's Irish work presents, then, is the extent to which it is 'unoriginal' even while it is greeted as innovative. As Chris Morash notes, the conventions of the Irish play with its cast of Irish character types and settings were already established in the late eighteenth century, and grew increasingly popular throughout the nineteenth. Representational authenticity was not a major concern; neither was originality. Baldly stated by Dion Boucicault: 'Playmaking is a trade like carpenting. Originality [. . .] is a quality that never existed.' Morash concludes: 'Freed from the constraints of originality and representation, the Irish play in the nineteenth century proliferated, and became a globalised form.'[15] McDonagh dovetails aspects of this popular mainstream tradition with elements of the peasant play—a form conceived to a large extent as corrective of the excesses of the Irish play, and which was to become prevalent in Irish theatre during the first half of the twentieth century. Unsurprisingly, then, there is much that is conventionally and symbolically overdetermined in McDonagh's drama: the settings and the fictive Hiberno-English speech of their characters cannot but recall the work of John Millington Synge, while the renovating of cultural stereotypes evokes Dion Boucicault. Set in the familiar, apparently realistically presented, interior spaces of the cottage kitchen or rural shop, these dramas nod to the scenographic patterns of the peasant play,

[13]   Mary Luckhurst, '*Lieutenant of Inishmore*: Selling (-Out) to the English', in Lilian Chambers and Eamonn Jordan (eds.), *The Theatre of Martin McDonagh: A World of Savage Stories* (Dublin: Carysfort Press, 2006), 117.

[14]   See Clare Wallace, *Suspect Cultures: Narrative, Identity and Citation in 1990s New Drama* (Prague: Litteraria Pragensia, 2006), 131–84.

[15]   Christopher Morash, 'Irish Theatre', in Joe Cleary and Claire Connolly (eds.), *The Cambridge Companion to Modern Irish Culture* (Cambridge: Cambridge University Press, 2005), 324–5.

while the melodramatic device of the letter (lost, found, forged, destroyed, or read aloud) makes frequent appearances: in *The Cripple of Inishmaan*, *The Beauty Queen of Leenane*, *The Lonesome West*, and in a slightly varied form as the confession (written and then destroyed) in *A Skull in Connemara*.

Aligned, these elements invite certain expectations that are then warped: the 'defamiliarizing poetic effect' of Synge's coined Hiberno-English mutates into 'uncouth, ungainly and deflationary' speech;[16] the scenographic citations fail to undergird a sense of realism but serve as ironic amplification. The extent to which McDonagh was aware of these expectations at the start of his career is difficult to ascertain. However, the director and co-founder of Galway's Druid Theatre, Garry Hynes, was definitely conscious of their potential. Hynes bought the rights to première *The Leenane Trilogy* in 1995, and her role not only in launching McDonagh's career but also in shaping the plays with a view to the debates they might catalyse among audiences and critics was decisive.[17] Hynes's discussion of the staging of *The Beauty Queen of Leenane* is particularly illuminating. Her casting decisions and staging deliberately played with the familiar, to segue into the unfamiliar: 'That was part of the whole cheat [...] We *wanted* them to think they were seeing John B. Keane play [...] But a half an hour later they're watching something completely different.'[18]

Humour is a core component of the unease generated by the work. In contrast to the plays that followed, *The Beauty Queen of Leenane* is acutely tragicomic; the plight of Maureen Folan, sole carer for her recalcitrant mother, Mag, is pitiful even though the tone of the play is comic. McDonagh builds sympathy for Maureen by gradually revealing Mag as callous, slow-witted, and vindictively devious. Jokes about brands of biscuits, the Irish language, and the boredom of rural life deck the dialogue. Mag's habit of emptying her chamber pot in the sink works as a piece of disgustingly hilarious stage business. However, the humour is displaced by a destructiveness that suddenly erupts into the domestic scene. The revelation of Maureen's history of mental illness, her physical abuse, and, ultimately, murder of her elderly mother forces a complete reappraisal of the preceding comic bickering. The subtleties of *The Beauty Queen*, however, diminish as the configuration of comedy and violence in a farcical arrangement becomes the dominant mode for *A Skull in Connemara*, *The Lonesome West*, and *The Lieutenant of Inishmore*, which infamously features on-stage torture and dismemberment. The remix of Synge, Punch and Judy, Grand Guignol, and Quentin Tarantino is certainly entertaining, but the broadside humour, improbable twists of plot, and reliance upon violent action come, predictably, at the expense of multidimensional characters and emotional depth.

A proliferation of eclectically assembled references is evident in all McDonagh's work, but is most structurally significant in *The Cripple of Inishmaan*, the play's parodic wit being chiefly underwritten by its intertext—Robert Flaherty's famous 'documentary' film, *Man of Aran* (1934). Here McDonagh openly takes on traditions of representation,

---

[16] Nicholas Grene, 'Ireland in Two Minds: Martin McDonagh and Conor McPherson', in Chambers and Jordan, *Theatre of Martin McDonagh*, 53.

[17] Patrick Lonergan discusses Hynes's significance in detail in *The Theatre and Films of Martin McDonagh* (London: Methuen, 2012), 46–9.

[18] Patrick Lonergan, '"Monstrous Children": Garry Hynes in Conversation', in *Theatre and Films of Martin McDonagh*, 159.

though it is significant that they are not theatrical in origin. Flaherty's film presented an apparently authentic vision of peasant life of the western seaboard through selective editing and strategic fictionalization; McDonagh's play takes a postmodern sledgehammer to those pretences and, by extension, to the values they imply. In doing so, the play seems to illustrate Fredric Jameson's understanding of 'intertextuality as a deliberate, built in feature of the aesthetic effect, and as the operator of a new connotation of "pastness" and pseudo-historical depth, in which the history of aesthetic styles displaces "real" history.'[19] McDonagh takes evident pleasure in dramatically unmasking the liberties Flaherty took with historical accuracy and mocking nationalist clichés, but his goal is pointedly not corrective accuracy. Lonergan sums up the play's approach as 'a damning critique of Flaherty's documentary, which is attacked for misrepresenting life on the Aran Islands. Yet rather than presenting an alternative vision of that life—rather than revealing "the truth"—McDonagh instead criticises *all* forms of representation that lay claim to authenticity.'[20]

The ironic register of the plays shields them from the implications of their involvement with the conventions they parody and pastiche; it also permits the coupling of an apparently critical stance with an indulgence in what might be the very target of critique. This is most clearly evidenced in *The Lieutenant of Inishmore*, a play that riffs on the subject of Irish Republican violence and terrorism and has divided critics as to whether it works as incisive political satire, or whether it is merely meretricious. According to McDonagh, *The Lieutenant* 'came from a position of what you might call pacifist rage. [. . . I]t's a violent play that is wholeheartedly anti-violence.'[21] Such impetus notwithstanding, the play itself is governed by a 'straw man' approach, making such exaggerated fun of its fictional terrorists that cheap laughs and grotesquely violent action encroach upon any space of reflection and render any political agenda in vague terms at best. The subject of the Troubles is recognizably political in a manner distinct from the debates prompted by the previous works, and the presentation of such a subject in unabashedly comic form proved difficult to place. McDonagh accused both the National Theatre and Royal Court of cowardice and censorship for rejecting the play (notably Druid also passed); however, their reservations may well have derived more from artistic concerns than alleged anxieties about the Northern peace process and the risk of terrorist retribution.

Lonergan argues that McDonagh's amoral stage worlds oblige their audiences to take up the baton of responsibility,[22] but the question lingers as to whether ironic violence, like ironic sexism, can function critically, or if it merely reintroduces and normalizes regressive attitudes under cover of knowing detachment or popular entertainment. The sense of having one's cake and eating it remains an ambivalent element to McDonagh's aesthetics—one that is much more openly acknowledged in his meta-cinematic films *In Bruges* (2008) and *Seven Psychopaths* (2012).

---

[19] Fredric Jameson, 'Postmodernism, or the Cultural Logic of Late Capitalism', in Thomas Docherty (ed.), *Postmodernism: A Reader* (Brighton: Harvester Wheatsheaf, 1993), 76.

[20] Lonergan, *Theatre and Films of Martin McDonagh*, 58–9.

[21] Sean O'Hagan, 'The Wild West', *Guardian*, 24 Mar. 2001.

[22] Lonergan, *Theatre and Films of Martin McDonagh*, 230.

Conor McPherson: Stories and Spectres

Involved in writing and directing while a student at University College Dublin, Conor McPherson won the Stewart Parker Award for *The Good Thief* at the Dublin Theatre Festival in 1994. The success of *This Lime Tree Bower* in 1995 led to a transfer to the Bush Theatre in London in 1996, and by 1997 McPherson had secured a major reputation with *St Nicholas* and *The Weir*, both of which opened in London. His subsequent work for theatre includes the plays *Dublin Carol* (2000), *Port Authority* (2001), *Come on Over* (2001), *Shining City* (2004), *The Seafarer* (2006), *The Birds* (2009), *The Veil* (2011), and *The Night Alive* (2013). Although lacking the incendiary impact of McDonagh's drama, McPherson's is delicately textured and manifests an evolving engagement with theatre as artistic practice. Early in his career McPherson distanced himself from the determining discourses of national identity:

> Although I had never set out to write consciously about my own country, my work seemed to suggest Irish issues to certain critics. [. . .] This may be true for some people, but all I was trying to do was to write plays that hold your attention, make you laugh and hopefully engender a sense of community between the work and the audience. I wasn't concerned with geography or politics.[23]

This predilection is confirmed by his preference to première his plays, whenever possible, in London rather than in Dublin—a practice unusual in modern Irish theatre history. Chiming with these apparently post-national aspirations is a profound sense of metaphysical dislocation that is vital to understanding McPherson's contribution to the theatre of the 1990s and 2000s. These plays are sensitive barometers of a wider cultural condition; in form and content they register some of the spatial, temporal, and ethical disorientations of the period.

McPherson's theatre is a model of subtle formal realignment as opposed to ludic and manic excess. His most widely produced play of the 1990s, *The Weir*—greeted enthusiastically as the epitome of cultural authenticity and traditional dramatic craftsmanship— indeed seems, at first sight, on a continuum with a highly traditional mode of Irish lyrical naturalism with a familiar emphasis on storytelling. But it is a backward glance that is complicated by a self-consciousness of the doubtful veracity of its own images. Jordan challenges the understanding of *The Weir* as exemplary of Irish dramatic conventions by reading the play as a 'meta-pastoral' that 'offers a space where the charade of authenticity is contested'.[24] Clearly, McPherson's treatment of space and form has far-reaching implications that ripple out across the apparently placid surfaces of the work.

Just as the dominant questions of parody and authenticity in McDonagh's drama centre the discourse around it, so too McPherson's frequent recourse to monologue and the implications of the form remain distinctive features of his 1990s writing that have drawn critical

---

[23] Quoted in David Edgar, *State of Play: Playwrights on Playwriting* (London: Faber & Faber, 1999), 100.

[24] Eamonn Jordan, 'Narrating Authenticities in Conor McPherson's *The Weir*', *Irish University Review* 34, no. 2 (2004), 366–7. Jordan elaborates this argument further in *Dissident Dramaturgies*.

attention, even though since then he has largely moved beyond it. In interview with Gerald C. Wood in *Imagining Mischief* (2003), McPherson claimed that the monologue form freed him to 'to tell smaller stories in a bigger way'.[25] It has also allowed him to explore the collusive and mischievous aspects of the theatre experience in collaboration with some fine performers. McPherson's three most significant monologue plays—*St Nicholas, This Lime Tree Bower*, and *Port Authority*—craft a form of performative storytelling that is not only distant from the abstract experimentalism of Beckettian monologue but also distinct from the lyricism of Friel's monologue plays *Faith Healer* (1979) and *Molly Sweeney* (1994).

McPherson was, of course, only one of a number of new writers who turned to the monologue format in the 1990s, and critics have subsequently sought to explain the significance of this development in various ways. Rooting his analysis in a sociopolitical context, Brian Singleton argues that monologue served primarily as a space for the articulation of contemporary Irish masculinities in crisis[26]—a convincing approach not only to McPherson but to O'Rowe's work as well. Crucially, too, McPherson's monologue work spotlights the communicative and epistemological role of story at a time when the established narratives of Irish identity were undergoing massive transformation.

McPherson's monologue plays fuse a heightened attention to diegesis with an anti-illusionistic acknowledgement of the theatre space; in *Port Authority*, stage directions make this explicit: 'The play is set in a theatre.'[27] Words are given priority and, as director of most of his own work, McPherson exerts strict control over the extent to which actors might invest their roles with physical action. The result is not an unequivocal affirmation of narrative truth, but rather its inconclusiveness. *St Nicholas* enacts a convoluted, self-reflexive game with the audience around questions of credulity and theatricality, as the theatre critic protagonist unfolds a tall tale of self-destructive conduct and vampires. *This Lime Tree Bower* advances this game of doubtful confidence and bad behaviour with a collage narrative. Finally, *Port Authority* assembles parallel, isolated stories of failure presented by three Dublin men of different generations. The dominant feeling left by each of these thematically divergent pieces is of dramatic narrative untethered from its usual contextual or formal coordinates.

One of the characteristics of the monologue form is the way in which the space of each character's story is as extensive or as confined as the character's perspective on their world. As Sara Keating points out, although the Irish monologue play might tend 'to eschew rather than embrace the social context informing its characters' world-views', the form itself may point to 'the increasingly individualistic reality of late-capitalist Celtic Tiger Ireland, a society where traditional communities had been shattered by urban migration and the swell of social housing on Ireland's cities' outskirts'.[28] The progressive sense of ambivalence across these plays points to a discomfort with the shadowy social realities and contingent

---

[25]   Quoted in Gerald C. Wood, *Conor McPherson: Imagining Mischief* (Dublin: Liffey, 2003), 128.

[26]   Brian Singleton, '"Am I Talking to Myself?" Men, Masculinities and the Monologue in Contemporary Irish Theatre', in Clare Wallace (ed.), *Monologues: Theatre, Performance, Subjectivity* (Prague: Litteraria Pragensia, 2006), 260–77.

[27]   Conor McPherson, *Plays: Two* (London: Nick Hern, 2004), 132.

[28]   Sara Keating, 'The Geography of Conor McPherson's Plays: The City as Salvation or Hell', in Lilian Chambers and Eamonn Jordan (eds.), *The Theatre of Conor McPherson* (Dublin: Carysfort Press, 2012), 32.

values that exist beyond their stories, yet from which they indirectly emerge. Nicholas Grene is wary of the potential emotional universalism of *Port Authority*; highlighting the significance of the absence of 'any amplifying echo-chamber of myth or archetype' he suggests: 'it is in this that McPherson's storytelling represents such a notable divergence from the practices of his Irish dramatic predecessors.'[29]

However, it is important to note that between 2000 and 2006, in addition to his monologue work McPherson wrote *Dublin Carol, Shining City*, and *The Seafarer*—three Dublin dramas that excavate a contemporary urban/suburban experience. Here too one might index his engagement with Irish dramatic tradition. If in 2000 Declan Hughes was to complain of the figurative exhaustion of rural experience in Irish theatre and its failure to engage with contemporary life,[30] then McPherson is one of a generation of writers who began to invest the sub/urban with a comparable symbolic valence, to envision such spaces as the norm rather than the exception. Prominent in each of these plays are motifs of confession, crisis, and haunting, and their settings are pivotal to the elaboration of this set of motifs. *Dublin Carol* takes place in an undertaker's office located on the north side of the city, *Shining City* in a therapist's office near the city centre, and *The Seafarer* in a house in a Northside suburb of Dublin. Both *Dublin Carol* and *The Seafarer* are deliberately set on Christmas Eve, and exploit the anticipatory potential of the season with a deep sense of irony. Each of these plays is governed by a morbid and at times painfully poignant humour applied to male characters who are failures as a result of alcoholism, loss of faith, or emotional detachment.

Allusions here do serve, to use Grene's words, as 'amplifying echo-chamber[s]'. *Dublin Carol* reprises Charles Dickens's *Christmas Carol* with its shades of past, present, and future. *Shining City* recalls Tom Murphy's *The Gigli Concert*: both plays probe the possibilities of confession in a setting where religious faith is a dissipated force; both conclude with a dramatic preternatural transference from patient to therapist. *The Seafarer* is built upon the myth of Faust. These allusions, however, reverberate in the space of the contemporary, and their acoustics can be productively understood in terms of present concerns. Thus, rather than the sentimental resolution of the Victorian fable or the peculiarly transcendent musical climax of Murphy's drama, more sombre tones of mortality and profound uncertainty colour the potentially redemptive moments in *Dublin Carol* and *Shining City*. In contrast to Faust, Sharky, the protagonist in *The Seafarer*, seems to evade his fate by lucky accident. McPherson exploits the financial resonances of the Faustian pact. His devil, the well-dressed Mr Lockhart, arrives at the Christmas Eve card game of semi-alcoholics and ne'er-do-wells to claim a debt. Sharky's promised route to hell is 'through the hole in the wall'[31]—an Irish expression for a cash-dispensing machine. Indeed, just as the excesses of the Celtic Tiger seem somewhat far-fetched in the cold light of day, so too does Sharky's predicament as the sun rises at the play's conclusion. Lonergan notes how McPherson is one of several contemporary Irish writers who draw upon the Faust myth in order to reflect upon Ireland's current state of post-Celtic Tiger insecurity,[32] and suggests that *The Seafarer*

[29] Nicholas Grene, 'Stories in Shallow Space: *Port Authority*', *Irish Review* 29 (2002), 82.
[30] Declan Hughes, 'Who the Hell Do We Think We Still Are?', in Eamonn Jordan (ed.), *Theatre Stuff: Critical Essays on Contemporary Irish Theatre* (Dublin: Carysfort Press, 2000), 8–15.
[31] Conor McPherson, *The Seafarer* (London: Nick Hern Books, 2006), 48.
[32] Patrick Lonergan, 'Irish Theatre and Globalisation: A Faustian Pact?', in Eamon Maher (ed.), *Cultural Perspectives on Ireland and Globalisation* (Bern: Peter Lang, 2009), 177–90.

might be seen to offer a palliative message to its audiences at a time of global financial crisis: that 'the spiritual or transcendent can survive in an excessively materialistic culture'.[33]

McPherson's sensitivity to storytelling, the subtle rhythms of everyday speech, personal psychology complemented by dramaturgical confinement, and avoidance of naturalistically presented sociopolitical realities in many respects do not mark a radical break with the tendencies traceable in modern Irish theatre. Rather, what he brings to those tendencies is a very contemporary sense of the ordinary, the urban, and the secular dogged by the metaphysical and the inexplicable. Indeed, as his work has developed, the otherworldly remainder emerges as a motif of increasing significance. The mundane, tangible world is haunted by something that cannot be dispatched by reason or logic. Recalling Jacques Derrida's coinage, 'hauntology'—used to express the afterlife of Marxism following the demise of Communism—McPherson's work similarly embodies a sense that '"time is out of joint": time is disarticulated, dislocated, dislodged'[34] in the space between the economic boom and its endgame. McPherson's exploration of the undead begins in comic, metatheatrical provocation with St Nicholas's referencing of Dracula, but evolves into a reflective engagement with the ghosts of the past in narrative and symbolic terms. In doing so, his work evokes an indeterminate sense of personal and communal identity at the turn of the century and beyond.

Mark O'Rowe: Poetic Violence

Mark O'Rowe's first play, The Aspidistra Code, was among the winning entries in the National Association for Youth Drama's Young Playwright's Scheme competition, and received a rehearsed reading directed by Gerry Stembridge at the Peacock Theatre in Dublin in 1995. His next work From Both Hips, which he describes as a 'kitchen-sink-crime-comedy-drama',[35] was staged by Fishamble Theatre Company in 1997. However, it was Howie the Rookie, first performed in the Bush Theatre, London, in 1999, that brought O'Rowe to wider attention, riding the wave of 'in-yer-face' theatre in the UK. Made in China (2001), Crestfall (2003), Terminus (2007), and Our Few and Evil Days (2014) are his other plays to date. Like McDonagh, O'Rowe is a writer who professed an ignorance of theatre and a preference for film culture early in his career. In conversation with Stembridge in 2001, he stated:

> [The tradition of Abbey writing] means nothing to me [. . .] I've never felt part of it and I've never really wanted to be part of it. What actually happens, when you have a successful play like Howie the Rookie, people start making you [. . .] part of it. [. . .] The Irish literary tradition—this is not meant to sound arrogant because I'm not talking about my own writing here, I'm talking about the kind of stuff I like—never impressed me that much. I'm much more of a fan of American literature.[36]

---

[33] Ibid. 189.   [34] Jacques Derrida, Specters of Marx (New York: Routledge, 1994), 20.
[35] Mark O'Rowe, 'Foreword', in Plays: One (London: Nick Hern, 2011), vii.
[36] Julie Cronin, 'Chinese Whispers: Gerry Stembridge in Conversation with Mark O'Rowe', 9 Feb. 2001, www.nayd.ie/content/files/Whispers.pdf. Accessed 15 May 2014.

O'Rowe is also a writer whose imagined world is sub/urban yet abstract, inviting interpretation at a figurative rather than literal level. This effect is galvanized by his repeated reliance on forms of monologue in which, as has already been noted with regard to McPherson's work, place is conjured only through the characters' words which hover in a minimalistically conceived stage space. Above all, O'Rowe's theatre is unsettling because of the centrality of violence to its operations. As he says himself:

> I don't think I'd ever say I want to deal with violence or do a study of violence, but I know it's what entertains me. In the end you write for an audience, but you write to please yourself as well in terms of what interests you. I love violence in its literary form, its cinematic form.[37]

Howie the Rookie is a pair of rollercoaster monologues delivered sequentially by two working-class Dublin young men who enact all the roles in their stories. The brutal, primal worlds of Howie Lee and Rookie Lee collide in a vortex of macho energy, politically incorrect attitudes, and violent death that provides a compelling example of what Brian Singleton describes as toxic masculinity.[38] As is also clear in *Made in China*, the gaping absence of any higher values or capacity for reflection among the characters is plugged with vague notions of a thug's code of honour, and fantasies of 'hard-body' masculinity[39] derived from popular culture. In *Howie the Rookie* 'the dead, mythologized film actor Bruce Lee, star of martial arts movies',[40] is the figure to whom both characters turn for a heroic role model, yet the manoeuvre is fundamentally disempowering. Monologue is wielded by O'Rowe in *Howie the Rookie*, *Crestfall*, and *Terminus*, not to achieve some cathartic purpose, but rather to channel visceral and self-destructive impulses. For Jordan, despite the performative energies of the play, *Howie the Rookie* 'escorts an audience [...] into the terrorism of a world where actions have no significance beyond the immediate, because it is a world without resonance or connection'.[41]

Indeed this nihilistic conclusion seems only to be confirmed by O'Rowe's most confronting works, *Crestfall* and *Terminus*, both of which feature a litany of vicious, semi-pornographic, and vicarious micro-narratives, again in monologue format set in a contemporary no-man's-land. With *Crestfall*, O'Rowe departs from his habitual all-male territory to explore a fantastically dystopian tale narrated by three women 'about motherhood [. . . in] a society so calcified by violence that people are reduced to the most basic of activities: having sex, killing, and shooting up'.[42] Despite the playwright's assertion in his foreword to *Plays: One* that some glimmer of hope might be spotted at its conclusion, the values beneath the veneer of experiment are undisguisable. Contrasting the exuberant celebration of male kinship of his preceding works, Cathy Leeney comments on the fact that the characters in *Crestfall* can only 'report their own victimization, their "perpetual crestfall." Where the only possible agency is participation in savage, meaningless brutality,

[37] Ibid.
[38] See Brian Singleton, *Masculinities and the Contemporary Irish Theatre* (Basingstoke: Palgrave, 2011).
[39] Singleton, 'Am I Talking to Myself?', 264.
[40] Eamonn Jordan, 'Project Mayhem: Mark O'Rowe's *Howie the Rookie*', *Irish Review* 35 (2007), 119.
[41] Ibid., 127.
[42] Karen Fricker, 'Crestfall', *Guardian*, 24 May 2003. http://www.theguardian.com/stage/2003/may/24/theatre.artsfeatures1. Accessed 10 May 2012.

passivity is the only expression of resistance.'[43] Accordingly, while *Crestfall* is deliberately taboo-busting in some all too palpable ways, it harbours a troublingly conservative message. The lurid cataloguing of fantastically macabre events continues in *Terminus*, leavened just a little with humour. The play reprises the motif of the Faustian pact with the devil, but augments the nightmare resonances of its predecessor with plot elements that involve the attempt to abort a baby a month before term, slasher violence, and the disembowelling of a woman during sex (lifted straight from *American Psycho*, 1991). If considered as parables of contemporary Ireland, the messages of these plays are bleak in the extreme, leaving audiences feeling perhaps just as gutted as some of their protagonists.

Both plays use a poeticized language that engineers a dissonance between what is narrated and how it is narrated. Speaking of *Terminus* in 2011, O'Rowe describes it as 'a muscular poetic rhyming style' that works as 'a safety net or suit of armour for the content of the play which is very, very over the top'.[44] Arguably, the reliance on rhyming couplets and relentless sound patterning does have an anaesthetizing, distracting effect. Critics have habitually found some safe haven in the discussion of O'Rowe's command of language, but perhaps cannot completely dispel the inkling that his poetry for the theatre is a heady cocktail of Brett Easton Ellis and Pam Ayres.

Back in 1995, Paul Taylor reviewed a play that sent shudders through the British theatre reviewing establishment; the show was 'a little like having your face rammed into an overflowing ash tray [. . .] and then having your whole head held down in a bucket of offal'. That infamous play was Sarah Kane's *Blasted*, and the visceral energies of O'Rowe's work recall something of her early work. But the rest of Taylor's statement is often omitted; he goes on to explain: 'As a theatrical experience, there's nothing wrong in principle with either of these ordeals. Provided, that is, you can feel there's something happening to your heart and mind as well as to your nervous system as a result.'[45] Representations of graphic violence verbally and physically are as old as theatre itself, and reacting to those representations is a necessary and vital dimension of an audience's relationship to performance. The ethically disquieting questions of form and content embodied by O'Rowe's work are difficult to resolve precisely because, so far, he seems primarily concerned with the nervous system.

Enda Walsh: Verbal Alchemy

A Dubliner who relocated first to Cork and later to London, Walsh began to work with the Corcadorca Theatre Company in the early 1990s and, in cooperation with director Pat Kiernan, penned *Disco Pigs* (1996)—a play that went on to win the Stewart Parker and George Devine Awards in 1997. *Sucking Dublin* (1997), *Misterman* (1999), *Bedbound* (2000), *Chatroom* (2005), *The Small Things* (2005), *The Walworth Farce* (2006), *The New Electric Ballroom* (2008), *Penelope* (2010), the stage adaptation of *Once* (2011), a revised version of

[43] Cathy Leeney, 'Men in No-Man's Land: Performing Urban Liminal Spaces in Two Plays by Mark O'Rowe', *Irish Review* 35, 'Irish Feminisms' (2007), 115.

[44] 'Mark O'Rowe on *Terminus*', citizenstheatre, YouTube, 14 Apr. 2011, http://www.youtube.com/watch?v=sIBeOIFsoes. Accessed 15 May 2014.

[45] Paul Taylor, 'Courting Disaster', *Independent*, 20 Jan. 1995.

Misterman (2011), and *Ballyturk* (2014)—the last two extending his creative relationship with actor Cillian Murphy, who performed in *Disco Pigs*—are among the most notable of his theatre projects since. The nature of Walsh's intervention in theatre tradition has recognizable appeal in continental Europe (in particular in Germany, thanks to cooperations with dramaturg Tilman Raabke), but until recently has been under-appreciated by Irish studies scholars. Here is a theatre-maker whose work radically distorts the coordinates of Irish drama proposed by Christopher Murray—history, identity, and home—with such experimental vigour that it becomes difficult to situate it on that map.

Walsh's theatre is marked by an acute awareness of language, linguistic dysfunction, and idiosyncrasy. As early as 2002, he remarked:

> I have this serious hang-up about being inarticulate. I went through years of speech therapy. I had a stammer. That has largely impacted on everything I have done: the sort of characters, the structure of my writing and the style of my writing. It is the poetry of being inarticulate.[46]

His breakthrough play, *Disco Pigs*, is a testament to this fusion of dysfunction and loquaciousness. As Lisa Fitzpatrick describes: 'The play is probably most renowned for its creation of a dialect, an almost incomprehensible patois that combines urban Cork with baby talk, animal noises and teenage slang.'[47] Its two characters, Pig and Runt, enact their fast-paced tale using a private language that lends a poetic and fantastical inflection to their pent-up, antisocial rage, which might otherwise come across as just a bad bout of teenage angst. Speed is a vital feature of the verbal performance of this distorted coming of age narrative. Pig and Runt begin with the story of their own births, and then hurtle forward to the present catalogue of violent games they play in a night world of clubs and off-licences in 'Pork Sity'. If at first their shared language seems to hermetically seal them off from the emotional and physical consequences of their actions, and to permit a cartoonish attitude to violence, it is evident that both characters are dangerously out of control. The climax of the play comes when Pig beats a man to death, and Runt, in horror, abandons both him and their shared parallel universe. Runt's progress to self-awareness, if not to accountability, is signalled by a transformation in speech, a stumbling revision of dialect into standard vocabulary that closes the play. Walsh's subsequent plays have remained intensely attuned to the potential of private worlds of storytelling, even though the pyrotechnics of dialect disappear. *Bedbound, Misterman, The Small Things*, and *The Walworth Farce* share a focus on aberrant narrative performance and, in the case of *Bedbound* and *The Walworth Farce*, compulsive re-enactment.

Walsh's dramaturgy has been consistently anti-naturalistic, and in important formal respects is indebted to absurdism and expressionism. 'Theatre', he tells Aleks Sierz in an interview for *Theatre Voice*, 'does not come from a real place for me.'[48] His interest is not in weaving current affairs into his work, nor about representing a real world. Rather, his

---

[46] Niamh Thornton and Padraic White, 'Interview with Enda Walsh', *Film and Film Culture* 1 (2002), 20.

[47] Lisa Fitzpatrick, 'Enda Walsh', in Martin Middeke and Peter Paul Schnierer (eds.), *The Methuen Drama Guide to Contemporary Irish Playwrights* (London: Methuen, 2010), 440.

[48] Aleks Sierz, 'Enda Walsh and *The Walworth Farce*', *Theatre Voice*, 3 Nov. 2008, http://www. theatrevoice.com/audio/enda-walsh-and-the-walworth-farce/. Accessed 20 Sept. 2014.

theatre repeatedly excavates states of obsessive interiority, linguistic hyperawareness, and spaces of dark fantasy. At points, its tonal qualities or thematic motifs invite comparison with those of Samuel Beckett (in particular the contours of *Bedbound*, the use of the tape recorder in *Misterman*) or with that of Harold Pinter (the narrative of *The Small Things* recalls something of *Ashes to Ashes*), but a knowing intertextual exchange or recycling of these writers' works is not the engine of his work.

The centrality of stage images of entrapment is counterpointed with characters that exist through frenetic and/or obsessive performance to stave off silence and, by extension, complete collapse. One consequence of this is the tantalizing disjunctions between these spaces and the spaces of the 'real' world. The objective locations of Cork, Dublin, and London referenced in these plays hover near the parallel subjective worlds the characters lead us through, but they never coincide. Another outcome is a heightened consciousness of the physicality of the performer in these spaces. As Jesse Weaver notes: 'Despite protestations that he's not a director, Walsh writes with a kind of directorial intention, one that seeks to define the play not just in terms of an expression of narrative, but as an event as well.'[49] The kinetic energy of Pig and Runt's acting out their story, the filthy bed and crippled form of the daughter in *Bedbound*, the symbolic objects in *The Small Things*, and the escalating chaotic performance of *The Walworth Farce* indicate the extent to which Walsh's work is physically as well as verbally conceived.

In charting Walsh's development as a playwright, it is clear that the manic energies of physical storytelling so vital to *Disco Pigs*, *Sucking Dublin*, *Misterman*, and *Bedbound* mutate into profoundly equivocal, uncanny scenarios and nuanced forms of experiment, exemplified by *The Small Things* and *The Walworth Farce*. *The Walworth Farce* is of particular interest for the ways in which it folds theatre in upon itself in a metatheatrical game. Although superficially they share a ludic and ultimately iconoclastic attitude to their Irish thematics, Walsh's use of farce differs from McDonagh's, both in terms of geographical reference—the symbolically charged west of Ireland places of McDonagh's plays are replaced with the comparative anonymity of a London council flat—and with respect to the complexity with which he freights it. Walsh approached farce as a tradition unfamiliar in Irish theatre, and while this point is debatable, certainly there is no equivalent to Joe Orton's plays of the 1960s or Michael Frayn's *Noises Off* (1982). With *The Walworth Farce*, he unites the self-conscious theatricality and menace intrinsic to the genre. However, he bends the genre to his own purposes by gesturing towards patterns of representation of Irish experience of exile and diaspora, while at the same time implying that these are just as exhausted as nostalgic idealizations of the rural: 'I knew I wanted to write the play that every Irish playwright has to write—the old Irish people in London—but [I knew] I ha[d] to explode that kind of play and bring it somewhere else.'[50] An immediate point of reference in Irish theatre is Tom Murphy's *A Whistle in the Dark* (1961); Jordan contends that Walsh 'is contesting the very sensibility of the world of Murphy's drama, deeming it to bear no resemblance to the reality of Ireland in the new millennium'.[51] Yet, if Murphy is a

---

[49] Jesse Weaver, '"The Words Look After Themselves": The Practice of Enda Walsh', in Nicholas Grene and Patrick Lonergan (eds.), *Irish Drama: Local and Global Perspectives* (Dublin: Carysfort Press, 2012), 139.

[50] Colin Murphy, 'An Irish Farce in London', *Village*, 30 Mar. 2006, quoted in Jordan, '"Stuff from Back Home": Enda Walsh's *The Walworth Farce*', *Ilha do Desterro* 58 (2010), 353.

[51] Jordan, *Dissident Dramaturgies*, 244.

perspective point then *The Walworth Farce* equally, if perhaps unintentionally, also inverts *Conversations on a Homecoming* and ironizes the iconic and tragic narrative performance of *Bailegangaire*.

The Walworth Farce presents audiences with an unstable mixture of possible perspectives that ultimately can only be reconciled at a symbolic level. Dinny and his sons Sean and Blake are discovered in a dingy flat on the Walworth Road. The décor of this space suggests it has changed little since the 1970s, and as the play unfolds it becomes clear that the three characters live in a bizarre nostalgic time warp, desperately attempting to make a fiction of the past live on through performance. Their obsessively maintained parallel universe is radically altered by the appearance of a character from the 'real' world: the young black Tesco employee, Haley. In consequence, Blake stabs Dinny and Sean kills Blake, but Walsh refuses to collapse farce into realism. As Haley flees this absurd but gory scene, contemporary London is again closed out and Sean prepares to 'lose himself in a new story'.[52]

The world of a play in which three adult men compulsively re-enact the story of a murder and escape to London from Cork on a daily basis in order to compete for an acting trophy patently refuses to be understood in terms of sociological realities or a televisual aesthetic. 'It is', as Jordan aptly describes, 'a world [. . .] malformed by a twist of the curious and dangerous imagination of Walsh, as nothing is "integrated", no closure is possible, [there remains only] the failure of resistance to the inevitability of history or farce, or history as farce, farce as history'.[53] Simultaneous with the rather gloomy message that history is confounded by spectacle is the competing suggestion applicable to Walsh's work in general— that at a more abstract level performance is all, and that audiences play a vital role in any theatrical situation. The layered dramatic situation alters fundamentally, if not redemptively, when an audience accidentally appears. The presence of Haley oxygenates the flow of farce, allowing another more tragic perspective to temporarily bubble through its circuit before it is co-opted by the last surviving performer.

CONCLUSION

In *The Haunted Stage*, Marvin Carlson reasons that while theatre may be a 'repository of cultural memory' it is also 'subject to continual adjustment and modification […] in new circumstances and contexts'.[54] Clearly in the 1990s circumstances and contexts in Ireland altered with a rapidity hitherto unknown. Each of the writers under consideration has contributed to the remaking of contemporary Irish theatre, and has been instrumental in the transformation of the reach of Irish theatre in the twenty-first century. It seems no accident too that, in the careers of all of these writers, film-making has played a significant role;[55] for O'Rowe and McDonagh, film in particular is the medium to which they seem more

---

[52] Enda Walsh, *The Walworth Farce* (London: Nick Hern Books, 2007), 85.

[53] Jordan, '"Stuff from Back Home"', 354.

[54] Marvin Carlson, *The Haunted Stage: The Theatre as Memory Machine* (Ann Arbor, MI: University of Michigan Press, 2001), 2.

[55] Notably, too, the equivalent does not hold for women playwrights of the period.

committed, while McPherson and Walsh have spoken on numerous occasions of their love of live performance.

Their disruptions of the representational patterns of Irish theatre are diverse but marked. McDonagh's crowning role in Irish theatre since the 1990s has been to put postmodern irony on the map with all its attendant difficulties. O'Rowe's desire 'to push Irish theatre on to the next level'[56] seems wedded to a verbal homage to violence that may be self-consuming. The prioritizing of personal temporalities apparently unanchored by historical, geographical, or sociological specificities links the otherwise dissimilar work of McPherson, Walsh, and O'Rowe. Taken together, such propensities are suggestive of the disaggregation of visions of Irish identity and lived experience in the period. Characterized by diverse and complex processes of rejection and reinvention, appropriation and re-enactment, their work speaks to and of the changing, dislocated cultural conditions of Irish theatre.

---

[56] Cronin, 'Chinese Whispers', n.p.

CHAPTER 33

SHADOW AND SUBSTANCE

Women, Feminism, and Irish Theatre
after 1980

MELISSA SIHRA

CONTEXTS

THE immense range of women's achievements in all aspects of Irish theatre since the early twentieth century, so long subsumed within a skewed historical perspective, continues to grow and to be revealed. This chapter will explore the evolving processes of women working in theatre in Ireland since the 1980s, when social awareness of the inequities of gender and effects of patriarchal conservatism began to infiltrate what was undoubtedly a male-dominated profession. This was a period of growth in feminist activism, and looking back, we can see how the emergent histories of women and Irish theatre mirror the complex and changing relationship between women and the feminist movement itself.

Women's relationship with feminism has been notoriously ambivalent since the second wave of activism for equal rights from the 1970s, where identification either with or against feminism parallels complex processes of exclusion from mainstream theatre production. Women's work in theatre has predominantly sought to renegotiate the terms of patriarchal systems of meaning-making, either in form or content, or both. While women frequently create alternatives to Aristotelian structures, offering multiple spaces of unreconciled indeterminacy with regard to place, language, plot and/or character, their positivist identification with a feminist theatre-making strategy is in constant process, having shifted remarkably in the last twenty years. While feminism sought to emancipate women and highlight their secondary status in theatre and everyday life, many women working in theatre in the 1980s and 1990s were ironically less inclined to self-identify as feminist for fear of further marginalization of their work.

Hesitancy around the word 'feminist' is plain to see when Mike Murphy, discussing the character Portia Coughlan in an interview in 2000, says to Marina Carr, 'I do not see a strong feminist line in your writing, despite the fact that your female characters are so strong.'¹ Carr's reply reveals the innate feminism at the heart of her work, while at the same time articulating women's reluctance to identify with the label:

> I think people are confused about the whole feminist thing. If something isn't polemical, they tend to think it isn't feminist. Feminism has become a dirty word and people are afraid of it. Women writers are afraid of their work being tagged as 'feminist'. I don't consciously set out with a feminist agenda, but I do happen to believe that we're as equal as the rest, given the world and how unequal and different everybody is.²

There is an important distinction to be made between theatre (and art in general) that is polemically feminist or 'issue-based', where the work serves as a political means to an end, and theatre that instinctively challenges heteropatriarchy through the very nature of its form and content.

I situate the work of many women in Irish theatre according to the latter sensibility, whereby an organic feminist feeling and affect is intrinsic to their work, from Teresa Deevy and Margaret O'Leary through to Marina Carr among others. In the same interview with Murphy, Carr elaborates on her female protagonists and, perhaps, on her own position and other rural women at the time:

> Most of the women I write about would be natural feminists, but they would never have read a book on feminism. They would feel their worth, and know their rights, and naturally have a sense of themselves. Women in the country are like that as well. They don't have the polemical dictionary or the related vocabulary, but they have a certain strength and sense of themselves.³

Working in the UK in the 1980s and 1990s, prominent radical lesbian feminist playwright Sarah Daniels expresses similar discomfort in her 1991 disclaimer: 'Feminism is now, like "panty-girdle", a very embarrassing word. Once seen as liberating, it is now considered to be restrictive, passé, and undesirable to wear. I didn't set out to further the cause of feminism. However, I am proud if some of my plays have added to its influence.'⁴ Jill Dolan puts her finger on the problem for many women working in theatre who actively resist the feminist appellation in order to survive economically and have their work considered in universal terms, where 'their desire to become part of the system that has historically excluded them forces some liberal feminists in theatre to acquiesce to their erasure as women'.⁵

Women's contribution to their own erasure is not a new concept in Irish theatre, perhaps most infamously going back to 1902, when Augusta Gregory relinquished her co-authorship of *Cathleen ni Houlihan* to W. B. Yeats. Differing generational attitudes can be identified when we consider Marina Carr's response:

> [It was] actually her play, which Yeats revised and then added to the last scene [. . .] she wrote the play and Yeats gave his name to it, and then took it over. Yeats called himself the author

¹ Clíodhna Ní Anluain (ed.), *Reading the Future: Irish Writers in Conversation with Mike Murphy* (Dublin: Lilliput, 2000), 51.
² Ibid., 51–2.   ³ Ibid., 52.
⁴ Sarah Daniels, *Plays: One* (London: Methuen Drama, 1991), xii.
⁵ Jill Dolan, *The Feminist Spectator as Critic* (Ann Arbor, MI: University of Michigan Press, 1991), 5.

of *Cathleen ni Houlihan* in front of the public [. . .] Lady Gregory says it was particularly hard for her, but she let it go. I do not understand why she let it go, but that was another generation.[6]

Women have held centre stage as performers since the inception of the Irish Literary Theatre in 1899 and foundation of the Abbey Theatre in 1904, in iconic roles which variously symbolize 'Woman' as 'Mother' and/or 'Ireland', embodying the anticolonial imaginary as *Eire* or *aisling*, which goes back at least to the time of the Penal Laws. On the other hand, real women's achievements as playwrights, directors, designers, and producers have either languished in the margins or, when successful, been deemed the 'extraordinary' exception to the rule. From the birth of the Irish Dramatic Renaissance up until the first decade of the twenty-first century, women have essentially been regarded as making theatre despite themselves, and have been measured against a normalized 'universal' (male) standard. Women's gender identity has persisted as a categorizing process, perpetuating the phenomenon of 'female playwrights' and so-called 'women's theatre', positioning the work of women as a genre or sub-category of the (male) norm. Looking back at Irish theatre history and criticism, we can see how, time and again, women's work is situated in a negative relationship to the 'canonical' values of the 'classical', perpetuating the notion that theatre by women is of less significance to humanity as a whole. 'Women's theatre' or 'women's play-writing' are thus pejorative terms, trivialized into categories of the 'private and domestic', deemed a 'minority interest' where subject matter such as the family, children, home, and motherhood are insidiously feminized vis-à-vis transcendent patriarchal representation.

If Irish theatre and folk culture has traditionally been one of ghosts, hauntings, and otherworlds, it is women who are the true spectres of this landscape, roaming shadows without substance. As we interrogate inequities of the past, we follow the roughly beaten tracks of the original women of the Irish theatre: Augusta Gregory, Dorothy Macardle, Alice Milligan, Helen Wadell, Maud Gonne, Constance Markievicz, Geraldine Cummins, Susanne Day, Eva Gore-Booth, Teresa Deevy, Margaret O'Leary, Mary Manning, Máiréad Ní Ghráda, and Christine Longford, to name only these. Co-founder of the Abbey Theatre and author of over forty plays in addition to performing and designing for the stage, Augusta Gregory was known predominantly during her life as a theatre manager, and has been afforded due critical recognition as an artist only since the 1980s. She poignantly embodies the contradiction of shadow and substance for women in Irish theatre, during her lifetime and since. In a metatheatrical moment of self-reflexive ghosting, Gregory haunted her own play when she stepped in to perform the role of the Poor Old Woman in a production of *Cathleen ni Houlihan* at the last minute at the Abbey in 1919. Highlighting women's symbolic centrality and subjective disavowal, Gregory's enunciation of the dialogue that she had 'ghost-written' led to her growing bitterness as the years went by concerning the attribution to Yeats alone of the play that she had co-written. As a member of the Anglo-Irish ascendancy, Gregory experienced a painful cultural eviction of her own, invisibly roaming the margins of her co-authored

---

[6] Maria Kurdi, ' "I Was Tired of the Sentimental Portrayal of Mothers": An Interview with Marina Carr', *Modern Filológiai Közlemények* 5, no. 2 (2003), 96–7.

play, resentfully annotating in the margins the passages she had written: 'All this mine alone A.G.'[7]

Unfortunately, Lady Gregory's sidelining from mainstream practice and historiographies of Irish theatre is no mere footnote of Irish theatre history but continued into this millennium. For the AbbeyOneHundred Centenary Celebrations Programme in 2004, not one of Gregory's plays was produced on either of the two stages of the National Theatre during the extensive twelve-month programme. The centenary celebrations were divided into five 'identifiable themes': The Abbey and Europe; The Abbey and New Writing; Summer at the Abbey; the Abbey and Ireland; and The Abbey on Tour. Out of the twelve full-scale productions on the main stage, no play by a woman was produced and no Irish woman directed on the Abbey stage.[8] Artistic director Ben Barnes's programme note for the 'The Abbey and Ireland' theme tells us:

> In celebrating the rich diversity of the Abbey repertoire with these 18 plays[9] we advert to the many hundreds of plays which constitute the Abbey repertoire and represent a body of dramatic literature which continues to be regularly re-animated and is a unique resource unparalleled in the theatre of Europe or North America.[10]

Gregory's popular *Spreading the News* was given a one-off rehearsed reading in the small top-floor rehearsal room for the Reading the Decades reading series on 28 September 2004. All the other writers in the Reading the Decades programme were male, and each one was afforded a dedicated afternoon slot with the exception of Gregory. Betraying the underlying judgement that her plays did not merit a presentation of their own, her play reading was shared with G. B. Shaw's *The Shewing-up of Blanco Posnet*.[11]

In terms of stage productions for AbbeyOneHundred, the only Irish women to have their work produced were, predictably, Marina Carr, whose *Portia Coughlan* was given a run on the Peacock stage during 'The Abbey and Ireland' section, and Paula Meehan's *The Wolf of Winter*, also on the Peacock stage for 'The Abbey and New Writing' section. No other play by a woman was represented at the National Theatre during the centenary celebrations. Women's minority status as directors and writers is explicit throughout the programming. Lynne Parker directed *Heavenly Bodies* and Andrea Ainsworth directed Meehan's new play, both at the Peacock. Women were also given the opportunity to direct six out of the ten staged readings in the rehearsal room for the Reading the Decades programme, highlighting women's secondary position as (partial) directors. They were: Jo Mangan, *Spreading the News*; Roisin McBrinn, *The Passing Day*; Audrey Devereux, *Home is the Hero*; Judy Hegarty-Lovett, *The Great Hunger*; Anabelle Comyn, *Prayers of Sherkin*; Rachel West, *Give Me Your Answer, Do!* Carr's position as the ostensible natural inheritor to Lady Gregory is highly limiting, excluding as it does the myriad of women's voices

[7] See James Pethica, '"Our Kathleen": Yeats's Collaboration with Lady Gregory in the Writing of *Cathleen ni Houlihan*', in Deirdre Toomey (ed.), *Yeats and Women*, 2nd edn. (Basingstoke: Macmillan, 1997), 209.
[8] The Canadian director Lorraine Pintal directed Seamus Heaney's *The Burial at Thebes* in April that year.
[9] Eight stage productions and eleven rehearsed readings during the Dublin Theatre Festival.
[10] Ben Barnes, 'The Abbey and Ireland Through the Decades', AbbeyOneHundred programme, http://www.abbeytheatre.ie/archives/production_detail/5022. Accessed 5 May 2015.
[11] http://www.abbeytheatre.ie/archives/production_detail/5023. Accessed 5 May 2015.

from Irish theatre history and reducing both Gregory and Carr to sufficient representation of 'Irish women playwrights'. It is ironic that in the 'AbbeyOneHundred: The Abbey and Ireland' programme, the then-President of Ireland, Mary McAleese observed:

> The names of [the Abbey's] champions are legendary and it is fascinating to see among them the names of so many women, among them Maud Gonne, Augusta Gregory and the English philanthropist Annie Horniman, each a sign of contradiction and a powerful revelation of how much our world benefits when it no longer wastes or corrals the talents of significant groups of human beings.[12]

The most powerfully contradictory sign that can be identified in the centenary project is the blinding omission of women from key artistic roles throughout the entire process. Typically, the symbolic centrality and actual disavowal of women was maintained, with Marina Carr's attractive image positioned largest and central on the glossy souvenir booklet, surrounded by a circle of male playwrights and Lady Gregory.[13]

A chapter-length study cannot offer equal or adequate attention to all of the work of women in Irish theatre since the 1980s, nor should it aim to do so. It is neither possible nor desirable to explore the full range and depth of work by women in theatre on the island over the last forty years within a single chapter, where listing and name-checking would further perpetuate a tokenistic categorization. Therefore, this chapter will explore some of the key issues at stake for women working in theatre through the overlapping practices of Charabanc Theatre Company founded in Belfast in 1983, and the plays of Marina Carr from 1989 in the Republic. The problematic positioning of Carr as Ireland's 'most prolific female playwright' or Charabanc as the 'most successful all-women theatre company' continues to determine reductive critical attitudes which inherently naturalize women's place and creativity as secondary to the universal male. Carr has been repeatedly asked about the 'issue' of 'Irish women playwrights' over the last thirty years—a question that ironically perpetuates inverted sexism, maintaining the separatist categorization of women as gendered artists while safeguarding the male as playwright. In exploring the approaches and achievements of Charabanc, Marie Jones, and Carr, some of the key issues that women have grappled with in Irish theatre production in recent decades can be illuminated.

CHARABANC AND MARIE JONES

The fraught relationship between women and theatre in Ireland is a mirror of the complex relationship between women and the feminist movement itself, and can be explored through the evolving creative process of the five-member women's collective Charabanc Theatre Company from 1983. A juxtaposition of Charabanc with the almost

[12] Mary McAleese, 'Message from the President', AbbeyOneHundred Programme.
[13] At the time of this volume going to print the Abbey Theatre launched its 1916 Centenary Programme, 'Waking the Nation', with 90% male-playwrights. An unprecedented national and international outcry at the lack of gender balance immediately gained momentum on social media named #WakingTheFeminists led by Lian Bell. On 12 Nov. 2015 #WakingTheFeminists hosted a rally at the Abbey articulating women's exclusion from mainstream theatre and pay inequities, calling for strategic implementation of gender equality across the arts.

contemporaneous activity of Field Day Theatre Company, co-founded by Stephen Rea and Brian Friel in 1980, usefully illuminates diverse approaches to creative practice which can be considered retrospectively in terms of gendered internalizations of authority and self-worth, in which single authorship is synonymous with masculinity, while collaboration or group work is commonly associated with the 'feminine'. With an all-male directorate, Field Day produced and published one male-authored play per year as well as publishing scholarly pamphlets on a range of academic, political, and philosophical subjects by leading Irish and international (predominantly male) writers, in addition to the further acts of cultural definition expressed in the first three volumes of the *Field Day Anthology of Irish Writing* (1991). Charabanc, on the other hand, epitomized the 'collective' spirit of the feminist movement of the 1980s, where single authorship was often eschewed in favour of plurality and publication did not take place.

Ironically, but typically for the time, Charabanc sought to distance itself from feminist politics. As noted above, for many women, the label 'feminist' was seen as troublesome and, at worst, detrimental to their advancement within mainstream culture. Feminism was often regarded as misandrist, with polemic, 'issue drama' associations, and therefore to be of limited value in terms of creative vision and notions of universality. Charabanc was not unusual in that they did not wish to further alienate their audience—male or female—with a label that might be deemed to place them within a non-commercial (anti-male) niche. Jones says: 'There is no doubt that we were feminists in the sense that we were presenting women, and very strong women, who always formed the centre of the plays, which were about empowering women. That's feminism.'[14] However, the company did not state an explicit feminist agenda at the time: 'we didn't want to put [people] off by having any kind of labels, we just wanted to say that this is a play about ordinary people.'[15]

Disillusioned by the lack of any substantial roles for women, Marie Jones co-founded Charabanc Theatre Company in Belfast in 1983 with four other out-of-work actors—Brenda Winter, Maureen McCauley, Eleanor Methven, and Carol Scanlon (Moore). The company was active for twelve years (1983–95), and during that time produced an extraordinarily popular body of twenty-four original shows, which toured across the sectarian divide as well as to the US and Russia. 'Charabanc', meaning an open-top day-trip bus, produced plays that were written collaboratively by its members; however, Jones's play-writing talent quickly became apparent within the group, and she went on to hold the position of writer-in-residence. The genesis of the company was wholly feminist, without being named as such, as the five women sought to redress the balance by self-authoring roles which would also serve to express the previously occluded voices of Northern Irish women on the stage as well as practically providing them with work of substance as actors. Brenda Winter reflects: 'The employment prospects for actresses living and working in Belfast at this time were truly dire. It was indignation that galvanized the founders of Charabanc into doing something about their disempowered situation.'[16]

[14] Imelda Foley, *The Girls in the Big Picture: Gender in Contemporary Ulster Theatre* (Belfast: Blackstaff Press, 2003), 30.

[15] Ibid.

[16] Brenda Winter, 'Introduction', in Martin Lynch and The Charabanc Theatre Company, *Lay Up Your Ends: A 25th Anniversary Edition* (Belfast: Lagan Press, 2008), 20.

Mobilizing their lack of agency through creative collective action, the five women sought to find stories that they could perform, and approached established playwright Martin Lynch to write sketches for them. Lynch immediately identified the irony; he insisted instead that they write the scenes themselves and that he would help them. Thus began the dawn of an extraordinary output of plays in a rich collaborative process where, every Sunday in Marie Jones's home, a group of theatre-makers gathered to collect ideas, interviews, and research, shaping and reshaping material that engaged with the women's identities and with the diverse social histories of their mothers and grandmothers. In Belfast Central Library the women first read about the 1911 Belfast mill-girls' strike. Some of these 'millies' were still alive in the 1980s, and the actresses interviewed them as material for their first play *Lay Up Your Ends*. A huge success, *Lay Up Your Ends* sets the tone of dynamism, professionalism, and theatricality that became the hallmarks of Charabanc's creative practice. Winter observes: 'there is no doubt that the actresses equated their own sense of powerlessness with that of their subjects. Although they most certainly did not endure the grinding poverty of physical deprivation of the mill-women, they certainly did share their marginality and invisibility as women.'[17] *Lay Up Your Ends* was first performed at the Belfast Arts Theatre in May 1983, and there were queues around the block. Imelda Foley notes: 'it may have begun as an experimental act of faith but it ended up playing to 12,000 people.'[18] Charabanc's plays, and subsequently those of Marie Jones, are known for vocalizing a sense of meaning, relevance, and humour arising out of the lives and experience of everyday situations and people's lives in Northern Ireland, particularly those of the underrepresented working classes and women in particular.

Although written in 1983, *Lay Up Your Ends* was only first published twenty-five years later, and here we can identify a major difference with Field Day. It is clear that lack of publication leads to obscurity, non-canonicity, fewer productions, and occlusion from university drama and literature courses on the island and internationally. This has resulted in a paucity of critical attention to Charabanc's creative output, unlike that afforded to Field Day, who combined theatrical production with an ambitious publishing enterprise.[19]

Charabanc's plays developed collaboratively from collecting lesser-known oral histories and focused on working-class concerns of people of all backgrounds, and Jones's skill at writing for the stage became quickly apparent. Of the early days, she says:

> Then I didn't recognise myself as a writer—I was just somebody who wanted to act and I wanted to do plays that were relevant to me and the people around me, and so, in retrospect, it was a way of finding a voice and getting a place to start from. It was years before I would even call myself a writer. Even though I was penning all the material and I loved doing it, it was very much a function in order to allow me and the company to perform material which was real and important to us as actresses in Northern Ireland at the time.[20]

Jones is known for the 'broad liberalism' of her work, which sets out to question personal and political borders and boundaries, refusing definitions, agendas, or allegiances.[21] One

---

[17] Ibid., 26.   [18] Foley, *Girls in the Big Picture*, 37.

[19] It was not until 2006 that the first collection of Charabanc plays was published: Claudia W. Harris (ed.), *The Charabanc Theatre Company: Four Plays, Inventing Women's Work* (Gerrards Cross: Colin Smythe, 2006).

[20] Foley, *Girls in the Big Picture*, 30.   [21] Ibid., 34.

of the effects of Charabanc's creative process, which, due to lack of resources, necessitated the actresses playing multiple, often cross-gender roles, was that an inherent theatricality of non-realist performativity was born. Jones reflects upon the significance of this for her development as a playwright:

> Sometimes I think there has been a form and a style that have been imposed upon me because of the economics of theatre and I don't know if I could write a play with twelve characters, or thirteen or fourteen. Because I am so used to saying that I have three people here who can play everyone, I actually have to think that I can't have *that* person talking to *that* person because they are playing *that* person. They are playing both characters, so in a sense that restricts you, but it is also a good thing because it's a discipline.[22]

Oul Delph and False Teeth (Arts Theatre, 1984), Charabanc's next play after *Lay Up Your Ends*, expressed a non-sectarian socialist ideology alongside a celebration of women, while *Now You're Talkin'* (Arts Theatre, 1985) focused on the contemporary lives of women and issues of class. *The Girls in the Big Picture* (Ardhowen Theatre, Enniskillen, 1986) foregrounded the lives of women, marriage, and the matriarchal sphere, bringing up questions of agency and changing social values and expectations across generations. Set on the balcony of one of the nationalist Divis flats, *Somewhere Over the Balcony* is an excellent example of Jones's unfolding formal theatricality and the company's only play to address the Troubles. The play opened at the Belfast Arts Theatre in November 1987 to a mixed response due to what could be perceived as an ostensible trivialization of the sectarian conflict, at least partly because the show opened just after the Remembrance Sunday bombing in Enniskillen and sensitivities were high amongst audiences. In this drama we encounter an absurdist rendering of the invasive, dehumanizing effects of war upon the family. All 'normal' expectations are inverted or suspended as the riotous becomes acceptable, enabling an 'institutionalised insanity'.[23] With lyrical dialect and a complex soundscape, the play is both a hilarious send-up of and poignant observation upon the anarchic realities of living in a war zone. All of the action is retold through the multiple perspectives of the three female protagonists, Kate, Rose, and Ceely. In this world, men lack individuation—sharing the same pet-name 'Tucker'—while the women comment upon, mediate, and filter the action. Violence is not permitted on stage, and so is not fetishized or objectified.

The Hamster Wheel (Arts Theatre Belfast, 1990), Jones's only sole-authored play whilst a member of Charabanc, explores women's roles in looking after disabled and sick people within the family and community. Jones parted ways with Charabanc in 1990. Her 1995 play *Women on the Verge of HRT* (West Belfast Féile an Phobail) focuses on the themes of ageing and women's sense of redundancy and invisibility in the face of the menopause and related issues of sexual attractiveness and relationships. The play charts the emotional journeys of its protagonists, Vera and Anna, and the cultural conditions of femininity and desire. *A Night in November* is Jones's one-man show in which the Protestant male protagonist, Kenneth McCallister, sets out on a spiritual journey, encountering sectarian division along the way as he recognizes his own sense of bigotry and achieves a more open-minded state of being. The play was first produced by DubbelJoint for the West Belfast Festival, Whiterock in 1994, and toured extensively North and South. Actor Dan Gordon memorably created

---

[22] Ibid., 35.   [23] Ibid., 44.

the role of McCallister in a tour de force performance which showcased Jones's brilliant theatricality. This was followed up by the unprecedented international critical success of *Stones in his Pockets*, in which two actors play a multitude of roles. *Stones in his Pockets* was first performed at Whiterock, West Belfast, in 1996, and again at the Lyric Theatre Belfast, in 1999, directed by Ian McElhinney with Conleth Hill and Sean Campion as the performers. The show toured extensively nationally and internationally, and was nominated for two Olivier Awards (Best New Comedy and Best Actor) in the West End and three Tony Awards (Best Actor for both performers and Best Director) on Broadway in 2001. The play is a hilarious and clever deconstruction of commodifications of 'Irishness', where two extras on a Hollywood film being shot in Kerry, *The Quiet Land*, decide to make their own film as an authentic counter-narrative. Yet, in spite of the huge success of Jones as solo author, her work, like that of the Charabanc company out of which it emerged, has still attracted far less critical attention than contemporary male playwrights Martin McDonagh, Conor McPherson, or Enda Walsh.

MARINA CARR

Marina Carr, who grew up on the Bog of Allen by the banks of Pallas Lake in Co. Offaly in the 1970s, appeared as an atypically confident 25-year-old woman in the 1989 Dublin Theatre Festival with a rehearsed reading of her first play, the absurdist two-hander *Ullaloo*. The irreverent tone and experimental theatricality of Carr's early plays were attractive to independent theatre companies in the late 1980s and early 1990s. *Low in the Dark* was first performed at the Project Arts Centre in 1989; Sarah Jane Scaife, who played the character of Binder, recalls in rehearsals how 'even at that early stage in her career, Marina was absolutely sure of her theatrical voice'.[24] *Ullaloo*, an old Gaelic word meaning 'funeral lament', was subsequently given a full production in the Peacock with Olwen Fouéré and Mark Lambert in 1991. Besides *Ullaloo* and *Low in the Dark*, other early, unpublished works are *The Deer's Surrender* (Gaiety School of Acting 1990) and *This Love Thing* (1991), which was an unprecedented cross-border North–South co-production between Tinderbox in the Old Museum Arts Centre, Belfast, and Pigsback in the Project Arts Centre, Dublin. The genesis of Carr's theatrical voice can be identified in these works, where her innate sense of irreverence, humour, and lyricism shine through the Beckettian absurdist experimental style, along with slapstick, role-play, and gender-bending. A strong feminist sensibility can be felt at this early point in Carr's career, particularly in *This Love Thing*, which depicts famous icons and religious figures such as Jesus and artists such as Leonardo da Vinci from tongue-in-cheek perspectives. Underlying all of these early works are the themes, existential questioning, and emotional landscapes of men and women that will be developed in her later works. *Ullaloo* closed early due to poor ticket sales, but this was a defining moment for Carr: 'I went straight into the Abbey. Garry Hynes was the Artistic Director at the time and

[24] Sarah Jane Scaife, 'Mutual Beginnings: Marina Carr's *Low in the Dark*', in Anna McMullan and Cathy Leeney (eds.), *The Theatre of Marina Carr: 'Before Rules Was Made'* (Dublin: Carysfort Press, 2003), 6.

I asked her for money [and] she said "No, I can't give you money." I said, "Well, will you give me a commission or something", and she did.'[25] With this commission Carr moved to Inishnee, Co. Galway, and wrote her breakthrough drama, *The Mai*.

Carr's emergence as a playwright in the late 1980s coincided with increasing visibility of women in Irish culture, politics, and many other spheres of public activity. In some respects, 1991 can be seen as a key moment in terms of women's artistry and activism. The newly inaugurated President of Ireland, Mary Robinson, made a speech at the press launch of Carr's new play *This Love Thing* at the Project Arts Centre in 1991, signalling a vital new energy and (symbolic rather than executive) presence in public life for '*mná na hÉireann*' (a phrase much associated with the Robinson presidency). The late 1980s was a period of transformation, leading out of recession to legislative reform in the early to mid-1990s. The decriminalization of homosexuality (1993) and legalization of divorce (1995) heralded a new era, as did the onset of what became known as 'the Celtic Tiger' in those same years, when Ireland became one of the fastest-growing economies in the world. The 1990s also saw the rapid decline of the authority of the Catholic Church, against a background of revelations of the horrendous sexual abuse of children by the Irish clergy resulting in a Redress Board being set up in 1999 which paid €850 million in compensation to survivors. Evidence of church and state collusion in abuse began to emerge in the 1990s, regarding the protection of paedophile priests within the Catholic Church and the truth about the church and state-run 'Magdalene Laundries', which incarcerated unmarried pregnant women as unpaid laundry workers, in some cases resulting in the illegal, often enforced, sale of their babies to families in the United States. With such a period of social flux, the emergence of Carr's socially confrontational voice marks a meaningful interrogation of the atrocities against Irish citizens, and against women and children in particular, which are part of Ireland's current negotiation with a darkly repressive and abusive past.

Like the work of earlier women of the twentieth century, Carr's plays express female dis-affection with the terms of motherhood, the family, and society at large, where the oppres-siveness of patriarchy is set against questions of women's agency. Many of Carr's plays after 1994 are set in rural, domestic settings and inherently challenge cultural assumptions of femininity, with a strong emphasis on nature and landscape as a re-politicized site of female agency, history, and creativity. Carr's relationship and identification with feminist politics has transformed over the decades, just as her plays, from the beginning, have been intrinsically feminist both in form and in content, continually testing the borders of patri-archal authority. While an experiential feminism has always been at the heart of her thea-tre, she explicitly identified her work as 'feminist' in 2014 when asked about her adaptation of the Phaedra myth in *Phaedra Backwards*.[26]

Carr's Midlands Trilogy from 1994 to 1998 explores unresolved female displacement, where the protagonist takes her own life in each case. Whilst some critics have expressed dissatisfaction that there are no 'positive outcomes' for the female protagonists in these plays, the power of Carr's voice lies in her de-idealized acknowledgement that painful

---

[25] Ní Anluain, *Reading the Future*, 55.
[26] Marina Carr, public play-reading in honour of John McGahern, St Patrick's College, Drumcondra, June 2014.

narratives must be addressed before transformation can occur. Again, there is an inverted sexism here, in the expectation that Carr should only represent positive 'female role models' whilst no such gendered onus is placed on a male writer in terms of their protagonists. For Carr, as for the earlier dramatists of the twentieth century, the importance lies in the creation of complex women who authentically vocalize their discontent whilst negotiating the limitations of society, forming part of the progress of society as a whole. Skipping over unappealing realities in order to showcase a happy ending might on one level seem desirable, but it does not function to interrogate the fundamental realities of inequity and abuse at the core of modern Ireland.

While Carr's earliest plays are absurdist in form, her engagement with Beckett moves to a deeper level in her Midlands plays, where themes of waiting, abandonment, and dehumanizing repetition lie at the core of the dramatic (in)action. In *The Mai* the eponymous character sits at the window waiting for someone to return, just as her mother, grandmother, and great-grandmother did before her. 'We repeat and we repeat, the orchestration may be different but the tune is always the same,' says 100-year-old Grandma Fraochlan.[27] In *The Mai* we witness four generations of richly woven female characters against the poetic backdrop of Owl Lake—a site of solace, fulfilment, and eventual death for the Mai. Combining poetic monologues incorporating folklore and rich nature imagery with contemporary dialogue and dialect interspersed with humour, the play offers major roles for seven women on stage. The drama focuses upon the life of 40-year-old Mai, her failing marriage, and her relationship with her extended family, while the omnipresent narrator of the play, Mai's daughter Millie, offers a reflective overview of the action in a doubly feminized authorial structure that revises Brian Friel's 1990 play *Dancing at Lughnasa*, with its framing device as a memory play.

Portia Coughlan (1996) was directed by Garry Hynes in a co-production with Druid and the Royal Court Theatre, and is written phonetically in a strongly expressed Midlands dialect. The play focuses on the life and death of 30-year-old Portia and her sense of alienation from the roles of wife, mother, and daughter. In the play, Portia's connection to nature, the outdoors, and the Belmont River is in strong contrast to the stultifying landlocked village of Belmont. Portia compares life at home to a living death: 'The pair of us might as well be dead for all the joy we knock out of one another. The kids is asleep, the house creakin' like a coffin, all them wooden doors and floors. Sometimes I can't breathe anymore.'[28] Carr wrote the play in a top-floor room of the National Maternity Hospital, which commissioned the script, and in an interesting reflexivity of place and thematic content, the work viscerally sifts through complexities of motherhood, radically demythologizing the so-called 'maternal instinct' and vociferously challenging oppressive patriarchy. Portia expresses resistance to stifling associations of womanhood with motherhood as inscribed within the 1937 Irish Constitution:

> Don'nen ya understan'! Jaysus! Ya thinche ah don wish ah chould be a natural mother, mindin' me children, playin' wud thim, doin' all tha things a mother is asposed ta do. Whin ah looche at my sons Raphael ah sees knives an' accidents an' terrible muhilations. Their toys

---

[27] Marina Carr, *Plays One* (London: Faber & Faber, 2000), 123.   [28] Ibid., 207.

is weapons for me ta hurt thim wud, givin' thim a bath is a place where ah chould drown thim.[29]

The richly evoked physical terrains in Carr's plays, such as bogs, rivers, lakes, forts, and farmlands, resonate with meaning, preserving cultural memories and (with)holding multiple hidden histories. *By the Bog of Cats* (1998), probably Carr's best-known and most widely produced play, is a loose reworking of Euripides's *Medea*, set in contemporary rural Ireland, with the Traveller Hester Swane dramatizing female exile and alienation. The play's action, set on the bog at crepuscular transitions of otherness, is attuned to the reverberating sensuality of nature's energies. Nature, like humanity, is violated in Carr's next play, *On Raftery's Hill*, also directed by Garry Hynes, which toured to the 'Island: Arts for Ireland' Festival in the Kennedy Center for the Performing Arts, Washington, in 2000. Perhaps Carr's most controversial work, this play, set in a farmhouse kitchen in the present day, opens up the brutal realities of incest and sexual abuse in the Irish family. Its circularity of form reflects the ontological repetition and non-transformation typical of Carr's mature plays, echoing the legacy of Beckettian dramaturgy that was more obvious in her earliest work. Exhuming legacies of darkness, *On Raftery's Hill* takes the theme of arrested development to an extreme, where incestuous cycles reveal purgatorial stasis. The cultural rage that is manifest in *On Raftery's Hill* gives expression to previously silenced anxieties of family and home through its enactment of patterns of sexual abuse, shattering idealized notions of the family and functioning as a critique of the Irish state's empty pledge to protect all of its citizens. The single-set kitchen is a deconstructive critique of Irish theatre and culture where the collusion and delusion of sex abuse and incest in Ireland is confronted. One-dimensional moralistic binaries of victim/perpetrator are avoided as the troubling complexity of violation, mutual dependency, and the intricate cause and effects of sexual abuse within the family are enacted.

Ghosts, fantastical beings, mythological archetypes, and Gothic traces recur in Carr's plays such as *Ariel*, a version of Aeschylus's *Oresteia* (Abbey Theatre, 2002), *Woman and Scarecrow* (Royal Court 2006), *Marble* (Abbey Theatre 2009), *The Cordelia Dream* (Royal Shakespeare Company, 2009), and *The Giant Blue Hand* (The Ark, Dublin, 2009). The latter three plays move between dream-states and the mundane, where the unconscious life powerfully determines everyday reality. In *16 Possible Glimpses* (Abbey Theatre, 2011), Carr explores her major themes through imagined mirrored shards or 'glimpses' into the life of Anton Chekhov, while *Phaedra Backwards* (McCarter Theater, Princeton, 2011) is a return to the Greek world, this time in a non-geographically specific reimagining of the Phaedra–Hippolytus myth, which offers a powerful feminist renegotiation of both the form and content of classical tragedy. In challenging conservative patriarchy, Carr's plays contest realism, foregrounding a sense of intrinsic otherness, which like her landscapes is never fully real and never purely fictional. As was the case with earlier plays by women, landscape, nature, and sites of water offer alternative realms of ontological resonance, particularly for the central female characters. Carr's poetic language and engagement with realms of death, dreams, memory, the soul, and the transformative power of storytelling express alternative modes of processing experience. Such imaginative engagements operate with visceral

---

[29] Marina Carr, *Portia Coughlan* (London: Faber & Faber, 1996), 42.

expressions of explicit social commentary in recognizably Irish contexts to contest conservative values and aesthetics.

Carr's plays are palimpsests of historical traces, sedimented like layers of the bog itself, in the unearthed seams of our cultural consciousness. In each play the ordinary is bathed in transformational light, lapping in darkness to illuminate possibilities for change, where the sacred and the tragic move towards transcendence linked to suffering. The necessary search to articulate the mysterious divine within the self as a mode of redemption runs through Carr's work, as the unbearable tragedy of lack of fulfilment marks a long running theme. In her 2006 play *Woman and Scarecrow*, Woman says:

> I know as well as the next that the arc of our time here bends to tragedy. How can it be otherwise when we think where we are going. But we must mark those moments, those passionate moments, however small. I looked up 'passionate' in the dictionary once because I thought I had never known it. [. . .] Well, I said to myself, if that's the definition of passion then I have known passion. More. I have lived a passionate life.[30]

Conclusion

If Irish women's work in theatre has historically been regarded as the exception to the male norm, such embedded perceptions have only begun to shift in the last decade or so. For the most recent generation of theatre-makers, gender equality is regarded as both a right and an expectation, even though it has not yet been achieved. Directors have been much more in evidence in particular. Well-established figures such as Garry Hynes and Lynne Parker continue to lead Druid and Rough Magic, Selina Cartmell and Anabelle Comyn direct high-profile main-stage productions at the Abbey and the Gate, and the innovative work of Louise Lowe with ANU Productions and Annie Ryan with Corn Exchange are two examples of a welcome diversification of Irish theatre. There are still not nearly enough women playwrights, but Hilary Fannin, Stacey Gregg, Nancy Harris, Abbie Spallen, and Elaine Murphy have all had plays commissioned by the Abbey in recent years. The increased presence of women working in theatre today has much to do with the growth in professional theatre training and the many tertiary drama and theatre studies degree courses available on the island, whose classes include a high proportion of women. Modules on feminism, gender, and queer studies have become integral to much tertiary education since the late 1990s, articulating and theorizing women's historic elision and enabling new processes of subjectivity and creativity. Unlike many women during the 1980s and 1990s, the younger generation of women in theatre now largely self-identify as feminists, due in part to the integration of feminist discourse in education, the visibility and vocalization of LGBTQ groups, the dismantling of its misogynist, bra-burning, 'man-hating' associations, and the move towards equality for all. There is a sense of self-worth and entitlement in this generation of women which was not inherent in the previous generation. Since the publication of *Women in Irish Drama* (2007), which sought to

---

[30] Marina Carr, *Woman and Scarecrow* (London: Faber & Faber, 2006), 76.

bring together voices to identify and critically engage with the contributions of women, a new generation of practitioners has emerged on the island, for whom being a woman is, arguably for the first time, not an extraordinary factor in terms of working in theatre. A more evenly distributed role for women in all aspects of theatre-making is now identifiable, although the situation is still far from equal in term of the production of plays by women or plays directed by women, as can be seen in the 2016 Abbey Theatre 'Waking the Nation' programme.

....

CHAPTER 34

IRISH THEATRE DEVISED

....

BRIAN SINGLETON

HISTORIES of Irish theatre since the beginning of the twentieth century for the most part have centred on the production and reception of play texts. Many of those histories have also contextualized the play texts of Ireland's historical avant-garde (especially those premièred by the Abbey Theatre) as being synonymous with the political revolution that led to independence, and thus Irish theatre became indelibly linked to the nationalist movement. Further, in the subsequent postcolonial decades, stage representations of anything Irish have invariably been read as markers of the state of the nation. 'The idea of "nation",' Shaun Richards contends, 'as both theme and setting, has haunted the development of Irish theatre.'[1] Even when Brian Friel rose to fame with the production in 1964 of his play *Philadelphia, Here I Come!*—a play that marked in many senses the failures of the postcolonial state represented in the play through intergenerational miscommunication and the emotional impact of emigration—the contestation of the national narrative was in the form of the dramatic text.

Irish theatre in the twentieth century largely eschewed the directors' and designers' theatres that had dominated the European theatrical avant-garde since the end of the nineteenth century (from André Antoine and Lugné-Poe to Adolphe Appia and Edward Gordon Craig). Successive generations of Irish youth—that constituency in which the avant-garde reconstitutes itself—never had the opportunity to have an impact on the production of the new in their home theatre, given the successive waves of emigration that blighted the country in the twentieth century. The strict morality of the new Irish state also drove Ireland's avant-garde practitioners into exile. Few and far between are theatre practices in Ireland until the 1980s that did not emanate from a script, or were not composed according to the strict hierarchy of a producing house, director, designer, and actors. From the 1980s, however, training for the theatre became more established both inside and outside the university system, and it became more commonplace for theatre practitioners to train abroad, but mostly in the non-verbal forms of dance, movement, clowning, and mime—training, in other words, that was not readily available in Ireland. The emergence of drama departments, first in Trinity College in 1984 and then in most tertiary institutions

---

[1] Shaun Richards, 'Plays of (Ever) Changing Ireland', in Shaun Richards (ed.), *The Cambridge Companion to Twentieth-Century Irish Drama* (Cambridge: Cambridge University Press, 2004), 1.

in Ireland, had a direct impact on the refocusing of generations of students as much on the form of performance in a live context, actor–spectator relationships, and the languages of the stage as on the meanings inherent in the play text. Further, the annual importation of non-Irish theatre with the establishment of the Dublin Theatre Festival in 1957 and beyond also exposed both practitioners and audiences to nonverbal forms of theatre.[2] But these forms were battling the imprint of the demarcation of performative forms of culture in the Irish psyche, delimited also by the strictures of funding by the Arts Council between dance and theatre. Indeed, such strictures still exist today.

Emerging companies in the 1980s and 1990s that questioned those strict demarcations found it difficult to attract Arts Council funding, as their work fell between several stools. Nevertheless, eleven decades after the establishment of one of the world's leading 'writers' theatres' of the historical avant-garde (the Abbey Theatre), it is fair to say that most of the innovative, provocative, political, and interdisciplinary work that stands at the front rank of Irish theatre is devised performance; some of it verbal, some non-verbal; some of it in theatres, some of it not; some of it realistic, some highly stylized. Its impact, though, is not predicated on a challenge to the written word per se, but on its challenge to the hierarchies of theatre process, theatre production, and theatre reception. Many of the practitioners who work in contemporary Irish theatre do not subscribe to the terminology that delimits their role in production. Directors, designers, and actors in the twenty-first century are embraced within the generic nomenclature of 'theatre-makers', who share tasks and are collaboratively engaged in creating what they often call 'performance' that is not necessarily theatrical, dramatic, or even taking place in theatre buildings.

'Devising' is the term most commonly associated nowadays with the process of making performance that does not necessarily begin with a play script. Nevertheless, various forms of texts other than play scripts may be in the rehearsal room from the outset, such as prose, poetry, print and online journalism, notes, philosophy, politics, and written and transcribed oral histories. Texts in a more metaphorical sense also exist in the rehearsal room, such as the notion of the body as text with its kinaesthetic memories and its life markers; sounds and music as texts with or without scores; visual imagery as texts that might predate rehearsal or indeed emanate from the improvisation of the performers in the room. In all of these ways, texts are present from the outset.

Perhaps the most significant characteristic of the theatre devising process historically is the prevalence in many companies internationally of breaking down the hierarchies of theatre production. This form of devising is known as collaborative. Most companies have roles according to the specialisms of the individuals who make up the companies. There are those in the companies who perform and those who do not, but in the rehearsal room all contribute equally to the process in terms of research and the improvisation around that research. Improvisation is one of the most frequently used tools for devising, and this is where devised performance intersects most directly with other arts practices in its use of found objects, stories, images, and sounds that provide the stimuli for the actor's exploration. In their study of improvisation in performance, Frost and Yarrow identify three strands of the practice that are useful in understanding Irish theatre's devising process: '(a)

---

[2] See Nicholas Grene and Patrick Lonergan, with Lilian Chambers (eds.), *Interactions: Dublin Theatre Festival 1957–2007* (Dublin: Carysfort Press, 2008).

the *application* of improvisation to the purposes of the traditional play; (b) the use of *pure* improvisation in the creation of an 'alternative' kind of theatre experience; and (c) the extension of improvisatory principles beyond the theatre itself.[3] While there are overlaps between these strands in the work of the Irish companies that will be examined presently, these strands productively can be mapped onto three specific characteristics of devised performance historically, described by Heddon and Milling:

> theatre predominantly concerned with the actor, acting and story; [. . .] theatre closely linked to art practices, which dramaturgically place the image as equal to the spoken text and which therefore pays close attention to the visual potentials inherent in the stage 'picture' [. . .]; and theatre predominantly concerned with its impact in a political and/or social context.[4]

As with the improvisation strands, these devising categorizations are never neatly configurative of Irish theatre practices, but again are useful markers of how Irish devised performance negotiates text, image, and politics within theatre structures, as well as negotiating new actor–audience relationships.

Devised theatre in Ireland has no historical beginning in the strictest sense of devising configured in terms of improvisation. Improvisation occurs at some stage of most theatre processes, including with a play script. But such processes are largely invisible to the historian, and no real visibility occurs in the archives until a late twentieth-century avant-garde appears, in an interdisciplinary form, with the establishment of the Project Arts Centre in Dublin in 1967. The Arts Centre as we know it emerged from a three-week festival at the Gate Theatre in 1966, with a mixture of readings, plays, recitals, teach-ins, and exhibitions. Such was the impetus that the project established itself more permanently in Lower Abbey Street, though suspending its theatre production in the early years in favour of exhibitions. By the time it became established in its premises in an old warehouse at the back of the Olympia Theatre in 1974 (in East Essex Street, Temple Bar), European influences on its theatrical output were in evidence. Noel and Peter Sheridan took over the running of this artists' cooperative, and brought to it a social and political engagement for the artistic work, as well as a commitment to the nurturing of new music. The project also became synonymous with new, young theatre companies—especially in the 1980s—such as Rough Magic and Operating Theatre. While Rough Magic cut their teeth on the canonical as well as contemporary play texts, Operating Theatre, led by actress Olwen Fouéré and composer Roger Doyle, worked at the intersection of several arts disciplines, and thus is an interesting first example to analyse.

Theatre as Arts Practice: Postmodern to Postdramatic

Operating Theatre was set up in 1980 by Fouéré and Doyle and produced new, challenging work for the subsequent twenty-eight years. Arguably their first major critical impact on

---

[3] Anthony Frost and Ralph Yarrow, *Improvisation in Drama* (Basingstoke: Macmillan, 1990), 15.
[4] Deirdre Heddon and Jane Milling, *Devising Performance: A Critical History* (Basingstoke: Palgrave Macmillan, 2006), 27.

the arts scene was a play called *The Diamond Body*, scripted by Aidan Mathews in collaboration with the company, and performed at the Project Arts Centre in 1984. It featured Fouéré performing solo as Stephanos, the hermaphrodite owner of a gay bar on a Greek island, facing the increasing revulsion of the island community—a revulsion that turned to violence. Preceding the decriminalization of homosexuality in 1993, this performance was one of the few in Ireland that had tackled the subject of homophobia.[5] Operating Theatre's work, though, was not directly political; their interest was in exploring new possibilities of theatre communication and the creation of character beyond words. This was seen most notably in their 1999 production, *Angel/Babel*, in Project @ The Mint, which featured Fouéré attached to custom-made sensory software that responded to the kinaesthetic impulses of the actor and reproduced those impulses through computer-generated sound, challenging notions of character and the dramatic and of refracting or reassembling words.[6] In *Passades* in 2004 Fouéré emerged into an abandoned warehouse as a lone explorer whose sounds were captured by software in temporal freeze frame but who eschewed words altogether. These critically acclaimed productions moved their performances into found spaces, to warehouses and galleries, and later a hotel room, all focusing on presence and absence, the body in space, and the intersection of image and sound.

Operating Theatre's final work for the theatre, *Here Lies* (2005), was a performative response to French theatre philosopher and actor Antonin Artaud's correspondence about his fateful trip to Ireland in 1937. Its first iteration was in the Imperial Hotel in Galway, where Artaud stayed en route to Inis Mór (off the west coast of Ireland) on his quest for premodern European culture. Spectators wore headsets as they entered the hotel room and listened to Fouéré's voice narrating the letter Artaud wrote subsequently about his experiences in Ireland to Art O'Briain at the Irish Legation in Paris. Artaud had been arrested in Dublin for being destitute and delirious in search of mescaline, to which he was addicted, and was deported and incarcerated in France for the next eight years of France's turbulent history. The whispering words of Artaud through the headsets were disembodied from the performer, who was trapped, cell-like, in a museum exhibition case furnished only with a single bed and a small writing desk, disconcerting the audience in the representation of time and space. There was no direct connection between the disembodied voice and the body in the case. It appeared as if we were hearing Artaud's unspoken thoughts. For most of the performance, Fouéré/Artaud ignored the spectators until at one point s/he pressed her face to the glass case and looked out at us, bringing us into the reality of the present and confronting our voyeurism of the historical character as exhibit. This moment caused the gallery attendant (played by Doyle) to switch on his torch and aggressively usher us out of the building. Working with director Selina Cartmell and lighting designer Paul Keogan, this was an installation in which Fouéré performed Artaud's imagined conspiracy of the forces of authority in Ireland against him, the whispering tones adding to a performative sense of threat. Disembodied and exhibited, Artaud could not communicate directly with audiences; all the while, audiences were challenged to conceive theatre not

[5] See, however, Ch. 21 for the analyis of an earlier example in Thomas Kilroy's *The Death and Resurrection of Mr Roche*.

[6] See Christopher Morash, *A History of Irish Theatre, 1601–2000* (Cambridge: Cambridge University Press, 2002), 272–3.

as entertainment but as an almost scopic Othering of the subjects of history. As a mime based on an original letter from the archives, taking place outside a theatre building, and with a lighting and sound installation that eschewed the dramatic, *Here Lies*, like much of Operating Theatre's preceding work, challenged the notions of theatre and theatricality. As such, it is emblematic of much recent Irish devised performance, in that it focuses on the body in relation to found text rather than play text and on the ethical relationship between performance and spectator.[7]

Countering the narratives of the canon—albeit not the Irish canon—and challenging its original form has been one of the hallmarks of Pan Pan Theatre Company, which emerged from Trinity College's Drama Department in 1991 under the leadership of director Gavin Quinn and designer Aedin Cosgrove. Its earliest formation worked in the field of deaf-hearing theatre, but increasing travels abroad—particularly to the theatre festivals of central Europe—saw the motivation and the aesthetic of the company change from what was considered in the 1990s to be postmodern to what today, under the influence of German theorist Hans-Thiess Lehmann, might be termed the 'postdramatic'.[8] While the postmodern is readily understood nowadays, after Lyotard and Baudrillard, to mean the disruption of grand narratives, bricolage, and non-linearity, the postdramatic might well be understood to signify specifically in theatre terms the elements of the avant-garde that focus on the relationships between the material in the performance and the materiality of the performance in relationship to the theatre as both event and space. Thus the principal characteristics of the postdramatic include the evacuation of the intentionality of an autonomous subject (character) and the foregrounding of the theatre machine as a primary producer of meaning.

Pan Pan Theatre Company came to prominence with a Best Overall Production award at the Dublin Fringe Festival in 1995 for *A Bronze Twist of Your Serpent Muscles*, described by irishplayography.com as '[a] study of decay, madness, erotic perversion and complex psychopathic personalities told through mime, dance and music'.[9] Like much of the early devised work of Pan Pan, this was a troubling production, non-linear in aspect, multi-focused, and way ahead of its time in an Irish context. Similar work, such as *Deflowerfucked* (2001), mixed genres such as live music video and an absurdist cookery demonstration without food, pointing to the loneliness of the individual in an increasingly globalized world, though even such a description does not encapsulate the eclectic nature and the unstable meanings of what was presented. But such productions must be seen in the context of another branch of Pan Pan's work—its annual Dublin International Theatre Symposia, first at the Samuel Beckett Centre and later at the Project Arts Centre in Dublin. The annual symposia took place between 1997 and 2003 and were held in January, at a fallow time theatrically, and far away from other festivals featuring many of Europe's leading avant-garde theatre companies. The symposia featured talks and, crucially, performance

[7] For further analysis of this production, see Brian Singleton, 'Performing Artaud in Ireland', *Études irlandaises* 33, no. 2 (2008), 43–52. See also Christopher Morash and Shaun Richards, *Mapping Irish Theatre: Theories of Space and Place* (Cambridge: Cambridge University Press, 2013), 169.

[8] See Hans-Thies Lehmann, *Postdramatic Theatre*, trans. Karen Jürs-Munby (London: Routledge, 2006), 26–7.

[9] See 'A Bronze Twist of Your Serpent Muscles', Irish Theatre Institute, Playography Ireland, http://www.irishplayography.com/play.aspx?playid=221. Accessed 20 Sept. 2014.

demonstrations and workshops, some of which had showings at the end of the symposia. The aim was for a new generation of theatre-makers in Ireland to be exposed to the practices of various European theatre traditions that contested the literary tradition of Irish theatre. And it is in the context of such companies as Mandala and Scena Plastyczna KUL, as well as Theatre of the Eighth Day from Poland, Teater Tyst from Sweden, and Ultima Vez from Belgium, that Pan Pan's devised work should be viewed and analysed. Such work had yet to be curated in Dublin's theatre festivals, as the theatrical language of some of the companies had yet to find its audience in an Irish context.

In the second decade of the company's existence, the focus moved to canonical texts and their deconstruction. Shakespeare's plays became a particular focus of the company, and their 2004 production *Mac-Beth 7* sought to stage the play's relationship with its audience, from first encounter in school as both literature and a rite of passage into adulthood, to subsequent encounters over time. The setting was a school classroom with pupils in uniform and at desks, the text at times forensically examined through microscope projection. And all the while the very constructedness of the theatre was on display, with the stage manager and director, Gavin Quinn, on stage the whole time, moving the production along, visibly being and playing director simultaneously. In a sense, this and subsequent productions of canonical plays were poststructuralist refractions of textual sources. In 2006, the company presented *Oedipus Loves You*, a new version of the Oedipus myth by Simon Doyle and Gavin Quinn, which took versions of the myth from Seneca and Sophocles and fused them with the writings of Freud to present a surburban family in need of therapy, whose self-help came in the form of their own garage band. Performed Dogme-style, in deadpan delivery, the drama of the myth was evacuated to reveal a contemporary malaise as a connecting point with the original mythological family. In their award-winning and widely toured *The Rehearsal: Playing the Dane* (2010) at the Samuel Beckett Theatre, spectators viewed as the first part of the production a staging of the pre-rehearsal process, from scholarly analysis to the casting of an actor in the role of Hamlet. An academic (the real-life English lecturer Dr Amanda Piesse from Trinity College), holding a live Great Dane (perhaps as visual metaphor of authority, or simply a dog-pun), gave a lecture on the play followed by a rendition of Greensleeves. As part of the production, Quinn and his casting director auditioned three very different actors with versions of Hamlet infused with the personality of the actors. Spectators were then asked to choose which actor should play the role. The second half of the production featured a truncated version of the play in monochrome in which Elsinore was represented by a series of dustbins, Hamlet was in an Elizabethan ruff—the only nod to the original context of the play—and the players were schoolchildren in contemporary uniform, playing not the play within the play, but the play *Hamlet* itself. Here the play was the play within the play.

> Before a single line of iambic pentameter is uttered, the play is academically addressed by Amanda Piesse of the School of English at Trinity College, who reads aloud an essay which describes the variables and ambiguities suggested by the conflicting contents of the 'Quartos' or drafts of the original. Piesse's conclusion is that *Hamlet* is a text which is indefinite in nature, and her hypotheses suggests that the philosophical enquiry of 'meaning' cannot find source in the characters' facts and mission statements but rather in the degree of self-conscious performance that they allege to. Thus, Pan Pan presents us with their masterful conceit: *Hamlet* as 'audition'. The audience find themselves privy to the casting process, as Quinn (in attendance himself, along with his stage manager and casting director) has three contenders perform their monologues to secure the role of Hamlet: an introverted but

loyal Derrick Devine; Conor Madden, who is authentic in his insecurities and wild in spirit; and solid and confident Garret Lombard. The three perform not only for the director but for us as well.[10]

Latterly, Pan Pan has continued its engagement with canonical plays in *Everyone is King Lear in his Own Home* (2012), domesticating the epic to a contemporary urban apartment, and Ibsen's *A Doll House* [*sic*] (2012), which distilled the text and setting to key moments in a marriage break-up, most notably in its non-staging of Nora's final door-slamming; the final lines were whispered by the actors playing Nora and Torvald, lying on the stage, immobile and apart. The company continue to garner critical and popular acclaim with staging of Beckett's non-theatre work, namely his radio plays: *All That Fall* (2011) was staged as immersive theatre, with the audience separated in rocking chairs experiencing a sound and light show; *Embers* (2013) as a front-on installation featuring a live performance of the text emanating from a giant skull. It is through the deconstruction of texts and their representation of text as simply text, with other texts being staged to inform the play text and contest the singularity of meaning in performance, that Pan Pan has made the most impact in terms of devised theatre in Ireland. What is more, the company's European influences have infused its work with the notion of visual imagery as a theatrical language and challenged the notion of theatre performance as dramatic.

Actors, Acting, and New Forms: Storytelling as Corporeal Practice

The 1990s witnessed an explosion of devised theatre, principally in the theatres of Dublin, appealing to young audiences with their new forms and extraordinary physicality; and even though their subjects might have dealt with the past, their representation of that past was one with a clear and confident sense of where Ireland and Irish theatre were placed culturally and socially at the end of the twentieth century. One of the most notable of those early productions was a devised play entitled *True Lines*, collaboratively written by director John Crowley and his cast (Cathy Belton, Gwynne McElveen, Tom Murphy, and Stuart Townsend). It was produced by Bickerstaffe theatre company in Kilkenny at Cleere's Theatre in April 1994, and transferred to great acclaim to the upstairs studio at Andrews Lane Theatre. The play features the stories of four Irish people in their 20s simultaneously in four different locations in the world: on a highway in Arizona, following Aboriginal songlines in Australia, in a hotel bedroom in Berlin, and somewhere in Africa. They are following 'lines' or paths to destinations as yet unknown, and during their journeying they question themselves and their own identities, as well as their culture (now displaced). The simultaneity of journeying with a global reach spoke much of the impact of emigration on generations of young people who had felt the need to emigrate. But this was not a

[10] Chris McCormack, *Musings in Intermissions* blog, 11 Oct. 2010, http://musingsinintermissions. blogspot.ie/2010/10/pan-pan-rehearsal-playing-dane-bins.html. Accessed 6 Apr. 2016.

production of nostalgia or a theatrical lament for a lost identity, but a visually arresting and formally innovative play. The characters were very much present in an Irish context, and seemed to be representing the Irish diaspora that was not necessarily forced to emigrate but may well have embarked on journeys of self-discovery. It was also a play that signalled how Irish theatre was about to transform through a generation of theatre-makers who were not going to leave the country, but were already connected through their theatre education to international forms of theatre now visible on the Irish stage. Structurally, the play was groundbreaking in an Irish context, as it interwove four disparate locations and narratives in a coherent and simultaneous space following literal and graphic lines in design terms and in a postmodern form. But these were young actors who were brought together for a one-off production. They would all continue to have successful careers at home, though the director would eventually move to the UK, for a successful career in theatre and film, and no longer contribute to the changing face of Irish theatre, nor even work in such a devised form again. For those who witnessed the production, however, a defining moment in Irish theatre had been reached.

True Lines would be indicative of the kind of work of undertaken by those wishing to push the boundaries of Irish theatre in the early 1990s. Similar work was also being carried out elsewhere in Ireland in those years by companies that, while they may have differed in the style and form of their devised work, shared a focus on storytelling as a corporeal practice. For instance, Blue Raincoat set up home in The Factory performance space in Sligo in 1991. Led by director Niall Henry, the company is collaborative in nature, and is influenced in terms of the form of their work by the corporeal mime of Étienne Decroux. Henry had trained with Corinne Soum (a former student of Decroux) and his son Maximilien Decroux. Though they began with classical texts, their work in later years focused primarily on the application of their form to modern European drama, as well as to adaptations and new writing. Not only does the style and form of their work owe much to the twentieth-century traditions of French theatre, but the operation of the company as an ongoing training ensemble is directly inspired by the French companies with whom Decroux trained and worked, namely Jacques Copeau (arguably the father of modern French theatre) and his Théâtre du Vieux-Colombier, and his successor, Charles Dullin and his Théâtre de l'Atelier. Both French visionaries—and many of their successors, who reinvigorated the French stage through physical training and often mime and non-verbal performance—believed in the notion of a company that not only performed but also trained for life on an ongoing basis. Blue Raincoat operates in similar school fashion, and also offers and facilitates workshops for actors not in their company who are interested in their style and form. The company now operates a repertory system with stock productions available for touring, all the while adding to the repertory with new work. One of their most notable successes is the transformation of the theatre of Eugène Ionesco from its word-bound origins into highly physicalized and imaginative corporeal experiences, such as in *The Bald Soprano* (1950), *The Chairs* (1952), and *Rhinoceros* (1961), staged by Blue Raincoat in 2004, 2005, and 2010, respectively. Following Decroux's original principles, the corporeal mime is not used to embellish stories; the stories themselves begin with the body, and the body moves through space, creating images full of narrative meaning in themselves.

Another theatre company to emerge in the early 1990s, Barabbas ... the Company (now Barabbas Theatre Company), also began their theatre-making primarily through the body. Raymond Keane, who had a background in mime, Veronica Coburn, who had a background in clowning, and Mikel Murfi, who trained at the École Jacques Lecoq, began to work together in 1993 and burst onto the Irish theatre scene with what they described as Theatre of Clown in a devised production entitled *Come Down From the Mountain, John Clown, John Clown*. Performed in red nose, this almost wordless play about contemporary Ireland featured three characters: Veronica Clown as a former entrepreneur, Mikel Clown as a political correspondent, and Raymond Clown, unemployed. Both characters and the scenes in which they played focused in great detail on the peculiarities of Irish life, and presaged the boom and bust society into which Ireland was about to transform. This was followed in 1994 with another devised production entitled *Half Eight Mass of a Tuesday*, featuring again the ordinary people of Ireland congregating at a rural church for a weekday Mass. Developing their physical craft still further, Barabbas used shadow play, miniatures, and puppets to tell the stories of ten fictional characters, with a focus once more on the minutiae of a life that is distinctly Irish, made all the more unusual by characters who make the trek to Mass and not just on a Sunday. Both productions in many ways were wordless chronicles of the times, sharp in social observation, universally resonant, and harbingers of an Irish life that was about to be challenged in mind and spirit.

Barabbas Theatre Company also was not averse to words. Their 1996 devised show *Strokehauling* focused on the singular life of a small-town draper's assistant, Liam, who is socially and physically awkward, but whose mind explodes with a plethora of imagined and imaginative action as he runs the country roads of Ireland on heroic adventures. Liam, played by Murfi, moves during the course of the play from being the taciturn clerk to one of the Fianna, a mythical hero of superhuman exploits, via a long sequence in which he runs and runs and occasionally hurls, testing the endurance of both actor and audience. A study in Irish masculinity revealing 'the secret life of the Irish male', as Adrian Turpin described it,[11] the production pointed out the disparity between the myth of an idealized masculinity made possible through the national sport of hurling, but belying the reality of a humdrum and socially awkward masculinity of rural Ireland. The company's inventive and physical storytelling was also used on numerous occasions to tackle some canonical texts, such as *Macbeth*—also in 1994, reducing the play to three witches, Macbeth, and his wife—and the most celebrated of all, Lennox Robinson's 1916 play *The Whiteheaded Boy*, which premièred in 1997 before touring Ireland and internationally for the next three years. Played by the three company members, and with Louis Lovett in the title role, the production was notable for its deconstruction of the text and its performance of the text as text rather than as an imagined real. For instance, the play began with the actors examining a model box of the set, speaking the stage directions, and slowly embodying the characters on the life-size set. Performing multiple roles, the actors' virtuoso display of physical comedy reimagined the text in a postmodern form and metatheatrical style that was to become their trademark for a decade to come. Arguably, the company reached their theatrical apogee in their 2007 production entitled *Circus*, which brought to life the popular traditions from which the company emerged in a theatrical version of a big top, complete with trapeze, escapology, knife-throwing, and rope acts.

---

[11] Adrian Turpin, 'Review: Of Mime and Men', *Independent*, 22 Jan. 1997, http://www.independent.co.uk/arts-entertainment/review-of-mime-and-men-1284519.html. Accessed 17 Sept. 2014.

In the wake of the 2010 Arts Council cuts to funding for eleven independent theatre companies in Ireland, Barabbas was threatened with extinction. But, pared down to just Keane himself, the company's 2011 touring production[12] of City of Clowns eschewed the conventions of theatre by ushering its audience away from auditoria and into a warehouse-like backstage containing a multitude of cardboard boxes of varying sizes. There was not a sound to be heard until eventually one of the boxes began to move, and from within emerged Keane as 'Fibril' Clown, who struggled to control his own environment; he disconnected the electricity but could not switch off the lights; he reordered boxes to no avail as the cardboard city appeared to have no exit. But in the midst of the absurd world around him, Fibril cuddled and rocked a small box as if it were a baby, until suddenly a shaft of light illuminated the room as the boxes parted, and a small boy entered and gestured for Fibril to follow. Follow he did, with the audience in tow, through the bowels of the theatres and into a room full of clowns. Fibril clown was no longer alone. He, like we, found comfort in a clown collective, and although this collective may be assembled and disconnected, their assembly provided a new cityscape for the futile gestures of other lonely clowns. In many senses this production saw the company turn full circle, from clowning the Irish everyman on the cusp of an economic transformation in Come Down from the Mountain to everyman's futile struggle to alter the course of destiny as a redemptive assembly of strangers in collective solidarity in City of Clowns. And, of course, all of this was built upon acts of the everyday, performed almost without words. According to Chris McCormack: 'Keane has a presence that can replace the audience's laughter with sympathetic silence instantly, and the Barabbas portrayal of 'clowns' as individuals not invincible to human loss and longing continues to be a very interesting psychology.[13]

The physicality of Barabbas is mirrored in the work of a company that emerged from Trinity College Dublin in the early 1990s and was established in 1995: the Corn Exchange, founded by director Annie Ryan. Ryan forged a new acting style that was a hybrid of commedia dell'arte and storytelling. As in commedia, the actors speak directly to the audience while the non-speaking actors look to their speaking counterpart. This shifting focus, especially in narrative theatre, creates a constantly evolving focus and energy for the stage picture that has filmic connotations to its practice. It resembles most closely the acting style developed by French director Ariane Mnouchkine at the Théâtre du Soleil known as jouer frontal, 'playing out front', inspired by forms such as commedia, Lecoq, and traditional Asian theatres.[14] Throughout its history, Corn Exchange has collaborated with writer Michael West as well as a company of actors who train in their particular non-realistic style. Much of their work is characterized by the interpretation of existing play texts in their unique acting style—a style that challenges the emotionalism of the 'real'

[12] The production, directed by Maria Fleming, was premièred in Dunamaise Arts Centre, Portlaoise (June 2011), where Raymond Keane was artist in residence, and subsequently toured to the Junction Festival in Clonmel and the Earagail Festival at An Grianán, Letterkenny. It was revived at The Complex, Smithfield, Dublin, in Nov. 2011.

[13] Chris McCormack, Musings in Intermissions blog, 1 July 2011, http://musingsinintermissions.blogspot.ie/2011/07/barabbas-city-of-clowns-back-to-basics.html. Accessed 7 Apr. 2016.

[14] Annie Ryan and Michael West, 'Annie Ryan and Michael West in Conversation with Luke Clancy', in Lilian Chambers, Ger FitzGibbon, and Eamonn Jordan (eds.), Theatre Talk: Voices of Irish Theatre Practitioners (Dublin: Carysfort Press, 2001), 424–31.

in theatre and exposes realism as a construction, through a style that makes their theatre self-consciously fabricated. Distancing audiences from realism, Ryan and her actors come much closer to establishing the emotional truth of characters, since the work derives from mask, and is influenced by the Lecoq/Mnouchkine tradition of characters' emotional 'states'. These 'states' are default emotions which actors build into a vocabulary and play at different levels and registers. Though much less pronounced or even visible than Mnouchkine's vocabulary, the style cuts through realism to arrive much more quickly at an emotional truth in a scene, a character, or a particular situation.

Corn Exchange's style has been applied to canonical plays such as Anton Chekhov's *The Seagull* in 1999 in a new version by Michael West, Tennessee Williams's *Cat on a Hot Tin Roof* in 2008, and Samuel Beckett's *Happy Days* in 2010. The acting style, with its garish, accentuated, mask-like make-up (white pancake with bold colours of the facial lines) has also been applied to new writing by Michael West, such as the play that launched his student career, *Play on Two Chairs* (1990), *Foley* (2000), and *Dublin by Lamplight* (2004). The latter play brought huge accolades and critical attention to the company for its fictional portrayal of a spoof theatre society attempting to represent the nation in 1904. That fictional company (the Irish National Theatre of Ireland) seeks to emerge triumphant from the murky streets of Dublin with a unified vision of the nation, to hilarious effect. Using their trademark style, figures of the real story of the early Abbey Theatre—such as Lady Gregory as Eva St John, Willie Fay and W. B. Yeats as the composite character of Willie Hayes, and Edward Martyn as Martyn Wallace—emerged larger than life though highly recognizable. The play and production offered a hilarious critique of the national theatre project by the 'Irish National Theatre of Ireland', whose romantic theatrical figures end up failing to alter the course of Ireland or its theatre. Performed at the time by one of the nation's leading independent theatre companies, this highly stylized performance—a product of the internationalization of Irish theatre—subjected the real national theatre project (that was celebrating its first hundred years in 2004) to the scrutiny of an invented and imported theatre form. Indeed, when by the end of 2004 the Abbey's actual centenary celebrations ran aground amid revelations of financial mismanagement, Corn Exchange's staging of the failure of a fictional national theatre company may well have appeared to be a prescient rebuke.

Corn Exchange followed up this popular and critical success with *Everyday* (2006), a play also by West and in collaboration with the company of actors and the director Ryan, featuring vignettes of everyday life in Dublin. With its character-driven snapshots, the tone of *Everyday* differed from its predecessor, with less slapstick and more social observation. On a bare stage characters came and went, some in isolation, some in pairs, some overlapping, building a picture of a city slowly coming to life. Collectively they performed both memories and fantasies, all the while struggling with the strictures of their lives. These were the unmarked of the city, made remarkable by actors whose physical storytelling pushed them into the spotlight. Some of the scenes were comments on contemporary culture, such as a lonely character listening to music, all the while recreating an Apple iPod advertisement; another recognizable scene featured actors Mark O'Halloran and Tom Murphy playing two Dublin wastrels in tracksuits—an obvious homage to their pairing in O'Halloran's celebrated film (directed by Lenny Abrahamson) *Adam & Paul*, which had premièred two years earlier. Just as the close observational Theatre of Clown by Barrabas had focused on the unremarkable in Ireland, so too did Corn Exchange in this production counter the metanarrative of the preceding canonical Irish theatre in its self-perpetuating complex and need to signify the nation or a national context. Collaborative, devised, and physicalized Irish people in these productions told a more accurate story of quotidian Ireland.

PERFORMANCE AND THE SOCIOPOLITICAL

If the 1990s saw the retention of avant-garde Irish theatre makers within the native industry who placed their work within an international rather than national context, it was also within an economic context of prosperity and unprecedented levels of state funding for the arts, particularly for independent theatre companies. Concomitantly, successive years of graduates from an ever-increasing pool of tertiary courses throughout the island helped to push the boundaries of what was generally accepted to be theatre. The economic crash in 2007 and the resulting recession at the end of the 2000s saw a retrenchment in state funding for theatre but an increasing politicization of performance, particularly within devised work. Three new companies emerged from this period to achieve critical acclaim and an international reputation. Brokentalkers, led by directors Feidlim Cannon and Gary Keegan, was formed in 2001 to 'explore new forms that challenge traditional ideologies of text-based theatre'. Their working method is 'founded on a collaborative process that draws from the skills and experiences of a large group of contributors of different disciplines and backgrounds'[15] to explore 'different ways of writing [...] [w]riting through improvization, as an ensemble, writing through action and movement'.[16] Their breakthrough performance—and their shift from devised work as art practice to the sociopolitical—was a commission from the Bealtaine Festival (celebrating creativity in older age) of *Silver Stars* (2008), a song cycle by singer-songwriter Seán Millar based on interviews with older gay men about their experiences of growing up in Ireland when their sexuality was criminalized, and about the escape of some to foreign shores.[17] Apart from one actor, the show was performed by many of the men who had been interviewed, who had little or no performance experience. In many respects it compared to the work of the celebrated German company Rimini Protokoll, which has produced work with various communities of non-actors. But it was Brokentalkers' 2011 devised performance *Blue Boy* that was to bring them international recognition, focusing on the abuse of one of Ireland's most notorious 'industrial schools' at Artane in north Dublin, next to which director Gary Keegan—whose grandfather would have been called in his profession of undertaker to make coffins for the boys who died there—grew up. As well as live testimony from Keegan himself, the production featured documentary footage, television recordings of the famous boys' band that acted as an acceptable front for the abuse in the reform school, and abstract dance of the ghosts of the boys who died there. Performing masked, the dancers represented the voiceless mass of the state-sanctioned abuse of children through dance that 'splinters the causes and effects of the abuse into convulsive moments'.[18]

[15] See: http://www.brokentalkers.ie. Accessed 26 May 2014.
[16] Gary Keegan, 'A Dance You Associate with Your Family', in Fintan Walsh (ed.), *'That Was Us': Contemporary Irish Theatre and Performance* (London: Oberon Books, 2013), 229.
[17] Homosexuality was decriminalized in the Republic of Ireland in 1993.
[18] Eithne Shortall, 'Theatre Review: *The Blue Boy*', *Sunday Times*, 16 Oct. 2011, http://www.thesundaytimes.co.uk/sto/news/ireland/_culture/arts/article797410.ece. Accessed 7 Apr. 2016.

Performed in Studio One of the Lir in Dublin, the dancers were separated from the audience by a scrim, on which was projected the documentary footage. The scrim appeared to act as a guardian to memory, projecting the failure of society to expose the abuse until long after the school had been closed down. Gary Keegan took his position on the audience side of the scrim along with live musicians, while the silent dancers performed their pain in choreographic sequences invoking pathos and horror. Coming two years after the Report by the Commission to Inquire into Child Abuse (known as the Ryan Report),[19] the performance was a reflection on the mediatization of the abuse in light of the report, as well as commenting on the failure of those charged with the protection of children in the care of the state at the time. The silence of the dancers pointed to the failure of successive generations of politicians to give voice to both victims and survivors. The politics of the performance lay in its exposure of the culture of silence, and it met the silence with a silence, inviting spectators of contemporary society to speak out for redress.

The exposure of societal ills and crimes of the past was a significant feature of arts and culture more generally in recession Ireland, now that the dominant narrative of economic success had been exposed as a sham that drowned out alternative voices and masked the abuses of the past. In the theatre, another company emerged in the same period that not only confronted the ills of the past but did so outside theatres in the original sites in Dublin city that were either neglected or forgotten in the narrative of the geography of Dublin as an international commercial and trading hub. ANU Productions' tetralogy of performances entitled the Monto Cycle took place over five years between 2009 and 2014 in the quarter-mile district of north inner-city Dublin colloquially known as the Monto, immortalized in song by The Dubliners. The area took its name from Montgomery Street (now Foley Street) that was the centre of Dublin's notorious red-light district of the late nineteenth and early twentieth century. After the establishment of the Irish Free State, the sex trade was systematically closed down by Dublin's police commissioner, supported by the very active Catholic organization the Legion of Mary. On the north end of the district stood the Gloucester Street Laundry, run by the Sisters of Our Lady of Charity, colloquially known as a Magdalene Laundry, in which prostitutes were incarcerated, as well as unmarried mothers and other women whose families deemed their behaviour inappropriate. It was one of the repositories of an increasingly puritanical society that hid its shame in the confines of a convent whose incarcerated women were put to work in laundries for no pay. While drug abuse was rife in the era of the area's brothels, its impact on society reached its apogee in the late 1970s and 1980s with the arrival of heroin to Dublin, bringing with it the spread of HIV and related deaths from shared needle use, effectively wiping out a generation in some communities. And then in the 2000s, with the arrival of new communities of workers from Eastern Europe, came a new form of the sex trade, but without the visibility of the shop as brothel or the madame or streetwalkers as visible traders. Instead the prostitution network was international, importing and exporting sex workers with increasing frequency, along trade routes that were imperceptible. These were the subjects of the Monto tetralogy.

[19] See 'The Commission to Inquire into Child Abuse': http://www.childabusecommission.ie/rpt/. Accessed 17 Sept. 2014.

FIG. 34.1 Sorcha Kenny in ANU Productions, *Laundry* (25 September 2011).

Photo: Pat Redmond. Courtesy of ANU Productions.

The principal company members of ANU Productions, including director Louise Lowe and visual artist Owen Boss, had direct family links with the area, and their work over four productions stemmed from personal connections and a shared social history. Their working methodology involves direct contact with communities, historical research, and improvisation, and the work responds to the area's sites, both inside and outside build-ings. Histories of place and both oral and written work formed textual starting points for performative creation, as well as 'the material fabric of the city's buildings and streets'.[20] The first production of the cycle, *World's End Lane* (2010), took place around Dublin City Council's arts office—the LAB, on the corner of Foley Street—and accommodated three spectators at a time but separated as individuals encountering characters from the past in a mock-up of a brothel, as well as more disturbingly contemporary characters on the sur-rounding streets who blended out of and back into the real world with disturbing ease, leav-ing spectators unsure of what was and was not part of the performance and a heightened awareness of the performativity of the real world vis-a-vis the sex trade. The second per-formance, *Laundry* (2011), took place in the now disused Gloucester Street Laundry. Again created for three spectators at a time, audience members as individuals encountered the harsh reality of the women being committed, before meeting more of the women in com-plex and emotionally charged scenes in a bathroom, chapel, confessional, and other rooms in the building that harboured the sounds of children and ghostly images of those who had passed on. The principal dramaturgical device of the performance featured individual

[20] Morash and Richards, *Mapping Irish Theatre*, 179.

spectators being cajoled into helping one of the women escape. While the escape was thrilling, as the consequences of being caught were unknown, that thrill was soon dissipated as the escapee returned each time voluntarily to the convent, while spectators were taken off in a taxi and put to work in a real-life launderette, encountering the past this time through a radio documentary, while meeting locals who dropped in and reflected on the laundry. The third part of the cycle, *The Boys of Foley Street* (2012), immersed spectators in pairs into the world of drug trafficking and substance abuse. In the streets, spectators encountered street dealers and pushers before being driven at speed to a council flat, where they were immersed in the climate of psychosexual abuse of a drug-dealing family. In every scene, spectators were implicated in the world, some by recording an act of violence on a mobile phone, and being recorded recording it, others by unwittingly giving the name of a pusher to a vigilante and then having to deal with the pusher's mother after he had been attacked; all spectators were photographed leaving the drug baron's flat, later to find their photographs posted on a wall as suspects in the criminal underworld.

In all three productions,[21] spectators were interpellated not just as spectators in the contemporary world but as contributors to the performed scenes of the past, and were invited to make choices whether to help the performers/characters in the world or not. Many times during the performance the boundaries between performance and reality were obscured, and so the stakes were even higher for spectators; but at all times the spectators' sense of thrill of being immersed in a community not their own, with its criminality, violence, and abuse, was challenged and even arrested by the ethical choices they were asked to make. While all theatre-makers address the question of who their audience is, ANU Productions literally address their spectators as individuals and force them to confront their own politics, ethics, and even the very act of spectatorship itself.[22]

One of the founding members of ANU Productions, Sophie Motley, formed her own company, Willfredd, in 2010, and brought with her similar questions about communities and spectatorship. Very quickly the company established itself as a leading force in Irish theatre. Their first production, *FOLLOW* (2011), featured Shane O'Reilly as solo performer exploring his own life growing up as a hearing child to deaf parents, in a sophisticated mix of sign language, physical theatre, and projected text. Their second production, *FARM* (2012), featured multiple farm environments, together with very real attendant sights and smells of hay, manure, horses, and ducks recreated in a disused industrial warehouse in which spectators encountered perambulatory scenes of community bonding, loneliness, and the daily grind of Ireland's farming community. And in their 2014 production, *CARE*, audiences witnessed a one-hour devised show based on the work and coping strategies of hospice care workers dealing with end-of-life issues. In all their productions, deep research in the communities they represent is paramount, and their working methodologies centre around that research as source material as well as found text, interviews, and improvisation. And as their reputation has emerged, and the community audiences have broadened, one of the defining features of their work now is the choice of locations in which they play,

---

[21] The fourth production, originally entitled *VardoCorner*, was in development at the time of writing. It was performed as *Vardo* at the Oonagh Young Gallery (23 Sept.–12 Oct. 2014).

[22] For more analysis of ANU's work, see Brian Singleton, 'ANU Productions and Site-Specific Performance: The Politics of Space and Place', in Walsh, 'That Was Us', 21–36. See also Morash and Richards, *Mapping Irish Theatre*, 145–74.

and also how they communicate the issues of one community to the spectators of another. *FARM*, for instance, was relocated to the Lir's Studio One theatre in a revival, while the performance had to take account of their deaf audience that had been built up since *FOLLOW*. And *CARE* was resurrected not only in a hospice after its original production in Project Upstairs but also at a conference of care workers.

With all of the companies above, the defining state of devised theatre in Ireland in the 2010s is political, with its politics emanating from communities but challenging audiences to examine their viewing position both inside and outside those communities. Reviewing the history of devised theatre in Ireland over the past three decades and more, it appears to have moved directly along the trajectory defined by Heddon and Milling as quoted above, and now focuses on theatre 'predominantly concerned with its impact in a political and/or social context'.[23] The politics in the work of the latter three companies is 'soft' in that the message is not always the primary emphasis of the experience, but the medium in which the political is evoked is of paramount importance. Whether immersed or witnessing performance front-on in a theatre space, this form of political performance challenges audiences' viewing positions as political positions. And thus it is in the act of spectatorship that the political challenge to audiences of contemporary Irish devised performance primarily resides.

---

[23] Heddon and Milling, *Devising Performance*, 27.

PART XI

IRELAND AND THE WORLD

....

CHAPTER 35

GLOBAL BECKETT

....

RÓNÁN MCDONALD

THE BECKETT BRAND

....

'BECKETT is the first dramatist of the space-age. In his plays, set on the edge of nowhere, society does not exist and man is in a void. The dramatic astronaut views life on earth with a wry sadness through vistas of space.'[1] So opined the theatre historian Micheál Ó hAodha of the Abbey Theatre's 1969 revival of *Waiting for Godot*, starring Peter O'Toole and Donal McCann. The Abbey had just moved into a new building and was eager to shake off its 'peasant drama' associations, to cloak itself with modernity and intellectual fashion. Beckett, who had just been awarded the Nobel Prize, was established not just as a successful Irish dramatist abroad but as a global figure who happened to be from Ireland. Earlier that year, the world was flushed with the excitement of the first manned landings on the moon, with many heralding a new era of rockets, astronauts, and star-trekking. Looking back, this space-age rhetoric seems winsome and quaint. Precisely in its enthusiasm for novelty, and for an escape from existing society, these remarks seem dated and inextricably meshed in their own time and place. Yet the idea of Beckett as a writer for the globe, writing at a distance from history or geography, above the humdrum concerns of the here and now, of political and social circumstances, is a recognizable, deeply entrenched aspect of his popular image. It has been widely queried by commentators suspicious of the idea that an artist ever would, could, or should write as if society 'does not exist'. All art, even the most abstract or seemingly deracinated, comes from history, from inside the world not outside it, and is also received at a particular moment and place. Perhaps more than any other art form, theatre happens *in situ*, as an event, a performance, unique and unrepeatable, intimate with its moment of actualization. There may be lines of connection between the nodes of creation and reception, continuities from the culture that created a work of art to the one that receives it. But there is no socially uncontaminated ur-stage in which theatre can escape from the world, viewing it from space. Yet that abstraction of Beckett's theatre work, its

---

[1] Quoted in John P. Harrington, *The Irish Beckett* (Syracuse, NY: Syracuse University Press, 1991), 177.

lack of definite geographical or specific referents, has led to a tenacious discourse of universalism. This discourse has created a Beckett myth that chimes with many of the values of mid-twentieth-century literary criticism, including the growth in studies of comparative and world literature in the USA in the postwar period, which tended to promulgate a universal over a national or nationalist idea of literary value. Yet, some decades after his death, Beckett's appeal endures not because his plays ascend above the social world so much as because of their capacity to move between diverse cultures and social moments. Beckett's importance has increasingly come to seem not as a transhistorical, universal dramatist but as a transnational, adaptable one—one who shifts between cultures rather than rising above them.

Beckett is arguably the most significant dramatist of the twentieth century. His success has relied on cultural mechanisms of transmission, as well as his own genius as a writer who has explored and expanded the possibilities of every form he has used, including stage, novel, radio, and television, creating artworks of unique beauty, craft, wit, and radiance. Unsurprisingly, his fame and renown on a public level is strongly associated with his first major breakthrough, *Waiting for Godot* (1953), which in some countries—such as China—remains virtually the only text of Beckett that is well known.[2] *Endgame*, which famously has two of the characters in dustbins, is also deeply etched into the theatrical imagination, though not so deeply as the two men in bowler hats waiting beside a tree. Through numerous avenues, these images have spread through the cultural atmosphere.

He has also given us an adjective. 'Beckettian', like 'Dickensian' or 'Kafkaesque', has a distinctive matrix of cultural associations and implications: demanding drama, high culture, 'deep' theatre, albeit leavened with mordant humour. 'Godot' has entered the language as a figure of non-arrival, a ready metaphor as likely to pop up in discussion of a bus timetable as of intellectual drama. He is now the stuff of journalistic rhetoric and political oratory, a coinage akin to 'Big Brother' or 'Scrooge', circulating outside their literary origins. Audiences may variously be impressed, intimidated, or scornful of the Beckett brand, but they cannot ignore or sidestep it. Just as we can no longer see 'Shakespeare' without the huge weight of cultural and historical baggage that now accompanies the author of *Hamlet*, so we must see Beckett's plays through his aura, through the prestige that he has accrued and the skein of connotations that the word 'Beckettian' has accrued.

While Beckett generally refused to give interviews, he often allowed himself to be photographed, with the result that his face has become one of the cultural and intellectual icons of the twentieth century. His gaunt, craggy, handsome head, with its steely spiked hair and 'gull-blue' eyes, is a globally recognizable visage, an emblem of expressive bravery, tragicomic profundity, supreme artistic achievement. When in the late 1990s Apple Inc chose to use his face, alongside that of other twentieth-century icons like Albert Einstein and Pablo Picasso, in its 'Think Different' advertising campaign, it demonstrated how intellectual chic and cultural capital could also be used to support a commercial brand. There is no other writer of the modern era whose face is so well known, while his voice (though there are a few rare recordings available on the Internet) is so rarely heard. The celebrity of this face even reached the pages of a 2007 commemorative issue of *GQ* magazine, where

---

[2] Mark Nixon and Matthew Feldman (eds.), *The International Reception of Samuel Beckett* (London: Continuum, 2009).

he was listed alongside Elvis Presley and George Clooney as one of the most stylish men of the last fifty years: 'Beckett himself looked like something from the void. A timeless figure, both ancient and modern, traditional and (whether he liked it or not) hip, he favored black (which ignited his blue eyes) and wool or tweed coats that could have come from any number of centuries.'³

We may feel misgiving at the way this modernist and avant-garde figure has been commodified and branded by corporate culture, his subversive challenge to hegemonic modes of thought rendered toothless and impotent.⁴ But the severance between popular and cliché Beckett and the 'real' writer, studied in universities and understood by fellow intellectuals, can be exaggerated. Beckett's theatre work, like his striking face, lends itself to branding, intentionally or not. Part of the reason for its permeability into a wider culture comes, like the association with universal themes, from its abstraction and sparseness, the instantly recognizable stage settings that lend themselves to imitation and parody. So the bare tree and derelict tramps or the two old people in dustbins have often appeared in newspaper cartoons and satirical sketches, even featuring in a skit on Sesame Street, entitled *Waiting for Elmo* ('A modern masterpiece. A play so modern, and so brilliant, it makes absolutely no sense to anybody'⁵). These often searing visual imprints are one of the most striking qualities to Beckett's work: two old people in dustbins (*Endgame*, 1957), a desperate old man crouched over a tape recorder (*Krapp's Last Tape*, 1958), a middle-aged woman dressed in finery buried up to her waist in a mound (*Happy Days*, 1961), a man and two women in urns (*Play*, 1963), a woman's mouth, gabbling out of the darkness (*Not I*, 1973), a head with flailing white hair (*That Time*, 1976), an old woman in a rocking chair (*Rockaby*, 1981). These images circulate within the cultural atmosphere to an extent unique among modern dramatists. They are all the more sharp and resonant because of their sparseness and concentration. Beckett's work, especially his later 'dramaticules', often includes striking tableaux, with strong painterly or visual qualities. Like his face, his stage images have often been reproduced by photographers, including the Royal Court Theatre's official photographer, John Haynes.⁶ That Beckett's manifold influence on later poets, novelists, and playwrights also extends to contemporary installation artists, photographers, film-makers, and contemporary dancers illustrates these visual qualities. As Michael D'Arcy points out, the problem of identifying Beckett's influence on later artists is how to speak of something that is both pervasive and elusive, omnipresent in the culture in a way that exceeds empirical analysis.⁷

³ http://www.gq.com/how-to/fashion/200709/cary-grant-paul-newman-andre-3000-george-clooney-slideshow#slide=21. Accessed 12 June 2014.

⁴ For an eloquent elaboration of this argument see S. E. Gontarski, 'Viva, Sam Beckett, or Flogging the Avant-Garde', *Journal of Beckett Studies* 16, nos. 1 and 2 (2006/7), 1–11.

⁵ http://www.openculture.com/2012/11/monsterpiece_theatre_presents_waiting_for_godot_elmo.html. Accessed 17 June 2014.

⁶ James Knowlson and John Haynes, *Images of Beckett* (Cambridge: Cambridge University Press, 2003).

⁷ Michael D'Arcy, 'Influence', in Anthony Uhlmann (ed.), *Samuel Beckett in Context* (Cambridge: Cambridge University Press, 2013), 407. See also Peter Boxall, *Since Beckett: Contemporary Writing in the Wake of Modernism* (London: Continuum, 2009), and Matthew Feldman and Mark Nixon, *Beckett's Literary Legacies* (Newcastle upon Tyne: Cambridge Scholars, 2007).

In that respect, and counterintuitively, one of the reasons for Beckett's global power is his simplicity: his work often pares down stage settings, dialogue, and dramaturgy to its spare and economical rudiments. Examination of the manuscripts of Beckett's works, and indeed his own directorial practices, reveals a tendency to pare away references or allusions that were geographically or historically recognizable.[8] But this radical simplicity supports an extraordinary, even revolutionary sense of theatre, affording formal and dramaturgical innovations that could probe the expressive possibilities of the medium. Kenneth Tynan, reviewing for the *Observer*, proclaimed that *Waiting for Godot* 'forced me to re-examine the rules which have hitherto governed the drama; and, having done so, to pronounce them not elastic enough'.[9] That Beckett could make effective theatre of such scant material, that he could thwart so skilfully the rules of what would allow dramatic conflict and tension, underlies his artistic achievement and his immense influence on subsequent playwrights. But 'Global Beckett' is not only an outcome of a singular talent. It is also a result of timing, contingency, good luck, cultural capital, complex cultural networks, and well-marketed intellectual chic.

THE EMERGENCE OF BECKETT

The story of how Beckett moved from obscurity to success is well known. Irish-born and living in France, he had garnered moderate notoriety as a writer of fiction, including his novels *Murphy* (1939) and *Watt* (1953), the latter a heavily experimental novel, written while he was a French Resistance member on the run from the Gestapo in Vichy France. The work that would secure Beckett's place in literary history was penned, in French, in a 'frenzy of writing' between 1947 and 1950. In these years, when money was extremely scarce and his health ailing, he wrote, 'like a man freed from demons'.[10] His celebrated trilogy of novels, *Molloy* (1951, English version 1955), *Malone Meurt* (1951; *Malone Dies*, 1958) and *L'innommable* (1953; *The Unnamable*, 1959), and *En attendant Godot* (1953; *Waiting for Godot*, 1955) all come from this period.

Beckett was transformed from an avant-garde, experimental novelist to a global star through this single play, written between October 1948 and January 1949 as a diversion from the more taxing (as he saw it) business of prose composition. The first production was brought to stage by the avant-garde director Roger Blin in the small Théâtre de Babylone in Paris on 5 January 1953. *En attendant Godot*, clearly belonging to a recognizably experimental theatrical style, performed to small and often bemused audiences. Yet the play seems to have struck a nerve in the postwar atmosphere of early 1950s Paris, a world of cafés

---

[8] For an account of this self-winnowing, see S. E. Gontarski, *The Intent of Undoing in Samuel Beckett's Dramatic Texts* (Bloomington, IN: Indiana University Press, 1985). For Beckett's directorial work and the changes he made to manuscripts of his plays, see James Knowlson (gen. ed.), *The Theatrical Notebooks of Samuel Beckett* (4 vols., London: Faber & Faber, 1992–9).

[9] *Observer*, 7 Aug. 1955, quoted in Lawrence Graver and Raymond Federman, *Samuel Beckett: The Critical Heritage* (London: Routledge & Kegan Paul, 1978), 97.

[10] James Knowlson, *Damned to Fame: The Life of Samuel Beckett* (London: Bloomsbury, 1996), 359, 355.

and existentialists. It became a talking point, buoyed by the support of esteemed intellectuals and reviewers. Its notoriety quickly became international. Eight productions of the German translation, *Warten auf Godot*, were performed in West Germany over 1953, heralding the deep and abiding affinity Beckett would have with German theatre audiences. For English speakers, the inaugural moment came with Peter Hall's London première in the Arts Theatre on 3 August 1955. The initial performances were greeted with catcalls and the early notices were poor. English theatregoers were not to be taken in by French pretension. However, the tide turned in London when the more eminent Sunday newspaper reviewers praised the play, proclaiming it a watershed in the dramatic arts. These imprimaturs and, in England, much practical support from the theatre critic Harold Hobson helped the play to accrue glamour, respectability, and intellectual and cultural weight, even from those who were not initially well disposed. Yet it was still capable of evoking confusion and hostility, especially when the production was badly located and marketed. The first American production—though directed by Alan Schneider, who would go on to be a trusted interpreter of Beckett's stage works—was unwisely put on by the producers in Miami Beach, and billed as 'the laugh hit of two continents'. Miami holidaymakers, in search of seaside entertainment, walked out in droves, demanding refunds.[11] Beckett's universal message was not appreciated universally, at least initially. However, as his reputation grew in Europe, America took note and his work was staged in more appropriate, culturally aspirational venues, such as off-Broadway theatres. He became an intellectual talking point in the USA and, in due course and thanks to the support of leading American academics such as Hugh Kenner, a staple figure on American university syllabi.

It takes nothing away from the merits of Beckett's work to acknowledge that his success has much to do with simple good luck and loyal friends. Literary history owes a debt of gratitude to Beckett's companion Suzanne Déchevaux-Dumesnil, who tirelessly sought out a publisher for his work. Eventually, the French publisher Jérôme Lindon of Éditions de Minuit would become his lifelong defender and friend, as later would his American publisher and promoter, Barney Rossett, a brilliant builder and marketer of Beckett's avant-garde reputation in the USA. It was not inevitable that Roger Blin, with his high-profile and extensive networks in the theatrical avant-garde around Europe, would put on *En attendant Godot* in 1953, choosing it above the much less innovative, and still unperformed, seventeen-hander *Eleutheria*, which Beckett offered for his consideration at the same time. The attention of well-connected impresarios, intellectuals, publishers, critics, and academics built, sustained, and disseminated Beckett's aura and prestige, which would later be enhanced by journalists, reviewers, and cartoonists.

Despite the anti-establishment, anti-capitalist self-positioning of European modernism, recent scholarship has demonstrated its deep reliance on complex systems of branding and marketing.[12] While it spurns mainstream or popular culture, high modernism nevertheless

---

[11] Ibid., 419–21.

[12] The relationship between marketing and modernism has received extensive scholarly attention in recent years, with Lawrence Rainey's *Institutions of Modernism: Literary Elites and Public Culture* (New Haven, CT: Yale University Press, 1998) the seminal work. Stephen Dilks's *Samuel Beckett in the Literary Marketplace* (Syracuse, NY: Syracuse University Press, 2011) emerges from this critical field, but questionably ascribes Beckett's image to a wholly intentional and choreographed project, orchestrated by Beckett himself for gullible acolytes in the 'Beckett industry'.

comes from the artistic centre, reliant on a sort of anti-commercial commodification, an alternative to the easy assimilability of popular culture, yet trading off its exclusive, intellectual, bohemian aura. Modernist art, like other forms of high culture, is steeped in cultural capital, even as it ostensibly disavows the formulaic modes and tawdry pleasures of the cultural marketplace.[13] An association with Beckett's work bespeaks artistic seriousness and cultural sophistication in a theatre actor, director, or spectator, and no doubt this cultural chic in part explains its huge attraction and enduring successes, notwithstanding the importance of Beckett's artistic achievements themselves and the associations they have with dissent.

Yet, for all his success in the far reaches of the globe, it is no coincidence that Beckett's reputation emerged and grew in the cultural centres of Europe and America: in Paris, London, Berlin, and New York, specifically in the arty, intellectual, and bohemian seams of these cities' cultural life. It is hard to imagine *Waiting for Godot* gaining its global traction had it been launched into the world from the West Bank rather than the Left Bank, from Gary, Indiana, rather than Greenwich Village. If *Waiting for Godot* was a *succès de scandale*, it was so in a way that is familiar for 'shocking' avant-garde art and music, from Manet to Stravinsky to Jackson Pollock, where an initial bemusement or hostility gets overtaken by critical expertise that heralds a new and culturally vital artwork. For all its countercultural aura, Beckett's work started in the metropolitan cultural centres, and accrued prestige because of the imprimatur of official cultural figures and institutions, albeit allied to bohemia rather than the bourgeoisie. The publicity generated by initial controversy only spurred its success. It travelled around the world quickly, facilitated initially by the formidable international networks of Blin, but soon by its huge success in London and New York. Beckett's plays would go on to become greatly popular in the most marginal and unexpected places: in prisons and war zones, in Eastern Europe, part of Africa, Korea, and Iran. We can speculate on the reasons in each case, and there are distinct reception histories to be traced in particular countries, each with its own cultural and intellectual milieu and social circumstance.[14] But the prestige and approval of the European cultural elite drove the work's global penetration, especially as it gained additional associations of dissidence and subversion when it ran foul of state control and censorship. In China and behind the Iron Curtain during the Cold War, Beckett's work was often banned, and thus became a favourite of intellectuals seeking extended freedoms and democracy. Beckett's work, with its depictions of arbitrary power and persecution, seemed deeply resonant in political situations where secret police subjected the artistic world to surveillance and censorship. It was a relationship that Beckett acknowledged through his practical support for directors seeking to put on his work in Communist Europe and in the dedication of, arguably, his most overtly political play, *Catastrophe* (1982), to the imprisoned Czech dissident, playwright, and, later president Václav Havel.

Surely these political resonances of Beckett's work, its structural relationship to situations of power and persecution, derive in part from Beckett's own experiences of European fascism in the 1940s. Nonetheless, there was a critical impulse to read transhistorical

---

[13] Pierre Bourdieu, 'The Forms of Capital', in John C. Richardson (ed.), *Handbook of Theory and Research for the Sociology of Education* (New York: Greenwood Press, 1986), 241–58.

[14] Nixon and Feldman, *International Reception of Samuel Beckett*, 1–2.

profundity in his work alongside its specific historical meanings. It seemed to many that these plays articulate a feature of the 'human condition' (as opposed to particular instances of life, in social and political context): a constant and unfulfilled waiting between cradle and grave; and all we on this blighted earth can do is to distract ourselves with pointless games and futile banter. Vladimir ponders on Pozzo's call for assistance when he is prostrate in Act II: 'To all mankind they were addressed, those cries for help still ringing in our ears! But at this place, at this moment of time, all mankind is us, whether we like it or not.'[15] Inspired by passages like these, and denied a clear meaning or interpretation, commentators often read the play as expressing a pessimistic view of existence that applies to all of us, outside history, politics, or social situation. Writing in the early 1970s, Hugh Kenner holds that Beckett's lack of geographical or historical specificity gives his drama a timeless quality, unlike the more historically located work of a compatriot: 'Sean O'Casey's plays being "about" the Irish troubles, slide rapidly into the past, period pieces like the photos in old magazines. *Waiting for Godot* in the 1970s is little changed from what it was the day it was first performed in 1953, a play about a mysterious world where two men wait.'[16] Of course, drama that is written in response to a particular historical crisis does not automatically become a period piece, and Kenner grossly misrepresents the currency of O'Casey's trilogy (which Beckett admired). But his remarks are illustrative: Beckett's abstractions have fuelled the tendency, especially in Anglophone and French criticism, to depict Beckett in ahistorical terms, whether the humanist assumptions of Kenner ('everyone everywhere has wondered and wondered why he waited') or the philosophical nihilism of the French intellectuals.[17]

Admittedly, Beckett himself tended to favour that strand of modernism that disdained provincial, local, or propagandistic concerns. He set his face against the agendas of the Irish revival, and disagreed with his friend Thomas MacGreevy that the painter Jack B. Yeats, brother of the poet, was significant for any national reasons. Rather, for Beckett, 'he brings light, as only the great dare to bring light, to the issueless predicament of existence'.[18] But yet for all his prewar insistence on the universal and issueless relevance of art, for all the deracinated and rootless qualities of his own work, a writer inevitably emerges from a context. As Beckett recedes from us into the past, and as more historical research is undertaken into his cultural and intellectual influences, we have come to recognize his enmeshment in his own time and place. This process has been greatly aided first by James Knowlson's landmark 1996 authorized biography and subsequently by a slew of historically orientated, often archival works that focus on Beckett's notebooks and diaries and, most recently, by the ongoing publication of Beckett's letters.[19] Of course it is not irrelevant or coincidental

[15] Samuel Beckett, *Waiting for Godot/En attendant Godot* (London: Faber & Faber, 2006), 155.
[16] Hugh Kenner, *A Reader's Guide to Samuel Beckett* (London: Thames & Hudson, 1973), 31.
[17] Criticism in Germany, perhaps most famously that of the Marxist critical theorist Theodor Adorno, tended to be less apolitical than that produced by the humanist American critics and the French *philosophes*: P. J. Murphy et al. (eds.), *Critique of Beckett Criticism: A Guide to Research in English, French, and German* (Columbia, SC: Camden House, 1994); Nixon and Feldman, *International Reception of Samuel Beckett*.
[18] Samuel Beckett, *Disjecta, Miscellaneous Writings and a Dramatic Fragment*, ed. Ruby Cohn (London: John Calder, 1983), 97.
[19] Knowlson, *Damned to Fame*; Mathew Feldman, *Beckett's Books: A Cultural History of the Interwar Notes* (London: Continuum, 2009); Samuel Beckett, *Letters*, vol. 1: 1929–40, ed. Martha Dow

that Beckett lived through—indeed, that his life was almost concurrent with—the darkest and most brutalized global period in recorded history. For Theodor Adorno, in his influential essay on *Endgame*, Beckett's work is singularly attuned to its historical moment:

> In Beckett, history devours existentialism. In *Endgame*, a historical moment is revealed [. . .] everything is destroyed, even resurrected culture, without knowing it; humanity vegetates along, crawling, after events which even the survivors cannot really survive, on a pile of ruins which even renders futile self-reflection of one's own battered state.[20]

The catastrophes of the twentieth century generate an infecting miasma within the morale and outlook of Western culture, and seep into its cultural, intellectual, philosophical, and critical temper. Beckett's work resonated with the pessimistic philosophy current in France in the aftermath of the Second World War, the existentialism of Sartre and Camus and the 'literature of the absurd'. But he was also central to the radical literary experimentation that accompanied this crisis of Western civilization, a descendant of the modernist movements that had opened up radical literary experimentation in the aftermath of the First World War. Beckett was engaging directly in theatrical and prose modes that addressed the intellectual crises of late modernity and the problems of expression and articulation they presented. He crafted unique and singular forms of formidable artistic integrity true to the 'mess' that he discerned.

THE 'RORSCHACH TEST'

Another reason why Beckett has prompted so much critical fascination is because his work can be persuaded to fit into any number of models or systems. His stripped-back stages and rootless contexts have resulted in his enlistment into many critical or theoretical movements over the last fifty years. It was almost as if the deracinated settings turned Beckett's work into a mirror in which a multitude of critical methods and schools could find their own reflections. Existentialists found a concern with human isolation and the absurdity of the universe, while narrative theorists pointed at the metatextual interest in the construction and unravelling of stories. Poststructuralists celebrated in Beckett the self-reflexive consciousness of textuality and a concern with shape, repetition, the forming and deforming aspects of language, while hermeneuticists pored over the abiding concern with interpretation and how meaning is generated from language and the world. Religious critics focused on the concern with spirituality and the deployment of religious and even mystical language, while psychoanalytic critics found a first-person narrator gabbling out memories like a patient to a therapist.

Beckett remarked that 'the keyword in my plays is "perhaps"'.[21] Certainty, the arrival of clear meaning is a Godot that we as spectators must perpetually await. Part of the success

Fehsenfeld and Lois Overbeck (Cambridge: Cambridge University Press, 2009); vol. 2: *1941–1956*, ed. George Craig et al. (2011); vol. 3: *1957–1965*, ed. George Craig et al. (2014).

[20] Theodor W. Adorno, 'Trying to Understand *Endgame*', *New German Critique* 26 (1982), 122.

[21] Quoted in Alec Reid, *All I Can Manage, More Than I Could: An Approach to the Plays of Samuel Beckett* (Dublin: Dolmen Press, 1968), 11.

of Beckett may be ascribable to this absence into which spectators, readers, and critics can insert their own readings and meanings. If Beckett's art resonates easily with a variety of different critical movements and moods, it is because its indefiniteness allows it to be endlessly suggestive and open to various interpretations. What is true for critical movements is also so for individuals. An early commentator described Beckett's drama as a sort of 'Rorschach test', the ink blot which psychiatrists present to patients to see what they might discern there.[22]

We could extend this semantic flexibility also to the diverse contexts in which the plays are produced. Productions and performances seem freshly relevant to multiple situations around the world because they instantiate variously and diversely. *Waiting for Godot* at one moment resonates with the prisoners in San Quentin jail, at another with those trapped during the siege of Sarajevo. This is not because it speaks directly to an ahistorical human condition but rather because, chameleon-like, it adapts to the colour of the context in which it is produced. This is so despite the often inflexible control that was exerted by the Beckett Estate, which, seeking to honour Beckett's own dismay at unauthorized deviations from his stage directions, took a strong line against directorial innovations. While Beckett himself was inconsistent about his strictures and tended to make allowances for friends and those he trusted, the Estate has often prohibited experimental productions. Yet, like any drama, Beckett's plays do not survive in aspic, nor in recycling productions that simply reproduce what the 'author intended'. The production history of Beckett's plays reveals the deep importance of the various contexts of performance, to which an innovative director can respond. This is one of the fundamental ironies about this body of work. While Beckett's deracinated stage settings seem to transcend the national, a play like *Waiting for Godot* speaks forcefully to particular social or political circumstances—apartheid South Africa, war-torn Sarajevo, flood-afflicted New Orleans. Beckett's drama, like a skeleton key, seems newly relevant to manifold and divergent moments of history. 'Global Beckett' does not gain relevance by setting the dramatic canvas outside history, but rather from the capacity of these plays to be freshly relevant to particular conditions, especially those of historical extremity and crisis. It is a different sort of 'timelessness', one based on reanimation rather than deracination.

This was evident quite early in productions of Beckett's work. The way it was perceived in Ireland, for instance, took on local colour from the very first production, inaugurating an ongoing controversy about whether emphasizing Irish dimensions in his plays might thwart their putatively universal import. The first Irish production of *Waiting for Godot*, in the Pike Theatre, Dublin, on 28 October 1955, was a great success, enjoying the longest continuous run of any play in Irish history up to that point, belying 'the image of Ireland in the 1950s as an intellectually timid cultural wasteland'.[23] One of the reasons that the play found an Irish audience was because the Irish elements, implicit in the English translation, were brought out here. Estragon and Vladimir speak with a Dublin argot—'Get up till I embrace you', 'your man', 'Oh I say'—while Pozzo speaks like an Anglo-Irish landowner: 'my good

[22] Vivian Mercier, *Beckett/Beckett* (London: Souvenir Press, 1990), vii.
[23] Christopher Morash, *A History of Irish Theatre, 1601–2000* (Cambridge: Cambridge University Press, 2002), 206. See also Alan Simpson, *Beckett and Behan and a Theatre in Dublin* (London: Routledge & Kegan Paul, 1962).

man'.[24] The themes of power and exploitation in the play adopt a particular Irish class con-figuration with this emphasis that spoke strongly to the Irish audience, familiar with the argot of Synge and O'Casey. If this lent dramatic power for some audiences, and showed how the class differences in the play operate, for other commentators it distorted the play's universal import. Beckett's friend A. J. Leventhal, already familiar with the French première, praised the Pike production but raised misgivings about its Irishness, claiming that 'the author had in mind a universal rather than a regional application of his vision of mankind in perpetual expectation'.[25] This tension between universal and particular has endured in those voices that have been raised against more recent efforts to 'green' Beckett's work, such as the Dublin Gate Theatre's 1991 Beckett Festival (examined elsewhere in this volume), which was a deliberate attempt to situate Beckett within an Irish dramatic tradi-tion, partly inspired by the absence of an Irish element from the 80th birthday celebrations in 1986. Michael Colgan was the impresario behind the festival, which toured interna-tionally and would evolve into the 'Beckett on Film' project (2001), the hugely ambitious attempt to bring all nineteen of Beckett's stage plays to the screen. Both these enterprises had many admirers, and 'Beckett on Film' is certainly a landmark in making Beckett's drama more widely known and studied around the world. But there have also been wary voices, concerned that emphasizing the Irish aspects of Beckett might draw attention away from his profound indebtedness to European and metropolitan intellectual and cultural currents. [26] That more recent objections to the posthumous embrace of Beckett by Ireland tend to target not its provincialism but rather the tacky corporatism and commodification of literary culture speaks a great deal about the shifts in official Ireland's relationship to modernity and national branding.

TRANSNATIONAL THEATRE

Yet the Pike Theatre case indicated early that Beckett's plays in performance break down and subvert any opposition between universal and local, centre and periphery. Abstract works like *Waiting for Godot* or *Endgame* take on their meanings and ramifications in con-crete situations. They do so not by forcing allegorical significance into the play through heavily signalled changes to stage directions, dialogue, or costumes. Beckett's plays are not (or not yet) like Shakespeare's *Henry V*, a work which takes on contemporary relevance when overtly brought to bear on contemporary military conflict. The least successful pro-ductions have often been those which hammer home the significance in a contemporary setting by experimenting with new dramaturgy or changing the dialogue; the most suc-cessful are those which allow the play to resonate in each singular context, without loading

---

[24] Beckett, *Waiting for Godot*, 3, 29, 39, 43. Morash points out that Simpson, on his own initiative, very much increased the number of such Hibernicisms in the script he used for his production: *History of Irish Theatre*, 199–200.

[25] A. J. Leventhal, 'Dramatic Commentary', *Dublin Magazine* 31, no. 4 (Jan.–Mar. 1956), 52.

[26] Graham Saunders, 'Reclaiming Sam for Ireland: The Beckett on Film Project', in Richard Cave and Ben Levitas (eds.), *Irish Theatre in England* (Dublin: Carysfort Press, 2007), 79–96.

down its spare and abstract power with extra dramatic accoutrements designed to tele-graph its message.[27]

Waiting for Godot made Beckett a globally famous figure, and it is still the play for which he is best known and the one that is most often revived. It could be that the hype around *Godot* has overshadowed Beckett's other work. Beckett himself was rather bemused by its success though, despite the image sometimes promulgated of the saintly, non-materialist artist, certainly not displeased by it. He felt that it was the result of a 'misunderstanding' and was dismayed by the attempts of actors, directors, and critics to find a message or a moral in the play.[28] In particular, he chafed against the critical and popular habit of steering his play into a philosophical discourse, away from the domain of art, shape, structure. 'The early success of *Waiting for Godot*', Beckett declared 'was based on a fundamental misunderstanding, critics and public alike insisted on inter-preting in allegorical or symbolic terms a play which was striving all the time to avoid definition.'[29] When asked by a young producer planning to broadcast readings from *En attendant Godot* on French radio for his ideas about the play, he responded, as he always did, with an insistence on the sufficiency of words and actions of the characters: 'All that I have been able to understand I have shown. It is not much. But it is enough, and more than enough for me.' Furthermore, the attempt to extract meanings was for him wrong-headed: 'As for wanting to find in all this a wider and loftier meaning to take away after the show, along with the programme and the choc-ice, I am unable to see the point of it. But it must be possible.'[30]

His next play, *Endgame*, is both more bleak and (arguably) less readable in philosophi-cal terms than *Waiting for Godot*. This one-act play concentrates the stasis and entropy of the stage action while also reducing even the lingering comforts of fellow-feeling and camaraderie which partially salve the pessimism of its predecessor. *Waiting for Godot* also withholds certainty, but there are reflections on time, habit, desire, and so on, where a critic can gain a precarious grip. *Endgame* poses the sheerer challenge. It is as if, frustrated by the philosophical interpretations of *Waiting for Godot*, a 'play struggling at all times to avoid definition', Beckett has produced a new play immune to explanation in 'allegorical or sym-bolic terms'. Adorno praises it precisely for dramatizing an incoherent situation, untrans-latable into the language of rationality and conceptuality:

> The interpretation of *Endgame* therefore cannot chase the chimera of expressing its mean-ing with the help of philosophical mediation. Understanding it can mean nothing other than understanding its incomprehensibility, or concretely reconstructing its meaning structure—that it has none.[31]

Rather than simply asserting a lack of 'meaning', the play actually demonstrates it. This is why Adorno held that the play was so much more powerful than the existentialist phi-losophy with which Beckett was sometimes associated. In abstract philosophy, what we

[27] David Bradby, *Beckett: Waiting for Godot* (Cambridge: Cambridge University Press, 2001); Jonathan Kalb, *Beckett in Performance* (Cambridge: Cambridge University Press, 1989).
[28] Beckett, *Letters*, vol. 2, 594.
[29] Quoted in Graver and Federman, *Samuel Beckett: The Critical Heritage*, 9.
[30] Beckett, *Letters*, vol. 2, 316.   [31] Adorno, 'Trying to Understand *Endgame*', 120.

understand only occurs at the level of complexity and ideas. *Endgame* claws at deeper and darker levels of experience and intuition.

Perhaps because he eschews critics who find in his work portentous messages, Beckett had an affinity with those who could relate to it viscerally, rather than intellectually, to the inmates in prisons who wrote to him about their experience of his plays, feeling affinity with its themes of entrapment and continual waiting, for release, for parole, for a pardon. The most famous such prison encounter occurred when the San Francisco Actors' Workshop took Herbert Blau's production of *Waiting for Godot* into San Quentin's maximum security prison in 1957. Thus began a long and productive relationship between Beckett and the San Quentin drama workshop. Under the directorship of inmate Rick Cluchey, the workshop would put on several of Beckett's plays both inside the prison and, later, as a professional troupe outside it.

The affinity of *Waiting for Godot* with conditions of extremity was also manifest in many well-known productions during periods of political or social crisis, when it appeared that confusion, uncertainty, waiting, hope were pressing with particular and material immediacy. Celebrated examples in the history of its staging history include Donald Howarth's 1980 Cape Town production in apartheid South Africa, Ilan Ronen's 1984 Haifa production, and Susan Sontag's 1993 Sarajevo production, during the Bosnian War. In Howarth's *Godot* black actors played Estragon and Vladimir, white actors Pozzo and Lucky, which activated the play's concern with power relations in the immediate context of the racial conditions in South Africa. Ronen's Haifa production also mobilized the play's surrounding politics, using language rather than race as the marker of difference. In this Arab–Israeli version, Estragon and Vladimir spoke colloquial Arabic to each other, but Hebrew to Pozzo; Pozzo spoke Hebrew to Estragon and Vladimir, but bad Arabic to Lucky; and Lucky spoke academic Arabic. Some of these markers of class and social power were embryonic in earlier productions, such as the Dublin première in the Pike theatre, but the transferability of the play to different political contexts is brought out strikingly in these productions. Susan Sontag also sought to activate the relevance and resonance of the play during the siege of Sarajevo. This production was moulded by the difficulty and pressure of the circumstances. Faced with an intense interest of Sarajevo's acting community, Sontag used multiple pairings of Vladimir and Estragon (as well as the original male–male pair, she also placed male–female and female–female ones onstage). She decided to perform only the first act because of the pressures on rehearsals and timing. Despite these limitations, Sontag explained her choice to stage *Waiting for Godot* by claiming that 'Beckett's play, written over forty years ago, seems written for and about Sarajevo'.[32]

The fame of the play and its celebrated director (Sontag was one of New York's most famous public intellectuals) no doubt explains part of its appeal in Sarajevo, which welcomed high cultural attention when it seemed that the world had forgotten it politically. There is a self-perpetuating cycle at work here: Beckett's play comes to peripheral locales swathed in associations of profundity, and then gains extra dimensions and cultural capital through its instantiation in a new locale. One recent production that might be taken as an instance, or perhaps a culmination, of the political productions of this play took place in New Orleans in 2007. Beckett, we know, was greatly enthusiastic about productions of his play with black actors, when they were put on in segregated USA in the 1950s or in South Africa in 1980, and would surely have approved of Harlem's Classical Theater 2006

[32] Susan Sontag, 'Godot Comes to Sarajevo', *New York Review of Books*, 21 Oct. 1993.

FIG. 35.1 *Waiting for Godot* by Samuel Beckett, directed by Christopher McElroen (Artistic Director, Paul Chan) (Gentilly, New Orleans, 9 November 2007). From left to right: T. Ryder Smith as Pozzo, J. Kyle Manzay as Estragon, Wendell Pierce as Vladimir, and Mark McLaughlin as Lucky.

Photo: Frank Aymami. Courtesy of Frank Aymami Photography.

production starring New Orleans natives Wendell Pierce and J. Kyle Manzay, staged on a simulated New Orleans rooftop in Harlem, New York.

In 2007 the visual artist and political activist Paul Chan persuaded the director Christopher McElroen and the arts organization Creative Time to take the show to the place itself. *Waiting for Godot in New Orleans* has quickly become a landmark production, perhaps the most significant production of the new century. The *New York Times* listed the project as one of the top ten national art events of 2007. The archives from the production have been acquired for the permanent collection of the Museum of Modern Art (MOMA). This production took *Godot* out of its conventional theatrical space and staged it outdoors, free for those who wanted to attend, in the Lower Ninth Ward and Gentilly, communities which had been ravaged by Hurricane Katrina in 2005. Part of the attraction of the play in New Orleans, and part of the attention the project received nationally and internationally, stemmed from the attempt to mount an original production in such an unlikely setting of a modern classic, a highpoint of European drama with an unmistakable aura of profundity and cultural capital. But, if that was the initial impetus, the production was able to subvert many of the hieratic and forbidding connotations of the play. It broke down the barrier between mandarin modernist culture and popular street performance, between autonomous art and political activism, between global brand and local event. *Waiting for Godot in New Orleans* emphasized the reality that insofar as theatre is always of its place and time, it always involves cross-cultural or transnational movements. Chan and his collaborators spent months seeking to enmesh themselves in the community. They organized social events, discussion groups, and classes in order to consult with locals in an effort to ensure that, even as the play took place in the streets of the city, it also had an organic connection with its values, perspectives, and problems.

It was an intriguing meeting of high modernism and street performance, of art and activism, which nonetheless was a consistent addition to the cultural impact of other productions of Beckett, which use the abstract setting of the play to speak powerfully to highly particular social, historical, and political issues. Alys Moody convincingly argues that this potential is deep within the text itself, suggesting that the Chan production reveals 'less the universality of *Waiting for Godot* than the way that abstraction can open itself to a cyclical process of decontextualization and recontextualization that reimagines the abstract through the local (and vice versa), and that speaks to the transnational potential of abstraction'.[33]

Importantly, though, the New Orleans production may indicate that what we value about Beckett's play has shifted or expanded. If the earlier critics prized the universal and timeless significance of *Waiting for Godot*, modern scholars tend to find such humanist and essentialist categories ideologically dangerous, eliding the specific and historical conditions that produce so much human suffering. It is not the ability of *Waiting for Godot* to transcend history that is now valued, but rather its capacity to recontextualize vividly in different moments, without sliding into allegory or one-on-one correspondence.

Beckett is inextricably caught up in a globalized culture, branded and consumed around the world. His global success was initially fuelled by the prestige and cultural capital his work, initially *Waiting for Godot*, later his other plays and prose works, accrued in the European metropolitan centres. Yet at the same time he is hailed for being above the marketplace, for his uncompromising—and unmarketable—recognition of difficulty and dissatisfaction. There is a contradiction between the Beckett brand—global, instantly identifiable, intellectually chic— and the fractiousness, difficulty, and opacity of much of his work. This is a paradox at the heart of the cultural impact of Beckett as a twentieth-century artist. It is a distinct if analogous paradox to that between the discourses of universalism and particularism that marks the critical reception of his work, which ironically his art has always acted to subvert. It subverts it from the beginning by the deep investment of the play in the ordinary, the everyday and the particular, the boots, carrots, bodily smells and functions, which contribute to the deflation of Pozzo's lofty theatrics or the intellectual rhetoric of Lucky's 'think'. At a metatheatrical level, too, this subversion operates as the play speaks powerfully to both the metropolitan centre and the neglected margins, to the denizens of the West End and to the wretched of the earth.

GLOCAL BECKETT

Even as we celebrate the chameleonic power and potential of Beckett's work, we must also acknowledge that its global circulation is caught up in systems of cultural capital, prestige,

---

[33] Alys Moody, '*Waiting for Godot* in New Orleans: Modernist Autonomy and Transnational Performance in Paul Chan's Beckett', *Theatre Journal* 65, no. 4 (2013), 539.

and reputational advantage that are not always enabling. His cultural prestige is one reason why his most famous works commands attention in New Orleans and Sarajevo. But at the same time, the commodification of Beckett as 'high culture', the circulation of his image and that of his stage plays into the iconography of global branding, has arguably also had the effect of defanging or domesticating a writer who challenges our most deeply seated ideologies and values. Late capitalism has proved remarkably skilled at recuperating and marketing those forces that would seek to challenge its hegemony, through assimilating the dissident and intellectual. Simon Critchley's remarks about this figure are pertinent to the cultural construction of 'Samuel Beckett':

> Is the intellectual (described with the figures of nomad, exile or agent of hybridity) really a course of resistance to late capitalism, or do these figures rather suggest a troubling complicity with that which the intellectual intends to oppose? That is to say, might not hybridity, exile and nomadism better describe the deterritorializing force and the speculative flows of late capitalism [. . .] rather than constituting any resistance to it?[34]

This may explain why one of Ireland's most expensive and exclusive hotels, the Shelbourne on Stephen's Green, has adorned its lobby with frescoes from Gate Theatre's 1990s production of *Waiting for Godot*, or why—in an ironic meeting of cultural capital and the conventional variety—the Irish Central Bank issued a commemorative 20-euro coin in the year of Beckett's centenary. The use of Beckett in modern Ireland, in general, is instructive, and its corporate tone was anticipated when Michael Colgan of the Gate declared that 'Samuel Beckett belongs to Ireland inc., as opposed to a theatre at the end of O'Connell St'.[35] Beckett took a scornful view of many policies of the Irish Free State, and chose famously to live in France at war rather than Ireland at peace; during much of his life, the Irish state took scant interest in its late modernist son. But in the two decades since Beckett's death, Ireland has sought strenuously to reclaim Beckett's prestige and reputation, alongside its other major modernist exile James Joyce. It is a vivid example of one of the tendencies of globalized culture in which Ireland re-imports (based on international success) flattened versions of its own culture in order to leverage its international reputation as a 'land of writers'. This culminated in the 2006 celebrations of the centenary of Beckett's birth, where Beckett was celebrated in conferences, symposia, and exhibitions around the world, and where the Irish state, enjoying the soon to be obliterated economic successes of the Celtic Tiger, featured prominently.

Do we see this recuperation of 'Beckett' as the sign of a new, sleek, globalized Ireland that has sloughed off the provincialism and small-mindedness that he deplored in his lifetime? Or do we see this uprooted, decontextualized laureate of postnationalist Ireland as founded on a shallow, empty commodification of his achievement? Does branding Beckett democratize 'high' culture, or does it simply allow people to feel that they can buy into the prestige of its difficulty? To be celebrated or treated with cynicism? Has the sign of Beckett lost or gained its power to represent anything countercultural by being styled as/trading off that image? If branding is associated with global capitalism, has it democratized Beckett

---

[34] Simon Critchley, *Ethics–Politics–Subjectivity: Essays on Derrida, Levinas and Contemporary French Thought* (London: Verso, 1999), 139.

[35] Quoted by Sean Kennedy, 'The Reception of Beckett in Ireland', in Nixon and Feldman, *The International Reception of Samuel Beckett*, 72.

or has it delinked him from other forms of association? Indeed, one could argue that the branding of Beckett has reinforced the tendency to dissociate his work from place or history, releasing him into the amnesiac surfaces of the market, with its concocted, plastic identities.

If Beckett is to retain into the twenty-first century the hold on the stage he enjoyed in the twentieth, his work will need to break beyond the shallow universal images that have secured the success of his brand, and reach the deeper transnational potential that his plays in performance actualize. It may be true that the former produces the latter: the reason Beckett gets a hearing in the peripheries is because of his huge prestige, which (as I have argued) is produced by mechanisms of branding and commodification. But peripheral productions nonetheless work against such branding, refreshing the capacity of Beckett's work to speak to particular circumstances. This occurs when the global brand cedes to the glocal instantiation. The Beckett Estate needs to step back, to free up producers and directors to take experimental production decisions, even if that risks misfires and travesties. There will need to be innovative, disruptive performances such as occurred in New Orleans, a less reverent and hieratic attitude to Beckett's cultural prestige. This could profitably also mean shifting the spotlight away from the firmly canonical *Waiting for Godot* on to the later drama and the prose works. Beckett needs to be liberated: from the aspic of universalism, from the iron grip of the Beckett Estate, from the shiny modernity of his contemporary branding.

CHAPTER 36

IRISH THEATRE AND THE UNITED STATES

JOHN P. HARRINGTON

THE complex interrelations between Irish theatre and the United States can be illustrated using two examples of transatlantic cultural transfer, one presented by an Irish writer and one by an American writer. In the first example, Fintan O'Toole begins his biography of the eighteenth-century Irish playwright Richard Brinsley Sheridan with a consideration of the playwright's American connections. During Sheridan's celebrated London career, his works were performed in the United States as a challenge to the Puritan-inspired censorship of theatre in colonial America. O'Toole traces productions of *The School for Scandal* (1777) and *The Rivals* (1775) in the 1780s from Jamaica, to New York (with George Washington in the audience), to Baltimore, and to that epicentre of colonial disdain for performance and other vanities, Philadelphia. The productions all occurred with some communication with, and influence on, the playwright in London. O'Toole concludes that 'it is but a small exaggeration to say that America pushed Sheridan into politics while Sheridan reconciled America to theatre', and that 'Sheridan's plays were important in re-establishing the theatre itself in post-revolutionary America'.[1]

The second example is found in that most American novel, *Main Street* (1920), by that most American of novelists, Sinclair Lewis. *Main Street* was lauded immediately and has been ever since as a pitiless anatomy of small-town life in the American Midwest. In it, Carol Milford of Gopher Prairie, Minnesota, marries a doctor, has aspirations, and collides with the deep-set pettiness and vindictiveness of her town. Among her aspirations is that of cultural improvement through the arts. The narrator tells us:

> The Little Theaters, which were to give piquancy to American drama three or four years later, were only in embryo. But of this fast-coming revolt Carol had premonitions. She knew from some lost magazine article that in Dublin were innovators called The Irish Players. She knew confusedly that a man named Gordon Craig had painted scenery—or had he written plays? She felt that in the turbulence of the drama she was discovering a history more important than the commonplace chronicles which dealt with senators and their pompous puerilities.[2]

---

[1] Fintan O'Toole, *A Traitor's Kiss: The Life of Richard Brinsley Sheridan* (New York: Farrar, Straus, & Giroux, 1998), xiii, xvi.

[2] Sinclair Lewis, *Main Street* (New York: Barnes & Noble, 2003), 215.

This leads her to a 'Cosmos School of Music, Oratory, and Dramatic Art' in Minneapolis and its programme of one-act plays by Shaw, Yeats, and Dunsany. Her husband is much more interested in another show, 'Lottie of Two-Gun Rancho', but Carol drags him to what appears to have been a very dreary performance of Lord Dunsany's *The Queen's Enemies*.

THE DYNAMICS OF IRISH THEATRE IN THE US

These examples suggest some of the multiple dynamics of Irish theatre in the United States. The performance history of Sheridan in early America demonstrates some of the potential subversiveness of theatre from an Irish playwright performed for American audiences, and the playwright's awareness of the same. The novelistic aside from Lewis demonstrates the perception in America of Irish theatre as innovative and the capacity of American performance to undo that subversive novelty. Together, they suggest something of the complexity of cultural transactions in an Irish theatrical diaspora. Irish theatre is not the only cultural counterpart to the many human migrations to America. Nor is it the only literary tradition to be affected by importation to America. Irving Howe famously inveighed against the transformation of Sholem Aleichem's stories into the Broadway musical *Fiddler on the Roof* (1964). For Howe, the process was 'corrupted by the trivial paraphernalia of a "lavish production"' and 'burst[ing] with quaintness and local color and the condescension that usually goes along. The condescension is affectionate, though not innocent.'[3] Similarly, one effect of the production of Irish theatre in the United States is a focus on local colour and authenticity that, however affectionate, may not be innocent in practice. Because of the priority of authenticity over other performance values, there are more Irish productions of Irish theatre in America than American productions of the Irish dramatic literature. Among cultural products exported to the United States, Irish theatre is singular in seeming to demand a far higher proportion of authentic, Irish, imported productions. American companies seem much less likely to mount their own productions of the works of Irish playwrights than they are of Chekhov, Brecht, Dario Fo, or Václav Havel.

Modern Irish theatre is famously influential in North America and elsewhere internationally. However, the diasporic narrative is not solely from Ireland to America in influence or in production. Abbey Theatre visits to America inspired whole companies, and the long shadow of Samuel Beckett is readily acknowledged by American playwrights such as Edward Albee. But at the same time, contemporary Irish playwrights such as Conor McPherson and Martin McDonagh point to the influence on their work of the American playwright David Mamet, while the Abbey, the national theatre of Ireland, has itself drawn inspiration and artistic vigour from many works by Americans including Eugene O'Neill and Tennessee Williams. The complexity of the history of modern Irish theatre and the United States includes these dynamics: subversiveness and its sublimation; a sometimes limiting emphasis on authenticity; and narratives from both east to west and west to east.

---

[3] Irving Howe, 'Tevye on Broadway', *Commentary* 38 (1964), 73, 74.

Pre-modern Irish Theatre and the US

As the prominence of Sheridan in Colonial America indicates, the history of Irish theatre in the United States is a long one, and Irish performance professionals of all kinds have often been complicit in the condescension stemming from an emphasis on 'local colour', however affectionate. For example, among the many Irish professionals working stages in the antebellum United States, John Brougham from Dublin had enormous audience contact through prolific authorship, popular performances, and tenacious touring. In early 1844 alone he appeared in theatres across the American south, giving performances as historical figures such as Daniel O'Connell and Father Theobald Mathew, as well as fictional ones from Sheridan's comedies and his own plays. For this, he was praised in the mainstream American press for managing 'to elevate the Irish character, and to dispel the prejudice which exists against our fellow citizens of Irish character'.[4] This was a press that was not itself free from prejudice concerning Irish character: its celebration of elevating perceptions of Irish character in the nineteenth century was equalled by its condemnation of what it perceived to be attacks on Irish character by Irish playwrights in the twentieth century.

After the American Civil War, stages across the country featured the work of Dion Boucicault, who, after a storied stage career in London and in New York, happily took full credit for inventing 'the Irish play' in America in works such as *The Colleen Bawn* (1860) and *The Shaughraun* (1874). After touring them across the United States, he later exported them, west to east, to Dublin and London. In the Irish plays, which were extraordinary visual displays of local colour and special stage effects, simultaneously authentic and contrived, he did not eschew sentiment but managed it to superb effect. As Patrick Lonergan has written, 'this involved use of "stage interpreters" such as the English gentlemen who populate Boucicault's Irish plays: characters whose interaction with feckless Irishness was not just the occasion of comedy, but also fulfilled an interpretative and mediative function for non-Irish audiences.'[5] Thus, by the time modern Irish theatre made its entrance into America in the twentieth century, an infrastructure of dramatic expectations of stage Irishness had been constructed and further integrated into popular culture by Irish theatre professionals. This included, in addition to playwrights, performers such as the writing and performing team Harrigan and Hart, the marquee star Tyrone Power, producers such as Augustine Daly, and musicians such as Chauncey Olcott or George M. Cohan.

Modern Irish Theatre and 'Little Theatre' in the US

It was precisely its contrast with that previous stage Irishness and elevation of Irish character that gave modern Irish theatre its novelty and influence in America. The Little Theatres

---

[4] Pat M. Ryan, 'The Hibernian Experience: John Brougham's Irish-American Plays', *MELUS* 10, no. 2 (1983), 35, 37.

[5] Patrick Lonergan, ' "The Laughter Will Come of Itself. The Tears Are Inevitable": Martin McDonagh, Globalization, and Irish Theatre Criticism', *Modern Drama* 47, no. 4 (2004), 646.

referred to by Sinclair were very much inspired by the Irish Players company sent from the Abbey Theatre to tour thirty-one American cities and small towns in 1911. By early 1915 the Abbey company's direct influence had led to the creation of three non-commercial companies fundamental to the history of modern drama in America. The Neighborhood Playhouse opened in February 1915 and promoted a theatre mission tied closely to social welfare and the mission of its sponsoring corporation, the Henry Street Settlement in lower Manhattan. One week later, the Washington Square Players opened in mid-town; the company, with emphasis on actors and performance, would evolve into the Theatre Guild. In the same month the third company, the Provincetown Players, which defined itself as a playwright's theatre, was being organized in Cape Cod around Eugene O'Neill. These and less notable companies, non-commercial and frequently amateur, were, like the Abbey, a reaction to spectacle theatre in huge urban venues, an attempt at decentralization of entertainment in major cities, and—as in the famous formulation for the Irish Literary Theatre—of 'a high ambition'.[6] Little Theatres in America often produced the work of playwrights singled out by Lewis—Shaw, Yeats, and Dunsany. There were some notable successes, but issues with both performance quality and financial resources eroded the movement. The phenomenon is treated much more critically by Lewis in other novels, such as *Ann Vickers* (1933). The brief flourishing, the ambition, and the not uncommon lunacies also inspired some effective stage satires in the American dramatic literature, including *The Torch-Bearers* (1923) by George Kelly, first produced three years after *Main Street* was published. American companies frequently fell short of the Abbey example from 1911. So did some Irish companies, such as the Ulster Literary Theatre, which toured America in 1912 with Rutherford Mayne's *The Drone* (1912). They were generally ignored as far west as Chicago and closed, without a performance in New York, on New Year's Eve.

IMMEDIATE INFLUENCE: MODERN IRISH THEATRE IN THE US

One of W. B. Yeats's most-rehearsed statements for the press in his five lecture tours of America (1903, 1911, 1914, 1920, and 1932) was this: 'we advocates of the new school believe we should submit the actual life of Ireland herself to the analysis of the stage.[7] This model was to have a long-term influence on American theatre, even though Yeats had no evident interest in applying his vision of the new school to American theatres. For that matter, he apparently had very little interest in anything else in America, with the notable exceptions of séances and the make of his limousines. Yeats instead sought to influence Ireland from America—and that is another complexity of the influences and transatlantic cultural transactions in modern Irish theatre and the United States. But in America his model was admired and applied by others.

---

[6] Augusta Gregory, *Our Irish Theatre: A Chapter of Autobiography*, 3rd edn. (Gerrards Cross: Colin Smythe, 1972), 20.

[7] 'The New Ireland Analysed by W. Butler Yeats', *New York Times*, 22 Oct. 1911.

Among the very early proponents of the Abbey model was Sheldon Cheney, trained at Berkeley and Harvard, and a prolific author on the idea of Little Theatre in America in several books such as *The New Movement in the Theater* in 1914. Cheney stressed the originality of 'The Irish School of playwrights' because 'there is a distinct difference: the universal social message is less stressed, the racial peculiarities are noticeable, and there is a poetic conception.'[8] In 'racial peculiarities', Cheney saw what Irving Howe had called local colour and only slightly less vehemently deplored it. He was not alone in his own time, and the issue of authenticity is embedded in the reception of modern Irish theatre in America from its introduction. Another American historian and theorist of theatre of the time, Branders Matthews, in 1917 also used that sense, slightly recast by Matthews to 'provincial peculiarities',[9] and so it very likely had some currency beyond these individual writers.

The impact of the Irish model was quite immediate and quite widespread. In 1919, George Pierce Baker published in the *Quarterly Journal of Speech Education* an account of his famous 47 Workshop at Harvard, which was and has remained famed for the influence of its alumni playwrights on American theatre history. For Baker, the 47 Workshop 'probably would never have been founded [without] the Abbey Theatre, Dublin, under the brilliant and wise guidance of W. B. Yeats and Lady Gregory'. He articulated how his 'laboratory' programme, as he liked to call it, adapted the Abbey model, and he further traced the Abbey influence to new studio approaches in New York, Chicago, and at Vassar College.[10] Another tribute came in 1916 from *Theatre Arts Magazine*, a very popular and expensive national magazine edited by Sheldon Cheney. Vocal in its elevation of arts over all commercial enterprises, the magazine was not immune to quantifiable assessment. In it, Stephen Allard ranked 'Plays for Little Theatres', and the Irish assessment was quite positive: four of the top ten and eight of the top twenty-five. The top twenty-five included three Dunsany works, two by Yeats, and one each by Synge and Lady Gregory.[11]

EARLY PRACTITIONERS OF MODERN IRISH THEATRE IN THE US

The influence and popularity of Irish theatre in America demanded practitioners, and many migrated east to west in the conventional diasporic narrative. Much has been made lately of the seduction of Irish stage artists from the Abbey Theatre by the corruption and vulgarity of Hollywood—a seduction to which they seem to have submitted readily enough. However, a great deal of the theatrical expertise that came to America from Ireland remained loyal to the stage. Notable examples include the English actor and director Ben Iden Payne. After serving as stage director at the Abbey, and after being detailed by Annie Horniman to Manchester, he spent fifty years from 1914 in association with the theatre department at Carnegie Mellon (originally Carnegie Institute) in Pittsburgh, which

---

[8] Sheldon Cheney, *The New Movement in the Theatre* (New York: Michael Kennelley, 1914), 85.

[9] Brander Matthews, 'Irish Plays and Irish Playwrights', *Scribner's Magazine* 61, no. 1 (1917), 85.

[10] George Pierce Baker, 'The 47 Workshop', *Quarterly Journal of Speech Education* 5, no. 3 (1919), 192.

[11] Stephen Allard, 'Plays for Little Theatres', *Theatre Arts Magazine* 1, no. 4 (1917), 175–7.

made him something of a trailblazer for the many others in Irish theatre who were welcomed into American university theatres and so had pervasive influence throughout the careers of their alumni. A less notable émigré from the Abbey to American theatre would be J. Augustus Keogh. R. F. Foster recounts how Yeats, looking for an Abbey director to succeed St John Ervine, considered the extraordinarily American poet Ezra Pound. In 1916 Yeats passed over 'the Idaho Kid' for Keogh, who lasted only a few months.[12] Keogh turned up in New York in 1926 in a minor role in a production of *Juno and the Paycock*, but by 1936 he had organized in New York an Irish Repertory Players company, with Paul Vincent Carroll and Padraic Colum on his advisory committee and himself as director. According to its prospectus, the company was 'composed of native Irish living in New York as well as of Irish-Americans'.[13] This sort of organization—an American company producing Irish plays, as distinct from an Irish touring company—was very popular in America. There was an Irish Guild Players in New York in 1928, and the name appears in Chicago in the 1950s. Effectiveness may not have been the reason for imitation. The first Irish Guild Players were reviewed by the *New York Times*, which chose its words carefully: 'it cannot be denied that the attempt was a whole-hearted one', but the lead in William Boyle's *The Building Fund* 'did not know more than half his lines'.[14]

EUGENE O'NEILL IN IRISH AND AMERICAN THEATRE

That Irish Guild Players production of *The Building Fund* was in Greenwich Village at the Provincetown Playhouse. The Provincetown Players had gone through several reorganizations by 1928, but even the indirect connection with Eugene O'Neill helps illustrate some of the complexity of Irish and American theatre interrelations in the first half of the twentieth century. O'Neill had been inspired to become a playwright by the Irish Players from the Abbey in their first tour in 1911, and subsequently always acknowledged that. He adopted the Abbey style in one-act form and realistic dialogue, and so Eugene and his father, James, legendary performer of melodrama, are in themselves very representative examples of the differences between Irish theatre in America in the nineteenth and the twentieth centuries. But Eugene O'Neill's work also migrated west to east, America to Ireland, and had its influences as an extended counternarrative to the conventional diasporic narrative. The production of *The Emperor Jones* (written 1920; Abbey 1927) by the Dublin Drama League raised O'Neill's visibility—and, by extension, that of American theatre in Ireland—considerably. The play's characters were not the Irish Americans common in other O'Neill works, and so they required a considerable stretch for the Irish cast in Dublin, especially the lead, played by Rutherford Mayne. The production was welcomed in the press and, according to the Dublin theatre diarist Joseph Holloway, whose entry on the play is laced

[12] R. F. Foster, *W. B. Yeats: A Life*, vol. 2: *The Arch-Poet* (Oxford: Oxford University Press, 2003), 53.
[13] Irish Repertory Players, Playbill, clippings, in New York, New York Public Library for the Performing Arts (NYPLPA), Billy Rose Theatre Collection, n.p.
[14] 'Irish Guild Shows Promise', *New York Times*, 6 June 1928.

with the N-word, 'a truly great audience thronged the Abbey' at the opening. Interestingly, the second one-act on the evening programme was Susan Glaspell's *Trifles* (written 1916; Abbey 1927) an American play ranked at number two (second only to Dunsany) on the Stephen Allard ranking of plays for Little Theatre companies. *The Emperor Jones* was not the first but was a particularly influential play without obvious Irish context exported from American theatre to the National Theatre of Ireland in the first part of the twentieth century. Some of the cross-cultural reception of the 1927 production features issues that were to remain in debate in the early twenty-first century. Holloway was disappointed in the American accents of some of the cast of *Trifles*, which they 'overdid'.[15] In contrast, from the American perspective, the *New York Times* correspondent in Dublin, J. J. Hayes, wrote of Mayne that 'his knowledge of the colored man was very superficial' and that in performance 'he frequently slipped away from the "negro speech"' and that 'he ceased to be a negro and became the white man playing the part of a negro in the white man's way'.[16] Mayne has been called the first white actor to play the black role, but from the American perspective the performance was rather more black-face than black. Both commentators on the performance, Holloway and Hayes, focus on the 'peculiarities' of the American play in Ireland: a form of characterization, of local colour as distinct from any broader empathetic and intellectual engagement in the performance or intentions of the playwright. For these two writers, the success or failure of theatre is limited to national 'peculiarities' as the sole test of production. The plays were celebrated, but, as Irving Howe observed in the very different context of *The Fiddler on the Roof*, celebration can be condescending in a way that may not be innocent.

Denis Johnston wrote that this 1927 production of *The Emperor Jones* was 'the first true invasion of the modern into the national theatre [of Ireland]'.[17] Johnston is an excellent reminder of another dimension in this dynamic of Irish and American theatre. As there is a diaspora of works, like *The Emperor Jones*, and a diaspora that moves from America to Ireland as well as from Ireland to America, so there is a diaspora of artists, not all of whom follow the narrative of an Iden Ben Payne or J. Augustus Keogh. There is another narrative of Irish playwrights who had formative artistic experiences in America and returned to work in Ireland and to shape performance history there. Johnston went to America in 1923, at the age of 22, to study law at Harvard.

> I was always a theatregoer, but I became interested in theatrical production when I went to America. I read a lot of plays when maybe I should have been reading law. Eugene O'Neill was being discovered about that time and I had discovered Shaw. [...] When I came back from America and began studying at King's Inns I joined the Dublin Drama League.[18]

And, presumably, he promoted O'Neill there. Examples of this are too numerous to recount, but these kinds of experiences and their effects are worth exploring. Another example from the first half of the twentieth century would be Ria Mooney, who, after touring in Irish

---

[15] Joseph Holloway, *Joseph Holloway's Irish Theatre*, vol. 1: *1926–1931*, ed. Robert Hogan and Michael J. O'Neill (Dixon, CA: Proscenium Press, 1968), 21.

[16] J. J. Hayes, 'An Irish "Emperor Jones"', *New York Times*, 13 Feb. 1927.

[17] Gene A. Barnett, *Denis Johnston* (Boston, MA: Twayne, 1978), 17.

[18] Des Hickey and Gus Smith (eds.), *Flight from the Celtic Twilight* (Indianapolis, IN: Bobbs-Merrill, 1973), 62.

travelling companies in the American Midwest, returned to New York and spent two years in Eva Le Gallienne's Civic Repertory Company. Le Gallienne must certainly have been a model for Mooney not only as an actor, or as director, but as an artistic director and company leader, all of which Mooney subsequently became in Ireland. The baggage from this American experience may not always have been welcomed by everyone. Seán O'Casey is known to have deplored Mooney's experience with Le Gallienne and its effect: Christopher Murray quotes O'Casey writing to others that Mooney worked with Le Gallienne '& [she] knows it'.[19]

THE RISE OF AMERICAN REGIONAL THEATRE

In the later half of the twentieth century, American theatre evolved in ways that equally served Irish theatre professionals and performances of Irish plays in the United States. As Little Theatre faded in the 1930s and 1940s, a new model for non-commercial theatre emerged in resident or regional theatre stock companies in cities as a local, autonomous alternative to touring shows from New York. Leading examples were launched through the 1960s, and those still in operation include the Mark Taper Forum in Los Angeles (1967), the Seattle Repertory (1963), the Long Wharf in New Haven (1965), and the Arena Stage in Washington, DC (1950).[20] The first model for regional theatre was developed by Margo Jones in her Theatre '47 (founded in 1947) in Dallas. She took as a model the Abbey Theatre, along with the Moscow Art Theatre and the Old Vic in London. However, she insisted that, like those models, her theatre would create new work: 'I believe it is imperative in creating new resident professional companies to take a violent stand about the choice of plays. Personally I believe in the production of classics and new scripts, with the emphasis on new scripts.'[21] The emphasis on new scripts also prioritized American plays, in intention and in effect.

A second model was conceived in Ireland by Tyrone Guthrie, who, in *A New Theatre*, described how at his home in Ireland, Annaghmakerig, he formulated a plan to locate a company in America outside New York. He wished to escape prescribed, restrictive professional practices in the theatre industry based there, which are described in a chapter entitled 'Give My Regards to Broadway'. The company opened in Minneapolis in 1963, to realize Guthrie's vision: 'Our program would be classical; only those plays would be chosen which had seemed, to discriminating people for several generations, to have serious merit; which had, in fact, stood the test of time.'[22] Thus his formula for an American theatre, defined in Ireland, had an emphasis that excluded modern Irish theatre. But Irish dramatic literature did play an important part in the establishment of American regional theatre: Herbert Blau's Actors Workshop, founded in 1952 in San Francisco, featured *The Playboy of the Western World* (1907) in its first season, and the Long Wharf Theatre featured Brendan Behan's *The Hostage* (1958) in its first season of 1965–6. The Guthrie Theatre in

[19] Christopher Murray, *Seán O'Casey, Writer at Work: A Biography* (Dublin: Gill & Macmillan, 2004), 286.

[20] See Joseph Wesley Zeigler, *Regional Theatre: The Revolutionary Stage* (Minneapolis, MN: University of Minnesota Press, 1973).

[21] Margo Jones, *Theatre-in-the-Round* (New York: McGraw-Hill, 1965), 55–6.

[22] Tyrone Guthrie, *A New Theatre* (New York: McGraw-Hill, 1964), 41.

Minneapolis also became an important venue for Irish theatre under artistic director Joe Dowling, who featured Brian Friel's *Philadelphia, Here I Come!* (1964) in his first season of 1996–7.

Many Irish playwrights, as well as Irish plays, found support in the American regional theatre system. Brian Friel, in particular, was forthright about his debt to the invitation from Tyrone Guthrie to spend time in his theatre in Minneapolis in 1963:

> I learned a great deal about the iron discipline of theatre [and] those months in America gave me a sense of liberation—remember, this was my first parole from inbred, claustrophobic Ireland—and that liberation conferred on me a valuable self-confidence, and a necessary perspective so that the first play I wrote immediately after I came home—*Philadelphia, Here I Come!*—was a lot more assured than anything I had attempted before.[23]

In Friel's long history on American stages, he criticized his work's productions on Broadway. He vented much of this criticism at the invitation of an American regional theatre company, the Actors Theatre of Louisville, Kentucky, in the form of a bitter monologue, *American Welcome*.[24] Moreover, Friel and his plays have a greater artistic history in America in regional theatres, such as the first American production of *The Freedom of the City* (1973) at the Goodman Theatre in Chicago in 1973.

Like Friel, Garry Hynes has described American experience as enabling her work in Irish theatre. She told an interviewer:

> You get a different kind of culture fuel in America. Different fuel in the engine. I was weaned on American theatre. I spent time in NY as a student, from 1971–75. [. . .] I spent 4–5 months of each year there, and saw everything. Theatre in Ireland seemed very remote. The fact that theatre could be made in small rooms, about people my age, that's what drove me! That's where I cut my teeth. For me it was like a series of explosions. When I went in and saw (Sam Shepard's) Tooth of Crime at the Performing Garage, in an environment where the audience followed the action around—it blew my head away. Joe Chaikin's performance in Woyczek also blew my head open. When I went back to Ireland then, I helped found Druid. To a large extent, Druid was founded to recreate that energy and excitement. Only in later years did I begin to explore Irish work.[25]

That is another, different, and complementary lineage compared to the one we usually recognize for the foundation of Druid with a legendary production in Galway of *The Playboy of the Western World* in 1975.

American Theatre in Ireland

Just as Irish theatre featured in productions in American regional theatre, American theatre has often been produced in Ireland. Eugene O'Neill has been presented on the Irish

[23] Paul Delaney (ed.), *Brian Friel in Conversation* (Ann Arbor, MI: University of Michigan Press, 2000), 104.

[24] Brian Friel, 'American Welcome', in Stanley Richards (ed.), *The Best Short Plays of 1981* (New Radnor, PA: Chilton Books, 1981), 112–14.

[25] Gwen Orel, 'Interview with Garry Hynes', CelticCafe.com, http://www.celticcafe.com/celticcafe/Theatre/Shows/Juno/Juno_02.html. Accessed 10 Oct. 2014.

National Theatre stage more than any other American playwright, and much has been written about the cultural connection embedded in the work of the playwright as the son of an emigrant to America. The playwright never visited Ireland himself, but his work did so frequently. In the 1930s, in the decade after *The Emperor Jones* at the Abbey, the Gate Theatre launched productions of *Where the Cross is Made* (1918) in 1931, *Before Breakfast* (1916) in 1934, *Ah, Wilderness* (1933) in 1936, and *Mourning Becomes Electra* (1931) in 1938.[26] In 1934, the Abbey produced *Days Without End* (1934) just after its opening on Broadway and just after Yeats's return from an American speaking tour promoting the Irish Academy of Letters. The play is a drama about a somewhat tortured character, represented on stage by two actors, rather like *Philadelphia, Here I Come!*, attempting to resolve his conflicting commitments to Catholic dogma and to family. In New York it was very poorly received—one review described it as being 'as heavy-handed and pretentious as only its author can be in his less fortunate efforts'[27]—and led to a general decline in American productions of O'Neill's work. Not so in Dublin. Yeats wrote back to a supporter in New York:

> I got a telegram from my wife with these words 'Great Success, magnificent acting, good production.' [. . .] Every seat is, I gather, taken each night. The success of this perfectly orthodox play has come at the right moment for us, as we are having some trouble with the government the echoes of which may have reached you.[28]

Thus O'Neill's American play could provide support for the Abbey and a defence of its work in the 1930s—a turbulent time in its history. Later, O'Neill's work could bring other benefits. Joe Dowling has described theatre in Dublin in the 1950s and early 1960s as 'a constant diet of mediocre plays, with occasional productions of Eugene O'Neill to leaven the tedium'[29]. At the Abbey, *Long Day's Journey into Night* (1956) was produced in 1959 and revived three times. *A Moon for the Misbegotten* (1947) was produced in 1990 for an American tour. The transatlantic reciprocity was also evident in 1992, when an Abbey production of *The Iceman Cometh* (1946) was directed by Robert Falls, long-term artistic director of Chicago's Goodman Theater.

Some, though not all, of O'Neill's work represents the Irish in America, notably the Tyrone family in *Long Day's Journey into Night*. In general, however, the work of twentieth-century Irish American playwrights or works about Irish Americans by American playwrights are not often produced in Ireland, while, ironically, the work once most dismissed as stage Irish buffoonery, such as Boucicault's Irish plays, are. In the twentieth century, notable Irish American playwrights include Philip Barry, a graduate of George Pierce Baker's 47 Workshop, whose work, such as *The Philadelphia Story* (1939), focuses on dramas of successful assimilation. Other Irish American playwrights scarcely referenced Ireland at all. These include George Kelly, most notable for satirical treatments of theatre culture such as *The Torch-Bearers* (1922) and *Philip Goes Forth* (1931). Prominent work on Irish American

[26] See Edward L. Shaughnessy, *Eugene O'Neill in Ireland: The Critical Reception* (Westport, CT: Greenwood Press, 1988).

[27] Arthur Gelb and Barbara Gelb, *O'Neill* (New York: Harper, 1960), 781.

[28] Quoted in John Unterecker (ed.), *Yeats and Patrick McCartan: A Fenian Friendship* (Dublin: Dolmen Press, 1967), 364.

[29] Joe Dowling, 'A View from the Mississippi', in Christopher Fitz-Simon (ed.), *Players and Painted Stage: Aspects of Twentieth Century Theatre in Ireland* (Dublin: New Island, 2004), 104.

family life, such as Frank Gilroy's *The Subject Was Roses* (1964), or Irish American politics, such as William Alfred's *Hogan's Goat* (1965), have not attracted Irish attention. Of contemporary Irish American playwrights, the most prominent is John Patrick Shanley, whose play *Doubt* (2004) was produced at the Abbey in 2006 before it was adapted by the playwright for a major motion picture. However, his many other plays have not attracted Irish attention, and his first work to represent Irish life, *Outside Mullingar* (2014), as produced on Broadway, was not reviewed positively in Ireland. Americans have not been absent from the Irish stage: Arthur Miller, Tennessee Williams, Thornton Wilder, David Mamet, and Beth Henley all have production histories in Ireland. Sam Shepard's *Ages of the Moon* (2009) opened at the Peacock Theatre in that spring and then reopened at the Abbey Theatre that autumn before travelling to the Atlantic Theater Company in New York later that winter with the same cast. But the interest in Irish America for Irish plays is not matched by an interest in Ireland for Irish American plays.

Contemporary Irish Theatre in the US

Sam Shepard and his work in Ireland and America may be an example of a new kind of accessibility and transportability: his *A Particle of Dread (Oedipus Variations)* (2013) was produced by the legendary cross-border Irish company Field Day for the Derry/Londonderry City of Culture celebration in that year. That choice of playwright and play may suggest a new, more international and less localized conception of what culture is and how theatre functions within it. For the most part, however, Irish theatre in the United States continues to be viewed as Irish theatre rather than theatre. That identity can on occasions be enabling, and on other occasions it can be limiting. It might be said that the long quest to change the perception of Irish characters on the American stage continues: that is, to lift them to the status of characters, and not just Irish characters, in works that are plays, and not just Irish plays. Two examples represent the kinds of reception likely in America to greet Irish work that disregard the kinds of expectations usually associated with Irish playwrights and attempt something new.

The first is the production of Brendan Behan's *The Hostage* (1958) that toured before opening on Broadway on September 20, 1960. Behan was with the play, and a major sideshow to it at performances and in the media. But many of the literary intelligentsia welcomed Behan and the play as innovation, as a welcome dismantling of tired conventions into a highly energized, improvisatory, and so newly performative work of a kind not often staged on as mainstream a venue as Broadway. For Howard Taubman, the lead critic of the *New York Times*, '[b]eing an expansive Irishman—and a rebellious and imaginative one—Mr Behan refuses to be confined within the boundaries of conventional dramaturgy. That is his privilege. He wishes his stage to erupt in unexpected ways, and it does.'[30] The play was very well received. However, similar combinations of new work and standing expectations were also in position nearly thirty years later, when the Abbey Theatre 'World Tour' production of Tom Mac Intyre's *The Great Hunger* (1983–6) reached New York. Conceived

[30] Howard Taubman, 'The Theatre: Behan Buffoonery', *New York Times*, 21 Sept. 1960.

FIG. 36.1 Seán McGinley and Stephen Rea in *Ages of the Moon*, by Sam Shepard. Directed by Jimmy Fay (Atlantic Theater Company at the Linda Gross Theater, New York, 27 October 2010).

Photo: Ari Mintz. Courtesy of Atlantic Theater Company.

for performative value and expressiveness by extratextual means, like much of Mac Intyre's work, it was greeted in New York as being very familiar, and as not being exotic or peculiar enough. For a (by then) different critic of the *New York Times*, Mel Gussow, 'the play seems to contradict the founding principles of the Abbey Theatre as home for the eloquence of such writers as Yeats, Synge, and O'Casey.' What it presents instead fails 'not so much with its dearth of poetry as with the familiarity and the ingenuousness of the performance techniques. As produced by the Abbey's experimental theater lab, the play is an artifact of the 1960s. It is as if the Open Theater and Jerzy Grotowski's Polish Lab had never existed.'[31] For the Behan production, departure from the usual, controlled Abbey craft was welcome because of the power of the novelty that replaced it; for the Mac Intyre production, departure from the usual Abbey craft disappointed because of the familiarity of what replaced it. It is very difficult to reconstruct the performance history to judge the validity of these claims. But whether warranted in these examples or not, these kinds of reaction are representative of many other judgements over many years noting the risk to Irish theatre in departure from its known, familiar identities. The known identity of familiar Irish theatre remains a dimension in contemporary work travelling east to west such as that of Martin McDonagh, Enda Walsh, or the multi-play productions of DruidSynge and DruidMurphy.

---

[31] Mel Gussow, '"Great Hunger" a Dearth of Words', *New York Times*, 18 Mar. 1988.

As an alternative production route, there are many American companies across the United States that define themselves through Irish theatre. Representative current examples include the Irish Classical Theatre Company in Buffalo, the Irish American Theater Company in Cincinnati, the American Irish Ensemble Company in Portland, Maine, the Seanachaí Theatre Company in Chicago, the Pittsburgh Irish and Classical Theatre, both Inis Nua Theatre Company and the Irish Heritage Theatre in Philadelphia, and, perhaps most notable, the Irish Repertory Theatre of New York. There are many more, and there are frequent launches and closings.

In addition, there are the resident companies in America not defined by an Irish repertory who produce new Irish work. Again, two examples may serve to represent some of the many issues raised by Irish plays in new productions by American companies. Conor McPherson is as popular in America as elsewhere. Lately his play *The Seafarer* (2006) has been in the top ten of productions in non-commercial theatre per year. *The Weir* (1997) is also produced frequently in American theatres, and in spring 2011 there were actually two productions nearly overlapping in Washington, DC, during the St Patrick's Day season, one by the Keegan Theatre Company and one by the Scena Company. Keegan has been in existence for fifteen years, and usually it has one Irish play in every season of four to six plays: Friel, Behan, McDonagh, and Marie Jones have been produced there in recent years. Keegan has toured Ireland with its production of Sam Shepard's *Fool for Love* (1983), and in America it produced the world première of Irish playwright Rosemary Jenkinson's *Basra Boy* (2010), both in the 2010–11 season. The company's artistic mission cites among its core artistic beliefs 'that American audiences can be profoundly enhanced by the richness and depth of Ireland's theatrical tradition—and vice versa'.[32] Its all-American cast production of *The Weir*, directed by Mark Rhea, was described in the press as somewhat remarkable for 'no Irish boyo', as lacking in 'all the crackling mayhem of Martin McDonagh', and, ultimately, as 'unnerving'.[33] Only a few days after it closed, Scena opened its production of *The Weir*. The company was in its twenty-fifth year, and its mission statement emphasizes classical Greek tragedy and contemporary international drama. Its production of *The Weir*, directed by Robert McNamara, was conceived as 'a genuine Irish production', with Irish actors in three of five roles, and publicity focused on its presentation of 'McPherson's chilling ghost stories as told by real Irishmen'[34]. In the terms of Sheldon Cheney and Brander Matthews, the first production, at Keegan, would seem to be linked to 'poetics' and the second, at Scena, to 'peculiarities'.

PROSPECTS FOR IRISH THEATRE IN THE US

More recently, on the occasion of a new production of one of his works, *The Night Alive* (London 2013; New York 2014), moving from London to New York, McPherson has said:

[32] 'Keegan Theatre: Full Vision Statement', http://keegantheatre.com/about/. Accessed 4 May 2014.

[33] Nelson Pressley, 'Theatre Review: "The Weir" Presented by Keegan Theatre', *Washington Post*, 23 Feb. 2011: http://www.washingtonpost.com/wp-dyn/content/article/2011/02/22/AR2011022206778.html. Accessed 10 Oct. 2014.

[34] 'Scena's Authentic Irish Production': http://www.scenatheater.org/TheWeirPR.htm. Accessed 27 June 2013.

We haven't really changed it for all the Americans sitting out there watching in the dark. I flatter myself, of course, that my plays go over well there because they have such good taste. Less flatteringly, one might also say they see it through the prism of an idea of Irishness.[35]

The Night Alive is a not entirely unprecedented example in the late twentieth and early twenty-first centuries of an Irish play that opened in London and travelled to New York before ever being performed in Ireland—of Irish theatre now appearing on the world stage before appearing on the Irish stage. This configuration in many ways reconstitutes the production systems familiar to Richard Brinsley Sheridan. But more acutely than before—at least as McPherson defines it—it also the raises the question of whether that 'prism' neutralizes the subversive qualities of powerful theatre, and whether that 'prism' refracts what might seem affectionate reception of Irish identity into a condescending, patronizing, and unrealistic 'idea of Irishness'. Because there is such a long, complex, and dynamic history of Irish theatre in the United States, because it is an Anglophone cultural transaction, and because it is less fraught with postcolonial relations than Irish theatre in England, Irish theatre in the United States may continue to serve as a revealing example of how Irish theatre functions in a more globalized culture and society. Modern Irish theatre as defined by Gregory and Yeats for the Irish Literary Theatre is thus far a twentieth-century phenomenon; it did not exist as we know it in the nineteenth century or before, and it is possible that it will not exist as we know it in the twenty-first century. But it is also quite possible that a new configuration will emerge of local and global qualities, of the peculiar and the poetic dimensions of performance, or of audience expectations for Irish theatre as theatre and not exclusively as Irish theatre. In that way modern Irish theatre in America and elsewhere can stand as a revealing test case and a productive research area within the broader theoretic conceptions of world literature. If Irish theatre in an international context manages to construct an identity rooted and localized without rendering itself merely exotic or essentially irrelevant to international audiences, it will fulfil those qualities of world literature described by literary theorists such as David Damrosch: as 'at once local and translocal' and as 'the simultaneous localization of the global and globalization of the local.'[36]

---

[35] Cited in Vanessa Thorpe, 'Conor McPherson: "TV is Where the Creative Work Happens Now"', *Guardian*, 12 Jan. 2014: http://www.theguardian.com/stage/2014/jan/12/conor-mcpherson-tv-drama. Accessed 10 Oct. 2014.

[36] David Damrosch, 'Toward a History of World Literature', *New Literary History* 39, no. 3 (2008), 491–2.

CHAPTER 37

···

IRISH THEATRE IN BRITAIN

···

JAMES MORAN

THE SHAUGHRAUN

···

IN 2004, during a troubled centenary year, the Abbey Theatre experienced a number of
well-publicized box office failures. However, one ray of light came from a production of
The Shaughraun, a 128-year-old melodrama by Dion Boucicault. In contrast with the rest of
the centenary programme, *The Shaughraun* exceeded all marketing projections and, during a long initial run of almost seventy performances between 27 May and 31 July, played
at 67% of capacity.[1] Unsurprisingly, four months later the Abbey revived the production
for another long run, clocking up almost another hundred performances between 23
November 2004 and 26 February 2005. By September 2004 the director of *The Shaughraun*,
John McColgan, anticipated that the production would soon tour the US, boasting: 'We're
looking at Broadway, and Broadway is looking at us.' Newspapers reported that the William
Morris Agency had already received an enthusiastic response from North American ven-
ues about the prospect of hosting the play, with the tour expected to begin at the Guthrie
Theater in Minnesota, and then to proceed to Chicago, Toronto, Boston, and the Kennedy
Center in Washington, DC.[2]

Unfortunately for the Abbey, this North American tour never materialized. The reason
was that, rather than going straight from Dublin to Minnesota, the production first travelled from Dublin to London's West End. As John McColgan declared: 'We had an opportunity to do an American tour in the early part of next year, but we decided for planning
reasons to go to the West End instead. Of course the fact that it will be in a West End theatre for eighteen weeks will make it even more attractive to American promoters.'[3] Here

---

[1] For more detail see Ben Barnes, *Plays and Controversies: Abbey Theatre Diaries 2000–2005*
(Dublin: Carysfort Press, 2008), 346.

[2] John Burns, 'Abbey's Shaughraun takes the Riverdance Route to America', *Sunday Times*, 12 Sept.
2004: http://www.thesundaytimes.co.uk/sto/news/world_news/article238046.ece. Accessed 15 Apr. 2014.

[3] Jerome Reilly, 'Shaughraun Coup Confounds Luvvies', *Irish Independent*, 27 Feb. 2005: http://
www.independent.ie/opinion/analysis/shaughraun-coup-confounds-luvvies-26205265.html.
Accessed 15 Apr. 2014.

McColgan attempted to emulate what he had done when he directed the *Riverdance* show in the previous decade, when the show had been staged strategically at locations in Dublin and the British capital (notably for Prince Charles at London's Coliseum, and for the Queen at the Royal College of Music). By the time the show reached the USA, the *New York Times* therefore hailed the arrival of *Riverdance* with a review that made no mention of the work's Eurovision origins but instead began by describing the production as having enjoyed 'phenomenal success in Dublin and London over the last two years'.⁴ In this way, London had provided a shop-window to attract other global consumers, particularly those of New York, to the realm of Irish performance.

The example of *The Shaughraun*, however, showed that London could also provide a 'reverse Midas' effect. For the last two weeks of that show's Dublin run, crowds had queued outside the Abbey for cancellations.⁵ By contrast, at London's Albery (now the Noël Coward) Theatre, audiences for *The Shaughraun* were rarely to be found. Before performances, the dispirited actors trod the pavements outside the theatre, trying to coax spectators inside. The London run opened on 8 June, and had been booked to continue until 24 September, but attendances proved so poor—particularly after the 7/7 bombings of London's public transport network—that the show closed two months early on 30 July. Even the dog playing the part of Patch started to look homesick and needed to be sent home to Dublin after two weeks in the British capital.⁶

Before the London opening, the Abbey's production of *The Shaughraun* had often been discussed in terms of box office success, US tours, and—in one enthusiastic review—of creating a theatrical 'revolution' that would revive the Abbey.⁷ Yet, after its first appearance in the British capital, the production was more frequently described as artistically bankrupt, inauthentic, and damaging to the Abbey Theatre at a particularly vulnerable time.⁸ When Ben Barnes later edited his diaries for publication, he made the notable claim that, long before the London opening, he had been worried about exposing the play which 'worked well with home audiences' to 'sophisticated theatre markets' where it would be 'crucified', and he went on to describe the London reaction as 'the expected critical drubbing'.⁹

This chapter will consider the determining role played by London in much recent Irish drama. I want to point to the ways in which, although—as shown above—the city can pose certain problems for the products of the Irish stage, the British capital is also a key centre for the mounting, developing, and showcasing of Irish work. In addition, although the chapter will give a set of localized readings from the last fifteen years rather than attempting a comprehensive overview, I want to look beyond the capital city to think about the

⁴ Anna Kisselgoff, 'Irish Steps and their Kin', *New York Times*, 15 Mar. 1996.
⁵ Reilly, 'Shaughraun Coup Confounds Luvvies'.
⁶ Eugene Moloney, 'Life's Too Doggone Ruff for Patch in West End', *Irish Independent*, 8 June 2005: http://www.independent.ie/irish-news/lifes-too-doggone-ruff-for-patch-in-west-end-25979384.html. Accessed 15 Apr. 2014.
⁷ Gwen Halley, 'We Want Less Theatre and Some More Plays', *Irish Independent*, 1 Aug. 2004: http://www.independent.ie/entertainment/books-arts/we-want-less-theatre-and-some-more-plays-26223055.html. Accessed 15 Apr. 2014.
⁸ See e.g. Angelique Chrisafis, 'How a Backstage Farce Nearly Ruined the Abbey Theatre', *Guardian*, 22 July 2005.
⁹ Barnes, *Plays and Controversies*, 416–17.

possibilities offered by Irish theatre elsewhere in Britain. London is key to the theatrical culture of these islands—it does, after all, contain over a quarter of the professional theatres in the UK.[10] But the Irish have migrated in significant numbers to British locations outside London, and so it is important when considering Irish performance in Britain to avoid what Claire Cochrane calls the theatre historian's 'unexamined prejudice' of assuming 'that everything important in British theatre happened in London'.[11] In thinking about Ireland's theatre in Britain, then, this chapter will move on to show what theatrical performances in other locations have revealed about the anxieties and affiliations of those Irish communities outside the capital. Although the geographical spread of those communities is wider than can be discussed and described in this short chapter (a full study would naturally require detailed examination of Scotland, Wales, and many other parts of England), my work here will include indicative examples of the way that Irish shows in two British cities outside London—Liverpool and Birmingham—have been able to engage with the particularities of Irish experience in these locations, and have articulated a distinct set of local concerns.

London Calling

To state the obvious, London is one of the world's major theatre centres. Part of this is explained by the size and profile of the city: almost double the number of people live in the area over which the mayor of London and London Assembly have jurisdiction than live in the whole of the Republic of Ireland, and the city uses its playhouses to attract a significant number of visitors. More than 20 million tourists visited London in 1994, and a survey during the same decade found that more than one in ten overseas tourists visited the city solely to see its theatres.[12] In 2009, the Society of London Theatre reported that London's playhouses attracted audiences in excess of fourteen million, earning revenue of £504 million. The society estimated that this activity kept 41,000 people in employment and generated almost £2 billion for the UK's economy.[13] Furthermore, London currently receives a disproportionate amount of the UK's arts subsidies. The independent report 'Rebalancing Our Cultural Capital' (2013) showed that, although Londoners' levels of engagement with the arts broadly matches the national average, in 2012–13 the UK taxpayer provided each Londoner with a cultural benefit of £68.99 per head, compared to £4.58 per head in the rest

---

[10] Howard L. Hughes, 'Theatre in London and the Inter-relationship with Tourism', *Tourism Management* 19, no. 5 (1998), 447.

[11] Claire Cochrane, *Twentieth-Century British Theatre: Industry, Art and Empire* (Cambridge: Cambridge University Press, 2011), 2–3.

[12] At the time of the 2011 census, 8.17 million lived in London: (http://www.londoncouncils.gov.uk/londonfacts/default.htm?category=2). Accessed 15 Apr. 2014. The census in the Republic during the same year described a population of 4.6 million: (http://www.cso.ie/Quicktables/GetQuickTables.aspx?FileName=CNA13.asp&TableName=Population+1901+-+2011&StatisticalProduct=DB_CN). Accessed 15 Apr. 2014. The tourist survey is described by Hughes, 'Theatre in London', 447–8.

[13] Nica Burns, 'Foreword', *Solt Annual Report 2009* (London: Solt, 2009), 1: http://www.solt.co.uk/downloads/pdfs/reports/2009-annual-report.pdf. Accessed 15 Apr. 2014.

of England.[14] That ratio is fifteen to one in favour of London, and the disparity would grow wider if private-sector arts funding were taken into account, as 82% of the £660 million awarded by the private sector in 2011–12 also went to London.[15]

Ireland has long felt the centripetal pull of Britain's well-resourced capital city, with Irish dramatists producing work in London since at least the Restoration, and there has hardly been a major Irish playwright, actor, or director who has not at some point been involved in a London production. In our own day, the city provides rich opportunities to find audiences, publicity, and skilled theatre-makers, in a way rivalled by few other locations across the world. As the Cork-born and RADA-trained actress Fiona Shaw declared, shortly before she played the title role in *Richard II* at London's National Theatre in 1995, 'I love London and there are people and places where this kind of experimentation that I am doing can be served.'[16] In the following decade she declared, 'The effect of London on Dublin has been enormous. It's the jumping-off ground isn't it? It's the Ellis Island of Irish culture.'[17]

In the important volume *Irish Theatre in England*, Richard Cave and Ben Levitas explain:

> The situation has a long history that is as true of James Shirley and George Farquhar in the seventeenth century as it is of Peg Woffington in the eighteenth or Tyrone Power in the nineteenth; Yeats and Lady Gregory were not content with the establishing of their proto-national theatre until the troupe had found acclaim in London and Oxbridge; and even today there are dramatists who prefer to première their works on English stages and actors who choose to harness their talents to London performers' agencies till Hollywood calls and cinematic success brings an income allowing a triumphant return to the homeland.[18]

As we have seen with the example of *The Shaughraun*, some visiting companies do slip when using London's playhouses as a stepping stone between Dublin and the USA; yet the British capital has nonetheless continually attracted Irish performers. In addition to hosting productions developed in Ireland, London has seen many of its own producing houses mounting Irish plays as a significant part of their repertory, and these theatres have influenced the history of modern Irish drama by premièring important works. During the past fifteen years, such playhouses have included the following five key venues:

1. The Tricycle Theatre: premièred Frank McGuinness's *Greta Garbo Came to Donegal* (2010) and Richard Norton-Taylor's verbatim piece *Bloody Sunday: Scenes from the Saville Enquiry* (2011), as well as producing revivals of work by contemporary writers such as Billy Roche.

---

[14] 63% of Londoners said they engaged three times or more annually with the arts, which was the same as the national average. Peter Stark, Christopher Gordon, and David Powell, *Rebalancing Our Cultural Capital: A Contribution to the Debate on National Policy for the Arts and Culture in England* (2013): http://www.theroccreport.co.uk/downloads/Rebalancing_FINAL_3mb.pdf, 13–14 (8). Accessed 15 Apr. 2014.

[15] Ibid., 11.

[16] Georgina Brown, 'And She's Not Bad at Tennis, Either', *Independent*, 26 May 1995.

[17] Fiona Shaw, in Richard Eyre (ed.), *Talking Theatre: Interviews with Theatre People* (London: Nick Hern Books, 2009), 78.

[18] Richard Cave and Ben Levitas, 'Introduction: Irish Theatre in England', in Richard Cave and Ben Levitas (eds.), *Irish Theatre in England* (Dublin: Carysfort Press, 2007), 1.

2. The Bush Theatre: premièred Mark O'Rowe's *Howie the Rookie* (1999), which followed the earlier première of Conor McPherson's *St Nicholas* (1997) and the English première of Enda Walsh's *Disco Pigs* (1997).
3. The Donmar Warehouse: premièred Frank McGuinness's interpretation of *Phaedra* (2006); Conor McPherson's version of *The Dance of Death* at Trafalgar Studios (2012); and McPherson's *The Night Alive* (2013).
4. The National Theatre: premièred Colin Teevan's *The Walls* (2001); Owen McCafferty's *Closing Time* (2002) and his *Scenes from the Big Picture* (2003); Martin McDonagh's *The Pillowman* (2003); Frank McGuinness's *Oedipus* (2008); and Conor McPherson's plays *The Seafarer* (2006) and *The Veil* (2011).
5. The Royal Court Theatre: premièred Conor McPherson's *The Weir* (1997) and famously collaborated with Druid in 1996–97 to bring Martin McDonagh's work to the stage, before giving the first productions of McPherson's plays *Dublin Carol* (2000) and *Shining City* (2004); Gary Mitchell's trio of work, *Trust* (1999), *The Force of Change* (2000), and *Loyal Women* (2003); as well as Tom Murphy's *Alice Trilogy* (2005), Stella Feehily's *O Go My Man* (2006), and Marina Carr's *Woman and Scarecrow* (2006).

The list of premières at these theatres is a reasonably diverse one. Admittedly, the list is male-dominated—with writers like O'Rowe, Walsh, and McPherson often favouring the monologue—but there is no fixed template for the Irish play in London. Such work might well discuss the politics of Northern Ireland or contemporary Irish social problems, but might also consist of surreal fairy tales or vampire stories.

The resourcing for such new works has also varied, although it might be noted that the average cast for the London premières listed above consisted of eight actors, a size that many regional theatres in the UK would be incapable of matching when producing new work. In addition, the list does not name any particular revivals or remountings of Irish drama in London. Yet such work has been consistently and often lavishly produced. In 2014, for example, the version of Seán O'Casey's *The Silver Tassie* at the National Theatre's Lyttleton space included a cast of twenty-five, and solved the script's awkward transition between first and second acts by featuring a tenement set that exploded in a moment of auditory and pyrotechnic overload.

When the Lyttleton remounted Enda Walsh's *Misterman* in 2011, Jamie Vartan's stage design provided a breathtakingly vast and technically accomplished set for a play that was essentially a one-man monologue, with the National Theatre gaining special permission from Lambeth Council to open the up-stage scene dock area (usually closed off, because of fire regulations) in order to deepen the space: hence, in contrast with the play's earlier stagings in Galway and New York, the London production included a second mezzanine structure and collapsible ceiling, and as Vartan puts it 'The NT was totally committed to providing the necessary back up and technical support to make it all work.'[19] Similarly, in 2008 the Old Vic theatre staged Brian Friel's *Dancing at Lughnasa* (with Andrea Corr, Niamh Cusack, and Michelle Fairley) and achieved a brilliant sense of domestic intimacy

---

[19] I am grateful to Jamie Vartan for permission to reproduce these comments from private correspondence.

FIG. 37.1 Jamie Vartan, model set design, *Misterman* by Enda Walsh (18 April 2012, Lyttleton Theatre).

Courtesy of the set and costume designer Jamie Vartan.

by staging the play in the round—something facilitated by the sponsorship of an asset management company that paid for the proscenium arch auditorium to be entirely reconfigured for the season.

Furthermore, the cultural and economic cachet of London—and its proximity to film and television makers—means that revivals of Irish plays in London are often able to draw upon some of the best, and best-known, actors on the planet. Hence London audiences have watched Holly Hunter in Marina Carr's *By the Bog of Cats* (Wyndham's Theatre, 2004), Simon Russell Beale in Boucicault's *London Assurance* (National Theatre, 2010), and Daniel Radcliffe in Martin McDonagh's *The Cripple of Inishmaan* (Noel Coward Theatre, 2013). Such actorly and material resources evidently allow Irish playwrights to explore creative avenues that would be available in few other cities: Frank McGuinness, for example, premièred a 2008 version of *Oedipus Rex* with a cast of twenty-eight, including Ralph Fiennes, at the National Theatre, before going on to create a full operatic version of Sophocles' work for English National Opera in 2014.

The role of the London theatrical agent is also central to the success of Irish drama on the British stage. In particular, Nick Marston (of A. P. Watt, and later Curtis Brown) has played a crucial, if underexplored, part in the recent flourishing of new Irish work. Marston began attending the Dublin Theatre Festival during the 1980s, at a time when writers expressed surprise at seeing a London agent at the event. He saw Declan Hughes' *Digging for Fire* there in 1992, and contacted Dominic Dromgoole (then artistic director of London's Bush Theatre) to arrange a transfer to the Bush. As well as hosting the transfer, the Bush subsequently premièred Hughes' *New Morning* in 1993. Next, in 1995, Marston watched Conor McPherson's *This Lime Tree Bower* at Dublin's Crypt Theatre, and arranged a 1996 transfer to the Bush, which then commissioned McPherson's 1997 play *St Nicholas*. (At almost exactly the same time as Marston's discovery of McPherson, the talents of Martin McDonagh were first being uncovered by Marston's friend and colleague at A. P. Watt, Rod Hall). Marston felt similarly impressed by Enda Walsh's *Disco Pigs* at Dublin's Da Club in 1996, and arranged for the work to appear at the Bush in 1997; and when he read Mark O'Rowe's *Howie the Rookie* Marston again organized the première at the Bush, which happened in 1999.

Marston describes his role in nurturing such talent:

> These are wonderful writers. So my job is mostly about providing encouragement and support. For example, after initially bringing McPherson's work to London, I introduced him to Ian Rickson [the artistic director of the Royal Court from 1998 to 2006], and Rickson commissioned *The Weir*, and also took *Dublin Carol*, which was the play that opened the new Royal Court in 2000. And more recently, McPherson wrote *The Night Alive*, which I arranged for production at the Donmar Warehouse. I think it's always been important for the Irish writers I've championed to have their stage and film work seen outside Dublin: they are also international writers, and it's important for the work to be accessed by different audiences.[20]

London's theatre managers have also sought to stage work that explores some of the nuances of Irish identity in the city itself. One venue, the Tricycle Theatre—according to its artistic director from 1984 to 2012, Nicholas Kent—specifically set about 'doing Irish work at a time when this area was known as County Kilburn'.[21] The theatre served its diverse community by equally promoting black theatre, and some of its most notable work considered the interaction between black and Irish cultures (famously Mustapha Matura's *The Playboy of the West Indies* in 1984). With such a history, in more recent years the Tricycle has continued to explore the way that Irishness might be malleable and prone to invention: most notably in Marie Jones's *Stones in His Pockets* (1999, 2000, 2011); Shaw's *John Bull's Other Island* (2003); and Jimmy Murphy's *The Kings of the Kilburn High Road* (2001).

At other times and places in London, similar questions about Irish affiliation have also been raised, both with the staging of work set in the city (such as McPherson's *St Nicholas* or Murphy's *The Kings of the Kilburn High Road*) and with the production of scripts by Irish writers who were born in, or who are long-term residents of, London. Martin McDonagh and Enda Walsh, for instance, have shown a repeated concern about the authenticity and societal effect of different kinds of Irish identity. Indeed, one of the most critically and commercially successful Irish plays on the London stage in recent years has been Enda Walsh's *The Walworth Farce* (National Theatre, 2008), which presents the story of a family who are long-term residents of England but remain holed up in a flat in London's Walworth Road, continually acting out fictionalized scenes from their old life in Cork and deeply wary of any engagement with the city in which they actually live.

---

[20] I am grateful to Nick Marston for his permission to reproduce these comments from our discussions of 22 May 2014.

[21] Quoted by Terry Stoller, *Tales of the Tricycle Theatre* (London: Bloomsbury, 2013), 95.

PITFALLS

There are, of course, a number of problematic aspects to be identified in London's prominent position in the Irish theatrical world. For one thing, the battles of the Irish revolution in the early twentieth century were fought—in large part—in order to wrest political control of the country away from London, and Cave and Levitas point to a nationalist suspicion that Irish theatre practitioners working in London constitute 'a long roll-call of renegade talent'.[22] Victor Merriman has argued that post-1922 Ireland might in many respects be considered a 'successor state' to the previous colonial one, and the fact that Irish theatre-makers have continued to seek London as a goal may emphasize just how pre-existing notions of cultural prestige have proved difficult to overhaul.[23] Indeed, in the years since Irish political independence, London-based critics have demonstrated a longstanding condescension towards the Irish. In 1948 T. S. Eliot, in *Notes towards the Definition of Culture*, described Ireland, Scotland, and Wales as 'satellite cultures' dependent on England as a gravitational centre, a centre that benefits in turn from their peripheral influences.[24] Eight years later, Kenneth Tynan famously rearticulated this viewpoint, when he commented that 'it is Ireland's sacred duty to send over, every few years, a playwright to save the English theatre from inarticulate glumness'.[25] When the Abbey Theatre's version of *The Shaughraun* tanked in 2005, a similar sense of condescension could be found in some high-profile reviews: the *Observer*'s Susannah Clapp, for example, lapsed into her own cod-Irish when she complained that the show 'must have lost edge in its transfer from Dublin, where it went down a storaum' [*sic*].[26] As Stuart Hall notes, such a perspective tends to read the particularities of the most economically prosperous and politically dominant part of Britain as providing the apparently timeless standards by which the rest of the world might be judged, whilst doing little to uncover or challenge the historical peculiarities of those hegemonic formations.[27]

In addition, with London exerting such an influence, there is a risk of Irish theatre playing it safe by emulating past successes, and so avoiding the avant-garde or experimental. London's theatre industry is fundamentally connected to the city's broader tourist industry, and this has an effect upon what is performed there, as Howard Hughes argues: 'In order to satisfy consumer demand and enable effective signification to the consumer, both the tourist and arts industries have standardized their products. They are made "safe: and predictable through packaging and they require limited consumer involvement.'[28] Despite the diversity we have noted in Irish plays at a number of London venues, the attitude that Hughes

[22] Cave and Levitas, *Irish Theatre in England*, 1.

[23] Victor Merriman, *Because We Are Poor: Irish Theatre in the 1990s* (Dublin: Carysfort Press, 2011), 26.

[24] T. S. Eliot, *Notes Towards the Definition of Culture* (London: Faber & Faber, 1948), 54–5.

[25] Kenneth Tynan, 'The End of the Noose', *Observer*, 27 May 1956.

[26] Susannah Clapp, 'Forest's Grump', *Observer*, 12 June 2005.

[27] Stuart Hall, 'Political Belonging in a World of Multiple Identities', in Steven Vertovec and Robin Cohen (eds.), *Conceiving Cosmopolitanism: Theory, Context, and Practice* (Oxford: Oxford University Press, 2002), 28–9.

[28] Hughes, 'Theatre in London', 446.

identifies can affect the content of shows produced by Irish theatre-makers in London—for example, when a musical version of Roddy Doyle's *The Commitments* opened at the Palace Theatre in 2014, the material was quickly adjusted after negative spectator response (one cast member observed that 'The swear words have been toned down a bit').[29] Such worries may also affect the overall packaging and perception of work that arrives in the city after being developed elsewhere: for instance, when *The Shaughraun* came to London in 2005, its connection to McColgan's previous show, *Riverdance*, was prominently emphasized in the opening pages of the Albery's theatre programme, even though the almost identical programme sold at the Abbey's most recent run of the same show had made no mention of *Riverdance*.[30]

The broader creative effect of such tendencies towards standardization were observed by Nicholas Grene and Patrick Lonergan, who hosted a meeting of the Irish Theatrical Diaspora network at Galway in 2009, and subsequently wrote:

> It is often assumed that the success of an Irish play on Broadway or in London's West End must be of benefit for theatre within Ireland itself, we had noted—and to a great extent we found that assumption borne out by the evidence. Yet we also discovered some evidence of an impoverishment of theatre in parts of Ireland: a homogenization of the kinds of plays being produced, a reduction in the number of new works by leading authors being premièred in Ireland, and a gradual decline or disappearance of companies with strong links to their localities.[31]

An Irish playwright or touring company seeking to confront audiences with surprising and counterintuitive themes may indeed be hindered by a marketing strategy aimed at London and New York. For, as John P. Harrington has pointed out, when Irish theatre-makers arrive in New York, their attempts to move outside a 'nitch' risks 'the "Coals-to-Newcastle" complaint: if the Irish National Theatre comes to New York with work inspired by Grotowski or Peter Brook instead of Synge or Friel, they are viewed as strangers from afar bearing nothing but what America already had.'[32] Concerns about this 'nitch' may become increasingly urgent as London's tourist industry pivots away from the Anglosphere and towards the Far East, bringing the question of whether the spoken-word dramas at which the Irish have excelled will retain a cultural pre-eminence.

MADE IN LIVERPOOL

London remains the best-known and best-resourced theatrical destination in Britain, but, as we shall now see, during the last decade and a half, the new plays staged in the country's

---

[29] Mark Hennessy, 'A Strong Commitment: Deco Wins Over the West End', *Irish Times*, 28 Jan. 2013: http://www.irishtimes.com/life-and-style/people/a-strong-commitment-deco-wins-over-the-west-end-1.1669723. Accessed 15 Apr. 2014.

[30] Abbey Theatre, *The Shaughraun*, programme of 23 Nov. 2004; Albery Theatre, *The Shaughraun*, programme of 8 June 2005.

[31] Nicholas Grene and Patrick Lonergan, 'Introduction', in Nicholas Grene and Patrick Lonergan (eds.), *Irish Drama: Local and Global Perspectives* (Dublin: Carysfort Press, 2012), 1.

[32] John Harrington, 'Introduction', in John Harrington (ed.), *Irish Theater in America: Essays on Irish Theatrical Diaspora* (Syracuse, NY: Syracuse University Press, 2009), xv.

other cities have repeatedly investigated forms of Irish identity that involve specific local attachments, associations, and affiliations.

From 2003, the Everyman and Playhouse theatres in Liverpool premièred at least twenty-three new scripts by local writers in the play series 'Made in Liverpool'. This series presented work that originated in Liverpool, was produced by the Liverpool Everyman and Playhouse, and had been specifically written for those spaces by dramatists from or in the region. Audiences watched new work by Laurence Wilson, Esther Wilson, and Jonathan Harvey, but one of the striking features of this series was the Irish content of some of its most prominent productions. According to the current literary associate of the Everyman and Playhouse, Lindsay Rodden (herself from Donegal), there was no explicit intention to make 'Made in Liverpool' address Irish themes, but the idea of Ireland emerged as something that is 'naturally there, knitted into the fabric of the city for many writers'.[33] After all, Liverpool has long been home to an extraordinarily large Irish population: the first modern census of the country, in 1841, records 49,639 Irish-born people in Liverpool, or 17.3% of the city's population.[34] Thus, as the former dramaturge and literary manager at the Liverpool Everyman and Playhouse, Suzanne Bell, puts it, although ideas of nationality and cultural identity were not 'discussed as a starting point' for any of the 'Made in Liverpool' plays:

> The history of the Irish communities in Liverpool and the associated notion of storytelling, community, drama and an oral tradition is something that was certainly discussed within wider groups of playwrights, including the playwrights that you mention [those involved in 'Made in Liverpool'], and there is perhaps something about the energy, atmosphere and tone of Liverpool that I would suggest is very particular to the identity of the city and its artists that one could perhaps suggest derived from the Irish ancestry of the city.[35]

One such play from the 'Made in Liverpool' series is the 2006 piece by Chloë Moss, *The Way Home*, which is set in and around an Irish Travellers' site in the city. Moss's plot works within a specific local context: not only are there numerous expressions and phrases that locate the play in Liverpool ('It would've been boss, that'; 'Go 'ead then') but the Travellers' site depicted on stage is a recognizable version of the real-life Tara Park, a location set up for Irish Travellers by Liverpool City Council in the 1970s, and which had been brought to regional prominence shortly before the production by the council's decision to modernize the site at a cost of £800,000.[36] The play therefore describes how Irish Travellers might provoke ire but also affection from others, and ultimately shows that both the Travellers and those in the wider community might feel equally uprooted and unsettled at different times. In making this point, Moss's script pulls apart any easy binary assumptions about national identity. At one moment, for example, the English character of Bobby and the

[33] I am grateful to Lindsay Rodden for these email comments. I am also indebted to Vic Merriman for his invaluable advice about Irish theatre in Liverpool.
[34] John Belchem, *Irish, Catholic and Scouse: The History of the Liverpool Irish 1800–1939* (Liverpool: Liverpool University Press, 2007), 7.
[35] I am grateful to Suzanne Bell for permission to reproduce these comments from private correspondence.
[36] Chloë Moss, *The Way Home* (London: Nick Hern Books, 2006), 15, 32; 'All Mod Cons at Travellers' Camp', *Liverpool Echo*, 14 Aug. 2003: http://www.liverpoolecho.co.uk/news/liverpool-news/mod-cons-travellers-camp-3552334. Accessed 15 Apr. 2014.

Irish Traveller character of Daniel talk to one another, with Bobby making a surprising discovery:

BOBBY.   Where yer from?
DANIEL.   Here.
BOBBY.   Liverpool?
DANIEL.   Here.
BOBBY.   Yer speak . . . Irish, isn't it? Yer accent like.
DANIEL.   I was born here.[37]

Thus, Moss complicates any simplistic notions about belonging, by pointing out that, in parts of Liverpool at least, people may speak with an apparently Irish voice in spite of having been born and raised in the English city. Such an emphasis draws attention to what Mary Hickman suggests is the dominant 'myth of homogeneity' in Britain, which has 'assumed that all people who were white smoothly assimilated into the "British way of life"', and which has presented particular problems for those suggesting alternative forms of allegiance.[38]

A similar point was made in 2007 when 'Made in Liverpool' premièred Stephen Sharkey's play *The May Queen*. Sharkey's work is set during the Liverpool Blitz of 1941, and tells the story of how Frank Donohue has been murdered by his wife's lover, with her two children subsequently seeking revenge. The play avoids revealing the place of birth or precise nationality of its protagonists, but—in addition to the fact that the play is suffused with a Marian piety—the characters have Irish names (Vinnie Phelan, Eileen McGrath, Father Quiggan, and so forth); the matriarch of the piece describes how her incontinent son 'could shit for Ireland, that one'; and at one point the characters sing 'a sentimental Irish song'.[39] Yet these characters are all shown inhabiting specific parts of Liverpool, and make little mention of Irish places or personalities. How, then, should such people be described? Are they English or Irish, or something else entirely? Can you really be 'diasporic' if you have little notion of yourself as having a homeland to which you wish to return? Notably, the play's only character to talk specifically about going to Ireland is the only on-stage character who comes from outside this Liverpool community altogether, the German Jewish Liliane, who describes how her dead brother wanted 'to go to Ireland. He was very romantic about it. He read too many poems about dark-eyed girls, and death, and the hungry sea.'[40]

Thus, in *The May Queen*, the idea of journeying to Ireland comes only from an inappropriate cooption of Jewish experience, with the Donohues and Collinses of Liverpool having little connection to such narratives of diasporic exile. At one of the most telling points in the play, Sharkey illuminates these questions of belonging with a biblical example:

THERESA.   Jesus was a Jew.
ANGELA.   How d'yer work that one out?
THERESA.   On the cross, wasn't it. King of the Jews.

---

[37] Moss, *The Way Home*, 22.
[38] Mary J. Hickman, 'Reconstructing Deconstructing "Race": British Political Discourses about the Irish in Britain', *Ethnic and Racial Studies* 21, no. 2 (1998), 305.
[39] Stephen Sharkey, *The May Queen* (London: Methuen, 2007), 68, 67.   [40] Ibid., 65.

PHELAN.   Aye, yeah, that's what the Romans called him, like—
THERESA.   He was born a Jew. His mother was Jewish.
ANGELA.   Go 'way. Our Lady?[41]

Amongst other things, this passage raises the question of what kind of cultural identity children might inherit from their parents. After all, the play's murdered husband apparently spent his time trying to persuade his son and his son's friend to 'join the IRA', but has done so in vain, with both boys ending up in the British army.[42] Despite that failure, a whole set of other cultural behaviours has been inherited from Ireland by these Liverpool-based characters, and Sharkey underscores this point at a formal level in the fact that this part of the play is a rewriting of one of the best-known moments from the most canonical work of Irish literature. Sharkey's script echoes the point in the 'Cyclops' episode of Joyce's *Ulysses* when Bloom angrily declares that 'the Saviour was a jew and his father was a jew'.[43] Through this emulation of Joyce, Sharkey develops the play's recurring question about the morality of Irish wartime neutrality in the face of the Holocaust, but also emphasizes how the behaviour of those in Liverpool might rely on a deep engagement with Irish precedents.

In 2007, 'Made in Liverpool' premièred Lizzie Nunnery's *Intemperance*, a play that again revolves around the examination of a particular kind of Irish identity in the city. This drama, set in 1854, describes the family of Fergal Monahan, who once lived in Omeath, Co. Louth, but who subsequently moved to Dublin, where his daughter Millie lived as a toddler. This duo then moved to Liverpool, where Millie's child Ruari was born and raised. Yet, although the Liverpudlian Ruari boasts that 'I was born here', he still realizes that he has an outsiderly status, knowing that he is seen as 'a Mick'; failing to recall the name of the English patron saint ('What is it? English guy. Dragon-killer'); and realizing that his sister is perceived as an 'Irish whore'.[44] Just as in Stephen Sharkey's *The May Queen*, Nunnery's play asks how an Irish cultural identity might be manifested in those who do not live in Ireland. In theme, the play explores how Ruari might be 'The bleedin ghost of yer bleedin Da'; whilst at a formal level Nunnery's play broadly echoes the storyline of Seán O'Casey's *Juno and the Paycock*, with members of an impoverished family living in the slums, surrounded by child death, but behaving as though they are about to transcend their current circumstances because of the false expectation of future wealth.[45]

Of course, these plays by Stephen Sharkey, Chloë Moss, and Lizzie Nunnery cannot straightforwardly be labelled 'Irish drama'. The scripts are each set in England, and are written by playwrights who were all born and raised in and around Liverpool. Yet each of these works seeks to analyse and disturb such straightforward notions of categorization, asking: how do we describe an individual's national identity if that identity is profoundly shaped by Ireland, not as a result of living in Ireland, but by having that culture passed down through family members and other acquaintances in the city of Liverpool? As Lizzie Nunnery puts it:

I am of Irish descent but a far way back. My great grandparents on both sides were Irish and in exploring Irish immigration through *Intemperance* I couldn't help but reflect on what

---

[41] Ibid., 25.   [42] Ibid., 7.   [43] James Joyce, *Ulysses* (1922) (London: Penguin, 1992), 445.
[44] Lizzie Nunnery, *Intemperance* (London: Faber & Faber, 2007), 37, 83, 36, 86.
[45] Ibid., 50.

their experience might have been. I was very interested in the idea of Liverpool as a cultural melting pot [. . .]. The characters in *Intemperance* identify themselves as Irish even though members of the younger generation have spent the vast majority of their lives in Liverpool. I think Liverpool today retains some of that sense of otherness—its inhabitants are often hesitant to call themselves English, and I tried to show the roots of this in my play.[46]

Stephen Sharkey has similarly commented, 'judging by the Irishness of my surname I do believe my family on my father's father's side is descended from Irish stock', and, '[i]n setting out to write *The May Queen* I wanted to reflect some of the murk and ambiguity of Liverpool's position in the War—a major strategic port (and therefore a target for German bombing), but also steeped in Irish culture, and therefore face to face with Irish neutrality and all its complexities.'[47]

BIRMINGHAM

At the same time as the Liverpool Everyman and Playhouse theatres explored the nuances of local Irish identity in 'Made in Liverpool', the Birmingham Repertory Theatre set about something similar. In 1998 the Birmingham playhouse opened a new studio space, 'The Door', which was intended to focus on new work that addressed contemporary concerns. As Robert Leach puts it, 'The policy here was to present work by new writers, many of them radical and from minority groups [. . .]. It was a space for new ideas and different approaches.'[48] Within its first six years, 'The Door' had premièred new work by more than fifteen different writers (including, most famously, Gurpreet Kaur Bhatti's *Behzti*),[49] and these premières included drama that gave a provocative interrogation of Irish identity.

Like Liverpool, Birmingham had long been a focus for Irish migration to the UK, with many people in the Midlands city boasting an Irish heritage. Indeed, in the mid-1960s, 16.5% of people born in Birmingham had at least one Irish-born parent.[50] Since the late 1990s, the city has hosted what is claimed as the third-largest St Patrick's Day parade in the world. But, in addition, Birmingham was also the site of the most lethal bombing planned by the IRA during the Troubles, when in 1974 bombs detonated in two city-centre pubs, injuring 162 and killing 21 (four of the dead being Irish citizens). The expression of Irish identity in Birmingham therefore became, during the late twentieth century, something problematic and controversial.[51] And at the dawn of the twenty-first century, it was the complex nature of this local Irish identity that was probed by new work at 'The Door'.

[46] I am grateful to Lizzie Nunnery for her permission to reproduce this quotation from private correspondence.
[47] I am grateful to Stephen Sharkey for his permission to reproduce this quotation from private correspondence.
[48] Robert Leach, *Theatre Studies: The Basics*, 2nd edn. (London: Routledge, 2013), 99.
[49] The 2004 production of *Bezhti* (Punjabi, 'Dishonour') had to be cancelled by the Birmingham Repertory Theatre, following protests by the local Sikh community.
[50] Corporate Statistician, Library of Birmingham, 'The Nationality of Children Born in 1964, Table 11' and 'Trends, the Nationality of Children Born in 1965', in *Ethnic Origins of Birmingham Children 1966–81*, Birmingham Central Statistical Office, LF 40–1.
[51] For a full discussion, see James Moran, *Irish Birmingham: A History* (Liverpool: Liverpool University Press, 2010), 185–210.

In February 1999 'The Door' premièred a play by a 36-year-old Dubliner, Declan Croghan, called *Paddy Irishman, Paddy Englishman and Paddy . . . ?* Croghan intended the script to focus particularly on the experience of the Irish outside Ireland, as he put it: 'this is written from the perspective of an Irish person in Britain'.[52] He described how 'There was a great freedom about coming to England — it was a place to grow. But each time there was a bombing on the mainland the community would withdraw into itself. Even intelligent middle-class English people, they wouldn't say anything, but you felt it.'[53] Croghan therefore constructed a play that broadly echoes the plot of Seán O'Casey's *The Shadow of a Gunman*, but updated the action so that a hardline IRA man who objects to the Good Friday Agreement leaves a bomb with two unknowing Irish immigrants in a London bedsit. The play includes descriptions of death and killing that had a particular resonance when delivered so close to the site of the 1974 attacks in Birmingham. At one point in *Paddy Irishman*, for example, one of the flatmates realizes 'There has been a big shoot out down in the pub', describing how an acquaintance has committed mass murder in a bar, where 'He storms in and wipes out the whole lot of them'.[54] Such descriptions of an IRA pub massacre conjured up disturbing memories for members of an audience in Birmingham, particularly when, a few moments later, the same flatmate realizes that he has been left with a bomb and sarcastically contemplates whether to 'plant the bomb and then we will phone up and give them a warning'.[55]

Croghan thus presented the audience with a kind of warped and distorted version of the 1974 attack; and he was not the only new writer in Birmingham's playhouse to do so. The subject of Irish terrorism appeared in another première at 'The Door' in 2005, when the theatre staged Billy Cowan's *Smilin' Through*. Cowan came from a working-class family in Newtownards in Co. Down, but had trained part-time as an actor at the Birmingham School of Speech and Drama, and for about a year was a member of the Birmingham Rep Youth Theatre, performing in Berkoff's *Agamemnon*. Cowan's own tongue-in-cheek play depicts a terrorist from the 'Irish Queer Liberation Army':

TERRORIST.   [. . .] We're a newly formed organisation of men and women dedicated to the cause—complete liberation of all queers in Ireland. We use whatever means are necessary to secure our rights to self determination.
KYLE.   You're serious?
TERRORIST.   Of course I'm bloody serious. Don't you think it's about time the people in this country were forced to recognise the rights of us Queers? [. . .] The armalite is the only language the people of this island recognise.[56]

As with the earlier work at 'The Door', Cowan's work set about refiguring the familiar imagery associated with the Irish bomber. Here, the terrorist is a figure who does 'kill people', but who is also accused of wearing 'combats as a fashion statement'. When premièred at 'The Door', these plays by Croghan and Cowan issued a challenge to local spectators: might

[52] Quoted by Terry Grimley, 'Gunpowder and Glamour', *Birmingham Post*, 3 Feb. 1999, 15.
[53] Ibid.
[54] Declan Croghan, *Paddy Irishman, Paddy Englishman, and Paddy ...?* (London: Faber & Faber, 1999), 55.
[55] Ibid., 60.
[56] I am grateful to Billy Cowan for permission to quote from the performance script of *Smilin' Through*.

it now be time to reconsider, and even to laugh at, a comedy involving the area's most bitter ideas about Irishness?

The year after staging Croghan's work, the Birmingham Repertory Theatre premièred a drama that addressed the legacy of the pub bombings still more directly. The play *Belonging* was written by Kaite O'Reilly, who had been born and grew up in Birmingham, and who had been 10 years old at the time of the terrorist attacks of 1974. O'Reilly has described how, although she had lived in Birmingham, she viewed her parents' home in Dublin as where she really belonged: 'In my family we always talked about going home for the summer and meant Ireland. I never really saw Birmingham as my home.'[57] As a writer, she began to wonder, 'Can you feel homesick for a place you've never lived?', and decided

> to write about the complex relationship between the English West Midlands and its Irish community. Growing up Irish in Birmingham in the 1970s was a formative and defining experience. I'm sure like many immigrants from other parts of the world I was constantly aware of my duality—English in Ireland and Irish in England—yet this identity was further complicated by the effects of the 1974 IRA bombing campaign, when a war was carried out— literally—on our doorstop.[58]

In *Belonging*, O'Reilly therefore tells the story of an elderly Irish-born woman, who by the 1990s has lived for many years in Birmingham but who longs to return home, in large part because of what happened during the Troubles. This character angrily tells her daughter:

> I'll tell you about the heart being blown out of the city we helped build. I'll tell you what it was like to be spat at in the street, having names hurled after you if you so much as opened your mouth and they heard the accent. Made guilty by association.[59]

The daughter has a very different sense of identity, although her allegiances are no less vexed. She was born in Birmingham rather than Ireland, and despite the fact that she desperately strives to be Irish, she constantly fails to achieve the authenticity she craves. She therefore describes the disorienting feeling of being a second-generation Irishwoman: 'I have the parentage, citizenship—bank account. I know my history, culture—I'm even learning the bloody language—but I'm still Plastic Paddy, hand-crafted in Digbeth.'[60] Here the play comes close to articulating the problem described by Aidan Arrowsmith, who observes that the second-generation Irish in Britain may feel particularly saddled by the remit of '[e]xclusive nationalisms', framed as 'doubly inauthentic: not quite English, neither are they "truly" Irish'.[61]

CONCLUSION

Of course, the Irish shows of 'The Door' and 'Made in Liverpool' have not gained widespread name recognition. But what they do indicate, along with the better-known work first

---

[57] Alison Jones, 'A Touch of the Irish at Home or Away', *Birmingham Post*, 4 Dec. 2000.
[58] Kaite O'Reilly, Author's Note, programme for *Belonging* (Birmingham Repertory Theatre, 2000).
[59] Kaite O'Reilly, *Belonging* (London: Faber & Faber, 2000), 76.
[60] Ibid., 88.
[61] Aidan Arrowsmith, 'Plastic Paddy: Negotiating Identity in Second-Generation "Irish-English" Writing', *Irish Studies Review* 8, no. 1 (2000), 35.

staged at London venues including the Royal Court, National Theatre, and Tricycle, is that the British theatre, when staging work on Irish themes, is willing to go beyond familiar stereotypes and explore provocative new theatrical realms—including those of the Irish Traveller, the gay Irish terrorist, or the disorientated second-generation Irishwoman. Impressively, much new work premièred in London, Liverpool, and Birmingham has avoided simplistic conceptions of Irishness, employing national paradigms but consistently highlighting the way that various rifts and differences might traverse such conceptions of nation. And although it has been beyond the scope of this chapter to survey Irish theatre in Wales and Scotland (including the important Edinburgh Traverse), the fact that the distinctive Irish identity of locations such as Kilburn, Digbeth, or Tara Park has been articulated onstage offers a promising sign that, in an era of increased devolution, the theatre has the potential to continue speaking of the particularities of Irish experience in diverse places across these islands.

When London hosted the Olympic Games in 2012, the event began with a theatrical ceremony that was labelled internationally as 'Very British', and yet depended upon the participation of those with significant Irish connections.[62] The contribution of theatre-makers including director Danny Boyle, writer Frank Cottrell Boyce, and actor Kenneth Branagh indicated just how much the British stage has been enriched by Irish migration to the country, and demonstrated that Irish theatre is by no means confined to the island of Ireland. But it is not only in such a lavishly funded theatrical jamboree, aimed largely at international viewers, that such an Irish dynamic can be seen. In small-scale London venues such as the Bush and the Tricycle, and in regional theatres such as those of Liverpool and Birmingham, the playhouse stage has been facilitating a dynamic process of interchange between cultures, and allowing surprising new perspectives to emerge. There are dangers, to be sure, in the prominent part played by Britain on the Irish theatrical scene—not least the risk of Irish productions being homogenized by commercial pressures and of being judged according to (the sometimes outmoded or inaccurate) perceptions and prejudices that prevail in the old imperial centre—but there is also much to be gained for an Irish theatre that utilizes connections with the diversity of modern Britain in order to find new audiences, new collaborative possibilities, and new ways of engaging with the world.

[62] For details, see Paul Edmondson, Paul Prescott, and Erin Sullivan (eds.), *A Year of Shakespeare: Re-living the World Shakespeare Festival* (London: Bloomsbury, 2013). For the perceived 'Britishness' of the Olympic opening, see Evan Osnos, 'The Ceremony and the Swimmer: China Watches the Olympics', *New Yorker*, 31 July 2012: http://www.newyorker.com/online/blogs/evanosnos/2012/07/china-opening-ceremonies-and-swimmer-ye-shiwen.html. Accessed 14 Apr. 2014.

....

CHAPTER 38

IRISH THEATRE IN EUROPE

....

ONDŘEJ PILNÝ

WRITING in 1999, Nicholas Grene asserted that Irish theatre was 'a distinct and distinctly marketable phenomenon'.[1] While this was and still remains a very apt comment as regards the UK, the US, and other areas of the Anglophone world which feature a significant Irish diaspora, evidence from Continental Europe shows that the situation there has been different, or at least much more complex. As has been the case in English-speaking countries, the work of Irish playwrights has enjoyed an enthusiastic reception in Continental theatres for more than a century; however, the reflection of Irish drama or theatre as a distinct phenomenon has been minimal. Together with a mapping of what kind of Irish plays have fared well in various parts of Europe and why, the present chapter will thus attempt to unravel the reasons for the overall lack of engagement with the specifics of Irish theatre.

IRISH OR BRITISH? POSTCOLONIAL OR ANGLOPHONE?

In the early decades of the twentieth century, plays by Oscar Wilde and Bernard Shaw became extremely popular across Europe. The production histories of these plays vary from country to country, depending on theatrical tradition and audience tastes. Productions of *Salomé* were often associated with Decadent or avant-garde artists and poets, but it is Wilde's comedies that have been in constant demand in the opulent theatres of cities such as Vienna. Shaw's plays of ideas were a particular favourite in Spain before the Civil War as well as in pre-Second World War Czechoslovakia, where Shaw was held in high regard not only as a playwright but also as a prominent public intellectual whose views were frequently reported by national dailies. A remarkable resurgence of his work occurred in German-speaking countries in the 1960s. This was in contrast to the virtual disappearance of Shaw's political dramas from Eastern Europe, especially after 1989, where the obligation to view art through a prism of ideology had finally been lifted, and as a result, a general disinclination

---

[1] Nicholas Grene, *The Politics of Irish Drama: Plays in Context from Boucicault to Friel* (Cambridge: Cambridge University Press, 1999), 262.

to have theatre discuss political issues prevailed. Regardless of the country and the decade, however, Wilde and Shaw have almost universally been perceived as English. This tendency has been recurrent in Europe also in the case of more recent playwrights, and as Werner Huber has pointed out, for instance, in relation to German-speaking countries, even the most contemporary Irish drama is 'more often than not (and more often than is legitimate) subsumed under the general rubric of "British/English Theatre"'.[2] The inclination towards an 'Englishing' of Wilde and Shaw is easily explained, given their association with the London theatre scene and their residence in England, together with the absence of an independent Irish state (all too often identified as the primary sign of the existence of an autonomous national culture) at the moment when their reputations were being forged, and perhaps most importantly by the absence of Irish themes, characters, or settings in their work. On the other hand, the regular failure to regard the Irish origin of contemporary plays or authors as significant is a more intricate issue. Clearly, the fading importance of the national in the context of globalization has been an important factor in the reception of playwrights such as Martin McDonagh, whose dark comedies—notwithstanding the rural Irish setting and a version of Irish dialect present in the first five—have been viewed rather in the context of British In-Yer-Face theatre,[3] and associated with the grotesque humour featured in US and British gangland films so popular in the 1990s. Furthermore, the trend among new Irish authors of McDonagh's generation and younger to put less emphasis on typical Irish subject matter or setting, and to turn away from the traditional naturalism of Irish theatre, has made the identification of their work with a national culture a matter of secondary importance for international audiences.

As regards the lack of a perception of Irish theatre as a distinct phenomenon, the single major exception in its modern history is provided by the activities of the Abbey Theatre, particularly in the early decades of its existence, when the efforts of W. B. Yeats, Lady Gregory, and J. M. Synge to set up a national theatre were widely reported on the Continent. As a matter of fact, the reputation of the Abbey as an outstanding and autonomous cultural venture was furthered through the promotion of Synge's plays by enthusiastic European practitioners, translators, and critics. These included Karel Mušek in Bohemia, who made the first translation of *The Shadow of the Glen* and produced it in Prague (1906), and followed it with the translation of Synge's other plays, a series of detailed articles on the Abbey and on Irish theatre, and the publication of most of Synge's work in Czechoslovakia; Max Meyerfeld in Germany, whose first translation of *The Well of the Saints* may have met with a tepid response from the audience in Berlin (also in 1906) but still placed Synge at the forefront of a generation of international playwrights with critics and theatre-makers in Europe; and Maurice Bourgeois, an early promoter of Synge in France and author of the first critical study dedicated to the playwright, whose translation of *The Playboy of the Western World* was produced at the Théâtre de l'Oeuvre in Paris in 1913.[4] While the

---

[2] Werner Huber, 'Contemporary Irish Theatre in German-Speaking Countries', in Nicholas Grene and Patrick Lonergan (eds.), *Irish Drama: Local and Global Perspectives* (Dublin: Carysfort Press, 2012), 83.

[3] Ibid., 83–4.

[4] See Ondřej Pilný, 'The Translator's Playwright: Karel Mušek and J. M. Synge', in Patrick Lonergan (ed.), *Synge and His Influences* (Dublin: Carysfort Press, 2011), 153–80, 295–9; Anthony Roche. 'Synge, Brecht, and the Hiberno-German Connection', *Hungarian Journal of English and American Studies*

attention given to Synge and the Abbey in these countries was due to the originality of their work, and in part also to the stormy reception of the initial productions of Synge's plays in Dublin, it was the cultural nationalism of the new Dublin theatre and of the Irish Literary Revival in general that drew the attention of commentators in Galicia, Catalonia, and the Basque Country in the 1920s because of its appeal to the nationalist movements there.[5]

The political context in the target country has been of significance also in Hungary, where modern Irish drama has hardly ever been 'subsumed under the general rubric of "British/ English Theatre"', to return to Huber's phrase. When the Treaty of Trianon (1920) determined the borders of Hungary after the defeat of the Austro-Hungarian Monarchy in the First World War , Hungary lost over 70% of its prewar territory, and over 30% of ethnic Hungarians who had previously lived in the Hungarian Kingdom found themselves outside the borders of the new state. The Treaty of Trianon left a considerable scar on the national consciousness, and, as Mária Kurdi has put it, the perceived injustice 'strengthened Hungarians' sensitivity to the troubled historical experience of other small nations as well as national and cultural minorities'.[6] This also explains the rise in interest in the decolonization of Ireland and its culture. Parallels that were being made between Hungary and Ireland as small nations became more emphatic due to the deplorable treatment of ethnic Hungarians in the surrounding states of Slovakia, Yugoslavia, and Romania, the latter particularly in the region of Transylvania after the communist dictator Nicolae Ceauşescu had taken over. The Hungarian language and culture were actively suppressed, and policies of forceful assimilation were pursued in all these countries. This situation encouraged Hungarian scholars to develop analogies between Hungarian and Irish culture in regard to colonialism and its aftermath; indeed, postcolonial approaches have been prevalent in the work of recent Hungarian commentators on Irish drama and theatre, such as Csilla Bertha and Mária Kurdi.[7] Moreover, the colonial/postcolonial analogies have become a focal point for Hungarian theatre practitioners working outside the borders of the Hungarian republic, that is, in areas that have been involved in an effort to revive their culture and reclaim their right to use their language after the fall of the Iron Curtain: for instance, Brian Friel's *Translations* has had two remarkable productions in the towns of Cluj (Kolozsvár) and Oradea (Nagyvárad) in 2000 and 2006 respectively, with a new translation of the play into the Transylvanian dialect of Hungarian commissioned for the Cluj production.[8]

10, nos. 1 and 2 (2004), 19–25; Maurice Bourgeois, *John Millington Synge and the Irish Theatre* (London: Constable, 1913).

[5] For details, see Antonio Raúl de Toro Santos and David Clark, *British and Irish Writers in the Spanish Periodical Press/Escritores británicos e irlandeses en la prensa periódica española, 1900–1965* (A Coruña: Netbiblo, 2007), and Antonio Raúl de Toro Santos, *La literatura irlandesa en España* [Irish Literature in Spain] (A Coruña: Netbiblo, 2007).

[6] Mária Kurdi, 'Transplanting the Work of "That Rooted Man": The Reception of John Millington Synge's Drama in Hungary', *Comparative Drama* 41, no. 2 (2007), 221.

[7] For a representative example, see Mária Kurdi and Csilla Bertha, 'Hungarian Perspectives on Brian Friel's Theatre after *Dancing at Lughnasa*', in Dermot Bolger (ed.), *Druids, Dudes and Beauty Queens: The Changing Face of Irish Theatre* (Dublin: New Island, 2001), 173–95. In this essay, Bertha also mentions having to smuggle copies of Irish plays in Hungarian translation and her work on Yeats to Transylvania in the 1980s.

[8] See Csilla Bertha, 'Brian Friel Performances in Hungarian Theatres: Problems in Theatrical Adaptation', in Mária Kurdi (ed.), *Literary and Cultural Relations: Ireland, Hungary, and Central and Eastern Europe* (Dublin: Carysfort Press, 2009), 90–1, 94–8.

Nevertheless, the focus on Irish theatre and drama in terms of the culture of a small nation that is perceived and studied separately from English or British culture, and linked with the culture of other small or minority peoples, has been rather a rarity than a rule in Europe. This is in regrettable accord with the general scarcity of any substantial commentaries on the life of Irish drama on the Continent. In most countries where the work of Irish playwrights has been staged to acclaim and on a regular basis, one is hard put to find even a single article that would summarize the local reception of Irish drama. There are a couple of outstanding exceptions, to be sure: the work of the late Paulo Eduardo Carvalho, whose 600-page volume on Irish plays in Portugal is a landmark not only in reception studies but also in Irish theatre criticism, and the research of Barry Keane, whose book on Irish drama in Poland is forthcoming. Apart from that, there have been individual volumes dedicated to the reception of Oscar Wilde and W. B. Yeats in Europe, and an edited collection on the international reception of Samuel Beckett; these may be complemented by a scattering of articles discussing productions of individual playwrights or plays in a particular country.[9] Monographs on canonical authors, such as Bernard Shaw or Seán O'Casey, by non-Anglophone European scholars have been relatively numerous, but these rarely discuss the plays in the context of the target country. Reviews of more recent productions are mostly available, of course, but using these as primary sources of information is notoriously problematic. A helpful development has been the creation of production databases by theatre institutes, university departments, and publishers of plays, which has allowed the basic picture to be established for a number of countries as to what has been staged and when—the proviso being that some of these sources are as yet incomplete. Production databases may be complemented by online archives of major theatre festivals, for instance the Berliner Theatertreffen/Festspiele or the Avignon festival, and the databases of periodicals such as *DIALOG*—an indispensable Polish theatre journal which has featured the publication of complete play scripts in translation since 1956, thereby often helping to introduce Irish playwrights to Polish practitioners—or the representative German monthly *Theater heute*.[10] Nonetheless, information for some parts of Europe still remains buried across a range of archives, and is waiting to be uncovered on location. It is with these limitations in mind that a consideration of the principal issues relating to the staging of Irish plays in Europe is offered in what follows.

TRANSFERABILITY

The first set of observations concerns the ways in which Irish plays have found their way to Continental theatres. Mostly, Irish plays tend to be produced after they have had a

---

[9] Paulo Eduardo Carvalho, *Identidades reescribes: figurações da Irlanda no teatro português* [Rewritten Identities: Representations of Ireland in Portuguese Theatre] (Porto: Edições Afrontamento/Instituto de Literatura Comparada Margarida Losa, 2009); Barry Keane, *Irish Drama in Poland: Staging and Reception, 1900–2000* (Chicago, IL: University of Chicago Press/Intellect, forthcoming). Details of the volumes on Wilde, Yeats, and Beckett are as follows: Stefano Evangelista (ed.), *The Reception of Oscar Wilde in Europe* (London: Continuum, 2010); Klaus Peter Jochum (ed.), *The Reception of W. B. Yeats in Europe* (London: Continuum, 2006); Mark Nixon and Matthew Feldman (eds.), *The International Reception of Samuel Beckett* (London: Continuum, 2009).

[10] A list of selected databases is appended to this chapter.

successful run in London, which has been a customary focal point for international practitioners and critics. In recent years, theatres and events outside London have begun to play a role as well, particularly the Edinburgh Festival, with the increasing number of European critics, dramaturges, and agents that it has been attracting. Occasionally, a play would be staged in a neighbouring country following a noteworthy production in Germany or France, particularly if it had been toured there. Such was the case with *Disco Pigs* by Enda Walsh in the Czech Republic, for instance, where a visiting German production created something of a generational controversy in 1999 and triggered the first staging of the play in Czech (2002).[11] At the same time, numerous excellent premières have been initiated by translators or local Irish-drama specialists, some of whom have made a concerted effort to provide their compatriots with a balanced sampling of the work of Irish playwrights. An exemplary instance here is Paulo Eduardo Carvalho again: an accomplished translator of contemporary Irish and British drama, Carvalho co-founded the Assédio theatre in Porto in 1998, where he started working as a dramaturge. Over the remaining twelve years of Carvalho's life, Assédio created what largely were first Portuguese productions of plays by Brian Friel, Conor McPherson, Marie Jones, Jennifer Johnston, Mark O'Rowe, Samuel Beckett, and Tom Murphy, mostly in Carvalho's translation. While Irish drama had not been unknown in Portugal before, it was Carvalho's work with Assédio that placed contemporary Irish plays firmly on the map of Portuguese theatre. Sporadically, notable moments for Irish drama arose as a result of fortuitous coincidence, such as the availability of funding on the occasion of Ireland's 2013 EU presidency which helped the Centro Dramático Nacional in Madrid to produce rehearsed readings of Synge's *Deirdre of the Sorrows*, Tom Murphy's *Conversations on a Homecoming*, and Marina Carr's *Marble*, with all three plays translated for the occasion and Marina Carr invited to a debate with Spanish practitioners. Some remarkable stagings occurred due to mere chance, as in the case of the celebrated productions of Martin McDonagh's plays in Prague by director (and translator) Ondřej Sokol, who came across his favourite author via an article in *Time* magazine.

As with any other foreign culture, a significant part of the canon will not travel easily. The embeddedness of most Irish drama up to the late 1990s in Irish locales, which has often been accompanied by a concern with issues of Irish history and politics, has represented a major obstacle in terms of its transferability into other cultures. Whereas European critics and practitioners were quick to recognize the originality of J. M. Synge, early audiences found the archaic world of the Irish countryside presented in his plays too exotic to relate to. This made his German translator Max Meyerfeld eventually complain to the playwright that his plays were simply 'too Irish', and to venture the following opinion: 'it seems very doubtful to me whether you will ever be able to conquer the world by dealing exclusively with Irish peasants.'[12] The Dublin plays by Seán O'Casey, which were the acme of Irish theatre in the 1920s and which saved the Abbey from bankruptcy, took decades to be presented in most European countries, with first productions occurring only after the success of O'Casey's later plays, such as *The Silver Tassie, Red Roses for Me*, or *Cock-a-Doodle Dandy* (and sometimes never). In an article promoting the work of Brian Friel, translator,

---

[11] See Ondřej Pilný, ' "Suitably Relevant": Irish Drama and Theatre in the Czech Republic, 2000–2007', in Kurdi, *Literary and Cultural Relations*, 68.

[12] Quoted in Anthony Roche, *Synge and the Making of Modern Irish Drama* (Dublin: Carysfort Press, 2013), 57.

dramaturge, and theatre scholar Michael Raab observed: 'The greatest difficulty perhaps in trying to win German theatre to Friel is less one concerning form […] but much more one of content. As with O'Casey's plays about the Irish Civil War, the local audience lacks the knowledge of details of Irish history, which it is impossible to compensate, were it even in the form of programme notes.'[13] It is indeed the amount of specific historical detail that has delayed or even completely prevented the production of a major part of Friel's work outside the Anglophone world, as with O'Casey's Dublin plays earlier. This has been particularly true of *Translations*, swiftly established as a masterpiece in Ireland, the UK, and the US, subsequent to its first production by Field Day Theatre Company in 1980. In most countries where it was staged at all, productions came only after the international success of the more accessible *Dancing at Lughnasa*: *Translations* was premièred in 1996 in Portugal and Hungary (though the latter was an English-language student production), in 1997 in Germany and the Czech Republic, and in 1999 in Poland (subsequent to a 1995 production at a Polish theatre in the town of Český Těšín, located in the Czech Republic); the 1984 French adaptation by Pierre Laville (entitled *La Dernière Classe*) seems to mark the earliest appearance of the play outside English-speaking countries. Equally, most of the drama from or about Northern Ireland has remained unproduced in Continental Europe due to fears of the audiences' inability to relate to the complex historical situation, perhaps apart from the scant stagings of Friel's *The Freedom of the City* in the 1970s and 1980s—a period in which producers could at least rely on the kind of familiarity with Northern Ireland that would be gathered from tragic newspaper headlines.

Irish plays from the 1990s onward have fared considerably better. Martin McDonagh in particular has ranked among the most frequently produced foreign authors across the entire continent of Europe in the late 1990s and the 2000s. As I have noted above, the significance of the Irish setting of most of McDonagh's work for the stage has largely been ignored abroad, and the same holds true for the intertextual links in McDonagh's plays to canonical authors such as Synge, Friel, or Tom Murphy, which are besides hard to reproduce in translation, since very few spectators will know the work of the earlier playwrights in detail, or indeed at all. What has held more currency is the affinity of McDonagh's characters, language, and humour to contemporary cinema, including echoes of films by Quentin Tarantino, Danny Boyle, or David Lynch, and in general the ubiquitous appetite for black comedy in this period. The kinship of McDonagh's plays with other favourites of popular culture has also been noted, as in the characterization of *The Pillowman* as 'Artaud reinterpreted by Homer Simpson' from a Spanish reviewer.[14] The only Irish playwright who has come to rival McDonagh's fame in Europe in the last decade or so is Enda Walsh. Walsh's career has been unique in that, while it has been regular enough for an Irish playwright's reputation to be forged in London, Walsh's international recognition has originated to a large extent through the production of his plays in Germany; as for Ireland, it was not really until the acclaimed Druid Theatre production of *The Walworth Farce* in 2006 that Walsh received a suitable acknowledgement from critics (notwithstanding the

---

[13] Michael Raab, 'Ballybeg ist überall. Brian Friel: *Aristokraten*' [Ballybeg Is Everywhere. Brian Friel: *Aristocrats*], *Die Deutsche Bühne* 1 (1991), 39, my translation.

[14] Javier Vallejo, 'Irlanda cuenta cuentos' [Ireland Tells Tales], *El País*, 6 Dec. 2008, my translation: http://elpais.com/diario/2008/12/06/babelia/1228521973_850215.html. Accessed 30 May 2014.

early praise for *Disco Pigs* from reviewers). Walsh's popularity in Germany was somewhat unexpectedly triggered by the early play *Disco Pigs* (1996); as Werner Huber has observed, with forty-two productions between 1998 and 2001 alone, *Disco Pigs* 'has undoubtedly been the darling of German-speaking theatre directors and dramaturges', and its production statistics were 'rivalled only by Patrick Marber's *Closer*'.[15] Even though very specifically set in Cork and couched in a local dialect, the urban setting and clubbing experience outlined in the play have been easy to transpose to the urban milieu of German-speaking cities; in fact, numerous popular productions of *Disco Pigs* were staged in clubs and discos, which were considered a natural space for the piece. Subsequently, a number of Walsh's dramas were premièred in Continental Europe or received major early productions there: *How These Desperate Men Talk* opened in Zurich in 2004, *Lynndie's Gotta Gun* was premièred in Lisbon in 2005; of the major plays, *The New Electric Ballroom* received its première at the Münchner Kammerspiele theatre in Munich on 30 September 2004, almost four years before the first English-language production by Druid, and *Penelope* was commissioned by and first staged at Theater Oberhausen in 2010, six months before its Druid production in Galway. Moreover, *The New Electric Ballroom* was not only commissioned by the Münchner Kammerspiele but also developed by Walsh jointly with his German dramaturge, Tilman Raabke, under the provisional title 'The Fishmonger's Tale'. Walsh has also been honoured by having as many as three of his plays published in the prestigious journal *Theatre heute* (*Disco Pigs* 1998, *Bedbound* 2002, and *The New Electric Ballroom* 2004). Walsh's long-term collaboration with German-language theatres is still waiting to be factored into the assessment of his work by Irish-drama criticism.

The success of McDonagh's and Walsh's plays, clearly assisted by the absence of references and settings that could be deemed too exotic or impenetrable for a foreign audience, has been further attested by *The Pillowman, Bedbound,* and *The New Electric Ballroom* being designated the best foreign play in German-speaking countries (seasons of 2003/4, 2001/2 and 2004/5 respectively).[16] In contrast, the work of Marina Carr—whose status at the forefront of a generation of playwrights was established in Ireland at the same time as that of Martin McDonagh—has received considerably less attention. The importance of the Irish locale in her most successful plays dating from the mid- to late 1990s may be at fault; however, the frequency with which productions of Carr's plays have turned out to be creaky or alternately lacklustre (including some in Ireland and the UK) seems to indicate that directors have had substantial difficulties trying to find an adequate production style for her unique modern-day tragedies.

TRANSLATION AND THEATRICAL TRADITION

Another matter that must be taken into account when attempting to explain the lack of engagement in Europe with Irish drama as a phenomenon is the effect of translation, particularly in the sense of erasing differences. At least up to the middle of the twentieth century there was a widespread trend to domesticate foreign proper nouns or items

---

[15] Huber, 'Contemporary Irish Theatre in German-Speaking Countries', 84.   [16] Ibid.

absent in the target culture. This is now rare, which means that an appropriate flavour, so to speak, of Ireland is retained in more recent translations (though any spectators with a knowledge of the pronunciation of Irish personal or place names often find themselves shuddering at the sound given to these by ill-instructed actors). However, what continues to be levelled in most translations is dialect. To put it simply, no European language features a dialect that would create similar connotations to those associated in the Anglophone world with Hiberno-English (not to speak of its individual varieties, including synthetic ones, like those crafted by J. M. Synge or Martin McDonagh). Any distinct dialects that may be available in the target language are bound to be burdened with a subtext, together with regional stereotypes. Consequently, any time a play written in Irish English is translated into, for instance, the brand of Italian spoken in Sicily, or the German of rural Saxony, its characters are to a significant extent bound to turn into Sicilians or the inhabitants of Saxony for the audience, with the appropriate connotations in tow. While such a parallel may at times be actively sought by a translator for the purpose of highlighting historical analogies (as in the translation of Friel's play into the variety of Hungarian spoken in Transylvania mentioned earlier in this chapter), or alternatively for comic effect (as in dialectal translations of Martin McDonagh, of which there have been some), the nature of the cultural shift involved has mostly been deemed undesirable. As a result, Irish drama is largely translated into the standard form of the vernacular, which is embellished with various forms of ad hoc estrangement at best. The linguistic difference between Irish and British plays (which are of course subject to the same constraints as regards the translation of dialect) is thereby cancelled out, and their identification is potentially encouraged.

The selection of plays for translation and/or production has been determined not only by their accessibility in respect of setting and content but, importantly, also by local staging traditions. On the whole, the role of the director has been much stronger in Europe than in Ireland, where theatre has been dominated by the playwright. The prevalence of director's theatre has been particularly strong in France and in Germany. Here is a succinct outline of the situation in Germany by Michael Raab:

> German theatre is dominated by the director. Many leading representatives of this profession tend to value plays in terms of how much of their own vision and personality they can project into them. [. . .] Well-made plays are not particularly appealing to directors who are keen to demonstrate their own uniqueness. In their attempts to be original they will be supported by reviewers who welcome any kind of transgression and are likely to refer to a very good production of a tightly constructed text as being 'merely solid'.[17]

The appeal to producers of twentieth-century Irish drama, with its canon consisting mostly of well-made plays, is thereby considerably lessened. Moreover, most areas of Europe have had their own tradition of formally conservative plays, and when looking for material to import, conventional drama is low on the list of priorities. A curator of a prominent Finnish festival has recently made this point simply: 'What we are looking for from abroad are

---

[17] Michael Raab, 'Directors and Actors in Modern and Contemporary German Theatre, 1945–2006', in Simon Williams and Maik Hamburger (eds.), *A History of German Theatre* (Cambridge: Cambridge University Press, 2008), 332.

productions that differ from what we have already.'¹⁸ While he was referring to productions by Irish or British theatres, this has been true of Irish plays in translation as well. Palpable evidence is provided by data from two of the most prestigious annual ventures on the Continent: the Berliner Theatertreffen and the Avignon festival. Founded in 1964, the Berliner Theatertreffen/Festspiele issues invitations to generally ten productions from German-speaking countries which have been judged by an independent jury as the most remarkable of the season. Over the years, invited productions have included one of a play by Shaw (1976) and Wilde (1998), four by O'Casey (1968, 1971, 1985, 1992), one by Brendan Behan (1964), and one went to a Joycean adaptation by Hugh Leonard (1964). No Irish plays have appeared at the festival since 1998, and if we exclude Wilde, when an Irish drama was last seen at the Theatertreffen moves back to 1985. The Festival d'Avignon was founded in 1947; the first production of an Irish play—*Cock-a-Doodle Dandy* by Sean O'Casey—did not take place until 1975. With no other Irish work staged until the end of the century, the position has altered somewhat in the 2000s, reflecting primarily the major shifts in the nature of contemporary Irish drama: there have been productions of *Observe the Sons of Ulster Marching Towards the Somme* by Frank McGuinness (2001), *The Lonesome West* by Martin McDonagh (2002), a German guest production of *Disco Pigs* by Enda Walsh (2004), and rehearsed readings of Walsh's *Bedbound* (2004) and Mark O'Rowe's *Terminus* (2008).

This list omits the Irish playwright who has had the greatest impact on European theatre since the Second World War, Samuel Beckett, productions of whose work were presented both at Berlin and at Avignon on a fairly regular basis. As Beckett is treated in detail elsewhere in this volume, and as the appropriation of his work for a particular national tradition is a matter for debate, I will merely point out that his plays provide a remarkable example of the impact that radically diverse political circumstances have had on the interpretation of international art. The reception of Beckett's early absurdist drama in Western Europe has been well mapped, ranging from outrage at its alleged nihilism to an eager approval of the work as the most adequate reflection of the postwar collapse of all (meta)narratives. In the context of the totalitarian regimes obtaining in the Eastern Bloc, however, Beckett's work was often interpreted as hyperrealistic, mirroring the absurdity and unrelenting sameness of existence in an oppressive state. The communist authorities were quick to react, discouraging productions or even preventing them from happening outright—as in Czechoslovakia, where the situation was aggravated by the involvement of prominent dissidents like Václav Havel.¹⁹

POLITICS OF PRODUCTION: O'CASEY AND BEHAN

Seán O'Casey represents another instance of the divergent reasons for staging the work of a particular author and of the differences in its reception. The scarcity of productions of his early Dublin plays in Europe has already been discussed above. Yet O'Casey's later work has

¹⁸ Jukka-Pekka Pajunen speaking at a 2009 Irish Theatre Institute conference, quoted in Peter Crawley, 'Viewed from Afar: Contemporary Irish Theatre on the World's Stages', in Fintan Walsh (ed.), *'That Was Us': Contemporary Irish Theatre and Performance* (London: Oberon Books, 2013), 221.
¹⁹ There were only two professional productions of Beckett's plays up to 1990 in Czechoslovakia, and both were of *Waiting for Godot* (1964, 1970), with Havel secretly acting as dramaturge for the first

arguably had as much of a life in translation as in the original English; in fact, *Oak Leaves and Lavender* even received its world première at the Helsingfors Stadsteater in Helsinki (1946). In France and Germany, it was the theatrical experimentalism of *Cock-a-Doodle Dandy* and *The Silver Tassie* which has been attractive to directors, and especially Peter Zadek's productions of *The Silver Tassie* (1968 Wuppertal, 1971 Stuttgart, both selected for the Berliner Theatertreffen and the latter also televised) resulted in sustained interest in O'Casey's work throughout the 1970s and 1980s. In contrast, the more ideological side of O'Casey, manifest in plays like *The Star Turns Red, Red Roses for Me*, or indeed *Oak Leaves and Lavender*, was officially celebrated in the 1950s in Hungary, despite the author's provenance from the 'capitalist West'; similarly, the numerous productions of a range of O'Casey's plays in East Germany were the result of the author being hailed as a representative of 'people's theatre'. Curiously enough, the favourable disposition of the communist authorities towards O'Casey found little reflection in Poland or Czechoslovakia, where the production history of his full-length plays has been negligible. A point of convergence in the otherwise contrasting image of O'Casey on the opposite sides of the Iron Curtain is the popularity of his more or less insubstantial one-acts, particularly in the 1960s and onward; successful productions of these have resulted in popular TV adaptations in Denmark, Finland, Poland, Czechoslovakia, West Germany, and Portugal (East Germany, on the other hand, saw a whole array of O'Casey's full-length plays televised).

The last example offered here to show the range of motivations for staging an Irish play, and to highlight the crucial influence of the political context on interpretation, concerns *The Hostage* by Brendan Behan. *The Hostage* was given a truly landmark production by director Peter Zadek in 1961, which had considerable impact on the shape of German theatre and has led to regular revivals of Behan's work in German-speaking countries. The son of Jewish parents who were forced to emigrate to the UK, Zadek came back to West Germany with an extensive experience of British theatre, having studied at London's Old Vic Theatre School and directed his first productions there and in repertory theatres in Wales. Zadek's style of directing reinvigorated the solemn scene in Germany; in Raab's words, 'Zadek brought an English sense of showmanship and revue to the German theatre, which was unusual for an artistic institution that was strongly marked as educational, in the sense expounded by Schiller.'[20] While using a realistic set for *The Hostage* at the Municipal Theatre in Ulm, the director put together a cast of classically trained German actors, a star of the local operetta scene, and American and British dancers with experience of acting and singing in musicals. The result was a veritable feast of theatre, characterized by improvisation every night but firmly held together by the director's vision. Comparing Behan's work with Brecht, Zadek wrote at the time:

> Behan replaces Brecht's idealism, which still originated in the nineteenth century, as well as his call for security and order, with a glorification of chaos, anarchy and unbridled vitality. Brecht's victims voice bitter accusations; in Behan they unleash devilish laughter. Between

staging. Apart from a single night's guest performance of *Oh les beaux jours* (in French) by the Théâtre de France in 1965, Czech and Slovak audiences were not allowed to see Beckett until the collapse of the regime. See Ondřej Pilný, 'Irish Drama in the Czech Lands, *c.* 1900–2013', in Gerald Power and Ondřej Pilný (eds.), *Ireland and the Czech Lands: Contacts and Comparisons in History and Culture* (Bern: Peter Lang, 2014), 214–17.

[20] Raab, 'Directors and Actors in Modern and Contemporary German Theatre', 339.

Brecht and Behan lies our realization that metaphysics cannot be substituted with bread, and that when the globe explodes around us, a joke may provide more solace than an ideal.[21]

In other words, Zadek asserts that the experience of the Second World War and its aftermath has unravelled Brecht's desire to do away with metaphysics as an unachievable ideal pertaining to a previous era, which has been appropriately replaced in Behan with unrestrained glee in the face of catastrophe. Moreover, Zadek's reference to an impending annihilation is indicative of the atmosphere in which he staged *The Hostage*; the menacing backdrop of the height of the Cold War was also listed as a primary motivation behind the production by the general director of the Ulm theatre, Kurt Hübner, who spoke of a world threatened by the H-bomb and 'dancing, boozing and loving on a volcano'.[22] The production generated a heated argument at the local municipality: many of the magistrates were scandalized by its alleged blasphemy and obscenity, and threatened to pull the play; regardless of that, Zadek's staging of *The Hostage* was a triumphant success with audiences and critics alike, who acknowledged its relevance very much in the terms outlined by its producers. For instance, Ernst Wendt in *Theater heute* praised what he saw as the production's social realism and its foregrounding of the grotesque, and likened it to the style of Charlie Chaplin in *City Lights*. *The Hostage* travelled from Ulm to Munich, Bremen, and Berlin, and Zadek followed it with a second production in Berlin and Bochum, which had originated as an experimental three-and-a-half-hour television piece (1975, stage version 1976).[23]

As in Germany, the première of *The Hostage* in Czechoslovakia (1963) made for a notable event in the history of local theatre, despite the Czech staging being distinctly more modest than Peter Zadek's. Behan's play was put on in Prague in the small but at the time very energetic S. K. Neumann Theatre. The production was preceded by the publication of a large part of the play text with the translator's comments in the journal *Divadlo* (Theatre), and was widely regarded by reviewers as the best play of the season. *The Hostage* was chosen by the theatre due to the success of Joan Littlewood's first presentation of the play at Stratford East in 1958 (which Zadek saw as well); in Czechoslovakia, this caused Behan to be classed among the Angry Young Men of British theatre, notwithstanding the fact that his Irish origin was simultaneously noted.[24] Both the translator, Jiří Mucha, and the director, Svatopluk Papež, indicated a political intent behind their venture. Mucha emphasized in his introduction to the published play that the once 'progressive struggle of Irish nationalists has degenerated into a plaything of a small group that has turned fascist', indicating an analogy with communist Czechoslovakia.[25] In the programme notes, Papež went even further, characterizing Behan's moral as follows:

it is time to stop wasting blood in the restitution of expired ideological programmes [. . .] any programme that has become separated from the interests for which it was created, and

---

[21] Quoted in Volker Canaris, *Peter Zadek: Der Theatermann und Filmemacher* [Peter Zadek: Theatre Practitioner and Filmmaker] (Munich: Hanser Verlag, 1979), 59–60, my translation.

[22] Letter to the editor of the *Donauzeitung*, in Canaris, *Peter Zadek*, 59, my translation.

[23] Cf. Canaris, *Peter Zadek*, 59, 66–7, 138, 246, 259.

[24] For details, see Pilný, 'Irish Drama in the Czech Lands', 212–13.

[25] Jiří Mucha, 'Behanova rozmarná tragédie' [Behan's Capricious Tragedy], *Divadlo* 2 (Feb. 1962), 46, my translation.

that has been surviving only due to injections of irate prestige, will transform its nutrient substances into poison and end up exterminating its own carriers.[26]

It appears that the message came across as intended by the producers, because, despite the success of the Prague production, *The Hostage* appeared in Czech only one more time (in the city of Brno in 1970), and subsequently would not be revived for almost two decades. Moreover, the Prague staging of Behan's tragicomedy influenced a whole generation of critics in their interpretation of modern Irish drama as having a distinctly anti-ideological and anti-nationalist slant.[27]

IRISH THEATRES IN EUROPE

Finally, a note is due concerning how much Irish theatre practice has been shown in Continental Europe. The answer is simple: sadly, very little, although there has been some positive development of late. The high costs involved in touring a production over a long distance, combined with language barriers, have understandably been perceived as serious problems. Even in a European metropolis, the number of potential spectators for an English-language performance (albeit with translation provided) will be limited, preventing any show from being presented for more than literally a couple of nights. The only Irish theatre which decided to tackle these obstacles fairly consistently was the Gate under Hilton Edwards and Micheál Mac Liammóir; the Gate successfully visited Malta (1937, 1938 together with Athens, and 1956), made a tour of the Yugoslav countries, Greece, Bulgaria, and Romania in 1939, of Germany and France in 1949, of Switzerland, Luxembourg, Belgium, and Holland in 1962, and staged *Hamlet* at Elsinore Castle in Denmark (1952). However, during the largest of these endeavours, the 1939 tour of the Balkans, the company were more often than not regarded as British, largely because the trip was organized and funded by the British Council. The Irish—as opposed to British—identity of the performers was appreciated only in Slovenia and Croatia, where people were making analogies in private between the British and the Serbs; be that as it may, no comparisons of Irish versus English styles of theatrical presentation seem to have been entered into.[28] The Abbey Theatre has ventured out of the Anglophone zone rather rarely (given its status and budget), with the remarkable exception of touring several productions by Patrick Mason and Ben Barnes in the 1980s and 1990s. In 1955, *The Plough and the Stars* was shown to acclaim at the Théâtre des Nations Festival in Paris, and the Abbey returned to Paris a number of times (1969, 1986, 1996, 2001, and 2004);

---

[26] Svatopluk Papež, 'Slovo k inscenaci' [A Note on the Production], programme notes to Brendan Behan, *Rukojmí* [The Hostage] (Prague: Divadlo S. K. Neumanna v Praze, 1963), my translation.

[27] See Pilný, '"Suitably Relevant"', 71.

[28] See Christopher Fitz-Simon, *The Boys: A Biography of Micheál MacLíammóir and Hilton Edwards* (1994) (Dublin: New Island Books, 2002), 111–20, 259–63, and the listing of the Gate seasons in Peter Luke, *Enter Certain Players: Edwards, Mac Liammóir and the Gate, 1928–1978* (Dublin: Dolmen Press, 1978).

other destinations have included Florence (1968), Greece (1985), Moscow and Leningrad (1988), Rome and Agen sur Gironde (1989), Brussels and Bonn (1996), and Tampere (2011), while Patrick Mason's staging of *Translations* was presented in Ludwigshafen, Barcelona, Paris, Prague, and Budapest in 2001. For smaller theatres, who were largely struggling to exist in Ireland up until the 1990s, touring outside places which did not guarantee sufficient revenue to cover expenses was simply not viable. However, the availability of Irish government funding, minimal as it may seem in relative terms, has made for a notable improvement in the last couple of decades; particularly through the grants provided by Culture Ireland, a number of Irish productions have toured to festivals across the European continent. The challenge of presenting work in English has remained a crucial impediment, as Rough Magic can unhappily testify. A theatre company which has been consistently looking to the Continent for material and inspiration, their first performance in a non-English-speaking country fell miserably flat. Rough Magic chose to present the witty, sparkling musical *Improbable Frequency*, which was a genuine highlight of Irish theatre of the 2000s, at the Kontakt festival in the Polish city of Toruń in 2006. Peter Crawley relates that the play was presented in English with simultaneous translation into Polish and Russian provided by 'a solitary male speaker who delivered every line and lyric of the performance in a manful monotone, heroically uninfluenced by the live music'. To make matters worse, the translation failed to convey any of the puns which are essential to the piece. Not only were there no laughs in the audience, but the critics tore the show apart, calling the play 'a vulgar farce' or 'a pitiful and at times embarrassing musical comedy'.[29] While the way the production was promoted to the audience may have been at fault as well, the lack of attention given to translation issues clearly made this particular tour a missed opportunity for the presentation of innovative Irish theatre. Fortunately, there have also been moments of remarkable success, such as 'The Full Irish', a ten-day festival of Irish theatre and performance hosted by the English Theatre Berlin in 2013, which featured productions by Brokentalkers, Gare St Lazare Players, and The Company, together with staged readings of four contemporary Irish plays. Moreover, a retrospective exhibition of Irish stage and sound design was presented to the wide community of European practitioners at the Prague Quadrennial, the world's largest exhibition of stage design and theatre architecture, in 2007.[30] These have been the first signs of putting contemporary Irish theatre practice on the larger map of Europe, alongside the popular and inspiring work of Irish dramatists.[31]

[29] Crawley, 'Viewed from Afar', 212.
[30] For a brief assessment, see Pilný, ' "Suitably Relevant" ', 73–5.
[31] I would like to thank numerous friends and colleagues for generously providing information and sharing their work with me, particularly Michael Raab, Werner Huber, Martine Pelletier, Filomena Louro, Mária Kurdi, Antonio de Toro, David Clark, Małgorzata Semil, Michał Lachman, Sandra Mayer, and Justin Quinn.

APPENDIX: SELECTED DATABASES OF PRODUCTIONS, PUBLISHED TRANSLATIONS AND REVIEWS

Berliner Theatertreffen—Festspiele Archive, https://www.berlinerfestspiele.de/en/aktuell/festivals/theatertreffen/archiv_tt/archiv_tt_1.php.

CETBase—Teatro em Portugal, Centro de Estudos de Teatro, Faculdade de Lettras Universidade de Lisboa, http://ww3.fl.ul.pt/CETbase/.

Culture Ireland, 'Outcome Grants', http://www.cultureireland.ie/applications/index.php?r=reports/outcomeGrants.

'Czech–Irish Relations: A Bibliography of Books and Articles', database compiled by Daniel Samek, Centre for Irish Studies at Charles University, Prague, http://ualk.ff.cuni.cz/ibibliography/index.htm.

Dialog, index of authors and plays printed in the journal (1956–2010), http://www.dialog.waw.pl/index.php?cmd=show&menu=main&id=4&lang=pl.

e-teatr.pl—Polski Portal Teatralny, Institut Teatralny im. Zbigniewa Raszewskiego (The Zbigniew Raszewski Theatre Institute), database of productions, http://www.e-teatr.pl/pl/realizacje/lista.html.

Festival d'Avignon, archive of productions, http://www.festival-avignon.com/en/.

Institut del Teatre—Diputació Barcelona/Centre de Documentació i Museu de les Arts Escèniques, http://www.cdmae.cat/ca/el-mae/presentacio/196; database of productions, http://www.cdmae.cat/ca/recursos/bd-despectacles.

Institut umění—Divadelní ústav (Arts and Theatre Institute), Prague, database of productions, http://vis.idu.cz/Productions.aspx.

The Internationalisation of Irish Drama, 1975–2005—Abbey International Tours 1975–2005 database, http://www.irishtheatricaldiaspora.net/databases/abbeysearch.php#totalto.

Theadok—Inszenierungsdatenbank, Vienna Society for Theatre Research and the Department of Theatre, Film and Media Studies, University of Vienna, http://www.theadok.at/home/index.php.

Theater heute Archiv, http://www.kultiversum.de/Theaterheute/Theater-heute-Archiv.html.

VDB: Verband Deutscher Bühnen- und Medienverlage (Association of German Theatre and Media Publishers) database, http://www.theatertexte.de/data.

Weltbühne Wien (World Stage Vienna), including a Performance Database, http://www.univie.ac.at/weltbuehne_wien/home_en.html.

CHAPTER 39

....

'FEAST AND CELEBRATION'
The Theatre Festival and Modern Irish Theatre

....

PATRICK LONERGAN

THEATRE festivals do not just host performances: they are themselves forms of performance—staged events that communicate a meaningful narrative to an audience. Festivals have allowed Ireland to perform new ideas about itself to the world: ideas about internationalization, Europeanization, tourism, economic prosperity, regionalism, history, the Troubles, the body, secularism—and about Irish theatre itself (among many other subjects). As performance events, festivals allow Irish playwrights and theatre-makers to accomplish objectives that are sometimes difficult to realize within the conventional theatre: to reach new and unusual audiences, to interact with non-Irish performance traditions, and to take risks.

Yet festivals are also marketplaces, spaces in which theatre companies and writers aim to attract opportunities to tour their work internationally. And they are, furthermore, examples of 'nation branding': events that aim to have an economic impact by performing a positive image of the host city or state before an audience of tourists, multinational corporations, ratings agencies, and other international institutions. The theatre festival is therefore a space in which the creative and commercial elements of theatre production overlap with what Erin Hurley has termed 'national performance': the use of 'cultural production to vouch for [a nation's] status'.[1] As such, they offer a useful space in which to analyse and investigate the changing status of theatre in an increasingly globalized environment.

THE ABBEY THEATRE FESTIVAL, 1938

....

The first significant modern Irish theatre festival took place in August 1938, when the Abbey Theatre staged a two-week event to celebrate its achievements during the previous

---

[1] Erin Hurley, *National Performance: Representing Quebec from Expo 67 to Celine Dion* (Toronto: University of Toronto Press, 2010), 21.

thirty-four years. Curated by Lennox Robinson, the 'Abbey Theatre Festival' staged seventeen plays over twelve days, and was accompanied by a series of lectures that were later collected as *The Irish Theatre* (1939). That event is now remembered mainly for premièring Yeats's *Purgatory* (1938), but it also established patterns and conventions that would prove important throughout the rest of the twentieth century

News of the Abbey Theatre Festival was announced in January 1938, and it was immediately clear what its primary objective would be: 'it is expected that there will be a considerable influx of visitors from all parts of the world,' wrote the *Irish Times* approvingly.[2] In seeking to attract an international audience, the Abbey was inspired by the success of festivals elsewhere. The Shakespeare Festival at Stratford-upon-Avon had been recently reinvigorated, first by the appointment of William Bridges-Adams in 1919, and then by the opening of the new Memorial Theatre in 1932. In Germany, Hitler's enthusiasm for Wagner had brought about a boost to the resources and profile of the Bayreuth Festival—though the Nazis were less enthusiastic about the Salzburg Festival in Austria, which suffered a decline in fortunes after the 1938 *Anschluss*. By imitating those public celebrations of Shakespeare, Wagner, and Mozart, the Abbey Festival was implicitly asserting the international significance of the Irish dramatic movement.

That message about the Abbey was directed towards audiences both within and beyond the Irish nation. The Festival included events that were self-evidently intended to appeal to international visitors: there was a tour to Glendalough, and delegates were brought to see the Book of Kells at Trinity College Dublin. The event also featured an afternoon garden party in Sorrento Cottage (then the home of Lennox Robinson and now the home of U2's The Edge) in Dalkey, a wealthy suburb that presents beautiful views over Dublin Bay. So it is apparent that the Abbey directors wanted to stage the Festival in a touristic context; the Irish dramatic movement was presenting itself as a form of heritage that could be consumed by overseas visitors.

Yet the Festival also aimed to assert the Abbey's importance before a somewhat sceptical Irish public. At the opening event at Dublin's Municipal Gallery on 6 August 1938, Robinson alluded to the presence of several international guests: the ambassadors of France, Italy, Germany, America, and Belgium, and the consul-generals for Holland, Czechoslovakia, Sweden, and Switzerland. His message was obvious: the Irish dramatic movement—and, by extension, the Abbey itself—must be worthy of national support, given its ability to command international attention. And that message was conveyed not just to the guests at the opening event but (potentially) to the entire nation: the Abbey had taken care to ensure that the opening ceremony would be broadcast on Irish radio.

That dual awareness of internal and external audiences was partly informed by financial considerations. Since 1911, income from the Abbey's tours of North America had safeguarded the theatre's viability, and there was a determination to ensure that those tours would continue. There was also a need to generate support for the Abbey within Ireland. On 5 August 1938—the day before the Festival began—Ernest Blythe had led a delegation of Abbey directors to a meeting with the minister for finance, Seán MacEntee, who pledged to provide £100,000 to build a new theatre in Dublin. The space would have three auditoria of 700, 400, and 300 seats, which would house the Abbey, the Gate, and An Comhar

---

[2] 'Abbey Theatre Festival', *Irish Times*, 24 Jan. 1938.

Drámaíochta respectively.[3] The minister asked that this commitment be treated as confidential, but the Abbey clearly hoped that a successful festival would generate popular support for the redevelopment of the theatre.

Although the announcement of the Festival was well received, the Abbey soon encountered obstacles. The proposed programme of lectures had to be reorganized when Seán O'Faolain stated that he would deliver a paper only on the condition that one of his plays be included in the Festival—an ultimatum that the Abbey felt compelled to reject, choosing to invite Micheál MacLiammóir to speak instead. The Abbey Company also proved resistant to the proposed programme. Hugh Hunt urged the Board to reduce the number of plays from seventeen to eight, worrying about the demands being placed upon the actors; shortly after his request was denied, Hunt informed the Board that he would resign from the company in order to return to England—though he gave a commitment not to do so until after the Festival had concluded. The Abbey's rising star Cyril Cusack was also made unhappy when his request for leave of absence to appear in a feature film was denied: he would be needed for too many roles in the Festival, he was told.

More seriously, Frank O'Connor resigned from the Abbey Board in a dispute about the programme, objecting particularly to the inclusion of Shaw's *The Shewing-up of Blanco Posnet* (1909). That play had been included to mark Shaw's many contributions to the Abbey, and also to commemorate the 1909 dispute with Dublin Castle that had resulted in the Abbey giving Shaw's play its première. Yet O'Connor considered the decision to remount it 'disgraceful' and 'directly contrary to my idea of a national theatre'.[4] The Abbey Board reluctantly accepted O'Connor's resignation, and *Blanco Posnet* stayed in the programme. O'Connor's decision was soon reversed, however: a day after the Festival concluded, he agreed to take up his seat on the Board again.

Those controversies would soon be eclipsed by what Roy Foster has termed Yeats's 'last great scene at the Abbey':[5] the première of *Purgatory* on 9 August 1938. As Foster writes:

> Facing the Abbey audience for the last time, after a success nearly as controversial as Synge's or O'Casey's, [Yeats] made the most of it. 'I wish to say that I have put into this play not many thoughts that are picturesque,' he told them, 'but my own beliefs about this world and the next.'[6]

Yet despite Yeats's celebratory mood, *Purgatory* encountered hostility almost immediately. Father Terrence Connolly, a Jesuit from Boston College, criticized the play at a Festival lecture given by F. R. Higgins on 10 August, the day after its première. Yeats was forced to defend himself in an *Irish Times* interview, in which he summarily dismissed Connolly's criticisms ('my plot is my meaning,' he stated), and spoke approvingly of Nazi Germany's recently enacted laws relating to eugenics.[7]

Behind the scenes, however, Yeats was furious. At a Board meeting hastily convened on 12 August 1938, he queried how Father Connolly had read the script of *Purgatory*, pointing

[3] Abbey Theatre, '5 August 1938', *Abbey Theatre Minute Books*, Abbey Theatre Digital Archive at NUI Galway.
[4] Ibid., '3 June 1938'.
[5] R. F. Foster, *W. B. Yeats: A Life*, vol. 2: *The Arch-Poet* (Oxford: Oxford University Press, 2003), 627.
[6] Ibid., 628. [7] 'The Plot is the Meaning', *Irish Times*, 13 Aug. 1938.

out that, because the play had not been published, it must have been given to the priest by a member of the Abbey company. A week later, the Board met again, and F. R. Higgins reported that the culprit had been found: F. J. McCormick had borrowed the script from Hugh Hunt, and had in turn lent it to Father Connolly. McCormick stated that 'he had given the script to Fr. Connolly in all good faith', but acknowledged that he 'might have been guilty of a technical breach in confidence'.[8] Perhaps owing to the importance of McCormick to the company, the Board limited themselves to posting a statement of the company's rules and regulations to the actors' noticeboard.

In that same Board meeting of 19 August 1938, the directors noted that the Festival had been a success 'by reason of the great publicity it had gained the theatre'.[9] But the proposal to have a second Festival in 1939 was dismissed: it 'could not be considered owing to the uncertainty as to when the theatre would be available in view of the reconstruction proposals,' state the Minutes. That proposed reconstruction came to nothing, of course. With the outbreak of war in 1939, a new minister for finance was appointed, the Abbey's international tours ceased, and the rebuilding project was quietly forgotten until after the theatre burned down in 1951.

The Abbey Theatre Festival is mostly forgotten now, but it allows for the identification of three major patterns that would recur in subsequent Irish festivals. First, the Festival in its entirety was a performance of the significance of the Abbey, based not just on its past—its repertoire of classics such as Synge's *The Playboy of the Western World* (1907) and O'Casey's *The Plough and the Stars* (1926)—but also on its ability to stage new plays such as *Purgatory*. It was not necessary for a member of the Irish public actually to be present at the theatre to understand the meaning of that 'performance', which was carried out in newspaper profiles, radio broadcasts, and in other media.

Second, that performance had an international as well as a national audience: it specifically set out to attract visitors from abroad, positioning attendance at plays within a range of activities related to tourism and cultural heritage. If one task of the tourist is to accumulate 'authentic' Irish experiences (such as seeing the Book of Kells), the Abbey was implying that no trip to Ireland would be complete without a visit to the national theatre. The resulting international interest was in turn retransmitted to the Irish public, the implication being that the Abbey must be worthy of support since it was viewed so favourably outside Ireland.

Finally, because the Abbey Theatre Festival was such a prestigious event, it provoked anxieties, jealousies, and controversies amongst a range of people—not just Abbey personnel such as Hunt, Cusack, and O'Connor, but also in writers such as O'Faolain. More importantly, the intervention of Father Connolly demonstrates how festivalized spaces can be appropriated, both by audience members and by institutions, who can then use those spaces for their own public performances and protests. The Abbey Festival thus gave rise to a public conflict that can now be seen as part of the battle for Catholic hegemony over the Abbey and, by extension, Irish theatre generally. That battle would recur at various times in the twentieth century, notably with the establishment of the Dublin Theatre Festival in 1957.

[8] Abbey Theatre, '19 August 1938', Minutes.   [9] Ibid.

THE FOUNDATION OF THE DUBLIN
THEATRE FESTIVAL

In the aftermath of the Second World War, arts festivals were established around the world (or reinvigorated, as in Salzburg). Those events aimed not only to capitalize on the growth of tourism internationally but also (in a spirit of postwar optimism) to help to foster a new era of transnational cooperation and exchange. The Edinburgh Festival was established in 1947 with a remit of 'inviting the world's best artists and companies to perform, whatever their nationality' in order to provide 'a platform for the flowering of the human spirit'.[10] In the same year, Jean Vilar created a new theatre festival in Avignon. Both events soon established themselves as the leading international theatre festivals—roles they continue to occupy.

In Ireland, similar developments were under way, albeit on a much smaller scale. The isolationism of the 'Emergency' era had given way to a growing attitude of openness, and a realization that, because economic self-sufficiency had proved impossible, it was necessary to attract investment from abroad. That attitude was gradually being reflected in government policy. Bord Fáilte, the Irish tourism development agency, was established in 1955, aiming to target the US market; and in 1958, T. K. Whitaker's *Programme for Economic Expansion* was published, arguing for the need to attract foreign investment, again with a focus on America.

Accompanying such developments was an incipient shifting of attitudes towards Ireland's literary heritage. Some of those changes were driven by writers themselves. The first public celebration of Bloomsday in Dublin, for example, was organized by Patrick Kavanagh and Flann O'Brien; many years would pass before the Irish state would publicly associate itself with Joyce. Yet there was certainly a growing awareness at government level that culture could be reimagined—not as a destabilizing force that needed to be controlled and (if necessary) censored, but as a commodity: a consumable product that could boost tourism and differentiate the country from its competitors for multinational investment. As a result of that change in attitude, state agencies proved more willing to support new artistic initiatives.

The first major event to benefit from this shift was the Wexford Festival Opera, established in 1951 with the aim of staging rarely produced works; it quickly became popular with opera-lovers internationally, and remains an important fixture in the Irish cultural calendar. An annual event called An Tóstal was initiated in 1953, with the remit of targeting the US market; its objective was to stage festivals around the country in order to attract tourists to Ireland during the late spring. An Tóstal hosted a variety of events: its first year featured an enormous pageant about St Patrick, which was directed by Hilton Edwards and written by Mícheál MacLiammóir; it also included chess and hairdressing competitions, as well as numerous sporting events. An Tóstal continued annually until 1958, when it was quietly abandoned in most areas (though it has continued in Drumshambo, Co. Leitrim,

---

[10] Edinburgh International Festival, 'About Us', http://www.eif.co.uk/about-us/our-mission-and-history. Accessed 12 May 2014.

FIG. 39.1 Poster for 1953 An Tóstal Festival pageant.

Courtesy of James Hardiman Library, NUI Galway.

into the present). Yet it had a lasting legacy. The Rose of Tralee Festival—a Hibernicized Miss World equivalent in which Irishness appears to be prized over beauty—originated in An Tóstal, as did the Cork Film Festival. And so too did the Dublin Theatre Festival.

Originally called the Dublin International Theatre Festival (henceforth DTF), the event was created in 1957 by Brendan Smith, a producer who ran an acting academy and managed the Olympia Theatre in Dublin. The Irish Arts Council declined to fund the Festival at first; it was instead supported by Bord Fáilte. So, as had been the case with the Abbey Festival of 1938, the DTF was founded with a focus on attracting international visitors rather than Irish theatregoers.

That prioritization of tourism should not, however, create the impression that Smith was attempting only to restage Irish cultural heritage. On the contrary, his first Festival offered a range of performances from high-profile international companies, which had

FIG. 39.2 Poster for 1956 An Tóstal festival pageant.

Courtesy of James Hardiman Library, NUI Galway.

been invited with the aim of stimulating new developments within Ireland. Ninette de Valois returned to Dublin with the Royal Ballet, which staged new work by Arthur Bliss and Frederick Ashton, while also performing a popular *Swan Lake*. Perhaps most impressively, Smith signalled his intention to position the DTF as a major international festival by inviting Jean Vilar to Dublin: his Théâtre National Populaire (TNP) staged Molière's *Le Malade imaginaire* and Balzac's *Le Faiseur*, both at the Olympia. That experience was an unhappy one for the TNP: Christopher Fitz-Simon recalls Vilar complaining that 'never, on their worst provincial tours, had [he] come across such a scruffy and ill-equipped *salle-de-théâtre*' as the Olympia.[11] Nevertheless, the productions were successfully staged, and

[11] Nicholas Grene and Patrick Lonergan (eds.), *Interactions: Dublin Theatre Festival 1957–2007* (Dublin: Carysfort Press, 2008), 210.

they had a lasting impact on those who saw them—not just because they displayed a level of professional and technical accomplishment that was mostly absent from the Dublin stages, but also because Smith's decision to invite the founder of the Avignon Festival was seen as a serious statement of his own ambitions.

By comparison, the offerings from the established Irish theatres seemed rather unimaginative. The Gate presented the play that had made its name almost thirty years earlier, Denis Johnston's *The Old Lady Says No!,* and at the Abbey Ria Mooney dutifully presented *The Playboy of the Western World* and *Juno and the Paycock* (1924), while Tomás Mac Anna directed Douglas Hyde's *An Pósadh* (1911). Both theatres thus used the Festival to celebrate their own histories rather than seeking to create anything new.

Yet there was evidence of daring from some of the smaller Irish companies. A young Jim Fitzgerald (later an important figure in Irish theatre) staged a season of seven of Yeats's plays, adopting an innovative approach to them that persuaded audiences that Yeats's drama could have a life beyond the Abbey (which had almost entirely removed Yeats from its repertoire after his death in 1939).

Also significant was the staging of an adaptation of Brian Merriman's poem *Cúirt an Mheán Oíche* (1780) in a late-night revue at the Pocket Theatre, by the Irish language company An Compántas. Frank O'Connor's English translation *The Midnight Court* (1945) had been banned by the Irish censor only twelve years earlier (one of the absurdities of Irish censorship was that the Irish original remained available). Yet, according to Brian Ó Conchubhair, the company included English and well as Irish excerpts in their performance.[12] An Compántas was apparently flouting Irish law but, perhaps because they advertised themselves using the poem's Irish title, they managed to avoid trouble.

Sadly, the same could not be said for Alan Simpson and Carolyn Swift, whose Pike Theatre staged Tennessee Williams's *The Rose Tattoo* (1951) in 1957. That production was accused of obscenity when, following complaints from members of the public, the Irish police claimed that the Pike had shown a contraceptive on stage, and duly brought Simpson and Swift to trial. As John Devitt recalls, the policeman at the centre of the case was being put under severe pressure by his superiors. He was 'frigid with embarrassment' and did not know whether he had seen the condom or not: to admit to knowing what a condom looked like would risk social disgrace, but to deny that he had seen one would collapse the case against the Pike, risking professional ruin.[13] Rather like Father Connolly's intervention after the staging of *Purgatory* in 1938, this attack on Williams's play on the basis of Catholic morality was widely perceived as an embarrassment and a joke. But it was not felt as such by Simpson and Swift: it first destroyed their theatre, and then destroyed their marriage.

Worse was to follow. The first DTF had been sufficiently successful to justify a second edition, so in early 1958 Smith announced a programme that was to have included an adaptation of Joyce's *Ulysses* by Alan McClelland, a new play called *The Drums of Father Ned* by Seán O'Casey, and short plays by Samuel Beckett. The archbishop of Dublin, John Charles McQuaid, objected to the inclusion of Joyce and O'Casey's work, and refused to

[12] Brian Merriman, *The Midnight Court/Cúirt an Mheán Oíche*, ed. Brian Ó Conchubhair (Syracuse, NY: Syracuse University Press, 2011), 111.

[13] John Devitt in conversation with Nicholas Grene and Christopher Morash, *Shifting Scenes: Irish Theatre-Going, 1955–1985* (Dublin: Carysfort Press, 2008), 48.

allow an opening mass for the Festival to go ahead. Learning of McQuaid's objections, the Irish Jesuit Provincial then gave instructions that the St Francis Xavier Hall was to withdraw permission to stage the Beckett plays at that venue, while Dublin Corporation, acting in support of McQuaid's position, then threatened to withdraw its grant of £3,000 to the Festival.

That controversy soon became internationalized. Members of the Catholic hierarchy in the United States were approached by two Irish bishops, who requested that the Americans use their influence to persuade the Irish government to extend censorship laws to include the theatre (Ireland at that time was one of the few countries in the West that did not operate theatre censorship). The Irish government stood firm and, in retaliation for their refusal to comply, the Catholic church 'encouraged a boycott of pilgrimages to Ireland [. . .]: a tremendous blow to the tourist industry of an ailing economy,' states John Cooney.[14] That decision had also been influenced by Ireland's recent decision to ignore the Catholic hierarchy's demands to vote against the admission of China to the United Nations—an indicator of how Irish theatre was at the centre of the country's re-examination of its status within the international community.

If the 1958 Festival caused tension between the Irish theatre and the Catholic Church, it also temporarily undermined Ireland's relationship with O'Casey and Beckett. 'After the revolting boycott of Joyce and O'Casey I don't want to have anything to do with the Dublin Theatre "Festival",'[15] Beckett wrote, refusing permission for any further Irish performances of his works. O'Casey likewise banned all professional performances of his work in Ireland—a blow to the Abbey, which remained financially dependent upon the plays. Characteristically, O'Casey announced his decision with several letters to newspapers in Ireland and Britain, bringing a great deal of attention to the case. Brendan Smith soon bowed to pressure and the 1958 Festival was 'postponed'.

Those two controversies—the case of the *Rose Tattoo* and the cancellation of the 1958 event—are sometimes presented as evidence of the conservatism of Ireland at this time. Yet the situation was more complex than that. The inclusion of work such as *Cúirt an Mheán Oíche* in the inaugural Dublin Theatre Festival showed a willingness to circumvent Irish censorship, to use the Irish language to create a space within the DTF that could allow banned work to be seen and heard. Brendan Smith's decision during the following year to produce Joyce and O'Casey reveals a desire to continue to open Irish culture to elements that had been suppressed during the recent past. His inclusion of work by Vilar also reveals his desire to place Irish drama in dialogue with the best international work.

The reaction of the Catholic hierarchy to Smith's programme shows that the festival space was perceived by both sides as a battleground in which could be enacted a struggle for control over Irish culture. In that context, Smith's choice of the word 'postponement' rather than 'cancellation' to describe the DTF's failure to appear in 1958 was telling: he was acceding to demands from McQuaid and others—but only temporarily. The DTF returned in 1959, and soon established a reputation for the production of new Irish work. And Smith

[14] John Cooney, *John Charles McQuaid* (Dublin: O'Brien Press, 2003), 330.
[15] Beckett to Alan Simpson, 17 Feb. 1958, cited in James Knowlson, *Damned to Fame: The Life of Samuel Beckett* (London: Bloomsbury, 1996), 447–8. I am grateful to Trish McTigue for identifying this quotation.

would quickly ensure that external interference would be unable to undermine future Festivals.

Coming of Age: The 1964 Dublin Theatre Festival

After the debacle of 1958, Smith had sought to avoid controversy in the following years, allowing the DTF time to establish itself gradually. Visits from non-Irish companies and performers continued. Orson Welles performed in the Festival in 1959, a year which also saw the first performances at the DTF of work by Harold Pinter; there were also visits from the Old Vic Theatre company and the Compagnie de Rigault during that period.

There were signs too that Irish companies were beginning to programme specifically for the Festival. John B. Keane's *The Highest House on the Mountain* (1960) and *No More in Dust* (1961) both premièred at the DTF—a significant step for a writer whose previous works had first appeared in Cork and Kerry. Things were changing at the Abbey, too. Whereas in 1957 the theatre had merely revived three classics, by 1961 it had decided to create a programme specifically for the Festival. Called *Plays in the Abbey Tradition*, the season revived work by Robinson and Louis D'Alton, premièred Tomás Coffey's *The Long Sorrow*, and brought back Richard Johnson's *The Evidence I Shall Give*—an unexpected success from earlier that year, and the first Irish drama to criticize the treatment of young people in institutions run by the Catholic Church. As the title of its season made clear, the Abbey was looking both backwards and forwards: using its tradition to stimulate the development of new writing, some of which (as in the case of Johnson's play) was both courageous and prescient.

In 1962, the DTF dropped the word 'international' from its title. This change can be related to the Festival's growing reputation: its organizers no longer felt the need to use the word 'international' to boost their credentials. The event was thus sufficiently well established to again risk provoking a reaction from the Catholic hierarchy. Beckett had reversed his decision to ban the production of his work in Ireland, though O'Casey remained obstinate in his refusal to follow suit. Even so, including a play by either writer in the DTF could have been seen as a provocation. Smith, resourceful as ever, found a way to include the pair in that year's DTF anyway: *Waiting for Godot* (1955) appeared in an amateur production by Portora Royal School, while O'Casey's autobiographical novel *Pictures in the Hallway* (1942) was adapted for a staged reading by Paul Shyre. Joyce's work made a comeback too, albeit in the form of an adaptation of *A Portrait of the Artist as a Young Man* and *Stephen Hero* by Hugh Leonard—which was, perhaps wisely, given a new title: *Stephen D.* Leonard's success with *Stephen D.* showed that the DTF was gaining a reputation as a space in which Irish writers could take risks—not only in terms of subject matter (as Leonard had done by adapting Joyce) but also with form (Leonard's play was theatrically ambitious, avoiding naturalism and using techniques derived from contemporary European practice).[16]

The potential evident in the success of *Stephen D.* was abundantly realized in 1964, which is now recalled as the year in which the DTF came of age. The Festival opened that year with

---

[16] For a fuller discussion of the significance of *Stephen D.*, see Ch. 27.

a new play called *The Wooing of Duvessa*, a rather conventional Abbey comedy by the popular Galway author M. J. Molloy. It was soon followed, however, by the première of three challenging plays: *The King of the Castle* by Eugene McCabe, *Philadelphia, Here I Come!* by Brian Friel, and *An Triail* by Máiréad Ní Ghráda.

Like Molloy's play, *The King of the Castle* was set in rural Ireland, but there were few other resemblances with the Abbey production. McCabe's play was seeking to present a rigorous exploration of Irish sexuality in a plot involving impotence, adultery, and the pursuit of property, while also enacting his view that Irish Catholicism had lost sight of the basic tenets of Christianity. At a symposium dedicated to new Irish writing at that year's Festival, McCabe was forced to defend himself against the accusation that his play was 'pornographic', even as he acknowledged that it was 'ugly and unlikeable'. 'It refers to basic facts and functions,' he said, glumly adding, 'I would imagine that my play would have a very dampening effect on sex.' [17]

Key figures came to the defence of the play. The critic Niall Montgomery, alluding to McCabe's exploration of Christianity and sex, described him as a 'Catholic on a hot tin roof', while Mícheál MacLiammóir said that McCabe had made the 'terrible discovery' that 'Kathleen Ni Houlihan had legs under her skirt'.[18] Those remarks probably reveal more about their speakers' desire to say something witty than they do about McCabe's achievement, but both Montgomery and MacLiammóir were trying to praise *King of the Castle* for bringing a new frankness to the representation of Irish sexuality. Crucially, they saw McCabe's candour as arising from his exposure to international writing: not just to Tennessee Williams, but also to O'Neill and Pinter.

Perhaps surprisingly, given Friel's subsequent career, *Philadelphia, Here I Come!* received less attention than McCabe's play. It was praised for its comical elements, and Friel's decision to split Gar O'Donnell into a Public and Private self was admired without being widely discussed. But *Philadelphia* was also seen as a straightforward Irish play. 'One wondered', wrote the *Irish Times* critic, 'why [everything in the play] hadn't all been said years ago, and at the Abbey, which is [. . .] its proper place.'[19] What went unappreciated in 1964 was the extent to which Friel's play was intended to mark a break from the past, rather than any kind of continuation of the Abbey tradition. He had been inspired to write the play during his now famous visit to Minneapolis, where he observed Tyrone Guthrie at work—a visit that 'gave me a sense of liberation', wrote Friel: 'Remember, this was my first parole from inbred, claustrophobic Ireland—and that sense of liberation conferred on me a valuable self-confidence and a necessary perspective so that [. . .] *Philadelphia, Here I Come!* was a lot more assured than anything I had written before.'[20] Like McCabe, Friel was attempting to change Irish theatre by importing ideas from America.

Friel's fortunes began to shift when his play drew international attention. In a sign of the DTF's burgeoning reputation abroad, the English critics had come to Dublin in 1964, and Harold Hobson had praised *Philadelphia* warmly. 'It is immensely desirable that the play should be seen in London,' he wrote. 'The best drama is rooted in the soil from whence it sprung and this play is all Ireland.'[21] An English production of *Philadelphia* would take

---

[17] Quoted in 'Irish Theatre in a Scramble to Survive', *Irish Times*, 30 Sept. 1964.   [18] Ibid.

[19] 'Brian Friel's Sadly Comic Story', *Irish Times*, 29 Sept. 1964.

[20] Paul Delaney (ed.), *Brian Friel In Conversation* (Ann Arbor, MI: University of Michigan Press, 2000), 104.

[21] 'Festival Killing Irish Drama?', *Irish Times*, 5 Oct. 1964.

another three years to arrive, but Friel's play made its way to Broadway in 1966. The DTF had thus established itself not only as a place where new Irish plays could be produced but also as a gateway to international production.

Yet the DTF was also intended specifically for Irish audiences, as was perhaps most evident in its production of Máiréad Ní Ghráda's *An Triail*. Ní Ghráda was well established at the Abbey, where her Irish-language plays had been staged successfully since the mid-1940s, often as curtain-raisers for longer works. But *An Triail* was different from the work usually staged at the Abbey, focusing on the fate of a young woman who had become pregnant outside marriage, and thus making explicit some of the issues that Richard Johnson had only been able to imply in *The Evidence I Shall Give*. Just as the 1957 Festival had been able to use the Irish language to stage *Cúirt an Mheán Oíche*, a work that was banned in English, so Ní Ghráda was able to write in Irish to explore an issue that would not be the subject of an original play in English until 1992, when Patricia Burke Brogan's *Eclipsed* premièred (to great hostility from some sectors of Irish society). Ní Ghráda also made use of a Brechtian aesthetic and performance style, which was doubtless encouraged and enhanced by the direction of Tomás Mac Anna. It is notable that the DTF offered an Abbey playwright and an Abbey director the space to explore a topic that would have been considered too dangerous to stage at Ireland's national theatre—and it is notable too that it was Brecht, rather than an Irish model, who provided the vehicle for the transmission of Ní Ghráda's critique.

The 1964 Festival fixed in place a pattern that would continue for much of the DTF's history. McCabe and Ní Ghráda had shown that, far from presenting an idealized, tourist-friendly version of Ireland, the DTF could be a space to reveal Ireland's most troubling truths to itself. And the success of *Philadelphia* had shown that, if Ireland was talking to itself, it was also engaged in a dialogue with the rest of the world. That dialogue was with writers such as Brecht, Williams, Pinter, and O'Neill—and it was also with international critics and theatre producers, all of whom would use their experiences at the DTF to bring Irish drama to the attention of audiences around the world. Those characteristics have remained evident at the DTF ever since. In 1968, the Festival would again show its capacity to place Irish drama in an international dialogue when the Moscow Art Theatre's Maria Knebel directed the Abbey company in *The Cherry Orchard*, while in the Peacock the première of Tom Murphy's *Famine* was given a Brechtian production by Tomás Mac Anna. The Abbey used those plays to show that its new building (opened in 1966) would facilitate new ways of working: the decision to situate Irish drama in the context of both Brecht and Chekhov was a statement of intent.

Similarly, Irish dramatists would continue to follow the example of Ní Ghráda by using the DTF as a space in which to reveal truths to Irish society—as, for example, when Thomas Kilroy's *The Death and Resurrection of Mr Roche* and Brian Friel's *The Gentle Island* became the first Irish plays to explore homosexuality when they premièred at the 1968 and 1971 festivals respectively. And there would be one final battle with the Catholic Church when, in 1975, Tom Murphy's *The Sanctuary Lamp* attracted a hostile reaction due to its anticlericalism. But times had changed: in 1958, a negative intervention from the archbishop of Dublin had led to the postponement of the DTF, but Murphy's new play instead attracted official support. At a debate organized by the Abbey to discuss the controversy about *The Sanctuary Lamp*, the Irish president, Cearbhaill Ó Dálaigh, made a point of attending, and used the privilege of his position to have the first word. Murphy's play, he said, 'ranks in the first three of the great plays of this theatre: *The Playboy of the Western World, Juno and the Paycock*, and *The Sanctuary Lamp*'.[22] Ó Dálaigh's speech was arguably a more signifi- cant public act than the Abbey's decision to stage the play in the first place: here was the president of Ireland defending the rights of the artist over the sensitivities of the Catholic Church. As the Festival entered its eighteenth year, then, there were signs of a new maturity in the wider society too.

Festivalization and Irish Theatre
since the 1970s

The Dublin Theatre Festival has continued to achieve success by staging new Irish plays and by hosting the best international work. It has premièred many major Irish dramas: Stewart Parker's *Northern Star* (1985), Thomas Kilroy's *The Secret Fall of Constance Wilde* (1997), Marina Carr's *By the Bog of Cats* (1998), and Fabulous Beast's *The Bull* (2005), among many others. It has also brought many of the world's leading theatre-makers and companies to Ireland: Anne Bogart, Peter Brook, Romeo Castellucci, Robert Lepage, Katie Mitchell, Thomas Ostermeier, Robert Wilson, and others—not to mention such companies as Cheek by Jowl, Elevator Repair Service, Footsbarn, Propeller, the Royal Shakespeare Company, the Schiller Theatre, Théâtre de Complicité, Wrocław Contemporary Theatre, and so on. By 1983, the Festival was celebrating its twenty-fifth anniversary by confidently describing itself as 'both feast and celebration: a feast of international shows and a celebration of the creative talents of Irish artists'. [23] That description remains apt in the present.

The success of the DTF inspired the development of other events. The Belfast Festival at Queen's was established in 1962, and is now a key platform for the staging of new plays in Northern Ireland. Similarly, an Arts Festival began in Kilkenny in 1973, and although it ini- tially prioritized classical music and literature, it soon hosted theatre too. This in turn had the impact of stimulating new theatre locally, as when Theatre Unlimited emerged in 1986, bringing an acclaimed pseudo-Shakespearean production called *The Murder of Gonzago* to Dublin and Edinburgh. In Galway, a cultural renaissance had begun in the mid-1970s— first with the foundation of Druid in 1975, and then with the establishment of the Galway Arts Festival (GAF) in 1978. That event made a virtue of Galway's lack of performance ven- ues by supporting street theatre, which it encouraged by bringing major European troupes to the city. Those visits in turn stimulated the development of the local company Macnas, which was founded in 1986 and is now itself a leading European street performance group.

In the 1990s, the Celtic Tiger period led to an expansion in activity across all art forms, and new festivals emerged as a result. Some were dedicated to individual writers: the Gate staged several festivals dedicated to Beckett and Pinter; a Brian Friel Festival was held in

---

[22] 'President's Praise for Tom's Play', *Sunday Press*, 12 Oct. 1975.
[23] Dublin Theatre Festival, clippings, Billy Rose Theatre Collection, New York Public Library. Cited by John P. Harrington, 'Festivals National and International: The Beckett Festival', in Grene and Lonergan, *Interactions*, 134.

1999 (organized by the Abbey, the Gate, and the Lyric); and the Abbey arranged a Tom Murphy Festival in 2001. A key aim of those events was to promote a vision of Ireland as a home of great writers. Yet there were also signs of a desire to foster the development of a new generation of playwrights too, notably with the emergence of a Dublin Fringe Festival in 1995. Originally intended to run simultaneously with the Dublin Theatre Festival, the Fringe provided valuable experience to writers such as Conor McPherson, Mark O'Rowe, Elaine Murphy, Grace Dyas, and Shaun Dunne. By designating work as occupying a 'fringe', the event gives practitioners permission to experiment, and a freedom to fail that is not as readily available in a prestigious international event such as the DTF.

The Fringe and the DTF have now settled into a symbiotic relationship. The Fringe is able to take risks with emerging companies, whose work can range in quality from the exhilarating to the inadequate. But the devised work of those young companies has been heavily influenced by groups that were brought to Ireland by the DTF: Belgium's Victoria and Ontroerend Goed, Germany's Rimini Protokol, Poland's TR Warszawa, and so on. Yet the Fringe also feeds into the DTF, most successfully in the case of Louise Lowe's ANU Productions. That group's 'Monto Cycle' of site-specific participative performances began in the Dublin Fringe with *At World's End Lane* (2010) and *Laundry* (2011), before being completed at the DTF with *The Boys of Foley Street* (2012) and *Vardo* (2014). It is now regarded as one of the major Irish performance events of the early twenty-first century. The Fringe has thus become a kind of laboratory for the main festival, operating much as the small theatres like the Pike and the Pocket did in the late 1950s.

Irish theatre companies are also strongly focused on the international festival market—on opportunities to tour work to international events—and by far the most important of these are, of course, the festivals at Edinburgh. As early as 1951, the director Shelah Richards brought a production of *The Playboy of the Western World* to the Festival, giving Siobhán McKenna her first opportunity to play Pegeen Mike.[24] In 1956, a group of students from Belfast and Dublin banded together and took part in the Fringe, calling themselves (rather grandly) the Irish Festival Players. They soon attracted positive notices with their unconventional stagings of canonical Irish work, especially the plays of Yeats. That group never professionalized, but many of its members went on to have an involvement in the theatre: David Nowlan, for example, became lead theatre critic of the *Irish Times*; Louis Lentin became a director (and was responsible for the first Irish productions of Beckett's *Endgame* and *Krapp's Last Tape*); Neil McCarthy enjoyed a modestly successful career acting in British films; and Kathleen Watkins (together with her husband, the TV personality Gay Byrne) would become a strong advocate for Irish theatre. The Irish Festival Players established attendance at the Fringe as an important rite of passage for young Irish theatre-makers. In subsequent decades many Irish writers and actors have made their name at Edinburgh: for instance, only a year after its Cork premiere, Enda Walsh's *Disco Pigs* was a huge success there in 1997, making Walsh one of Ireland's most successful dramatists internationally, while launching the career of Cillian Murphy, who took one of that play's two leading roles.

---

[24] See Margaret Mac Curtain, 'Siobhán McKenna', in *Dictionary of Irish Biography* (Cambridge: Cambridge University Press, 2010).

Indeed, from the 1980s onwards, many Irish companies and writers would announce themselves by being successful not in Ireland but in Edinburgh. That, for example, was the path taken by Druid, whose much-celebrated Edinburgh productions of *Playboy of the Western World* in 1980 and 1982 did much to establish the company's reputation within Ireland (while also continuing the tradition of Irish companies surprising Scottish audiences by providing a radical reappraisal of an Irish writer). Similarly, Patrick Mason faced down criticism during his tenure as Abbey artistic director (1994–99) by bringing Synge's *The Well of the Saints*, Kilroy's *The Secret Fall of Constance Wilde*, and Tom Murphy's *The Wake* to Edinburgh in 1996, 1998, and 1999 respectively. Those productions had been only moderately successful with the critics during their Abbey runs; but by making a success of them abroad, Mason was able to imply that the problem was not with the Abbey but with the sensitivity and responsiveness of the Abbey's critics, who were left looking rather parochial and out of touch.

Attendance at Festivals also makes possible a scale of production that would otherwise be impossible. Garry Hynes's *DruidSynge* cycle (2005) staged all of Synge's plays (with the exception of *When the Moon Has Set*) during a single day—a feat that was accomplished only because the company knew that its costs would be offset by their attendance at the Galway Arts Festival, the Edinburgh International Festival, and the Lincoln Center Festival in New York. Similarly, the Abbey used a co-production model with the Edinburgh International Festival to première Frank McGuinness's adaptation of *Barbaric Comedies* by Ramon Maria del Valle-Inclan at the Dublin and Edinburgh festival of 2000. That was a five-hour production with a cast of more than twenty actors, and a plot that included necrophilia, incest, and a variety of other obscenities and blasphemies—all tied together by Calixto Bieito, one of Europe's the most notorious young directors. In a sign of how much things had changed since 1958, the production failed to attract either controversy or an audience. But in scale if not in substance it provided a model of festivalized co-production that would later be emulated by other Irish theatre companies, notably Druid and the Gate, the latter of which would produce a Beckett Festival with Edinburgh (2013) and the Lincoln Center (2008).

Festivals in Europe have also been important, especially since the mid-1990s. Ireland's leading post-dramatic theatre company, Pan Pan, has been heavily influenced by cross-cultural European encounters: its approach to text, its prioritization of visual impact over textual meaning, and its playful approach to canonical texts all have their roots in the European festival network, which tends to stage work that will be seen as iconoclastic (a necessary method of attracting attention from jaded festival directors), while also being able to circumvent linguistic barriers by emphasizing sound and spectacle over spoken words. Through organizing a series of international symposiums in Dublin, Pan Pan has in turn brought those ideas into Irish contexts.

Conclusions

The aim of the Abbey's founders was to create a national dramatic tradition for Ireland. and from an early stage in that theatre's development a debate arose about whether Irish drama would be healthier if quarantined from international influences. Consequently, international drama was often held apart within Irish theatre during the early twentieth century: the plays of Pirandello, Calderón, or Claudel may have been performed on the Abbey stage, but only under the auspices of the Dublin Drama League.

The postwar movement towards festivalization was also a movement towards internationalization—which might have prompted fears that Irish drama would lose its national focus. Yet as the Abbey Theatre Festival of 1938 had demonstrated, the country's theatre could be most 'Irish' when attracting an international audience: Irishness is what made the work distinctive, and what made international audiences view it as authentic. Far from diluting the national characteristics of Irish drama, international festivals have worked to protect the legacies of the Abbey Theatre, creating strong expectations amongst international audiences about how Irish plays should be seen and produced. Those expectations have complex consequences: they have certainly allowed many Irish actors, directors, and writers to make a living, by introducing them to international audiences—yet they have sometimes limited Irish drama to a small set of defining characteristics: rural settings, a whimsical form of gallows humour, lyrical speech, and so on.

A second significant characteristic of the festival is its relationship with the state. As noted above, the Dublin Theatre Festival was supported by Bord Fáilte before it was supported by the Arts Council—showing how its remit was partially determined by the need to attract visitors to Ireland, perhaps by producing positive consumable images of the country. Yet Irish writers and directors were quick to resist any pressure to romanticize their nation, choosing to explore those elements of Irish life that the state most wished to ignore: the inhibition of Irish sexuality and the hypocrisies associated with it, the impact of emigration, the declining influence of Catholicism, the problem of homophobia, and so on. This clash between 'official' and 'real' Irelands provides a revealing perspective on the longstanding debate about whether government support allows theatres the freedom to challenge the state's most treasured delusions about itself.

Those features reveal another significant impact of festivals on Irish drama: its development of new writing. Hence, we find Brian Friel transforming Irish dramatic form with *Philadelphia, Here I Come!* in 1964—just as later writers such as Kilroy, Parker, Carr, and many others would enjoy the freedom that festivals offer to push beyond formal and thematic boundaries. For that reason, it would probably be more accurate to see the development of Irish drama after 1950 as being directed not just by individual theatres such as the Abbey but also by festivalization. That development has also been inspired by the kinds of international exchange made possible within festivals. The evolution of Irish drama and theatre practice since 1950 has been substantially influenced by the tours to Ireland of major world figures such as Robert Lepage and Anne Bogart (among many others), and also by such playwrights as Williams, Brecht, and O'Neill.

Theatre festivals are, as the Dublin Theatre Festival put it in 1983, both a feast and a celebration. They are a feast in that they compress an extraordinary variety of productions into small periods, and they are a celebration in that they have allowed Irish drama to present the best of itself to the world. But that celebration has never been uncritical, and has never been fully appropriated by national or religious agencies. Certainly, Irish festivals have faced obstacles—from unruly Jesuits in 1938 to intolerant archbishops in 1958 to funding difficulties in the 1980s, and so on. Yet festivals are also public events that have consequences far beyond the stage, and far beyond the auditorium—inspiring surprising (and sometimes reactionary) interventions, raising the profile of Ireland internationally, and allowing audiences to imagine the possibility of societal and personal change. The festival has thus become one of the key spaces in which Ireland has learned to perform itself, for audiences both within and beyond the nation.

CHAPTER 40

REINSCRIBING THE CLASSICS, ANCIENT AND MODERN
The Sharp Diagonal of Adaptation

CHRISTINA HUNT MAHONY

IN 1906 the Abbey Theatre's third season included Lady Gregory's *The Doctor in Spite of Himself*, an adaptation of Molière's *Le Médecin malgré lui*. For twenty years Gregory continued to reinterpret the great French playwright's work and that of other European dramatists. In 1926, just as Gregory's *The Would-Be Gentleman* was staged, her co-founder and director, W. B. Yeats, was beginning his adaptation of Sophocles' *Oedipus Rex*, pursuing an interest that predated the founding of the theatre. Yeats and Gregory both sought dramatic models for Irish writers to emulate and a means of circumventing English dramatic tradition as part of a broader nationalist agenda. As Michael Cronin has observed, 'Lady Gregory's translation work was conceived of primarily as an act of cultural self-confidence.' Yeats, like the writers of 'Tudor England, Classical France, and Romantic Germany[,] considered the translation of Greek and Roman classics to be part of the process of nation building'.[1]

Whatever its impetus or purpose, translation is an artistic undertaking very much of its time. Like original works of art, a translation aspires to permanence, but must also prioritize the needs of its era. Irish theatregoers throughout the twentieth century had no shortage of drama in translation on offer, even if the aims of the Abbey founders were not evident in other productions. In his *History of the Irish Theatre, 1601–2000*, Christopher Morash surveys the range of modern European drama on Irish stages, and confirms broad Irish access to such works often shortly after they debuted in their native countries.[2] Playwright Edward Martyn's Irish Theatre staged *Uncle Vanya* (1915) in Dublin, a production involving writer/revolutionaries Thomas MacDonagh and Joseph Plunkett. Writer Frank O'Connor played Lopakhin in the Cork production of his *The Cherry Orchard* (1928). Chekhov's *The*

---

[1] Michael Cronin, *Translation and Globalization* (London: Routledge, 2003), 154.
[2] Christopher Morash, *A History of Irish Theatre, 1601–2000* (Cambridge: Cambridge University Press, 2002), 118–20.

Bear was staged in Dublin in 1923 and 1924, *The Proposal* in an Irish-language version in Galway at An Taibhdhearc (1929).[3] Despite such exposure to theatre from different traditions, it was only many decades after the deaths of the Abbey founders that Irish playwrights began to produce significant theatrical adaptations from other languages.

In the 1980s, audiences in Ireland, and throughout the Anglophone world, witnessed the start of a proliferation of Irish versions of European modern classics. A generation of Irish playwrights had emerged who were sufficiently secure in their original work to aspire to reinscribe Continental classics, while others refashioned ancient Greek drama. Some did both. A dramatic phenomenon was emerging that bridged the gap of cultures, languages, and decades.

It is necessary to establish that none of the works discussed here is a translation in the true sense. None of the playwrights has sufficient facility in the relevant second language, and none worked directly from source texts. Rather, these texts are adaptations or versions, written either in collaboration with a translator whose work is acknowledged to varying degrees or by drawing upon previous English-language translations. In adapting these plays, Irish writers were rejecting the prevailing British (and to a lesser extent American) cultural assumptions of previous translators, and thus altering the linguistic landscape. On both sides of the footlights, standard acting versions in English were considered obstacles to Irish audiences, with Irish actors using an English not their own. Recent Irish versions of these canonical works should be seen, then, not as the continuation of Yeats's and Gregory's early efforts at nation-building, but as examples of a postcolonial sensibility reflective of the cultural and critical priorities of their time. Here too is evidence of cultural confidence, but with a different historical and social context, expressed in a contemporary artistic register.

The adaptation of modern classics is ongoing, comprising multiple versions of Chekhov, Ibsen, Strindberg, Pirandello, Brecht, and other plays dating from the 1880s to the mid-twentieth century.[4] The foremost Irish interpreters are Brian Friel, Frank McGuinness, Thomas Kilroy, and Tom Murphy. All began by writing indirectly in 'tribute to their inspirational sources', but progressed to adapting those source texts.[5] The versions from the Greek, written from the 1980s onward, returned once again to realpolitik, mainly in Northern Ireland, where a group of established poets turned to stage adaptation. Most of the work was produced by the Field Day Theatre Company in the Guildhall in Derry. For these writers, Greek tragedy, with its stark content and spare execution, served to bear witness to the social and political realities of their province. It also meant working in a very public genre new to most of them. The dramatic adaptations of poets Seamus Heaney and Tom Paulin were among the most prominent; however, playwright Brian Friel emerged as, and remained, a pivotal figure in both dramatic

---

[3] Robert Tracy, 'Chekhov in Ireland', programme note, *Uncle Vanya by Anton Chekhov, a Version by Frank McGuinness* (Derry: The Guildhall, Field Day Theatre Company, Feb. 1995). See also his 'Rehearsing the 1916 Rising: Theatre Politics and Political Theatre', in Ros Dixon and Irina Ruppo Malone (eds.), *Ibsen and Chekhov on the Irish Stage* (Dublin: Carysfort Press, 2012), 127–38.

[4] Only Derek Mahon would follow Lady Gregory's lead with Molière. His *High Time (after Molière)* (1984) reworked *L'École des maris* for Field Day in a double bill with Tom Paulin's *The Riot Act*. Mahon's *A School for Wives: after Molière* (1989) appeared as part of the Dublin Theatre Festival.

[5] Catherine Piola, 'Stage Adaptations and the Dublin Theatre Festival', in Thierry Dubost (ed.), *Drama Reinvented: Theatre Adaptation in Ireland (1970–2007)* (Bern: Peter Lang, 2007), 37–43.

flowerings under consideration here. Friel was the first to open a dialogue with Chekhov, and also produced versions of Turgenev and Ibsen. Although he did no adaptations of Greek tragedy, as director of Field Day Friel was instrumental in commissioning several new versions from that canon. As the result of such industry by Irish playwrights, audiences have seen an Irish Nora in Ibsen's *A Doll's House*, an Irish Arkadina in Chekhov's *The Seagull*, and figures from the Trojan Wars reciting verse in unmistakeably Northern Irish rhythms. These adaptations appealed to Irish audiences, but the degree of their success abroad requires further examination. Writers elsewhere were producing excellent adaptations in English—one need only point to David Mamet's superb *Vanya on 42nd St.*[6] So why the demand for Irish adaptations?

We must recognize that these adaptations became artistic currency not only because of the writerly skill involved, but also because of a confluence of cultural factors. Irish dramatic adaptations were in demand as Irish poets and novelists became prominent among the nominees and winners of literary prizes, such as the Booker, Whitbread (later Costa), and T. S. Eliot prizes. Two Irish poets were appointed during this period to the prestigious Chair of Poetry at Oxford. Original Irish plays, actors, and directors were garnering Oliviers in London and Tonys on Broadway. Irish filmmakers and actors were recognized with BAFTAs and Oscars. Nor can the success of Irish musicians worldwide be underestimated, or the international phenomenon that was Riverdance. Irish culture was enjoying a period of unprecedented popularity, and the world wanted more.

In theatre circles, playwrights Brian Friel, Frank McGuinness, Sebastian Barry, Martin McDonagh, and Conor McPherson were now established names abroad. With such recognition came money: financial backers seized upon opportunities to invest in future productions. So when producers and directors were looking for writers to adapt classics (with their own proven lucrative history) it was good business, both artistically and financially, to seek out an Irish writer for the job. The 'Irish play', an elusive but already identifiable concept abroad, marked by linguistic agility and beauty and edifying themes, expanded conceptually to embrace Irish adaptations of other great dramatists.[7]

Another explanation for the number of adaptations (often of the same plays) issuing from Ireland in the past forty years is the country's small artistic milieu. Irish playwrights have a documented history of writing plays in echo and response to those of their colleagues (two such pairings are Brian Friel's *Philadelphia, Here I Come!* (1964) and Tom Murphy's *A Crucial Week in the Life of a Grocer's Assistant* (1969), and Murphy's *Sanctuary Lamp* (1975) and Friel's *Faith Healer* (1979)). Their artistic environment is thus indirectly collaborative, making for an unacknowledged literary movement of sorts. Such conditions, perhaps unique to Ireland, provide opportunities for encouraging more and better dramatic reinscription to suit the demands of the international Anglophone world. The attractions are even strong enough to threaten the flow of original drama.

---

[6] At the Freeman Studio in New York, director André Gregory devised an *Uncle Vanya* workshop from 1990 to 1994, which evolved into the film *Vanya on 42nd St*, directed by Louis Malle, produced by Fred Berner, 1994: http://www.thefreemanstudio.com/#!andre-gregory-lecture/c1u3o. Accessed 18 Aug. 2014.

[7] See Christina Hunt Mahony, 'The Irish Play: Beyond the Generic?', in John P. Harrington (ed.), *Irish Theater in America: Essays on Irish Theatrical Diaspora* (Syracuse, NY: Syracuse University Press, 2009), 163–76.

Commissioned plays introduce another element into the creative process that can alter its dynamic. Writers used to finding initial inspiration from within before entering into the collaborative process of theatre-making must collaborate on commissioned projects from the outset. Notable Irish examples of commissioned adaptations include Thomas Kilroy's *The Seagull* (1981), John McGahern's *The Power of Darkness* (1991), and Frank McGuinness's *Peer Gynt* (1988), all the result of recognition of latent artistic connections between writer and source material. This essential ingredient for successful reinterpretation can be conveyed variously as simple affinity, absorptive appropriation, or lateral affiliation.[8]

Parallel themes, language, or characters in a writer's world and that of another era or culture can often act as a catalyst, or as an entry point, for adaptation. Poet Aidan Carl Mathews, explaining the process in relation to his version of *Antigone* (1984), described his approach as making 'its way into the source text at a sharp diagonal'.[9] His phrase can signify both the translator's tool and his angle of vision. It acknowledges the acuity and individuality inherent in successful adaptation, making what was great theatre both great and new. That diagonal also recalls the final apt exhortation of James Joyce at the end of Seamus Heaney's visionary poem 'Station Island', published in the same year as Mathews's play: 'Keep at a tangent […] fill the element with signatures on your own frequency.'[10] Joyce's advice, cast as though from one writer to another, is really that of a writer to himself, and a particular challenge for the adaptive artist.

AFFINITIES

True affinity between writers is often apparent early in a writing career. Brian Friel and Frank McGuinness may have adapted the works of a number of writers, but each man's strong affinity for a single playwright emerged quickly and overtook all others.

Friel's period working in Minneapolis with Tyrone Guthrie, another theatre-maker from Northern Ireland, occasioned his initial exposure to Chekhovian productions, including Guthrie's production of *Three Sisters* (1963).[11] The influence of this experience became apparent first in Friel's *Living Quarters* (1977). Acknowledged to be 'after Hippolytus', its Phaedra-like plot and characters also adhere closely to Chekhov's *Three Sisters*—a play which Friel would translate several years later from English-language sources.[12] Absorptive use of Chekhov's originals continued in *Aristocrats* (1979), which mirrors the plot of *The Cherry Orchard*—a family's failure to maintain its property and status. Much has been

---

[8] Kilroy's *Seagull* is discussed below. McGahern's *The Power of Darkness*, from Tolstoy's play of the same title, was originally commissioned by the BBC, McGuinness's version of Ibsen's *Peer Gynt* by Michael Colgan at the Gate.

[9] Christopher Murray, 'Three Irish *Antigones*', in Jacqueline Genet and Richard Allen Cave (eds.), *Perspectives of Irish Drama and Theatre* (Gerrards Cross: Colin Smythe, 1991), 125.

[10] Seamus Heaney, 'Station Island', in *Station Island* (London: Faber & Faber, 1994), 93–4.

[11] Nicholas Grene, 'Chekhov and the Irish Big House', in Dixon and Malone, *Ibsen and Chekhov on the Irish Stage*, 140.

[12] Marilynn J. Richtarik, *Acting Between the Lines: The Field Day Theatre Company and Irish Cultural Politics 1980–1984* (Oxford: Clarendon Press, 1994), 109.

written on the social affinities between Russia and Ireland in the period in which Chekhov's plays are set, usually revolving around the periphery aspiring to the metropolis, the lingering strictures imposed upon a fraying upper class forced to maintain grand houses and large estates, and the resulting stagnation and defeat. Less has been written on the attachment, verging on obsession, to the land and the home place which informed consciousness across generations in both countries. Friel fixes on this connection in both *Living Quarters* and *Aristocrats*, even before he reinscribes Chekhov's works directly.

Chekhov for Friel is not the intimidating presence he can be for others. This is Friel's most significant contribution to Irish writers' ongoing engagement with the Russian master, and possibly with the whole adaptive undertaking in Ireland. In Russia, and in theatres worldwide, Chekhov's work is approached with a reverence that cannot be overstated. Friel's unusual ease with this iconic *oeuvre* freed him to take broad interpretive approaches with the plays (and some of Chekhov's stories), and opened the door for others in Ireland. His is never an insouciant approach, although critical reaction has been varied. Michael Billington takes issue with what he sees as Friel's tendency to make obvious what Chekhov chooses to leave open to interpretation, or to make ribald elements of dialogue not as baldly humorous in Russian or other English-language versions.[13] It may be that Friel's Chekhov is simply too Irish for Billington, but this view is shared by purists, especially in light of Friel's retention of the plays' Russian settings. The counter-argument to Billington's is that by constructing real dialogue, in which speakers respond to each other (as they often do not in Chekhov), Friel shifted the emotive landscape from the solipsistic to a speculative and discursive frame more suited to Irish sensibility.[14]

Neither of these responses, however, seems fully alive to the possibility that what may *seem* dialogic in Friel is merely Irish banter or blather just as ineffectual as speech in the Russian original. Are Irina and Chebutykin really conversing when Friel breaks up Irina's monologue on the value of work?

IRINA.   Dear, darling, dopey Doctor!
CHEBUTYKIN.   My own little sweetheart—what is it?
IRINA.   You'll know the answer.
CHEBUTYKIN.   The answer to what?
IRINA.   Why am I so happy today?[15]

The scene continues thus before Irina's real monologue begins, but Chebutykin's part in the dialogue is formulaic. The dialogue does, however, have a function. With these exchanges Friel picks up the tempo on stage effectively, increases movement, and allows for more interaction between characters. Such small changes lessen the burden of a long monologue, with its inherent demand on actor and audience alike. This is something of a signature of Friel's Chekhovian interpretations. Friel's extended original stage directions also provide

---

[13] Helen Rappaport, 'Chekhov in the Theatre: The Role of the Translator in New Versions', in Gunilla M. Anderman (ed.), *Voices in Translation: Bridging Cultural Divides* (Bristol: Multilingual Matters, 2007), 73–4.

[14] Robert Tracy, 'The Russian Connection: Friel and Chekhov', *Irish University Review* 29(1) (1999), 64–77.

[15] Brian Friel, *Three Sisters* (Oldcastle: Gallery Press, 1981), 15.

additional or altered rhythm. In Act II, Chebutykin reads aloud from the newspaper a bit of news which Friel renders metrically in dactylic English—'Balzac was married in Berdichev town'. After the potentially playful possibilities of this phrase are mimicked by Irina and Fedotik, Friel inserts:

> Pause. There is a sense that this moment could blossom, an expectancy that suddenly every-body might join in the chorus—and dance.[16]

The opportunity is missed, though, and 'the moment is lost'. The faltering piano music and the 'atmosphere of vague embarrassment' are non-linguistic sublimations of the non-sequiturs, unfinished sentences, and half-expressed thoughts of the original text.

Despite the natural affinity between these two writers, or indeed because of it, Friel rec-ognized an impediment for Irish actors approaching Chekhov, making access 'more and more remote'. 'They have to pretend, first of all, that they're English and then that they're Russians.'[17] His provision of an Irish blas '(literally, 'taste' or 'flavour') does much to restore the cosy and familiar relationship between characters found in the original, and is in keep-ing with both Chekhovian and Irish society of the same stratum. Friel's language thus stands in contrast to that used in other, more formal English translations. The language of the play also suited the artistic aims of Field Day, which mounted the play in its second season after the success of the playwright's Translations. Such claims as 'For the Russians,' the division between the characters and unavoidable changes is essential, whereas for Friel, interaction, continuity and even a shared lamentation are at the core of his dramatic work' must be challenged.[18] Friel's versions leave the possibility for a more positive reading at play's end, even though they are situated within the same claustrophobic and static con-fines ever-present in Chekhov.

Friel's adaptation of Uncle Vanya (1998) has had perhaps more productions than any of the other adaptations discussed here. The first of these, at the Gate, featured Eamon Morrissey as Telegin, in the type of expanded comic role favoured by Friel's Chekhov. The running references to Telegin's unexplained and (in context) bizarre predilection for Germans and German culture, and his awkward recurring references to personal hygiene, are not found in Chekhov. (Telegin turns to Elena rather early in the play and asks the young lady 'Do you sweat much yourself?')[19] Both additions elicited a broadly comic response, but there is little context for the former, while the latter overbalances the degree of familiarity between classes and genders that Friel captured so adroitly in Three Sisters. Telegin's speech in Friel's adaptation seems to operate in a different register from the other roles, an isolated example of flat-footedness in an otherwise agile dramatist. The provision of a linguistic tic, a verbal leitmotif, for Vershinin in Three Sisters, whose lines are padded with self-deprecating fillers such as 'What I'm suggesting is' or 'The point I'm trying to

[16] Ibid., 55.

[17] Brian Friel quoted in Marilynn Richtarik, 'The Field Day Theatre Company', in Shaun Richards (ed.), The Cambridge Companion to Twentieth-Century Irish Drama (Cambridge: Cambridge University Press, 2004), 197.

[18] Virginia Roche-Tiengo, 'Brian Friel's Theatrical Adaptations of Chekhov's Works', in Dubost, Drama Reinvented, 97–110.

[19] Brian Friel, Uncle Vanya: A Version of the Play by Anton Chekhov (New York: Dramatists Play Service, 1998), 12.

make is', serve to enhance the comedy. Vershinin endears himself to the audience, whereas Telegin's given tics invite derision.

That Friel's *Vanya* appeared nearly two decades after his *Three Sisters* is crucial to our understanding of his approach to the play, and the resultant version. Importantly, and unlike the process for *Three Sisters*, Friel was then working from a literal translation from the Russian, which seemed to restrain his earlier brio. He was also writing in a Northern Ireland suffering from years of violence, with tentative feelers of hope only just emerging. Field Day too had changed from primarily a theatre company to more of a publishing venture, a fact which influenced Friel's decision to première the play at the Gate.

If Brian Friel has been called 'the Irish Chekhov', then Frank McGuinness may deserve the sobriquet 'the Irish Ibsen'. He has now adapted all of Ibsen's major works and sees the task as being complete—'[I]t's been a 20-year love affair. I still love him. I'll always love him. But we are not going to have any more children.'[20] McGuinness works from literal translations commissioned from native speakers who are credited, both in published texts and theatre programmes, and provide him with insight into the register and stylistic signatures of Ibsen. The translators are not the playwright's competitors, but collaborators whose work provides a space where his original text is created for contemporary audiences.

McGuinness's years of Nordic study have been rewarded. His version of *A Doll's House* (1996), in a London production directed by Anthony Page, went on the following year to sweep Tonys for best revival, leading actress, supporting actor, and director. McGuinness's Nora Helmer, magnificently well served by Janet McTeer, is influenced by his upbringing in Buncrana, Co. Donegal, a town where factory work made women independent to a degree, but within a male-dominated society without parity of esteem. Nora's adult status is variously undercut, notably in early scenes with her husband, Torvald. The on-stage presence of her childhood nanny, now minding Nora's own children, intensifies her infantilization. McGuinness's text subtly links the language used to address Nora and the children. Torvald's string of diminutives in apostrophe to his wife as a 'skylark chirping' and a 'squirrel', and the frequent repetition of the word 'little' are all assonantal choices which gather in intensity, relating to his child-wife, and parroted in turn by Nora:

HELMER.   There are *little birds* that like to *fritter* money. What do you call them?
NORA.   *Little fritter birds*, yes. [italics mine][21]

In Act II the nanny, Anne-Marie, picks up the same sounds when she calls her mistress first 'little Nora', then switches to 'Mrs Nora'—forms of address which are aurally almost interchangeable. Nora's dialogue with her children noticeably echoes Torvald's with her, in its exaggerated and repetitive baby talk: 'My little doll, my sweet baby'; 'Doggies don't bite lovely baby dolls.' McGuinness's interpretation might have 'emotional consistency and logic', but McTeer's performance and McGuinness's wording expose the gap between the assertion that Nora's lot is like that of all married women in her society and the specific

[20] 'A happy marriage', interview with John O'Mahony, 24 Apr. 2008: http://www.theguardian.com/stage/2008/apr/24/theatre1. Accessed 13 Aug. 2014.

[21] Frank McGuinness, *Henrik Ibsen,* A Doll's House: *A New Version by Frank McGuinness from a Literal Translation by Charlotte Barslund* (London: Faber & Faber, 1996), 5.

FIG. 40.1 Janet McTeer as Nora in Frank McGuinness's version of Ibsen's *A Doll's House* (Playhouse Theatre, London, 1996).

Courtesy of Victoria and Albert Museum.

domestic reality of the Helmer household.[22] McTeer's height, bearing, and voice helped to assert the power of McGuinness's text. Ultimately this imposing physicality lent credence to Nora's clear-eyed determination to save her husband's life at all costs, and rendered hers a demonstrably independent adult decision. Torvald's obtuse response at the play's end is striking in McGuinness's pointed use of short, sharp sentences, as when Nora's debt to Krogstad is forgiven: 'We're both saved, you and me. Look. Your contract, he's returning it. He regrets, he repents, he says.' Thus McGuinness's adaptation makes way for Nora's famous final speeches, which swell as her husband's power and speech wane.

[22] Ben Brantley, 'The Doll House Brings Down the House', *New York Times*, 3 Apr. 1997: http://www. nytimes.com/1997/04/03/theater/the-doll-brings-down-the-house.html. Accessed 13 Aug. 2014.

McGuinness's recent interpretation of Ibsen's *John Gabriel Borkman* (2010) reached the Abbey stage and the Dublin Theatre Festival at a time of financial crisis throughout the European Union. Post-boom Ireland, still reeling from its descent from the giddy heights of Celtic Tiger prosperity, was highly receptive to the retributive tale of Ibsen's failed banker (with Alan Rickman in the title role). Borkman had given up all, including the woman he loved, for wealth. Present-day parallels were reinforced by 'Show Related Talks', including journalist Martina Devlin discussing her bestseller about the Irish banking collapse, *Banksters*.[23] A bleak snow-laden set, presaging one of the worst winters in Irish history, rendered even more elemental the domestic tragedy in which father, son, wife, and sisters chafe against their fates and each other. Fiona Shaw, as Borkman's wife, and second choice as mate, gave a grim dignity to the role. While her performance spoke to contemporary audiences, Shaw subtly conveyed the graver historic implications of social and economic ruin among the bourgeoisie in Ibsen's era.

McGuinness's primary motivation in adapting Ibsen's middle-class drama is to fully realize the source texts with which he has innate affinity. He has become the go-to dramatist for West End and Broadway adaptations, which is both lucrative and artistically rewarding. His Ibsen work serves the modern theatre well, with his skilful slashing through layers of formality and evangelical rectitude to assert Ibsen's pragmatism, his clear-eyed exposition of base motives, and credible glimpses into imperfect marriages and relationships. This Ibsen shows us the evils of greed and ambition, but with a jaundiced view of the power of reforming zeal. Some of Ibsen's high drama and rhetoric, based on démodé views of honour, the finality of scandal, bespoiled virtue, or financial skulduggery no longer speak to modern audiences; however, underlying immorality and injustice do. This same appeal to fundamental morality, shorn of rhetorical niceties or cultural custom, also limns McGuinness's version of Ibsen's radically different verse fable, *Peer Gynt*, and his adaptations of Brecht, especially *The Caucasian Chalk Circle* (National Theatre, 2007). In these peasant plays there is an earthier and more identifiably Irish register at play, far from the comfort zone of the middle-class drawing room, but one which also displays the breadth of McGuinness's adaptive talent.

Appropriations

Despite the scope of Brian Friel's Chekhovian engagement, it was his Field Day colleague Thomas Kilroy who would remake the Russian's great work *The Seagull* (1981) as an Irish play. Produced at the Royal Court in London several months before Friel's *Three Sisters* appeared in Derry, it is set in the west of Ireland. Max Stafford-Clark commissioned the adaptation, due to his interest in the Anglo-Irish as a social caste in decline, one quite different from their English counterparts. Kilroy has written of the collaboration: 'Max felt, and I agreed with him, that some English-language productions of Chekhov tended toward a very English gentility where the socially specific Chekhov tended to be lost in polite vagueness.'[24]

[23] 'Show Related Talks': http://www.abbeytheatre.ie/whats_on/event/john_gabriel_borkman/. Accessed 13 Aug. 2014.

[24] Thomas Kilroy, '*The Seagull*: An Adaptation', in Vera Gottlieb and Paul Allain (eds.), *The Cambridge Companion to Chekhov* (Cambridge: Cambridge University Press, 2000), 80.

FIG. 40.2 Thomas Kilroy's version of Chekhov's *The Seagull*, directed by Max Stafford-Clark (Royal Court, 8 April 1981).

Courtesy of Victoria and Albert Museum.

That social specificity is captured by Kilroy's interweaving elements from *The Cherry Orchard* into his text, adumbrating historical issues from a later period into his version to reflect relevant conditions in Ireland. It is an artistic decision which meshes well with Kilroy's readily recognizable borrowings from Yeats, Joyce, and O'Casey. The most obvious of these is his devising an arch rendering of a Celtic Twilight play, a Yeatsian pastiche, for Chekhov's esoteric symbolist drama. Like Treplyov's in the original, it is avant-garde, with symbolist roots, and ripe for derision. Constantine/Treplyov's play also emerges from the 'suppressed culture' of Ireland, making this adaptation more overtly political than the original while retaining its historicity.[25] Kilroy goes on subtly to connect Chekhov's fictional lake with that at Coole Park, Lady Gregory's estate. He borrows characters' names from Joyce's *Dubliners*, and serves up an Uncle Peter (Chekhov's Sorin) smuggled in from O'Casey's *The Plough and the Stars*. In this Irish version, the doctor's name is Hickey (from the Irish word for healer, *iceadh*, a name long linked with the medical profession). The melodramatic, self-regarding heroine (Chekhov's Arkadina) is Isobel Desmond, suggestive of the iconic performance of Gloria Swanson as fading diva Norma Desmond in the film *Sunset Boulevard*.[26] The Royal Court's production thus presented itself before English

---

[25] Ibid., 84.
[26] Billy Wilder's classic film noir explores the delusional state of an ageing, outré actor whose extravagance results in the decay of her grand house. The film is narrated by a struggling young writer whom she first spoils but in the end kills.

audiences culturally and historically laden—a condition which epitomizes the layered accretion through which Russian audiences must access Chekhov.

Kilroy has also fashioned versions of Pirandello's work, but has more recently found a *fin-de-siècle* German playwright whose plays anticipate the thematic preoccupations of his own original work. *Christ Deliver Us!* (2010) is based on Frank Wedekind's *Frühlings Erwachen* (*Spring Awakening*), a work which challenged bourgeois German sexual mores in the 1890s. In Kilroy's adaptation, set in 1950s small-town Ireland, church and state combine to repress sexual expression. The vacuum of ignorance and misinformation that results causes the death of three innocent teenagers. Kilroy's message is no less an indictment than Wedekind's, and the authorial match in this adaptation is a fortunate one.

Kilroy's young heroine, Winnie Butler, does not know what to do with her budding sexuality, and no one will tell her. She resists growing up because, as she looks about her, she sees the adult female world as one of unrelieved burden. The play emphasizes the separated worlds of gender and age in the town as a microcosm of Irish society. When these worlds intersect it can be with calamitous effect. In *Christ Deliver Us!* sexual innocence is not endearing, but dangerous. Kilroy retains nearly all the particulars of Wedekind's original, and its condemnatory stance, although the Irish playwright's alterations are significant. For Kilroy's play is severely class-conscious, with all the inequity that that suggests, and it is also laced with violence. Children are beaten at home and in school for showing any signs of sexual awakening. Perhaps Kilroy's most shocking dramatic borrowing from Wedekind is to have Winnie masochistically confuse being beaten with the onset of sexual feeling. As an indirect result she becomes pregnant by a young boy, Michael Grainger, who is not much better informed than she. Mossie, a friend of Michael's, hangs himself after being expelled from school, in part because of a sexual misdemeanour involving Michael. For both his transgressions Michael is consigned to a reformatory, and Winnie dies alone on a riverbank with her stillborn child.[27]

Christ Deliver Us! reflects contemporary Irish audiences' acknowledgement of institutional abuse dating from the period in which the play is set; it also captures the national zeitgeist in the wake of multiple legal cases of rape, pregnancy, and abortion in the 1980s and 1990s, often involving underage women.[28] In adapting Wedekind, Thomas Kilroy, more than his contemporaries, found a playwright whose primary dramatic impetus seems akin to his own. From the outset of his career, with *The Death and Resurrection of Mr Roche* (1968), through *Double Cross* (1986), *The Madame MacAdam Travelling Theatre Company* (1991), and *The Secret Fall of Constance Wilde* (1997), Kilroy has written of the societal consequences of sexual ignorance, repression, and shame, all central to an understanding of Wedekind's corpus.

Powerful Irish adaptations of classics are thus continuing into this century; and recently there has been no more striking evidence of Brian Friel's imaginative approach to Chekhov than his recent reworking of the much-anthologized short story 'The Lady with the Dog'.

---

[27] Winnie's death evokes that of 15-year-old Ann Lovett in Granard, Co. Longford, in 1984. The shocking circumstances of this case continue to be the subject of media investigation and artistic representation.

[28] The 'Kerry Babies' case also occurred in 1984. Two newborns were found dead in County Kerry, and the unmarried mother of one child was accused of having killed both. The case became notorious in its mishandling, a byword for the conflict of changing mores in Ireland at the time. See Nell McCafferty, *The Kerry Babies Case* (Cork: Cork University Press, 2010).

Friel's dramatic retelling, *The Yalta Game* (2001), achieves what is usually only aspirational in adaptation, becoming a parallel art form equal to its source. This level of appropriation is more familiar in opera, where original stories are rare, but musical retellings serve as heightened responses to the original. Friel's equally inventive decision to conjoin two characters from separate Chekhov plays—Sonya Serebriakova from *Uncle Vanya* and Andrey Prozorov from *Three Sisters*—in *Afterplay* (2002) confirms a writer working with supreme confidence and skill. Such artistic splicing (echoing Kilroy's earlier fusing of two Chekhovian time-frames in *The Seagull*) partakes of a literary vogue more the province of fiction writers. Imagining on-stage afterlives for fictional characters is a far riskier undertaking. Friel succeeds brilliantly, illuminating Chekhov in an entirely original light.

In *The Yalta Game* Friel exploits the quintessentially dramatic nature of the story set in a seaside resort where residents seek to leave the constraints of their real lives behind. Chekhov provided his holidaymakers with staged entrances and exits, allowed them the performative possibilities of the nightly promenade, and provided the costuming essential to maintain illusion while they played the game. Friel both refracts and compresses the story. Chekhov's Gurov is a misogynist and predator, with a prematurely ageing wife whom he loathes and fears. He sets out to corrupt the young Anna, who despises her 'flunkey' husband. Friel's Gurov is more roué than misogynist, playfully articulating preposterous imagined lives for the Yalta denizens for Anna's benefit. Friel seizes upon the hats in the story, using them as real or imagined props on stage. His imagined dog is a tour de force, especially as Gurov breaks the fourth wall in reference to its debated existence. Friel's reimagining of the story is lighter and wittier than the original, but he artfully comes to a very similar moral resolve that leaves frivolity behind.

In his preface to *Afterplay*, which takes place twenty years after the events in Chekhov, Friel describes his role as adaptor:

> Had I created these characters in the first place I would feel free now to reshape them as I wished. But they are not mine alone. I am something less than a parent but I know I am something more than a foster parent. Maybe something closer to a godparent who takes his responsibilities scrupulously.[29]

This diagonal approach acknowledges the intimate boundaries which reinscribing another's work requires. Friel's godfatherly stance towards Chekhov's characters places him in a similar frame with McGuinness's metaphorical regret that he and Ibsen will have no more children, and gives a nod to the historical importance of godparents in Russian society. Friel's wards, Sonya and Andrey, exist in a Chekhovian afterlife vacillating wildly between reality and layers of illusion, or perhaps delusion. They contradict themselves consistently as Friel toys with the audience's anticipation. Both the limitations imposed upon them and the mistakes they made in their original roles play out here in a grim cautionary tale. The ripple effects of Andrey's ill-advised marriage to Natasha are particularly harshly conceived. She left him for better prospects with Protopopov, while their indulged children, now grown, have come to dire ends. Friel uses post-Soviet names for the provincial hinterlands of Chekhov's original plays to resonate better with his contemporary audience. The impoverished Andrey, along with an Uzbek companion, busks in Moscow to finance

---

[29] Brian Friel, *Three Plays After* (London: Faber & Faber, 2002), 75.

visits to his son in jail. His daughter, burdened by many children, is marooned in far-off Kazakhstan. The ruination of drink saturates *Afterplay*—Sonya sneaks vodka into her tea, Andrey admits losing ten years to alcoholism, the drunken Doctor Astrov, now married to the widowed Elena, returns occasionally to torment Sonya with the impossibility of a relationship. The wit that is in Friel's imagined sequel is far outweighed by the squalor of failure in both these lives. The tug between reality and illusion pales against what Sonya recognizes as the difference between courage—a virtue for the young and impetuous—and fortitude—the strength needed to carry on in the face of futility. Friel leaves only the faintest hope at the end, as Andrey scribbles a desperate letter to Sonya after she has sworn never to return to Moscow.

Playwright Tom Murphy's experience of Chekhov shares characteristics with that of Friel, as his own plays bear the mark of influence long before he attempts adaptation. His sole effort in the latter case is his version of *The Cherry Orchard* (2004), a late entry into the field. Although not considered a success, the version exhibited a facility for Hibernicizing Russian domestic speech, especially Chekhov's many endearments and religious apostrophes.[30] Murphy's debt to Chekhov is far better displayed in his original play *The House* (2000), which found delayed success in 2012 under Annabelle Comyn's direction.[31] The play succeeds both because of its resemblance to and productive divergence from Chekhov's original. Murphy has always shared Chekhov's penchant for leaving sentences half-articulated, knowing well that some thoughts, if given full expression, might have grave and lasting consequences. However, Murphy never shies away from very un-Chekhovian acts of violence performed on stage. Christy Cavanagh (Murphy's Lopakhin), who idolizes the upper-crust de Burca family, is also capable of beating a man senseless—a thuggish act for which there is no warning. This on-stage violence is of a piece with the actions of other Irishmen in Murphy's work who feel despised and react by abusing others. Murphy's female characters would be far more at home in a Chekhovian drawing room, the trio of de Burca daughters especially—spinster Marie, histrionic Suzanne, and caged-bird Louise.

In Murphy's *The Last Days of a Reluctant Tyrant* (2009), also premièred at the Abbey, the playwright worked from a translation of Mikhail Saltykov-Shchedrin's novel *The Golovlyov Family*, about a woman who has married above her station and slaves in vain to accumulate and maintain family wealth. As the source text is little known in the Anglophone world, theatregoers approach Murphy's play with few preconceptions. 'Sprawling' is a word that is used for the original Russian novel, which ranged across decades, and could also be applied to Murphy's play. The hardened matriarch and widow, Arina, might be cast in a favourable light as a survivor, but Murphy's play remains true to the original's emphasis on Arina's destructive qualities, which undermine her children or drive them away. Her single-minded pursuit and husbanding of land, power, and money infects her every interaction, and in this character Murphy probes a common theme in the work of playwright John B. Keane, making it an effortless fit into the Irish theatrical panoply. Marie Mullen's portrayal, harsh and unforgiving, is one that needed little adjustment to transition from

---

[30] Zsuzsa Csikai, 'Tom Murphy's *The Cherry Orchard* in the Context of Irish Rewritings of Chekhov', in Dixon and Malone, *Ibsen and Chekhov on the Irish Stage*, 168–9.

[31] The 2000 production, also at the Abbey, and directed by Conal Morrison, met with little critical acclaim.

another culture. In a development which underscores the aptness of Murphy's choice of source text, *The Last Days of a Reluctant Tyrant* was translated into Irish by Macdara Ó Fátharta as *An Tíoránach Drogallach* (2013), and mounted at An Taibhdhearc as part of the Galway Arts Festival. The Irish version avoided some of the intrusive contemporary cross-references in Murphy's play, but writing at a third remove—an Irish-language play, translated from an English-language play, based on an English-language translation of a Russian novel—left a script lacking the vitality of Murphy's work.[32]

APPLICATIONS

Although initially Field Day featured Chekhovian adaptations, they also commissioned versions of Greek drama. One tragedy which unsurprisingly resonated amid the sectarian violence in Northern Ireland was Sophocles' *Antigone*. The play was performed on Irish stages in three versions in 1984 alone, with more to follow.[33]

Field Day director and poet Tom Paulin's *The Riot Act* (1984) is written partially in verse, and relies on Northern Irish vernacular to locate the drama. Paulin's championing of vernaculars is a longstanding passion, a linguistic choice suited to the stage and to conveying a timeless story,[34] even though the play's allusions to T. S. Eliot and Yeats place it firmly within the mainstream English-language tradition. Paulin's poetic diction can be arresting, as in this passage recited by the Chorus before Antigone is immured:

> It's love has done this. Love's responsible. But what is it,
> Love, would you tell me?
> You've seen the air tremble on a hot day—a clemmed shimmer, like chains?
> You've seen a wide snowy field when it's dayligone
> and the sky violet?
> You've seen a dead light on the sea of astronomers? A bruised peach, blood-orange—a padded cell,
>   a frazzled moth?—aye, well, you've known love.[35]

Equally striking, although of a totally different timbre, is Tiresias' speech warning Creon of the gods' refusal of their sacrifices:

> I had to tell
> What's waiting on us;

---

[32] Brendan Daly, review, *An Tíorganách Drogallach/The Last Days of a Reluctant Tyrant*, 16 July 2013: http://www.scoop.it/t/irish-literature/p/4005136777/2013/07/24/irish-theatre-magazine-an-tiorganach-drogallach-the-last-days-of-a-reluctant-tyrant-tom-murphy. Accessed 8 Apr. 2016.

[33] *Anne Devlin*, a film directed by Pat Murphy, also appeared in 1984, the true story of an Irish woman who risked her life in the 1798 Rebellion to obtain the body of a fellow prisoner for burial. In 1986, while Brendan Kennelly's *Antigone* appeared at the Project Arts Theatre in Dublin, across the city the Gate mounted Athol Fugard's *The Island*, with its rehearsal of Sophocles' play by two male prisoners in Robben Island prison in South Africa. Director/playwright Conall Morrison's *Antigone* appeared in 2003 in Galway and subsequently toured.

[34] Paulin edited *The Faber Book of Vernacular Verse* (London: Faber & Faber, 1990). Earlier he urged the compilation of an Irish–English vernacular dictionary in his Field Day pamphlet *A New Look at the Language Question* (Notre Dame, IN: University of Notre Dame Press, 1986).

[35] Tom Paulin, *The Riot Act* (London: Faber & Faber, 1985), 43–4.

> To finger guts
> And poke at shite—
> that's evidence.
> A bird scritched someplace—
> That was strange
> And then a clack of choughs
> Flew at each other[36]

In these two passages alone the dialectic, colloquial and vulgar—'clemmed', 'dayligone', 'shite', 'scritched', and 'clack of choughs'—resound very differently from 'the sea of astronomers' and 'bruised peach'.

Regardless of its poetic diction, *The Riot Act* is an overtly political play. High ideals are sidelined at the outset by factionalism. Initial stage directions indicate the display of Masonic symbols associated with the Orange Order. In Creon's first appearance he delivers a lengthy speech at a press conference in empty rhetorical prose. Thus a regal figure is reduced to a politician, and not one easily mistaken for a statesman.

Paulin's Antigone drew on the figure of independent nationalist MP Bernadette Devlin McAliskey, an iconic figure in Northern Ireland, viewed by many as a fearless witness to the violation of Catholic civil rights there. Local audiences, more than used to scenes of burial rituals in the media, could easily associate McAliskey with the defiant sister of the slain Polynices. Paulin's own nationalist views informed and intensified this portrayal. But *The Riot Act*, despite its relevance to its audience, fails in its disregard for the essential balance of responsibilities to the state and the individual on which the Sophoclean original rests. Paulin's Creon is more grubby politician than monarch, easily replaceable and answerable only to the cohort who elected him. His stature is further reduced when Paulin belabours the linguistic link between the concept of loyalty at the heart of Sophocles' drama and Loyalism in its uniquely Northern Irish context. Sophocles' posing of the requirements of competing allegiances to state and kin, of public and private morality, is not central here. Sophocles' Creon, because he is a king, not only wields power but also bears a great responsibility to all within his state. Also, as king, obedience is his due. When the final tragedy unfolds, Paulin's Creon is a broken man who has lost his son and wife, but the tragedy has been rendered solely a private matter, not a crisis of state. His behaviour has been so arbitrary and capricious that Antigone, despite Paulin's linking her to Bernadette McAliskey, becomes far too much a victim. Her victimization is intensified by the author's larding of the text with a vicious misogyny—an element not remarked in the critical reception of the play at the time. The slurs do not begin until the play is well under way, when Ismene fails in her attempt at solidarity with her sister, and then they are mild enough and predictable. Creon, in exasperation, vows:

> As long as I draw breath
> I'll not be bested by a woman.[37]

Simple chauvinism then devolves quickly into abuse. Creon calls Antigone 'a hard bitch', 'hard-nosed bitch', and 'dirty bitch',[38] and makes vulgar sexual remarks about a woman who is, after all, his son's intended bride. Finally, Creon denies Antigone a gender at all by referring to her as 'it'. Although one could argue that Paulin is replicating the language

---

[36] Ibid., 50.   [37] Ibid., 30.   [38] Ibid., 34, 36, 42.

of contemporary paramilitary intimidation, the male–female dynamic has irrevocably parted ways with the original. Poet/playwright Paulin's subtext also must be considered as part of his ongoing polemic with former government minister Conor Cruise O'Brien, who had effectively banned the IRA from the airwaves in the Republic.[39]

Although an *Antigone* set in Northern Ireland in 1984 seems a logical artistic response to an intractable political conflict, versions of the Sophoclean tragedy written and performed south of the border offered very different contemporary interpretations and were well received. Poet Aidan Carl Mathews's metatheatrical experiment staged in the same year (*The Antigone*, 1984) is set in a post-apocalyptic police state where a troupe of actors are fated to perform the play on a loop despite having lost faith in its message. Mathews's overtly violent play leaves no doubt about the effect of unchecked authoritarianism. His weak and ailing Antigone is no match for Creon, his enforcer son Hemon, or the single male figure who serves both as the Chorus and the director, exerting his authority in a roughshod way.[40] This existential and despairing rendition of the play mirrored the repressive social and political conditions in the Republic of the day, especially the looming passage of the Criminal Justice Bill.[41]

Seamus Heaney, another of Field Day's directors, also turned his hand to writing for the stage with his version of another Sophoclean tragedy, *Philoctetes*. *The Cure at Troy* (1990) included the stanza:

> History says, don't hope
> On this side of the grave.
> But then, once in a lifetime
> The longed-for tidal wave
> Of justice can rise up,
> And hope and history rhyme.[42]

Often quoted in Ireland and abroad, Heaney's lines are now part of the wider political lexicon beyond that of the Northern Irish peace process. Along with its applicability to the local political climate, Heaney found in the story of the abandoned warrior called back to serve with those who had exiled him echoes of the life of Nelson Mandela and South Africa's civil rights history. What these events shared, apart from the denial of human rights, is their lengthy duration. By 1990 Northern Ireland had been pummelled by conflict, and there was still no promise of a peace. After his first adaptation from Sophocles,

---

[39] Paulin sets out his argument in 'The Making of a Loyalist', in *Ireland and the English Crisis* (Newcastle: Bloodaxe, 1984), 23–38, challenging, in particular, Cruise O'Brien's preference in *States of Ireland* (London: Hutchison, 1972) for Ismene, advocate of civil conformity, over the rebellious Antigone, in his application of Sophocles' play to the Northern Irish crisis.

[40] Aidan Carl Mathews, *The Antigone*, directed by Michael Scott (Dublin: Project Arts Centre, 1984). The text of the Criminal Justice Bill, yet to become law, was read aloud in the theatre during the interval. See Marianne McDonald, 'Classics as Celtic Firebrand: Greek Tragedy, Irish Playwrights and Colonialism', in Eamonn Jordan (ed.), *Theatre Stuff: Critical Essays on Contemporary Irish Theatre* (Dublin: Carysfort Press, 2000), 21.

[41] Murray, 'Three Irish *Antigones*'. Murray also refers to Anthony Roche's 'Ireland's *Antigones*: Tragedy North and South', in Michael Kenneally (ed.), *Cultural Contexts and Literary Idioms in Contemporary Irish Literature* (Gerrards Cross: Colin Smythe, 1988), 221–50.

[42] Seamus Heaney, *The Cure at Troy* (London: Faber & Faber, 1991), 77.

Heaney would not approach *Antigone* for many years. *The Burial at Thebes* (2004) was first staged not in Derry, but at the Abbey in Dublin, where the choice of Québécoise director Lorraine Pintal could only reinforce an understanding of the intractable nature of provincial strife as a global reality.[43]

The many recent Irish adaptations of both modern and ancient drama were written in a period of profound cultural change. The world press shone a light on thirty years of civil strife in Northern Ireland and, beginning in the 1990s, on Ireland's unprecedented financial boom. At the same time that Ireland was coming to terms with its new European Union identity, its writers were finding resonances in the ancient classical canon—a recurring historical means of approaching subjects still raw and too dangerous to be discussed without a distancing mechanism. The reinscription of modern classics also worked in tandem with the academic and critical discourse which predominated in Irish public life. The longstanding dialogic practice of Irish playwrights, reworking similar themes and parallel structuring principles, is even more relevant. It has yielded the unforeseen benefit of giving these writers the flexibility, the adaptability one might say, to create new work for the stage with one eye on the work of others. Irish playwrights adjusted easily to the art of adaptation from this productive working culture. In turn they have also become the beneficiaries of translations and adaptations of their original work. Finally, then, the flow of Irish theatre adaptations in the last four decades is best considered not as an isolated phenomenon, but as part of a long and fruitful tradition of artistic discourse.

[43] In 2014 Pintal stood as separatist Parti québécois candidate for local office in Montreal, coming second in the election. Verdun election results: http://www.cbc.ca/elections/quebecvotes2014/ridings/view/riding-122. Accessed 13 Aug. 2014.

PART XII

CRITICAL RESPONSES

CHAPTER 41

IRISH THEATRE AND HISTORIOGRAPHY

EAMONN JORDAN

INTRODUCTION

IRELAND has produced playwrights of world standing, most of whom have had complicated dealings with the Abbey Theatre as a national institution, whether through acceptance, rejection, or disassociation. Predominantly playwright-led, text-based, and context-acknowledged scholarship informed the traditional responses to the works of these playwrights. Over the last twenty-five years in particular there has been a huge upsurge in critical evaluation.[1] A new scholarly research network, the Irish Theatrical Diaspora (ITD), a new society, the Irish Society for Theatre Research (ISTR),[2] numerous summer schools, conferences, symposia, colloquia, and public fora initiated by theatre companies and festivals have variously contributed to the debates.[3] The critical platform provided by the International Association for the Study of Irish Literatures (IASIL) is also notable.

Journal articles and special journal issues dedicated to Irish theatre have been numerous; monographs, collections of essays, and more recently, performance-related and practice-as-research-informed scholarship have brought additional and often rigorous academic scrutiny to bear on theatre practices and the material conditions surrounding these. Attention has been given not only to drafts of scripts, published texts, and their revised editions, but also to rehearsal processes and prompt books, and the inputs of directors, actors, and lighting, sound, costume, and stage designers. The archival holdings of libraries, theatre

---

[1] Today the critical mass of scholarship is prompted by an increase in direct disciplinary or subject-specific teaching at undergraduate and graduate levels in the area of drama/theatre, by the expansion in numbers undertaking self-funded and funded graduate work, and by the increasing number of academic appointments made in the discipline.

[2] The ITD has published numerous collections of essays, and the ISTR's *Irish Theatre International* has three issues to date.

[3] State agency reports prepared for the Irish Arts Council (An Chomhairle Ealaíon) are also important.

companies, theatre critics, theatre-makers, and diarists, and the records of state agencies—particularly those that fund and promote the theatre sector—have been effectively exercised.

In this chapter I can but deal with some of the dominant methodological dispositions and note significant variations. I single out examples of what I regard as being typical of key critical approaches, and evaluate the suppositions and implications of such methodologies, ever alert to the fact that many of the points I make are summative, and exist without the opportunity to tease out implications or to qualify remarks. I regret that I cannot deal in greater detail with the work of more scholars. I have also opted to engage with the more recent scholarship, as it has built on the many methodological approaches of prior generations. (I would also like to signal from the start the relative dearth of scholarship on directors, designers, actors, and administrators.) Theoretical framings of theatrical and performance practices offer reflections, explorations, connections, and reinterpretations. Critical commentary identifies commonalities, anomalies, and the significance of various contextualizations. I hope to capture some of the conscious and unconscious dialogues, tensions, and disagreements that have emerged between different scholars writing about theatre. Many factors—including era, age, gender, sexual orientation, race, class, education, training, and institutional associations—determine scholarly approaches, but most scholars do not openly set out their critical stall or ideological affiliations, so to speak.[4]

Landmark scholarship by Helen Burke, Richard Allen Cave, Una Ellis-Fermor, James Flannery, Adrian Frazier, John Harrington, Robert Hogan, D. E. S Maxwell, Vivian Mercier, Stephen Watt, S. E. Wilmer, and Katharine Worth have contributed to the documentation of Irish theatre history and the evolution of critical methodologies.[5] It was not until the end of the twentieth century that a number of survey monographs appeared, covering large parts of the twentieth century's Irish theatre tradition; work by Susan Cannon Harris,[6] Nicholas Grene,[7] Mária Kurdi,[8] Christopher Morash,[9] Morash and Shaun Richards,[10] Christopher Murray,[11] Lionel Pilkington,[12] Mary Trotter,[13] and Robert

---

[4] Elizabeth Butler Cullingford is one of the few critics who is explicit about her own critical practices and ideological positioning. See her *Ireland's Others: Ethnicity and Gender in Irish Literature and Popular Culture* (Cork: Cork University Press, 2001), 1–9.

[5] In order to save on space, and given that the works of these scholars are so well known, I have decided only to reference the work of the scholars I cite, or those that speak directly to a specific issue or circumstance.

[6] Susan Cannon Harris, *Gender and Modern Irish Drama* (Bloomington, IN: Indiana University Press, 2002).

[7] Nicholas Grene, *The Politics of Irish Drama: Plays in Context from Boucicault to Friel* (Cambridge: Cambridge University Press, 1999).

[8] Mária Kurdi, *Representations of Gender and Female Subjectivity in Contemporary Irish Drama by Women* (Lewiston, NY: Edwin Mellen Press, 2010).

[9] Christopher Morash, *A History of Irish Theatre: 1601–2000* (Cambridge: Cambridge University Press, 2002).

[10] Christopher Morash and Shaun Richards, *Mapping Irish Theatre: Theories of Space and Place* (Cambridge: Cambridge University Press, 2014).

[11] Christopher Murray, *Twentieth-Century Irish Drama: Mirror Up to Nation* (Manchester: Manchester University Press, 1997).

[12] Lionel Pilkington, *Theatre and the State in Twentieth-Century Ireland: Cultivating the People* (London: Routledge, 2001).

[13] Mary Trotter, *Modern Irish Theatre* (Cambridge: Polity Press, 2008).

Welch[14] are exemplary of a cross-twentieth-century and early twenty-first-century approach. Cathy Leeney's work covers 1900–1939;[15] Anthony Roche's era is post-Second World War,[16] as is that of Michael Etherton and Margaret Llewellyn-Jones; monographs by Helen Heusner Lojek,[17] Eamonn Jordan, Mária Kurdi, Patrick Lonergan,[18] Victor Merriman,[19] Anne F. O'Reilly,[20] Ondřej Pilný,[21] Brian Singleton,[22] Bernadette Sweeney,[23] Clare Wallace,[24] and Fintan Walsh[25] deal in the main with the later decades of the twentieth century and beyond.

Specific epoch-related work by Ben Levitas, P. J. Mathews, Irina Ruppo Malone, Paige Reynolds,[26] and Paul Murphy[27] cover political and artistic developments from the start of the century. Ian R. Walsh covers the 1930s to the 1950s. Joan Fitzpatrick Dean writes about public censorship,[28] and Lauren Arrington demonstrates the effectiveness of institutional self-censorship, whilst complicating simplistic notions of artistic freedom.[29] Books by Imelda Foley, Tom Maguire, and Eugene McNulty[30] offer comprehensive studies on Northern Irish Theatre, as does Mark Phelan's work across a range of publications, including essays, chapters in edited collections, and volumes dedicated to the work of a single

[14] Robert Welch, *The Abbey Theatre 1899–1999: Form and Pressure* (Oxford: Oxford University Press, 1999).

[15] Cathy Leeney, *Irish Women Playwrights,1900–1939: Gender and Violence on Stage* (New York: Peter Lang, 2010).

[16] Anthony Roche, *Contemporary Irish Drama*, 2nd edn. (Basingstoke: Palgrave Macmillan, 2009).

[17] Helen Heusner Lojek, *The Spaces of Irish Drama: Stage and Place in Contemporary Plays* (Basingstoke: Palgrave Macmillan, 2011).

[18] Patrick Lonergan, *Theatre and Globalization: Irish Drama in the Celtic Tiger Era* (Basingstoke: Palgrave Macmillan, 2008).

[19] Victor Merriman, *Because We Are Poor: Irish Theatre in the 1990s* (Dublin: Carysfort Press, 2011).

[20] Anne F. O'Reilly, *Sacred Play: Soul-Journeys in Contemporary Irish Drama* (Dublin: Carysfort Press, 2004).

[21] Ondřej Pilný, *Irony and Identity in Modern Irish Drama* (Prague: Literaria Pragensia, 2006).

[22] Brian Singleton, *Masculinities and the Contemporary Irish Theatre* (Basingstoke: Palgrave Macmillan, 2011).

[23] Bernadette Sweeney, *Performing the Body in Irish Theatre* (Basingstoke: Palgrave Macmillan, 2008).

[24] Clare Wallace, *Suspect Cultures: Narrative, Identity and Citation in 1990s New Drama* (Prague: Litteraria Pragensia, 2006).

[25] Fintan Walsh, *Male Trouble: Masculinity and the Performance of Crisis* (Basingstoke: Palgrave Macmillan, 2011).

[26] Paige Reynolds, *Modernism, Drama, and the Audience for Irish Spectacle* (Cambridge: Cambridge University Press, 2007).

[27] Paul Murphy, *Hegemony and Fantasy in Irish Drama, 1899–1949* (Basingstoke: Palgrave Macmillan, 2008).

[28] Joan Fitzpatrick Dean, *Riot and Great Anger: Stage Censorship in Twentieth-Century Ireland* (Madison, WI: University of Wisconsin Press, 2004).

[29] Lauren Arrington, *W. B. Yeats, the Abbey Theatre, Censorship, and the Irish State: Adding the Half-Pence to the Pence* (Oxford: Oxford University Press, 2010).

[30] Imelda Foley, *The Girls in the Big Picture: Gender in Contemporary Ulster Theatre* (Belfast: Blackstaff Press, 2003); Tom Maguire, *Making Theatre in Northern Ireland: Through and Beyond the Troubles* (Exeter: Exeter University Press, 2006); Eugene McNulty, *The Ulster Literary Theatre and the Northern Revival* (Cork: Cork University Press, 2008).

writer.[31] By isolating a number of broad and loose clusters of critical dispositions, I will illustrate how different historiographical approaches determine base knowledge, working methodologies inform the ways that scholars speak or fail to speak to each other, and discursive practices evolve over time.

LIBERALISM, HUMANISM, PATRIARCHY, AND SOCIAL DEMOCRACY

Ideological differences and critical dispositions vary considerably, as almost all scholarly work takes Ireland's colonial history and its sociopolitical aftermaths through to the Celtic Tiger period of the mid-1990s to 2006/7 as the foundational and springboard conditions for what happened throughout the century. Starting with Dion Boucicault's *The Shaughraun* (1874) and ending effectively with Conor McPherson's *The Weir* (1997)—both works that premièred outside Ireland—Grene's 1999 *The Politics of Irish Drama* opens with a chronology, where the dates for the productions of key theatre events are given in one column and a list of the monumental historical incidents that occurred over the period of analysis in another. Grene's chronology is indicative of the relationship between politics, contexts, audiences, and the plays that he discusses—without necessarily affirming their absolute standing or canonical status. He writes about these works non-chronologically. The agenda is set by his opening comment: 'As long as there has been a distinct Irish drama it has been so closely bound up with national politics that the one has often been considered more or less a reflection of the other.' This is a mimetic default setting which Grene's work consistently interrogates—or, in his words, 'there is more to the politics of Irish drama than merely a theatrical mimesis of the national narrative.'[32]

Grene's methodological disposition is to analyse the 'political interplay of dramatic text and context' with 'the idea that Ireland is out there to be represented, analysed, interpreted for audiences at home and *abroad*' (my emphasis). The dramatized Ireland 'is a world elsewhere', distinctive in its 'otherness'. Grene opts to focus on work that both has 'specific political contexts' and is 'written as a more-or-less direct, more-or-less self-conscious, intervention in that context', thus leaving himself free to select widely and exclude easily. Further, he concentrates on the importance of characters whose role is to interpret 'between characters, between stage and audience, reading and explaining Ireland on behalf of the dramatist creator'.[33] In that way, theatre has an interrogative function, as well as holding open the possibilities of individual characters critiquing and shifting perspectives, thus illustrating potentially new perspectives for audiences.

The debate about cultural intervention and the challenges of representation was kickstarted by the manifesto written for the Irish Literary Theatre in 1897 by Edward Martyn, W. B. Yeats, and Lady Gregory.[34] Grene captures both the obsessions with and delusions

---

[31] See e.g. Phelan's introduction to Owen McCafferty, *Plays 1* (London: Faber & Faber, 2013).

[32] Grene, *Politics of Irish Drama*, 1.   [33] Ibid., 3, 71, 262, 268, 6, 7.

[34] Augusta Gregory, *Our Irish Theatre: A Chapter in Autobiography*, 3rd edn. (Gerrards Cross: Colin Smythe, 1972), 20.

of writers cyclically focusing on 'unprecedentedly authentic Ireland' in the face of an Ireland that had previously been 'misrepresented, travestied, rendered in sentimental cliché or political caricature'. Further, Grene lays down an important critical marker, suggesting that evidence-based, close, or concentrated readings of 'selected dramatic texts' tend to be more beneficial than 'more theoretically inflected analyses of broader cultural manifestations'.[35]

Murray's *Twentieth-Century Irish Drama: Mirror Up to Nation* includes a far wider range of playwrights and plays than Grene, covering playwrights from Yeats, Gregory, and J. M. Synge to Seán O'Casey, George Shiels, and Teresa Deevy; from Tom Murphy, Brian Friel, Hugh Leonard, and Tom Kilroy to Sebastian Barry, Marina Carr, Anne Devlin, Frank McGuinness, Tom Mac Intyre, and Stewart Parker. Again he is foregrounding the interfaces between audiences, politics, and society. As with Grene, here politics is evident in economic and cultural conditions, in political and in institutional practices, emerging bourgeois culture, repression, religious consciousness, emigration, unemployment, secularism, the urban/rural divide, language, connections with place, the English–Irish relationship, and Northern Ireland. Direct challenges to puritanism and censorship, shared moral and social codes, identity constraints, and gender inequalities are cogently identified.

For Murray, drama and theatre 'were both instrumental in defining and sustaining national consciousness'; what is being negotiated is 'belief, identity, freedom', or more generally, 'the conditions of Irish experience'.[36] The divide between writer and society was 'unprecedented' from the 1930s onwards, Murray suggests. Accordingly, Irish drama, rather than simply reflecting, 'helps society find its bearings; it both ritualises and interrogates national identity'. As it ritualizes, it also demythologizes identity; and as it interrogates, it also iterates possibility. Murray takes inspiration from Raymond Williams's notion of the artist who provides 'a structure of feeling', and potentially new modes of perception, acknowledgement, and attribution.[37] The generation of writers who emerged in the late 1950s/early 1960s were 'conditioned by circumstances of penury and inhibition' and fought against such circumstances, thus benefiting audiences. The verbal and gestural articulations are critical in redefining contexts and delivering the potential of change, even when an 'individual's freedom is rendered suspect'. Murray then appropriately shifts the frame: '[I]n Irish drama the mirror does not give back the real; it gives back *images* of a perceived reality. [...] The thing is fluid and proleptic.'[38]

Prompted by his reading of productions of Brendan Behan's *The Quare Fellow* and Samuel Beckett's *Waiting for Godot* at the Pike Theatre in 1954 and 1955 respectively, Roche in *Contemporary Irish Drama* suggests that 'in a situation where most forms of agency are directed or proscribed, the emphasis is thrown on talk, on the orality of speech as a site of potential freedom and self-realisation'.[39] He argues that 'playwrights and all those involved

---

[35] Grene, *Politics of Irish Drama*, 6, 2–3.

[36] Murray, *Twentieth-Century Irish Drama*, 3. Trotter sees 'theatre as a vehicle for cultural definition and social change' (*Modern Irish Theatre*, 2), and Welch sees 'the Abbey as an arena in which the latent forces, and energies, and pressures of modern Irish consciousness manifest themselves; and on the plays in which these pressures are given imaginative form' (*Abbey Theatre*, vii).

[37] Raymond Williams, *Drama from Ibsen to Brecht* (London: Chatto, 1986), 11. Cited in Murray, *Twentieth-Century Irish Drama*, 10.

[38] Ibid., 7, 9, 164, 8, 9.   [39] Roche, *Contemporary Irish Drama*, 38.

in the act of theatre have attempted to create a space in which some kind of meaningful dialogue can be enacted, in which the limitations of language can be both demonstrated and gone beyond [. . .] characters are displaced from their original affiliations into potentially new groupings and proto-communities'. Interestingly, while there are debates and often quarrels, Roche notes: 'the argument in Irish plays tends to have no overt or immediate social application.'

For Roche, 'creative contradiction' is at the core of the tradition, and 'not just when one play provokes another by way of response, but within the individual plays themselves'. This principle of creative contradiction 'extends to the audience, who are drawn into the process of questioning what is being represented'; an interrogative process that 'registers and is resisted'.[40] For Grene, Murray, and Roche, drama is not simply a manifestation of sociopolitical circumstances but an act of re-mediation, a place where the past can be reimagined and contested, and a future potentially devised.

Although often less publicly visible and acknowledged, women playwrights engaged, as their men counterparts had, with the major events on the political landscape, pre- and post-Independence. Recent, specifically gender-related scholarship—by some men, but predominantly by women[41]—more often than not has the Abbey in its sights, in relation not only to what the theatre decided to perform and how it performed it, but how others sidestepped or were rejected by the institution. In *Irish Women Playwrights, 1900–1939* Cathy Leeney describes the Abbey as an 'unrivalled arbiter of playwrights' careers'.[42] Most Irish feminist criticism, while focused on patriarchal dynamics and male dominance, still has more in common with a liberal/social democratic ethos than with Marxist/materialist or postcolonial framings, even if such criticism has incorporated the theoretical perspectives offered by the wide spectrum of radical, cultural, and socialist feminism.

Critics have made numerous attempts to address the implications and practices of a broad range of gender disparities, giving rise to discussions on social inequality of participative democracy on the one hand and, on the other, reflections on canonical exclusions and inclusions of women writers. Commentators also sought out evidence of counter-narratives, challenging theatrical practices and anti-mimetic strategies. Questions are asked about where women characters sit on the spectrum of agency relative to their male counterparts, and most importantly the connections between alienation, hegemony, and inequality in relation to the imperatives of patriarchy. Through rituals, myths, cultures, histories, politics, and practices in social and personal spheres, patriarchy gives masculinity centrality and focus, while simultaneously normalizing the subjugation of women. In addition, patriarchy essentializes gender differences, even when social transactions appear to be based on similar access to rights, freedoms, and opportunities.

[40]   Ibid., 159, 38, 11, 12.

[41]   Apart from those directly mentioned here, numerous women scholars, including Helen Carr, Jacqueline Genet, Claire Gleitman, Miriam Haughton, Charlotte Headrick, Lynda Henderson, Cheryl Herr, Marjorie Howes, Christina Hunt Mahony, C. L. Innes, Marie Kelly, Brenda Liddy, Sheila McCormick, Lucy McDiarmid, Audrey McNamara, Gerardine Meany, Emma Meehan, Hiroko Mikami, Riana O'Dwyer, Siobhán O'Gorman, Martine Pelletier, Ann Saddlemyer, Ailbhe Smyth, Carolyn Swift, Maureen Waters, and Clair Wills have been active in the field.

[42]   Leeney, *Irish Women Playwrights*, 164.

Internationally renowned theorists and critics such as Elaine Aston, Catherine Belsey, Judith Butler, Sue-Ellen Case, Una Chaudhuri, Jill Dolan, Gail Finney, Elizabeth Grosz, Luce Irigaray, Lynda Hart, Eve Kosofsky Sedgwick, Julia Kristeva, Gay McAuley, Janelle Reinelt, Hanna Scolnicov, Elaine Showalter, and Lib Taylor all are drawn upon to bolster, frame, inform, and substantiate arguments. Most of this scholarship deals with key figures like Teresa Deevy, Eva Gore-Booth, Lady Gregory, Dorothy Macardle, Mary Manning, Alice Milligan, and then more recently professionally produced writers such as Geraldine Aron, Patricia Burke-Brogan, Mary Elizabeth Burke-Kennedy, Anne Devlin, Grace Dyas, Emma Donoghue, Stacey Gregg, Hilary Fannin, Stella Feehily, Jennifer Johnston, Marie Jones, Deirdre Kinahan, Liz Kuti, Ena May, Gina Moxley, Elaine Murphy, Éilís Ní Dhuibhne, Edna O'Brien, Máiréad Ní Ghráda, Christina Reid, Carmel Winters, and work by the likes of Charabanc theatre company.[43] Many of the arguments turn to Marina Carr's work,[44] and the more contemporary scholarship has focused considerably on the site-specific/immersive works of Louise Lowe and Owen Boss's ANU Productions.

The criticism has been predominantly playwright-led, but it also delves into the careers of renowned companies—for example, Inghinidhe na hÉireann, formed by Maud Gonne—and women actors, producers, directors, and administrators, such as Sara and Molly Allgood, Lelia Doolan, Olwen Fouéré, Christine Longford, Paula McFetridge, Siobhán McKenna, Ria Mooney, Marie Mullen, Deirdre O'Connell, Mary O'Malley, Lynne Parker, Shelah Richards, Phyllis Ryan, and Carolyn Swift.[45] The Tony Award-winning director Garry Hynes, most associated with Druid Theatre Company during her forty-year professional career (and a short spell at the Abbey Theatre as artistic director) is the most acclaimed.

The relationship between colonial practices, patriarchy, and the objectification of women is captured in Kurdi's comments in *Representations of Gender and Female Subjectivity in Contemporary Irish Drama by Women* as to how 'a version of Irishness was produced that emphasised the presence of exaggerated feminine qualities like hypersensitivity, dependency, sexual pathology, and neurotic unreliability with the potential of hidden aggression'.[46] For Melissa Sihra in *Women in Irish Drama* there is a combination of the 'symbolic centrality' (*Sean Bhean Bhocht*, Cathleen ní Houlihan, and Róisín Dúbh) and 'subjective disavowal' as both colonial ideology and nationalist movements promoted feminized concepts of the nation, while subordinating women in everyday life'.[47] Anna McMullan's conceptualizations include both women's association with homeland and the domestic, kitchen space. Thus, 'in the Irish theatrical canon women often figure as lost, damaged or barren home/land/womb'.[48]

---

[43] Sometimes there is a sense of token inclusion of writing by women in anthologies, in some Irish theatre historiographies, and during commemorative events. See Melissa Sihra's analysis in her introduction to Melissa Sihra (ed.), *Women in Irish Drama: A Century of Authorship and Representation* (Basingstoke: Palgrave Macmillan, 2007), 1–22. This book includes an appendix that lists over 250 Irish women playwrights.

[44] Work on Carr includes numerous articles and theses, and two excellent publications: Cathy Leeney and Anna McMullan (eds.), *The Theatre of Marina Carr: Before Rules Was Made* (Dublin: Carysfort Press, 2003) and Rhona Trench, *Bloody Living: The Loss of Selfhood in the Plays of Marina Carr* (Bern: Lang, 2010).

[45] See Sihra, *Women in Irish Drama*, 91–3.   [46] Kurdi, *Representations of Gender*, 2.

[47] Sihra, *Women in Irish Drama*, 1.

[48] Anna McMullan, 'Unhomely Stages: Women Taking (a) Place in Irish Theatre', in Dermot Bolger (ed.), *Druids, Dudes and Beauty Queens: The Changing Face of Irish Theatre* (Dublin: New Island, 2001), 72.

Thus the recovering, evaluating, and contextualizing of plays by women are, as Sihra notes, 'crucial to the re-negotiation and pluralizing of Irish theatrical traditions, that many in their original historiographies paid scant attention'.[49] Leeney's exemplary work establishes the complex contributions of Gregory, Gore-Booth, Macardle, Manning, and Deevy to Irish theatre. She argues that their work 'tests how women's experiences and insights might inform theatrical aesthetics, how the woman's point of view might, or might not be accommodated within theatrical forms and conventions that were available to those creating theatre in that period'. Leeney identifies how these women interacted with writing traditions and practices (nationally and internationally), how they evolved dramaturgical and performance strategies that challenged conventional wisdom and the social and psychological imperatives inscribed by dramatic forms, and really changed 'the paradigms used to describe the development of Irish theatre from its early formation'. These writers establish a 'counter-tradition that disrupts the totalizing canon of male authors', and illustrate how 'the agenda of the nation compromised Irish women's agenda'.[50]

Much scholarship identifies the significances of legislative and constitutional practices.[51] There is of course the infamous Article 41.2 of the 1937 Constitution. Lisa Fitzpatrick references how the Women's Prisoners Defence League, in the publication *Prison Bars*, objected to the constitutional article as to how it sanctioned, idealized, confined, and marginalized women.[52] This retrograde constitution contrasted sharply with the egalitarian values of the Proclamation of 1916 and Article 3 of the 1922 Free State constitution that, as Sihra reports, stated: 'every person, without distinction of sex, shall ... enjoy the privileges and be subject to the obligations of such citizenship.'[53] Unemployment, poverty, rampant emigration, forced adoptions and labour, clerical sexual abuse, industrial schools, imprisonment in Magdalene Laundries and mental institutions were some of the horrors of the sociopolitical landscape from the 1940s onwards that affected the poor and, in particular, women.

Gender inequalities slowly began to be addressed, initiated by the Irish Women's Liberation Movement of the 1970s that foregrounded issues of employment rights, contraception, divorce legislation, abortion, the deaths of young women in childbirth, unmarried mothers, the situation of deserted wives, the separated and widowed, and the issue of homosexuality.[54] It is through acts of social protest and resistance, Fitzpatrick argues, that these women were 'performing a new idea of Irish womanhood as active, challenging, and taking control', by trying out new roles, and inspiring others 'to explore roles and behaviour that were previously prohibited'.[55] This 'radical re-ordering' of society, in terms

[49] Sihra, *Women in Irish Drama*, 1.   [50] Leeney, *Irish Women Playwrights*, 1, 11, 4, 46.

[51] See e.g. Leeney's comments on the '1927 Juries Bill (which meant that women had to apply specifically to be considered for jury duty while men were automatically called), the 1932 public service marriage bar (whereby women had to leave the civil service and later national teaching once they married), Section 16 of the 1935 Conditions of Employment Bill (A Government minister could limit numbers of women in any one sector)': ibid., 168.

[52] Lisa Fitzpatrick, 'Taking Their Own Road: The Female Protagonists in Three Irish Plays by Women' in Sihra, *Women in Irish Drama*, 70.

[53] Ibid., 2.

[54] The establishment of the 'National Council of Women, the Joint Committee of Women's Societies and Social Workers, the Irish Countrywomen's Association and the Irish Housewives' Association enabled some sense of a collective identity and outlet for women': ibid., 88.

[55] Lisa Fitzpatrick, 'Introduction', in Lisa Fitzpatrick (ed.), *Performing Feminisms in Contemporary Ireland* (Dublin: Carysfort Press, 2013), 1.

of freedoms, sexuality, employment, and greater opportunities for women, was something to which the later generation of women playwrights spoke.

Dramaturgically and in performance, gender differences in the work of men and women writers can be blatant, obvious, or subtle. Helen Heusner Lojek singles out a very specific gender distinction in Frank McGuinness's work, where 'male artists launch their quests horizontally across the surface of the earth; the female artists quest vertically, exploring the depths of place and self'.[56] Trotter signals how, traditionally, 'Female characters provide the [male] protagonist with emotional support, a source of conflict, or a sexual interest, but the real attention in the family memory drama centres on the patrilineal relationships.'[57] For Anne F. O'Reilly in *Sacred Play*, 'the colonization of the female body either as a site for male meaning or carrier of repressed aspects of the cultural unconscious must be addressed by theatre audiences and practitioners.'[58] And gendered bodies are central to Bernadette Sweeney's monograph *Performing the Body in Irish Theatre*. Dance/theatre is a new area of study with Finola Cronin,[59] Aoife McGrath,[60] and others making vital interventions in terms of embodiment, performance, space, and place. Using Adrienne Rich's ideas as to how value is placed on the mother–son relationship 'as the eternal, determinative dyad', Kurdi demonstrates how the mother–daughter relationship is 'minimized and trivialized', as often are relationships between women.[61] Gendered objectification ties in with textual and performance spaces. Kurdi cites McAuley's suggestion: 'If we can understand the spatial system, we can unravel the philosophical and ideological content of play and production.'[62]

Gender-related scholarship also considers how 'hegemonic, heteronormative, masculinity' (R. W. Connell's much-cited term) operates, as Singleton in *Masculinities and Contemporary Irish Theatre* notes, 'through a performance of patriarchy'. Singleton further emphasizes the substances of subordinate, 'non-hegemonic masculinities' evident in illustrations of diverse sexualities and in class, religious, race, and ethnic differentiations.[63] In different ways, the writings of David Cregan and Fintan Walsh have addressed masculinities and homosexualities in complex ways, and in particular the body, performances, and the subversion of crisis masculinities. The male characters in the plays of O'Casey, Murphy, or McPherson seem to be less than unyielding agents of patriarchy or significant benefactors of its dividends. Such dividends often include 'material benefits' (sexual and

---

[56] Helen Heusner Lojek, *Contexts for Frank McGuinness's Drama* (Washington, DC: Catholic University of America Press, 2004), 102.

[57] Mary Trotter, 'Translating Women into Irish Theatre History', in Stephen Watt, Eileen Morgan, and Shakir Mustafa (eds.), *A Century of Irish Drama: Widening the Stage* (Bloomington, IN: Indiana University Press, 2000), 165.

[58] O'Reilly, *Sacred Play*, 313.

[59] Finola Cronin, 'The Choreography of Place in Irish Dance Theatre' (PhD dissertation, University College Dublin, 2013).

[60] Aoife McGrath, *Dance Theatre in Ireland: Revolutionary Moves* (Basingstoke: Palgrave Macmillan, 2013).

[61] Adrienne Rich, *Of Woman Born: Motherhood as an Experience and an Institution* (London: Virago, 1977), 226; cited in Kurdi, *Representations of Gender*, 30.

[62] Gay McAuley, *Space in Performance: Making Meaning in the Theatre* (Ann Arbor, MI: University of Michigan Press, 1999), 22–3; cited in Kurdi, *Representations of Gender*, 188.

[63] Singleton, *Masculinities*, 10, 8.

economic), 'social status' (psychological and existential), and the 'honour, prestige, and the right to command' (cultural and political) that Connell identifies.[64]

Employing the work of Slavoj Žižek and Jacques Lacan to inform Antonio Gramsci's writings on subaltern figures, Paul Murphy in *Hegemony and Fantasy in Irish Drama, 1899–1949* links the 'Peasant, Tramp, Pauper, Landless Labourer, Proletariat, Small Farmers, Cottiers, Unemployed', with 'the gendered subaltern as Women, Wife, Mother, [and] Fallen Woman' characters. Murphy explains '*how* the subaltern is essentialised as a fantasy object which is symbolically central to dramatic and ideological representation', but marginalized socially, and that such centrality is designed 'to repress the continuing existence of class and gender hierarchies', and to conjure up an 'amnesia concerning inequality'.[65]

The above scholarship is predominantly prompted by a liberal/humanist and social democratic disposition. Such writing supports a combination of potential self-actualization and collective realization, where a multitude of social failures are the fault of a repressive religious ethos and conservative social and economic politics. The injustices of the state are not necessarily failings of democratic ideology per se, more a not seeing through on the duties and obligations of citizenship. Theatre practices are trusted to bear the burden of contradictions and anomalies, but more importantly to signal and devise social change. Although these approaches deal with the impacts of colonization, imperialism is incorporated very differently by those who frame the writing and performances of the last hundred years or so in terms of cultural materialist, postcolonial, anticolonial, and neo-colonial theories.

DOMINANT STATES: MATERIALIST AND POST-COLONIAL PERSPECTIVES

Lionel Pilkington's cultural-materialist orientated *Theatre and the State in Twentieth-Century Ireland* interrogates the writings and public pronouncements of Yeats and Lady Gregory, not as Grene and Murray have done, but to demonstrate how these literary figures advanced the values of 'fin de siècle southern Irish unionism', of former and current Ascendancy elites, of a 'constructive unionism'—which was 'conservative and ameliorative in its objectives' in terms of 'reform and conciliation'—and of 'peasant proprietorship' and the views of the dominant and emerging Catholic elites. For Pilkington, the Abbey Theatre, shaped by Gregory and Yeats and many others, was fundamentally 'an act of quasi-Ascendancy philanthropy' intent on 'moderating the traumatic prospects of majority rule', and thus paving the way for a new Catholic elite. Opposing these elites were those associated with what were disingenuously regarded as the common scourges of 'socialism and agrarian insurgency', Republican and 'trade union militancy'.[66]

Not only does Pilkington trace a strong anti-Catholic rhetoric and a negative attitude towards collective projects, but he also demonstrates how theatre practices aligned

---

[64] R. W. Connell, 'The Social Organisation of Masculinity', in Stephen M. Whitehead and Frank Barrett (eds.), *The Masculinities Reader* (Cambridge: Polity Press, 2001), 40–3.

[65] Murphy, *Hegemony and Fantasy*, 12, 10, 26.

[66] Pilkington, *Theatre and the State*, 2, 13, 10, 4, 14, 86.

themselves with the modernist project of individualism and later with a tactical and embryonic, constitutional nationalism. Pilkington's work also demonstrates how by the 1920s the Abbey Theatre had negotiated its way from receiving donations and subscriptions from 'titled guarantors' and senior figures in the British administration to modest state funding of £850 by 1925. He argues that revolt is framed only as 'individual conscience' and 'individual volition' in works by J. W. Whitbread, Yeats, and Gregory. He emphasizes how the '[p]olitical elements deemed recalcitrant to that authority, such as the legacies of anti-colonial militancy, are portrayed as dangerously recidivist or as urgently requiring reassessment and revision'. O'Casey's Dublin Trilogy is accused of sentimentalizing Dublin working-class culture in ways that are beneficial 'to the increasingly middle-class and business orientated interests'. (Paul Murphy also validates this opinion, whereas Murray opposes this perspective.) Pilkington argues that republicanism in O'Casey is portrayed 'as fundamentally antithetical to domestic value, and thus as ethically deleterious'.[67] (Seamus Deane had previously espoused a similar argument in *Celtic Revivals*.)[68]

For Pilkington, the plays of the '1950s expose not only a concern with the de-politicization of Irish republican militancy, but also a compelling need for an adjustment of nationalist ideology to the exigencies of foreign capital'. After the new Abbey Theatre building was opened in 1966, he notes a more 'ambitious cultural agenda' with 'its championing of Brechtian dramaturgy at the Peacock, its attempts to establish a working-class theatre project in the Cabra area of Dublin in 1967, and the strong socialist emphasis of the newly established Abbey Theatre Playwright's Workshop'. (The Pike Theatre, as an alternative cultural site, founded by Alan Simpson and Carolyn Swift, gets some praise for innovation and radicalism.) Broadening focus, Pilkington also considers the Northern Irish state and the theatrical responses to the emergence of 'The Troubles'. The Abbey Theatre's production of Friel's *The Freedom of the City* (1973), not long after the events of Bloody Sunday (1972), is confronted by Pilkington because of how the play seemingly foregrounds an 'inscrutable individuality' at the expense of collective political protest.[69] Friel's *Translations* (1980) is read as underlining 'the need for a *via media* of political accommodation based on the acceptance of inherited political and cultural realities, and, to this extent, constitutes a rebuttal of republican militancy', through the marginalization of insurgency in the form of the Donnelly twins.[70]

Pilkington's book ends with a short analysis of Frank McGuinness's *Observe the Sons of Ulster Marching Towards the Somme*, which premièred at the Peacock, the Abbey's sister theatre, in 1985. On the one hand, McGuinness's work is accused of conforming to

[67] Ibid., 7, 18, 4, 95, 94.

[68] Seamus Deane, *Celtic Revivals: Essays in Modern Irish Literature* (London: Faber & Faber, 1985), 108–22.

[69] Eva Urban contests Pilkington's analysis of a play like John Boyd's *The Flats* (1974). Urban's work, informed by the utopian thinking of Jill Dolan and Ernst Bloch and the existential Marxism of Jean-Paul Sartre, Henri Lefebvre, and Guy Debord, argues for a more positive approach to be given to the cross-sectarian alignments between the working classes. See Eva Urban, *Community Politics and the Peace Process in Contemporary Northern Irish Drama* (Bern: Peter Lang, 2011), 23–4.

[70] Pilkington, *Theatre and the State*, 150, 191, 151–2, 201, 220. This last point would put him very much at odds with two of the more recent books on Friel: Anthony Roche, *Brian Friel: Theatre and Politics* (Basingstoke: Palgrave Macmillan, 2011) and Christopher Murray, *The Theatre of Brian Friel: Tradition and Modernity* (London: Bloomsbury, 2014).

the broader consensus politics of the Anglo-Irish Agreement of 1985, and on the other, of accommodating excess and inclusivity, particularly in the framing of a libidinous surplus in the form of homosexuality—Pilkington acknowledges how licentiousness and excess exceed the reach of the state. His analysis recognizes a dramaturgical acceptance of Loyalism and difference in McGuinness's play, but McGuinness's attempts to address his own 'bigotry' towards the Loyalist community, and his absolute contestation of tribal and sectarian blood sacrifice, are elided.

For Pilkington, most institutional theatre in Ireland is about 'educating its nation's citizenry by consolidating and extending the authority'[71] of either a British or Irish state. Institutional theatre's role is not to nurture citizenship, but to serve as a weapon of subjugation, and offers none of the potentials for disruption and transformation that others have championed. Pilkington rejects the notion of arts practices as ever being beyond or uncompromised by politics, or the idea that the arts can be a source of essential truths, as Yeats and Gregory would have wanted to suggest. While he engages with notions of excess and libidinous energies, these are not integrated into an analysis that is determined to demonstrate the negative conditions of ideological cultivation and the coercive relationships between the elite and marginalized classes. Elsewhere, Pilkington's comment that a more passive performance of Irishness 'is full of traits that emulate eccentricities of behaviour of the oppressed'[72] sits alongside a more transgressive relationship with performativity and mimicry, as discussed by Helen Gilbert and Joanne Tompkins,[73] and Homi Bhabha's general writings in relation to postcolonial theory.

Postcolonial theories evolved predominantly in relation to the experiences, conditions, and consequences of colonization in Africa, the Americas, Asia, and the Middle East, and these conceptualizations were then variously applied to Ireland's political contexts starting in the 1980s, as these theories evolved.[74] Ania Loomba's work on the practices of colonization links the impacts of trade, plunder, warfare, genocide, enslavement, rebellion, and political negotiation with 'cultural decimation and political exclusion'.[75] In particular, she notes the simultaneity of myths of mutuality and reciprocity, and the collusions and oppressions of indigenous populations. She also highlights the pathologizing of rebellion and the impacts on the mindsets of indigenous populations.

Early postcolonial-informed theorizations came from Shaun Richards and David Cairns[76] and also from those central to the Field Day Project (1980–),[77] who were variously

[71] Pilkington, *Theatre and the State*, 4.

[72] Lionel Pilkington, *Theatre and Ireland* (Basingstoke: Palgrave Macmillan, 2010), x.

[73] This wide-ranging and hugely informative study could be used a great deal more to inform contemporary Irish critical practices: Helen Gilbert and Joanne Tompkins, *Post-colonial Drama: Theory, Practice, Politics* (London: Routledge, 1996).

[74] Scott Boltwood and F. C. McGrath apply postcolonial theory in their responses to the work of Brian Friel: Scott Boltwood, *Brian Friel, Ireland and the North* (Cambridge: Cambridge University Press, 2007); F. C. McGrath, *Brian Friel's (Post)Colonial Drama: Language, Illusion, and Politics* (Syracuse, NY: Syracuse University Press, 1999).

[75] Ania Loomba, *Colonialism/Postcolonialism* (London: Routledge, 1998), 10.

[76] See Shaun Richards and David Cairns, *Writing Ireland: Colonisation, Nationalism and Culture* (Manchester: Manchester University Press, 1988).

[77] See Marilynn J. Richtarik, *Acting Between the Lines: The Field Day Theatre Company and Irish Cultural Politics 1980–1984* (Oxford: Clarendon Press, 1994) and Carmen Szabo, *Clearing the*

inspired by the work of Bhabha, Frantz Fanon, Ashis Nandy, Edward Said, Gayatri Spivak, and many others. Declan Kiberd set the benchmark with his landmark publication *Inventing Ireland*, as he illustrated how the notion of Ireland became 'patented as not-England', and how Ireland functioned traditionally as England's 'unconscious'.[78] Kiberd did much to articulate the formation of stereotypes associated with the Irish,[79] including the labelling of them as uncivilized, irrational, violent, drunken, and childlike, concurrent with the feminization of Ireland—something other scholarship addresses differently. Later, Dawn Duncan, Colin Graham,[80] Richard Kirkland, Gerry Smyth, and many others entered the critical fray, engaging in robust dialogues. Joe Cleary's later work establishes links between colonization and imperial and globalized capital flows.[81]

Loomba wisely broadens focus, demonstrating the ways that '[c]olonialism intensified patriarchal relations in colonised lands, often because native men, increasingly disenfranchised and excluded from the public sphere, became more tyrannical at home. They seized upon the home and the woman as emblems of their culture and nationality.' She also notes the inclusion of women and the working classes in imperial cultures within the similar frames of prejudice and subjugation afforded to colonized cultures. The prefix 'post' in postcolonialism implies an aftermath, in terms of time, as in 'coming after', but also as 'ideological, as in supplanting', but 'if the inequities of colonial rule have not been erased, it is perhaps premature to proclaim the demise', Loomba advises.[82]

Situating the writings of Cleary, Seamus Deane, Luke Gibbons, David Lloyd, Kiberd, Peadar Kirby, Joe Lee, Smyth, and Cairns and Richards alongside the work of Bhabha, Said, Wole Soyinka, and Awam Amkpa especially, Merriman in *Because We Are Poor* takes a different look at independent Ireland. Merriman argues that Ireland never followed through on the radical aspirations of its early political leaderships; instead, the state colluded in the transitioning of British power to Irish elites, perpetuating most of the inequalities and horrors of colonization in a neocolonial form. Independent Ireland brought a continuity of ranked relationships, effectively leading to a 'postponed decolonization'. For Merriman, this neocolonial society resulted in 'disillusion, voluntary exile and even persecution for some of the most radical persons and groups in the successor state'. Thus neocolonialism 'is a bourgeois social project, effectively nameless as a state of being, and almost never acknowledged in public discourse'. [83]

In some respects, Merriman and Pilkington are similar in their tracing of how modernism and neoliberalism place false emphasis on egalitarianism—by implication a clear-cut rejection of a liberal democratic reading—whilst the state, at the behest of dominant elites (local

Ground: The Field Day Theatre Company and the Construction of Irish Identities (Newcastle upon Tyne: Cambridge Scholars, 2007).

[78] Declan Kiberd, *Inventing Ireland: The Literature of the Modern Nation* (London: Vintage, 1996), 9, 17.

[79] See Kathleen Heininge, *Buffoonery in Irish Drama: Staging Twentieth-Century Postcolonial Stereotypes* (New York: Peter Lang, 2009).

[80] See the hugely influential Colin Graham, *Deconstructing Ireland: Ireland, Theory, Culture* (Edinburgh: Edinburgh University Press, 2001).

[81] Joe Cleary, *Outrageous Fortune: Capital and Culture in Modern Ireland* (Derry: Field Day, 2006).

[82] Loomba, *Colonialism/Postcolonialism*, 168, 7.

[83] Merriman, *Because We Are Poor*, 4, 1, 20.

and international), perpetuate their privileges. Merriman's championing of the 'segregated, marginalized or suppressed in the existing social order'—the homeless person, Traveller, refugee/asylum seeker, cultural workers, and the working classes—are as impassioned as they are deliberate. He promotes a postcolonial desire, not for a neo-Marxist state, but for a vigorous system of 'social solidarity' and 'democratic citizenship' in terms of advocacy, pluralism, wealth distribution, and ethical trading, and highlights the potential of theatre as 'interventionist witness'. In Merriman's model, some writing passes the test of social inclusion and transformation by not offering 'homogenizing fantasies'. Companies like Wet Paint and Calypso, the hosting venue Project Arts Centre, and contemporary writers like Dermot Bolger, Charlie O'Neill, and Donal O'Kelly do well, while Marina Carr and Martin McDonagh are noted for offering 'benighted dystopias', travestying the experiences of the poor.[84]

HOME AND AWAY RULES:
PERFORMANCE AND SPECTATORSHIP

The traditional approach of those inclined towards textual analysis was to acknowledge the significant experience of a performance or multi-performances of the same work, whose impact would be absorbed as part of the critical processing. Further feature pieces, reviews,[85] interviews, programme notes, marketing campaigns, prompt books, costume and design, and some production stills were variously used to substantiate some distilled essence of a performance. (Archived video recordings have helped in various ways.) When more extensive details of a performance were deployed, they primarily served to reinforce textual analysis rather than being seen as a chance to discuss how a *mise-en-scène* might have disputed consensual assumptions about a text and genre frame or contested the ideology or authority of the text.[86] While such critical approaches are no longer to the fore, what still remains inadequate is any consistent theorization of the relationships between texts and performances,[87] and not much work has been done on subsequent performances of plays by different companies, in dissimilar spaces and cultures.[88]

---

[84]   Ibid., 216, 12, 222, 225, 11, 195.

[85]   Newspaper criticism of performances by writers and papers of standing are seldom the objective record that they are often held up to be. The exception is Fintan O'Toole's brilliant work as a critic evident in *Critical Moments: Fintan O'Toole on Modern Irish Theatre*, ed. Julia Furay and Redmond O'Hanlon (Dublin: Carysfort Press, 2003). The *Irish Theatre Magazine* afforded journalists and academics the chance to write extended reviews that, while not performance analyses, still offered an opportunity to engage more critically with the elements of performance.

[86]   Anthony Roche in *Contemporary Irish Drama* is excellent on Garry Hynes's 1987 production of Murphy's *Whistle in the Dark* at the Abbey and her Gate production of *The Weir* in 2008. He also superbly compares Hynes's 1985 Druid production of *Conversations on a Homecoming* to her 1991 production at the Abbey.

[87]   See Patrice Pavis, *Analyzing Performance: Theatre, Dance, and Film*, trans. David Williams (Ann Arbor, MI: University of Michigan Press, 2004). See also W. B. Worthen, 'Drama, Performativity, and Performance', *PMLA* 113, no. 5 (1998), 1093–1107.

[88]   Texts are sometimes used to construct imaginatively the potential performance parameters of work whose traces are lost, or of work that remains currently unperformed.

For Morash in *A History of Irish Theatre: 1601–2000* a theatre history is not only about writers and plays, but also must account for actors, designers, directors, 'the architects who build those stages, and the managers, entrepreneurs', patrons, and audiences: '[W]ho they were, how much they paid for their tickets, where they sat, whether they watched reverentially or threw oranges at the orchestra.' By interfacing personal journals, critical responses, letters to papers, collective and individual ideologies, and judicial findings with the artistic policies, repertoire management, and the administration of theatres, Morash's study moves towards a different critical paradigm. He illustrates the impacts of cutting out 'half price tickets after nine fifteen', how the darkening of auditoria modified audience behaviours by eliminating noisy interactions and interruptions; for an audience accustomed to melodrama in the popular Queen's Theatre, such restrictions 'would have been considered the equivalent of a custodial sentence'. [89]

When the Abbey Theatre set itself up in the Mechanics' Institute, its footprint made it smaller in scale to its rival theatres, but also its tiered pricing structure effectively 'excluded the sixpenny audience from the theatre'—an audience who could be catered for in both the Queen's and Gaiety Theatres.[90] (This price insensitivity is something the theatre would later address.) As Morash notes, the Abbey's design by Joseph Holloway took little from the pioneering ideas of 'Wagner's Festspielhaus in Bayreuth', as Annie Horniman had wished, but instead was configured to be predominantly representational in emphasis. From the opening of the Abbey Theatre on 27 December 1904 to the end of 1910, 'forty-nine shows (out of a total of sixty-three) would use box-set interiors, putting the Abbey firmly on the road to a realistic production style which would dominate until the early 1960s.' Clearly, Yeats did not get the theatre that he wanted.

Morash's reconstructed nights at the theatre are a 'reasonably accurate picture of what those vanished audiences expected, and of what they saw on those now-darkened stages'.[91] The reception of *The Playboy of the Western World* (1907) and *The Plough and the Stars* (1926) appear on most critical radars. In these events, Morash distinguishes between the premeditated crying down of a performance for political purposes and spontaneous responses when alleged misrepresentations occurred that seemingly challenged conventional values.

In *Modernism, Drama, and the Audience for Irish Spectacle*, Paige Reynolds puts an even greater emphasis on audiences. Reynolds's case studies also include *Playboy* and *The Plough*, but also more public events like the Dublin Suffrage Week, the Tailteann Games of 1924, and the death of Terence MacSwiney. She wishes to capture how the '[i]nterface between revivalism and international modernism' determined 'a distinctly Irish modernism', which synthesized both. She illustrates how some critics in their challenges to both revivalism and modernism 'assume that the state or nationalist culture is necessarily pernicious, seeking largely, if not exclusively, to delude or oppress its subjects', and argues: 'These appraisals leave little room for an Irish modernism that allows for—or even encourages—positive and productive engagements with mainstream culture and the pleasures generated by a feeling of belonging.' So to Reynolds's mind audiences are not simply passive absorbers, always unaware of how they are being seduced or indoctrinated; they are alert to the impact of genre and rhythm, to the operation of empathy, and to

---

[89] Morash, *History*, 1, 131.   [90] Ibid., 126.   [91] Ibid., 128, 1.

their own susceptibility. Secondly, while audiences are a collective presence, they are never a homogeneous unit.

Thus reflecting on and responding to David Lloyd's work, Reynolds suggests that she cannot accept 'the individuals who compose popular social bodies as merely transparent objects of manipulation, estranged from themselves as a consequence of the abuses proffered by the state and other structures of power'. [92] She argues: 'according to Lloyd, mainstream culture offers no legitimate subject position, let alone relief or pleasure, for its participants, because "one principal and consistent dynamic of identity formation has been the negation of recalcitrant or unassimilable elements in Irish society".[93] Irish modernism allowed and even promoted 'competing receptive practices' that led to a combination of 'riotous resistance and delighted acquiescence'. She argues, as do Grene, Murray, and Roche, that literature and theatre play a crucial role in 'consolidating and disrupting the perceptions of identity employed by a real national community, the audience'.[94]

The Abbey Theatre toured nationally and internationally from the beginning.[95] Today, work by Irish writers can première in London at the Royal Court,[96] National Theatre, or Donmar Warehouse, or tour to London, Edinburgh, New York,[97] Chicago, Perth, or Toronto. (Both the Arts Council and Culture Ireland have supported touring.) Writing is commissioned, adapted, translated, and produced in various international contexts.[98] Contemporary playwrights are less dependent on the Abbey to perform new work.

Patrick Lonergan's work, on Martin McDonagh in particular[99] and on globalization more broadly, demonstrates that texts in the context of their marketing, performance, and reception do not necessarily have global or universal meanings, but ones that are localized. Lonergan suggests in *Theatre and Globalization* that 'branding,' 'reflexivity', and 'an audience's enjoyment of a theatrical production is determined by that audience's capacity to relate the action to their own preoccupations and interests, as those preoccupations and interests are determined locally'. He adds: 'Irishness acts as a deterritorialized space in which audiences may explore local preoccupations.' [100]

[92] Reynolds, *Modernism, Drama*, 13, 15, 18.

[93] David Lloyd, *Anomalous States: Irish Writing and the Post-Colonial Moment* (Dublin, Lilliput Press; Durham, NC: Duke University Press, 1993), 6. Cited in Reynolds, *Modernism, Drama*, 18–19.

[94] Ibid., 15.

[95] According to Richard Allen Cave, when the Abbey Theatre first toured in 1906 the company produced a series of 'Irish plays' in London, which provided 'a kind of constellation of specific terms and epithets' that 'steadily defines the company's claim to originality as lying in its concern for a scrupulous authenticity', as audiences were assured that locals had been consulted in order to confirm the exactness of the details of the space, costumes, language, and accent. See Richard Allen Cave, 'The Abbey Tours in England', in Nicholas Grene and Christopher Morash (eds.), *Irish Theatre on Tour* (Dublin: Carysfort Press, 2005), 15.

[96] Peter James Harris, *From Stage to Page: Critical Reception of Irish Plays in the London Theatre, 1925–1996* (Bern: Peter Lang, 2011).

[97] A good example is John P. Harrington's Introduction to his edited collection, *Irish Theater in America: Essays on Irish Theatrical Diaspora* (Syracuse, NY: Syracuse University Press, 2009), xi–xix.

[98] See Clare Wallace's address of the need to consider criticism determined by work produced outside Ireland in 'Irish Theatre Criticism: De-territorialisation and Integration', *Modern Drama* 47, no. 4 (2004), 659–70.

[99] Patrick Lonergan, *The Theatre and Films of Martin McDonagh* (London: Methuen, 2012).

[100] Lonergan, *Theatre and Globalization*, 87.

The success of the Abbey's *Dancing at Lughnasa* (1990) is central to Lonergan's argument. Most aspects of any work will be inevitably localized, but sometimes that which is strangely foreign or Other can be maintained; the stereotyping, commodification, reproduction, and enrichment of the concept of Irishness are thus countered by erasures, depletions, and subversions.[101] (Amanda Third stresses that Irishness 'offers a way of *performing whiteness* with legitimacy' (my italics), and, as I have proposed elsewhere, also with illegitimacy.[102]) Further in terms of reception, the relationships between textual, conceptual, and scenographic space are increasingly vital ones. Critics like Csilla Bertha, Cave, Leeney, Donald Morse, McMullan, Sihra, Roche, and particularly Enrica Cerquoni[103] have offered various reflections on textual and scenographic space, prompted by work by Marvin Carlson, Una Chaudhuri, Michel Foucault, Michael Issacharoff, Gay McAuley, Hanna Scolnicov, Gerry Smyth, and others. More recent publications by Lojek (*The Spaces of Irish Drama*) and Morash and Richards (*Mapping Irish Theatre*) have applied the work of Gaston Bachelard, Edward Casey, Henri Lefebvre, Doreen Massey, Edward Soja, Yi-Fu Tuan, and others to the configurations and implications of theatre architecture and performance, and the relationships between and the production/construction of place and space. Detailed performance-related scholarship is seen in work as varied as Eric Weitz's work on Raymond Keane's clowning,[104] where theories of clowning and analysis of performance are conjoined to telling effect, and the reflections of Miriam Haughton, Sara Keating, Charlotte McIvor, Morash and Richards, Emilie Pine, and Brian Singleton on ANU Productions' site-specific/immersive performances.[105] Consideration of the rehearsal process is a vital emerging field, especially in relation to devised work by companies like Performance Corporation, Corn Exchange, and Pan Pan.[106] While Irish theatre historiography has been primarily focused on Irish plays in Irish performance contexts, and primarily on relationships between writers within this tradition, there is an emerging but insufficient body of work that looks at dramaturgical and performance practices alongside work by international writers. There is far less work done on Irish productions of writing originating abroad.

Additionally, a Richard Schechner-inspired performance studies perspective has afforded the inclusion of spectacles, rituals, protests, and other public events within the frames of analysis.[107] Fitzpatrick's *Performing Feminisms*[108] includes the representations

[101] Within American popular culture, Diane Negra broadens the scope of things by identifying the relationship between Irishness, performance, and enriched whiteness. See 'Introduction', in Diane Negra (ed.), *The Irish in Us: Irishness, Performativity and Popular Culture* (Durham, NC: Duke University Press, 2006), 1.

[102] Amanda Third, ' "Does the Rug Match the Carpet?": Race, Gender and the Redheaded Woman', in Negra, *The Irish in Us*, 224.

[103] See esp. Enrica Cerquoni, 'Ways of Seeing and the Womb-Theatre: Theatrical Space and Scenic Presentation in Marina Carr's Ariel', in Rhona Trench (ed.), *Staging Thought: Essays on Irish Theatre, Scholarship and Practice* (Bern: Peter Lang, 2012), 73–92. Trench's collection is very strong on performance and practice.

[104] Eric Weitz, 'Failure as Success: On Clowns and Laughing Bodies', *Performance Research* 17, no. 1 (2012), 79–87.

[105] See Eamonn Jordan, *From Leenane to LA: The Theatre and Cinema of Martin McDonagh* (Dublin: Irish Academic Press, 2014), which includes performance analysis.

[106] See Noelia Ruiz's work on rehearsal processes in 'Contemporary Creative Processes in Contemporary Irish Theatre and Performance' (PhD. dissertation, University College Dublin, 2013).

[107] See also Sara Brady and Fintan Walsh (eds.), *Crossroads: Performance Studies and Irish Culture* (Basingstoke: Palgrave Macmillan, 2009).

[108] See Fitzpatrick, *Performing Feminisms*.

and the performance of gender, in theatre performances, in stand-up comedy,[109] and in the everyday, alongside community and activist initiatives and rights campaigns. In Northern Ireland, the overlap between theatre and political and cultural performances such as parades, mural memorialization, and paramilitary cortèges is far more pointed, and is something that many of the essays in Fitzpatrick's *Performing Violence in Contemporary Ireland* clearly demonstrate.[110] Pilkington's work raises important issues in relation to counterperformances, which include traditional indigenous performance events as noted by Alan Fletcher,[111] such as jesting, poetry recital, and satire, which can be added to practices of mumming, patterns, and wake games. Pilkington emphasizes street marches, blanket protests, and hunger strikes by Republican prisoners in the later 1970s and early 1980s. Mark Phelan's work looks at the kidnapping, torturing, executions, and burial of 'the disappeared' as other forms of spectacular and vanishing performances.[112]

Mutual Dissonance

The applications of theoretical approaches developed in the fields of literature, history, politics, anthropology, sociology, cultural materialism, gender, psychology, sexuality, and subaltern and class studies have informed the numerous approaches of Irish theatre historiography. Critical practices have strengths, prejudices, self-deceptions, and ideologically shaped blind spots.[113] Those writing from a liberal/democratic and sometimes humanist perspective tend to respond easily to given socioeconomic circumstances, accommodate social, cultural, and gender differences, and put down political failings to individual misjudgement, unconscionable actions, or systemic irregularities or corruption that can be changed. This rationale is based on creative and evolving systems of rights, freedoms, and access to justice. The artist/writer as revolutionary and visionary is never far behind. Art is not just a response to a shared and perceived reality, but it is also likely to be ideologically conditioned, and less free than it is imagined to be—and this is said without considering the impact of funding environments and patronage.

Gender-aware criticism, predominantly informed by feminist discourses, has given great emphasis to the workings of patriarchy, and the challenges are seen in terms of the

[109] See Susanne Colleary, *Performance and Identity in Irish Stand-Up Comedy: The Comic 'I'* (Basingstoke: Palgrave Macmillan, 2015).

[110] See Lisa Fitzpatrick (ed.), *Performing Violence in Contemporary Ireland* (Dublin: Carysfort Press, 2009).

[111] Alan J. Fletcher, *Drama and the Performing Arts in Pre-Cromwellian Ireland: A Repertory of Sources and Documents from the Earliest Times* (Cambridge: D. S. Brewer, 2001), 6. Cited in Pilkington, *Theatre and Ireland*, 26–7.

[112] See Mark Phelan, 'Not So Innocent Landscapes: Remembrance, Representation and the Disappeared', in Patrick Anderson and Jisha Menon (eds.), *Violence Performed: Local Roots and Global Routes of Conflict* (Basingstoke: Palgrave Macmillan, 2011), 285–316.

[113] While performance is gaining more and more attention, and academics are working more with theatre companies, it must be accepted that a great deal of work has to be done before the theatre community is less dismissive of—or more comfortable with—academia.

material and the symbolic.[114] In terms of sexualities, Frank McGuinness's work has done a great amount to foreground predominantly male homosexuality; Emma Donoghue or Amy Conroy are good examples of playwrights that deal with lesbianism, but it seems that male–male relationships are more visible.[115] The International Dublin Gay Theatre Festival was founded in 2004 and is ongoing.

Irish theatre has dealt in complex enough ways with poverty: while characters may have little access to political capital, they tend to have significant access to social capital, and to awareness of the performance of their own disadvantages. Much criticism has shown a lack of confidence in dealing with class-related issues. The oppressions, criminality, and exploitation endemic to many working-class communities are airbrushed out of much criticism: the differences between the corrupt developer/businessperson and the tradesperson who will fleece the naive customer are often just a matter of scale. The working classes do not view themselves as any more 'decent' or 'ordinary' than anyone else—unless it is to their advantage. For class-related bad behaviour there are far too many explanations and apologies circulated, and positive actions are sometimes unduly romanticized.

Working-class men's access to patriarchal privilege is complex, but whatever their rewards, these are modest relative to middle-class men. Currently, working-class women are tending to be more socially mobile; males were hit far harder by unemployment during the collapse of the Celtic Tiger, because their skill sets were more tied in with the sectors worst hit by economic collapse. Income equality is not the norm in any economy. There is a growing realization that patriarchal dividends are also differently available to wealthy gay people, for example, thus complicating a simplistic non-hegemonic categorization. The socioeconomic rewards of women amongst the more privileged classes can be suppressed in some critical analysis. The unwillingness at times of both men and women to enable others outside their social rank, ethnicity, or race, and the challenges posed by individual and collective rivalries or competitiveness, cannot be excluded from contextual evaluations. There are classes within classes, groups within groups, aspects that often go unrecognized in attempts to compartmentalize the non-hegemonic marginalized, whether they are male or female, heterosexual or homosexual. Given that across all categories people can be radical on specific issues and deeply conservative on others, the allotment of an all-embracing 'non-hegemonic' status should be treated with caution. Better integration of gender, class, sexuality, ethnicity, and race issues,[116] plus an acceptance that the man/woman, hegemonic/non-hegemonic, heteronormative/homosexual binaries must evolve, will lead to more constructive critical models.

Materialist and postcolonial readings illustrate the collusion of imperial and global capital with establishment elites and the various instruments of state. Anne Fogarty has

[114] For a thorough interrogation of the relationship between feminism and post-colonial theory, see Claire Connolly, 'Theorising Ireland', *Irish Studies Review* 9, no. 3 (2001), 301–15.

[115] See David Cregan (ed.), *Deviant Acts: Essays on Queer Performance* (Dublin: Carysfort Press, 2009); *Irish University Review* 43, no. 1 (May 2013) (special issue: 'Queering the Issue', ed. Anne Mulhall); and Fintan Walsh, *Queer Notions: New Plays and Performances from Ireland* (Cork: Cork University Press, 2010).

[116] Race remains almost absent from critical discourse. Bisi Adigun's Arambe Theatre Company produced work by Wole Soyinka and Derek Walcott, and also *The Butcher Babes* (2010), which was conceptualized as white-face production.

queried postcolonial theories' spawning of 'false universals and ahistorical abstractions that impede rather than further literary analysis'. Further, she finds deeply problematic a 'fixating on liminal spaces and hybrid identities'.[117] Eoin Flannery notes Graham's interrogation of Lloyd's theoretical failure 'to sanction any telos other than perpetual discontinuity and fragmentation': 'Lloyd constructs a corollary fetish of the subaltern itself by "ethically endowing" the notion of subalternity.'[118] An obsession with subaltern violation can lead to forms of ahistorically conceived superiority.[119]

There are also the challenges posed by those who write about militant republicanism, armed resistance, and the conflict in Northern Ireland, who often see freedom fighting and paramilitarism as the inevitable consequences of British rule. It is not that Republican ideology and actions are given impunity by most scholars, but sometimes they are not accorded the rigour applied elsewhere. Cogent demonstrations as to how the British state manipulates history and frames armed resistance as barbaric are matched by failures to address how Republicanism engages in sometimes similar and disingenuous propagandist strategies. Occasionally constitutional politics are all too easily dismissed, and challenges to Republican thinking or actions are labelled as pro-British. Despite the impassioned focus on injustices and inequality, the absence of any clearly articulated, viable solutions invites caution in the face of much of the more radical scholarly expression and discourse.

More recently, criticism that deals with rampant and early (not 'late') liberal capitalism points to how the state, large corporations, and financial markets are never just simplistic allies, and how a small state like Ireland cannot be seen in isolation but instead operates within a network of first-world democracies. (Postmodernist frameworks that reflect on the collapse of grand narratives have been dealt with brilliantly by Clare Wallace in her book *Suspect Cultures*.[120]) The anti-establishment, anti-big business, and anti-market rhetoric of much of Irish theatre historiography leaves unaddressed—or at least underacknowledged—the reality that many academics are based in mainstream universities, are on reasonably high salaries, have permanent, tenured contracts, sometimes chase down competitive research funding, and are encouraged to attract 'non-exchequer income'— all activities that enhance career value and further employment prospects and chances of promotion. Academics, like all cultural practitioners, are neither hermetically nor hermeneutically sealed off from neocapitalist practices. Participative privileges do not dispel the potential of radicalism or beneficial insights of public intellectuals or creative artists, but incite associated challenges—few get to bite the hand that feeds for long. Not all failings can be placed at the door of colonialism, neocolonialism, and neoliberalism. Additionally,

---

[117] Anne Fogarty, 'Other Spaces: Postcolonialism and the Politics of Truth in Kate O'Brien's *That Lady*', *European Journal of English Studies* 3, no. 3 (1999), 342–4.

[118] Colin Graham, 'Subalternity and Gender: Problems of Post-colonial Irishness', *Journal of Gender Studies* 5, no. 3 (1996), 367, cited in Eoin Flannery, 'Outside in the Theory Machine: Ireland in the World of Post-Colonial Studies', *Studies: An Irish Quarterly Review* 92, no. 368 (2003), 363.

[119] 'Irish drama has yet to establish a new role outside of the comfort zone of postcolonial criticism and soft-centred Celtic Tiger critique and engage with the position it occupies in a state which now has the power to "translate"—its own as well as other subjects—rather than being always "translated"': Shaun Richards, 'To Me, Here Is More Like There', *Irish Studies Review* 15, no. 1 (2007), 12.

[120] See also José Lanters, ' "Like Tottenham": Martin McDonagh's Postmodern Morality Tales', in Lonergan, *The Theatre and Films of Martin McDonagh*, 168.

Ireland is not poor even by first-world standards, and this needs to be effectively addressed more fully in critical debates. In Irish theatre criticism, there is not enough of sociological history and economic science, a point made by many people of late: perhaps there is too much of psychoanalysis and philosophy, and not enough about hedge funds, interbank Libor rates, and wealth injustices globally. The failure of so many plays, and even more of criticism, to engage with the flow, circulation, and impact of money is staggering in its own right.

Far more analysis is needed of the relationship between theatres and funding regimes. Audience-based research, eco-criticism, biopolitics, cognitive and evolutionary psychology, popular culture, genre-framing,[121] interculturalism, comparative studies, and diaspora studies will all need greater attention. In increasingly hurried and frantic academic environments and in the rush to get ahead, outlier theatrical practices become all too easily institutionalized.

Conclusion

The academic/practitioner divide has not been really surmounted as it has in other jurisdictions, despite many efforts through conferences, publications that combine the two disciplines, practitioner-taught academic modules, and partnerships between theatre companies and academics. A generation of theatre practitioners who did not fully welcome the practices of academia is being replaced by a cohort far more open to dialogue, and to scholars attending rehearsals. More and more early-career scholars combine practice-informed scholarship with their academic-inflected training.

The number of publishing outlets that provide the discursive opportunities for critical endeavours have also increased over the last fifteen years, and their commercial and strategic objectives are always worth recognizing. At the same time, while publishers like to encourage and promote claims of originality and are fixated on paradigm shifting, these claims need to be strenuously stress-tested. Critical dispositions could be more attentive to their own orthodoxies and self-contradictory ideas, alert to potential counterarguments, and more forthright about what are often not explicit ideological positions. Critical practices must be willing to contest assumed wisdoms, avoid being ad hoc, or too creatively eclectic, and must avoid regurgitating tired methodologies. Equally, by robustly engaging with and contesting the work of others, there are opportunities to evolve knowledge and critical frameworks. Thus horizons of expectation are broadened and discursive possibilities heightened in relation to the rich and complex body of work created by the Irish theatre community over the past century.

---

[121] Ondřej Pilný's impressive work on irony and satire and Eric Weitz's work on comic framing have been consistent in giving appropriate consideration to genre, form, and idiom.

Bibliography

Abdel, Aaty Mohamed, and Mona El Halawany (eds.), *Proceedings of the Seventh International Symposium on Comparative Literature* (Cairo: Cairo University, 2003).

Allain, Paul, and Vera Gottlieb (eds.), *The Cambridge Companion to Chekhov* (Cambridge: Cambridge University Press, 2000).

Allen, Nicholas, *Modernism, Ireland and Civil War* (Cambridge: Cambridge University Press, 2009).

Anderman, Gunilla M. (ed.), *Voices in Translation: Bridging Cultural Divides* (Clevedon: Multilingual Matters, 2007).

Anderson, Benedict, *Imagined Communities* (London: Verso, 1983).

Anderson, Patrick, and Jisha Menon (eds.), *Violence Performed: Local Roots and Global Routes of Conflict* (Basingstoke: Palgrave Macmillan, 2011).

Arrington, Lauren, *W. B. Yeats, the Abbey Theatre, Censorship, and the Irish State: Adding the Half-Pence to the Pence* (Oxford: Oxford University Press, 2010).

Augusteijn, Joost, *Patrick Pearse: The Making of a Revolutionary* (Basingstoke: Palgrave Macmillan, 2010).

Ayling, Ronald (ed.), *Sean O'Casey: Modern Judgements* (London: Macmillan, 1969).

Barfoot, C. C., and Rias van den Doel (eds.), *Ritual Remembering: History, Myth and Politics in Anglo-Irish Drama* (Amsterdam: Rodopi, 1995).

Barnes, Ben, *Plays and Controversies: Abbey Theatre Diaries 2000–2005* (Dublin: Carysfort Press, 2008).

Barnett, Gene A., *Denis Johnston* (Boston, MA: Twayne, 1978).

Barrett, Frank, and Stephen M. Whitehead (eds.), *Masculinities Reader* (Cambridge: Polity Press, 2001).

Barry, Sebastian, *The Steward of Christendom* (London: Methuen, 1996).

Barsacq, André, et al., *Architecture et dramaturgie* (Paris: Flammarion, 1950).

Beckett, Samuel, *Disjecta, Miscellaneous Writings and a Dramatic Fragment*, ed. Ruby Cohn (London: John Calder, 1983).

Beckett, Samuel, *Letters*, vol. 1: *1929–40*, ed. Martha Dow Fehsenfeld and Lois Overbeck (Cambridge: Cambridge University Press, 2009).

Beckett, Samuel, *Letters*, vol 2: *1941–1956*, ed. George Craig et al. (Cambridge: Cambridge University Press, 2011).

Beckett, Samuel, *Letters*, vol. 3: *1957–1965*, ed. George Craig et al. (Cambridge: Cambridge University Press, 2014).

Beckett, Samuel, *Waiting for Godot/En attendant Godot* (London: Faber & Faber, 2006).

Beckson, Karl (ed.), *Oscar Wilde: The Critical Heritage* (London: Routledge, 1974).

Beitchman, Philip, *The Theatre of Naturalism: Disappearing Act* (New York: Peter Lang, 2011).

Behan, Brendan, *Poems and a Play in Irish* (Dublin: Gallery Books, 1981).

Belchem, John, *Irish, Catholic and Scouse: The History of the Liverpool Irish 1800–1939* (Liverpool: Liverpool University Press, 2007).

Belsey, Catherine, *Critical Practice* (London: Routledge, 1980).

Blanchard, Mary Warner, *Oscar Wilde's America: Counterculture in the Gilded Age* (New Haven, CT: Yale University Press, 1998).

Blau, Herbert, *The Audience* (Baltimore, MD: Johns Hopkins University Press, 1990).

Bolger, Dermot (ed.), *Druids, Dudes and Beauty Queens: The Changing Face of Irish Theatre* (Dublin: New Island, 2001).

Bolger, Dermot, *The Parting Glass* (Dublin: New Island, 2011).

Boltwood, Scott, *Brian Friel, Ireland and the North* (Cambridge: Cambridge University Press, 2007).

Booth, J. B., *Sporting Times: The 'Pink 'Un' World* (London: T. Werner Laurie, 1938).

Booth, Michael R., *Prefaces to English Nineteenth-Century Theatre* (Manchester: Manchester University Press, 1980).

Boucicault, Dion, *Selected Plays*, ed. Andrew Parkin (Gerrards Cross/Washington, DC: Colin Smythe/Catholic University Press of America, 1987).

Bourgeois, Maurice, *John Millington Synge and the Irish Theatre* (London: Constable, 1913).

Bourke, Angela, *The Burning of Bridget Cleary* (London: Pimlico, 1999).

Boylan, Patricia, *Gaps of Brightness* (Dublin: A. & A. Farmar, 2003).

Boxall, Peter, *Since Beckett: Contemporary Writing in the Wake of Modernism* (London: Continuum, 2009).

Bradbury, Malcolm, and James McFarlane (eds.), *Modernism: A Guide to European Literature 1890–1930* (Harmondsworth: Penguin, 1976).

Bradby, David, *Beckett: Waiting for Godot* (Cambridge: Cambridge University Press, 2001).

Brady, Sara, and Fintan Walsh (eds.), *Crossroads: Performance Studies and Irish Culture* (Basingstoke: Palgrave Macmillan, 2009).

Braidotti, Rosi, *Patterns of Dissonance* (Cambridge: Polity Press, 1991).

Brandes, Georg, *Friedrich Nietzsche*, trans. A. G. Chater (London: William Heinemann, 1914).

Bratton, J. S., et al., *Acts of Supremacy: The British Empire and the Stage, 1790–1930* (Manchester: Manchester University Press, 1991).

Bratton, J. S., *Terence Gray and the Cambridge Festival Theatre* (Cambridge: Chadwyck-Healey, 1980).

Brennan-Whitmore, W. J., *Dublin Burning: The Easter Rising from Behind the Barricades* (Dublin: Gill & Macmillan, 2013).

Brewster, Scott, and Michael Parker (eds.), *Irish Literature Since 1990: Diverse Voices* (Manchester: Manchester University Press, 2009).

Brook, Peter, *The Empty Space* (London: MacGibbon & Kee, 1968).

Brooker, Peter, Andrzej Gasiorek, Deborah Longworth, and Andrew Thacker (eds.), *The Oxford Handbook of Modernisms* (Oxford: Oxford University Press, 2010).

Brooks, Peter, *The Melodramatic Imagination: Balzac, Henry James, Melodrama, and the Mode of Excess* (New York: Columbia University Press, 1985).

Brown, Terence, *Ireland: A Social and Cultural History 1922–1985* (London: Fontana, 1981).

Brown, Terence, *Ireland: A Social and Cultural History 1922–2002* (London: Harper Perennial, 2004).

Brown, Terence, *The Literature of Ireland: Culture and Criticism* (Cambridge: Cambridge University Press, 2010).

Bull, Philip, *Land, Politics and Nationalism* (Dublin: Gill & Macmillan, 1996).

Burke, Mary, *'Tinkers': Synge and the Cultural History of the Irish Traveller* (Oxford: Oxford University Press, 2009).

Burke Brogan, Patricia, *Eclipsed* (Knockeven: Salmon Publishing, 1994).

Burnham, Richard, and Robert Hogan (eds.), *The Cork Dramatic Society: Lost Plays of the Irish Renaissance*, vol. 3 (Newark, DE: Proscenium Press, 1984).

Bushrui, S. B. (ed.), *A Centenary Tribute to John Millington Synge, 1871–1909: Sunshine and the Moon's Delight* (New York: Barnes & Noble, 1972).

Butler, Christopher, *Modernism: A Very Short Introduction* (Oxford: Oxford University Press, 2010).

Butler, Judith, *Excitable Speech: A Politics of the Performative* (London: Routledge, 1997).

Byrne, Ophelia, *State of Play: The Theatre and Cultural Identity in Twentieth Century Ulster* (Belfast: Linen Hall Library, 2002).

Canaris, Volker, *Peter Zadek: Der Theatermann und Filmemacher* [Peter Zadek: Theatre Practitioner and Film-Maker] (Munich: Hanser, 1979).

Carlson, Marvin, *The Haunted Stage: The Theatre as Memory Machine* (Ann Arbor, MI: University of Michigan Press, 2001).

Carlson, Marvin, *Places of Performance: The Semiotics of Theatre Architecture* (New York: Cornell University Press, 1989).

Carr, Marina, *Plays One* (London: Faber & Faber, 2000).

Carr, Marina, *Portia Coughlan* (London: Faber & Faber, 1996).

Carr, Marina, *Woman and Scarecrow* (London: Faber & Faber, 2006).

Carvalho, Paulo Eduardo, *Identidades reescribes: figurações da Irlanda no teatro português* [Rewritten Identities: Representations of Ireland in Portuguese Theatre] (Porto: Edições Afrontamento/Instituto de Literatura Comparada Margarida Losa, 2009).

Carville, Darargh, *Convictions* (Belfast: Tinderbox, 2000).

Casanova, Pascale, *The World Republic of Letters* (Cambridge, MA: Harvard University Press, 2004).

Case, Sue-Ellen, *Feminism and Theatre* (Basingstoke: Palgrave Macmillan, 2008).

Cave, Richard Allen, *Collaborations: Ninette de Valois and William Butler Yeats* (Alton: Dance Books, 2011).

Cave, Richard Allen, *Terence Gray and the Cambridge Festival Theatre* (Cambridge: Chadwyck-Healey, 1980).

Cave, Richard Allen, and Ben Levitas (eds.), *Irish Theatre in England* (Dublin: Carysfort Press, 2007).

Chambers, Lilian, Ger FitzGibbon, and Eamonn Jordan (eds.), *Theatre Talk: Voices of Irish Theatre Practitioners* (Dublin: Carysfort Press, 2001).

Chambers, Lilian, and Eamonn Jordan (eds.), *The Theatre of Conor McPherson* (Dublin: Carysfort Press, 2012).

Chambers, Lilian, and Eamonn Jordan (eds.), *The Theatre of Martin McDonagh: A World of Savage Stories* (Dublin: Carysfort Press, 2006).

Chansky, Dorothy, *Composing Ourselves: The Little Theatre Movement and the American Audience* (Carbondale, IL: Southern Illinois Press, 2004).

Chaudhuri, Una, *Staging Place: The Geography of Modern Drama* (Ann Arbor, MI: University of Michigan Press, 1997).

Cheney, Sheldon, *The New Movement in the Theatre* (New York: Michael Kennelley, 1914)

Chesterton, G. K., *Christendom in Dublin* (London: Sheed & Ward, 1932).

Clarke, Brenna Katz, *The Emergence of the Irish Peasant Play at the Abbey Theatre* (Ann Arbor, MI: UMI Research Press, 1982).

Clarke, Brenna Katz, and Harold Ferrar, *The Dublin Drama League: 1919–1941* (Dublin: Dolmen Press, 1979).

Cleary, Joe, *Outrageous Fortune: Capital and Culture in Modern Ireland* (Derry: Field Day, 2006).

Cleary, Joe, and Claire Connolly (eds.), *The Cambridge Companion to Modern Irish Culture* (Cambridge: Cambridge University Press, 2005).

Clery, Arthur, *The Idea of a Nation*, ed. Patrick Maume (Dublin: University College Dublin Press, 2002).

Cochrane, Claire, *Twentieth-Century British Theatre: Industry, Art and Empire* (Cambridge: Cambridge University Press, 2011).

Cole, Catherine, *Performing South Africa's Truth Commission: Stages of Translation* (Bloomington, IN: Indiana University Press, 2010).

Colleary, Susanne, *Performance and Identity in Irish Stand-Up Comedy: The Comic 'I'* (Basingstoke: Palgrave Macmillan, 2015).

Colum, Padraic, *The Fiddler's House* (Dublin: Maunsel, 1907).

Colum, Padraic, *The Road Round Ireland* (New York: Macmillan, 1930).

Colum, Padraic, *Selected Plays*, ed. Sanford Sternlicht (Syracuse, NY: Syracuse University Press, 2006).

Colum, Padraic, *Selected Poems*, ed. Sanford Sternlicht (Syracuse, NY: Syracuse University Press, 1989).

Colum, Padraic, *Three Plays: The Fiddler's House, The Land, Thomas Muskerry* (Boston, MA: Little, Brown, 1916).

Cooney, John, *John Charles McQuaid* (Dublin: O'Brien Press, 2003).

Corkery, Daniel, *Synge and Anglo-Irish Literature* (Cork: Cork University Press, 1947).

Cousins, James H., and Margaret E. Cousins, *We Two Together* (Madras: Ganesh, 1950).

Cowell, John, *No Profit but the Name: The Longfords and the Gate Theatre* (Dublin: O'Brien Press, 1988).

Craft, Robert, *Conversations with Igor Stravinsky* (New York: Doubleday, 1959).

Cregan, David (ed.), *Deviant Acts: Essays on Queer Performance* (Dublin: Carysfort Press, 2009).

Critchley, Simon, *Ethics—Politics—Subjectivity: Essays on Derrida, Levinas and Contemporary French Thought* (London: Verso, 1999).

Croghan, Declan, *Paddy Irishman, Paddy Englishman, and Paddy …?* (London: Faber & Faber, 1999).

Cronin, Michael G., *Impure Thoughts: Sexuality, Catholicism and Literature in Twentieth-Century Ireland* (Manchester: Manchester University Press, 2012).

Cronin, Michael, *Translation and Globalization* (London: Routledge, 2003).

Cruise O'Brien, Conor, *States of Ireland* (London: Hutchinson, 1972).

Cullingford, Elizabeth Butler, *Ireland's Others: Ethnicity and Gender in Irish Literature and Popular Culture* (Cork: Cork University Press, 2001).

D'Alton, Louis, *Death Is So Fair* (New York: Doubleday, Doran, 1938).

D'Alton, Louis, *They Got What They Wanted* (Dundalk: Dundalgan Press, 1962).

D'Alton, Louis, *This Other Eden* (Dublin: P. J. Bourke, 1954).

Daniels, Sarah, *Plays: One* (London: Methuen Drama, 1991).

D'Arcy, Margaretta, *Loose Theatre: Memoirs of a Guerrilla Theatre Activist* (Victoria, BC: Trafford, 2005).

Darley, Emmanuel, *Tuesdays at Tesco's* [*Mardi à Monoprix*], trans. Matthew Hurt and Sarah Vermande (London: Nick Hern, 2011).

Darwin, John, *The Empire Project: The Rise and Fall of the British World-System, 1830–1970*, rev. edn. (Cambridge: Cambridge University Press, 2011).

Dawe, Gerald, Darryl Jones, and Nora Pelizzari (eds.), *Beautiful Strangers: Ireland and the World in the 1950s* (Oxford: Peter Lang, 2013).

Dawe, Gerald, and Jonathan Williams (eds.), *Krino 1986–1996: An Anthology of Modern Irish Writing* (Dublin: Gill & Macmillan, 1996).

de Búrca, Séamus, *The Queen's Royal Theatre Dublin 1829–1969* (Dublin: Séamus de Búrca, 1983).

de Toro Santos, Antonio Raúl, *La literatura irlandesa en España* [Irish Literature in Spain] (A Coruña: Netbiblo, 2007).

de Toro Santos, Antonio Raúl, and David Clark, *British and Irish Writers in the Spanish Periodical Press/Escritores británicos e irlandeses en la prensa periódica española, 1900–1965* (A Coruña: Netbiblo, 2007).

Dean, Joan Fitzpatrick, *All Dressed Up: Modern Irish Historical Pageantry* (Syracuse, NY: Syracuse University Press, 2014).

Dean, Joan Fitzpatrick, *Riot and Great Anger: Stage Censorship in Twentieth-Century Ireland* (Madison, WI: University of Wisconsin Press, 2004).

Deane, Seamus, *Celtic Revivals: Essays in Modern Irish Literature* (London: Faber & Faber, 1985).

Deane, Seamus (ed.), *The Field Day Anthology of Irish Writing* (3 vols., Derry: Field Day, 1991).

Deevy, Teresa, *Teresa Deevy Reclaimed*, vol. 1, ed. Jonathan Bank, John P. Harrington, and Christopher Morash (New York: Mint Theater Company, 2011).

Delaney, Paul (ed.), *Brian Friel in Conversation* (Ann Arbor, MI: University of Michigan Press, 2000).

Delgado, Maria M., and Dan Rebellato (eds.), *Contemporary European Theatre Directors* (London: Routledge, 2010).

Derrida, Jacques, *Specters of Marx* (New York: Routledge, 1994).

Devitt, John, with Nicholas Grene and Chris Morash (eds.), *Shifting Scenes: Irish Theatre-Going, 1955–1985* (Dublin: Carysfort Press, 2008).

Dickson, David, *Dublin: The Making of a Capital City* (London: Profile Books, 2014).

Dilks, Stephen, *Samuel Beckett in the Literary Marketplace* (Syracuse, NY: Syracuse University Press, 2011).

Dixon, Ros, and Irina Ruppo Malone (eds.), *Ibsen and Chekhov on the Irish Stage* (Dublin: Carysfort Press, 2012).

Docherty, Thomas (ed.), *Postmodernism: A Reader* (Brighton: Harvester Wheatsheaf, 1993).

Dolan, Jill, *The Feminist Spectator as Critic* (Ann Arbor, MI: University of Michigan Press, 1991).

Dorgan, Theo, and Máirín Ní Dhonnchadha (eds.), *Revising the Rising* (Derry: Field Day, 1991).

Dorn, Karen, *Players and Painted Stage: The Theatre of W. B. Yeats* (Brighton: Harvester, 1984).

Dubost, Thierry (ed.), *Drama Reinvented: Theatre Adaptation in Ireland, 1970–2000* (Bern: Peter Lang, 2007).

Dumbleton, William, *James Cousins* (Boston, MA: Twayne, 1980).

Dunleavy, Janet Egleson, and Gareth W. Dunleavy, *Douglas Hyde: A Maker of Modern Ireland* (Berkeley, CA: University of California Press, 1991).

Durcan, Paul, *A Snail in My Prime: New and Selected Poems* (London: Harvill, 1993).

Eakin, David B., and Michael Case (eds.), *Selected Plays of George Moore and Edward Martyn* (Gerrards Cross: Colin Smythe, 1995).

Edelstein, T. J., et al., *The Stage is All the World: The Theatrical Designs of Tanya Moiseiwitsch* (Chicago, IL: Smart Museum of Art, 1994).

Edgar, David, *State of Play: Playwrights on Playwriting* (London: Faber & Faber, 1999).

Edmondson, Paul, Paul Prescott, and Erin Sullivan (eds.), *A Year of Shakespeare: Re-living the World Shakespeare Festival* (London: Bloomsbury, 2013).

Edwards, Ruth Dudley, *Patrick Pearse: The Triumph of Failure* (London: Victor Gollancz, 1977).

Eglinton, John, W. B. Yeats, Æ, and William Larminie, *Literary Ideals in Ireland* (Dublin: T. Fisher Unwin, 1899).

Eliot, T. S., *Notes Towards the Definition of Culture* (London: Faber & Faber, 1948).

Ellmann, Richard, *Oscar Wilde* (London: Hamish Hamilton, 1987).

Ervine, St John, *Bernard Shaw: His Life, Work and Friends* (London: Constable, 1956).

Ervine, St John, *How to Write a Play* (London: George Allen & Unwin, 1928).

Ervine, St John, *Mixed Marriage* (Dublin: Maunsel, 1911).

Ervine, St John G., *Some Impressions of My Elders* (London: George Allen & Unwin, 1923).

Ervine, St John, *The Theatre in My Time* (London: Rich & Cowan, 1933).

Evangelista, Stefano (ed.), *The Reception of Oscar Wilde in Europe* (London: Continuum, 2010).

Eyre, Richard (ed.), *Talking Theatre: Interviews with Theatre People* (London: Nick Hern, 2011).

Fallon, Brian, *An Age of Innocence: Irish Culture 1930–1960* (Dublin: Gill & Macmillan, 1998).

Fallon, Gabriel, *The Abbey and the Actor* (Dublin: National Theatre Society, 1969).

Fallon, Gabriel, *Sean O'Casey: The Man I Knew* (London: Routledge & Kegan Paul; Boston, MA: Little, Brown, 1965).

Fanon, Frantz, *The Wretched of the Earth* (Harmondsworth: Penguin, 1967).

Farley, Fidelma, *This Other Eden* (Cork: Cork University Press, 2001).

Fay, Frank J., *Towards a National Theatre: The Dramatic Criticism of Frank J. Fay*, ed. Robert Hogan (Dublin: Dolmen Press, 1970).

Fay, Gerard, *The Abbey Theatre, Cradle of Genius* (Dublin: Clonmore & Reynolds, 1958).

Fay, W. G., and Catherine Carswell, *The Fays of the Abbey Theatre: An Autobiographical Record* (New York: Harcourt Brace; London: Rich & Cowan, 1935).

Feldman, Matthew, *Beckett's Books: A Cultural History of the Interwar Notes* (London: Continuum, 2009).

Feldman, Matthew, and Mark Nixon, *Beckett's Literary Legacies* (Newcastle upon Tyne: Cambridge Scholars, 2007).

Ferriter, Diarmaid, *The Transformation of Ireland 1900–2000* (London: Profile Books, 2005).

Finn, Tomás, *Tuairim: Intellectual Debate and Policy Formation: Rethinking Ireland, 1954–1975* (Manchester: Manchester University Press, 2012).

Fischer-Lichte, Erika, *The Show and the Gaze of Theatre: A European Perspective* (Iowa City, IA: University of Iowa Press, 1997).

Fischer-Lichte, Erika, *The Transformative Power of Performance: A New Aesthetics* (London: Routledge, 2008).

Fischer-Lichte, Erika, and Benjamin Wihstutz (eds.), *Performance and the Politics of Space: Theatre and Topology* (London: Routledge, 2013).

Fisher, Judith L., and Stephen Watt (eds.), *When They Weren't Doing Shakespeare: Essays on Nineteenth Century British and American Theatre*, 2nd edn. (Athens, GA: University of Georgia Press, 2011).

Fitzpatrick, Lisa (ed.), *Performing Violence in Contemporary Ireland* (Dublin: Carysfort Press, 2009).

Fitzpatrick, Maurice, *The Boys of St. Columb's* (Dublin: Liffey, 2010).

Fitz-Simon, Christopher, *The Boys: A Biography of Micheál Mac Liammóir and Hilton Edwards* (Dublin: Gill & Macmillan, 1994; repr. Dublin: New Island Books, 2002).

Fitz-Simon, Christopher, *'Buffoonery and Easy Sentiment': Popular Irish Plays in the Decade Prior to the Opening of the Abbey Theatre* (Dublin: Carysfort Press, 2011).

Fitz-Simon, Christopher, *The Irish Theatre* (London: Thames & Hudson, 1983).

Fitz-Simon, Christopher (ed.), *Players and Painted Stage: Aspects of Twentieth Century Theatre in Ireland* (Dublin: New Island, 2004).

Flannery, James, *W. B. Yeats and the Idea of a Theatre: The Early Abbey Theatre in Theory and Practice* (New Haven, CT: Yale University Press, 1976).

Fletcher, Alan J. (ed.), *Drama and the Performing Arts in Pre-Cromwellian Ireland: A Repertory of Sources and Documents from the Earliest Times* (Cambridge: D. S. Brewer, 2001).

Fletcher, Alan J., *Drama, Performance and Polity in Pre-Cromwellian Ireland* (Cork: Cork University Press, 2000).

Foley, Imelda, *The Girls in the Big Picture: Gender in Contemporary Ulster Theatre* (Belfast: Blackstaff Press, 2003).

Forster, E. M., *Maurice* (Harmondsworth: Penguin, 1972).

Foster, R. F., *Luck and the Irish: A Brief History of Change, 1970–2000* (London: Allen Lane, 2007).

Foster, R. F., *Modern Ireland 1600–1972* (London: Penguin, 1988), 517

Foster, R. F., *W. B. Yeats: A Life*, vol. 1: *The Apprentice Mage 1865–1914* (Oxford: Oxford University Press, 1997).

Foster, R. F., *W. B. Yeats: A Life*, vol. 2: *The Arch-Poet* (Oxford: Oxford University Press, 2003).

Foucault, Michel, *Discipline and Punish: The Birth of the Prison*, trans. Alan Sheridan (London: Penguin, 1991).

Frazier, Adrian, *Behind the Scenes: Yeats, Horniman and the Struggle for the Abbey Theatre* (Berkeley, CA: University of California Press, 1990).

Frazier, Adrian, *George Moore, 1852–1933* (New Haven, CT: Yale University Press, 2000).

Frazier, Adrian, *Hollywood Irish: John Ford, Abbey Actors, and the Irish Revival in Hollywood* (Dublin: Lilliput Press, 2011).

Freeman, Elizabeth, *Time Binds: Queer Temporalities, Queer Histories* (Durham, NC: Duke University Press, 2010).

Friel, Brian, *Brian Friel in Conversation*, ed. Paul Delaney (Ann Arbor, MI: University of Michigan Press, 2000).

Friel, Brian, *Essays, Diaries, Interviews: 1964–1999*, ed. Christopher Murray (London: Faber & Faber, 1999).

Friel, Brian, *The Loves of Cass McGuire* (Dublin: Gallery Books, 1984).

Friel, Brian, *Plays 1* (London: Faber & Faber, 1996).

Friel, Brian, *Plays 2* (London: Faber & Faber, 1996).

Friel, Brian, *Plays 3* (London: Faber & Faber, 2014).

Friel, Brian, *Three Plays After* (London: Faber & Faber, 2002).

Friel, Brian, *Three Sisters* (Oldcastle: Gallery Press, 1981).

Friel, Brian, *Uncle Vanya: A Version of the Play by Anton Chekhov* (New York: Dramatists Play Service, 1998).

Frost, Anthony, and Ralph Yarrow, *Improvisation in Drama* (Basingstoke: Macmillan, 1990).

Gelb, Arthur, and Barbara Gelb, *O'Neill* (New York: Harper, 1960).

Genet, Jacqueline, and Richard Allen Cave (eds.), *Perspectives of Irish Drama and Theatre* (Gerrards Cross: Colin Smythe, 1991).

Gilbert, Helen, and Joanne Tompkins, *Postcolonial Drama: Theory, Practice, Politics* (London: Routledge, 1996).

Girard, René, *Violence and the Sacred*, trans. Patrick Gregory (Baltimore, MD: Johns Hopkins University Press, 1977).

Gogarty, Oliver St John, *Plays*, ed. James F. Carens (Newark, DE: Proscenium Press, 1971).

Gogarty, Oliver St John, *Poems and Plays*, ed. A. Norman Jeffares (Gerrards Cross: Colin Smythe, 2001).

Goldstone, Herbert, *In Search of Community: The Achievement of Seán O'Casey* (Cork: Mercier Press, 1972).

Gontarski, S. E., *The Intent of Undoing in Samuel Beckett's Dramatic Texts* (Bloomington, IN: Indiana University Press, 1985).

Gonzalez-Perez, Margaret (ed.), *Women and Terrorism: Female Activity in Domestic and International Terror* (London: Routledge, 2008).

Gore-Booth, Eva, *Plays*, ed. Frederick Lapisardi (San Francisco, CA: EMText, 1991).

Gore-Booth, Eva, *Poems*, ed. Esther Roper (London: Longman Green, 1929).

Gough, Kathleen M., *Kinship and Performance in the Black and Green Atlantic: Haptic Allegories* (London: Routledge, 2014).

Graham, Colin, *Deconstructing Ireland: Ireland, Theory, Culture* (Edinburgh: Edinburgh University Press, 2001).

Graver, Lawrence, and Raymond Federman (eds.), *Samuel Beckett: The Critical Heritage* (London: Routledge & Kegan Paul, 1978).

Greene, David H., and Edward M. Stephens, *J. M. Synge 1871–1909* (New York: New York University Press, 1989).

Gregory, Augusta, *Journals*, ed. Daniel J. Murphy, vol. 1 (Gerrards Cross: Colin Smythe, 1978).

Gregory, Augusta, *Journals*, ed. Daniel J. Murphy, vol. 2 (Gerrards Cross: Colin Smythe, 1987).

Gregory, Augusta, *Our Irish Theatre : A Chapter of Autobiography* (New York: Capricorn Books, 1965); 3rd edn. (Gerrards Cross: Colin Smythe, 1972).

Gregory, Augusta, *Selected Plays*, ed. Mary Fitzgerald (Gerrards Cross: Colin Smythe, 1983).

Gregory, Augusta, *Selected Writings*, ed. Lucy McDiarmid and Maureen Waters (Harmondsworth: Penguin, 1995).

Grene, Nicholas, *The Politics of Irish Drama: Plays in Context from Boucicault to Friel* (Cambridge: Cambridge University Press, 1999).

Grene, Nicholas, *Synge: A Critical Study of the Plays* (London: Macmillan, 1975).

Grene, Nicholas (ed.), *Talking About Tom Murphy* (Dublin: Carysfort Press, 2002).

Grene, Nicholas, and Patrick Lonergan (eds.), *Irish Drama: Local and Global Perspectives* (Dublin: Carysfort Press, 2012).

Grene, Nicholas, and Patrick Lonergan, with Lilian Chambers (eds.), *Interactions: Dublin Theatre Festival 1957–2007* (Dublin: Carysfort Press, 2008).

Grene, Nicholas, and Christopher Morash (eds.), *Irish Theatre on Tour* (Dublin: Carysfort Press, 2005).

Guérin, Jean-Yves, *Le Théâtre en France de 1914 à 1950* (Paris: Honoré Champion, 2007).

Guthrie, Tyrone, *A New Theatre* (New York: McGraw-Hill, 1964).

Hadfield, D. A., and Jean Reynolds (eds.), *Shaw and Feminisms: On Stage and Off* (Gainesville, FL: University Press of Florida, 2013).

Hadley, Elaine, *Melodramatic Tactics: Theatricalized Dissent in the English Marketplace, 1800–1885* (Stanford, CA: Stanford University Press, 1995).

Haedicke, S. C., et al. (eds.), *Political Performances: Theory and Practice* (Amsterdam: Rodopi, 2009).

Hanna Bell, Sam, *The Theatre in Ulster: A Survey of the Dramatic Movement in Ulster from 1902 until the Present Day* (Dublin: Gill & Macmillan, 1972).

Harmon, Maurice (ed.), *J. M. Synge Centenary Papers, 1971* (Dublin: Dolmen Press, 1972).

Harmon, Maurice (ed.), *The Irish Writer and the City* (Gerrards Cross: Colin Smythe; Totowa, NJ: Barnes & Noble, 1984).

Harrington, John P., *The Irish Beckett* (Syracuse, NY: Syracuse University Press, 1991).

Harrington, John P., *The Irish Play on the New York Stage* (Lexington, KY: University of Kentucky Press, 1997).

Harrington, John P. (ed.), *Irish Theater in America: Essays on Irish Theatrical Diaspora* (Syracuse, NY: Syracuse University Press, 2009).

Harrington, John P. (ed.), *Modern and Contemporary Irish Drama*, 2nd edn. (New York: Norton, 2009).

Harris, Claudia W. (ed.), *The Charabanc Theatre Company: Four Plays, Inventing Women's Work* (Gerrards Cross: Colin Smythe, 2006).

Harris, Peter James, *From Stage to Page: Critical Reception of Irish Plays in the London Theatre, 1925–1996* (Bern: Peter Lang, 2011).

Harris, Susan Cannon, *Gender and Modern Irish Drama* (Bloomington, IN: Indiana University Press, 2002).

Hatton, Joseph, *Henry Irving's Impressions of America*, vol. 1 (London: Sampson, Low, Marston, Searle, & Livingston, 1884).

Hay, Marnie, *Bulmer Hobson and the Nationalist Movement in Twentieth-Century Ireland* (Manchester: Manchester University Press, 2009).

Heaney, Seamus, *The Cure at Troy* (London: Faber & Faber, 1991).

Heaney, Seamus, *Station Island* (London: Faber & Faber, 1994).

Heaney, Seamus, *Sweeney Astray: A Version from the Irish* (London: Faber & Faber, 1983).

Heddon, Deirdre, and Jane Milling, *Devising Performance: A Critical History* (Basingstoke: Palgrave Macmillan, 2006).

Heininge, Kathleen, *Buffoonery in Irish Drama: Staging Twentieth-Century Postcolonial Stereotypes* (New York: Peter Lang, 2009).

Herr, Cheryl (ed.), *For the Land They Loved: Irish Political Melodramas, 1890–1925* (Syracuse, NY: Syracuse University Press, 1991).

Hickey, Des, and Gus Smith (eds.), *Flight from the Celtic Twilight* (Indianapolis, IN: Bobbs-Merrill, 1973).

Hickey, Des, and Gus Smith (eds.), *A Paler Shade of Green* (London: Leslie Frewin, 1972).

Hickey, Raymond, *A Dictionary of Varieties of Language* (Oxford: Wiley–Blackwell, 2014).

Hobson, Bulmer (ed.), *The Gate Theatre, Dublin* (Dublin: Gate Theatre, 1934).

Hoehn, Matthew, *Catholic Authors: Contemporary Biographical Sketches* (Newark, NJ: St Mary's Abbey, 1952).

Hogan, Robert, *After the Irish Renaissance: A Critical History of the Irish Drama since 'The Plough and the Stars'* (Minneapolis, MN: University of Minnesota Press, 1967).

Hogan, Robert, and Richard Burnham, *The Modern Irish Drama*, vol. 6: *The Years of O'Casey, 1921–1926: A Documentary History* (Gerrards Cross: Colin Smythe, 1992).

Hogan, Robert, Richard Burnham, and Daniel P. Poteet (eds.), *The Modern Irish Drama*, vol. 4: *The Rise of the Realists 1910–1915* (Dublin: Dolmen Press, 1979).

Hogan, Robert, and James Kilroy (eds.), *The Abbey Theatre: The Years of Synge, 1904–1909* (Dublin: Dolmen Press, 1978).

Hogan, Robert, and James Kilroy (eds.), *Lost Plays of the Irish Renaissance* (Newark, DE: Proscenium Press, 1970).

Holloway, Joseph, *Joseph Holloway's Abbey Theatre: A Selection from his Unpublished Journal 'Impressions of an Irish Playgoer'*, ed. Robert Hogan and Michael J. O'Neill (Carbondale, IL: Southern Illinois University Press, 1967).

Holloway, Joseph, *Joseph Holloway's Irish Theatre*, vol. 1: *1926–1931*, ed. Robert Hogan and Michael J. O'Neill (Dixon, CA: Proscenium Press, 1968).

Holloway, Joseph, *Souvenir of the Twenty-Fifth Anniversary of the Opening of the Gaiety Theatre, 27th November, 1871* (Dublin: Dollard, 1896).

Holroyd, Michael, *A Strange Eventful History: The Dramatic Lives of Ellen Terry, Henry Irving, and Their Remarkable Families* (London: Chatto & Windus, 2008).

Hughes, Derek, *Culture and Sacrifice: Rituals in Literature and Opera* (Cambridge: Cambridge University Press, 2007).

Humphries, Madeleine, *The Life and Times of Edward Martyn: An Aristocratic Bohemian* (Dublin: Irish Academic Press, 2007).

Hunt, Hugh, *The Abbey: Ireland's National Theatre, 1904–1979* (Dublin: Gill & Macmillan; New York: Columbia University Press, 1979).

Hurley, Erin, *National Performance: Representing Quebec from Expo 67 to Celine Dion* (Toronto: University of Toronto Press, 2010).

Huxley, Aldous, *Brave New World* (London: Granada, 1977).

Hyde, Douglas, *Selected Plays*, ed. Gareth W. Dunleavy and Janet Egleson Dunleavy (Washington, DC: Catholic University of America Press, 1991).

Hynes, Jerome (ed.), *Druid: The First Ten Years* (Galway: Druid Performing Arts and Galway Arts Festival, 1985).

Innes, Christopher (ed.), *Cambridge Companion to George Bernard Shaw* (Cambridge: Cambridge University Press, 1998).

Innes, Christopher, *Modern British Drama: The Twentieth Century* (Cambridge: Cambridge University Press, 2002).

Ireland, David, *Can't Forget About You* (London: Bloomsbury, 2013).

Izarra, Laura P. Z., and Munira H. Mutran (eds.), *Kaleidoscopic Views of Ireland* (São Paulo: Universidade de São Paulo, 2003).

Jameson, Frederic, *A Singular Modernity: Essay on the Ontology of the Present* (New York: Verso, 2002).

Jeffares, A. Norman, and Anna MacBride White (eds.), *The Gonne–Yeats Letters 1893–1938* (London: Hutchinson, 1992; Syracuse, NY: Syracuse University Press, 1994).

Jochum, Klaus Peter (ed.), *The Reception of W. B. Yeats in Europe* (London: Continuum, 2006).

Johnson, Josephine, *Florence Farr: Bernard Shaw's 'New Woman'* (Totowa, NJ: Rowman & Littlefield, 1975).

Johnston, Denis, *Dramatic Works*, vol. 2 (Gerrards Cross: Colin Smythe, 1979).

Johnston, Denis, *The Old Lady Says 'No!' and Other Plays* (Boston, MA: Little, Brown, 1960).

Johnston, Denis, *Selected Plays*, ed. Joseph Ronsley (Gerrards Cross: Colin Smythe, 1983).

Jones, Margo, *Theatre-in-the-Round* (New York: McGraw-Hill, 1965).

Jones, Nesta, *File on Synge* (London: Methuen Drama, 1994).

Jordan, Eamonn, *Dissident Dramaturgies* (Dublin: Irish Academic Press, 2009).

Jordan, Eamonn, *The Feast of Famine: The Plays of Frank McGuinness* (Bern: Peter Lang, 1997).

Jordan, Eamonn, *From Leenane to LA: The Theatre and Cinema of Martin McDonagh* (Dublin: Irish Academic Press, 2014).

Jordan, Eamonn (ed.), *Theatre Stuff: Critical Essays on Contemporary Irish Theatre* (Dublin: Carysfort Press, 2000).

Josipovici, Gabriel, *The Lessons of Modernism* (Basingstoke: Macmillan, 1977).

Joyce, James, *The Dead*, ed. Daniel R. Schwarz (New York: Bedford/St Martins, 1994).

Joyce, James, *Finnegans Wake*, 3rd edn. (London: Faber & Faber, 1964).

Joyce, James, *A Portrait of the Artist as a Young Man* (Harmondsworth: Penguin, 1960).

Joyce, James, *Ulysses* (London: Penguin, 1992).

Joyce, James, *Ulysses* (London: Alma Press, 2012).

Joyce, Stanislaus, *My Brother's Keeper* (London: Faber & Faber, 1982 [1958]).

Kaiser, Matthew, *The World in Play: Portrait of a Victorian Concept* (Stanford, CA: Stanford University Press, 2012).

Kalb, Jonathan, *Beckett in Performance* (Cambridge: Cambridge University Press, 1989).

Kalb, Jonathan, *Great Lengths: Seven Works of Marathon Theater* (Ann Arbor, MI: University of Michigan Press, 2011).

Kavanagh, Peter, *The Story of the Abbey Theatre* (Orono: National Poetry Foundation, 1976).

Keane, Barry, *Irish Drama in Poland: Staging and Reception, 1900–2000* (Chicago, IL: Chicago University Press/Intellect, forthcoming).

Keane, John B., *Three Plays: Sive, The Field, Big Maggie* (Cork: Mercier Press, 1990).

Kearney, Colbert, *The Glamour of Grammar: Orality and Politics and the Emergence of Sean O'Casey* (Westport, CT: Greenwood Press, 2000).

Kearns, Kevin C., *Dublin Tenement Life: An Oral History* (London: Penguin, 2000).

Keenan, Brian, *An Evil Cradling* (New York: Viking, 1993).

Kenneally, Michael (ed.), *Cultural Contexts and Literary Idioms in Contemporary Irish Literature* (Gerrards Cross: Colin Smythe, 1988).

Kennedy, Dennis, *Granville Barker and the Dream of Theatre* (Cambridge: Cambridge University Press, 1985).

Kennedy, Dennis (ed.), *The Oxford Companion to Theatre and Performance* (Oxford: Oxford University Press, 2010).

Kennedy, S. B., *The White Stag Group* (Dublin: IMMA, n.d. [2005])

Kennedy-Andrews, Elmer, *The Art of Brian Friel: Neither Reality Nor Dreams* (Basingstoke: Macmillan, 1995).

Kenner, Hugh, *A Reader's Guide to Samuel Beckett* (London: Thames & Hudson, 1973).

Keown, Edwina, and Carol Taaffe (eds.), *Irish Modernism: Origins, Contexts, Publics* (Bern: Peter Lang, 2009).

Kerrigan, Anthony (ed.), *Yeats and the Noh: Types of Japanese Beauty and their Reflection in Yeats's Plays* (Dublin: Dolmen Press, 1966).

Kiberd, Declan, *Inventing Ireland: The Literature of the Modern Nation* (London: Jonathan Cape, 1995).

Kiberd, Declan, *Irish Classics* (Cambridge, MA: Harvard University Press, 2001).

Kiberd, Declan, *Ulysses and Us: The Art of Everyday Living* (London: Faber & Faber, 2009).

Kilroy, Thomas, *The Death and Resurrection of Mr Roche* (Oldcastle: Gallery Press, 2002).

Kilroy, Thomas, *My Scandalous Life* (Oldcastle: Gallery Press, 2004).

Kilroy, Thomas, *The O'Neill* (Oldcastle: Gallery Press, 1995).

Kilroy, Thomas (ed.), *Sean O'Casey: A Collection of Critical Essays* (Englewood Cliffs, NJ: Prentice-Hall, 1975).

Kilroy, Thomas, *Talbot's Box* (Oldcastle: Gallery Press, 1997).

Kilroy, Thomas, *Tea and Sex and Shakespeare* (Oldcastle: Gallery Press, 1998).

King, Linda, and Elaine Sisson (eds.), *Ireland, Design, and Visual Culture: Negotiating Modernity, 1922–1992* (Cork: Cork University Press, 2011).

Klaus, H. Gustav, *Strong Words Brave Deeds: The Poetry, Life and Times of Thomas O'Brien Volunteer in the Spanish Civil War* (Dublin: O'Brien Press, 1994).

Knapp, Bettina L., *The Reign of the Theatrical Director: French Theatre 1887–1924* (Troy, NY: Whitston Press, 1988).

Knowles, Ric, *Reading the Material Theatre* (Cambridge: Cambridge University Press, 2004).

Knowlson, James, *Damned to Fame: The Life of Samuel Beckett* (London: Bloomsbury, 1996).

Knowlson, James (gen. ed.), *The Theatrical Notebooks of Samuel Beck*ett (4 vols., London: Faber & Faber, 1999).

Knowlson, James, and John Haynes, *Images of Beckett* (Cambridge: Cambridge University Press, 2003).

Kosok, Heinz, *O'Casey the Dramatist* (Gerrards Cross: Colin Smythe; Totowa, NJ: Barnes & Noble, 1985).

Kristeva, Julia, *The Kristeva Reader*, ed. Toril Moi (Oxford: Blackwell, 1986).

Kurdi, Mária (ed.), *Literary and Cultural Relations: Ireland, Hungary, and Central and Eastern Europe* (Dublin: Carysfort Press, 2009).

Kurdi, Mária, *Representations of Gender and Female Subjectivity in Contemporary Irish Drama by Women* (Lewiston, NY: Edwin Mellen Press, 2010).

Lacey, Brian, *'Terrible Queer Creatures': A History of Homosexuality in Ireland* (Dublin: Wordwell, 2008).

Laurence, Dan H., and Nicholas Grene (eds.), *Shaw, Lady Gregory and the Abbey: A Correspondence and a Record* (Gerrards Cross: Colin Smythe, 1993).

Leach, Robert, *Theatre Studies: The Basics*, 2nd edn. (London: Routledge, 2013).

Lee, J. J., *Ireland 1912–1985* (Cambridge: Cambridge University Press, 1989).

Lee, Laurie, *Cider with Rosie* (London: Hogarth Press, 1959).

Leeney, Cathy, *Irish Women Playwrights, 1900–1939: Gender and Violence on Stage* (New York: Peter Lang, 2010).

Leeney, Cathy, and Anna McMullan (eds.), *The Theatre of Marina Carr: Before Rules Was Made* (Dublin: Carysfort Press, 2003).

Leerssen, Joep, *Mere Irish and Fíor-Ghael: Studies in the Idea of Irish Nationality, Its Development, and Literary Expression Prior to the Nineteenth Century* (Amsterdam: Benjamins, 1986).

Lehmann, Hans-Thies, *Postdramatic Theatre*, trans. Karen Jürs-Munby (London: Routledge, 2006).

Leonard, Hugh, *Selected Plays* (Gerrards Cross: Colin Smythe, 1988).

Levenson, Michael (ed.), *The Cambridge Companion to Modernism*, 2nd edn. (Cambridge: Cambridge University Press, 2011).

Levenson, Samuel, *Maud Gonne* (London: Cassell, 1976).

Levinas, Emmanuel, *Totality and Infinity: An Essay on Exteriority*, trans. Alphonso Lingis (Dordrecht: Kluwer Academic, 1991).

Levitas, Ben, *The Theatre of Nation: Irish Drama and Cultural Nationalism, 1890–1916* (Oxford: Clarendon Press, 2002).

Lewis, Sinclair, *Main Street* (New York: Barnes & Noble, 2003).

Lloyd, David, *Anomalous States: Irish Writing and the Postcolonial Moment* (Dublin: Lilliput Press; Durham, NC: Duke University Press, 1993).

Lloyd, David, *Irish Times: Temporalities of Modernity* (Dublin: Field Day, 2008).

Loizeaux, Elizabeth Bergmann, *Yeats and the Visual Arts* (Syracuse, NY: Syracuse University Press, 2003).

Lojek, Helen Heusner, *Contexts for Frank McGuinness's Drama* (Washington, DC: Catholic University of America Press, 2004).

Lojek, Helen Heusner, *The Spaces of Irish Drama: Stage and Place in Contemporary Plays* (Basingstoke: Palgrave Macmillan, 2011).

Lonergan, Patrick (ed.), *Synge and His Influences* (Dublin: Carysfort Press, 2011).

Lonergan, Patrick, *The Theatre and Films of Martin McDonagh* (London: Methuen, 2012).

Lonergan, Patrick, *Theatre and Globalisation: Irish Drama in the Celtic Tiger Era* (Basingstoke: Palgrave Macmillan, 2009).

Lonergan, Patrick, and Riana O'Dwyer (eds.), *Echoes Down the Corridor: Irish Theatre—Past, Present and Future* (Dublin: Carysfort Press, 2007).

Longenbach, James, *Stone Cottage: Pound, Yeats, and Modernism* (Oxford: Oxford University Press, 1988).

Loomba, Ania, *Colonialism/Postcolonialism* (London: Routledge, 1998).

Lowery, Robert G. (ed.), *A Whirlwind in Dublin: The Plough and the Stars Riots* (Westport, CT: Greenwood Press, 1984).

Luckhurst, Mary (ed.), *A Companion to Modern British and Irish Drama, 1880–2005* (Oxford: Blackwell, 2006).

Luke, Peter (ed.), *Enter Certain Players: Edwards, Mac Liammóir, and the Gate 1928–1978* (Dublin: Dolmen Press, 1978).

Lynch, Martin and The Charabanc Theatre Company, *Lay Up your Ends: A 25th Anniversary Edition* (Belfast: Lagan Press, 2008).

Mac Anna, Tomás, *Fallaing Aonghusa: Saol Amharclainne* (Indreabhán: Cló Iar-Chonnacht, 2000).

Macardle, Dorothy, *Witch's Brew: A Drama in One Act* (London: H. F. W. Deane, 1931).

MacDonagh, Thomas, *When the Dawn is Come* (Dublin: Maunsel, 1908).

Macgowan, Kenneth, and Robert Edmund Jones, *Continental Stagecraft* (New York: Harcourt, Brace, 1922).

Mac Intyre, Tom, *What Happened Bridgie Cleary* (Dublin: New Island, 2005).

Mackintosh, Iain, *Architecture, Actor and Audience* (London: Routledge, 1993).

Mac Liammóir, Micheál, *All for Hecuba* (London: Methuen, 1947; rev. edn., Dublin: Progress Press, 1961); repr. Boston, MA: Brayden Press, 1967.

Mac Liammóir, Micheál, *Each Actor on His Ass* (London: Routledge & Kegan Paul, 1961).

Mac Liammóir, Micheál, *An Oscar of No Importance* (London: Heinemann, 1968).

Mac Liammóir, Micheál, *Theatre in Ireland* (Dublin: Three Castles, 1964).

Maguire, Tom, *Making Theatre in Northern Ireland: Through and Beyond the Troubles* (Exeter: University of Exeter Press, 2006).

Maher, Eamon (ed.), *Cultural Perspectives on Ireland and Globalisation* (Bern: Peter Lang, 2009).

Manfull, Helen, *Taking Stage: Women Directors on Directing* (London: Methuen, 1999).

Marshall, Gail (ed.), *The Cambridge Companion to the Fin de Siècle* (Cambridge: Cambridge University Press, 2007).

Marshall, Norman, *The Other Theatre* (London: John Lehmann, 1947).

Martin, F. X. (ed.), *Leaders and Men of the Easter Rising: Dublin 1916* (London: Methuen, 1967).

Martin, Peter, *Censorship in the Two Irelands, 1922–1939* (Dublin: Irish Academic Press, 2006).

Marx, Karl, *Selected Writings*, ed. David McLellan (Oxford: Oxford University Press, 1977).

Mason, Patrick, *The National Theatre: Artistic Policy* (Dublin: Abbey Theatre, 1996).

Matejka, Ladislav, and Krystyn Pomoska (eds.), *Readings in Russian Poetics: Formalist and Structuralist Views* (Cambridge, MA: MIT Press, 1971).

Mathews, P. J. (ed.), *The Cambridge Companion to J. M. Synge* (Cambridge: Cambridge University Press, 2009).

Mathews, P. J., *Revival: The Abbey Theatre, Sinn Féin, the Gaelic League and the Cooperative Movement* (Cork: Cork University Press in association with Field Day, 2003).

Maxwell, D. E. S., *A Critical History of Modern Irish Drama 1890–1980* (Cambridge: Cambridge University Press, 1984).

Mc Intyre, Alice, *Women in Belfast: How Violence Shapes Identity* (Westport, CT: Praeger, 2004).

McAuley, Gay, *Space in Performance: Making Meaning in the Theatre* (Ann Arbor, MI: University of Michigan Press, 1999).

McCafferty, Nell, *The Kerry Babies Case* (Cork: Cork University Press, 2010).

McCafferty, Owen, *Antigone* (London: Nick Hern, 2008).

McCafferty, Owen, *Plays 1* (London: Faber & Faber, 2013).

McCafferty, Owen, *Quietly* (London: Faber & Faber, 2012).

McCarthy, John, and Jill Morrell, *Some Other Rainbow* (New York: Bantam, 1993).

McClintock, Henry, *Old Irish and Highland Dress and That of the Isle of Man* (Dundalk: Dundalgan, 1950).

McCormack, Jerusha (ed.), *Wilde the Irishman* (New Haven, CT: Yale University Press, 1998).

McCrum, Elizabeth, *Fabric and Form: Irish Fashion since 1950* (Stroud: Alan Sutton, 1996).

McDonnell, Bill, *Theatres of the Troubles: Theatre, Resistance and Liberation in Ireland* (Exeter: University of Exeter Press, 2008).

McFeely, Deirdre, *Dion Boucicault: Irish Identity on Stage* (Cambridge: Cambridge University Press, 2012).

McGarry, Fearghal, *The Rising. Ireland: Easter 1916* (Oxford: Oxford University Press, 2001).

McGlone, James P., *Ria Mooney: The Life and Times of the Artistic Director of the Abbey Theatre, 1948–1963* (London: McFarland, 2002).

McGrath, Aoife, *Dance Theatre in Ireland: Revolutionary Moves* (Basingstoke: Palgrave Macmillan, 2013).

McGrath, F. C., *Brian Friel's (Post)Colonial Drama: Language, Illusion, and Politics* (Syracuse, NY: Syracuse University Press, 1999).

McGuinness, Frank, *Carthaginians and Baglady* (London: Faber & Faber, 1988).

McGuinness, Frank, *Gates of Gold* (London: Faber & Faber, 2002).

McGuinness, Frank, *Henrik Ibsen, A Doll's House: A New Version by Frank McGuinness from a Literal Translation by Charlotte Barslund* (London: Faber & Faber, 1996).

McGuinness, Frank, *Mutabilitie* (London: Faber & Faber, 1997).

McGuinness, Frank, *Plays 1* (London: Faber & Faber, 1996).

McGuinness, Frank, *Plays 2* (London: Faber & Faber, 2002).

McMillan, Dougald, and Martha Fehsenfeld, *Beckett in the Theatre* (London: John Calder, 1988).

McMinn, Joseph (ed.), *The Internationalism of Irish Literature and Drama* (Gerrards Cross: Colin Smythe, 1992).

McNulty, Eugene, *The Ulster Literary Theatre and the Northern Revival* (Cork: Cork University Press, 2008).

McPherson, Conor, *Plays: Two* (London: Nick Hern, 2004).

McPherson, Conor, *The Seafarer* (London: Nick Hern, 2006).

McPherson, D. A. J., *Women and the Irish Nation: Gender, Culture, and Irish Identity, 1890–1940* (Basingstoke: Palgrave Macmillan, 2012).

Mercier, Vivian, *Beckett/Beckett* (London: Souvenir Press, 1990).

Merriman, Brian, *The Midnight Court/Cúirt an Mheán Oíche*, ed. Brian Ó Conchubhair (Syracuse, NY: Syracuse University Press, 2011).

Merriman, Victor, *Because We Are Poor: Irish Theatre in the 1990s* (Dublin: Carysfort Press, 2011).

Middeke, Martin, and Peter Paul Schnierer (eds.), *The Methuen Drama Guide to Contemporary Irish Playwrights* (London: Methuen, 2010).

Mikhail, E. H. (ed.), *The Abbey Theatre: Interviews and Recollections* (London: Macmillan, 1988).

Mikhail, E. H. (ed.), *Oscar Wilde: Interviews and Recollections* (2 vols., London: Macmillan, 1979).

Miller, Kerby A., *Ireland and Irish America: Culture, Class, and Transatlantic Migration* (Dublin: Field Day, 2008).

Miller, Liam, *The Noble Drama of W. B. Yeats* (Dublin: Dolmen Press, 1976).

Milligan, Alice, *The Last Feast of the Fianna* (London: David Nutt, 1900).

Molloy, M. J., *Selected Plays*, ed. Robert O'Driscoll (Gerrards Cross: Colin Smythe, 1998).

Montague, C. E., *Dramatic Values* (New York: Macmillan, 1911).

Moore, George, *Hail and Farewell!* (3 vols. [1911, 1912, 1914]), 2nd edn., ed. Richard Allen Cave (Gerrards Cross: Colin Smythe, 1985).

Moore, George, and Edward Martyn, *Selected Plays*, ed. David B. Eakin and Michael Case (Gerrards Cross; Colin Smythe, 1995).

Moore, John Rees, *Masks of Love and Death: Yeats as Dramatist* (Ithaca, NY: Cornell University Press, 1971).

Moran, James (ed.), *Four Irish Rebel Plays*, ed. James Moran (Dublin: Irish Academic Press, 2007).

Moran, James, *Irish Birmingham: A History* (Liverpool: Liverpool University Press, 2010).

Moran, James, *The Theatre of Seán O'Casey* (London: Bloomsbury, 2013).

Moran, James, *Staging the Easter Rising: 1916 as Theatre* (Cork: Cork University Press, 2005).

Morash, Christopher, *A History of Irish Theatre 1601–2000* (Cambridge: Cambridge University Press, 2002).

Morash, Christopher, and Shaun Richards, *Mapping Irish Theatre: Theories of Space and Place* (Cambridge: Cambridge University Press, 2013).

Morris, Catherine, *Alice Milligan and the Irish Cultural Revival* (Dublin: Four Courts Press, 2012).

Morrison, Bill, *Flying Blind* (London: Faber & Faber, 1978).

Morse, Donald, Csilla Bertha, and Mária Kurdi (eds.), *Brian Friel's Dramatic Artistry: 'The Work Has Value'* (Dublin: Carysfort Press, 2006).

Moss, Chloë, *The Way Home* (London: Nick Hern, 2006).

Mulrooney, Deirdre, *An Illustrated History of Dance and Physical Theatre in Ireland* (Dublin: Liffey Press, 2006).

Mumford, Lewis, *The City in History: Its Origins, its Transformations, and its Prospects* (Harmondsworth: Penguin, 1966).

Murphy, P. J., et al. (eds.), *Critique of Beckett Criticism: A Guide to Research in English, French, and German* (Columbia, SC: Camden House, 1994).

Murphy, Paul, *Hegemony and Fantasy in Irish Drama, 1899–1949* (Basingstoke: Palgrave Macmillan, 2008).

Murphy, Tom, *Bailegangaire* (Dublin: Gallery Press, 1986).

Murphy, Tom, *Plays: 3* (London: Methuen Drama, 1997).

Murphy, Tom, *Plays: 4* (London: Methuen Drama, 1997).

Murphy, Tom, *The House* (London: Methuen, 2000).

Murray, Christopher, *Seán O'Casey, Writer at Work: A Biography* (Dublin: Gill & Macmillan, 2004).

Murray, Christopher, *The Theatre of Brian Friel: Tradition and Modernity* (London: Bloomsbury, 2014).

Murray, Christopher, *Twentieth-Century Irish Drama: Mirror Up to Nation* (Manchester: Manchester University Press, 1997).

Murray, T. C., *Selected Plays*, ed. Richard Allen Cave (Gerrards Cross: Colin Smythe, 1998).

Nagler, A. M., *A Source Book in Theatrical History* (New York: Dover, 1959).

Nagy, Peter, Phillippe Rouyer, and Don Rubin (eds.), *World Encyclopaedia of Contemporary Theatre*, vol. 1: *Europe* (London: Routledge, 1994).

Negra, Diane (ed.), *The Irish in Us: Irishness, Performativity and Popular Culture* (Durham, NC: Duke University Press, 2006).

Nevin, Donal, *James Connolly: 'A Full Life'* (Dublin: Gill & Macmillan, 2005).

Ní Anluain, Clíodhna (ed.), *Reading the Future: Irish Writers in Conversation with Mike Murphy* (Dublin: Lilliput, 2000).

Ní Aoláin, Fionnuala, Dina Francesca Haynes, and Naomi Cahn, *On the Frontlines: Gender, War and the Post-Conflict Process* (New York: Oxford University Press, 2011).

Ní Chinnéide, Mairéad, *An Damer: Stair Amharclainne* (Dublin: Gael Linn, 2008).

Ní Chinnéide, Mairéad, *Scéal Ghael-Linn* (Indreabhán: Cló Iar-Chonnacht, 2013).

Ní Ghráda, Mairéad, *Breithiúnas: Dráma Dhá Ghníomh* (Dublin: An Gúm, 1996).

Nic Shiubhlaigh, Máire, *The Splendid Years: Recollections of Máire Nic Shiubhlaigh as Told to Edward Kenny* (Dublin: Duffy, 1955).

Nietzsche, Friedrich, *The Case of Wagner; Nietzsche Contra Wagner; Selected Aphorisms*, 3rd edn., ed. and trans. Anthony M. Ludovici (London: T. N. Foulis, 1911).

Nixon, Mark, and Matthew Feldman (eds.), *The International Reception of Samuel Beckett* (London: Continuum, 2009).

Nochlin, Linda, *Realism* (Harmondsworth: Penguin, 1990).

Nolan, Jerry, *Six Essays on Edward Martyn (1859–1923), Irish Cultural Revivalist* (Lampeter: Edwin Mellen Press, 2004).

Nora, Pierre, *Realms of Memory*, ed. Lawrence D. Kritzman, trans. Arthur Goldhammer (New York: Columbia University Press, 1996).

Nunnery, Lizzie, *Intemperance* (London: Faber & Faber, 2007).

O'Brien, Kate, *My Ireland* (London: B. T. Batsford, 1962).

O'Brien, Victoria, *A History of Irish Ballet from 1927 to 1963* (Bern: Peter Lang, 2011).

O'Casey, Eileen, *Cheerio, Titan: The Friendship between George Bernard Shaw and Eileen and Sean O'Casey* (London: Papermac, 1991).

O'Casey, Sean, *Autobiographies* (2 vols., London: Macmillan, 1963).

O'Casey, Sean, *Autobiographies*, vol. 1 (New York: Carroll & Graf, 1984).

O'Casey, Sean, *Blasts and Benedictions*, ed. Ronald Ayling (London: Macmillan, 1967).

O'Casey, Sean, *Collected Plays*, vol. 2 (London: Macmillan, 1949).

O'Casey, Sean, *Complete Plays* (5 vols., London: Macmillan, 1984).

O'Casey, Sean, *The Flying Wasp* (London: Macmillan, 1937).

O'Casey, Sean, *The Green Crow* (London: W. H. Allen, 1987).

O'Casey, Sean, *Inishfallen, Fare Thee Well* (London: Macmillan, 1954).

O'Casey, Sean, *The Letters of Sean O'Casey*, vol. 1: *1910–1941*, ed. David Krause (New York: Macmillan, 1975).

O'Casey, Sean, *The Letters of Sean O'Casey*, vol. 2: *1942–54*, ed. David Krause (New York: Macmillan, 1980).

O'Casey, Sean, *Plays 1* (London: Faber & Faber, 1998).

O'Casey, Sean, *Plays 2* (London: Faber & Faber, 1998).

O'Casey, Sean, *The Story of the Irish Citizen Army* [1919] (London: Journeyman Chapbook, 1980).

O'Casey, Sean, *Three Dublin Plays*, ed. Christopher Murray (London: Faber & Faber, 1998).

O'Casey, Sean, *Under a Colored Cap: Articles Merry and Mournful with Comments and a Song* (London: Macmillan, 1963).

O'Connor, Emmet, *James Larkin* (Cork: Cork University Press, 2002).

O'Connor, Frank, *My Father's Son* (London: Macmillan, 1968).

O'Connor, Ulick, *Celtic Dawn: A Portrait of the Irish Literary Renaissance* (London: Hamish Hamilton, 1984).

Odling-Smee, Hugh (ed.), *Its Own Way of Things:* The Enthusiast *by Lewis Purcell and* Thompson in Tir-nan-Og *by Gerald MacNamara* (Belfast: Lagan Press, 2004).

O'Donoghue, Helen, *Scene Change: One Hundred Years of Theatre Design at the Abbey* (Dublin: Irish Museum of Modern Art, 2004).

O'Donovan, Patrick, and Laura Rascaroli (eds.), *The Cause of Cosmopolitanism: Dispositions, Models, Transformations* (Bern: Peter Lang, 2011).

O'Driscoll, Robert (ed.), *Theatre and Nationalism in Twentieth-Century Ireland* (London: Oxford University Press, 1971).

O'Driscoll, Robert, and Lorna Reynolds (eds.), *Yeats and the Theatre* (Toronto: Macmillan, 1975).

Ó Duibhne, Cormac, *The Field Day Archive* (Dublin: Field Day, 2007).

O'Dwyer, Rory, *The Eucharistic Congress, Dublin 1932: An Illustrated History* (Dublin: Nonsuch, 2009).

O'Farrell, Ciara, *Louis D'Alton and the Abbey Theatre* (Dublin: Four Courts Press, 2004).

O'Flaherty, Liam, *Darkness* (Dublin: Arlen House, 2014).

O'Flynn, *Criostoir: A Writer's Life* (Dublin: Obelisk Books, 2001).

Ó hAnnracháin, Stiofán, *An Comhchaidreamh: Crann a Chraobhaigh* (Dublin: An Clóchomhar Tta, 1985).

Ó hAodha, Micheál, *The Importance of Being Micheál: A Portrait of MacLiammóir* (Kerry: Brandon Press, 1990).

Ó hAodha, Micheál, *Siobhán: A Memoir of an Actress* (Dingle: Brandon, 1994).

O'Kelly, Seamus, *The Bribe* (Dublin: Maunsel, 1914).

O'Leary, Philip, *Gaelic Prose in the Irish Free State 1922–1939* (Dublin: UCD Press, 2004).

O'Leary, Philip, *The Prose Literature of the Gaelic Revival, 1881–1921: Ideology and Innovation* (University Park, PA: Pennsylvania State University Press, 1994).

O'Leary, Philip, *Writing Beyond the Revival: Facing the Future in Gaelic Prose 1940–1951* (Dublin: UCD Press, 2011).

Ó Lochlainn, Gearóid, *Ealaíon na hAmharclainne* (Dublin: Clódhanta Teo, 1984).

O'Malley, Aidan, *Field Day and the Translation of Irish Identities: Performing Contradictions* (Basingstoke: Palgrave Macmillan, 2011).

O'Malley, Conor, *A Poet's Theatre* (Dublin: Elo Press, 1988).

O'Malley, Mary, *Never Shake Hands with the Devil* (Dublin: Elo Press, 1990).

Ó Morónaigh, Seán (ed.), *Drámaíocht ó Dhúchas* (An Comhlachas Náisiúnta Drámaíochta, 2005).

O'Regan, John (ed.), *Michael Scott 1905–1989* (Kinsale: Gandon, 1993).

O'Reilly, Anne F., *Sacred Play: Soul-Journeys in Contemporary Irish Drama* (Dublin: Carysfort Press, 2004).

O'Rowe, Mark, *Plays: One* (London: Nick Hern, 2011).

Ó Siadhail, Pádraig, *An Béaslaíoch* (Dublin: Coiscéim, 2007).

Ó Siadhail, Pádraig, *Stair Dhrámaíocht na Gaeilge 1900–1970* (Indreabhán: Cló Iar-Chonnachta, 1993).

O'Toole, Fintan, *Critical Moments: Fintan O'Toole on Modern Irish Theatre*, ed. Julia Furay and Redmond O'Hanlon (Dublin: Carysfort Press, 2003).

O'Toole, Fintan, *Ship of Fools: How Stupidity and Corruption Sank the Celtic Tiger* (London: Faber & Faber, 2010).

O'Toole, Fintan, *Tom Murphy: The Politics of Magic* (Dublin: New Island, 1994).

O'Toole, Fintan, *A Traitor's Kiss: The Life of Richard Brinsley Sheridan* (New York: Farrar, Straus, & Giroux, 1998).

Owens, Rosemary Cullen, *A Social History of Women in Ireland 1870–1970* (Dublin: Gill & Macmillan, 2005).

Parker, Stewart, *Dramatis Personae* (Belfast: John Malone Memorial Committee, 1986).

Parker, Stewart, *Plays: 2* (London: Methuen Drama, 2000).

Paulin, Tom (ed.), *The Faber Book of Vernacular Verse* (London: Faber & Faber, 1990).

Paulin, Tom, *Ireland and the English Crisis* (Newcastle upon Tyne: Bloodaxe, 1984).

Paulin, Tom, *The Riot Act* (London: Faber & Faber, 1985).

Pavis, Patrice, *Analyzing Performance: Theatre, Dance, and Film*, trans. David Williams (Ann Arbor, MI: University of Michigan Press, 2004).

Pavis, Patrice, *Dictionary of Theatre: Terms, Concepts, and Analysis* (Toronto: University of Toronto Press, 1998).

Peacock, Alan J. (ed.), *The Achievement of Brian Friel* (Gerrards Cross: Colin Smythe, 1992).

Pearse, Patrick, *Collected Plays: Drámaí an Phiarsaigh*, ed. Róisín Ní Ghairbhí and Eugene McNulty (Dublin: Irish Academic Press, 2013).

Pearse, Patrick, *The Coming Revolution: The Political Writings of Patrick Pearse* (Cork: Mercier Press, 2012).

Pearse, Patrick, *The Letters of P. H. Pearse*, ed. Seamus O Buachalla (Gerrards Cross: Colin Smythe, 1980).

Phoenix, Eamon, Pádraic Ó Cléireacháin, Eileen McAuley, and Nuala McSparran (eds.), *Feis na nGleann: A Century of Gaelic Culture in the Antrim Glens* (Belfast: Stair Uladh, 2005).

Pilkington, Lionel, *Theatre and Ireland* (London: Palgrave Macmillan, 2010).

Pilkington, Lionel, *Theatre and the State in Twentieth-Century Ireland: Cultivating the People* (London: Routledge, 2001).

Pilný, Ondřej, *Irony and Identity in Modern Irish Drama* (Prague: Literaria Pragensia, 2006).

Pilný, Ondřej, and Gerald Power (eds.), *Ireland and the Czech Lands: Contacts and Comparisons in History and Culture* (Bern: Peter Lang, 2014).

Pine, Richard, *The Diviner: The Art of Brian Friel* (Dublin: University College Dublin Press, 1999).

Pine, Richard (with Richard Cave), *The Dublin Gate Theatre* (Cambridge: Chadwyck-Healey, 1984).

Pinter, Harold, *Mac* (London: Pendragon, 1968).

Póirtéir, Cathal (ed.), *The Great Irish Famine* (Dublin: Mercier Press, 1995).

Powell, Kerry, *Oscar Wilde and the Theatre of the 1890s* (Cambridge: Cambridge University Press, 1990).

Powell, Kerry, and Peter Raby (eds.), *Oscar Wilde in Context* (Cambridge: Cambridge University Press, 2013).

Presenting Architecture: An Exhibition of Twentieth-Century Drawings and Models (Dublin: Irish Architectural Archive, 2005).

Quinn, Antoinette, *Patrick Kavanagh: A Biography* (Dublin: Gill & Macmillan, 2001).

Rainey, Lawrence, *Institutions of Modernism: Literary Elites and Public Culture* (New Haven, CT: Yale University Press, 1998).

Rebellato, Dan, *1956 and All That* (London: Routledge, 1998).

Redmond, James (ed.), *The Theatrical Space* (Cambridge: Cambridge University Press, 1987).

Regan, John, *The Irish Counter-Revolution 1921–1936: Treatyite Politics and Settlement in Independent Ireland* (Dublin: Gill & Macmillan, 1999).

Reid, Alec, *All I Can Manage, More Than I Could: An Approach to the Plays of Samuel Beckett* (Dublin: Dolmen Press, 1968).

Reynolds, Paige, *Modernism, Drama and the Audience for Irish Spectacle* (Cambridge: Cambridge University Press, 2007).

Rich, Adrienne, *Of Woman Born: Motherhood as an Experience and an Institution* (London: Virago, 1977).

Richards, Shaun (ed.), *The Cambridge Companion to Twentieth-Century Irish Drama* (Cambridge: Cambridge University Press, 2004).

Richards, Shaun, and David Cairns, *Writing Ireland: Colonisation, Nationalism and Culture* (Manchester: Manchester University Press, 1988).

Richards, Stanley (ed.), *Best Short Plays of 1981* (New Radnor, PA: Chilton Books, 1981).

Richardson, John C. (ed.), *Handbook of Theory and Research for the Sociology of Education* (New York: Greenwood Press, 1986).

Richtarik, Marilynn, *Acting Between the Lines: The Field Day Theatre Company and Irish Cultural Politics 1980–1984* (Oxford: Oxford University Press, 1994).

Richtarik, Marilynn, *Stewart Parker: A Life* (Oxford: Oxford University Press, 2012).

Ritschel, Nelson Ó Ceallaigh, *Shaw, Synge, Connolly, and the Socialist Provocation* (Gainesville, FL: University Press of Florida, 2011).

Roberts, Philip, and Max Stafford-Clark, *Taking Stock: The Theatre of Max Stafford-Clark* (London: Nick Hern, 2007).

Robinson, Lennox, *Curtain Up: An Autobiography* (London: Michael Joseph, 1942).

Robinson, Lennox, *Ireland's Abbey Theatre: A History 1899–1951* (London: Sidgwick & Jackson, 1951).

Robinson, Lennox, *Selected Plays*, ed. Christopher Murray (Gerrards Cross: Colin Smythe, 1982).

Robinson, Lennox, *Towards an Appreciation of the Theatre* (Dublin: Metropolitan Publishing, 1945).

Robinson, Lennox, *Two Plays: Harvest; The Clancy Name* (Dublin: Maunsel, 1911).

Roche, Anthony, *Brian Friel: Theatre and Politics* (Basingstoke: Palgrave Macmillan, 2011).

Roche, Anthony (ed.), *The Cambridge Companion to Brian Friel* (Cambridge: Cambridge University Press, 2006).

Roche, Anthony, *Contemporary Irish Drama: From Beckett to McGuinness* (Dublin: Gill & Macmillan, 1994).

Roche, Anthony, *Contemporary Irish Drama*, 2nd edn. (Basingstoke: Palgrave Macmillan, 2009).

Roche, Anthony, *The Irish Dramatic Revival 1899–1939* (London: Bloomsbury, 2015).

Roche, Anthony, *Synge and the Making of Modern Irish Drama* (Dublin: Carysfort Press, 2013).

Roche, Billy, *The Wexford Trilogy* (London: Nick Hern, 1992).

Ryan, Frederick, *The Laying of the Foundations* in *Lost Plays of the Irish Renaissance*, ed. Robert Hogan and James Kilroy (Newark, DE: Proscenium Press, 1970).

Ryan, Louise, *Gender, Identity, and the Irish Press 1922–1937* (Lewiston, NY: Edwin Mellen Press, 2002).

Ryan, Phyllis, *The Company I Kept* (Dublin: Town House, 1996).

Ryan, Vera, *Dan Donovan: An Everyman's Life* (Cork: Collins Press, 2008).

Saddlemyer, Ann (ed.), *Theatre Business: The Correspondence of the First Abbey Directors: William Butler Yeats, Lady Gregory and J. M. Synge* (Gerrards Cross: Colin Smythe, 1982).

Said, Edward, *Covering Islam* (New York: Vintage, 1997).

Said, Edward, *Reflections on Exile and Other Literary and Cultural Essays* (London: Granta Books, 2000).

Samuel, Raphael (ed.), *People's History and Socialist Theory* (London: Routledge & Kegan Paul, 1981).

Sanderson, Michael, *From Irving to Olivier: A Social History of the Acting Profession in England 1880–1983* (London: Athlone Press, 1985).

Schechner, Richard, *Essays on Performance Theory 1970–1976* (New York: Drama Book Specialists, 1977).

Sekine, Masaru, and Christopher Murray (eds.), *Yeats and the Noh: A Comparative Study* (Gerrards Cross: Colin Smythe, 1990).

Sharkey, Stephen, *The May Queen* (London: Methuen, 2007).

Shaughnessy, Edward L., *Eugene O'Neill in Ireland: The Critical Reception* (Westport, CT: Greenwood Press, 1988).

Shaw, Bernard, *Back to Methuselah* (London: Constable, 1930).

Shaw, Bernard, *Collected Letters, 1911–1925*, ed. Dan H. Laurence (London: Max Reinhardt, 1985).

Shaw, Bernard, *The Doctor's Dilemma; Getting Married; The Shewing-up of Blanco Posnet* (London: Constable, 1930).

Shaw, Bernard, *Heartbreak House; Great Catherine; Playlets of the War* (London: Constable, 1930).

Shaw, Bernard, *Immaturity* (London: Constable, 1931).

Shaw, Bernard, *John Bull's Other Island; How He Lied to Her Husband; Major Barbara* (London: Constable, 1930).

Shaw, Bernard, *Major Critical Essays* (London: Penguin, 1989).

Shaw, Bernard, *The Matter with Ireland*, ed. David H. Greene and Dan H. Laurence (London: Rupert Hart-Davis, 1962).

Shaw, Bernard, *Our Theatres in the Nineties*, vol. 1 (London: Constable, 1932).

Shaw, Bernard, *The Quintessence of Ibsenism: Now Completed to the Death of Ibsen* (London: Constable, 1913).

Shaw, Bernard, *Saint Joan; The Apple Cart* (London: Constable, 1930).

Shaw, Bernard, *Shaw on Theatre*, ed. E. J. West (London: MacGibbon & Kee, 1958).

Shaw, Bernard, *Sixteen Self-Sketches* (London: Constable, 1949).

Sheehy, Michael, *Is Ireland Dying? Culture and the Church in Modern Ireland* (London: Hollis & Carter, 1968).

Shellard, Dominic, *British Theatre Since the War* (New Haven, CT: Yale University Press, 2000).

Shepherd-Barr, Kirsten, *Ibsen and Early Modernist Theatre, 1890–1900* (London: Greenwood Press, 1997).

Sierz, Aleks, *In-Yer-Face Theatre: British Drama Today* (London: Faber & Faber, 2001).

Sihra, Melissa (ed.), *Women in Irish Drama: A Century of Authorship and Representation* (Basingstoke: Palgrave Macmillan, 2007).

Simpson, Alan, *Beckett and Behan and a Theatre in Dublin* (London: Routledge & Kegan Paul, 1962).

Sinfield, Alan, *Out On Stage* (New Haven, CT: Yale University Press, 1999).

Singer, Ben, *Melodrama and Modernity: Early Sensational Cinema and Its Contexts* (New York: Columbia University Press, 2001).

Singleton, Brian, *Masculinities and the Contemporary Irish Theatre* (Basingstoke: Palgrave Macmillan, 2011).

Sisson, Elaine, *Pearse's Patriots: St Enda's and the Cult of Boyhood* (Cork: Cork University Press, 2004).

Slowey, Desmond, *The Radicalization of Irish Drama 1600–1900: The Rise and Fall of Ascendancy Theatre* (Dublin: Irish Academic Press, 2008).

Soja, Edward, *Thirdspace: Journeys to Los Angeles and Other Real-and-Imagined Places* (Malden, MA: Blackwell, 1996).

Spallen, Abbie, *Pumpgirl* (London: Faber & Faber, 2006).

Spencer, Stewart, and Barry Millington (eds.), *Wagner's Ring of the Nibelung: A Companion* (London: Thames & Hudson, 1993).

Steele, Karen, *Women, Press and Politics during the Irish Revival* (Syracuse, NY: Syracuse University Press, 2007).

Stoller, Terry, *Tales of the Tricycle Theatre* (London: Bloomsbury, 2013).

Sweeney, Bernadette, *Performing the Body in Irish Theatre* (Basingstoke: Palgrave Macmillan, 2008).

Swift, Carolyn, *Stage by Stage* (Dublin: Poolbeg, 1985).

Symons, Arthur, *Plays, Acting, and Music: A Book of Theory* (London: Constable, 1909).

Synge, John Millington, *Collected Letters*, ed. Ann Saddlemyer (2 vols., Oxford: Clarendon, 1983, 1984).

Synge, John Millington, *Collected Works*, gen. ed. Robin Skelton (4 vols., London: Oxford University Press, 1962–8).

Synge, John Millington, *Letters to Molly: John Millington Synge to Maire O'Neill, 1906-1909*, ed. Ann Saddlemyer (Cambridge, MA: Harvard University Press, 1971).

Syssoyeva, Kathryn, and Scott Proudfit (eds.), *Women, Collective Creation, and Devised Theatre* (Basingstoke: Palgrave Macmillan, 2015).

Szabo, Carmen, *Clearing the Ground: The Field Day Theatre Company and the Construction of Irish Identities* (Newcastle upon Tyne: Cambridge Scholars, 2007).

Taylor, Richard, *The Drama of W. B. Yeats: Irish Myth and Japanese Nō* (New Haven, CT: Yale University Press, 1976).

Taylor, Richard, *A Reader's Guide to the Plays of W. B. Yeats* (New York: St Martin's Press, 1984).

Tétreault, Mary Ann, and Robin L. Teske (eds.), *Partial Truths and the Politics of Community* (Columbia, SC: University of South Carolina Press, 2003).

Titley, Alan, *Nailing Theses* (Belfast: Lagan Press, 2011).

Tóibín, Colm, *Love in a Dark Time* (Sydney: Pan Macmillan, 2001).

Townshend, Charles, *Easter 1916: The Irish Rebellion* (London: Allen Lane, 2005).

Trench, Rhona, *Bloody Living: The Loss of Selfhood in the Plays of Marina Carr* (Bern: Peter Lang, 2010).

Trench, Rhona (ed.), *Staging Thought: Essays on Irish Theatre, Scholarship and Practice* (Bern: Peter Lang, 2012).

Trotter, Mary, *Ireland's National Theaters: Political Performance and the Origins of the Irish Dramatic Movement* (Syracuse, NY: Syracuse University Press, 2001).

Trotter, Mary, *Modern Irish Theatre* (Cambridge: Polity Press, 2008).

Uhlmann, Anthony (ed.), *Samuel Beckett in Context* (Cambridge: Cambridge University Press, 2013).

Unterecker, John (ed.), *Yeats and Patrick McCartan: A Fenian Friendship* (Dublin: Dolmen Press, 1967).

Urban, Eva, *Community Politics and the Peace Process in Contemporary Northern Irish Drama* (Bern: Peter Lang, 2011).

Valente, Joseph, *The Myth of Manliness in Irish Nationalist Culture, 1880–1922* (Champaign–Urbana, IL: University of Illinois Press, 2011).

van den Toorn, Pieter, *Stravinsky and the Rite of Spring: The Beginnings of a Musical Language* (Berkeley, CA: University of California Press, 1987).

Vaněk, Joe, *Scene Change: One Hundred Years of Theatre Design at the Abbey* (Dublin: Irish Museum of Modern Art, 2005).

Vertovec, Steven, and Robin Cohen (eds.), *Conceiving Cosmopolitanism: Theory, Context, and Practice* (Oxford: Oxford University Press, 2002).

Views of Theatre in Ireland (Dublin: An Chomhairle Ealaíon, 1995).

Wagner, Richard, *Prose Works*, vol. 4: *Art and Politics* (London: Kegan Paul, 1895).

Walker, Dorothy, *Michael Scott, Architect in (Casual) Conversation with Dorothy Walker* (Kinsale: Gandon, 1995).

Wallace, Clare (ed.), *Monologues: Theatre, Performance, Subjectivity* (Prague: Litteraria Pragensia, 2006).

Wallace, Clare, *Suspect Cultures: Narrative, Identity and Citation in 1990s New Drama* (Prague: Litteraria Pragensia, 2006).

Walsh, Enda, *The Walworth Farce* (London: Nick Hern, 2007).

Walsh, Fintan, *Male Trouble: Masculinity and the Performance of Crisis* (Basingstoke: Palgrave Macmillan, 2011).

Walsh, Fintan (ed.), *Queer Notions: New Plays and Performances from Ireland* (Cork: Cork University Press, 2010).

Walsh, Fintan (ed.), *'That Was Us': Contemporary Irish Theatre and Performance* (London: Oberon Books, 2013).

Walsh, Ian R., *Experimental Irish Theatre: After W. B. Yeats* (Basingstoke: Palgrave Macmillan, 2012).

Walshe, Eibhear, *Oscar's Shadow* (Cork: Cork University Press, 2011).

Walter, Macken, *Home Is the Hero* (New York: Macmillan, 1953).

Ward, Margaret, *In Their Own Voice: Women and Irish Nationalism* (Dublin: Attic Press, 2005).

Ward, Margaret, *Unmanageable Revolutionaries* (Dingle: Brandon; London: Pluto, 1983).

Watson, G. J., *Irish Identity and the Irish Literary Revival: Synge, Yeats, Joyce and O'Casey*, 2nd edn. (Washington, DC: Catholic University of America Press, 1994).

Watt, Stephen, *Joyce, O'Casey, and the Irish Popular Theater* (Syracuse, NY: Syracuse University Press, 1991).

Watt, Stephen, Eileen Morgan, and Shakir Mustafa (eds.), *A Century of Irish Drama: Widening the Stage* (Bloomington, IN: Indiana University Press, 2000).

Welch, Robert, *The Abbey Theatre 1899–1999: Form and Pressure* (Oxford: Oxford University Press, 1999).

Weygand, Cornelius, *Irish Plays and Playwrights* (London: Constable, 1913).

Whelan, Gerard, with Carolyn Swift, *Spiked: Church–State Intrigue and The Rose Tattoo* (Dublin: New Island Books, 2002).

Whitbread, J. W., *The Nationalist* (Dublin: W. J. Alley, 1892).

Wilde, Oscar, *Complete Letters*, ed. Merlin Holland and Rupert Hart-Davis (New York: Henry Holt, 2000).

Wilde, Oscar, *The Complete Plays* (London: Methuen, 1988).

Wilde, Oscar, *De Profundis and Other Writings*, 1949 edn., ed. Vyvyan Holland (London: Penguin, 1973).

Wilde, Oscar, *Impressions of America*, ed. Stuart Mason (Sunderland: Keystone Press, 1906).

Wilde, Oscar, *Oscar Wilde: A Life in Letters*, ed. Merlin Holland (New York: Carroll & Graf, 2007).

Wilde, Oscar, *The Picture of Dorian Gray*, ed. Robert Mighall (London: Penguin, 2000).

Wilde, Oscar, *Selected Letters*, ed. Rupert Hart-Davis, 2nd edn. (Oxford: Oxford University Press, 1979).

Williams, Raymond, *Drama from Ibsen to Brecht* (London: Chatto, 1986).

Williams, Raymond, *Drama from Ibsen to Brecht* (London: Pelican Books, 1973).

Williams, Simon, and Maik Hamburger (eds.), *A History of German Theatre* (Cambridge: Cambridge University Press, 2008).

Williams, Tennessee, *The Rose Tattoo and Other Plays* (London: Penguin, 2001).

Wilmer, S. E. (ed.), *National Theatres in a Changing Europe* (Basingstoke: Palgrave Macmillan, 2008).

Winwar, Frances, *Oscar Wilde and the Yellow 'Nineties* (New York: Blue Ribbon Books, 1941).

Wood, Gerald C., *Conor McPherson: Imagining Mischief* (Dublin: Liffey, 2003).

Worth, Katharine, *The Irish Drama of Europe from Yeats to Beckett* (London: Athlone Press, 1978).

Wright, Julia (ed.), *A Companion to Irish Literature*, vol. 2 (Chichester: Wiley-Blackwell, 2010).

Yeates, Pádraig, *A City in Wartime: Dublin 1914–18* (Dublin: Gill & Macmillan, 2011).

Yeates, Pádraig, *Lockout: Dublin 1913* (Dublin: Gill & Macmillan, 2000).

Yeats, W. B., *Autobiographies* (London: Macmillan, 1955).

Yeats, W. B., *Collected Letters*, ed. John Kelly et al. (4 vols., Clarendon Press: Oxford, 1986–2005).

Yeats, W. B. *Collected Letters: Electronic Edition* InteLex: http://www.nix.com/collections/130

Yeats, W. B., *Collected Works*, vol. 1: *Poems*, ed. Richard Finneran, 2nd edn. (London: Macmillan, 1997).

Yeats, W. B., *Collected Works*, vol. 2: *The Plays*, ed. David R. Clark and Rosalind E. Clark (New York: Scribner, 2001).

Yeats, W. B., *Collected Works*, vol. 3: *Autobiographies*, ed. Douglas Archibald and William O'Donnell (New York: Scribner, 1999).

Yeats, W. B., *Collected Works*, vol. 4: *Early Essays*, ed. Richard J. Finneran and George Bornstein (New York: Scribner, 2007).

Yeats, W. B., *Collected Works*, vol. 8: *The Irish Dramatic Movement*, ed. Mary FitzGerald and Richard J. Finneran (NewYork: Scribner, 2003).

Yeats, W. B., *Collected Works*, vol. 10: *Later Articles and Reviews*, ed. Colton Johnson (New York: Scribner, 2000).

Yeats, W. B., *The Cutting of an Agate* (London: Macmillan, 1919).

Yeats, W. B., *Essays and Introductions* (London: Macmillan, 1961).

Yeats, W. B., *Explorations* (London: Macmillan, 1962).

Yeats, W. B., *Four Plays for Dancers* (London: Macmillan, 1921).

Yeats, W. B., *Letters*, ed. Allan Wade (London: Hart-Davis, 1954).

Yeats, W. B., *Memoirs*, ed. Denis Donoghue (London: Macmillan, 1972).

Yeats, W. B., *Selected Plays*, ed. Richard Allen Cave (Harmondsworth: Penguin Books, 1997).

Yeats, W. B., *Uncollected Prose*, ed. John P. Frayne, vol. 2 (London: Macmillan, 1975).

Yeats, W. B., *The Variorum Edition of the Plays of W. B. Yeats*, ed. Russell K. Alspach (London: Macmillan, 1966).

Yeats, W. B., *The Variorum Edition of the Poems of W. B. Yeats*, ed. Peter Allt and Russell K. Alspach (New York: Macmillan, 1956).

Zeigler, Joseph Wesley, *Regional Theatre: The Revolutionary Stage* (Minneapolis, MN: University of Minnesota Press, 1973).

Zimmerman, Claire, *Mies van der Rohe* (Hohenzollerning: Taschen, 2006).

Zola, Emile, *The Experimental Novel and Other Essays*, trans. Belle M. Sherman (New York: Haskell House, 1964).

INDEX

Note: The method of alphabetical ordering used is letter-by-letter; titles of plays are indexed under name of playwright; bibliographical references and titles of academic books/commentaries are not included. Page references in **bold** denote principal entries; references in *italics* denote illustrations.

A. P. Watt 612–13
Abbey School of Acting 206, 263, 278, 452
Abbey School of Ballet 246, 278–9
Abbey Theatre (Dublin) 1–3, 5, 62, 64–6,
    77, 85, 99, 105, 127, 129, 134, 147–9,
    156, 158, 165, 172, 184, 210, 218, 223,
    276, 286, 291, 300, 307–9, 322, 332, 337,
    400, 407, 425, 442, 448, *502*, 526, 528,
    560, 597, 599–604, 614–15, 624–5, 627,
    650–2, 654–5, 666, 670, 673, 678–9,
    682–3, 689
  'AbbeyOneHundred' (centenary
    celebrations) 548–9, 569, 607
  actors and acting 2, 3, 55, 67, 92–4, 116,
    166n.37, 179–80, 231, **234–45**, 246;
    see also Abbey School of Acting; post-1950s
    459–60, *461*, 461–2, 463–6, 469, 476–7
  archives 5, 398
  building and venues 51, 172, 182, **427–31**,
    431, 432, 435, 687; *see also* Peacock
    Theatre; fire (1951) 278, 294, 425–6, 435;
    plans for new theatre 439–41, *440*,
    638–9; rebuilding (1966) 435–6, 439
  development of National Theatre 1–2,
    42–57, 214, 569; *see also* Irish Literary
    Theatre; Irish National Theatre Society;
    establishment (1904) 1, 13, **51–3**, 58, 124,
    138, 271, 687; patent 52–3; patronage 63;
    reorganization 53, 63–4, 113
  direction and design 2, 79, *119*, 148–9,
    201–8, 211–13, *212*, 277–9, 447–9,
    449–52, 456–7, 458, 517
  disturbances: *Playboy* (1907) 52,
    88–90, 96, 144, 178, 192, 254, 431;

Plough and the Stars (1926) 57, 89,
    166, 174–6, 187, 192, 206, 254, 431
  festivals 485; Abbey Festival (1938)
    637–40, 642, 652; Dublin Theatre
    Festival contributions 404n.5, 644–8;
    Tom Murphy Festival (2001) 650
  Irish-language productions 70–1, 171–2,
    252, **253–9**, 294, 398, 447–8
  and the Irish State **169–82**, 393, 638;
    annual subsidy 56, 169, 170–2, 174–80,
    254–6, 390
  nationalist melodrama 21–2
  1916 Centenary Programme, 'Waking the
    Nation' 549
  pantomimes 255–6, 259, 447–8
  peasant plays **91–4**, 204, 316, 431, 448, 577
  productions (by playwright); *see also*
    Gregory, Augusta; O'Casey, Seán; Synge,
    John Millington; Yeats, William Butler;
    Beckett 481–3, 577; Friel 333, 339, 362,
    365, 370–1, 515, *516*; Keane 313, 316–17;
    Kilroy 340, 347–50, *349*, 446; Leonard
    317; Molloy 308–9, 313; Murphy 404n.5,
    408, 417–18, 524, 650; Shaw 139, 141–6;
    Wilde 221, 229
  realists 113–17
  tours 110, 112, 144, 177–80, 247, 277, 594,
    596, 598, 603–4, 607–8, 634–5, 638, 688
  women and 271, 276–80, 283–4, 547, 549,
    553, 556–7, 559
Abbey Theatre Festival (1938) **637–40**,
    642, 652
Abbey Theatre Playwright's Workshop 683
Abdo, Diya M. *502*

Abrahamson, Lenny 569
absurdism 85, 123, 541, 543, 552–3, 563, 568,
    584, 631
Académie de Danse (Paris) 290
Academy of Choreographic Arts
    (London) 278
Achill Island, Co Mayo
    open-air theatre 432, *433*, 433–4, *434*,
    435, 442
activism 58–71
actors and acting 2–4, 9, 49, 69–71, 93,
    166n.37, 173, 253, 290–1, 292, 492,
    493, 560
    actor-managers 232, 245–6, 460
    devised theatre **565–9**
    early twentieth century **231–47**; Abbey
    234–45; Gate 245–7
    post-1950s **459–77**
    presentational acting 134–5, *135*
    training and professionalism 3–4, 232,
    268, 278, 477
Actors Theatre (Louisville) 601
Actors' Workshop (San Francisco) 588, 600
Adam, Bernard 447
Adam & Paul (film) 569
adaptation **654–70**
Adigun, Bisi 524, 691n.116
Adorno, Theodor 323, 583, 587
Aer Lingus 489
Aeschylus: *Oresteia* 556
Africa 582
Afternoon Theatre Company 96n.38
Agate, James 462
Agen sur Gironde (France) 635
Ahern, Bertie 529
Ainley, Henry 134
Ainsworth, Andrea 548
Aisling Ghéar (Belfast) 262, 266, *267*,
    268, 398
Aisteoirí Bulfin 262, 268
Aisteoirí Loch Con Aortha 256n.32
Albee, Edward 489, 594
Albery Theatre (London) 608, 615
Aleichem, Sholem 594
Alexander II, Czar 25
Alexandra College (Dublin) 280
Alfred, William
    Hogan's Goat 603

Allard, Stephen 597, 599
Allgood, Molly, *see* O'Neill, Maire
Allgood, Sara 2, 49, 54, 189, 233–4, 238–41,
    245, 679
Alliance and Dublin Consumers' Gas
    Company 288
amateur drama 47, 71, 73, 109, 128, 136, 171,
    202, 235, 247, 252–3, 262, 268, 277, 288–
    9, 290–1, 299–300, 307, 309–10, 316–17,
    321, 596, 646
    All-Ireland Amateur Drama Festival 313,
    407, 482
    funding 391–2, 394
American Civil War 595
American Ireland Fund 369
American Irish Ensemble Company
    (Portland, Maine) 605
American Psycho (film) 540
American theatre, *see under* United States
Amharclann de hÍde 262, 268
Amkpa, Awam 685
An Chomhairle Ealaíon, *see* Arts Council
An Claidheamh Soluis 69, 70, 198, 254
An Comhar Drámaíochta 71, 254–6,
    259–60, 638–9
An Compántas 644
An Damer (Dublin) 255, 259–61, 398
Anderson, Benedict 498
Anderson, Sarah Pia 451
Andrews Lane Theatre (Dublin) 565
Andreyev, Leonid 127
Anglo-Irish 140, 185, 340–1, 547
Anglo-Irish Agreement (1985) 684
Anglo-Irish Treaty (1921) 143, 164, 166,
    169n.2, 191
An Lab (The Lab) 266n.90
Anne Devlin (film) 667n.33
Anouilh, Jean 218
    Antigone 290
An Seabhac
    Jimín 261
An Taibhdhearc (Galway) 2, 207, 245, 254–5,
    262–4, 268, 398, 464–5, 655, 667
An Taibhsín (Galway) 263
Antient Concert Rooms (Dublin) 59, 147,
    252, 427–8
Antoine, André 42, 108–11, 234, 430, 559
An Tóstal 215–16, 641–2, *642*, *643*

ANU Productions 4, 426, 457, 557, 571–3,
    650, 679, 689
  The Boys of Foley Street 573, 650
  Laundry 526, *572*, 572–3, 650
  Monto Cycle 571–3, 650
  Vardo 573n.21, 650
  At World's End Lane 572, 650
Aonach Tailteann 214
Aonach Thír Chonaill (1898) 251
Apollo Theatre (London) 129
Appia, Adolphe 2, 204–5, 208, 559
Apple Inc 578
Arabs 505–8
Arambe Theatre Company 691n.116
Aran Islands, Co Galway 19, 49, 59, 100,
    101n.66, 406, 419, 442, 532, 534
Áras Éanna (Inisheer) 442
Archer, Kane 350
Archer, William 109
Árd-Chúirt na hÉigse 70
Arden, John 338
Ardhowen Theatre (Enniskillen) 552
Arena Stage (Washington DC) 600
Arikha, Avigdor 484
Aristotle
  Ethics 32
  Poetics 376
Ark (Dublin) 556
Armstrong, Laura 72
Aron, Geraldine 679
  Bar and Ger 406
  A Galway Girl 406, 408
  Same Old Moon 408
Aronson, Jack 291
Arrington, Lauren 675
Arrow 50
Arrowsmith, Aidan 621
Artane Industrial School (Dublin) 570–1
Artaud, Antonin 121, 350, 562, 628
Arts Acts 391, 393–4, 402
Arts Centre Theatre Company
    (Wexford) 395
Arts Council 3, 361, 402–3, 560, 568, 642,
    652, 673n.3, 688
  establishment 391–2
  Project 67 392–5
Arts Council of Northern Ireland 359,
    402, 447

Arts Plan 1993–1995 397
Arts Theatre (London) 581
Ashton, Frederick 643
Asmus, Walter 478, 491
Assédio theatre (Porto) 627
Aston, Elaine 679
Athens (Greece) 634
Atlantic Theater Company (New York) 603
Atlantis 362
Auden, W. H. 289
Auditoria project (Arts Council) 402–3
Augusteijn, Joost 26n.7
Augustine, St
  City of God 198
Australia 239, 257, 409, 411, 499
Austro-Hungarian Empire 30–1, 38, 625
Avedon, Richard 486–7, 492
Avenue Theatre (London) 26, 32, 42, 138
Avignon Festival 626, 631, 641, 644
axis theatre (Ballymun, Dublin) 398,
    400, 442
Ayckbourn, Alan
  How the Other Half Loves 318
Ayling, Ronald 184

Bachelard, Gaston 689
Back to the Cradle (RTÉ) 406
BAFTAs 656
Baker, George Pierce 597, 602
Bakst, Léon 209
Balanchine, George 279
Balcombe, Florence 33
Balfour, Arthur 143
Balkans 634
Ballaghaderreen, Co Roscommon 253
Ballagh, Robert *186, 228*, 455, *455*
ballet 88, 221, 246, 278–90, 643
Ballets Russes 209, 246, 278
Ballybofey, Co Donegal 407, 442
Ballymun (Dublin), *see* axis theatre
Ballyshannon, Co Donegal 407
Balor Theatre (Ballybofey) 442
Baltimore (USA) 593
Balzac, Honoré de
  Le Faiseur 643
Bancroft, Effie 232, 245
Bancroft, Squire 232, 245
Banville, John 286

Barabbas Theatre Company 457, **566–9**
  Circus 567
  City of Clowns 568
  *Come Down From the Mountain, John
    Clown, John Clown* 567, 568
  Half Eight Mass of a Tuesday 567
  Strokehauling 567
Barber, John 416
Barbican (London) 492
Barcelona 635
Barker, Howard 399
Barlow, Jane
  A Bunch of Lavender 68
Barlow, Seaghan 203, 206, 436
Barnes, Ben 316–7, 396, 418, 548, 608, 634
Barnes, Clive 470–1
Barratt, William 41
Barrault, Jean-Louis 350
Barrett, Wilson 232
Barrie, Sir James 164
  Peter Pan 164
  Shakespeare's Legacy 164
Barry, Philip 602
  The Philadelphia Story 602
Barry, Sebastian 4, 473, 515, 656, 677
  Fanny Hawke Goes to the Mainland Forever
    524n.17
  Prayers of Sherkin 524–5, 548
  The Pride of Parnell Street 520
  The Steward of Christendom 168,
    471–3, 518–19
  Tales of Ballycumber 518
Barry, William Spranger 231
Basque Country 625
Baudrillard, Jean 97, 563
Baugh, Christopher 449
Bayreuth Festival 38, 638
Bayreuth Theatre 44, 430, 687
BBC Northern Ireland 380
BBC television 469
Beale, Simon Russell 612
Bealtaine Festival 570
Beardsley, Aubrey 27, 31
Béaslaí, Piaras 70–1, 253–4
  Beirt na Bodhaire Bréige 70
Beckett Centenary Festival (Gate, 2006)
    483n.16
Beckett Estate 585, 592

Beckett Festival (Gate, 1991) 4, **478–89**,
    586, 651
  reception and aftermath 489–94
Beckett on Film 4, 492–3, 586
Beckett, Samuel 1, 4, 5, 27, 123, 262, 268, 311,
    318, 376, 389, 439, 500, 514, 542, 594,
    626–7, 631, 644, 645, 646, 649
  at the Gate 294, **478–93**, 487, 488, 586, 651
  as global figure **577–92**; emergence 580–4;
    'Rorschach test' 584–6; transnational
    theatre 586–90
  historical research into 583
  in Irish imagination 481–4
  Irish-language productions 262, 263, 268
  Act Without Words II 490
  All That Fall 488, 565
  Breath 493
  … but the clouds 84
  Catastrophe 492, 582
  Eh Joe 486
  Eleutheria 581
  Embers 565
  Endgame 359, 478–9, 486, 578–9, 584,
    586–8, 650
  Fall 451
  Footfalls 451, 479, 486, 490
  Ghost Trio 84
  Happy Days 478–9, 486, 489, 493,
    569, 579
  Krapp's Last Tape 262n.80, 478–9, 486, 492,
    579, 650
  L'innommable (The Unnamable) 580
  Malone meurt (Malone Dies) 580
  Molloy 580
  Murphy 580
  Not I 451, 490–1, 492–3, 579
  Ohio Impromptu 486
  Play 451, 492–3, 579
  Rockaby 490, *490*, 579
  That Time 579
  Waiting for Godot 84, 213, 294, 451, 469,
    478, 481–2, 486, 489, 491, *491*, 493,
    577–8, 580–3, 585–6, **586–90**, 592, 646,
    677; Irish-language production 263; in
    New Orleans *589*, 589–90; Pike Theatre
    (1955) 123, 294, 295
  Watt 458, 580
Beerbohm, Max 31, 92–3

Beerbohm-Tree, Herbert 28–9, 109–10, 207,
    219, 232
Behan, Brendan 376, 605, 631
    An Giall/ The Hostage 167, 259–60,
        263, 338–9, 445n.7, 600, 603–4; in
        Europe 632–4
    Borstal Boy 449
    Lá Breá sa Roilig 260
    The Quare Fellow 213, 2945, 338, 376, 677
Behan, John 392
Beirut 506
Beitchmann, Philip 106
Béjart, Maurice 350–1
Belfast 12, 29, 59– 61, 114–15, 149, 165, 251–2,
        281, 288, 376, 378, 380–2, 385–6, 437,
        442, 446, 519, 549–53, 650; *see also* Lyric
        Theatre
    Irish-language theatre 266–8
    peace walls 374
    Wedding Community Play 374–5
Belfast Arts Festival 406, 649
Belfast Arts Theatre 406, 551–2
Bel Geddes, Norman 209
Belgium 499, 564, 634, 650
Bell, Colin 378
Bell Helicopter 458
Bell, Lian 549n.13
Bell, Sam Hanna 60n.4
Bell, Suzanne 616
Belltable Arts Centre, Limerick 395
Belsey, Catherine 282, 679
Beltaine 44
Belton, Cathy 565
Benavente, Jacinto 127
Bengal 158
Benson, Constance 232
Benson, Frank 232
Bentley, Eric 16n.31
Ben-Zvi, Linda 489
Bergen (Norway) 47
Berger-Hammerschalg, Alice 447n.15
Berkeley, George 140
Berkoff, Steven 227–8, 455
    Agamemnon 620
Berlin 42, 108, 136, 449, 582, 624, 631,
        633, 635
Berliner Ensemble 448–9
Berliner Theatertreffen/Festspiele 626, 631–2

Berlin Volksbühne 129n.16
Bernadette Players ('Bernos') 290–1, 302
Bernard, Claude 107
Bernhardt, Sarah 233–4, 236, 428
Bertha, Csilla 625, 689
Betti, Ugo 445
Bewick, Pauline 302
Bhabha, Homi 684–5
Bhatti, Gurpreet Kaur
    Behzti 619
Bhreathnach, Micheál 263
Bible 184, 505–8
Bickerstaffe theatre company 395, 565
Bieito, Calixto 651
Biggar, Joseph 30
Bigger, Francis Joseph 59
Billington, Michael 418, 476, 491, 658
Binchy, Kate 297
Bin Laden, Osama 268
Birmingham 609, 619–21
Birmingham Repertory Theatre: 'The Door'
        studio **619–21**
Birmingham Rep Youth Theatre 620
Birmingham School of Speech and
        Drama 620
Bismarck, Otto von 30, 38
Black Box (Galway) 264
Blackrock (Dublin) 251
Blackshaw, Basil 447n.15
Blair, Les 491
Blakeley, Colin 459
Blake, William
    The Marriage of Heaven and Hell 151
Blanchard, Mary Warner 28n.17
Blasket Islands, Co Kerry 96n.39
Blau, Herbert 588, 600
Blin, Roger 580–2
Bliss, Arthur 643
Bloch, Ernest 683n.69
Bloody Sunday (Derry, 1972) 501–3, 683
Bloomsday 641
Blue Angel Films 492
Blue Raincoat Theatre Company (Sligo) 4,
        395, 401, 457, 566
Blythe, Ernest 59, 171–2, 175–8, 213, 245,
        253n.11, 254–6, 260, 262–3, 278, 286,
        316–17, 339–40, 407, 436, 449, 638
Boal, Augusto 375

Bochum (Germany) 633
Bodkin, James 391
Boer War 46, 214
Bogart, Anne 649, 652
Bohemia 624
Boland, Eavan 223
Bolger, Dermot 392, 522, 524, 686
    In High Germany 268, 523
    The Lament for Arthur Cleary 400
    The Parting Glass 523
Boltwood, Scott 325, 364
Bonn 635
Booker Prize 656
Book of Kells 638, 640
Booth, Edwin 231, 459
Booth, J. B. 232
Boothman, Denis 291
Booth, Michael 16n.31
Bord Fáilte 299, 489, 641–2, 652
Borthwick, Norma 251
Bosnian War 588
Boss, Owen 572, 679
Boston 12, 607
Boston College 639
Boston Evening Transcript 239
Boucicault, Dion 4, 12, 14–17, 20–2, 47, 97,
    102, 123, 139, 184, 189, 231, 246, 376, 389,
    428, 519, 532, 595, 602
    Arrah-na-Pogue 11, 13n.15, 15, 17
    The Colleen Bawn 10–11, 13n.15,
        15–18, 251n.2, 257n.41,
        258n.50, 595
    London Assurance 612
    The Octoroon; or, Life in
        Louisiana 10–12, 15–16
    Robert Emmet 17
    The Shaughraun 11, 13n.15, 15–17, 97, 460,
        461, 463, 469, 476, 595, 614–15, 676; in
        London 607–9, 610
Boucicault, Dion, Jr 149
Bourgeois, Maurice 101, 624
Bourke, Brian 484
Bourke, P. J.
    When Wexford Rose 113
Bourke, Siobhán 402
Boyce, Frank Cottrell 622
Boydell, Brian 433
Boyd, Ernest 206

Boyd, John
    The Flats 373, 683n.69
Boyd, Marie and Edna 447n.15
Boyd, Nigel 455
Boylan, Patricia 463
Boyle, Consolata 453
Boyle, Danny 622, 628
Boyle, William
    The Building Fund 598
Brady, Erina 288–90
Brahm, Otto 42, 108
Braidotti, Rosi 276
Branagh, Kenneth 386, 459, 622
Brandes, Georg 32
Brecht, Bertolt 121, 375, 408, 448, 453, 594,
        632–3, 648, 652, 655, 683
    The Caucasian Chalk Circle 662
    The Life of Galileo 212, 448
    Mother Courage/Mutter Courage 102, 337
    The Resistible Rise of Arturo Ui 448
Bremen 633
Brennan, Bríd 459, 516
Brennan, Stephen 349
Brennan-Whitmore, W. J. 194
Brian Friel Festival (1999) 649–50
Bridges-Adams, William 638
Brieux, Eugène 147
Bringing Up Baby (film) 238
Briscoe, Eamon 434
Britain/England 13, 33–4, 38, 43, 58, 73, 111,
        121, 123, 155, 160, 164, 168, 219–20, 239,
        277–8, 288, 314, 317, 359, 406, 418, 455,
        500, 510, 531, 546, 566, 609, 628, 632,
        645, 685
    actors and acting 231–3, 234, 246, 466, 476
    English touring companies in Ireland 201
    Irish in, as dramatic subject 323–4, 328–
        31, 336, 410, 523–4
    Irish theatre in 5, 26–7, 85, 139, 144, 291,
        462, 581, 606, 607–22, 623; see also
        Birmingham; Liverpool; London
    Irish writers in 130, 138–9, 322, 338–9,
        522, 624
    Modernism 134
    realism, drama of 108–9
    Venezuela crisis 27–8, 31
British army 144, 155, 163, 270, 501
British Association 237–8

British Council 634
British Empire 166, 280
British Empire Shakespeare Society 165
British Guiana 27
British Library 228
British Pathé 242–3
British Red Cross Society 156, 165
Brno (Czech Republic) 634
Broadway, *see* New York
Brogan, Patricia Burke 679
    Eclipsed 648
Brokentalkers 457, 570–1, 635
    The Blue Boy 526, 570
    Silver Stars 570
Brookfield, Charles
    The Poet and the Puppets (with James
        Glover) 24
Brook, Peter 350, 353, 443, 458, 615, 649
Brooks, Peter 10, 15, 16n.31, 22
Brophy, Robert J., *see* Ray, R. J.
Brougham, John 14, 595
Brown, Deborah 447n.15
Browne, John
    Craving (with Johnny Hanrahan) 401
Brown, Terence 89n.5, 220, 223
Brugha, Cathal 253n.11
Brussels 635
Brustein, Robert 9
Bryant, Marie 293
Bucharest 221
Büchner, Georg 127, 206
Buckstone, John Baldwin
    The Green Bushes 13n.15
Budapest 635
Buffalo (USA) 605
Build 435
Bulfin, William 97
Bulgaria 634
Bull, Ole 109
Bull, Philip 91
Buncrana, Co Donegal 660
Burke Brogan, Patricia 526
    Eclipsed 526–8
Burke, Helen 674
Burke-Kennedy, Mary Elizabeth 401, 679
Bush Theatre (London) 535, 538, 611–13, 622
Butler, Judith 679
Byrne, Catherine *516*

Byrne, David 398, 402
Byrne, Gabriel 459
Byrne, Gay 650
Byrne, Jason 457–8
Byrne, John Keyes, *see* Leonard, Hugh

Cabinet of Irish Literature 367–8
Cabra (Dublin) 683
Cairns, David 684–5
Cairo 221
Calderón, Pedro 652
Caldwell, Lucy 386
California (USA) 418
Calypso Productions 398–400, 686
Cambridge Festival Theatre 134, 278
Cambridge University 283n.55, 362
Campbell, Beatrice 206, 232
Campbell, Brian 378
    A Cold House (with Laurence
        McKeown) 385
Campbell, Gordon, Lord Glenavy 208
Campbell, John and Joseph 59
Campbell, Mrs Patrick (Stella) 9, 54, 124n.5,
    237, 240
Campion, Sean 553
Camus, Albert 584
Canada 417, 499
Cannon, Feidlim 570
Cannon, John
    The Dentist/An Fiaclóir (with Michael
        Rogers) 251
caoineadh (keening) 273–4
Cape Town 588
Capuchin Annual 245
Carlisle, Bob 393n.22
Carlson, Marvin 426, 427, 429–30, 543, 689
Carmichael, Coralie 245
Carnegie Mellon (Pittsburgh) 597–8
Carrickfergus, Co Antrim 60
Carr, Marina 1, 4, 458, 530, 545–9, **553–7**,
    629, 652, 677, 679, 686
    Ariel 556
    By the Bog of Cats 526, 556, 612, 649
    The Cordelia Dream 556
    The Deer's Surrender 553
    The Giant Blue Hand 556
    Low in the Dark 553
    The Mai 554, 555

Carr, Marina (*cont.*)
  Marble 556, 627
  Phaedra Backwards 554, 556
  Portia Coughlan 526, 548, 555
  On Raftery's Hill 526, 556
  16 Possible Glimpses 556
  This Love Thing 553–4
  Ullaloo 553
  Woman and Scarecrow 521, 556–7, 611
Carroll, Paul Vincent 598
  Shadow and Substance 212
  The White Steed 182
Cartmell, Selina 458, 557, 562
Carty, Ciaran 479
Carvalho, Paulo Eduardo 626–7
Carville, Daragh
  Male Toilets 380–1
Casanova, Pascale 107, 115
Casement, Roger 59, 146
Case, Sue-Ellen 679
Casey, Edward 689
Cassin, Barry 256, 291
Casson, Bronwen 3, 449–50
Castellucci, Romeo 649
Catalonia 625
Cathal Brugha Barracks (Dublin) 263
Catholic Bulletin 171, 173, 175, 181
Catholic Church/Catholicism 16, 50, 84, 173,
    182, 215, 220, 296, 302, 312–13, 338, 344,
    353, 364, 508–10, 571, 602
  as dramatic subject 130–1, 314–16, 325,
    334–5, 525–7, 567, 646, 664
  and Easter Rising (1960) 160
  and the Irish state 170, 307, 325; decline in
    power 333, 554
  and Irish theatre 639–40, 644–5,
    647–9, 652
Catholics 93–4, 99, 115, 155, 177–8, 180–1,
    185, 192, 215, 236, 300, 316, 330, 333, 335,
    361, 363, 364, 376, 379, 385, 387, 497, 498,
    503, 508, 509–10, 511, 518, 525, 668, 682
Catholic Truth Society 170
Catholic Young Men's Association 174
Cavendish, Lord Frederick 30n.27
Cave, Richard Allen 79, 85–6, 203, 610, 614,
    674, 688n.95, 689
Ceaușescu, Nicolae 625
Cecchetti, Enrico 278

Celtic Literary Society 42
Celtic Tiger 228, 266, 326, 419, 520, 523–4,
    528–30, 536–7, 554, 591, 649, 662, 691
Celtic Twilight 219, 223, 663
censorship 144, 149, 169, 173 5, 182, 220,
    226, 284–5, 288, 296, 582, 644–5
Central Bank of Ireland 591
Central School of Arts and Crafts
    (London) 277
Central School of Speech and Drama
    (London) 454
Centro Dramático Nacional (Madrid) 627
Cerquoni, Enrica 689
Chaikin, Joe 456
Channel 4 492
Chan, Paul 589–90
Chaplin, Charlie 213, 633
Charabanc Theatre Company 4, 373,
    377–8, 399, 549, **549–53**, 679; *see also*
    Jones, Marie
  The Girls in the Big Picture 552
  Lay Up Your Ends (with Martin
    Lynch) 377–8, 551, 552
  Oul Delph and False Teeth 552
  Somewhere Over the Balcony 552
Charles, Prince 608
Chaudhuri, Una 409, 679, 689
Cheek by Jowl 649
Chekhov, Anton 5, 127, 263, 594, 648, 654–9,
    663, 664, 665–6
  The Bear 654–5
  The Cherry Orchard 146, 464, 466, 648,
    654, 657, 663, 666
  The Proposal 655
  The Seagull 73, 569, 656–7, 662–4, *663*, 665
  Three Sisters 365, 463, 485, 657,
    659–60, 665
  Uncle Vanya 371, 654, 656n.6, 665
Cheney, Sheldon 597, 605
Chicago 215, 435, 492, 596–8, 601–2, 605,
    607, 688
Chicago *Mail* 238
child abuse 554, 570–1, 646, 664
Chimes at Midnight (film) 211
China 578, 582, 645
Christians 506–7
Churchill, Caryl 399
Cincinnati (USA) 605

cinema 211, 245, 393, 459, 464, 466, 531, 534, 543–4, 610, 628
  Beckett on Film project 4, 492–3
Citizen Kane (film) 211
City Lights (film) 633
Civic Repertory Theatre (New York) 213, 277–8, 600
Civic Theatre (Tallaght) 442
Civil War 20, 146, 164–5, 176, 191–2, 264, 461, 623, 628
Clapp, Susannah 614
Clarence Place Hall (Belfast) 61
Clark, David 635
Clarke, Austin 288–90, 296, 299–300, 301, 446
Clarke, Brenna Katz 92–4
Clarke, Jocelyn 401n.56
Clark, Mary 287
Classical Theater (Harlem) 588–9
classics 5, 254, 375, **654–70**
Claudel, Paul 121, 127, 652
Cleary, Bridget 517
Cleary, Joe 374, 685
Cleere's Theatre (Kilkenny) 565
Clery, Arthur 178–9
Clifden, Co Galway 405, 419
Clonmel, Co Tipperary 395
Clooney, George 579
Clubhouse (London) 73
Cluchey, Rick 588
Cluj (Kolozsvár) 625
Coburn, Veronica 566–7
Cochrane, Charles 129
Cochrane, Claire 609
Cocteau, Jean 127
Coffey, Tomás
  The Long Sorrow 646
Cogley, Daisy Bannard (Helen Carter) 208, 281, 302
Cohan, George M. 595
Cold War 582, 633
Cole, Catherine 384
Colgan, Eileen *349*
Colgan, Michael 4, 217, 227, 432, 470, 586, 591
  and Beckett Festival (1991) 478, 480–9, *487*, 492–4
Coliseum (London) 608

Colonial America 595
Colum, Mary 270
Colum, Padraic 53–4, 64, 66, 68, 91, 99–100, 102, 111, 112, 598
  'An Old Woman of the Roads' 100
  Broken Soil 48, 67, 99
  The Fiddler's House 67, 99–100
  The Land 48, 98, 99–100, 112
  The Miracle of the Corn 67
  The Road Round Ireland 100, 299
  The Saxon Shillin' 48
  Thomas Muskerry 115–18
Comédie Française 232, 236
Commission to Inquire into Child Abuse, *see* Ryan Report
Commitments (musical) 615
community theatre 65, 71, 374–5, 377–8, 457
Compagnie de Rigault 646
Compántas Amharclainne na Gaeilge 255
Compántas Chorcaí 261, 287, 290
The Company 635
Complex (Smithfield, Dublin) 568n.12
Comyn, Annabelle 548, 557, 666
Congreve, William 139
Connell, R. W. 681–2
Connemara, Co Galway 264, 268, 415, 532
Connolly, Darach 299
Connolly, James 156, 162, 164–6, 168, 187, 193–4, 198
  Under Which Flag? 162–3
Connolly, Sean 163
Connolly, Fr Terrence 639–40, 644
Conradh na Gaeilge, *see* Gaelic League
Conroy, Amy 691
Constitution of Ireland (1937) 180n.54, 274, 516, 555, 680
Constitution of the Irish Free State (1922) 680
Consultative Group on the Past 378–9
Conway, Frank 3, 415–16, 449, 451–2, 456
Coole Park, Co Galway 144, 251–2, 663
Cooney, John 645
Copeau, Jacques 566
Copenhagen 254
Coquelin, Benoît-Constant 233, 428
Corcadorca Theatre Company 395, 401, 540
Cork 12, 114, 150, 177–8, 253, 287, 290, 316, 394–5, 401, 406, 418–19, 442, 540–2, 629, 646, 650

Cork Dramatic Society 50, 113–14
Corkery, Daniel 139–40
    Embers 114
Cork Examiner 417
Cork Film Festival 642
Cork Opera House 316, 395, 436–7, *437*
Cork Realists 105, 114, 118
Corn Exchange 4, 457, 557, 568–70, 689
Corr, Andrea 611
Corrie, John 266n.90
Cosgrave, Liam 394
Cosgrave, W. T. 170–1, 181, 391
Cosgrove, Aedin 457n.54, 458, 563
Costello, John A. 391
Cousins, James 59, 64, 66, 270
    The Racing Lug 59, 60–1, 65
    The Sleep of the King 112
    Sold 48, 65
Cousins, Margaret 270
Cowan, Billy
    Smilin' Through 620
Coward, Noel 218, 281
Coyne, Joseph Stirling 27
Craig, Edward Gordon 2, 79, 204–5, 208,
    430, 559, 593
Craigie, Ingrid *349*
Craig, May 174, 241, 243
Crawley, Peter 635
Creative Time 589
Creed, Tom 458
Cregan, David 500, 511, 681
Crilly, Joseph
    McQuillan's Hill 379
    Second Hand Thunder 379
Critchley, Simon 591
critical evaluation, *see* historiography
Croatia 634
Croghan, Declan 621
    *Paddy Irishman, Paddy Englishman and
        Paddy ...?* 620
Cromwell, James 246, 475
Cronin, Finola 681
Cronin, Michael 287, 654
Crosby, Bing 243
Crowe, Eileen 173–4, *244*, 245, 462
Crowley, John 418
    True Lines (collaboration) 565–6
Crypt Theatre (Dublin) 613

Cuchulain (mythological figure) 77–80, 82,
    84, 86, 125, 309
Cullen, Charles 392
Culleton, Jim 457
Cullingford, Elizabeth Butler 674n 4
Cultural Development Incentive Scheme
    (CDIS) 402–3
Culture Ireland 635, 688
Cumann na mBan 68, 174–6, 192, 214, 258
Cumann na nGaedheal (society) 71, 235
Cumann na nGaedheal government 214
    and Abbey Theatre 169–78
Cummin, Alyson 385
Cummins, Geraldine 547
Cunard, Lady 82
Cunnane, Noreen and Kevin 291
Curragh Barracks, Co Kildare 224
Curran, C. P. 209, 222
Curran, Sarah 132
Curtis Brown 612
Cusack, Alice Violet 460
Cusack, Catherine 460n.2
Cusack, Cyril 3, 102, 317, 459, *461*, 464–6,
    469, 473, 476–7, 485, 639, 640
    acting career **460–4**
Cusack, Niamh 611
Cusack, Sinéad 459, 460n.2, 464
Cú Uladh (Peadar Toner Mac Fhionnlaoich)
    Eilís agus an Bhean Déirce 251–2
Cyrano de Bergerac (film) 233
Cyril Cusack Productions 460
Czech lands 5, 582, 623, 624, 627–8, 631–4

Da Club (Dublin) 613
Daily Dispatch 240
Daily Express 107–8
Daily Telegraph 416
Dali, Salvador 133
Dalkey, Co Dublin 318
Dallas (Texas) 600
Dalton, Frank 12n.11
D'Alton, Louis 14, 22, 150, 646
    Death is So Fair 23
    They Got What They Wanted 22
    This Other Eden 21–3, 150
Daly, Augustine 595
Daly, Fr Edward 502
Daly, Jane 402

Daly, Jim 401
Damer Hall (Dublin) 259
Damrosch, David 606
Daniels, Sarah 399, 546
Danio Biofilm 254
Dante's *Inferno* 129, 133
D'Arbois de Jubainville, Henri 101
D'Arcy, Margaretta 287–8, 291–2
D'Arcy, Michael 579
Dargent, Sabine 457n.54
Darley, Emmanuel
    *Mardi à Monoprix/Tuesdays at
        Tesco's* 387–8
Darragh, Florence 124n.5
Daughter of Darkness (film) 464, 466
Davis, Thomas 64
Day, Susanne 547
Deane, Ciarán 358
Deane, Seamus 188, 192, 434, 683, 685
    and Field Day 357, 358, 361–6, 368–70, 371
    Rumours 363
Dean, Joan Fitzpatrick 221, 225, 297, 675
De Beauvoir, Simone 291
De Bhilmot, Séamus
    Baintighearna an Ghorta 255
Debord, Guy 683n.69
De Bosis, Lauro: *Icaro* 300
De Brun, Seosamh 165
De Búrca, Seamus 11
Déchevaux-Dumesnil, Suzanne 581
Decroux, Étienne 401, 566
Decroux, Maximilien 566
De Danaan 406
Deevy, Teresa 2, 150, 281–3, 461, 546–7,
    677, 679–80
    A Disciple/In Search of Valour 282–4
    Katie Roche 278, 282–4
    The King of Spain's Daughter 283
    Light Falling 278
    Wife to James Whelan 278
De Faoilte, Seamus
    Harrigan's Girl 292
De Fréine, Celine
    Nára Turas é in Aistear 262
Deilt Productions 261–2, 395
De Jongh, Nicholas 416
Delaney, Pauline 291
Delgado, Eduard 397

De Max, Edouard 236
Democratic Unionist Party 379
Denisoff, Dennis 36
Denmark 632
Department of Arts, Culture and the
    Gaeltacht 403
Dermody, Frank 255, 259–60, 263
Derrida, Jacques 538
Derry 3, 61, 322, 357, 361, 363–5, 378, 381,
    383, 389, 406, 497, 501–3, 655, 670; *see
    also* Guildhall
Derry/Londonderry City of Culture 603
design, *see* direction and design
De Toro, Antonio 635
De Valera, Éamon *90*, 180–2, 195, 319, 325,
    391, 516
De Valera, Síle 441
De Valois, Ninette 134, 206, 246, 278–9,
    281, 643
Devereux, Audrey 548
Devine, George 338
devised theatre 450, **559–74**
Devitt, John 287, 311, 350–1, 448, 644
Devlin, Anne 373, 677, 679
    Ourselves Alone 378
Devlin, Anne (1798) 667n.33
Devlin, Martina
    Banksters 662
Devlin McAliskey, Bernadette 668
Diaghilev, Sergei 89–90, 246, 279
DIALOG 626
Dickens, Charles
    Christmas Carol 537
Diderot, Denis 42
Digbeth (Birmingham) 621–2
Digges, Dudley 60, 233, 235, 245
Dingle, Co Kerry 266n.90
direction and design 2, 3, *119, 126, 132*, 148–9,
    201–13, *212, 450–1, 455*, 480, 492, 548,
    557, 560, *612*
    playwright-directors 458
    post-1960 **443–58**; styles 457–8; theatrical
        complexity 452–7
    presentational theatre 134–5, *135, 136*
    spectacle and pageantry 213–16
    training and professionalism 268,
        277–9, 449
discussion plays 2, 141, 143, 147

disruptions (1990–2007) 529–44

Divadlo 633

diversification **389–403**, 557

Dobbins, Gregory 102

Doherty, Brian 420, *421*

Doherty, Gerry 381

Dolan, Jill 546, 679, 683n.69

Dolan, Michael 173–4

Dolmen Press 292

Domville, Eric 75

Donegal, county 365, 515, 522, 527

Donlon, Phelim 402–3

Donmar Warehouse (London) 406n.11, 413, 416, 468, 474n.53, 611, 688

Donnelly, Donal 290–1

Donnybrook (Dublin) 89

Donoghue, Emma 399, 679, 691

Donovan, Dan 287

Doolan, Lelia 679

Doran, Charles 207

Douglas, Lord Alfred ('Bosie') 225

Dowey, Mary 489

Dowling, Clare 399

Dowling, Joe 283n.55, 452–4, 460n.2, 469, 470, 473, 477, 480, 601–2

Downes, J. Neil 437–9, 441

Doyle, Roddy 524, 615

Doyle, Roger 227, 561, 562

Doyle, Simon
    Oedipus Loves you (with Gavin Quinn) 564

Draíocht (Blanchardstown) 442

Dramick 128

Dresden 290

Dromgoole, Dominic 612

Druid Lane Theatre (Galway) 262, 264, 394–5, 405

Druid Theatre Company 3–4, 246, 332, 390, 394, 396, 400, **404–21**, 442, 451–2, 456, 468, 473–5, 477, 533, 557, 601, 611, 628–9, 649, 651, 679
    DruidMurphy 404–5, 418–21, *420*, *421*, 604
    DruidSynge 418, 456, 475, 485, 604, 651

Drumshambo, Co Leitrim 641

Dubbeljoint Theatre Company 381, 552

Dublin 3, 11–13, 42, 93–4, 101–2, 140, 160, 219, 253, 318, 395, 398, 407, 414, 418, 429, 442, 542, 602; *see also* Dublin Theatre Festival; Easter Rising (1916); *individual theatres* (Abbey, Gate, etc)
    City of Culture (1991) 484
    Civic Weeks 215
    Irish-language theatre 254–62
    little theatres 288–99
    Lockout (1913) 114, 162, 186, *186*, 193, 348, 447
    O'Casey 183–98

Dublin Arts Theatre 290

Dublin Castle 163, 639

Dublin City Council 572

Dublin Corporation 256, 645

Dublin Dance Theatre Club 288–90

Dublin Drama League 56, 127, 133, 172, 206, 210, 598–9, 652

Dubliners (folk group) 571

Dublin Evening Mail 19n.43, 297

Dublin Fringe Festival 563, 650

Dublin Gay Theatre Festival 229, 691

Dublin Horse Show 177

Dublin Industrial Development Association 175

Dublin International Theatre Symposia 563

Dublin Players Club 110

Dublin Suffrage Week 687

Dublin Theatre Festival 5, 260–1, 317, 341, 347, 349, 393, 396, 404n.5, 406–8, 444–5, 458, 535, 553, 612, 640, 650, 652, 662
    foundation 560, **641–6**
    1964 festival 646–9

Dublin Verse Speaking Society 288–90

Dublin Writers' Museum 484

Dublin Youth Theatre 401

Dudley Edwards, Ruth 158, 159n.16

Duggan, Dave 378
    AH6905 385
    Makaronik 267

Duggan, Garry
    Shibari 451, 452

Duke, Mike
    Revenge 385

Duke of York's Theatre (London) 148–9

Dulac, Edmund *126*, 204

Dullin, Charles 566

Dumas, Alexandre *fils*
    La Femme de Claude 9n.2

Du Maurier World Stage Festival
    (Toronto) 417
Dunamaise Arts Centre (Portaloise) 568n.12
Duncan, Dawn 685
Dunlop, John 376
Dunne, Michael 291
Dunne, Phil 353
Dunne, Shaun 650
Dunsany, Lord (Edward Plunkett) 127, 594,
    596–7, 599
    *King Argimines and the Unknown
    Warrior* 205
Durcan, Paul 484
Dürrenmatt, Friedrich
    The Visit 393
Duse, Eleonora 9
Dyas, Grace 650, 679

Earagail Festival (Letterkenny) 568n.12
Eastern Europe 582, 623–4, 631
Easter Rising (1916) 20, 23, 68, 71, 83, 150,
    155–68, 174–5, 186, 198, 206, 214–15,
    241, 253, 274, 441, 456, 499
    centenary: Abbey Centenary Programme
    'Waking the Nation' 549
    as dramatic subject 166–8, 192–4
    fiftieth anniversary 327
    legacy 155
East Germany 632
East Wall (Dublin) 185
Eblana Theatre (Dublin) 261, 286, 288
Echegaray, Jose 44
École Jacques Lecoq (Paris) 567
Edgeworth, Maria
    Castle Rackrent 97
Edinburgh 418, 651, 688
Edinburgh Festival 227, 465, 526, 627,
    641, 649–51
Edinburgh Festival Fringe 405–6
Edinburgh Traverse 622
Éditions de Minuit 581
Edmondson, Adrian 491
Edwards, Hilton 134, 137, **207**, 209, *218*,
    218–19, 339–40, 344, 512, 634, 641
    collaboration with MacLiammóir/
    Gate Theatre. *see under* Gate Theatre
    (Dublin)
    and Irish-language theatre 245, 262

Edward VII 143
Eglinton, John 107
Egoyan, Atom 492
Einstein, Albert 578
Electricity Supply Board 299
Elevator Repair Service 649
Eliot, T. S. 81–2, 127, 614, 667
    The Waste Land 85
Elizabeth II 608
Ellis-Fermor, Una 674
Ellis, Havelock 32
Elsinore Castle (Denmark) 634
emigration 14, 98, 149, 231, 308, **323**, 389,
    498, 565–6, 652, 680; *see also* exile
    as dramatic subject 11, 112, 116, 145,
    163, 308–11, 314, 323–33, 336, 339,
    407, 410–11, 414, 416, 419–20, 517,
    522–4, 559
Emmet, Robert 23, 131–2, 210
Emory University (USA) 357–8
Empire Palace (Dublin) 429
Encumbered Estates Act 1849 91
England, *see* Britain/England; London
English National Opera 612
English Theatre (Berlin) 635
Enniskillen, Co Fermanagh 229, 552
Epic Theatre 408
Equal Status Act (2000) 498n.4
Ervine, St John 149, 241, 461, 598
    Jane Clegg 149
    John Ferguson 149
    Mixed Marriage 115, 118, 149
    Some Impressions of My Elders 151
Esmonde, Osmond 175
Esposito, Vera 49
Etherege, George
    The Man of Mode 475
Etherton, Michael 675
ethnicity 4, 42, 681
Eucharistic Congress (1932) 215
Euripides 127
    Medea 556
Europe 5, 581–2
    Irish theatre in **623–36**; transferability
    626–9; translation 629–31
European Union 627, 662, 670
Evening Herald 174, 178, 341, 488
Everyman (Jedermann) 133

Everyman Playhouse (Cork) 287, 394–5
Everyman Theatre (Liverpool) 616, 619
exile 130, 225, 261, **322–36**, 521, 524–5, 542,
    556, 559, 591; *see also* emigration
    internal exiles 525–8
existentialism 213, 291, 581, 584, 587
experimental theatre 48, 79, 102, 131, 172,
    207–8, 213, 260, 264, 281, 290, 333, 338,
    446, 479, 482, 533, 604, 632
    Beckett 580, 585, 592
    Dublin (1920–1930) 127–8
    Yeats 73–4, 77, 80, 82–3, 85, 127

Fabbri, Diego
    Processo a Gesù 261
Fabian Society 140, 149
Fabulous Beast
    The Bull 649
Factory (Sligo) 566
Fagan, James B. 143
Fairley, Michelle 611
Fallon, Gabriel 188, 239
Falls, Robert 602
Fanning, A. P.
    Vigil 461
Fannin, Hilary 557, 679
Fanon, Frantz 685
    The Wretched of the Earth 118
Farquhar, George 139, 455, 610
Farrell, Bernard 401
Farrell, Patrick 181
Farr, Florence 73–5, 202
    The Music of Speech 75
Fay brothers (Frank and William) 48–9,
    54, 60, 63, 93–4, 110, 112, 237, 241, 246,
    252, 254, 476
Fay, Frank 2, 13, 47, 49, 69n.42, 92–4, 107–10,
    202, 204, 234–6, 239, 428
    and acting 231–4
Fay, William 2, 13, 47, 54–5, 59, 69, 91–2, 94,
    97, 102, 109, 201–3, 235, 238, 569
    resignation from Abbey 238
Feehily, Stella 679
    O Go My Man 611
Fehling, Jürgen 129n.16
Feiseanna 252
feminism 29–30, 46, 270–1, 276, 284, 316,
    377–8, 399, 545–6, 549–50, 553–4,
    556–7, 678, 689–90

Fenians 11, 27
Fenollosa, Ernest 81
Ferguson, Samuel
    The Fairy Thorn 290
Fernald, John 465
Ferriter, Diarmaid 323, 333
Festival d'Avignon, *see* Avignon Festival
festivals, *see* theatre festivals
Fianna Fáil 170, 172, 296, 325, 391
    and Abbey Theatre 171, 176, **178–82**
Fianna Fáil, Incorporated (USA) 179–81
Fíbín 264–6, 268
    Réiltín 259
    *Stair na gCeilteach/History of the
        Celts* 265–6, *266*
Fiddler on the Roof (musical) 594, 599
*Field Day Anthology of Irish
        Writing* 368–70, 550
Field Day Archive 357–8, 360
Field Day Theatre Company 3, 56, 357–71,
    373, 380, 400, 453, 515, 550–1, 603, 628,
    655–6, 659, 662, 667, 669, 684–5
    publishing projects 367–70
Fiennes, Ralph 493, 612
Fine Gael 391
Finland 632
Finnbogadóttir, Vigdís 485
Finney, Gail 679
First World War 127, 129–30, 144–5, 155,
    160, 163, 194–5, 274, 499, 518, 584, 625
Firth, Roger 416
Fishamble Theatre Company 457, 538
Fitzgerald, Barry 2, 189, 238, 240–1, *242*,
    243–4, *244*, 245, 459, 462
FitzGerald, Desmond 171
Fitzgerald, Lord Edward 23
Fitzgerald, Jim 337, 341, 392, 393n.22,
    444–6, 644
Fitzgibbon, Emelie 401
Fitzmaurice, George 313
Fitzpatrick, Kathleen
    Expiation 68
Fitzpatrick, Lisa 279–80, 541, 680, 689–90
Fitz-Simon, Christopher 11–12, 224, 287,
    460n.2, 463, 643–4
Flaherty, Robert
    Man of Aran 533–4
Flanagan, Terence 447n.15
Flannery, Eoin 692

Flannery, James 74, 674
Flaubert, Gustave
    La Tentation de Saint Antoine 350
Flecker, James Elroy 127
Fleming, Maria 568n.12
Fletcher, Alan 690
Florence 634
Flynn, Mannix
    James X 526
Fo'castle Theatre (Galway) 390, 405
Fo, Dario 594
Fogarty, Anne 691–2
Foley, Imelda 551, 675
folk drama 4, 25–6, 44, 65–6, 69, 74, 77, 87,
    97, 178, 252–3, 308–9, 316, 521, 555
Footsbarn 649
Forbes-Robertson, Johnston 149, 232
Ford, John 240, 245
Forester's Hall (Dublin) 160
Forman, Ross 34
Forster, E. M., *Maurice* 223
Fort, Paul 43
47 Workshop (Harvard) 597, 602
Foster, Roy 220, 529–30, 598, 639
Foucault, Michel 283, 689
Fouéré, Olwen 227, 553, 561–2, 679
France 27, 45, 100, 106, 108, 174, 483, 499,
    566, 580, 591, 624, 627, 630, 632, 634; *see
    also* Paris
    actors and acting 233–4
Frawley, Bernard 291
Frawley, Maureen (neé Foley) 287, 290
Frawley, Monica 457n.54
Frawley, Oona 287
Frayn, Michael
    Noises Off 542
Frazer, Sir James George
    The Golden Bough 85
Frazier, Adrian 111, 674
Freeman's Journal 12, 98, 105, 113, 115
Freie Bühne (Berlin) 42, 108, 109
French Revolution 510
Freud, Sigmund 133, 564
Freyer, Major Dermot 432–3
Friel, Brian 3–5, 211, 286–7, 319–20, 322–3,
    333, 338–9, 343, 389, 438, 446, 454, 457,
    460n.2, 468, 473, 480, 500, 515–16, 522,
    550, 605, 615, 627–8, 630, 647, 655–6,
    662, 677

and Field Day **357–71**
    Brian Friel Festival 649–50
    Chekhov adaptations **657–60**, 664–6
    Afterplay 665–6
    American Welcome 601
    Aristocrats 333, 359, 363–4, 451–2,
        522n.10, 657–8
    Crystal and Fox 463
    Dancing at Lughnasa 19, 84, 320, 323,
        370–1, 454, 515–16, *516*, 517, 519, 523–4,
        526–8, 555, 611–12, 628, 689
    The Enemy Within 339, 362
    Faith Healer 84, 333–6, 363, 452, 469–70,
        471, 510, 519, 536, 656
    The Freedom of the City 333, 358, 362, 499,
        601, 628, 683
    The Gentle Island 332, 343, 648
    Give Me Your Answer, Do! 548
    The Home Place 517, 522–3
    La Dernière Classe (Translations) 628
    Living Quarters 333, 451–2, 657–8
    The Loves of Cass McGuire 326–7, 405, 466
    Making History 515–17, 522
    Molly Sweeney 519, 536
    Philadelphia, Here I Come! 260, 318, 320,
        322, 324–6, 328, 330, 336, 339, 341, 362,
        559, 601–2, 647–8, 652, 656
    Three Sisters (adaptation) 657, 659–60, 662
    Translations 264, 268, 323, 332, 359–61,
        363, 366, 370, 374, 389, 453, 515, 517, 522,
        625, 628, 635, 659, 683
    Uncle Vanya (adaptation) 659–60
    Volunteers 333, 363, 451
    The Yalta Game 665
Friel, Deirdre 258
Friel, Judy 283n.55
Frier, Michael 291
Friers, Rowel 447n.15
Frohman, Charles 148–9, 206, 238
Frost, Anthony 560–1
Fryer, June 289–90, 302
Fuchs, Dieter 37
Fugard, Athol
    The Island 505, 667n.33
Funge, Josephine 302

Gaelic Athletic Association 170, 293
Gaelic League 42, 46, 69, 70–1, 139–40, 148,
    158, 170, 251–4

Gaelic Movement 139
Gaelic Players 171
Gael Linn 259
Gaiety School of Acting 246, 278, 452n.38, 477, 553
Gaiety Theatre (Dublin) 13n.15, 47, 52, 224, 23–3, 252, 254–5, 291, 297, 316, 414, 416–17, 428–9, 463, 469, 687
Galicia 625
Gallery Press 365, 409
Gallipoli (Turkey) 163
Gallowglass (Clonmel) 395
Galvin, Patrick 446
    Nightfall to Belfast 373
Galway 3, 207, 253–4, 262–6, 308, 332, 394–5, 398, 405–6, 408, 411, 415–16, 418, 442, 456, 468, 562, 601, 611, 615, 629, 649; *see also* An Taibhdhearc; Druid Theatre Company
Galway Arts Festival 264, 418, 649, 651, 667
Gambon, Michael 493
Garda Síochána 192, 296
Gare St Lazare Players 635
Garfield, James A. 25
Garvey, Máire 49
Gas Company Theatre (Dun Laoghaire) 286, 288
Gate Theatre (Dublin) 1, 4, 56, 182, 208–9, 214, 246, 261, 278, 280–1, 284, 286, 291, 293–4, 298, 339, 393, 396, 426–7, 439, 441, 446, 470–2, 512, 557, 561, 591, 602, 638, 644, 649–51, 659–60, 667n.33
    actors and acting 245–7, 465, *467*, 470, *472*
    Beckett festivals: (1991) **478–93**, 586, 651; (2006) 483n.16
    building 209–10, 431–2, 435
    decline 480
    direction and design 2, 128, 131, *132*, *135*, *136*, **207–11**, 215, 432, 445, 452–3
    Edwards/Mac Liammóir collaboration 133n.24, 207–11, 218–20, 226, 246, 284, 337
    establishment (1928) 128, 134, 136, 172, 208, 218
    The Importance of Being Oscar 217, 220, 223–6
    Irish-language plays 254, 256, 398

Modernism 131, *132*, 133–4, *135*, 135–7
    pageants: *The Ford of the Hurdles* 215; 'Pageant of the Celt' 215
    Project 67 392–3, 446
    Saint Joan 465
    tours 215, 225, 634
    Wilde's plays **217–30**, 455, *455*
Gate Theatre Studio (London) 128–9, 134, 208–9
'The Gathering' (2013) 216
Gemini Productions 281, 287, 302, 316, 396, 445
gender identity 46, 229, 269, 275, 281, 387–8, 498–9, 503, 505–6, 511, 547, 557, 668
gender politics 30, 55, 167, 378
Gentleman's Magazine 98
George Devine Awards 540
George, Henry 140
Geraghty, Clive *349*
German expressionism 130–1, 135, 207, 284
Germany 5, 30, 38, 155, 164, 174, 499, 541, 581, 624, 627–34, 638, 650
Gibbon, John 291
Gibbons, Luke 685
Gielgud, John 492
Gilbert, Helen 684
Gillespie, Elgy 345
Gillespie, Kathleen 383
Gillespie, Patsy 383
Gill, Michael 362
Gilmour, Alexander 421
Gilroy, Frank
    The Subject Was Roses 603
Giraudoux, Jean
    Amphytron 38 261
Gladstone, William Ewart 58
Glaspell, Susan 127
    Trifles 599
Glasshouse Productions 398–400, 402
Gleeson, Brendan 456, 459
Glenaan, Kenneth
    The Business of Blood (with Donal O'Kelly) 399
Glenarm, Co Antrim 59
Glendalough, Co Wicklow 638
Glendenning, Robin 378
Glenroe (tv drama) 414n.29

Globe Theatre (Dun Laoghaire) 287–8, 337, 445
Gloucester Street Laundry (Dublin) 571–2
Glover, James
   The Poet and the Puppets (with Charles Brookfield) 24
Godfrey, Peter 128, 134, 209
Godfrey Quigley Productions 396
Goethe, Johann Wolfgang von
   Faust 137, 164n.33
Gogarty, Oliver St John
   Blight 147, 191
Going My Way (film) 243–4
Golden Dawn, Order of 75
Goldsmith, Oliver 139–40
   The Vicar of Wakefield 418
Gonne, Iseult 83
Gonne, Maud 46, 48, 50, 60, 76, 83, 132, 235, 244, 272, 547, 549, 679
Good Friday Agreement (1998) 3, 373, 378–9, 385, 620
Goodman Theater (Chicago) 601–2
Gordon Craig, Edward, *see* Craig, Edward Gordon
Gordon, Dan 552–3
Gore-Booth, Eva 2, 272, 274–6, 547, 679, 680
   The Buried Life of Deirdre 272, 275
Gorman, Damian 378
Gorman, Declan 397
   Féile Fáilte 399
Gough, Kathleen 389
GQ (magazine) 578–9
Graffiti Theatre in Education Company (Cork) 401
Graham, Colin 685, 692
Graham Medal 317
Gramsci, Antonio 682
Granada Television 317, 339
Grand Opera House (Belfast) 149
Granville Barker, Harley 143–4, 149, 206
Gray, Terence 134, 136n.29, 278
Great Dublin Lockout Tapestry 186
Great Famine 120, 323, 419
Great War, *see* First World War
Greece 183, 634
Greek classics 375, 654–6, 667–70
Greenwich Village (New York) 598

Gregg, Roger 401
Gregg, Stacey 378, 557, 679
Gregory, André 656n.6
Gregory, Lady (Augusta) 1–2, 13, 48, 58–9, 65–6, 69, 76, 105–6, 113, 124, 144–5, 148, 173–4, 178, 210, 217, 237, 251, 263, 270, 272, 281, 549, 569, 606, 610, 624, 655, 663, 676–7, 679–80, 682–4
   and Abbey Theatre 52–4, 63, 94, 169–71, 173, 176–7, 182, 202–3, 239–40, 597; Irish Literary Theatre/INTS 43, 93, 108, 202, 253, 428
   sidelining of 546–8
   The Canavans 54
   Cathleen ni Houlihan (with Yeats). *see under* Yeats, William Butler
   Cuchulain of Muirthemne 77, 98
   The Deliverer 205
   Dervorgilla 26, 54
   The Doctor in Spite of Himself (adaptation) 654
   The Gaol Gate 54, 256n.32, 272–4
   Grania 276–7
   Hyacinth Halvey 54
   The Image 203
   The Jackdaw 54
   Kincora 54, 203
   The Rising of the Moon 54, 162, 177, 236
   The Rogueries of Scapin (adaptation) 239
   Spreading the News 240, 548
   Twenty-Five 98
   The White Cockade 54
   The Would-Be Gentleman (adaptation) 654
Gregory, Robert 168, 202–3
Grein, J. T. 42–3, 108, 111
Grene, Nicholas 350, 537, 615, 623, 674, 676–7, 678, 682, 688
Grieg, Edvard 209
Griffin, Revd E. M. 185
Griffith, Arthur 47, 48–9, 71, 101, 178
Griffiths, Trevor 359
Grosvenor, Charles H. 28
Grosz, Elizabeth 679
Grotowski, Jerzy 604, 615
Groundwork Productions 396
Guardian 261, 416, 418, 491
Guildhall (Derry) 361, 381, 389, 406, 655

Gussow, Mel 604
Guthanna Binne Síoraí 262n.80
Guthrie Theater (Minneapolis) 322, 325, 339, 362, 438, 452n.38, 453, 600–1, 607
Guthrie, Tyrone 212, 277, 322, 325, 339, 362, 466, 600–1, 647, 657
Gwynn, Stephen 64

Hadley, Elaine 13–14
Haifa 588
Haire, Wilson John
    Bloom of the Diamond Stone 374
    Within Two Shadows 373
Hallinan Flood, Frank 453
Hall, Kenneth 432
Hall, Peter 359, 581
Hall, Rod 613
Hall, Stuart 14n.21, 614
Hamilton, Malcolm 401
Hammond, David 357, 366, 367–8, 371
Hankin, St John 127
Hanna, Gillian 393n.22
Hanrahan, Johnny
    Craving (with John Browne) 401
Harcourt Street Studio (Dublin) 289
Hardwicke, Cecil 240
Hardwicke Street Theatre (Dublin), *see* Irish Theatre
Harkin, Margo
    The Far Side of Revenge (film) *383*
Harlem (New York) 588–9
Harrigan, Edward 595
Harrington, John 615, 674
Harris, Claudia 490–1
Harris, Nancy 557
Harrison, Rex 240
Harris, Susan Cannon 196, 674
Hart, Lynda 679
Hart, Tony 595
Harvard University (USA) 597, 599
Harvey, Jonathan 616
Harvey's Irish Theatre Award 408
Haughey, Charles 485–6
Haughton, Miriam 689
Hauptmann, Gerard 44, 49, 127n.10
Havel, Václav 489, 582, 594, 631
Hawke, Fanny 524n.17

Hawkes, Jacquetta
    Dragon's Mouth (with J. B. Priestley) 293
Hawk's Well Theatre (Sligo) 395
Hayes, J. J. 599
Hayes, Katy 399
Hayes, Richard 182
Hayes, Trudy 399
Haymarket Company 232
Haymarket Theatre (London) 27–30
Haynes, John 579
Hayter, S. W. 484
Healing Through Remembering 378
Heaney, Seamus 357, 362, 365–9, 371, 509, 655, 669–70
    The Burial at Thebes 548n.8, 670
    The Cure at Troy 371, 375, 379, 669
    'Station Island' 657
Heath, Caroline 232
Heddon, Deirdre 561, 574
Hegarty-Lovett, Judy 548
Helsingfors Stadsteater (Helsinki) 632
Henderson, Cathy *186*
Henley, Beth 603
Hennessy, Ben 401
Hennique, Léon 108
Henry, Niall 401, 566
Henry Street Settlement (New York) 596
Herder, Johann Gottfried 42
Hickey, Tom 450, 454
Hickman, Mary 617
Higgins, F. R. 462, 639–40
    A Deuce o' Jacks 212
Higgins, Michael D. 264, 397–8, 402–3
Hill, Conleth 553
Hillery, Patrick 263
Hingerty, Kay 417
Hirsch, Edward 97
historical melodrama 10–12, 15, 17–18
historiography 5, 271, 276, 548, **673–93**
    gender-related 678–82
    little theatres 286–7
    performance and spectatorship 686–90
    post-colonial 684–6, 691–2
history plays 11, 20, 77–8, **517–18**, 526, 528
Hitchcock, Alfred 240, 241, 244
Hitler, Adolf 638
Hoare, Kieran 287

Hobson, Bulmer 59–60
Hobson, Harold 261, 581, 647–8
Hogan, Robert 674
Holland 634
Holloway, Joseph 46–7, 49, 51–2, 66–7, 92,
    157, 174, 182, 202, 212, 235, 430, 441,
    461n.7, 598–9, 687
Hollywood (California) 245, 459, 597
Holocaust 618
Holroyd, Michael 140
Home Rule Bills 58, 156
Home Rule crisis (1912) 59, 62, 68, 71
homophobia 340, 342, 562, 652
homosexuality 217–18, 220, 223–6, 288, 302,
    387, 497, 501–3, 512, 557, 570, 680, 691;
    see also Wilde, Oscar
  decriminalization 229, 498n.4, 554, 562,
    570n.17
  as dramatic subject 226, 229–30, 333,
    341–5, 500–1, 512–14, 527, 620, 648, 681,
    684, 691
Honan, T. V. 401
Honest Ulsterman 372
Horniman, Annie 51–3, 56, 63–4, 91, 138,
    203, 236, 238, 240, 430, 549, 597, 687
Houlihan, Barry 287
Howarth, Donald 588
Howe, Irving 594, 597
How Green Was My Valley (film) 240
Howth, Co Dublin 72–3
Huber, Werner 624–5, 629, 635
Hübner, Kurt 633
Hughes, Barnard 318
Hughes, Declan 347, 350, 537
  Digging for Fire 612
  New Morning 613
Hughes, Derek 36
Hughes, Howard 614–15
Hugo, Victor 156n.6
Humphreys, R. A. 28n.14
Hungary 625, 628
Hunter, Holly 612
Hunt, Hugh 21n.50, 124n.5, 211–12, 277, 452,
    639, 640
Hurley, Erin 637
Hurricane Katrina (2005) 589
Hurt, John 492–3

Hurt, Matthew 388n.46
Huxley, Aldous
  Brave New World 529
Hyde, Douglas 66, 69, 251, 262–3
  An Pósadh 257, 644
  An Tincéar agus An tSídheog 113, 255
  Casadh an tSúgáin 65–6, 69, 252, 255,
    398, 428
  Love Songs of Connacht 95
Hynes, Garry 3, 396, 400, 402, 404–6, 408,
    416–18, 452, 456–7, 474, 480, 533, 553–7,
    601, 651, 679, 686n.86; see also Druid
    Theatre Company
  Island Protected by a Bridge of Glass 406
  The Pursuit of Pleasure 405–6

Ibraheem, Noha 509
Ibsen, Henrik 5, 9–10, 44–5, 49, 65–7, 97, 106,
    109, 139–41, 218, 252, 655–6, 665
  An Enemy of the People 29, 42, 109–10
  Brand 65–6
  A Doll's House 48, 107, 110, 140, 276, 565,
    656, 660–1, 661
  Ghosts 42, 109
  Hedda Gabler 140
  John Gabriel Borkman 662
  Peer Gynt 44, 133, 136, 137, 209, 221, 246,
    657, 662
identity 497–8; see also gender identity;
    national identity
immigration 14n.21, 330, 498, 522, 618–19;
    see also emigration
Imperial Hotel (Dublin) 194
Imperial Hotel (Galway) 562
Imprimatur Productions 393
Improbable Films (Madrid) 265, 266
In Bruges (film) 534
Inchovea, Co Clare 310
Independent Theatre (London) 42–3,
    108–9, 111
In Dublin 415
Inghinidhe na hÉireann 46, 60, 214, 235,
    271, 679
Inglis, Tom 220
Inisheer, Co Galway 442
Inishmaan, Co Galway 19
Inishnee, Co Galway 554

Inis Nua Theatre Company
    (Philadelphia) 605
International Association for the Study of
    Irish Literatures (IASIL) 673
International Commission of English in the
    Liturgy 333
Ionesco, Eugène 566
    The Bald Soprano 566
    The Chairs 566
    Rhinoceros 566
Iran 582
Ireland, David 378, 386
    Can't Forget About You 387–8
    Everything Between Us 384–5
Irigaray, Luce 679
Irish Academy of Letters 180, 602
Irish Actors Equity 402–3, 447
Irish-Americans 100, 181, 369, 598, 603
Irish American Theater Company
    (Cincinnati) 605
Irish and Classical Theatre (Pittsburgh) 605
Irish Ballet Company 393
Irish Citizens' Army 162, 186, 193
Irish Classical Theatre Company
    (Buffalo) 605
Irish Countrywomen's Association 680n.54
Irish Farmers Journal 93
Irish Ferries 229
Irish Festival Players 650
Irish Film Board 492
Irish Free State 165–6, 196, 210, 220, 270,
    279, 517–18, 571, 591
    and Abbey Theatre **169–82**
    and Irish-language theatre 254
    spectacle and pageantry 214–15
Irish Free State Army 176, 262, 263
Irish Guild Players 598
Irish Heritage Theatre (Philadelphia) 605
Irish Housewives' Association 680n.54
Irish identity, *see* national identity
Irish Independent 100–1, 224, 488
Irish International Advertising 487–8
Irish-language opera 264
Irish-language theatre 1–2, 65–7, 69–71, 158,
    171–2, 207, **251–68**, 398, 447–8, 465,
    644–5, 648, 655, 667
    Belfast 266–7

Dublin 254–62, 294; *see also* An Damer
    Galway 262–6; *see also* An Taibhdhearc
Irish-Language Theatre Company 255
Irish Legation (Paris) 562
Irish Literary Revival 38, 58 9, 69, 101, 130,
    169–70, 219, 432, 583, 625
    Irish-language theatre **251–4**
Irish Literary Supplement 491–2
Irish Literary Theatre (ILT) 2, 12, 38, 42–7,
    59, 63, 66, 69, 75, 108–9, 111, 124, 138–9,
    142, 202, 252–3, 361, 427–9, 547, 596, 606
    manifesto (1897) 1, 43, 56, 61, 73, 93, 108,
    460, 522n.9
    Ulster branch 59–60
Irish Museum of Modern Art (Dublin) 484
Irish National Dramatic Company 59, 63,
    147, 202
Irish National Theatre, *see* Abbey Theatre;
    Irish Literary Theatre; Irish National
    Theatre Society
Irish National Theatre Society 13, 42, 47–51,
    53, 56, 59–60, 63–5, 67, 109, 111, 113, 147,
    182, 389, 391, 429; *see also* Abbey Theatre
    acting 236–7, 239
Irish Parliamentary Party 30, 41–2, 58, 155
Irish Patriotic Children's Treat 214
Irish Peasant 93
'Irish play' **11–14**, 231, 688n.95
Irish Players 149, 593, 596
Irish Press 180, 224, 257, 297, 434
Irish Repertory Players 598
Irish Repertory Theatre (New York) 605
Irish Republic 176
    spectacle and pageantry 215–16
Irish Republican Army (IRA) 191,
    618–19, 669
Irish Republican Brotherhood (IRB) 68, 157,
    164, 257
Irish Research Council 404n.1
Irish School of Dance Art 290
Irish Society for Theatre Research
    (ISTR) 673
Irish State, and the theatre 192, 390–403; *see
    also* Abbey Theatre; Arts Council
Irish Theatre (Hardwicke Street, Dublin) 70,
    157, 161, 207, 654
Irish Theatre (New York) 181

Irish Theatre Company (ITC) 391, 393, 402–3, 462
Irish Theatre Institute 398, 402
Irish Theatre Magazine 686n.85
Irish Theatrical Diaspora (ITD) 615, 673
Irish Times 96–7, 115, 117, 175–6, 197, 205, 224, 227, 229, 259–60, 289, 294, 350, 406, 441, 460, 465, 480, 483–4, 486, 490, 638–9, 647, 650
Irish Volunteers 68, 155–7, 162
Irish Women's Liberation Movement 680
Irish Workers' Dramatic Club 189
Irisleabhar na Gaedhilge/The Gaelic Journal 251
Iron Curtain 582, 625, 632
Irving, Sir Henry 33, 72, 205, 232, 236
Isherwood, Christopher 289
Ishibashi, Hiro 84
Islam 506–8
Island (Limerick) 395
Island: Arts for Ireland Festival (Washington) 556
Issacharoff, Michael 689
Ito, Michio 81

Jackson, Barry 150
Jakobson, Roman 106
Jamaica 593
James, Henry 26
Japan 81; *see also* Noh theatre
Jarman, Derek 491
Jarry, Alfred
    Ubu Roi 49, 108
Jellett, Bay 209
Jenkinson, Biddy
    Mise, Subhó agus Maccó 266
    Ó Rajerum 266
Jenkinson, Rosemary 378, 386
    Basra Boy 605
Jerrold, Douglas
    Black Ey'd Susan 13n.15
Jessner, Leopold 136
Jesuits 645
Jews 507
Jew Suss 208
Joan of Arc 10
John, Augustus 129n.18

John F Kennedy Center (Washington), *see* Kennedy Center for the Performing Arts
Johns, Jasper 484
Johnson, Josephine 75
Johnson, Richard
    The Evidence I Shall Give 646, 648
Johnson, Thomas 177
Johnston, Anna 59
Johnston, Denis 128–9, 131–3, 137, 150–1, 208, 211, 222, 284, 348, 599
    Blind Man's Buff 131
    A Bride for the Unicorn 131, 133, 135, 211
    The Dreaming Dust 131
    The Golden Cuckoo 131, 289
    The Moon in the Yellow River 131, 151
    The Old Lady Says No! 131–2, *132*, 133, 135, *135*, 210, 256, 337, 644
    The Scythe and the Sunset 131, 150–1, 167
    Storm Song 131
    Strange Occurrence on Ireland's Eye 131
Johnston, Jennifer 627, 679
Joint Committee of Women's Societies and Social Workers 680n.54
Joint Stock (UK) 399
Jones, Margo 600
Jones, Marie 4, 377–8, 519, **549–53**, 605, 627, 679; *see also* Charabanc Theatre Company
    The Hamster Wheel 552
    A Night in November 519, 552–3
    Stones in His Pockets 520, 553, 613
    Women on the Verge of HRT 520, 552
Jones, Robert Edmond 134
Jordan, Eamonn 507, 530, 535, 539, 542–3, 675
Jordan, Neil 492–3
Jordan, Wayne 458
Joyce, James 9–10, 88, 102, 183, 191, 198, 318, 322, 348, 591, 641, 645, 657, 663
    Dubliners 197, 663; 'Ivy Day in the Committee Room' 211; 'The Dead' 428
    Finnegans Wake 102, 197, 211
    A Portrait of the Artist as a Young Man 339, 445, 523, 646
    Stephen Hero 339, 646
    Ulysses 132–3, 164, 429, 618, 644
Joyce, Stanislaus 184

Junction Festival (Clonmel) 568n.12
Jung, Carl 133
Juno and the Paycock (film) 240–1, 244
Juries Bill 1927 680n.51

Kabosh Theatre Company (Belfast) 386, 457
Kaiser, Georg
    From Morn to Midnight 129
Kaiser, Matthew 14–15
Kalb, Jonathan 418
Kane, Aidan 287
Kane, Michael 392
Kane, Sarah
    Blasted 540
Kantor, Tadeusz 444
Kaut-Howson, Helena 397
Kavanagh, John 453
Kavanagh, Patrick 293, 641
    The Great Hunger 450
    Tarry Flynn 457, 469
Keane, Barry 626
Keane, John B. 3, 56, 287, 307, **313–17**, 321,
    338, 533, 666
    Big Maggie 314, 316
    The Chastitute 314, 316
    The Field 308, 314–15, 317
    The Highest House on the Mountain 646
    Hut 42 314
    Many Young Men of Twenty 524n.15
    No More in Dust 646
    Sharon's Grave 314
    Sive 313, 315, 339
Keane, Raymond 566, 568, 689
Kearney, Colbert 188
Kearney, Richard 368
Kearns, Kevin C. 187–8
Keating, Ruth 277
Keating, Sara 536, 689
Keating, Sean 212
Keegan, Gary 570, 571
Keegan Theatre Company 605
Keel, Co Mayo 434
Keenan, Brian
    An Evil Cradling 504n.33
Kelly, George 602
    Philip Goes Forth 602
    The Torch-Bearers 596, 602

Kelly, John 75, 392
Kelly, Seamus 289, 348, 460, 465
Kennedy, Brian 393
Kennedy Center for the Performing Arts
    (Washington DC) 419, 556, 607
Kennedy, Douglas 480
Kennedy, Jackie 225
Kennedy, John F. 332, 411
Kennedy, Marie 287
Kennelly, Brendan
    Antigone 667n.33
Kenner, Hugh 581, 583
Kenny, Sorcha *572*
Kent, Nicholas 613
Kent (England) 522
Keogan, Paul 562
Keogh, Garrett 469, 470
Keogh, J. Augustus 145, 598–9
Keohler, Thomas 64
Kerrigan, J. M. 238–9, 241, 245
'Kerry Babies' case 664n.28
Kerry, county 96n.39, 646
Kettle, Thomas 64
Kiberd, Declan 26n.9, 33, 156, 160, 192, 260,
    368, 685
Kiernan, Pat 540
Kilburn (London) 613, 622
Kilkenny 395, 565
Kilkenny Arts Festival 649
Killeedy, Co Limerick 310
Kilroy, Thomas 3–5, 287, 301, 357, 371, 374,
    454, 652, 655, 677
    adaptations 662–4
    and the idea of a theatre **337–
        53**; 'Groundwork for an Irish
        Theatre' 338–9
    Christ Deliver Us! 526, 528, 664
    *The Death and Resurrection of Mr
        Roche* 340, **341–5**, 346–7, 445–6,
        562n.5, 648, 664
    Double Cross 370, 453, 664
    *The Madame MacAdam Travelling Theatre
        Company* 371, 664
    The O'Neill **339–41**
    The Seagull (adaptation) 657, 662–4, *663*
    The Secret Fall of Constance Wilde 455,
        526, 649, 651, 664

Talbot's Box 317, **348–53**, *349*, 451, 526
Tea and Sex and Shakespeare **345–8**, *346*
Kiltartan, Co Galway 59
Kinahan, Deirdre 679
King, Adele ('Twink') 490
Kirby, Peadar 685
Kirkland, Richard 685
Kiss of the Spider Woman (film) 505
Knebel, Maria 464, 648
Knowles, Ric 426
Knowlson, James 583
Kontakt festival (Poland) 635
Koran 505–8
Kosok, Heinz 184–5
Krause, David 192
Kristeva, Julia 679
Kurdi, Mária 625, 635, 674–5, 679, 681
Kuti, Elizabeth 515, 679
  The Sugar Wife 518

LAB (Dublin City Council arts office) 572
Labour movement 111, 148, 162, 185–6, 193
Labour Party (Britain) 226, 432
Labour Party (Ireland) 398
Lacan, Jacques 682
Lachman, Michał 635
Laffan, Kevin
  It's a Two-Foot-Six-Inches-Above-the-Ground World 405
Laffan, Pat 480
Laird, Helen, *see* Lavelle, Honor
Lally, Mick 405, 442, 456, 474
Lambert, J. W. 343
Lambert, Mark 553
Lambeth Council (London) 611
Lancashire school 106
Land Act1903 (Wyndham Act) 53, 91, 112, 142
Land Commission 317
Lang, Jack 483n.16
Langtry, Lily 225
Lanternscope 299, 302
Lantern Theatre Club (Dublin) 287, 289, 291, **299**, 302
Lappin, Arthur 396, 403
Larkin, Delia 189
Larkin, James 184–7, 193, 196

Laura Keene Theatre (New York) 11
Lavelle, Honor (Helen Laird) 64, 68, 203, 239
Laverty, Maura 281, 284–5
  Lift Up Your Gates/Liffey Lane 284–5
Laville, Pierre 628
Lawrence, W. J. 205
Leach, Robert 619
Leader 115, 293
Lebanon 502, 504, 508
Le Brocquy, Louis 206, 484, 492
Lecoq, Jacques 568–9
Le Corbusier 435
Lee, Bruce 539
Lee, Joe 685
Lee, Laurie 185
Leeney, Cathy 539–40, 675, 678–80, 689
Lees, Georgie Hyde (George Yeats) 83
Lefebvre, Henri 683n.69, 689
Le Gallienne, Eva 212–13, 246, 277–8, 600
Le Gallienne, Richard 31
Legion of Mary 571
Lehmann, Hans-Thiess 563
Leigh, Vivien 240
Lemaître, Jules 430
Lemass, Seán 286
Leningrad 634
Lennon, Peter 261
Lenormand, Henri-René 127
Lentin, Louis 650
Leonard, Hugh 3, 307, **317–21**, 338, 454, 631, 646, 677
  The Big Birthday (Nightingale in the Branches) 317
  Da 318, 320
  Home Before Night 317
  The Italian Road 317
  A Life 318–19, 320, 463
  Out After Dark 317
  The Patrick Pearse Motel 168, 316
  Stephen D 339, 341, 445–6, 646
Lepage, Robert 444, 649, 652
Letterkenny, Co Donegal 251
Leventhal, A. J. 586
Lever, Nora 291, 302
Levinas, Emmanuel 497
Levitas, Ben 113, 117, 157, 610, 614, 675
Lewisholm, Alice 430

Lewis, Sinclair 594, 596
  Ann Vickers 596
  Main Street 593–4, 596
Liberty Hall (Dublin) 189, 194
Life magazine 466
Limerick 395
Lincoln Center (New York) 492
Lincoln Center Festival (New York) 419, 651
Lindon, Jérôme 581
Linehan, Fergus 299
Linehan, Rosaleen *50*, 493
Lir Academy 477
Lir: Studio One Theatre (Dublin) 571, 574
Lisdoonvarna, Co Galway 407
Lissadell, Co Sligo 274
Listowel, Co Kerry 313, 405
Little, Patrick 391
Little Red Kettle (Waterford) 395
little theatres 1–3, 44, 136–7, 208, 281,
    286–303
  in America. *see under* United States
Little Theatre Society (Cork) 290
Littlewood, Joan 259–60, 338, 445, 633
Liverpool 149, 160, 261, 609,
    615–19, 622
Liverpool City Council 616
Liverpool Repertory Theatre 149
Living Age 98
Llewellyn-Jones, Margaret 675
Lloyd, David 685, 688, 692
Loane, Tim 378–80
  To Be Sure 379
  Caught Red Handed 379
Local Government (Ireland) Act 1898 52
Lojek, Helen Heusner 675, 681, 689
London 5, 10, 44, 72–3, 75, 82, 92, 98, 107–8,
    139, 142, 149, 206, 218–19, 221, 225,
    231, 236, 244, 263, 277, 279, 282, 292–3,
    396, 430, 449, 529, 531, 540, 542, 553,
    593, 595
  club theatres 288
  Irish drama in 11–12, 26, 74, 96n.38,
    116, 129, 138, 143, 198, 202, 204, 240,
    283n.55, 322, 338, 349, 406n.11, 454, 460,
    462, 465–6, 468–9, 535, 538, 606–15,
    609–15, 622, 624, 626–7, 647, 662, 688;
  see also individual London theatres;

  awards 656; Beckett 490, 492, 581–2;
    McGuinness 504, 508–9, 660, *661*;
    Murphy 407–8, 411, *413*, 414, 416–19;
    Wilde 24, 26, 30, 33, 42–3
  O'Casey in 128, 194–5
  Olympic Games (2012) 622
London 2012 Cultural Olympiad 419
London Assembly 609
London Library 121
Lonergan, Patrick 530, 534, 537–8, 595, 615,
    675, 688–9
Longford, Christine 547, 679
Longford, Lord 291, 298, 445
Longford Productions 393
Long Wharf Theatre (New Haven) 600
Loomba, Ania 684–5
Loose Canon 457–8
Lopokova, Lydia 278
Lorca, Federico García 121, 445
  Yerma 448
Los Angeles 600
Louisville (USA) 601
Louro, Filomena 635
Lovett, Ann 664n.27
Lovett, Louis 567
Lowe, Louise 557, 572, 650, 679
Loyalism 668, 684
Luckhurst, Mary 532
Ludwigshafen 635
Lugné-Poe, Aurélien 45, 47, 108, 559
Luxembourg 634
Lyceum Theatre (London) 33
Lyceum Theatre (New York) 225
Lynch, David 628
Lynch, Martin 373, 378, 551
  Chronicles of Long Kesh 381
  *History of the Troubles (Accordin' to my
    Da)* 381
  Lay Up Your Ends (with
    Charabanc) 377–8, 551–2
Lyotard, Jean-Francois 563
Lyric Theatre (Belfast) 281, 287–9, **299–300**,
    302, 374, 387, 437–9, *438*, 441, 446–7,
    449, 553, 650
Lyric Theatre Company (Dublin) 288–90,
    296, 299, 301, 446
Lyttleton Theatre (London) 611, *612*

McAleavey, Jimmy 378
McAleese, Mary 228, 549
McAlpine (Sir Alfred) and Sons
    (Belfast) 439
McAnally, Ray 459
Mac Anna, Tomás 3, 130n.20, 212–13, 257,
    260, 340, 439, 446–9, 452–3, 644, 648
Macardle, Dorothy 547, 679, 680
    Ann Kavanagh 280
    The Old Man 280
    Witch's Brew 280
McAuley, Gay 679, 689
McAuley, Maureen 377
MacBride, John 50, 83
McBrinn, Roisin 548
McCabe, Eugene 648
    The King of the Castle 260, 647
McCafferty, Owen 373, 378, 382
    The Absence of Women 386
    Antigone (adaptation) 375–6
    Closing Time 611
    Courtroom No. 1 380
    Quietly 385–6
    Scenes from the Big Picture 382, 386, 611
McCann, Donal 3, 346, 347, 452–3, 459,
    471–2, 476–7, 482, 577
    acting career **469–73**
McCann, John 469
    Put a Beggar on Horseback 469n.39
McCarter Theater (Princeton) 556
McCarthy, John 504n.33
McCarthy, Neil 650
McCarthy, Sean 480
McCarthy, Seán
    Bullaí Mhártain (adaptation) 261–2
McCauley, Maureen 550
McClelland, Alan 644
McColgan, John 607–8, 615
Mac Con Iomaire, Darach 264
McCormack, John 215
McCormick, F. J. 2, 22, 166n.37, 173, 188–9,
    239, 241, 243, 243, 244–5, 425, 459, 462,
    464, 470, 477, 640
McCullough-Mulvin (architects) 439–41
Mac Curtain, Margaret 460n.2, 468
McDaniel, James 504
McDiarmid, Lucy 273

MacDonagh, Donagh 301
    Happy as Larry 289, 296, 299
McDonagh, Martin 1, 4–5, 396, 418, 457, 530,
    531–4, 535, 538, 542–4, 553, 594, 604–5,
    611, 613, 624, 627–8, 630, 656, 686, 688
    The Beauty Queen of Leenane 418, 457,
        475, 531–3
    A Behanding in Spokane 531
    The Cripple of Inishmaan 531, 533–4, 612
    Hangman 531
    In Bruges (film) 534
    Leenane Trilogy 395, 396, 418, 533
    The Lieutenant of Inishmore 531–4
    The Lonesome West 531, 631
    The Pillowman 531, 611, 628
    Seven Psychopaths (film) 534
    A Skull in Connemara 531, 533
MacDonagh, Thomas 68, 156, 163–6,
    168, 654
    Literature in Ireland 163
    Metempsychosis 68
    When the Dawn is Come 163–5
McDonald, Chris 291
McDonald, Frank 441
McDonald, Rónán 372, 481
McElhinney, Ian 553
McElligott, J. J. 180
McElroen, Christopher 589
McElveen, Gwynne 565
MacEntee, Seán 638
McEvoy, Mary 414
McFeely, Deirdre 11
McFetridge, Paula 679
McGahern, John
    The Power of Darkness (after
        Tolstoy) 657
McGarry, Fearghal 155
McGarry, Patsy 257
McGinley, Sean 604
Mac Góráin, Roibeárd 259
McGovern, Barry 491–2, 491
    I'll Go On 481, 484
Macgowan, Kenneth 134
MacGowran, Jack 465
McGrath, Aoife 289, 681
McGrath, John 42
MacGreevy, Thomas 583

McGuinness, Frank 4, 371, 401, 454, 458,
    497–514, 527, 655–6, 677, 681, 684, 691
  Ibsen adaptations 657, **660–2**, 665
  Barbaric Comedies (adaptation) 651
  Carthaginians 378, 451, 497, **501–4**,
    502, 504–5
  The Caucasian Chalk Circle
    (adaptation) 662
  A Doll's House (adaptation) 660–1, *661*
  Dolly West's Kitchen 454n.45, 498, 504, 511,
    513, 527–8
  The Factory Girls 417, 454n.45, 498–9, 505
  Gates of Gold 454n.45, 497, **512–14**
  Greta Garbo Came to Donegal 610
  The Hanging Gardens 454n.45, 513
  John Gabriel Borkman (adaptation) 662
  Mutabilitie 497, **508–11**, 514
  *Observe the Sons of Ulster Marching
    Towards the Somme* 84, 454n.45, 455,
    497, **499–501**, 501–2, 504–5, 507, 510,
    512, 631, 683–4
  Oedipus Rex 611–12
  Peer Gynt (adaptation) 657, 662
  Phaedra (adaptation) 611
  Someone Who'll Watch Over Me 497 8,
    504–8, 510, 527
  There Came a Gypsy Riding 513
McGuinness, Norah 206, 277
Mac Intyre, Tom 450, 454, 458, 515,
    604, 677
  Caoineadh Airt Uí Laoghaire
    (adaptation) 258–9
  Cúirt an Mheán Oíche
    (adaptation) 258–60
  The Great Hunger 548, 603–4
  What Happened Bridgie Cleary 517–18
McIvor, Charlotte 689
McKenna, Siobhán 3, 257n.41, 293, 409n.20,
    413–14, 459, 462, *467*, 469, 473, *474*,
    476–7, 650, 679
  acting career **464–8**
  Here are Ladies 466
  San Siobhán (translation of Shaw, *Saint
    Joan*) 263, 465
McKenna, T. P. 245, 459
Macken, Walter 14, 22n.50, 263
  Home is the Hero 21–3, 548

McKeown, Laurence 378
  A Cold House (with Brian Campbell) 385
  The Official Version 381
Mackintosh, Iain 427, 430, 439
Macklin, Charles 519
McLaughlin, Mark *589*
Mac Liammóir, Micheál *132*, **207**, 209, 215,
    218, **218–19**, 220, 222–7, 230, 432, 462,
    512, 639, 641, 647
  collaboration with Edwards/Gate Theatre.
    see Gate Theatre (Dublin)
  and Irish-language theatre 245, 254,
    262–3, 266
  All for Hecuba (memoir) 223
  An Oscar of No Importance (memoir) 220,
    222, 226
  Diarmuid and Grainne 207, 223,
    262–3, 266
  I Must Be Talking to my Friends 223
  Prelude in Kazbek Street 226
  Prunella 262
  Put Money in Thy Purse 211
  Theatre in Ireland 223
  W. B. Yeats and his World (with Eavan
    Boland) 223
McMahon, Frank 449
McMaster, Anew 207, 219, 245–7
Mac Mathúna, Seán
  Hulla Hul (Duilleoga Tae) 264
  *The Winter Thief / Gadaí Géar na Geamh
    Oíche* 257, 259
McMullan, Anna 679, 689
MacNamara, Brinsley
  Look at the Heffernans 177
MacNamara, Gerald (Harry Morrow) 94
  The Mist that Does be on the Bog 62, 94
  Thompson in Tir-na-nOg 62
McNamara, Robert 605
Macnas 395, 649
MacNeill, Eoin 59, 64, 171
McNulty, Edward
  The Lord Mayor 147
McNulty, Eugene 675
McPherson, Conor 4, 458, 519–20, 530,
    535–8, 539, 544, 553, 594, 611, 627, 650,
    656, 681
  The Birds 535

Come on Over 535
The Dance of Death 611
Dublin Carol 535, 537, 611
The Good Thief 535
The Night Alive 535, 605–6, 611
Port Authority 535–7
The Seafarer 535, 537–8, 605, 611
Shining City 535, 537, 611
St Nicholas 535–6, 538, 611, 613
This Lime Tree Bower 535–6, 613
The Veil 535, 611
The Weir 520–1, 522, 528, 535, 605, 611,
    676, 686n.86
McQuaid, John Charles 296, 325, 644–5
McSharry, Deirdre 293
McSwiney, Paul
    An Bord'gus an Fó 251
MacSwiney, Terence 687
McTeer, Janet 660–1, *661*
MAC Theatre (Belfast) 387–8
McWilliams, Monica 377
Madrid 627
Maeterlinck, Maurice 44–5, 12–2, 124, 275
    Pelléas et Mélisande 47
    The Treasure of the Humble 44
Magdalene laundries 526, 554, 571–3, 680
Magee, Lisa 386
Magee, W. K. ('John Eglinton') 44–5
Magennis, William 180–1
Maguire, Tom 675
Mahon, Derek 27, 362
    High Time (after Molière) 655n.4
    A School for Wives (after Molière) 655n.4
Mair, George 241
Malone, Irina Ruppo 675
Malta 634
Malvern Festival 150
Mamet, David 492, 594, 603, 656
Manahan, Anna 291–2, *295*, 297, 302, 396
Manchester 452, 524, 597
Manchester Courier 240
Manchester Guardian 96, 262
Manchester University 454
Mandala Theatre Company 564
Mandela, Nelson 669
Manet, Édouard 582
Mangan, Jo 548

Manning, Mary 2, 210–11, 280–1, 284, 347,
    547, 679, 680
    Youth's the Season? 280–1
Mannion, Elizabeth 191
Man of Aran (film) 533–4
Manzay, J. Kyle 589, *589*
Marber, Patrick
    Closer 629
Markievicz, Constance 68, 270, 272,
    274, 547
Mark Taper Forum (Los Angeles) 600
Marlowe, Christopher
    Doctor Faustus 124, 133
Marshall, Frank 17
Marston, Nick 612–13
Martin, Augustine 81
Martínez Sierra, Gregorio 263
Martyn, Edward 13, 38, 43, 54, 64, 66, 70,
    93, 108, 110, 124, 202, 207, 253–4, 569,
    654, 676
    The Heather Field 45, 108, 139
    Maeve 67, 111
    The Tale of a Town 111
Marxism 130, 538, 678, 683n.69
Marx, Karl 35
Mary Wigman School (Dresden) 290
Mason, Patrick 3, 348, 350–1, 397, 400, 402,
    439, 450–1, 454–5, 460n.2, 463, 480,
    634–5, 651
Massey, Doreen 689
Massine, Léonide 278–9
Mathews, Aidan Carl 669
    The Antigone (adaptation) 657, 669
    The Diamond Body 562
Mathews, P. J. 108, 675
Mathew, Fr Theobald 595
Matthews and Lane (publishers) 27
Matthews, Brander 597, 605
Maxwell, D. E. S. 196, 313, 674
Mayall, Rik 491
May, Ena 679
Mayer, Sandra 635
Mayne, Rutherford 62, 598–9
    The Drone 596
    The Turn of the Road 114
Maynooth University 404n.
Mays, J. C. C. 481

Maze/Long Kesh prison (Northern Ireland) 381, 385
Mazhar, Amal Aly 506–8
Mechanics' Institute (Dublin) 51–2, 429–30, 687
Meehan, Felix 287
Meehan, Paula
   Cell 399
   The Wolf of Winter 548
Melbourne 492
Meldon, Maurice 292, 301
   Aisling 256, 292
Melfi, Leonard
   Birdbath 405
melodrama 1, **9–23**, 41, 48, 110, 113, 123, 131, 140, 146, 150, 189, 241, 316, 460, 533, 607, 687
Memorial Theatre (Stratford-upon-Avon) 638
memory plays 4, 379, 426, 441, **515–18**, 555
Mercier, Paul
   Setanta 259, 265, *265*
Mercier, Vivian 674
Mercury Theatre (London) 462
Meridian (Cork) 395, 401
Merriman, Brian
   Cúirt an Mheán Oíche 644–5, 648
Merriman, Victor 614, 675, 685–6
Methven, Eleanor 377, 550
Metropole Theatre (Glasgow) 19n.43
Meyerfield, Max 624, 627
Meyerhold, Vsevolod Emilevich 453
Meyer, Mary K. 383
Miami Beach (Florida) 581
Michelangelo 17
Middleton, Colin 447
Mies van der Rohe, Ludwig 435
Millar, Séan
   Song Cycle 570
Miller, Arthur 445, 603
Miller, Jonathan 485
Miller, Josephine 292
Miller, Liam 292
Miller, Sam 378
Milligan, Alice 59–61, 68, 270, 547, 679
   The Last Feast of the Fianna 59, 67, 111, 271
Milling, Jane 561, 574

Milltown, Co Galway 407
Minghella, Anthony 492–3
Minneapolis 418, 600, 647, 657; *see also* Guthrie Theater
Mitchell, Gary 373, 378 80
   Demented 379
   The Force of Change 611
   Loyal Women 611
   Re-Energise 379
   Tearing the Loom 379
   Trust 611
Mitchell, Ian Priestley 263
Mitchell, Katie 649
Mitchell, Tom 484
Mnouchkine, Ariane 449, 568–9
modernism 2, 13, 44, 54–6, 89–90, 102, **121–37**, 139, 246, 260, 288, 428–30, 432–3, 435, 439, 441, 579, 581–4, 589–91
   definition 121–2
   experimental theatre in Dublin 127–8
   performance 134–5
   playwrights: Johnston131–3; O'Casey 128–31; Yeats 124–7
Moffett, Noel 433–5
Moinaux, Jules: *Les deux sourds* 70
Moiseiwitsch, Tanya 2, *119*, 124n.5, 211–12, *212*, 277
Molesworth Hall (Dublin) 66, 428–9
Molière, Jean-Baptiste Poquelin 263, 655n.4
   Le Malade imaginaire 643
   Le Médecin malgré lui 654
   Les Précieuses ridicules 233
   Tartuffe 47
Molloy, John *349*, 350
Molloy, M. J. 3, 307, **308–13**, 314, 321, 323
   The King of Friday's Men 308–10, 313
   Old Road 308
   The Paddy Pedlar 309–11, 313
   Petticoat Loose 309n.3
   The Visiting House 308
   The Wood of the Whispering 309–14, 400, 406–8
   The Wooing of Duvessa 647
Molnár, Ferenc 127
Moloney, Alan 492

Monk, Meredith 456
monologue drama 316, 334, 382, 470, 499,
    520–3, 536–7, 539, 611
Montague, C. E. 236
Monte Carlo 221
Montgomery, James 174
Montgomery, Niall 647
Monto district (Dublin) 571
Moody, Alys 590
Mooney, Ria 2, 212, 246, 277–8, 281, 283n.55,
    448, 462, 599–600, 644, 679
Moonfish 264
Moore, George 38, 66, 69, 91n.15, 108, 110,
    202, 232, 235–6, 239
  and Irish realism 110–11
  The Bending of the Bough 111
  Diarmuid and Grania (with Yeats) 428
  The Strike at Arlingford 111
Moore Institute 404n.1
Moore, Julianne 492
Moore, Meriel *132*
Moore, Thomas 522–3
Moore, T. Sturge 202
Moran, D. P. 108, 167n.41
Moran, James 185, 389
Morash, Christopher 293–4, 317–18,
    401–2, 453, 481–2, 499, 512, 532, 654,
    674, 687, 689
Morell, Jill 504n.33
Morgan, Sydney 239
Morrison, Bill
  Flying Blind 374
Morrison, Conall 229, 457
Morrison, Danny 378
Morrison, Toni
  Beloved 510–11
Morrissey, Eamon 659
Morrow, Harry, *see* MacNamara, Gerald
Morse, Donald 689
Mortimer, Mark 101
Moscow 634
Moscow Art Theatre 73, 209, 600, 648
Moss, Chloë
  The Way Home 616–18
Mossop, Henry 231
Motley 210–11, 432
Motley, Sophie 573

Mouth on Fire 262, 268
Moxley, Gina 679
Moynihan, Áine 266n.90
Mozart, Wolfgang Amadeus 263, 638
Mucha, Jirí 633
Mullan, Eilis 401
Mullen, Marie 3–4, 246, 405, 414, 416, 456,
    459, 460n.2, 468, *474, 476,* 666–7, 679
  acting career **473–7**
Mumford, Lewis 183, 187, 197–8
Münchner Kammerspiele (Munich) 629
Munich 44, 629, 633
Municipal Gallery (Dublin) 101, 638
municipal politics 111–12, 147
Municipal Theatre (Ulm) 632–3
Murfi, Mikel 418, 457–8, 567
Murphy, Brenda 378
Murphy, Cillian 541, 650
Murphy, Elaine 557, 650, 679
Murphy, Jack 323–4
Murphy, Jimmy
  *The Kings of the Kilburn High
    Road* 329, 613
Murphy, Johnny 491–2
Murphy, Fr Mick 290
Murphy, Mike 545–6
Murphy, Pat 667n.33
Murphy, Paul 675, 682–3
Murphy, Tom 3–5, 119, 287, 313, 320, 322–4,
    338, 404–5, 454, 456, 460n.2, 467–8, 485,
    515, 522–5, 542–3, 565, 569, 627–8, 655,
    677, 681
  Abbey Festival (2001) 650
  adaptations 666–7
  and Druid Theatre Company **407–21**
  Alice Trilogy 418, 521, 611
  Bailegangaire 404, 410–12, *412–14,* 415–19,
    452, 456, 466–8, 473–4, *474,* 475, 517,
    523, 543
  The Blue Macushla 408, 418, 469
  Brigit 404n.5
  The Cherry Orchard (adaptation) 666
  The Contest (retitled *A Thief of a
    Christmas*) 404–5n.5
  Conversations on a Homecoming 323–4,
    332, 404, 406n.11, 409, 411, 417–9, 452,
    456, 523, 543, 627, 686n.86

Murphy, Tom (*cont.*)
  A Crucial Week in the Life of a Grocer's
    Assistant 322, 324, 330–2, 339, 408,
    523, 656
  Famine 268, 322, 404, 408–10, 417, 419–21,
    421, 449, 648
  The Fooleen (A Crucial Week in the Life of a
    Grocer's Assistant) 339
  The Gigli Concert 408, 418, 427, 537
  The House 324, 523–4, 528, 666
  The Iron Men (A Whistle in the
    Dark) 338–9, 407–8
  The J. Arthur Maginnis Story 408
  The Last Days of a Reluctant Tyrant 666–7
  The Morning After Optimism 331, 333, 408
  On the Outside 327–9, 407, 409, 415, 417
  The Sanctuary Lamp 317, 333–6, 408, 449–
    50, *450*, 648–9, 656
  She Stoops to Folly (adaptation) 418
  The Wake 523, 651
  A Whistle in the Dark 322, 324, 329–30,
    339, 404, 407–8, 416–17, 419, 449, 523,
    542, 686n.86
  The White House 332, 404n.5
Murray, Christopher 344, 358, 374, 482, 530,
    541, 600, 674, 677–8, 682–3, 688
Murray, Rupert 485
Murray, T. C. 56, 106
  Autumn Fire 177
  Birthright 117, 203
Mušek, Karel 624
Museum of Irish Art (New York) 181
Museum of Modern Art (New York) 589
Mussolini, Benito 174
Mutura, Mustapha
  The Playboy of the West Indies 613

Na Cluicheoirí 252–4
Na Fánaithe 261–2, 264–5, 268
Na hAisteoirí **70–1**, 253–4
Nandy, Ashis 685
Nation 177
National Association of Youth Drama
    (NAYD) 393, 401, 538
National College of Art and Design
    (Dublin) 449
National Council of Women 680n.54

National Folk Theatre (Tralee) 394
national identity 49, 56, 101, 178, 220, 271,
    281, 300, 313, 497–8, 503, 511, 535,
    536, 544
  in Irish theatre internationally 603–5, 613,
    616–19, 621–2, 670
nationalism 15, 18, 22, 27, 42–3, 46–9, 55,
    62, 64, 68, 89, 94, 101, 108, 128, 142, 144,
    148, 159–60, 163, 185, 187, 193, 217, 253,
    257, 300, 307–8, 338, 342, 368, 400, 497,
    614, 625; *see also* Irish Parliamentary
    Party; Irish Volunteers
  core values 109
  political and military activism 58–9, 71,
    155–7, 162
  women and 270, 272–4
nationalist drama 15, 17–18, 50, 54, 56, 59,
    156–67, 210, 213–14, 300; *see also* Irish-
    language theatre
  dramatic societies 71
  melodrama 12, 15, 20–3
National Library of Ireland
    (Dublin) 357–8, 429
National Lottery 489
National Maternity Hospital (Dublin) 555
National Musical Hall (Dublin) 51
National Players 50
National Student 117
National Theatre (Ireland), *see* Abbey
    Theatre; Irish National Theatre Society
National Theatre (London) 359, 478, 534,
    610–13, 622, 688
National Theatre Archive 398
National Theatre Society Ltd 64, 180
National Touring Agency 402
nautical melodrama 10, 13n.15
Navan, Co Meath 93n.27, 442
Nazi Germany 638–9
Neeson, Liam 459, 493
Negra, Diane 689n.101
Neighbourhood Playhouse
    (New York) 430, 596
Newgrange, Co Meath 442
Newman Society (Queen's University
    Belfast) 300
New Orleans 585, 588–91, 592
New Players 128, 207

New Theatre Group (Dublin) 288–9, 300, 444, 446
New York 10–12, 21, 25, 29, 181, 198, 213, 225, 231, 246, 277, 283n.55, 341–2, 344–5, 368, 409, 418–19, 430, 456, 466, 471, 492, 519, 582, 588–9, 593, 595–8, 600, 602, 606, 608, 611, 615, 651, 688
    Broadway 449, 452, 454, 475, 581, 602, 607, 615, 648, 656, 662
New York Herald 25n.4
New York Society for the Preservation of the Irish Language 251
New York Times 25n.4, 29, 589, 598–9, 603–4, 608
Niblock, Robert 'Beano' 378, 381
    A Reason to Believe 381
Ní Chinnéide, Mairéad 253n.11
Nic Shiubhlaigh, Máire (Mary Walker) 49, 51, 64, 66n.34, 67–8, 71, 201, 203, 206, 233, 253–4
Ní Dhiscín, Brighid 70
Ní Dhiscín, Máire 70
Ní Dhomhnaill, Nuala 258
    Jimín (adaptation) 261
Ní Dhuibhne, Éilís 679
    Milseog an tSamhraidh 262
Nietzsche, Friedrich 32, 36–7, 50
Ní Ghráda, Mairéad 281, 547, 679
    An Triail 260–1, 263, 398, 448, 647–8
    Breithiúnas 258n.50, 260
Nijinsky, Vaslav 246, 279
Ní Mhurchadha, Eilís
    Beart Nótaí (with M. Ní Shíthe) 70
Ní Neachtain, Bríd *516*
Ní Neill, Nuala: *The Fadgies* 266
Ní Shíthe, Máire
    Beart Nótaí (with E. Ní Mhurchadha) 70
Nobel Prize 482, 484, 577
Nochlin, Linda 106
Noel Coward Theatre (London) 608, 612
Noel Pearson Productions 396
Noh theatre (Japan) 54, 81–4, 121, 124–5, 124n.9, 204
Nolan, Jim 395, 401
    The Salvage Shop 525
Nolan, Melissa 262
Nolan, Patrick 289, *295*

Nolan, Thomas 175
Nora, Pierre 425
Norris, David 441, 512
Northern Ireland 300, 357, 359, 364, 406, 497, 499, 504, 507, 510, 519–20, 527, 551, 611, 628, 649, 655, 657, 675, 677
    peace process 378–80, 388, 505, 520, 528, 534, 669
    sectarian divide 149, 359, 498, 499, 507
    theatre in **372–88**; *see also* Belfast; Derry; community theatre 374–5377–8; post-conflict theatre 375, 378–88; 'Troubles play' **372–7**; women and 377–8, 382–4
    Troubles 3, 333, 362–3, 366, 372, 380–2, 387, 447, 497, 501–3, 508–9, 511, 534, 552, 619, 621, 660, 667, 668–70, 683, 690, 692
Northern Ireland Women's Coalition 377
Norton, Elliot 466
Norton-Taylor, Richard
    Bloody Sunday: Scenes from the Saville Enquiry 610
Norton, W. W. 368
Norwegian National Theatre 109
Nowlan, David 650
NUI Galway 404n., 413, 421
Nunnery, Lizzie 618–19
    Intemperance 618–19

Ó Baoill, Niall 398, 402
Ó Beirn, Séamus 263
O'Briain, Art 562
O Briain, Colm 392–3, 403, 446, 490
Ó Briain, Liam 257n.41, 263
Ó Briain, Noel 261
O'Briain, Ruth 456
O'Brien, Conor Cruise 669
O'Brien, Edna 393, 679
O'Brien, Eugene 519
    Eden 520, 528
O'Brien, Flann 348, 641
O'Brien, George 172–3, 175, 179
O'Brien, James 163
O'Brien, Kate 150
O'Brien, Michael 287
O'Brien, Victoria 279
Ó Broin, Seán
    Daoine ar an Dart 261

Observer 98, 580, 614

Ó Cadhain, Máirtín
  Cré na Cille (adaptation by M. Ó
    Fátharta) 258–9, 264
Ó Cairealláin, Gearóid
  In Ainm an Rí 266
  The Wheelchair Monologues 266–7, *267*
O'Casey, Eileen 151
O'Casey, Isaac 10n.6
O'Casey, Seán 2, 5, 10–11, 13–14, 20–2, 62,
    115, 128, 132, 137, 141, 148–9, 151, 157,
    162–3, 204, 244, 253n.11, 318, 334, 338,
    376, 389, 429, 431, 444, 446, 452, 583,
    586, 600, 604, 626–7, 628, 645–6, 663,
    677, 681, 683
  and Dublin **183–98**; Dublin trilogy 118,
    157, **165–8**, 184–5, *186*, 187, 448, 683;
    language and politics 188–94
  as Modernist playwright 128–31, 134
  in Europe 631–2
  Bedtime Story 195
  Behind the Green Curtains 191
  Cock-a-Doodle Dandy 448–9, 627, 631–2
  The Cooing of Doves 193
  The Drums of Father Ned 644
  Hall of Healing 195
  The Harvest Festival 184–90, 196–7
  Juno and the Paycock 20–2, 128, 166, 177,
    179, 181, 184, 190–2, 194–5, 237, 242,
    242, 243, *243*, 445, 452–3, 470–1, *472*,
    477, 490, 504, 598, 618, 644, 649
  Oak Leaves and Lavender 632
  The Plough and the Stars 20, 128–9, 150,
    163, 166–7, **172–7**, 181–2, 184, 187, **192–
    4**, 195, 197, 206–7, 212–13, 244, 254,
    278, 317, 458, 464, 640, 663; Abbey riots
    (1926) 57, 89, 166, 174–6, 192, 206, 431,
    687; Hynes's production (1991) 452, 456–
    7; Paris (1955) 634
  Purple Dust 21, 448–9
  Red Roses for Me 184–5, 187, 196–8, 447,
    627, 632; poster for first production *195*
  The Shadow of a Gunman 20, 128, 148,
    166, 181, 184, 188–91, 620
  The Silver Tassie 129–30, 148, 190, 194–5,
    197–8, 276, 611, 627, 632
  The Star Turns Red 130–1, 196, 448–9, 632

  The Story of the Irish Citizen Army 193
  Within the Gates 130–1, 184, 195
  writings: *Inishfallen, Fare Thee Well*
    (autobiography)194; *Pictures in the
    Hallway* (autobiography) 196–7, 646;
    Three Shouts on a Hill (essays) 148
Ó Ceallaigh, Colm 297
Ó Ceallaigh Ritschel, Nelson 19
Ó Ceallaigh, Tomás 263
Ó Cearbhaill, Eoin S: *Brian Boroimhe* 251
Ó Clochartaigh, Trevor 264
Ó Coileáin, Conchubhar 70
Ó Conaire, Pádraic 263
  Bairbre Ruadh 252
Ó Conchubhair, Brian 644
Ó Conghaile, Micheál
  Cúigear Chonamara 264
  Go dTaga do Ríocht 264
  Jude 264
O'Connell, Daniel 595
O'Connell, Deirdre 679
O'Connor, Carroll 465
O'Connor, Francis 457
O'Connor, Frank 639, 640, 654
  Guests of the Nation 211
  The Midnight Court 644
  My Father's Son 182
  Time's Pocket 119
O'Connor, Joseph
  Star of the Sea 264
O'Connor, Joseph (lawyer) 147n.44
O'Connor, Ulick 446
O'Connor, Una 245
Ó Dálaigh, Cearbhaill 648–9
O'Daly, Cormac
  The Silver Jubilee 174, 182
Odd Man Out (film) 245
O'Dea, Jimmy 482
Odets, Clifford
  Awake and Sing 289
  Waiting for Lefty 289
Ó Domhnaill, Aodh
  Idir an Dá Shúil 258
O'Donnell and Tuomey (architects) 441
O'Donnell, Peadar 151
O'Donoghue, Noel 407
O'Donovan, Fred 145, 239

O'Driscoll, Robert 308
O'Dwyer, Paddy 401
Oedipus myth 564
O'Faolain, Sean 149–50, 512, 639, 640
   The Great O'Neill 340
   She Had to Do Something 150
Ó Faracháin, Roibéard 288
O'Farrell, Ciara 12n.11, 23n.58
Ó Fátharta, Macdara 667
   Cré na Cille (adaptation) 258–9, 264
O'Flaherty, Liam
   Dorchada (Darkness) 254
   The Informer 408
Ó Flaithearta, Tomás 259
Ó Flaithearta, Tom Sailí 264
Ó Flatharta, Antoine
   An Fear Bréige 261
   An Solas Dearg 258–9
   Gaeilgeoirí 258–9
   Imeachtaí na Saoirse 258
Ó Floinn, Críostóir
   An Spailpín Fánach 263
   Cluichí Cleamhnais 263
   Cóta Bán Chríost 261
O'Flynn, Philip 469, 476
Ó Garbhaigh, Micheál 259
O'Gorman, Siobhán 302
O'Grady, Hubert 11–12, 231
   Emigration 11
   Eviction 11, 12n.11
   The Famine 11–12, 13n.15,
     16–19
   The Fenian 11
Ó Gramhnaigh, Eoin
   Imtheacht Chonaill 251
O'Halloran, Mark 569
   Adam & Paul (film) 569
Ó hAodha, Micheál 224, 436, 577
Ó hAodha, Séamus
   Donnchadh Ruadh 255
O'Hara, Maureen 240
Oireachtas na Gaeilge 268
O'Kelly, Aideen 346
O'Kelly, Donal 524, 686
   The Business of Blood (with Kenneth
     Glenaan) 399
   Farawayan 399

   Hughie on the Wires 399
   Trickledown Town 399
O'Kelly, Seumas 118
   The Bribe 114–16, 118
   The Flame on the Hearth/The
     Stranger 67
   The Matchmakers 67
   The Shuiler's Child 67–8
O'Kelly, Revd Thomas 69
Olcott, Chauncey 595
Old Museum Arts Centre (Belfast) 553
Old Vic Theatre (London) 212, 277, 279, 600,
   611–12, 646
Old Vic Theatre School (London) 632
O'Leary, David 290
O'Leary, Margaret 546–7
   The Woman 279–80
O'Leary, Lance-Corporal Michael 145
O'Leary, Philip 69, 139
Olivier Awards 553, 656
Olivier, Laurence 246
Ó Lochlainn, Gearóid 71, 208, 254, 256
Ó Loingsigh, Fionán 70
Olympia Theatre (Dublin) 189, *195*, 339, 429,
   446, 561, 642–3
O'Malley, Aidan 358, 370–1
O'Malley, Ellen 146
O'Malley, Mary 281, 288–9, 299–300, 302,
   437, 439, 446–7, 679
O'Malley, Pearse 288, 299–300, 437, 439
Ó Muircheartaigh, Tomás 258n.50
Ó Murchú, Liam
   Fear an Tae 262
   Spéir Thoirní 261
Ó Neachtain, Joe Steve 264
Ó Neachtain, Seán 251n.2
O'Neill, Charlie 524, 686
   Rosie and Starwars 399
O'Neill, Chris 396
O'Neill, Eugene 9, 127, 172, 218, 594, 596,
   598–600, 601–2, 647–8, 652
   Ah, Wilderness 602
   Before Breakfast 602
   Days WIthout End 602
   The Emperor Jones 133, 206, 598–9, 602
   The Hairy Ape 210
   The Iceman Cometh 602

O'Neill, Eugene (*cont.*)
  Long Day's Journey into Night 231, 246,
    475, 602
  A Moon for the Misbegotten 602
  Mourning Becomes Electra 602
  Where the Cross is Made 602
O'Neill, Hugh 340–1
O'Neill, James 231, 598
O'Neill, Maire (Molly Allgood) 54, 236, 239,
  241, 465, 679
O'Neill, Michael C. 457
Ó Néill, Pádraic 259
Oonagh Young Gallery 573n.21
Open Theater 604
opera 36–8, 234, 264, 395, 454, 612, 641, 665;
  see also Wagner, Richard
Operating Theatre 561–3
  Angel/Babel 562
  Here Lies 562–3
  Passades 562
Oradea (Nagyvárad) 625
Orange Order 668
Order of Golden Dawn 75
O'Reilly, Anne F. 675, 681
O'Reilly, Kaite
  Belonging 621
O'Reilly, Shane 573
O'Riordan, John 416
Ormonde Dramatic Society 252
Ormsby, Frank 372
O'Rorke, Breffni 460, 461n.7
O'Rourke, Pat 290
O'Rowe, Mark 4, 458, 530, 536, **538–40**, 543,
  544, 611, 627, 650
  The Aspidistra Code 538
  From Both Hips 538
  Crestfall 538–40
  Howie the Rookie 538–9, 611, 613
  Made in China 538–9
  Our Few and Evil Days 538
  Terminus 538–40, 631
Orton, Joe 542
O'Ruitleis, Padraig 176
Osborne, John 338
Oscars 656
Oscar Wilde (ship) 229
Oscar Wilde Festival (Enniskillen) 229

Ó Scolaí, Darach
  An Braon Aníos 268
  An tSeanbhróg 268
  Coinneáil Orainn 268
O'Shea, Katharine 41, 140
O'Shea, Milo 245, 291, 293–4, 297, 462n.11
O'Shea, Sean 213
Ó Snodaigh, Pádraig
  Leaba Dhiarmada 266
Ostermeier, Thomas 649
Ó Suilleabháin, Gearóid 70
O'Sullivan, Maureen 245
O'Sullivan, Seumas 64
Ó Tarpaigh, Seán 264
Othello (film) 211
O'Toole, Fintan 141, 258, 312–13, 320, 323–4,
  327, 333, 344–5, 348, 400, 415, 419, 421,
  463, 468, 480, 593, 686n.85
O'Toole, Peter 469, 482, 577
Ó Tuairisc, Eoghan
  De Réir Rubricí 260
  Lá Féile Mhicíl 260
Out of Joint Productions 472
Oxford Playhouse 419
Oxford University: Chair of
  Poetry 656

pacifism 272, 274–5, 534
Page, Anthony 660
pageants, *see* spectacle and pageantry
Paget, Dorothy 74
Pakenham, Christine 208
Pakenham, Edward, Lord Longford 208
Palace Theatre (London) 615
Pallisers, the (BBC) 469
Pan Pan Theatre Company 4, 458, 563–5,
  651, 689
  *A Bronze Twist of Your Serpent
    Muscles* 563
  Deflowerfucked 563
  *Everyone is King Lear in his Own
    Home* 565
  Mac-Beth 7 564
  The Rehearsal: Playing the Dane 564–5
pantomime 13n.15, 255–6, 259, 264–5, 291,
  302, 447–8, 482
Papez, Svatopluk 633–4

Paris 25, 27, 42–5, 49, 73, 88–9, 108, 290, 292,
       350, 430, 478, 483, 580, 582, 624, 634–5
    Beckett in 580–1
    Playboy productions 102
    Rite of Spring riot (1913) 88–90
    Synge in 100–2
    théâtres de poche 287–8
Paris Commune 106
Paris Conservatoire 232–3
Paris Theatre Festival (1954) 102, 462, 465
Park, David
    The Truth Commissioner 384
Parker, Lynne 402, 458, 548, 557, 679
Parker, Stewart 359, 380, 390, 652, 677
    Heavenly Bodies 548
    The Iceberg 376–7
    Northern Star 376, 380, 649
    Pentecost 370, 374, 376–7
    Spokesong 376–7
Parkhill, David 59–60
Parnell, Charles Stewart 27, 30, 34, 41,
       58, 140–1
Passion Machine 3
Patrick, St 641
Paulin, Tom 357–8, 366, 368–9, 371, 655, 669
    The Riot Act 375, 655n.4, 667–8
Pavilion Theatre (Dun Laoghaire) 442
Pavis, Patrice 106
Payne, Ben Iden 54, 124n.5, 597–9
peace and reconciliation 384–6
peace process, *see under* Northern Ireland
Peacock Theatre (Dublin) 56, 128n.12,
       133n.24, 137, 172, 209, 222, 246, 254,
       256–7, 265, 283n.55, 290, 318, 322, 330,
       340, 348–9, 386, 390, 398, 401n.56, 436,
       440–1, 446, 452, 454, 458, 480–3, 499,
       538, 548, 553, 603, 648, 683
    experimental theatre 213
    stage design *136*, 449–51, *451*, 452
Pearse, Patrick 26, 54, 59, 64, 69–70, 163–8,
       184, 187, 193, 197–8, 207, 214, 244,
       254, 441
    and drama of self-sacrifice 156–8
    and Easter Rising 155, 156, 194
    The King 158–60
    The Master 161
    The Singer 26, 158, 160–2

Pearson, Noel 396
peasant plays **91–100**, 102, 204, 316, 431,
       532, 577
Pelletier, Martine 635
Pepsico Summer Festival (New York) 409
Performance Corporation 457, 689
performers, *see* actors and acting
Performing Garage (New York) 456
Perth 688
Phelan, Jim 299
Phelan, Mark 675–6, 690
Philadelphia 593, 605
Phoenix Park (Dublin) 30n.27, 177, 214, 215
Picasso, Pablo 578
Pierce, Wendell 589, *589*
Piesse, Amanda 564
Pigott, E. F. S. 24
Pigsback 395, 553
Pike Newsletter 292–4
Pike Theatre (Herbert Lane, Dublin) 56, 213,
       281, 287–9, 291, **292–4**, 302, 337, 481–2,
       585–6, 588, 644, 650, 677, 683
    The Follies of Herbert Lane 293, 294, 302
    The Rose Tattoo controversy
       (1957) **295–8**, 337
Pike Theatre Defence Fund 298
Pilgrim, James 14
Pilkington, Lionel 373–5, 674, 682–6, 690
Pilkington, Lorraine 456
Pilný, Ondřej 530, 675, 693n.121
Pine, Emilie 530, 689
Pine, Richard 221
Pintal, Lorraine 548n.8, 670
Pinter, Harold 245, 480, 492, 646–9
    Ashes to Ashes 542
    The Lover 393
Pirandello, Luigi 121, 127, 206, 210, 218, 652,
       655, 664
Pittsburgh 605
places of performance, *see* theatres
Playgoers' Circle 289
Playhouse Theatre (Liverpool) 616, 619
Playhouse Theatre (London) *661*
Playography na Gaeilge 1901–2010 398
Plays and Players 416
Plays International 484
Playwrights and Actors Company 395

Plough and the Stars (film) 245
Plunkett, Edward, Baron Dunsany, *see*
    Dunsany, Lord
Plunkett, Horace 61
Plunkett, Joseph 654
Pocket Theatre (Dublin) 287, 644, 650
pocket theatres, *see* little theatres
Pocket Youth Theatre Company
    (Wexford) 395
Poets' Theatre 211
Poland 564, 626, 628, 632, 635, 650
Polish Lab 604
Pollock, Jackson 582
Portland (USA) 605
Portora Royal School (Enniskillen) 229, 646
Portugal 626–8, 632
posters and flyers 12, *195*, *265*, *267*, 411–12,
    413, *414*, *642*, *643*
Potter, Maureen 490, *490*
Pound, Ezra 54, 81, 121, 598
poverty 20, 49, 140, 147, 166–7, 175, 215, 285,
    308, 311, 314, 352, 377, 456, 470, 691
Powell, Kerry 24
Power, Tyrone 123, 595, 610
Prague 489, *624*, 633–5
Prague Quadrennial (2007) 635
presentational theatre 134–5, *135*, *136*
Presley, Elvis 579
Priestley, J. B: *Dragon's Mouth* (with Jacquetta
    Hawkes) 293
Prison Bars 680
Proclamation of the Irish Republic
    (1916) 155, 157, 165, 680
professional theatre 3–4, 65, 261–2, 277, 390–1,
    394–5, 402, 442, 449, 457n.54, 477, 557
Programme for Economic Expansion
    (1959) 392
Project 67 392–5, 446
Project Arts Centre (Dublin) 393, 395, 405,
    408, 446, 553–4, 561, 563, 667n.33, 686
Project Gallery 393
Project Upstairs 574
Propeller 649
Protestant National Association 59
Protestants 53, 115, 173, 185–6, 241, 243–5,
    359, 368, 374–5, 376, 387, 498–9, 503,
    507–10, 519, 552
Provincetown Players 208, 596, 598

Provincetown Playhouse (Greenwich
    Village) 598
Provisional Government (1922) 169–71
Provisional IRA 508
publishing 367–70, 550 1, 660, 673, 693
Punch (magazine) 27
Purcell, Lewis
    The Enthusiast 61–2
Purser, Sarah 51

Quarshie, Hugh 504
Quarterly Journal of Speech Education 597
Queen's Theatre (Dublin) 11–12, 13n.15,
    19n.43, 50, 52, 189, 241, 256n.32, 278,
    283n.55, 294, 429, 448, 687
Queen's University Belfast 300, 361, 649
Quest Productions 466
Quiet Man (film) 459
Quigley, Godfrey 288, 297, 408, 445
Quigley, Peter 388
Quill, Siân 399–400
Quin, James 231
Quinn, Bob 287, 291
Quinn, Cathal 262
Quinn, Gavin 458, 56–4
    Oedipus Loves you (with Simon Doyle) 565
Quinn, Justin 635
Quinn, Maire 60, 235

Raabke, Tilman 541, 629
Raab, Michael 628, 630, 632, 632n.20, 635
race issues 681, 691
Radcliffe, Daniel 612
Radio Forth awards 406
Radley, Lynda 458
Raftery, Mary
    No Escape 526
Rakoczi, Basil 432–3
Ray, R. J. (Robert J. Brophy) 106, 116–18
    The Casting Out of Martin Whelan 116–17
    The Gombeen Man 116–18
realism 2, 45, 48, 56, 62, 67, 85, 91, 99–100,
    105–20, 125, 128, 131, 137, 188, 196, 335,
    339–40, 569
    decline of 118–20
    Synge's 'failed realism' 94–8
Rea, Stephen 3, 452, 459, 550, *604*
    and Field Day 357, 358–61, 365–6, 370–1

Rebellato, Dan 302
rebellion of 1798 11, 146, 162, 376, 380
rebellion of 1916, *see* Easter Rising (1916)
Reddin, Norman 208
Red Kettle Theatre Company
    (Waterford) 395, 401
Redmond, John 163
Red Rex 408
Rees Moore, John 84–5
Regent Street Polytechnic (London) 449
Rehan, Ada 231
Reid, Christina 378, 679
    The Belle of Belfast City 378
    Did You Hear the One about the
        Irishman? 374
Reid, Graham 373, 378
    Love Billy 386
    Remembrance 374, 378
Reinelt, Janelle 679
Reinhardt, Max 133–4
Réjane, Gabrielle 233
Rellis, Liam 401
repertory theatre 2, 118, 136, 143, 148–9, 237,
    277–8, 395, 566, 632
Repertory Theatre of Galway, *see* Druid
    Theatre Company
republicanism 26, 160, 174, 271, 683, 692
Return to Glenascaul (film) 211
Review of Theatre in Ireland
    (1995–96) 397–8, 403
Reynolds, Horace 10–11
Reynolds, Paige 89, 271, 675, 687–8
Rhea, Mark 605
Rice, Elmer
    The Adding Machine 291
Rich, Adrienne 681
Richards, Shaun 334, 375, 401–2, 499, 512,
    559, 674, 684–5, 689
Richards, Shelah 2, 206, 464–5, 650, 679
Ricketts, Charles 204
Rickman, Alan 492, 662
Riff Raff Theatre 395
Rimini Protokol (Germany) 650
Riordan, Arthur 458
rituals of performance **72–86**
    masks 79–80
Riverdance 608, 615, 656
Roberts, George 64

Robinson, Jacqueline 289–90
Robinson, Lennox 56, 106, 114, 118–19, 127,
    149, 169, 171–4, 180, 191, 204, 206, 425–
    7, 638, 646
    and Irish realism 112–13
    The Big House 177–8
    The Clancy Name 105, 112–13
    Crabbed Youth and Age 149
    The Cross Roads 113, 117
    The Drama at Inish 118
    The Far Off Hills/Is Glas Iad na Cnuic
        258n.50
    Harvest 117–18
    Killycreggs in Twilight 119
    Patriots 150
    The Whiteheaded Boy 106, 118, 567
Robinson, Mary 397–8, 485, 515–17, 554
Roche, Anthony 349–50, 352, 373, 484–6,
    492–4, 675, 677–8, 688–9
Roche, Billy 395, 525, 610
    Belfry 525–6
    The Cavalcaders 525
    A Handful of Stars 525
    Lay Me Down Softly 525
    Poor Beast in the Rain 525
Rodden, Lindsay 616
Roddy McSorley Social Club (Belfast) 381
Rodway, Norman 291–2
Rogers, Cathleen 209
Rogers, Michael
    The Dentist/An Fiaclóir (with John
        Cannon) 251
Roinn na Gaeltachta 394
Rolling Stones 525
Roman Catholic Relief Act 1829 122–3
Roman classics 654
Romania 625, 634
Rome 635
Ronen, Ilan 588
Rose & Crown Bar (Belfast) 385
Rosemary Street Presbyterian Church
    (Belfast) 380
Rosenstock, Gabriel 262n.80
Rose of Tralee Festival 642
Rosicrucianism 73, 75
Rosmuc, Co Galway 59
Ros na Rún (TG4) 398
Rossaveal, Co Galway 407

Rossett, Barney 581
Rostand, Edmond
    Cyrano de Bergerac 233
Rothenstein, William 24
Rotunda (Dublin) 99, 209, 431
Rouen 10
Rough Magic 3, 347, 350, 395, 458, 557,
    561, 635
    Improbable Frequency 458, 635
Rousseau, Jean-Jacques 42
Royal Academy of Dramatic Art 232
Royal Ballet Company 279, 643
Royal College of Music (London) 608
Royal Court Theatre (London) 116, 143, 338,
    349–50, 358–9, 418, 493, 534, 555–6, 579,
    611, 622, 662–4, 688
Royal Court Upstairs 472
Royal Dublin Society 177
Royal Irish Academy 429
Royal Shakespeare Company 449, 475,
    556, 649
Royal University 158
Rozema, Patricia 492
RTÉ 398, 405n.5, 406, 435, 478, 483–4, 486,
    492, 523n.12
Rushe, Desmond 348
Russell, George (AE) 44, 59–61, 64–5, 105,
    162, 173
    Deirdre 59, 67, 69, 202, 234, 428
Russia 25, 35, 73, 317, 550, 658–9, 665
Ruttledge, Paul (George Moore) 110
Ryan, Annie 457–8, 557, 568–9
Ryan, Frederick 66, 111
    The Laying of the Foundations 111–12, 147
Ryan, Phyllis 281, 302, 396, 402, 445, 679
Ryan Report (2009) 526, 571
Ryman, Robert 484

Sadler's Wells (London) 279, 449
Said, Edward 323, 506, 685
St Barnabas's church (East Wall, Dublin) 185
St Enda's School (Dublin) 70, 158
St Francis Xavier Hall (Dublin) 645
St Laurence O'Toole's Club (Dublin) 189
St Patrick's College (Maynooth) 326
St Petersburg 25, 73
St Teresa's Hall (Dublin) 63, 65, 235, 428–9

Salacrou, Armand
    Les nuits de la colère 261
Salamander 268
Salkeld, Blanaid 127
Salkeld, Cecil ffrench 459
    Berlin Dusk 292
Salonika 163
Saltykov-Shchedrin, Mikhail
    The Golovlyov Family 666
Salzburg Festival 133, 638, 641
Samhain 50
Samuel Beckett Centre (Dublin) 563–4
San Francisco 27, 588, 600
San Quentin prison (USA) 585, 588
Sarah Bernhardt Theatre (Paris) 102
Sarajevo 585, 588
Sardou, Victorien 141
Sartre, Jean-Paul 291, 584, 683n.69
Saturday Review 9
Saunders, James
    Double Double 393
Scanlon, Carol (now Moore) 377, 550
Scannell, Raymond 401
Scena Company 605
Scena Plastyczna KUL 564
Schauspielhaus (Berlin) 136
Schechner, Richard 429, 689
Schiller, Friedrich 632
Schiller Theatre 649
Schisgal, Murray
    The Tiger 393
Schneider, Alan 581
Schnitzler, Arthur 127
Schramm, Jan-Melissa 37
Scolnicov, Hanna 426, 679, 689
Scotland 614, 622
Scotsman Fringe First Awards 406
Scott, Michael 432–3, 435–6, 439, 441, 480,
    669n.40
Scott, Patrick 433
Scott Tallon Walker (architects) 435
Scott-Thomas, Kristin 492
Scribe, Eugène 141
Scruggs, William Lindsay 28n.14
Seanachaí Theatre Company (Chicago) 605
Sears, David
    The Dead Ride Fast 211

Seattle Repertory 600

Second World War 255, 323, 584, 633, 641

sectarianism 3, 61–2, 115, 149, 185, 359, 374,
        376–8, 385, 447, 498–500, 503, 507, 552,
        667, 684

Sedgwick, Eve Kosofsky 679

self-doubt, dramas of 162–5

self-sacrifice, drama of 156–8

Selim, Heba-T-Allah Ahmed 506–8

Semil, Malgorzata 635

Sepinuck, Teya 383

Seven Psychopaths (film) 534

sexuality/sexual identity 4, 219–20, 296;
        see also gender identity;
        homosexuality

Shakespearean Company 207

Shakespeare Festival
        (Stratford-upon-Avon) 638

Shakespeare, William 77–8, 164–5, 184, 189,
        232, 246, 300, 466, 508–9, 564, 638
    As You Like It 376
    Coriolanus 212, 449
    Hamlet 72, 136, 164–5, 564–5, 578, 634
    Henry IV 190
    Henry V 511, 586
    Julius Caesar 165, 210, 337
    King Lear 115, 136n.29, 211, 475
    Macbeth 79, 461, 510, 567
    Measure for Measure 240
    A Midsummer Night's Dream 107
    Othello 136
    Richard II 610
    Richard III 136
    Romeo and Juliet 36, 245
    The Tempest 529

Shanley, John Patrick
    Doubt 603
    Outside Mullingar 603

Sharkey, Stephen 619
    The May Queen 617–19

Shaw, Fiona 459, 610, 662

Shaw, George Bernard 1, 5, 9, 33, 42, 47, 107,
        121, 123–4, 127, 129, 132, 138–40, 206,
        217, 246, 252, 319, 376, 389, 455, 462, 594,
        596, 623–4, 626, 631
    impact on Irish letters **146–51**
    Irish contexts of plays **140–6**

Arms and the Man 26, 33, 42, 138, 145,
        202, 469

Back to Methuselah 123, 145–6

Candida 145, 461

Common Sense About the War 144

The Devil's Disciple 146, 149, 173, 459

The Doctor's Dilemma 145, 148

Getting Married 141

Heartbreak House 123, 146, 150, 282, 289

The Inca of Perusalem 145

John Bull's Other Island 123, 141–3, 145,
        148, 150, 177, 319, 462–3, 613

Major Barbara 123

Man and Superman 123, 141, 145, 150

Misalliance 141

O'Flaherty V.C. 144

The Perfect Wagnerite 139

The Quintessence of Ibsenism 9n.2, 139

Saint Joan 146, 149, 263, 293, 465–6, 467

The Shewing Up of Blanco Posnet 53, 144–
        5, 149, 548, 639; British ban 144

Sixteen Self-Sketches 150

Too True to be Good 123

A Village Wooing 212

Widowers' Houses 123, 140, 145

You Never Can Tell 462, 463

Shea, Wendy 449–51, 453

Sheehy, Michael 286

Sheehy-Skeffington, Francis 149, 163

Sheehy-Skeffington, Hannah 174–5

Sheen, Martin 318

Shelbourne Hotel (Dublin) 591

Shelley, Percy Bysshe: 'Mutability' 510

Shepard, Sam 359
    Ages of the Moon 603, 604
    Fool for Love 605
    *A Particle of Dread (Oedipus
        Variations)* 603

Shepherd-Barr, Kirsten 29

Sheridan, Jim 401

Sheridan, Noel and Peter 561

Sheridan, Richard Brinsley 139–40, 231, 376,
        455, 593–5, 606
    The Rivals 233, 406, 593
    The School for Scandal 593

Sheridan, Thomas 231, 431

Sherkin Island, Co Cork 524

Shields, Arthur 95, 239–41, 243, *244*,
    245, 462
Shiel, Matthew Phipps
    The Yellow Danger 34
Shiels, George 313, 461, 677
    The Passing Day 548
    Paul Twyning 173
    The Rugged Path 92n.18
Shirley, James 610
Showalter, Elaine 679
Shyre, Paul 646
Siamsa Tíre 394, 395
Sierz, Aleks 541
Sihra, Melissa 679–80, 689
Simpson, Alan 213, 263, 292–9, 337, 644, 683
Sinclair, Arthur 238, 239, 241
Singleton, Brian 536, 539, 675, 681, 689
Sinn Féin 48, 157, 379
Sinn Féin 66, 115
Sisters of Our Lady of Charity 571
66 Theatre Club 287–8
S. K. Neumann Theatre (Prague) 633
Slade School of Fine Art 219
Sligo 59, 395, 401, 406, 566
Slovakia 625
Slovenia 634
Smith, Brendan 445, 642–6
Smith, Gretta 209
Smith, Gus 482
Smith, T. Ryder *589*
Smock Alley Theatre (Dublin) 395, 432
Smyth, Ailbhe 274
Smyth, Gerry 685, 689
Society of London Theatre 609
Sofia 221
Soja, Edward 415, 689
Sokol, Ondrej 627
Solstice Arts Centre (Navan) 442
Sonrel, Pierre 435
Sontag, Susan 588
Sophocles
    Antigone 375, 667–70
    Oedipus Rex 612, 654
    Philoctetes 669
Sorrento Cottage (Dalkey) 638
Soum, Corinne 566
South Africa 585, 588, 667n.33, 669

South African Truth and Reconciliation
    Commission 384
South Armagh 382
South Coast Repertory Theatre
    (California) 418
South Pacific (musical) 505
Soyinka, Wole 685, 691n.116
Spain 623
Spallen, Abbie 378, 386, 557
    Pumpgirl 382–3
Spanish Civil War 517
spectacle and pageantry 2, 213–16, 252, 641,
    642, 643
Spellbound (film) 238
Spenser, Edmund 509, 510
    View of the Present State of Ireland 508
Spivak, Gayatri 685
Stabb, Dinah 393n.22
Stafford-Clark, Max 347, 460n.2, 472–3, 662
Stafford, Maeliosa 474
stage design, *see* direction and design
Stage Society 140
Standard Life 488
Stanford, Alan 227, 229
Stanislavski, Constantin 209, 453
Starkie, Walter 179–80
Steinway Hall (New York) 251
Stembridge, Gerry 538
Stephens, James 68, 206
    The Crock of Gold 68
Stevenson, Juliet 492
Stewart Parker Awards 535, 540
Stoker, Bram: *Dracula* 33
A Storm in a Teacup (film) 240
storytelling 4, 515, **519–21**, 528, 536–8, 541–
    2, 556–7, 566–9, 616
Stratford (Ontario) 466
Stratford East (London) 445; *see also*
    Theatre Royal
Stratford-on-Avon (England) 77, 638
Stravinsky, Igor *90*, 100, 582
    The Rite of Spring: Paris protests
    (1913) 87–90, 102
Strindberg, August 9, 44, 121, 127, 206,
    276, 655
    To Damascus I 44
Studies 338, 353

Studio Theatre Club (Dublin) 281n.45, 288, 302
Stuttgart 632
Sudermann, Hermann 49, 127
  Magda 9
Suez Canal 31
Sunday Independent 257, 317, 482, 488
Sunday Press 483–4, 490
Sunday Times 182, 343
Sunday Tribune 479
Sunset Boulevard (film) 663
Sun, Yue 458
Swan Lake (ballet) 643
Swanson, Gloria 663
Sweden 564
Sweeney, Bernadette 675, 681
Sweetman, Alicia 212
Swift, Carolyn 213, 281, 292–4, 296–9, 302, 644, 679, 683
Swift, Jonathan 85, 131, 140
Swift, Tom 426
  Lizzy Lavelle and the Vanishing of Emlyclough 426
Switzerland 634
Sydney (Australia) 418
Sydney Festival 417
Symbolism 122, 124
Symons, Arthur 31, 73, 101n.66, 233
Synge, John Millington 1–3, 5, 19, 58–9, 62, 67, 87, 89n.5, 93, 144, 241, 282, 308, 313, 318, 334, 338, 376, 418, 425, 444, 475, 532–3, 586, 597, 604, 615, 624–5, 627–8, 630, 677
  and Abbey Theatre/INTS 13, 48–55, 63, 94–8
  'failed realism' 94–8
  Paris sojourn 100–2
  peasant plays 92, 94–8
  The Aran Islands 93
  Deirdre of the Sorrows 263, 476, 627
  In the Glens of Rathvanna (compilation) 405
  The Playboy of the Western World 54–6, 95, 95, 98–9, 102, 177–9, 181, 203, 212, 237, 239, 241, 244, 282–3, 330, 359, 405–6, 409, 413, 417, 456, 462, 464–5, 474–7, 600–1, 624, 640, 644, 649–51, 687; Abbey

riots (1907) 52, 88–90, 96–7, 99, 144, 192, 254, 431; Chinese translation 458; Peacock production (2001) 401n.56
  Riders to the Sea 49, 60, 86, 88, 102, 181, 204, 239, 259, 475; Irish-language version: Chun an Farraige Síos 258n.50, 264
  The Shadow of the Glen 48–9, 94n.32, 95–9, 101, 178–9, 181, 206, 236, 264, 405–6, 624
  The Tinker's Wedding 95–6, 98, 100, 109, 405, 475, 476
  The Well of the Saints 96–9, 181, 204, 212, 475, 624, 651
  When the Moon Has Set 101, 651
Syrett, Netta 31–2

tableaux vivants 214–15, 271
Tagore, Rabindranath 127n.10
  The Post Office 158
Tailteann Games 214, 687
Talbot, Matt 348–53
Tallon, Ronnie 435–6
Tampere (Finland) 635
Tarantino, Quentin 628
Tara Park (Liverpool) 616, 622
Taubman, Howard 603
Tawain Island, Co Galway 263
Taylor, Lib 679
Taylor, Paul 540
Taylor, Richard 74, 81
TEAM Educational Theatre Company (Dublin) 401
Teater Tyst (Sweden) 564
Teevan, Colin: The Walls 611
Teilifís Éireann 261
Teilifís na Gaeilge 398
Telecom Éireann 488
terrorism, Irish 534, 620–1
Terry, Ellen 33, 204, 232
Tesín, Cesky 628
TG4 268, 398
Theater heute 626, 629, 633
Theater Oberhausen (Germany) 629
Theatre '47 (Dallas, USA) 600
Theatre Arts Magazine 597
Theatre Arts Monthly 136n.31

Theatreclub 457
theatre companies 3–4, 64–8, **259–61**, 262, **288–91**, 390–1, **395**, 457–8, **561–74**, 649, 679; *see also* Irish National Theatre Society; *individual companies*
  commercial production companies 396
Théâtre d'Art (Paris) 43
Théâtre de Babylone (Paris) 580
Théâtre de Complicité 649
Théâtre de France 632n.19
Théâtre de l'Atelier 566
Théâtre de L'Oeuvre (Paris) 45, 108, 624
Théâtre des Champs-Élysées (Paris)
  Rite of Spring riots 88, 89–90, 102
Théâtre des Nations Festival (Paris, 1955) 634
Théâtre du Soleil 449, 568
Théâtre du Vieux-Colombier 566
theatre festivals 5, **637–53**; *see also* Abbey Theatre Festival; Beckett Festival; Dublin Theatre Festival
Theatre Forum 398
Theatre Guild 596
Theatre Journal 490
Théâtre Libre (Paris) 42, 108–9, 111, 234, 430
Théâtre Mogador (Paris) 290
Théâtre National Populaire (TNP) 643
Theatre of Ireland (Cluithcheoiri-na-hÉireann) 53, 63, **63–8**, 69, 71, 99, 113, 253–4
TheatreofplucK 378, 387–8
Theatre of the Eighth Day (Poland) 564
Theatre of the Nation 401
Theatre of Witness (Derry) *383*
  I Once Knew a Girl 383–4
  We Carried Your Secrets 384
Theatre Projects Consultants 439
Theatre Royal (Dublin) 9, 13n.15, 47, 52, 429
Theatre Royal (Stratford East) 260, 338–9, 408
theatres 394; *see also individual theatres*
  buildings and plans 425–42; *see also* Abbey Theatre
  definition 426
  expansion and diversity 400–3
  Irish theatres in Europe 634–5
  little theatres 286–303

open-air theatre (Achill Island) 432–4, *434*
  State support 390–6, 401–2; Abbey 169–82
Theatre Shop 398
Theatre Unlimited
  The Murder of Gonzago 649
Theatre Voice 541
Theatre Workshop (Stratford East) 338–9, 445
Third, Amanda 689
37 Theatre Club (Dublin) 256, 287–90, **291–2**, 302
thisispopbaby 457
Thorndike, Sybil 149
Threshold 300
Tidy Towns competition 216
TiE (theatre-in-education) 401
Time magazine 627
Times 47n.27, 261, 416
Tinderbox 380, 553
Titanic 376
Titley, Alan 258
  An Ghráin agus an Ghruaim 262
  Tagann Godot 257
Todhunter, John
  A Sicilian Idyll 73
Tóibín, Colm 416, 470, 519
  Testament 521, 527
Tóibín, Niall 449
Toller, Ernst 127, 129, 133
  The Blind Goddess 131
  Hoppla! 133
  Masses and Man 129
Tolstoy, Leo
  The Power of Darkness 657n.8
Tomelty, Frances 516
Tompkins, Joanne 684
Tony awards 449, 454, 456–7, 475, 553, 656, 660, 679
Toronto 417, 492, 607, 688
Torún (Poland) 635
tourism 176–7, 214–16, 456, 522, 609, 614–15, 640–2, 645
Town Hall Theatre (Galway) 395
Townsend, Stuart 565
Townshend, Charles 194
Trafalgar Studios (London) 611

Tralee, Co Kerry 394
translation 268, 654–5; *see also* Irish-
    language theatre
    Irish theatre in Europe 624, 627, **629–31**,
        633, 635
Transylvania 625, 630
Travelling community 67, 616–17, 622
travelling theatre companies 12n.11, 207, 219,
    245, 252n.3, 599–600
Travers-Smith, Dorothy 2, 206, 211, 277
Tricycle Theatre (London) 417, 430, 610,
    613, 622
Trimble, David 385
Trinity College Dublin 165, 216, 458, 479,
    481–6, 492, 564, 568, 638
    Drama Department 559, 563
Trollope, Anthony 469
Trotter, Mary 12, 253, 270–1, 674, 681
Trouble and Strife (UK) 399
'Troubles,' *see under* Northern Ireland
'Troubles play' **372–7**, 380
TR Warszawa 650
T. S. Eliot Prize 656
Tuam, Co Galway 313, 323, 407–8,
    415, 419
Tuan, Yi-Fu 689
Turgenev, Ivan 656
Turpin, Adrian 567
Tynan, Katharine 72
Tynan, Kenneth 580, 614

U2 638
Ua Duinnín, Pádraig 253n.11
Ulad (magazine) 61
Ulm (Germany) 632–3
Ulster Defence Association (UDA) 379
Ulster Literary Theatre (ULT) 50, **59–62**, 65,
    71, 94, 113–14, 596
Ulster Revivalism 59
Ulsterville House (Belfast) 288
Ulster Volunteer Force (UVF) 381, 385
Ulster Volunteers 68
Ulster Workers' Council strike (1974) 374,
    376, 447
unionists 43, 61–2, 300, 302, 361, 368–9, 385,
    498–9, 510, 519, 682
United Ireland 42

United Irishman 13, 47, 64, 69n.42,
    231–2, 234
United Irishmen 11, 19, 59, 380
United Nations 645
United States 112, 174, 277, 290, 322, 369,
    466, 499, 504–5, 550, 578, 608, 610, 624,
    628, 641; *see also* New York
    American theatre 127–8, 134, 137, 208,
        231, 277–8, 322, 337, 394, 595–6, 598–
        601, 647; in Ireland 601–2
    Irish theatre in 5, 11–12, 14, 144, 179–81,
        211, 215, 224–5, 238–9, 409, 581–2, 588–
        90, **593–606**, 607, 615, 623, 638, 645;
        modern theatre 595–8; contemporary
        theatre 603–5; prospects 605–6
    Little Theatre movement 208, 290, 593,
        595–7, 600
    regional theatre 600–1
    Venezuela crisis (1895) 27–8, 31
Unity Theatre 445
University College Dublin 338, 481,
    497, 535
University College Galway 405, 456, 464
University of California (Berkeley) 362
University of Notre Dame (Indiana) 180–1
Unusual Rural Tour 407
urban and rural theatre **307–21**
Urban, Eva 683n.69

Valente, Joseph 513
Valle-Inclan, Ramon Maria del
    Barbaric Comedies 651
Vaněk, Joe 3, 450, 454–5, 515
Vanya on 42nd St (film) 656
Vartan, Jamie 611–12, *612*
Vassar College (USA) 597
Vedrenne, J. E. 143
Venezuelan crisis (1895) 27–8, 31
Vermande, Sarah 388n.46
Vernon, Emma 64
Vichy France 580
Victims' Commission (NI) 379
Victoria and Ontroerend Goed (theatre
    company) 650
Victoria, Queen 37, 46, 214, 271
Vienna 30, 44, 623
Vilar, Jean 641, 643–5

Villiers de L'Isle Adam, Comte
    Auguste 44–5, 122
    Axel 73
Viney, Michael 260

Wadell, Helen 547
Wade, Virginia 505
Wagner, Richard 36–7, 38, 44–5, 50, 139,
    204, 638
    Götterdämmerung 36, 38
    Lohengrin 36–8
    Parsifal 37–8, 50
    Tristan and Isolde 38
Waiting for Elmo (Sesame Street) 579
Waiting for Godot in New Orleans 589–91
Wakefield, Tony 350
Walcott, Derek 691n.116
Wales 614, 622, 632
Walker, Frank 64
Walker, Mary 49; *see also* Nic
    Shiubhlaigh, Máire
Walker, Robin 435–7, 439
Wallace, Clare 530, 675, 692
Wallace, Neil 397
Waller, Lewis 30
Walshe, Eibhear 512
    Oscar's Shadow 217
Walsh, Enda 1, 4, 5, 401, 458, 530, **540–3**,
    544, 553, 604, 611, 613, 628–9, 650
    Ballyturk 541
    Bedbound 540–2, 629, 631
    Chatroom 540
    Disco Pigs 401, 540–2, 611, 613, 627, 629,
        631, 650
    The Ginger Ale Boy 401
    How These Desperate Men Talk 629
    Lynndie's Gotta Gun 629
    Misterman 540–2, 611, *612*
    The New Electric Ballroom 540, 629
    Once 540
    Penelope 540, 629
    The Small Things 540–2
    Sucking Dublin 540, 542
    The Walworth Farce 329, 540–3, 613, 628
Walsh, Fintan 512, 675, 681
    Queer Notions 229–30
Walsh, Ian 291, 301, 675

Walsh, J. P. 179–80
Walter Kerr Theatre (Broadway) 418
Ward, William Humbel, Lord Dudley 52
War Illustrated 163
War of Independence 146, 165, 257, 258
Washington DC 25, 225, 419, 556, 600, 607
Washington, George 593
Washington Square Players (New York) 596
Waterford 395, 397, 401
Waterford Arts for All 395
Waterford Spraoi 395
Waters, Maureen 273
Watkins, Kathleen 650
Watson, George 192
Watt, Stephen 674
WAVE 378
Weaver, Jesse 542
Wedekind, Frank 121
    *Frühlings Erwachen (Spring
        Awakening)* 526, 664
Weiss, Peter
    Marat/Sade 350
Weitz, Eric 689, 693n.121
Welch, Robert 258, 316, 439, 500–1,
    511, 674–5
Welles, Orson 208, 211, 215, 646
Wendt, Ernst 633
Wesker, Arnold 338
West Belfast Festival 552
West, Derek 568
West, Michael 401, 568, 569
    Dublin by Lamplight 569
    Everyday 569
    Foley 569
    Play on Two Chairs 569
Westminster Theatre (London) 277
Westport, Co Mayo 407
West, Rachel 548
Wet Paint Arts 398–9, 402
Wet Paint Theatre Company 398–400, 686
Wexford 395
Wexford Opera Festival 641
Wexford Theatre Workshop 395
Whelan, Gerard 296
Whelan, Kevin 119–20
Whitaker, T. K. 286, 299, 301, 641
Whitbread, J. W. 11–13, 683

The Insurgent Chief 11
The Irishman 13n.15, 201
Lord Edward or '98 11, 13n.15, 17
The Nationalist 17–18
Sarsfield 17
The Ulster Hero 19
Wolfe Tone 11–12, 13n.15, 17
Whitbred Prize 656
White, James 403
Whitelaw, Billie 489–90, 493
Whiterock (Belfast) 552–3
White Stag Group 432–3
White, Victoria 29
Wickham, John 449
Wilde, Constance 29, 225
Wilde, Oscar 1, 5, **24–38**, 42, 121, 123–4, 127,
    138–9, 239, 281, 376, 406, 455, 623–4,
    626, 631
  at the Gate **217–27**, 246; reinvention and
    renewal 227–30
  geo-politics **27–34**
  homosexuality 26, 217, 220–1, 223–7
  An Ideal Husband 27, **30–4**, 123, 221,
    227, 229
  The Ballad of Reading Gaol 225
  De Profundis 37–8, 224–5
  The Doer of Good 225
  The Importance of Being Earnest 31, 34–8,
    42, 217, 221, 227, 229, 455, *455*
  Lady Windermere's Fan 24–6, 123,
    221, 229
  The Picture of Dorian Gray 30n.27, 36, 38,
    221, 225, 229
  Salomé 25–7, 29, 85, 217, 221–2, 225, 227,
    228, 229, 455, 623
  Vera, Or the Nihilists 25–6, 29, 35–6
  A Woman of No Importance 27–30,
    123, 229
Wilder, Billy 663n.26
Wilder, Thornton 603
Willfredd 573–4
  CARE 573–4
  FARM 573–4
  FOLLOW 573–4
William Morris Agency 607
Williams, Caroline 399
Williams, Raymond 188, 677

Williams, Tennessee 445, 594, 603,
    647–8, 652
  Cat on a Hot Tin Roof 569
  The Glass Menagerie 499, 501
  The Rose Tattoo 295, 295–8, 337, 644–5
  Summer and Smoke 293
Willmore, Alfred, *see* Mac Liammóir,
    Micheál
Willmore, Marjorie 245
Wilmer, S. E. 674
Wilson, A. P.
  Slough 191
  Victims 191
Wilson, Esther 616
Wilson, Laurence 616
Wilson, Robert 444, 649
Wimbledon championship (1977) 505
Winter, Brenda 377, 550–1
Winter Garden (London) 293
Winters, Carmel 679
Winwar, Frances 31
Woffington, Peg 231, 431
Wolf, Matt 490, 492
women 1–2, 4, **269–85**, 302, **545–58**, 659,
    678; *see also* feminism
  historiography 271, 678–81
  and nationalism 270, 272–4
  Northern Ireland 377–8, 382–4
  training and professionalism 277–9
Women's Prisoners Defence League 680
Wood, Gerald C. 536
Wood, Mrs. Henry
  East Lynne 12, 13n.15
Woods, Vincent
  At the Black Pig's Dyke 417
World Cup (1994) 519
Worth, Katharine 84, 674
Wright, Udolphus 234
Wroclaw Contemporary Theatre 649
Wuppertal (Germany) 632
Wyndham Act, *see* Land Act 1903
Wyndham Theatre (London) 612

Yarrow, Ralph 560–1
Yeates, Pádraig 186
Yeates, Ray 261
Yeats, Anne 212–13, 277

Yeats family 72–3

Yeats, Jack B. 583

Yeats, William Butler 1–2, 27, 38, 42, 48, 50–
1, 53, 58–61, 64–5, 68, 71–3, 91, 105, 111,
127, 137, 139–40, 173–4, 202, 217, 219,
222–3, 235–6, 252, 270, 272, 281, 300,
318, 441, 444–7, 546, 569, 594, 596, 598,
604, 606, 610, 624, 626, 644, 650, 655,
663, 667, 676–7, 682–4
    and Abbey Theatre 52–3, 56, 63, 94, 105,
        134, 139, 148, 169, 170–1, 176, 179–2, 280,
        429–30, 597, 639, 687; acting style 237–8,
        241, 246; direction and design 201, 204–
        6; disturbances 57, 173, 175, 192, 254;
        reorganization 63–4, 113
    and Dublin Drama League 172, 206
    and Easter Rising 68, 83, 156n.6, 198
    and Irish Literary Theatre/INTS 13, 43–5,
        48, 51, 63–4, 93, 108, 124, 202, 253, 428
    and other playwrights: O'Casey 129, 187,
        197; Shaw 138–9, 141; Synge 49–51,
        96–7, 100–1
    as dramatist 73–4, 76–7, 80, 82–3,
        85, 127, 337; interest in Noh theatre
        54, 81–3, 124–5, 204; Modernist
        playwright 121–2, 124–7, 134; rituals of
        performance **72–86**
    lecture tours in America 179, 181, 596, 602
    At the Hawk's Well 54, 81–4, 125, *126*, 204,
        279, 309
    Calvary 84–5, 125
    Cathleen ni Houlihan (with Gregory) 25–7,
        37, 46–9, 59–60, 63, 65, 67, 69, 76–7, 92,
        132, 202, 244, 272–3, 300, 428, 468,
        546–8; first performance **234–8**
    The Countess Cathleen 32, 45, 73, 75–6,
        108, 202, 427–8
    The Death of Cuchulain 78n.22, 86, 205
    Deirdre 54, 124, 237, 240, 275
    Diarmuid and Grania (with George
        Moore) 428

The Dreaming of the Bones 83, 125, 213, 279
Fighting the Waves (ballet) 178, 278–9
Four Plays for Dancers 57, 81, 84, 125, *126*,
    127, 278–9, 350
A Full Moon in March 85
The Green Helmet 80, 85, 446
The Herne's Egg 85, 182, 446
The Hour-Glass 77, 124, 202–3, 205
The King of the Great Clock Tower 85, 127,
    279, 446
The King's Threshold 51, 203–4, 239
The Land of Heart's Desire 26–7, 32, 42,
    74–5, 121–2, 138, 202
Oedipus the King (adaptation) 459, 654
The Only Jealousy of Emer 26, 78n.22, 84,
    105, 125, 206
On Baile's Strand 51, 77–9, 84, 86, 124, 203
The Pot of Broth 77
Purgatory 85–6, 446, 638–40, 644
The Resurrection 85
The Shadowy Waters 54, 122, 203
Sophocles' King Oedipus 180
The Trembling of the Veil 73
Vivien and Time 72–3
Where There is Nothing 91n.14
The Words Upon the Window-Pane 85, 127
writings and poems 105, 107, 168; 'Certain
    Noble Plays of Japan' 124; 'Cuchulain
    comforted' 86; 'Easter 1916' 68; 'The
    Circus Animals' Desertion' 77; 'The
    Reform of the Theatre' 202; 'The
    Wanderings of Oisin' 38
The Yellow Book (magazine) 31
Young Abbey 452
Young Irelanders 64
Yugoslavia 625, 634

Zadek, Peter 632–3
Žižek, Slavoj 682
Zola, Émile 106–9, 184
Zurich 88, 629

Printed and bound by CPI Group (UK) Ltd, Croydon, CR0 4YY